In the Richness of the Earth

In the Richness of the Earth

A History of the Archdiocese of Milwaukee 1843–1958

by

Steven M. Avella

Marquette University Press

CABRINI COLLEGE LIBRARY
610 KING OF PRUSSIA ROAD
RADNOR, PA 19087

#4898917

Urban Life Series
No. 1

Library of Congress Cataloguing in Publication

Avella, Steven M.
In the richness of the earth : a history of the Archdiocese of Milwaukee, 1843-1958 / by Steven M. Avella.
p. cm. — (Urban life series ; no. 1)
Includes bibliographical references and index.
ISBN 0-87462-076-7 (alk. paper) — ISBN 0-87462-077-5 (pbk. : alk. paper)
1. Catholic Church. Archdiocese of Milwaukee (Wis.)—History.
2. Milwaukee Region (Wis.)—Church history.
I. Title. II. Urban life series (Milwaukee, Wis.) ; no. 1.
BX1417.M5 .A84 2002
282'.7759—dc21

2002001423

© Steven M. Avella
2002

Co-published by Marquette University Press and the Archdiocese of Milwaukee

Table of Contents

To Archbishop Rembert G. Weakland, O.S.B.
Ninth Archbishop of Milwaukee, 1977–2002

Et cum haec feceritis, oculi mei super vos et aures meae ad preces vestras; et antequam me invocetis, dicam vobis: Ecce Adsum.
Quid dulcius nobis ab hac voce Domini invitantis nos, fratres carissimi?
Ecce pietate sua demonstrat nobis Dominus viam vitae.

—**Regula Monachorum**

And when you have done these things, my eyes will be upon you and my ears open unto your prayers. And before you call upon me, I shall say to you, "Lo, here I am."
What can be sweeter to us, dearest brethren, than this voice of our Lord inviting us?
Behold in his loving mercy the Lord showeth us the way of life.

—**The Rule of St. Benedict**

Abbreviations*

AAB: Archives of the Archdiocese of Baltimore, Baltimore, Md.
AAC: Archives of the Archdiocese of Chicago, Chicago, Ill.
AAM: Archives of the Archdiocese of Milwaukee, Milwaukee, Wi.
ACSA: Archives of the Congregation of Sisters of St. Agnes, Fond du Lac, Wi.
AOP/PA: Archives of Propaganda/Propaganda Archives, Rome, Italy
AOP-Racine: Archives of the Dominican Sisters of Racine, Racine, Wi.
AOP-Sin: Archives of the Dominican Sisters of Sinsinawa, Sinsinawa Mound, Wi.
AOSF: Archives of the Sisters of St. Francis, St. Francis, Wi.
ASAC: Archives of the Pallottine Fathers & Brothers
ASDS: M: Archives of the Salvatorian Fathers and Brothers, Milwaukee, Wi.
ASDS: W: Archives of the Sisters of the Divine Savior, Milwaukee, Wi.
ASND: Archives of the School Sisters of Notre Dame, Elm Grove, Wi.
ASSF: Archives of the School Sisters of St. Francis, Milwaukee, Wi.
ASV: Archivio Segreto Vaticano, Vatican City
ICCA: Italian Community Center Archives
MCHS: Milwaukee County Historical Society, Milwaukee, Wi.
MUA: Marquette University Archives
SCHRC: Sheboygan County Historical Research Center
SCHS: Sheboygan County Historical Society, Sheboygan, Wi.
SHSW: State Historical Society of Wisconsin, Madison, Wi.
SVdPSA: St. Vincent de Paul Society Archives

*Abbreviations are used in captions in square brackets, thus: [AAB]

Introduction

In the Richness of the Earth is the first effort to compile a comprehensive history of the Roman Catholic archdiocese of Milwaukee, Wisconsin. This ecclesiastical jurisdiction was officially created by the bull *In Suprema Militantis* issued by Pope Gregory XVI on November 28, 1843. Although the boundaries of the Milwaukee See have shifted over the course of time, the history of the archdiocese has been the history of the Catholic Church in Wisconsin.

The boundaries of an archdiocese are arbitrary lines imposed on an often complex social and physical environment. It is also a series of overlapping jurisdictions that continually interact with each other bringing the universal to the local and vice versa. An archdiocese, for example, is a subsidiary of the larger Roman Catholic communion which recognizes the Pope, the Bishop of Rome, as its spiritual leader. At the same time however, it is also a quasi-independent entity under the direction of a local bishop who commands his clergy, religious, laity and an array of spiritual institutions. A diocesan bishop administrates personnel and property, and his decisions directly affect the lives of thousands of men and women who live within his boundaries. Undergirding these visible, institutional features is its identity as a spiritual institution. In fact its juridical and institutional features serve primarily to propagate the spiritual values, teachings, and discipline of the Roman Catholic Church. It is the visible expression of the religious faith and identity of a significant number of people. It is a context for the religious experience of men and women.

The history of an archdiocese is also affected by national, state and local events. It exercises its specific functions under a particular set of circumstances. The Archdiocese of Milwaukee is part of the wider social, economic and political forces that have shaped the American Midwest. Its spiritual and temporal task have been directly affected by the development of the state of Wisconsin. Because of the nature of the sources, this account tends to focus more on the internal dynamics of Catholic life and development. But it also attempts to situate each epoch of Catholic life in the wider framework of Wisconsin history. It is on Wisconsin soil that Catholicism became visible.

The title of this book, *In the Richness of the Earth*, is taken from the motto selected by Archbishop Sebastian Messmer for the first official crest of the Archdiocese of Milwaukee. Messmer, who was a sincere, if not altogether successful, agent of archdiocesan unity, chose the symbols of Wisconsin's productivity, Lake Michigan, represented by fish, and the fertile Wisconsin soil, represented by sheaves of wheat to express visibly the deeper meaning of being a Catholic in Wisconsin. He chose the Latin motto *In Ubertate Terrae*—In the Richness of the Earth—to encapsulate the dynamic interchange between the proclamation of the Catholic faith and its acceptance by the people of Wisconsin. Messmer had a strong sense of the history of the local Church and his optimistic view of the progress of Catholicity was not without merit. Catholicism in Wisconsin had grown substantially in the years since the diocese of Milwaukee was created in 1843. By the time Messmer came to Milwaukee in 1904, a dense network of schools, churches, sisterhoods, a thriving seminary, health care and other social welfare institutions and a still vibrant set of ethnic subcultures gave witness to the richness of the Catholic presence, especially in the cities of Wisconsin, but also in its agricultural hinterlands.

Messmer understood the archdiocesan vision as a summons to greater efforts to evangelize and "Catholicize" Wisconsin. Social historians would perhaps be more comfortable stressing a language of "encounter" when speaking of the interaction of the Catholic Church and Wisconsin. Catholicism had and still has a "universal" character–its creed, cult and code are essentially the same throughout the world. But the Church of Rome has also learned to adapt to local social and spatial realities. Wisconsin's geography, climate, demographic and social composition, its economic and political life provided a prism through which the Catholic experience was refracted. This history is an effort to capture at least some of the various expressions of that experience.

In the Richness of the Earth stops deliberately at the end of Albert Meyer's brief episcopate in 1958. The reason for this demarcation is that the year 1959 not only brought a new archbishop, former Peoria Ordinary William E. Cousins, to Milwaukee, but it is also the year that Pope John XXIII made his first call for Vatican II. These events set in motion a whole new epoch of archdiocesan life and in my estimation the implications of these years have not matured sufficiently to offer much by way of perspective. Moreover, they also constitute an important part of my own personal experience and hence historical objectivity (never perfect when writing about any epoch of history) is even more difficult here.

Gathering all of these diverse threads into a comprehensive narrative has been a daunting task. Mindful of the original mandate given to be "inclusive" of as many aspects of the Wisconsin Catholic experience as possible, the account covers much ground. As the reader will note, sources are generally stronger for the institutional aspects of archdiocesan life. Other areas of the Catholic experience are not as well documented. The desire to include as many aspects of archdiocesan life and culture as possible also runs the risk of having the history sound like a mere cataloguing of events and persons such as compiler Henry Heming attempted with his massive *History of the Catholic Church in Wisconsin* (1888). There is an effort to include a lot of data, but often, the text then "samples" a particular person, place or event as a general example of larger trends. The use of pictures scattered throughout the text is intended to amplify and even extend the narrative.

The earliest portions of this history stand on the shoulders of the work of prior historians, especially Monsignor Peter Leo Johnson, longtime historian on the faculty of St. Francis Seminary, and Father Benjamin Blied, a minor seminary professor who used his personal fortune to self-publish a number of works that were of great help. Franciscan Sister of

Perpetual Adoration, M. Mileta Ludwig, who wrote an exhaustively researched biography of Archbishop Michael Heiss, also provided a great deal of solid information. A number of archdiocesan institutions and religious communities of men and women have written their stories. Some of these accounts are dated, but most of them are very good. Although my perspectives and emphases differ at times from these early giants of Wisconsin Catholic history, their contributions form a "firm foundation" for the remainder of this account. In addition, this text also incorporates some of the best new scholarship coming from the ranks of religious sisterhoods concerning the 19th century origins of their communities in Wisconsin. Some episodes, such as the Polish "Church War" have already been covered by capable scholars. This account draws heavily on their work as well.

The second half of the work (parts 3 and 4) represents my own original research in twentieth century archdiocesan Catholicism. My doctoral dissertation on the life and times of Cardinal Albert G. Meyer was my first foray into the world of archdiocesan history. Father Jerry Hauser, editor of the seminary quarterly *Salesianum* in the 1980s, allowed me to present nuggets of research on the pages of that magazine—a practice I consciously imitated from the example of Monsignor Peter Leo Johnson and Father Benjamin Blied. I wrote substantial histories of the Salvatorian Fathers and the Pallottines, as well as shorter encyclopedia pieces for the *American National Biography*, the *Encyclopedia of American Catholic History*, *Milwaukee History*, the *U. S. Catholic Historian*, and *Records.* Papers that I delivered at various conferences also found their way into this account. The archdiocesan sesquicentennial in 1993 offered a good opportunity for a gathering of materials. I was called on to give presentations to various groups in the archdiocese: priests, Catholic educators, musicians, and women's groups. This plunged me into records and documents that covered a wide array of topics. During my years on the faculty at St. Francis Seminary and at Marquette University, various of my students did original research and wrote papers worthy of mention. These include works by Francis X. Malloy, Debra Honore, Donald Hying, Michael Petrie, Jerome Herda, Charles Gallagher, Michael Jacobs and the late Henry Mueller. They followed a generation of St. Francis and Marquette scholars who produced similar works for professors of another generation in the form of bachelor's, master and Ph.D. theses. Other student research assistants at Marquette include Sherry Knutson, James Bohl, Paula Dicks, Edward Schmit, Gretchen Cochrane, Catherine Sanders, Amy Bedford, Gayle Kiszely, and Stephanie Ferguson.

Dating back to the time of my original doctoral research, I managed to interview a number of important players in the history of Milwaukee Catholicism, some of whom have returned to the Maker of All Things. These included: Bishops Leo Brust, John Grellinger, and Cletus F. O'Donnell; Monsignors Joseph Emmenegger, Joseph Holleran, and Vernon Kuehn; Fathers Mark Lyons and Fran Eschweiler; Franciscan Sisters Patrice

McNamara and Frederick Lochemes were most helpful as well. Among the living include Monsignor John Donovan and Fathers John M. Murphy, Paul Esser, and Robert Skeris. Mr. Eugene Bleidorn and Mary Agnes Blonien provided critical information about the origins of lay movements in Milwaukee. Racine Dominican Sister Suzanne Noffke gave me a tutorial on her research about the origins of her community in America.

Indispensable to the completion of the work has been the unlimited access to materials given me by Archbishop Rembert G. Weakland, O.S.B., and Chancellors Ralph Gross and Barbara Anne Cusack. My researches in the Milwaukee archives are or ought to be the envy of my colleagues in the historical field. Access was complete and generous. Archbishop Weakland, like many other enlightened prelates past and present, believes in the dictum of Pope Leo XIII, "the church has nothing to fear from the truth." For his trust, and the trust of the archdiocese, I am deeply grateful.

Implementing the archbishop's will has been one of the best archivists I have ever had the privilege of working with, Timothy Cary. Appointed in 1987 as the first professional archivist of the archdiocese, Tim built on the work of Fathers Robert Sampon and Thomas Fait in gathering and organizing the huge documentary record of the Archdiocese of Milwaukee. He has been a support, a friend, and a research assistant. Words cannot express the gratitude and affection I feel for him and without him this work would never have been completed. Milwaukee's archives are the best source of information about the archdiocese. Especially helpful was the complete microfilm run of the various archdiocesan newspapers which helped provide a skeleton for the basic narrative. Documentary sources include a considerable number of letters of archbishops Henni, Heiss, Katzer, Messmer, Stritch, Kiley, and Meyer as well as the files of institutions, parishes, and deceased priests. On top of this the archdiocese has an excellent iconographic collection which details many interesting aspects of church life.

Other archives and archivists have supplemented the work with documents and pictures. Sister Marjorie Buttner and her staff at the Archives of the Sinsinawa Dominicans was the soul of helpfulness. Sister Suzanne Renee Sobczynski of the Notre Dame archives worked me into her busy schedule. Sister Connie Halbur and Sister Corrine Dais of the School Sisters of St. Francis were always generous with their time, as was the curator of their extensive photo collection Sister Luan Noecker. Sister Jeremy Quinn of the Agnesians, Sister Aquin Gilles of the Salvatorians, Amy Levinthal of the Sisters of Mercy, Matthew Blessing, Susan Stawicki-Vrobel and Phil Runkel of the Marquette University archives, Father James Wolf of the Capuchin Archives, and Abbot Edmund Boyce of the Benedictines of St. Benedict's Abbey all provided important records and photos. Earlier research projects brought me to the archives of the Diocese of Superior, Green Bay, and the Archdioceses of Chicago, Cincinnati and Baltimore. I discovered a particularly rich treasure trove of materials during a 1993 research trip to the Secret Vatican Archives. Other archival collections consulted included the Milwaukee County Historical Association, the State Historical Society of Wisconsin, and the Marquette University Archives. My priest-brothers Father Michael Petrie and Father Kevin Wester gladly shared their knowledge of "remote" areas of archdiocesan life and introduced me to the beauties of the Catholic presence in the Fond du Lac/Washington County "Holy Land." They also shared their magnificent picture collections for this work.

The only archives I was not permitted to consult were the records of the Diocese of Madison. A frustrating turn of events had excluded me from using these documents when I was working on a history of the Pallottine community. Letters of inquiry about the reasons for this were directed to the highest authorities of the diocese, but went unanswered. Fortunately the secretaries of the various Madison parishes were good enough to send on whatever materials they had at hand, and Monsignor Daniel Ganshert of St. Raphael's Cathedral was quite helpful in providing information about his church. Other sources about Catholicism in Madison had to be derived from newspapers and other ancillary sources. If the material on Madison is not as rich as it could have been, it is not due to a lack of effort.

Drafts of the text were read and commented on by Mr. Leon Unruh, a journalist in the employ of the McClatchy Newspapers in Alaska. In addition Fathers John Michael Murphy, Thomas Fait, and Donald Hying, along with Dr. Jack Augenstein, read the text. My ever-generous colleague, John Buenker of the University of Wisconsin-Parkside also set aside time from his sabbatical to read and comment. These good men accepted this massive draft without flinching (although they no doubt privately cursed themselves for agreeing to be readers). I am deeply grateful to them for preserving me from grammatical and factual errors. My dear friend, Susan Silva, volunteered to do the proofreading for the final draft. Like the other readers, her name is blessed. The remaining mistakes are, of course, mine.

The Archdiocese of Milwaukee has been generous in their support of this project. They have supplied financial and travel support for the research. They have released Tim Cary from a portion of his duties so that he could tend to helping me complete this project. Marquette University allowed me two sabbaticals that gave me important time and research assistants to work on this book. My chairman, Dr. Lance Grahn was understanding about arranging my class schedule to maximize my research and writing time. Jerry Topczewski, archdiocesan director of communications, took hold of the production end of the project in its final phases. Andrew Tallon, my colleague at Marquette University and the head of the University Press, has done a superb job in bringing this book to print.

Of the revelation of Christ, the evangelist John tells us, there are many things he did not record, because if he did "there would not be room enough in the whole world to hold the books to contain them." The history of the Archdiocese of Milwaukee cannot make quite the same theological claims. Yet there are many more things that this history could relate and much more sense could be made of the general sweep of its history than I have time, pages or basic talent to do. Many of my colleagues in the field of American Catholic history have long abandoned the genre of diocesan history, claiming that earlier works reflected a rather narrow "institutional" view of the church long since superceded by the ecclesiologies of Vatican II. Cultural historians find the medley of religious experiences far too numerous to describe and link together in some sort of coherent narrative. The few historians who have written superb diocesan histories in this new historiographical climate such as Leslie Woodcock Tentler's history of Detroit or Brother Thomas Spalding's account of the Archdiocese of Baltimore, are scholars of exceptional talents—head and shoulders above many of us in the field.

I frankly admit that after I accepted the task of writing this book from Archbishop Weakland I had a severe case of "buyer's remorse." The wealth of the material and the insistence on inclusivity brought my talents to their frontier early on. As time went by, occasional queries about the progress of the book came from interested parties, lay and clerical, many of whom had a genuine interest in history. Occasionally there were those who claimed expertise in research and writing and wondered why the history couldn't just be "popped out." These queries received the attention they deserved.

Gentle hints from Milwaukee's gentlemanly auxiliary bishop, Richard Sklba, in the form of gifts of other diocesan histories sent to him by his episcopal colleagues, provoked bouts of anxiety. Even Archbishop Weakland wondered publicly when this book would be done. Since a word given to the archbishop could not easily be retracted, I decided to adopt presidential candidate Ross Perot's solution to ending the federal deficit, and "just do it." The result is this book.

With all of this lengthy apologia, I submit this work to you, gentle reader, imperfect as it is, realizing that there is far more to this history than I have researched and written. Like all tasks that require discipline and patience, the writing of this book will hopefully produce virtues that will overcome my other defects of character. If I have one lingering regret in this work, it was that I could never really climb like Moses to the top of the historian's Mount Pisgah and see the panorama of the historical Promised Land. What follows is in many cases, boilerplate, a first draft, a gathering of sources and episodes that certainly has more nuances and interconnections than I was able to see. I was in the forest far too long to see the trees. Perhaps future generations will see more than I saw in doing all this. May that future Joshua "bring the people into their heritage."

Steven M. Avella
November 28, 2001

Part I
Becoming Visible
1843–1868

The Catholic Counter Reformation created the nexus of forces that gave birth to Catholic life in Wisconsin. In part, this sweeping movement was a response to the challenges posed by the Protestant reformers in the 16th century. It prompted a doctrinal sharpening that retooled the truths of Catholicism for combat, intellectual and spiritual. However, the rejuvenation of Catholic life was not only a reaction. Catholicism was also caught up in a more far-ranging renewal impulse that had been building since the end of the Middle Ages. The new energies released by the forces of internal reform found outlets in new religious communities, more effective episcopal leadership, a rejuvenated clerical life, and lay devotionalism. It also took visible form in the glories and excesses of baroque art and architecture.[1] The Council of Trent (1545-1563), which ratified and codified many of these reforming impulses, also imposed a stricter organizational unity on Catholic life. Diocesan structures and leadership were strengthened during this period. Likewise, the parish church and the Mass were accentuated as the centering points of Catholic life. Although the full implementation of Trent's decrees took several generations, these structures were intended to provide a new unity which restored confidence to a Catholic Church reeling from the challenges of the Protestant reformers.[2]

The epicenter of Catholic identity was Rome. Since Medieval times, Roman pontiffs had played a decisive role in the unfolding of life, law, governance, and culture in the west. However, the Catholic Reformation reinforced the image of the Eternal City as the "hub of Christendom" and the touchstone for Catholic identity. Further, to project Catholic influence far and wide, it reaffirmed the dimension of Catholic identity that the Reformers had denied and stripped away as they purged churches of their "Romish" visibility. Catholicism's presence in the world was to be deliberately, even at times garishly, visible. Catholicism was a religion that took the Incarnation quite seriously. To be Catholic was to believe that the world of creation

The first Chapter of the 25th Council of Trent, Venetian School, c. 1630 by Italian School (17th century). PFA83066 [Phillips, *The International Fine Art Auctioneers*, UK/Bridgeman Art Library]

was the chief vehicle of divine revelation. In the *Credo* sung at every High Mass, priests and people knelt in homage at the words *et homo factus est* (and the Word became flesh). Not only did they reaffirm their belief in the doctrine of the Incarnation: they proclaimed with their entire body the ongoing reality of God's embrace of the world. Wherever the Catholic faith went, it was to be visible.

The desire to spread the Catholic faith and to make it visible in all places took as its scriptural warrant of Matthew 28:19-20: *Euntes ergo docete* (Go ye therefore and make disciples of all nations). But the impulse of missionary activity was far more complex. There existed already in the DNA of Catholic life a cultural legacy derived in part from Christianity's absorption of the culture of Imperial Rome. Like the great Empire whose roads stretched from the Eternal City to the distant corners of the world, so too the Roman Church was destined to spread its influence to the farthest corners of the earth. Although the corporate energy to fulfill this genetic inheritance ebbed and flowed throughout the life of the church, in fact no one doubted that Christianity was of its very nature missionary. When the new power of Catholic Reformation ideology hit the turbines of Catholic life and action, a new burst of energy and creativity resulted that recreated the Catholic presence in new places and times, even to Wisconsin.

As historian Kenneth Scott Latourette observed, "Religious revival coincided with geographic discoveries, political conquests, and the subjugation and exploitation of the native races of America."[3] Indeed, the desire to move, expand and grow was also fueled by revolutionary changes in commerce, transportation technology, and the rising force of nationalism. Western civilization itself had no hesitation about spreading itself far and wide and recreating its culture in strange new lands. If the trader sought new markets and the conquistador new conquests for national glory, Catholicism demanded that all know Christ and submit to the teachings of his visible church. This missionary impulse was the cutting edge for much church activity between the 15th and 20th centuries.[4] In the 16th century, colleges and centers for the training of missionaries were opening up all over Rome. On Epiphany in 1622, by the bull *Inscrutabili divinae providentiae arcano*, Pope Gregory XV established the *Sacra Congregatione Propaganda Fidei* (Sacred Congregation for the Propagation of the Faith). Known throughout history simply as "Propaganda," this office of the Roman curia (papal bureaucracy) made sure that missionary expansion remained under Roman control. This office maintained oversight of the church in the United States (especially the selection of bishops) until 1908. In 1627, Pope Urban VIII created a special missionary training college near the Spanish steps.[5] Seminarians from all over the world came to this center for priestly formation. Milwaukee would one day attend classes in the *Propaganda* college.

Entering and Encountering a New World

Catholic expansion shared in the nationally inspired voyages of encounter and exploration of the Western hemisphere that began in earnest in the 15th century. Spanish and Portuguese navigators claimed much of the Caribbean and Central and South America for their nations and the Catholic Church. Spain's colonial policy reflected better than most the symbiosis of national gain and glory with the demands for aggressive, visible Catholic proselytization. The Catholic Reformation's most fascinating historical artifacts are the remains of this Iberian Catholicism transplanted, modified, and reinterpreted visibly on American soil.[6] Catholic clerics accompanied voyagers and deployed a number of strategies to convert native inhabitants. They built visible institutions to reflect theological, social and economic priorities. Great Cathedrals, distinctive religious art, devotions that syncretized Indian religious systems with Christian icons, adobe missions and brown robed padres—all these constituted the visible inheritance of the transplanted Catholic faith. The legacy of their spiritual conquest has been revisited often in the historiographical debates of the 20th century.[7] Missionaries brought disease, cultural disruption, and intolerance as they strove to plant the gospel, erect churches and schools, and bring "stability" to the lives of the Indians. They also at times shielded native inhabitants from the worst depredations of soldiers and colonial administrators, provided tools and clothing that genuinely improved the quality of life and showed Indians more effective uses of the lands they possessed. The legacy of exchange was and is bitter fruit to some. To others it represents the triumph of truth. It remains a complex and diverse reality that defies easy generalization.

France followed Spain in these paths. Eager too for colonial spoils, a pathway to the

A missionary in America [Richard Brennan. *A Church History,* Benziger Brothers, 1881, p. 68]

riches of Asia and an active role in the geo-politics of 16th and 17th century Western Europe, France sent colonists and developers to tap the new sources of furs and pelts that abounded in the St. Lawrence River Valley and in the vast North American hinterland.[8] As in the case of Spain, the Catholic Reformation inspired zealous missionaries committed to a gospel of visibility. The French Catholics were perhaps even more zealous and sharp-edged because of the internal struggles in France with Calvinists (Huguenots) and other "reforming pests" from nearby Switzerland and beyond the Rhine. The missionaries accompanied the forces of commercial exploitation and plunged into the ever-expanding fur trading frontier that would for a time be called New France. The worldview of these missionaries (allowing for the Gallic interpretation of Counter Reformation decrees and the shifting geo-politics of early modern times which occasionally put the pope at loggerheads with the French monarchy) was essentially the same as the Spanish: doctrinal clarity, spiritual rejuvenation, and visibility.[9] Indeed being present physically was the crucible of effective spiritual presence. It is significant that their first acts were to enhance the visible presence of the church among the native peoples. They constructed lean-to chapels into which they transported altar vessels, prayer cards and liturgical books. Even the vesture of the clerics themselves—the blackrobes—became the emblem of Catholic presence and identity.

The hallmarks of this visibility would often be the mere replication of European forms and standards on the new soils. European-style cathedrals and seminaries were to be found in New Spain and New France. But this impulse toward visibility also had built into it a certain degree of flexibility. Visibility took the shape and form of local customs and conditions. The Catholic presence drew on the local environment and the folkways of the people. It both shaped and was shaped by the new environment. The history of Catholicism in Wisconsin reflected this dialectic of encounter, transformation, and synthesis, creating yet again and again a visible church in a continually changing physical, social, economic and cultural environment.

Catholic life in Wisconsin naturally corresponded to the contours of physical and human geography. The lands of Wisconsin were affected by ancient glaciers that contoured the land, knocking down mountains and leaving gentle hills and fertile soils. As its land form settled, it nestled within the right-angle embrace of two of the great inland seas, Lakes Michigan and Superior. Both lakes would prove a vital source of the state's earliest development. The last state of the Old Northwest was heavily forested, with an ample supply of water and, south of the axis formed by the Fox and Wisconsin Rivers, a rich farming land. Deposits of lead in the southwestern corner of the state would set off one of the first mining rushes in U. S. history.

Human forces interacting with the land began with the tribes of American Indians:

Winnebagoes, Menominee, Potawatomi, Chippewa were among the original inhabitants. Later relocations of tribes like the Stockbridge and the Oneida created localized Indian cultures. Each of these tribal groups developed their own religious systems: their cosmogonies, creation and flood stories, stories about spirits and the life beyond and various rituals to accompany important transitions in life.

Catholic life in New France began in 1615 when French explorer Samuel de Champlain brought the Franciscan Recollects to establish mission outposts. The demands of the frontiers brought an invitation to the Society of Jesus in 1625. By 1632, responsibility for the entire Catholic presence in New France had been given to the Jesuits, and this included the future state of Wisconsin.[10] The fur trading frontier brought merchants and trappers of New France into Wisconsin with Jean Nicolet in 1634.[11] Following in their wake were the Jesuits who devoted themselves to conversion of the Indians and maintaining the religious loyalty of the handful of French trappers and traders. In 1660, Jesuit René Menard was the first missionary to establish Catholic visibility in the areas later known as Wisconsin. He helped to set up rugged outposts on the shore of Lake Superior and Green Bay. Later, when he disappeared into the wilderness attempting to reach a starving Huron tribe in Black River, all that was left of the Catholic presence were bits of his tattered blackrobe.[12] In 1665 another Jesuit, Claude Allouez, arrived in Chequamegon (near present-day Ashland)

A Menomonee Indian Village [Susan Burdick Davis. *Wisconsin Lore for Boys and Girls*, p. 80]

and eventually settled in Green Bay in 1669, founding missions there and along the Fox River.[13] The Jesuits soon settled on the trading post of Sault Ste. Marie as a central headquarters and used it as a staging-base for future penetration of the Wisconsin wilderness. Father Claude Dablon arrived in 1669 to head the mission.

In 1673, French Jesuit Jacques Marquette left the Sault Ste. Marie base to accompany explorer Louis Jolliet along the Fox and Wisconsin Rivers (with a transfer at Portage) to

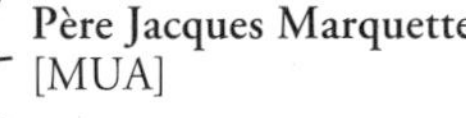

Père Jacques Marquette [MUA]

the Mississippi. Marquette and his band traveled as far as the mouth of the Arkansas River before turning back north. The following year Marquette left on his last missionary journey, and on the way to preach to the Illinois Indians he put ashore for a time on its banks in the heart of where a large city would arise. Here he probably celebrated Mass.[14] Plying the inland streams of Wisconsin with the voyageurs and setting up camp with them, came a cavalcade of Jesuit missionaries. These early Jesuits framed the first, if ultimately ephemeral, reality of Catholic visibility in Wisconsin. Missionary outposts at Sault Ste. Marie, La Pointe, and Green Bay provided an organizational framework for Catholic evangelical activities. The visibility of Catholicism in early Wisconsin provided glimpses of efforts at native evangelization and the first reports of the land, people and the prospects for the church. As noted earlier, the Jesuits dominated the missionary field. But other religious orders, including the Franciscan Recollects represented by Father Louis Hennepin, contributed their part to the Christianization of Wisconsin. The missionaries also provided some of the first important information about the geography and topography of the state as well as records of the lives of the early inhabitants.

Ultimately, however, this first wave of Catholic life in Wisconsin faded as New France's claims to the American interior were ended by the British victory on the Plains of Abraham in 1761 during the Seven Years War. This defeat pushed French social and cultural institutions back to the old Canadian cities of Quebec and Montreal and undercut institutional support for missions. The suppression of the Jesuits in 1773, an event that had many ramifications for Catholic life and development in America, added an additional death blow to the once promising French outposts in Wisconsin. The last Jesuit in the region, Peter Potier, valiantly remained at his post until his death in 1781, eight years after the Society of Jesus had been suppressed.

The era of French dominance in early Wisconsin left its imprint on the state's own understanding of itself, and Catholic history must take account of it. Indeed, French Catholicism shaped the character of Catholic life in certain Wisconsin localities for many years after the French were banished by Britain. Green Bay, De Pere, Milwaukee, Fond du Lac and Prairie du Chien as well as scattered settlements in Door County and elsewhere all continued to have French Catholic populations sizeable enough to merit parishes and local clergy. The remnants of French Catholic life are found in old churches like St. Louis in Fond du Lac or in the ministry of the French-speaking Oblates of Mary Immaculate in Door County.

But French Catholicism's impact on Wisconsin's life and culture is best assessed by evaluating its impact on the reconstruction of the state's past. Indeed, while the accomplishments of the French missionaries, along with the traders and voyageurs, were real, the memories of them have taken on a romantic luster that more reflects the needs of late 19th century historians and "myth-makers" than the fruits of serious scholarship. During the

19th century, Wisconsin, like many other states, drew from historic images of the past to create a founding myth that accentuated the state's "antiquity." The French presence, marked by names like René Menard and Claude Dablon, and places like Green Bay, La Pointe, Prairie du Chien, and Butte des Mortes became an important part of Wisconsin's heroic past. Wisconsinites of all denominations came to cherish and revere the doughty "blackrobes" in much the same way that Californians embraced the Franciscan padres and rebuilt the missions they had once staffed.[15] When the old U. S. House of Representatives chamber was transformed into a statuary hall, and states were invited to send a statue of their most prominent citizen, Wisconsin, like California (who selected Franciscan Junipero Serra), chose an ancient missionary, Father Jacques Marquette, to represent itself. State Catholics were naturally supportive of this. However, although the process of finally getting sculptor Gaetano Trentanove's "Père Jacques Marquette" to the national capital was arduous (it took 17 years of effort), the initial decision to include Marquette won approval from Wisconsinites of all denominations as "an appropriate symbol of the courage and resourcefulness of the state's early pioneers."[16] When all is said and done, however, French Catholicism played a comparatively small role in defining Wisconsin's Catholic life and identity. After the withdrawal of France, Catholic life was carried on only by a handful of French trader families like the Langlades, the Vieaus, the Grignons, and the Juneaus as well as Catholicized Indians. These groups kept the embers of Catholicism alive until a new wave of settlers would cause it to burst into flame once again.

Louis Grignon and his family were typical of the French Canadian Catholics that inhabited Green Bay. Grignon was the grandson of Charles de Langlade who was among the founders of the Green Bay settlement in 1745. Louis's father, Pierre Grignon, had been one of those who kept the embers of Catholicism glowing for his children. Missionary Florimond Bonduel noted that Catholics of Green Bay "lived sometimes ten, twenty, and thirty years without seeing a priest." But he found that Catholicism was still alive because, "Certain pious persons had, however, taken particular pains to instruct their children in Christian doctrine."[17] Louis had learned well from his father and went on to a successful career. He married several times, had a very large family and inherited the prosperous fur trade from his grandfather. The Louis Grignon home became a place of culture and perpetuated Catholic life and tradition through a "home religion."

The Grignons taught their children the Creed and the commandments. They also used the festivals of the liturgical year as a framework for family life. From Christmas to Ash Wednesday, one historian observes, Green Bay was "rife with feasting, dancing, and merry-making." Once Lent began, "festivity ceased and was suspended until Easter." During Advent, it was the custom of the Grignons and other French Catholics to gather once a week at a home and sing hymns "to praise the Lord." On New Year's Day, the family gathered at the home of Grignon's mother, Madame Langevin, for a prayer service and a supper. Madame Langevin presided at funeral services, having the mortal remains of a deceased person brought to her house for prayer and accompanying it to the place of burial.[18] So strong was the religious character of this family that two daughters served the church: Elizabeth Grignon as a lay catechist and Ursule Grignon as a nun. Although priests would eventually make the parish and the weekly Eucharist the center and touchstone of Catholic life, families like the Grignons reflected the persistence of a pre-Catholic Reformation religious identity that made the home and the extended family the chief locus of religious life.

The Return of Visibility

Although various priests remained in the territory, Catholicism as a visible presence in the region slowly evaporated with the expulsion of the French Jesuits. Green Bay and Prairie du Chien remained as remote trading outposts with some nominal Catholics.[19] The geopolitics of Wisconsin were largely quiet until the American Revolution when the trans-Allegheny frontier was wrested from British hands. The fur-trading frontier had never really ceased and British and American merchants squabbled over the acquisition and sale of the still abundant peltry in the rivers and streams of the interior waterways.

It would require many years for actual American sovereignty to be established in the Old Northwest. Through conflicts and treaties with the native peoples, lands along the Ohio Valley and the upper Great Lakes gradually fell into United States control. Land fever seized the American spirit with malarial intensity. In the great drive to subdue the vast American wilderness, the real movers and shakers were not the buckskinned explorers and flannel-shirted miners, but the well-dressed real estate speculators and those to whom they sold a piece of the land. Even in the relatively mild form of governance the early United States chose for its first organic law (the Articles of Confederation), one of

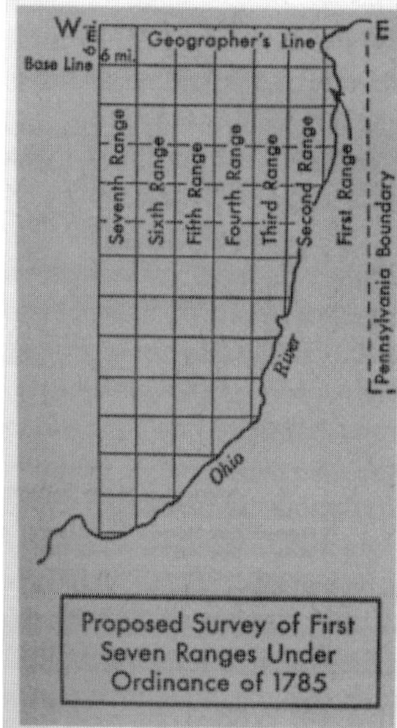

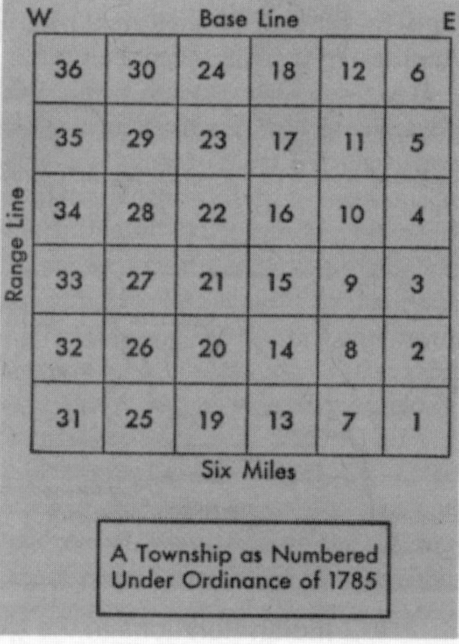

Northwest Ordinance, Township & Range System [Ray Allen Billington. *Westward Expansion,* Macmillan Pub. Co. 1974, p. 205]

the few things the independent minded former colonies could agree on was the need to regularize and order land ownership and to arrange for the orderly integration of rapidly filling lands into the federal union. The Land Ordinance of 1785 imposed a relentless grid-iron template on the vast land of the Old Northwest. Americans were unwilling to tolerate colonies on their borders, and the Northwest Ordinance of 1787 provided a phased-in program for the integration of new lands and peoples into the growing American union of states. Later, the federal constitution of 1789 defined with greater specificity the relationship between a state and the federal government. In these formulations, the lands that would become the state of Wisconsin were considered to be part of the Northwest—and America's frontier.

It was a professor at the University of Wisconsin, Frederick Jackson Turner, who pointed to the significance of the West, especially the availability of vast amounts of land, as a defining feature of American life. While many today quibble with his arguments and conclusions, Turner's thought-provoking words have led American historians in all fields to assess the impact of the physical and social environment on the various people and institutions that have moved into America's varying "Wests." Likewise, the lure of the West is also an important factor in assessing the development of the United States. The West was always more than a physical location; it was a projection of the deepest dreams and aspirations of Americans. It was a place to advance and prosper, to succeed and to fail; it was the repository of the limitless dreams that came to make up the ethos of American life in the 19th century. Wisconsin was once on the cutting edge of this "westering" drive—its lakefront, farm and forest lands, its mineral deposits, and inland waters were all seen as focal points for development and personal and social advance. Everyone who came to Wisconsin bought into this dream—and this included church members who sometimes were the greatest boosters of the rolling lands, the "salubrious" climate and the sparking waters of the territory lying west of Lake Michigan.

Connecting the development of Catholic life with the special conditions on the ever-shifting American frontier is a task historians are only beginning to undertake.[20] To be sure, the Catholic Church was not immune from the social and intellectual forces that shaped the rest of a nation that was moving steadily west. For the Catholic Church, the lure of the West simply added fuel to its already well-established expansionist impulses. With new settlements, cities, farms and industries, came churches, schools and social welfare institutions. Catholic visibility fit harmoniously into the expansive "westering" of the American people.

Wanting more land was fueled by important technological breakthroughs. First, came the construction of canals that connected the inland waterways with the vast Great Lakes and all of them to ocean trade. The opening of the Erie Canal in 1825 had a powerful impact on American life and economic vitality, and opened the Great Lakes to new waves of development. The development of steam-powered vessels that could ply the inland waters created a boom. Later, another steam driven mode of transportation, the railroad, superceded the ditch-like water ways, the rough plank roads and the overland trails, and even the lake and river traffic, further accelerating population growth and commercial activity. Land hunger compelled changes in the economy as more and more people demanded more surveyed lands. The areas of the Old Northwest, the lands north of the Ohio River, soon filled up. Each of them soon became a state: Ohio, 1803; Indiana, 1816; Illinois, 1818; and Michigan, 1837.[21] All that was left was Wisconsin.

Fort Winnebago in 1834
[Henry C. Campbell. *Wisconsin in Three Centuries,* Century History Co. 1906]

Land hunger created the state of Wisconsin.[22] Renewed interest in the region was evidenced by the placement of federal forts at the two terminal points along the Fox/Wisconsin axis, Green Bay's Fort Howard and Prairie du Chien's Fort Crawford. At the portage between the two rivers, Fort Atkinson provided protection and stability to a frontier about to burst into growth. These outposts provided some stimulus for the forces of organized religion, and were convenient gathering places for traveling missionaries. However, interest in Wisconsin was fairly minimal until the existence of lead deposits in the southwestern portion of the territory became widely known.[23] The existence of lead ore had been known for a long time and had been exploited by early settlers like Julien Dubuque as early as 1788. The increasing need for lead for paint, printer's type and bullets created a huge demand. Wisconsin was the largest lead producer in the nation. Beginning in the 1820s, a major rush brought scores of miners

Shot tower at a lead mine Old Helena, 1836
[Henry C. Campbell. *Wisconsin in Three Centuries,* Century History Co. 1906]

and their families to the region. Towns such as New Diggings, Hardscrabble (Hazel Green), Benton, Gratiot Grove, Shullsburg, Platteville, Mineral Point, Dodgeville and Potosi were created by the lead rush. The mining frontier brought scores of Cornish immigrants to Wisconsin, many of them having mining skills from their native England. It also brought large numbers of Irish immigrants as the great migration from Ireland began.[24] Each of these groups replicated the distinct social and cultural institutions of their homelands—including their churches.

However, by 1829, the main bulk of the lead rush was over, and miners either left the region or settled into the cheap and fertile farming lands around Wisconsin. The rapid influx of white people in mining rushes set off tensions with the Indian tribes living in Wisconsin. Difficulties over land claims and other disagreements led to the Blackhawk War in 1832.[25] By 1833, virtually all the land south of the Fox/Wisconsin axis had been swept clear of Indian titles. In 1836, Wisconsin had enough white residents to be declared a territory of the United States, beginning its process of assimilation into the Union and regularizing its laws, landholding and civic life. The creation of the Wisconsin Territory with Governor Henry Dodge as the first governor commenced the second act of Catholic visibility in Wisconsin, which came through a new wave of missionary activity, launched not from far-off France or Quebec, but from the contiguous states of the Old Northwest that had matured sufficiently to be able to develop economic and social interests in adjoining lands. This new phase of the Catholic presence did not build on distant memories of a Catholic culture across the ocean. By this time the Catholic Church in America was a settled institution with a record of creating its place in the sometimes precarious but always receptive American environment.

Bishop John Carroll, first bishop in the United States
[AAB]

The Return of Visibility: Organizational Structures

Catholics kept pace with the rapid development of the new nation with the establishment of the first diocese in 1789 at Baltimore headed by a former Jesuit, John Carroll.[26] The first boundaries of his Baltimore See stretched from the Atlantic Ocean to the inland empire bounded by the River Mississippi. What would become Wisconsin years later was first under his ecclesiastical control, but there was little he could do to oversee it (and there were relatively few Catholics living in the region). Even though Carroll never visited Wisconsin, his actions in establishing Catholic visibility within his immediate sphere of influence along the Eastern seaboard provided the model for future bishops who were charged with creating dioceses. Carroll's priority was the Catholic Reformation mandate to build parish churches and staff them with priests. Likewise, the need to create a centrally directed and unified diocesan structure led him to value the establishment of an indigenous clergy. By a stroke of good luck, Carroll secured the services of the Sulpicians who established a seminary in his new diocese.[27] Likewise, to feed the seminary, he also brought into being other educational institutions that helped shape a unified Catholic community.[28] Carroll's institutional accomplishments provided a role model for subsequent "missionary" bishops sent to other areas of the hinterland to create new dioceses out of scattered population centers. A cathedral, a seminary, a "college" (a boys boarding school), the importation of religious sisterhoods and later a native clergy—these were the main components of diocesan formation and would serve as models for other dioceses.

Bishop Benedict Flaget of Bardstown Kentucky [Martin Marty, OSB. *Dr. John Martin Henni, First Bishop and Archbishop of Milwaukee,* Benziger Bros., 1888, p. 43]

Superimposed on the map of the American Republic was a rapidly growing array of emerging jurisdictions: dioceses and archdioceses split off from the vast territories of the original Baltimore See. Wisconsin changed hands several times. In 1805 the first diocese west of the Appalachians was erected at Bardstown, Kentucky, and was given to a long-lived Sulpician missionary, Benedict Joseph Flaget. However, the vast distances between Bardstown and the handful of Catholics on the Wisconsin frontier meant that there was little done by way of church organization.[29] In 1821, a new diocese erected in Cincinnati assumed control over the lands that would become the states of Michigan and Wisconsin.[30] Also in 1821, the legendary Michigan Sulpician, Gabriel Richard, visited the old Catholic center of Green Bay and began a church there. Earlier, in 1817, Marie Joseph Dunand, a Trappist from Moncks Mound near St. Louis visited Prairie du Chien and organized St. Gabriel's Church for the French Canadian residents of the tiny village.[31] In 1825, Father Vincent Badin, a priest of Detroit, arrived in Green Bay and completed the church, which served about 60 congregants. Two years later; Badin also visited Prairie du Chien where he baptized inhabitants and erected a small log chapel. In these villages Badin found a combination of French Canadian and mixed Indian/French settlers (métis) who had maintained their Catholic faith.

A Religious Revival and Interdenominational Rivalry on the Frontier

The renewal of Catholic visibility in Wisconsin was also a result of the revival of Catholic life and presence in Europe in the 19th century.[32] After the end of the Napoleonic Wars in 1815 and the shifting politics of an ill-fated effort at a pre-revolutionary restoration, there emerged a strong resurgence of interest in the Catholic Church and an expansion of its presence and influence in Western Europe. Part of this was fired by the forces that created the Romantic movement in literature and general culture. The "medievalism" of Catholic life and church architecture caught the fancy of many in the 19th century. Moreover, clashes between church leaders and liberals (many of whom were quite anticlerical and eager to exclude religion from social and political influence) produced an equally strong Catholic backlash that quickened church life all over Europe. New religious congregations devoted to charity, religious education, and service in foreign missions arose at this time. Many of the priests and sisters who would come to Wisconsin were caught up in this European religious revival. The perennial appeal of Catholic symbols, the clarity of doctrine, and the clear lines of hierarchical authority inspired many. Parish life flourished as well. Internal motivation was high. But there were other factors as well. Two important features of this revival that had a direct bearing on the Catholic church in Wisconsin were the revival of missionary efforts and the rejuvenation of Catholic life in the German-speaking areas of Western Europe.

Thousands of European and American Catholics read René de Chateaubriand's *Le Génie du Christianisme* (1802) and heard his eloquent appeal for the church to rouse itself against the rationalism of the Enlightenment era and linked a revived Christianity with an increase in missionary activity. New religious orders dedicated to mission work began to develop in France and elsewhere, and French clerics, like Benedict Joseph Flaget, came to America riding the tide of this new interest in missions. French Catholics also began to raise money for the propagation and support of missions. In Lyons, the Association for the Spreading of the Faith was formed in 1822. It collected money from members, and pledges of prayer and spiritual support, and directed them toward missionaries. American bishops would beat a path to the Lyons offices of this organization. In 1814, the Jesuit Order, suppressed in 1769, was formally reinstated, thereby releasing a new burst of energy into missionary work. In 1831, a former head of the Propaganda Fidei, Cardinal Mauro

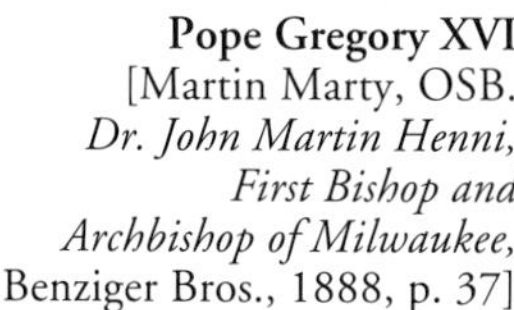

Pope Gregory XVI
[Martin Marty, OSB. *Dr. John Martin Henni, First Bishop and Archbishop of Milwaukee,* Benziger Bros., 1888, p. 37]

Cappellari, was elected Pope Gregory XVI. Deeply interested in the missions because of his previous work, he brought the full prestige of the papacy behind the efforts to expand Catholic life to the farthest corners of the world. It would be Cappellari who would be a source of personal inspiration to men like John Martin Henni, Martin Kundig, and Samuel Mazzuchelli. He would officially establish the Diocese of Milwaukee in 1843. The increasing interest in the missions and the willingness of so many men and women to abandon their homes and families to establish the church on the "rim of Christendom"—be that Africa, China, Oceania, or the Americas—is understandable against the backdrop of this wider revival.[33]

The 19th century revival also had its own peculiar regional manifestations. Elements of a quickened pace of Catholic life were found in the building of churches, the increases of vocations in seminaries, convents, and monasteries, and a surge in popular devotional activity. In the German-speaking areas of Europe (Germany as a geopolitical entity did not exist until 1871) the forces of Romanticism were in full flower by the early to mid-19th century. Specifically, the "rediscovery" and renewed appreciation of the Middle Ages led to a rebirth of interest in the Catholic Church, especially its legacy of art, music, and architecture. Just as importantly, Christians of all denominations rose in a common reaction against the excessive rationalism and aridity of the Enlightenment (at least some portions of it), and began to reclaim an earlier, richer heritage associated with their own soil and emerging national identity. The center of German Romanticism was Vienna, Austria and the impact of the legendary Redemptorist, Clemens Maria Hofbauer (1751-1820), in stirring up new zeal for Catholic expansion and missionary activity is important to note. Hofbauer's efforts were strongest in Warsaw and Vienna, but he yearned to expand the Redemptorist order to America. Although he died in 1820, several of his religious "sons" came to the Great Lakes.[34] Likewise, also the Crown Prince, later King Ludwig of Bavaria, put himself at the center of a circle of Bavarian Catholic scholars and enthusiasts and contributed substantially to the rejuvenation of Catholic institutions in southern Germany. Switzerland too experienced a quickening of Catholic life spearheaded by orders like the Capuchins. There were differences among the German Catholic revivalists. But collectively, they provided emotional, intellectual, and financial strength for a renewed and energetic Catholic life. Like their French counterparts, German-speaking Catholics formed organizations that helped to spread and support Catholic missions around the world. All of them contributed substantially to the shaping of the Catholic culture of Wisconsin.[35]

The presence of other denominations in Wisconsin provides an important backdrop for understanding the nature of Catholic presence and identity in Wisconsin. Catholics and Lutherans would eventually come to be the dominant religious traditions of most Wisconsinites. But in these early years of Wisconsin's development, a lively rivalry existed with other denominations for converts, choice land for building churches and schools, and also for social, cultural and political dominance. Religious institutions played an important if under-studied force in the shaping of Wisconsin's state and urban culture.

Catholics had indeed maintained the "foothold" in the state's religious geography from the days of French hegemony. But the lead rush in the 1820s brought scores of Protestant missionaries and church members into the region. In Green Bay the first recorded Protestant services were conducted by an Indian agent in 1820.[36] The military posts also recorded periodic religious services by 1826. In 1829, the Catholic Church in Wisconsin had its first religious competition in Green Bay when the Protestant Episcopal Church was organized. The settlement of Wisconsin was taking place as the fires of the Second Great Awakening were building to peak under the revival fervor of Charles Grandison Finney.[37] The quickening of Protestant missionary fervor was reflected in the creation of the inter-denominational Home Missionary Societies which recruited and funded ministers to preach the gospel to frontier lands. In 1830, the Congregational minister Reverend Cutting Marsh was sent to pastor to the Stockbridge Tribe (who had fled Congregational Massachusetts) at Kaukauna. Marsh also established a Presbyterian church in Green Bay in 1835 and in 1837 helped Milwaukee's Presbyterian community organize.

Rev. Cutting Marsh
[WHS (x3) 28364]

Perhaps the best equipped Protestant denomination on the frontier were the Methodists with their circuit riding ministers who easily set up shop at remote outposts and large cities. Methodist circuit riders arrived in 1828-1829 and in 1832, Methodist John Clark set up shop in Kaukauna to minister to Indians who had been moved to Wisconsin from New York. A Methodist society was founded in Platteville in 1833 and in 1834, Method-

Bishop Edward Fenwick, OP, of Cincinnati
[Martin Marty, OSB. *Dr. John Martin Henni, First Bishop and Archbishop of Milwaukee,* Benziger Bros., 1888, p. 57]

ists claimed the honor of erecting the first Protestant church building in Wisconsin at the lead mining region's epicenter, Mineral Point. Methodist missionaries found an eager reception for their efforts from the increasing number of Cornish miners. Baptists came into the territory via the lead region as well, creating a network of communities around the state. Likewise their evangelical cousins, the Disciples of Christ made significant gains in the state. Wisconsin also had its encounter with Mormonism, begun in the famous "Burned Over District" of upstate New York, when a break-off group under James Jesse Strang founded a Mormon "stake" near Burlington. Later, as we shall see, thousands of German-speaking and Scandinavian Lutherans would add to the diversity of Wisconsin's religious population.

The first systematic concern for the well-being of Catholics, largely Indians, living in far-off Wisconsin came from Dominican Bishop Edward Fenwick of Cincinnati. Fenwick, in many respects, would be a kind of spiritual godfather to Wisconsin Catholicism.[38] Fenwick was an American-born Dominican who had studied abroad and had returned to the United States in 1804 to help establish the Dominican Order in the United States. After creating a Dominican center in Springfield, Kentucky, he set out on missionary work in Kentucky and Ohio. With the cessation of Indian resistance to the westward movement of American settlers, the Ohio Valley soon began to fill up with settlers and Cincinnati became one of the leading population centers along the lengthy Ohio River. In 1821 Fenwick was appointed the first bishop of Cincinnati. The vast jurisdiction included not only the state of Ohio, but Michigan and Wisconsin. When the Erie Canal opened a direct commercial link between the Great Lakes and the Port of New York, population grew even more rapidly and Fenwick was soon challenged to provide churches, priests, and schools for his vast diocese.

The need for German-speaking priests was especially acute since many of the newcomers were from the German-speaking areas of Europe. Through the persuasiveness of Hanoverian-born Father Frederick Résé, Fenwick recruited priests for his new diocese, which began to grow substantially. Résé's convincing words and lyrical descriptions of the challenges and the rewards of ministering in far off America found a ready audience among European youth caught up in the religious revival of the 19th century. His efforts brought three who would have a defining impact on the Catholic Church in Wisconsin: John Martin Henni (1805-1881), Martin Kundig (1805-1879), and Samuel Mazzuchelli (1806-1864). Mazzuchelli, who arrived in the United States after the two others, was the first of a series of Catholic priests sent to rekindle Catholic life in the long fallow Wisconsin soil.

A native of Milan, Mazzuchelli entered the Order of Preachers (Dominicans) in 1823 and was educated in Rome at the Order's Santa Sabina House of Studies.[39] Mazzuchelli's education made him enthusiastic for work abroad. Likewise, aforementioned Romantic impulses that brought about a Catholic revival also touched his own Dominican Order which was eager to re-establish a place for itself as a missionary band.[40] The call to make the church visible on "the rim of Christendom" was enough for the dynamic young Mazzuchelli who accepted the invitation to America and received priestly ordination at the hands of his confrere Fenwick in Cincinnati in 1830.

Fenwick's concerns about the growing Wisconsin territory were real. The Catholic populations of Green Bay and Prairie du Chien were increasing, and the demands and necessity for a full-time priestly ministry were strong. The need to minister to the scattered French Catholics, métis and Indians in Wisconsin and also concerns to preserve Catholics from the "contamination" of heresy led Fenwick to dispatch Mazzuchelli to the Upper Peninsula of Michigan and Wisconsin. Mazzuchelli took up residence at Mackinac Island in late 1830. He used the Mackinac assignment as a base for missionary activities in the Wisconsin territory, i.e., Green Bay. At Mackinac, he worked strenuously to make converts and established a girls school for Indians which lasted for 150 years. He also contended with a local Protestant minister over doctrinal issues and scriptural interpretation. In 1833, after the Diocese of Detroit

Rev. Samuel Mazzuchelli, OP [AOP-Sin]

had been formed, the new Bishop, Frederick Résé, assigned the Slovenian cleric, Frederick Baraga, stationed at Arbre Croche on the Upper Peninsula, to Mackinac. He assumed control of the Michigan part of the territory. In 1835 Baraga set up a chapel at La Pointe, being the first priest to visit the area since René Menard in 1661.[41]

Mazzuchelli moved to Green Bay in 1833, where he built a church in honor of St. John the Evangelist. Adept at winning all kinds of people to his cause, he worked closely with John Lawe, a Jewish trader from England who had come over to work in the fur trade, and also with Louis Grignon. As we have seen, Louis Grignon was active in a number of areas of Green Bay's life. He also provided shelter and support to the various priests who visited the city. When Mazzuchelli arrived and began to build a new church, Grignon was his "straw boss," overseeing the details of the financing and construction when the missionary was away. This church was eventually turned over to a group of Austrian Redemptorists under Father Simon Saenderl.[42]

Mazzuchelli then turned to efforts with the French-Canadians and later the Woodland tribes of Ojibwa, Ottawa, Menominee, and Winnebago. Eventually he focused his energies on the Menominee around Green Bay and the Winnebago in western and southern Wisconsin.

The First Efforts: Working with the Indians

The task of working with the Indians, once the cutting edge of the earlier missionary work in Wisconsin, was resumed. But this time, Catholics found themselves in vigorous competition with other denominations. Historian Michael Stevens, who compared the efforts of Catholic and Protestant missionaries during the territorial period of Wisconsin history, characterizes missionary endeavors as well-intentioned but "at times misguided, often ethnocentric and usually ineffective."[43] Nonetheless the rivalry that existed between the Catholic and Protestant missionaries could be seen in the exchange of Dominican Theodore J. Van den Broek and Congregational minister, Cutting Marsh. When Marsh came on Van den Broek teaching a large group of Indians to sing, the Dominican wrote to Elizabeth Grignon, "He [Marsh] was greatly surprised to see them, and asked me whether I always had so many people." He observed acidly, "I believe that he was jealous, because he had hoped to convert some of them to his own Religion."[44]

Stevens notes that while both sides sought to alter the Indians' culture and religious systems, the Catholics seemed a tad more respectful of native cultures. Specifically, he cites the identification the foreign-born missionaries had with being an "alien" culture in an American environment. Likewise, Catholic efforts to start a school for Indians in Green Bay floundered time and again. Frederick Baraga's efforts at La Pointe and Van den Broek's efforts at Little Chute seemed a bit more successful.[45] However, Stevens notes that Mazzuchelli had criticized Protestant evangelical techniques as "too intellectual" and not flexible enough to permit a more gradual adaptation to a new religion. Protestants scorned Catholic efforts as superficial.

Indeed a reading of Mazzuchelli's journals and letters confirms Stevens' judgement. Mazzuchelli adapted well to the demands of ministering to these peoples, learning their religious systems and relying on native catechists to help him preach the gospel. One of his companions in ministering to the Winnebago whose language he did not understand was Elizabeth Grignon, who received her father's permission to accompany the young Dominican to Portage where the tribe resided. This "unseemly" pairing of the celibate Mazzuchelli and the unmarried young woman aroused the suspicions and gossip of some. Elizabeth's sister, Ursule, and Van den Broek, reported the incident to Mazzuchelli's Dominican superiors in Ohio. They in turn called him to Ohio for an accounting. Mazzuchelli took his time in replying to the command to return and eventually secured support from other circles to sidestep the charges of inappropriate behavior.[46] He opened schools for the native inhabitants, but failed in his efforts to secure government money to fund them and they soon failed. Mazzuchelli's own education among the Indians was important. Not only did he adapt well to the demands of language, food, culture, and custom, but he also picked up even more important lessons about the nature of American life and the specific language, thought-worlds and cultural value systems of the settlers pouring into the territory. Keeping a foot in both the world of the Indians and the world of the aggressive land speculators, politicians and entrepreneurs, he soon plighted his troth to the latter and moved away from Indian ministry. But he never forgot his love and affection for the native peoples.

Another kind of cultural accommodation can be found in the work of Dutch-born Theodore J. Van den Broek. In 1833 he arrived in Green Bay, where he remained until the Redemptorists relieved him. He then moved to Little Chute in 1835 to work among the Menominee Indians.[47] There, his vigorous advocacy of Indian rights enhanced his respect among the tribe. At Little Chute,

Rev. Theodore Van den Broek, OP
[AOP-Rac]

Rev. Florimond J. Bonduel [AAM]

Van den Broek built what one historian described as a "semi-theocratic community" modeled to some extent after the Jesuit Reductions in Paraguay.[48] Like the Jesuits, he taught the Indians music. For the administration of Confirmation at his mission church in 1839 by Detroit Bishop Peter Paul Lefevre, he taught the Indians to sing the Latin anthems *Ecce Sacerdos Magnus* and *Veni Creator* in their own language. Likewise, he taught them the Ordinary parts of the Mass (*Kyrie* and *Gloria*) and even schooled them in chants of solemn vespers, "You never hear a finer harmony than this, in which the Indians who sang, sang in Gregorian chant."[49] At Little Chute, Van den Broek relied heavily on the Grignon family, including Elizabeth whose trip with Mazzuchelli he had reported to Dominican superiors. As time went on, the enterprising Van den Broek opened up a network of mission stations along the Fox/Wisconsin axis all the way to Prairie du Chien. At Kaukauna he built a modest mission church and opened a school for the Indians. In 1846, the advent of white farmers compelled the Menominees to move from Little Chute and Kaukauna to a new settlement at the Neenah River near Lake Poygan. It is unclear whether Van den Broek followed them to this site, but he continued to make reports to the local Indian agent about conditions among the Menominees until 1848. In 1848, stricken with homesickness, he left for Holland with the intention of remaining there. Within two years, however, he was back in Wisconsin, where he died in 1852 and was buried at Little Chute. By this time, the tribe had been transferred to a reservation in Keshena and the ministry to the Menominees was carried on for a time by a Belgian missionary, Father Florimond Bonduel.

Bonduel was a native of Comines, Belgium.[50] He arrived in Detroit in 1831 and was ordained in 1834.[51] At some point in 1835 he made a quick trip to Milwaukee where he celebrated what many consider the first Mass in the future metropolis, in the home of the city's putative founder, Solomon Juneau. He spent six years as pastor in busy Mackinac from 1837 to 1843 and also served at St. John's Church in Green Bay, replacing the Redemptorists. Bonduel suffered from grandiose visions of his role on the Wisconsin frontier, reflected in his occasional penchant for conferring titles on himself in letters, such as accentuating his status by appending to his letters the title "First Ordained in Detroit," or "Apostolic Missionary." At one point he even dubbed himself the "Bishop-Elect of Prairie du Chien." Nonetheless, he was a zealous and hard-working priest. In 1843, he began to serve in some capacity at the Keshena Menominee Reservation, taking over the full ministry when Van den Broek returned to Holland. His faithful co-workers were Mrs. Rosalie Dousman and her daughters, Kate and Jane. It was Bonduel who advised the Menominees to reject the government offer of removal to lands in Minnesota that were unsuitable for farming and to seek to remain in Wisconsin. Bonduel's emphasis on the Indians developing settled agricultural traits (they had been food-gatherers and hunters rather than farmers) and his railing against drunkenness soon brought a great deal of opposition from those who traded with the Indians. This included the famous Grignon family. The Grignons stirred up considerable opposition to the priest and induced the non-Christian chieftain Oshkosh to appear naked one night at the priest's door to threaten him and the Dousman women with physical injury.[52] Nonetheless, he remained at Keshena until 1854 when he returned to Belgium for a long visit. He eventually came back, serving in pastorates until his death in 1861.

Father Otto Skolla, a Slovenian-born Franciscan, had also come to Wisconsin by way of Detroit in 1841.[53] After a brief tenure in a Detroit parish, he was sent north to assist Baraga. After three years of working with Baraga, he debarked for La Pointe and joined the Diocese of Milwaukee. Skolla worked among the Chippewa people until they were removed in the 1850s. In 1853 Henni reassigned him to the station at Keshena among the Menominee. At Keshena, he was summoned to the deathbed of Solomon Juneau. In his death agonies, Juneau, "made a general confession of his whole life and left none of his sins untouched in order to become repentent [sic] for them." Skolla was moved by the sincerity of Juneau's confession, "With deep consolation and astonishment, I was surprised at it and I consoled and excited him with gentle words to hope in God and repent over his sins."[54]

Rev. Otto Skolla, OSF
[Antoine I. Rezak. *History of the Diocese of Sault Ste. Marie and Marquette,* Houghton MI, 1906]

The work of Van den Broek, Bonduel, Skolla, and Baraga is important to the understanding of the return of Catholic visibility in Wisconsin. Ministry to Indian tribes would be an important and ongoing part of the state's Catholic culture. But in terms of subsequent demographic shifts, the resumption of work among the Indians was soon overwhelmed by an even greater demand made by floods of newcomers from eastern states and from Europe. This new phase of Catholic presence led directly to the creation of the Diocese of Milwaukee, and Samuel Mazzuchelli would be at its cutting edge.

Lead Mining, Indian Warfare, and a New Detroit Jurisdiction

By the time Mazzuchelli was relieved of his duties in Green Bay, there were about 1,000 Catholics living in that community and another 600 in Prairie du Chien.[55] In

1835, the Dominican appeared in the lead mining town of Galena, Illinois, and began to open churches for the growing number of largely Irish settlers. The area of the Mississippi Valley where Iowa, Illinois, and Wisconsin all come together was the first staging ground for this new phase of Mazzuchelli's career. By the time Matthias Loras arrived in 1839, carrying the bull of appointment as the first bishop of Dubuque, Mazzuchelli had founded four churches in his new jurisdiction, St. Raphael's in Dubuque, St. Michael's in Galena, St. Thomas's in Potosi, and St. Anthony's in Davenport.[56] Mazzuchelli remained under Loras's direction for six years and ranged freely around Iowa, Illinois, and Wisconsin. Loras paid a series of pastoral visits to Catholics in Wisconsin in 1839, 1841, and 1842, at each step visiting scattered Catholics in various portions of the state (although it was under the jurisdiction of Detroit) and encouraging the development of Catholic life through the building of churches. In Prairie du Chien the Trappist Dunand's church was replaced with the rock-fortress St. Gabriel in 1840. Other Wisconsin foundations include St. Matthew's in Shullsberg (1841), St. Paul's in Mineral Point (1841), and St. Augustine's in Sinsinawa (1842). In 1843, Mazzuchelli's health broke and he returned to his native Milan to recuperate. But there he wrote glowingly about the American mission; he returned in 1844, free from service to Dubuque, and encouraged by his Dominican superiors to create a new branch of the Order of Preachers in the American wilderness. Mazzuchelli continued to found churches in Southwestern Wisconsin at Platteville (1845), Potosi (1845 and 1848), Beetown (1846), Hazel Green (1848), St. Augustine's in New Diggings (1846), St. Patrick's in Benton (1847), and Calamine (1850). In 1847, Mazzuchelli's newly ordained nephew, Father Francis Mazzuchelli, joined his uncle briefly in serving the churches of the southwestern portion of the territory.[57]

Bishop Matthias Loras of Dubuque [AOP-Sin]

Mazzuchelli's long and heroic career, draped in the language of pioneer myth, is replete with stories of encounters with rowdy miners, efforts to administer the sacraments in the extremes of Midwestern weather (he died in February 1864 after contracting pneumonia after visiting two shut-in parishioners), and the establishment of churches with little or no means of visible support. Nearly 40 churches claimed him as their founder, as did an order of teaching sisters (the Sinsinawa Dominicans). Mazzuchelli was committed to making the Catholic Church visible on the soil of Wisconsin, Illinois, and Iowa.

Mazzuchelli was one of the first to break with the old Indian missionary role and to concentrate his efforts on the new demographic realities of Wisconsin in the 1830s. Just as important as this transition were Maz-

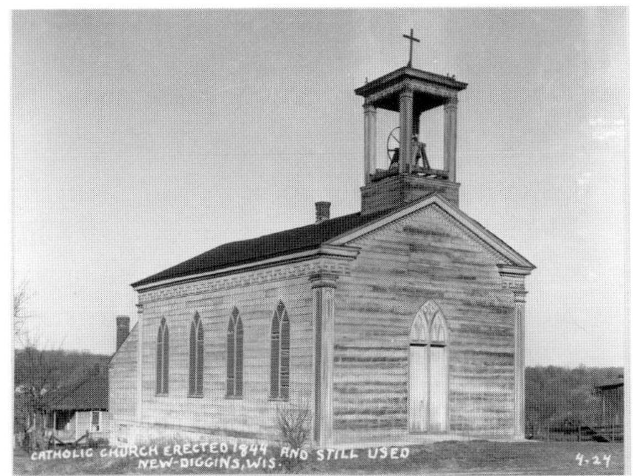

St. Augustine Church, New Diggings
[Leo Rummel, O Praem. *History of the Catholic Church in Wisconsin,* Knights of Columbus, 1976, p. 38]

zuchelli's evangelical methods. Mazzuchelli immersed himself in a variety of areas that were not strictly related to the "sacred ministry" but that were calculated to help him make the church visible in the new environment. For example, Mazzuchelli was active in the formation of the Wisconsin territorial government and served as the first chaplain to the Wisconsin legislature. His skills as an architect were used not only in building church structures but, some insist, also in designing secular buildings such as the Iowa state house. As noted earlier, when illness sidetracked him in 1843, and he spent a lengthy recovery period in Italy, Mazzuchelli turned his pen to writing his memoirs. These lively and apologetic tracts were not only the account of the unfolding of Catholicism in Wisconsin and the Upper Mississippi Valley, but were also paeans to the beauty, attractiveness, and salubrity of Wisconsin, as well as to the beneficence of American institutions. They were, in short, booster publications, intended to draw newcomers to Wisconsin. Mazzuchelli sought to integrate the church into the rapidly transforming frontier economy. He was priest and promoter. Archbishop John Ireland, in an effusive introduction to the 1915 edition of Mazzuchelli's memoirs, summed up the missionary's ability to adapt to his native land when he wrote, "Mazzuchelli understood with singular clearness the principles of American law and life and conformed himself to them in heartfelt loyalty. There lay one of the chief causes of the influence allowed him by his fellow-citizens of all classes, and of the remarkable success with which his ministry was rewarded. He was a foreigner by birth and education .... Yet he was American to the core of his heart, to the tip of his finger."[58]

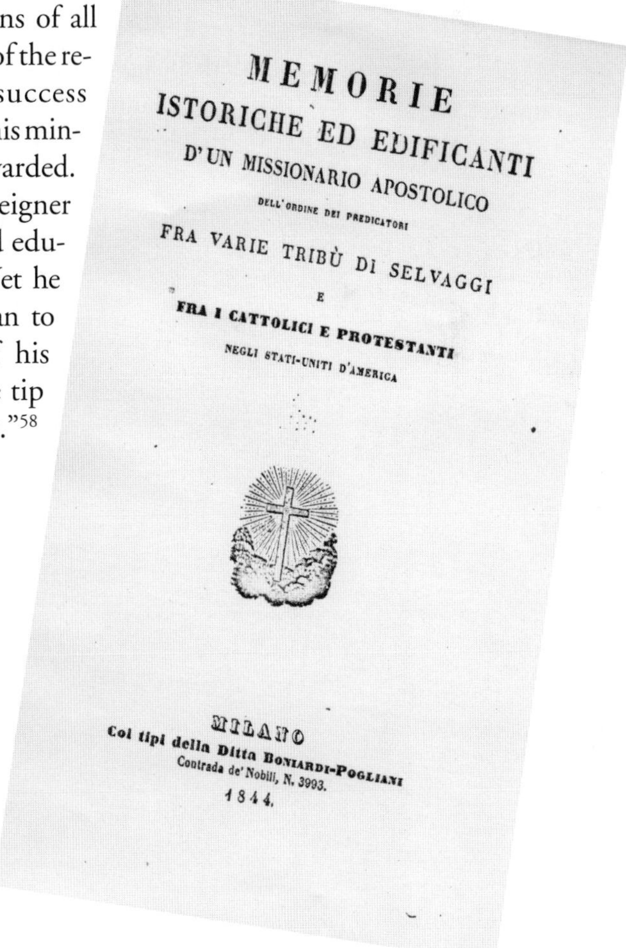
MEMORIE
ISTORICHE ED EDIFICANTI
D'UN MISSIONARIO APOSTOLICO
DELL'ORDINE DEI PREDICATORI
FRA VARIE TRIBÙ DI SELVAGGI
E
FRA I CATTOLICI E PROTESTANTI
NEGLI STATI-UNITI D'AMERICA

MILANO
Col tipi della Ditta Boniardi-Pogliani
Contrada de' Nobili, N. 3993.
1844.

Detroit Takes Control—Creating Milwaukee As a Central Outpost

Mazzuchelli's successes won the notice of other church officials. The next phase of Wisconsin's Catholic development was affected by further organizational moves by the Holy See which detached the Michigan and Wisconsin portions of the Diocese of Cincinnati to form the Diocese of Detroit in 1833.[59] For 10 years, Catholic affairs in Wisconsin would be the concern of the bishop of Detroit and his clergy. The Detroit jurisdiction was the final chapter in Wisconsin's "missionary" status; an identification that stretched back, at least in the popular imagination, to the first landings of the French missionaries in the 17th century.[60]

Bishop Frederick Rese of Detroit [AAD]

Detroit's first bishop was Fenwick's protégé Father Frederick Résé. Since he had been Fenwick's vicar general for Michigan and Wisconsin, the appointment seemed natural and few knew more than he about the demands of the new territories under his jurisdiction. While his episcopal tenure was troubled (he suffered a serious mental breakdown and was compelled to accept a coadjutor bishop in 1841), Résé and his successor, Belgian-born Peter Paul Lefevre, devoted some attention to the needs of the growing number of Catholics migrating into Wisconsin in the 1830s and 1840s.

Clearly for both bishops, the areas of greatest growth and natural prominence were the growing settlements that would come to form Milwaukee. The growth in Milwaukee was spectacular.[61] In 1835 the first settler in the future metropolis, Solomon Juneau, together with financier Morgan Martin, began to organize a settlement east of the Milwaukee River, an area referred to later as "Juneauville." Many of the earliest Catholic institutions would be located there.

Juneau was not alone. The money to be made from developing lands along the bustling lakefront enticed two other avid speculators, Byron Kilbourn and Gilbert Walker, to start rival settlements to the west and south of Juneau's community. Although a period of internecine rivalry kept these three settlements, conveniently divided by the three rivers that transected the area, from working together, eventually the logic of cooperation rather than competition set in. In 1846, the city of Milwaukee was chartered, and what would become Wisconsin's largest and most dynamic city was founded. The forces of city development accelerated, once rivalry was exchanged for interdependence. New England and New York Protestant families (Yankees and Yorkers) established themselves as the first social and economic elite and began to raise the city's financial, social and political infrastructure.[62]

City building took place next along the new commercial frontier on the west banks of Lake Michigan. Through the bustling ports, Wisconsin's interior riches were now more easily marketed. This symbiosis of city and hinterland provided the crucible for social and cultural developments that followed. Religious institutions were part of the larger package of dynamic growth that began in the 1830s and continued through the 19th century.[63]

As the number of Catholics moving to Wisconsin increased, Detroit diocesan officials became more active in providing Catholic ministry especially in the rapidly growing eastern portion of the state. Itinerant priests, the advance guard of organized Catholicism on the frontier began to appear. Some missionaries remained in the coastal cities that were forming at strategic points along Lake Michigan's shore. Others made for the agricultural hinterlands.

Historian Peter Leo Johnson devoted considerable efforts to discover when the first Mass was held in the future see city of Wisconsin. Ignoring the Mass celebrated by Père Marquette, Johnson could not come up with the "definitive moment." But the strongest evidence suggests that Belgian missionary Florimond Bonduel, a priest of Detroit, celebrated Mass at the home of Solomon Juneau some time in 1835.[64] At that time he may have elicited a promise of land for a Catholic church, but the record is not clear. Some sources suggest that the Indian missionary Theodore J. Van den Broek, who also visited and ministered in Milwaukee in 1836, may have received the pledge of land. Regardless of when Catholicism made its formal entrance into Milwaukee, it is clear that there were enough Catholics to warrant the establishment of a permanent church building by the end of the 1830s.

Solomon Juneau
[John G. Gregory *History of Milwaukee, Wisconsin,* S.J. Clarke Pub. Co., 1931, p. 131]

In 1837, Bishop Peter Paul Lefevre sent Father Patrick O'Kelley, the pastor at Ann Arbor, Michigan, to start a church in the rapidly growing town.[65] The Irish-born O'Kelley had come to the United States after completing studies at St. Kieran's College in County Kilkenny. He emigrated to the United States in 1820 and was ordained by Bishop Luke Connolly of New York in 1821. He migrated to Michigan and was active in pastoral work for about 10 years before being sent to Milwaukee. O'Kelley "commuted" between Wisconsin and Michigan at first, arriving in May 1837 and celebrating Mass in the Milwaukee County Court House. At this time he may have secured the lots on the northwest corners of Jackson and Martin Streets (today East State Street) that had been promised to either Bonduel or Van den Broek. Records show him returning briefly to Michigan and then coming back to Wisconsin for more church building in 1839.

Accompanying O'Kelley was another Irish-born priest, Father Thomas Morrissey. A native of County Waterford, he had arrived in Michigan in the 1830s. He assisted O'Kelley at Ann Arbor, and later accompanied him across Lake Michigan. Morrissey road the circuit while O'Kelley remained in Milwaukee. To Morrissey is given the credit for celebrating the Eucharist for the first time in Burlington, Brighton, Geneva, Oak Creek, and Racine in 1838. After a return to Michigan, he came back in 1839 and helped O'Kelley launch the new St. Luke's in Milwaukee.

Rev. Patrick O'Kelley [AAD]

The "Circuit"

As vibrant and "upstart" as early Milwaukee was, there were other concentrations of population and Catholics that required attention. These were to be found in scattered agricultural settlements, often dominated by one or the other ethnic group, as well as in the various towns that saw the first stirrings of life along rivers. These areas also quickened as more and more people moved to Wisconsin, especially after federal land surveys and sales began in 1835, and even more so in 1836 when Wisconsin became a territory. Following up on the initial contacts made by his friend Morrissey, Father Patrick O'Kelley began to circuit ride around what would become "Greater Milwaukee" visiting the port of Racine and its environs: Mount Pleasant Township, Rochester, Burlington, and the equally active lake city of Southport (Kenosha), and its adjuncts, Pleasant Prairie, and Salem. Closer to Milwaukee he traveled south to Oak Creek, north to Granville, and west to Greenfield. In two locations he organized congregations and helped erect small churches.

At Oak Creek, O'Kelley found a contingent of Irish farmers and began saying Mass for them in 1839. By 1841, enough were gathered to establish a log cabin chapel on lands donated by James and Bridget Oherrn [sic] which was finished in 1842 and named "St. Matthew, "perhaps after the evangelist but, as the parish history suggests, more likely in honor of Father Theobald Matthew, the Irish temperance advocate who was a great hero of O'Kelley's.[66] In Greenfield, O'Kelley built another log chapel named St. Mary's Mission. O'Kelley did not have the financial resources to build permanent churches in these locations, but he dropped the seeds that later sprouted into permanent, visible churches.

Morrissey also continued to minister to Catholics far and wide in places such as East Troy, Lannon, Pewaukee, Watertown, and Platteville. The indefatigable Morrissey spent the rest of his life in Wisconsin, eventually dying in Spring Prairie in 1850. By mid-1842, there were only six church buildings in Wisconsin: Prairie du Chien, La Pointe, Green Bay, Little Chute, Milwaukee, and Potosi. But the promise of future development was great, particularly in the rapidly growing eastern part of the Wisconsin territory.

The work of O'Kelley and Morrissey gave ecclesiastical affirmation to an important shift in the demographic and social realities of Wisconsin: the center of development had shifted from the lead mining region of the state to the coastal areas of Lake Michigan and to the farming communities that would be carved out of the rich lands in the southeastern portion of the state. O'Kelley had been the first to project Catholic visibility into the continuum of development between lake city and rural inland. The next stage in the promotion of the Catholic presence in this area fell to O'Kelley's successor Martin Kundig. Few people were better equipped temperamentally, culturally, and intellectually to sink Catholic roots deeply into Wisconsin's southeastern quadrant than Kundig.

The Kundig Accomplishment

By the eve of the establishment of the Milwaukee Diocese, events were coming together that would bring about a new religious structure for Catholics in Wisconsin. Shortly after taking over for the broken Bishop Frederick Résé, Bishop Peter Paul Lefevre of Detroit began to take an active interest in the Wisconsin portion of his domain. In 1842, he took one of his priests, Martin Kundig, on an important visitation of the eastern portion of the Wisconsin vineyard. Part of the reason for this tour was part of the ritual of "taking over" that Lefevre and other bishops routinely did when they assumed new duties. Part of it was to investigate complaints against O'Kelley that had emanated from some seriously disgruntled Milwaukee Catholics—including the city's most prominent Catholic lay person, Solomon Juneau. The decision to take Kundig was an important step in the process of creating the Catholic Church in Wisconsin and forming the diocese of Milwaukee.

Rev. Martin Kundig [AAM]

Kundig, a native of Canton Schwyz, was born November 19, 1805. Historian George Pare observed that Kundig, who was gifted with a sweet soprano singing voice "sang his way into the affections of influential friends."[67] At the age of 13 he was sent to the elite monastery academy of the Benedictine Abbey of Einsiedeln to study music. He also learned to play the flute and piano. His gift for music would be a great asset in his pastoral ministry. There also he discovered a vocation to the priesthood. After four years, he began studies at a diocesan college in Lucerne.[68] In 1827, with his fellow Swiss, John Martin Henni, he went to Rome to complete his seminary studies at Sapienza University. That same year, he and Henni were swayed by the romantic tales of Father Frederick Résé, the agent of Dominican Bishop Edward Fenwick of Cincinnati, and both men volunteered to go to Ohio. They were warmly received by Fenwick who sent them to St. Thomas Seminary in nearby Bardstown, Kentucky, for a year. Kundig was ordained to the priesthood by Fenwick after a year of study in Ohio. Kundig remained in Ohio only briefly before moving to Detroit in 1833, the year it was created as a diocese. There he joined Frederick Résé who had been appointed the first bishop.

Bishop Peter Paul Lefevre of Detroit [AAD]

Kundig's years in Detroit, 1833-1842, saw him undertake a wide array of duties.[69] He was first assigned to the city's proto-church, St. Anne. The growing church kept him busy, as did the many mission stations attached to it. Kundig formed and directed a choir, which included Protestants as well. At the parish school, Kundig and his fellow cleric, Florimond Bonduel, taught music and French and put on musical entertainments which attracted many. With a winning way, a gift for music, and an ability to speak several languages, Kundig endeared himself to some of the most prominent Detroit families. In 1834, Résé made him pastor of a new parish for the English-speaking in Detroit named Holy Trinity. Later that same year a serious cholera epidemic broke out and Kundig threw open the new church for use as a hospital and organized a Catholic Female Association to help nurse the sick.

In July 1834, Kundig took a "secular" job as the superintendent of the poor for Wayne County. The task was daunting primarily because expenses for the poor and the sick who came to the house were never adequately covered by the appropriations of the Wayne County government. Kundig did what he could to keep the house clean and orderly, and ran up debts to cover the shortfalls between appropriations and actual expenses. At the same time, he expanded operations by establishing an orphanage near the poorhouse. Eighteen orphans were taken in, but promises of contributions from Catholic churches and other charitable agencies were never fulfilled. Kundig did what he could to raise money, including fairs and bazaars and even a scheme to run a bathhouse. But all to no avail. Even efforts to retrieve his expenses from the Michigan legislature (Michigan entered the Union in 1837) failed. In 1839, Kundig was replaced as superintendent of the poor. Moreover, he had a difficult time disbanding the orphanage he had started, and found it nearly impossible to place all the orphans elsewhere. After the poor house and orphanage failures, Kundig returned full-time to parish work, serving again at Holy Trinity and helping to found a new church of St. Mary in Detroit. He also was appointed to be a regent for the University of Michigan in 1841. His pastoral labors took him to Saginaw where he helped to found a Catholic church. But Kundig was ready to move to greener pastures. The embarrassment of the situation, his heavy debts, as well as problems stemming from the breakdown of Bishop Résé may have contributed to all of this.[70] When, Résé's successor, Bishop Peter Paul Lefevre asked him to accompany him to Wisconsin in the spring of 1842, Kundig readily agreed.

St. Anne Church, Detroit
[AAD]

The 1842 journey gave them both an overview of the condition of Wisconsin Catholicism on the eve of the creation of the diocese of Milwaukee. Following the time-worn route, they departed Detroit for Mackinac, then proceeded to Green Bay. Down the Fox River they met Van den Broek at Little Chute and then went overland to Fond du Lac and on to Milwaukee. As mentioned above, Lefevre's and Kundig's visit had come in part as the result of complaints made by Solomon Juneau about the conduct and character of Milwaukee's Father Patrick O'Kelley. For reasons not completely clear, discontent with the Irish-born pastor had developed. Some have suggested that his frequent absences from Milwaukee created tensions. Others disliked his harping on temperance, destined to be a controversial issue among Wisconsin Catholics. O'Kelley did not have a facility with languages other than English and could not easily minister to the polyglot of nationalities soon taking up residence in the parish, especially German speakers. O'Kelley's disgruntled congregation, including no less a figure than Milwaukee founder Solomon Juneau, expressed their displeasure to Detroit and also by withholding funds for the building of the church.[71] When Kundig and Lefevre arrived in 1842, it was clear that O'Kelley was slated for transfer. He ended his days as a pastor in Ann Arbor. Martin Kundig was given "temporary" leadership of the fledgling Milwaukee church. When Peter Paul Lefevre bid him farewell, the bishop fully expected to see his clerical "subject" back in Michigan. As Kundig waved farewell, he no doubt knew better.

St. Peter Cathedral, Milwaukee [AAM]

The Kundig Accomplishment: Ethnic Accommodation

Visibility was the first priority for the 37 year old Kundig. "When we arrived at Milwaukee," Kundig wrote a friend, "we found Catholic affairs not a little neglected."[72] He quickly finished off the partially completed St. Luke's (which had been under roof since 1839 but woefully ill-equipped and cramped), obsequiously renaming it St. Peter's in honor of the patron of his bishop in Detroit. In 1844, as the Catholic population of Milwaukee flourished, the church was enlarged by a full 40 feet, making it one of the largest worship sites in early Milwaukee. To the great delight of the congregation, he installed a church bell he had purchased from a local Presbyterian church. "Last Sunday, amid universal rejoicing, we rang for the first time from our tower the Presbyterian bell of Milwaukee."[73]

The significance of this accomplishment is well worth our consideration, given the fact that throughout its existence this structure has had an important preeminence in the historical memory of Catholicism in the Archdiocese of Milwaukee. This church served as a worship site for Milwaukee Catholics until the construction of St. John's Cathedral in 1853. Its four walls would house a number of other diocesan institutions, schools, storage, and even a school for social justice. In 1892, a sentimental (and wealthy) Monsignor Leonard Batz would move the old structure to the site of his newly founded parish of Ss. Peter and Paul on Milwaukee's east side. The *Catholic Citizen* lauded the generous Batz and called to mind the "cluster [of] remembrances of privations endured by the sturdy Catholic pioneers of a half-century ago."[74] In 1939, the Milwaukee Archdiocesan Council of Catholic Women paid to have it relocated once again, this time to the woods next to St. Francis Seminary.[75] In 1975 the pioneer church, stripped down to its essentials, made its final move to an outdoor museum park called Old World Wisconsin in the tiny community of Eagle. The deep interest and concern for the well-being of this building reflected the importance associated with its very structure to the people of the archdiocese. As humble and inadequate as it was, it was the first visible sign of Catholic identity in the city of Milwaukee. Like the statue of Marquette, which was sculpted at the time the church was first saved from destruction, it constituted a visible reminder of a heroic, pioneer past. It was preserved by a generation now removed from the struggles of the earlier days and as part of a general effort to cultivate memory of a distant and glorious past. Old St. Peter's (ironically placed in the heart of "colonial village" in the outdoor park) still continues to be a living reminder of the value Catholics put on their first effort to stake out a claim on the soil of Wisconsin and in Milwaukee in particular.

As he had done in Michigan, Kundig finished the church and additions by borrowing. Others would be left to pay the bills after he left. Financial troubles notwithstanding, Kundig's skills as an ethnic peacemaker were soon tested. He quelled discontent by providing separate services for his parishioners, using his competence in German, English, and French. This immediately undercut anxieties that one group was going to be neglected by the church. Separate organizations for German and English speakers were founded for church support and benevolence. St. Mary's Female Benevolent Society was created for the English-speaking, while St. Ann's Female Benevolent society was established for the German-speaking. To calm tensions further, he diplomatically soft-pedaled his own protemperance feelings—at least to the point that he did not offend those who resented efforts to deprive them of spirits. "Since my arrival the triple parish (French, English and German nationalities) has become nicely united."[76] In August 1842, with a unified parish behind him, Kundig opened a school for girls in a house on the east side of Jefferson Street under the tutelage of a Miss Murray and Catherine Shea. In the fall a school for

Sisters' House Academy and Orphanage, Milwaukee
[Peter Leo Johnson. *Daughters of Charity in Milwaukee, 1846-1946,* Daughters of Charity, 1946]

boys was opened as well with two separate instructors for English-speaking and German-speaking boys. This became the nucleus of the first Catholic school in Milwaukee.

Later, in 1846, the Daughters of Charity accepted the request of Bishop Henni for co-workers to found schools and provide for female orphans.[77] Three sisters arrived in Milwaukee and were quickly put to work at a free school he had founded in the basement of St. Peter's Church in 1842. When the sisters took over new quarters at North Van Buren Street, they were able to turn one wing of that school into an academy and another into an orphanage. As such they became the chief educators of the children of the cathedral parish until 1905 when they withdrew from school work altogether to concentrate on St. Mary's Hospital.

After settling affairs at St. Peter's, Kundig mounted his horse and made a remarkable journey that not only followed up on O'Kelley's and Morrissey's earlier itineracy, but also plowed new ground in church formation.

Revisiting the Circuit

Kundig took to the road as soon as Morrissey returned to Milwaukee and offered to take care of St. Peter's. Kundig retraced O'Kelley's and Morrissey's circuit and even went farther to the territorial capital in Madison. Here too he sought to adapt to the ethnic realities which were creating single-language parishes of Irish or Germans, but where neither dominated. Here he was able to bring both sides together (at least for a time) in establishing a visible Catholic presence.

Land sales kept the population booming and the pace of change rapid. The Janesville Plank Road was the main artery to the southwest, and going straight to a number of small villages were important agricultural crossroads west of Milwaukee. Kundig traveled first to Greenfield and then branched out to Hales Corners, New Berlin, Mukwonago and Troy, and in another direction between Little and Big Muskego Lakes via Wind Lake, and Rochester to Burlington. On another journey he traveled southbound along the old Chicago Road on to Racine and Kenosha.

The nuclei of Catholic life outside the settlement of Milwaukee were the log chapels in Oak Creek and Greenfield that had been started by O'Kelley. But Wisconsin was bursting with growth, and small communities of Catholics that O'Kelley had visited were now of sufficient size and strength to begin their own modest structures. Heading due south, Kundig entered Racine where he built a small Catholic church in honor of St. Luke. In Southport (Kenosha), he found 100 families that he organized into St. Mark's parish and built an expensive brick church. Fifteen miles east of the city, he found a group of multiethnic Catholics in Brighton, who had been ministered to by O'Kelley in 1841; in 1845, Kundig helped them build a log church. St. Patrick's Church in Brighton (later St. Francis Xavier) was given a permanent pastor in 1848. In Franklin Township, a German land speculator named Nuekirch brought together a mixture of German- and English-speaking families that was ministered to by priests at St. Mary's. Thirty families comprised St. Andrew's Church in Yorkville in 1842, a church that would become a "ghost church" later on. In Muskego, he found another dependency of the Greenfield church with 24 families (named then for St. Joseph). In Burlington 40 families had services once a month while in a little burg named Spring Prairie, six miles from Burlington, 10 families required ministry. In Geneva he found 36 families, but in Prairieville (Waukesha) he was unable to determine the Catholic population since it was "widely scattered." Ten miles south of Waukesha was a church in Mukwonago with 20 families. At Marcy, near present day Brookfield, he found 20 families in "Mr. Raferty's settlement." In Erin, he found a handful of Irish families and gathered them together for Mass. Shortly afterwards they built a log chapel in Monches dedicated to St. John.

St. Mary Church, Hales Corners
[*St. Mary's, Hales Corners, 125th Anniversary* [no publ.], 1967]

Kundig's peregrinations included visits to German Catholics in Fussville (Menominee Falls), Grafton, Granville, Cedarburg, Mequon, West Granville, Oak Creek, and New Coeln. The most remarkable facet of this journey was his sojourn into the territorial capital where he made the acquaintance of Governor James Doty who, according to tradition, was so taken with Kundig's charm that he presented the priest with two lots for the first Catholic church in the city, St. Raphael's, land on which the governor had earlier determined to build his own residence.

The Promoter

Like Mazzuchelli, Kundig had a feel for the heterogeneity of American life and knew that Catholics and non-Catholics could coexist peacefully and work for the common good in Wisconsin as they had in Michigan. As a promoter of Wisconsin, he wrote regularly for English- and German-language publications, extolling in terms most eloquent (if at times a bit mendacious) the beauty, appeal, and healthfulness of the Wisconsin territory. But even if many of Kundig's audiences were German Catholics, he did not envision the new land as a new Munich, Linz, or St. Gallen. Instead, he attempted to convey the sense of wider opportunity and attractiveness of the land that would bring "respectable" and monied people to the state. It was in this context that his well-known advocacy of temperance, a *bête noire* to his German-speaking colleagues, is best understood. Knowing that the respectable Yankees and Yorkers were often staunch advocates of temperance, Kundig courted their favor by echoing their calls for temperance and even abstinence from spirits.

Kundig's observations of the rapidly growing character of Wisconsin Catholic life were widely disseminated. In his journey of 1842, Kundig kept copious notes and wrote to his friend John Martin Henni of Cincinnati and others about conditions in Wisconsin. His assertion that he had founded 20 parishes during the journey was reprinted in German on the pages of *Der Wahrheits-Freund* and twice in English for the *Western Catholic Register* (Detroit) and the *United States Magazine* (Baltimore). Kundig's glowing accounts of Catholic possibilities in rapidly expanding Wisconsin were particularly intriguing to Henni who was, as we shall see, immersed in an ambitious project to create a German-language seminary.[78]

Kundig and the Creation of a New Diocese

Kundig's boosterism played some role in the decision to create a diocesan headquarters in the city of Milwaukee. To be sure, the decision to create a new diocese in Wisconsin was in response to the growing needs of an increasing number of Catholics who poured into the territory. When the ill-effects of the Panic of 1837 began to lift in 1840, population surged especially in the lake-port city of Milwaukee. In other parts of the territory, settlements began to fill in the lands south of the Fox/Wisconsin axis, lakefront cities like Racine and Kenosha, and towns along the Rock River (Madison, Watertown, Janesville and Beloit). Likewise farming villages and outposts also began to rise. Wisconsin's population surged from 11,683 in 1836 to 305,390 by the 1850 census, a 2,514 percent increase.

On the Catholic front, the efforts at church visibility were well underway, thanks to the efforts of the second wave of Catholic missionaries. Indeed, priests like Mazzuchelli, Kundig and others made sure that the seedlings of Catholic growth were now growing south of the Fox/Wisconsin axis. As reports of Wisconsin's Catholic development filled eastern newspapers and traveling priests and bishops related stories of development on the Wisconsin frontier, the church's organizational machinery for coping with the growth cranked into gear.

An important agency of organizational life for the American church were the various Provincial and Plenary Councils that were held throughout the 19th century. At these gatherings of the growing number of U.S. bishops, local problems were discussed, church discipline was regularized, and above all the demands of the church on the frontier were resolved. Detroit, beset by its own dynamic growth, found it impossible to care for the rapidly growing Catholic contingent in Wisconsin. As a result, the Fifth Provincial Council which met at Baltimore in May 1843 took up the question of new diocesan establishments in the Midwest and elsewhere. With regards to Wisconsin, the question soon came down to the location of the new diocese—either the "upstart" city of Milwaukee on the thriving eastern side or the old Catholic center of Prairie du Chien on the west.

It is possible that eastern bishops with antiquated geographical knowledge and little by way of reliable reports about demographic and social trends in Wisconsin might have thought that Prairie du Chien was the best place. All that many bishops may have known would have been the writings and reputation of Samuel Mazzuchelli who was centered in the southwestern portion of the state. But if there were doubts, Martin Kundig's boosterism of Milwaukee quickly dispelled them. There were few rivals to Milwaukee in Wisconsin by 1843. It was already the center of active land speculation and commercial activity. Kundig's writings boasted of a thriving Catholic church, St. Peter's, which had been in existence since 1839, and a rudimentary school that had been commenced in the church basement in 1842. Moreover, the overcrowded conditions at St. Peter's suggested the rapid growth of a substantial Catholic population, wealthy enough to build a fitting cathedral.

To bring home his point, Kundig used the one-year anniversary of the Catholic Temperance Societies on March 17, 1843; he contrived to assemble 3,000 Catholics, and many non-Catholics, for a Mass on the steps of the courthouse. Historian James S. Buck, who witnessed the event, wrote, "I shall never forget the spectacle of people kneeling in the snow."[79] After the Mass, the assembled multitudes with banners flying from their respective parishes marched in procession through the city streets. It would be on that very day that Milwaukeeans heard the news that Congress had approved funds to straighten and widen the sand-filled harbor of the city. This decision, which helped to cement Milwaukee's already strong position as the leading Wisconsin port on Lake Michigan, set off a wave of general rejoicing for a public works project that people in the 21st century would find difficult to understand. In the general celebrations planned to celebrate the good news, Kundig again helped mobilize Catholics for yet another civic celebration that highlighted the presence of Catholics in the city (and also their commitment to urban development).

Mounted on a spirited horse, Kundig led banner-bearing German speakers through the city. Later, he saw to it that news of these huge demonstrations reached the ears of bishops in

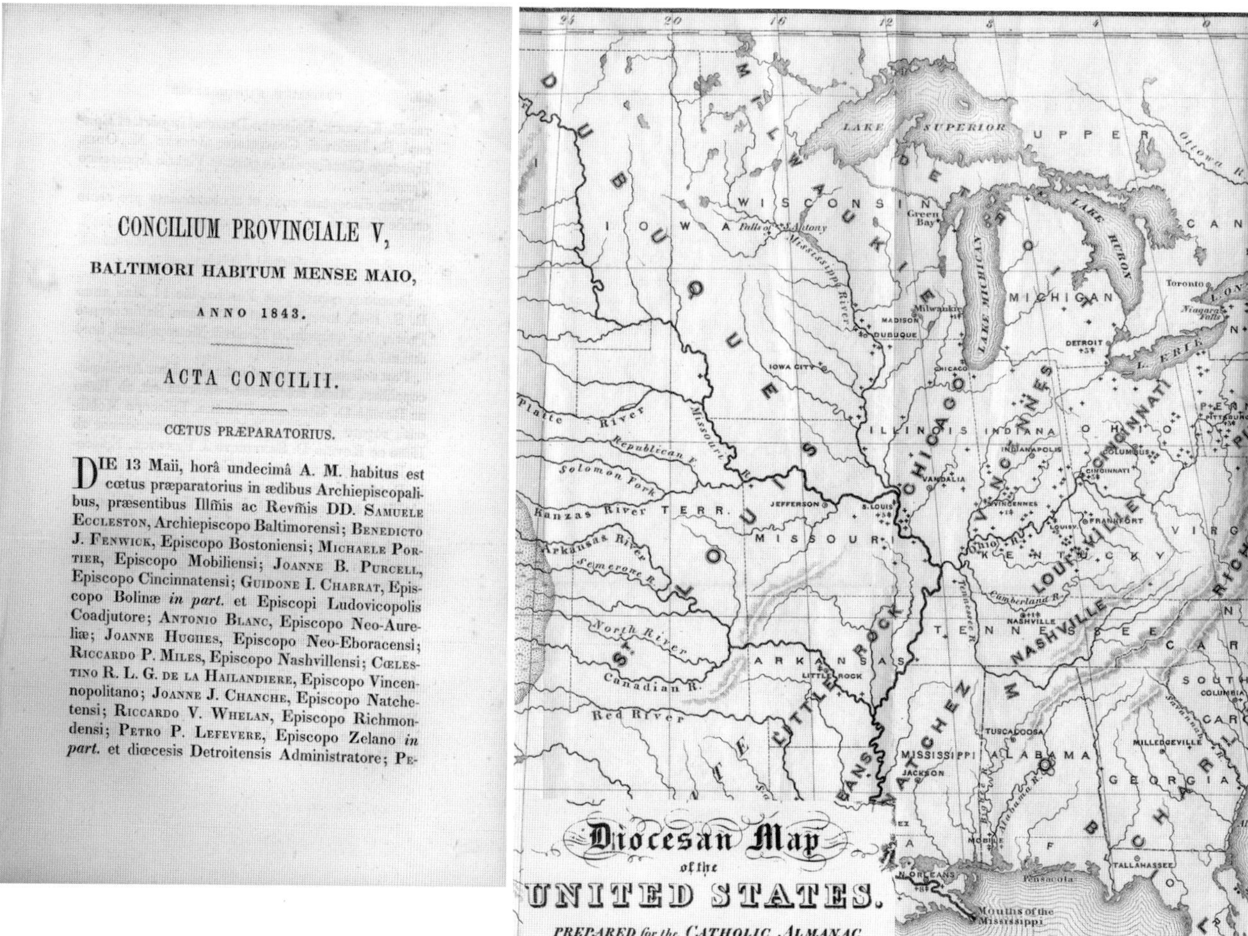

CONCILIUM PROVINCIALE V,

BALTIMORI HABITUM MENSE MAIO,

ANNO 1843.

ACTA CONCILII.

CŒTUS PRÆPARATORIUS.

Die 13 Maii, horâ undecimâ A. M. habitus est cœtus præparatorius in ædibus Archiepiscopalibus, præsentibus Illmis ac Revmis DD. Samuele Eccleston, Archiepiscopo Baltimorensi; Benedicto J. Fenwick, Episcopo Bostoniensi; Michaele Portier, Episcopo Mobiliensi; Joanne B. Purcell, Episcopo Cincinnatensi; Guidone I. Chabrat, Episcopo Bolinæ *in part.* et Episcopi Ludovicopolis Coadjutore; Antonio Blanc, Episcopo Neo-Aureliæ; Joanne Hughes, Episcopo Neo-Eboracensi; Riccardo P. Miles, Episcopo Nashvillensi; Cœlestino R. L. G. de la Hailandiere, Episcopo Vincennopolitano; Joanne J. Chanche, Episcopo Natchetensi; Riccardo V. Whelan, Episcopo Richmondensi; Petro P. Lefevere, Episcopo Zelano *in part.* et diœcesis Detroitensis Administratore; Pe-

Acts of the Provincial Council of Baltimore, from 1843 [*Provincial Councils of Baltimore, from 1829-1849*, Baltimore, 1851]

1845 Diocesan Map [*Metropolitan Catholic Almanac and Laity's Directory for 1845*, Lucas Field, Jr., 1845]

the east who were planning the Fifth Provincial Council of Baltimore. Kundig's celebrations—their size and ostentation—brought home a new reality to those who may have not paid attention to the developments on the Wisconsin frontier. The present and future number of Catholics had now reached the threshold required for a new diocese.

When the Provincial Council met in May 1843, a number of bishops and their theological advisors may have secured enough information about events in Wisconsin territory to make an informed recommendation. Certainly the one who knew the most was Kundig's correspondent, Father John Martin Henni, who had accompanied his bishop, John Baptist Purcell, to the council as a theological advisor. A number of rapidly growing areas in the American West were laid before the council fathers, and recommendations for the erection of new dioceses were conveyed to Propaganda in Rome. On November 28, 1843, Pope Gregory XVI issued the bull *In Suprema militantis* formally establishing the diocese of Milwaukee; it consisted of the entire state of Wisconsin, together with a small slice of present-day Minnesota east of the Mississippi River. By the same bull, Roman authorities created dioceses in Bridgeport, Connecticut; Little Rock, Arkansas; and Chicago, Illinois.

To head the new territory, Propaganda followed the suggestion of the Fifth Plenary Council and appointed Henni of Cincinnati as proto-bishop. On the Feast of St. Joseph, March 19, 1844, the Swiss-born Henni was consecrated by Bishop John B. Purcell of Cincinnati, assisted by Bishops Michael O'Connell of Pittsburgh and Richard Pius Miles, O.P., of Nashville. After tearful farewells from Cincinnati's Germans, he traveled via Great Lakes steamers with Bavarian Father Michael Heiss and arrived at the pier on Third Street in Milwaukee on May 4 or 5, 1844. This began a 37-year reign that would not only establish a network of churches and institutions to accommodate the state's growing Catholic population, but would also attempt to create a homogeneous Catholic culture for the people of Wisconsin.

Another Type of Visibility: The Work of John Martin Henni and the Rise of Ethnic Catholicism

Peter Leo Johnson's classic account of Henni's life and career, *Crosier on the Frontier,* was a faithful retelling of the peripatetic career of the first bishop (later archbishop) of Milwaukee. Although framed in the conventional filiopietism that characterized episcopal biographies of those days (1958), Johnson's book was published by the Historical Society of Wisconsin, whose editors straightened out his occasionally convoluted prose and chronology and gave the book a scholarly style that sets it apart from many others of the time. Even more importantly, *Crosier* was exhaustively researched and rested on a foundation of solid primary and secondary sources.[80]

Bishop John Martin Henni of Milwaukee [Martin Marty, OSB. *Dr. John Martin Henni, First Bishop and Archbishop of Milwaukee,* Benziger Bros., 1888]

Henni was born in 1805 in the village of Misanenga in the Swiss canton of Obersaxen. He grew to maturity in the context of the religiously heterogeneous culture of the federation of cantons. Swiss Catholicism was both remarkably strong and yet also sufficiently flexible to coexist peaceably with the other religious traditions in Switzerland. By the time Henni was born, combating the hangovers of Reformation polemics was a part of the "territory" of Swiss Catholicism. Just as important, Swiss Catholics (and other German-speaking nationalities) also waged intellectual war on the forces of the Enlightenment and the excesses of modern liberalism which scorned and sought to marginalize religious influence in public affairs as well as attack religious doctrines. The religious revival in 19th century Europe, alluded to earlier, took firm root in the Catholic cantons of Switzerland. Swiss Catholicism strongly embraced the teachings of the Council of Trent, renewed local religious communities, accentuated its loyalty and devotion to the pope, and was imbued with a deep missionary spirit.

Henni's studies for the priesthood began when at 10 years of age he was sent to live with an uncle who was a priest. He was further mentored by another cleric, Father John Peter Mirer, whom Johnson characterizes as an "accomplished scholar in the fields of theology, canon and civil law, and philosophy."[81] With Mirer's patronage, Henni was admitted to higher studies at the magnificent monastery of St. Gallen in 1820, a place of scholarship and knowledge destined to have an impact on two Milwaukee bishops, Henni and Sebastian Messmer. As previously noted, in 1826, he and Martin Kundig moved to Rome where they pursued their studies for the priesthood at the Sapienza University. Henni's Roman years were important ones for the Catholic Church. In the aftermath of the Napoleonic Wars, a revived papacy began to assert itself as the single most important Roman Catholic institution in the world.[82] Likewise, as we have seen, Rome also was the center for a renewed burst of interest in missionary activity.[83] In 1827 Father Frederick Résé of Cincinnati visited the Sapienza and convinced the two Swiss seminarians, Henni and Kundig, that there was plenty of work to do, especially for the growing number of German-speaking Catholics in Ohio. The two men left their families and decamped for America in late 1827. As noted earlier, Fenwick greeted them warmly and after a brief period in an American seminary at Bardstown, Kentucky, ordained the two men in February 1829.

Bishop Johann Peter Mirer of St. Gallen [Martin Marty, OSB. *Dr. John Martin Henni, First Bishop and Archbishop of Milwaukee,* Benziger Bros., 1888, p. 381]

At this point the two men went in separate directions. Kundig, as we have seen, soon moved to the western reaches of Ohio, ending up in Michigan and, later, Wisconsin. Henni remained in Ohio at first seeking out scattered German Catholics and circuit-riding as far east as Canton which became his base of operations.[84] Both Kundig and Henni helped raise the infrastructure of Catholic life in their areas of missionary endeavor, but an important difference between them emerged from the outset. Kundig soon accommodated himself to the socially fluid character of frontier life and threw himself into the task of city and community building. Henni soon identified his role as preserving and expanding German Catholic identity in America. Although it is a bit of an oversimplification, for Henni the link between German culture and Catholicism was important to maintain, while Kundig seemed to shed the cultural shell of German-speaking Catholicism in order to adapt the church to its new environment.

A German "Las Casas"

In his declining years, Henni was hailed by Father Ludwig Mueller, the administrator of an important missionary fund-raising organization, as the "Las Casas" of the Germans in America. This comparison to the courageous Dominican Bartolmeo de las Casas who passionately defended the rights of the Indian peoples, suggested that Henni was a bulwark against the onslaughts of a culture that sought to deprive people of their native tongue and religion. Although the comparison is hyperbolic, Henni did focus the beam of his pastoral ministry and church building on the maintenance of the religio-cultural synthesis that characterized most German-speaking Catholics in America.

Eventually, his days as a missionary in eastern Ohio ended, and Henni came back to Cincinnati. Here the traces of Henni's career as a German-advocate are most clearly seen. Cincinnati's place on the Ohio River made it a leading entrepot for the growing state's agriculture and manufacturing industries. Eager settlers poured into the Ohio Valley and fanned north through rich farmlands to the Great Lakes. In the 1830s, Cincinnati's population was swollen by immigrants, most notably the Germans.[85] Henni's special affection for the German people stemmed from two sources. First he loved the ways in which his native culture sustained and encouraged a Catholic way of life (a sensibility perhaps sharpened by nostalgia for the homeland and also the "indifference" of many Americans about choosing a denomination). German culture was not just an idiom of the faith, it was part of the faith itself, especially the German language. Secondly, he feared that if German speakers weren't satisfied by the official Catholic response to their needs, other churches, namely the Lutherans, would fill the void. Henni soon identified his chief pastoral task as preserving the German cultural shell of Catholicism. Catholic visibility and ethnic preservation went hand-in-hand. The famous saying, "language preserves faith," used by scores of German clerics, may have originated with Henni. Virtually any historical overview of German-speaking immigration to America, especially to Wisconsin, mentions Henni and his reputation as a promoter and defender of German Catholic life in America. Henni was pretty clear about the suitability of Wisconsin for Germans. He wrote in 1844, "A good half of the Catholics here are German, but many of them have settled at quite a distance in the interior of the land on the very rich wheat soil and to those places daily many others follow, because here the soil and the climate are especially suitable to Germans."[86] Indeed, Milwaukee's proto-bishop was an important "pull factor" of German-speaking immigration to America and especially to Wisconsin.[87]

European Aid to Wisconsin Catholicism

Henni's "vision of ministry" was strongly supported by missionary support societies that developed in German-speaking areas of Europe. Integrally woven into the history of the archdiocese of Milwaukee are the histories of the various missionary support agencies that literally sent thousands of dollars as well as material objects necessary for church life (vestments, liturgical and music books, bells, art work, altars, etc.) to Henni's new diocese in Wisconsin. Just as important, these organizations provided missionary personnel who generously came to America to staff churches, schools, and social welfare organizations.

As noted earlier, the oldest of these organizations was the Society for the Propagation of the Faith founded in Lyons in 1822.[88] Winning critical episcopal and papal support, the organization recruited funds from Catholics around Europe by a successful combination of devotional activities, interesting stories of mission life from abroad, and periodic begging campaigns directed by priests associated with the organization. The Propagation of the Faith was naturally interested in areas of America inhabited by French Catholics, and dioceses all over America received tidy sums of money and religious goods for their endeavors. Henni first engaged the organization in 1835, when he traveled abroad at the behest of Bishop John Purcell and secured money for Cincinnati. Milwaukee would receive a share of Propagation monies throughout the years.

Of even greater importance to Milwaukee's life were the two German-speaking missionary support organizations, the Vienna-based *Leopoldinen Stiftung* and the Munich-based *Ludwig-Missionsverein.* The Austrian organization was formed in 1829 through the efforts of Father Frederick Résé, who, as we have seen, was Bishop Edward Fenwick's chief recruiter for German needs in Ohio. Résé had visited the Propagation headquarters in 1824 with Fenwick and noted the structure and organization. In 1827-1828, on the same trip where he recruited Henni and Kundig, Résé visited Vienna and began begging alms for the missions in Ohio. Through a stroke of luck, he was introduced to Leopold Maximilian, Prince Archbishop of Vienna, who in turn brought him to the court of the Hapsburg Emperor, Francis I. Résé urged the introduction of the Propagation of the Faith in Austria, but the Austrians urged Résé to found a local version of the operation. Named for the daughter of Emperor Francis I, Leopoldine (then Empress of Brazil) who had died in 1827, the organization began in May 1829 and received papal approbation from Pope Leo XII, who conceded a variety of indulgences to those who undertook the spiritual exercises of the organization. Interest in the organization was stimulated by pamphlets and sermons, but in 1831, the society hit on the idea of reporting events in America. This series of reports, called *Berichte*, were published annually until 1914. Administration of the organization was left to the Archbishops of Vienna, who delegated day-to-day operations to a priest secretary. In 1835 as well, Henni began his long association with the *Leopoldinen Stiftung* by establishing contact with Archbishop Vincent Milde of Vienna.[89]

Résé took a hand in the formation of a Bavarian missionary society, the *Ludwig-Missionsverein*. In a manner similar to those in Austria, Résé secured permission to raise money and recruit priests and seminarians for American missions. A steady flow of money from Bavarian Catholics began to come to selected American dioceses. In 1836, Henni went to Munich looking for money and met with Canon Speth who had a deep interest in American affairs. Speth induced Henni to write a lengthy report of conditions in the diocese of Cincinnati, which Henni did: *Ein Blick in's Thal des Ohio oder Briefe uber den Kampf und das Wiederaufleben der katolischen Kirche im fernen Western der Vereiningten Staaten Nordamerika's* (A Glance at the Valley of the Ohio or Letters Concerning the Struggle and the Renascence of the Catholic Church in the Far West of the United States of North America). Speth had 3,000 copies of this tract printed and distributed throughout Bavaria, which paved the way for a renewed effort by Résé to found a missionary fund-raising organization in Munich. In 1838, Résé, now bishop of Detroit, approached King Ludwig I of Bavaria with the request to start an organization. Ludwig, deeply sympathetic and interested in the fate of German Catholics abroad, approved Résé's request, and by December 1838 the constitution of

King Ludwig I of Bavaria
[Bruce Seymour. *Lola Montez: A Life,* Vail-Ballou Press, 1996]

Holy Trinity Church, Cincinnati [Martin Marty, OSB. *Dr. John Martin Henni, First Bishop and Archbishop of Milwaukee,* Benziger Bros., 1888, p. 77]

the *Ludwig-Missionsverein* was approved. Like its French and Austrian counterparts, the Bavarian organization recruited members through devotional tracts. Deeply jealous and suspicious of the activities of the French Propagation, King Ludwig took a direct hand in the affairs of the *Missionsverein,* and its collecting area was largely restricted to Bavaria. Nonetheless, the generous monarch funneled money, art, and people to the German-speaking Catholics of the United States, and Milwaukee received an important share of this largesse.[90] In all, Milwaukee received a grand total of $86,000 in cash gifts from generous European Catholics as well as art works, vestments, missals, and other church accouterments.[91]

With the help of these organizations, Henni and others were able to minister effectively to German-speaking Catholics in the Midwest. Moreover, the stories of his activities, reprinted in the *Berichte* and the Propagation *Annales* not only informed and entertained European audiences, eager for information about the American missions, but may have actually played a role in bringing German-speaking immigrants to Wisconsin.

These organizations were more than just a cash cow for the American missions; they also performed a critical function as a clearinghouse for missionaries anxious to come to a new location. For example, Father Joseph Ferdinand Mueller, secretary and chaplain of the *Ludwig-Missionsverein,* helped to facilitate the movement of a number of religious orders to Wisconsin. It was he who alerted the Abbey of Wilten in Innsbruck to the needs of German-speaking Catholics in America, and they sent the scholarly Father Adalbert Inama. He also played a role in settling the Capuchins, the Racine Dominicans, the Sisters of St. Francis, and the School Sisters of Notre Dame in Wisconsin. It was Mueller who brought Henni's attention to a Third Order Franciscan group of men and women located in Ettenbeuren. All of these communities came to Wisconsin and all received at least some measure of support from the generous king.

Henni in Cincinnati

Henni soon became the right-hand man for German affairs for Bishop John Baptist Purcell, who succeeded Fenwick in 1834. Purcell had a special sensitivity to German speakers and had founded Holy Trinity parish in Cincinnati's west end to accommodate the growing German populace in the queen city.[92] Holy Trinity Church located in the "Over the Rhine" area of Cincinnati had erected its first church in 1834, one of the first German Catholic churches established in the west. It first pastor, Father Damian Juncker (later bishop of Alton, Illinois) was unable to manage affairs, so Purcell turned over the parish to John Martin Henni in 1836.

After Juncker's departure, Henni calmed internal tensions. He then set to work creating a model ethnic parish that soon put the church at the center of the spiritual, social, and cultural life of Cincinnati's growing German community. With strong support from his church members, he enlarged and decorated the church. He proved his administrative mettle by surmounting trustee problems, and expanded his school and stabilized its faculty by recruiting the Sisters of Charity and capable male teachers. Adult education for German-speaking adults was begun in the church basement. In order to prevent German orphans from being placed in a Presbyterian public institution or in the asylum of English-speaking Catholics, Henni formed a German orphanage in 1837, replete with a fund-raising society. To reinforce bonds of German solidarity and to help raise funds for the orphanage, Henni founded *Der Wahrheits-Freund* in 1837, the first German-Catholic newspaper in the country. He turned over day-to-day editorial affairs to Bavarian Franciscan Francis L. Huber (who succeeded Henni in the Holy Trinity pastorate in 1844). The paper grew in circulation, providing ample religious instruction and warnings about defection from the Catholic Church. One liberal German, H. A. Ratterman, lauded

"Der Wahrheits-Freund," 1837
[Martin Marty, OSB. *Dr. John Martin Henni, First Bishop and Archbishop of Milwaukee,* Benziger Bros., 1888, p. 119]

Bedingungen. Der Wahrheits-Freund erscheint wöchentlich einmal und zwar am Donnerstag. — Der Preis für den ganzen Jahrgang ist: zwei Dollars und fünfzig Cents, Vorausbezahlung während des ersten halben Jahrganges. — Bezahlung während des zweiten halben, und nach Verlauf des ganzen Jahrganges, drei Dollars. — Wer während des ersten halben Viertel Jahres abonnirt, hat den vollen Jahrgang, während des zweiten, drei viertheile, und während der beiden letzten, die Hälfte, des Jahrganges zu bezahlen. — Wer zwey Nummern des Wahrheitsfreundes annimmt, verbindet sich dadurch zur Annahme und Bezahlung eines vollen Jahrganges — Aufkündigungen werden nur dann berücksichtiget, wenn sie einen Monat vor dem Anfange eines neuen Jahrganges geschehen sind, und der Aufkündiger alle Rückstände bezahlt hat. — Auswärtigen Unterschreibern wird der Wahrheitsfreund auf ihre Kosten durch die Post zugesandt. — Alle Briefe, Mittheilungen und Anzeigen, müssen portofrei (post paid) eingesandt werden, an

Rev. Mr. J. M. Henni.

„Stehet fest in einem Geiste, eines Sinnes mitkämpfend für den Glauben des Evangeliums, und laßt euch in keinem Stücke abschrecken durch die Widersacher, welches ihnen Anzeige des Verderbens, euch aber des Hasses ist." — Phil. 1.

Mögen die Glieder eurer Kirche in Amerika, vom reinen Geiste des Christenthums nur beseelt — und sich stets als getreue Unterthanen unserer Regierung bewährend, — allen Segen zeitlichen und geistlichen Wohles genießen!

Georg Washington.
Adr. an die Kath. der Ver. Staaten.

Der Wahrheits-Freund.

Herausgegeben von einem Waisen-Vereine in Cincinnati, Hamilton Cty, Ohio.

Jahrgang 1. — Donnerstag, den 20. Juli, 1837. — No. 1.

Prospectus.

Der Wahrheits-Freund.

Ein wöchentliches Blatt unter obigem Titel.

Herausgegeben von einem teutschen Waisen-Vereine.

Wer den erstaunlichen Zuwachs der teutsch-katholischen Bevölkerung in diesen Vereinigten Staaten betrachtet, und besonders dem Strome der Auswanderung, der in vielarmiger Richtung sich nach den westlichen Prairies und Waldungen bewegt, mit still beobachtendem Auge folgt, und bedenkt — daß da vor Allen nicht nur der auf wissenschaftliche Bildung Anspruch machende Teutsche fast allen Mitteln einer ordentlichen Lektür in seiner Muttersprache entblößt, und wie abgeschlossen lebt; sondern daß da auch der nüchterne und industriöse Landmann, der Gesetze dieses Landes fremd, der üblichen Sprache unkundig, fern von Lehrern, fern oft von einem Altare — die leeren Stunden, selbst des Sabaths, entweder einsam oder gruppenweise zu Familien betrauert, und nicht selten untröstlich in seinen Nachkommen die im Teutschland begonnene Bildung, statt selbe fester zu begründen, aus Mangel christlicher oder sonst nützlicher Unterhaltungsquellen, allmählig abnehmend und erlöschend erblickt; wer über dies ein Zeuge ist des seit einiger Zeit reggewordenen und lebhaft gefühlten Interesse aller Teutschen für Selbstständigkeit und Sprache: der kann wahrlich nicht umhin die Bedürfniße, besonders der teutschen Katholiken, die nicht in jeder Hütte selbstberufene Prediger finden — lebhaft zu fühlen, und lebhafter den Wunsch zu hegen — daß doch nach Maaßgabe der Zeit und Mittel, ihre Lage erleichtert, Bildung und Religion nach Kräften aufrecht erhalten, und möglichst befördert werden möchte!

Solcher Erwägung zufolge, glauben wir dem Wunsche aller Gutgesinnten am ehesten zu entsprechen durch die Herausgabe eines Blattes, wodurch wir einerseits (als Katholiken) die Religion unserer Väter, wie sie ist — nicht wie selbe fälschlich und boshaft uns angedichtet wird, als die Eine, Wahre, ihrem Wesen nach Unveränderliche, für alle Länder und Zeiten Passende — erklären, und wenn nöthig rechtfertigen wollen: anderseits gedenken wir auch jedesmal das Resultat, oder Ergebniß der Zeit, und besonders die Ereignisse unserer Tage — in Europa sowohl als in Amerika, aus zuverläßigen Quellen zu sammeln, und was einer Erwähnung werth, den Lesern des Wahrheits-Freundes vorzulegen. Somit eröffnet dieses Blatt (in zwei Hälften getheilt) dem geehrten Leser ein doppeltes Gebiet — das religiöse, und das weltliche.

Der Wahrheitsfreund im Religiösen verspricht:

1, eine einfache und deutliche Darstellung über den ganzen Umfang der christlichen Lehre zu geben — wie selbe nämlich von Christus, ihrem Stifter, und dessen Aposteln vorgetragen, dessen Nachfolgern überliefert worden, und wie selbe fortdauern muß „bis an's Ende der Welt." — Math. 28. 20.

2, Wird auf den Kampf und Sieg dieser Lehre, auf ihren wohlthätigsten Einfluß auf alle Moral angespielt, begleitet mit treffenden Auszügen aus der Geschichte der Kirche, besonders über Leben und Wirken großer Personen in derselben.

3, Folgen Obigen zu Zeiten authentische Nachrichten neuester Denkwürdigkeiten, als Missionsberichte &c. und was überhaupt im äußern Leben und gegenwärtigen Wirken unserer heiligen Kirche, so weit sie sich erstreckt, merkwürdig ist.

Der Wahrheitsfreund im Weltlichen sammelt:

1, In möglichster Eile und Tagesordnung, die wichtigsten politischen Ereignisse, sowohl die einheimischen, als fremden, d. h. alle vorzüglichen Neuigkeiten der alten Welt — mit besonderem Rückblick auf unsere alte Heimath — ganz Teutschland und die Schweiz. — Bei Erwähnung der einheimisch politischen Ereignissen oder parteilichen Umtrieben aber versprechen wir feierlich — uns an keine sogenannte politische Partei anzuschließen, oder im Mindesten deren Werkzeug zu werden. Jedoch als Freunde der Wahrheit und öffentlichen Ruhe, gebrauchen wir — Allen hier zugestandenes Recht — die Tendenz nämlich irgend eine Parteiung zu prüfen, und nach Verdienst zu preisen oder zu rügen.

2, Uebersetzungen oder Erklärungen jener bürgerlichen Gesetze, welche Allen, die Amerika als ihr Vaterland adoptirt haben, zu wissen nöthig sind, ferner statistische Nachrichten, geschichtliche Auszüge, Leben und Denkwürdigkeiten ausgezeichneter Charaktere, kurz, Gegenstände, welche den meisten als nützlich und unterhaltend erachtet werden, beschließen dieses Blatt.

Gegebenem Umrisse nun so nahe als möglich tretend, und mit angedeutetem Inhalte ausgestattet — sollte der Wahrheitsfreund jedem biederen Katholiken, dem Gott und die Grundsätze seiner Väter heilig sind, als stiller, prunkloser Gefährte zur Hand stehen; er darf mit Recht als lehrreicher Gast dem Kreise einer jeglichen Familie, der es noch um Bildung und moralischen Bestand zu thun, sich nahen; ja — der Wahrheitsfreund sollte darum schon, bei Allen, (Katholiken wenigstens) einer Prüfung und gütigen Aufnahme werth sein, weil er in ganz Amerika als der einzige katholische Bote unter seinen Teutschen aufzutreten wagt, und wahrlich — kein anderes Interesse kennt, als zu belehren, zu erbauen und Waisen zu helfen.

Wir sagen: Waisen zu helfen — weil nach Abzug nöthigster Auslagen, aller Gewinn welcher aus der Publikation dieses Blattes hervorgehen mag, in die Kaße des hl. Aloysius Waisen-Vereins treulich verabfolgt werden wird; indem auch aus derselben die Unkosten bestritten werden. Damit wäre also der Zweck dieses Blattes ausgesprochen — ein Zweck der gewiß von allen gutgesinnten Teutschen gebilligt werden muß: denn es gilt für ihre Sprache — für ihre Religion — und für die Wohlfahrt der Waisen. —

☞ Diejenigen, und besonders die Herrn des geistlichen Standes, — welchen der Plan und Geist des Wahrheitsfreundes zusagt, ersuchen wir freundschaftlichst, uns in unserm wohlgemeinten Unternehmen mit gefälligen Beiträgen zu unterstützen.

Hirtenbrief.

Des Hochwürdigsten Erzbischofes von Baltimore und der übrigen während dem letzten April daselbst in einem Provincial-Concilium versammelten Bischöfe der kath. Kirche in den Vereinigten Staaten von Amerika — an alle Geistlichen und Laien ihrer Sprengel.

„Um deß willen ich auch dieses leide; aber ich „schäme mich dessen nicht; denn ich weis an Wen ich „geglaubt habe, und bin gewiß, daß Er vermöge das „Pfand so ich Ihm anvertraut habe, zu bewahren „auf jenen Tag."

2 Tim. 1. 12.

Unter ihnen sind jene, welche in die Häuser schlei„chen, und wie Gefangene an sich ziehen die Weib„lein, die mit Sünden beladen sind, und von mancherlei Lüsten umgetrieben. —

Aber sie werden nicht lange gedeihen, denn ihr „Frevelsinn wird Allen kund werden. — —

Du aber hast erfasset meine Lehre; mein Verfah„ren, mein Bestreben, meinen Glauben, meine Sanft„muth, Liebe, Geduld, meine Verfolgungen, meine „Leiden.

2. Tim. 3. K. 6, 9, 10, 11. Vs.

Hochwürdige Brüder!

Theure Mitchristen!

Friede Euch, und Glaube mit der Liebe von Gott dem Vater, und dem Herrn Jesus Christus, sammt den Tröstungen des heiligen Geistes.

Zur Berathschlagung für das Wohl jenes Theiles

the newspaper, praising Henni as one who "gave new inspiration and life to German literature in the United States." Ratterman noted, "the spirit and zeal of Henni radiated to the German Catholics in widely scattered settlements, and his innumerable contributions to the civic and religious life of Cincinnati laid a basis for its cultural development."[93]

In 1838, Henni's accomplishments merited him appointment as an "ethnic" vicar general to Bishop Purcell. He encouraged bilingual education, even in the city's public schools, secured the services of a reputable Catholic book-selling firm for the community, and facilitated the formation of a church music association that would provide appropriate music for liturgical celebrations. In 1840, the modest Holy Trinity had grown so big that a second German parish, St. Mary's, was founded at Henni's direction. Ultimately from the seedbed of Holy Trinity an entire network of 12 German Catholic churches, as well as schools and institutions, was created—a veritable phalanx of German Catholic strength. Henni's work at Holy Trinity was singled out as an important exception to the generally poor assessment of American Catholic life rendered by the *Leopoldinen Stiftung* agent Canon Joseph Salzbacher, who was sent to the United States by a suspicious Austrian hierarchy in 1843 to inspect what was happening with *Leopoldinen Stiftung* funds. Even the dour Salzbacher took note of the dynamo of effective activity that emanated from Cincinnati's Holy Trinity, and the mind that was behind it.[94] At Holy Trinity, Henni's efforts at forming a Catholic subculture within a busy city and against challenges posed by other claimants to the loyalties of German Americans, provide an important backdrop for understanding his efforts in the Diocese of Milwaukee. The pattern of its development and the philosophy of its growth was, in some respects, nothing more than Holy Trinity writ large.

Transition to Milwaukee

Henni's pastoral success and his highly visible efforts to minister to German Catholics played some role in his appointment to the see of Milwaukee.[95] His most controversial move was to press for the creation of a seminary for German speakers that would supply needed priests. This idea was proposed by Bishop Purcell, at Henni's urging, at the Fourth Provincial Council of Baltimore in 1840. The plan aroused suspicions and outright opposition. John Bernard Stallo, an outspoken advocate of German-American presence, wrote this for the weekly *Die Freisinnegen* of Cincinnati: "The Irish bishops opposed the erection of institutions for training German priests in order to have a pretext to be satisfied with the dregs, the trash of German seminaries; in a word, the candidates who, on account of their dullness, will become tools of the Irish leaders."[96] Although, as Johnson notes, Stallo was refuted by the *Wahrheits-Freund*, some have speculated that Henni's advocacy of this controversial plan meant that his appointment to Milwaukee was an "exile."

However, the seminary was not an albatross around Henni's neck. Indeed, the seminary project was actively opposed by some Irish bishops and a panel of scholars headed by Sulpician seminary rector Louis R. Deluol, and with Purcell's support Henni managed to secure land for the project in nearby Covington. At the Fifth Provincial Council of Baltimore in May 1843, the bishops approved the controversial plan as long as it was under the direction of a religious order. At that same council they endorsed the creation of a new diocese in Wisconsin and petitioned for Henni's appointment as bishop. Johnson properly argues that although Milwaukee may have been perceived as far distant as another planet, Henni would not have been promoted to episcopal orders if he had been perceived as some sort of nationalist rabble-rouser or potential disrupter. Banishment could have taken far more subtle forms. Whatever misgivings any bishop may have had over the seminary project, they were far overshadowed by Henni's reputation as a skilled administrator, practical pastor, and newspaper editor. In the relatively small pool of competent American priests of the early 19th century, Henni clearly was a clerical star.

Henni decamped for Wisconsin in company with Father Michael Heiss.[97] The Bavarian-born Heiss had come to America in 1843 and immediately associated himself with Henni's plan for a German-speaking seminary. Installing himself at *Muttergottes* (Mother of God) Church in Covington, Heiss did pastoral work until the call arrived to accompany Henni. The two arrived in Milwaukee during the early morning hours of May 4th or 5th, 1844, and proceeded directly to St. Peter's Church, where Kundig was celebrating Mass. When he turned from the altar to impart the final blessing and utter the *Ite Missa est* (Go the Mass is ended) he recognized his new superior and Father Heiss. The joyful reunion brought the three men to the city's first episcopal house on Martin and Juneau Streets and a welcome breakfast.

It was at this breakfast that Henni confronted the distaff side of Kundig's church building activities. Kundig had bought the house as a shell and contracted for the finishing of the interior on credit. The furnishing and decoration were provided by the women of the new church. However, a knock at the door during Henni's first meal brought Luther Wood, "the proprietor of the very lot on which Rev. Kundig built or rather shaped a house," who wanted "a bargain or money from the Bishop whose arrival he so long expected." Henni was compelled to give up $475 of the $500 he had received as a gift from the people of Holy Trinity. "I had therefore to buy the whole concern, lest I should lose even the money expended by Mr. Kundig and the congregation upon it."[98] Henni then discovered other debts that still hung over the adjacent ladies academy, built next to his home and on the church itself. He complained to Bishop Lefevre, "The old debt on the church remains, as I fear, still unpaid .... Yet they bought a bell and an organ." Henni for the first time recognized the difference between the hyperbolic letters sent from his clerical comrade of old and the stark realities of administering the new, but growing diocese. He groused, "Indeed, I do not see that the good Mr. Kundig has ever learned prudence by his ... experience at Detroit."[99]

Henni's surprise at receiving a bill on the first day of his presence in Milwaukee was his first cultural shock. Wisconsin's population skyrocketed between 1842 and 1875. Beginning with fewer than 50,000 people in the year prior to the establishment of the diocese of Milwaukee, the population of the state had surpassed one million by the time Roman authorities created it a metropolitan see in 1875. The rapid growth affected every aspect of Wisconsin's settled areas. It would put special stress on the development of Catholic life. The demands of this rapidly growing diocese came home to Henni, not only amid the clanging of hammers and the rush of building in the see city, but especially from an inspection tour he began shortly after his arrival.

St. Mark Church, Kenosha [AAM]

The year of Henni's arrival witnessed a burst of church development that began to blanket the areas south of the Fox/Wisconsin axis. These parishes grew up in association with the configuration of economic life in the state. The easternmost counties, stretching from the Lake Michigan shore to the rough line that is the western boundary of Green, Dane, and Sauk counties, were oriented toward the commerce developing on the lake. The natural outlets for this activity were the cities of the lakeshore. Iowa, Richland, Crawford, and Lafayette counties were more oriented to lead mining, and later to commerce generated by Mississippi River traffic and the growing significance of Minneapolis-St. Paul.

Henni knew from his experiences in Ohio that the task of creating a viable diocesan infrastructure required a substantial transfusion of funds from abroad. To acquaint himself and potential European benefactors with the needs of his diocese, Henni planned an extensive tour of his new domain. He also made sure that European audiences would have a clear idea of his needs. In a short article for the Benedictine periodical *Der Pilger* Henni announced, "Next week, if God wills, I will begin the visitation of my diocese. I am firmly resolved to visit all villages and settlements wherever Catholics are found in groups in order to obtain an accurate insight into the conditions and the wants of my diocese."[100] He stayed with his new flock to celebrate the Feast of Pentecost (May 26, 1844). A few days later he set out to inspect his new jurisdiction.[101]

The Visitation of 1844

Henni's visitation revealed the pockets of Catholic settlement that had preceded the erection of the new diocese. First he inspected the work of O'Kelley and Kundig in the area south and east of Milwaukee. He headed directly southeast, stopping first at Sac Creek (Oak Creek) "a strong settlement of Irish Catholics about fourteen miles distant from Milwaukee." He proceeded from there to Racine and Kenosha, "two rapidly flourishing towns in Racine county (Kenosha county had not yet been established), both having a considerable number of Catholics especially in and around Southport." He stopped long enough to inspect St. Mark's Church, "a real pretty church built of brick and 80 feet long" erected by his friend Kundig. He noted as well that a frame church was being erected in Racine, "where more than half are German Catholics," as well as in Burlington. Henni pressed on to Salem, Geneva, and Yorkville, where he observed, "all settlements having a great number of Catholics." He then inspected the foundations in Greenfield, Menominee, Granville, Monches, Lake Five, Newland, and Watertown. St. Boniface's in Town 10, Goldenthal (Germantown) also received an episcopal visitation. In June, Henni regrouped and began a journey to the western districts of the diocese by way of Madison. Stopping for a time at the territorial capital, he admired the "charming view" afforded by the new capital. "God willing, I hope to see the erection of a Catholic Church also in this town."[102]

He ascended the ridge of the Blue Mounds leading westerly toward the lead mining area. Here he became very much aware of the influence of Catholic priests from nearby Dubuque. He viewed the lead mines and "whitish yellow piles of ground" as he approached the Mississippi. He paused in the village of Mineral Point where he selected the plot of land on which the new Catholic church would be erected. He noted that among the new parishioners of the church were the two Catholic daughters of Governor James Duane Doty.

He moved next to Grant County, abutting the Mississippi River, and found several settlements of Catholics. Two villages, Platteville and Potosi, both had small churches. Farther west he entered into the missionary domain of Dominican Samuel Mazzuchelli in Benton, New Diggings, Shullsberg, and Sinsinawa. Of the latter he wrote effusively, "a solitary hilltop which like a veritable new Tabor rises from the level of a wide prairie, crowned by a beautiful forest." All had new churches built by Mazzuchelli, who also was laying plans for a college "dedicated to religion and science" on eight hundred acres purchased from a former military man with a Catholic wife.[103]

Heading northward, beyond the Wisconsin River, Henni entered into the more sparsely populated lands of the new diocese. In Crawford County he paused among the largely French-Canadian Catholic flock at Prairie du Chien's St. Gabriel Church, which he noted was "burdened with a debt of $3,000 dollars." Reminded of Kundig's penchant for overspending, he noted, "How and why such a building could be undertaken is beyond my comprehension." Yet he noted that the stone construction of St. Gabriel's "is and always will remain an imposing, durable structure."[104] Administering Confirmation at a ceremony that brought out not only Catholics, but also Protestants and soldiers from the nearby garrison, he completed his tour there with a visit from the Winnebago tribe's chieftain, Core. Core's "imposing figure and posture" called to mind "a race, at one time possessing power over America, now nearly exterminated or perishing from inner causes."[105]

The visit with Core, who was a Catholic, stimulated Henni's interest in the other tribes residing in Wisconsin and by the end of July he found his way to Green Bay, from where he launched into the northern reaches of Wisconsin. At Green Bay he was met by several Indians who conveyed him by canoe up the Fox River, passing the Rapides des Pères, where a century and a half before, the Jesuits had built a wooden chapel. His first stop was at Little Chute where he met the Dutch Dominican Theodore J. Van den Broek, who had been in Wisconsin since 1833, and had moved to Little Chute in December 1835. As we have seen Van den Broeck had established a successful missionary circuit along the trails and waterways of the Fox/Wisconsin valleys. With the Dominican and four Indians, Henni ascended the Fox River, crossing Lake Winnebago to inspect the new relocation site for the recently moved Menominees. After sleeping the night in an Indian wigwam, Henni and his party proceeded to the center of the new Indian settlement and in an arbor chapel presided over divine services. Meeting with the Indians, he gave permission for the erection of a chapel at the new site and then proceeded to Portage, and on to Butte des Mortes where he stayed at the home of Augustin Grignon, a French settler who had settled and married an Indian wife.

Continued curiosity about the Indians brought Henni to Sault Ste. Marie and, from there, by difficult passage along Lake Superior, to La Pointe where he met with Father Frederick Baraga in August of 1844. Baraga had just returned from a missionary trip to L'Anse where his efforts at converting the Indians had been highly successful ("to the intense irritation of the Methodists, their agents and helper"). He escorted Henni to St. Joseph's Chapel, where the prelate was overwhelmed by the warmth of the reception by the Chippewas. He stayed up half the night receiving Indians who wanted "to receive a blessing from the Great Black-Robe."[106]

Henni celebrated the Feast of the Assumption, preaching to the Indians as Baraga "repeated point by point in the soft Chippewa language."[107] He confirmed 122 and left reluctantly only because the vessel back to Sault Ste. Marie would not wait. He was unable to visit the colonies of Fond du Lac and Grand Portage, Minnesota. Baraga would later move to the Upper Peninsula of Michigan and his work would be picked up by Franciscan Father Otto Skolla.

Henni arrived home on September 23, in time to greet a new priest, Father Adalbert Inama, who would soon labor to bring Catholicity to Dane County and its surrounding areas. Safely settled in his new home, Henni met with his clerical comrades—Heiss, Kundig, and Thomas Morrissey—who shared the small episcopal residence with him. He now began in earnest nearly 40 years of labor to establish, develop, and spread the Catholic Church throughout Wisconsin. As appealing as he found the missions to the Indians, he devoted the lion's share of his energies and resources to accommodating the flood of European settlers coming to Wisconsin.

Bishop Frederick Baraga of Marquette
[Martin Marty, OSB. *Dr. John Martin Henni, First Bishop and Archbishop of Milwaukee,* Benziger Bros., 1881, p. 169]

The "Catholicisms" of Wisconsin

The task faced by Henni, and most American bishops, was daunting. On the one hand, they were obliged to uphold episcopal authority and prerogatives and to serve as a source of ecclesial unity. Bishops had to direct both the temporal and spiritual aspects of diocesan life, serve as overseers of the local clergy, and represent the church to civil authorities. Doing this required not only the support of church law and clergy, but also the less tangible skills of inspiring respect and genuine leadership. Throughout his long career, Henni managed to make episcopal authority visible, respected, and effective in the cause of archdiocesan unity. He was a nearly picture perfect model of the kind of bishop envisioned by the reformers of the Council of Trent.

But the mandate of unity was also confronted by the reality of significant ethnic differences. In fact, there was not just one "Catholicism" in Wisconsin, but really multiple "Catholicisms" based largely on ethnic differences. The observation made by Italian scholar Antonio Gramsci is applicable to the history of the archdiocese of Milwaukee: "Every religion, even Catholicism (in fact especially Catholicism, precisely because of its efforts to maintain a superficial unity and not allow itself to be fragmented into national churches or along class lines), is really a multiplicity of religions that are distinct and often contradictory."[108]

Archdiocesan history is, to some degree, a history of "Catholicisms" generated by the forces of ethnicity. At nearly every stage of its history, ethnic considerations have played an important and often defining role in archdiocesan life. Ethnic issues have shaped episcopal selections, the formation of local clergy, the recruitment of sisterhoods, the scope and content of Catholic education, the use of urban space, the character of public celebrations and the provision of social services. Ethnicity is the "second language" of Catholic identity, augmenting the "official" parlance of liturgical, doctrinal, and creedal statements with an argot of "popular" religion.

In the first round of coping with these various "Catholicisms," German-speaking Catholics established hegemony in parish establishments and institutions of social provision, constituted the bulk of the religious professionals (priests, nuns, and choral directors), and impressed their own distinctive cultural imprints on that elusive category called archdiocesan "character." German dominance of Milwaukee is what made the See distinct among many American dioceses of similar size and strength. Milwaukee was known nationally and even internationally as "a German diocese" with a German bishop and a German seminary. It was the central headquarters for several large and influential German sisterhoods, the home base for German-language newspapers, and the source of many of the German-speaking priests who served in Wisconsin and throughout the Midwest. This was made possible by the sheer numbers of foreign-born Germans who created dense social networks that made the church a major focus for social, cultural, and intellectual life.

The only group capable of challenging German hegemony were Irish and English-speaking Catholics, who weren't so numerous as the Teutons, but who nonetheless developed rival institutions, their own professional cadre and a voice in Catholic affairs. The English-speaking were not passive. Although never as numerous as the German-speakers, they managed to hold their own in diocesan affairs, and then some. Symbolically, they controlled the cathedral church of the diocese, had their own orphanages and newspapers, and relied on their own teaching sisterhoods and religious orders of men. They also built, as money became available, churches of supreme elegance.

Balancing the competing claims and desires of these two "Catholicisms" occupied much of Bishop Henni's time (and that of several of his successors). These tasks would become more complicated as other "Catholicisms" made their home in Wisconsin, but in the first generations of Catholic history in Wisconsin, the focus was on the Germans and English-speaking.

The English-Speaking Catholics of Wisconsin: The Irish

The largest group of English-speaking Catholics were Irish, and they played a major role in shaping Catholic life in Wisconsin.[109] Their presence was "relatively isolated and sporadic" in the upper Midwest until the 1820s "lead rush" in southwestern Wisconsin. After the opening of large-scale U. S. settlement in Wisconsin following the Blackhawk War of 1832, a small number of Irish immigrants entered the Wisconsin Territory. In the 1840s, the lure of Wisconsin land attracted a number of Irish who had already settled in the East, and some also escaping Ireland's disastrous famine (1845-1850). Interestingly, the first foreign-born Catholic group to dominate Wisconsin were the Irish who reported 21,043 in the census of 1850.[110] However, this did not last long. By 1860, there were 50,000 Irish-born residents in Wisconsin or 6.4 percent of the state's population, making them briefly the second largest foreign-born group in the state. The Irish-born numbers declined after that, until by 1900 they were only 1 percent of the state's foreign-born. Historians note that there was "never a large cohesive Irish community in Wisconsin as there was in New York, Boston or Chicago."[111] A large number of the Irish immigrants enumerated in 1860 lived in rural areas, and most Irish-born men were involved in farm work. Irish Catholicism eventually gave way to a more generic English-speaking Catholicism.

Irish settlers entered Wisconsin as lead miners, railroad builders, laborers, and craftsmen of all kinds. Naturally, residence followed jobs. The Irish Catholic presence in Wisconsin was first strong in the lead mines of the southwestern part of the state. Small towns like Benton, Darlington, Gratiot, Kendall, Seymour, Shullsberg, and Willow Springs in Lafayette County were still predominately Irish as late as 1890.[112] By 1860 the lakeshore communities of Milwaukee, Racine and Kenosha, had strong Irish enclaves. So also did Waukesha County. Railroad construction brought in many Irish laborers to the town of Janesville. Irish farming communities developed after the lead mining and railroad building jobs dried up. Irish farmers had a strong foothold in rural Dodge, Washington, and even a foothold in heavily German Ozaukee County. Eden and Osceola in Fond du Lac County had a heavy concentration of Irish settlers. The town of Mitchell in Sheboygan County was also known as an Irish domain. Indeed, Irish-born Catholics were found in virtually every corner of the state.

One particularly strong and accomplished Irish family lived in the Walworth County town of East Troy. Thomas Cleary had come to the United States from Balinskill, County Galway in 1848 to escape the famine and arrived in Wisconsin in 1850. Settling in East Troy, Cleary devoted himself to manual labor but was an omnivorous reader and poured his love of learning into his sons. Among his offspring were a priest son, James Cleary, and several sons who distinguished themselves in careers in medicine, politics, and the law. The elder Cleary was typical of many Wisconsin

Irish. He kept one foot on the "old sod" by perpetuating the Gaelic tongue and keeping abreast of conditions in Ireland through the troubled years of the 19th century. However, he also invested himself totally in American life and culture. Each of his sons embraced the American way of life wholeheartedly, especially James Cleary who aligned himself with like-minded Irish-Americans in the Milwaukee clergy in calling for more cultural accommodation on the part of Wisconsin Catholics and less ethnic separatism. Thomas Cleary lived to the ripe old age of 90 and was buried in the East Troy cemetery in 1908.[113]

We know comparatively little of the quality and depth of Irish Catholic practice in Wisconsin. Perhaps some immigrants brought over the pre-famine religiosity described by sociologist Michael Carrol. This form of Irish religious practice borrowed extensively from the Celtic past and reflected itself in popular customs such as "rounding rituals" (ritualized walks around devotional shrines) and visits to penitential spots and holy wells.[114] More likely however, the religious practices of Wisconsin's Catholics reflected the impact of the "Devotional Revolution," a religious revival that swept Ireland between 1850-1875. The remote origins of this Irish movement took root during the Catholic Reformation when clerics sought to revive the parish church and the Sunday Mass as the center of Catholic life and identity as they had been in the 16th century. These efforts, of course, were hampered by the harsh British penal laws that forbade public Catholic practice. The period of the Enlightenment also contributed to a generally low level of Irish religious practice, religious vocations, and public devotion. Irish religious culture changed dramatically, however, during the 19th century religious revival, when Cardinal Paul Cullen helped to bring about a "devotional revolution" in Ireland. A combination of techniques, spearheaded by the Roman-trained Cullen, soon made Irish Catholic life the envy of the western world. Religious life quickened in Ireland, resulting in an abundance of vocations to the priesthood and religious life, a spate of church-building to accommodate new crowds coming to weekly Mass, and the cultivation of a host of Roman devotions (e.g., the rosary, use of the scapular, various Marian devotions, 40 Hours, etc.) that soon defined the new face of Irish religion.[115]

Cardinal Paul Cullen [AAM]

Irish Catholicism in Wisconsin would replicate many of these traits. Irish Catholic parishes in Milwaukee, Kenosha, and Racine developed a rich devotional life, in many respects replicas of the devotional practices of Ireland. However, because of the large presence of ethnic-German speakers, and also the relatively small number of foreign-born Irish who settled in Wisconsin, Irish Catholics assimilated quickly into American society. As one historian noted, "The Irish need for self-protective settlement diminished, allowing the gradual blending of these enclaves into the country's mainstream. Today little remains of their former existence other than the eroded gravestones of their founders."[116] Irish Catholic churches then soon became English-speaking churches, dominated no doubt by people and priests with Irish surnames, who in many cases considered themselves more "American" than "Irish."

The English-speaking were sizeable enough in most Wisconsin cities and counties to bring about the formation of a parish for their needs.[117] Henni visited Irish seminaries like Maynooth to recruit Irish-born priests to minister to their countrymen in rural missions. Most of these parishes began with log chapels, which were replaced by more sturdy frame or stone churches in the late 19th century. Stained glass windows, statuary and other improvements followed, although as a rule these Irish chapels were never as elaborately decorated as their German counterparts. Other religious institutions contributed to the development of the English-speaking presence in Wisconsin Catholicism. This included religious sisterhoods.

Any consideration of the sisterhoods involves some discussion of the origins of Catholic schools. In 1842, Kundig began the school in St. Peter's basement. In 1846, the same year that ground was broken for the German church, Henni welcomed the first contingent of the Sisters of Charity, an American community based in Emmitsburg, Maryland. These sisters came at the behest of Henni, who appealed to them in 1845 "to get up a school for female children of my congregation, a thing which is very urgent indeed."[118] On July 15, 1846, the pioneer sisters, Mary Simeon, Mary Paul and Frances Agnes arrived with Kundig. By the end of August the basement of St. Peter's was set up to receive girls. Other schools were begun in 1845 when Kundig opened a school at St. Mark's in Kenosha and in 1847, when Samuel Mazzuchelli's school began at Sinsinawa Mound and St. Regina opened its doors in Madison. The origins of religious communities of women in the Milwaukee diocese, as elsewhere, is bound tightly with the formation of Catholic schools.

English-Speaking Sisterhoods

In response to the need for English-speaking sisters to begin an educational center in Kenosha, two members of the Irish-based Sisters of St. Brigid arrived in that city in early 1851.[119] This community, founded in the city of Tullow, was of rather recent vintage, taking their lead from the other popular orders of Irish teaching women, the Sisters of the Presentation and the Sisters of Mercy. Like these two communities, the Brigidines followed the Irish diaspora around the world, taking missions in Australia and New Zealand. They were brought to Kenosha by Irish-born Father Michael McFaul, who had been ordained for Milwaukee by Henni in the fall of 1847. Events were promising at first, with the small group of sisters opening a female academy under the auspices of St. Mark's parish. However, the inability of the community to sustain the enterprise led to the withdrawal of the sisters. They were eventually suppressed in 1869.

To the west, a Wisconsin-based sisterhood was shaping up under the hand of

St. Clara Academy, Benton WI [AOP-Sin]

Samuel Charles Mazzuchelli.[120] The ambitious Dominican had helped raise the framework of organized life on the western frontier of Wisconsin, northwestern Illinois and northeastern Iowa. In 1844, he conceived a scheme to create a mini-Dominican empire in the heart of his endeavors. He secured permission from his Dominican superiors in Rome to create a new province, named for St. Charles, with headquarters in western Wisconsin.[121]

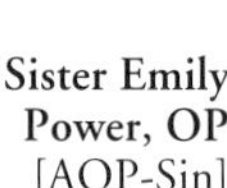

Sister Emily Power, OP [AOP-Sin]

For the center of this new Dominican province, he purchased property on a high promontory called Sinsinawa Mound, owned by former soldier Edgar Wallace. Wallace was eager to sell the Mound and Mazzuchelli managed to secure enough of the $6,500 price from wealthy friends abroad. In 1846 he began to raise buildings on its southern face that would be the center of new province of St. Charles, a men's college and a school for younger children. In 1847, he invested four young women with the habit of the Dominican order and set them to work forming a community and helping to staff the fledgling school. In 1849, these women took their first vows. But that same year, an exhausted Mazzuchelli quit the entire enterprise and turned over the Mound to the Kentucky Dominicans, retiring to a parish he had founded in Benton, 14 miles east of the site. The new Dominican male leadership, sharing little of Mazzuchelli's dreams for a sisterhood of educators, transformed the sisters into housekeepers for themselves and the college. When the sisters balked at this, Mazzuchelli welcomed them to his parish at Benton in 1852. There they established a convent and opened a girls school, St. Clara's Academy.

Mazzuchelli then devoted more attention to the sisters and began to draw up a rule of life based on the principles of the Dominican Third Order rather than on the rule for contemplative Dominican nuns. The sisters embraced the Third Order rule, enhanced by observance of the equally flexible Rule of St. Augustine. Like all other communities, the sisters had a difficult time attracting new members and suffered the inevitable losses of membership that threatened their existence. In a Sinsinawa Dominican version of a story quite common among religious orders, a moment of crisis was reached when the group seemed on the verge of dissolution. At this point, the decision to go forward or disband was left in the hands of the youngest member, who urged the sisters to remain together.[122]

In 1858, Mazzuchelli cherished some hopes of restarting the ill-fated Province of St. Charles, but received no support or encouragement from Rome. When he learned that his Dominican confreres on the Mound had plans to close the college and sell the property, Mazzuchelli used his contacts with the Wisconsin legislature to wrest control of the college and its property from the hands of the Dominicans living there. A friendly legislator, J. Earnest, complied with his request, and had a law passed in March 1864, setting up a new corporation for the Sinsinawa College which Mazzuchelli planned to dominate.[123] However, by the time the bill became law, Mazzuchelli had died of pneumonia contracted while answering a sick call. The new board provided by law was never constituted, and the departing priests sold the land and its buildings in 1866 to a sympathetic lay couple, the Ryans. The sisters, who by this time had built up a respectable girls academy in Benton, voted to purchase the property and begged the Ryans to sell the land to them. Deeds were executed in late March 1867 and shortly afterward the community prepared to move back to their "ancestral" home. By this time, they were led by a newly-elected superior, Sister Emily Power. Power, a native of Ireland, had grown up in southwestern Wisconsin, and through force of will and exceptional leadership skills she built the Sinsinawa Dominicans, as they would be called, into one of the largest religious communities of women in the United States.[124] By the time of her death in 1909, the Sinsinawa Mound was a thriving motherhouse, academy, and college. The Dominican Sisters of Sinsinawa would be among the leading educators of children in the English-speaking parish schools and high schools of the Milwaukee church.

The Jesuits

From the outset of his term as bishop, Henni struggled to secure a teaching order of men to open a college in his jurisdiction. He tried first in 1844, when after returning from his lengthy visitation he encountered Norbertine Father Adalbert Inama and requested that he and his community begin a college in Green Bay. Inama's demurral was just the first of a series of disappointments. Henni was deeply disappointed when Mazzuchelli's plan for a college on the Sinsinawa Mound faltered and he encouraged the

Rev. Joseph Anderledy, SJ [AAM]

Dominican's efforts to renew it in 1858 and 1864. Henni cultivated Benedictine Abbot Boniface Wimmer of St. Vincent's Archabbey in Latrobe, even endorsing the Pennsylvania monastery's petition for independent status with Roman authorities.[125] However, efforts to recruit the Benedictines of Latrobe to come to his diocese were rebuffed as was a similar request in 1847 to the monks of Einsiedeln in his native Switzerland.[126]

While on his fund-raising trip to Europe, in 1848-1849, Henni met Father Anthony Minoux, superior of the German and Swiss Jesuits. He asked that recently exiled Swiss Jesuits living in Missouri come to Milwaukee to open a boys school.[127] On that trip, he had received a modest gift of 75,000 francs ($16,000) from the Chevalier William Joseph DeBoey of Antwerp to underwrite a Jesuit foundation in Milwaukee. DeBoey was described by Jesuit historian Gilbert Garraghan as a member of the "petite bourgeoisie" of Belgium, who made a small fortune as a clerk and merchant for wealthy Antwerp traders. Generous to a fault, he was deeply devoted to American missionary Jesuit Father Peter de Smet.[128] The news of DeBoey's benefaction was communicated from Minoux to the Jesuit Provincial of Missouri, Father John A. Elet. Elet was skeptical of thc Henni offer. He questioned whether Henni was a friend to the Jesuits, dismissed the 75,000 francs as barely enough to build a house for the professors, and warned of the impecunious habits of the Milwaukee clergy: "We advanced $1700 to [Henni's] vicar general, [Kundig] to prevent the sale of one of his churches."[129] However, after a personal visit with Henni in June 1849, Elet changed his mind about Milwaukee's prospects. Moreover, the Swiss Jesuits under his control wished to come to Milwaukee. Two Jesuits did come in August 1849, Anthony Anderledy (who later became the Jesuit General) and Frederick Huebner. Huebner died ten days after coming to Milwaukee (and had the grim distinction of being the first priest interred in the newly founded diocesan cemetery off Grand Avenue—his remains were later transferred to Calvary Cemetery which was founded in 1857). Another Jesuit, Joseph Brunner, was sent to take his place. Anderledy negotiated with Henni for the new school and Brunner even promised that a corps of "brilliant professors" would be in Milwaukee by the next year. Since neither man was fluent in English, they both were sent to care for St. John the Evangelist Church in Green Bay, a bilingual parish, until they felt comfortable enough with the American tongue to start a parish and a school in Milwaukee. Anderledy, it seems, had every intention of beginning the boys school requested by Henni. In August 1849, Henni purchased a home on Van Buren Street and eight adjoining lots for the new school. But Anderledy was recalled to Europe, where he was later elected the Jesuit

General. Brunner also left Wisconsin. There would be no Jesuit school.

In 1853, Henni renewed his desire for a Jesuit college when Fathers John Gleizal, S.J., and Isidore Boudreaux came to Milwaukee to conduct a retreat for the clergy. To "sweeten the pot" and to give the Jesuits a stable source of income until a school could be organized, Henni also offered them the pastorate of St. Gall's parish on the west bank of the Milwaukee River at Second and Sycamore Streets.[130] St. Gall's, founded in 1849, was named for Henni's beloved canton and seminary in Switzerland. It had been a troubled parish from the outset. A succession of English-speaking pastors had passed through its leadership from 1849 until 1855 when the ever-faithful Kundig took over for a short spell. In September 1855, Father Peter DeSmet and Francis Xavier DeCoen were sent to lead the parish. The site of St. Gall's sat on swampy, marshy ground. However, city developers raised the level of the "low-lying and miasma-breeding blocks" an average of twenty-two feet. By 1856, a new rectory and a new church were built. Unable to start a "college" immediately due to lack of funds and professors, in 1857 a boys academy named for St. Aloysius was opened. This would be the nucleus of a high school and Milwaukee's first Catholic university.

In 1861, one of Milwaukee's most celebrated English-speaking clergymen, Father Stanislaus Petit, later surnamed Lalumiere, was assigned to the pastorate of St. Gall's.[131] Lalumiere was born in Vincennes, Indiana in 1822. Educated at St. Mary's College in Kentucky, he "read law" at Vandalia, Illinois and then went on to Springfield, Illinois to become a clerk for the United States court. One of his examiners on the rather informal bar examinations of those days was Abraham Lincoln, then a young lawyer. Lalumiere had been assigned to St. Gall's to direct the fledgling St. Aloysius Academy. Under his leadership the parish soon became an important center for English-speaking Catholics. He was able to bring the Little Sisters of the Poor to Milwaukee to open their care facilities for the elderly poor. This French religious community came to Milwaukee in February 1876 and took up residence in two rented houses that Lalumiere had secured. The next year he helped find new property at Twentieth and Wells Streets where they built a convent and a home for the elderly.[132] He also oversaw the establishment of the House of the Good Shepherd for "wayward girls." Lalumiere remained in the city until 1889 when he was transferred to Cincinnati, visiting the city only once more to attend the cornerstone laying for the new Gesu Church. He died in Cincinnati in 1895.[133]

Rev. Stanislaus Laumiere, SJ
[AAM]

The Jesuits were the most important religious community of men for English-speaking Catholics in Milwaukee. In 1868, the Jesuits began the erection of a new and even larger St. Gall's, a mammoth church that seated 1,000 people. Henni's original site for a Jesuit College, the Van Buren Street property, was deemed too close to the cathedral and its attendant schools to make a good Jesuit foundation. In 1855-1856, Henni sold it and both he and the Jesuits secured the entire block bounded by Tenth, Eleventh, Prairie and State Streets, popularly known as "the Hill." Continued delays for money and professors, and wrangles with Henni over the ownership of the property allowed it to remain vacant until 1875 when a new Jesuit church, Holy Name, was erected on part of it. Finally in August 1880, Coadjutor Bishop Michael Heiss laid the cornerstone of the long-awaited Marquette College. On September 5, 1881, the new school opened its doors.

The Culture of English-Speaking Catholicism

Irish and other English-speaking Catholics cut less of a profile than their German counterparts. One reason for this was a tragic accident, the sinking of the pleasure steamer *Lady Elgin*, which single-handedly wiped out nearly 300 Irish Milwaukeeans on September 7, 1860. St. John's Cathedral was the site of the funerals of the unfortunates, and the disaster was a turning point for the Irish community in Milwaukee. "What makes this catastrophe doubly afflicting," wrote Jesuit Father Francis X. DeCoen of St. Gall's Church, "is that almost without exception, they [the deceased] were Catholics and of the first families of the town. Scarcely a Catholic family but mourns over one of its members or a near relative."[134] DeCoen could have easily substituted the word "Irish" for "Catholic." By 1861, Irish immigration had all but stopped. Irish Milwaukeeans soon began to assimilate into the city's mainstream and left the Third Ward, which had been their main ethnic enclave. The Milwaukee Irish rallied themselves during the Civil War to support the Union cause and formed an Irish Regiment, the 17th, which drew recruits from Irish-Americans in Kenosha, Sheboygan, Dodge, Milwaukee, Fond du Lac, Outagamie, and Racine counties. At about the same time, the Irish nationalist movement, the Fenians, began to recruit actively among the Wisconsin Irish.

The "Lady Elgin" was struck and sank on September 8, 1860 [John G. Gregory *History of Milwaukee, Wisconsin,* S.J. Clarke Co., 1931, p. 723]

The Fenian Society had first been organized by Irish refugees intent on using America as a staging base for the overthrow of British rule in Ireland. Its leaders looked to the young Irish men, trained for duty in the Civil War, to form the core of an army that would one day take on the hated British. The 17th was visited by Fenian representatives during the war, and sympathy for their goals was high. A local Irish leader, Jeremiah Quinn, was Milwaukee's representative to the first national convention of the Fenian Brotherhood in Chicago in 1863. Fenian visibility and power grew in Milwaukee after the war. Church response to Fenianism was negative. Its support of violent revolution, its resemblance to banned "secret societies" and the occasional anti-clerical outbursts of its members led bishops in cities like Boston, New York, and Chicago (all with large Irish populations) to condemn the movement and forbid Catholic participation. Selected Irish-American clergy in Wisconsin joined in this condemnation and Henni attempted to discourage it with speeches and articles. His warnings had little effect and Irish Milwaukeeans joined in the failed efforts to invade Canada. They also raised money for Irish causes.[135]

Fenianism eventually died away, but its presence in Milwaukee contributed to a renewed sense of Irish solidarity, even as their numbers were diminishing. For the rest of its history, Milwaukee and Wisconsin would continued to have a healthy, if not large, Irish subculture which found expression in part through religious activities.

The annual celebration of St. Patrick's Day with parades, dancing, and feasting reflected the ongoing reality of Irish national consciousness in Milwaukee and throughout Wisconsin, even in the midst of a sea of German speakers. For example in 1888, celebrations took place in most major cities of the archdiocese. In Milwaukee "no less than five evening demonstrations were held ...in honor of Ireland's patron saint." In Madison, the home of Mr. and Mrs. J. R. Melvin (the founders of the Catholic ministry to the University of Wisconsin) was transformed into an Irish national shrine with garlands and Irish flags. Serious papers, toasts, and an elaborate banquet commemorated the event. Similar celebrations were held in Bay View, Watertown, Menasha, and Eau Claire.[136] Likewise, among the Irish an intense devotion to the cause of temperance became an important defining mark of the community. Temperance or even total abstinence from alcohol seemed to be the cause that united most of them.[137]

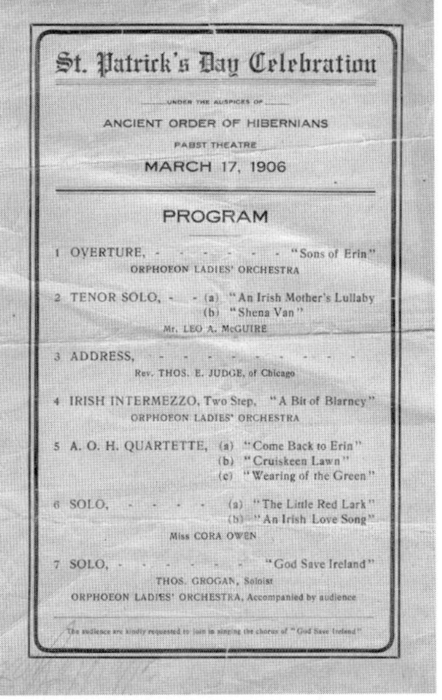

St. Patrick's Day Celebration

UNDER THE AUSPICES OF

ANCIENT ORDER OF HIBERNIANS

PABST THEATRE

MARCH 17, 1906

PROGRAM

1 OVERTURE, - - - - - - - "Sons of Erin"
ORPHOEON LADIES' ORCHESTRA

2 TENOR SOLO, - - (a) "An Irish Mother's Lullaby
(b) "Shena Van"
Mr. LEO A. McGUIRE

3 ADDRESS, - - - - - - - - - - -
Rev. THOS. E. JUDGE, of Chicago

4 IRISH INTERMEZZO, Two Step, "A Bit of Blarney"
ORPHOEON LADIES' ORCHESTRA

5 A. O. H. QUARTETTE, (a) "Come Back to Erin"
(b) "Cruiskeen Lawn"
(c) "Wearing of the Green"

6 SOLO, - - - - - (a) "The Little Red Lark"
(b) "An Irish Love Song"
Miss CORA OWEN

7 SOLO, - - - - - - - - "God Save Ireland"
THOS. GROGAN, Soloist
ORPHOEON LADIES' ORCHESTRA, Accompanied by audience

The audience are kindly requested to join in singing the chorus of "God Save Ireland"

St. Patrick's Day Program at Pabst Theater [AAM]

Catholic interest in temperance, generally acknowledged as a Protestant reform, took root with the preaching of a charismatic Irish priest, Father Theobald Matthew. Matthew's preaching and his insistence that reformed drinkers "take the pledge" caught on in Ireland and spread through the United States. It took particularly strong root among communities of Irish Americans. In 1842, young Irish Catholics in Milwaukee organized a branch of the Catholic Total Abstinence Society. Under the auspices of a cathedral curate, another organization, Father Donahoe's Temperance Society, was organized between 1857 and 1866. As we shall see in subsequent chapters, temperance became an especially sensitive point in the relations between German-speaking and English-speaking Catholics, as the former viewed the production and consumption of beer and other spirits as part of their native culture.

Bernard Durward [AAM]

Nonetheless, the early and growing advocacy of temperance became a defining feature of the English-speaking Catholic contingent.

Emphasis on temperance may have also been stressed by a number of converts to the Catholic faith who also contributed to English-speaking Catholicism's vitality in Wisconsin. A number of convert-priests, including Fathers John Ives, George Willard, and Hiram Fairbanks became important leaders of the English-speaking community in Wisconsin. Likewise, Bernard Durward, a Scottish convert who was baptized by Henni, and joined the seminary faculty in 1856. Teaching English and elocution, he augmented his pitifully small salary by portrait painting and sketching and by giving drawing lessons to students. Durward developed a national reputation as a writer and poet.[138] His contribution to Milwaukee Catholic history was a lengthy sketch of the life of Martin Kundig that was later edited and annotated by Archbishop Sebastian Messmer in a series of articles in the seminary publication *Salesianum.*[139] His career at the seminary did not last long (he served two different short stints on the faculty) but his profile as an English-speaking Catholic reflected the complex layers of Catholic life in Wisconsin. His family retired to a rural retreat near Portage called Durward's Glen and his son John was ordained a priest of the Archdiocese of Milwaukee in 1871.[140]

Although Irish citizens were scattered throughout the rapidly developing area of Milwaukee, most of them resided in the Third Ward, just south of the cathedral. The proximity of the Irish Catholics to the church etched its identity for many years as an "Irish" church. In Milwaukee, Irish and French-speaking Catholics made common cause to dominate the cathedral parish, thereby causing one of the first German withdrawals in the diocese. English-speaking priests reinforced the work with English-speaking Catholics, although, as we shall see, the number of English speakers who came and went in the increasingly Teutonic diocese became a matter of singular controversy.

The German Accomplishment

Wisconsin's "first wave" of immigrants were "Yankees and Yorkers" who took advantage of their wealth and knowledge of American land acquisition to establish a beachhead on Wisconsin soil.[141] Milwaukee's early history was dominated by these speculators and wealthy types. Immigrants of all kinds, many of them Catholics, began to arrive at the time the state was developing. German-speaking migrants already were on the way as early as 1839 when a group of "Old Lutherans," reacting negatively to efforts of the "efficient" Prussian state to blend them into the Reformed Prussian state church, moved to America. Some of them ended up in Mequon (known then as "Freistadt" or Free State). German-speaking groups began to trickle in and then picked up to a crescendo in the 1850s. Ebbs and flows of German-speaking immigration continued throughout the 19th century.

This German-speaking group was quite diverse. It included people from all regions of yet to be unified Germany—northern Germans tending to be Lutherans or evangelicals—while southern Germans, Bavarians, and others tended to be Catholic. Southern German leaders included men like Michael Heiss, Mother Caroline Friess, and the foundresses of the Racine Dominicans and the School Sisters of St. Francis. German-speaking Catholics also included Austrians—a group that would provide important leaders for the local church in the persons of men like Joseph Salzmann, Michael Wisbauer, Capuchin Fabian Bermadinger, and Frederick X. Katzer. Austrian Catholicism, like south German Catholicism, had benefitted widely from the religious revival described earlier. Two Milwaukee bishops, Henni and Messmer were Swiss-born. Swiss Catholics were in evidence throughout the state, but especially in Green County's New Glarus Township and the city of Monroe.

The Duchy of Luxemburg was a small territory with an enormous Catholic population. Luxemburg-born Catholics came in numbers significant enough to stamp their own identity on parishes and certain members of the local clergy. Among their number were the Thill brothers, Nicholas and Dominic, who dominated Sheboygan Catholic life for years; and Kilian Flasch, a future rector of the seminary and bishop of La Crosse, who was the first of several Flaschs in Wisconsin Catholic life. Significant numbers of Luxemburger Catholics were found in Ozaukee County. An especially strong bastion was Dacada, where strong ethnic and religious ties precluded mixed marriages for 92 years.[142]

Finally, German speakers also hailed from sections of central Europe. For example a number of Bohemian Catholics knew and spoke German. So later did some Lithuanians. The German language may have provided a common tongue, yet the group's history, culture, and religious background were all quite different.

German-speaking immigration picked up in the 1850s in part because of the active efforts of the state of Wisconsin to fill the vacant lands. A law of 1852 established a commissioner of emigration with an office in New York. A law the next year allowed a traveling agent to promote the state.[143] Responding to published accounts of rich farm land, good climate and the presence of fellow-nationals, immigrants from the German-speaking areas of Europe and others who had temporarily settled in the east, made their

St. Nicholas Church, Dacada [Courtesy of Michael Petrie]

kee County held the bulk of the new immigrants, with 40 percent of the county's population being foreign-born German speakers.[146]

The tremendous growth of the state in the 1850s reflected itself in the growth of urban communities of 2500 or more. Twenty-four Wisconsin communities fell into this category in 1860—most of them southwest of the Fox/Wisconsin Rivers axis: Milwaukee (45,246), Racine (7882), Janesville (7,703) Madison (6,611), Oshkosh (6,086), Fond du Lac (5,450), Watertown (5,302), Sheboygan (4,262), and Beloit (4,098). Only one of the 24—La Crosse (3,860)— lay to the north of the axis. Only two—Platteville (2,865) and Hazel Green (2,543)—were in the old lead mining area that had been Father Mazzuchelli's sphere of influence.[147]

St. Joseph Chapel, Convent of the School Sisters of St. Francis [ASSF]

way to Wisconsin by stagecoach, lake steamer and railroad (or a combination of all of them). Of the 123,879 foreign-born residents of Wisconsin in 1860 (over half of the state, making it one of the largest foreign-born populations in the American union) nearly 53,000 came from Prussia, and 4,722 from Switzerland.[144] German immigration ebbed and flowed from 1850 to 1870. Between 1860 and 1870 the number of German-speaking people in Wisconsin rose by 39 percent (116,798 to 162,234). When added to those born in Wisconsin of German parentage, the number of people of German-speaking background constituted nearly one-third of the state's population.[145] Richard Current observes that this percentage is higher when one factors in German speakers from the polyglot Austro-Hungarian empire, including Austrians and Bohemians. Milwau-

German Catholics played a dominant role in the history of the Archdiocese of Milwaukee. Historian James Berquist observes: "The Germans were one of the most successful ethnic groups in establishing a tangible presence in America's cities that went beyond a mere collection of institutions to advance ethnicity, and became instead a community in the fullest sense ... a network of institutions of both a formal and informal nature, based upon a sense of mutuality, and extensive enough to enable those within it to carry on a continual pattern of social interactions mostly within that network."[148] Catholic Germans in Wisconsin were deeply committed to the marriage of their culture and faith. Indeed, one could not be seen apart from the other—it was as though the German language itself bore the only acceptable idiom for the proper and effective transmission of the true Catholic faith. The Catholicism of German speakers of the 19th century was not some free-floating Platonic "form." For them it took explicit, almost scandalously particular form, in distinctive styles of music, architecture, church decoration, organizational life, and personal association. The inner core of the German Catholic experience that came to Wisconsin in the 19th century was a baroque faith—redolent with expansive scenes and crowded canvasses. German Catholics built, decorated, organized, sang, marched, and gave expression to the deepest aspirations of the human heart.

German-speaking Catholics played an important role in defining the German "place" in Wisconsin's life and culture. The archdiocese of Milwaukee with its German bishops, priests and sisters provided the framework for the maintenance of ethnic solidarity for Germans—and Germans generously supported church building of the highest caliber, gave their sons and daughters to the ranks of priests, brothers, and sisters, and loyally identified with the larger mission and goals of the church. An examination of this complex yet vital German Catholic heritage begins with a look at some of its chief representatives, the ranks of German clergy and sisterhoods.

Within three years of the establishment of the diocese of Milwaukee, a parish church for German Catholics was established a few blocks from St. Peter's Cathedral. Designed by the architect Victor Schulte, destined to be an important figure in Catholic church-building, St. Mary's had been approved by Henni in response to the demands of German Catholics at St. Peter's for a worship site of their own. In 1846, the new structure was dedicated and placed under the pastorate of Father Michael Heiss. From this church came other German congregations throughout the city of Milwaukee and around the diocese. Clergy would be needed for these new German-speaking congregations.

German Clergy

The role of German-speaking bishops is covered at length in this text. German clergy of the first generation of Milwaukee established an important framework for religious life and continually articulated the needs and values of German-speaking Catholicism in Wisconsin. Hundreds of German-speaking clerics could be cited as exemplars of the character of German identity in Milwaukee. Above them all were Father Joseph Salzmann and the remarkable cadre of Austrians that came with him to America in 1847. Salzmann did more to build up the sense of German identity in the diocese than any other priest except Henni.

Joseph Salzmann was born August 17, 1819 in the village of Munzbach, Austria. Winning a scholarship to the gymnasium at Linz from his home parish, he attended school in the city. Since he sent the scholarship money home to his impoverished parents, he supported himself by doing odd jobs and by literally begging for his supper door-to-door.[149] At Linz he discovered a vocation to the priesthood. While studying philosophy he confessed weekly to Father Francis X.

Rev. Joseph Salzmann
[Joseph Rainer. *A Noble Priest: Joseph Salzmann,* Olinger & Schwartz,1903]

Weninger, who later became a Jesuit and an important advocate for German Catholics in America.

He was ordained in August 1842. He undertook advanced studies after his ordination and did some brief pastoral work. As a curate, he became associated with the activities of the *Leopoldinen Stiftung* and from them heard stories of German missions in America. He also had a classmate, Father Caspar Rehrl, who had been the first Austrian priest to come to Wisconsin. In July 1847, inspired by a desire to serve in the missions, Salzmann departed Austria for Milwaukee in company with Capuchin Father Fabian Bermadinger, Father Michael Wisbauer, Father Antony Urbanek, a curate in Maria Laach, and seminarians Matthias Gernbauer and Francis Fusseder. All of them would make an important mark on the Catholic life of Wisconsin.

Rev. Fabian Bermadinger
[AOP-Rac]

The group arrived in the United States in September, and by early October 1847 were warmly received by Henni. In that first interview with Henni, Salzmann related, "We had so many questions to ask and answer that days seemed like hours; the more so since the Right Reverend Bishop showed us about all day long and told us of his plans for the future, especially regarding the welfare of the many Germans in his diocese."[150] The first evening Henni assigned Bermadinger to join Rehrl in Calumet County. Urbanek was sent to St. Anthony parish "in town 8" (Fussville/Menominee Falls). Wisbauer began his lifelong stay in Burlington, and Salzmann assumed control of St. Boniface in Germantown, Washington County, with a string of mission parishes. Accompanying him were seminarians Gernbauer and Fusseder, and a third, Peter Deberge, all of whom Salzmann instructed in preparation for their ordinations to the priesthood.

In 1849, Heiss's health broke down, requiring a long recuperation in Bavaria. Salzmann returned to Milwaukee, where he took over Heiss's tasks as the pastor of St. Mary's and also assisted in the foundation of a second German church in Milwaukee, Holy Trinity Church in Walker's Point.[151] He contracted architect Victor Schulte, who made plans very similar to those he made for St. Mary's Church. In September the magnificent new church was dedicated, long to be a second bastion of German strength in the city, and one of the parishes of the original German three that would undergo the process of ethnic succession, adapting each time to a new congregation.

To help pay for the new church, Salzmann began the first of a series of begging trips around the city, going door-to-door to solicit funds, and visiting benefactors in the East. In company with bookseller Christian Ott, he made his way into what he believed to be friendly German dioceses, where he met mixed results. In Cleveland, Bishop Amadeus Rappe refused him permission to preach. In Buffalo, the large German contingent met a friendlier reception from Bishop John Timon. The tour took him as far east as New York and then back through Kentucky, Ohio, Michigan, and Illinois. He arrived home with a purse large enough to help retire the large Holy Trinity debt.

As it turned out, this fund-raising expedition would be the first of many made on both sides of the Atlantic by the engaging Salzmann. Salzmann's role as the chief fund-raiser for the seminary, his close association with the School Sisters of Notre Dame, his pugnacious response to local anti-Catholic bigots, and his efforts to expand and develop the influence of Catholic education will all be considered later. However, his own personal commitment to keep faith and culture united is central to his life's work. In the many accomplishments of his life—the formation of Holy Trinity Church, the erection and funding of the seminary, his work with local sisterhoods, and his emphasis on church music— he sought to advance and strengthen the German Catholic presence in Wisconsin.

Salzmann stood at the center of a German-speaking contingent in the diocese, which of course included the bishops, but also other friends. He became deeply enmeshed in the activities of the School Sisters of Notre Dame and became so personally friendly with Mother Caroline Friess that rumor circulated that the two were having a torrid affair. Local anti-Catholics—skilled at the coarse and often scatological invective typical of other clerical pornographers of the time—publicized the ugly rumors of "blamable intercourse" between the priest and the nun, and at one point, heaved a pile of infant clothes over the convent wall, shouting, "Here is something for the Superior's and Dr. Salzmann's child."[152]

The public attacks had no discernible effect on Salzmann, except to sharpen his appeal as a fund-raiser. He refused to back away from his open assistance of the School Sisters and directed Father Anthony Urbanek to become their chaplain. Urbanek, who had had an indifferent career as a parish priest, seemed to like the work, and although he was a bit on the dour side, managed to bring some mirth into the lives of the early sisters. Urbanek was a skilled musician who played various instruments and even composed hymns which he taught the nuns and sang enthusiastically himself. The nuns wrote of Urbanek, "Although himself of a strict disposition he nevertheless loved good humor and cheerfulness and could not endure melancholy in them [the sisters]."[153] In 1858, Urbanek took an inspection tour of a Notre Dame foundation in New Orleans in company with Mother Caroline. On the return trip, the steamer exploded, killing Urbanek. The

Rev. Anton Urbanek
[ASND]

heartbroken sisters implored Salzmann to help them find a new chaplain, and when Mother Caroline gave him a $1000 loan for one of his projects, he personally traveled to Buffalo to recruit Father Francis X. Krautbauer, who agreed to take the post. Krautbauer eventually became the bishop of Green Bay, and when he left, the sisters acquired the service of Father Peter Abbelen.[154]

In Burlington in Racine County, Salzmann's companion, Father Michael Wisbauer, took up the cause of German Catholic identity.[155] Wisbauer had been assigned to serve in Burlington the very night in 1847 he and Salzmann arrived in Milwaukee, and he remained there until his death in 1889.[156] Located on the conflux of the White and Fox Rivers, Burlington began its history as a milling station for the grain growers of the region. Later, the flowing water helped to move turbines and machines and helped the community make the transition to a minor industrial community. As early as 1838, Father Thomas Morrissey had celebrated Mass for a small number of Catholics in the area. Father O'Kelley also included this community on his circuit. But Martin Kundig arrived in 1842, and in 1843-1844 he commenced the building of a 30 by 40 foot (modest by the standards of later churches) church named in honor of the martyr St. Sebastian. A series of visiting priests rode in and out of Burlington to keep the Catholic faith alive. Two resident pastors, Francis Henry Kendeler and Karl Schraudenbach, served the church between 1844 and 1847.

St. Sebastian Church, Burlington [AAM]

In 1847, Wisbauer arrived and set to work immediately to put German Catholicism "on the map." Following the example of Heiss and Salzmann, Wisbauer also employed Victor Schulte to design an elegant church. This neo-Gothic structure became the major site on Burlington's skyline, its tower spiking high above the growing community. It was dedicated by Henni in December 1859. At that time, popular enthusiasm over the recent definition of the doctrine of the Immaculate Conception inspired Wisbauer to rename the church St. Mary's of the Immaculate Conception (St. Sebastian's would be resurrected in the 20th century for a new Milwaukee parish).

Once the church was completed, Wisbauer invited the School Sisters of Notre Dame to take up residence in the former rectory; they assumed control over a school that had been opened at some point in the 1850s, with a lay male teacher directing the boys. The sisters arrived in December 1860 and received a chilly welcome from some of the parishioners, who were strong supporters of the male teacher and who proceeded to send their children to the private school he had opened in town. The challenges of teaching in this rural environment were not easy for the sisters. The needs of the farming economy made attendance at school erratic. Moreover, their efforts to discipline the young people aroused the ire of their parents. "Hardly anyone can satisfy them [the parents]," huffed one of the nuns. "The children are supposed to learn much and behave well, but are not to be looked at crossly, and above all are not to be punished. The people are crude, rough and unlikeable, very stingy and extremely proud. The children are very disrespectful toward the sisters, that is the majority of them." In the harvest month of October, one sister complained, "school attendance was very poor. Daily about two-thirds of the children were absent. Those who did attend the school were difficult to handle, so that the sisters had to resort to punishment every day." One instance of student misconduct included, "in the primary grades, one of the boys during class banged another boy over the head with his slate board, causing a hole in his head."So intense did the ill-will toward the sisters become that someone even poisoned the convent's pet dog, "Lion."[157]

However, these unpleasantries notwithstanding, the parish flourished under lovable "Papa" Wisbauer, and German Catholicism put down strong roots in the far end of Racine County. Wisbauer lived to a ripe old age and began his slow physical decline in 1888. His health broke down when his home was broken into by three men who blew open a safe with explosives and bound and gagged the resisting priest. He never recovered from the shock and physical abuse of the break-in, and in 1889 he died. For a generation and more of Burlington Catholics he had been the only pastor they had ever known, and he was the last link with the founding years of Catholic life in the Archdiocese of Milwaukee.

Rev. Michael Wisbauer [AAM]

The Character of German Parishes

German Catholic priests made parish churches the center of spiritual, cultural, and social life for their flocks. As churches for the German-speaking began to dot the Wisconsin landscape and contribute to the emerging

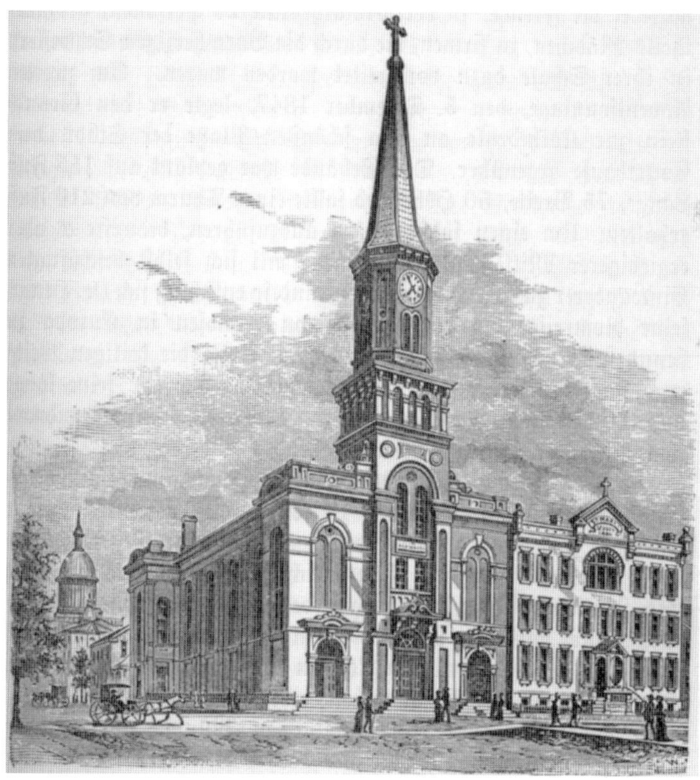

"Old" St. Mary Church, Milwaukee [AAM]

skylines of the state's largest cities, their special characteristics stood out.

German Catholic churches soon distinguished themselves by the elegance of their architecture and their rich interior decor. Milwaukee's St. Mary's Church led the way. Its elaborate interior was focused around a gift of King Ludwig of Bavaria, a magnificent oil painting of the Annunciation executed by the Bavarian artist Heinrich Von Gluenck. In the continual lists of requests sent over by Henni and Salzmann to the missionary societies were pleas for paintings, decorated altars, statuary, and elaborate vestments. One artist who contributed substantially to the rich decoration of Wisconsin German churches was Martin John Pitzer. He had come over with Salzmann and his company in 1847. While the clerics moved on to Milwaukee, Pitzer remained for several months in Baltimore and then arrived in Milwaukee in late 1847. He was given a room in the basement of St. Mary's Church where he began instructing young men in the arts of drawing, painting, and gilding. Likewise, he set himself to the task of restoring old or damaged altar pieces, paintings, and religious objects that had been brought over from Europe. Pitzer's artistic skills were soon on display in new German churches of the diocese. He helped to decorate Wisbauer's church in Burlington, contributed to the beautification of St. Mary's in Greenfield, Holy Trinity in Milwaukee, and St. Martin's in Granville. Pitzer noted the powerful effect of his art work and its contribution to the cause of Catholic visibility. "In this region I have restored, with God's grace and blessing, and to my joy and edification, many old and new church pictures as well as altars," he wrote to benefactors in Europe. "The altars in the first, second, and third churches, which are ten to thirty-five miles apart, are already famous far and wide. People came from great distances to see them and expressed their desire to have similar ones."[158] Pitzer returned to Austria in 1854, but continued to send artwork to Milwaukee at Henni's commission.

Artwork helped to inspire and shape the religious faith of German-speaking Catholics. Social provision, manifested in parish organizations, also reinforced bonds of ethnic loyalty. One example in the Burlington parish was the *St. Eustachius Kranken-Unterstuetzungs Verein.* This mutual aid society was formed by 34 men "to help whenever illness or the Grim Reaper of death enters a home."[159] Paying a lump sum death benefit of $200 to cover funeral costs and a stipend of $3.00 per week for someone who was sick, the group flourished and gathered excess funds to purchase the first St. Sebastian's Church as their meeting hall. St. Mary's in Milwaukee had the *St. Pius Kranken-Unterstuetzungs Verein* which served the same function. A number of societies paid the standard $200 burial fee, but they varied on the weekly disability payment (in some Milwaukee parishes it was $8.00).[160]

Other organizations were formed to support the school and provide funds for church decoration and the purchase of linens, flowers, candles and other necessities of the sacred liturgy. While most of the money for these groups came from the annual or monthly dues that members paid to the common treasure, these groups also ran endless series of fund-raisers: card parties, dances, "pound" parties and entertainments of various sorts. These entertainments provided another ligament of community building that brought parishioners to church halls for social interaction. The history of church entertainments merits at least a few words. Entertainments ran the gamut of events, with choral groups, instrumentalists, public lectures on interesting topics (a special treat were the travelogues of priests who had visited Rome or the Holy Land), magic lantern shows, live tableaux, and later films.

St. Elizabeth Church, Milwaukee theater production, 1912 [AAM]

Far and away, the most popular form of entertainment was the parish theatrical. James Grummer notes in his study of German parish life, that most of the plays performed in parish halls (a necessity in a German parish), often involved twin bills: a serious play with a religious theme and a farce. In Milwaukee's St. Joseph parish, the St. Aloysius Young Men's Society presented *Der taubstumme Waisenknaben oder der Abbe de l'Epee* (*The Deaf-Mute Orphan Boy*) and a farce *Die Drei Musikanten* (*The Three Musicians*) on Wednesday, November 10, 1880 at 8 P.M. Medieval themes were often highlighted. Both St. Joseph's and Holy Trinity performed *Das Vater's Fluch* (*The Father's Curse*), a piece set in the crusades. Men dominated the acting, but women also had their own plays. In 1908, the St. Mary's Society of Holy Ghost parish put on a three-act play, *Koenigin von Gottes Gnaden* (*Queen of God's Grace*).[161]

Religious and devotional life, apart from the Mass and the sacraments, had a distinctive flair in German churches. The popularity of the parish mission, Catholic revivals characterized by a series of intense, soul-searching talks that culminated in the renewal of baptismal promises, were fostered extensively by Jesuit Francis X. Weninger.[162]

Weninger was born in 1805 near Wildhaus, Styria, a province of Austria. He began his theological studies and was ordained a diocesan priest in Marburg in 1827 and took advanced degrees in preparation for an academic career. By 1830, he was prefect of studies at the episcopal seminary in Gratz (Graz), Austria. But two years later he joined the Jesuits who dispatched him to the University of Innsbruck where he served between 1834 and 1848. In addition to his teaching, Weninger soon cultivated his skill at giving missions.

Rev. Francis Xavier Weninger, SJ [Martin Marty, OSB. *John Martin Henni, First Bishop and Archbishop of Milwaukee,* Benziger Bros., 1888, p. 211]

Weninger may have learned the methods and themes of missions from the Austrian Redemptorists who adopted it as a special work of their order. In the wake of the suppression of the Jesuit order in Austria after revolutionary upheavals in 1848, Weninger followed his Jesuit colleagues to America where he initially set up residence in Cincinnati. In December 1848, he gave his first parish mission at Oldenburg, Indiana, drawing "tears of repentance and consolation from the eyes of his hearers."[163] Weninger soon began to travel the country far and wide, preaching missions in German parishes, but he found himself in special demand in the heavily German areas of the Midwest. Between January 1853 and January 1854, Weininger's superior reported that the missionary had been in 5 dioceses and 27 parishes; gave 32 missions, planted 32 [mission] crosses; heard 3,000 confessions; preached 900 sermons, converted 50 Protestants, and had given a clergy retreat.[164] In addition to his preaching, he authored a popular book of lives of the saints, a devotional tract in honor of the Sacred Heart, a popular apologetic text, *Manual of Christian Doctrine,* and a companion work, *Protestantism and Infidelity.* These he sold on his mission tours.

Weninger preached in both German and English, but his popular *Volksmissionen* registered its strongest impact with his fellow Germans. His mission technique, elaborately detailed by seminarian Carl Wagner in a 1936 master's thesis, described in detail the dramatic effects Weninger used to accompany his fiery preaching. Weninger brandished a large crucifix with a 15- to 18-inch corpus as he preached. Wagner related, quoting Weininger's words, "This gives the sermon the singular character of a mission sermon and has a powerful effect."[165] He made elaborate arrangements for the lighting of the churches (he preferred dim candlelight), and insisted on the presence of images of the Blessed Mother and the Sacred Heart. Likewise, he made sure that the parish choir was in fine fettle and ready to break into song at the appropriate moment. Each pastor was to arrange for sufficient confessors and confessionals to shrive the various age and gender groups that came to the sacrament of penance. Once the mission was over, a permanent reminder of the "soul changing" impact of the mission was to be left in the church in the form of a mission cross that had inscribed at its top "He Who Perseveres to the End Shall Be Saved."

Weninger's spiritual mission was also accompanied by an ethnic task: reinforcing the German Catholic identity of parishes and encouraging them to advance organizationally. One of Weninger's standard sermon themes harped on the evils of the public schools and the need for Catholic schools. Such was his message in 1852 when he descended on St. George's German parish in Kenosha, where he broke a logjam over the formation of the school that had divided the parish since its beginning in 1848. In his wake, fellow Austrian Father George Rehrl, pastor of the parish, commenced the operation of a school under the headship of a lay school master. However, efforts to form a stable Catholic school were unsuccessful until 1857 when the School Sisters of Notre Dame arrived.[166] Weininger's efforts were major factors in the development and perpetuation of German religious subculture in Milwaukee.

Devotional and public religious life of the German community flourished in other contexts. Historian James Grummer's study of German parish life between 1840 and 1920, relates in great detail the high ceremony and pomp associated with the blessing of church bells. In 1868, 22 years after the parish's founding, the *Jugenfrau Verein* of St. Mary's, Milwaukee, raised $2,500 to purchase bells for the church tower. An elaborate account on the front page of the *Milwaukee Sentinel* told readers that the 2,700 pound, 1,400 pound and 900 pound bells, cast at a Cincinnati foundry, were tuned to the notes G, B, and A and named *Maria, Maria Anna, and Maria Magdalena.*[167] Another popular blessing that reflected the religious world of Germans was the blessing of church banners. These elaborate flags carried the parish name and organization and were hoisted aloft by the proud members of societies for the many parades that took place in German parishes and for participation in larger civic or ethnic functions. Many of the most beautiful and elaborate used in archdiocesan history were made by the seamstresses of the School Sisters of Notre Dame. Grummer notes that this transplanted practice, frequent in the winding streets and close-knit villages and towns of Europe was soon dropped in Wisconsin, but the banners themselves were a popular icon of solidarity and collective pride.

German Catholic celebration also provided a window into their spiritual world. For example, the liturgical celebration of Christmas took place generally in German congregations at four in the morning rather than at

A Corpus Christi procession at the School Sisters of Notre Dame Motherhouse, Milwaukee, 1950s [ASND]

the "traditional" midnight Mass. It would be the Capuchins at St. Francis parish who would begin the celebration of the Lord's Nativity at midnight in 1882. In 1895, Archbishop Katzer reluctantly gave permission for the Sinsinawa Dominicans to celebrate midnight Mass (although he insisted that "no seculars be permitted" to attend and no one could receive communion).[168] Nonetheless, the custom, fanned by the Victorian romanticization of Christmas, became a desideratum of local Catholics, and by 1904 Archbishop Sebastian Messmer gave his permission to extend this mode of celebration to the rest of the archdiocese's parishes.[169]

One celebration that distinguished German Catholics was the celebration of the Feast of Corpus Christi. Held on the Thursday after the Feast of the Holy Trinity, the most elaborate form of this celebration involved an outdoor procession with the Blessed Sacrament, accompanied by music, children strewing rose petals, vested servers and parish organizations marching in procession to three separate altar shrines where Benediction of the Blessed Sacrament would be given. The first one described in Milwaukee took place at St. Mary's Church in 1851 and used a modified form of the celebration consisting of a novena of Masses, litanies, and religious ceremonies within the church. The Capuchins introduced the practice of the procession using their own ample grounds and drafting the brown-habited and bearded young friars to perform the liturgical chanting to add solemnity to the event.

Other German churches, priests and institutions will be highlighted in this study, but the role of the clergy and the German influence of the seminary were pervasive. So also was the role of the sisters.

The German Sisterhoods: Franciscan Sisters of Penance and Charity

Three groups of German sisters came to Wisconsin in the founding period and rose to high prominence in Wisconsin Catholic life: the Franciscan Sisters of Penance and Charity, the School Sisters of Notre Dame and the Racine Dominicans. Each of these sisterhoods was born in the religious revival of early 19th century Germany, and all of them came to have a defining influence on some very important areas of diocesan life.

The first group, eventually known as the Franciscan Sisters of Penance and Charity, began as a mixed community (men and women) of devout, even apocalyptic, communitarians, caught up in the full sway of German Romanticism. They were drawn together by a popular parish priest, Joseph Keppler, and his assistant Matthias Steiger, and on December 8, 1848, were formed as a lay Franciscan brotherhood and sisterhood in Ettenbeuren, Bavaria, a small town on the Kammback River, 25 miles west of Augsburg.[170] Keppler and Steiger were taken with dreams of a commune in America and drew a farmer's daughter, Ottilie Dir, to the association. She entered into an arranged and chaste marriage with Joseph Zahler of the group. Through the good offices of the *Ludwig-Missionsverein* Henni agreed to welcome them to Milwaukee in 1849. On June 11, 1849, these Tertiaries purchased from Heinrich and Eva Gross 35.67 acres of a small property called by the Indian name "Nojoshing" for $1,000. Immediately the group set to work to develop the property, building separate cottages for the brothers and the sisters. Ottilie Zahler became "Mother Aemiliana" and Keppeler and Steiger helped support the community by providing liturgical service to surrounding communities. Keppeler served as the local priest at nearby New Coeln, where a community of Germans had helped create St. Stephen's Church. Steiger also rendered service in early Wisconsin, and for a year served as chaplain to the School Sisters of Notre Dame in Baltimore. When he returned he started a church on Beloit Road called "Holy Cross," but it would later be renamed for his patron St. Matthias.

Tragedy befell the community. Keppeler finished building the new church at New Coeln and promptly succumbed to cholera in September 1851. A few days later Steiger died as well. In 1852, Henni then remanded the sisters (the brothers were slowly dying out) to the care of his close friend and confidant, Father Michael Heiss, newly returned from a two-year sick leave in Germany where he had served as chaplain to a convent of Visitation Sisters at Ditramzell, 25 miles south of Munich. Heiss attempted to impose order on the community by devising a religious rule, habit, and central leadership for the women under Mother Aemiliana Zahler. Their first work was to receive the care of German orphan boys who had initially been cared for by the Sisters of Charity and the School Sisters of Notre Dame. (The origins of St. Aemillian's Orphanage will be covered later.) The

Mother Aemiliana Zahler, OSF
[AOSF]

key work of the women's community, however, soon became the housekeeping for the new diocesan seminary that rose on the grounds next to their early convent in 1856.

When St. Francis Seminary opened and Heiss assumed full-time duties as rector, he turned over the supervision of the community to Bavarian-born Father Leonard Batz, a faculty member. The history written by Franciscan Sister Eunice Hanousek, rather gently characterized Batz as "overzealous" in insisting on the details of their religious life. Benjamin Blied was more blunt when he suggested that Batz was "more devastating than cholera" to the sisters.[171] Batz insisted on absolute obedience and demanded that the single women of the community either leave or be married. By 1860, the sister founders had had enough of Batz's tyranny and they withdrew from the convent. This included Aemiliana Zahler who left her husband dumbfounded. Heiss was mortified by the departure and Batz lost his seminary professorship over the incident. Regretting his role in pushing the sisters to the limits, Batz then graciously made accommodations for them from his own considerable fortune. Known as the "Father Batz Sisters," they remained at his side providing housekeeping help wherever he was. Ottilie/Aemilliana Zahler spent her final days with an offshoot of the community that opened a new motherhouse in La Crosse, dying in 1904. The male branch of the community continued to live on the grounds in the "brother house" (remodeled years later into the residence of the archbishop of Milwaukee). Joseph Zahler remained, pious, devout, and utterly irascible until his death in 1878. Other brothers remained as workers. One, Leo Seuss, ended his days with a similar lay community in St. Nazianz.

Mother Antonia Zimmer, OSF [AOSF]

A new mother superior, Antonia Herb Zimmer, soon sought to get out from under the "condemnation" of seminary housekeeping and began asking Bishop Henni for permission to teach. Henni resisted, needing the small community to care for the seminary and insisting that they had no proper training to be school teachers. Zimmer persisted nonetheless and in September 1862 intensified her desire to "declare independence" of the regime at Nojoshing, and transferred the site of the community's motherhouse (St. Colletta's Convent) to the city of Jefferson in Walworth County. Eventually schools were given to Mother Antonia's sisters. They provided teachers for St. Lawrence and St. John's schools in Milwaukee. Teachers were also sent to Cross Plains, Janesville, Franklin, Germantown, and also to Watertown, Golden Lake, Fussville, Cazenovia, and Prairie du Chien. By 1871 the growing cadre of teaching sisters even had houses in Ohio. Eventually Mother Antonia decided to move the motherhouse to La Crosse, the jurisdiction of Bishop Michael

Heiss. A split developed among the sisters and the result was the separation of the congregation. Mother Antonia took a number of sisters to La Crosse where they renamed themselves the Franciscan Sisters of Perpetual Adoration and built a large convent on land donated to them. The sisters who remained at the seminary were the Franciscan Sisters of Penance and Charity, referred to henceforth in this work as the Franciscans of St. Francis.[172]

School Sisters of Notre Dame

One of the largest and most influential of the German sisterhoods in Wisconsin, the Poor School Sisters of Notre Dame, traces its origins to the 16th century work of St. Peter Fourier. Their original founding was suppressed in the secularization of the revolutionary era. In the 1830s, the community was reconstituted under the leadership of Mother Teresa of Jesus Gerhardinger, and a new title, the Poor School Sisters of Notre Dame, was bestowed on the foundation.[173] A motherhouse was established in Munich and the sisters were first enticed to come to America by the Redemptorists, a male congregation of priests and brothers who had carved an important niche for themselves as ministers to the growing numbers of German immigrant Catholics in the United States. At some point, the sisters were taken into a Catholic colonizing scheme in rural southwestern Pennsylvania spearheaded by the company of Benziger and Eschback, a church goods supplier of Einsiedeln, Switzerland, that was given credibility by a protégé of Pope Pius IX, Baron von Schroeder. Additional enticement for the sisters was provided by the *Ludwig-Missionsverein* which offered to pay their way over and support them in the colony, which by 1847 had about 200 families.

Gerhardinger and a cadre of sisters, including Sister Caroline Friess, then made the journey to the United States. After stopping briefly in Philadelphia to consult the Redemptorist provincial, John Neumann, (later the bishop), they made the arduous trip to the region. To their dismay, they found not the glowing city promised by Von Schroeder and the publicists, but a barely civilized swamp. Gerhardinger refused to begin a foundation there, but did leave sisters behind to teach in the school. She made her way back to Neumann, who offered her and the sisters a place in Baltimore near the Redemptorist parishes. The sisters remained in Baltimore, but a complex series of conversations and actions ensued that eventually caused them to relocate their motherhouse to Milwaukee.

In June of 1848, Neumann, Gerhardinger, and Friess journeyed by steamer and stage to Milwaukee to survey the prospects for a foundation there. Henni was on a trip to Europe when they came, but knowing of their visit, he used his opportunity in Europe to press for the sisters to come to Milwaukee. His first efforts were with the *Ludwig-Missionsverein*, which also assisted the sisters, urging the leaders of the organization to press the nuns to come to his diocese. The organization, through its general secretary Joseph Ferdinand Mueller, played an important role in urging the School Sisters to come to Milwaukee, and paid many of their bills. By the time Henni got to Munich, Gerhardinger had returned from America, and he personally urged her to send sisters, suggesting that such an enterprise would win the assistance of King Ludwig of Bavaria. Henni continued to woo the nuns after his return. When the sisters in Baltimore lost their chaplain, Henni dispatched Father Matthias Steiger, one of the chaplains to the Franciscan Tertiaries in Nojoshing , to serve as chaplain for a year. In 1850, Gerhardinger agreed to move the general headquarters of her American foundation to Milwaukee under the leadership of Caroline Friess.[174]

Mother Caroline Friess, SSND [ASND]

Friess, who had accompanied the group over in 1848, had taken to American conditions and worked hard to expand the community's membership and teaching assignments throughout the East. Because the demands of school work often clashed with rigorous convent community and liturgical life, Caroline had also taken a strong hand in re-working the cloister-bound rules of the congregation to make them more responsive to the demands of an active life. She insisted, for example, that the sisters be permitted to attend Mass in parishes and not in the convent. She sought other mitigations of the exact letter of the European convent rule that would make it easier to serve the increasing number of parishes that the community was accepting. In pursuit of her plans, Friess made a controversial trip to the Munich motherhouse. Her major sin appeared to be the fact that she traveled without a companion, a clear violation of community regulations. When she arrived at the door of the convent, she was treated as a "fugitive" (the technical term to refer to someone who leaves their religious house without permission). After laying her case before Archbishop Ernest von Reisach of Munich, however, she convinced him of the purity of her motives and he pressed the reluctant Mother Teresa to receive her "erring daughter." Her near defeat turned into victory and Gerhardinger not only agreed to the mitigation of convent rules, but gave Friess a broad grant of authority to act in her name by appointing her a vicar of the Superior General. The permission may have been tentative, because von

Reisach warned her "Now get back to America, or you will stay here altogether."[175]

Friess wasted no time. She secured additional help for her new plans when she agreed to escort Henni's niece, Miss Agnes Casanova, back to America. By December 15, 1850, four School Sisters of Notre Dame arrived in Milwaukee with Casanova and were given hospitality by the Sisters of Charity. Few religious congregations had as soft a landing as they did. They moved into a house that had been purchased with the funds made available by King Ludwig I on Milwaukee and Knapp Streets. This would be the nucleus of one of the largest motherhouses of sisters in Milwaukee. By December 30, 1850, they had received their first recruit, Catherine Flasch, or Sister Mary Laurentia as she would be known, one of many religious vocations that would come from the very large and very Catholic Flasch family. By January 2, 1851, they had begun teaching the 130 pupils that had already been gathered at St. Mary's parochial school. Friess soon added an annex to the small house. In October 1851, it became the home of St. Mary's Institute, which welcomed resident and day students of all creeds. By 1864 she had encompassed the entire block bounded by Milwaukee, Jefferson, Knapp, and Ogden Streets. The huge convent that faced Milwaukee Street stood on that spot until its demolition in 1959.

Branch houses began to be founded—at first with limited personnel, but as the nexus of schools and convent "kicked in," scores of young women poured into the Milwaukee motherhouse. Sisters added to their favor with the Milwaukee clergy by making altar linens and providing the delicate lace that stood inside tabernacle interiors. New houses appeared in Milwaukee (Holy Trinity School, 1854, and St. Joseph, 1860), Port Washington (1857), Watertown (1857), Kenosha (1858), Sheboygan and Lacrosse (1858), Burlington (St. Sebastian's, 1860), Beaver Dam (St. Peter's, 1862), Green Bay (St. Mary's, 1862), St. Kilian (St. Kilian's, 1867).

Friess wrote to her supporters at the *Ludwig-Missionsverein* in April 1858, "A decade has passed since our congregation was transplanted to America .... The tiny mustard seeds planted by our universally loved Mother General Mary Theresa of Jesus [Gerhardinger], warmed by the rays of divine grace, and supported by the generous donations from our unforgettable fatherland, is slowly bearing fruit." Friess reported that the congregation had taken in 50 candidates, 24 novices, and had witnessed 11 sisters profess

The "House of Four Chimneys," the site of the beginning of the School Sisters of Notre Dame Motherhouse [ASND]

their vows.[176] Their rising numbers suggest the importance of the heavy German immigration of the 1850s. Their strong presence and stable leadership allowed them to move forward quickly.

Mother Caroline's ten-year report to the Bavarian mission society revealed many things about the German community's adaptation to American soil. Seeking more money, she gave an account of the expansion of the community to New Orleans, Philadelphia, Rochester, and Detroit. "Here in Milwaukee and Wisconsin we still recognize our German country men," she wrote appreciatively, and spoke tenderly of the goodness of those who presented themselves at the schools run by the sisters or who sought admission to the convent.[177] However, she also noted immediately that among the "adversities and trials" faced by the congregation was the difficulty of getting American candidates habituated for the community, with their "exuberance for freedom," to come around to "the voluntary renunciation of self-will" required by the Notre Dame way of life. "How difficult therefore," she wrote, "the task to mold daughters of this free country into true religious!"[178] But Friess was realistic. In dealing with the young girls who came to Notre Dame schools for instruction, the superior urged each teaching sister to "use her influence indirectly … on account of the attitude of the parents—who resent a fancied invasion of their authority …. Compulsion must not be used." Instead she urged a more gentle and easy-going approach to American pupils, "What cannot be achieved by kindness is unattainable, at least in the average case."[179] Henni appended a note to the request for funds, assuring the directors of the *Missionsverein* that Friess gave "a true picture of the situation" and lauding their work with the steadily increasing German population of the state.[180]

Mother Caroline sat at the pivot of this expansion, and her own role as mother general of the community continued to grow. In many ways, her strength of character, her stability, and her ability to manage what eventually became an ethnically diverse and rapidly growing sisterhood made her one of the leading figures in the first generation of Catholic life in Wisconsin. Her contributions, although often cloaked behind a rhetoric of piety and "submission," were clearly equal to those of most of the clergy and the equivalent in some respects of the bishops. Certainly only the bishops had both financial and administrative burdens equal to hers.

Racine Dominicans

Adding to the growing contingent of German sisterhoods was yet another Third Order group affiliated with one of the mendicant orders. This time it was the Dominicans. The Cloister of the Holy Cross in Regensburg was the site for a renewed presence of the German Dominican sisterhoods of the 19th century. The active and growing cloister was a part of the general religious reawakening of southern Germany after the Napoleonic era and the end of secularization. The sisters of this community had also formed a Third Order outreach and established a teaching sisterhood in Williamsburg, New York. The spearhead of this renewed Dominican presence had been Mother Benedicta Bauer and her faithful companion, Thomasina Ginker.[181]

Like all strong leaders, Bauer had both inspired and created controversy. A long-fought lawsuit launched by a disgruntled former sister who had been expelled from the community by Bauer had eventually been decided against the Dominican prioress. In anger in 1859, she came to the United States "in exile" and began looking for a new life after the embarrassment and humiliation of Holy Cross. Her first stop, after a visit in Williamsburg, was to the diocese of Nashville, where Dominican Bishop James Whelan had invited her to come to establish a Catholic school program in his rural diocese. As with the experience of the Sisters of Notre Dame in Pennsylvania, the prelate's glowing descriptions of life in Tennessee did not match the realities. Moreover, Bauer and Ginker, accustomed to the more bracing climate of Regensburg, found the heat and humidity of Nashville more than they could bear. Bauer next traveled to Green Bay and established a convent, pondering whether that would be the site of a new motherhouse. Through the work of a diocesan priest, Michael Diesenreider, the sisters were urged to share their plans with Bishop Henni. In 1863, at his urging, they opened a community house in the Lake Michigan port city of Racine. Another community was opened along Lake Michigan at Port Washington. But Racine was the location where Bauer decided to be "rooted," and the community secured land on Racine's south side near the German-speaking St. Mary's Church. The land, marked out between 12th and Park Streets would be the site of a mother house that would dominate the south side of the city until it was torn down in 1973.

In 1865, Bauer accepted a school at the Norbertine stronghold of Roxbury, near Madison. When she died on October 13, 1865, she left behind a small but close-knit community that was already beginning to adapt the regulations of the cloistered Dominican life to the demands of a busy apostolate. Subsequent community leaders would steadily expand the ambit of the teaching sisterhood. Using the Catholic schools of Racine as their main base, the Dominicans eventually branched out to the Fox River Valley, near Madison, and into other areas in the diocese.

Mother Benedicta Bauer, OP [AOP-Rac]

St. Catherine Convent, first convent occupied by Racine Dominicans, 1862 [AOP-Rac]

All of these Wisconsin sisterhoods established an ever-wider scope of Catholic visibility and influence in the state. Historian Florence Deacon has accentuated the social significance of religious sisterhoods in Wisconsin. Her study notes in great detail the major financial investments the sisters made in Wisconsin land and services. Further, as "autonomous women" they proved to be one of the most important outlets for women's activism in early Wisconsin. Few Wisconsin women had as much control over financial assets, made decisions that affected hundreds of people and jousted as effectively with male church authorities as these nuns.[182] In their teaching roles, sisters created the framework of the major system of Catholic schools in the state, and sometimes, in rural areas, they also taught in the emerging public school system.

A Wisconsin Holy Land: Father Caspar Rehrl and the Sisters of St. Agnes

Caspar Rehrl, who would engage in church-planting north of Milwaukee, was born in Aigen, a suburb of Salzburg, Austria, in December 1809.[183] Strong Catholic faith produced three vocations to the priesthood from the Rehrl family; and two of the brothers, Caspar and George, came to America. Caspar Rehrl was ordained to the priesthood on September 20, 1832, for the archdiocese of Salzburg. A prodigious intellect, Rehrl knew nine ancient and modern languages, held a doctorate in theology, and was a master of homeopathic medicine. He served 10 years as an assistant in a Salzburg church, which prepared him for pastoral ministry. He came to maturity in the 1840s and like many German-speaking priests, Rehrl heard of the exploits of his co-religionists in far-off America. These accounts, popularized by the dramatic writing of people like Henni and Kundig, were circulated by the *Leopoldinen Stiftung* in Vienna and stirred Rehrl's imagination.

Rehrl arrived in the United States in early 1845. After stays at New Orleans and St. Louis, he made straight for Wisconsin. Arriving in Milwaukee in May 1845, he met with Henni. "He [Rehrl] came unannounced and unexpected, but he was very welcome."[184] Henni assigned him to the districts north along the Milwaukee River. In August 1845, he offered Mass in the home of Alban Kent in Sheboygan. In September 1845, he arrived at

Rev. Casper Rehrl [AAM]

Johnsburg, where a church had begun under Father Constantine Carabin. Johnsburg became Rehrl's base of operations, and he established a school where his brother George taught.[185] From Johnsburg he fanned out over 170 miles to the north and west engulfing seven Wisconsin counties. In all he founded twelve churches and visited twenty parishes in Calumet, Fond du Lac, Sheboygan and Washington Counties.

In 1858 at Barton, Wisconsin, in Washington County, Rehrl began a young ladies society to assist him in catechetical work. He dedicated this group to the patronage of St. Agnes, an early Christian martyr, whose tomb he visited in Rome. The first three recruits were Katherine Goetz, Madgalene Hapfer, and Gertrude Rehberg. After a few months, they made a profession of vows for one year. Rehrl recruited mostly children and young teenagers for this new group. The next year, the Agnesian chronicle reports, "twelve children, ages 11 to 13 received the white veil, after a few months several of these children received the black veil."[186] By 1860, the St. Agnes Society had 18 members. The chronicler further noted, "the rule was very defective and community life not well-ordered." Rehrl did not closely supervise the young women and their religious training and formation was haphazard at best. Eventually, however, Rehrl began to come under some pressure from Bishop Henni and others to provide more of a regular structure of religious life (i.e., habit, rule, convent cloister, etc.) for this young group. At Henni's urging, he agreed to allow the sisters to elect their own leader.

In 1864, four of the five sisters able to vote elected young 17-year-old Agnes Hazotte as their mother superior. Hazotte, a native of Buffalo, New York, had only entered the community the year before. She set to work and numbers began to grow. Before long the small band had accepted seven rural Catholic schools. Hazotte's determination to keep the community alive led her to the spiritual care of the nearby Capuchins, who played a major role in the next phase of the community's existence. Mother Agnes moved to Barton and attempted to work with Rehrl, and immediately conflict arose. Hazotte wished to

Mother Agnes Hazotte (left), CSA
[M. Vera Naber, CSA *With All Devotedness*, Kenedy & Sons, 1959]

take more time to train and form young recruits to the community, but Rehrl insisted that they move quickly into new apostolates. "I did not established a convent for contemplatives," he huffed to Hazotte, "but a pious Society to teach the ignorant."[187] As relations between Rehrl and his sisterhood grew increasingly tense, Rehrl's Austrian priest-friends, including Salzmann, urged him to disband the sisterhood.

Hazotte's "salvation" came from the nearby Capuchins.[188] In early 1870, she had met Father Francis Haas, one of the founders of the Order (more later) at a mission at St. Bridget's Church in Washington County. On this occasion she discussed her plight, and Haas urged her to move the community to a new location in Fond du Lac. In this small city there was a rail link, available land, and parishes that needed teaching sisters. Hazotte traveled to Fond du Lac, and received a warm reception from the pastor of St. Mary's (German) Church in the city. In June 1870, she purchased twelve city lots on East Division Street, which included a two-story frame house.

When this happened, Rehrl withdrew his support, and jurisdiction for the sisters reverted to Martin Kundig, vicar general of the diocese in charge of affairs while Henni was attending Vatican Council I. Viewing the relative disorganization and lack of structure of the Agnesians, Kundig ordered the sisters to spend no more money and contemplated the dissolution of the community due to the lack of a rule. Once again, at Hazotte's request, the Capuchins intervened. At a retreat in Barton in July 1870, Hazotte asked Father Haas to draft a rule that would be acceptable to diocesan authorities. Haas immediately set to work, extending the length of the retreat by a few days, and produced a written constitution that provided a framework for religious life for the community. Haas also argued with Kundig, who had actually shown up with a decree of dissolution, and assured him that he would oversee the community. The sisters themselves, now 32 in number, voted to accept the rule that Haas had hastily drafted during their community retreat. When Henni returned, he was not happy with the decision to continue the community, but allowed it to go forward. Some sisters remained with Rehrl at Barton.

Nonetheless, with the rule and the support of the more stable Capuchins, the sisters re-established themselves firmly in Fond du Lac, where they built a motherhouse, a sanitarium, a girls academy, and a hospital. In 1874, four sisters began work at St. Thomas parish in Beloit where their chronicle noted, "The parishioners were chiefly pioneers who had emigrated from Ireland .... The children were docile, humorous, and promising."[189] With these stable apostolic works the community soon settled into a healthy existence. In the meantime, the sisters devoted themselves heavily to the education of young people in the growing number of parishes in the Fond du Lac/Washington County area. The Agnesian presence was especially strong among the German-speaking communities of the region. German was spoken among the sisters and was part of their common prayer life until the 1920s.

The Capuchins

The role of the Capuchins in the "rescue" of the Sisters of St. Agnes demonstrates the close links that existed among the religious communities of men and women in Wisconsin—especially among those who spoke German. This cooperative spirit existed to a lesser extent between religious order priests and diocesan priests. The most prominent German-speaking community of men in Wisconsin were the Capuchins, who established their American roots in the archdiocese of Milwaukee.

The Capuchin Order, a reform of the Franciscans, had been founded in Europe in the 17th century. Although various groups of Capuchins abroad thought of creating a Capuchin province in America, the task fell to two Swiss diocesan priests, Gregory Haas and John Frey. Haas had attended the University of Tübingen, and Frey completed his studies at the Benedictine house in Einsiedeln. The two met in 1850 at the University of Freiburg in Baden and the two of them began to share their mutual dreams of priestly service in mission lands. Capuchin historian Celestine Bittle characterized Haas, the elder, as more staid, conservative and reserved. Frey was younger, more voluble, and more willing to take risks.[190] It would be Frey who would take most of the initiative in literally building the Capuchin presence in the United States.

Haas was ordained in his home diocese of Basle in 1851. Three years later, Frey was ordained by Henni's old friend and mentor, Bishop Peter Mirer of St. Gall. While at a parish assignment in Sirnach in the Canton of Thurgau, Frey met a man who had temporarily returned from a visit to America. Enthused by the man's descriptions of the American frontier, Frey supposedly asked if the Capuchin order was to be found over there. When he learned that it was not, he contacted Haas and another Swiss priest, Ferdinand Zuber, and the three decided to transplant the Capuchin Order to the United States.

The fact that they were secular priests and not even Franciscans did not deter them from approaching Capuchin Father Theodosius Florentini, who tried to dissuade them and urged them to work in their native Switzerland to reclaim "lost" Protestants. Temporarily dissuaded by Florentini's arguments, they stayed for a time, but eventually their fervor for the project returned. They knew from Mirer about the needs of Henni's new diocese in Wisconsin and they boldly went back to Florentini and asked him to inform Bishop Henni of their coming. Further plans were hatched at a conference in Zurich, where another possible cooperator, Aloysius Stocker, was invited to join the band. When the time came to actually cross the ocean, however, only Haas and Frey were able to

Rev. Francis Haas, OFM
[AOP-Rac]

go—the two other Swiss priests were anchored by their own pastoral and financial commitments. Haas and Frey contacted Capuchin officials in Switzerland and secured a conditional promise of cooperation, with the proviso that a bishop could be found to take them in. The Capuchin provincial wrote a letter of introduction that the two priests would present to Henni. On July 16, 1856, they set sail from Antwerp. Landing in New York, they took eight days to get to Wisconsin.

When they finally made contact with Henni, he assured them "I have work for you in abundance."[191] He set them to work at different German-speaking churches in the diocese; Haas was dispatched to St. George Church in Kenosha, and Frey to St. Mary's in Milwaukee. The two men shared their hopes of recreating the Capuchin Order on Wisconsin soil. However, Henni too attempted to dissuade the priests from undertaking such a project without money. Haas and Frey were unwilling to change their plans and Henni acceded. In fact it was Henni who suggested in the fall of 1856 a hilly location along Lake Winnebago in Fond du Lac County as "the first bride of the Order." Each of these hills would be marked by a religious name. There they linked up with the School Sisters of Notre Dame, who had come to a hill called Mount Carmel five years earlier. On the top of the highest of the hills, Mount Calvary, already existed a rude chapel and dwelling that had been left by Caspar Rehrl. There, the two priests began to build the Capuchin monastery.

Haas traveled back to Europe to secure funds, but he met a stony reception from the Swiss Capuchins, who had seemed to endorse the work earlier. Haas's request for a Capuchin to join them in America was at first turned down. Later, however, he was given tentative approval, provided he could secure permission from Capuchin superiors in Rome. Haas repaired to the Eternal City to press his case with the highest officials of the Order. After much tugging and pulling, Haas received the permission to establish a branch of the order in America and with the support of the Capuchin authorities approached both the *Ludwig-Missionsverein* and the *Leopoldinen Stiftung* for money. Haas took with him a small collection from these and other sources and a contingent consisting of two seminarians, a candidate for the brotherhood, Haas's sister, Agatha, who entered the Notre Dame convent, and two professed Capuchin brothers. One of the Capuchins, Anthony Maria Cachet, was to come as novice master for Haas and Frey, who still were not formal members of the community they aspired to create in the United States.

After their arrival in America in November 1857, Haas, Frey and the lay brother candidate (also named Frey) received the Franciscan habit. In keeping with the customs of religious life, Hass was renamed "Francis" and Frey "Bonaventure." Both men played key roles in establishing the Capuchins on a firm basis in Wisconsin. Haas was elected a definitor (general counselor) of the Capuchin Order in 1878 and moved to Rome in that year. He returned to the states in 1893 in ill-health and died in 1895.[192] When the Capuchin membership attained a sufficient number in 1881, it was given the status of an independent province of the worldwide order, and Frey was chosen as first provincial. He expanded the order's holdings in America, building the large St. Bonaventure Monastery in Detroit which eventually became its central headquarters. He lived until 1912.[193]

After surmounting financial and internal crises, the Capuchins branched out to other dioceses and locations, beginning with Our Lady of Sorrows Church in New York. Capuchins soon began to supplement their income by helping out at local parishes. Eventually they ran a few of their own in Fond du Lac County, St. Anne, Johnsburg, and Forest, a region of Wisconsin already known for its large concentration of Catholics. They also received benefactions from the German-speaking missionary associations and undertook their own begging tours in Canada and elsewhere.

At Mount Calvary the Capuchins ran a parish and monastery and in 1860 opened a school for four boys who resided at the monastery. A larger monastery church was built and dedicated in July 1863. The growing number of students (20 by 1863) resulted in the addition of a student wing. In 1866, Francis Haas commenced another building project for a new and larger school. Bricks were produced in the thousands for the new complex of church, school and monastery that was essentially completed in 1868. Disaster struck on Christmas and the next morning as the new buildings (except the granary and the chapel) disappeared in flames. The School Sisters of Notre Dame on nearby Mount Carmel lent the homeless Capuchins their own convent while they sought lodgings with neighbors. For eight months they lived in the cramped convent until a new structure was raised on the ruins of the older one. Eventually, the Mount Calvary site would become a strong Capuchin center.

Efforts to come to Milwaukee were difficult at first. Henni had invited them in 1865 to establish a parish in the see city. However, these first efforts laid bare the rivalry that often existed between diocesan priests and religious orders. The trouble started when Haas purchased a lot from one Peter Gerstner at 9th and Walnut Streets. On this property the friars believed they could establish a monastery using the old shell of a brewery that still stood on a portion of the grounds. Interestingly, objections to the presence of the friars emanated from worried German-speaking diocesan clergy such as Ludwig Conrad of

St. Lawrence College, Mt. Calvary
[Courtesy of Kevin Wester]

Holy Trinity parish, Leonard Batz of St. Mary's and especially the corpulent Joseph Holzhauer, whose church of St. Joseph was located only a few blocks from the new Capuchin site. Although the Capuchins intended to begin a monastery and not a parish church, the worried clerics knew that local German-speaking Catholics would flock to the Capuchin chapel for Sunday Mass. The loss of parishioners would put a strain on the finances of the local churches. Moreover, the Capuchins who were known as good preachers, tender confessors, and down-to-earth pastors, would have to do no more than be themselves to attract parishioners. Henni himself later expressed some misgivings for having invited them: "Here in Milwaukee there is great commotion against your monastery, The chief objection is that it will be situated right in the middle of the city among existing parishes—while such monasteries, namely those of the Capuchins, are placed only in suburbs. I must confess that I myself had never expected, when I granted permission, that you would build so close to St. Joseph's [parish]."[194] But the opposition of diocesan clergy paled when Haas discovered that Gerstner did not have clear title to the property he sold to the Capuchins. In the ensuing legal battle the judgement went against Gerstner and Haas forfeited $2,000 on the deal.

St. Francis Church, Milwaukee [AAM]

With the property at 9th and Walnut lost for their monastery, the chaplain of the School Sisters of Notre Dame, Francis X. Krautbauer, pointed out an area in the so-called Sherman's Addition of the city—an area north of the downtown on the corner of 4th and Brown Streets (of sufficient distance from any other German diocesan parish). For $5,350, Frey bought a block of city property. "It overlooks the city and the lake and has a large Catholic population," wrote an excited Bonaventure Frey to the treasurer of the *Ludwig-Missions-verein.* "Providence has helped us to acquire a better location through these difficulties."[195] However, the Capuchins lacked the money to build on the new property until July 1869, when Father Ivo Prass arrived in Milwaukee. By this time, the growing order was looking for a new site for their young candidates, separate from their novitiate at Mount Calvary. The new foundation at Milwaukee, named St. Francis, was designated as the site of a theological seminary. Remembering the objections raised by the German pastors when Haas bought the first piece of property, the Capuchins insisted that they would not open a parish. Indeed, the desire to maintain some cloister for their theologians made that decision even wiser. However, as the Sherman's Addition section became Milwaukee's Sixth Ward, houses, businesses and rival churches began to be founded in the area. Catholic laymen in the community approached both the friars and Henni for permission to create a church, and Ivo Prass added an additional church to the construction of the monastery chapel that could be used for "seculars." The church was dedicated July 31, 1870.

The formal establishment of the parish waited until Henni's return from Vatican I, and in April 1871 the new parish was announced. Shortly after the building of the church, the Capuchins and their parishioners began constructing a frame schoolhouse and invited the School Sisters of Notre Dame to take over. Because of the continued presence of the theological seminary, the parishioners were often treated to the spectacle of various ordinations to major and minor orders—ceremonies generally confined to seminary chapels. In the first 25 years of the parish 57 men were ordained priests and 48 of them had their first Mass at St. Francis.

The growth of the parish required the Capuchins to build a more capacious and beautiful structure to replace the frame church. William Schickel, a New York architect known to the friars, designed a basilica-style structure 140 feet long and 61 feet wide seating nearly 800 worshipers. The church, built in 1876 of Milwaukee's famous cream brick, was a showpiece of the decorative skills of Milwaukee's German-speaking Catholics.[196]

The Norbertine Contribution

Yet another religious community of men that made a home in Wisconsin were the Canons Regular of Premontre, known as the Norbertines. The most famous Norbertine in the state was Father Adalbert Inama, a native of the Tyrol and a member of the Abbey of Wilten, a famous Norbertine center in the city of Innsbruck, Austria.[197] For 14 years prior to coming to America he served as a pastor and professor of classical languages at the University of Innsbruck.

In 1843, he emigrated to New York and was enticed by Bishop John Hughes to remain in the "empire state" to minister to German Catholics. Inama must have felt like a star as he received offers from the diocese of Cincinnati (where then Vicar General John Martin Henni attempted to recruit him and his order for his seminary project there). The Norbertine remained in New York, helping to establish a parish at Syracuse. But Inama's goal was to establish a stable monastery for his own community. In the fall of 1844 he visited Chicago, where he was warmly welcomed by Bishop William Quarter. In September he traveled to Milwaukee. Henni was still gone on his initial inspection tour, but Inama met Martin Kundig who filled him with excitement about the prospects for the Church in Wisconsin.

Rev. Adalbert Inama, O Praem [AOP-Rac]

When Henni returned, he attempted to convince Inama to establish a college staffed by the Norbertines at Green Bay. Inama demurred, but he did agree to take his own inspection tour of the western areas of the diocese to see where a future establishment might be located. It was on the trip to Sac Prairie that he met the famous Hungarian Count Agostin Haraszthy, who had settled in the town and held vast holdings in south central Wisconsin along the Wisconsin River. Haraszthy offered him 100 acres for a Norbertine abbey that would sponsor a school. Inama returned to New York to fulfill his obligations to Hughes, but he returned to Wisconsin in 1845 and began operations at the city of Haraszthy (later Sauk City) and ministered to Catholics in Mineral Point, Green Lake, and Stevens Point. Haraszthy was as good as his word, donating not only the 100 acres, but two lots in Sauk City on which Inama built a church. Inama bought 80 more acres on credit, an additional 80 financed by his abbot in Wilten, and held an option on 160 more. On these 420 acres, Inama planned a mission center for the education of priests and laity.

The new abbey was to be in the city of Roxbury. In 1846, Inama was joined by fellow Norbertines from the Abbey of Wilten including Father Maximilian Gaertner and several lay brothers.[198] Later, Father Francis X. Sailer joined the group. Other additions to the contingent and generous gifts from German relief societies allowed the purchase of more land.[199] During the first five years of the Roxbury foundation, Inama and Gaertner traveled the circuit of Portage, Columbia, Juneau, Sauk, Marquette, Green Lake, Iowa, Dane, and Jefferson counties.[200] However, under the burden of pastoral care assumed by the Norbertines, any hope of creating a stable abbey fell apart. The unordained brothers complained frequently about the absence of priests for prayer and daily Mass. Inama himself, accustomed to living independently, found it hard to re-acclimate himself to the burdens of communal living. Moreover, even though Inama was flush with funds from Europe and donations of land (1,260 acres), he was unable to administrate them effectively to the support of his Roxbury abbey. In 1858, the Abbey of Wilten recalled Gaertner. Inama then turned over the property to the Dominican Sisters of Racine and lived as a hermit until his death in 1879.

The Emerging Wisconsin Church: German-Irish Realities

Perhaps no public official other than the governor of the state had a first-hand sense of the range and diversity of Wisconsin's climate, geography, and demography as did Henni following his initial pastoral tour of his new diocese. Each region had a particular character to it. Within his administrative purview were the rapidly growing coastal counties, the bustling interior towns along the Rock River and the state capital, which itself had a particular culture relative to its diverse population. Heavily forested areas of the north, rural farming communities, and pockets of French, Irish and German Catholics all required attention.

The demographic realities placed special burdens on those entrusted with the pastoral ministry. As early as 1839, Dutch Dominican Theodore J. Van den Broek wrote, "Wisconsin is gradually becoming more and more populated, especially by Germans and Irish." Van den Broek spoke of the challenges he faced as he traveled to various churches and mission stations filling up with new settlers, "My labor is incredibly great. Sunday forenoon I usually preach in French, English and the High German languages, in the afternoon in the Indians [language]."[201]

From the 1830s through the 1870s (and even afterward) virtually everyone in Wisconsin (and this included those who lived in the growing cities along the lake) depended on the expansion of the farming economy. Wisconsin, like many of the agricultural states of the upper Midwest, benefitted from a transportation revolution that allowed agricultural products to be transported quickly to market. A series of roads crisscrossed the state. Later, the railroad would provide even more rapid and less expensive transportation for people and products. This provided a steady economy that attracted immigrants—and this brought even more dynamic population growth in the 1850s. These demographic realities provided the crucible of Catholic life in the first generation. Virtually everything broke down according to German and Irish lines, beginning with the two key diocesan institutions: the cathedral and the seminary. One would be dominated by the Irish, the second by the Germans.

Cathedral and Seminary: Irish and German Divisions

Early St. Peter's was a polyglot church—composed of Germans, French and English, all of whom had been corralled into a rough unity by the efforts of Martin Kundig. But the growth of the German population in Milwaukee in the 1840s soon made these conditions difficult to sustain. The result was a parochial division based on ethnic lines. This was begun by the Germans at St. Peter's, and in particular through their St. Anna *Frauenverein* which began to collect money for a new German church. As noted earlier, in 1846, Henni gave permission for the first German church in Milwaukee when he approved the construction of St. Mary's Church a few blocks southwest of the St. Peter's site. Left with the decrepit St. Peter's as his cathedral, Henni desired to build a more elegant symbol of diocesan presence and prestige in Wisconsin's largest city. This began a long and arduous process which took nearly six years to complete. In August 1847, land was procured opposite Milwaukee's court house square in block 78. Subsequent sales and confiscations added to the property. Henni was so impressed with the architectural job done on St. Mary's by Victor Schulte that he commissioned him as the architect for the cathedral. Henni also took a large role in its design.

Victor Schulte left an indelible mark on the Catholic Church in Wisconsin. His elegant designs of St. Mary's, Holy Trinity, St. Francis Seminary, and St. Mary's in Burlington played a major role in defining a clear

Catholic niche in the state's emerging urban communities. The most elegant of all these buildings was the Cathedral of St. John the Evangelist. Schulte was a native of Westphalia. He emigrated to the United States and lived for a time in Pennsylvania where he learned the arts of carpentry. In 1840 he came to Milwaukee and, finding no work, spent a brief time in Janesville. Typical of early architects of the day, he learned his trade by being a practical engineer and specialized in building railroad bridges. He returned to Milwaukee after a year and received a commission to build a bridge over the Milwaukee River on Chestnut Street (Juneau Avenue). Subsequent bridge contracts were given to construct spans for Spring and Oneida Streets. Schulte found himself in the middle of Milwaukee's famous "Bridge War," as his son recalled the builder confronting a mob intent on tearing down the west half of the Oneida and Chestnut Street bridges by informing them that the bridges were not paid for and that if they destroyed them they would be responsible for the debt.[202] Schulte's shop between River and East Water Streets employed 13 men. In addition to bridges he built a few dwellings including the family home on East Water Street. But his real love was big buildings like churches.

Holy Trinity Church, Milwaukee [AAM]

A brilliant autodidact, Henni learned the elements of style and design by poring over books of great buildings and making his own observations of various structures. He was apparently quite taken by the clean, sharp lines of the so-called "federalist" style which seemed to borrow from the archetype of the New England meeting house. Sharp steeples and corners, simple facades, and a kind of spartan dignity was evident in the design of Milwaukee's earliest churches and the seminary buildings.[203]

The laying of the cornerstone took place in horrid weather on December 5, 1847. A large group gathered to hear Henni and acting pastor Peter McLaughlin formally launch the cathedral building, which was to be 154 feet long and 74 feet wide and was priced at $20,000 to $30,000. Working closely with Schulte, Henni himself pored over architectural designs, supposedly drawing from ideas contained in the work of German architect, Johann Frederick Penther. Henni may have also consulted with Father Samuel Mazzuchelli, himself an architect of note. James Douglas, a local architect and builder, was the superintendent of the building. The walls of the new structure were made of local materials. Waukesha limestone helped to set the foundation, while Milwaukee's famous cream brick, pressed at the yards of the Burnham brothers, was used for the walls.[204] Schulte's son recalled of the supporting beams of the church, "Father used no steel beams like those which hold arches today. He used great oak timber which he cut himself at North Point and hauled down to his shop on the river to be trimmed." Stucco for the interior of the cathedral was mixed in the Schulte's basement.[205]

The problem that Henni faced, not only with the cathedral, but with all his plans to raise a visible Catholic presence in Wisconsin, was money. Johnson notes that shortly after his inspection tour of 1844, Henni was so overcome by the challenges and the lack of resources that he wept bitterly to Kundig as the two men walked along Lake Michigan one day—daunted by "the magnitude of his task and his lack of means."[206] Raising money for the cathedral was not easy. Since the German speakers had pulled out of the cathedral parish when they began St. Mary's, Henni had to rely on the largely working-class Irish who remained. Unfortunately, collections from them generated at best $700 a year, far short of the funds necessary to build a church the size of Henni's and Schulte's projections. Funds would have to be raised from other sources, for due to lack of money, by the middle of 1848 the project stopped after the basement walls were set. Overall, it took four years to raise enough money to complete the cathedral. Henni was compelled to go begging in a number of different places to support his project.

The long-term result of these difficult origins was to give the cathedral a somewhat ambiguous position vis-à-vis other churches in Milwaukee. Since the numerous and well-heeled Germans had their own churches, they paid little attention to the cathedral, seeing it as just another "Irish" church. Few large diocesan-wide ceremonies were held in its precincts, apart from the formal installation of bishops. Ordinations were held at the seminary and eventually bishops even quit living near the church. Few, it appears, regarded the huge structure as a source of diocesan unity. In the Catholicisms of Milwaukee, the Cathedral of St. John was part of the Irish or English-speaking league.

The Need for Money: A European Pipeline for Germans

But the reception of the cathedral was far into the future. Henni was faced with the need of funding this large project and many others in his growing diocese. Thrown back on his resources, Henni sought to replicate his formula for success at Holy Trinity—

heartfelt appeals to German Catholics in Europe to supply material and financial shortfalls. However, this avenue was blocked in a letter waiting for him when he returned from the northern inspection tour. Mueller of the *Ludwig-Missionsverein* urged the prelate to remain home, warning him that Europeans were feeling "indignant" at the presence of wandering missionaries among them, and wondered "how shepherds could leave their flocks if there was such a shortage of money and priests."[207] Henni was not daunted. Sending a "pretty long list" to the group, he noted in a letter to his former superior, Bishop Purcell, "if they could not supply me conveniently with them [the items] I would be obliged to get them by going over myself."[208] In 1848, he went abroad, seeking money. Part of this tour we have reviewed earlier. It was at this time he made efforts to secure the School Sisters of Notre Dame and received money for a later Jesuit foundation. But in addition, support for his new cathedral and the securing of additional priests were on his agenda.

In January 1848, Henni departed east, briefly revisiting his old haunts in Cincinnati, preaching to groups of German Catholics in New York and Baltimore and recruiting an American seminarian, John William Norris, for service in Wisconsin. Norris accompanied Henni to Europe, where the prelate undertook an active fund-raising campaign. Landing in England on March 7, 1848 Henni made straight for Rome. (Europe was convulsed with revolutionary disorders in 1848.) Leaving behind Norris, who began studies there, he reported on the growth of the church to Roman officials at the Propaganda and had an audience with Pope Pius IX. After quick visits to the tomb of St. Francis de Sales in Annecy and to his home in Switzerland, he turned to serious recruitment and fund-raising. His first stop was the venerable Benedictine abbey of Einsiedeln to recruit monks to teach in his proposed new seminary. Here, as we have seen, the monks turned him down.

In Munich, despite Mueller's warnings, he called on the *Ludwig-Missionsverein.* Henni received a cordial welcome from King Ludwig of Bavaria, who gave 4,000 florins for the School Sisters of Notre Dame and another 4,000 florins for the other German educational institutions of the diocese. Determined however that his money should only go to Germans, the Bavarian monarch refused to give to the ethnically-mixed cathedral. In all, the Bavarian society gave more than $15,000 before 1851 in addition to funds allotted for other projects in the diocese. In all, Henni would receive $56,432 from Munich.[209]

Henni avoided Vienna, a hotbed of revolutionary activity, and skipped a visit with the headquarters of the *Leopoldinen Stiftung,* but he did repair to Lyons where he called on the officials of the Propagation of the Faith. Here he stressed the large numbers of French Canadians at Prairie du Chien and Green Bay and carried with him an appeal written by Father Florimond Bonduel. Henni made it clear he would do all he could to promote the work of the Propagation in America and they rewarded him with a gift of 26,000 francs for the years 1849 and 1850. In Cologne he forged close ties with local bishops and priests and recruited seminarians from the dioceses of Muenster, Wurzburg and Limberg. He also drew some inspiration from the example of a bilingual seminary in Strasbourg. On a visit to Kitzingen in Bavaria, Henni persuaded bookseller Christian Ott to transplant his business to Milwaukee.[210]

Upon his return to America, Henni attended the Seventh Provincial Council of Baltimore in May and was drafted by the council fathers to write a letter of gratitude to the *Leopoldinen Stiftung*. Construction on the cathedral resumed and the building was soon under roof; however, cost overruns soon dried up the money Henni brought back from Europe. In 1851, he traveled to Cuba and Mexico to secure additional resources. Henni secured permission from the Bishop of Havana to take up a collection, and was able to do the same in Mexico City, pleading for money to complete his cathedral church.

By 1852, Henni had enough money to finish the cathedral. To bring the project to conclusion, Henni relied on the scholarly convert-priest, Father John M. Ives, who had come to Milwaukee from New York in 1850 and was made pastor of St. Peter's. Ives apparently knew enough about architecture and building to complete the task. A "polished and cultured preacher," Ives "became a favorite with the leading Americans of the city" and specialized in explaining the Inquisition to sometimes hostile Protestant audiences.[211] Ives apparently expected that the reward for his labors would be an appointment as pastor of the cathedral. However, when the building was done, Henni appointed the recently ordained John Norris to the coveted post, and Ives quit the city. He may have abandoned the priesthood for a time, but after the Civil War he re-emerged in Rome and was reinstated by Pope Pius IX who allowed him to devote himself to literary endeavors while residing at monasteries in France and Ireland. His writings found an outlet in such prestigious journals as the *London Tablet* and the *Dublin Review*. Ives spent the remainder of his days in Darlington, England where he succumbed to diphtheria in January 1891.[212]

Cathedral of St. John the Evangelist, Milwaukee
[AAM]

By 1852 funds were secured to finish the interior of the great church, and the formal dedication of the building was undertaken in the summer of 1853 by Archbishop Gaetano Bedini, the visiting apostolic delegate, together with bishops John Hughes of New York, John B. Purcell of Cincinnati, Peter Kenrick of St. Louis, and Henni's old associates, Peter Paul Lefevre of Detroit, Michael O'Connor of Pittsburgh and James van de Velde of Chicago. The Cathedral of St. John the Evangelist was in an incomplete state on the day Bedini consecrated it. A handsome altar and a circular window depicting the Holy Spirit were about the only items of decor in the new structure. Outside, the plans for a high clock tower were also stymied by the lack of funds. But the cathedral of St. John did have a distinctive "Zwiebelturm" [onion shaped] tower for the first thirty years of its existence. When this dome deteriorated and had to be taken down, the structure seemed incomplete until 1892-1893, when enough money was available for the erection of a brick tower. Historian Kathleen Neils Conzen best summed up the social significance of the cathedral for the city. Observing the church building in a new way, she accentuated the church as "a Counter Reformation symbol of assertive Catholicism triumphant, erected by a Swiss bishop in a Yankee-Yorker city with strong German Lutheran and freethinking, as well as Catholic elements." Conzen further noted, "This was not a reticent classical republican temple like nearby Chicago's first Catholic cathedral .... Milwaukee's St. John's Cathedral was a militant instrument of aggressive Catholic revival of the period."[213] The same thing could be said of the new seminary Henni built.

St. Francis Seminary

Cathedrals and seminaries shared important significance in the Tridentine world of post-Reformation Catholicism. The cathedral and its attendant buildings reinforced the centrality of the bishop and the cause of diocesan unity around his leadership. Likewise, the mandates of the Council of Trent had stipulated the formation of a well-educated clergy. Like all other endeavors in the creation of dioceses, the formation of educational institutions of any sort were tremendously costly. Unlike parishes they could not bring in revenue to defray their own costs.

Henni was in desperate need of priests to tend to the veritable flood of immigrants who came to Wisconsin in the 1850s. His various trips abroad included talks and personal pleas to seminarians or priests to join him in Wisconsin. For example, on the way to Europe in 1848, he met John Norris, a native of Washington, D.C., and a graduate of Georgetown Academy. Norris was well into his studies at Baltimore's St. Mary's Seminary when he heard Henni's appeal for priests. Dropping his Baltimore studies, he immediately joined the Milwaukee prelate on a trip abroad and completed his studies at the Propaganda in Rome. Other seminarians came from the famous Irish training center at Maynooth or from various universities in German-speaking areas of Europe. In all, between 1845 and 1855, Henni recruited 112 clerics for the new diocese, and of these he ordained 29. Of the 29, sixteen were born in Germany and eleven in Ireland.[214]

Pioneer bishops in America's West recognized the need for seminaries and often began them in their own homes. Henni was no exception. As noted earlier, in 1845, with the help of a generous grant from the *Ludwig-Missionsverein,* he too began a seminary in his own residence on Jefferson Street in Milwaukee.[215] The first three seminarians, Francis Mazzuchelli, Francis X. Obermuller, and Patrick McKernan were educated there (although they had begun studies elsewhere). Mazzuchelli, ordained in June 1845, was the first Henni raised to the priesthood in Wisconsin (and one of the first to leave the ordained ministry). Henni added rooms to his home and welcomed more seminarians. The small group of aspiring clerics used St. Peter's Church as their chapel, and Henni sought to enhance the intellectual reputation of his seminary by collecting a small library. However, the number of seminarians fluctuated, and when Henni went to Europe in 1848 and later Heiss returned to Bavaria, the house seminary lost its faculty and was then transferred to St. Boniface Church in Germantown where, as we have seen, Father Joseph Salzmann piloted the theological training of Father Francis Fusseder, and seminarians Peter DeBerge and Matthias Gernbauer.

The Germantown seminary moved back to Milwaukee when Salzmann became pastor of St. Mary's in 1850. Efforts were made to renew a form of early seminary training at the houses attached to the old St. Peter's site, and between 1852-1853, St. Peter's Academy, a boarding school for seminarians and lay students, was created with something resembling a respectable faculty. It closed after a year, but by that time Heiss returned, and together with Father John Ives, efforts were made to continue the education of students for the priesthood. Although cultured and literate men, like Henni and Ives, were able to give the seminarians some formal instruction, the demands of a busy parish and the informality of the surroundings provided little by way of the substantive theological and spiritual training required by Trent and insisted on by the American bishops at their various provincial councils. Moreover, Wisconsin's population was soaring. Between 1844 and 1853, the number of people living in the Milwaukee diocese grew from 20,000 to 100,000. The old log chapels of the early 1840s were giving way to substantial stone or frame churches. Fifteen new churches were built and 25 more were under construction in 1853. It was in that year, after his cathedral was finally built, that Henni turned his full attention to the need for a stable seminary, and the need to recruit and train native vocations.

The dedication of the cathedral provided the first opportunity for serious fund-raising for a new permanent seminary, and a subscription drive began during the retreat of the German priests held at St. Mary's in anticipation of the cathedral dedication in July 1853.[216] Twenty-two diocesan and two religious order priests subscribed $3,145 for the seminary. At the top of the list was Joseph Salzmann with a subscription of over $1,000.

By this time as well, the need for a special seminary for Germans was pressing. Not only was there substantial growth in the German-speaking population of Wisconsin, but local Catholics took quite seriously the "threat" of the so-called "Forty-Eighters," virulently anticlerical German liberals who had made Milwaukee one of their centers. With the return of Henni's colleague, Michael Heiss, to active duty in the diocese in 1852, plans went forward for a new special seminary for German youth. Assisting Heiss were Salzmann and Father F. X. Paulhuber. Paulhuber, a native of Bavaria and graduate of the University of Wurzberg, had come to Wisconsin in 1848 at Henni's invitation. Broadly educated in the study of scripture, church history, and science, Paulhuber was a perfect choice to help create a new and more respectable seminary. Paulhuber was also deeply suspicious of American culture, equating "Yankeeism" with unbelief. Paulhuber would remain in America only five years and then return to his native land.[217] The three men were often like oil and water: Salzmann, still passionate, emotional, and sentimental, Heiss, slow, methodical, and occasionally obdurate, and Paulhuber, ill-at-ease in America, but practical minded, pedantic, and hypersensitive.[218] Nonetheless, the fruit of their labors was St. Francis de Sales seminary.

Original building at St. Francis Seminary, 1856 [AAM]

At first, the special seminary, more like a boys prep school, was located downtown at the St. Peter's site. Paulhuber, who replaced Salzmann as pastor of St. Mary's, oversaw the instruction. But already before the priest's retreat in 1853, Heiss and Salzmann had purchased 52 acres adjoining the Nojoshing property of the Ettenbeuren Tertiaries. Heiss then overcame Paulhuber's opposition, and relocated the school to the old brother's house on the property. The property was soon expanded by the purchase of an additional 53 acres and became the site for the new diocesan seminary, which even at its Jefferson Street location was already called the "Seminary of St. Francis de Sales" or the Salesianum.

Erecting the Salesianum

From September 1853 to September 1854, Paulhuber was the superintendent of the seminary project. He saw to the practicalities of construction by erecting a brick-making operation near the new building, digging wells, foundations, and cellars. He added to the lands under cultivation and purchased lumber for the infrastructure. In early 1854, he also began to construct the first St. Aemillian's orphanage on the seminary property. However, Paulhuber's association with the seminary ended abruptly in 1854. His fears of contracting the dreaded cholera and his distaste for American life and culture culminated in his departure. In August of 1855 he moved to Buffalo and in 1856 he returned to Bavaria. Salzmann, with whom he had quarreled bitterly, rejoiced in his departure, commenting that he had finally come to his senses.[219]

Paulhuber later maintained that he had laid out the basic design of the seminary building; however credit for this goes to Victor Schulte, who designed the three-story, "federalist" building which began to be erected in the spring of 1855. Schulte moved to the site, purchasing a farm not far from the building. A kiln was erected to make bricks from the clay on the site. His son and grandchildren continued to live there for many years. Aiding the workers were the Franciscan Tertiaries, who provided food, labor and other support for the project. In gratitude for his service, Henni gave Schulte a ring that was passed down through generations the family.

As the building rose, both Henni and Salzmann's efforts to pay for it intensified. Henni begged and importuned the mission societies for money, and eventually received $6,000 from the *Ludwig-Missionsverein* for the new structure.[220] Moreover, gifts of art, lighting fixtures, and other elements of decor were contributed by European Catholics. Salzmann became the most ardent champion of the seminary, trumpeting its prospects in the newly-founded newspaper *Der Seebote,* and traveling extensively all over Wisconsin and the nation in search of donations. Johnson relates the details of the nearly 10,000 names carefully inscribed in a "cash memo" in

Rev. Joseph Salzmann
[AAM]

Salzmann's papers. Salzmann formed a society, the Salesian Society, for the support of the institution. Members of the Salesians donated anywhere from 15 cents to $20 and were promised a remembrance at the Holy Masses to be offered by the seminary. Prayer books, like Francis de Sales's *Philothea*, and popular devotional books such as *Der Pilgerstrab,* were given out as part of the promotion. After the Civil War, Salzmann traveled to Europe where he received grants from King Ludwig of Bavaria, Emperor Franz Joseph of Austria-Hungary, and the Duke of Modena. At the famed Benedictine abbeys where he sought shelter and hospitality, he secured boxes of books. These were added to the many tomes Henni had collected to form the seminary library.

Salzmann's most famous sermon, given in his own parish church of St. Mary in 1853, knit together the various themes of an impending priest shortage, the dangers of infidelity, the special needs of Germans, and the role of the seminary as a socially useful institution for the entire state of Wisconsin. "At this day there are in all Wisconsin but seventy priests." He warned of the encroachments of foreign ideologies: "This enemy is not Lutheranism nor Methodism, nor any other of the countless sects ... but a sham enlightenment, a sham free thought, a sham humanitarianism, atheism and indifferentism and by whatever names these false systems may designate themselves." In words aimed at his German-speaking audience, he reminded them of the Catholic culture of the homeland and its difficult political conditions: "Not one of you ... would desire to bring over here the political institutions of the old country, the burgomaster, the many clerks, the whole swarm of petty officials, the soldiery, the whole system of government; but many a one yearns for his old pastor." He drove home the importance of the appeal by linking the cause of the priesthood with additional German immigration: "I have no hesitation in claiming for this institution, the Salesianum, that it will add greatly to the prosperity of the state of Wisconsin. If Wisconsin is once provided with priests, undoubtedly, a great number of Catholic families will settle in the state. If you praise the state for its fertility and its German settlers, I praise it as a rich field for the Catholic Church. Yes, this will attract Catholic immigrants more than good harbors, good roads, and all other material advantages."[221] Salzmann eventually came to head the seminary he had literally helped build. When he died in 1874, his personal property was raffled for the benefit of St. Francis.[222]

On the 15th of July 1855, the formal laying of the cornerstone took place. Heiss was the principal German speaker of the day, while Father George Riordan of the cathedral clergy spoke in English. Henni himself, wilting under the midday heat, uttered words that sharply etched the nature of the institution as a Germanizing agent: "What I have accomplished in my diocese I owe to God and my German priests."[223] The new St. Francis Seminary was dedicated on January 29, 1856. Literally thousands of young men would be educated for the priesthood within its walls. For many years, St. Francis developed a reputation as the premier seminary for German-speaking youth in the United States. The first recruits were from Milwaukee, but soon other dioceses with German-speaking seminarians sent them to the Milwaukee seminary. In 1865, the seminary ordained 25 men. Half of them were from Milwaukee, the others came from St. Louis, Dubuque, St. Paul, or Detroit. Aspirants to the priesthood soon hailed from all over the country.

Yet, although much was made of the German character of the seminary, from the outset it always took in English-speaking students and provided niches on the faculty for English-speaking priests. Later students and professors of other nationalities would find a welcome place at the seminary. In some respects, the seminary became a mirror of the ethnic diversity of the diocese, and managed, with some success, to negotiate ethnic differences.

Unable to secure a religious community to staff the seminary, Henni then relied on diocesan priests to educate clerical aspirants. The effect of this was to create a body of clerical scholars that enhanced the overall quality of the Milwaukee priesthood for generations.[224] Early seminary scholars were recruited from the ranks of classically trained priests from German uni-

Seminary Chapel
[AAM]

versities. Many of these men had a breadth of knowledge in everything from theology to mathematics, languages and natural science. The first rector, Michael Heiss, would establish a seminary reputation for scholarship by his published works on matrimony and the four gospels. It became one of the premier institutions of clerical training in the country.

The early seminary contained a wide spectrum of age groups. Included within its walls were teenaged boys who were part of a preparatory seminary program required by the Council of Trent, as well as young adult men who were finishing their studies for ordination. The course work of the younger men included languages (classical and modern), mathematics, science, literature, and writing. After completion of these classes, seminarians were then advanced to the study of philosophy; and then, in the final years, an intense study of various branches of theology. A division was made between the lower and upper classes when the seminarian received "tonsure," a ritual cutting of hair that admitted a man to the "clerical state." The clerics were then required to wear the long black Roman cassock as part of their daily attire. Subsequent "minor orders" of porter, lector, exorcist, and acolyte, were successively bestowed on the young men who persevered. Finally, major orders of sub-diaconate, diaconate, and priesthood were conferred at the end of the course of study. The different academic programs of the seminary required housing the seminarians in separate wings to accentuate the difference in their ages, study, and levels of maturity. As time went on, the seminary academic program came to resemble more and more the traditional high school, college, and professional school separations of secular institutions. Eventually, the younger men would be moved from the same building as the older seminarians, as separate high school and college arrangements were made. Likewise, separate faculties were developed for each of the institutions. At first however, the professors of the seminary floated among the various age groups and taught a variety of subjects. Sometimes, as was the case with future archbishop Frederick X. Katzer, older seminarians helped defray some of their tuition by teaching the younger men. Katzer taught mathematics. He remained on the seminary faculty after ordination, and taught

Seminary high school students [AAM]

philosophy and even directed dramatic performances.

In 1866, Rector Heiss purchased an additional 160 acres to the west of the seminary for $10,000. The timber on the land was used for future construction and it was also good for some small agricultural endeavors that helped to feed the growing number of seminarians. On this property would eventually be built the Holy Family Normal School, St. John's School for the Deaf and Sacred Heart Church. One of the most beautiful structures on the property was a devotional chapel built in honor of the Visitation of the Blessed Virgin known as the Chapel of the Woods. Erected in 1867 by a nostalgic Father Matthias Gernbauer, it evoked memories of similar shrines in his native Austria. Gernbauer enlarged the structure in 1874 and it became a site of special pilgrimage especially after papal delegate Cesar Roncetti brought a special indult granting a plenary indulgence for those who visited the chapel.[225]

Cathedral and seminary were the two most visible institutions of Henni's desire to promote a visible Catholic subculture in Wisconsin. Huddled along the lakeshore, the twin institutions would anchor and expand Catholic visibility. The cathedral's location directly across from the court house had the effect of linking the Church with the very center of Milwaukee's political and social life. The seminary also became one of Milwaukee's and Wisconsin's growing centers of culture and intellectual refinement, and its picture and description occasionally graced booster publications as signs that Milwaukee had the accouterments of civilized society. Together with the Franciscan convent, and later the Normal School, St. Francis Seminary carved out a sizeable niche of prime acreage along or near Lake Michigan that shaped the development of the little village of St. Francis.

But, after the creation of churches, no accomplishment of the founding generation had a more long-lasting influence on the expansion of church life in Wisconsin than St. Francis Seminary. Not only did it provide priests to celebrate the sacraments—the very well-spring of Catholic life and identity—but just as importantly it provided a steady flow of native-born priests. This meant that Milwaukee quickly slipped the bonds of missionary existence early in its ecclesiastical history and was strong enough to generate its own local leaders. More populous Chicago had to wait until the 20th century to create a successful major seminary. Other dioceses, with far fewer Catholics, and lacking the resources or the bold leaders that Milwaukee had, may have looked with envy on its thriving seminary. A continual flow of local men embraced the priesthood and spent their entire lives serving the people of the state. Catholicism in Wisconsin was qualitatively better because it had native priests.

The same property also hosted other Catholic institutions devoted to the care of the poor.

English-Speaking and German Orphanages

In addition to schools, Roman Catholic sisterhoods staffed asylums for the care of the

St. Rose Orphanage [Peter Leo Johnson. *Daughters of Charity in Milwaukee, 1846-1946,* Daughters of Charity, 1946]

indigent and ill. The Sisters of Charity and the other sisterhoods who came to Wisconsin at Henni's invitation provided a network of Catholic social services that cared for the "stranger and the alien" through the corporal works of mercy. The need for these institutions was evident when Milwaukee bloomed from a rural village of 1700 to over 20,000 people. Other cities grew rapidly as well. With every increase of population, the social welfare needs of the community grew proportionately.

Care of dependent children, as well as other "unfortunates" in society, had been formalized in 19th century American society by the rise of asylums.[226] Although the word is generally applied to mental institutions, the reformers who proposed this model of social care believed that mental and physical health could be restored only in an atmosphere of peace and restful calm. Asylums for the mentally ill were, of course, the prototype, but the asylum concept soon influenced the rise of the penal system (the original ideas behind penitentiaries), and the care of dependent children.

The rise of the orphanage in America dated back to colonial foundling societies, but as American cities grew in size and complexity, the care of dependent children became a more pressing issue. Ultimately county governments established orphanages for infants and young children. The care of dependent youth came to the Catholic Church almost naturally, since religious houses in Europe had often taken in needy children. The Catholic Church of the diocese of Milwaukee committed itself early on to this corporal work of mercy and erected a number of institutions for little children.

Henni's experiences with dependent Catholic children in Cincinnati provided the prototype for diocesan development. In his years as pastor of Holy Trinity Henni had taken the care of orphan children under the expansive wings of his growing parish. The establishment of the St. Aloysius Orphan Society began to generate revenues to pay for the erection of a Catholic boys orphanage under German auspices in Cincinnati. Henni hoped to recreate this in Milwaukee. But it

St. Rose Orphanage in 1940s [Peter Leo Johnson. *Daughters of Charity in Milwaukee, 1846-1946,* Daughters of Charity, 1946]

was not until the Sisters of Charity, who had arrived in 1846, actually took in an orphan girl in 1848 that diocesan care of dependent children began. Despite a legend that the bishop himself brought the first orphan to the sisters, it was Father Peter McLaughlin of St. Peter's Church who left a young Irish immigrant girl, Katie Colfer, with the Sisters of Charity. This was the remote origin of St. Rose Orphanage.[227] Housed in the south wing of their convent on Van Buren Street, by 1851 the sisters eventually took in 31 orphans.

Eventually, Henni planned a new facility on property on Jackson Street adjacent to the Cathedral of St. John. On his 1851 fund-raising trip to Mexico, Cuba, and Europe he also included an appeal for the orphanage. In 1853, a brick building was built on the north side of the cathedral. Funding of the orphanage proved to be a problem at first. However, by 1863 it managed to run a small surplus. St. Rose had times when its facilities were overwhelmed. One such moment was after the sinking of the steamer *Lady Elgin* in September 1860. As noted earlier, this tragic accident, which occurred during a fund-raiser for an Irish Civil War regiment, claimed the lives of many Irish Milwaukeeans and left many children behind.

The Sisters of Charity were also called to fill the void in city social welfare services. In September 1860, the Milwaukee Common Council voted to deed nearly four acres of land to the sisters on the proviso that they erect an orphanage on the spot within two years. Conveniently located north of the city on prime land near the sister's new St. Mary's Hospital, the sisters built a two-story brick house in 1861 which they named St. Joseph's Orphanage. There they transferred younger girls.[228] St. Rose and St. Joseph's were dedicated to the care of dependent girls. As with all diocesan institutions, ethnicity played a role in orphanages. St. Rose and St. Joseph were dominated by Irish-surnamed children. German-speaking boys had another institution.

The care of orphan boys was entrusted to the Sisters of Charity at first. But they, like many other religious communities, became reluctant to keep the boys who often grew restless and rebellious as they got older.[229] Moreover there were language difficulties posed by the influx of German immigrants. As we have seen, Martin Kundig knew something about the care of dependent children from his days in Michigan. In Milwaukee, he found himself with seven orphans on his hands after he promised a dying mother he would care for them. The seven children lived with him for a time, but he soon realized that he had to make other provisions for their care. Henni helped him secure a small home on Van Buren Street in 1849 for the care of the children, and Kundig's two sisters took care of them. In the meantime, Henni's chief fund-raiser, Joseph Salzmann, added appeals for the orphanage to his efforts to raise monies for the cathedral and the seminary. The new orphanage was put under the patronage of St. Jerome Emiliani, a 16th century Italian cleric who founded orphanages in his homeland, and the new institution was given the

St. Aemilian Boys' Orphanage, c. 1905 [AAM]

latinized name of "Aemillianum." Henni continued to scour for funds and a full-time staff to care for the growing number of children who sought assistance at the house. A new supporting society, called the "St. Jerome Aemillian Society," recruited members who would raise funds for the maintenance of orphans.

The Sisters of Notre Dame undertook the task of caring for the orphan boys at their own motherhouse. However, by 1853 Mother Caroline's plans for the expansion of the motherhouse and the taking of new missions strapped the new congregation. They asked Henni to be relieved of the task of caring for the orphan boys. It was at this point that the Franciscan Tertiaries, now formed into something resembling a religious congregation, agreed to care for orphan boys. In 1854, the Tertiaries, erected a frame house on the corner of their Nojoshing property, near the seminary. The new orphanage was called St. Aemillian's.

Fire was the everlasting enemy of the orphanage on the seminary grounds, as a conflagration destroyed the small home. In four weeks they raised enough money to replace the house, this time in brick. By sometime in 1856 the construction was complete and 49 orphans were welcomed. Growth was swift and in 1861 an addition was made to the building. The *Lady Elgin* disaster and the Civil War caused the number of orphan boys to grow to 85 by 1866. In 1869 a north wing was added, and in 1872, the center building, the original structure, was torn down and a three-story edifice was added. Later a chapel was set aside for the boys and further additions were made to the building.

The orphanage became home to scores of boys and the presence of the German-speaking nuns and priests who oversaw operations assured its German character. Funding the operation was nearly a full-time task. Until state law prohibited it in 1876, some money came to Catholic orphanages in Wisconsin from the state. Milwaukee County also provided some limited funding and support.[230] These funds were supplemented by private fund-raising by the diocese. Through a support society established for the orphanage, German Catholics gave 25 cents a month for the support of the boys at St. Aemillian's. Until his death in 1874, Father Salzmann preached "in season and out" for the support of the place. The sisters ran an annual picnic, held special collections on Christmas, Easter, and patronal feasts, and solicited donations and bequests from their increasingly large circle of friends. Later, a general collection from the German parishes provided regular support. In 1911, Archbishop Sebastian Messmer imposed a collection on all parishes for the support of the orphanage.

Although the orphanage was funded by contributions from German parishes, and was considered a German facility, it took in boys of all nationalities. As time went on, Milwaukee's denominational divisions became more sharply etched and Catholic leaders insisted on separate institutions for Catholic youth. Moreover, the various counties of the state began to erect separate institutions for the care of the poor, sick, and dependent children. There were always non-Catholic youth in diocesan child care facilities, but the Catholic character of the institutions grew more pronounced with time. In addition to providing bed and board to their young charges, the sisters instructed the orphans in the Catholic faith and made them attend regular religious services. Seminary professors became occasional instructors of the young men, as did seminarians (perhaps an early form of contemporary "internships"). In 1893, Archbishop Katzer appointed a former protégé from Green Bay, Father Norbert Kersten, to be the first full-time priest, chaplain, and superintendent of St. Aemillian's. On December 11, 1895, the orphanage was once again destroyed by a disastrous kerosene fire that erupted in the print shop. As before, Milwaukee Catholics responded generously and a new structure quickly replaced the fire-charred ruins.

In 1878, state law required the founding of boys homes for vagrant and wayward youth. This gave rise to the creation of industrial schools (or reform schools, as they were known). St. Aemillian's also created an industrial school under Catholic auspices, and instructors taught the older boys woodworking, printing and other practical skills.

First Holy Communion at St. Aemilian Orphanage, June 1899 [AAM]

Parochial Explosion: The German-Irish Competition

The competing Catholicisms of Wisconsin were most obvious in the creation of separate parishes for English-speaking and German-speaking Catholics. Diocesan parochial development tended to follow two patterns. In one pattern, one ethnic group dominated the other, and the only church (and/or school) was for the dominant group. The

St. Joseph Church, Milwaukee [Martin Marty, OSB. *Dr. John Martin Henni, First Bishop and Archbishop of Milwaukee,* Benziger Bros., 1888, p. 237]

other pattern that was common in cities large enough to support more than one parish had one church for English speakers and the other for the German-speaking.

The city of Milwaukee pioneered the creation of ethnic parishes. Germans dedicated St. Mary's Church, which was the mother German church for all other German congregations in the city in 1847. Two other important churches followed: Holy Trinity on the south side in Walker's Point in 1850, and St. Joseph's in 1855 west of the city. By 1920 there were 14 German parishes in the city of Milwaukee alone.[231] As noted earlier, to provide for the growing number of English-speaking Catholics, the bishop established St. Gall in 1849. In 1853, the Cathedral of St. John the Evangelist became the most important church for the English-speaking of the city.

Other settlements of size followed suit. Racine's proto-parish was named in honor of St. Luke in 1840 and like Milwaukee's St. Peter's was open to all comers, regardless of nationality. When Racine grew explosively in the 1840s, German and Irish Catholics demanded and received their own separate parishes. In 1845, a church dedicated to St. Ignatius (later relocated and renamed St. Mary's) was opened for the Germans and St. Patrick's Church was founded for the city's Irish. In the county, the river town of Burlington accommodated the Germans when Father Michael Wisbauer took over St. Sebastian Church. Three years later a parish named in honor of St. Thomas Aquinas opened for the English-speaking in nearby Waterford.

In Southport, later Kenosha, the first Catholic Church, St. Mark's, was founded in 1840 and encompassed all the Catholics in the small town. But here too, Kenosha's growing German community eventually demanded its own parish. In 1849 St. George opened at a site not far from the lakefront. St. Mark's, later renamed St. James, remained an Irish bastion well into the 20th century.

Other examples of this German-Irish rivalry abound. Ozaukee County, directly to the north of Milwaukee, boomed as the possibilities of lakeshore commerce tantalized the founders of Port Washington. Ozaukee county's first Catholic church, founded by German immigrants and named in honor of

St. James, was located in the village of Mequon in 1845. A string of German-speaking parishes dotted the rural county. Farther north in Cedarburg, St. Francis Borgia opened its doors in 1846. In Grafton, St. Francis Xavier (later St. Joseph) began in 1848, and in 1849 Port Washington welcomed another parish, St. Mary's. Yet despite the Teutonic domination of Ozaukee County, a small Irish contingent founded the church of St. Finbar in Saukville in 1850. This small church eventually joined the register of "ghost" churches, but its tiny cemetery still exists and holds the remains of one of the most influential Irish Catholics of archdiocesan history, newspaper publisher and editor, Humphrey J. Desmond.

In the state capital of Madison, the same dynamic of parish development took place. Martin Kundig first came to Madison in 1842 and celebrated Mass. Kundig ingratiated himself with the territorial governor, James Duane Doty, who on impulse donated two lots to the Catholic Church that he had originally purchased for a future governor's mansion. This became the site of St. Raphael's Church. It was not until 1848 that a resident pastor was assigned to Madison and a church was constructed in the 1850s. This future Cathedral of the diocese of Madison soon became a center of Irish Catholicism. By 1856, German Catholics in Madison grew restive at the Irish St. Raphael's and Henni himself came in September of that year to announce plans for the creation of a new German congregation, Holy Redeemer, to be opened on the growing city's west side.[232]

St. Francis Xavier Church, Grafton [AAM]

Examples can be multiplied of the patterns of this German-Irish dyad throughout the counties of the archdiocese. But there were exceptions. For example, in Waukesha County Irish and German Catholics existed, for the most part, in a kind of peaceful coexistence. Waukesha County developed gradually, its population rising slowly despite the fact that the famed Blue Mound Road, and later rail connections, opened it to commercial development early on. Waukesha's first Catholic church was named in honor of St. Joseph and opened in 1842. Five years later, a mission station was founded a few miles east in rural Marcy (Brookfield) and named in honor of St. Dominic. Both of these communities had English- and German-speaking parishioners who worshiped together in relative peace for many years.

In some instances, the Irish had a free rein within a region, as did the Germans. Two examples that bore the imprint of dominance were a triangular Irish area that encompassed land in two counties, and a communal colony that was totally German.

An Irish Center in Rural Wisconsin

Six hundred Irish families lived in adjoining townships in Sheboygan and Fond du Lac counties in an irregular triangle that stretched from Kennedy's Corners in Lima to St. John's Church in Byron.[233] The Fond du Lac County section of these parishes was overseen by visiting priests from Fond du Lac which, since 1847, operated from St. Louis Mission for the French-speaking. Irish churches like St. John's in Byron (1848) and St. James (1849) in Eden developed. In Armstrong, Osceola Township, Father Louis Dael of Fond du Lac established St. Matthew's Church (1856), later renamed Our Lady of the Angels. Sacred Heart in Dundee (1874) was built for that town's growing Irish community.

Rev. Ambrose Oschwald, SDS [ASDS-M]

In Sheboygan County, a series of German-speaking priests helped provide a foothold for Irish parishes. Austrian immigrant priest Caspar Rehrl had established St. Mary Magdalen's Church in Sheboygan in 1845. His successors, Capuchin Fabian Bermadinger, Matthias Gerend, Francis Fusseder and Peter DeBerge attempted to reach out to the Irish farmers in the western parts of the county. St. Mary Magdalen's was the parent of St. Patrick's in Cascade (1853), St. Michael's in Mitchell (1854), St. Mary's in Lyndon (1854), Blessed Virgin Mary of Carmel in Abbott (1854), St. Rose's in Lima (1861), and St. Fridolin's in Glenbeulah (1865). This cluster of parishes, set within German, French, and Dutch communities, stands out as one important concentration of Irish Catholic life in rural Wisconsin.

A German Catholic Commune: Ambrose Oschwald and the St. Nazianz Colony

Although new parishes in urban and rural centers were the foci of German growth in Wisconsin, one important communal experiment sponsored by and for German Catholics is worth noting. This was the effort of Baden priest Ambrose Oschwald to create what one historian has called a "chiliastic" or "apocalyptic" community in the virgin forest of Manitowoc colony.[234]

The Oschwald foundation began in discontent among a number of German lay persons in their rapidly secularizing portion of southern Germany. Under the guidance of a charismatic local priest, Ambrose Oschwald, a large group of devotees migrated to the United States in August 1854 and laid claim to 1500 acres in rural Manitowoc County.

According to historian Jerome Schommer, the small community was not a replica of the utopian experiments like Brook Farm or New Harmony that flourished briefly in the 19th century, but rather their intention was to replicate a particular form of German Catholic religiosity popular in Baden in Southern Germany. St. Nazianz was, in Schommer's words, "completely Catholic and completely German."[235] Composed of married and unmarried members, the Oschwald colony devoted itself to communal life, prayer, and an anxious waiting for the return of Christ. They managed to make the effort self-sustaining by farming. They built a log chapel and common living quarters. Each day's activities were punctuated by times of common prayer. By 1855, 70 people had gathered on the site and the colony had four residences, a common kitchen, stable, blacksmith shop, and smokehouse. Still the group continued to grow. By 1859, 200 people had settled on the property. When Bishop Henni inspected the site in 1860, he found 56 houses and 48 family heads in the village. Married and unmarried members were separated into their own living quarters and each group was to recite the Roman breviary in German. In addition, colony members were to engage in acts of charity: caring for the sick, orphans and widows, and providing religious instruction, devotions and services for those who required them. The colony endured bouts with malaria, bad planting and harvesting years, and continual shortfalls of money, which Oschwald repeatedly seemed to remedy. But when the priest died of pneumonia in 1873, the fate of the colony tottered until the property was transferred to the priests and brothers of the Society of the Divine Savior in 1896. Before its collapse, however, the St. Nazianz Colony provided about as pure an example of the character and influence of German Catholicism as was ever seen on Wisconsin soil. To enter into the living quarters and life of the community was, to some degree, like going back to Baden.

General Patterns of Parochial Development

On May 29, 1848, Wisconsin entered the Union as the 30th state. The establishment of a popularly elected state government and the settling of social conditions clarified the forces of state development and encouraged even heavier immigration. The population of Wisconsin more than doubled in the 1850s surging from 305, 390 to 775,881 by 1860. By 1870, Wisconsin surpassed the million mark, with a population of 1,054,670.

Parochial development in this epoch became increasingly more complex and drew on many more names and people to account for the proliferation. Using the same breakdown of counties and adding additional counties north of the Fox/Wisconsin axis, we see the corresponding settlement of the Church upon the land. There were six areas of settlement: the lakeshore counties (Milwaukee, Racine, Kenosha, Ozaukee, and Sheboygan); a "second tier" (Walworth, Waukesha, Washington, and Fond du Lac); the north lakeshore/Lake Winnebago counties (Calumet, Brown, Outagamie, Kewaunee, Door, and Winnebago); the "third tier" (Rock, Green, Dane, Jefferson, Dodge, Columbia, Green Lake, Marquette, Waushara, Portage, and Juneau); the mining counties (Grant, Crawford, Vernon, Richland, Iowa, and Lafayette); the north counties (LaCrosse, Trempeleau, Monroe, Jackson, Buffalo, Piece, St. Croix, Pepin, Dunn, Chippewa, Eau Claire, Clark, Wood, Marathon, Portage, Waupaca, Shawano, Menominee, Oconto, and Marinette). The development of parish life in these areas is noted in the Appendix.

Although there was not a Catholic church in every county by the end of this period, strong growth continued in the southeastern quadrant of the state, complemented by dynamic expansion to the northeast and northwest, stretching like an arc from Green Bay, through Stevens Point to Hudson in St. Croix County. Indeed, the strongest growth in Wisconsin was in the farming areas. Eventually the population of the northeastern and southwestern portions of the state resulted in the division of Wisconsin into three dioceses with newer headquarters at LaCrosse on the Mississippi River and Green Bay on Lake Michigan. The reduced area of the diocese of Milwaukee would remain, with a minor adjustment of its northern boundaries in 1905 and the formation of the diocese of Madison after World War II.

Catholic Acceptance in Wisconsin: Social Provision, Accommodation and Rejection

As original participants in the settling of Midwestern cities and the shaping of local culture, Catholics were "present" at the creation of most Wisconsin cities. In contrast to their co-religionists in the east, Catholics had comparatively fewer obstacles in winning acceptance, and few barriers to their civic, economic, or social mobility. Moreover, certain forms of Catholic social provision, especially hospitals and schools, played an important role in the development of local community.[236] Non-Catholics frequented Catholic hospitals, sent their sons and daughters to Catholic schools, and relied on the generosity of church figures to contribute to the common good and welfare of developing cities. The presence of elegant church buildings, for example, was often used by promoters and boosters of various Wisconsin localities as an incentive for people to settle.

What often kept hospitals full were outbreaks of plague-like illnesses that ended the lives of adults in an eye-blink. Milwaukee's reputation for public health was poor in its earliest days.[237] Like most instant cities, it grew more rapidly than its facilities could handle. As in most large cities, the close living of people from different parts of the world encouraged contagious disease. The disastrous impact of cholera and typhus offered the proximate cause for the establishment of Catholic hospitals. Already in 1844, Henni had witnessed devastating outbreaks of these dreaded, waterborne illnesses in Milwaukee's foul port. In the territorial days, no state legislature existed to charter county-institutions and asylums, so the need to do something about the sick, the poor, and the orphaned fell to religious institutions.

The Sisters of Charity took the lead in providing for this important civic need. In 1848, the sisters took over a newly-built two-story frame building on the southeast corner of Jackson and Wells and named it St. John's Infirmary. The new facility opened on May 15, 1848 and Henni, who had purchased the building, continued to provide financial support. From the start, the facility was to be open to all comers and singularly devoid of any overt religious identity. In the broadside announcing the Infirmary, the sisters declared: "... no minister, whether Protestant or Catholic, will be permitted to preach to, pray aloud before, or interfere with, such patients as do not ask for the exercise of this office. The rights of conscience must be held paramount to all others."[238] Local members of the newly founded Milwaukee Medical Association endorsed the new project.

Before long St. John's Infirmary was overwhelmed with victims of cholera and typhus. Unable to mount their own public hospital, the city and county used the facility for the indigent, and officials reimbursed the sisters for the care of public charges that they took in. Later, the city forestalled the admission of cholera-bearing passengers onboard ships full of immigrants by setting up a way station in government buildings at Jones Island and removing sick passengers. To nurse them, city Mayor Don A. J. Upham requested and received the services of the sisters.[239] After the cholera crisis passed, the sisters were entreated by the treasury department of the United States to care for sick or disabled seamen. Even though they lost the federal contract for a year, the sisters regained it and devoted a ward of their hospital to the care of sailors and naval veterans.

The demands on the initial St. John's Infirmary were such that the sisters needed larger quarters. Henni's old home on Jefferson Street was apparently more capacious. (In 1854 he moved into the new cathedral rectory which would be his home for the next 25 years.) The old house had been not only an episcopal residence, but also the first seminary, and a short-lived academy for boys. The Jefferson Street house was dubbed "the Crystal Palace" by the sisters because it was so difficult to heat and so damp that frost covered its walls and windows and icicles hung from the ceilings.[240] At any rate , the building did not last long, as Henni was compelled to sell it to meet pressing debts.

In 1858 the sisters moved to a new hospital which they named St. Mary's located on three acres donated to them by the Milwaukee Common Council for a charitable hospital. The site was on the grounds of a former city poor farm on Prospect and North Avenues. City fathers reckoned that having a charitable hospital built by private resources would inevitably benefit their poorhouse. The sisters had already begun gathering money for this. Although fund-raising was set back by the Panic of 1857, the cornerstone was laid on May 11, 1857. The sisters transferred to the hospital on November 24, 1858. Standing a bit north of the present day hospital, the all brick St. Mary's had three stories, six wards, 10 private rooms, parlors, offices, and quarters for the sisters. It was prepared to hold 55 patients. Its best years of business were the first years of the Civil War, when nearby Camp Siegel transferred wounded veterans to the sisters.[241] Other hospitals rose to fill Milwaukee's need for health care—especially the county hospital which was built in Wauwatosa in 1860.

Original St. Mary' Hospital, Milwaukee, 1858 [Peter Leo Johnson. *Daughters of Charity in Milwaukee, 1846-1946,* (Daughters of Charity, 1946)]

Apart from their intrinsic significance as healers of the sick, these early Catholic hospitals reflected as well an early form of ecumenical amity. Catholics and non-Catholics alike availed themselves of the ministrations of the Sisters of Charity. Public officials felt comfortable entrusting the religious community with public funds and relied on them to help shoulder important civic responsibilities.

However, the respect for the sisters and the willingness to share public funds with them was not a universal sentiment. In Milwaukee, as elsewhere, Catholics would face serious questions, and open challenges to their presence, their doctrines, and their loyalty to America. In the 1850s, especially, the organized forces of anti-Catholicism mounted serious opposition to Catholics in Milwaukee and throughout the state.[242]

Nativist Anti-Catholicism

Long-standing theological differences with the Roman Church over such things as the papacy, the sacraments, various church disciplines and other issues occasionally spilled over into public discourse and even public battle. At the very time Wisconsin was being settled in the 1830s and 1840s, yet another cauldron of anti-Catholic sentiment was preparing to boil over.[243] Stoked by the evangelical revival known as the Second Great Awakening, anti-Catholic outbursts had occurred in Massachusetts with the burning of an Ursuline convent in Charlestown in 1836, in Philadelphia in 1844 when riots broke out between Catholics and Protestants in the suburb of Kensington, and elsewhere. Anti-Catholic literature, like the scurrilous *Awful Disclosures of the Hotel Dieu Nunnery* hit the stands in 1836, relaying lurid tales of sexual activity between priests and nuns and blood-curdling tales of infanticide in convent basements. Earlier Samuel F. B. Morse's "Appeal for the West" (1834) warned loyal Americans of an impending Catholic takeover of the Mississippi Valley.

Anti-Catholic sentiment made common cause with nativist feelings and joined hands in the 1840s to create the Know-Nothing or American Party. Garnering substantial popular support, this party spread throughout the nation and registered significant electoral gains on the local and state levels, and even began to run candidates for federal office. But, the American Party's growth was stymied by the rise of the slavery issue which ultimately engulfed it. With this kind of agitation in the air, it was likely that there would be some anti-Catholic outbursts in Wisconsin, given the fact that some of its earliest denizens came from heavily Protestant areas of New York.

According to historian Leonard Koerber, there were two distinct phases of anti-Catholic outbursts that took place in Wisconsin in the 1840s and 1850s.[244] The first shared in the general national suspicion of foreigners that swept the nation at the time. Anti-Catholicism was linked to a wider xenophobia that mistrusted foreigners and viewed them as incapable of understanding or supporting American values, ideals, and institutions. The second kind of anti-Catholicism was more localized to the Wisconsin environment (and other areas of the country with high percentages of German speakers). This brand was generated by liberal anti-clerical Germans, the Forty-Eighters, who came to Wisconsin in numbers carrying with them a strong distaste for "reactionary" institutions, especially the Roman Catholic Church.[245] Both of these movements and the Catholic response found public expression in an explosion of newspaper activity. Bitter invectives were often hurled in person and on the street, but more often came through the partisans of one side or another in the press.

The "nativist" or anti-foreign brand of anti-Catholicism flared only briefly and somewhat ineffectually in Wisconsin state politics during the 1850s. Nativist influences had already begun to be felt in Wisconsin, especially in counties that had a high number of U.S.-born citizens. But Wisconsin also had a large immigrant flood and many of them

Anti Catholic diatribe [William L. Stone. *Maria Monk and the Nunnery of the Hotel Dieu*, Howe & Bates, 1836]

were Catholic. The chaplain of the School Sisters of Notre Dame, Father Anthony Urbanek, estimated that by 1852, the Catholic population of Milwaukee was between 8,000 and 9,000.[246] The rising Catholic presence in the city had been noted with some concern by non-Catholics. For example, Lutheran layman, Johann Carl Pritzlaff, the founder of a successful hardware enterprise, complained about the growing visibility of Catholics. "As far as church matters go, I cannot write much that is good," wrote Pritzlaff to relations abroad, "for the Anti-Christ [the Catholic Church] has also set up his See in America."[247] Local Protestant leaders initially held the upper hand and marshaled their collective forces to bring about the defeat of John White, a Catholic who ran for sheriff in the 1844 elections. White had been defeated in part because he had advocated a more liberal grant of the franchise to immigrants. To be able to vote, all that was required was six months residency in the territory. This did not sit well with many of the American-born, who feared that the immigrant vote could be easily manipulated. Moreover, immigrants seemed to show little interest in two areas that reform-minded Protestant clergy harped on continually: abolitionism and temperance.

The most noted outburst of anti-Catholic nativism took place in Milwaukee shortly before Henni's first Christmas in his See. On December 12, 1844, the pastor of the First Congregational Church, Reverend John J. Miter, delivered a Thanksgiving Day speech that began with an appropriate tone of Thanksgiving, but ended with a bitter onslaught against immigrant voting and indicted the Catholic Church as an agent of persecution and repression. Although the rhetoric was hot and even inflammatory in part, Miter's assault on the Catholic Church was reasoned and based on facts, as he understood them. In the manner of other Protestant critics of Roman Catholicism, Miter appealed to historical episodes, such as the Inquisition, to highlight the repressive nature of the Catholic Church. Miter especially singled out Catholic devotion to the pope, who was at that time a temporal ruler, as evidence of their divided national allegiances. They could not possibly be loyal to the Roman Church and to the American Republic. Consequently, Miter argued, extending the franchise to Catholic immigrants was ill-considered and ultimately destructive to the United States. Miter's lengthy comments were reprinted some weeks after he delivered the sermon on the pages of the *Milwaukee Sentinel.* Opposition to Miter's comments and his aspersions on Catholic loyalty came from several quarters, but most dramatically from Bishop John Martin Henni, who faced his first test of public leadership.

Barely in Wisconsin a year, Henni, with the help of Dr. James Johnson, a local physician and a close friend and benefactor of the prelate, drafted a 174-page reply to Miter. Called "Facts Against Assertions," it was published under the pseudonym "Philalethos" [truth-lover] in the Catholic-friendly newspaper, *Milwaukee Courier.* He then had his comments reprinted in pamphlet form titled

"Facts Against Assertions or a Vindication of Catholic Principle." Henni replied to what he considered Miter's distortions of historical evidence and fact, noting that, although Miter's diatribe was called a "Thanksgiving Sermon," "Did he conceive a single thought or utter a single word of 'thanksgiving' throughout his whole sermon—save the last sentence but one, after he had worked and sweated, through all the curses of Tristram Shandy."[248] In rhetoric that would one day seem ironic, given Henni's reputation as a strong proponent of German cultural preservation in America, the prelate defended at length the patriotism and civic pride of Catholic Americans. He refuted Miter's historical examples of Catholic repression by equally strong examples of Catholic patriotism. He invoked the Catholic heroes who had helped American win its independence, Lafayette, DeKalb, and Pulaski. Henni, according to his biographer, won much esteem for the nature of his response.

Milwaukee also hosted its share of anti-Catholic speakers. Giuseppe Garibaldi's chaplain, the former priest Alessandro Gavazzi, who had become a Methodist, visited the city and, with arms flailing, denounced the pope as an enemy to liberty. But by the 1850s, Catholics had grown in such numbers that such lecturers came at their peril. Irish Catholics wrecked vengeance on the church building where an ex-Dominican by the name of DeHelle, a Scot who "calumniated religion, the clergy, and convents,"[249] spoke. The most famous case of Catholic counter-violence to an anti-Catholic speaker came in 1851, when a so-called ex-monk, Edward Leahy, delivered a diatribe against the Catholic Church at the Spring Street Methodist Church. Leahy, a popular nativist preacher, came to Milwaukee prepared to reveal pornographic secrets about the lives of priests and nuns—a genre of anti-Catholic diatribe made popular by Maria Monk's *Awful Disclosures*. However, Leahy had never been a priest or a monk and Catholic Milwaukeeans were ready for him when he arrived. His speech was interrupted by shouts and catcalls that soon evolved to a full-blown riot. Leahy managed to escape without harm (aided by Sheriff John White, a Catholic who had finally been elected to the office he sought in 1844). Leahy left Milwaukee in one piece, and in 1851 he became involved in a sexual scandal himself when he murdered his wife's lover. During a prison term, he repented of his anti-Catholic ways and when released undertook a lecture tour to defend the Church.[250] One final blast of convent erotica made headlines in Milwaukee when an article in an anti-Catholic periodical, the *Christian Statesman*, repeated lurid tales of drinking and lewd conduct in the Notre Dame convent. This time, a lawsuit was launched by lawyer-priest Stanislaus Lalumiere, together with journalists P. V. Deuster and Valentine Zimmerman. The long legal battle was fought to a draw in 1873.[251]

Ultimately, anti-Catholic nativism never took off in Wisconsin as it had elsewhere. Nativism had entered Wisconsin politics under the umbrella of "Free Soil" beliefs—those who wished to keep Wisconsin free from slavery.[252] When Wisconsin entered the Union in 1848, its votes in the first presidential election favored the Democratic candidate Lewis Cass by a plurality, but there was strong sentiment for the Free Soil candidacy of Martin Van Buren. Wisconsin might have been ripe for a strong nativist uprising because it had a large foreign-born population, but the drafters of Wisconsin's constitution had essentially continued the liberal proviso of the territorial regime by allowing the foreign-born to vote. The only modification they made simply extended the time of residency to a complete year, provided they had declared their intention of becoming citizens. As a result of this, and because foreign-born numbers were so high, nativist movements could never get the political traction necessary to win an election. Moreover, the two major parties—the Democrats and the Republicans (who had come into existence in 1854 from the remnants of the old Whig and Free Soil parties)—were both reluctant to accept support from the cadre of nativists in Wisconsin. Efforts on the part of local nativists to affect the outcome of a gubernatorial election in 1855 were minimal. Even though the Germans and Irish were divided in many ways, their common status as immigrants and Catholics generally kept them aligned to the Democratic party, which had sponsored the liberal voting provisions and which had played no part in the nativist efforts in the east or at home.

European Anti-Catholicism Transplanted: The Forty-Eighters

The second form of anti-Catholicism was far more serious and distressing to Wisconsin Catholics. This emanated from a small but vocal cadre of German liberals who had fled to Wisconsin after the failed liberal revolution in Germany in 1848. These "Forty-Eighters," as they were known, were a highly educated and upwardly mobile group among Wisconsin's large and diverse German population. They were the sponsors of cultural and literary organizations and had introduced a popular gymnastic club, the *Turnverein,* to Milwaukee and other areas of German strength. In the Turner Hall, tumbling and acrobatic exercises were held, as were public meetings, smokers and other public gatherings. They had several newspapers—the *Wiskonsin Banner*, the *Volksfreund* and the *Flugblatter*—a school, a volunteer fire brigade and fund-raising organizations.

The Forty-eighters brought to America a strong dose of anti-clericalism. It stemmed in part from their own embrace of the militantly secular Enlightenment, and accentuated by their disdain for the Catholic Church's embrace of reactionary, restorationist regimes. The typical Forty-Eighter stood for freedom of speech, the press, civil liberties, and economic individualism. Militant "free-thinkers," as they called themselves, German Forty-Eighters were often the source of caustic criticism of the Church. Local churchmen, who bore no love for "the filth of the country and rubbish of the people," responded in kind. Father Michael Heiss of St. Mary's

Church had denounced the anti-clerical revolutionaries from his pulpit and had refused burial to one of their number who had died in Milwaukee. Similarly, when anti-Catholic elements sponsored a performance of Haydn's "Creation" and asked that it be held in St. Mary's Church in 1851, Henni initially agreed until he discovered the sponsors of the concert. The offer of St. Mary's was summarily withdrawn.[253] Henni and his clergy replied tit for tat to the attacks that emanated from Forty-Eighter lodges, like the Sons of Hermann, refusing to allow this anti-Catholic group to wear lodge regalia in Catholic churches. One of the Forty-Eighter organs, *Flugblatter*, edited by Bohemian Vojta Naprstek, fired regular salvos at the local Catholic clergy. It took particular glee in targeting Father Joseph Salzmann, who succeeded Heiss as pastor of St. Mary's, drawing unflattering caricatures, fabricating letters and encouraging street urchins to verbally assail him on the street. In one incident, Salzmann was heckled for riding in a carriage instead of traveling by jackass as had Jesus. To this came the acerbic reply, "I know, but what can I do? There are no more asses on the market, they have all become 'radicals.'"[254]

As noted earlier, some of the worst insults to Salzmann came when he was accused of "blamable intercourse" with the mother general of the School Sisters of Notre Dame, Caroline Friess. Indeed, the sisters too took their share of Forty-Eighter baiting since they were highly visible symbols of Catholicism in Milwaukee. The sisters were deeply sensitive to the rudeness, disrespect and bullying by German liberals, who publicly insulted them and made them feel odd and nervous apart from the safety of the convent. Indeed, in the early years of their residency in Milwaukee the sisters were actually dispensed from wearing parts of the religious habit (the veil) to keep from being annoyed or verbally attacked.

The sisters cordially reciprocated the sentiments. In a rather unusual departure from their normally charitable and euphemistic ways of describing conflicts or difficult situations, the chronicler of the Notre Dame motherhouse related their encounter with the Forty-Eighters: "The fifties (1850s) were very evil years." Speaking of the migrants from Germany, "they were the filth of the country and the rubbish of the people.... They were called 'Radicals.'" Since many of

Motherhouse of School Sisters of Notre Dame [ASND]

the assailants were themselves former Catholics, they knew just how to hurl invectives that would attack the most sensitive areas of Catholic life and ritual. The chronicler relates, "the convent of the Poor School Sisters were [*sic*] often the target of their religious hate and mocking. On public streets they frequently called after priests, 'Kyrie Eleison! Dominus Vobiscum' [Lord Have Mercy, The Lord Be With You—parts of the Mass]." In a prank that must have totally horrified the sisters, the local "radicals" brought to the front of the convent yard a cow which they ceremoniously "baptized." "The cow was baptized 'Marianne,'" a disgusted sister chronicler noted, "[and] even Latin church songs resounded jeeringly at the top of their voices."[255]

As in the case of the nativist assault, Catholics were not passive. Henni, Heiss, Salzmann, and Mother Caroline fought back. Henni in particular felt it important to offer the citizens of Milwaukee an alternative to the press monopoly of the Forty-Eighters, and began a new German language paper called *Der Seebote* in 1851. Though controlled by an independent board of directors and overseen by Salzmann, it printed church news and eventually gained a solid journalistic reputation when in 1857 it was handed over to the editorship of Peter V. Deuster, who transformed it into an even more secular journal. In 1873, another German Catholic paper, *Columbia* began publication under the editorship of diocesan priest John Gmeiner.[256]

Dealing with Other Denominations

Relations between the Catholic Church and their neighbors are worth noting. Catholics became a dominant force in Wisconsin—thanks largely to the heavy German migration. But other denominations, initially Congregationalists and Presbyterians, as well as Methodists and Baptists, filled out the religious geography of the state. Far and away the closest competitor with Catholics for the religious loyalties in the state were German Lutherans. Replicating a similar parochial/school nexus of visibility, Lutheran churches, schools, and social services provided an important context for the presence of the Catholic Church. They also attempted to rival the Church in appealing to immigrant communities. The religious geography of Wisconsin resembled to some degree the religious settlement of Switzerland with its Protestant and Catholic cantons. Certainly some counties had a preponderance of one religion over another. Racine County, which attracted heavy concentrations of Danes, Scandinavians, and some Northern Germans, had a heavy Lutheran flavor. Fond du Lac and Dodge counties tended to be heavily Catholic. Large cities like Milwaukee found some rough parity between Lutherans and Catholics, and enough Protestants to leaven the population. Each denomination regarded the other warily as competitors for the religiously transient. They did share a common disdain for the irreverent, and both employed architects that built grand and glorious churches in the prevailing neo-Gothic style of the 19th century. Catholics were, however, more numerous and more influential. Likewise the public expressions of their Catholic faith were inspired by the kind of baroque excesses that defined their religious identity. Other cities had similar mixtures of religious faiths. Catholic life, nonetheless, seemed to permeate its local communities, striking the right balance between the development of a vibrant subculture with enough sensitivity to remain open to the larger environment.

Catholics and the Civil War

The outbreak of the war between the states in April 1861 placed the Catholic community in Wisconsin in a strained position. Few Catholics associated themselves with the strong abolitionist positions of the Protestant evangelicals and reformers in the north. In addition, anti-slavery elements fused with the remnants of the old Know-Nothing Party to form the Republicans in the 1850s. If Catholics were not inclined to support abolition, they were less enamored of the Republicans, who still carried with them the whiff of anti-foreign/anti-Catholic sentiments.[257] Nonetheless, Republicans triumphed in state elections. In 1860, Republican governor Alexander Randall attempted to disband the largely Irish Catholic Union Guards as a state militia regiment. The move was condemned by the Catholic *Seebote* as an act of Know-Nothing prejudice. The guards determined to keep themselves together as an independent unit, and to raise funds, chartered a pleasure cruise aboard the triple-decked lake steamer *Lady Elgin*. As aforementioned, this vessel, with its 400 largely Irish Catholic passengers, was sunk in Lake Michigan in early September 1860.[258]

In the electoral race of 1860, Wisconsin Catholics voted in large numbers for Democratic candidate Stephen A. Douglas, but Lincoln carried the state handily with a 20,000 vote plurality.[259]

Lincoln's election prompted the withdrawal of the states of the lower south in the great "secession winter" of 1860-1861. Lincoln played a careful waiting game until the Southerners attacked a federal fort in Charleston Harbor in April 1861. When the president called out volunteers to suppress the rebellion, most of the states of the upper south seceded, and the Civil War was on. Enthusiasm for the Union ran high in Wisconsin. One of the first Catholic voices raised in defense of the Union was Father Florimond Bonduel from Bay Settlement, who claimed he was for "asserting the power of the Government with Bible in one hand and the sword in the other."[260]

But other Wisconsin Catholics were not so enthusiastic to support the "Republican War." One group of Hibernian Guards in Fond du Lac disbanded rather than join the volunteers flocking to eastern battle fields. Prussian-born Frederick Horn of Cedarburg, the commander of the Cedarburg Rifles, openly expressed his fear that the war "might turn into an anti-Catholic crusade." Eventually however, Catholic recruits began to fill the ranks of the state regiments destined for duty in the bloody conflict. The most famous was the heavily Irish Wisconsin 17th Infantry.

In 1862, Congress passed the Militia Act which required governors to impose quotas on counties to fill the Union armies. When shortfalls in recruitment developed in counties with strong German Catholic constituencies, recruiting officers approached Father Francis Fusseder, pastor of St. Mary's Church in Port Washington, to ask why. Fusseder explained that existing Wisconsin regiments did not offer Catholic recruits the "consolations of his religion in the hour of danger and death." Fusseder believed that German Catholics would volunteer if there were a German-speaking Catholic chaplain attached to their units. When a heavily German-speaking unit, the 24th Infantry was formed, Fusseder received a commission on September 3, 1862 as its chaplain, the first Milwaukee priest to serve in this capacity.[261] Fusseder served with distinction, but came away from the war with permanently weakened eyesight.

Rev. Francis Fusseder [AAM]

But even as their numbers were increasing in the army, German Catholics in Wisconsin continued to hold Lincoln in deep suspicion. Likewise, they were unenthusiastic about abolition—linking it to the militant Protestants who interlarded their appeals for black freedom with denunciations of "Romanism" and "popishness." Serious opposition to the draft manifested itself among Wisconsin's Catholic constituencies in 1862. In Brown County, Belgian farmers, armed with blunt farming instruments, marched to the home of Senator Timothy Howe in Green Bay, blaming him for conscription. In West Bend, Germans attacked a draft officer and sent him packing. In Ozaukee County a major riot erupted when a local draft commissioner, William Pors, a German, who was also a Democrat and a Mason, was accused of exempting his Masonic lodge friends from the draft and attempting to fill the quota with the sons of the county's Luxemburger population. Pors was beaten within an inch of his life, and eight companies of the 28th regiment had to be sent to restore order.[262]

Draft opposition did not just occur among disgruntled farmers. When a more serious conscription act was passed in 1863, considerable draft dodging took place among the students of St. Francis Seminary. Some theological students coughed up the $300 exemption fee provided for in the law. However, many escaped to Canada. Twelve left in one night in 1863. When Congress passed another conscription act in May 1864, about half of the St. Francis student body moved to the Dominion.[263] Seminary disobedience to the draft laws even extended to providing safe harbors for fleeing students and a system of signals to alert potential inductees that officials were on the way.

If seminary students and rural Catholics disparaged Lincoln and the war, they were certainly not gainsaid by their religious leader. Scot convert Bernard I. Durward was sympathetic to the Confederate cause. Joseph Salzmann bitterly criticized the 16th president. "For the last four years," he wrote to the *Ludwig-Missionsverein* during the presidential campaign of 1864, Lincoln has been the worst kind of a misfortune, and unbelievable as it may be, and awful to say, this scamp has the best chance for re-election."[264] Two years before he had lamented, "The right of Habeas Corpus is suspended and newspaper editors are imprisoned. Corruption runs into hundreds of thousands; indeed to many, the war is continued only to enrich a few contractors."[265]

Still Catholics supported the war, focusing exclusively on the need to preserve the Union. Henni shared the misgivings of his German-speaking brethren, but nonetheless displayed the flag at St. John's Cathedral tower.[266] Even more importantly, Catholics fought in the Union armies that suffered heavy casualties on battlefields in the east. Of the 80,595 men Wisconsin gave to the Union army, 11,000 died of wounds or disease or were reported missing in action. Of those who returned, 15,000 suffered disabilities.[267] The remains of Catholic lads were sometimes brought home for burial. Henni presided at the funeral of Captain Moses O'Brien in the summer of 1862 and delivered a sermon that even the critical *Milwaukee Sentinel* described as "one of the most impressive and eloquent that we ever listened to." In his remarks, Henni voiced his support for the Union cause and urged people to come forward and enlist.[268] Many Catholic priests served as chaplains, and religious sisters worked in the charnel house, Civil War surgery tents and field hospitals. Fusseder said little of his Civil War service after his return. When the war ended, people were anxious to get on with life. St. Francis Seminary once again ran at full numbers and the political passions of the era subsided.

The pivotal first generation of Catholic life in Wisconsin was drawing to a close after the Civil War ended in 1865. In the Second Plenary Council of Baltimore, the assembled American bishops gathered to assess the direction of the Church after the bitter conflict. Glowing words promoting sectional healing and well-intentioned promises to establish a Catholic University and build more Catholic schools were made. In the final Mass and *Te Deum* at the end of the council, President Andrew Johnson sat dour-faced in the first pew of St. Mary's Cathedral in Baltimore. Under these more formal deliberations, bishops also conferred on the need to create new dioceses. In Wisconsin, the first of many divisions of the diocese of Milwaukee would be proposed and then sent on to Propaganda in Rome for approval. In 1868, Bishop Henni received word that a new era of Milwaukee Catholicism was about to begin.

Notes

1 Hubert Jedin, "Origin and Breakthrough of the Catholic Reform," pp. 431-498 and "Religious Forces and Intellectual Content of the Catholic Renewal," pp. 535-574, in Hubert Jedin (ed.) *History of the Church: Reformation and Counter Reformation* (*Handbuch des Kirchengeschichte* trans. Anselm Biggs and Peter W. Becker) vol. 5 (New York: Seabury Press, 1980). See also Owen Chadwick, *The Reformation* (Baltimore: Penguin Books, 1972), pp. 251-320 and Marvin R. O'Connell, *The Counter Reformation, 1559-1610* (New York: Harper and Row, 1974), pp. 83-172.

2 Hubert Jedin, "The Papacy and the Implementation of the Council of Trent (1565-1605)," in Jedin, *History of the Church.*

3 Kenneth Scott Latourette, *A History of the Expansion of Christianity: Three Centuries of Advance, A.D. 1500-A.D. 1800* vol. 3, (New York: Harper and Brothers, 1939), pp. 21-22.

4 Jedin, pp. 575-614.

5 Latourette, pp.33-35.

6 David J. Weber, *The Spanish Frontier in North America* (New Haven: Yale University Press, 1992), pp. 92-121.

7 A variety of historical books have been written on the strengths and failures of the Spanish mission system. One of the most critical is Robert H. Jackson and Edward Castillo, *Indians, Franciscans, and Spanish Colonization* (Albuquerque: University of New Mexico Press, 1995). Mission defenders include Maynard Geiger, *The Life and Times of Junipero Serra* 2 vols. (Washington D.C.: Academy of American Franciscan History, 1959); *Franciscan Missionaries in Hispanic California, 1769-1848* (San Marino: Huntington Library, 1969); and Francis Guest, O.F.M., "An Examination of the Thesis of S. F. Cook on the Forced Conversion of Indians in the California Missions," *Southern California Quarterly* 61 (1979): pp. 1-77.

8 Important works on French expansion include, H. P. Biggar (ed.) *The Works of Samuel de Champlain* 6 vols. (Toronto, 1922-1936); W. J. Eccles, *The Canadian Frontier, 1534-1760* (New York, 1969); George M. Wrong, *The Rise and Fall of New France* 2 vols. (New York, 1928); Francis Parkman, *Pioneers of France in the New World* (Boston, 1885).

9 Jedin, pp. 513-516.

10 Alice E. Smith, *History of Wisconsin: From Exploration to Statehood,* vol. 1 (Madison: State Historical Society of Wisconsin, 1973), pp. 10-11.

11 The best overview of the French presence in Wisconsin is still Louise P. Kellogg, *The French Regime in Wisconsin and the Northwest* (Madison, 1925). See also Louise P. Kellogg, "The Story of Wisconsin, 1634-1848, Chapter II: The Red Men and the Fur Trade," *Wisconsin Magazine of History* 2 (1918-1919): pp. 413-430; Rhoda R. Gilman, "The Fur Trade in the Upper Mississippi Valley, 1630-1850," *Wisconsin Magazine of History* 58 (August 1974): 2-18.

12 Louise P. Kellogg, "The First Missionary in Wisconsin," *Wisconsin Magazine of History* 4 (1920-1921): pp. 417-425; A.A.A. Schmirler, "Wisconsin's Lost Missionary: The Mystery of Father Rene Menard," *Wisconsin Magazine of History* 45 (Winter 1961-1962): pp. 99-114; Smith, *History of Wisconsin,* p. 26.

13 Hjalmar R. Holand, "Claude Allouez, The Indomitable Missionary," *Salesianum* 50 (April 1955): pp. 64-75.

14 Joseph P. Donnelly, S.J., *Jacques Marquette* (Chicago: Loyola University Press, 1985); Francis Borgia Steck, *Marquette Legends* (New York: Pageant Press, 1960); "French Colonial Attitudes and the Exploration of Jolliet and Marquette," *Wisconsin Magazine of History* 56 (Summer 1973): pp. 300-310.

15 For one introduction to the mission myth in California see Kevin Starr, *Americans and the California Dream, 1850-1915* (New York: Oxford University Press, 1973), pp. 395-401.

16 E. David Cronon, "Father Marquette Goes to Washington: The Marquette Statue Controversy," *Wisconsin Magazine of History* 56 (Summer 1973): pp. 266-283.

17 Quoted in M. Lucy Geegan, F.S.P.A., "The Louis Grignon Family: Catholic Pioneers of Wisconsin," (unpublished M. A. thesis, St. Louis University, 1943), p. 27.

18 Geegan, pp.39-41.

19 P. L. Scanlan, "Pioneer Priests at Prairie du Chien," *Wisconsin Magazine of History* 13 (December 1929):

pp. 97-106; and William V. Groessel, "The Early History of Prairie du Chien, 1750-1850," (unpublished M.A. thesis, St. Francis Seminary, 1925).

20 One fine example of this, albeit from the perspective of the "Old" Western history, is Thomas W. Spalding, "Frontier Catholicism," *Catholic Historical Review* 77 (1991): pp. 470-484. An earlier historian who grappled with this subject was Thomas T. McAvoy, C.S.C., "Americanism and Frontier Catholicism," *Review of Politics* 5 (1943): pp. 275-301.

21 Ray Allen Billington and Martin Ridge, *Westward Expansion: A History of the American Frontier* 5th ed. (New York: Macmillan, 1982), pp. 294-300.

22 Smith, pp. 162-198.

23 Ibid., pp. 182-188. See also Dale Roger Fatzinger, "Historical Geography of Lead and Zinc Mining in Southwest Wisconsin, 1839-1861," (unpublished Ph.D. diss., Michigan State University, 1971).

24 Janet M. Welsh, "Where the Spirit Dwells: Catholic and Protestant Women and the Development of Christianity in the Upper Mississippi River Valley Lead Region, 1830-1870," (unpublished Ph.D. dissertation, University of Notre Dame, 1995), pp. 106-149.

25 Anthony F.C. Wallace, "Prelude to Disaster: The Course of Indian-White Relations Which Led to the Blackhawk War of 1830," *Wisconsin Magazine of History* 65 (Summer 1982): 247-288.

26 Peter Guilday, *The Life and Times of John Carroll, Archbishop of Baltimore (1735-1815)* (New York, 1922); Annabelle M. Melville, *John Carroll of Baltimore: Founder of the American Catholic Hierarchy* (New York, 1955). The best synthesis of scholarship on Carroll and the origins of the first American diocese can be found in Thomas W. Spalding, *The Premier See: A History of the Archdiocese of Baltimore, 1789-1989* (Baltimore, 1989).

27 The significance of the founding of St. Mary's Seminary in Baltimore for subsequent Catholic seminary history is laid out by Joseph M. White, *The Diocesan Seminary in the United States: A History from the 1780s to the Present* (Notre Dame: University of Notre Dame Press, 1989), pp. 27-47.

28 Philip Gleason, "The Main Sheet Anchor: John Carroll and Catholic Higher Education," *Review of Politics* 38 (October 1976): pp. 576-613.

29 Martin J. Spalding, *Sketches of the Life, Times, and Character of the Rt. Rev. Benedict Joseph Flaget, First Bishop of Louisville* (Louisville: Webb and Levering, 1852. Reprint. New York: Arno Press, 1969).

30 A dated history of Cincinnati's Catholic roots is John H. Lamott, *History of the Archdiocese of Cincinnati* (Cincinnati: Frederick Pustet, 1921). The sections on Bishop Edward Fenwick are helpful, pp. 39-70.

31 Scanlan, "Pioneer Priests at Prairie du Chien,"pp. 97-99.

32 The full range of this 19th century Catholic revival is summarized in Roger Aubert and Rudolf Lill, "The Awakening of Catholic Vitality," in Hubert Jedin (ed.) *History of the Church: The Church Between the Revolution and Restoration* vol.7 (New York: Crossroad, 1981), pp. 206-260.

33 Johannes Beckmann, "The Resumption of Missionary Work," in Jedin, vol. 7, pp. 189-205.

34 B. J. Blied, "Two Tombstones Tell A Tale," *Salesianum* 50 (October 1955): pp. 161-169.

35 Roger Aubert, "The Beginnings of the Catholic Movement in Germany and Switzerland," in Jedin, *History of the Church* vol. 7, pp. 216-227. See also Jonathan Sperber, *Popular Catholicism in Nineteenth Century Germany* (Princeton: Princeton University Press, 1984).

36 Mark Wyman, *The Wisconsin Frontier* (Bloomington: Indiana University Press, 1998), pp. 202-204.

37 The power and impact of the Second Great Awakening in 19th century America is ably discussed in Whitney R. Cross, *The Burned-Over District: The Social and Intellectual History of Enthusiastic Religion in Western New York, 1800-1850* (Ithaca: Cornell University, 1950).

38 Loretta Petit, *Friar in the Wilderness: Edward Dominic Fenwick* (Chicago: Opus, 1994). A dated biography of Fenwick is Victor F. O'Daniel, O.P., *The Right Rev. Edward Dominic Fenwick, O.P.: Founder of the Dominicans in the United States* (New York: Frederick Pustet, 1920). See also, Reginald M. Coffey, O. P., *The American Dominicans: A History of Saint Joseph's Province* (New York: Saint Martin De Porres Guild, 1969), passim.

39 The most complete single source on Samuel Mazzuchelli is Mary Nona McGreal's "Samuel Mazzuchelli, O.P., Missionary to the United States:

A Documentary Account of His Life, Virtues and Reputation for Holiness," *Positio* submitted for the Canonization of the Servant of God, Charles Samuel Mazzuchelli, O.P., 1989. (Hereafter McGreal.) Copy in Op-Sin. Other works include, McGreal, "Samuel Mazzuchelli: Participant in Frontier Democracy," *Records of the American Catholic Historical Association* 87 (March-December 1976): pp. 99-114; Joseph T. McQuestion, "The Personality of Mazzuchelli The Builder," (unpublished M. A. thesis, St. Francis Seminary, n.d.). A more jaundiced view of the Dominican is recorded in Coffey, pp. 228-236. Sister Maria Michele Armato, O.P., and Sister Mary Jeremy Finnegan, O.P., (trans.), *The Memoirs of Father Samuel Mazzuchelli, O.P.* (Chicago: Priory, 1967) provides a well-translated account in Mazzuchelli's own words.

[40] William A. Hinnebusch, O.P., *The Dominicans: A Short History* (New York: Alba House, 1975), pp. 151-163.

[41] A dated biography of Baraga, who is a candidate for beatification, is Joseph Grigorich, *The Apostle to the Chippewas: The Life of the Most Rev. Frederick Baraga* (Chicago: Bishop Baraga Association, 1932).

[42] For Saenderl's career see John Lenhart, "Rev. Simon Saenderl, C.Ss.R., Indian Missionary," *Social Justice Review* 34 (1941): 130-132 ff.

[43] Michael E. Stevens, "Catholic and Protestant Missionaries Among the Wisconsin Indians: The Territorial Period," *Wisconsin Magazine of History* 58 (Winter 1974-1975): pp. 140-148.

[44] Van den Broek to Elizabeth Grignon, December 27, 1835, quoted in Joseph R. Jansen, "The Life of the Reverend Theodore J. Van den Broek," (unpublished M.A. thesis, St. Francis Seminary, 1937), pp. 13-14.

[45] Nicholas Langenfeld, "Catholic Indian Education In Early Wisconsin, 1671-1848," (unpublished M.A. thesis, St. Francis Seminary, 1925).

[46] McGreal, *Positio*, pp. 133-140.

[47] Joseph W. Jansen, "The Life of the Reverend Theodore J. Van den Broek, O.P.," (unpublished M.A. thesis, St. Francis Seminary, 1937).

[48] Coffey, p. 227.

[49] Quoted in Jansen, p. 17.

[50] A full biography of Bonduel is Malcolm Rosholt and John Britten Gehl, *Florimond J. Bonduel: Missionary to Wisconsin Territory* (Rosholt: Rosholt House, 1976). See also, S.G. Messmer, "The Reverend Florimond Joseph Bonduel, Wisconsin Pioneer Missionary," *Salesianum* 19 (April 1924): 1-16; (July 1924): 1-21; (October 1924): pp. 1-26.

[51] Raymond C. Miller, "Father Bonduel: Pioneer Missionary of Wisconsin," (unpublished M.A. thesis, St. Francis Seminary, 1931).

[52] Albert G. Ellis, Indian Subagent to William Medill, Commissioner of Indian Affairs, Green Bay, August 10, 1848, reprinted in "Documents," *Salesianum* 54 (July 1959): pp. 107-113.

[53] Gerard J. Esser, "Rev. Otto Skolla, Indian Missionary," (unpublished M.A. thesis, St. Francis Seminary, 1936).

[54] Otto Skolla to Henni, November 19, 1856, Henni Papers, Box 4, Folder 3, AAM.

[55] M. Paschala O'Connor, O.P., "Some Mazzuchellian 'Firsts'," *Salesianum* 49 (October 1954): pp. 161-169.

[56] Louis de Cailly, *Memoirs of Bishop Loras, First Bishop of Dubuque, Iowa and Member of His Family, 1792-1858* (New York: Christian Press, 1897); Thomas E. Auge, "This Savage Land," in Mary Kevin Gallagher, BVM, *Seed/Harvest: A History of the Archdiocese of Dubuque* (Dubuque: Archdiocese of Dubuque Press, 1987), pp. 1-24.

[57] Francis Mazzuchelli was ordained in 1847 by Bishop John Martin Henni. However, his priestly career was brief. By 1849, he left the diocese and returned to his native Northern Italy. Coffey suggests that he left the priesthood and even the Catholic faith. McGreal notes that young Francis simply disappears from the scene with some scandal, but after a period of time with Bishop Anthony Blanc in New Orleans, mends his ways and by 1859 is serving as a priest again in Milan. See Coffey, p. 234, fn. 34. McGreal, *Positio*, pp. 264-265.

[58] *Memoirs of Father Samuel Mazzuchelli, O.P.*, p. 327.

[59] Benjamin J. Blied, "Precursors of Bishop Henni," *Salesianum* 43 (October 1948): pp. 148-155.

[60] Milwaukee's years under Detroit's jurisdiction are covered only briefly in two sources. George Pare, *The Catholic Church in Detroit, 1701-1888* (Detroit: Gabriel Richard Press, 1951), pp. 418-419. Leslie Woodcock Tentler, *Seasons of Grace: A His-*

tory of the Archdiocese of Detroit (Detroit: Wayne State University Press, 1990), pp. 16-17.

[61] For the origins of Milwaukee see Bayrd Still, *Milwaukee: The History of a City* (Madison: State Historical Society of Wisconsin, 1948), pp. 3-51 and John Gurda, *The Making of Milwaukee* (Milwaukee: Milwaukee County Historical Society, 1999), pp. 23-58.

[62] Gurda, pp. 43-57.

[63] For a good overview of the religious diversity of early Milwaukee see Annabel Douglas McArthur, "Religion in Early Milwaukee," (Milwaukee: Religious Committee of the Milwaukee Centennial Celebration, 1946).

[64] Peter Leo Johnson, "Milwaukee's First Mass," in Johnson, *Centennial Essays for the Milwaukee Archdiocese, 1843-1943* (Milwaukee: Archdiocese of Milwaukee, 1943), pp. 13-18.

[65] Peter Leo Johnson, "First Catholic Church in Milwaukee: St. Peter's 1839," *Salesianum* 33 (July 1938): pp. 123-131; Peter Leo Johnson, "Reverend Patrick O'Kelley, First Resident Catholic Pastor of Milwaukee," *Salesianum* 45 (July 1950): pp. 108-113; Peter Leo Johnson, "Unofficial Beginnings of the Milwaukee Catholic Diocese," *Wisconsin Magazine of History* 23 (September 1939): pp. 1-16.

[66] Juanita Hartung and Betty Maier (eds.), *St. Matthew's Church, 1841-1991* (St. Matthew, Oak Creek, 1991), parish history file, Archives of the Archdiocese of Milwaukee (hereafter AAM). Monsignor George Radant discovered that the parish corporation had no actual title to the St. Matthew property donated by the Oherrn's and that it remained in the hands of the bishops of Detroit "and their successors." With much difficulty Radant had the title cleared in December 1955. "Oak Creek Parish Title, Over 100 Years in Detroit Name," *Catholic Herald Citizen*, 24 December 1955.

[67] Pare, p. 395.

[68] Peter Leo Johnson, *Stuffed Saddlebags: The Life of Martin Kundig, Priest, 1805-1879* (Milwaukee: Bruce Publishing Co., 1942).

[69] Marguerite Schuler, S.C., "Mission Life of Father Martin Kundig," (unpublished M.A. thesis, University of Notre Dame, 1940), pp. 69-104. Johnson, *Stuffed Saddlebags,* pp. 73-162.

[70] Johnson, *Stuffed Saddlebags*, pp. 159-162.

[71] Johnson, *Stuffed Saddlebags*, p. 175.

[72] Quoted in Sebastian Messmer, "Chips for a Kundig Block," *Salesianum* 14 (January 1919): pp. 1-33.

[73] Ibid.

[74] "Old St. Peter's Church," *Catholic Citizen*, 21 May 1892.

[75] "You're Invited to Cornerstone Laying at First Cathedral," *Catholic Herald Citizen*, 26 August 1939; "Academy of Church History Erected," *Catholic Herald Citizen*, 2 September 1939.

[76] Ibid.

[77] Peter Leo Johnson, *The Daughters of Charity in Milwaukee, 1846-1946* (Milwaukee: Daughters of Charity, 1946), pp. 13-26.

[78] Johnson, *Crosier on the Frontier,* pp. 66-68.

[79] Quoted in Leonard G. Koerber, "Anti-Catholic Agitation in Milwaukee, 1843-1860," (unpublished M.A. thesis, Marquette University, 1960), p. 13.

[80] Peter Leo Johnson, *Crosier on the Frontier: A Life of John Martin Henni* (Madison: State Historical Society of Wisconsin, 1958) is the best single source for the prelate's life. See also Martin Marty, *Dr. Johann Martin Henni* (New York, 1888).

[81] Johnson, *Crosier on the Frontier*, p. 10.

[82] Derek Holmes, *The Triumph of the Holy See: A Short History of the Papacy in the Nineteenth Century* (London: Burns and Oates, 1978), pp. 59-100 and passim.

[83] Kenneth Scott Latourette, *The Great Century in Europe and the United States of America, A.D. 1800-A.D. 1914,* (New York: Harper and Brothers, 1941), pp. 22-33, 47-64.

[84] Johnson, *Crosier on the Frontier*, pp. 34-37.

[85] A solid account of German religious life in Cincinnati is Joseph M. White, "Religion and Community: Cincinnati's Germans, 1814-1870," (unpublished Ph.D. dissertation, University of Notre Dame, 1980).

[86] "Documents-Letters of Bishop Henni," *Salesianum* 24 (July 1929): pp. 30-33.

[87] Robert C. Nesbit, *The History of Wisconsin, Urbanization and Industrialization, 1873-1893* vol. III (Madison: State Historical Society of Wisconsin, 1985), p. 288. See also Johnson, *Crosier on the Frontier,* pp. 77-82 and Kathleen N. Conzen, *Immigrant Milwaukee, 1836-1869: Accommodation*

and Community in a Frontier City (Cambridge, 1976), p. 29.

[88] Theodore Roemer, *Ten Decades of Alms* (St. Louis: B. Herder Book Co., 1942), pp. 15-31.

[89] The most comprehensive work on the origins and activities of the Austrian society is Benjamin Blied's, *Austrian Aid to American Catholics, 1830-1860* (Milwaukee, 1944). Roemer, *Ten Decades*, pp. 32-46.

[90] The comprehensive history of the origins of the Bavarian organization is Theodore Roemer, *The Ludwig-Missionsverein and the Church in the United States (1838-1918)* (Washington, D.C., 1933), pp. 1-28. See also Roemer, *Ten Decades*, pp. 47-61. Roemer makes no mention of the fact that Ludwig was publicly involved with an American courtesan named Lola Montez and sought to procure Bavarian citizenship for her. Ludwig was toppled in the revolutions of 1848. His son Ludwig II (Ludwig the Mad) came to power in 1868.

[91] "Cathedral Shared Gifts of $86,000," *Catholic Herald Citizen*, 13 March 1942.

[92] Henni's work in Cincinnati is covered in White, "Religion and Community," pp. 162-170.

[93] Johnson, *Crosier on the Frontier*, p. 51.

[94] Joseph Salzbacher, *Meine Reise nach Nord-Amerika im Jahre 1842* (Vienna, 1845), pp. 184-185.

[95] Johnson, *Crosier on the Frontier*, pp. 56-57.

[96] Quoted in Johnson, *Crosier on the Frontier*, p. 56.

[97] M. Mileta Ludwig, F.S.P.A., *Right Hand Glove Uplifted: A Biography of Archbishop Michael Heiss* (New York: Pageant Press, 1968), pp. 103-142.

[98] Henni to Lefevre, May 13, 1844, in "Documents," *Salesianum* 43 (April 1948): pp. 63-65.

[99] Ibid.

[100] Ibid.

[101] Henni to Editor of *Wahrheitsfreund*, January 7, 1845, in "Letter of Bishop Henni," *Salesianum* 23 (April 1928): pp. 30-43.

[102] Ibid., and Johnson, *Crosier on the Frontier*, p. 71.

[103] Johnson, *Crosier on the Frontier*, p. 72.

[104] Ibid.

[105] Ibid.

[106] "Letter of Bishop Henni, 1844," *Salesianum* 23 (July 1928): pp. 15-25.

[107] Ibid.

[108] Quoted in Michael P. Carroll, *Irish Pilgrimage: Holy Well and Popular Catholic Devotion* (Baltimore: Johns Hopkins University Press, 1999), p.12.

[109] M. Justille McDonald, *History of the Irish in Wisconsin* (Washington D.C.: The Catholic University of America, 1954), pp. 194-254 and passim.

[110] Smith, p. 489.

[111] "Wisconsin," in Michael Glazier (ed.) *Encyclopedia of the Irish in America* (Notre Dame: University of Notre Dame Press, 1999), pp. 958-962.

[112] McDonald, p. 46.

[113] Obituary Notes, *Catholic Citizen*, 27 June 1908.

[114] Carroll, passim.

[115] Emmet Larkin, "The Devotional Revolution in Ireland, 1850-1875," in Larkin, *The Historical Dimensions of Irish Catholicism* (Washington, D.C., The Catholic University of America Press, 1984), pp. 57-89.

[116] Bernard Michaels, *A Bit of the Old Sod, The Account of the Byron-Lima Settlement* (Bernard Michaels, 1999), p. 29.

[117] Humphrey J. Desmond, "Early Irish Settlers of Milwaukee," *Wisconsin Magazine of History* 13 (June 1930): pp. 365-374 and Robert G. Carroon, "John Gregory and the Irish Immigration to Milwaukee," *Historical Messenger* 27 (June 1971): pp. 51-64.

[118] Quoted in David J. O'Hearn, *Fifty Years at Saint John's Cathedral: Being a History of the Parish, Its Clergy, Schools and Societies with Illustrations* (Milwaukee, 1897), p. 34, parish history file, AAM. Johnson, *Daughters of Charity*, pp. 16-26.

[119] Peter Leo Johnson, "The American Odyssey of the Irish Brigidines," *Salesianum* 39 (April 1944): pp. 61-67.

[120] M. Paschala O'Connor, *Five Decades: History of the Congregation of the Most Holy Rosary, Sinsinawa, Wisconsin, 1849-1899* (Sinsinawa Mound: Sinsinawa Press, 1954); M. Eva McCarty, *The Sinsinawa Dominicans: Outline of Twentieth Century Development, 1901-1949* (Sinsinawa: St. Clara Convent, 1952).

[121] Coffey, pp. 230-234.

[122] O'Connor, pp. 35-36.

[123] Coffey, pp. 235-236.

[124] Although hagiographic in tone, Mary Synon's, *Mother Emily of Sinsinawa: American Pioneer* (Mil-

waukee: Bruce Publishing, 1954) is a solid overview of the life and times of Power who could in fact be called a foundress of the Sinsinawa Dominicans.

[125] Jerome Oetgen, *An American Abbot: Boniface Wimmer, O.S.B.* (Latrobe: The Archabbey Press, 1976), pp. 88-89.

[126] Jerome Oetgen, *Mission to America: A History of Saint Vincent Archabbey, The First Benedictine Monastery in the United States* (Washington, D.C., The Catholic University of America Press, 2000), p.109.

[127] Raphael Hamilton, S. J., *The Story of Marquette University* (Milwaukee: Marquette University Press, 1953), pp. 1-16.

[128] Gilbert J. Garraghan, S.J., *The Jesuits of the Middle United States* Vol. III (reprint Chicago: Loyola University Press, 1984), pp. 353-354.

[129] Garraghan, p. 356.

[130] Garraghan, pp. 379-388.

[131] There is no biography of Lalumiere. Sketches of his life are found in clippings in the Marquette University Archives. See, "An Honored Priest," (1895 clipping) and "Plans Abandoned in 1850 Led to Establishing Marquette Academy," (clipping *Milwaukee Journal*, 7 December 1925), "Lalumiere, Stanislaus P., S.J., Biographical Data," UNIV, D-2, Series 1, Box 1, Marquette University Archives.

[132] Charles M. Scanlan, "Little Sisters of the Poor: Milwaukee," *Salesianum* 32 (July 1937): pp. 107-111.

[133] "Is Mourned by Many," *Catholic Citizen*, 30 March 1895.

[134] Garraghan, Vol. III, p. 383.

[135] Richard N. Current, *The History of Wisconsin: The Civil War Era, 1848-1873* (Madison: State Historical Society, 1976), p. 551.

[136] A compendium of St. Patrick's day celebrations in the various cities of the Archdiocese of Milwaukee can be found in "St. Patrick's Day," *Catholic Citizen*, 24 March 1888.

[137] John F. Quinn, "Father Matthew's Disciples: American Catholic Support for Temperance, 1840-1920," *Church History* 65 (December 1996): pp. 624-640.

[138] Ronald J. Rindo, "Bernard I. Durward: Poet and Painter of Frontier Milwaukee," *Milwaukee History* 10 (1987): pp. 129-139.

[139] S. G. Messmer, "Chips for a Kundig Block," *Salesianum* 13 (January 1918): pp. 1-26; (April 1918): pp. 1-17; (July 1918): pp. 1-27; vol. 14 (October 1918): pp. 1-16; (January 1919): pp. 1-11; (April 1919): pp. 1-22; (July 1919): pp. 1-28; (October 1919): pp. 1-28.

[140] J. J. Barry, "The Durward Letters," *Salesianum* 28 (October 1933): 27-31; "The Durward Letters II," *Salesianum* 28 (January 1934): pp. 11-16.

[141] Edward P. Alexander, "Wisconsin, New York's Daughter State," *Wisconsin Magazine of History* 30 (September 1946): pp. 11-30.

[142] "Parish Has No Mixed Marriages in 92 Years—Policy of 'Insulation not Isolation' Follows at St. Nicholas Church Since Year 1849 Gets Outstanding Results," clipping from *Register* Archives of the School Sisters of St. Francis, 2011, Box 6, F23.

[143] Current, pp. 43-45.

[144] Current, p. 78.

[145] Current, pp. 419-422.

[146] Theodore Mueller, "Milwaukee's German Heritage," *Historical Messenger 62* (September 1966): pp. 112-119.

[147] Current, p. 77.

[148] James M. Berquist, "German Communities in American Cities: An Interpretation of the Nineteenth Century Experience," *Journal of American Ethnic History* 4 (Fall 1984): pp. 9-30.

[149] M. M. Gerend, "Dr. Salzmann in His Youth," *Salesianum* 31 (July 1936): pp. 113-115.

[150] Joseph Rainer, *A Noble Priest: Joseph Salzmann, D.D., Founder of the Salesianum* (trans. Joseph Berg), (Milwaukee: Olinger and Schwartz 1903), p. 43.

[151] William Geo. Bruce, K.S.G., *The Story of Holy Trinity Parish, 1850-1950* (Milwaukee: Holy Trinity Centennial Committee, 1950), parish history file, AAM.

[152] Chronicles of the School Sisters of Notre Dame, vol. 1833-1876, Archives of the Schools Sisters of Notre Dame (hereafter ASND).

[153] Ibid.

[154] Salzmann to Wisbauer, October 31, 1858, reprinted in "Correspondence of Archbishop John Martin Henni, et al.," (Milwaukee: SSND Heritage Resource Publications, 1986), pp. 260-261, #38.

[155] Herbert J. Wagner, "The Reverend Michael Wisbauer," (unpublished M.A. thesis, St. Francis Seminary, 1933).
[156] Richard R. Dolezal and Thomas G. Fait, *Saint Mary's Community of Faith,* parish history file, AAM.
[157] Chronicle of St. Mary Church, Burlington, Wisconsin, ASND.
[158] Martin Pitzer to Joseph Mueller, June 4, 1848, trans. Henry Hargarten.
[159] "Diamond Jubilee of St. Mary's Parish, Burlington," parish history file, AAM.
[160] For additional information about Milwaukee based German mutual aid societies see Grummer, pp. 79-84.
[161] James Grummer, "The Parish Life of German-Speaking Roman Catholics in Milwaukee, Wisconsin, 1840-1920," (unpublished Ph.D. dissertation, University of Notre Dame, 1989), pp. 98-100.
[162] Jay P. Dolan, *Catholic Revivalism: The American Experience, 1830-1900* (Notre Dame: University of Notre Dame Press, 1978) is the best discussion of the methods and impact of the Catholic Mission.
[163] Gilbert J. Garraghan, S. J., *The Jesuits of the Middle United States* Vol. II (reprint Chicago: Loyola University Press, 1984), pp. 54.
[164] Garraghan, Vol. II, pp. 60-61.
[165] Quoted in Carl J. Wagner, "Mission and Methods of F.X. Weininger, S. J.," (unpublished M. A. thesis, St. Francis Seminary, 1936), p. 2.
[166] Steven M. Avella, "The People of Kenosha Were Rejoiced: Catholic Education in Kenosha, 1858-1868), in Nicholas C. Burkel (ed.) *Kenosha: Historical Sketches* (Kenosha: Kenosha County History Committee, 1986), pp. 68-69.
[167] Cited in Grummer, p. 120.
[168] Frederick X. Katzer to Emily Powers, December 16, 1895, GA-11, Box 6, 12b, (Milwaukee, 1880-1890), Archives of the Dominican Sisters of Sinsinawa (hereafter AOP-Sin).
[169] Grummer, pp. 128-129.
[170] M. Eunice Hanousek, *A New Assisi: The First Hundred Years of the Sisters of St. Francis of Assisi,* (Milwaukee: Bruce Publishing Co., 1949), pp. 1-54.
[171] Blied, "Two Tombstones," p. 166.
[172] The story of the split is told in M. Mileta Ludwig, *A Chapter of Franciscan History: The Sisters of the Third Order of St. Francis of Perpetual Adoration, 1849-1949* (New York: Bookman, 1949), pp. 156-191.
[173] *Mother Caroline and the School Sisters of Notre Dame* 2 vols. (St. Louis: Woodward and Tiernan, 1928).
[174] A summary of the origins and development of the School Sisters of Notre Dame in America can be found in a letter from Sister Caroline Friess to Joseph Ferdinand Mueller, secretary of the *Ludwig-Missionsverein,* June 18, 1850, in Barbara Brumleve (ed.), *The Letters of Mother Caroline Friess, School Sisters of Notre Dame* (Winona: School Sisters of Notre Dame, 1991), pp. 23-48.
[175] *Mother Caroline,* V. 1, p. 50.
[176] Ibid., pp. 80-81.
[177] Ibid., pp. 81-89.
[178] Ibid., p. 80.
[179] Ibid., pp. 80-81.
[180] Ibid., pp. 89-90.
[181] M. Hortense Kohler, *Rooted in Hope: The Story of the Dominican Sisters of Racine, Wisconsin* (Milwaukee: Bruce Publishing, 1962) and *Life and Work of Mother Benedicta Bauer* (Milwaukee: Bruce Publishing Co., 1937).
[182] Florence Deacon, "Handmaids or Autonomous Women: The Charitable Activities, Institution Building and Communal Relationships of Catholic Sisters in the Nineteenth Century Wisconsin," (unpublished Ph.D. dissertation, University of Wisconsin, Madison, 1989).
[183] Imogene Palen, *Fieldstones '76: The Story of the Founders of the Sisters of Saint Agnes* (Oshkosh Printers, 1976).
[184] M. Vera Naber, C.S.A., *With All Devotedness: Chronicles of the Sisters of Saint Agnes,* (New York: P. J. Kennedy, 1959), p. 11.
[185] Benjamin F. Blied, *A History of St. John the Baptist Congregation, Johnsburg, Wis* 2nd ed. (Johnsburg, St. John the Baptist Parish, 1980), parish history file, AAM.
[186] "Record of the First Beginning in Barton until the First General Chapter in Fond du Lac," Archives of the Sisters of St. Agnes, Fond du Lac, Wisconsin (hereafter ACSA).

[187] Quoted in Celestine Bittle, *A Romance of Lady Poverty: The History of the Province of St. Joseph of the Capuchin Order in the United States* (Milwaukee: Bruce Publishing, 1933), p. 203.

[188] The story of the Capuchins and Agnesians is discussed at length in Bittle, pp. 200-216.

[189] "Record of First Beginnings," ACSA.

[190] Bittle, pp. 5-8.

[191] Bittle, p. 25.

[192] "A Noted Capuchin Passes Away," *Catholic Citizen*, 29 June 1895.

[193] Bittle, pp. 290, 296, 408.

[194] Quoted in James Fleischmann, O.F.M., Cap., *St. Francis Church, 1871-1946, The History of the Parish Compiled for the Occasion of Its Diamond Jubilee,* (Milwaukee: St. Francis Parish, 1946), pp. 2-3.

[195] Bonaventure Frey to Treasurer of the *Ludwig-Missionsverein*. September 17, 1865 in Theodore Roemer (trans. and ed.) "Pioneer Capuchin Letters," *Franciscan Studies* 16 (January 1936): pp. 24-26.

[196] The elaborate stained glass windows were designed and executed by the Mittermaier Studios of Brooklyn. Within the walls were adorned with oil paintings by William Lamprecht and frescoes executed by a New York artist named Muer. The altars were also works of art. The high altar and five side altars designed and built by Milwaukee architect Erhard Brielmaier. On its dedication day, the visual richness of the interior was complimented by the lush "Caecilian" music of Milwaukee's own Catholic composer and organist, Johann Singenberger who premiered his "Litaniae Laurentanae" at the dedication. Fleischmann, pp. 29-31.

[197] Cornelius James Kirkfleet, O. Praem, *The White Canons of St. Norbert: A History of the Praemonstratensian Order in the British Isles and America* (De Pere: St. Norbert Abbey, 1943), pp. 206-220; "Letters of the Reverend Adalbert Inama, O. Praem.," *Wisconsin Magazine of History* 11 & 12 (1927-1928). For a solid treatment of Norbertine activities in America see Heinrich K. Halder, O. Praem., *Die Wiltener Mission in den USA im 19 Jahrhundert* (Diplomarbeit zur Erlangung des akademischen Grades eines Magisters der Theologie an der Theologischen Fakultat der Leopold-Franzens-Universitate Innsbruck, Mai, 1996).

[198] Joseph P. Springob, "The Reverend Maximilian Gaertner, O. Praem., Missionary," (unpublished M. A. thesis, St. Francis Seminary, 1934).

[199] Blied, *Austrian Aid*, pp. 174-177.

[200] "First Mass Offered in East Bristol Area 100 Years Ago," *Catholic Herald Citizen*, 25 January 1947.

[201] Quoted in Jansen, p. 16.

[202] "He Helped His Father Build Saint John's" undated clipping, Milwaukee County Historical Society.

[203] Alexander Carl Guth, "Early Day Architects in Milwaukee," *Wisconsin Magazine of History* 10 (1926-1927): 18-23; "Early Day Architects in Wisconsin," ibid. 18 (1934-1935): pp. 141-144; B. J. Blied, "The Seminary Architect," *Salesianum* 41 (July 1946): pp. 150-154.

[204] Johnson, *Crosier on the Frontier*, pp. 159-160.

[205] "He Helped His Father," 9 see note 202 above.

[206] Johnson, *Crosier on the Frontier*, p. 75.

[207] Johnson, *Crosier on the Frontier*, p. 76.

[208] Ibid.

[209] Roemer, *Ten Decades*, pp. 120-121, 104-105.

[210] Johnson, *Crosier on the Frontier*, p. 92.

[211] David J. O'Hearn, *Fifty Years at St. John's Cathedral, Being a History of the Parish, its Clergy, Schools and Societies with Illustrations,* (Milwaukee: St. John's Cathedral, 1897), pp. 35-36, parish history file, AAM.

[212] "A Former Milwaukee Priest," *Catholic Citizen*, 16 May 1891.

[213] Kathleen Neils Conzen, "Forum: The Place of Religion in Urban and Community Studies," *Religion and American Culture* 6 (Summer 1996): pp. 108-114.

[214] Peter Leo Johnson, *Halcyon Days, The Story of St. Francis Seminary, 1856-1956* (Milwaukee: Bruce Publishing Co., 1956), p. 46.

[215] Roemer, *Ludwig-Missionsverein*, pp. 48-49.

[216] Johnson, *Halcyon Days,* pp. 54-55.

[217] Johnson, *Halcyon Days*, p. 44.

[218] Heiss characterized the trio in a letter to his friend Kilian Kleiner reprinted in *Salesianum* 10 (April 1915): pp. 18-19.

[219] Johnson, *Halcyon Days*, p. 61.

[220] Roemer, *Ludwig-Missionsverein*, pp. 48-49.

[221] Rainer, pp. 94-95.
[222] *Milwaukee Sentinel*, 27 June 1874.
[223] Quoted in Johnson, *Halcyon Days*, p. 68.
[224] Robert Massey, "St. Francis Seminary, 1855-1981: One Hundred and Twenty-Five Years of Continuity and Change," (St. Francis: Salesianum Alumni Association, 1981), pp. 18-28.
[225] Johnson, *Halcyon Days*, 85, 125.
[226] The use of the term "asylum" reflects the Catholic use of a common program of social provision used throughout 19th century America. See David J. Rothman, *The Discovery of the Asylum: Social Order and Disorder in the New Republic* (Boston: Little, Brown, 1971).
[227] Johnson, *Daughters of Charity*, pp. 137-192; George L. Huber, "St. Rose's Orphanage of Milwaukee, 1848-1900" (unpublished B.A. thesis, St. Francis Seminary, 1948).
[228] Johnson, *Daughters of Charity*, p. 154.
[229] Anthony William Fischer, "History of St. Aemillian's Orphan Asylum, 1849-1928." (Unpublished M. A. thesis, St. Francis Seminary, 1928).
[230] Johnson relates these funding schemes in *Daughters of Charity*, p. 184.
[231] William George Bruce, K.S.C., *St. Mary's Church Milwaukee: History of a Pioneer Copy* (Diamond Jubilee Publication, October 1921), *The Story of Holy Trinity Parish, 1850-1950* (Holy Trinity Centennial Committee, 1950), parish history file, AAM. "St. Joseph's Pioneer Milwaukee Parish, Nears Centennial Day," *Catholic Herald Citizen*, 22 October 1955.
[232] "Rededication of St. Raphael Cathedral," Memorial Pamphlet, date unknown, St. Raphael parish Madison. See also, Leo Belda, "History of the Catholic Church in Dane County, 1842-1941," (unpublished M.A. thesis, St. Francis Seminary, 1941).
[233] Bernard Michaels, *A Bit of the Old Sod: The Account of the Byron-Lima Settlement* (Privately published, 1999).
[234] "Introductory Note to the History of St. Nazianz," *Wisconsin Magazine of History* 31 (September 1947): pp. 84-91. See also Jerome Schommer, *The Moment of Grace: One Hundred Years of Salvatorian Life and Ministry in the United States* vol. 1 (1892-1947) (Milwaukee: Society of the Divine Savior, 1994), pp. 62-65.
[235] Schommer, p. 64.
[236] Timothy Walch, "Catholic Social Institutions and Urban Developments: The View from Nineteenth Century Chicago and Milwaukee," *Catholic Historical Review* 64 (1978): 16-32.
[237] Judith Walzer Leavitt, *The Healthiest City: Milwaukee and the Politics of Health Reform* (Madison: University of Wisconsin Press, 1996).
[238] Johnson, *Daughters of Charity*, pp. 38-39.
[239] Ibid., pp. 46-52.
[240] Johnson, *Halcyon Days,* p. 27. This building had previously served as a seminary.
[241] Ibid., pp. 78-97.
[242] Ray Allen Billington, *The Protestant Crusade, 1800-1860: A Study of the Origins of American Nativism* (New York: Macmillan, 1938).
[243] James Hennesey, *American Catholics: A History of the Roman Catholic Community in the United States* (New York: Oxford University Press, 1981), pp. 117-127.
[244] Leonard G. Koerber, "Anti-Catholic Agitation in Milwaukee, 1843-1860," (unpublished M.A. thesis, Marquette University, 1960).
[245] M. Hedwigis Overmoehle, "The Anti-Clerical Activities of the Forty-Eighters in Wisconsin, 1848-1860, A Study in German-American Liberalism," (unpublished Ph.D. dissertation, St. Louis University, 1941).
[246] Emmet H. Rothan, "The German Catholic Immigrant in the United States, 1830-1860," (unpublished Ph.D. dissertation, Catholic University of America, 1946), p. 63.
[247] Quoted in John Murphy, "Catholic and Protestant Conflict in Milwaukee During the 1840s: The Miter-Henni Debate in Historical Perspective," (unpublished paper, 2001 in possession of author), p. 4.
[248] John Martin Henni [Philalethos] "Facts Against Assertions: Or a Vindication of Catholic Principles Against Misrepresentations, Calumnies and Falsehoods, Embodied in the 'Thanksgiving Sermon.' Delivered by J. J. Miter in the Congregational Church of Milwaukee, December 12, 1844," (Milwaukee, 1845), p. 9.
[249] Ibid.

[250] Johnson, *Crosier on the Frontier*, p. 130.
[251] Motherhouse Chronicle, May 1, 1873, ASND.
[252] Joseph Schaefer, "Know Nothingism in Wisconsin," *Wisconsin Magazine of History* 8 (1924-1925): pp. 1-21.
[253] Johnson, *Crosier on the Frontier*, p. 166.
[254] Quoted in Koerber, p. 69.
[255] Chronicle of the Mother House of the School Sisters of Notre Dame, vol. 1, p. 41, ASND.
[256] Thomas T. Brundage, "The Development of Catholic Journalism in the Milwaukee Archdiocese," (unpublished paper, St. Francis Seminary, 1985).
[257] For Catholic views on the slavery issue see Hennesey, pp. 145-157. Wisconsin Catholics expressed their disdain for the Republican party in the 1857 elections by refusing to vote for former Forty-eighter Carl Schurz for lieutenant governor. Richard N. Current, *The History of Wisconsin: The Civil War Era, 1848-1873* vol. 2 (Madison: State Historical Society of Wisconsin, 1976), p. 266.
[258] Current, pp. 276-281.
[259] Ibid. p. 287.
[260] Quoted in Current, p. 297.
[261] Peter Leo Johnson, "Port Washington Draft Riot of 1862," *Mid-America* 1 (January 1930): pp. 219-222.
[262] Lawrence H. Larsen, "Draft Riot in Wisconsin, 1862," *Civil War History* 7 (1961): pp. 421-427; Current, p. 316.
[263] Massey, p. 25.
[264] Salzmann to *Ludwig-Missionsverein*, October 3, 1864, in Brumleve, #45, pp. 269-270.
[265] Salzmann to Msgr. Paul Kagerer September 23, 1862, in Brumeleve, #42, pp. 266-267.
[266] Johnson, *Crosier on the Frontier*, pp. 154-155.
[267] Current, p. 355.
[268] Quoted in Frank Brickl, "Catholic War Attitudes in the Milwaukee Sentinel for 1863," (unpublished M.A. thesis, St. Francis Seminary, n.d.), p. 15.

Part II
How Firm a Foundation
1868–1903

The first epoch of the Wisconsin Church story ended in 1868 when Bishop Henni's 25 years of work in the state brought about the separation of the dioceses. Days of arduous travel, fund-raising, and efforts to recruit new priests and religious for the diocese had born fruit. Henni had also created a German bastion in the upper Midwest, visibly present in a strong seminary, a network of German parishes and organizations, and in the membership of the clergy and the religious orders. Henni's was a strong voice in behalf of the pastoral needs of Germans nationwide, and he used the opportunities such as those presented at occasional provincial councils in St. Louis to emphasize the importance of taking care of the Teutonic populace of the Midwest.

By the mid-1860s the Catholic population of Wisconsin had soared to 300,000 or roughly one-third of the state's population. The largest growth continued in the lakeshore counties, but cities along the Rock River Valley from Madison to Beloit also grew. Likewise a more visible and prosperous Catholic presence flourished in Green Bay and La Crosse. Even as early as 1859, plans for a new diocese were circulating, with Milwaukee as the metropolitan see. Bishop Henni had already labored in the diocese for 15 years and was growing weary of the long travel and the increasing complexity of the problems and challenges that crossed his desk. Rumors abounded for a time that Henni was to be sent back to his Swiss homeland to become the Archbishop of Chur.[1] However, this prospect never materialized and the question of subdividing the large Wisconsin diocese was discussed at the Second Plenary Council of Baltimore, which met in May 1866. Council fathers petitioned Propaganda to reorder Wisconsin's ecclesiastical boundaries, creating a metropolitan See at Milwaukee, with suffragan dioceses at Green Bay and La Crosse. In reply, Rome readily carved two new dioceses for Green Bay and La Crosse, but deferring to the aged and often testy Archbishop Peter Richard Kenrick of St. Louis, Milwaukee was denied metropolitan status. Milwaukee would not become an archdiocese until 1875.

The new dioceses were created using the boundary lines of the rivers and not the counties. They were reordered in this fashion in 1905 when a further diocesan boundary adjustment was made. To the north of the Fox River emerged a new see with headquarters at Green Bay. Spurred not only by lakeshore development, but also by the stirrings of the lumber industry that would eventually create enormous wealth, the counties of Brown, Calumet, Door, Florence, Forest, Kewaunee, Langlade, Marinette, Menominee, Oconto, Outagamie, Shawano, Waupaca, Waushara, and Winnebago as well as the northern half of Manitowoc County were detached on March 3, 1868. This effectively transferred to the administration of first Bishop Joseph Melcher more than sixty parishes and mission stations that had been formed between 1833 and 1867.[2]

A second diocese, headquartered on the banks of the Mississippi at the city of La Crosse was established with Michael Heiss as its first bishop. This new diocese took away the counties of Crawford, Richland, Vernon, La Crosse, Monroe, Jackson, Trempeleau, Buffalo, Pepin, Eau Claire, Clark, Chippewa, Taylor, Price, Juneau, Sauk, Iron, Ashland, Bayfield, Douglas, Burnett, Washburn, Sawyer, Polk, Barron, Rusk, St. Croix, and Pierce. It also included portions of Vilas, Oneida, Lincoln, Marathon, Wood, and Portage.[3]

After the 1868 partition, the Diocese of Milwaukee was left with only 21 counties: Kenosha, Racine, Walworth, Rock, Green, LaFayette, Grant, Iowa, Dane, Jefferson, Waukesha, Milwaukee, Ozaukee, Washington, Dodge, Columbia, Marquette, Adams, Green Lake, Fond du Lac, and Sheboygan. Although sheared of land, it contained the heaviest concentration of Catholics in Wisconsin. Indeed, in the latter part of the 19th century, the Catholic Church became the single largest religious denomination in Wisconsin. This growth reflected the rapid maturation of the Church within a generation of its pioneer beginnings. Literally thousands of new communicants flocked to the increasing numbers of churches and schools that dotted the urban and rural landscapes of the state. Scores of new priests and religious, many of them born and reared in Wisconsin, staffed the new facilities.

Since the end of the Second Plenary Council it had been rumored that Milwaukee was about to be made a metropolitan see and Henni its archbishop. The occasion of the divisions came and went in 1868 and no such status was granted. Likewise, all of Wisconsin celebrated Henni's 25th anniversary of episcopal consecration in March 1869. Henni's close friend, Dr. James Johnson led the festivities with a florid tribute to the aging prelate, whom he compared to St. Joseph. Yet on that occasion, the long-sought archiepiscopal pallium was still denied. Historian Peter Leo Johnson speculates that the delay

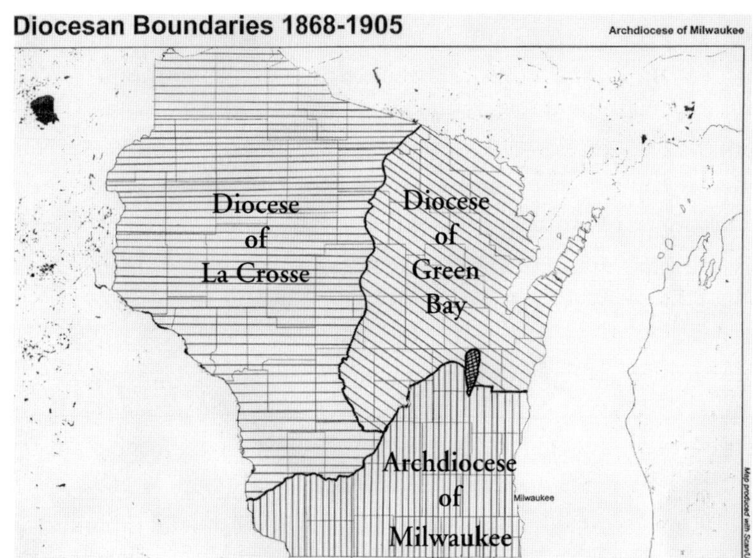

in granting metropolitan status to Milwaukee was tied to a delicate matter in Chicago. By 1866, Chicago had over a quarter of a million Catholics and certainly merited elevation to the rank of archdiocese. Unfortunately, the bishop of Chicago, James Duggan, was in the early stages of a tragic mental breakdown that ultimately resulted in his removal from office and placement in an mental asylum. Since Chicago's ailing ordinary could not be made an archbishop, it seemed implausible to make Milwaukee a metropolitan see.[4] Henni's promotion was also affected by the shifting fortunes of the papacy.

Henni's ties with the Roman See had been strong throughout his career. But during his lifetime, the role, influence, and direct jurisdiction of the Roman papacy over the affairs of the universal church grew substantially.[5] Henni may have already been aware of the changes underway when he traveled in 1862 with Archbishop John Purcell and Bishop James Duggan of Chicago to Rome to witness the canonizations of Franciscans who had been martyred in Japan. The journey to Rome by the world's bishops had been mandated by Pope Pius IX (1846-1878)—also known as "Pio Nono." The pontiff, a unique blend of authoritarian megalomania and genuine piety, brought bishops from around the world to visit the Holy City in order to reinforce their ties of personal loyalty to him. He also hoped to strengthen his international prestige vis-à-vis the Italian nationalists who were demanding surrender of the Papal states and even the city of Rome as the natural birthright of a new Italian nation state.[6] Henni and his traveling companions were touched by the goodness of the pontiff whom he met in person for the first time in an audience on June 3. Pius IX spared no efforts to impress on his fellow prelates the necessity of his office, even quoting Anglican Bishop William Wilberforce: "If the Pope were done away with, there would be no basis for social order and security on earth."[7] He had a plaque made to commemorate the canonizations, bestowed specially-struck medals on the visiting prelates, and had them all declared assistants at the pontifical throne and patricians of the city of Rome, which he

Pope Pius IX [Martin Marty, OSB. *Dr. John Martin Henni, First Bishop and Archbishop of Milwaukee,* Benziger Bros., 1888, p. 305]

governed temporally as well as spiritually. He then revealed his plans to convene a General Council of the Church in 1869 (Vatican I). Henni was no doubt swept away by the emotion of the moment and, like most bishops, became a bit dewy-eyed in the presence of the charismatic, lovable Pio Nono. But as he steamed away from Rome, back to Milwaukee, he doubtlessly spoke with other bishops and questioned the theological basis for the growing power of the papacy.

Although Pius IX did not mention it during the gathering, the question of declaring papal infallibility was percolating among the scholars at various theological schools and universities.[8] Two factions emerged among the international hierarchy. One, led by the Jesuits and Cardinal Henry Edward Manning of Westminster, advocated a conciliar definition of papal infallibility. Another, spearheaded by bishops like Felix Dupanloup of Orleans, France, and intellectuals like historian Johann Döllinger, argued that such a definition could not be sustained by an appeal to the scriptures and the tradition of the Church. Between the "infallibilist" and "non-infallibilist" positions were a spectrum of other views. Infallibilists naturally enjoyed the favor of Pope Pius IX, who encouraged their efforts. Those who opposed such a definition generally did so on the basis that it would be "inopportune" to make such a declaration at this time.

Archbishop Peter Richard Kenrick of St. Louis
[Martin Marty, OSB. *Dr. John Martin Henni, First Bishop and Archbishop of Milwaukee,* Benziger Bros., 1888, p. 243]

American bishops reflected the same divisions on the issue.[9] Many American bishops, such as St. Louis's Archbishop Peter Richard Kenrick, opposed the idea of papal infallibility on theological grounds. Other bishops realized that such a definition, even if carefully phrased and nuanced, would be derided by hostile Protestant ministers, journalists, and others as proof that Catholics believed that the pope was above the scriptures and the long-standing tradition of the Church. Others, suspicious of the loyalties of Catholics, would see such a definition as evidence of further papal autocracy and yet another instance of Catholic resistance to principles of democracy and republicanism.[10] Some bishops, like Martin Spalding of Baltimore, came to Rome opposed to the definition, but changed his mind once he got there.

Wisconsin's bishops made a distinct contribution to Vatican I. Bishop Michael Heiss was from the outset of the council a strong proponent of a definition of papal infallibility.[11] In this he was supported by another priest with Wisconsin ties, Jesuit Francis X.

Weininger (who had written two books in 1869 to support such a definition). Bishop Joseph Melcher of Green Bay, by contrast, was opposed to the definition and allied himself with that faction of the council. Caught in the middle was Henni. Initially, Henni's beliefs on infallibility were closer to those of the "inopportunists." In fact, in replying to the anti-Catholic diatribe of John Miter at the Congregational Church in "Facts Against Assertions," he had refuted Miter's claim that the pope himself claimed personal infallibility.[12]

In October 1869, Henni traveled with Heiss and joined 700 bishops for the opening of the council. The council got off to a slow start, encumbered by complicated procedures that gave individual bishops unlimited time to filibuster on issues dear to their hearts. In addition, bad living accommodations and illness created by the damp rooms and poor food in Rome contributed to the initial difficulties. In early 1870, fearful that Vatican I might collapse from the weight of its procedures, infallibilist bishops pressed to reorganize proceedings so that they could advance the discussion of infallibility to the top of the conciliar agenda. Heiss took a lead in drafting a petition to reorganize. The opposing sides squared off in this procedural matter, and in the subsequent debate. Henni joined 17 other American bishops in voting against its repositioning.[13] However, once the question of papal infallibility was taken up, Henni voted with the majority on every one of the subsequent votes that eventually led to the definition.[14] Bishop Melcher had left the council in February 1870, after the relocation of the infallibility debate.

Bishop Joseph Melcher of Green Bay [Martin Marty, OSB. *Dr. John Martin Henni, First Bishop and Archbishop of Milwaukee,* Benziger Bros., 1888, p. 273]

The council ended abruptly when the Franco-Prussian War erupted in the summer of 1870, and by October Henni was safely back in Milwaukee. A huge demonstration, staged by local Catholics, turned out five thousand people at the Milwaukee railroad depot to catch a glimpse of the returning prelate. To cheering throngs and booming cannon he mounted a carriage to St. John's Cathedral where his entrance was marked by a sonorous organ and an all male chorus singing Schnabel's *Herr Unser Gott,* and then the solemn *Te Deum Laudamus.* Mayor Joseph Philips welcomed him home. Henni replied: "During my entire absence, I thought of Milwaukee and prayed for my people .... I love you all, you inhabitants of this city who have been so kind and good to me during my stay here. I hope in the future to see you all with me in the Heavenly Paradise."[15] Henni came back from the council apparently in good health, at least as far as he was concerned. He was now 65-years-old and in his 26th year as bishop. He wrote to Mother Emily Power of the Sinsinawa Dominicans who inquired about his well-being, "Yes, thanks to heaven, I have constantly been in great health. Indeed, I made an exception in the midst of all other bishops as to health."[16] But despite his own reports of "good health" from Rome, the rigors of travel and the years of administration had taken their toll. In the next 10 years, his last full decade of leadership, Henni's health and vitality would steadily deteriorate.

Archiepiscopal Status

When he got back home, Henni demonstrated again and again his loyalty to the Holy See. When Rome was taken by Italian revolutionaries and Pio Nono became the "prisoner of the Vatican," Henni dispatched a letter of support for the beleaguered pontiff. He also directed celebrations be made for the pontiff's silver jubilee on the throne of St. Peter in June 1871, and it was then that a branch of the newly-founded Holy Family Normal School at St. Francis was named "Pio Nono." He even concurred in efforts to name a post office in Mitchell Township in Sheboygan County for the pontiff. (This was done through the efforts of local official Thomas Herarty.[17] One can imagine the pontiff, upon hearing of this, poring over a map of the United States seeking to locate Sheboygan County!) At the same time Henni also conveyed that a collection be taken up for the Holy See.

Despite this public display of support for Pio Nono, delays in the request for archiepiscopal status for Milwaukee dragged on for several more years. Finally, on Lincoln's birthday in 1875, Henni received the news that he was created archbishop of the new metropolitan see of Milwaukee (the letters arrived on April 21, 1875). In June, huge public celebrations attended the conferral of the lamb's wool pallium by papal delegate Caesare Roncetti. Over 4,000 men marched in a torchlight procession, as bishops from around the Midwest, seminarians, clerics, and local sisterhoods took a conspicuous part in the celebrations.[18] The boundaries embraced a territory that included the dioceses of Wisconsin, as well as St. Paul, Minnesota, the upper Michigan diocese of Marquette, the vicariate apostolic of Northern Minnesota with its headquarters at St. Cloud (this reached into the Dakota Territory), and the diocese of Fort Wayne, Indiana.

Henni's Decline

But by the time Roncetti arrived with the pallium, Henni was on the decline. Already in 1874 Henni's physical health had begun to falter—and was reflected in the deterioration of his generally legible handwriting. Heart disease and perhaps some form of mental confusion began to overtake the prelate.

The slowdown came at an unfortunate time, for the population growth in Wisconsin meant that important tasks were ahead. In 1868, a new addition to the seminary was required, and 10 years later another addition expanded the main building to its present proportions. In 1871 a new Catholic Normal School was constructed west of the seminary. Henni was struck a blow in 1874 when his chief fund-raiser died, the indefatigable Father Joseph Salzmann. Without Salzmann working his fund-raising charms, the cash flow into the diocese began to suffer, while the bills run up by institutions such as the seminary and orphanages began to mount. Likewise, the cathedral began to accumulate a substantial debt. In 1872, the cathedral built a meeting center called Bishop's Hall, and efforts were made to enlarge the school buildings. All of this was done on credit. Between 1871 and 1880, 15 new parishes were constructed, 7 of them in Milwaukee, but others in growing industrial cities like Racine, Fond du Lac, and Beaver Dam were all established. Since parish revenues did not keep up with expenses, by 1879 the diocese was deeply in debt. But an increasingly befuddled and isolated Henni could do little about it. Henni would not even order diocesan-wide collections for the needs of the diocesan institutions such as the orphanages and the seminary.

Henni's inattentiveness to his episcopal duties and to the condition of the diocese/archdiocese began to be manifested in other ways. For example, Henni steadfastly refused to delegate authority to priests in outlying regions by creating a system of deaneries for the growing diocese. As Johnson notes, he preferred "to discharge the function of direct supervision himself." But distances and his own weariness with adjudicating quarrels and sorting through competing claims simply meant that some problems were left unattended.[19]

Rev. Joseph Salzmann [AAM]

Despite the hagiographical renderings of his life as the "patriarch of the Northwest," Henni's declining years were ones marked by growing irritability and eccentricity. Father Dominic Thill, ordained by Henni in 1868, and longtime pastor in Sheboygan, recalled in 1922, that Henni "was a pleasing speaker," but would now and then erupt in unexpected rage ("pathos and ire" as Thill gently put it) that would startle the congregation and inevitably strain his weakened nerves. Thill also recalled Henni's cleanliness and grace of gesture. (Henni was in fact a bit of a dandy, walking the streets of Milwaukee with a silk hat, flowing cape, and tapping cane.[20]) But he developed an obsession with the attire of other clerics, which led him to rudely inspect the clothing of others and occasionally chide clerics and seminarians if so much as a button were missing or improperly fastened on their clerical cassock. He could also be "quick tempered and impetuous," Thill remembered. Thill told a variation of an old tale regarding the ceremonial custom of putting on and taking off the episcopal miter during solemn ceremonies—long the bane of many an episcopal secretary and priest. On one occasion in Saukville, a hapless priest had the misfortune to plant the miter on Henni's head while he was reciting the prayers at the foot of the altar. In disgust Henni took the pointed hat off and flung it on the altar platform with the audible rebuke "You old fart." At the Capuchin church, Henni was overcome with giggles during a service when his assistant placed the book of the prayers from which Henni was to chant on his pot belly (*promontorium* Thill called it). Most embarrassing of all was the episode in which Henni asked Michael Heiss to assist him in putting on his sandals during some liturgical service (perhaps Good Friday), Heiss did not know what the bishop wanted, and proceeded to take off Henni's stockings. Enraged, Henni simply applied his free foot to Heiss's rear end and pushed the priest over.[21]

These embarrassing though humorous episodes were probably the sign of the crotchetiness of old age, or perhaps the effects of mini-strokes that affected portions of the brain controlling his emotions. In the summer of 1878, Henni was taken seriously ill when a severe heat wave in July downed him in the midst of a confirmation tour. He lay unconscious and motionless for two days until a mixture of ice water and liquor revived him.[22] From that time on he grew increasingly enfeebled. A stroke of "apoplexy" at Christmas 1879 induced paralysis (the left side of his face was never shown in portraits again because of the disfiguring effects of the stroke). In the meantime, diocesan affairs languished.[23]

Archbishop John Martin Henni [AAM]

Ethno-Cultural Conflict in the Archdiocese

Yet another disquieting feature of Henni's stewardship was the question of adjusting to the ethno-cultural realities. Here the story is mixed. As we have seen, Henni relished the reputation (if not the title) "Las Casas" of the Germans. His decision to create a bastion of German-speaking Catholicism in Wisconsin was a deliberate policy given voice by his famous utterance at the 1855 seminary cornerstone laying, "What I have accomplished in my diocese I owe to God and my German priests." Indeed, although he referred to the clergy on that day, he could easily have substituted the word "priests" with "sisterhoods," "missionary societies," or "lay persons."

But Henni was also reacting to the actual realities of Wisconsin life. As we have seen, Wisconsin, and especially Milwaukee, had some of the highest concentrations of German-speaking inhabitants in the nation. German speakers were indeed different: Swiss, Austrians, Bavarians, Luxemburgers, and others were in fact representatives of quite different strains of the same German culture. However, under the homogenizing pressure of American life, they blended together. German-speaking churches for a German-speaking people were quite understandable.

But discontent with this policy probably always rippled beneath the surface of Catholic life. Misgivings about the perpetuation of "foreignism" had rumbled in Wisconsin politics since territorial days. As noted earlier, immigrants were given the privilege of voting even before they were naturalized. Nativist elements in Wisconsin society as well as members of the early Republican party formed in the state (Ripon is one of the birthplaces of the Grand Old Party) shared a common distaste for immigrant participation in American political life. To this disdain was added a suspicion of Catholic voters who, in addition to their foreign status, were also seen as products of an illiberal and undemocratic church regime. In addition the Republicans associated themselves with the cause of moral reform, pressing for abolitionism and temperance. The religious aspects of Wisconsin's electoral politics were quite clear. Protestants, or "pietists," as they are identified by some political scientists, readily signed on to the anti-foreign/anti-Catholic/pro-reform platform embodied in the state Republican party. Catholics, or "ritualists" and/or "liturgicals," tended to side with the more immigrant-friendly Democratic party and held the "reforming" platform of their political foes in suspicion.[24] This division between Protestants and Catholics even had the effect of bringing the Irish and Germans, rivals within the Church, together when they approached the ballot box for national, state, and local elections.

In a strange turn of events, however, the ethno-cultural divisions that marked secular politics made a modified entry into the precincts of the Catholic Church in Wisconsin. Indeed, many of the issues that polarized Catholics and Protestants in their electoral behavior, such as support or opposition to temperance, and the degree to which the church ought to retain a "foreign" public image, were publicly pressed by different groups within the Catholic fold.

The Temperance Issue

Catholics of Irish ethnicity were somewhat sympathetic to the causes of secular reformers. It was among the Irish, for example, that temperance organizations flourished and the Irish themselves were much better suited linguistically and culturally to "fit-in" with American society. The question of temperance and prohibition had been debated for many years in Wisconsin and elsewhere.[25] Largely pushed by the evangelical churches, the desire to regulate or even ban the consumption of alcohol had been an important part of Protestant revivalism and also the reform efforts of Wisconsin women. Ethnic groups, most importantly the Germans, resisted these efforts, in part because they were sponsored by their political en-

Father Matthew's Hall, Racine [AAM]

Rev. James M. Cleary [AOP-Sin]

emies, Know-Nothings and Republicans. Even more importantly, they constituted an invasion of privacy and challenged cultural practices that honored the moderate consumption of alcoholic beverages as a way of life. Milwaukee and other Wisconsin cities had an active "beer culture" and the famous beer gardens of Milwaukee and elsewhere were important social outlets for families.[26] Germans and other opponents of temperance and prohibition regarded efforts to curtail drink as insulting and foolish.

As we have seen, within the Catholic Church temperance found a foothold primarily through the Irish and other English-speaking clergy. Patrick O'Kelley, the founder of St. Peter's in Milwaukee, spoke often to the press about Catholic temperance activities. A follower of the famed Irish apostle of temperance Father Theobald Matthew, O'Kelley had formed Milwaukee's first Catholic Temperance Society in February 1841 and boasted a membership of 250. Following Matthew's methods, O'Kelley was quite successful in getting rambunctious Milwaukee Catholics to "take the pledge," and the membership jumped to 700 before he was transferred back to Detroit.[27] Martin Kundig had also come to be a proponent of temperance, especially in his years of working with the poor in Wayne County, Michigan. It was at a temperance parade that he turned to various Catholic temperance groups around the state to march for Milwaukee's candidacy as the see city in 1843. Other Catholic temperance advocates included Milwaukee priest Father George Willard, who was a founder and popular speaker for the Catholic Total Abstinence Association. Father Hiram Fairbanks, another convert priest, who had become Catholic after his studies at the Protestant Lawrence College, organized the St. Patrick's Catholic Total Abstinence Society at his parish in Whitewater, Wisconsin.[28] These organizations charged dues, held lectures, participated in parades and publicized their efforts with printed materials and lectures far and wide. One of the most potent voices in favor of temperance was Father James Cleary. Cleary rose to national prominence as a lecturer on the temperance circuit and became a popular pastor in Kenosha, where he rebuilt old St. Mark's Church. Cleary's pro-temperance activities received little or no support from the archbishops of Milwaukee. In 1892, he left the archdiocese of Milwaukee and incardinated into the archdiocese of St. Paul, where the strongly pro-temperance Archbishop Ireland welcomed him with open arms.[29]

Archbishop Michael Heiss refused to endorse temperance activities, realizing that it was merely a front to attack German Catholics. He also did not allow priests to participate in a crusade to close saloons on Sunday (a popular Protestant-backed cause with some Catholic adherents). He even refused to receive a complimentary copy of the main organ of Catholic temperance advocates. "Please don't send your paper to my address," he noted, "for though it may be valuable in itself, I cannot find time to read it."[30]

However, all of Milwaukee's archbishops who dealt with the temperance issue balanced their opposition to restrictions on liquor with equally firm denunciations of saloons and the unsavory atmosphere of taverns. At a diocesan synod in 1892, Archbishop Frederick Katzer astounded priests when he threatened to suspend them if they went into a tavern.[31] Archbishop Messmer also publicly denounced saloons and threw his weight behind efforts to have them removed from residential districts, near churches or schools.

Moving to Action

As Henni's term drew to a close, discontent with his pro-German policies came into the open. This came from an assortment of clergy, mostly Irish-born priests, who came to believe that there were more possibilities for English-speaking Catholics than Henni or his German advisors had envisioned.

In the spring of 1878, Henni attempted to anoint his protégé, Bishop Michael Heiss of La Crosse, as coadjutor bishop with right of succession.

Archbishop Michael Heiss [AAM]

Rev. George Willard [AAM]

The temperamentally gloomy Heiss (already beset by chronic illness, depression, and general melancholia) fretted about the matter, but he did not hesitate to accept Henni's invitation. The aging prelate placed two more names on the *terna* or list of three to be sent to Rome, Bishop Joseph Dwenger, C.Pp.S., of Fort Wayne, and Bishop Francis Krautbauer of Green Bay. He then informed the archbishops of the country of his selections, and requested them to submit their opinions to Rome.

When news of this leaked out, German priests, especially on the seminary faculty, were glad of the news. Heiss, who had been the seminary's first rector, was a man with a decent scholarly reputation, and possessed sufficient administrative skills to tackle the floundering state of diocesan affairs. Moreover, he had Henni's confidence. English-speaking priests, however, seized the moment of Milwaukee's first episcopal transition to try to change the direction of the diocese and perhaps reorient it to a more "Americanized" identity. Their chief spokesman was Fond du Lac pastor, George Willard.

A native of New York, Willard had converted to Catholicism from the Episcopal faith, and had been received into the Catholic Church by Henni. In 1865, Henni ordained him to the priesthood after he completed his studies at St. Francis Seminary. Willard helped advance the cause of Catholic journalism in Wisconsin when he purchased the *Catholic Vindicator* and transformed it into the *Catholic Citizen.* This periodical, ultimately purchased by journalist Humphrey Desmond, would become the chief mouthpiece for English-speaking Catholics in Wisconsin and elsewhere. Willard was also a passionate advocate for temperance. Although he never wavered in his Catholic faith, Willard often proclaimed his "Yankee" credentials, bragging that his family had fought in the American Revolution and been a part of the founding generation of America. Unfortunately, he never really lost much of his Protestant disdain for immigrants and for "foreign" religion. Like other prominent converts of the time, such as Paulist founder Isaac Hecker, he was highly optimistic that American culture could be a good breeding ground for future converts, and did not believe that the future of the Catholic Church in America was inextricably linked to the perpetuation of ethnicity.

Willard's pastoral career included a brief stint on the faculty of the seminary, and later pastoral assignments in East Troy, Waupun and the pastorate of St. Joseph's parish in Fond du Lac. From these perches he refined his own ideas about the future of the diocese and viewed with alarm the growing strength of the German-speaking phalanx in Wisconsin. He knew full well, no doubt through conversations with such men as Father Thomas Fagan and layman Bernard Durward (both of whom taught seminarians), of the strength of the German coalition on the seminary faculty, and their ability to influence the bishop. Like many other priests of the diocese he heard rumors that Mother Caroline Friess of the School Sisters of Notre Dame also exercised powerful influence over the declining Henni. Finally, Willard himself spoke German and was often invited to gatherings of the Teutonic clergy. Over the years he had accumulated a good bit of information on the ways his German-speaking confreres thought and acted. Hearing of Henni's efforts to secure the Heiss nomination, Willard and his clerical allies appealed to Archbishop James Gibbons of Baltimore, who as the head of the oldest American diocese (the premier see), was responsible for forwarding episcopal nominations to Propaganda in Rome.

In a remarkable letter to Gibbons in May 1878, Willard put to paper what must have been his own pent-up frustrations as well as those of other English-speaking priests and laity.[32] Setting aside the nearly ritualistic respect tendered the aging Henni, Willard attacked and even ridiculed every aspect of the archbishop's Germanizing activities, characterizing them as a "conspiracy." He insisted that Henni had literally made his declaration that Wisconsin was the German-speaking heartland come true by somehow altering the "laws" of immigration and encouraging a disproportionate number of Germans to come. Willard accused his clerical comrades of discouraging vocations among deserving English-speaking lads, and accused the German priests of being more interested in perpetuating their ethnic identity than preaching the gospel and making converts among the willing Americans. In an oft-quoted phrase, Willard opined: "So long as these priests care more for sauerkraut and its concomitants than they do for the souls of the Americans they are not very likely to convert them. And this practically one great object of the existence of the church of God here is frustrated." He had nothing but contempt for Mother Caroline, "the superioress of a large German congregation."

Willard attempted to provide Gibbons and Roman authorities with a more accurate picture of the real needs of Wisconsin Catholics. He challenged the prevailing wisdom that the archdiocese of Milwaukee was an impregnable German-speaking redoubt, noting that the annual reporting of ecclesiastical statistics had been skewed by calling a church "German" if the pastor was German, and ignoring the fact that he may have been assigned to a largely English-speaking flock. He emphatically noted, "The great majority of the Catholics speak English." As a counter to the "Germans-only" pastoral approach of the Teutonic presbyterate, he insisted that there were more potential Catholic converts among the English-speaking than had been imagined (perhaps something he had seen at his temperance lectures). "Over one half (by far) of the inhabitants of our state are Americans and Protestants ...." He reiterated: "The work of the church here is twofold: to convert the Americans and preserve our own." Willard could come to no other conclusion but that Milwaukee required an English-speaking bishop. A few days later, Willard sent a similar letter of protest directly to Propaganda,

Rev. James J. Keogh [AAM]

assuring raised eyebrows in Rome of the Milwaukee situation by linking the attitudes of the German clergy with the ideas of heretics and church persecutors such as John Calvin, Johann Döllinger (a schismatic church historian), and Prussian Chancellor Otto von Bismarck.[33] An even lengthier petition to Gibbons was drafted and signed by a cadre of English-speaking priests, reiterating Willard's arguments and amplifying them with statistics, anecdotes, and a sense of urgency. "We have determined to remain silent no longer," proclaimed the clerics. They asked him to "put an end in this Province to the rule of excessive nationality, not only so un-Catholic but so un-American." Willard's name was also on the second letter, together with fellow convert-priest Hiram Fairbanks of Whitewater, Patrick Pettit of Madison, Joseph Keenan at Pio Nono College, young James Keogh of the cathedral (who lived with Henni) and Thomas Fagan of the seminary faculty.[34]

Fortunately for the English-speaking "conspirators," Henni's efforts to nominate Heiss hit procedural snags. Not only did the archbishops decide to take the complaints seriously, and look closely at the successor to Henni, but Propaganda also sent the nomination back, claiming that Henni had skipped the important step of polling his suffragans for candidates for the *terna.* Henni had five suffragans, Bishop Heiss of La Crosse, Bishop Francis Krautbauer of Green Bay, Bishop Thomas Langton Grace, O.P., of St. Paul, Minnesota, Bishop Martin Marty, Vicar Apostolic of the

Bishop John Lancaster Spalding [*Souvenir of the Episcopal Silver Jubilee of the Rt. Rev. J.L. Spalding, D.D.,* Press of Hollister Bros., 1903]

Dakotas, and Bishop Ignatius Mrak of Marquette, Michigan. In September 1878, Henni convened his suffragans. Heiss once again came in first, Dwenger was dropped, and Krautbauer moved to second place. But this time the English-speaking Grace was present, and with the encouragement of Father Martin Kundig, insisted that the name of Father John Lancaster Spalding be added to the *terna.* John Lancaster Spalding, a Kentucky priest and a nephew of the deceased archbishop, Martin John Spalding of Baltimore, was a Louvain-trained cleric, of impeccable "American" credentials, who also spoke German fluently. Since 1876, he had been the bishop of Peoria, Illinois.[35] Grace seemed to reinforce some of the observations of the Milwaukee English-speaking clergy when he suggested in a letter to Gibbons that Milwaukee was ready now for a non-German ordinary.[36] Grace's observations were reinforced by Fathers Martin Kundig, Patrick Donohoe, James Keogh of the cathedral and Father Edward P. Lonigan, who wrote to Cardinal John McCloskey of New York who also endorsed Spalding. "His thorough knowledge of German would make him acceptable to the German element, and from all accounts he is the first choice of all the English speaking Catholics," they informed the cardinal. "His advent to Milwaukee would usher in a new era of prosperity for the Church in the North West which has for so long been laboring under foreign rule."[37] To Archbishop Gibbons they also voiced their support of Spalding's candidacy asserting that he would be an attractive choice to non-Catholics, "who were numerous and well-disposed and on the threshold of the Faith, but ignored up to then."[38] Gibbons was in favor of Spalding and noted in his diary that he wrote to Cardinal Simeoni in Rome in his favor. As it turned out, Henni had once more ignored procedure and sent the new *terna* to Rome without consulting the archbishops. The patient officials at Propaganda informed him once again of the proper procedure.

The dispute now reached a critical phase when the English-speaking priests attempted to drum up support for Spalding by a press campaign. "Leaks" of the dispute reached the editorial desks of the occasionally anti-Catholic *Milwaukee Sentinel*, which had for years fanned the flames of suspicion about the foreign and illiberal nature of the Catholic Church. The source of these leaks was Father Thomas Fagan, a member of the seminary faculty whose own gifts with pen were well known (he started the seminary publication *Salesianum*). Fagan ridiculed Heiss's nomination, jeering at his inability to speak uninflected English. Fagan's animus toward

Rev. Thomas Fagan
[AAM]

Germans was perhaps even sharper than his colleagues, in part because he witnessed the "discouraging" of American seminarians and perhaps because the Germans may have chastised Fagan for his occasional over-indulgence in alcohol. Fagan did have serious "issues" with seminary rector Christopher Wapelhorst, whom Henni had brought from St. Louis to replace Salzmann in 1874. In a strong letter to Cardinal Simeoni in 1878, Fagan scored Wapelhorst's administration of the seminary, pointing to the fact that it had resulted in the resignation of a number of faculty. This included future Milwaukee archbishop Frederick X. Katzer, who told Fagan he had accepted a post as secretary to the bishop of Green Bay "on account of Father Wapelhorst."[39] Fagan declared, "Now he wants to get me away and so far as I know for personal reasons and he told me if I did not go, he would tell the archbishop he would go." Fagan pleaded with Simeoni to keep his seminary post, "German influence prevails in the diocese .... I have a poor chance of being heard .... I am accustomed to a teaching life ... a forced removal from the seminary would seriously injure my reputation."[40] Fagan fought hard against Wapelhorst and his German allies (of whom he presumed Heiss was one). In addition to letting the public know about the efforts to appoint Heiss, Fagan also launched a campaign to remove seminary rector Wapelhorst by circulating a petition demanding his resignation.[41] The *Sentinel* needed no encouragement to fan suspicions about the "foreign" nature of the Catholic Church and suggested that a German conspiracy was at work.[42] German priests rebutted the accusation.[43] In the meantime, Wapelhorst, fed up with the feuding and conflict on the seminary faculty (some of it of his own manufacture) "retired" to the German Franciscans in Teutopolis, Illinois, in August 1879 where he took the name "Innocent." Father Kilian Flasch replaced him as rector and Fagan was dismissed from the seminary faculty. When Fagan appealed for his reinstatement, angry German priests petitioned Simeoni not to allow him back and affixed to their document a letter from a local physician who swore that all during 1877 and in early 1878, he was "frequently called upon to give medical treatment to Reverend Thomas Fagan ... in the course of time it became evident to me that his illness was owing to the continued and excessive use of alcoholic beverages."[44] Henni also sent a long memorial condemning Fagan in September 1879.[45] Fagan was never permitted back to the faculty and spent the rest of his life as pastor of Immaculate Conception in Bay View, where his intemperance and choleric traits grew worse.[46]

The appearance of the dispute in the columns of the secular *Milwaukee Sentinel* both mortified and enraged Henni. He arose from the miasma of his own confusion and ill-health to publicly denounce the press campaign and threatened sanctions against any and all who gave it aid and comfort.[47] Willard (who was not close to Fagan) distanced himself from the press controversy, noting, "As far as the Coadjutorship itself is concerned, the newspaper controversy in Milwaukee can have no more to do with the appointment ... than a debate on the same subject in Africa."[48] Likewise, he paid tribute to Henni, "at whose hands we had the happiness to receive the two powerful sacraments of confirmation and holy orders."[49] But he also noted that German priests had also dared to wade into the controversy and attempted to affect the outcome. He related a gathering of mostly German priests at Sauk (*viz.*, Sauk City) for the blessing of an altar by Heiss. At the social afterwards, the priests spoke forcefully on the need for a German coadjutor and proposed a petition. Heiss attempted to dissuade them by observing that it was probably too late. Nonetheless, the petition was drafted and circulated.[50] Not all the German priests signed it, but it clearly expressed the views of most. Because of this, Willard drew a sharp distinction between the unfortunate airing of internal difficulties of the Church in the public press and the legitimate right of Catholics to inform Rome of local conditions. He strongly insisted that nationality politics play no role whatever in the selection of bishops, "If there be any country in the world where foreign nationalities should be cast aside, and the church appear in her true light as *Catholic—universal*—for all nations, that country is America."[51]

In February 1879, the celebration of Henni and Kundig's 50th anniversary of ordination did not see a respite from the factionalism, since the English-speaking priests avoided the general diocesan reception and went *en bloc* to a local hotel for a private dinner party. Some refused to donate to the purse for Henni.[52] The Golden Jubilee also made clear the urgency of resolving the dispute.[53] Henni

Revs. Christopher (Innocent) Wapelhorst and Kilian Flasch [AAM]

Rev. Martin Kundig [AAM]

was physically spent from the exertion of the celebration, and shortly afterwards took ill and had to be taken to St. Mary's Hospital. One month after the celebration, Kundig suffered a major heart attack and died. Henni, stricken with grief, rose from his hospital bed to attend the obsequies for his old companion but he fainted in the sanctuary during the lengthy services.[54]

The nomination of Heiss languished throughout 1879 as the archbishops took their time in evaluating the Milwaukee selections. When it finally did reach Rome, cardinals at Propaganda, perhaps given pause by Gibbons's respectful listening to the dissidents, could not arrive at a clear answer. Other American archbishops such as John Williams of Boston and James Wood of Philadelphia, and Bishop John Foley of Chicago added to their indecision by urging the Spalding nomination. On the other side, a priest of the diocese of La Crosse, Father Edward Fitzpatrick, wrote a scathing letter to Leopold Moczygemba, a Conventual Franciscan on the staff of Propaganda. In the letter he bitterly denounced Fagan as the source of the difficulties. "Pride, self-conceit and drink have been the cause of his ruin." He further indicted the priests who sided with Fagan, scoring their motives as full of "national spirit, revenge, partisanship, rebellion—motives as base as Father Fagan's." He dismissed each one individually: "Rev. Willard, a convert who has been too much petted, a sly worker, an open calumniator of the seminary, a dangerous and suspect character; Rev. J. J. Keenan, a shrewd schemer [considered] by all unworthy of credence; Rev. J. J. Keogh, a bitter antagonist in this unjust war ... Rev. [M. J.] Ward, a Fennian [*sic*] blaster, Rev. Petit a *minus habens;* Rev. Matthews, suspected of drink ... Rev. Doyle, charged with dishonorable practices; Rev. Fairbanks, a convert and imprudent." He concluded, "I would have it understood that I am an Irishman and I know the vindictiveness of these Irish priests."[55] On May 17, 1879, Cardinal Giovanni Simeoni of Propaganda wrote to Henni, suggesting that Heiss could not be spared from La Crosse. The cardinal asked if Henni would accept Spalding.[56] Hearing of the indecision of Rome, Krautbauer and Spalding withdrew their names from consideration. Heiss himself was tempted to pull back, but at Henni's urging remained.[57] Henni then nominated Heiss once again, and on the new list included two new names: Father Kilian Flasch of the seminary faculty and English-speaking Bishop James O'Connor of Omaha, Nebraska. When Henni suffered yet another stroke after Christmas in 1879, concerned parties in Milwaukee attempted to break the logjam that had set in over the Heiss nomination.

The chief actors in this final stage were Mother Caroline Friess and Father Peter Abbelen. Henni held Friess and Abbelen in high regard, and there may have been some truth to the rumors circulated by Willard and others that Friess exercised a great deal of control over the mentally deteriorating Henni. Evidence for this is found in 1891 when Capuchin founder, Father Francis Haas, who knew both Henni and Friess, attempted to destroy a note from some sisters in North Dakota who spoke of when, "Sister Caroline rule[d] the diocese and shape[d] the bishop."58 Already in February 1880, Mother Caroline noted in a letter to the convent spiritual director, "The Most Reverend Archbishop [Henni] is really childish now."[59] Alarmed that continued inaction could further damage the economic and spiritual well-being of the archdiocese, Friess sent her chaplain to Rome to personally petition the order's "cardinal protector," Joseph Hergrenrother, to intervene on behalf of the stalled Heiss nomination.[60] Although we have no record of what Abbelen said, no doubt he painted a dire picture of Henni's health and mental capacities as well as the need to protect the well-being of German Catholics in America. Hergenrother's intervention was decisive, and informal word was sent that Heiss had received the nomination. Milwaukee Catholics received the news via a cablegram reprinted in the local press in late March 1880.[61] On May 9, 1880, Heiss took up his new duties in Milwaukee, and on May 11, 1880 the apostolic brief appointing Heiss coadjutor with right of succession arrived. As this controversy came to a close, Henni himself floated in and out of reality. He rallied a bit during the summer months, but he remained bedridden and muddled of mind. Finally, in November 1880, Henni turned over complete jurisdiction of the archdiocese to his hand-picked successor. On September 7, 1881, the aging prelate died in Milwaukee and was buried at the cathedral.[62]

Did Heiss want the job, especially knowing the intensity of opposition to his nomination and the fact that he literally owed the position to the efforts of Mother Caroline and Abbelen? His sympathetic biographer, Sister M. Mileta Ludwig, depicts Heiss as piously awaiting the decision of Rome as his fate unfolded.63 But his humble bearing notwithstanding, Heiss did indeed want to be the archbishop of Milwaukee and neither stopped nor discouraged anyone who made efforts on his behalf. As he wrote to his dear friend Kilian Kleiner, "The opposition party which had powerful patrons in Rome tried everything to prevent my appointment .... The opposition is silenced ...."[64]

Mother Caroline Friess, SSND
[ASND]

Just in case their minds were not changed, he took pains to purge the diocese of the chief participants of the anti-Heiss faction. Willard left the diocese in 1882 and assumed a post in the Dakotas with the Bureau of American Catholic Indian Missions. Although he occasionally returned to Milwaukee for visits, the convert-priest seemed to find a "niche" in work with Indians and moved steadily westward, dying in Banning, California in July, 1890.65 Fagan's punishment, as we have seen, was removal from the seminary faculty. The rest of the conspirators received the common clerical punishment of "exile" from the large see city and "banishment" to the pastorates of remote churches. Patrick Pettit, who might have been "promoted," remained in Madison until his death in 1895. Joseph Keenan was dispatched to Fond du Lac, where he continued to do battle with local German clergy. Former Methodist Hiram Fairbanks of distant Whitewater was more quickly "rehabilitated" and was welcomed back to Milwaukee in 1881 to assume the pastorate of prestigious St. Patrick's Church. James Keogh attempted to withdraw from Milwaukee in 1880, alleging difficulties with his health, but a petition signed by 400 cathedral parishioners insisted that he remain, and Henni agreed.[66] Indeed, as a gesture to soothe the hurt feelings of the English speakers, Henni appointed Father Patrick Donohoe to the pastorate of St. John's Cathedral to replace the deceased Kundig, thereby establishing the custom of having the mother church led by an Irish-surnamed cleric (the seminary rector was always a German until 1976 when Slovak Father Richard Sklba became its head).[67] Keogh worked with Donohoe and then became rector himself. He managed to work well under Heiss. Together they managed to erase the indebtedness left behind by Henni.

Rev. Patrick Donohoe [AAM]

However, the aftermath of the bitter struggle left its wounds. English-speaking clergy always felt like second-class citizens in Milwaukee, with one priest lamenting in 1889, "Although I have one of the best parishes in the state, I have been so unfortunate as to be settled under this excessive and exclusive German rule, which precludes all chance of worldly preferment."[68] English-speaking clergy seemed to withdraw into their own separate world, tending to their parishes and responsibilities and accepting the reality that their voices were not taken seriously in any matter of import dealing with the whole archdiocese. As late as 1911, English-speaking priests still felt marginalized. When the relatively small number of Irish-surnamed clergy caused editor Humphrey Desmond to wonder if English-speaking parishes were doing their bit to encourage vocations, Father Thomas Johnson of St. Raphael's parish in Madison produced a list of 25 Irish-surnamed Milwaukee lads that abandoned the diocese for service elsewhere, suggesting that this exodus was because of German dominance in Milwaukee. He added, "The list does not include the thirty or more Irish American young men who have entered into the Vincentian, Servite, Dominican, Jesuit and Holy Cross orders ... older priests could add a few more names to the list."[69] Seminary procurator Louis Peschong attempted to refute Johnson's allegations by noting that some priests "left" Milwaukee because of diocesan boundary changes, but tacitly acknowledged that there were relatively few vocations from English-speaking families.[70] Heiss lived his entire episcopate under the shadow of the embarrassing events that had propelled him to power. He was so sure that ethno-cultural tensions would erupt again among his clergy that he foreswore an *ad limina* visit to Rome in 1882 after he had received the pallium. Nonetheless, his nine-year episcopate left its mark on the archdiocese.

Archbishop Michael Heiss (1880-1890)

Michael Heiss was born in Pfahldorf, Bavaria on April 12, 1818, the fourth son of Joseph Heiss and Gertrude Frey.[71] His parents were prosperous farmers and his father served as Mayor of Pfahldorf. In 1823, the local parish priest welcomed Heiss to his school and offered him instruction in Latin. News of his excellence in studies reached the ears of the Bishop of Eichstatt, the diocesan headquarters, and at the age of 11 young Heiss was sent to school in the see city. After further education at a gymnasium in Neuberg, Heiss began studies at the University of Munich in 1835. The university, with its excellent classical and theological faculties, was one of the intellectual centers of Europe at that time. Amply endowed by the royal family of Bavaria and blessed by papal approval, the university exposed Heiss to an array of subjects and teachers that developed further his own native intelligence. In 1837, he decided to study for the priesthood and

Archbishop Michael Heiss [AAM]

took up residence in the seminary on the University of Munich grounds called the Georgianum. In his years of theological study, he met great scholars such as Johann Adam Möhler and Johann Döllinger, destined to play important roles in the theological debates of the 19th century. He was also at the center of serious debates over the rights of the Church in Bavaria as the reconfiguration of the relations between church and state continued throughout Europe in the first third of the 19th century. It was an exciting time and place to be. The years away at school also seemed to bring out Heiss's tendency to brood and lapse into long periods of melancholy, self-pity, and complaining. It was in these dark moments that he turned to his close friend, Kilian Kleiner, a classmate from Augsburg, with whom he shared everything.[72] Kleiner would remain Heiss's sounding board and tonic for life.

He returned to his home diocese of Eichstatt and on October 13, 1840, was ordained by Bishop August von Reisach. After an assignment in a parish, Heiss joined his fellow seminarian Karl Boeswald in plans to travel to America and serve German-speaking Catholics. This did not come out of the blue. In 1839, Bishop John B. Purcell of Cincinnati visited the Georgianum seeking German-speaking priests for his diocese. At that time Heiss indicated his interest, but he needed to wait until he was ordained. Once his priesthood had begun, Heiss renewed his interest in the American mission and he approached his bishop for permission. Boeswald would be delayed, but Bishop von Reisach permitted Heiss to go, and in December 1842, he arrived in New Orleans and made his way up the Mississippi and Ohio Rivers to Louisville, Kentucky, where he reported to Bishop Benedict Flaget and his coadjutor Guy Ignatius Chabrat.

Flaget assigned him to the brand-new *Muttergottes Kirche* (Mother of God Church) in Covington, directly across the river from Cincinnati. Heiss immediately took note of the greater number of German speakers across the Ohio River and petitioned Chabrat for permission to travel among them. Both Flaget and Chabrat were incensed at the young priest's rapid exit and simply dismissed him from the diocese. The arrival of Boeswald to take over the Covington pastorate freed Heiss to go to Ohio where he traveled far and wide seeking out and ministering to the pockets of German-speaking Catholics all over the state. He arrived just as Henni had received the news of the creation of the new Milwaukee See and in a moment of fervor agreed to accompany the new bishop to Wisconsin.

In May, 1844, Henni and Heiss arrived in Milwaukee and set to work creating the diocese of Milwaukee. In Milwaukee, Heiss's gifts of intellect and his passion for hard work were put to good use. Ministry "specialization" was unknown and impractical in those days, and Heiss held an array of jobs. He was at first a circuit-riding missionary. He wrote to Kleiner of the hazards of a trip to Burlington which included getting drenched in a rain shower, bitten by mosquitoes, and nearly drowning with his horse in a swollen stream. He further wrote that the natural beauty of the Wisconsin landscape reminded him of home: "Since I can only think of the homeland as the quintessence of everything beautiful .... I cannot see anything beautiful without thinking of it."[73] Heiss's missionary days ended when Henni appointed him the first resident pastor for the newly built St. Mary's Church in Milwaukee. He was fairly successful in administering the new congregation, but always felt unsettled in Milwaukee. After accompanying Henni to one of the provincial councils of Baltimore, he returned to Milwaukee with a heavy heart. "Although I am now used to the conditions of this country, know its customs and language," he related to Kleiner, "still I cannot rid myself of the feeling that this is not my home and that I live, so to say, in exile."[74] Heiss had already contemplated going back to Bavaria and Henni had given his permission, but he held back, fearing "to go counter to the designs of God."[75]

Heiss had indeed suffered physically from his initial brush with the Wisconsin frontier, contracting typhoid fever and complaining of liver trouble. In 1850, he resigned his pastorate at St. Mary's and departed for a two-year sick leave in Bavaria. After some rest, he became active in local parishes in the diocese of Eichstatt, reconnected with his parents and Kleiner, and was of great help to the *Ludwig-Missionsverein* in helping them to identify and fund new projects in America. He spent a brief time as well as the chaplain of a convent of Visitation nuns at Ditramzell. Despite strenuous efforts to keep him in Europe, Heiss went back to Milwaukee in 1852, where he set to work on a number of projects, most notably the building of the new seminary. Here his earlier experience as a seminary prefect in Eichstatt provided him a framework for the administration of the revived institution which opened in 1856.

Until his consecration as the first bishop of La Crosse in 1868, Heiss remained at St. Francis Seminary, watching it grow and pursuing his own scholarly interests. His natural aptitude for study and the world of ideas never ended. He read whatever he could get his hands on in the far-off missions, and authored works on matrimony, the four gospels, and the life of the Cistercian Peter Damian. Heiss could be forceful, decisive, and occasionally vindictive, but no one doubted his zeal or devotion to the Church. An intensely introspective man, he had a deeply spiritual life, and was harder on himself than anyone else.

Since his student days, Heiss brooded. Indeed, as he confided to Kleiner, and as was obvious to anyone who interacted with him, he was often in the "dumps," constantly beset by serious illness brought on by a combination of bad diet and overwork, not to mention his own overwrought temperament. Mother Caroline Friess, who occasionally referred to Heiss as a "sourpuss," seemed to suggest that he "enjoyed" ill health. Speaking of his occasional get-togethers with Bishop Francis X. Krautbauer of Green Bay (a former chaplain of the School Sisters), the doughty Friess (who had suffered her own share of slings and arrows) noted: "Because of his [Heiss] troubles he becomes ill frequently, but when the two Bavarian bishops and brothers-in-suffering get together and converse one must really laugh with them. It is really sad to see how grief and construction troubles can break these men. They are almost brought to the brink of insanity."[76]

But of all the archbishops of Milwaukee, it is Heiss who reveals the most about his inner life. As years went on, it is apparent that he had a David-Jonathan relationship with Kleiner. As he had done since student days, he poured out his soul again and again to Kleiner, lamenting his problems, lambasting his opposition, and often indicating his desire to "get even" or to settle scores. For example, when he was sent to La Crosse in 1868, he systematically targeted clerical opponents and made plans to remove them from the diocese, even if this meant that some churches would not have pastors. "In the city of La Crosse ... there is only one priest and unfortunately one whom I do not like to see there .... I expect to find similar conditions in at least seven other places where there are priests who know or suspect that I do not like to keep them. They remain only because they think that I need them owing to the scarcity of priests, but I am resolved to send those priests whom I cannot trust back to the diocese of Milwaukee where they belong even if some parishes should be without priests for some time." [77]

However, this "tough-guy" episcopal macho was also accompanied by an unseeming hypersensitivity that makes one wonder why he wanted to be any kind of ecclesiastical leader. Heiss could not abide being criticized and reacted with hurt feelings and pouting. Father Augustine Schinner characterized Heiss as: "Sensitive without being vindictive, he reminded one of those delicate plants that shrivel at a rough touch of wind or hand."[78]

In La Crosse this surfaced when he built an overly-large episcopal residence severely taxing the resources of the largely rural diocese and earning him the scorn of some of his priests. He had also ignored the larger and more suitable "English" church in La Crosse and spent heavily to build a new cathedral at the German church of St. Joseph.[79] Heiss's turmoil spilled out in his letters to Kleiner. "Sheer worry had practically destroyed my appetite," he lamented to Kleiner on one occasion, "and neither can I sleep well." In another letter he weeps, "Here there is no end of troubles. As soon as I think one problem is settled, I am confronted with another."[80]

Nonetheless, during his nine years as archbishop of Milwaukee, he made considerable headway on a number of issues that Henni had either neglected or chose to ignore: the solution to a serious fiscal crisis; the proper organization of parishes according to civil and canonical requirements; the development of the first diocesan bureaucracy; and the extension and unification of Catholic schools. He also boldly confronted the challenges posed by Wisconsin's political and social environment. Without a doubt he was deeply committed to Henni's program of preserving German-ethnic identity as the proper way to advance Catholic visibility in Wisconsin. In his time, the Church in Wisconsin matured, evidenced not only by larger numbers, but by the expansion of its services, and the construction of churches, schools, and other buildings of architectural elegance. There were in addition increased enrollment in parochial schools, swelling numbers of sisters and priests, and an aggressive clergy and laity willing to do battle at the ballot box and in the courts to assert Catholic rights.

An Organizational Revolution: Restoring Financial Stability

When Archbishop Heiss re-immersed himself in the affairs of the archdiocese his first task was finances. As noted earlier, archdiocesan finances had suffered from Henni's poor management and increasing incapacitation. In addition, the decade of the 1870s had seen a serious economic malaise in Wisconsin and across the nation as the United States suffered one of the first of its regular industrial depressions.[81] No one knows for certain the extent of the financial mess left behind by Henni, in part because good records were not kept. Heiss moved aggressively to sort out this spaghetti bowl of fiscal problems and at one point wrote to Bishop Martin Marty, vicar apostolic of the Dakotas, that the debts of the archdiocese required the payment of $3,000 a year in interest.[82] It was eventually determined that the archdiocese owed $77,000. Of this, $26,000 was the cathedral's debt alone.

The priority of dealing with the debt issue seemed even more ominous after 1878 when the entire American Church was rocked by the financial collapse of the archdiocese of Cincinnati. Here, a diocesan bank under the leadership of Archbishop John B. Purcell's brother had failed, plunging the se into deep debt. Indeed, so bad was Cincinnati's fiscal plight that its seminary was forced to go out of existence for a time.[83] Heiss was determined to avoid such a publicly embarrassing disaster in Milwaukee, and pressed ahead with debt restructuring and repayment. By late 1880, he had enough of a handle on the situation to write to the clergy that the diocesan income had not been meeting interest.[84] With the help of Vicar General Leonard Batz and cathedral rector Patrick Donohoe, Heiss separated diocesan bills from cathedral expenses. Heiss proposed a debt repayment schedule that could be met by requesting a voluntary contribution from the priests of a maximum of $50 a year for the next four

Rev. Leonard Batz [AAM]

years. While he left the amount each priest could pay up to himself, the first general fund appeal in archdiocesan history was quite successful. Within five years the total debt had been whittled down to nearly nothing. Later, the cathedral parish paid off its debt and positioned itself to make substantial improvements to the aging structure. In August 1885, Heiss introduced the *cathedraticum*—a diocesan tax that was devoted to the support of the central administration. He imposed an assessment on each parish of 25 cents per family, and a demand that clergy transmit 5 percent of the stole fees and all collections to him. He also introduced archdiocesan seminary and orphan collections.[85] With these funds he helped establish a more stable basis for diocesan administration, including a regular salary for himself, and a housing allowance and salaries for the few archdiocesan officials he kept.[86]

Burned by his experience in La Crosse, Heiss did not seek any funds to build an episcopal residence. After an unpleasant stint of living at the seminary ("paradise is not to be found on earth and especially not at the seminary"), he realized he had to have his own home.[87] Unwilling to burden the diocese, he purchased with his own funds a lot near old St. Peter's Church costing $5,000 and on it he erected a two-story brick veneer building for an additional $5,000. His faithful valet "Brother" Bernard Gerleman, a former Capuchin, lived with him, as did two Franciscan sisters from La Crosse. After his death, the house was sold and the proceeds distributed. His successor Katzer had to find a new home.

Heiss's careful management of archdiocesan monies was helped by the return of prosperity to Wisconsin and the nation in the 1880s. However, the ethno-cultural passions stirred by his appointment still festered. Their outlet shifted from the now settled episcopal succession to the parish level where there were several very antagonistic explosions of lay trusteeism.

Lay Trusteeism: Disaster at Sinsinawa and a New Corporation Law

As part of his program to bring order and rationality to the rapidly growing archdiocese, Heiss also undertook the tangled legal laws of the archdiocese. As had happened in many developing dioceses in U. S. Catholic history, arguments over the control of church property and even the placement of the clergy had taken place in Wisconsin. Although earlier historical treatments of this phenomenon regarded it as an "evil" or an act of lay disobedience, alternative historical perspectives by Patrick Carey and others have sought to give a wider context for lay-clerical struggles over the governance of parishes.[88] Carey identified lay efforts to control church affairs as a manifestation of American approaches to church life, and specifically the introduction of republican principles and democratic practices to the ecclesiastical sphere. Likewise, the struggles between laity and clergy over church property, finances, and clergy placement are also to be observed against the backdrop of actual conditions of church life in Wisconsin.

As we have seen, lay persons actually created some church communities and held them together during infrequent visits from itinerant priests. The boundaries between lay and clerical leadership were fluid in the earliest days of Wisconsin Catholicism. When clergy did become more available and attempted to establish themselves as the undisputed leaders of heretofore lay-led congregations, troubles erupted. In addition, various ethnic issues also became part of lay-clerical struggles. Sometimes, as we shall see at Sinsinawa Mound, there were struggles between two groups vying for power over the location of a parish church. Other times, European concepts of lay governance clashed with newer American patterns of episcopal centralization. Milwaukee's experiences with trustee problems fed into the larger pool of similar experiences that took place across the country.

One of the diocese's earliest lay-clerical flare-ups occurred between 1848-1851 at St. Joseph's Church in East Bristol, Walworth County, where two factions clashed over who would hold the title to a new church, the bishop or the trustees. For a time, the dissident faction secured their own priest and operated "independently" until order was restored. At St. Lawrence Church in Jefferson County, a bitter argument between the man who wished to deed land to the church and the parish trustees stalled the building of the church until Father Michael Haider was able to make peace. Serious problems developed in Beaver Dam when disaffected parishioners from St. Peter's Church broke away and formed a "schismatic" St. Mary's Church in the 1850s. They were not reconciled with ecclesiastical authorities until after the Civil War.[89] In Appleton in 1867, a nationality quarrel broke out between Irish and Germans when Germans wanted to create their own distinct parish and Archbishop Henni had to travel to the Fox River Valley city to untangle the competing claims for resources and property.[90] Trustee difficulties erupted all over the diocese, in part due to a lack of clarity on the legal incorporation of church property. These issues crystallized during Heiss's time with two very serious trustee problems. Heiss's experience with these, as well as the support of legislation from the provincial and plenary councils of Baltimore and Rome, led to permanent changes in the mode of handling church property. Both flare-ups began during the waning days of Henni's episcopate—one at Sinsinawa and the other at Fond du Lac.

The Sinsinawa troubles concerned St. Dominic's Church near Sinsinawa, which had been organized in 1842 by Father Samuel Mazzuchelli.[91] A flourishing parish developed, serving mostly Irish farmers; Dominicans from the Mound said Mass. In 1856, the small frame building was enlarged, and when the Dominican priests withdrew from the Mound in 1866, they conveyed to Henni the title to the church property. Henni continued to assign diocesan priests to serve St.

Dominic's. The difficulties began as early as 1871 when plans were discussed to build a new church. By this time a contingent of Germans living north of the site had moved in and wanted the church and a Catholic school built near their homes. The Dominican Sisters, now firmly ensconced on the hill, had a stake in the matter. Since the pastor of the church also doubled as a confessor and chaplain to the sisters, the sisters donated some land near the convent for the proposed new church. In 1878, Henni had appointed Father James Cleary to the pastorate. Cleary was eager to make his mark as a church builder (one that he would finally realize in Kenosha in the 1880s) and pressed for a new church building. Once again, however, German parishioners requested a new location and a school, while the English-speaking insisted that the new building be erected on the lands donated by the sisters. Cleary appealed for direction from some ecclesiastical authority. He wrote not to the incapacitated Henni but to Bishop Michael Heiss at La Crosse. Heiss urged him to do whatever two-thirds of the parishioners decided. The majority voted to keep the site donated by the sisters on the Mound. Cleary attempted to follow this advice, but the parish became more factionalized and so in August 1880 Cleary was transferred to Kenosha. Heiss in the interim had become the coadjutor of the Milwaukee See and the issue of the polarized parish was now his to contend with.

Rev. James M. Cleary [AOP-Sin]

A young German priest, Theodore Jacobs, replaced Cleary in the summer of 1880, but he had no more success than his predecessor in mending the rift over the location of the new church. In the summer of 1881, the matter was laid before archdiocesan officials, and Heiss dispatched Vicar General Leonard Batz to determine the facts and render a judgement. Batz, a practical financier, used the best financial advantage for the parish as his chief criterion. When he learned that the sisters had actually donated land—thereby relieving the congregation of the expense—that settled the matter for him. He hurried back to Milwaukee and informed Heiss that the traditional site at the Mound should be retained. Heiss informed Father Jacobs of the decision and ordered him to inform his parishioners by reading his letter to them from the pulpit at Sunday Mass.[92]

Jacobs received the letter, but did not read it to his flock as directed. Instead he aligned himself with the Germans who wanted to move the church, and began collecting money for the project, carefully avoiding any of his well-to-do Irish parishioners. He then made a personal representation to Archbishop Heiss, insisting not only that parish opinion had decisively shifted in favor of a new site, but also that those who wanted it were willing to pay for the new church. He suggested that Batz's cost-benefit analysis was wrong, and in fact, even though the sisters had donated land, the Irish parishioners were not going to contribute to the new church. The earnest Jacobs must have been convincing and Heiss abruptly reversed his earlier decision. He approved the plans of Jacobs and the minority. When the news of this reversal was read in church on July 15, 1881, the parish was thrown into turmoil as Irish parishioners sought to understand what had happened.

Throughout the fall and winter of 1881-1882, their efforts to address Heiss by mail failed. The prelate was simply turning over the letters unopened to Jacobs, who read them and then lashed his opponents from the pulpit. When a delegation went to visit Heiss about the matter he slammed the door in their faces and refused to see them. On January 24, 1882, Jacobs closed St. Dominic's Church and refused to offer Mass on the "dissident" location. He set up shop at an alternative site in a schoolhouse the Germans had built and insisted that all parishioners of St. Dominic's come there. This left two-thirds of the congregation, the entire convent and the girls academy, which the sisters operated, without divine services. This drove the nuns to a near frenzy of worry (especially since the sisters could not make their weekly confessions). "For the first time in the history of our community," Mother Emily Power explained to the distraught Dominicans, "we are to be deprived of Mass."[93] Although she counseled the sisters to be "charitable" and speak little of the imbroglio, it is clear that passions were stoked. Mother Emily was so infuriated with the decision that she made the over 100-mile trek to Milwaukee in the win-

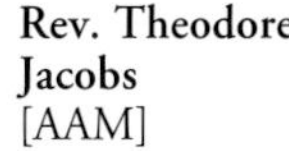
Rev. Theodore Jacobs
[AAM]

Mother Emily Power, OP [AOP-Sin]

ter to personally appeal to Heiss. He received her coldly and gave her no assurance.

The trustees of St. Dominic moved to refute Jacob's claim that they would not support a new church on the Mound site. As a sign of good faith they raised $6,850. But Heiss's ability to deal with the matter rationally was seriously impaired when former pastor James Cleary re-entered the fray with a controversial letter to a Galena, Illinois newspaper wondering "how the archbishop became so much opposed to the wishes of the majority ...?"[94] Cleary's tart words no doubt resurrected memories of the abuse Heiss had suffered in the public press from Fagan and others during the succession crisis. As a result, Heiss simply refused to deal with the trustees. Sick of appealing to Heiss, and anxious to show Jacobs they meant business, disgruntled Irish parishioners dismantled the old church and preserved portions of it for the new church they intended to build on the sisters property, with or without episcopal permission. This then triggered legal action. The church was not the property of the trustees, but belonged to Heiss who had received it from Henni upon the latter's death. Hence, the trustees were trespassing and dismantling property that was not in their legal possession.

Primed no doubt by Jacobs, Heiss attributed the actions of the trustees to the machinations of the Dominican sisters. In order to get at the trustees, Heiss ordered the sisters not to grant permission to build on their land.[95] At this point the sisters grew elusive: the builders of the new church were friends and neighbors. Moreover, the church provided religious services prescribed by their religious rule and also for the girls at the academy. Mother Emily was not about to take away the land and did what she could to explain things to Heiss. She wrote in June 1882, "The land desired was promised to the people by Father Cleary from the altar. That promise was repeated by Fr. Jacobs .... It was [given again] by Vicar General Very Rev. Fr. Batz when here last summer ...."[96] But her explanations only convinced Heiss that she and the entire community were deliberately flouting his authority.

Power and Heiss squared off for battle. Heiss was determined to make the sisters bend to his will, and demanded "Unless you stop that building, I will stop your convent." He also challenged the sisters to "go to law" [meaning, take it to court] if they disputed his right to order the affairs of the parish as he saw fit.[97] In retaliation, Power appealed for guidance from fellow Dominican Bishop Thomas Langton Grace, O.P., of St. Paul, and began to explore a new canonical status that would give her community a cardinal protector in Rome and liberation from Heiss's clutches. Grace replied sympathetically that he could not "account for the strange course of the archbishop except upon the ground that he might have been led to think or believe that the parties who were attempting to build a church in defiance of his authority were in some way encouraged in this by the community."[98] Eventually, through the help of the Dominican fathers, the Sinsinawa Dominicans managed to become a community of pontifical right, and escaped the direct jurisdiction of local Wisconsin bishops.

The standoff ended when Jacobs relented, heard the confessions, and celebrated Mass for the sisters and the academy girls. Mother Emily swore never to entrust the liturgical fate of her community to diocesan priests, and sought friendly Dominican priests to provide chaplaincy services to the sisters and the academy. Heiss continued to treat the sisters with coldness. He rejected an invitation to preside at the dedication of their new chapel in 1882, and petulantly refused to accord faculties (official permission granted by a bishop for the exercise of liturgical duties by another cleric) to any other bishop. This unkindly deprived the sisters of the kind of pomp and ceremony they relished on special occasions. In turning down the invitation to dedicate the new facility, Heiss noted curtly,

St. Mary Church, Fond du Lac [AAM]

"It is not necessary to state these reasons as I cannot think they are unknown to you."[99] Subsequent invitations to visit and inspect the convent were all turned down by an unforgiving Heiss.[100]

In the meantime, the men of the parish began to build the new St. Dominic's, a structure costing $10,500. Heiss, however, refused to allow the sacraments to be celebrated in the structure. In early 1883, he took the leader of the trustees, Joseph Vosberg, to court, claiming that the property they had despoiled was rightfully his. The case, *Heiss vs. Joseph Vosberg and others* was argued in the Grant County courthouse. At the same time both sides made an appeal to Rome. Heiss's lawyers insisted that even though the First

Plenary Council of Baltimore mandated that all church property be vested in the hands of the diocese, Heiss had a stronger claim in that he owned the property and building on the former St. Dominic site.[101] Heiss won his judgement in both civil and ecclesiastical courts, and the trustees were compelled to pay $200 in damages to the Milwaukee archbishop.[102] Heiss jubilantly informed the trustees that they would never receive a pastor. Efforts on the part of the trustees to appeal the original court decision and to seek redress from Rome met failure. The matter was unresolved when Heiss died in 1890. The next year, after having built a new church, Jacobs was transferred to Burlington. The church building on the Mound stood empty and unused until it was razed in 1912.[103]

Even worse were the difficulties that blew up at St. Mary's Church in Fond du Lac. Fond du Lac's Catholic community was growing and prospering. St. Patrick's Church was founded in 1855, St. Louis's in 1862, and a church for the Germans, St. Mary's, commenced in 1865.[104] Two religious orders living in the vicinity would also exercise an enormous sway over Fond du Lac's Catholic development: the Capuchin fathers and the Sisters of St. Agnes. The cause of trustee troubles in Fond du Lac came from the antagonism felt for the Capuchins by the pastor of St. Mary's Church, Father Nicholas Pickel. Pickel's animus against the Capuchins apparently related to their influence over the Agnesian sisters. Pickel lost no opportunity to heap scorn on the Capuchins—so much so that the friars protested to Henni, demanding retractions from the irascible Pickel. In 1879, after ignoring the name-calling for a while, Henni decided to act on the matter by removing Pickel and substituting Capuchin Father Haas—the chief object of Pickel's ire—as pastor of St. Mary's.

St. Dominic Church, Sinsinawa WI [AOP-Sin]

Haas accepted the assignment and sparks began to fly almost immediately, as the new pastor insisted on having the weekly collection turned over to his care. The parish trustees, partisans of Father Pickel, refused Haas's request. In retaliation, the Capuchins had the parish canonically transferred to their regime, thereby removing all doubt that parish revenues were rightfully theirs. The trustees fired back by incorporating the parish as a civil organization and thus out of the legal reach of the friars. Parish factions, already in place before the arrival of the Capuchins, hardened, and threats of violence at Sunday Mass prompted the need for policemen in the body of the church. Defiant parishioners held meetings forbidden by Father Haas, and in December 1879 Henni put the parish under interdict. Local pastors, like Joseph Keenan, fed the flames of antipathy toward the Capuchins by firing off letters to Henni accusing them of evil deeds. Henni made matters worse by constantly switching positions in the midst of the dispute. One reversal came when Henni asked the Capuchins to leave St. Mary's and to start another parish under their direction, promising them that he would not send a new priest to St. Mary's. The Capuchins evacuated the strife-torn parish and opened a new church, Sacred Heart, on the corner of Main and Merrill. However a confused Henni reversed himself and sent a new diocesan pastor, Father Sebastian Schwin, who took over St. Mary's and resumed verbal combat with the Capuchins. Finally, the Capuchins quit Sacred Heart, and Schwin was transferred. Peace soon returned to the Fond du Lac Catholic community.

The personal and legal battles which were waged over Sinsinawa and Fond du Lac, as well as the accumulated memories of other trustee "eruptions" of previous years, led Heiss to aggressively forestall any reoccurrence. In January 1883, a bill was introduced into the Wisconsin Legislature to incorporate churches according to a trustee arrangement that favored episcopal control.[105] This law was enacted in the summer of 1883, placing the archbishop, vicar general, pastor, and two lay trustees on the board of every parish.[106] Heiss then informed each parish of the new law and insisted that each one organize itself according to its demands.[107] He also devised a pamphlet laying out the new structures of governance. By August the *Catholic Citizen* reported, "We have it from reliable authority that with two exceptions, the Catholic congregations of all the large cities and towns in the archdiocese have applied for Articles of Incorporation." However it did note that "Some opposition is made by a few parties, but it is mainly due to a want of the proper understanding of the law."[108]

Rev. Joseph J. Keenan [AAM]

Indeed, some resistance to the new program continued. The trustees in Sinsinawa built the new church despite Heiss's orders not to do so.[109] St. Stanislaus in Milwaukee simply ignored the order to reorganize and incorporate themselves according to the new law. Nonetheless, by September 1883 Heiss managed to convince most of the parishes to incorporate and dispatched former seminary professor, Jodok Birkhauser, to the offices of the secretary of state in Madison with a large bundle of incorporation papers.[110]

These laws applied only to churches, however, and in the 1890s the need for a diocesan form of incorporation was made evident when Archbishop Frederick Katzer ran into tax problems related to his episcopal residence. If church buildings were not incorporated according to the law, they risked losing the tax-exempt status that many of them needed.[111] However, only when Katzer was on his deathbed and worried about the orderly transfer of property were steps taken to create a separate archdiocesan corporation with the archbishop, the vicar general and one of the consultors as members of the board of directors. Katzer also carefully listed the archdiocesan properties held in his name that were to be transferred to his successor.[112]

St. Rose Church, Racine [AAM]

The impact of these incorporation arrangements were helpful to the bishop in asserting legal rights over parishes. However, they also made the bishop liable for parish financial disasters. This became evident during the Depression era when a number of parishes that had borrowed heavily in the 1920s experienced serious difficulties paying their debts. Archbishop Samuel A. Stritch, archbishop from 1930 to 1940, explained to a fellow bishop the nature of the Milwaukee parish corporation system, "While each corporation was independent, the law did provide that the bishop of the diocese was a sort of underlying trustee for each parish. In trying to maintain the credit of the whole and to prevent the collapse of weak parishes, he experienced some difficulty and was not able to call on the resources in the treasuries of the strong parish corporations."[113]

There were occasional problems under the trustee system as well. One of the most widely publicized involved Father John B. Piette, pastor of St. Rose of Lima parish in Racine from 1921 to 1923. Piette had succeeded to the Irish church after the death of longtime pastor John M. Naughton. The Montreal-born Piette had come to Wisconsin and served at parishes in Chippewa Falls, Fond du Lac and Watertown. He had also served a stint as a chaplain in World War I. When he returned from service, he hoped to return to Watertown, but Messmer dispatched him to Racine. He later claimed that he was not interested in going to the church because other clergy had warned him that the parish was factionalized between Irish nationalists and "those who love the church."[114] Piette also came to Racine with a reputation of being a martinet. His unbending personality appeared already while he was stationed at Chippewa Falls. He cancelled the parish's Midnight Mass at Christmas in 1907 because town saloon keepers had refused to close their establishments during the service. Criticized by the local newspaper, Piette was soon compelled to leave town.[115] Disconsolate over the St. Rose assignment, he found all was not well in Racine. He claimed that the rectory and church were in a sorry state of repair and even more importantly he began to run into conflicts with the two trustees Dennis Fitzgerald and John Olle. Fitzgerald, who had also had run-ins with the late Father Naughton, withheld the books from the new pastor and when Piette grew insistent on seeing them, allegedly informed the priest, "No damned Frenchman will ever see the books of record of the church." Piette began to suspect that church finances were not in order and wanted an audit without Fitzgerald present. He noted as well what he perceived to be discrepancies in a collection taken for St. Benedict the Moor Mission. Tensions grew sharper between the pastor and the trustee and at one point when the priest went to wipe his brow after an argument with the trustee, Fitzgerald thought the priest was reaching for a revolver. From the pulpit Piette compared the dissident trustees to Judas and called them hypocrites. Fitzgerald sued the pastor and won a $16,000 judgement against him for libel in a Racine court.[116] Piette appealed the decision to the state Supreme Court and the parish remained in turmoil for an entire year. In a final act of defiance, the dissident trustees held an election and ordered Piette out of the parish. Messmer sent a notice to the parish calling for a new election and insisting that they find a peaceful solution.[117] Finally, in late June Piette was transferred to Portage and the dissident trustees withdrew.[118] Pastor-trustee controversies continued, but few with such drama.

Besides trustee issues, further administrative reforms were effected. These included the development of a small chancery operation, the holding of archives, the appointment of a full-time secretary to the prelate and the creation of a system of deaneries around the archdiocese that would help extend the administrative reach of Heiss.[119] Two major clusters of issues were at Heiss's door: ethnicity and schools. Both of them would pose serious challenges, but we shall examine them in detail later.

After the furor that engulfed the question of succession, Heiss's term was relatively devoid of major intra-diocesan conflicts. In part, most of the protagonists had left the diocese and the other "conspirators" were quiescent.[120] Other areas of archdiocesan life began to develop. The Milwaukee See matured rapidly. The emergence of a Catholic press was one sign.

The Catholic Press

German Catholic newspapers dominated the majority of Catholic reading in the archdiocese of Milwaukee. Milwaukee Catholics read Henni's *Der Wahrheits-Freund* which he had started in Cincinnati in 1837. In 1851, he launched another German Catholic paper, *Der Seebote*. In response to a more militant German secular press, German Catholics founded another paper, *Excelsior,* in January 1873, and in the same year *Columbia*. On the pages of these weeklies were chronicled events in German parishes, national issues, and serials, essays and commentary. To keep English speakers informed, Henni helped found the *Star of Bethlehem*, a monthly paper that first rolled off the presses in October 1869 under the direction of two brothers, George and Thomas St. Louis. This "review of Catholic news and events" lasted until 1871. Another paper, printed in Monroe by Father John Casey and a physician named David Nolan, was the more militant *Catholic Vindicator*. It first appeared in 1870 and became a vigorous champion of Irish causes. In October 1871, Edward Bray and R.B. Johnson took over the struggling *Star of Bethlehem* and merged it with the *Catholic Vindicator*, which they had already secured. Retaining both of the names on a single masthead at first, the paper had a mixed

Die Katholische Kirche

in den

Vereinigten Staaten.

(Ein Büchlein,
darinnen auch zwischen den Zeilen zu lesen.)

Von

J. Gmeiner,

Priester der Erzdiöcese Milwaukee und

Redakteur der

„Columbia“,

415 Ostwasserstraße, Milwaukee, Wis.

Preis dieser Schrift 20 Cents; portofrei nach irgend einem Orte in den Ver. Staaten.

Milwaukee, Wisconsin.
Columbia-Office, 415 Ostwasser-Straße.

ST. FRANCIS SEMINARY SALZMANN LIBRARY ST. FRANCIS, WIS.

[AAM]

[AAM]

THE CATHOLIC CITIZEN.

GOD AND OUR COUNTRY

VOL. X--NO. 33. MILWAUKEE, JULY 3, 1880. Price, 5 Cents.

board including Casey and Nolan as editors, Johnson as business manager and Bray as secretary. In 1874, Casey resigned from the paper, leaving all editorial duties to Nolan who dropped the *Star of Bethlehem* and simply called the paper the *Catholic Vindicator.* The paper reported on a variety of church events, but continued the special attention it had given to the cause of a free Ireland. In November 1878, Father George Willard and Bray took control of the paper and renamed it the *Catholic Citizen.* In this phase of the English-speaking paper's history, it served as an important medium of Willard's temperance activities. As we have seen, it also provided him a forum to discuss the ethno-cultural issues surrounding the Henni/Heiss succession.[121]

Humphrey J. Desmond, editor of the *Catholic Citizen* newspaper [Harry Heming (ed.). *Catholic Church in Wisconsin,* Catholic Historical Publishing Co., 1898, p. 1092]

The *Catholic Citizen* retained the *Vindicator's* strong interest in Irish affairs. It also inherited a strong circulation list of 8,500, which included subscriptions in Wisconsin, Illinois, Michigan, Iowa, Kansas, Nebraska and southern Minnesota. Following Willard's lead, the paper was also a strong proponent of temperance. In 1882 when Willard quit the diocese for South Dakota, Bray retained ownership and direction of the paper, although he kept Willard's name on the ownership masthead, and the paper continued to prosper, swelling the number of readers until it could boast it had the largest circulation for a Catholic paper west of New York.

In 1880, Humphrey J. Desmond joined the paper as the chief editorial writer. When the paper underwent a reorganization and incorporation in 1891, Desmond acquired control and became president and general manager of the Citizen Company. Over his nearly fifty years of editorial control, the *Catholic Citizen* became one of the leading Catholic newspapers in the country.[122] The paper maintained rugged independence and at the same time a healthy respect for the Catholic hierarchy, reflecting a common practice among Catholic journalists of the 19th and 20th centuries. Desmond wrote 15,000 editorial columns and 2,500 columns of brief news.[123]

Desmond was one of the best representatives of articulate and influential Catholic laity for over a generation. His roots were Irish. His grandfather, for whom he was named, arrived in the United States in 1829 and settled first in Canada, then in upstate New York, and finally in 1842 in Ozaukee

County, Wisconsin. Working a 160-acre farm, the Desmond family was occasionally the host to visiting priests who celebrated Mass for local Catholic settlers. Henni himself visited the house from time-to-time.

Humphrey's father, Thomas, married Johanna Bowe an Irish immigrant, and the two moved to Milwaukee in 1866, after producing three children. Thomas worked in a variety of clerical jobs, including clerk and secretary of the local public school board. When a Republican city vote swept the Democratic Desmond from office in 1880, he went to work as the Wisconsin manager for the Connecticut Mutual Life Insurance Company. The Desmonds became solid members of the Cathedral of St. John.

Young Humphrey, born September 14, 1858, grew up in an intellectually stimulating environment where issues of politics, Irish nationalism, and Catholicism were discussed at great length. Desmond attended public schools for all his life and received his college education at the University of Wisconsin where he took an active role in the popular debating society, Hesperia, and met, among others, the famed Wisconsin historian Frederick Jackson Turner. Desmond's editorial skills were first tried when he became the editor of the University Press, a bimonthly publication of the student body. Desmond received his degree in 1880, and in 1881 he was admitted to the Wisconsin Bar. His career in law and subsequently politics, allowed him to become a first-hand participant in two issues that directly affected Catholic life in Wisconsin. When he joined the law firm of Flanders and Bottum, he participated in the Edgerton Bible Case, a lawsuit filed by Catholics who objected to bible reading in public schools. In 1883, following the example of his father, he became a member of the Milwaukee School Board and remained there until he was elected to the Wisconsin Assembly in 1890. His brief legislative career allowed him to write the alternative compulsory education legislation that removed the offensive Bennett Law, which was seen as a blow to German-language private schools. He also assisted in the shaping of the Wisconsin Freedom of Worship Law. It was at about this time as well that he acquired the ownership of the *Catholic Citizen* and participated in the establishment of the Catholic Press Association.

Desmond married Susan Ryan of Oshkosh and the couple bore six children. As a young man, Desmond was deeply influenced by the ethos of progressive social reform that enveloped the University of Wisconsin campus and the state in the latter years of the 19th and the early years of the 20th century. This reforming impulse strongly affirmed the American way of life, and insisted on a program of reforms to make the country more democratic, efficient, and more thoroughly Americanized. Desmond adapted this Progressive ideology to his Catholic identity. In his editorial columns, and in particular in his understanding of the role of the Church in society, he was, as Richard Scheiber suggests, a thoroughgoing Americanist—one in sympathy with the sentiments of those who wanted to see a greater adaptation of Catholic life and practice to the American environment. Although not uncritical of certain government policies and programs, Desmond provides probably the best insight into the mind-set of a growing number of professional and middle class Catholic citizens.

Desmond continually expanded and improved the offerings of the paper, and provided a role model for other lay journalists around the country with whom he maintained an active correspondence and association through the Catholic Press Association. He emulated the practice of secular newspapers by providing specialized "departments" for various constituencies: one for youth, one for women and another for young men, sectional reports on various church activities, and serialized short stories that dramatized religious themes. For the historian of the archdiocese of Milwaukee, Desmond's viewpoints, expressed in the weekly column "Local Church News," provide virtually the only window into the non-German-speaking world of the local Catholic Church. His paper provided a strong counter-weight to the powerful German-language press that still flourished in the Wisconsin church until the 20th century. Desmond recruited writers from among popular American Catholic figures, such as literary giant and ambassador Maurice Francis Egan, an important figure in the emergence of lay Catholic journalism in America and an important Catholic voice in public affairs. The *Catholic Citizen* was a paper of, by, and for the laity; and Desmond intended it "to make, educate, and stimulate an intelligent, reasoning and loyal Catholic laity."[124]

Desmond settled down to full-time work with the paper after he left the Wisconsin Legislature in the 1890s. He also found time to author several books on various subjects. Blending his legal knowledge with his love for the Church, he wrote a book *The Church and the Law*, and took an especially careful look at anti-Catholicism through *The Know Nothing Party and The A.P.A. Movement: A Sketch* (1912). His Irish nationalism found expression in the playful *Why God Loves the Irish* (1918). Desmond showed his grasp of history with *Curious Chapters in American History* (1924) and published compilations of his editorials and ventured into moral exhortation with such works as *Your Better Self* (1918) and *Ways of Courage* (1927).

Under Desmond the paper grew dramatically, surpassing 26,000 subscribers by the time he died. As his financial condition improved, Desmond began absorbing other smaller Catholic newspapers to make them part of a Catholic journalism empire. In 1898 the *Citizen* took over the *Omaha Chronicle*. That was followed by the *Detroit Witness*, the *Catholic Review* from Brooklyn, and the *Catholic American* from New York. In 1902 he absorbed the *Catholic Voice* of Green Bay. Soon Desmond was able to adapt the *Catholic Citizen's* generic news reporting with the local interests of other markets, and a chain of papers developed under his direct control: the *Northwestern Chronicle* in St. Paul; the *New Century* in Washington, D.C.; the *Catholic Journal of the New South* in Memphis; and the *Iowa Catholic Citizen* headquartered in Sioux City. All of these papers ceased to exist when the *Citizen* merged with the archdiocese of Milwaukee's *Catholic Herald* in 1935. By that time, however, Humphrey J. Desmond was dead and the heyday of lay-controlled, independent Catholic newspapers was past. Nonetheless, Desmond and his papers would play a role in the unfolding issues of Catholic life for years to come.

Nationality and the Schools: Milwaukee in the National Eye

Archbishop Heiss's own unflinching support of German language preservation was joined at the hip by his equally strong support for Catholic schools.

The dispute that erupted over the succession to Henni between 1878 and 1866 turned out to be one of the first signs of a serious fissure between German- and English-speaking Catholics in American Catholic history. Heiss's struggle to perpetuate Henni's pro-German policy catapulted him into the national eye. The question of German bishops in the hierarchy, which had incited the activism of the English-speaking clergy of Milwaukee in 1878-1880, now engaged the Germans nationally. Although they felt secure in Milwaukee and a few other places around the country, overall, German Catholic leaders felt increasingly beleaguered when they compared their status and numbers in the hierarchy with those of other Catholic ethnic groups. In 1886 of the 69 bishops in the United States, 35 were Irish and 15 were German-speaking. The French had 11, the English 5, and the Dutch, Scots, and Spanish 1 apiece. The sense of being cheated of a proportional number of bishops relative to their numbers in the wider American Church began to grow among the Germans. When these feelings reached a critical mass, they did what they always did best: organize. The archbishops of Milwaukee became the de facto leaders of the German struggle for recognition and rights within the Church in the United States.

Rumblings of renewed nationality troubles involving Milwaukee Catholics began in St. Louis, where English-German tensions had been building for a time. In July 1883, Catholic journalist and historian, John Gilmary Shea, had published an inflammatory article in the *American Catholic Quarterly Review* entitled "Converts—Their Influence and Work in the Country."[125] In this lengthy piece, Shea lamented the fate of converts to the Catholic faith who found themselves isolated among their foreign-born coreligionists, especially Germans, unless they learned the language and culture of the foreign-born. He likewise worried that not enough American-born bishops were being appointed to represent the Church in America.

Response to the Shea article came from the pages of *Das Pastoral Blatt*, a monthly theological magazine. Founded by Heiss in Milwaukee in 1866, its first editor was Father Henry Muhlsiepen of St. Louis, a priest of the St. Louis archdiocese. The magazine was transferred to St. Louis, but drew heavily from the German-speaking faculty of St. Francis Seminary for many of its articles. In 1873, Father William Farber of St. Louis took over the periodical and made it an important mouthpiece for German concerns in the American Church. Two rebuttals were published to the Shea piece, one by Farber and another by former Milwaukee priest and seminary rector, Father Innocent (Christopher) Wapelhorst, O.F.M. Their two-part article entitled "Clerical Know Nothingism in the Catholic Church," compared Shea's criticisms with the attacks of the now discredited anti-Catholic movement of the 1850s. The article rebutted Shea's charges of German clannishness, and discounted fears that Germans were perpetuating their culture to an unhealthy degree. They turned Shea's argument of "leakage" from the Church against him, and said that the reason Catholics were abandoning the flock was that their cultural and linguistic needs were not being attended to properly. Farber and Wapelhorst urged a slower pace to inevitable Americanization: "How in the future different nationalities will unite harmoniously into one people, what is to become of different languages, of the German churches and schools, will all be arranged later on. Forcible, premature interference is always dangerous. 'In nature there is no leap.'"[126]

Both men took aim at the practice of St. Louis churches (since 1842) of assigning an inferior or "succursal" status to German ethnic churches while English-speaking churches had the status of regular parishes. The Germans came to resent the status of implied subservience (and the limitations on fund-raising) that occurred under this system. No German priest wanted to defer to an Irish pastor, much less account to him for funds raised and disbursed. *Pastoral Blatt* asked for full autonomy for German congregations.[127]

Three months after these articles appeared, 82 priests of the diocesan and religious clergy of St. Louis drew up a petition to present to Simeoni on the question of succursal parishes. Vicar General Henry Muhlsiepen, a well-known defender of German rights, supported the petition, and both he and Father Farber pressed it in Rome in the summer of 1884. Cardinal Simeoni referred the matter back to the archbishops of the United States. Cardinal Gibbons, who served as convener and papal delegate for the Third Plenary Council of Baltimore that met from November to December 1884, referred the German parish question to a committee that included Archbishop Heiss, but no mention was made of it in the conciliar deliberations. The council fathers decided to leave the matter to the resolution of each local bishop.

Although the succursal parish matter did not arise, it colored other issues raised at the plenary council. Heiss gave considerable attention to an issue that had ethnic overtones, the question of schools. He favored their expansion and supported strongly the council's most controversial policy that every parish have a school.[128] But the peaceful approach of the council fathers toward the nationality question belied its explosive importance, and failed to take notice of the growing polarization of the nationality issue in the American Church.

By the end of the Baltimore Council, American bishops Joseph Dwenger, C.Pp.S.,

.of Fort Wayne and John Moore of St. Augustine were sent to Rome to convey the decrees of the council to Roman authorities for final approval. They were later joined by Bishop Richard Gilmour of Cleveland. All of these bishops became intensely aware that the complaints of German priests and laity in America were receiving a sympathetic hearing in Rome. The key German advocate was Cardinal Joseph Hergenroether, who had helped to secure Heiss's nomination in 1880. Other pro-German bishops were the Jesuit Cardinal Johann Baptist Franzelin and Cardinals Paulus Melchers and Mieceslaus Ledochowski, both exiles of Otto von Bismarck's *kulturkampf.* Gilmour and Moore took the extraordinary step of writing a memorial (or position paper) on the status of the Germans in America, refuting allegations of discrimination against German-speaking Catholics and pointing out how Germans insisted that a parish be totally German, even if it contained other nationalities. Most notably they pointed to the provinces of Cincinnati and Milwaukee, "There are seventeen bishops, of whom nine are German and only one Irish, whilst at least half of the Catholic population in these two Provinces is Irish."[129] Milwaukee was again and again targeted as a prime example of all that was wrong with excessive German nationalism in the American Church. "We have heard it said and we regard it as true," Gilmour and Moore reported to Roman officials at Propaganda, "that the archbishop of Milwaukee, Msgr. [*sic*] Henni, asserted that no Irishman would ever occupy his throne."[130] Most damning was the assertion that the rector of St. Francis Seminary, science and mathematics teacher Monsignor Augustine Zeininger, "advised [English-speaking] students of that institution to be incardinated into other dioceses."[131]

Debate over Catholic Schools

Linked with the issue of ethnicity was a serious debate among Catholic bishops over Catholic schools.

Although Bishop John Carroll had made the creation of schools a priority in his work in Baltimore, Catholic schools associated with parishes only began to develop when the common or public school became a part of American life. In the 1840s in New York, Bishop John Hughes took an important stand for separate schools and insisted that Catholics be given a share of public monies collected for education. When this was denied, Catholics became even more fixed on providing alternatives to public education. The rise of concerted anti-Catholic movements, like the Know-Nothings, also contributed to the desire for Catholic schools. Common school teaching staff and boards of education often included many openly anti-Catholic members and evangelical Protestants who insisted on hymn singing and bible reading in public school classrooms and interpretations of world history that consistently portrayed the Catholic Church as an enemy of human freedom. In 1844, Catholic discontent with the reading of the King James version of the Bible in Philadelphia's public schools led to violent clashes with Protestants. Increasingly, through the legislation of the plenary councils of Baltimore (1851 and 1866), Catholic bishops urged their flocks to build Catholic schools. Teaching orders of women and men came to the United States and opened up schools in various dioceses. In 1876, Roman authorities urged that Catholics in the United States make the establishment of schools a priority, and pressed harder on Catholic parents to send their children to these schools.[132]

Thanks to Henni's successful recruitment of teaching sisterhoods, Milwaukee had a substantial investment in Catholic schools long before the 1876 decree. German parishes took the lead in this, viewing the Catholic school as the best means of perpetuating the faith through the retention of German cultural identity. In addition, battles with local Forty-Eighters and other advocates of public education led many German-speaking Catholics to view the public school system as a source of secularism. German-speaking bishops, priests and sisters insisted that Catholic schools were the best way to retain the loyalty of the young and resisted the encroachments of the state on their right to educate. This lasted a long time. Even in the 20th century Milwaukee Catholics looked askance on such programs as free textbooks. Archbishop Sebastian Messmer lobbied against a proposal to provide free textbooks and informed the governor: "I can assure you that Catholics as a body are strongly opposed to any such measure, which we consider socialistic in tendency, absolutely unjust to Catholic citizens, and entirely unnecessary."[133]

English-speaking Catholics did not reject Catholic schools, but did not see them as the pressing priority that German speakers did. In fact, a schism existed for many years over attendance at Catholic schools between the English-speaking and the Germans. Archbishop Michael Heiss had noted already in 1844, "If our Catholic Children are to be instructed in the catechism, the Catholics have to support their own schools .... But not all of our Catholics are zealous enough to make these sacrifices."[134] Father Joseph Salzmann too was worried: "The laity do not seem willing to entrust us with the young generation upon whom I build my hopes. Attendance at school and interest in educational matters is far from being what I desire."[135] English-speaking Catholics around the diocese continued to send their children to public schools believing the public institutions to be worthwhile, and resisting the Germanizing elements of Milwaukee's Catholic school network.

Archbishop Henni made some limited efforts to bring English-speaking Catholics more closely into the archdiocesan fold when he established the *Star of Bethlehem* in 1869. This paper, for English-speaking Catholics, began to press English-speaking parents to send their children to Catholic schools by attacking the common schools. Its successor the *Catholic Vindicator* (formed in 1871) kept up the drumfire of support for Catholic schools among the English-speaking, urging Catholic parents to support Catholic schools as a way to preserve the faith and culture of Catholicism in America. It urged Catholic parents to "cast off [their] lethargy and to reject the "flimsy arguments of liberal Catholicism," and to support the schools.[136] Further efforts were made by the *Vindicator's* successor, the *Catholic Citizen*, which even secured a benefactor who promised a $100 bonus to any parish that formed a Catholic school of brick or stone, had 75 pupils and taught classes in English. No one took the offer. English-speaking parents continued to be convinced of the adequacy, if not the superiority, of the common schools, and did not want the heavy financial burden of a school. Some simply resented the German domination of the schools and did not want "Dutch" sisters teaching their children.

Archbishop Michael Heiss also tried to use strong methods to shore up the schools. In August 1881 he resurrected a decree that Archbishop Henni had issued in 1875 mandating that the confirmation of all Catholic school children had to be preceded by at least one year's attendance in a Catholic school. The decree, issued before Henni's death, created some furor, including some stinging comments in the ever-critical *Milwaukee Sentinel.* Heiss quickly retreated, learning that it is was one thing to promulgate decrees and another to enforce them. School issues were paramount for him, however, and in 1883 he formed a school board "to examine the prospective teachers for Catholic schools, to regulate courses of study, and to promote high standards of education generally ...."[137] The board was urged to develop a uniform course of study throughout the diocese and to provide for graded transitions for each age group. The board met infrequently, and had limited influence over the highly localized practices of parish schools and the efforts of the various teaching communities to standardize and coordinate teaching practice. Later, efforts toward archdiocesan coordination of school endeavors took place with the establishment of a school superintendency in the 1920s.

The cause of Catholic education received an important boost in 1884 at the Third Plenary Council of Baltimore. In its most controversial mandate, each parish was expected to establish a school. In Milwaukee, Heiss enthusiastically embraced this decree and began to press for new Catholic schools, especially among the English-speaking parishes. Heiss and the other German-speaking bishops were strong in their support of this policy. But so also were bishops like Bernard McQuaid of Rochester and Michael Corrigan of New York. Disagreements over school policy would be an important part of internal church conflict.

Further Fallout

The growing antipathy between Irish and German elements in the hierarchy and the clergy found another flashpoint in Milwaukee in 1886 when Heiss convened his suffragans for a provincial council in Milwaukee.[138] This included the bishops of La Crosse and Green Bay, as well as the bishops of Minnesota, the vicar apostolic of the Dakotas, and one of the leaders of the "Americanist" faction of the hierarchy, John Ireland of St. Paul. The encounter was anything but pleasant. Ireland was restive under Heiss's leadership and was already scheming to detach St. Paul from Milwaukee jurisdiction in order to bring "discipline" to "unruly" German elements in Minnesota. Disturbing as well were the blunt criticisms by Bishop Martin Marty, vicar apostolic of the Dakotas (and the author of a complimentary biography of John Martin Henni), for Heiss's policy of using German in religious instruction. By this time, Marty complained, few American-born children of German families were capable of understanding the language (and in particular the nuances used in catechisms and biblical texts that are often difficult to discern in English). He commented sarcastically that because of the perpetuation of this practice "there was a lapsed German Catholic in every second house in Milwaukee."[139] Heiss acceded to the request for a new division of territories, and in 1888 the pallium of an archbishop was conferred on John Ireland. Martin Marty was now his suffragan and not Heiss's.[140]

The Abbelen Memorial: A Milwaukee Context

The simmering ethnic conflict now began to flare in public. Germans around the country mobilized to resist the Irish "Hibernarchy," while English-speaking bishops, priests and laity warned darkly of "foreign conspiracies" and "sauerkraut churches." After the 1886 provincial council, Heiss realized that strong leaders like Ireland could topple the hard-won accomplishments of German bishops, priests, and religious. Even German speakers, like Swiss-born Bishop Martin Marty, were "taken in" by arguments for greater Americanization. When news of the Moore-Gilmour Memorial of 1885 began to seep back to the United States, German-speaking priests and others began to consider a formal appeal to Propaganda on the question of parish rights. At the heart of their demands was an insistence that German-language parishes enjoy the same rights as English-language territorial parishes: fund-raising, status of pastors, rights to baptize and marry—and over all, a right to exist as a separate agency for the preservation of German Catholic faith. In the Milwaukee archdiocese this was no problem.

First Provincial Council, held in Milwaukee from May 23-30, 1886
[AAM]

Rev. Peter Abbelen [AAM]

German parishes and English-speaking parishes were treated equally in all these regards. Indeed, because of the demographic realities of Wisconsin, German parishes and priests enjoyed a hegemony not known in other areas of German strength in the United States. In fact, the archbishops of Milwaukee were seen as the leaders of the German Catholic cause.

Heiss took the lead in the defense of Germans, and he was assisted by the long-serving chaplain of the Notre Dame motherhouse, Father Peter Abbelen, who played an important role in articulating German parochial rights. Abbelen would pen an important memorial in 1886, with the blessing and even the assistance of Archbishop Heiss, that would attempt to refute the Gilmour-Moore efforts of the previous year. By bringing the needs of German Catholics in America to the attention of the Holy See, Abbelen found himself at the center of a nationwide discussion on the role and pace of ethnic identity in the American Catholic Church.

Abbelen was born in Duelke in the Rhineland on August 8, 1843. While a student at Muenster, he responded to a request from Father Salzmann and came to America in 1866. Ordained by Henni on January 24, 1868, Abbelen taught briefly in the seminary. When seminary rector Heiss was made bishop of La Crosse, he asked Abbelen to come with him to the new see, and Abbelen obliged, serving as a parish priest in Chippewa Falls, La Crosse and Prairie du Chien. The harsh Wisconsin climate nearly killed Abbelen and he was forced to recoup his health in Alabama. In 1876, after Father Francis X. Krautbauer, chaplain to the Notre Dame sisters, was made the second bishop of Green Bay, Abbelen was released by Heiss to replace him. Until his death in 1917 he was an important figure in the growing Notre Dame community. He became a close friend of Mother Caroline Friess and her inner circle and worked well with her. His primary work with the sisters was to provide spiritual direction and liturgical services. But the Notre Dame community was expanding in those days, and requests for new missions were pouring into the motherhouse daily. He often helped the sisters evaluate new offers for schools and assignments in various areas of the country. Abbelen traveled to New Orleans, Minnesota, to the west and to the east on behalf of the sisters. In the days when the sisters purchased and supplied their own convents on parish grounds, Abbelen helped to negotiate the property deals and the construction. He even helped oversee some of the building of additions to the Milwaukee motherhouse and added his own special legacy on the devotional life of the sisters with his design of the motherhouse's perpetual adoration chapel and its Marian shrine. Abbelen lived in a book-lined house on Jefferson Street where he authored short spiritual works, and a popular catechism. He also offered hospitality to visiting priests and bishops. His friendship with Heiss grew over the years, and as we have seen, he played a major role in securing the Milwaukee See for his old teacher and friend. Heiss, who often celebrated daily Mass at the Notre Dame convent, saw and spoke with Abbelen freely. In 1884, Abbelen accompanied Heiss as his personal theologian to the Third Plenary Council of Baltimore.

At the urging of the German priests in Milwaukee, Cincinnati, and St. Louis, and other places, Abbelen undertook a refutation of the Gilmour-Moore Memorial and wished to deliver his response to Cardinal Giovanni Simeoni at Propaganda in Rome. With Heiss's encouragement, and maybe his help, the chaplain drew up the famous "Abbelen Memorial" which argued vigorously on behalf of the rights of German priests and parishes.[141] Abbelen insisted that German parishes be independent entities with the rights and privileges of English-speaking territorial parishes, including a parity in the appointment of "irremovable rectors," permanent pastors approved by the Third Plenary Council of Baltimore.[142] He urged that special vicars general for Germans be appointed in dioceses where there was a sizeable number of German speakers and where neither the bishop nor vicar general spoke German. Overall, he urged a slower pace to Americanization and a healthy respect for the rights of foreign-born Catholics and those caught in the twilight zone of bilingual/bicultural identity. He argued for the retention of German churches, schools, priests, and sisters. "Wherever that most sad dictum 'let them learn English,' has prevailed or now prevails, there has been and there will be, a truly deplorable falling away of [Germans] from the church."[143]

Although the text reflected the experience of many German-speaking Catholics around the United States (and Abbelen had contact with many, since the Notre Dame sisters were quite widely scattered), it also reflected his experiences with German Catholicism within the archdiocese of Milwaukee. Few people other than the bishop had as much contact with the day-to-day affairs, needs, complaints and successes of German parishes in Milwaukee and the Midwest as did Abbelen. Years of patient listening to the reports of Mother Caroline Friess and the School Sisters of Notre Dame of conditions in Wisconsin and in other parts of the country revealed problems of opposition and turmoil over Catholic schools. He noted, with an obvious reference to the pesky Forty-Eighters, who still annoyed the School Sisters and howled catcalls at Catholic priests on the streets of Milwaukee, that Germans were threatened by "infidels" who spoke German and who did everything to lure German Catholics away from their loyalty to the Church.[144] Abbelen's memorial stirred up a hornet's nest of opposition from English-speaking bishops and clergy, and once again events that emanated in Milwaukee served as a flashpoint for building tensions around the country

At the same time that Abbelen was drafting his memorial, the question of the rights of

German parishes had been directly posed to Propaganda by Heiss's suffragan, Bishop Kilian Flasch of La Crosse. Flasch had asked whether there could be more than one parish in a given territory; and whether children born to parents of a given national origin should be obliged to attend national parishes as long as they remained under the jurisdiction of their parents.[145] Propaganda referred the matter to the American archbishops in 1886. These prelates, facing other ethnic groups besides the Germans, readily agreed to the proposal to establish national parishes that overlapped with territorial ones, and "wished only to preserve the right of the parents to send their children to the school of another parish and the right of grown children to choose to attend their territorial parish."[146] Indeed, before Abbelen brought his memorial to Rome, two of the items on his agenda had already been settled.

Yet difficulties for both Heiss and Abbelen were in the making. Heiss made no secret of his support for Abbelen's memorial and scratched *Legi et approbavi*—"I have read and approved"—on the top of the draft. In preparation for his trip to Rome, Abbelen traveled to Baltimore to secure the support of Archbishop Gibbons (newly created as a cardinal), who also gave his approval to the document and to Abbelen's plans to carry it to Propaganda.[147] However, once he got to Rome, trouble erupted.

Abbelen arrived in Rome while Bishop John Ireland and Bishop John Keane of Richmond were there discussing the charter of the proposed new Catholic University of America. Alerted to the petition, Ireland and Keane obtained a copy of the memorial and cabled warnings to Gibbons and others at home about it. Both prelates decried the "secrecy" of the proposal and insisted that it was part of a larger conspiracy of Germans of which Abbelen was "a secret emissary."[148] Ireland and Keane did not even wait to consult with other bishops; they simply drew up a counterblast that they submitted to Propaganda.[149] As they refuted the arguments of Abbelen and the "German clique" he represented, they made special allusions to conditions in the Milwaukee See. For example, they pointed out that not all German speakers felt so strongly about the perpetuation of German language as did Abbelen and Heiss, singling out Vicar General Leonard Batz as a representative of a moderate "German-American party that was increasing in the Milwaukee See from day to day."[150] They cited the membership of the School Sisters of Notre Dame, Abbelen's own charges. Of the 1,110 members of the congregation, Ireland and Keane noted that "several hundred are of Irish or American language." But despite this, "the language of the prayers, of the meditations, of the retreats, of all the spiritual exercises of these Sisters is German, although the order has been established in American for thirty-five years."[151] They noted other damning facts about the hegemony of Germans in Wisconsin: that Heiss had made the German church of St. Joseph his cathedral, rather than the existing English church of St. Mary's in La Crosse; in Green Bay, English was never heard from the cathedral pulpit. They repeated Henni's canard, given in the heat of the succession crisis, that "never would an Irishman sit upon his episcopal throne." Likewise, they declared that English-speaking young men were not welcome at St. Francis Seminary, that German speakers in churches drove away English speakers and potential converts to the faith. "It is a common saying in America, that in going to Milwaukee one goes to Germany."[152]

In a damning indictment of Heiss' mental acuity and political savvy, James Keane had written to Cardinal Henry Manning in February 1887, "Some German ecclesiastics, using the poor old Archbishop of Milwaukee as a tool, had secretly sent an emissary to represent the Hierarchy of the United States as hostile and unjust to German Catholics ...."[153] But despite Keane's disbelief that Heiss could actually do something like this, the Milwaukee prelate's support for German-speaking hegemony in Milwaukee was in fact unquestioned. For example, in Fond du Lac he implemented one of the proposals in the memorial when he insisted that no territorial parish could accept a member of a national parish without securing permission from the national pastor.[154] In fact, as historian Gerald Fogarty has noted, the Abbelen Memorial was warmly backed by a number of German bishops, including Bishop Frederick X. Katzer of Green Bay, who wrote to Propaganda asking them to accept all its propositions.[155]

The denouement of the Abbelen Memorial was somewhat anticlimactic. After the vigorous representations of Ireland and Keane, and the intervention of Gibbons (who was embarrassed that he gave Abbelen his approval to travel to Rome), Propaganda looked for a way to sidestep the document. As it turned out, two of the key issues, the status of parishes and the rights of school attendance, had been resolved even before Abbelen got to Rome. The other demands of the petition were set aside. Still the aftermath of the memorial left a legacy of raw feelings and bitterness between two factions in the hierarchy that had very different ideas about how best to maintain the vitality of the Catholic faith in the United States. The case of Milwaukee was preeminent in this serious debate as either a model of proper action or an example to be avoided.[156]

The Pamphlet and Rhetorical War

In the aftermath of the Abbelen memorial, battle lines hardened between English-speaking Americanizers and Germanizing conservatives. In February 1887, German priests mobilized to found their own clergy association, the *Deutsch-Amerikanischer Priester Verein,* which made plans to hold a meeting in September in conjunction with a national *Katholickentag* in Chicago. This organization included a number of Milwaukee priests. Ireland of St. Paul, already the chief source of complaints about the secretiveness of the Abbelen efforts, reacted with hostility to this development, and continued to agitate among his fellow bishops for a rebuttal to German activities. He continued a drumfire of criticism of the "secret" document by running selected excerpts in his diocesan paper the *Northwestern Chronicle,* decrying it as

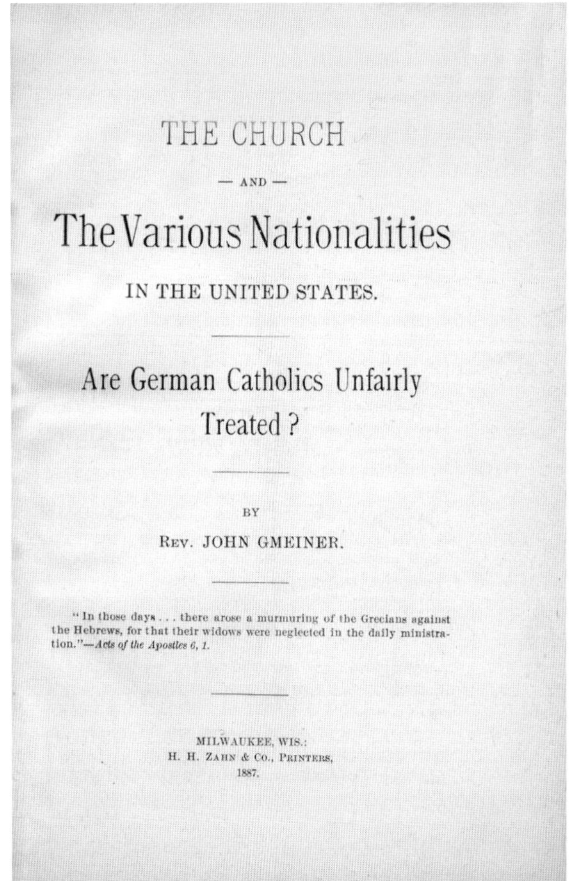
THE CHURCH

— AND —

The Various Nationalities

IN THE UNITED STATES.

Are German Catholics Unfairly Treated ?

BY

REV. JOHN GMEINER.

"In those days . . . there arose a murmuring of the Grecians against the Hebrews, for that their widows were neglected in the daily ministration."—*Acts of the Apostles 6, 1.*

MILWAUKEE, WIS.:
H. H. ZAHN & CO., PRINTERS,
1887.

[AAM]

a plea for "special rights." To Ireland's great delight, a German-born Milwaukee priest, John Gmeiner, also poured vitriol on the Abbelen Memorial.[157] Gmeiner had been ordained for Milwaukee in 1870. A skilled writer, he had been selected by Henni to reply to the anti-religious attacks of the Forty-Eighters. He was later appointed editor of the German paper *Der Seebote* and served on the faculty of St. Francis Seminary from 1883 to 1887. In a widely circulated pamphlet printed in Milwaukee, *The Church and The Various Nationalities in the United States: Are German Catholics Unfairly Treated?,* Gmeiner dismissed the Abbelen Memorial and harshly lectured his fellow Germans by pointing out the futility of retaining German language and culture in America. He urged them also not to try to conform the mission of the Church to their ethnic whims. "The Catholic Church is no literary club to foster peculiar linguistic tastes, nor any ethnological society to advance any particular national cause, but a divinely instituted organization to bring men of 'all nations and tribes, and peoples, and tongues,' to eternal salvation."[158] Gmeiner's words, "written in the camp of the enemy" warmed the heart of Archbishop John Ireland, who had exposed the Abbelen Memorial in his weekly paper and who welcomed Gmeiner to his diocese when he was no longer welcome in Milwaukee.[159]

Gmeiner's pamphlet opened up a floodgate of invective between both sides, some of it centered in Milwaukee. Abbelen chose to respond to Gmeiner on the pages of the German Catholic weekly *Columbia* in August 1887, insisting that Germans were not seeking "special privileges" but only equal rights.[160] Gmeiner replied with a pamphlet, *Calm Reason and Furor Teutonicus;* while Nicholas Gonner, a future president of the *Central Verein*, attacked not only Gmeiner but actually berated the English language by comparing it to the "barking of dogs," and urged corporal punishment of German-speaking children caught speaking English. He extolled German immigrant stock as superior to the "consumptive Yankees," and predicted that one day the Catholic Hapsburgs would dominate Europe and America.[161]

In the summer of 1887, Heiss himself threw fuel on the smouldering fires of the ethnic dispute. In anticipation of a *Central Verein* convention and *Katholikentag* (Catholic Day) in Chicago in 1887, a series of interviews were conducted with Midwestern bishops on the status of internal ethnic affairs by the *Northwestern Chronicle*, the official newspaper of the diocese of St. Paul. Heiss turned aside all questions about the passage of a rumored anti-Irish resolution at the convention.[162] But in a subsequent interview with the *Milwaukee Sentinel*, he seemed to endorse the idea of more Germans in the hierarchy and the perpetuation of German language in the United States. In the course of the interview he speculated that there were nearly 3 million German Catholics out of a total of 8 million U.S. Catholics, but that there were only a handful of German bishops and he alone was the only German archbishop. Likewise, he noted that the need for German-language ministry did not seem to be receding, "I have been forty-five years in America and the demand for the German language has been growing right along, although it was at first supposed, and I believed it myself, that it would disappear with the older immigrants."[163] "He Stands Alone" read the headline of the article which appeared on August 18, 1887, increasing suspicions that Heiss endorsed the sentiments of the rejected Abbelen Memorial. Opponents seized on the interview as proof of German plotting for additional episcopal appointments and the "upgrading" of their parochial status. They feared these policies would marginalize the Catholic Church in America by making it seem "foreign." Some urged Cardinal Gibbons to report Heiss to Rome, but the cardinal demurred.[164] German papers leapt to the prelate's defense, insisting that Heiss's words had been distorted by the *Sentinel* reporter.

Rev. John Gmeiner
[AAM]

The Edgerton Bible Case and the Bennett Law Controversy

The conflicting approaches of Germanizers and Americanists over the place of the Church in America were defined not only by their respective philosophical positions on the pace and scope of Americanization, but also by local experiences. In Wisconsin, two serious clashes over school issues took place that sharpened the fears of German speakers concerning the fate of these treasured institutions. The public controversies over the Edgerton Bible Case and the Bennett Law revealed Catholic support for their parochial schools.

Arguments over bible reading in public schools had been a regular flashpoint between Protestants and Catholics in the pre-Civil War period. In Wisconsin, the issue had been joined in 1876 when the school board of Bay View permitted Bible reading from the King James version in the public schools. Immaculate Conception parishioner James McIver led the fight against the practice and had it stopped.[165]

The Edgerton Bible case began in 1888 in the Rock County city of Edgerton where 30 Catholic parents protested that their children had to listen to readings and prayers taken from the King James version of the Bible.[166] When the school board of Rock County refused to stop the practice, the parents sought a writ of mandamus from the circuit court to order the board to act. The board's lawyers argued that when the offensive Bible reading took place, children could leave. Moreover, it challenged Catholic teaching that the Church was the proper interpreter of the scriptures, insisting that people could interpret the holy writ as they pleased. To stop the Bible reading, the board insisted, would be to give into Catholic sectarianism. It swept away Catholic objections to the King James version of the Bible by comparing the decision to read this version of the Bible with the decisions made about the selection of textbooks. Standing on rights given to local school boards in the state constitution, Rock County was free to choose whatever version of the Bible it desired.

Humphrey J. Desmond, who had recently taken over the *Catholic Citizen* and who was a lawyer, encouraged Catholic parents to protest. He lent his legal and journalistic expertise to the cause as the case made its way through the Wisconsin courts up to the state Supreme Court.[167] The case came before the circuit court in June 1888, and Judge John R. Bennett ruled (in November 1888) against the Catholic parents, declaring that the King James version was not a sectarian tract, that Bible reading was not coercive, and that to decide in their favor was to open the door to unending intrusiveness in textbook selection. Bennett lectured the Catholic parents from the bench, noting that they, not the Bible, were the troublemakers and suggested that it was they who wanted to impose their beliefs on others, not the other way around. In an argument redolent of the racialistic missionary Protestantism of the day, he extolled the superiority of those who read the Bible (his way) over others: "Of those nations, which in the highest degree enjoy its influence, it is not too much to affirm the differences, public and private, physical, moral and intellectual, are only less than what might have been expected from a diversity of species."[168]

Stung by the virulence of Bennett's decision, Desmond became even more passionate. He covered the various aspects of the case in the *Catholic Citizen* and helped raise funds to pay for the appeal. Within four months of Bennett's decision, Desmond had raised $806.30, the exact cost of the appeal. Desmond kept up the drumfire of agitation linking the whole matter to other offensive school textbook issues, such as history books that defamed the papacy or the Jesuits. Desmond entered a brief with the Wisconsin Supreme Court, which accepted the appeal of the Edgerton parents. He also joined in the oral arguments in their behalf. Desmond did not wish to exclude character formation from school instruction, but insisted repeatedly that the King James version-—or any version of the Bible—was sectarian in nature and thereby a violation of basic freedom of religion guaranteed under the state constitution. On March 18, 1890, the Supreme Court sided with the parents, ruling that the reading of the Bible was in fact sectarian instruction, an act of worship and an activity that illegally united the functions of church and state.

The Bennett Law

While Desmond and his various allies crowed over the victory, harsh words of condemnation for the Catholic Church came from sources like the Wisconsin Presbytery and a congregational convention. Warnings about the power and influence of Catholicism, and the "foreign" threat to American institutions, including the public school, began to be heard from various sources. These sentiments received an additional boost from yet another school case that would literally be fought up to Heiss's death. The battle was begun quietly when Republican Governor George Hoard attempted to tighten up an 1879 compulsory education law. He found an ally in State Senator Levi E. Pond of Westfield who introduced a bill requiring the compilation of statistics from both public and private schools. The bill carried a provision which mandated that those turning in the statistics should make a judgement as to whether the students had "received suitable elementary instruction in that language [English] that they are able to speak, and to write the same with reasonable ease and correctness."[169] The implications of this requirement for private schools where foreign language instruction was still carried on became evident right away. Heiss, among others, vigorously opposed the Pond Bill as German Catholics were reminded how German Chancellor Otto von Bismarck had demanded a

Governor William D. Hoard
[MCHS]

similar procedure when he sought to "Prussianize" the private schools of Germany. Thanks to lobbying by Heiss and others, the Pond Bill went down in defeat.

However, public school advocates in state government were not content to accept this defeat. In 1889, Assemblyman Michael J. Bennett, an Irish Catholic from rural Iowa County, introduced a compulsory education law mandating instruction for children between 7 and 14. Added to the bill was a proviso directing that the only kind of school where a Wisconsin child could comply with this law was one that " taught therein, as part of the elementary education of children, reading, writing, and arithmetic, and United States history in the English language."[170] The bill passed easily on April 13, 1889 and was signed by Governor Hoard who strongly supported it.

A Protest of the Catholic Bishops of Wisconsin

AGAINST THE

BENNETT LAW.

[AAM]

The outcry over the Bennett law was furious. Almost overnight, a polyglot coalition of opponents set to work to effect its repeal, and to punish the legislators and governor who had foisted it on the Wisconsin public. In the forefront were the Roman Catholics of the state, who with nearly 300 parochial schools felt the most threatened by the Bennett law. The English-language provisions of the law were not the issue. Most Wisconsin Catholic schools already had substantial English instruction. The question was even more fundamental: who had the right to educate, the state or parents? Even though he was in failing health, Heiss traveled to La Crosse to consult with Bishops Kilian Flasch of La Crosse and Frederick X. Katzer from Green Bay to plot a strategy and a response. With Katzer doing the majority of the writing, the three drafted "A Protest of the Catholic Bishops of Wisconsin Against the Bennett Law." Insisting that the Bennett Law was unnecessary, offensive and unjust, they declared, "After a calm and careful study of the Bennett law, we hold that it interferes with the rights of church and parents. We moreover conscientiously believe that the real object of this law is not so much to secure a greater amount of instruction in and knowledge of the English language, as rather to bring our parochial and private schools under the control of the state. And in this attempt, we cannot but apprehend the ultimate intention—gradually to destroy the parochial school system altogether."[171] Released to the public on March 12, 1890 the protest circulated rapidly and mobilized German Catholic forces.[172] They were joined in protest by German and even some Scandinavian Lutherans who likewise despised the law and through their synodal gatherings called for its repeal. A third player in the coalition was the state Democratic party. State Democrats had long been the friends of the foreign-born of Wisconsin, but while their strength among Catholics had been steady, they often lost large parts of the Wisconsin Lutheran vote. By aligning themselves with the anti-Bennett law forces, they found an opportunity to peel away a portion of Republican strength in the upcoming state elections in 1890.[173]

The first test of the new coalition came when the campaign for Milwaukee mayor in March 1890 focused almost totally on pro- and anti-Bennett Law candidates. Milwaukeeans voted heavily for the anti-Bennett law candidate, humorist George Washington Peck, who handily won the mayoral position. Peck hardly had time to warm his seat when he was chosen as the gubernatorial candidate of the Democratic party. Going head-to-head with incumbent Governor William Hoard, Peck swept to a stunning victory in November 1890.[174] Likewise, Democrats dominated the new state legislature. Among the winning candidates was Humphrey J. Desmond, who garnered a chair in the State Assembly and was empaneled as chair of the Assembly Education Committee. Desmond saw to it that the Bennett law's repeal was speedily drafted and it passed in 1891.

The effect of both of these struggles made many Wisconsin German-speaking Catholics wary of suggestions, whether from within or without the Church, to Americanize rapidly. Depending on how one viewed the need for Americanization, these events either reinforced an unfortunate siege mentality that was doomed to fail, or they provided a renewed commitment to sharpen Catholic identity and create an even more vibrant and stable Catholic subculture.

The Death of Heiss

Heiss's health, never good, failed seriously in the last months of 1889. In October he collapsed and lay on the floor helpless until he could summon his man-servant Brother Bernard. In November he recovered sufficiently to travel to Washington, D.C. for the centennial of the American Hierarchy and the opening of Catholic University. On Friday, November 22, 1889 he suffered another serious heart attack in Milwaukee and was down for a time. After a failed effort to get back to his work schedule, he decided to be hospitalized in La Crosse where he could be cared for by the Franciscan Sisters at St. Francis Hospital. Two days before Christmas he made his way to La Crosse by train. There he weakened and died on March 26, 1890 just 17 days before his 72nd birthday.[175] Father Augustine Zeininger, vicar general, was appointed administrator of the diocese—a post he would hold from March 1890 until June 1891.

Among those who kept the death vigil in LaCrosse were Bishop Kilian Flasch, whom Heiss hoped would succeed him in Milwaukee, various priests of the diocese, his secretary Father Charles Koetting, and the faithful Brother Bernard Gerleman. Also among those who paid a last call on the dying prelate was another colleague from the seminary, Frederick X. Katzer, the bishop of Green Bay whom Heiss had consecrated in 1886.

Frederick X. Katzer

Rev. Frederick Xavier Katzer [AAM]

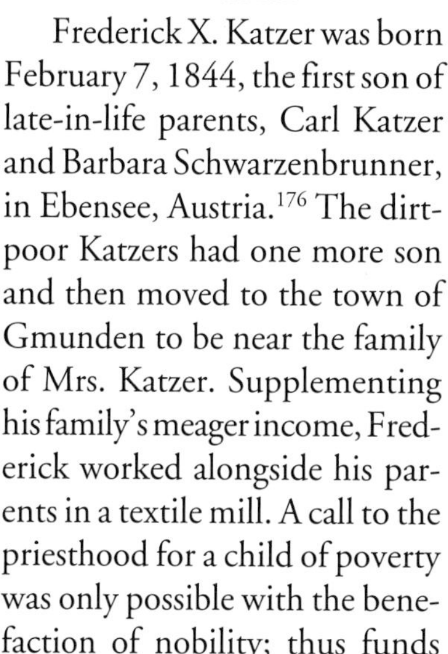

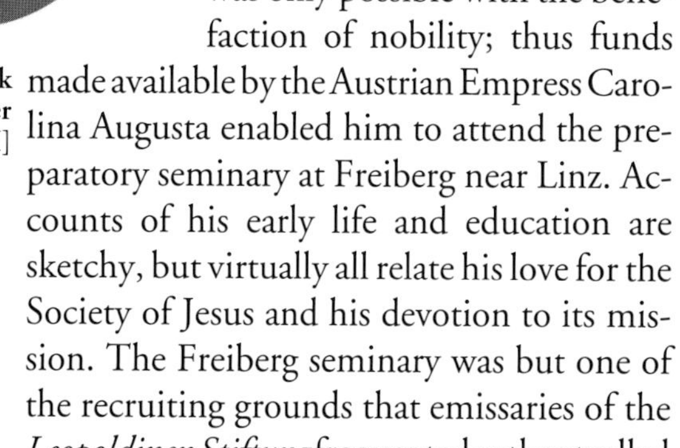

Frederick X. Katzer was born February 7, 1844, the first son of late-in-life parents, Carl Katzer and Barbara Schwarzenbrunner, in Ebensee, Austria.[176] The dirt-poor Katzers had one more son and then moved to the town of Gmunden to be near the family of Mrs. Katzer. Supplementing his family's meager income, Frederick worked alongside his parents in a textile mill. A call to the priesthood for a child of poverty was only possible with the benefaction of nobility; thus funds made available by the Austrian Empress Carolina Augusta enabled him to attend the preparatory seminary at Freiberg near Linz. Accounts of his early life and education are sketchy, but virtually all relate his love for the Society of Jesus and his devotion to its mission. The Freiberg seminary was but one of the recruiting grounds that emissaries of the *Leopoldinen Stiftung* frequented as they trolled for volunteers to come to America.

One of the American recruiters was Father Francis Pierz, an important figure in the history of Catholic life in Minnesota. For years Pierz wrote effusive letters about missionary life for the readers of *Der Wahrheits-Freund,* and more matter-of-fact reports for the *Berichte* of the *Leopoldinen Stiftung.*[177] Pierz had been ordained 22 years when Frederick Résé recruited him to come to Detroit and thence to the Indian missions of Upper Peninsula and Minnesota. In 1864, Pierz himself traveled abroad and cast his fisherman's net wide for new European recruits for Minnesota. He snared only one priest, Joseph Buh, who later became a legend in Minnesota Catholic circles, but managed to convince 15 students to come—one of whom was 22-year-old Frederick Katzer. Pierz's skills as recruiter outstripped the demand for priests in Minnesota (and the ability of Bishop Thomas Langton Grace of St. Paul to support them), and young Katzer was told he wasn't needed in Minnesota. Just as Katzer was toying with the idea of joining the Jesuits in Baltimore, Salzmann invited the young man to come to Milwaukee to join the rest of the Austrian diaspora. He moved to St. Francis Seminary where he soon joined the faculty, and in 1866 he was ordained by Bishop Henni.

Unlike Heiss, whose partings from his parents were stormy scenes of bitter farewell, Katzer moved his family with him when he got settled in Milwaukee. His parents took up abode on the seminary grounds in 1867. His younger brother Charles also came over and for many years was employed by the Wisconsin Bridge and Iron Works. His parents accompanied Frederick to Green Bay, where his father died in 1876; his mother died in the episcopal residence in Milwaukee in 1895. All of the Katzers are buried in the cemetery in the seminary woods.

The close-knit circle of Austrian priests in Wisconsin provided support for Katzer and helped account for his promotions. Katzer remained on the seminary faculty teaching mathematics, philosophy, and theology. He supported the work of Salzmann in creating the normal school by donating the proceeds of his one literary work, *Der Kampf der Gegenwart*, an allegorical play he wrote to glorify his Jesuit mentors.[178] It is in the composition of this play written in 1872 that we have one of the few pictures of the human face of Katzer. A former student, Mathias Gerend, recalled being a part of the production of the play which was, "the first dramatic production at the Seminary, as far as I know." Gerend, who played a minor role because he was "the smallest boy in the house" related how Katzer worked closely with future Bishop Joseph Koudelka, who designed the scenery for the play. Gerend recalled also how the often frosty Katzer would be seized by the muse of drama. "When the spirit moved him he would call some of the boys to his sanctum, then take his long German pipe and pace up and down the room, and while he was enveloped in clouds of smoke, he would dictate in perfect meter and rhyme parts of his drama; and he did it with such force and rapidity that it required a stenographer or a very rapid penman to follow him."[179]

But of all the archbishops of Milwaukee, Katzer revealed the least about his inner self. There is in his public utterances none of the sharpness or volubility of John Martin Henni, nor in his papers, anything resembling the emotional letters of Heiss to Kleiner. From the fragments of evidence we pick up from those who knew him, Katzer was reserved and aloof. In 1922, Dominic Thill recalled Katzer's studious traits. "He was above all things a professor, philosopher, poet and mathematician." But, he noted wryly, "Mathematicians as a rule, are not men of sentiment and great feeling. They become stern and cold as figures." Thill observed, "There surely was no sentimentality in Archbishop Katzer. He was a very able and brilliant man and almost scrupulously pious. He was lacking altogether in worldly and what we might call Yankee polish."[180] A woman recalled that he was "silent, almost austere when met upon the street."[181] Yet, the reserved and sober mien of Milwaukee's third archbishop also projected an image of authority and even nobility (for

Rev. Frederick Xavier Katzer
[AAM]

one born in such lowly social conditions). In 1895, a friend paid $1500 to have sculptor Gaetano Trentanove (the artist who designed the controversial statue of Jacques Marquette for Washington's Statuary Hall) execute a bust of Katzer. Acclaimed as "very life-like in its resemblance" the marble statue depicts a serenely self-confident Katzer, unafraid of the tasks of administration and leadership.[182]

Fortunately for him, the qualifications for episcopal advance in those days did not require a great deal of backslapping or glad-handing. While he was still on the seminary faculty, Katzer's career took another step up when the newly appointed bishop of Green Bay, Francis X. Krautbauer, took the young priest with him to serve both as his secretary and to help shepherd the construction of a new cathedral in Green Bay.

In 1879 Katzer was appointed vicar general of the Green Bay diocese and also as pastor of the cathedral church. Krautbauer died in his sleep unexpectedly on December 17, 1885, and Katzer was appointed administrator of the diocese in the interim. Heiss no doubt played a major role in the nomination of Katzer, and on September 21, 1886, consecrated him the third bishop of Green Bay.[183] Katzer spent only five years in Green Bay, devoting himself to the steady expansion of the diocese. During this episcopal novitiate, Katzer honed his reputation as a defender of German ethnic rights and as a strong proponent of Catholic schools. During the years of his episcopate he embarked on a vigorous school building campaign increasing the number of Catholic schools from 44 to 69, and enrollments from 5,292 to 10,785.[184] He was strong in his defense of the Abbelen Memorial and in 1888 had traveled to Rome to defend this cause before Church officials. As Heiss began to falter physically throughout 1889, it was the aggressive and sharp Katzer that picked up the torch of opposition to the Bennett Law. The defeat of the law and Katzer's high profile made him a natural for the Milwaukee See.

The Milwaukee Succession: Americanists versus Germanizers

Evidence suggests that Heiss preferred his successor in La Crosse, Bishop Kilian Flasch, to be his successor in Milwaukee. But Flasch was in poor health at the time of Katzer's death, and there is no evidence that he was seriously considered. Yet again, the Milwaukee succession became a flashpoint in the now escalating struggle between various factions of the U.S. hierarchy. The struggles of the 1880s and the outburst of yet another round of bitterness over the best care for ethnic Catholics further polarized feelings among the bishops.

Despite Heiss's wishes, Frederick X. Katzer would succeed to the Milwaukee See after yet another struggle among the members of the American hierarchy (again featuring the doomed candidacy of John Lancaster Spalding). When the consultors met after the burial of Heiss, they nominated Bishops Katzer, Kilian Flasch, and Henry Richter of the diocese of Grand Rapids, Michigan, for the *terna*. A change in the rules for proposing new candidates for episcopal office enacted at the Third Plenary Council of Baltimore now mandated that these nominations be sent directly to Propaganda without a vetting by the archbishops of the country—as had been the case with the Heiss nomination. Katzer's appointment seemed secure, until the archbishops of the country, prodded by Archbishop John Ireland of St. Paul, decided to make an issue of the matter.[185]

Ireland, since 1888 an archbishop and head of his own metropolitan province, moved aggressively to block the Katzer nomination as part of a larger strategy to challenge German power in the American Church. Ireland's ambiguous feelings towards foreign language in Catholic schools made him watch the efforts of the Wisconsin bishops with mixed feelings.[186] After the drafting of the *terna* by the priest consultors and its affirmation by the suffragans of the Milwaukee province, a cadre of English-speaking priests sent a protest to Gibbons and to the other American archbishops, insisting that this time Milwaukee should have an American-born archbishop. Ireland, who feared the more belligerent and sharper-edged Katzer, seized on the letter, and wrote to Gibbons, "The German consultors chose Bp. Katzer pro primo loco—[for first place on the terna] a man thoroughly German and thoroughly unfit to be an archbishop."[187] In his place he wished to place Bishop John Lancaster Spalding of Peoria. Willing to make a full-court press to affect the outcome in Milwaukee, Ireland urged Gibbons to help stall the nomination until a general meeting of the archbishops in July 1890. Gibbons concurred, and contacted Cardinal Simeoni at Propaganda to ask a delay in Milwaukee's succession. In the meantime, Ireland pressed Roman agent, Monsignor Denis O'Connell, to do what he could to affect the Milwaukee outcome, writing, "John Lancaster Spalding is the only man for Milwaukee."[188]

Ireland did everything he could to stop Katzer and he nearly succeeded. On the eve of the meeting of the archbishops in Boston in July 1890, he once again denounced Katzer to Archbishop Elder: "at the last meeting of the German societies he has said such bitter things and has shown such violence of temper that the American people have conceived a great dislike for him—the daily papers speak-

Archbishop Frederick Xavier Katzer
[AAM]

Archbishop John Ireland of St. Paul MN [AAM]

ing most harshly of him."[189] Ireland's aggressive lobbying succeeded in ejecting Katzer from the Milwaukee list altogether and replacing him with Spalding. He also managed to nominate for the second and third posts Bishop Martin Marty of the Dakotas and Bishop Henry Richter of Grand Rapids.[190] Although this body had no real canonical authority to pass on these nominations, Ireland hoped the endorsement of the metropolitans would provide the boost needed for Spalding's nomination and the ultimate breakup of the German dynasty. If Ireland had any doubt that his opposition was well-warranted, it was more than justified by reports that in September 1890, Katzer had attended a convention of the *Priesterverein*. This organization was viewed by Ireland as subversive.

As this new *terna* made its way through Roman channels, throughout the fall Ireland politicked incessantly for Spalding or Richter—but all to no avail. Historian Gerald Fogarty gives the best description of the Byzantine Roman politics that attended the Katzer nomination.[191] In the first place, Monsignor Denis O'Connell, who was to head the effort to secure Milwaukee for Spalding, was absent from Rome from November 1889 to July 1890. During his absence, Archbishop Michael Corrigan, soon to become a strong foe of Ireland and his faction, visited Rome and voiced his support for Katzer. Serious doubts about Spalding began to surface among Roman authorities, despite O'Connell's efforts to convince them that he was the right man for Milwaukee.[192] Still other prelates did not feel the alternatives, Richter or Marty, would be acceptable to the Milwaukee clergy. Katzer and Flasch learned of efforts to derail the original *terna* and lodged strong protests with Propaganda over the departure from established procedures. Consequently, as Fogarty notes, when Jesuit Cardinal Camillo Mazzella drew up the *ponenza* (or general report deliberation) on the Milwaukee succession, he not only questioned the right of the archbishops to draw up a new *terna*, but quite rightly noted that the issue was a "battle" between Germans who wanted a German, and non-Germans, who wanted an American. Mazzella himself may have been tilted to the support of Katzer by reports that the Green Bay bishop had studied with the Jesuits at Linz and had wanted to become a member of the Society of Jesus in his youth.[193] Rumors had begun to fly shortly after Heiss's death alleging that he had unsuccessfully petitioned Rome for a coadjutor.[194] Then in September a Catholic newspaper had reported that Bishop Winand Wigger of Newark had been offered the Milwaukee See and had declined.[195] The *Milwaukee Sentinel* linked the Milwaukee succession to the success of efforts in November to elect a state regime to overturn the Bennett Law. "A prominent Catholic priest says that if the German Catholics should be victorious in the elections this year, that would be the end of all the hopes of ever having an English-speaking bishop in the state."[196] On December 15, 1890, the cardinals of Propaganda voted and Katzer received the nomination. Introduced to Milwaukee Catholics as "Rome's Christmas Gift," the *Catholic Citizen* noted the 46-year-old Katzer's reputation for scholarship and conservatism and observed that in the struggle over the Bennett Law, "The Bishop was a better American than any of them [the proponents of the law].[197]

Milwaukee was spared the lengthy ordeal it had known in the Henni/Heiss succession crisis. Ireland and his fellow archbishops had simply over-stepped the boundaries of their authority. Moreover, as historians Fogarty and John Tracy Ellis note, Katzer himself had strong friends in Rome who worked overtime to secure his nomination.[198] His nomination may have been assured by his reported affection for the Jesuits. However, although support in Rome was helpful, there were other reasons for the success of the Katzer nomination. Although Ireland dismissed Katzer as "thoroughly German," the Green Bay bishop was perhaps better suited for the realities of leadership in rapidly changing Catholic Wisconsin than Ireland gave him credit for being.

Indeed, he was the choice of the state's still large German-speaking contingent, and his nomination gave a special lift to those who resented Ireland's continual meddling in their internal affairs. Father Francis Haas spoke for many when he reassured Mother Agnes Hazotte, "His choice as the Archbishop is a great triumph when everything Archbishop Ireland did to oppose him is considered. It is an answer to much prayer. It is also a sign of God's pleasure."[199] On the eve of Katzer's entry into Milwaukee, Haas was even more laudatory: "Archbishop Katzer, in my judgement, is the right man for the present circumstances. He may keep Bishop [*sic*] Ireland from error because he is superior to Ireland in knowledge and character."[200] Katzer maintained a continuity with the ethnic policies of his predecessors Henni and Heiss for he spoke mangled English and was always more at home with German speakers than with the English-speaking.

However, Katzer's strong support for the retention of national "Catholicisms" was consistently applied to all groups, not just his fellow German speakers. His record in Green Bay suggests he was highly responsive to other ethnic groups, especially the Poles, who were flooding in and demanding a niche in the emerging network of parishes and schools. As archbishop of Milwaukee, as we shall see,

Katzer did all that he could to encourage what many would consider a "healthy pluralism" among Wisconsin's various Catholic ethnic groups. This policy, guided by his associates, helped significantly to lower the level of ethnic bitterness in the archdiocese of Milwaukee during his years as its leader. Likewise, even though English-speaking priests regarded his coming with apprehension and formed an American Catholic Clerical Union for the province of Milwaukee, retribution and vengeance on American-born and English-speaking clergy did not take place.[201]

Cahenslyism and Katzer's Pallium

Unfortunately, Katzer's appearance in Milwaukee came at the same time as another highly controversial effort on the part of German speakers to secure more representation in clergy and bishops, and more equity in the status of their parishes. This movement, known popularly as "Cahenslyism," came just as Katzer was getting ready to take over the Milwaukee See, and it aroused strong antipathies among the Americanist bishops. It even arched the eyebrows of the President of the United States, Benjamin Harrison.

The storm center of this dispute was Peter Paul Cahensly, a wealthy merchant, a well-connected member of the German Center Party and a highly esteemed Catholic layman. Cahensly had taken a deep interest in the plight of German-speaking immigrants and helped found the *St. Raphael's Verein*, an organization that set up houses of hospitality in port cities and helped German-speaking immigrants to make a gentle transition to their new environment. In 1883, a branch of this organization opened in New York. In 1889 they opened the residence facility called "Leo House" and the Sisters of St. Agnes were invited to staff the new facility.[202] At a meeting of the organization in Lucerne, Switzerland in December 1890, a memorial was drafted that appeared to resurrect some of the features of the discredited Abbelen Memorial. It asked for more national parishes, priests, and catechetical instruction in the native tongue of immigrant groups.[203] It petitioned for equal rights for foreign-speaking clergy, and the sponsorship of seminaries to train priests to serve with immigrants. But the most explosive proposal was this: "It seems very desirable that the Catholics of each nationality, wherever it is deemed possible have, in the episcopate of the country where they immigrate, several bishops who are of the same origin. It seems that in this way, the organization of the church would be perfect, for in the assemblies of the bishops, every immigrant race would be represented, and its interests would be protected."[204] Peter Paul Cahensly and Marchese Giovanni Battista Volpe Landi, both representatives of the organization, were designated to present the declaration to Pope Leo XIII. Volpe Landi could not go, so Cahensly went alone and in an audience with the pontiff on April 16, 1891 formally presented him with the document.

Reactions were universally negative, even among more conservative American bishops, like New York's Michael Corrigan. Cahensly's name was a red flag to the Americanist faction of the hierarchy. Only eight years before, on an inspection tour of the United States, Katzer had lamented the poor treatment given to German Catholics. Given his reputation for strong support of many of the ideas of the Lucerne Memorial, some associated Katzer with it, and in fact he did embrace certain of its propositions. However, in a letter to Gibbons, inviting him to confer the pallium on him in Milwaukee, Katzer hastened to assure the Baltimore prelate that despite the association of his name with "this deplorable Cahensly affair," he knew nothing about it.[205]

The summer of 1891 was filled with Lucerne Memorial controversy. Cahensly himself set off another round when he sent a list of recommendations to the Holy See (at their request) citing even more difficulties for Germans in the United States. In this second document Cahensly insisted that great numbers of Germans were leaving the church because there were not enough organizations to keep them loyal, and that American public schools weaned children away from the faith.[206] These allegations brought angry denials from American prelates, and their assurance that Rome did not plan to act on the recommendations of the two memorials. But Catholic officials in America grew even more concerned when in a chance meeting at Cape May, New Jersey, in July 1891, President Benjamin Harrison confided to Cardinal Gibbons that he had followed the controversy in the papers with great concern because "foreign and unauthorized interference with American affairs cannot be viewed with indifference."[207] Gibbons, who had restrained militant bishops from lodging a formal protest over the Lucerne Memorial, was now quite eager to say something publicly about the loyalty of American Catholics to the American republic. The conferral of Katzer's pallium in August 1891 provided the perfect opportunity.

Katzer bid a long farewell from Green Bay, taking nearly seven months to tie up his affairs and make his way to Milwaukee.[208] A triumphal train tour on June 30, 1891, took him through the Green Bay diocese's major cities, where throngs of laity turned out to say good-bye. He finally arrived in Milwaukee at 8:30 in the evening and was met by a huge entourage that escorted his carriage. Mounted Kosciuscko guards carrying Chinese lanterns and other marching Catholic associations led the way from the Chicago and Northwestern depot on Wisconsin Street down illuminated streets to St. John's Cathedral. Only at 11:00 in the evening did Katzer enter the cathedral where the vicar general, Augustine Zeininger, conducted the formal ceremony of welcome and Katzer gave a brief speech in English. At 11:45, he waved his hand in blessing over the crowd and sent them home.[209]

In August, 1891, Gibbons arrived to confer the archiepiscopal pallium on Katzer and dropped a bombshell.[210] The soul of circumspection and "masterly inactivity," Gibbons rarely spoke harshly or forcefully on any subject. His restraint and gentility was much lauded by his sympathetic biographer John Tracy Ellis. But his contemporaries, like John Ireland, at times found it maddening. In his sermon in Milwaukee, he cast off all restraints and inveighed forcefully, in the very heart of the German citadel, against further ethnic divisiveness. He counseled Katzer not to launch any kind of retribution against any English-speaking clergy who had doubts about his candidacy. In his most pointed comments, he recalled the unity enjoyed by the 85 bishops who had met two years previously for the centenary of the hierarchy, and warned: "Woe to him, my brethren, who would destroy or impair this blessed harmony that reigns among us! Woe to him who would sow the tares of discord in the fair fields of the Church in America! Woe to him who would breed dissension among the leaders of Israel by introducing a spirit of nationalism into the camps of the Lord!" He lectured Katzer forcefully on the meaning of citizenship: "It matters not whether this is the land of our birth or of our adoption. It is the land of our destiny. Here we intend to live and here we hope to die. And when our brethren across the Atlantic resolve to come to our shores may they be animated by the sentiments of Ruth when she determined to join her husband's kindred in the land of Israel.... 'Whither thou has gone, I also shall go; where thou dwellest, I also shall dwell, thy people shall be my people and thy God my God."[211] Gibbons recalled the speech twenty years later, "When I finished, they [Katzer and the Germanizers in the hierarchy] were aghast, but I think the lesson had its effect."[212]

Cardinal James Gibbons, Archbishop of Baltimore
[*Trials and Triumphs of the Catholic Church in America*, J.S. Hyland Co., 1901]

Katzer was never able to shake the unfavorable feelings that Ireland and other Americanist prelates continued to feel for him. Once when it was rumored that Ireland and Katzer would be called to the Vatican to discuss both sides of the looming school issue, Ireland remarked snidely that he was appalled at the thought of debating with Katzer, "who knows as much of America as a Huron."[213] Serious efforts were also launched by members of the hierarchy to "break the Wisconsin Union." Archbishop William Henry Elder of Cincinnati, an opponent of Katzer's promotion, attempted to rally the archbishops to block a German from succeeding to the see of Green Bay. Gibbons threw cold water on this initiative, urging individual archbishops to lodge their own protests with the Holy See if they felt as strongly as Elder.[214] If anybody complained, they were not taken seriously. When Kilian Flasch died in 1891 the vacant see went to Katzer's selection, Luxemburg-born James Schwebach. In Green Bay, Katzer's successor was Sebastian G. Messmer, a German-speaking Swiss.[215]

Katzer and the School Question

Because of the Edgerton Bible case and the Bennett Law controversy, Catholic sensibilities on the school issue were raw. Added to this was the emergence of the anti-Catholic American Protective Association in 1887 which raised public doubts about the loyalty and social utility of Catholic schools.

Some Catholic leaders, however, took a different view regarding the public schools. Indeed, depending on the region of the country, Catholics got on quite well with local public school authorities. In Savannah, Georgia, Bishop Augustin Verot, S.S., had turned over Catholic schools to public instruction. In 1873, a facilities-sharing agreement was reached in Poughkeepsie, New York where Catholic school buildings were used as public schools during the day, and Catholic school children were instructed in religion after-hours. However, after the 1884 declaration of Baltimore III, further reflection on the relationship of Catholics to the public school system was necessary. In 1890, Archbishop John Ireland gave an important address to the National Education Association, the chief professional organization of public school educators, essentially extolling the public school and hoping that at some point public schools would admit the teaching of religion. He urged that state funds be given to parochial schools for teaching secular subjects. The most startling aspect of his speech was his acknowledgment that the state had a right to educate children—a concept some Catholic commentators had dismissed, insisting on the primacy of parents as educators.[216] In 1891, Ireland permitted a form of the Poughkeepsie plan to be implemented at two Catholic schools at Faribault and Stillwater, Minnesota.

These developments widened the rifts in the hierarchy on matters relative to nationality and Catholic identity. Ireland's ideas received a substantial boost by the appearance of a 31-page pamphlet by Catholic University professor Thomas Bouquillion, who argued in *Education: To Whom Does It Belong* that the state had an "intrinsic" right to educate. He was rebutted by Jesuit Rene Holaind in *The Parent First,* who challenged Bouquillion's bold assertion of state's rights. A tidal wave of articles, brochures, editorials and reviews ensued.[217]

Catholic leaders in Milwaukee had already weighed in on this issue with their clear insistence in the Bennett Law pastoral that the right to educate resided with the parents and the Church. They rejoiced when Ireland was called to Rome to explain his address and his seeming abandonment of Catholic education. Ireland managed to fend off the attacks and even won a grudging *tolerari potest* from authorities for the Faribault and Stillwater plans. Part of his defense was that Archbishop Katzer had eight such arrangements in his own archdiocese.[218] Ireland's school experiment faded, and Archbishop Katzer redoubled his efforts to build and staff Catholic schools and ended many of the embarrassing public/church school partnerships within his jurisdiction. With only a few ethnic exceptions (the Italians most notably), subsequent parochial establishments began with a combined church and school building.

The Finale

The controversy among the prelates raged on through the 1890s.[219] In 1892 an apostolic delegate, Francesco Satolli, was appointed to the United States. Satolli at first seemed favorably disposed to the arguments of Gibbons, Ireland and Keane, and seemed to tilt his decisions and his presence in their favor. However, Katzer and his allies in the American hierarchy, especially New York archbishop Michael Corrigan, bided their time. They eventually managed to bring Satolli and the pope himself around to their views of the proper relationship between the Church and American society.

Winds of the changing mood appeared first in a papal letter *Longinqua Oceani* (1895), which praised the growth of the Church in the United States and shared the gratitude of American Catholics that the state stayed out of its internal affairs. However, the pontiff warned, the American separation of church and state could hardly be upheld as the model for other societies.[220] In the same year, Satolli began to distance himself from the Americanizers. In April he appeared at the dedication of a German church in Pottsville, Pennsylvania where his address praised German Americans and suggested the ongoing need for more ethnic parishes. Glasses must have been clinking in Katzer's episcopal mansion when he heard reports of this address, but subsequent events gave him and his allies even more joy. In September, 1895, Propaganda demanded the resignation of Gibbons's and Ireland's agent in Rome, Father Denis O'Connell, rector of the North American College. Shortly afterward they rebuked Catholic participation in interdenominational congresses like the World Parliament of Religions held at the Columbian Exposition in Chicago in 1893. No less a personage than Cardinal Gibbons had been in attendance at this event.

When Satolli returned to Rome and received the scarlet of a cardinal he teamed with another ex-American, Jesuit Camillo Mazzella, to combat virtually anything Ireland, Gibbons, and Keane stood for. Keane was unceremoniously removed from the rectorship of the Catholic University in 1897. A year later, another leading Americanist personality, Notre Dame professor John A. Zahm, had his book *Evolution and Dogma* placed on the Index of Forbidden Books. Ultimately, a papal condemnation of "Americanism" came in the wake of dispute over a biography of Paulist founder, Isaac Hecker. Hecker's deeply held belief that Americans could be converted to Catholicism by a greater sensitivity to their language, culture and way of life (in many ways similar to the ideas advanced by Willard in the succession crisis of 1878-1880 in Milwaukee) became a point of contention to opposing sides of the issue.

An investigation of conditions in the American Church took place shortly after America's victory over Catholic Spain in the ten-week Spanish-American War of 1898. Spearheaded by Cardinals Satolli and Mazzella, now open opponents of Ireland and Gibbons, they convinced Pope Leo XIII to issue the encyclical letter *Testem Benevolentiae* in January 1899. In this document which condemned Americanism the pontiff warned against watering down the essential elements of the Catholic faith in order to make the faith intelligible to the modern age. He urged a greater reliance on the passive virtues of prayer, contemplation, and poverty to counterbalance the American penchant for excessive activity and endless organizing. As William Halsey put it, the pontiff condemned as heresy the "activist individualism, self-confident mystique and optimistic idealism of American civilization."[221] Katzer, Corrigan, McQuaid and their associates felt a sense of victory over their foes. When erroneous Associated Press reports included Katzer's name among those "who solemnly protested to the pope that the errors, which he designated as Americanism, had no place in the American Roman Catholic church," he immediately set the record straight. The report was "an absolute falsehood." He declared, "Had I written, it would have been a letter of sincere thanks and heartfelt congratulation for this most opportune letter."[222] The divisions ceased for a time and the differences between the two groups faded as immigration slowed and the Americanist values took hold in other ways. The end of these controversies removed Milwaukee from the center of national attention.

Pope Leo XIII
[Martin Marty, OSB. *Dr. John Martin Henni, First Bishop and Archbishop of Milwaukee,* Benziger Bros., 1888, p. 307]

Katzer's Administration

As the Americanist controversy came to a climax, Archbishop Katzer had to contend with the steady growth of his see city and the need for a new episcopal residence. Heiss had abandoned Henni's episcopal residence attached to the cathedral when he straightened out its tangled finances early in the 1880s. The modest brick home on Jackson Street he had built afterwards had never been held in the title of the diocese and had been sold at the time of his passing. This left Katzer without a place to reside. Desiring to live neither in the seminary with its clerical politics, nor with the largely Irish cathedral clergy, Katzer had the archdiocese purchase the former Lynde mansion at Chestnut and Twenty-Second Streets for the whopping sum of $62,000.[223] In the fall of 1892, renovations were complete and he moved in with his mother, his secretary and housekeeping sisters from St. Francis.[224]

Shortly after Katzer's accession to Milwaukee, Vicar General Augustine Zeininger's star, already in the ascendant with Heiss (despite the fact that Heiss had replaced him at St. Francis Seminary with Father Joseph Rainer) appeared to be rising even higher. Zeininger, a fellow Austrian and also someone recruited by Salzmann, returned frequently to his native land, occasionally in the company of Katzer. Zeininger was a good match for the somewhat unemotional and rational Katzer. Like Katzer, he had a deep love for mathematics, science, and gadgets. He also appeared to know the rudiments of financial administration and had paid off the 1875 south wing addition to the seminary and installed electric lights and other appliances. Historian Benjamin Blied put it mildly when he noted: "Father Zeininger's gifts apparently were along practical rather than speculative lines."[225]

But, despite all his gifts, Zeininger made a serious miscalculation by approving Father Wilhelm Grutza's grandiose plans to build St. Josaphat Basilica. This decision would have grievous implications for the parish, the Polish community of Milwaukee, and the entire archdiocese. When the weight of St. Josaphat's bills began to sink the parish and threaten archdiocesan finances, Zeininger returned to his native Austria in 1899, never to return. There he undertook limited pastoral

Rev. Augustine Zeininger [AAM]

Archbishop Katzer's residence [AAM]

work and was able to lend assistance to the local bishop in a major building project of the Linz Cathedral. He remained there, safe from the ravages of the St. Josaphat mess he had helped to create, until he died on March 25, 1920.[226]

After Zeininger faded from the scene, administrative decisions and the care of Katzer fell to a young priest who served as the prelate's secretary, Augustine Schinner.[227] Schinner was born May 1, 1863 in Milwaukee. Educated at St. Mary's school and St. Francis Seminary, he was ordained by Heiss on March 7, 1886. After a brief stint in a parish in Richfield in Washington County, he was drafted for the faculty of St. Francis Seminary. In 1892, when Father Charles Koetting departed to take over the pastorate of St. Joseph's Church in Racine, Katzer chose the young Schinner as his secretary.[228] After Zeininger resigned, Katzer anointed Schinner as his vicar general and would have liked to have him as his successor. Schinner was a remarkably popular choice among the clergy and to him goes the lion's share of credit for the ultimate success of Katzer's episcopate. Schinner was bilingual, able to speak German and English fluently (and as time went on managed to master enough Polish to carry on a conversation). He soon developed a reputation as a fair-minded and congenial diocesan functionary.

Rev. Augustine Schinner [AAM]

In 1895, Katzer suffered some sort of emotional and/or physical breakdown and took an eight month trip abroad in company with Zeininger and several other priests. His stops included Rome, where he had an audience with Pope Leo XIII and met with various cardinals.[229] Then to Egypt and a trip up the Nile. Afterwards he went into the Holy Land, through Turkey, Greece, and back to his native Austria. [230] The press portrayed this journey as something of a vacation and Katzer sent regular travelogue reports of his journeys abroad to the German-language *Columbia*. However, that the extended time away from the archdiocese was for recuperation was made known in a letter to Mother Ernesta Funke of the School Sisters of Notre Dame. To the nun, he confided that he hadn't "overcome my nervousness completely."[231] When Katzer returned, he found his mother in ill health and she died shortly after Christmas.[232]

Although he pushed on stoically, Katzer began to fade throughout the remainder of the 1890s. At least this was the observation of cathedral rector, Father James Keogh, who later pushed for Schinner as Katzer's successor, and lauded him as one "who has had practical charge of the archdiocese for nearly eight years, since he was made administrator during the absence of the archbishop."[233] As his health faded, Katzer began to farm out more work to his subordinates. A year before his death, he revivified the deanery system that Heiss had inaugurated in the 1880s and delegated the deans to visit the parishes in their deaneries annually and to establish local school boards in anticipation of the creation of an archdiocesan school system.[234] Schinner was to oversee all this work.

Bishop Augustine Schinner of Superior WI [AAM]

Despite a promising beginning Schinner's ecclesiastical career and life was a disaster after the death of his patron. He held the fort in Milwaukee until the appointment of Sebastian Messmer, and later was dispatched to head up the new diocese of Superior in 1905. Schinner went reluctantly to the far northern city which at that time had the good prospects of becoming a major trade and cultural center on the shores of Lake Superior. However, at the outset of his nine year tenure, Superior's hopes collapsed when Standard Oil mogul John D. Rockefeller withdrew critical support for the industrial growth planned there.[235] Schinner himself became bored and disillusioned with life in the remote diocese which encompassed 16 relatively unpopulated counties at the very top of Wisconsin.

Ultimately, his boredom turned to deep depression and he began to crack. He begged Roman officials to deliver him from the burden of the diocese . "I have not been hindered in my duties," he wrote, "but every mental effort is veritable drudgery, and I cannot do my work as I should like." He even offered to "de-consecrate" himself as bishop, asking at one point if he could be a simple parish priest. He volunteered to assist Bishop Denis Dougherty as a missionary in the far-off Philippines (then an American colony).[236]

Schinner's requests were not heeded but, after a short stint in an Indiana sanitarium, the Vatican transferred him in 1914 to the leadership of the newly created diocese of Spokane, Washington. He here remained for 11 years, and then resigned in 1925, accepting the titular See of Sala and becoming chaplain to the School Sisters of Notre Dame at Mankato, Minnesota. He ultimately got his dream of becoming a missionary when he served for a time in Bolivia. A few years in Bolivia were all he could take and he returned to the United States and found a home in Grand Rapids, Michigan, intending to take care of Mexicans coming into the United States. After "shopping" his services as chaplain and teacher around to several religious communities, he eventually found refuge with the Sisters of the Divine Savior who gave him quarters and care at St. Mary's Convent on 35th and Center Streets in Milwaukee.[237] There he celebrated his 50th anniversary as a priest in 1936 and on February 7, 1937, he died.[238]

The demographics of church life changed dramatically between 1868 and 1903. The Germans continued to hold sway, and dominated most areas of church life. However, a new medley of Catholic groups flooded into Wisconsin, largely attracted by the new industrial economy. Indeed, with the exception of the Scandinavians, who were by and large Lutheran, virtually every new ethnic group that came to Wisconsin in the final decades of the 19th century had a strong Catholic representation. Indeed, some, like the Poles, were virtually all Catholics. This diversity was reflected in new churches, the membership of sisterhoods, the ranks of seminarians, and most importantly in the new faces in the pews and schoolrooms of the Catholic Church. Virtually no other institution in Wisconsin's public life, with the exception of the public schools, held together such an amalgam of different cultures, languages, and ways of life. The "Catholicisms" of the state simply became more numerous. What brought these newcomers was a changing Wisconsin economy that required scores of new laborers.

The New Industrial Economy

Industrial-era realities gave shape to the nature and scope of Catholic visibility in this epoch. Although the Catholic life of the rural and town areas would remain in place (especially since Wisconsin had developed a highly diversified and very successful agricultural economy), most Catholics lived in large cities or near manufacturing operations. Industrial life defined the parameters of every aspect of life—including religion.

Wisconsin's industrial "takeoff" was stimulated by the same new technologies that were creating the larger American industrial revolution. These technologies made possible the mass production of numerous products and materials. A changing transportation system made possible the expansion of markets beyond manufacturing centers or regional areas. The advent of the railroad was a particularly important development for the emergence of the national economy. In Wisconsin, the development of rail lines took off at a rapid pace during the 1850s, greatly facilitating immigration, and subsequent improvements created important rail hubs. At these rail centers existing towns flourished or new towns were created. Communication links—telegraph and telephone—created even stronger bonds and forged closer links between diverse areas of the state. Finally, the new economy generated an abundance of wealth never before seen in Wisconsin. Not only did the rich get richer, but even the working class shared to some degree in the new bounty created by the expanding markets for industrial products. There were, however, also times when the industrial miracle stopped working. Wisconsin's economy exploded with growth between 1879 and 1883, turned down for a time and then resumed another period of robust expansion from the late 1880s until another crash in 1893.[239]

Industrial Milwaukee–Gettelman Brewing Co. [Milwaukee Real Estate Board. *Milwaukee. 100 Photogravures,* Art Gravure & Etching Co., 1892]

The new industrial economy created two interlinking realities that affected church life: an expansive urban growth and a numerous and diverse labor force. As Catholic visibility had adapted itself to the industries and settlement patterns of the founding epoch, so too Catholic life and identity were shaped by these new socioeconomic realities.

The Progress of Industrialization

Industrialization and urbanization were two sides of the same modernizing coin. In the early 1870s, a stream of engineers and developers with the right combination of entrepreneurial, managerial, and inventive skills began to remake the Wisconsin economy. Milwaukee led the way with machine shops, foundries, and breweries, but also in areas like mens clothes, shoes, hats and caps, and even trunks and valises. Racine and Kenosha, like Milwaukee, became major port cities and processors of the grain produced in their respective hinterlands. Neither of them attained the success of Milwaukee, but they did create successful local industries.[240]

In 1890 another burst of industrial expansion further developed the industrial foundations of Wisconsin.[241] Historian John Buenker calls this the "neo-technic" revolution, a term he uses to characterize the new technologies and processes that "spawn[ed] new industries, transform[ed] existing ones, and consign[ed] others to oblivion." In this period he observes, "Giant corporations and factories, highly mechanized mass production, specialized organization and elaborate nation-wide marketing systems appeared." He further notes, that during the heyday of this neotechnic revolution, "Wisconsin soon became a manufacturing Mecca of the Upper Midwest," and "an integral component of the Great Lakes metal and machinery belt that connected Buffalo, Cleveland, Detroit, Chicago, Milwaukee and Duluth-Superior."[242] Hand-in-hand with these developments was the growth of industrial neighborhoods in older cities and towns, and even the creation of all new "industrial suburbs"—towns like Bay View that arose from empty fields to serve a major industry that settled in the area. This shift of people and cities provides an important backdrop for Catholic development.

Milwaukee was the giant. If Eber Brock Ward had been Milwaukee's proto-industrialist, Edward P. Allis created the industry that would be the mainstay of industrial growth, the manufacture of small machines. In 1861 he purchased an old flour-milling equipment plant called the Reliance Works and transformed it into a machine shop. Later, he got a lucrative contract to replace the pipes of the Milwaukee water system, which nearly bankrupted him. Bouncing back, he moved aggressively into manufacturing engines for lumber mills, flour mills, mine ventilation, and water pumps.[243] Other industries and workers followed.

To accommodate the new workers, Milwaukee and its environs were resculpted into new industrial suburbs. West Allis grew up around the Allis-Chalmers Company: South Milwaukee was founded in 1891 in the shadow of the Bucyrus-Erie plant; the industrial suburb of Cudahy was created around a huge meat-packing plant also in 1891; West Milwaukee, incorporated in 1906, was dominated by the huge Pawling Harnifschweger operation.

Racine's industrial transformation began when it won federal help in dredging its "rather unpromising harbor." The new port could now receive important raw materials essential for industrial processing.[244] One of the most important industries to locate in the "Belle City" was founded by Jerome I. Case, who began to manufacture steam-driven farm equipment and became one of the largest manufacturers of threshing machines in the world. Case's success drew others to Racine, which by 1880 had 11 agricultural implement factories, 5 shops making carriages and wagons, and 3 foundry and machine shops. In addition it gained certain specialty operations like the Horlick Malted Milk Company and the S. C. Johnson Company which spe-

Industrial Milwaukee–Milwaukee Works of the Illinois Steel Co. [Milwaukee Real Estate Board. *Milwaukee. 100 Photogravures,* Art Gravure & Etching Co., 1892]

cialized in floor cleaning products. In the second phase, early industries expanded dramatically and new companies came into being. J. I. Case and Horlick were still major employers. But new companies such as Hamilton Beach, Racine Electric, the Dumore Company, and Western Publishing built a solid industrial core in the Belle City.[245]

Neighboring Kenosha took a longer time to develop its industrial system, but by 1886 was well on the road to success when the Chicago Brass company moved to the lake city. By the first part of the 1900s Kenosha's industrial transformation was well underway as scores of Kenoshans worked for the Bain Wagon company, Allen Tannery, Simmons Mattress and various clothing manufacturers. The purchase of the Jeffrey Bicycle Company by Henry Nash would eventually bring the automotive industry to Wisconsin.[246]

In the Rock River Valley, a combination of entrepreneurial skills, sufficient water power and linkage with the network of railroads accounted for the industrial growth of cities like Janesville and Beloit, Beaver Dam, and Watertown. In Beaver Dam, the J. S. Rowell manufacturing company founded the Beaver Dam Cotton Mills. Janesville began manufacturing bed sheets in 1873-1874. By 1885 Watertown had six flour mills, machine shops, a small cotton mill, a woodenware factory, and other industries.[247] When the forces of the neotechnic revolution hit these areas another major burst of industrial activity took place. Industrial growth was augmented by the rail linkage of Dane, Rock, Jefferson, and Walworth counties to Chicago via the city of Rockford.[248] Beloit soon emerged as a major producer of iron and steel products through the Fairbanks, Morse Company, which had been founded in the 1830s. Beloit Iron Works founded in the 1860s made papermaking equipment soon to be used in the Fox River Valley. Later it too specialized in steam and gas engines. Janesville, a few miles upriver from Beloit, made good use of the river's water power and transformed the tobacco grown in Rock and Dane counties into cigars and cigarettes. Parker fountain pens were already being made in the city in the 1880s. Janesville's industrial output also included plows, reapers, threshers and other farm implements (providing for a later transition to auto manufacturing). It also had cotton and woolen mills. The state capital kept industrial growth at bay, dominated as it was by the huge capitol complex and the University of Wisconsin. However, it too had some industrial development: machine tools, corsets, soap, beer, flour, lumper, printing presses, and telephones. It also hosted a regional railroad center and repair shops. Nearby Beaver Dam in Dodge County opened its major industrial site with the Malleable Iron Range works in 1901. A rival company, Beaver Dam Malleable Iron Company likewise grew.

The adjoining counties of Fond du Lac and Sheboygan also felt the winds of change. In Fond du Lac, efforts to become a lumber processing center had been edged out by Oshkosh. The city at the foot of Lake Winnebago turned to manufacturing with wood and metal working industries. Two of Fond du Lac's biggest employers were the Fred

Rueping Leather Company and Giddings and Lewis, a machine-tool maker. Sheboygan grew slowly, not establishing rail contact with Milwaukee until 1872. However, its Lake Michigan location gave it a niche in the emerging economy. Sheboygan manufactured chairs and later became the site of the Kohler Company. It continued its steady growth with specialization in plumbing supples, furniture, refrigerators, wooden ware, footwear, coal and salt docks. Nearby Two Rivers and Manitowoc developed the capacity to make aluminum. In Manitowoc, malt, aluminum cookware, and shipbuilding dominated the local economy.[249]

Patterns of Immigration: 1870-1890

Added to the industrial development were new patterns of immigration that directly affected the nature of Catholic life. By 1880, 30.8 percent of Wisconsin's population were foreign-born.[250]

The strongest foreign-born cohort were German-speaking.[251] They were especially strong in the counties of Racine, Milwaukee, Jefferson, Ozaukee, Washington, Dodge, Fond du Lac, Sheboygan, and Manitowoc. In Milwaukee in 1880, the German-born made up 7 out of 10 foreign-born and they constituted 40 percent of the city population. By 1890, Milwaukee County had a quarter of the state's German-born population. In Dodge County the German-born were 21.3 percent of the population, 17.6 percent in five cities and four incorporated villages, 22.9 percent in the rural areas; Sheboygan had 29.6 percent in the city and 7.4 percent in the remainder of the county. Madison had 7.3 percent German-born, and the rest of Dane County, 8.2 percent. The preponderance of German speakers were Catholics followed by Lutherans.[252]

The Irish-born, the second largest foreign group of Catholics in the state clustered in cities like Milwaukee, Madison and Janesville. The Irish would soon be eclipsed in numbers and in prominence by Poles, who began appearing in sizeable numbers after 1870. Like the Poles, the Bohemians existed as a linguistic and cultural group, but were subsumed into a multinational empire. Wisconsin became an important port of call for them as well. In 1890 the census recorded 1,999 Bohemians. Bohemians often settled close to Germans and an especially large contingent made their homes in Racine.[253] Earlier ethnic groups, Swiss, Belgians, and French Canadians, continued to hang on to their identity. This solid first tier of Catholics would be reinforced by a second wave of immigrants who remade the face of the Catholic Church even more dramatically.

Patterns of Population II: 1890-1920

In the period between 1890 and 1920, Wisconsin became more recognizably "American." Indeed, between 1890 and 1920, Wisconsin's population grew by more than 60 percent and the native born element increased in prominence. The proportion of Wisconsin citizens born in the United States jumped from 26 to 41 percent, and the percentage born in Wisconsin from 57 to 71 percent. In-migrants averaged between 11 and 13 percent per year. The largest segment of the state's population (42 percent) continued to be American-born children of immigrant or mixed parentage. The percentage of foreign-born residents declined from 31 percent to slightly over 17 percent, or from 519,199 to 460,485. Even so by 1920, Wisconsin still had the seventh highest foreign-stock population in the country, more than 58 percent of German ancestry and 15 percent Scandinavian.[254]

However, a new wave of largely Catholic southern and eastern Europeans made the biggest difference in Wisconsin and in the ethnic composition of the archdiocese of Milwaukee. In 1890 southern and eastern Europeans were only 4 percent of the state's foreign-born population. By 1920, the figure was over 30 percent. The biggest rush came between 1900 and 1914 when the Polish segment increased from 6 to 11 percent; Russian and Lithuanian from 1 to 5 percent; Italian, Hungarian and Finnish from virtually nothing to 2 percent each. Wisconsin had 8 percent of the country's Czechs and Slovaks, 6 percent of its Poles, 5 percent of its Slovenians, and 3 percent of its Serbs and Croats.[255]

The Poles were a minor presence until after 1880, but their presence was masked owing to the fact that Poland did not exist as an independent state. Most of Wisconsin's Poles came from Posen and Pomerania, areas under the control of Imperial Germany, and as such may have been counted as Germans. So too were Polish-speaking immigrants from Silesia and West Prussia. While the 1890 census enumerated 17,660 Poles in Wisconsin and 52,121 in 1900, some insisted that the actual numbers were far higher. Polish advocates, like Father Wenceslaus Kruszka, claimed the true number was closer to 200,000 in 1900. One-fourth of Wisconsin's Poles lived in Milwaukee. Other distinctly Polish settlements in the archdiocese were in Berlin, Manitowoc, and Beaver Dam. Racine and Kenosha also had Polish settlements. Poles soon surpassed Norwegians as the second largest immigrant group.[256]

Close behind came other Slavic peoples. Czechs (Bohemians) and Slovaks, shared a similar language, and after 1918 shared a country. There were about 12,000 Czechs in Wisconsin by 1890; by 1910, 16,301—a peak that declined afterwards. By 1910 there were 3,408 Slovak speakers, a number that doubled in the next decade. These western Slavs were joined by southern Slavs: in 1910, almost 4,300 immigrants were Slovenian speakers; in 1920, there were 5,559; 3,188 listed Serbo-Croatian as their nationality in 1910. By 1920, they numbered 4,888.[257]

Wisconsin's Lithuanian population went from 2,907 in 1910 to 4,642 in 1920. Fifty-six percent of the Lithuanians lived in Kenosha, Racine, and Milwaukee. Between 1890 and 1920 the state's Italian-born population jumped from 1,123 to 11,188. In 1920, 100,000 residents claimed Polish as their native language and there were 31,000 Czechs, 3,444 Slovaks, 2,936 Lithuanians, and 2,836 Magyars. Polish-speaking Wisconsinites represented over 10 percent of the state's first and second generation immigrant population. Only the Germans outnumbered them. Czechs, Italians, Slovaks, Slovenians, Serbo-Croatians, Lithuanians and Magyars represented about 20 percent of Wisconsin's foreign stock. "Thus within a single generation," notes historian John Buenker, "southern and eastern European immigrants and their children had become a substantial part of Wisconsin's people."[258]

Patterns of Settlement

Industrial expansion brought new demographic realities to the state. Wisconsin's urban population in 1870 was located in 27 centers. Milwaukee, the leading city, numbered 71,440. Only three cities, Milwaukee, Oshkosh, and Fond du Lac had populations over 10,000 in 1870.[259] By 1890, Milwaukee had a population of 204,315. Eleven other Wisconsin cities had populations over 10,000. Also by 1890, one-third of Wisconsinites lived in cities of 2,500 or more, and 42 percent lived in officially incorporated cities and villages. Catholic growth, reflected in the growing number of parishes, mirrored this growing population.

Even more significant the necessities of industrialism imposed their own template of values and virtues on the state. Because the life of the state was so tied up in industrial manufacturing, Wisconsin's populace was deeply committed to being a "productive" people in every way. Social and cultural institutions of all kinds constantly reinforced the requisite values for productivity: sobriety, a strong work ethic, and a balanced life. Residents were urged to be homeowners and to make an investment in local neighborhoods. Institutions, like churches, echoed these sentiments, reinforced them in moral and ethical training and benefitted from them. Wisconsin's magnificent Catholic churches, schools and social welfare institutions reflected these values.

In 1910 when the state was only 43 percent urban, 81 percent of Hungarians and Slovaks, and 67 percent of Poles lived in urban places, generally in southeastern industrial cities. In 1920 when the state was half urban, about 75 percent of Lithuanians, Italians, South Slavs, and Hungarians were urban dwellers. Only Czechs and Austrians were evenly distributed between rural and urban.

Poles, the largest contingent, continued to make Milwaukee County their main center and were to be found not only in the city itself, but in industrial suburbs such as South Milwaukee, Cudahy, and West Allis. Outside of Milwaukee they lived in two industrial counties, Racine and Kenosha. A substantial number resided in the rural counties of the north.

Until 1890, Czechs and Slovaks lived in both urban and rural areas. Arrivals after 1890 settled in southeast industrial cities. In seven of the state's nine largest cities, Czechs outnumbered Slovaks—except in Kenosha and Superior. By 1920, cities were home to 98 percent of the Czechoslovakians (mostly Slovaks) in Kenosha county, 80 percent in Racine County, and 78 percent in Milwaukee County. About 80 percent of the state's

Croatian and Slovenian immigrants were in Milwaukee, Sheboygan, Kenosha, or Racine counties.

Italians had different patterns. Early northern Italians settled in Fond du Lac County (Campbellsport). However, by the 1890s southern Italians settled in industrial cities. By 1920 over three-fourths lived in Milwaukee, Kenosha, Racine, Dane, Rock, or Waukesha counties. Nearly all of Madison's Italians and about two-thirds of Milwaukee's were Sicilians, while those who lived in Racine and Kenosha were heavily Calabrian. Over 70 percent of Hungarians resided in Milwaukee and Racine counties (over half in the city themselves), with sizeable populations in Dodge, Kenosha, and Waukesha counties. In 1920, 70 percent of Kenosha's foreign-born population had arrived after 1900, as had more than half of those in Racine, Sheboygan and Milwaukee.

The emergence of the industrial economy had tremendous implications for Catholicism in the remaining counties of the archdiocese of Milwaukee. It brought a tremendous burst of population to the cities of the state. As a result, Catholicism's meridian in Wisconsin was now definitively urban and working-class. By 1910, many immigrant Poles and Italians were recorded among the ranks of day laborers, street and railroad track layers, and dockhands. In Kenosha, Italian immigrants were a large part of the workforce of the local foundries. Polish citizens worked making cabinets.[260]

At the risk of over-simplifying the economic and social differences in the immigrant community in the archdiocese, one could subscribe to the observation of a Notre Dame sister who worked at St. Hyacinth parish in Milwaukee and wrote that the parents of her school children were, "Poor day-laborers, most of them fathers of families of many children."[261] A similar observation was made of West Allis, "The population consists mostly of factory laborers who with their families established themselves in the proximity of their means of living. Many of them are good Catholics, Germans as well as Irish, who had the erection of a house of God and a parochial school at heart."[262] Indeed the average immigrant worker in Milwaukee in 1908 made about $453 a year working 10-to-12 hours every day, six days a week.[263]

The strong Catholic presence among the ranks of the working classes was also evident in parochial formation. New parishes, many of them ethnic, grew up near the new factories and shops. Likewise, older generations of Catholics who benefitted from the new wealth by either owning new businesses or becoming part of the swelling white-collar middle management also built new churches and schools that reflected their status. Everything grew during this period: parishes, the seminary, the cathedral, social welfare, sisterhoods, and schools. By 1903, the gales of industrial wealth were blowing into the sails of Catholic life.

The Urban Parish: The Deeper Meaning

Viewed merely as social institutions, Roman Catholic parishes were a vital part of the process of urban community building. Commenting on the rapid development of parishes in Milwaukee during the 1880s, the *Catholic Citizen* observed: "Population still centers around churches in our cities. The churches exert an influence in persuading people where they shall center. So much so that shrewd owners of tracts, platted into lots, help the speedy sale of their property by giving free sites for churches."[264] The newspaper urged church planners to locate new parishes near land cheap enough for people to purchase their homes. "Otherwise they are not apt to prove reliable renters of pews." Likewise, the new churches should take into account, "the industrial advantages of the location, so that the men of the parish may have as good facilities for their work as circumstances permit."[265]

Although the *Citizen* had inverted the normal order of parish development following the pace of population shift (generally induced by the opening of new factories and commercial outlets in undeveloped parts of cities), it was quite right in describing the impact of Catholic movement into these areas. Catholic parishes in fact enhanced the quality of urban life in Milwaukee and elsewhere by creating what historian John McGreevy calls "dense social networks" which included often massive churches, schools, gymnasiums, and social halls.[266] Within the often disorienting conditions of urban life and work, Catholic parishes provided a sense of identity and belonging.[267] Such was expressed by Charles King, a Milwaukee writer who described the neighborhood surrounding St. Stanislaus parish for *Cosmopolitan Magazine* in 1891, "The twin towers of the Polish church stand like double sentries high in the air, and all around them, in that far away section, hundreds of comfortable little homes are grouped where one might wander for a week and hear no language but that of Kosciusko."[268] Milwaukee's parochial growth in this era reflected the new industrial realities. The growing diversity of the archdiocesan population gave birth to a new generation of ethnic parishes. In addition, the new wave of wealth provided resources to build churches even grander and more glorious than the first generation of Milwaukee churches. Sometimes the new ethnic churches were built along these lines—often exceeding the capacity of their largely working-class parishioners to sustain them.

The New Catholicisms: Parochial Growth

Between 1868 and 1903, the Catholic population of the archdiocese of Milwaukee grew from roughly 180,000 to nearly 240,000. As noted above, the primary cause of this growth was the huge influx of European immigrants who came to work in the state's growing industries.

Germans still dominated and their increasing visibility and power was manifested in both the size and scope of their parochial establishments. From the nucleus of the three German parishes of the first generation—St. Mary's, Holy Trinity, and St. Joseph's—came an array of even larger and more magnificent churches that adorned Milwaukee's skyline. New German Catholic communities began to be established to the west, including the Capuchin-run St. Francis of Assisi (1871), and to the south, St. Anthony's in 1873. In 1879, the Capuchins accepted a second Milwaukee parish, Holy Cross, located on Bluemound Road. Directly west of the new church were the growing county institutions (especially the county hospital and insane asylums) to which the sons of St. Francis also provided generous ministry over the years. Racine's Germans branched out from St. Mary's Church to found St. Joseph's in 1876 and Holy Name in 1885. In Sheboygan, the German St. Peter Claver opened its doors in 1889.

The Irish and English-speaking managed to keep pace. In Milwaukee, the nucleus of English-speaking Catholicism had been St. John's Cathedral and the Jesuit-run St. Gall Church at Third and State Streets. In 1872, Bay View's Immaculate Conception, an "industrial" parish, was unabashedly Irish in part because of its leadership by Father Thomas Fagan, an American-born priest of Irish extraction. A second Jesuit parish, Holy Name of Jesus, opened at 12th and State Streets in 1878 and would eventually replace the old St. Gall's (and then itself be replaced by the building of Gesu in 1894). St. Patrick's Church had been founded in 1876. In 1881 Father Hiram Fairbanks was appointed pastor and in 1895 he built a new church. Designed by J. J. Egan of Chicago, the charming English Gothic church soon dominated

Table 2-1

City	1870 Population	# of Parishes	1900 Population	# of Parishes
Milwaukee	71,440	10	285,315	27
Racine	9,330	2	29,102	7
Kenosha	4,309	2	11,606	2
Sheboygan	5,310	1	22,962	2
Manitowoc	5,168	1	11,786	2
Fond du Lac	12,764	3	15,110	5
Madison	9,176	2	19,164	3
Beaver Dam	3,265	3	5,128	4
Janesville	8,789	1	13,185	2
Beloit	4,396	1	10,436	1

its surroundings. Replete with "large and handsome tracery windows" its giant steeple soared 122 feet over the Menominee Valley and was topped by a Celtic cross. Flanking the church were a series of heavily ornamented buttresses. Oak pews and railings adorned the interior along with white marble altars and stained glass windows crafted by the famous Tyrolese Art Glass Studio of Innsbruck.[269] The same architect had earlier rebuilt the old Irish church of St. Mark's in Kenosha (renamed St. James in 1883 in honor of pastor, Father James Cleary). This elegant new church was Kenosha's most lovely church.[270] Holy Name, the cathedral, and St. Patrick's would vie for the dwindling number of Irish and English-speaking Catholics in the city and the competition could be tough. St. Patrick's first pastor, the volcanic John W. Vahey, regularly warned the Jesuit pastor, Stanislaus Lalumiere, to refrain from "poaching" on his ecclesiastical territory on the other side of the Menominee River. "Did St. Ignatius embody in his constitutions the right to invade the parishes of neighboring priests. If so, I doubt the wisdom of the church that pronounces him a saint."[271] Years later, St. Patrick parish would be handed over to the charge of the same Jesuit Fathers that Vahey had excoriated.

St. John's Cathedral: Irish Bastion

Clearly, the center of Irish and English-speaking Catholic activity in Milwaukee was the Cathedral of St. John. After the death of Kundig in 1879, Henni made Father Peter Donohoe, a former assistant at the cathedral, the pastor, thus establishing a long line of Irish-surnamed clerics who headed the premier church of the diocese. When ill health

St. James Church, Kenosha [AAM]

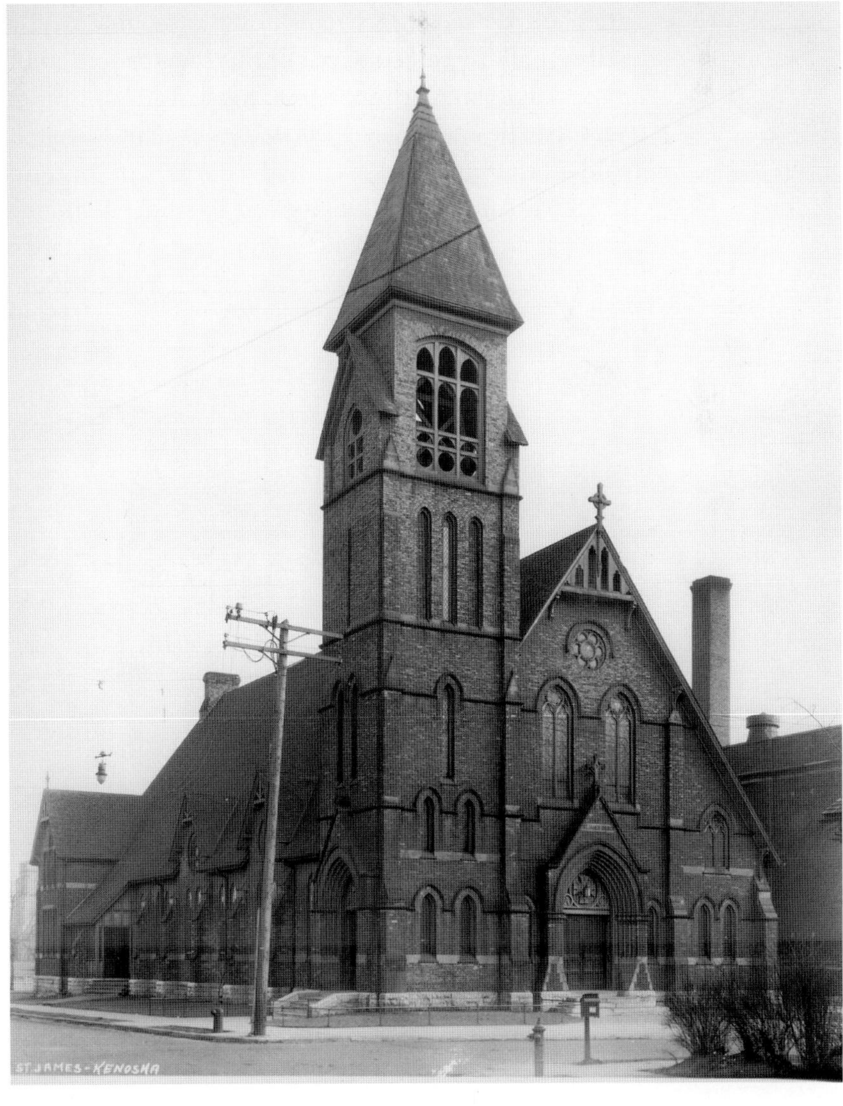

felled Donohoe in the 1880s, his popular curate, Father James Keogh, began a long reign as cathedral rector. Before he was through, Keogh substantially transformed the physical plant of the church and reinforced its urban-Irish identity. Henni's last years, as we have seen, saw a major physical and mental decline in the prelate, and the management of diocesan and cathedral finances had by then become hopelessly and disastrously intermingled. Between 1880 and 1885, Keogh helped pull the cathedral out of this financial morass. By 1885, he reported to his parishioners that he had retired the $26,000 debt, paid all the bills, and even had a surplus of $288.64. After 1885, he planned to undertake a massive series of improvements on the aging building, which included rebuilding the tower, a rich interior redecoration, the installation of a new organ and the construction of a new residence for the Brothers of the Holy Cross who taught in the Cathedral boys school.[272] Keogh's hope was to have a refurbished and renewed cathedral in time to celebrate the 50th anniversary of the laying of its cornerstone in 1897.

Rev. James J. Keogh [AAM]

By early 1892, Keogh had raised nearly $50,000 and opened bids on a major renovation of the interior for the church. The task went to the firm of Leibig and Gartner, a local interior decorator (who beat out the prestigious Tiffany Art Glass Works and Decorating Company of New York). The new inner decor was largely designed and executed by Thaddeus Zukotynski who was "said to be without peer in oil painting in which the Cathedral" would be finished throughout.[273] New images adorned the walls, depicting the theological virtues, symbols of the sacraments, and pictures of the four evangelists. In the sanctuary the half dome was decorated by stars presided over by an image of the Virgin Mary. The paintings of Munich masters that had been brought over by Henni were also rehung in the sanctuary. Complementing the interior painting was a series of 24 windows—two panels each—that depicted Old and New Testament scenes.[274] Keogh supplied the subject matter for the windows which were designed by Roger Watts of London and executed by the London-based John Hardman Company. The windows were not done at the time of the 1897 celebrations, but as money became available, all 24 windows were eventually installed.

The most visible outer sign of rejuvenation was the rebuilding of the tower. The old onion dome tower had presided over the neighborhood since the 1850s. But its wooden construction and the lack of an adequate drainage system around it had caused the structure to rot, and Father Donohue had taken it down in 1880. For 12 years the glorious building sat denuded of the tower that was necessary to make it whole. Finally in 1892, thanks to a $10,000 benefaction from former Mayor John Black, a new tower was erected. It was "intended to harmonize fully with the style of the body of the church ... with no suggestion of a modern addition to an old building."[275] The architectural firm of Ferry and Clas (who also built Milwaukee's *beaux arts* library and the majestic buildings of the State Historical Society in Madison) replicated the elegant tower of the Church of the Holy Trinity in Paris, an architectural masterpiece crafted in the 1860s by Theodore Ballu. Even the great apostle of America's Gothic revival architecture, Ralph Adams Cram, offered a backhanded compliment to the new tower, "In spite of its not being Gothic, it is the finest tower west of Philadelphia."[276]

Keogh's efforts to renew the cathedral hit two serious snags. The first was the establishment of a rival parish for English speakers, Holy Rosary, which was carved out of the former cathedral boundaries on the east side in 1884. The next year Milwaukee architect E. Townsend Mix designed a new structure for the church located on Oakland Avenue.[277] Later, Father Robert Roche became the full-time pastor. An excellent preacher and popular pastor, he soon began to woo people away from the cathedral.

Secondly, the residential neighborhood that once surrounded the great church began to fade away. The natural transition of downtown residents to more upscale housing to the north and west of the cathedral was accelerated when a devastating blaze, known as the "Third Ward fire," swept through the old neighborhoods adjacent to the cathedral on October 28, 1892. Before it was extinguished, it destroyed 20 square blocks in the ward and left nearly 2,000 homeless.[278] Keogh and the cathedral clergy worked in relief efforts and opened the cathedral that night for temporary quarters for the homeless. Arch-

Cathedral of St. John the Evangelist, Milwaukee [AAM]

bishop Frederick X. Katzer, along with other Catholic parishes and individuals, donated generously to the relief fund.[279] The Third Ward fire emptied the cathedral of many of its longtime parishioners. "The Irish of the Third Ward are disappearing and their homes and places are being filled by the members of the progressive Italian colony," declared A. G. Wright, the compiler of the city directory.[280] Eventually the cathedral would make pastoral arrangements for this new group of Catholics.

The decision of Archbishop Katzer to move his residence away from the cathedral and nearer the large churches going up on the west side, St. Michael's for the German-speaking and Gesu for the English-speaking, also had an impact on the cathedral. The *Catholic Citizen* acknowledged the significance of Katzer's move and what it might bode for the future of St. John's. It was not enough to merely invoke the titular preeminence of the cathedral as a reason for asserting its primacy and importance among the churches of Milwaukee. "The really determining considerations are the number, culture, affluence, and intelligence of the people making up the congregation," wrote editor Humphrey J. Desmond, who was certain that St. John's still possessed these traits. "But if the leadership ever passes away, the most likely candidate is the church of the Jesuits to be built on Grand Avenue."[281] Indeed, the high gothic steeples of the Jesuit Gesu Church soon soared high over the Milwaukee landscape. This church fit with the name of the street on which it was located: "Grand." When some wondered if Archbishop Katzer would make the newly built and elaborately decorated St. Michael's Church on 24th and Cherry his new cathedral, he denied it. "Rome alone has the power to do that."[282]

Cathedral of St. John the Evangelist, Milwaukee [AAM]

A New Generation of Parishes

Beginning in the 1880s, both German and Irish Catholics began to move out of the Catholic heartland on the east side of Milwaukee. As noted earlier, in 1885, Holy Rosary had been founded north of the cathedral. In 1889, the growing number of Irish railroad workers near the car repair yards of the Chicago Northwestern led to the establishment of St. Rose parish on Michigan.

Other "Irish" enclaves included St. Rose's in Racine in 1889 and St. Patrick's in Madison in the same year. Working-class Irish Catholics established St. Matthew's Church on the south side in 1893, a refuge for the dwindling number of south side Irish. Subsequent churches built farther west in Milwaukee included Holy Ghost (1902) and St. Thomas Aquinas (1902) which accommodated the needs of those moving farther west. Founding pastor Father Edward Blackwell, formerly of Fox Lake, was sent to establish the new St. Thomas Aquinas (which he tried hard to have named for his patron St. Edward).[283] In 1901 he built a church/school combination but worked diligently to raise funds for a new church. By 1912 he was able to secure the services of Wisconsin architect Alexander Eschweiler to design his new temple. Costing an enormous $100,000, St. Thomas Aquinas was done in Eschweiler's characteristic English-Gothic style. The interior had an "open tim-

Holy Ghost Church, Milwaukee, under construction [ASSF]

St. Thomas Aquinas Church, Milwaukee [*12th Annual Convention American Federation of Catholic Societies Souvenir*, Milwaukee, WI August 10th–14th, 1913, p. 69]

ber" roof and the sanctuary was marked off by a partial rood. At the center was an elaborate marble altar with two harts drinking depicting the Eucharistic interpretation of the psalm "As the Hind Longeth for Running Waters."[284] Of the interior of St. Thomas, a priest wrote, "Our parish church was not excessively ornate. Its chaste solemn simplicity was much like the pure doctrine and logical order of its Patron, St. Thomas Aquinas."[285] This "chaste solemn simplicity" stood in contrast to the new German churches.

In 1884, a new German parish at 24th and Cherry in Milwaukee, was carved out of the boundaries of St. Joseph's and named for St. Michael. In 1895, neighborhood growth had resulted in the opening of St. Anne at 35th and Wright. German-speaking parishes opened in every other direction as well. On the south side, St. Augustine on Howell Avenue appeared in 1888 and St. Lawrence on Greenfield Avenue the next year. On the growing north side of the city (destined to be a major center of German life in Milwaukee), St. Boniface on Clark Street opened its doors in 1888. In 1902 another German-speaking parish was split off from the rapidly growing St. Boniface and named for St. Elizabeth. With his personal fortune, Monsignor Leonard Batz opened Ss. Peter and Paul on the east side in 1889.[286]

St. Lawrence Church, Milwaukee [AAM]

Twin Towers of Excellence: St. Michael's and Gesu

Although the creation of the German and English parishes seemed to replicate the existing patterns of parochial development described earlier, there was something different about this next wave of parish growth. These new churches were larger and more architecturally elaborate than those of the first generation of Catholic life. The Germans led the way. Already in 1884, the parish of St. Michael at 24th and Cherry Streets had begun a cluster of buildings designed by the noted Milwaukee architect Henry Messmer. A combination church, school, and parish house served their needs until 1892, when plans for a new church were drawn by the architectural firm of Schnetzke and Liebert. The parishioners of St. Michael's spared no expense in building and decorating this huge neo-Gothic temple that left its mark on Milwaukee's emerging skyline. Carved wooden altars were

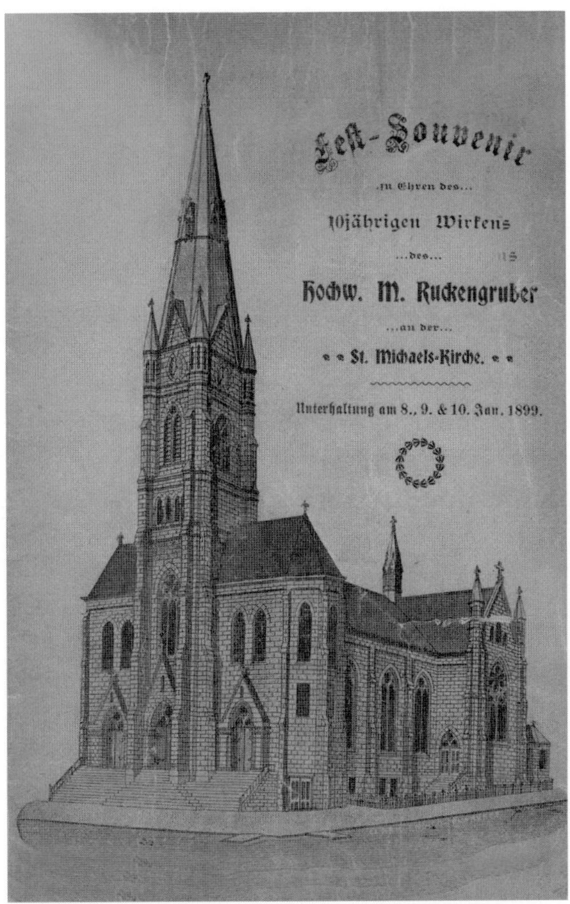

St. Michael Church, Milwaukee [AAM]

designed by master architect and builder Erhard Brielmaier, destined to play an important role in Milwaukee's architectural history. Parish member Paul N. Klose designed the interior adornments, and Thaddeus Zukotynski, who also worked on the interior of St. John's Cathedral, provided paintings. Five tower bells were hoisted into the huge steeple and rang out with joy as parishioners worshiped in a rich environment reminiscent of some of the finest churches of Europe.[287]

As noted earlier, the biggest Irish monument of all was the elegant Gesu, designed and erected in 1893-1894. The two Jesuit parishes of St. Gall's and Holy Name had merged quietly in 1889, soon taxing the limited resources of Holy Name's space. The Jesuits eventually disposed of the St. Gall property on 2nd and Sycamore (carefully storing the art treasures and altars that had adorned the church); and on land they had acquired at 12th and Grand, laid plans for the new church. They commissioned Hanover-born architect H. C. Koch, architect of Milwaukee city hall, to draw up plans for a Gothic church on the west side of Milwaukee. Excavations began in the fall of 1892 and the cornerstone was laid in May 1893 amidst a huge public parade in which 7,000 marched.[288] By mid-December 1894 Milwaukee had another architectural masterpiece adorning its main thoroughfare.[289] The new Gesu Church's facade soared 74 feet into the air and was 54 feet wide; it was reminiscent to some of the facade of the great cathedral of Chartres. Its two towers added to the elegance of the church, one reaching 252 feet and the other 215 feet. Into one of them a 2,800 pound bell was placed.

Within, some of the most magnificent decorations were provided by Harriet Barker Cramer, the well-to-do wife of Protestant William Cramer, owner of the *Evening Wisconsin*. Their lives are worth brief consideration. Harriet was a native of Fond du Lac and had married William Cramer, already a successful newspaper man. Flush with money, they traveled abroad and managed to get trapped in Paris in the summer of 1870 when

Gesu Church, Milwaukee, under construction [MUA]

Prussian armies besieged the city. Both of the Cramers were generous benefactors of the archdiocese of Milwaukee and were particularly close to Jesuit Father Stanislaus Lalumiere. In 1877, she and Lalumiere had played important roles in bringing the Sisters of the Good Shepherd to open a house for poor and delinquent girls. Harriet cajoled her husband into donating property for the House of the Good Shepherd on North Avenue. When the state attempted to charter a similar school at Sparta, she decamped to Madison and personally lobbied the legislature to stop the bill, fearing it would jeopardize the work of the Good Shepherd Sisters. Her passion for the religious training of delinquent children caused her to press for a Catholic ministry to the State Industrial School for Boys and Lalumiere served as its first chaplain. In 1883, the Cramers had the misfortune to be caught in the tragic Newhall House fire—in the posh hotel where they lived in Milwaukee. After suffering terrible burns, both barely escaped the blaze. Nonetheless, they continued to give. Harriet donated to the building of Our Lady of Pompeii in the Third Ward and gave a great deal of money to Marquette University. Her husband William, blind and deaf at the end of his life, converted to Catholicism on his deathbed in 1905.[290]

For the inside of Gesu, Cramer purchased polished Amberg granite columns that set off the aisle from the nave. She also saw to it that a magnificent depiction of the *Pietá* done by sculptor Giovanni Dupre, a gift she had given to St. Gall Church in 1867, was transferred to the church, along with paintings. Three altars from the old St. Gall's and two from Holy Name were transferred to the new church, but they were also eventually replaced with permanent marble ones. It took time to finish off the plans for the decoration of the interior, including the magnificent rose window which faced north on Grand Avenue. However, the empty window slots were soon filled with elegant stained glass windows, designed and executed by the Royal Bavarian Institute of Munich. English-speaking Catholics knew they had "arrived" when they entered the precincts of their new church by Christmas 1894, and they watched in awe as the ongoing process of completing the interior decor of the great church unfolded before their eyes.

In 1901, the final touch was added when Mrs. Margaretha Lonstorf donated $15,000 in memory of her son Eugene for a new portico to replace the shabby temporary entrance to the church. Picking up on the Gothic design of the building, the portico provided a grand entrance to the elaborate church. "This work will complete the exterior finish of the church edifice .... It is said that it will be one of the finest entrances to a church to be found in the northwest."[291] A chronicler of the School Sisters of Notre Dame summed up the meaning of these great buildings by noting in the motherhouse chronicle, "The grand contributions which made this undertaking possible, testify to both the wealth and liberality of many members of the parish."[292]

All of these churches soon became bastions of elegance in the growing archdiocese of Milwaukee, and reflected the growing preponderance of the Catholic presence in the see city. The nineteen German and Irish churches listed below (Table 2-2) reflect a major Catholic claim on increasingly precious urban space. The elegance of these buildings, and the amount of money needed to build, adorn, and sustain them represent one of the single most important private contributions to the development of Milwaukee in its history. By the time of the death of Frederick Katzer (1903), the Catholic identity of the community was even more sharply etched along the skyline of the city.

The Industrial Parishes

By the end of the 19th century, every major city or town in Wisconsin was an industrial city. Industrialists often assisted in the creation of churches from all denominations by donating land, money, and other resources.

Gesu Church, Milwaukee [MUA]

In the first phase of industrial development, the suburb of Bay View modeled the industrial parish. The opening of Immaculate Conception Church there in 1871 was the harbinger of the nature of diocesan development for the years to come. The new parish, established on the corner of Kinnickinnic and Russell Streets was built on lands donated by the Milwaukee Iron Company, which had been created by Detroit native Eber Brock Ward. Bay View, a small settlement in the Walker's Point section of Mil-

Table 2-2

Church	Year Established	Architect of Final Church Building
Immaculate Conception (I)	1872	Herman Buemming and Gustave Dick
St. Francis of Assisi (G)	1872	William Schickel
St. Anthony (G)	1873	Naescher and Heer
Holy Name (I)	1876	Unknown
St. Patrick (I)	1876	J. J. Egan
Holy Cross (G)	1880	Unknown
St. Michael (G)	1884	Schnetzke and Liebert
Holy Rosary (I)	1885	E. Townsend Mix
St. Augustine (G)	1889	Unknown
St. Boniface (G)	1888	August Riesch
St. Lawrence (G)	1889	Unknown
St. Rose (I)	1889	H. Paul Schnetzky
Ss. Peter and Paul (G)	1890	Unknown
St. Matthew (I)	1893	Herman Buemming and Gustave Dick
Gesu (I)	1895	H. C. Koch
Holy Redeemer (G)	1898	Unknown
Holy Ghost (I)	1902	Alexander Eschweiler
St. Elizabeth (G)	1902	Unknown
St. Thomas Aquinas (I)	1902	Alexander Eschweiler

waukee, was largely owned by banker Alexander Mitchell. Milwaukee Iron's progress was erratic at first. It flourished for a time and went out of existence temporarily after Ward's death in 1875. But it was revived in 1878 by the North Chicago Rolling Mills, and once again its payroll spiked up to nearly 1500. Immaculate Conception became one of the first Catholic parishes to be created in direct response to (and with the assistance of) Wisconsin's industrial "takeoff" in the 19th century. It survived the various vicissitudes of the company's financial fortune, interacted with the other denominations whose churches were built in proximity by the paternalistic factory owners, and experienced a continual shift in the demographics of its parish membership that reflected the changing workforce of the mill. Immaculate Conception mirrored in important ways the significant role an industrial plant played in the shape and nature of a Catholic parish.

In the second or "neo-technic" phase of industrialization, two areas south of Milwaukee became the sites of important industrial development. South Milwaukee was incorporated as a village in 1892. Dominated by the huge Bucyrus Erie and later Ladish plants, South Milwaukee rapidly filled up with working-class people of every nationality. Three parishes developed in the area: St. Mary's, for the English-speaking, founded in 1893, St. John for the Germans in 1894, and St. Adalbert for the Polish in 1898. Next door in the meat-packing center of Cudahy, three parishes were created as well: St. Frederick for the Germans in 1896, Holy Family for the Polish in 1902, and St. Joseph for the Slovaks in 1909.

On the north side of the city, the industrial suburb of North Milwaukee welcomed the foundation of Holy Redeemer parish in 1897. Substantial donations from local businessmen helped to cover a large portion of the $12,000 need to build the 50 by 100 foot church. At the cornerstone laying, Father Peter Theisen "paid an eloquent tribute to the North Milwaukee business men for their liberality in contributing to the erection of the church."[293]

Immaculate Conception Church, Milwaukee
[AAM]

Holy Redeemer Church Hall, Milwaukee [AAM]

Southwest of the city, the E. P. Allis and Chalmers Corporation of Chicago had merged in 1901 and decided to build a new plant on the vacant lands once called North Greenfield. The company was destined to become Wisconsin's largest private employer. Other large industrial firms located themselves on the abundant lands. These included Kearney and Trecker, Pressed Steel Tank Company, Prescott Steam Pump, Federal Malleable, Gerlinger Steel Casting, Wehr Steel, and Milwaukee Stamping. Cheap land was snapped up by enterprising workers and real estate agents; soon neighborhoods began to sprout. The suburb that developed acquired a distinctive working-class character, and it too began to sprout Catholic parishes to serve the medley of ethnic workers that moved to the community. Since the closest Catholic outpost was the Soldier's Home, Archbishop Katzer sent military chaplain Michael Huston to establish Holy Assumption parish. Huston did not stay long, but the new parish with 13 families was turned over to young Father Julius Burbach, an assistant priest at old St. Mary's on Broadway.[294] Although West Allis was filling up with a medley of ethnic Catholics, Burbach insisted that it would be known as a German church.[295] By 1902, he built a temporary church designed by Nicholas Dornbach for $18,000.[296] West Allis boomed as the new plant expanded. Burbach became not only a founding pastor, but also a highly influential figure in the development of West Allis itself. He was on good terms with all of the owners and executives of the huge company, and worked with other civic leaders to lay out parks, plan city hall, and develop a cultural and social life. He even wrote a highly respectable history of the community.[297] West Allis grew spatially and its demographic diversity increased apace. Burbach contributed substantially to the growth of the city's "downtown" by erecting a most unusual permanent (for the locale) "Spanish Mission" style brick church in 1916. Designed by architect A.C. Clas, the 150-foot structure sported a green tile roof and terra cotta trimmings. Burbach reigned over Holy Assumption until felled by ill health in the 1950s.[298]

The Church of the Holy Assumption was the mother community for the entire area, and the westward expansion of West Allis is reflected in the medley of new parishes that spun off the mother church, geared both to territorial and ethnic needs. In 1907, St. Mary Help of Christians Church was founded.

Rev. Julius Burbach [Courtesy of Eileen Krahn]

In 1909, Polish Catholics were invited to join the new St. Joseph parish. St. Aloysius Gonzaga was founded in 1920 and several years later St. Rita was opened. The tiny Italian community opened a chapel in honor of Our Lady of Mount Carmel in 1938-1939.

The lives of these parishes were intertwined with the well-being of the Allis Chalmers works. Company officials were generous to church needs and gave to building funds; industrial wages provided the sustenance of these communities. Another major difference was in schools. Here the German speakers perpetuated their practice of creating new schools simultaneously with the erection of the parish. The School Sisters of Notre Dame laid claim to the new German parish schools. But even more remarkably, the English-speaking parishes, now mandated to do so by the prescriptions of the Third Plenary Council of Baltimore and the unflinching insistence of the archbishops of Milwaukee, began to increase the number of their schools as well. Gesu, for example, inherited the schools from St. Gall's and Holy Name and built its own new school in 1899, staffed by the Sisters of Charity of the Blessed Virgin Mary, an English-speaking congregation from Dubuque. The Dominican Sisters of Sinsinawa took the lead as the major congregation staffing English-speaking schools, but other religious communities of women soon began to enter the ranks of Milwaukee's teaching sisterhoods.

Holy Assumption Church, West Allis [AAM]

The use of elegant and capacious church buildings and schools to establish a viable urban presence was not invented by the German- or English-speaking, but it was certainly replicated by other Catholic ethnic groups—most notably the Poles.

Polish Catholicism

As noted earlier, it is difficult to account with any degree of accuracy the actual number of Poles living in Wisconsin between 1860 and 1920. However, their numbers did increase substantially in this period.[299] Attracted largely to the lakeshore counties and to some rural areas, by 1880 the Poles made up one-third of the foreign-born population of Wisconsin. In 1890, the first year that foreign-born per county were enumerated, it was revealed that there were 17,660 Poles in Wisconsin: 10,066 in Milwaukee County alone and 2,100 in Portage. Trempeleau, Marathon, and Manitowoc counties had more than 500 Polish-born residents. The 1900 census further broke down Polish settlement by partition, and the population of the state's Poles surged to 31,103. In 1905, the census number was 36,285 Polish-born in the state, with 18,527 in Milwaukee.

Poland had been dissolved as a geopolitical entity at the end of the 18th century, so Poles were also enumerated by the part of the Polish partition where they were born (Germany, Austria, or Russia). In Wisconsin by 1900, 80 percent of the Polish-born were originally from the German partition, 11 percent from the Russian, 9 percent from Austrian or elsewhere. In the migration that came into the state between 1900-1905, the majority of Wisconsin Poles were still from the German partition (69.6 percent) but the number from Russia rose to 9.8 percent. In Milwaukee County in 1900, the percentage of German-born Poles declined from 88.3 percent to 80.2 percent. Likewise, the number of Russian Poles settling in Racine and Kenosha increased.

The 1910 census showed that there were about 128,915 first and second generation Poles. During the decade from 1911 to 1920, only Racine and Kenosha registered a sharp increase in foreign-born. The number of foreign-born and second generation Poles increased to 152,063. Milwaukee was still the leader of Polish Wisconsin with 70,238 Polish Americans, 24,374 of whom were foreign-born. Other archdiocesan cities with substantial Polish communities were Kenosha (3,227) and Racine (2,427).

However, scholars of the Polish presence in America almost universally agree that the Poles in America were undercounted by the census. The Polish language daily newspaper *Kuryer Polski*, founded in Milwaukee in 1888, began to monitor Polish numbers in the state. In 1896 they figured the number to be at 40,000 in Milwaukee and 115,000 for the whole state. By 1902, the paper insisted that there were 58,000 Poles in Milwaukee. In 1913 *Kuryer* reported there were 85,000 Poles in Milwaukee and by 1915 they claimed 100,000 Poles in Milwaukee County. The *Kuryer* statistics suggest that the true-Polish American population of Milwaukee was around 90,000. The actual statistics may never be known, although this study tends to favor more the *Kuryer* statistics than the occasionally erratic U. S. Census.

The significance of these numbers for the history of the Catholic presence in Wisconsin is evident. Most Poles were Catholics and their increasing numbers made them an important element of the diverse tapestry of archdiocesan groups. As with other ethnic groups, their main vehicle for religious-cultural expression was the ethnic parish. The *Kuryer Polski* noted in 1903, "Whoever is familiar with the history of these churches will know at the same time the history of Polish immigration in Milwaukee."[300]

Like all other ethnic groups, the visible sign of Polish identity was the ethnic church. Patterns of Polish settlement in the state tended initially to be in the agricultural areas that would later become part of the dioceses of Green Bay and La Crosse. In a fairly interesting example of local development and Catholic church formation, the efforts of land company baron John J. Hof who began selling land to Poles in Shawano County in 1877 are worth noting.[301] Perhaps taking a page from the Henni/Salzmann school of land boosterism, Hof recognized that churches enhanced the attractiveness of property for certain groups of immigrants. Hof shrewdly donated 23 acres for a church in Hofa Park and gave 100 acres for the formation of a Polish Franciscan Friary at Pulaski, Wisconsin, in 1888. Both the church at Hofa Park and the Franciscan monastery figured prominently in booster materials generated by Hof and Company. The Franciscan friars devoted themselves to work with Polish Wisconsinites, staffing missions, running a school, printing Polish devotional literature and keeping alive the flame of the Catholic Polish faith.

Another cluster of Polish development in the archdiocese was in Green Lake County, especially in the city of Berlin midway between Milwaukee and Stevens Point—two centers of Polish life—and two parishes catering to Poles were formed in 1873 and in 1894. Polish citizens in Northheim in Sheboygan County were numerous enough to build a church in 1868. In the Rock River Valley, Polish settlements in Beaver Dam, Ripon, and Princeton were to be found; and eventually parish churches.

But rural Polonia was far outstripped by the urban dwellers. Indeed, according to the famed government study of immigration overseen by the Dillingham Commission early in the 20th century, nearly 60 percent of Polish immigrants lived in cities. As suggested above, by 1900 nearly half of the state's Poles lived in Milwaukee County. Poles had been in Milwaukee since the 1840s. Initially the growth was slow so that only about 30 Polish families lived in Milwaukee by 1865, and most of these were located in Walker's Point or Jones Island on the south side of the city. These were in the main Poles from the Baltic region, "Kazubes." As suggested earlier, Poles from the German partition would soon become dominant in Wisconsin.

The Roots of Conflict

As their numbers increased, a distinctly Polish subculture emerged. Poles moved into the public professions of politics, law, medicine, journalism, and education. Likewise, within the church they began to demand a greater and more visible role.

A special condition was attached to the situation of Poles who came to Milwaukee. As noted earlier, although Polish language and cultural identity persisted, the Poles had been deprived of their homeland. Fears about the dilution of Polish identity flared after the unification of Germany in 1871. At that time Chancellor Otto von Bismarck made a strenuous effort to "Germanize" all the inhabitants of the new nation-state by insisting on German-language instruction in public schools, and mandating service in the German army for all males. Poles stuck in the German Reich bridled at these efforts. Many fled from Polish-speaking areas of Germany to Polish enclaves around the world—especially to American cities where industrial jobs were plentiful. Wisconsin's Polish immigrants carried with them a deep suspicion of Germans—right into the heart of the most German of Roman Catholic dioceses in the United States. As early as 1869, historian Anthony Kuzniewski notes, young Father Joseph Dombrowski wrote to friends in Rome concerning his fears of German-speaking domination over Milwaukee's Poles—fears that they would abandon their cultural heritage.[302] The Polish mistrust of the Germans manifested itself in many ways, but perhaps none so prominently as in the troubled history of the German and Polish relations in the archdiocese of Milwaukee.[303]

Since 1866, Polish Catholics in Milwaukee had had their own church. The onset of heavy Polish immigration to Wisconsin in the 1870s through the remainder of the century had increased the size, presence and visibility of Poles. As with other ethnic groups, their main vehicle for religious-cultural expression was the ethnic parish.[304]

Both Archbishops Heiss and Katzer were quite receptive to the expansion of Polish Catholic churches. After the Civil War, the number of Poles grew so rapidly that they were able to form St. Stanislaus parish in 1866 on South 5th and Mineral. This small brick edifice housed the growing Polish community until 1872 when a new church on Grove and Mitchell was erected. A companion Polish parish, St. Hedwig, was formed in 1872 on the north side. With the parish, they formed a grade school, staffed by the School Sisters of Notre Dame, which claims to be the first Polish Roman Catholic school in the United States.[305] During the 1870s and 1880s, the rate of Polish settlement in Milwaukee is reflected in parochial formation.

In the period under consideration, additional Polish parishes were formed in Berlin (1874), in Princeton (1876 later discontinued), in Beaver Dam (1877), in Kenosha (1898), in Cudahy (1903), in Racine (1908), and in Sheboygan (1909.

The growing number of Polish sons and daughters was also felt in religious communities in the city. Everyone of the major teaching sisterhoods with headquarters in Milwaukee began to receive Polish aspirants. At St. Francis Seminary, Polish young men were accepted into the heretofore strongly German seminary. In 1879 there were two young Poles in the seminary. By 1884, 12 Polish seminarians felt confident enough to found the St. Stanislaus Kostka Literary Society. In 1883 the faculty welcomed its first Polish faculty member, Father John Rodowicz, who taught Polish on a part-time basis. In 1899 Father Boleslaus Goral was recruited for the faculty and in 1906 he was joined by Father Casimir Olszewski.[306] Under the leadership of Father Joseph Rainer, Polish seminarians had been warmly welcomed into the "*cor diocesis*" (the heart of the diocese). Rainer had not only allowed the formation of Polish clubs and literary organizations, but he also had learned enough Polish to converse and even preach in the language. In 1906, the polyglot nature of the seminary community and the archdiocese was noted in the observance of the seminary's golden jubilee which presented speeches in English, German, Polish, and Bohemian.[307] Likewise, the School Sisters of Notre Dame had been similarly flexible in admitting and using Polish candidates in their schools. Polish-speaking sisters received their first charge under Mother Caroline when she sent them to the newly founded St. Stanislaus School in 1868. The Motherhouse Chronicle reported "The sisters were happy to be able to use their native language in the classroom."[308] The seminary and the Notre Dame convent were models of ethnic accommodation.

St. Stanislaus Church, Milwaukee [AAM]

Yet another factor common to all ethnic groups, but more noticeable with the Poles because of their size, was the presence of intra-ethnic rivalries. Wisconsin's Polish communities were occasionally wracked by internal tensions that pitted people against one another in sometimes very heated battles. Henni encountered these difficulties first in the Portage County town of Polonia in the

Table 2-3

Church	Year of Foundation	Architect
St. Stanislaus	1866	Leonard A. Schmidtner
St. Hedwig	1872	Henry Messmer
St. Hyacinth	1883	Henry Messmer
St. Josaphat	1889	Erhard Brielmaier
St. Vincent de Paul	1889	Bernard Kolpacki
Sts. Cyril and Methodius	1894	Bernard Kolpacki/additions by Anton Dohmen
St. Casimir	1895	Erhard Brielmaier
St. Adalbert, South Milwaukee	1899	Unknown

1870s where Polish Catholics eventually seceded from a parish in Sharon split along German and Polish lines. All the Poles were united in wishing a separation from the Germans, but they soon fell to quarreling among themselves over the location of the new Polish church. The feud between these two factions dragged on for many years (and was still simmering when Sebastian Messmer became bishop in 1891). In 1875, a major flare-up occurred at Milwaukee's St. Stanislaus parish when two families clashed over the ordering of a new clock and a parish organist. When fist fights and rock throwing broke out, Henni transferred the St. Stanislaus pastor, Lithuanian-born Pole, John Rodowicz, to the northside St. Hedwig parish, and sent St. Hedwig's pastor, Capuchin Xavier Kralczynski, to the embattled mother church of the Poles. St. Hedwig's erupted in a controversy over an organist in 1885 and this time too there was violence. Heiss at first refused to move Rodowicz and placed the parish under an 81 day interdict. Eventually, Rodowicz left for Baltimore and peace was secured by a new pastor.[309] Other disputes erupted within the diocese of Green Bay at Thorp (1891), Manitowoc (1893), Stevens Point (1894) and at Green Bay when the famous old Catholic bishop Rene Villatte attempted to form a schismatic church among the Green Bay Poles. Interestingly, the bishop who would contend with these various Polish "uprisings" was Messmer, who would face these issues with even greater fury during his years as archbishop of Milwaukee.

St. Hedwig Church, Milwaukee [AAM]

The Archdiocese of Milwaukee and the Polish Presence

Archbishop Frederick Katzer would be the first to acknowledge the prominence of archdiocesan Poles, by the gift of ecclesiastical patronage. In September 1891, Katzer appointed Father Hyacinth Gulski, the founder and pastor of St. Hyacinth's Church on Becher Street, to the office of Archdiocesan Consultor. Gulski, born in West Prussia in 1847 had begun his ecclesiastical life as a Franciscan. Ordained in 1873, he faced serious difficulties when his friary was suppressed by Bismarck's efforts to purge religious influence in the German Reich. He wandered for a time, escaping German police, and in 1875 came to Wisconsin and was made pastor to the Polish community at Berlin in Green Lake County. The next year he came to St. Stanislaus in Milwaukee, and in 1882 Archbishop Michael Heiss tapped him to found St. Hyacinth's parish. Like Kruszka, Gulski's stature as a local leader of Polish Catholics, and even his national profile, grew steadily. In 1890, it was already rumored when the priest took a trip abroad that he was being considered as a Polish auxiliary bishop.[310]

Another rising star of Milwaukee's Polonia was Michael Kruszka. Born to a prosperous farming family in Poznan in German Poland (the home of many Wisconsin Poles), he became politically

Rev. John Rodowicz [AAM]

active as a teenager in opposition to Chancellor Otto von Bismarck. Michael Kruszka soon discovered his gifts with words and began a career in journalism, writing strongly pro-nationalist articles for a variety of Polish newspapers. Arrested and held for a time by German authorities, he was released because of his youth (he wasn't even 18), and in 1880 he emigrated to the United States, settling first in New Jersey. In 1883 he came to Milwaukee. Kruszka learned English and worked as an insurance agent. In 1885 he bought a printing press and began to publish a small advertising tabloid in Polish. Milwaukee already had two Polish weeklies by this time. Forming a partnership with another Polish journalist, Kruszka formed *Krytka* (The Critic), which was strongly pro-labor. In 1885, after a few reverses, Kruszka mounted a successful Polish daily called *Kuryer Polski,* or *Kuryer* as it was popularly known. On the pages of this journal, Kruszka helped to maintain Polish solidarity, by reporting news of the homeland, local events, and his own considered views on current national, state, and local political issues. He was an ardent proponent of the perpetuation of Polish identity, and believed strongly that Polish nationalism was linked to the Catholic faith. In this position, he took a stand in the raging debate among America Poles over Polish identity in America. Kruszka sided with the Chicago-based Polish Roman Catholic Union which urged Poles to become good American citizens while at the same time preserving their ethnic and religious heritage. The opposing side, represented by the Polish National Alliance, also based in Chicago, pressed American Poles to put aside questions of assimilation and use the resources of American wealth to

Mr. Michael Kruszka [Harry Heming (ed.). *Catholic Church in Wisconsin*, Catholic Historical Publishing Co., 1898, p. 1108]

St. Hyacinth Church, Milwaukee [AAM]

send money over to Polish patriots struggling for independence.[311]

Kruszka plunged into the often tense labor politics of Milwaukee, which had seen serious violence in 1886 when workers at the Bay View Rolling Mills struck for an 8-hour day. The episode ended in the death of seven workers, and in its aftermath Kruszka counseled labor leaders to pursue their goals through negotiation rather than violence. In addition to journalism, Kruszka entered state politics for a time. In 1890, he ran as the Democratic candidate for the State Assembly's Twelfth District. Garnering the support of labor leaders and even of local priests, he pressed his campaign in Polish parishes where he was a welcome speaker. He won by a resounding plurality and became one of the most important spokesmen for Polish issues in the state legislature.

Although the clergy supported his candidacy and found the pages of *Kuryer* an important tool in building the local community, Michael Kruszka's relations with Polish priests were always a bit tense, in part because his strong pro-labor positions were at odds with initial church wariness of organized labor. An even more serious fissure opened up between Kruszka and the Polish clergy when *Kuryer* supported plans of the Polish Educational Society (PES) in 1896 to press the Milwaukee public schools to teach Polish language classes in high schools.[312] Fearing a siphoning off from their grade school population, the priests opposed the plan. Although the plan went through without either a great surge of Polish migration to the public schools or serious damage to Polish Catholic parochial schools, the issue stirred deep feelings—similar to those that had been seen in the violent disputes at St. Stanislaus and St. Hedwig parishes. In the wake of the PES efforts to woo Polish children away from Catholic schools, even the School Sisters of Notre Dame attacked the "corruptible sentiments" of the "liberals" and praised the "lion-like courage" of the Polish pastors. "With the help of God they gained a brilliant victory, whose trophies were seven new classes that had to be opened in September."[313] The arguments between the clergy and the editor set the stage for future difficulties. Michael Kruszka himself, although strongly attached to the importance of Catholicism to Polish character and identity, had no hesitancy in criticizing the church and church officials when certain of their actions harmed what he thought were the best interests of the larger cause of Polish nationalism and identity. As Polish pastors groused over his "disrespect" for the Holy See, Kruszka did not flinch from criticizing the clergy when they did things he considered wrong or unethical. The combination of Kruszka's occasionally inflammatory rhetoric and the hypersensitivity and over-reaction of the Polish clergy was a combustible combination.

But over all, according to Kuzniewski, Kruszka maintained a foot in both the secular and religious world. It helped that his brother, Francis, and half-brother, Wenceslaus, were priests. Both joined him Milwaukee. It was Wenceslaus who would rival his half-brother as an important leader of Milwaukee's Poles. As Anthony Kuzniewski observes, "Without doubt, the energetic presence of Wenceslaus Kruszka in Milwaukee increased the visibility and importance of the whole family in the Polish community in the city and the state. To Michael's leadership in the political field was added the growing possibility that Wenceslaus would eventually acquire some importance in the ecclesiastical field."[314]

Wenceslaus (Waclaw) Kruszka was born in 1868 and had entered the Jesuits in the 1880s.[315] Already his strong and somewhat forceful personality manifested itself, and he was temporarily ejected from the Society of Jesus, but later readmitted. Young Kruszka was a genuine scholar and like his half-brothers had a gift for writing. His first written works were lyrical descriptions of his travels abroad, including a classic called *Rzym* (Rome), which detailed his travels in the Eternal City for a few months in 1891, and had a powerful effect on Milwaukee. Joining his family in Milwaukee, Wenceslaus presented himself to Archbishop Katzer, who was anxious for Polish seminarians, and in 1895 he received priestly ordination at Katzer's hand. For a brief time he was assigned to assist Father Wilhelm Grutza, pastor of St. Josaphat's, which had split off from St. Hyacinth's in 1888.

Rev. Wenceslaus Kruszka [AAM]

St. Josaphat's Basilica: The Glory and the Travail

Michael Kruszka's penchant for attacking the mismanagement by the clergy found a ready target in the construction of one of Milwaukee's most magnificent churches, the basilica of St. Josaphat. The founding pastor Father Wilhelm Grutza had started the parish in a modest church/school building on 7th and Lincoln.[316] Grutza was a clerical entrepreneur of the first order. In addition to his parish building, he also founded a small high school that was attached to the church and helped create two Polish Catholic newspapers, *Katolik* and *Zrodlo*. After a disastrous fire wiped out the church in 1889 (Grutza's hands were severely burned as he rescued the Blessed Sacrament and vestments), Grutza rebuilt a new church/school combination by the end of the year. In 1890, the growing parish opened St. Josaphat's Polish Normal School, a high school for boys—a rare innovation at a time when few children went to school beyond the sixth grade. But a growing parish soon required a new church and the dreamy Grutza began to envision a temple that would be grander and more elegant than any ever built in Milwaukee. Ironically, the stimulus for his imagination was the book *Rzym* written by his newly-ordained assistant, Father Wenceslaus Kruszka, in 1895. Poring over the stories of the grand church of Christendom, Grutza wanted to build a replica on Milwaukee's south side.

He repaired to the offices of the architect, German-born Erhard Brielmaier. The now popular architect had been in Milwaukee since 1871 and had distinguished himself as a master of church interiors such as St. Michael's. Grutza laid out his dreams and with Brielmaier developed plans to build a

Latin cross church 128 feet by 212 feet and capped with a monumental dome. Brielmaier stoked the priest's imagination with plans for elaborate Carrara marble interiors and gilded altars. Grutza was convinced he could do this for $150,000 (roughly $2 million in 1999 dollars), a rather significant sum to be derived from the wages of his working-class flock, and as it turned out, far less than what the building would actually cost. In 1896, Grutza made one of the most audacious purchases of Milwaukee County architectural history when he acquired the walls and pillars of Chicago's federal Customs House (even to this day the door knobs of the church still sport the scale and keys—the emblems of the customs service). On 500 special railroad flatcars, he transported the granite walls, columns and capitals to Milwaukee. Grutza did this in the hope that these "pre-fabricated" materials would save him money (they cost $85,000), but the actual costs of the building soon skyrocketed beyond anything Grutza imagined. The burden that these new expenditures imposed on the struggling Polish community attracted the attention of Michael Kruszka, who worried aloud on the pages of his newspaper that the local community could not afford Grutza's dreams of grandeur. Nonetheless, the fire-scarred priest pushed on, and on July 4, 1897, Archbishop Katzer arrived to help lay the cornerstone. At that ceremony were the bishop of Green Bay, Sebastian Messmer, a young Polish priest from Grand Rapids, Edward Kozlowski, and Wenceslaus Kruszka—all destined to play a role in the aftermath of the building of this great church.

In July 1901, the massive building was ready to be consecrated.[317] Apostolic Delegate Sebastian Martinelli and Katzer presided (their presence was memorialized in bas reliefs to the side of a similar portrait of Pope Leo XIII that still adorn the rear portals of the nave) at a three-hour ceremony in which nearly 8,000 people participated. Grutza died of pneumonia one month after the dedication and at his funeral Katzer appointed Grutza's assistant, Father Anthony Prondyzinski as his successor.[318] One can imagine Prondyzinki's sinking feeling when he discovered that the indebtedness on the new church (which was undecorated inside) was not the $382,000 that had been shared with the public, but closer to $600,000 or even $800,000.[319] It may have dawned on him and

Rev. Wilhelm Grutza [AAM]

St. Josaphat Church, Milwaukee [AAM]

others, including Archbishop Katzer who had approved the church building, that Kruszka's public mutterings had been essentially correct: Grutza had left his parishioners and the archdiocese of Milwaukee with one enormous, but very beautiful, white elephant. The ensuing dispute over paying off this debt coalesced with a set of Polish demands for greater representation in leadership of the church in the archdiocese of Milwaukee. Michael Kruszka would make the pages of *Kuryer Polski* the chief outlet for this quarrel. However, the written word would be amplified by the able, articulate, and eloquent voice of his half-brother, Father Wenceslaus Kruszka.

St. Josaphat Church, Milwaukee [AAM]

The Rise of Wenceslaus Kruszka

Wenceslaus Kruszka was transferred from St. Josaphat's after spending only one year in the parish. His departure to Ripon, located in a far-off corner of Fond du Lac County, had come in the wake of allegations that he had sired an illegitimate child with his housekeeper at St. Josaphat's. Kruszka strenuously denied the allegations, but agreed to pay support to the mother and her child. He was sent to the city of Ripon (one of the birthplaces of the modern Republican party and the site of a prosperous liberal arts college). Here he founded St. Wenceslaus parish in 1896 and had several mission stations attached. Kruszka enjoyed the challenge at first, but the small town atmosphere and distance from Milwaukee's thriving Polish community began to wear on him. Always sensitive to "insults," he fired off letters of bitter complaint when Katzer transferred two of his mission stations, Springvale and El Dorado, to another pastor. In a nasty exchange of letters between Kruszka and Katzer, the prelate wondered if he had not been too hasty in taking the former Jesuit into his archdiocese.[320] Kruszka stewed as he watched priests with shorter tenures in the archdiocese receive choice Polish parishes ahead of him. Hypersensitive to any slight, Kruszka was also quick to link his personal problems with ethnic discrimination. However, as we shall see, some of his sharpest critics were not the

German- or English-speaking clergy, but his own Polish brethren. Dismissing the concern that his sexual past required that he be kept "on ice," he attributed his excessively long term in Ripon to the politics of petty vengeance practiced by his rivals in the Polish community and the Germans in archdiocesan leadership.

There might have been a different outcome if Katzer had transferred Kruszka to a more active parish. In the quiet of Ripon he had time to stew, plot and begin writing. Starting in 1901 he began to write a series of articles on the history of Poles in America that were published on the pages of *Kuryer*. These essays would later be gathered into a best-selling series of volumes, *History of Poles in America*. He also took note of things happening around him. For example, he watched from a distance as the German-speaking School Sisters of St. Francis expelled a number of Polish girls from their congregation. With the help of their pastor (and the approbation of Bishop Sebastian Messmer of Green Bay), these young women formed a new Polish sisterhood, the Sisters of St. Joseph of the Third Order of St. Francis, headquartered at Stevens Point, Wisconsin.[321] Likewise, he reacted with rage when he heard of the decree of Bishops Frederich Eis of Marquette, Michigan, and Sebastian Messmer of Green Bay that English sermons be preached at least twice a month in foreign-language parishes. Kruszka decried this edict as another variation of German efforts to deprive Poles of their culture.

Basilica of St. Josaphat, Milwaukee [AAM]

The Polish cleric began to burnish a reputation as the most effective spokesman for Polish Catholicism in Wisconsin. In 1899,

Kruszka turned his scholarly writing skills to the production of a history of Poles in America This 13 volume masterwork, *Historya Polska w Ameryce* (*History of Poles in America*), brimmed with statistics and the inner story of Polish life in America; and despite its lack of footnotes, its repetitious and sometimes polemical style, it is a valuable source for the early Polish experience in America.[322] On the pages of *Historya* Kruszka burned with indignation over the "subjugation" of Polish Catholics in America, and began to insist that Poles "receive their due" in the polyglot American Church by having members of their clergy elevated to positions of prominence in the American hierarchy. In 1901 he made his first public call for a Polish bishop in an article "Polyglot Bishops for Polyglot Dioceses," which appeared in the New York *Freeman's Journal*.[323] The next year he wrote in defense of Cahenslyism. And although Kruszka and Katzer continued to spar over the "exile" to Ripon, the prelate had come around to the fact that a Polish bishop was needed.

Rev. Wenceslaus Kruszka, Silver Jubilee [AAM]

Failure to Secure a Polish Bishop

Despite occasional wrangling between the two men over parish life and sermons, Kruszka found a sympathetic ear with Archbishop Katzer over the matter of a Polish bishop. The prelate was remarkably consistent in his earlier advocacy of ethnic diversity and supported efforts to have a Polish auxiliary bishop appointed to Milwaukee. In 1901, Kruszka and Father Jan Pitass, another Polish advocate from Buffalo, New York had planned to go to Rome to press the case personally with Church authorities.[324] Katzer dissuaded him from this and promised to do what he could to bring about a Polish appointment. In January 1902, Katzer wrote a lengthy letter to Propaganda laying out the reasons why the time was opportune for a Polish auxiliary in Milwaukee. He lauded the deep Catholicity of the Poles, extolling them as "numerous, generous, [and] the builders of the most beautiful churches. [They had] full schools." Just as importantly among them was a priest who could "most honorably wear the adornment of episcopal dignity: Hyacinth Gulski." More practically, he also noted that a Polish bishop would bring calm to the sometimes tumultuous Polish community, and be able to lift the huge debts on St. Josaphat's Church that he had dedicated only the previous summer. [325]

However, this analysis was not shared by Apostolic Delegate Sebastiano Martinelli. When he passed on Katzer's letter to Roman officials, he added his own warnings of caution, noting that although the Poles were numerous, "to appoint a Pole would arouse jealousy with the Germans and with the French Canadians [here he cited disturbances in Springfield, Massachusetts] and the Eastern Rites."[326] Heeding Martinelli, the Prefect of Propaganda, Cardinal Mieceslaus Ledochowski denied Katzer's request.[327] Discouraged but not undeterred, Katzer determined to use his final *ad limina* visit to Rome in 1902 to personally press for a Polish auxiliary with the Cardinal Prefect of Propaganda.[328] Traveling with Abbelen and Gulski he went first to Rome where he attempted to set up a meeting with Ledochowski. But the cardinal was ill and could not receive visitors. Katzer was urged by Ledochowski's subordinates to wait for a break in the cardinal's ill health but when prospects of recovery were slim, Katzer left Rome and there ended the hope of a Polish auxiliary.[329] In ill health himself, he made for his Austrian homeland and met up with his old friend Zeininger in Linz. In September he received an invitation to dine with the aging Emperor Franz Joseph at a dinner in Vienna. Although probably bound by the prescribed protocols attending such occasions, one wonders if the two aging and ill leaders may have commiserated over their burden of ruling multinational empires.[330] When Katzer returned to Milwaukee in October he was so spent that he could hardly endure the elaborate welcoming ceremonies planned by the clergy.

In 1903, Katzer began to fail badly, and Kruszka took up the standard of a Polish bishop and became the leading spokesman for the cause with Roman authorities. Endorsed by the influential Polish National Congress, he and Pitass resumed their earlier decision to lobby Roman officials for a Polish appointment.[331] In 1903 they secured the services of a former American ambassador Rowland Mahany, to accompany them to Rome. (The Protestant Mahany was included to assure skittish Roman authorities that the U.S. government would not object to a "foreign" bishop—a not inconsequential detail given President Benjamin Harrison's concerns over the Cahensly issue in 1891.) Wenceslaus Kruszka camped out for nearly 10 months in Rome. His efforts were delayed when Pope Leo died in July. Katzer's death at the same time also injected a note of uncertainty. However, Kruszka worked the circuit of cardinals and bishops until he could present his needs to the newly elected Pope Pius X.

Nonetheless all to no avail, it would be Katzer's successor, Sebastian Messmer, who would have to deal with the tangled skein of Polish Catholic concerns. Other ethnic groups began to resculpt archdiocesan life at this time as well.

The Italians

Towards the end of the 19th century, Italian immigrants began to make their presence felt in the Milwaukee archdiocese.[332] Pockets of Italian strength first appeared in the Third Ward, where heavily Sicilian numbers began to press on the old Irish settlement. Later, the industrial suburbs of West Allis and Bay View saw an increase in their Italian populations. Likewise, industrial development in Kenosha, Racine, and Beloit also attracted Italian colonies. The state capital, Madison, also welcomed Italians settlers into its midst. By 1886, close to 400 Italians had settled in Milwaukee. The numbers grew steadily in the 1890s with 800 by 1900 and 3,500 by 1910.

The needs of Italian Catholics rose steadily throughout the latter 1890s. Many of them in the Third Ward attended the nearby cathedral, while Bay View Italians made efforts to get into Immaculate Conception. In Racine and Kenosha, they attended local churches. However, the numbers soon grew large enough to merit their own churches. Two forces began to press for an archdiocesan response. The first was from the newly appointed apostolic delegates, themselves Italians, who passed on the concerns of Pope Leo XIII regarding the "leakage" of Italian Catholics in America, in part because they received limited pastoral attention. The appointment of Diomede Falconio as apostolic delegate in 1902 focused this issue for American bishops, as the delegate repeatedly reminded American prelates in areas of Italian growth that they had to provide for the newcomers—meaning securing native clergy and religious and eventually allowing them to build their own churches and schools.

Falconio knew of what he spoke. A member of the Franciscan Order, he had actually lived in the United States and was a naturalized U. S. citizen. He had attended his order's St. Bonaventure College in Allegheny County, New York from 1866 to 1885 and had been ordained there. Subsequent work in New Foundland eventually delivered him a leadership position with his order in Rome, and from there he was picked to be the apostolic delegate to Canada.[333] Falconio's experiences convinced him that ministry to the rapidly growing number of Italians had to be stepped up so as to prevent their loss to the Church.

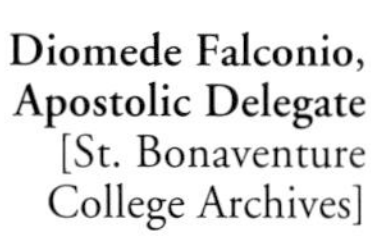

Diomede Falconio, Apostolic Delegate
[St. Bonaventure College Archives]

The second force pressing for better ministry to Italian Catholics was an unlikely supporter of ethnic ministry: *Catholic Citizen* editor Humphrey J. Desmond. Desmond, an unabashed friend of the Americanizers in the U. S. hierarchy, took up the cause of the Italians in Milwaukee, monitoring their growth while accentuating the need to do something about their situation.[334] Under Desmond's auspices, Italian organizers found a friendly advocate to promote a greater degree of specialization. With the encouragement and support of cathedral curate (and later rector) David J. O'Hearn (who had studied in Rome and was fluent in Italian), the cathedral parish was the first to welcome and encourage Italian Catholic aspirations.[335] O'Hearn was a great lover of all things Italian and cherished every opportunity to savor Italian food and culture. On one occasion when the famous composer Pietro Mascagni visited Milwaukee, O'Hearn attended a banquet in his honor at the home of the prominent Italian DeLorenzo family. O'Hearn welcomed Mascagni in flawless Italian and even entertained the maestro by his renditions of "O Sole Mio" and "O Maria, Mari." Mascagni was so taken with the effusive Irish cleric that he claimed that O'Hearn "could be taken for a born Roman."[336] With O'Hearn's support Italians were offered the use of cathedral resources to hold socials and other ethnocultural events that reinforced their group identity. However, the steady ingress of Italians into the nearby Third Ward and the inevitable desires for separation from the larger English-speaking body led to the formation of a small chapel a few blocks south of the cathedral at Jackson and Clybourn.

The spearhead for this was Sicilian-born Father Rosario Nasca who arrived in Milwaukee in 1898. After preaching a successful mission at the cathedral aimed at the Italians, he attracted enough interest in his work to purchase a two-story store at 189 Huron Street (today Clybourn). He transformed the lower part into a chapel called "Sacro Cuore" (Sacred Heart) and he resided upstairs. Nasca performed baptisms and religious services in the chapel and also taught classes in "Americanism" as well as in reading and writing. Nasca raised funds for a more capacious Italian church, and in one fund-raiser at the University Club managed to raise $500. In ill health Nasca left after two-years, dying shortly

Rev. David J. O'Hearn [AAM]

after arriving in New Orleans in November, 1900.

Nasca was replaced by another Sicilian priest, Bartolomeo Imburgia. Imburgia called together a building committee and gave the mission its name—Our Lady of Pompeii—and created a fund-raising society. Led by notables in the Italian community, the society's strongest force was educator Hanno Pestalozzi, who soon recruited about 1,000 members each paying a dollar a year to the fund. He also received ample support from *Catholic Citizen* publisher Humphrey Desmond, who advertised every fund-raising and cultural event sponsored by the mission. At one gala event, Cardinal-elect Sebastiano Martinelli, apostolic delegate to the United States, made a guest appearance at an event at the Pabst Theater where Imburgia recited a lengthy Latin poem from memory. Likewise, other well-to-do Milwaukeeans contributed to the mission, including industrialist Thomas Neacy and Judge Paul Carpenter. But the single largest donation came from cookie and cracker manufacturer Robert Johnston who donated the princely sum of $6,000. The astonished Italians could not believe it to be true and were suspicious of the industrialist's motives, but eventually were convinced of his sincerity and generosity. In 1902, Imburgia purchased a 40-by-120 foot lot on Jackson Street between Detroit and Huron (Clybourn and St. Paul), near the center of the Third Ward residential district.[337] An important moment for the Italian colony came when their chief advocate, the new Apostolic Delegate Diomede Falconio, visited the city, ostensibly to check on the failing health of Katzer. Falconio's public appearances included a highly publicized stop at "the little cramped storeroom"—the mission on Huron Street—early in the first full day of his tour. From a flower bedecked throne he addressed the participants for 25 minutes in Italian, commending their hard work and saying he "hoped the Italians would continue in the way they were going."[338] The Falconio visit must have encouraged the community. They needed it for what lay ahead.

1899 sketch of the interior of the Mission of Sacred Heart of Jesus, the first official Italian place of worship in Milwaukee [Judith A. Simonsen. "The Third Ward: Symbol of Ethnic Identity. *Milwaukee Hist.*, Vol. 10, No. 2, p. 64]

Shortly after Falconio's departure, Imburgia announced his decision to return to his native Sicily. Afflicted by "bronchial affection with which he has been troubled since his residence in Milwaukee," he decided to follow the advice of his doctors and return to Sicily's sunnier and drier climes. A tearful farewell ensued. [339]

His replacement between July and October was Father Giuseppe Angeletti, who arrived in Milwaukee as Imburgia left. A native of Perugia, Angeletti was 40-years-old and had served in parishes in Wichita, Kansas and Scranton, Pennsylvania (where he succeeded Rosario Nasca). His appearance seemed to fill the bill for a community now on the verge of building a new structure for themselves.[340] However, his northern Italian heritage was to bring complications to his work. Father Augustine Schinner (who was managing diocesan affairs as Katzer was in his death throes in Fond du Lac) was aware of the regional differences and assured the congregation that a Sicilian priest, Domenico Leone, currently serving in Louisville, Kentucky would also soon be joining the mission.

Angelleti arrived in time for the parish to not even miss one Mass. Shortly thereafter Leone arrived, but he was told by Angelleti that there was no room for him in the cramped mission. It is not clear whether Leone remained in Milwaukee or went back to Kentucky. However, word did get out into the community that he had been refused entrance. Augustine Schinner, appointed as administrator after the death of Katzer, must have hoped that things would right themselves, but as with most ethnic parishes, internal disputes soon became public.

Before long the Perugian-born Angeletti clashed with his Sicilian parishioners. Facing frustration in raising money, he soon made common cause with Hanno Pestalozzi and the two of them began to criticize the tepid response to their pleas for financial support. Pestalozzi complained publicly that Sicilians refused to donate telling the public that the common response he received from many non-supporters usually ran: "I have a church in my village at home. I am not going to stay here, I am not in the church building business. If Americans want to build a church for us, well and good, we won't do it."[341]

Angeletti's conflicts with his Sicilian parishioners resulted in defections from the church and public acrimony. By October, 1903 the parishioners were demanding his replacement with Father Leone, who sat by watching all this (perhaps encouraging it from the sidelines). The feuding spilled into the public press, as one of Angeletti's opponents shared: "Yes it is jealousy between Sicilians and Northerners," Salvatore Palise was quoted as saying, "Almost all of the people who go to church are Sicilians and we want a priest of our own race."[342] Schinner then intervened and removed Angeletti and Leone took over. Leone was only 27-years-old and ordained only four years when he came to Milwaukee. Born in America, he had studied for the priesthood in Italy and had begun his priesthood at St. Michael's Church in Louisville. Full of energy and well-suited for the Italian mission, Leone would eventually build the long-desired church, which would function as a hub of the Italian community of Milwaukee.

In April 1904, Leone drew plans for a larger church and increased the size of the lot that had been purchased by Imburgia the previous year. Brielmaier and Sons designed "a structure in the Roman style" that cost

Interior of Blessed Virgin of Pompeii, c. 1940s [ICC]

$10,000 and work began in August of that year.[343] In the meantime a host of fund-raisers and other community building events mobilized the colony. The cornerstone was laid in October 1904, and by Christmas 1904 the Church of Our Lady of Pompeii was up and running. This simple brick structure was 5,000 square feet and seated only 200 congregants. However, the interior was a veritable pantheon of popular religious figures, frescoes and ornamental plasterwork. The outside brick was eventually painted pink and Our Lady of Pompeii was known in Milwaukee's history as the "Little Pink Church."

Religious education of the growing number of young people was not accomplished by a parochial school (the Italian youth who wanted a Catholic school education probably attended the cathedral grade school), but by religious education classes. Dominican sisters and later Carmelites provided these services, especially to prepare the little ones for first communion or confirmation. In 1916, while Father Peter Dietz was temporarily assigned to shepherd the parish, the Catholic Instruction League made Pompeii the site of one of its city centers. For years, Catholic Instruction League teachers provided the religious training of the Italian young people.

The life of the Catholic community at Pompeii soon became an important part of the fabric of Milwaukee life. Mass attendance among Italian Catholics, especially males, was sporadic. Weekly Eucharist was not the heart of the religious experience of many Italian Catholics. Efforts to induce Italian school children to come to Mass were not often successful. In 1914, the Notre Dame sisters reported that 42 children left St. James parish school in Madison, "because we urged them to come to Mass on Sundays."[344] An important celebration of the Italian community, the *festa*, was first celebrated under the auspices of the Holy Crucifix Society on September 15 and 16, 1906 (near the feast of the Seven Dolors of Mary). The celebration was so successful and such an occasion of fun for the citizens that it was repeated again the next year with even greater size.[345] A key part of this celebration was the street festival, which bore a statue of

Blessed Virgin of Pompeii Church, Milwaukee [ICC]

was the potential for defection to Protestant denominations. Various ministers sensed that Italians, many of whom cherished deep grudges against the anti-nationalist policies of the papacy, would be easy pickings for active proselytization. Itinerant Italian Protestants received a cordial reception among their co-religionists in Milwaukee. In 1897, Giuseppe Silva, pastor of an evangelical church in Milan, received a respectful hearing from the members of Immanuel Presbyterian and Grand Avenue Congregational churches in Milwaukee when he informed them that "Thirty-five years ago, the Bible was not allowed in Italy," and he described at length how the Holy Writ was secretly produced and disseminated in the punitive environment of the dominant Roman

Members of a girls society from the Blessed Virgin of Pompeii [ICC]

the Holy Crucifix to which Italian devotees affixed monetary and votive offerings.

As did the German and Polish parishes, the Italian parish served as a gathering place for the organization of mutual benefit societies which paid out sick and burial benefits to premium payers. The nature of these organizations, and their sheer numbers, united *paesani* from the various villages in Sicily from which they had emigrated. Many of the Milwaukee Italians were from the village of Santo Stefano Camastra in Sicily.

An added incentive for further Catholic attention to the Italian colony

Catholic Church. His discourse was accompanied by a pitch for funds "to convert the benighted Italians.[346] Most Protestant evangelizing was also accompanied by social services. Near the "Pink Church" was St. Paul's Episcopal Chapel, sponsored by the All Saints Episcopal Church on Knapp and Marshall Streets. A cadre of Third Ward Italians became members of this church. In addition to services and religious instruction, St. Paul's offered a hall for rent, a pool and billiard room, and a bathroom equipped with tub and shower baths.

The outreach of evangelical churches was spearheaded by Katherine Eyerick, a young woman from Ohio who deeply wished to become a missionary to China. Denied this, she devoted herself to converting and helping Italians. She arrived in 1908 and opened the rather plain Evangelical Mission in an old storeroom on Huron Street. The vocal evangelist flayed the Roman church as a bastion of superstition, raged about devotion to the Virgin and the use of the rosary, and plugged her nose in disdain over the bacchanalian features of the annual festa. Nonetheless, as historian Alberto Meloni notes, she soon came to accept the Italians on their own terms. This was helped considerably when she visited Italy in 1910 and there met and married the Reverend Augusto Giuliani, a Catholic convert to Evangelicalism. She brought her new Italian husband home to the Third Ward in 1911 and the two of them continued to work for the conversion of Milwaukee's Italians.[347] The presence of active Protestant proselytizing in other cities quickened efforts to accommodate Italian Catholics with their own churches and to bring them religious education.

But almost as soon as the "Little Pink Church" was established and running, the demographic shift of the east side began. Italians lived in overcrowded housing—so bad that in 1910 government investigators declared "Little Italy to have the worst housing in Milwaukee."[348] Commercial and industrial development of the Third Ward area also took its toll on the local churches (Pompeii and the cathedral). In 1915, former priest Giorgio LaPiana, who had quit the clergy in the wake of the Modernist crisis of 1907, came to Milwaukee and studied conditions among the city's Italians. He predicted that the neighborhood would soon be emptied of its residents, "Day after day houses are disappearing to give way to big iron and concrete factories. In ten years this section will be a distinctly business district, and the Italians will be forced to move away."[349]

In 1907, the *Catholic Citizen* noted, "The Italians are now beginning to settle north of Wisconsin [Avenue] as far as Ogden Avenue."[350] By 1919, Pompeii began its own mission on the lower east side, where the largest number of Third Ward Italians had migrated. This mission was begun by Father Enrico Fadanelli, a Stigmatine Father. Fadanelli's term, according to the parish history, "was neither an agreeable nor a successful one for a number of reasons."[351] In 1925 the Pious Society of St. John Baptist Scalabrini, the Scalabrinians, assumed control of the mission. The Scalabrinians brought a new burst of energy for the Italian community, and the resources of a religious order to help finance future building. During the pastorate of Antonio Bainotti (1925-1935) Masses were added to the schedule to handle the crowds.

Added to the mix of Italian community building at this time was the introduction of an Italian sisterhood to Milwaukee, the Sisters of Charity of St. Joan Antida.[352] This Italian-based community was first invited to Milwaukee to assist the Camillan fathers in the domestic department of the hospital they had built on Bluemound Road. Five sisters reported for duty in September 1932 at the Camillan hospital. The next year, at Archbishop Stritch's request, a second contingent of sisters arrived to begin work at Our Lady of Pompeii. The sisters threw themselves into the tasks of organizing and training the choir, catechetical instruction, and the opening of a social center to teach music and the domestic arts. They also began a kindergarten, which was especially welcomed by working mothers who now had day care for their dependent children. Following the path of the Italian community as it expanded north, a group of four sisters opened a convent on Cass Street next to the St. Rita Mission. In 1937, the sisters opened a parochial school for Italian children. In 1939, when a group of Italian independents opened their own Mount Carmel mission in West Allis, Stritch sent the sisters to teach catechism. Stritch convinced the nuns to open a novitiate near the site. Here they remained, welcoming new members to their community until 1954 when the estate of Max A. Friedman on the north side of Milwaukee (Old Granville), near St. Catherine's Church and the Servite monastery, came on the market. The sisters purchased the Tudor-style structure and opened the Regina Mundi novitiate in 1955. Other social services were provided by the growing community, including a home for elderly women that opened in 1949.

In 1935, Bainotti was succeeded by the dynamic Ugo Cavicchi, a handsome, youthful priest who posed with his hand in his cassock vest like a young Napoleon waiting to conquer. Working closely with Italian consul Angelo Cerminara and other leaders of the community, Cavicchi built up the Italian community by means of social events, a newspaper called *Vita Parocchiale*, and the sheer dynamism of his personality. In fact he was so

Sisters of St. Joan Antida at dedication of Our Lady of Mt. Carmel Church, West Allis [AAM]

exuberant and of such powerful personality that Stritch had to gently chide him for taking too many things into his hands. "May I say," he gently lectured the priest, "that I am intensely interested in the progress of Religion among my Italian-children and that I am just as intensely opposed to over-concentration of authority as I am to a spread of it which makes for ineffectiveness." He recommended that in running the parish, "there should be a bit of home-rule which makes for better government. Especially here in the United States where we believe in salutary home-rule ...."[353]

Rev. Ugo Cavicchi, PSSC [AAM]

Cavicchi soon began raising funds for a new combination church/school building. Property at Cass and Pleasant Streets was purchased, but funds permitted only the erection of a basement church, which opened in 1937. Just as he hit his full stride, Cavicchi was transferred and replaced by Father Gregory Zanoni. Zanoni picked up the challenge and within a year, Stritch was present to lay the cornerstone for the $60,000 upper church designed by Alfred H. Siewert. [354] In June 1939, the dedication of the new church took place. On that bright morning, Zanoni "predicted St. Rita's to be the cradle of a bright future for Milwaukee's Italian population."[355]

South of Milwaukee, Italians also pushed into Bay View to work at the steel mill and to open shops and small businesses. A small Italian colony became visible along Russell Avenue with the small grocery store of Giocondo Groppi, which opened on the corner of Russell and Wentworth in 1912, as its centering place. The interaction of the Italian community with the church in Bay View was complicated by the antipathy of local church men, most notably Immaculate Conception pastor Thomas Fagan, to the presence and ideology of an Italian Nationalist club. The Garibaldi Club, which opened in 1908, was several blocks north of his church. Fagan had never been kindly disposed to the incoming Italians, whom he derisively referred to as "dagoes" and "wops." He liked even less their limited financial support of the church, since he had just built a large new structure for the parish in 1903. When members of the Garibaldi Club insisted on wearing their tri-color nationalists sashes and buttons at funerals, Fagan was incensed by the "insult" offered to the person and dignity of the pope and refused to allow them into the church.

Disgruntled Italian Catholics in Bay View who did not fall away from the church altogether, trekked to Pompeii for the sacraments of Baptism, First Communion, and Confirmation. They also chose the church for their weddings. When Fagan died in 1923, his successor Thomas Pierce was only slightly more open to Italians, simply refusing them the right to wear the Garibaldi attire in the church, but scaling back considerably the anti-Italian invective that had spewed occasionally and publicly from Thomas Fagan's mouth. At some point, during Fagan's last years and perhaps in the early years of Pierce, archdiocesan officials took note of the situation in Bay View and quietly dispatched priests who had been trained in Roman seminaries to celebrate Mass in rented quarters directly across from Giocondo Groppi's grocery store. By the time Father David Ryan took over for Pierce in 1950, the passions of Italian nationalism, the wearing of ceremonial sashes and buttons, and the antagonism toward Italian nationalists had become a thing of the past. Quietly, the Groppi family and the Richetta family among others joined the once Irish bastion—they sent their sons to the seminary in the 1940s and 1950s.

Kenosha was another center for archdiocesan Italians. After Father Angelleti had been pushed out of Pompeii, he bided his time in Milwaukee until Archbishop Sebastian Messmer sent him south to Kenosha. In August 1904 Angelleti arrived in Kenosha and took up residence at St. James Church. Gathering a small band of Italians around him and even before taking a census of the community, he purchased land at Howland and Pearl Streets for a new Italian parish. He found 43 families and on November 14, 1904, 500 people watched as he laid the cornerstone of Holy Rosary of Pompeii (another Pompeii church). Construction took time, however, and it was not until August 13, 1905 that Holy Rosary Church was ready for occupancy. A procession through the streets from St. James to the new site marked the first public demonstration of Kenosha's growing Italian Catholic community. Angelleti seemed to lose interest in the project and Kenosha soon after its completion. In 1908, he departed for Italy leaving the parish with a huge debt which his successor Augusto

Our Lady of the Holy Rosary of Pompeii Church, Kenosha [AAM]

Baudizzone worked day and night to pay off. Angelleti's poor handling of parish finances may have poisoned the well for his two successors, Father Baudizzone and Father Pietro Perardi. Both of them quarreled bitterly with their parishioners and Perardi's conflicts were so intense that he had to flee for his life when a mob stormed the church and rectory. The internal conflicts of the parish would continue into the 1930s.

In Madison and Beloit, colonies of Italians soon founded their own parishes. In 1914, Messmer created St. Joseph parish for Madison's Italians. The first resident pastor, Father Angelo Simeoni, erected a frame building at 20 S. Park Street. After Simeoni was replaced by Father Pietro Perardi, the church building was moved to an adjoining lot and a capacious first floor built under it to serve as a school. Where the first church stood, Perardi built a catechetical center called "St. Joseph's Institute," and a parsonage.[356] Perardi remained only three years in Madison, replaced by the Norbertines from DePere who relocated it in 1958. Italian outposts were also set up at St. Thomas parish in Beloit.

The Italian "Little Pink Church" of Milwaukee eventually became the symbol of many of the myths that held together Italian Catholics in the archdiocese of Milwaukee. Similarities can be seen between the "myth making" that attended the romanticization of the "French past" of Wisconsin Catholicism. Indeed, just as the first incursions of French Jesuits bearing Catholicism are historically noteworthy and important, so too the first Italian church was a major accomplishment for a struggling community. The attachment to Pompeii remained constant throughout its development, but seemed to grow in magnitude when the church was torn down for freeway construction in the 1960s. In a way similar to the activities of late 19th century Catholics who sought to romanticize the heroic exploits of "ancient" French missionaries, Italian Catholics and others wrapped a layer of romance around the small church. Italian-American citizens placed a memorial plaque at the exit ramp where the church once stood. The construction of the popular Italian Community Center in the 1980s was done in proximity to the old Third Ward church. Annually, visitors to the popular "Festa Italiana" on the city's lakefront festival park visit an elaborate display of the artifacts and images of the church. For many years, even Italian Catholics who migrated to newer areas of the city or to suburbs, faithfully came back for the church's annual festa, or to be married and have their children baptized. No doubt to regularize the administrative end of this continual demand for sacraments by people who really did not reside in the parish's boundaries, St. Rita's was raised to parochial status in 1942.

But in fact, church membership began to wane as the Third Ward emptied of residents. Certainly by the 1930s, more Italian Catholics attended Mass at St. Rita than at Pompeii. Even more, Italians moved away from the traditional areas of their dominance, and other areas of the diocese felt the presence of Italian Catholic life. Again, like the French of the 17th and 18th century, the long-term significance of the church was more symbolic than substantive. Italian Catholics did not wish to live near or regularly attend the "Little Pink Church," but held on to it as an icon of a heroic past—a past burnished especially by the revival of interest in ethnicity in the 1970s.

Other historical debates related to the history of immigration can be examined in the context of archdiocesan history. Did these parishes serve as "way stations" to Americanization or did they perpetuate ethnic identity for the "uprooted"? It is important to note that the answer is yes to both. Certainly, the structure and gathering space created by the huge Polish churches, thriving schools and public expressions of Catholicity helped keep the community together. The creation of the two Pompeii's—Milwaukee's and Kenosha's—were positive features in the perpetuation of what would have been a fairly difficult effort at group identity. But tensions did emerge. The ethnic story was not complete at this point. In some instances this second epoch of archdiocesan history was only the beginning.

Bohemians

One additional ethnic group in the diocese deserves treatment, the Bohemians or Czechs. This group actually predates the Poles and Italians, though not in size.[357] Bohemian (or Czech) immigrants poured into Wisconsin in their heaviest numbers between 1850 and 1880. Bohemian Catholics shadowed German immigration, coming mainly from the Pilsen and Budweis regions of southern Bohemia. Czechs were farmers and settled initially in farming regions of the lakeshore counties and in the far western part of the state. One of the first prominent areas of Czech settlement was in Racine County and in the township of Caledonia. Czech social life blossomed in Racine with a newspaper and a school. Czech settlers also planted roots in Manitowoc County and came to settle in cities like Kossuth, Kellnersville, Cooperstown, Francis Creek, Melnik, Tisch Mills, and Two Creeks. Similar incursions into Kewaunee County brought farms, schools, churches and other social institutions. In La Crosse, Bohemian life focused on the church of St. Vaclav (Wenceslaus).

Religiously the Czechs were seriously divided into two camps: one Roman Catholic the other Free Thought or *Svobodomyselene.* The latter emanated from the residue of the Hussite controversies of the 15th century as well as the collaboration of the Catholic Church in Bohemia with the Hapsburgs of Vienna. Bohemian nationalists scorned Vienna and its ally Rome, and according to one historian 50 to 70 percent of Czech immigrants to America defected from the Church "and found meaning in organized fraternalism and highly ritualized agnosticism."[358] Free Thought appeared to be the intellectual mainstay of most of Wisconsin's Czech social and intellectual leaders. Moreover, as historian Karel D. Bicha has demonstrated, the partisans of Free Thought among American Czechs, many of them former religious, actively sought to "de-Catholicize" the sometimes devout immigrants who came to Wisconsin.[359]

Bicha notes that the first organized Czech parish in Wisconsin was established in 1859 in Greenstreet in Manitowoc County. Other chapels were built in Cooperstown, Tisch Mills, and Kewaunee.[360] Organizational efforts among Milwaukee Czechs began in 1860 with a missionary association under the patronage of St. John de Nepomuc.[361] This local association found shelter at St. Joseph's parish in Milwaukee, but it dissolved in 1863 when Father Francis Zastera arrived and began using the vacant old St. Peter's Church near the cathedral. Zastera remained briefly and was followed by one of the earliest Czech missionaries in Wisconsin, Father Josef Maly. Maly, a native of Bohemia, was ordained in 1853. Two years later he entered Wisconsin and ministered all over the state to clusters of Bohemian Catholics. He took charge of the St. John de Nepomuc Church on Easter Sunday 1866 and purchased two lots on Fifth and Cherry Streets for $600. When a nearby Protestant church in the final stages of construction at Fourth and Cherry could not be completed, Maly sold the earlier purchase, paid the eager Protestants $5,500 for the unfinished church, and set to work completing the structure. Maly left and was succeeded by Father Joseph Maria Gartner.

Gartner, a native of Olmutz, Moravia must have been quite a self-promoter, having himself designated in the Catholic directory "Missionary of all Bohemians in the State of Wisconsin." Gartner had entered the priesthood late in life and studied at the University of Innsbruck. In August 1866 he came to St. Francis Seminary to complete his studies, and was ordained by Bishop John Martin Henni in April 1867. The departure of Maly in September 1867, left a pastoral need that Gartner filled (he had been originally assigned to teach at the seminary). He reported to St. John de Nepomuc in November and was there to witness the completion and dedication of the new church building three days before Christmas. The prospects for the new mission were not bright. "After a short time," he wrote in a report several years later, "I realized the lack of its viability." He complained that it was made up of "workers and day-laborers, who because ignorant of the language of the country, could scarcely earn the means for a miserable subsistence themselves," much less lift the now $10,000 burden that Maly had left behind. But the generosity of the people "who would occasionally give me their whole earnings and perhaps starve for a month ... on dry potatoes" touched his heart, as did his mission appeals to various Slavic peoples in rural areas cause him to "read the unmistakable Will of God to persevere."[362] Gartner refocused his energies, devoting himself not only to paying off the church, but also reaching out to all Slavic peoples, Bohemians, Slovenians, and Poles. He formed a loosely knit religious community called the Missionary Institute of the Sacred Heart, and proposed using the parish as the center of the new organization. He traveled hither and yon (even back to Europe) to solicit funds for what he thought would be a training center for the priests, called the Sacred Heart Mission House, but what his congregation thought was money to purchase a suitable rectory for the church. Gartner's new Gothic style home cost a whopping $3,000 (raised from the wages of rather poor workers) and was finished in 1869. This small monastery-like building never served its original purpose and the parish was compelled to purchase it in 1874.

By 1869, Gartner was a broken man, and retired from the parish. After a stint as chaplain to the School Sisters of Notre Dame, he ended up as a pastor in Hoka, Minnesota. Feeling guilty that he had encumbered St. John's with such a heavy debt, he tried to leave the proceeds of a $6000 life insurance policy to his former community, but was unable to do so. A small school was begun on the grounds, taken over in 1871 by the School Sisters of Notre Dame, who learned Bohemian, and the parish bought more property to the north and west. Creating a viable parish was no easy task. The sisters reported that in the first six years of their endeavors at the school, no children were presented for first communion.[363] A succession of short-term pastors tried to stabilize parish life, but all gave up when confronted with the heavy debts. It was not until a former Franciscan, Leo Suchy, came from La Crosse in 1873 that St. John's enjoyed solid leadership. Suchy came to St. John's and remained for 10 years. In 1883, Archbishop Michael Heiss directed him to start another mission to Czech Catholics on the south side of the city at 14th and Scott Streets, named for St. Wenceslaus. Because the specialized needs of Czech Catholics continually challenged the archbishops of Milwaukee to supply clergy, Suchy carried both parishes for two years until he resigned St. John's and became pastor of St. Wenceslaus. St. John's remained at the site (although serious discussions of its relocation took place in 1906) until 1926. In 1908, the opening of a parish for Slovaks who had attended St. John's put a crimp in membership. After efforts to rejuvenate the parish and additions to buildings, in 1926 the church relocated to a huge block between 37th and 38th Streets and Keefe Avenue in the center of Milwaukee's posh Sherman Park district.

St. Wenceslaus soon became a thriving center of Czech Catholic life. Under Suchy, a small church/school combination was built in 1883, and after the parish built a respectable priest's residence, Suchy came on "full-

Sacred Heart Church, Milwaukee [AAM]

time." The Notre Dame sisters took note of the building accomplishment, rare among Bohemian congregations, "That was an inexpressible joy … a regular jubilation for the Bohemians, who in this country with difficulty … slowly attain their end as regards buildings for religious purposes."[364] The school, begun under the School Sisters of Notre Dame, was eventually handed off to the School Sisters of St. Francis in 1904-1905. For a Franciscan, Suchy was a dapper figure who sported a silk hat and cane and had a flair for singing opera. A malignancy on his larynx rendered him mute, however, and he trained altar boys to read the parish announcements and lead the Stations of the Cross—perhaps inadvertently creating one of the first instances of lay presiding in the diocese.[365] After his death in 1894, a succession of pastors, garnered with some difficulty, held the reins at the south side church.

The fate of Catholicism among the Czechs in Racine County had languished, and for a time Czech Catholicism was extinguished in Caledonia. Nevertheless, a few embers were stirred in 1896 to form yet another parish named in honor of the Bohemian protector of the seal of confession. St. John Nepomuk parish in Racine was the third center for Czech life in the archdiocese. Racine's large Czech population found the church a welcome respite from the German St. Joseph's parish.[366] To each of the parishes, was attached a school that soon completed the circle of Catholic life in the area.

Schools

The industrial period brought dynamic growth to the Catholic population of the

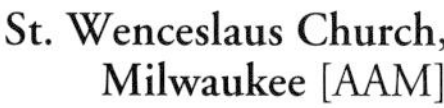

St. Wenceslaus Church, Milwaukee [AAM]

counties of the archdiocese. Efforts to improve the school system led to the creation of educational opportunities for the aging Catholic populace, and the increase in the number of religious sisters teaching in the schools. The increase in the number of schools, the quality of their physical plants, and the level of instruction were other by-products of the vitality of the Catholic community of southeastern Wisconsin.

Schools were an important part of the larger visible presence of the Catholic Church. The accounts of the teaching sisterhoods leave us some of the most complete records of the efforts to build, staff and maintain these institutions, which soon rivaled the public schools. They also leave us some impression of the kind of impact the school had on making Catholic culture visible in the industrial environment. In the archdiocese, the School Sisters of Notre Dame continued to be the leader in taking on new parish schools, largely among the Germans and the Polish. In 1884, the sisters arrived at the newly established St. Michael's Church and took up residence in the basement, where they also taught 270 students in three partitioned sections. By street car, the School Sisters commuted to the newly opened St. Augustine's in Bay View, teaching children from "five different sections of the city of Milwaukee and surrounding suburbs." The teaching conditions were not easy. "Many came from the public school and were wild, bold and un-

Holy Redeemer School, Milwaukee [AAM]

St. Anne School, Milwaukee [AAM]

ruly. It took days until with much trouble and effort they could be brought to some order and quiet."[367] The Agnesian sisters, who agreed to take over St. Thomas school in Beloit, by contrast found the children in the heavily Irish parish to be "docile, humorous and promising."[368]

In 1910, the School Sisters of Notre Dame opened St. Casimir's School in Kenosha and were welcomed to the new convent by cheering parishioners who sang out, "Witamy! Witamy! Welcome! Welcome!" The new Polish parishes found School Sisters ready and willing to adapt to the new cultural geography of the diocese. In 1868, several Polish-national sisters of the School Sisters were sent to open St. Stanislaus's School. Several years later, the sisters purchased their own convent at Polish St. Hedwig's on the north side and began instructing 80 children. Likewise, in 1915 the sisters found faculty members for Kenosha's Lithuanian parish.

The most dramatic impact of the Third Plenary Council's mandate for parish schools reflected itself in the English-speaking parishes in Milwaukee. The prime example of this was the re-making of the Catholic school at the Cathedral of St. John. Two schools occupied the property, one for girls run by the Daughters of Charity and another for boys run by the Brothers of the Holy Cross. Cathedral rector James Keogh eventually dismissed the Holy Cross brothers, whose penchant for corporal punishment got out of hand. The brothers themselves were distressed that Keogh had backed away from earlier promises to build them a new residence; they resented living in the two-story brick building the parish had purchased twenty years earlier. In 1895, Keogh cajoled Mother Emily Power to send a contingent of Sinsinawa Dominican sisters to take over the boys school. The sisters set to work in August 1895, taking over the cramped quarters of the Holy Cross brothers, which they were forced to endure (and did so more graciously than the brothers) until the construction of a new convent building in the 1920s.[369] The school had 320 children, "almost all being old for their grades."[370]

In 1905, the Daughters of Charity began to retrench from all their teaching assignments in Milwaukee in order to focus their energies on their growing hospital. They handed their notice to Keogh that they could no longer serve at the girls school. Scrambling to replace them, he pressed the Sinsinawa sisters to take over the operation of the entire school. Keogh announced the sister's departure to the cathedral parish and to the public at large, acknowledging the significant role the Daughters of Charity had played for nearly 60 years at the cathedral. Keogh, who genuinely loved the sisters, lamented, "None can regret or deplore this withdrawal more deeply than myself and none will feel their loss more keenly." He concluded "The parish owes them a debt of gratitude which it never can repay." But, he assured the parish as he announced the complete Dominican takeover of the school, "I have ... no hesitation in now giving them charge of the whole school with the fullest confidence in their ability to conduct it on the most progressive educational lines." Keogh ended the gender separation and combined the grade school children into mixed classes. He moved the high school out of the convent, leaving more room for the full contingent of Dominicans. And he even forced the hand of Mother Emily Power by announcing that the school would have "in addition to the usual curriculum … a school of music, art, and painting to which pupils from any part of the city will be admitted."[371] On his own, Keogh appointed the Dominican artist, Sister Angelico Dolan, to the teaching faculty of the school. The sisters were compelled to borrow to meet expenses at the school, and the tightfisted Keogh made them pay their own utility bills.[372]

Social Services and Benevolent Societies

Providing teachers for Catholic schools was an important priority. It was in 1873 that a new Milwaukee-based congregation of religious women appeared: the School Sisters of St. Francis.[373] This rapidly growing congregation had begun in Schwarzach near the Black Forest in Southern Germany as a local sisterhood set up by Father Francis Xavier Lender to care for the domestic and other needs of an orphanage in 1859. Bound together by a "rule" written by Lender and approved by the archbishop of Freiburg, the small sisterhood left a lasting impression and served as the seedbed for a much more ambi-

Sr. M. Angelico Dolan, OP, (left) and Sr. M. Catharine Wall, OP [AOP-Sin]

Mother Alexia Hoell, SSSF [ASSF]

to the United States. They came to be known as the School Sisters of St. Francis.

Landing in New York, the sisters scoured areas of the country looking for an opportunity to take over the administration of a new school. In 1874, they ended up at the door of Mother Caroline Friess of the School Sisters of Notre Dame, who took them in. She then introduced them to a local pastor, Father Anton Michels of the German New Cassel area about 40 miles north of Milwaukee. Michels immediately set himself up as their "father spiritual" and installed them as the teachers of St. Matthew's School in New Cassel. Eventually they opened a boarding school for the rural area. Rapid growth took place, as a flood of postulants from Germany and the United States sought admission into

tious project. In 1872, in the wake of the *Kulturkampf*, church authorities in Freiburg "dissolved" the vows of the 10 Schwarzach sisters that had gathered at Lender's popular orphanage. However, little changed in the life of the small community at Lender's parish—except that three of the sisters were growing restive under the relatively confined experience of the orphanage and sought a wider field of activity. Three women of the group, Alexia (Emma) Hoell (one of the first members of the early community), Clara (Helena) Seiter and Alfons (Paulina) Schmid used the occasion of the dissolution of their vows to uncouple from Lender's operation and strike out on their own. In 1873, the 35-year-old Hoell, together with the 23-year-old Schmid and Seiter (age unknown), migrated

Mother Alfons Schmid, SSSF [ASSF]

the new congregation. From a small motherhouse in New Cassell the sisters took in new recruits and encouraged young girls to come to their schools and to an orphanage they created. Attracted first to rural schools (German pastors in Wisconsin, Illinois and Minnesota deluged them with requests for teaching sisters), the sisters eventually turned to an urban ministry and a permanent headquarters in Milwaukee.

The path to Milwaukee was strewn with difficulties. The insistent demand of Minnesota Germans for bilingual education led the sisters in 1885 to build a new motherhouse in Winona, Minnesota in the diocese of St. Paul. Little did they expect that they would soon be under the administration of the hierarchy's chief opponent of German Catholic identity: John Ireland. The strong-willed prelate had a host of problems with the German sisters. First, the steady flow of new candidates from Germany upset him. An avid proponent of Americanization, Ireland was uneasy about the kind of bilingual education the School Sisters of St. Francis provided. Finally, Ireland felt that the sisters were poorly prepared to enter school work. In 1886 he sought to assume direct authority of the community by declaring it a diocesan sisterhood. The sisters balked at this and simply transferred their headquarters back to Wisconsin and away from Ireland's meddling. The building they had erected at great expense became a girls academy.

Meanwhile, the sisters received a warm welcome to build in Milwaukee. By 1887, they located land on 27th and Greenfield Avenues and built St. Joseph's Convent, which was completed and dedicated in 1888. The building burned in 1890 and a new structure was erected on the site. In 1917, the convent's elegant new chapel was completed and became one of the architectural gems of the city. Across the street from the motherhouse a new German Catholic congregation, St. Lawrence, was founded in 1888 under the pastorate of Father Ludwig (Louis) Barth.

The School Sisters of St. Francis, like the Notre Dames, grew rapidly and continued the flow of candidates from Germany and America. By 1895 they numbered 350 professed sisters, 50 novices, and 75 postulants. However, unlike the Notre Dames, they were

Rev. Anton Michels
[ASSF]

unable to negotiate the ethnic tensions within the community. Cultural and linguistic differences erupted between the German sisters and the Polish sisters—the latter making increasing application to the School Sisters, especially after the move back to Wisconsin. Painful incidents of exclusion and occasional comments about the intellectual and social "inferiority" of the Polish sisters, plus proscriptions on the use of the Polish tongue and devotional life among the sisters simmered until 1900, when six girls came from heavily Polish Stevens Point to enter the congregation. Fiery disputes led to the secession of 46 Polish-speaking Franciscan sisters back to Stevens Point, where a friendly cleric gave them shelter, protection, and freedom to form a new congregation, the Sisters of St. Joseph of the Third Order of St. Francis.[374] With the combination of rural and urban school education, as well as their place in health care in the archdiocese, the School Sisters of St. Francis soon assumed a rank in the archdiocese exceeded only by the more numerous Notre Dame Sisters.

Health Care

Catholics had already begun a history of health care service when the Daughters of Charity opened their hospital in the 1840s. However, hospitals of the 19th century were not seen as centers of healing or therapy, but rather as places to isolate sickness and provide an acceptable place to die. As a result, the early healthcare programs of archdiocesan Catholics focused on unique cures for chronically ill patients and home nursing.

In 1892, the School Sisters of St. Francis foundress Mother Alfons Schmid returned to Germany to restore her shattered health. While she was abroad she stumbled on a popular hydropathic cure then popular in Germany known as the Kneip Water Cure, at a resort in Woerishofen, Germany. A sickly cleric named Sebastian Kneip (1821-1897), a parish priest in Woerishofen, read an account by German physician J. S. Hahn describing the curative effect of the waters in that area. Kneip devised a therapy program of water baths and massage therapy, and soon the Woerishofen site became a mecca for those seeking cures. School Sisters of St. Francis Mother Alexia Hoell opened a hospital dedicated to this cure therapy in the Italian resort city of San Remo in 1895. Mother Alexia then directed her associate in America, Mother Alfons, to begin a Kneip Program in Milwaukee in a three-story health resort on the grounds of the new motherhouse. Other therapies were added to the Kneip Method: various water and sand baths, electrotherapy, massage and gymnastics—all used at various bath spas of Germany.[375]

When the sisters approached Katzer for permission to begin the new establishment, the archbishop demurred. Although he was a devotee of hydropathic cures (he took them up at the Agnesian sisters who also had a Kneip facility) he was somewhat skeptical of this divergence from the school work of the sisters. In the end, however, he gave his permission.[376] The Kneip Sanitarium was later renamed Sacred Heart Sanitarium. Under Mother Alfons, the Kneip cure center became a popular place to recover "shattered nerves" and even had a "resort" replete with swimming pool, horseback riding (with a stable of Kentucky horses) and indoor amusements of various sorts.

The Sacred Heart Sanitarium eventually became a favorite "drying out" spot for a number of American celebrities seeking a confidential cure and for alcoholic clergy, including some bishops. Numerous letters arrived from bishops around the country to the archbishop of Milwaukee of "pathetic" cases of broken and derelict clergy who needed therapy.[377] In some respects, Milwaukee became as much a clerical "refugium peccatorum" as did the Trappist Abbey of Gethsemani with its fabled "clerical jail" on the third floor of the old monastery building. In 1912, the School Sisters opened St. Mary's Hill Hospital for the mentally ill, and in 1937, they opened St. Joseph's Hospital in Beaver Dam.

The admission of the Franciscan Sisters Daughters of the Sacred Hearts of Jesus and Mary (also known as the Wheaton Franciscans) to the archdiocese constituted perhaps the most important contribution to Catholic health care in the history of the archdiocese of Milwaukee. Founded in 1859 in Paderborn, Germany, this community devoted itself to the care of the sick and orphans.[378] In 1872, a group of sisters came to St. Louis to help establish a hospital near a German parish. They were fortunate to meet Henry Spaunhorst, an officer of the *Central Verein*, who took them under his wing, gave them sound financial advice and coordinated

Sacred Heart Sanitarium, Milwaukee [ASSF]

St. Joseph Hospital, Milwaukee [MCHS]

their engagement with the network of German-speaking priests, religious and laity around the Midwest. More and more sisters came from the motherhouse in Salzkotten, Germany, and soon the congregation became well-known in German-speaking communities in St. Louis, Carondelet, and Cape Girardeau. Members of this German-speaking congregation were originally invited to Milwaukee by Father Theodore Breuner, the rector of the Pio Nono/Holy Family Normal Schools in 1874. Living in the basement of the building, the sisters cooked, did laundry and cared for the chapel. These same sisters played a role in the foundation of the School for the Deaf, begun by Breuner as a department of the Normal School.

St. Mary Hospital, Racine [AAM]

When the superior of the sisters, Mother Bernarda Passman, visited Henni in 1877, he tried to recruit her to establish a hospital and even more to provide home nursing services. Monsignor Leonard Batz reinforced Henni's invitation and urged the sisters to come to

Milwaukee.[379] The sisters could not come until 1879, and by that point Henni's mind and health were failing, and he asked them to devote themselves to home nursing. This the sisters did until 1881, when demand for their services required that they withdraw from Pio Nono and the deaf school. They secured property on 4th Street and Reservoir, near St. Francis Church, and built the 50-bed St. Joseph's Hospital, which opened in 1882. In 1897, the sisters accepted responsibility for the patients and staff of Milwaukee's Presbyterian Hospital. Attached to it was a College of Physicians and Surgeons. By 1900, its added staff and professional nursing school made St. Joseph's one of the leading health care institutions in the city.

The same year St. Joseph's began, Batz conveyed the request of the pastor of St. Mary's Church in Racine, Father I. M. Albers, to open a hospital in the growing port city. A local hotelier, anxious to be rid of his building, offered to "donate" it to the sisters (it was still encumbered with $1,200 in debt). With advice of their friend Henry Spaunhorst, they took over the building and had it moved to 16th and Grand Avenue in Racine where they began St. Mary's Hospital. The next year a tornado ripped through Racine causing much damage and loss of life, and the Franciscans stepped forward to help care for the injured and dispossessed. In 1889, the good will of the community gave them enough money to build a new St. Mary's Hospital. In 1910 a school of nursing opened; it lasted until 1933.

Building on their success in Milwaukee, the sisters went to Madison in 1886 to respond to the need for a Catholic health facility. Two sisters were dispatched to a rented house near Holy Redeemer parish and conducted home health care operations in what they called St. Anthony's Hospital. However, when the time came to build a full-fledged facility, the sisters ran into "unforeseen obstacles," and so withdrew. Madison would not have a Catholic hospital until 1912 when the Sisters of Mercy would open St. Mary's.

St. Nicholas Hospital, Sheboygan [AAM]

In 1890, another group of Franciscans, the Hospital Sisters of the Third Order of St. Francis, provided another link in the chain of archdiocesan health care when they opened St. Nicholas Hospital in Sheboygan. Begun in a private dwelling on 9th and Superior Avenue, the four founding sisters named the hospital for Father Nicholas Thill, pastor of Holy Name (brother of Father Dominic Thill a future pastor of the same church). These Franciscans devoted most of their early labors to home nursing, but as hospital facilities became more necessary, they managed to erect an imposing three-story brick structure costing $80,000 in 1908. This new hospital grew piecemeal, adding on service facilities, laboratories and x-ray rooms, and a new three -story wing with 45 more beds. In 1919, the Reiss family, wealthy coal merchants in Sheboygan, constructed a home for the aged next to St. Nicholas. In 1924, an entirely new hospital structure replaced the first one built in 1903.[380]

The Sisters of the Divine Savior also entered the archdiocese to provide home health care.[381] This religious congregation had been founded in Rome as the second effort of a Baden-born priest, Francis Jordan, who also founded the Catholic Teaching Society, later known as the Society of the Divine Savior (Salvatorians). After an aborted attempt to found a woman's congregation (later known as the Sisters of the Sorrowful Mother) Jordan tried again, this time working in greater harmony with a former German noblewoman, Mother Theresa von Wuellenweber.

Jordan had created the Sisters of the Divine Savior as a female branch of an international religious community, established in 1888 in the Italian city of Tivoli. In 1895, Archbishop Katzer made his *ad limina* to Rome and met with Francis Jordan and requested practical nurses to work among the Catholics in Wisconsin. Jordan took him to the convent on Via Lungara and there was made the selection of Sisters Raphaela Bonnheim, Walburga Sieghart and Agnes Weber for the new American foundation. Before leaving Rome in the late spring of 1895, the three selectees got a crash course in nursing from the Sisters of Mercy at the hospital of San Giacomo in Rome. They remained for a time at the Leo House in New York, run by the Wisconsin-based Agnesian Sisters, and on July 4th they arrived in Milwaukee, where they were given shelter by the School Sisters of St. Francis in Greenfield.

The three sisters began their work at the rapidly growing Sacred Heart Sanitarium, and calls for home nursing, from both Protestants and Catholics, flowed in. Bonnheim and her group remained three months with the Franciscans, and with the help of a clerical friend in Milwaukee, Father Ludwig Barth, eventually secured property near St. Anthony's parish on Second Avenue. Bonnheim had grandiose dreams of building a Catholic hospital and a school of nursing on the south side (a dream later realized by the Felician Sisters), but these gave way to more practical considerations.

Barth's association with the Salvatorians did not end with his kindness to the sisters.

He also played an important role in bringing the Salvatorian fathers and brothers to the United States. Barth had come to the German religious commune at St. Nazianz from Louisville in 1872. While he was there he helped to tend to Father Ambrose Oschwald in his last illness. Barth then went to St. Francis Seminary and was ordained in 1880. Even in the midst of a busy clerical career, he kept an eagle eye on the declining colony in St. Nazianz. Oschwald's successor Father Peter Mutz tried to keep the colony together, but by 1896, the founders were dying out. Barth pressed Raphaela Bonnheim to recruit Jordan and his company to take over the nearly 1500-acre Oschwald property. Bonnheim did so and urged Jordan to send her brother, Ephrem Bonnheim, who was one of Jordan's earliest recruits. Katzer also contacted the Salvatorian founder who assured him of his interest in the St. Nazianz property. Jordan arrived in Milwaukee in August 1896 and inspected the property, and he left behind Fathers Epiphanius Deible, Hermann Rogier and two brothers, who assumed control over the lands and the care of the last colonists.[382] In 1909, the Salvatorians opened a rival minor seminary in Wisconsin that would be a natural training place for rural youth in the confines of the Diocese of Green Bay, and even for some young men who could not attend school in the increasingly overcrowded Salesianum. A convent of Salvatorian sisters was also established at St. Nazianz.

Mother Raphaela Bonnheim, SDS
[ASDS-W]

The Salvatorian sisters under Bonnheim flourished in Milwaukee. Surmounting the inevitable tensions associated with beginning a new enterprise, the social nursing ministry of the Salvatorian sisters thrived as the number of patients requiring home nurses and housekeepers grew steadily. Outgrowing their convent home on Third Street (even when a second house was added), the sisters sought larger quarters for new sisters and postulants and better facilities for the sick. With Katzer's help, property was located at 35th and Center

St. Agnes Hospital, Fond du Lac [Courtesy of Kevin Wester]

Street in a rapidly expanding area of Milwaukee, and the sisters built St. Mary's Convent. Bonnheim's dream of a nursing home/hospital, however, was once again placed on the back burner as internal conflicts between the Salvatorians in Milwaukee and St. Nazianz hampered more prosperous growth. Nonetheless, the Salvatorian social nursing project proved a great success.

The establishment of St. Agnes Hospital in Fond du Lac followed on the heels of the failure of the sectarian St. Paul Hospital in 1887. Mother Agnes Hazotte was urged to start a new Catholic hospital by Dr. F. S. Wiley (a local physician), Father Joseph Keenan of St. Patrick's Church, and the community's leading benefactors, John and Henry Boyle. (The Boyle brothers had made an enormous fortune in a yeast foam company. They sold their assets and each pocketed more than a million dollars apiece.[383]) Katzer approved the plan, and Mother Agnes engaged William Schickel, who had built their convent, and Joseph Hutter, who was their favorite builder, to prepare blueprints. As the fund-raising for the $55,000 hospital went forward, Mother Agnes sent three sisters to learn nursing in Chicago. When the 50-bed hospital opened in 1896, a full complement of trained sisters was on hand to greet patients.[384]

Mother Agnes had also purchased a parcel of property some few miles outside the city, on the shores of Lake Winnebago. John Boyle called on Mother Agnes and offered to build a sanitarium on this site in 1901. She agreed, but the distance from the city made it difficult to maintain a sanitarium, so the sisters converted it to an academy called St. Mary Springs.

Henry Boyle, not to be outdone by his brother, offered a portion of a city block and built the Henry Boyle Catholic Home for the Aged, a three-story red brick building on North Park Avenue.

Care for the Deaf

Catholics in Wisconsin built even more institutions of social provision. In 1876, Father Theodore Breuner, rector of Pio Nono/Holy Family Normal School, founded a Catholic enterprise for the deaf and dumb.[385] A separate building for these students was erected in 1879, and deaf children from the archdiocese were admitted to the program. The combined school was called St. John's School for the Deaf. Breuner entered the Franciscan friars in Teutopolis, Illinois (the same group Father Christopher Wapelhorst had joined), and he was succeeded in his work by Father Charles Fessler. Fessler's tenure was financially disastrous for the institution, and it temporarily closed until 1889, when Father Mathias Gerend reconnected it with the work of the Normal School.[386] With a promise of support from Heiss and a donation of $1,000 from the estate of recently deceased Father Michael Wisbauer of Burlington, the enterprising Gerend built shops and purchased machinery to produce an array of church furniture: altars, confessionals, baptismal fonts, stations of the cross, pulpits and carved work that was used in pews and other church decorations. By 1890, the shops turned out $20,000 worth of merchandise.[387] Architect Erhard Brielmaier oversaw the industrial department, teaching the students woodworking skills and decorative arts. Gerend was able to raise enough money in 1893 to build a beautiful chapel dedicated to the memory of Archbishop Heiss. In 1895, Gerend resigned from the leadership of the Normal School and turned his full attention to the School for the Deaf. He too sought to improve the financial condition of the still-struggling school. Gifted with a witty writing style, he contributed to the support of the school with juvenile stories and a Christmas book called *The Good Child,* printed in the shops of the nearby St. Aemillian Orphanage. The sale of Gerend's book was temporarily slowed by the

Henry Boyle Catholic Home for the Aged, Fond du Lac [Courtesy of Kevin Wester]

St. John School for the Deaf, St. Francis [AAM]

Rev. Mathias Gerend [AAM]

St. John School for the Deaf [AAM]

1895 St. Aemillian fire which destroyed the manuscript. However, Gerend quickly rewrote it, and it became a best-seller. He later churned out other popular Catholic literature such as *Fireside Tales by Catholic Authors*; and the quarterly, *The Deaf-Mutes' Friend Family Library*. He continued his writing with *Our Young People*, a monthly magazine for the support of the deaf. Gerend's bouncy prose and personal kindness gave the school a firm foundation and a wonderful reputation throughout the country. When the Franciscan sisters from St. Louis and Mount Alverno Wisconsin withdrew in 1885, the St. Francis Franciscans and sisters took over housekeeping and teaching duties.

In 1906, Father Stephen Klopfer joined Gerend, and in 1909, Father Eugene Gehl also came aboard. Fire ravaged the school in 1907 and 1917, but its popularity was so widespread that Gerend had no trouble building a new structure. The Franciscan sisters

St. John School for the Deaf [AAM]

soon assumed the teaching and mentoring of the deaf and hard-of-hearing students. The expertise gained in this work added to their reputation as reading specialists in the Milwaukee archdiocese.[388] The school remained open until the 1980s when it was closed and many of its students transferred to the Wisconsin School for the Deaf in Delavan.

Benevolent Societies and Fraternalism

In the days before strong social safety nets, these kinds of benefits were absolutely indispensable for newcomers as the means by which they "mediated between the individual immigrant and the relatively strange social world in which he found himself."[389] As James Grummer notes, "These benevolent aid societies alleviated some of the tension felt by wage earners who feared that unemployment or death would deprive their families of crucial support. The societies provided insurance to assuage fears about an uncertain future, even if not as generously as the benefits of modern insurance policies. This function was particularly important for immigrants who had sundered the conventional Old World bonds of familial and communal support during times of crisis when they embarked for the New World."[390]

It seemed to follow that the farther away Catholic immigrants were from their home culture, the more they seemed to need and be active in organizing social safety nets. The Germans and the Polish were clearly the strongest in this regard, and the chief context for their work was the parish. On a parochial level, the provision of social welfare, especially among German parishes, is quite noteworthy. The powerful forces of associationalism helped to create important networks of social provision. Benevolent aid societies developed in most German parishes in the archdiocese. As early as 1849, an association for the care of the sick, *St. Pius Kranken Unterstuetzungs Verein* was created in St. Mary's parish, Milwaukee, to help families who had lost their principal wage earner.

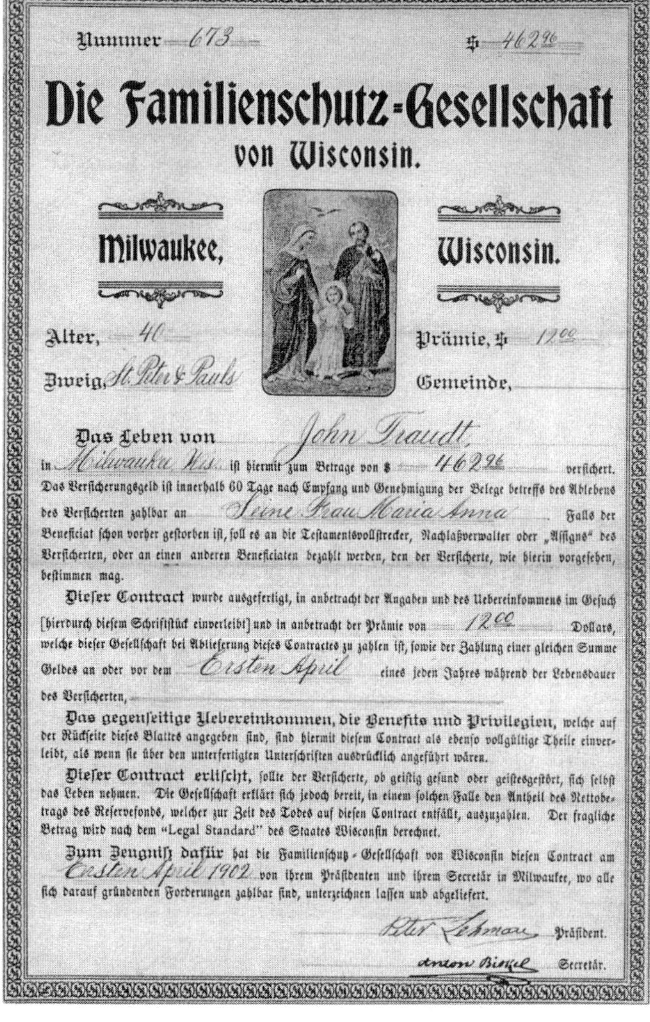
Nummer 673 $ 462.96

Die Familienschutz-Gesellschaft
von Wisconsin.

Milwaukee, Wisconsin.

Alter, 40 Prämie, $ 12.00

Zweig, St. Peter & Pauls Gemeinde,

Das Leben von John Traudt,
in Milwaukee Wis. ist hiermit zum Betrage von $ 462.96 versichert. Das Versicherungsgeld ist innerhalb 60 Tage nach Empfang und Genehmigung der Belege betreffs des Ablebens des Versicherten zahlbar an Seine Frau Maria Anna. Falls der Beneficiat schon vorher gestorben ist, soll es an die Testamentsvollstrecker, Nachlaßverwalter oder „Assigns" des Versicherten, oder an einen anderen Beneficiaten bezahlt werden, den der Versicherte, wie hierin vorgesehen, bestimmen mag.

Dieser Contract wurde ausgefertigt, in anbetracht der Angaben und des Uebereinkommens im Gesuch [hierdurch diesem Schriftstück einverleibt] und in anbetracht der Prämie von 12.00 Dollars, welche dieser Gesellschaft bei Ablieferung dieses Contractes zu zahlen ist, sowie der Zahlung einer gleichen Summe Geldes an oder vor dem Ersten April eines jeden Jahres während der Lebensdauer des Versicherten,

Das gegenseitige Uebereinkommen, die Benefits und Privilegien, welche auf der Rückseite dieses Blattes angegeben sind, sind hiermit diesem Contract als ebenso vollgültige Theile einverleibt, als wenn sie über den unterfertigten Unterschriften ausdrücklich angeführt wären.

Dieser Contract erlischt, sollte der Versicherte, ob geistig gesund oder geistesgestört, sich selbst das Leben nehmen. Die Gesellschaft erklärt sich jedoch bereit, in einem solchen Falle den Antheil des Nettobetrags des Reservefonds, welcher zur Zeit des Todes auf diesen Contract entfällt, auszuzahlen. Der fragliche Betrag wird nach dem "Legal Standard" des Staates Wisconsin berechnet.

Zum Zeugniß dafür hat die Familienschutz-Gesellschaft von Wisconsin diesen Contract am Ersten April 1902 von ihrem Präsidenten und ihrem Secretär in Milwaukee, wo alle sich darauf gründenden Forderungen zahlbar sind, unterzeichnen lassen und abgeliefert.

Peter Lehman Präsident.

Anton Birkel Secretär.

Catholic Family Life Insurance policy of John Traudt, the Society's first president [*Celebrating a Proud Past—Sharing the Challenges of the Future*, Catholic Family Life Insurance, 1993, p. 3]

Other societies, *St. Joseph's Kranken Unterstuetzungs Verein* and St. Peter's Benevolent society, performed similar functions for other parishes. The structures of these societies were fairly similar. Membership was voluntary and generally open to men from 18 to 45 who were practicing members of the church. An initiation fee was charged and the payment of dues (generally $.25 per month) entitled them to some limited benefits if they were sick or out of work. When a member died, all the others were expected to pony up $15 apiece for the burial and attend the funeral service. Polish parishes also developed analogous social welfare provisions. St. Hedwig's parish had the St. John Kanty Society, the Knights of St. Casimir and the Society of Jesus and Mary. All of them provided for widows and included burial benefits. At annual gatherings and group events, the members were permitted to wear badges or sashes indicating membership. Each organization had a beautiful banner that was held aloft during parades. Some of the groups had elaborate uniforms that members wore on special occasions.

Ultimately, mutual benefit societies branched out from their parishes. For example in 1872 some German-speaking priests formed the "Clerical Mutual Benefit Society of the Diocese of Milwaukee." German immigrants banded together to take care of newcomers, forming a German Immigration Association in 1880. The members of the St. George Society of St. Joseph parish, Milwaukee, formed an association to find jobs for unemployed workers. Gradually, the lessons learned on the parish level became wider and more consolidated.

The increased growth of the population soon made parish-based mutual aid societies incapable of dealing with the demands for insurance coverage. One of the first joint societies, the Catholic Family Protective Association, was called together by Henni in 1868 to respond to some of the lingering illnesses and economic dislocation caused by the Civil War. To the initial meeting Henni summoned 21 men from Milwaukee's seven largest benevolent societies and together they devised a new system of life insurance. (This group changed its name to Catholic Family Life Insurance in 1949). Under the leadership of dry goods merchant John Traudt, the Catholic Family Protective Association offered low-cost protection to men between the ages of 18 and 45. Later, when the need for more members was required by the growing pace of benefit payments, a separate death benefit for women was added in 1890. After a generation of struggle, Catholic Family Protective underwent a reorganization in 1902 under the direction of presidents Peter Lehman and Otto Seifriz that created an even stronger organization.[391]

A similar organization, the Catholic Knights of Wisconsin, was first known as "The Order of United Catholics." This was founded in 1877 in Nashville, Tennessee by James J. McLoughlin who claimed that the idea for the fraternal association came from a sermon given by Bishop Patrick Feehan of Nashville.[392] Feehan, who later became Archbishop of Chicago, encouraged McLoughlin, and the organization was chartered by the state of Tennessee. It changed its name to the more militant "Catholic Knights of America." Departing from the custom that only branches of a group would receive a charter, the Catholic Knights secured a charter for their national organization and began to expand.

By 1880, various branches of the organization had come to Wisconsin, and by 1885 a local state council had been organized. The secretary of that council, a former seminarian named William Mulholland of Manitowoc, discovered that Wisconsin members were not receiving a fair return for their premiums, so together with Green Bay attorney, John H. M. Wigman teamed up to press the national organization for regional rates that would equalize the premium and beneficiary burdens. At a tumultuous meeting, the national organization rejected this. Wigman and Mulholland returned to Wisconsin, seceded from the national body, and on January 21, 1885 chartered a new organization, the Order of the Catholic Knights of Wisconsin. The rest of the Wisconsin branches of the national organization seceded as well and joined the new fraternal. Establishing their general headquarters in Milwaukee, they soon grew into a strong organization that maintained close links with the archdiocese and had diocesan priests on their board. One of the first was Father James Keogh. Another was temperance advocate, Father M. J. Ward of Beloit, who tried to interest the association in his cause.

Various participants in the insurance programs of the Catholic Knights left the seminary as their beneficiary, and in 1912, Rector Joseph Rainer opened branch 231 of the Catholic Knights at St. Francis. In one of the first efforts to interest the laity at large to support the seminary, Messmer appealed to the Catholic Knights at their biennial convention held in Oshkosh in 1916 to help pay for improvements on the aging St. Francis Seminary. The students of branch 231, encouraged by seminary faculty member Father Joseph Lederer (who was also a delegate at the Oshkosh meeting), proposed the taking up of a collection for a recreation facility on the seminary campus. Although the collection was insufficient to build a small gym, it represented a link between an agency of the diocese and the prosperous insurance company.[393]

Catholic Knights Insurance Society
[Catholic Knights]

Catholic Order of Foresters, St. George Church, Kenosha [AAM]

Another organization, the Catholic Order of Foresters was founded in Chicago in 1883 by a group of men at Holy Family parish. It arrived in Wisconsin in 1887. Dedicated to principles of mutual help and protection, the organizational structure of the Foresters consisted in the formation of a series of "Courts" or local branches that recruited members and transferred premium and benefit payments to members. Illinois was the heartland of Forester activity with 322 courts by the time it celebrated 50 years. However, Wisconsin was number two with 220 courts and a membership of 18,933. Life insurance was the primary "product" of the Foresters, but they also sponsored social events, built halls and conducted collections for disaster relief. The Milwaukee court, number 17 grew to the point that it was able to purchase a new hall in 1895.[394]

Knights of Columbus retreat [Horton L. Roe. (ed.). *History of the Knights of Columbus in Wisconsin*, Knights of Columbus, 1952, p. 598]

Similar in name, but not in size, were the Knights of Columbus. This fraternal order of men (with a branch for women, the Daughters of Isabella) was founded in 1882 by Father Michael McGivney in New Haven, Connecticut.[395] McGivney's goal in founding the society and putting it under the patronage of Christopher Columbus was to emphasize the close association of Catholics with the founding ideals and heroes of the United States. Columbus was the most appropriate symbol of the union of Catholicism and Americanism. Group insurance was mandatory in the first ten years of the organization's existence, but in 1892 non-insurance or associate membership was established. The newly-retooled "Columbianism" planted strong roots in New England, and thanks to energetic promotion by its leaders, spread rapidly among Catholic men. The Columbian celebrations of 1892-1893 proved to be a particularly fertile time for their growth. The Knights developed a form of specialized ritual to mark initiation and promotion to the various degrees and ranks within the Order. They likewise became increasingly devoted to various works of charity, apologetics, and organizing that promoted the Catholic Church.

Wisconsin soon came under the Columbian spell, being the 23rd state to begin establishing local councils.[396] The first local coun-

cil in Wisconsin was founded in Superior (Superior Council No. 499) on June 17, 1900, spun off from a council in nearby Duluth, Minnesota. Just one week later, June 24, 51 Milwaukee men became Knights of Columbus and the new Milwaukee Council, No. 524, was begun. Subsequent councils began in Janesville (No. 596, August 1901), Beloit (September 1901), Appleton (November 1901), Green Bay (November 1901), and Oshkosh (1901). By the end of 1901, 600 men had joined the Knights. In January 1902, a Wisconsin State Council of the Knights of Columbus was formed at a meeting held in Milwaukee's Hotel Pfister. Henry T. Killea of Milwaukee was chosen the first state deputy. By 1904, Milwaukee had two councils (Père Marquette, No. 850, was started in February 1904). Growth of the order in the state's largest cities proceeded apace. By 1905, 625
Wisconsinites had signed up for the Knights insurance benefits and 2,170 had become associate members.

At their general convention held in Milwaukee, the Knights turned outward to begin dealing with issues of general import. Among their first joint actions was a commitment to helping the Indians on the Oneida Reservation near Green Bay by providing funds for church repairs and paying a resident priest. Subsequent endeavors of the Knights included donations to a chair of American history at the Catholic University of America and providing hotels with lists of churches and Mass times. The Knights sponsored a lecture bureau that brought prominent speakers like Catholic evangelist David Goldstein to Wisconsin. At their 1906 convention in Racine, the Knights heard from Father Henry Hengell, a priest from Madison, who told them about his plans to build a chapel and Catholic information center near the campus of the University of Wisconsin. Over the years, the Knights contributed nearly $26,000 to the building of the St. Paul Chapel. In appreciation, Hengell agreed to be state chaplain of the organization. Other good causes followed: the funding of a chaplaincy at the Wisconsin Industrial School for Boys in Waukesha County, and contributions to an endowment fund for Marquette University. During World War I, the Wisconsin Knights contributed heavily to liberty loan campaigns.

In 1916, the Knights transformed one of the old Plankinton mansions on Grand (Wisconsin) Avenue into their Milwaukee headquarters.[397] Felicitously given the address of "1492 Grand Avenue" an extensive addition was made to the old mansion that provided club rooms, an auditorium and places for banquets and large gatherings. Until Marquette University tore it down in campus renovations, "1492" was an important hub of archdiocesan Columbianism.

Creating an Educated Middle Class: Education for Men: Pio Nono and Sacred Heart College

The quickening of professional life in Wisconsin, brought on by the rapid industrialization of the state, provided opportunities for Catholics to offer professional training in fields associated with the professions or busi-

Knights of Columbus headquarters, 1492 W. Wisconsin Ave., Milwaukee [MUA]

ness. In the latter half of the 19th century, several new schools of "higher education" (high school and some college) specialized in certain kinds of professional training. This often involved taking a "commercial" course in some business-related field. But it also included formal training in pedagogy and music—two important needs of the archdiocese's parish and school network.

The idea of forming a Catholic normal school had been floated as early as 1851 by Archbishop Henni, who was quite anxious for a teacher's seminary. Various Catholic newspapers and German Catholic periodicals kept the question alive.[398] This was driven partly by the need for Catholic male schoolmasters, considered integral for the schools, since the rules of many sisterhoods forbade the teaching of boys. Equally important in German Milwaukee was the need for trained organists and choirmasters who could render the Catholic liturgy with appropriate solemnity. As early as 1864, Salzmann was eager to create a "teacher's seminary" and had designated the now abandoned brother's house on the seminary grounds for his plans. As always, the lack of funds and the unsettled conditions of American life created by the Civil War slowed plans. In 1865, Salzmann took yet another trip to Bavaria and was rewarded with 3,000 florins. However, his efforts to establish a normal school were sidetracked by his appointment as rector of St. Francis Seminary in 1868. In 1869 he resumed fund-raising and was particularly successful in pressing the case before the association of German societies known as the *Central Verein.* This organization contributed over $3,000 to the new enterprise between 1869 and 1872. By mid-1870 he had secured enough money to break ground for a four-story German Gothic-revival school to be named for the Holy Family, the primary patrons of the *Central Verein.* Bishop Joseph Melcher of Green Bay presided at the cornerstone laying, and thousands attended, many transported by a special Chicago and Northwestern train, whose ticket proceeds went to the new building. The building was ready for occupancy in January 1871 and Bishop Henni dedicated it on January 2. On September 14, 1871, the first students were welcomed.

The completion of Holy Family Normal School was part of Salzmann's plans for an interlocking network of German organizations and schools to reinforce German Catholic identity in the diocese.[399] He shared this in 1870 when the new structure had been designed and was being built. Speaking to a meeting of the *Central Verein* in Louisville he noted: "The Normal School (Teacher's Seminary) is by no means the crowning glory. My heart aims for a greater work; it desires to establish Fulda in America. In Fulda, at the tomb of St. Boniface, the German bishops decided to found a Catholic University. We also need a university; but first come the common schools, and then the university. If your sons wish to enter one of the professions, he need not then go to Europe or to one of the universities in this country, hotbeds of indifferentism, whence he returns to you filled with the spirit of irreligion. He need not become a priest. As an educated lay-man he can bring honor upon his church, and labor in her interests."[400]

Salzmann couldn't raise enough funds for the new school and it began its existence in deep debt. Consequently he had difficulty securing leadership for it (various accounts relate that he asked 14 priests). In order to increase income, he was compelled to form another institution within the same structure called Pio Nono College. This branch of the school, distinct from the normal school program, was intended to fill the building with more tuition-paying students. Its curriculum, which included a number of courses in business subjects, was calculated to fill the needs of southeastern Wisconsin's rapidly growing industrial society. It soon became more popular than the normal school, whose task was overshadowed by the proliferation of sisterhoods who moved into Catholic classrooms, displacing laymen and laywomen from the rostrum.

Pio Nono College, St. Francis [AAM]

The normal school course work took three years and involved a rather rigorous introduction to various branches of learning. One of the more fascinating of the course programs offered by Holy Family Normal began in 1872, when it started training organists. In that year, the college welcomed John Singenberger and Max Spiegler, professors of music from Regensburg (a center for German church music). The latter would remain only three years, but Singenberger would become a fixture of Milwaukee Catholic life until his death in 1924. For his efforts, Singenberger became the most decorated layperson in Milwaukee Catholic history. He was honored by the University of Notre Dame, received the papal medal "Pro Ecclesia et Pontifice" from Pope Pius X in 1905, and in 1906 the pontiff created him a Knight Commander of the Order of St. Sylvester. From then on he gloried in the title "Chevalier." On his deathbed, Singenberger was honored by Pope Pius XI who created him a Knight of St. Gregory, the highest title that could be conferred on a layman not of noble birth.[401]

Singenberger's role in training a generation of fine church musicians, took place against the backdrop of his work with the American branch of the Caecilian Society, an important church music organization.[402] The Caecilian Movement was begun in Germany under the leadership of choirmaster Franz X. Witt. Responding to a call for reform of church music, Witt helped to organize the Caecilian society in Regensburg in 1870. Dedicated to ending the "abuse" of long operatic music and the playing of elaborate orchestral pieces at Mass and the restoration of a "churchly atmosphere," Witt devised a program of reform. The Caecilians stood for a restoration of a form of Gregorian chant (called "Medicean" and not quite like the type that would come from the monastic revival of chant at Solesmes). They also called for the use of unaccompanied vocal polyphony in imitation of the works of Giovanni de Palestrina, and congregational singing, primarily for devotion and rarely in Mass. They emphasized the use of the organ as the chief musical medium. To propagate these ideas, Witt and his devotees published a popular magazine, held meetings, and trained scores of Catholic choirmasters at their school in Regensburg. Reams of Caecilian music, primarily for vespers and benediction, were turned out by composers influenced by this school.

Prof. John Singenberger [AAM]

When Henni traveled abroad looking for church musicians, Witt recommended Spiegler and Singenberger to Henni. As fate would have it, Singenberger was also a native of Canton St. Gallen and willingly came to America to work with his countryman Henni. Singenberger essentially replicated the Caecilian program in the archdiocese of Milwaukee. He turned out a magazine called *The Caecilian* which highlighted new musical scores and methods. His long composing career included the production of 23 Masses, 4 introits, 40 graduals, 17 offertories, 30 vespers, 30 hymns of vespers, 4 *Magnificats*, 4 antiphons in honor of the Blessed Virgin, 37 hymns in honor of the Blessed Sacrament, 55 collections of hymns, and 199 hymns in honor of the Holy Trinity and the Virgin Mary and the saints.[403] When the school year ended, Singenberger was in high demand to give lectures to eager students in other American cities. In addition, annual conventions of the Caecilians met in a variety of cities and always found Singenberger in attendance.[404] Singenberger's influence was felt in the convents of Milwaukee as well. In 1879, he was hired by the School Sisters of St. Francis to train convent organists and direct the sister's choir. In their long association, Singenberger composed music that was designed for the elaborate rituals of investiture and profession. One of his Franciscan pupils, Sister Cherubim Schaefer, continued to compose and eventually helped organize a college of music at the School Sisters' St. Joseph Convent. Other sister pupils included Sister Gisela Hornback, of the Notre Dame community, and sister musicians of the Agnesians of Fond du Lac.

A host of clerical and lay musicians came from the Singenberger school. Seminary professors Charles Becker and Fridolin Walter were well-known teachers and composers—devising music for special celebrations. Diocesan priest Joseph Pierron (who preached at Singenberger's funeral in 1924) composed the widely distributed *Ave Maria* hymnal in 1928. Published by the Bruce Company, this hymnal contained not only devotional hymns, but also texts for congregational singing after different moments of the Mass (e.g., hymns to be sung after the consecration, during communion, etc.). Singenberger choirmasters included men like Thomas Stemper of St. Boniface, who formed a magnificent boys choir whose melodic voices were heard on a Milwaukee radio station in the 1930s and 1940s. The typically trained product of Holy Family Normal School not only served as parish choirmaster and musician, but also functioned as church sacristan, opening and

1934 composition of Rev. Fridolin T. Walter [AAM]

closing the church and setting up for Mass, as well as serving as a school music teacher.

Singenberger's son Otto helped to perpetuate the Caecilian ideals after his father's death in 1924.[405] A competent church musician in his own right, Otto had loomed to national prominence when he was selected by Cardinal George Mundelein to lead the huge Mass choirs of children gathered to sing the beautiful *Missa de Angelis* during the Eucharistic Congress of 1926 held at Soldier's Field in Chicago. Otto Singenberger taught music at the Mundelein seminary and also served as a music consultant to the Milwaukee Catholic School Department, organizing Mass choirs for archdiocesan celebrations.

Otto Singenberger's success at the 1926 Eucharistic Congress made him something of an expert at the daunting task of training thousands of young school children to sing simple Gregorian Masses for "Field Masses"—outdoor celebrations of the Eucharist that drew large assemblies. At one Mass held on the playing field of Pio Nono College on Memorial Day 1932, Singenberger directed 2,500 children in a choral Eucharist that was described as "one of the most exquisitely beautiful experiences which could befall anyone." The author observed of the participants, "they heard the venerable chant restored to its rightful place in the liturgy, a satisfying proof that our youngest children hold in their hearts the seed of appreciation for a truly Catholic Church music."[406] The tradition of large children's choirs who sang simple Gregorian Masses continued for many years in the Milwaukee See. In one memorable Mass at St. Casimir's Church in Milwaukee, 1,200 children representing 20 parish schools directed by the School Sisters of Notre Dame chanted a Mass so beautifully that Archbishop Moses Kiley wept in the sanctuary.[407] The Singenberger family home, a 16-room mansion built of bricks made on the seminary grounds, sat directly across the street from the old Holy Family buildings. In 1958, Father Oswald Krusing of Sacred Heart parish razed the structure to make way for a new church/school building.[408] The Singenberger legacy of excellence in church music, and the reputation that many German parishes had for excellent church music directed by a skilled musician at the organ console, was the enduring legacy of the Caecilian Movement and the Holy Family School.

John Singenberger Family; Otto Singenberger is on far right [AAM]

Singenberger was not only a skilled musician, and an excellent teacher, but thoroughly conversant with the sometimes arcane world of liturgical observances, rubrics, and feasts. One of his students recalled his musical skills and expert knowledge of the liturgical jargon of the time (material that often befuddled young priests with four years of seminary training):

> Professor Singenberger's range went far beyond mere instrumental rendition of musical compositions, and he could transmit a healthy portion of his own ability to his students with a thoroughness which, in some cases, was almost marvelous. His raw material came from the farms and the common walks of life to which but little of worthwhile music ever penetrated, yet those who went forth from the Catholic Normal School from the fourth year of his course knew more than merely to strike the notes as they came due. They could harmonize a given air very creditably and complete a figured bass with comparative ease. They had learned how to use the Ordo insofar as ecclesiastical rules were concerned, as well as any priest. They knew all about first and second vespers, "commemoratio pracecendenti" and "de sequenti" and could tell at a glance whether the Ite Missa est was to be "de ea", "de beata", "duplex" or "duplex primae classis". He could transpose the response and harmonize it, in any key to which an exuberant predecessor had strayed in intoning it![409]

Both the Catholic Normal School and Pio Nono College coexisted on the same property until 1922. Pio Nono eventually changed into a traditional high school, while the normal school floundered. Enrollments were low as the need for male Catholic school teachers declined when the sisters began to accept the training of boys. From 1889-1895, Father Mathias Gerend was the rector and brought with him two talented priests, Fathers Michael Lochemes and Henry Ries.[410] Working without salary, Gerend, Lochemes, and Ries re-established fiscal soundness to the institution and upgraded its curricular and cultural offerings. Courses were offered in Polish (1894) and Greek (for those destined for the seminary). Greater curricular flexibility was introduced, including the traditional multiyear courses for the normal school and college students, as well as shorter business sequences and even winter sessions that drew idled farm boys to the urban school. The normal school "came to a painless end in 1922."[411]

Msgr. Michael Lochmes
[AOP-Rac]

Pio Nono remained, and efforts were made to turn it into a solid Catholic boys school. A long-needed gym was built in the 1920s by T. C. Esser. In 1931, Archbishop Samuel Stritch approved the building of another structure, Salzmann Hall, to house boarding students. The school proved to be an important peda-

Sacred Heart College, Watertown
[Charles J. Wallman. *Built on Irish Faith,* Edwards Bros., 1994]

gogical training ground for a number of young priests who were destined for the faculty of the diocesan seminary (and a seedbed of vocations, including Aloysius Gerken who became archbishop of Santa Fe, New Mexico). Some of the more illustrious graduates of the school included world-renowned photographer Edward Steichen, Milwaukee architect Peter Brust, and bankers Joseph Moser and Alfred Kliebhahn. In 1941 Archbishop Moses E. Kiley transformed the campus into a minor seminary.

Sacred Heart College

While Salzmann was assembling the components of the "New Fulda" on the shores of Lake Michigan, another enterprise for boys was being created in the Rock River village of Watertown.[412] Watertown was booming in 1871, with a population of 8,000. Two parishes, St. Bernard's for the English-speaking and St. Henry's for the Germans, had been established in 1844 and 1853 respectively. Both had parochial schools. To meet the needs of English-speaking Catholics, Bishop Henni invited the Fathers of the Holy Cross from South Bend, Indiana to take over St. Bernard's and he offered 51 acres on which to build a new college for boys. Negotiations with Father Henry Sorin, superior general of the Order at Notre Dame, led to the sale of the property for $12,000. The College of Our Lady of the Sacred Heart was opened on September 8, 1872 with an enrollment of 40 boys housed in an old farmhouse on the property. The leader of the new group was Father William Corby, a famed Civil War chaplain who had given general absolution to the Union forces at Gettysburg. In July 1873, Corby had begun construction of a new college building just a month after he began constructing an entirely new St. Bernard's Church. The three-story college building had thick brick walls, capacious study halls and adequate heating. In 1874, the "University of Our Lady of the Sacred Heart" received a charter from the state of Wisconsin.

Like the Holy Family/Pio Nono schools, it had a variety of programs from classical instruction to a business or commercial course, and consisted of day and residential scholars. The age groups included young lads from 7 to 13 (minims) to young adults. Enrollment in both peaked at around 60. In 1886, the Holy Cross community closed the college to all but aspirants to the brotherhood. This decision was reversed in 1888, however, and by 1890 the numbers were again up to 60. In November 1888, the decision was made to expand the facilities to attract more students, resulting in another three-story building. In 1891 a new dining hall and chapel were added and three years later a gymnasium and other service buildings were built. One paper noted that the now sprawling campus was one of the largest educational institutions in Wisconsin. The Watertown college sported athletic teams, musical programs, a cadet program and eventually peaked at 117 students hailing from seven states and Mexico in 1908-1909. After that, enrollments plummeted to 44 by 1912, and the Holy Cross brothers once again used it as a training site for their postulants. Today it is Marantha Baptist College.

Catholic Chautauqua

The celebrations attending the 400th anniversary of Columbus's landing were the occasion for a number of Catholic initiatives demonstrating allegiance to the country. A huge world's fair in Chicago invited active Catholic participation, and Milwaukee Catholic school children constructed displays for the event. Catholic priests and sisters visited the fair and were taken by its marvelous Great White Way, the illuminated Ferris Wheel and the display of Vatican maps brought by Archbishop Francesco Satolli, who visited Milwaukee in 1893.[413]

In 1889, a lay Catholic congress was held at Baltimore. This lively gathering hosted a series of popular speakers and sessions that proved immensely successful. A second congress was planned for the Columbian Exposition. It too was well received. One of the byproducts of the general celebration was a lay congress held in Washington, D.C. in 1894, at which a series of addresses and educational lectures were offered.[414] Out of the good will generated by the 1894 movement, Catholic intellectuals led by Notre Dame professor Maurice Francis Egan proposed to continue the event by devising a Catholic summer school based on the model of the popular summertime lectures and recreation events that took place at a camp ground in northwestern New York along Chautauqua Lake. The popularity of the speakers drew hundreds to the site and eventually the program was put on the road. Catholics in the east used the Chautauqua format at a summer session in New London, Connecticut. The combination of instruction, recreation and travel attracted large crowds, and in 1894, Professor Egan, who was one of its organizers, decided to arrange for a summer school in the "west," meaning the Midwest. Among the planners for the event were Sebastian Messmer, recently appointed bishop of Green Bay, Humphrey Desmond, William Onahan of the St. Vincent de Paul Societies, and assorted bishops and laypersons from Minne-

sota and Illinois. Seeking a middle ground for their various constituencies, they decided to locate the western summer school in the Wisconsin state capital of Madison. They drafted a constitution for their organization and chose Messmer as its head.[415]

Two prominent names highlighted the opening events of the summer school: literary figure Maurice Francis Egan and Holy Cross priest and scientist, John A. Zahm.[416] The sessions began in mid-July and extended until August 4th. The opening day began with 400 people in attendance at the sessions held at the Fuller Opera House. Notices of welcome were given by the governor and the head of the state university. Messmer assured the politicians and educators, "We are not going into politics," and "our Summer school will issue no declaration of war against science and modern theories of progress. Our church is in favor of all." Zahm's lecture on "Modern Scientific Errors" touched on the topic of evolution of plants, animals and men—subjects that would later earn his work a Vatican rebuke and their placement on the Index of Forbidden Books.[417] Egan provided a lighter touch, with some literary meanderings. The future editor of the *Catholic Encyclopedia* lectured on Florentine firebrand Girolamo Savonarola. Other archdiocesan priests such as Joseph LaBoule and Messmer himself offered sessions. Thousands attended the event and it garnered $1,500 for the sponsoring organization.[418]

However, controversy erupted shortly after the participants went home when the German language *Columbia* attacked Zahm for advocating Darwinian evolution with its emphasis on natural selection through the "survival of the fittest." Messmer rose to defend Zahm, whose presentation he insisted fell within the boundaries of Catholic orthodoxy. He further argued against the notion that a discussion of evolution and other controversial issues was somehow harmful to the Catholic faith of the "simple" people who attended the lectures. "It is simply nonsense," he declared, "to assert that such discussions belong within the circle of specialists and savants although they are brought before the public by press, in books and current literature."[419] Messmer's ringing defense of free intellectual debate also reflected his own years as a scholar and the hopes of many that the Church could enter the ranks of public debate on issues of importance. He appeared to have sincerely meant it when he assured state university officials that the Church was not at war with modern culture.

Nonetheless, the controversy had its effect. Although the 1896 summer school continued to attract record numbers, most of the topics hewed to safe ecclesiastical and literary lines, with few presentations on science, history, or any other topic likely to raise the hackles of conservatives. Messmer led off the events with a sermon in St. Raphael's Church in Madison on the subject of faith and reason—comparing them to the sun and moon, "Both are great lights," he declared to the congregation, "but faith is greater as the light of sun is greater than the light of the moon."[420] Although the 1896 gathering was a success, posting another surplus of $1500, a behind the scenes controversy further damaged its reputation when Messmer excluded Catholic University professor Edward A. Pace from the program. As a result, Catholic leaders lost interest in the interchange of ideas with their counterparts in the secular Chautauqua movement and in the academy.[421] In 1899, the Vatican condemned the accomodationist strategies of the liberals in the American hierarchy when Pope Leo XIII issued the encyclical *Testem Benevolentiae* scoring the heresy infelicitously named "Americanism." In the same general crackdown on Americanist bishops and their activities, Zahm's work, *Evolution and Dogma* was placed on the Index in 1899. In 1900 the summer school moved to Detroit, and Messmer stepped down from the presidency as well. Afterwards it floundered, moving again to St. Paul and each year drawing fewer and fewer crowds. In 1907 the papal condemnation put a chill on any kind of activity that encouraged free debate on controversial topics such as biblical studies, the historicity of dogma, and papal power.

In 1908, interest in the school revived at the suggestion of Humphrey Desmond to give the summer school a permanent home at Spring Bank, a resort area 28 miles from Milwaukee and easily accessible by trains that stopped at nearby Okauchee.[422] Although most bishops applauded the idea, few were willing to financially support it so local laypersons moved forward on their own. On July 4, 1908 a group of 150 Catholics including Desmond came to the site for a tour of the grounds and buildings, a ride on the nearby lake and a Sunday Mass celebrated on the grounds by Oconomowoc pastor Charles McBride.[423] The next year a consortium of Catholic laity formed the Spring Bank Corporation and sold bonds and began dickering for the land. They finally purchased 60 acres and began to transform the buildings into a resort and summer camp.[424] On July 4th another resort season began with prominent Catholic families squaring off against each other for baseball, tennis and other games. Dancing and evening fireworks, orchestral concerts and talks by prominent Catholic citizens marked the season.[425] In 1910, a gathering of ranking American archbishops and bishops filled the bill for the "Western Catholic Chautauqua" as it was called.[426] In 1912, the *Central Verein* held its social study classes on the grounds.[427]

Ultimately efforts to rekindle the summer school failed. The property was sold to the Catholic Health Association who used it briefly for nurse's training. However, the remoteness of the area and the need to be near a teaching hospital made this impractical. As late as 1925, however, Desmond and others, remembering the glory days of the 1890s, tried to resurrect the school.[428] However, by that time the need for adult education classes would later be filled by other forms of ongoing education, such as lecture bureaus sponsored by Catholic organizations or colleges.

Coping with Anti-Catholicism: The American Protective Association

The close identification of Catholicism with the foreign-born, and the increased visibility and power of Catholics in Wisconsin, provoked a backlash in the 1890s. The strong Catholic/Lutheran alliance to defeat the Bennett law reawakened the sleeping forces of anti-Catholicism once again. This time the vehicle was an organization founded in nearby Clinton, Iowa, the American Protective Association (APA).[429] The APA was a new incarnation of the nativist/anti-Catholic impulse that had been last seen in an organized form in the 1850s.

The origins of this new group were born out of anxieties of a potential Catholic "takeover" of local government, and the "stacking" of critical urban services, such as police and fire departments, as well as the ranks of public school teachers. In addition, the APA singled out Catholics as willing collaborators of monopolists and at the same time the source of anarchism and radicalism in the growing labor movement.[430] APA devotees refurbished old arguments about the incompatibility of Roman Catholic beliefs and organizational structures with American democracy and representative government. Unlike the nativists, the APA did not attempt to mount a parallel party apparatus in order to win elections, but instead directed support to candidates who endorsed their goals of limiting foreign and Catholic influence from all areas of public life. Interestingly, the organization flourished for a time, creating local branches in a number of Midwestern and Western states. Local APA enthusiasts circulated lists of acceptable candidates at election time and found sympathetic journalists and others, mainly Protestant ministers, who endorsed their cause as "reform." The APA presence in Wisconsin grew slowly, but by 1893, it had councils in a number of Wisconsin towns.[431] Milwaukee had nearly 500 members. Janesville, Portage, La Crosse, Kaukauna, Oregon, Stevens Point, and Elroy also recorded the growth of chapters. From the outset, Humphrey Desmond's *Catholic Citizen* gave warnings about the organization, reporting that 4,215 Wisconsinites were part of the organization. By 1894, Milwaukee had 20 councils, and other cities like Racine, Fond du Lac, Sheboygan, Manitowoc, Madison, Kenosha, and Janesville reported visible APA activity.[432] At its peak the organization numbered nearly 176,000 Wisconsinites out of a population of 2 million.[433] In Milwaukee, Desmond's criticism stirred up sufficient voting strength to thwart openly APA candidates for city or county office, and even managed to turn out 3,000 angry citizens at an anti-APA rally at the Academy of Music in March 1894.[434]

The existence of the APA posed a political and public policy threat to Catholics for at least a short time in Wisconsin. APA voting strength, though not decisive in itself, was able to exercise influence because it held the balance of power in the tightly balanced politics of Wisconsin in the late 19th century. The efforts of the APA also laid bare the divisions that existed between Catholics and Protestants in the state. This was most evident in a decade-long controversy over the placement of the statue of Father Jacques Marquette in Statuary Hall in the U. S. Capitol.

The Marquette statue controversy began in 1864 when Congress transformed the old House of Representative chamber into a memorial to the great citizens of each state called Statuary Hall.[435] It was not until 1887 that Wisconsin got around to nominating a representative figure. State Senator George Clay Ginty, a Republican of Chippewa Falls, suggested Father Marquette. Stressing Marquette's role as an explorer and pioneer in early Wisconsin more than his religious activities and identity, Ginty felt that he was the perfect exemplification of the state's heroic past, and the symbol of the progress and enterprise that reflected Wisconsin's present greatness. Ginty's proposal may have emanated from the purest motives of admiration and respect for the intrepid 17th century Jesuit pioneer, but he also had ambitions to be governor and believed this would help him with important segments of Wisconsin's electorate. Whatever the motive, Ginty's proposal was strongly endorsed by leading politicians and newspaper editors (the only sour note was the *Milwaukee Sentinel* who pointed out that Marquette was not a Wisconsin citizen), and his bill passed the state senate comfortably and the assembly by a narrow margin of 36 in favor, 29 against, and 35 abstaining. The votes broke primarily on party lines—Democrats in favor and Republicans against. These mirrored the political divisions in the state—Catholics were primarily Democrats and Protestants were Republicans.

The success of Ginty's bill was set back in 1888 when the superintendent of the capitol in Washington ruled that Marquette was ineligible since he was not a citizen. Efforts on the part of Wisconsin congressmen to secure a resolution to overturn the decision of the superintendent died in committee, and the subject became an even greater political liability when the Bennett law agitation began in 1889 and the elections of 1890 brought in a new Democratic regime headed by George Peck. Peck had warmly endorsed the statue on the pages of his *Wisconsin State Journal* in 1887. But now as governor, he faced a serious problem. Because of his opposition to the Bennett law he had been elected with strong Catholic support. But he had also managed to draw Wisconsin Lutherans into his winning coalition, and their interest in a statue of a Jesuit was minimal. Catholics began to

Mr. George C. Ginty [*History of Northern Wisconsin,* Western Historical Co., 1881, p. 209]

press Peck to push through the long-deferred statue which now had become a symbol of Catholic interests in state politics.

In 1892 the matter was rejoined when Congressman John L. Mitchell secured the passage of a resolution authorizing the statue. As the bill moved to the senate for approval, Catholics began to apply pressure on newly-elected Senator William F. Vilas to support the bill. Vilas hesitated. Although not directly elected by the people of the state (that would only happen after the enactment of the 17th amendment in 1913), Vilas did have to pay attention to the wider dynamics of state politics, especially in the legislature. When he hesitated to express strong support for the Marquette statue, the German language *Columbia* threatened to attack him publicly. At this point, state Democratic chairman, Edward Wall (a Catholic) intervened and secured the help of Archbishop Katzer in quieting potential Catholic outrage. Wall also convinced Vilas to not actively oppose the statue. In February 1893, the strongly Democratic legislature voted a joint resolution to urge the state's senators to move the Marquette bill out of committee. Humphrey Desmond also kept up a steady stream of support for the statue and informed Vilas that his growing chain of newspapers would spearhead a campaign to have the statue approved. Vilas finally moved and got the congress to concur with the house resolution. It made it to the desk of lame duck president Benjamin Harrison, who failed to sign it before leaving office, and it lapsed. In 1893, the resolution was introduced again in the House and the Senate, and it was finally passed and signed by President Grover Cleveland.

Back in Wisconsin, the once strong support of Governor Peck waned (he too feared a political backlash from Lutherans over the statue), but in early 1894, with Humphrey Desmond's prodding, he appointed a committee to find a sculptor for the statue. On this committee were Judge Joseph Loesey of La Crosse, attorney Robert LaFollette, Milwaukee meat packer Frederick Layton (also a connoisseur of fine art), Superior banker James Bardon and Archbishop Katzer. The new commission moved expeditiously and announced a competition for the statue. In November 1894, they chose the design of Florentine sculptor Gaetano Trentanove. Trentanove was known to Milwaukeeans for his busts of prominent people in Milwaukee (as previously noted he would also do one of Katzer and design the angels that adorned Our Lady of Pompeii Church as well as a statue of the Virgin Mary for St. Patrick's Church, and was involved with the sculptures at St. Josaphat's Basilica).[436]

As Trentanove began carving Marquette out of an eight-foot block of marble, additional complications set in when the American Protective Association of Wisconsin began to stir up trouble. In 1893 they had begun a widely-circulated journal, the *Wisconsin Patriot*, which stirred the opposition of the local councils of the APA and bitterly attacked Peck and other officials associated with the project. The statue once again became a symbol of ethno-cultural divisions in the state, and elected officials did what they could to avoid being drawn into the controversy, thereby alienating a portion of their electoral constituencies.

Trentanove seemed oblivious to all of this. When he finished the statue in early 1896, he planned a gala celebration for the transfer of the statue from his Milwaukee studio to the capitol and then an elaborate unveiling that would be attended not only by state and federal officers, but by Cardinal Gibbons, Apostolic Delegate Francesco Satolli, representatives of the Jesuits, and the French and Italian ambassadors. However, APA-generated opposition to the statue was so intense (replete with threats to blow it up) that a less ostentatious unveiling took place. A representative from Michigan, William S. Linton, the APA's chief point man in the House of Representatives, introduced a resolution to have "this statue of a zealous priest who never knew the meaning of the precious word 'liberty'" removed from the capitol and returned to Wisconsin. Linton, who met Trentanove one day while inspecting the statue, withdrew the resolution, but APA efforts in Wisconsin to get rid of the statue went on unabated.

Statue of Father Jacques Marquette, SJ, Gaetano Trentanove, sculptor [AAM]

One plan was to avoid attacking Marquette on religious grounds and to simply offer as substitutes two prominent Civil War veterans, Lucius Fairchild and Jeremiah Rusk. The Marquette statue was to be returned to Wisconsin to have an honored place in the newly-built State Historical Society in Madison. This plan, which had the backing of the state branch of the Grand Army of the Republic, a powerful Civil War veteran's organization, seemed to be the best way out of the impasse, but Catholic voices, like Bishop Sebastian Messmer of Green Bay, and the

Marquette College Alumni, saw through it and denounced it vigorously. The state legislature, caught in the cross fire, withdrew the plan to move Marquette to the State Historical Society and tried to submit all three statues for congressional approval. Eventually, however, the legislature killed the plans for the Rusk and Fairchild statues and just decided to leave things as they were.

The Marquette statue remained in Washington, and through the efforts of the Marquette Alumni, Congress formally accepted the statue in 1904 (this had never been done in the heat of the controversy). The collapse of APA efforts to stop the Marquette statue coincided with the decline of the APA in Wisconsin and elsewhere. In 1898, the U.S. government issued a postage stamp of Marquette in full Jesuit regalia. Wrote one gloating Catholic to an APA official, "Just think of the members of the great American Protective Association being compelled to lick the backside of Father Marquette every time they mail a piece of literature to enlighten the American people concerning the disloyalty of their Catholic fellow citizens."[437]

By late 1902, Katzer had lost much of his strength, and day-to-day affairs were being handled by his faithful secretary, Monsignor Augustine Schinner. Since 1901 he had been afflicted by fainting spells. After consulting a number of physicians (including the Mayo Brothers), he was diagnosed with pancreatic cancer, and in March 1903 retired to St. Agnes sanitarium in Fond du Lac, where he literally wasted away losing about three pounds a week. Ten days before his death, he was completely bedridden. He died on July 20, 1903.[438] Katzer's funeral was attended by two archbishops, ten bishops, 420 priests and representatives of state and city government, including Governor Robert LaFollette. Twelve plumed Knights of St. George stood as an honor guard over the remains of the prelate, and 200 carriages and conveyances accompanied the hearse. His old nemesis, Archbishop John Ireland, gave the final absolution.[439] After consigning Katzer to eternity in the seminary cemetery, diocesan consultors met to draft a *terna* for the new archbishop. Milwaukee would be *sede vacante* until Christmas and without someone living in the episcopal mansion until the next summer. Speculation about his successor began almost immediately and eyes turned north to Green Bay and Sebastian Messmer.[440]

Notes

1 Johnson, *Crosier on the Frontier*, p. 181.

2 There is as yet no comprehensive history of the diocese of Green Bay. See Gordon Gilsdorf and William Zimmer (eds.) *The Diocese of Green Bay: A Centennial, 1868-1968* (Diocese of Green Bay, 1968). Monsignor Orville Griese compiled a series of life sketched of the bishops and priests of the diocese of Green Bay, *In His Vineyard, 1868-1962* (diocese of Green Bay, 1962).

3 A very good history of the Diocese of La Crosse is Gerald Edward Fisher, *Dusk is My Dawn, The First Hundred Years of the Diocese of La Crosse, 1868-1968* (Diocese of La Crosse, 1969). Fisher also produced a compendium of diocesan facts on the occasion of the 125th anniversary of the diocese. See *257 Things You Should Know About the Diocese of La Crosse, 1868-1993* (Diocese of La Crosse, 1993).

4 Johnson, *Crosier on the Frontier*, pp. 182-183.

5 See Derek Holmes, *The Triumph of the Holy See: A Short History of the Papacy in the Nineteenth Century* (London: Burns & Oates, 1978).

6 A dated but still reliable source on Pio Nono is Roger Aubert, *Le pontificat de Pie IX (1846-1878)* (Paris: Bloud and Gay, 1952); One of the first biographies to use the recently opened papers of the pontiff is Frank J. Coppa, *Pope Pius IX, Crusader in a Secular Age* (Boston: Twayne Publishers, 1979). The recent beatification of the pontiff produced this extensive postulation document, *Città del Vaticano: Editrice la Postulazatione della Causa di Pio IX* (Libreria editrice Vaticana, 1968-1988). See also, Roger Aubert, "The Continuation of Catholic Renewal in Europe," pp. 3-56; Roger Aubert and Rudolph Lill, "The Ascension of Pius IX and The Crisis of 1848," pp. 57-87; "The Victory of the Ultramontanes," pp. 304-350 in Hubert Jedin (ed.) *History of the Church: The Church in the Age of Liberalism* vol. 8 (New York: Crossroad, 1981).

7 Quoted in Johnson, *Crosier on the Frontier*, p. 178.

8 Roger Aubert, "The Vatican Council," pp. 315-329 in Jedin, *History of the Church*.

9 The most trustworthy account of American participation at Vatican I is still James J. Hennesey, *The First Council of the Vatican: The American Experience* (New York: Herder and Herder, 1963).

10 For a good treatment of American Catholic perceptions of the papacy and their relationship to the sentiments of American Protestants see Sandra Yocum Mize "The Papacy in Mid-Nineteenth Century American Catholic Imagination," (unpublished Ph.D. dissertation, Marquette University, 1987).

11 Hennesey, pp. 34, 44, 48, 78, 88, 89, 91, 106, 159, 169, 202, 230, 274, 282.

12 "Philathelos," *Facts Against Assertions.*

13 Hennesey, p. 101.

14 Hennesey, pp. 159, 169, 281-282.

15 "Reception of Bishop Henni," *The Star of Bethlehem,* November 1870.

16 Henni to Emily Power, December 12, 1870, GA-11, Box 6, 12a, (Milwaukee, 1864-1882), AOP-Sin.

17 *Star of Bethlehem*, June 1871; *Milwaukee Sentinel*, 8 June 1871.

18 "The Investiture of the Most Rev. John M. Henni as Archbishop," *Milwaukee Sentinel*, 4 June 1875. The *Sentinel* devoted three full pages to the coverage of the celebration.

19 Johnson, *Crosier on the Frontier*, p. 181.

20 "Priest's Housekeeper, 69, Recalls Knowing Every Milwaukee Bishop," *Catholic Herald Citizen*, 28 October 1939.

21 "Milwaukee Bishops," *Catholic Herald*, 20 April 1922.

22 Chronicle of the Motherhouse, 1876-1886, p. 124, ASND; "Illness of Archbishop Henni," *Milwaukee Sentinel* 18 July 1878.

23 One additional sign that Henni's judgement was not perfect even before he became seriously impaired is to be found in the list of 77 "ghost parishes" that was later compiled by historian Peter Leo Johnson. Although the some of these church failures reflected the shifts in Wisconsin's demo-

graphics created by the new economic and transportation systems, some were just started by impulse and advanced due to Henni's unwillingness to exercise firm control over small but noisy minorities who wanted a church in their region. The amount of money lost on acceding to these demands is difficult to calculate. "Ghosts of 77 One-time Flourishing Churches Located by Dr. Johnson," *Catholic Herald Citizen*, 12 April 1941.

24 A fuller discussion of the religious dimension of the political world of Wisconsin and general Midwestern politics can be found in Paul Kleppner, *The Cross of Culture: A Social Analysis of Midwestern Politics, 1850-1890* (New York: Free Press, 1970) and Richard Jensen, *The Winning of the Midwest: Social and Political Conflict, 1888-1896* (Chicago: University of Chicago Press, 1971).

25 Nesbit, *History of Wisconsin,* pp. 142-143, 225, 549-550. I use the term "temperance" in a popular but not technically accurate way. As historian Ronald G. Walters notes in his chapter on drink in *American Reformers, 1815-1860* (New York: Hill and Wang, 1978), p. 123, "It is a catchall term—the lowest common denominator for the crusade against alcohol. Some people believed in temperate use of alcohol, others were for total abstinence, and some were for prohibiting its manufacture and sale."

26 Gurda, pp. 63-64.

27 "Documents," *Salesianum* 55 (April 1960): 63-66.

28 Peter Leo Johnson, "An Experiment in Adult Education," *Salesianum* 45 (October 1950): pp. 149-158. See also Harry H. Heming, *The Catholic Church in Wisconsin* (Milwaukee: Catholic Historical Publishing Company, 1895-1898), pp. 1078-1079.

29 "To Leave the Diocese," *Catholic Citizen*, 24 September 1892; "Father Cleary's New Field," *Catholic Citizen*, 1 October 1892.

30 Quoted in Blied, *Three Archbishops*, p. 42.

31 "Must Shun Saloons," *Evening Wisconsin*, 14 July 1892.

32 George W. Willard to James Gibbons, May 7, 1878, #7351, Archives of the Archdiocese of Baltimore (hereafter AAB).

33 Willard Letter to Propaganda Fidei, May 21, 1878, *Congressi America*, Vol. 29, pages unnumbered. See also Ludwig, n.14, p. 417.

34 Willard, Fagan, Fairbanks, Petit, Keenan, and Keogh to Gibbons, May 8, 1878, Gibbons Papers, AAB.

35 The best biography of Spalding is David Francis Sweeney, OFM, *The Life of John Lancaster Spalding, First Bishop of Peoria, 1840-1916* (New York: Herder and Herder, 1965), pp. 113-118.

36 Grace to Gibbons, September 8, 1878 quoted in Daniel F. Reilly, *The School Controversy, 1891-1893* (Washington, D.C.: The Catholic University of America, 1943), pp. 248-249. The news of Grace's "shift" reached the secular press in early January 1879, "The Catholic Coadjutorship," *Milwaukee Sentinel*, 20 January 1879.

37 Martin Kundig *et al* to John McCloskey, September 2, 1878, quoted in Sweeney, p. 116.

38 Kundig, Donohoe, Keogh, and Lonigan to Gibbons, September 23, 1878, Gibbons Papers, AAB.

39 Thomas Fagan to Giovanni Simeoni, July 5, 1878, Scritture e Referitte, 1878, Archives of the Propaganda (hereafter AOP).

40 Ibid.

41 Edward Fitzpatrick to Leopold Moczygemba, March 2, 1879, #641, Scritture e Referitte, AOP.

42 *Sentinel*, 21 December 1878.

43 "The Coadjutor to our Archbishop," *Catholic Citizen,* 21 December 1878; *Columbia* 26 December 1878 and 16 January 1879.

44 Moczygemba to Simeoni, March 5, 1879; Letter of E. Kramer, M.S., February 10, 1879, #646, Scritture e Referetti, 1879, AOP.

45 Henni to Simeoni, September 7, 1879, #657, Scritture e Referitte, 1879, AOP.

46 "Father Fagan Local Pastor Answers Call," *Catholic Citizen*, 11 October 1923.

47 Henni Circular, January 19, 1879, Henni Papers, AAM.

48 "The Coadjutorship," *Catholic Citizen*, 21 January 1879.

49 Ibid.

50 A copy of this defense of Heiss appeared in the secular press. "The Coadjutorship," *Milwaukee Sentinel*, 30 January 1879.

51 Ibid.

[52] Edward J. Fitzpatrick to Leopold Moczygemba, March 2, 1879, #641, Scritture e Referitte, AOP.

[53] "Fiftieth Anniversary of the Ordination of His Grace, Archbishop Henni to the Priesthood," *Catholic Citizen,* 18 January 1879; "The Golden Jubilee," *Catholic Citizen*, 8 February 1879; "The Golden Jubilee," *Catholic Citizen*, 15 February 1879.

[54] "A Page of Mourning," "Fainted in Sanctuary," *Catholic Citizen*, 15 March 1879.

[55] Edward J. Fitzpatrick to Leopold Moczygemba, March 2, 1879, #641, Scritture e Referitte, AOP.

[56] Simeoni to Henni, May 17, 1879, Henni Papers, AAM.

[57] Heiss relates the nature of Henni's insistence that he remain an active candidate for the coadjutorship in a letter to Kleiner. "At last the Roman authorities found a good way to get rid of me. It was reported that the Bishop of La Crosse, although otherwise eminently qualified for the position, was advanced in age and of feeble health....Thereupon the Archbishop [Henni] declared that things were different: the Bishop of La Crosse was strong and healthy and the fact that the diocese of La Crosse was in such good order had been his principle motive why he had made his selection and had proposed Bishop Heiss "primo loco." Heiss to Kleiner, July 16, 1879, Heiss-Kleiner Letters.

[58] Francis Haas to Mother Agnes Hazotte, June 23, 1891, ACSA.

[59] Mother Caroline Friess to Peter Abbelen, February 22, 1880, #135, p. 279, Brumleve.

[60] The meeting of Abbelen with Hergenroether and Propaganda is verified in Heiss to Kleiner, April 27, 1880, Heiss-Kleiner Letters.

[61] "Coadjutor of Archbishop Henni," *Catholic Citizen*, 20 March 1880.

[62] *Evening Wisconsin,* pp. 7,8,9, September 1881.

[63] M. Mileta Ludwig, *Right Hand Glove Uplifted: A Biography of Archbishop Michael Heiss* (New York: Pageant Press, 1967), pp. 394-416.

[64] Quoted in Blied, *Three Archbishops*, p. 27.

[65] "Father Willard Dead," *Catholic Citizen*, 2 August 1890; "Father Willard," *Catholic Citizen*, 16 August 1890. In 1957, St. Joseph pastor Henry G. Riordan named a parish building after Willard. "Fond du Lac Honors Memory of Pioneer Priest," *Catholic Herald Citizen*, 6 April 1957.

[66] One of the reasons for the groundswell in favor of Keogh was his work in reorganizing the cathedral schools. See, "The Cathedral Schools," *Catholic Citizen*, 30 August 1879. Ludwig, n22, pp. 438-439.

[67] McDonald, *Irish in Wisconsin*, p. 214.

[68] Quoted in Ludwig, p. 433.

[69] "Why Do English-Speaking Priests Seek Parishes outside the Diocese," *Catholic Citizen*, 19 August 1911.

[70] "Vocations to the Priesthood in Milwaukee Archdiocese," *Catholic Citizen*, 24 August 1911; "Father Johnson in Rejoinder," *Catholic Citizen*, 2 September 1911.

[71] The only substantial biography of Heiss is Sister M. Mileta Ludwig's *Right Hand Glove Uplifted.* Although its tone is hagiographical, Ludwig's research scholarship is excellent. Benjamin Blied provides a solid essay on the second archbishop in *Three Archbishops*, pp. 9-45.

[72] Peter Leo Johnson had the bulk of the Heiss-Kleiner letters translated and they appeared periodically in the seminary quarterly *Salesianum.* A complete run of these letters was compiled and edited by Barbara Brumleve, *Correspondence of Archbishop John Martin Henni, Archbishop Michael Heiss, Rev. Joseph Ferdinand Mueller, Dr. Joseph Salzmann and Assorted Other Persons* (School Sisters of Notre Dame: Heritage Resource Publication no. 38, 1986), pp. 1-217.

[73] Heiss to Kleiner, June 27, 1844, Heiss-Kleiner Letters, Brumeleve, #18, pp.115-116.

[74] Heiss to Kleiner, September 27, 1849, Heiss-Kleiner Letters, Brumleve, #19, pp.117-118.

[75] Ibid.

[76] Mother Caroline Friess to Sister Theophila Bauer, January 24, 1883, Brumleve, #162, pp. 326-27.

[77] Heiss to Kleiner, June 22, 1868, quoted in Blied, *Three Archbishops*, p. 21, fn. 26.

[78] Augustine F. Schinner, "The Catholic Church in Milwaukee," in Howard Louis Conard (ed.) *History of Milwaukee County From Its Settlement to the Year 1895* Vol. II (Chicago and New York: American Biographical Publishing Company, 1896), p. 156.

[79] Heiss's years as bishop of La Crosse are covered in Ludwig, pp. 309-394 and Fisher, *Dusk is My Dawn*, pp. 23-39.

[80] Quoted in Ludwig, p. 434.

[81] Richard N. Current, *History of Wisconsin* Vol. II (Madison: State Historical Society of Wisconsin, 1976), pp. 452-455.

[82] Blied, *Three Archbishops*, p. 27, n. 41.

[83] M. Edmund Hussey, "The 1878 Financial Failure of Archbishop Purcell," *Cincinnati Historical Society Bulletin* 36 (Spring 1978): 6-41.

[84] Blied, *Three Archbishops*, p. 28.

[85] "St. Rose's Orphan Asylum: Provision for Its Future Support," *Catholic Citizen*. 11 March 1882; "The Little Orphans," *Catholic Citizen*, 26 August 1882.

[86] Heiss, "Report on Debt Reduction," August 10, 1885, Heiss Papers, AAM.

[87] Quoted in Ludwig, p. 440.

[88] Patrick Carey, *People, Priests, and Prelates: Ecclesiastical Democracy and the Tensions of Trusteeism* (Notre Dame: University of Notre Dame Press, 1987).

[89] An abbreviated version of the Beaver Dam troubles is related in the Chronicle of St. Peter Church, Beaver Dam, ASND.

[90] These controversies are laid out in some detail in a dated but helpful M. A. thesis. See G. A. Brielmaier, "The Evils of Lay Trusteeism in Wisconsin," (unpublished M.A. thesis, St. Francis Seminary, 1936).

[91] M. Paschala O'Connor, *Five Decades: History of the Congregation of the Most Holy Rosary Sinsinawa, Wisconsin, 1849-1899,* (Sinsinawa: Sinsinawa Press, 1954), pp. 231-236.

[92] O'Connor, p. 232. Some doubt whether he ever read the letter.

[93] Ibid., p. 233.

[94] Quoted in O'Connor, p. 233.

[95] Heiss to Mother Emily Power, January 20, 1882, GA-2, Box 6, 12b, Emily Power Papers, AOP-Sin.

[96] Mother Emily Power to Heiss, June 26, 1882, GA-2, Box 6, 12b, Emily Power Papers, AOP-Sin.

[97] O'Connor, p. 234.

[98] Ibid.

[99] O'Connor, p. 236.

[100] Heiss to Power, October 5, 1882; Heiss to Power, March 22, 1883, GA-2, Box 6, 12b, Emily Power Papers, AOP-Sin.

[101] "The Church Troubles at Lancaster," *Catholic Citizen*, 24 February 1883. Legal papers related to this litigation are to be found in AOP-Sin.

[102] "Sustained by Rome," *Catholic Citizen*, 14 July 1883. This account gives a lengthy account of the controversy and its civil and canonical resolution.

[103] "Church Torn Down" unidentified clipping, 1912, in AOP-Sin. *Catholic Citizen* of April 20, 1912 reported in a brief note, "Old St. Dominic's Church at Sinsinawa Mound is being torn down and the material will be used in putting up buildings at St. Clara's College."

[104] Brielmaier, pp. 24-35; Mary Ann Wettstein, *150 Years of Catholic Faith in the Fond du Lac Area: Retracing the Steps* (Fond du Lac, 1998), pp. 75-77; John J. Schmitz, *More than Brick and Mortar: A History of St. Mary's Parish* (church history, copy in AAM).

[105] A copy of the text of this law is found in "Church Property," *Catholic Citizen*, 27 January 1883.

[106] Patrick J. Dignan, *A History of the Legal Incorporation of Catholic Church Property in the United States (1784-1932)* (New York: P. J. Kenedy and Sons, 1935), p. 261.

[107] "Incorporating Church Property," *Catholic Citizen*, 21 July 1883.

[108] *Catholic Citizen,* 18 August, 1883.

[109] Dignan, p. 232.

[110] *Catholic Citizen*, 5 September 1883.

[111] Dignan, pp. 235-236.

[112] "The Archdiocese Incorporated," *Catholic Citizen*, 16 May 1903.

[113] Stritch to Martin D. McNamara, June 14, 1949, Stritch Papers, Box 2994, Archives of the Archdiocese of Chicago.

[114] "Racial Clashed Called in Cause of Case in Court," May 1922, unidentified clipping St. Rose File, AAM.

[115] "Sustains Father Piette," *Catholic Citizen*, 2 February 1907.

[116] "St. Rose Pastor Ordered to Pay Heavy Damages," May 1922 (unidentified clipping) St. Rose File, AAM.

[117] "St. Rose Church Tries to Oust Its Own Pastor," June 1923, (unidentified clipping), St. Rose File, AAM.

[118] "Racine Trouble Settled; Father Piette Transferred," *Catholic Citizen*, 25 June 1923.

[119] "The Deaneries of the Archdiocese," *Catholic Citizen*, 11 December 1886; Ludwig, pp. 450-451.

[120] Marvin O'Connell's biography of Ireland says that the idea for the new province was Ireland's and it occurred to him at the first Provincial Council of Milwaukee in 1885. See Marvin O'Connell, *John Ireland and the American Catholic Church* (St. Paul: Minnesota Historical Society Press, 1988), p. 251. Ludwig suggests that Willard's hand was in it, especially since the Prefect Apostolic Martin Marty of the Dakotas had complained bitterly about German instruction in the catechism—a slap at the Germans in Wisconsin. The need to be free of German control must have had strong support or consultation from Father Willard.

[121] Thomas T. Brundage, "The Development of Catholic Journalism in the Milwaukee Archdiocese," (unpublished paper, St. Francis Seminary, 1985). See also Apollinaris Baumgartner, *Catholic Journalism, A Study of Its Development in the United States, 1789-1830* (New York: Columbia University Press, 1931), pp. 27, 29; Robert J. Baranow, "Nineteenth Century Wisconsin Catholic Newspapers and Periodicals: A Checklist," (unpublished B. A. thesis, St. Francis Seminary, 1958.)

[122] Richard Scheiber, "Humphrey J. Desmond, 'The Catholic Citizen' and Catholic Liberalism," (unpublished Ph.D. dissertation, Marquette University, 1990); John O. Geiger, "H. J. Desmond, Catholic, Citizen, Reformer: The Quest for Justice Through Educational and Social Reform," (unpublished Ph.D. dissertation, Marquette University, 1972); Richard J. Orsi, "Humphrey Joseph Desmond: A Case Study in American Catholic Liberalism," (unpublished M.A. thesis, University of Wisconsin, 1965).

[123] E. P. Willging and Herta Hatzfield, *Catholic Serials of the Nineteenth Century in the United States: Second Series: Part Two, Wisconsin* (Washington, D.C.: Catholic University Press, 1960), p. 52.

[124] Ibid.

[125] John Gilmary Shea, "Converts—Their Influence and Work in This Country," *American Catholic Quarterly Review* 8 (July, 1883): pp. 509-529.

[126] Quoted in Barry, p. 53.

[127] "Clerical Know-Nothingism in the Catholic Church," *Pastoral Blatt* (November 1883), pp. 121-131.

[128] Ludwig, p. 485; Blied, *Three Archbishops*, p. 31.

[129] *Memoriale sulla questione dei Tedeschi della Chiesa di America*, AAB.

[130] Quoted in Blied, *Three Archbishops*, pp. 37-38.

[131] Benjamin J. Blied, "The Unknown Rector," *Salesianum* 43 (April 1948): pp. 56-62.

[132] Jay P. Dolan, *The American Catholic Experience* (New York: Doubleday, 1985), pp. 262-293.

[133] Messmer to Blaine, April 6, 1921, Messmer Papers, AAM.

[134] Heiss to George Kellerman, May 23, 1844, quoted in Timothy Walch, "The Catholic Press and the Campaign for Parish Schools: Chicago and Milwaukee, 1850-1885."

[135] Salzmann to Michael Hansreidter, October 10, 1849, ibid.

[136] *Catholic Vindicator*, 2 March 1871.

[137] Ludwig p. 452; *Catholic Citizen*, 21 April 1883; "The New Catholic School Board," *Catholic Citizen*, 9 June 1883.

[138] "An Important Event," *Catholic Citizen*, 15 May 1886. Present at the gathering were Archbishop Michael Heiss, Bishops Kilian Flasch, John Ireland, Thomas Langton Grace, Rupert Seidenbusch, Martin Marty, and John Vertin. Father Frederick X. Katzer, administrator of the diocese of Green Bay was present as well.

[139] Ludwig describes the details of this tense Provincial Council. Heiss clearly was opposed to the division, and had apparently resisted earlier efforts to make St. Paul an archdiocese. Ludwig, pp. 494-496.

[140] "The Council," *Catholic Citizen*, 22 May 1886; "The Provincial Council," *Catholic Citizen*, 5 June 1886.

[141] The full text of the Abbelen Memorial is found in Barry, pp. 289-296.

[142] This practice was not introduced in Milwaukee at this time and hence no priest of any nationality or

parish-type (territorial or national) could have this status.

[143] Barry, Abbelen Memorial, p. 293.

[144] John Tracy Ellis, *The Life of James Cardinal Gibbons* 2 vols. (Milwaukee: Bruce Publishing Company, 1951), pp. 347-348.

[145] Gerald P. Fogarty, *The Vatican and the American Hierarchy From 1870 to 1965* (Wilmington: Michael Glazier Inc., 1982 and 1985), p. 46.

[146] Ibid.

[147] Ibid.

[148] Ibid., p. 47.

[149] "An Answer to the Memorial on the German Question in the United States Written by Rev. P. M. Abbelen, by Bishop John Ireland, of St. Paul, and Bishop John J. Keane, of Richmond, to His Eminence, Cardinal Giovanni Simeoni, Prefect of the Holy Congregation of the Propaganda, Rome, December 6, 1886," reprinted in Barry, pp. 296-312.

[150] Ibid., p. 299.

[151] Ibid., p. 301.

[152] Ibid., p. 302.

[153] Quoted in Ludwig, pp. 581-519.

[154] Fogarty, p. 48. This information had appeared in the *Catholic Citizen* in 1887 and was passed on to Propaganda by Father James Keogh of the cathedral.

[155] Ibid., p. 48.

[156] Ibid., pp. 48-49; Barry, pp. 71-74.

[157] "Necrology," *Salesianum* 9 (January 1914), p. 83.

[158] John Gmeiner, *The Church and The Various Nationalities in the United States: Are German Catholics Unfairly Treated?,* (Milwaukee: H. H. Zahn, 1887). Barry, pp. 77-79. In 1887, perhaps reeling from Gmeiner's pamphlet attack and eager to bring the entire seminary faculty "into line," Heiss attempted to recruit German-speaking Jesuits of the Buffalo mission (a kind of German-speaking *imperium in imperio* tied to the other German provinces of Jesuits rather than the other Jesuit provinces in the country) to take over the teaching at St. Francis Seminary. These efforts nearly succeeded until inter-Jesuit jurisdictional issues prevented the Buffalo Jesuits from working alongside the Missouri Jesuits at Gesu and Marquette College.

[159] O'Connell, p. 242.

[160] *Columbia,* 1 September 1887.

[161] Barry, n. 64, p. 81. Barry notes that Gonner's pamphlet was "among the most extreme statements made at the time and cannot be regarded as typical of the German position."

[162] *Northwestern Chronicle*, 18 August 1887.

[163] "He Stands Alone," *Milwaukee Sentinel*, 18 August 1887.

[164] Ellis, *Cardinal Gibbons*, pp. 361-364.

[165] "James McIver," in Henry Heming, *History of the Catholic Church in Wisconsin*, pp. 1116-1117.

[166] Nesbit, *History of Wisconsin,* pp. 611-612.

[167] John O. Geiger, "H. J. Desmond, Catholic, Citizen, Reformer: The Quest for Justice Through Educational and Social Reform" (unpublished Ph.D. diss., Marquette University, Milwaukee, 1972), pp. 215-245.

[168] Quoted in Geiger, p. 223.

[169] Quoted in Nesbit, *History of Wisconsin,* p. 605.

[170] Quoted in Louise P. Kellogg, "The Bennett Law in Wisconsin," *Wisconsin Magazine of History*, 2 (September 1918): p. 4.

[171] These quotes are found in Robert J. Ulrich, "The Bennett Law of 1889: Education and Politics in Wisconsin" (unpublished Ph.D. diss., University of Wisconsin, 1965), pp. 214-217.

[172] A copy of this is in the Heiss Papers, AAM.

[173] Roger E. Wyman, "Wisconsin Ethnic Groups and the Election of 1890," *Wisconsin Magazine of History* 51 (Summer 1968): pp. 269-293.

[174] "The Local Election," *Catholic Citizen* 8 November 1890.

[175] "The Archbishop Dead," *Catholic Citizen*, 29 March 1890; "The Dead Archbishop," *Catholic Citizen*, 5 April 1890.

[176] Blied, *Three Archbishops,*, pp. 46-81.

[177] Interesting translations of the Pierz letters to *Der Wahrheits-Freund* were done by John J. Miller in his St. Francis Seminary M.A. thesis in 1930. See, John J. Miller, "Letters of the Reverend Francis Xavier Pierz, 1954 to 1865" (unpublished M.A. thesis, St. Francis Seminary, 1930).

[178] Blied, *Three Archbishops*, p. 48.

[179] M. M. Gerend, "Memories of By-Gone Days," *Salesianum* VII (October 1911): pp. 1-8.

[180] "Milwaukee Bishops," *Catholic Herald*, 20 April 1922.

[181] "Priest's Housekeeper, 69, Recalls Knowing Every Milwaukee Bishop," *Catholic Herald Citizen*, 28 October 1939.

[182] "Bust of Archbishop Katzer," *Catholic Citizen*, 7 September 1895.

[183] "Green Bay Bishopric," *Catholic Citizen*, 5 June 1886; "Bishop Katzer," *Catholic Citizen*, 25 September 1886.

[184] Blied, *Three Archbishops*, p. 50.

[185] Fogarty, pp. 49-53; Barry, pp. 128-130.

[186] Ireland's biographer asserts that the prelate "would have looked benignly" on the Americanizing provisions of the Bennett law, and "did not quarrel with the state's right to impose on all schools, public and parochial, a minimum attendance requirement." But he was also committed to the program of the Third Plenary Council of Baltimore which had mandated a substantial expansion in parish schools. Moreover, he too feared that public education was dominated by secularists. O'Connell, pp. 290, 292.

[187] Ireland to Gibbons, quoted in O'Connell, p. 293.

[188] Ibid. However, Ireland also appeared to have pushed the candidacy of Bishop Camillus Maes of Covington, Kentucky until he found out that Maes could not preach in German. Sweeney, p. 195.

[189] Quoted in Sweeney, p. 195.

[190] Ellis, *Cardinal Gibbons,* pp. 364-365; O'Connell, p. 300.

[191] Fogarty, p. 51.

[192] Sweeney confirms this, see pp. 196-197.

[193] Ibid.

[194] "Authoritatively Denied," *Catholic Citizen*, 11 April 1890.

[195] "Milwaukee's Vacant See," *Catholic Citizen*, 20 September 1890.

[196] Quoted in *Catholic Citizen*, 27 September 1890.

[197] "Rome's Christmas Gift," "Archbishop Katzer," *Catholic Citizen*, 27 December 1890.

[198] Denis O'Connell, the chief Roman agent of Cardinal Gibbons "wrote ominously of a few intransigent cardinals in Propaganda who were determined to teach American bishops a lesson in docility toward the Holy See." He noted as well that Msgr. Donato Sbaretti, a high ranking official in Propaganda had regretted what happened in the Katzer case and "did not hesitate to say that German influences in Rome were invoked to win the miter for the Bishop of Green Bay." Ellis, *Cardinal Gibbons*, p. 366.

[199] Haas to Hazotte, January 22, 1891, ACSA.

[200] Haas to Hazotte, June 6, 1891, ACSA.

[201] The Milwaukee branch of the American Clerical Union enrolled 55 members of the Milwaukee clergy, including Hiram Fairbanks, James Keogh, James Cleary, and Thomas Fagan. *Catholic Citizen*, 14 February 1891.

[202] Sister Amadea Wirtz, C.S.A., *Haven for the Homeless: The Leo House, 1889-1989* (Fond du Lac, Sisters of St. Agnes, 1985), pp. 10-11.

[203] Fogarty, *The Vatican,* pp. 55-61; Ellis, *Cardinal Gibbons*, pp. 367-372.

[204] Quoted in Barry, p. 136. The full text of the Lucerne Memorial is found in Barry, pp. 313-315. It is interesting that despite the furor associated with the Lucerne Memorial, and especially the idea of having bishops for individual ethnic groups, in fact this became a regular feature of episcopal preferment. Wenceslaus Kruszka's quest for proper respect for Polish Catholics included warm words for the Cahensly Memorial as he sought the appointment of a Polish bishop. In Cleveland, Bishop Ignatius Horstmann appointed Joseph Koudelka, a multilingual Bohemian as a special bishop for ethnic groups. In more recent times, African American, Latino and American Indian Catholics have insisted on representation in the college of bishops. One Puerto Rican historian Anthony M. Stevens-Arroyo invoked the Cahensly episode in his argument for Hispanic bishops. Anthony M. Stevens-Arroyo, "Cahensly Revisited?: The National Pastoral Encounter of America's Hispanic Bishops," *Migration World Magazine* 10 (1987): pp. 16-19.

[205] Katzer to Gibbons, June 5, 1881, Gibbons Papers, AAB. See also Ellis, *Cardinal Gibbons*, p. 369.

[206] Barry, p. 316.

[207] Fogarty, p. 59.

[208] "The Coming of the Archbishop," *Catholic Citizen*, 20 June 1891.

[209] "Archbishop Katzer," *Catholic Citizen*, 4 July 1891.

[210] Ellis, *Cardinal Gibbons,* pp. 374-378.

[211] "Cardinal Gibbons, Full Text of His Admirable Address to the Archbishop at the Cathedral," *Catholic Citizen*, 28 August 1891.

[212] Ellis, *Cardinal Gibbons*, p. 378.

[213] O'Connell, p. 309.

[214] Ellis, *Cardinal Gibbons,* p. 375.

[215] "Both Bishops Named," *Catholic Citizen*, 19 December 1891.

[216] Ellis, *Cardinal Gibbons*, pp. 657-658. The argument over who has the right to educate sparked a pamphlet war between Catholic University professor Thomas Bouquillion, who insisted that the state had some rights, and Jesuit Rene Holaind and Sulpician Alphonse Magnien who upheld the rights of parents.

[217] O'Connell, pp. 328-330.

[218] O'Connell, p. 341. The identity of these eight schools is unknown, but most certainly they were in rural areas where sisters taught public school children and then instructed Catholic children after-hours in the catechism.

[219] The most complete account of the Americanist crisis is still Thomas T. McAvoy, *The Americanist Heresy in Roman Catholicism, 1895-1900* (Notre Dame: University of Notre Dame Press, 1963).

[220] Hennesey, p. 200.

[221] William M. Halsey, *The Survival of American Innocence: Catholicism in an Era of Disillusionment, 1920-1940* (Notre Dame: University of Notre Dame Press, 1981), pp. 4, 128.

[222] "Archbishop Katzer and the Papal Letter," *Catholic Citizen*, 6 May 1899.

[223] "Archbishop Katzer's Reasons for Acquiring the Lynde Property," *Catholic Citizen,* 2 January 1892.

[224] "City Brevities," *Catholic Citizen*, 22 October 1892.

[225] Blied, "The Forgotten Rector," p. 58.

[226] "Necrology," *Salesianum* 15 (April 1920): pp. 93-94.

[227] Henry L. Hargarten, "The Most Rev. Augustine F. Schinner, D.D.," *Salesianum* 32 (April 1937): pp. 100-101.

[228] "Father Koetting's Charge," "City Brevities," *Catholic Citizen*, 29 October 1892.

[229] "Will Start For Rome, *Catholic Citizen,* 26 January 1895; "Received By Leo XIII," *Catholic Citizen*, 16 March 1895.

[230] "Now in Austria," *Catholic Citizen*, 20 April 1895.

[231] Katzer to Mother Ernesta Funke, July 6, 1895, Papers of Commissary General, 2.1.2.2., ASND.

[232] "Death of Mrs. Katzer," *Catholic Citizen*, 28 December 1895.

[233] James Keogh to Diomede Falconio, August 10, 1903, Del. Ap. USA IV, #64, Archivio Segreto Vaticano (hereafter ASV).

[234] "Important Letter Issued by Archbishop Katzer," *Catholic Citizen*, 19 April 1902.

[235] John Buenker, *The History of Wisconsin: The Progressive Era, 1893-1914* (Madison: State Historical Society of Wisconsin, 1998), pp. 117-118.

[236] Schinner to Falconio, March 21, 1910, #4735-d, Del. Ap. IX Superior, ASV.

[237] One of the groups he contacted was the Sisters of St. Agnes in Fond du Lac. Schinner offered to provide for himself financially, but the sisters were unwilling to dislodge one of their own chaplains and graciously informed the prelate that they had no room. Annals of the Sisters of St. Agnes December 26, 1925, ACSA.

[238] "Native Bishop, A. F. Schinner Buried February 11," *Catholic Herald-Citizen*, 13 February 1937.

[239] Nesbit, p. 176.

[240] Nesbit, pp. 148-259.

[241] Buenker, pp. 80-125.

[242] Buenker, p. 97.

[243] Gurda, pp. 123-124; 164-165.

[244] Nesbit, p. 179.

[245] Richard H. Keehn, "Industry and Business," in Nicholas C. Burckel (ed.), *Racine: Growth and Change in a Wisconsin County* (Racine: Racine County Board of Supervisors, 1977), pp. 279-343.

[246] Richard H. Keehn, "Industry and Business," in John A. Neuenschwander (ed.), *Kenosha County in the Twentieth Century: A Topic History* (Kenosha: Kenosha County Bicentennial Commission, 1976), pp. 175-221.

[247] Nesbit, p. 183.

[248] Buenker, p. 115.

[249] Sheboygan County does not have an adequate history. A helpful overview is Janic Hildebrand, *Sheboygan County: 150 Years of Progress* (Northridge: Windsor Publication, 1988).

[250] Nesbit, pp. 266-267.

[251] Ibid., pp. 285-295.

[252] Ibid., pp. 290-291.

[253] Ibid., pp. 301-302.

[254] Buenker, pp. 179-186.

[255] Ibid., p. 203.

[256] Nesbit, p. 301; Buenker, pp, 205-206.

[257] Nesbit, pp. 301-302.

[258] Buenker, pp. 203-205.

[259] Nesbit, p. 275.

[260] Buenker, pp. 213-216.

[261] Chronicles of the Motherhouse, V. I, 1884, p. 162, ASND.

[262] Chronicles of the Motherhouse, Vol. II, 1902, p. 117, ASND.

[263] Buenker, p. 218.

[264] "New Parishes," *Catholic Citizen*, 10 October 1885.

[265] Ibid.

[266] John T. McGreevy, *Parish Boundaries: The Catholic Encounter With Race in the Twentieth Century Urban North* (Chicago: University of Chicago Press, 1996) p. 15.

[267] McGreevy, p. 18.

[268] Quoted in Gurda, p. 173.

[269] "St. Patrick's Church," *Catholic Citizen*, 4 May 1895.

[270] "Dedication of St. James Church, Kenosha," *Catholic Citizen*, 28 June 1884. Cleary financed the church by issuing bonds at six percent interest. These weighed heavily on the parish for many years until Kenosha businessman Zalmon G. Simmons offered to help the parish retire the debt by offering to match parish donations. "Generous Aid for Kenosha Church," *Catholic Citizen*, 23 March 1901.

[271] John Vahey to Stanislaus Lalumiere, February 28, 1877, LaLumiere Papers, Marquette University Archives.

[272] David J. O'Hearn, *Fifty Years at St. John's Cathedral: Being a History of the Parish, Its Clergy, Schools and Societies* (Milwaukee, St. John's Cathedral 1903), p. 82; "Subscriptions Amount to $15,000," *Catholic Citizen*, 6 February 1892.

[273] "The Bids Are Accepted," *Catholic Citizen* 30 July 1892.

[274] *Catholic Citizen*, 18 March 1893.

[275] Black, a longtime member of the parish had come to the community's rescue earlier on with a 1,000 donation to help alleviate its huge debt. "Subscriptions Amount to $15,000," *Catholic Citizen*, 6 February 1892; "Tower Design Adopted," *Catholic Citizen*, 26 March 1892.

[276] "St. John's Tower," *Catholic Citizen*, 19 February 1921.

[277] "St. John's Divided—The New Parish of the Holy Rosary," *Catholic Citizen*, 5 July 1884; "Church of the Holy Rosary," *Catholic Citizen*, 22 August 1885.

[278] Judith A. Simonsen, "The Third Ward: Symbol of Ethnic Identity," *Milwaukee History* 10 (1987): pp. 61-76.

[279] "The Milwaukee Fire," *Catholic Citizen*, 5 November 1892; "Fire's Awful Visit," ibid. Katzer gave $100, St. John's Cathedral gave $500, Holy Trinity, $302, School Sisters of Notre Dame, $100. Protestant churches gave "substantial aid." Indeed, the *Citizen* reported, "Religious barriers were lost sight of and Catholics and Protestants worked hand in hand in support of the common end."

[280] "Irish Moving Out of Third Ward," *Catholic Citizen*, 4 June 1903.

[281] "The Premier Congregation," *Catholic Citizen*, 2 January 1892.

[282] "Change of Residence," *Catholic Citizen*, 26 December 1891.

[283] The episode of naming this parish was quite interesting. Blackwell threw it open to the parishioners and a few names surfaced including St. Gall and Sacred Heart. But the chief competition was between St. Edward, Blackwell's patron, and St. Thomas Aquinas. A series of votes were taken and by a vote of 50 to 28, the "angelic doctor" won. "The women were allowed to vote on this question," the *Catholic Citizen* noted, "but they were barred from participating in the selection of officers." "To Be St. Thomas Church," *Catholic Citizen*, 2 March 1901.

[284] "Dedication of St. Thomas Church," *Catholic Citizen*, 13 March 1915. Blackwell was so proud of his church that he invited Bishop Thomas Conaty, rector of the Catholic University of America to preside at the dedication.

[285] Lawrence S. Brey, "St. Thomas Aquinas: Memories of My Home Parish, 1976," copy in St. Thomas Aquinas, Milwaukee Parish File, AAM.

[286] "Mgr. Leonard Batz Passes Away on Sunday," *Catholic Citizen*, 1 June 1901. Batz's personal fortune was said to have come "from relatives in Europe" and with it he purchased the square block between Bradford and Cramer Streets, erected the

church, moved old St. Peter's Church to the property and served the parish without salary. He also accumulated a 20,000 volume library which he donated on his death to the Vincentians in Kentucky. However, by his death, his fortune appears to have been exhausted. He left the paltry sums of $50 a piece to two orphanages and two hospitals, the Little Sisters of the Poor and an additional $50 for Masses at St. Mary's Church and St. Francis Seminary. "In Catholic Circles," *Catholic Citizen*, 8 June 1901.

[287] "History of St. Michael's Parish of Milwaukee," n.d. copy in AAM.

[288] "With Great Pomp," *Milwaukee Sentinel*, 22 May 1893.

[289] "Dedication of The Gesu, Dec. 16," *Catholic Citizen*, 1 December 1894.

[290] "William E. Cramer Ill," *Catholic Citizen*, 25 March 1905.

[291] "New Gesu Portico," *Catholic Citizen*, 25 May 1901; "New Gesu Portico," *Catholic Citizen*, 15 March 1902.

[292] Motherhouse Chronicles, 1886-1897, v. 1, p. 59, ASND.

[293] "Cornerstone Laid," *Catholic Citizen*, 31 July 1897.

[294] "Father Burbach Appointed Pastor," *Catholic Citizen*, 9 November 1901. Apparently there had been a squabble among parishioners over the site for the new church and school and Burbach had been able to negotiate the differences. Huston gladly handed over the leadership of the new parish to him. "The West Allis Church," *Catholic Citizen*, 7 December 1901.

[295] "It Will Be a German Parish," *Catholic Citizen*, 16 November 1901.

[296] "City Brevities," *Catholic Citizen*, 4 January 1902.

[297] Julius H. Burbach, *West Allis: 'A City of Marvelous Growth' in a Decade June 28, 1902-June 28, 1912.* Copy available in West Allis Library; "Telechron Clock Ticks Story of Priest's 43 Yesteryears," *Milwaukee Journal*, 30 July 1944.

[298] "New Holy Assumption Church," *Catholic Citizen*, 22 January 1916.

[299] The following synthesis of demographic information about Poles in the Archdiocese of Wisconsin is taken from Anthony F. Kuzniewski, "Faith and Fatherland: An Intellectual History of the Polish Immigrant Community in Wisconsin, 1838-1918," (unpublished Ph.D. dissertation, Harvard University, April 1973), pp. 88-97.

[300] Quoted in Kuzniewski diss., p. 115.

[301] For a comprehensive treatment of rural Polish communities see Dariusz Aleksander Ciemniewski, "The Other Polonia: Polish Rural Settlements in Central and Northern Wisconsin, 1850-1920," (unpublished Ph.D. dissertation, Marquette University, 1999).

[302] Quote in Kuzniewski diss., p. 127.

[303] The best source for this information is Anthony F. Kuzniewski's expansive dissertation, "Faith and Fatherland." Kuzniewski distilled this lengthy dissertation into a short monograph, *Faith and Fatherland: The Polish Church War in Wisconsin, 1896-1918* (Notre Dame: University of Notre Dame Press, 1980). Kuzniewski's account is as thorough as one could wish for. *In the Richness of the Earth's* rendering of the "church war" relies on his chronology, but it also adds newly unearthed information from the records of the Apostolic Delegation in the Vatican Archives in Rome. These new materials fill in some voids in Kuzniewski's account and give important background as to Messmer's thinking and role in this matter.

[304] Quoted in Kuzniewski diss., p. 115.

[305] "Diamond Jubilee of St. Stanislaus Church, 1866-1941," parish history files, AAM.

[306] Massey, "St. Francis Seminary," p. 34.

[307] Steven M. Avella, "The Seminary and Society," in Avella (ed.), *Sesquicentennial Essays* (St. Francis: St. Francis Seminary, 1997), p. 61.

[308] Motherhouse Chronicles, Vol. 1, 1833-1876, September 8, 1870, ASND.

[309] "Diamond Jubilee of St. Hedwig, 1871-1946," parish history file, AAM; "No Compromise," "Turbulent Polacks," unidentified clippings, 30 November 1885; Kuzniewski diss, pp. 130-141.

[310] Kuzniewski, diss. p. 178a.

[311] For a full discussion of the differences among Poles on issues related to support of a free Poland see Joseph John Parot, *Polish Catholics in Chicago, 1850-1920* (DeKalb: Northern Illinois University Press, 1981).

[312] Anthony J. Kuzniewski, "Milwaukee's Poles, 1866-1918: The Rise and Fall of a Model Community," *Milwaukee History*, 20 (1997): pp. 27-40.

[313] Chronicle of the Motherhouse, Vol 1, p. 69, ASND.

[314] Kuzniewski diss, p. 162.

[315] "Father Kruszka Dies Tuesday; At St. Adalbert's 28 Years," *Catholic Herald Citizen* (4 December 1937); "Necrology," *Salesianum* 38 (January 1938): pp. 46-47.

[316] John Gurda, *Basilica of Saint Josaphat: Centennial of Faith, 1888-1988*, parish history, copy in AAM.

[317] "St. Josaphat's Church," *Catholic Citizen*, 13 April 1901; "The New St. Josaphat's Church to be Dedicated Next Sunday," *Catholic Citizen*, 20 July 1901.

[318] Grutza had been in failing health before the dedication. *Catholic Citizen*, 15 June, 1901. See also "Death of Father Grutza," *Catholic Citizen*, 24 August 1901.

[319] The actual amount of the debt is hard to pin down. Kuzniewski reports that Messmer claimed the debt was $400,000 while *Kuryer* insisted it was closer to $700,000, Kuzniewski, diss., p. 316.

[320] Kuzniewski, *Faith and Fatherland*, p. 43.

[321] Josephine Marie Peplinski, SSJ-TOSF, *A Fitting Response: The History of the Sisters of St. Joseph of the Third Order of St. Francis* 3 vols. (South Bend: Sisters of St. Joseph of the Third Order of St. Francis, 1982).

[322] James S. Pula, "Waclaw Kruszka: A Polonia Historian in Perspective," *Polish American Studies* 44 (1987): 57-69.

[323] A distillation of the article in the *Freeman's Journal* appeared in the *Catholic Citizen*, "Poles Want a Bishop: Father Kruszka's Argument," *Catholic Citizen*, 17 August 1901.

[324] "Wants a Polish Bishop," *Catholic Citizen*, 7 December 1901.

[325] Frederick Katzer to Prefect of Propaganda, Miecieslaus Ledochowski, January 30, 1902, #125-132, Vol. 230, Propaganda Archives (hereafter PA).

[326] Sebastiano Martinelli to Miecielaus Ledochowski, February 28, 1902, #1969, Vol. 289, PA.

[327] Ledochowski to Katzer, March 22, 1902, #153, Vol. 289, PA.

[328] "Archbishop Katzer Leaves Tuesday," *Catholic Citizen*, 5 April 1902, "Will We Have an Auxiliary Bishop," *Catholic Citizen*, 7 June 1902.

[329] "Archbishop Katzer's Return," *Catholic Citizen*, 18 October 1902.

[330] "Archbishop Katzer Dines with Emperor," *Catholic Citizen*, 13 September 1902.

[331] "Want a Polish Bishop," *Catholic Citizen*, 18 June 1902.

[332] Alberto Cosimo Melone, "Milwaukee's 'Little Italy,' 1900-1910: A Study in the Origins and Struggles of an Italian Immigrant Colony," (unpublished M.A. thesis, University of Wisconsin, Milwaukee, 1969); Mario A. Carini, with Austin Goodrich, *Milwaukee's Italians: The Early Years* (Milwaukee: The Italian Community Center, 1999).

[333] "Msgr. Falconio Pleased," *Catholic Citizen*, 4 July 1903.

[334] "Italian Colony Prospering," *Catholic Citizen*, 18 April 1903. Desmond noted that many of the Italians worked for the railroads while others were carving an important niche in grocery and green grocer trades—he mentions in particular the Catalano Brothers.

[335] O'Hearn was a native of Milwaukee and grew up in the cathedral parish pastored by his uncle, James Keogh. He entered St. Francis Seminary in 1882 and would have been ready for ordination in June 1889 but did not attain the canonical age of 25 until November when he was finally raised to the priesthood. At the urging of his uncle he was sent away to higher studies at the newly-opened Catholic University of America and returned in 1892 and worked at the cathedral. In 1898, Katzer sent him to Rome to study canon law and in 1901 he secured a doctorate in the subject—making him one of only two Americans to have such a degree. He returned to St. John's in the Fall of 1901. "Rev. David J. O'Hearn, J.C.L.," *Catholic Citizen*, 3 August 1901.

[336] "Father O'Hearn Meets Mascagni," *Catholic Citizen*, 24 January 1903.

[337] "New Italian Mission Site," *Catholic Citizen*, 17 January 1903.

[338] "Msgr. Falconio Greeted in Wisconsin," *Catholic Citizen*, 4 July 1903.

[339] "Father Imburgia Leaves," *Catholic Citizen*, 11 July 1903.
[340] "New Priest at Italian Mission," *Catholic Citizen*, 18 July 1903.
[341] Henry Mueller, "Italian Catholics in Milwaukee," (unpublished paper, St. Francis Seminary, 1986), p. 28.
[342] "Trouble at the Italian Mission," *Catholic Citizen,* 17 October 1903.
[343] "Italian Mission Church," *Catholic Citizen*, 20 August 1904.
[344] Chronicles of the Convent of St. James, Madison, ASND.
[345] Meloni, p. 58.
[346] "Nursery Yarns for Adults," *Catholic Citizen*, 13 March 1897.
[347] Meloni, pp. 61-65.
[348] John Andreozzi, "*Contadini* and *Pescatori* in Milwaukee: Assimilation and Voluntary Associations," (unpublished M.A. thesis, University of Wisconsin, Milwaukee, 1974), p. 39ff.
[349] George LaPiana, *The Italians in Milwaukee* (Milwaukee: Associated Charities, 1915), p. 14. LaPiana later quit Milwaukee and ended his days as a respected professor of languages at Harvard University.
[350] *Catholic Citizen*, 27 June 1907.
[351] "Souvenir Program, Solemn Dedication of St. Rita's Church and School, June 11th, 1939," copy in AAM.
[352] "25th Anniversary, Sisters of Charity of St. Joan Antida, 1932-1957," memorial booklet, copy in AAM.
[353] Stritch to Ugo Cavicchi, March 24, 1937, St. Rita File, AAM.
[354] "New Church on Cass Street for St. Rita's Mission," *Catholic Herald Citizen*, 22 October 1938.
[355] "35 Years Sees Dedication of Second Italian Church in City—New St. Rita's," *Catholic Herald Citizen*, 24 June 1939.
[356] "Monsignor Traudt Dedicates Madison Institute Sunday," *Catholic Herald*, 15 March 1925.
[357] Karel D. Bicha, "The Czechs in Wisconsin History," *Wisconsin Magazine of History* 53 (Spring 1970): pp. 194-203; Herbert W. Kuhm, "Milwaukee's Early Bohemians: *Ze Zaslych Dob*—From Times Past," *Milwaukee History* 18 (1995): pp. 81-98.
[358] Bicha, "Czechs in Wisconsin," p. 201.
[359] Karel D. Bicha, "Settling Accounts With an Old Adversary: The Decatholicization of Czech Immigrants in America," *Social History* IV (November 1972): pp. 45-60.
[360] Bicha, "Czechs in Wisconsin," p. 202.
[361] "A Resume of the History of St. John de Nepomuc Parish," *Souvenir and Dedication Book, St. John de Nepomuc School Addition and Auditorium* (October 9, 1955), copy in AAM.
[362] "Public Report About the Slavic Mission Institute in Milwaukee, Wisconsin, by the Rev. Fr. John M. Gartner, vicar general and missionary of the Sacred Heart, July 20, 187-1873," reprinted in Barbara Brumleve, (ed.) *Correspondence of Various Persons Significant in the Early History of the School Sisters of Notre Dame in North America* (School Sisters of Notre Dame, Heritage Resource Publications No. 30, 1986), p. 52.
[363] Chronicle of the Motherhouse, Vol 1, p. 4, ASND.
[364] Chronicle of the Motherhouse, Vol. 1, p. 161, ASND.
[365] "St. Wenceslaus Church, Commemorating the Diamond Jubilee, 1883-1958," in parish history file, AAM.
[366] "Golden Jubilee of St. John Nepomucene Congregation, Racine Wisconsin, 1896-1946," in parish history file, AAM.
[367] Chronicle of the Motherhouse, Vol. 1, p. 12, ASND.
[368] "Record of the First Beginning in Barton, Until the First General Chapter, (1874)," Archives of the Sisters of St. Agnes, Fond du Lac, WI.
[369] "New Corps of Teachers," *Catholic Citizen*, 24 August 1895.
[370] Annals of the Convent of St. John, AOP-Sin.
[371] "The Change at the Cathedral School, The Sisters of Charity Recalled, Statement by Father Keogh," copy in Annals of St. John Cathedral Convent, AOP-Sin.
[372] Annals of the Convent of St. John, AOP-Sin.
[373] Sister JoAnn Euper, O.S.F., *Century of Service: School Sisters of St. Francis* (Milwaukee: School Sisters of St. Francis, 1976), pp. 2-13.

[374] Josephine Marie Peplinski, *A Fitting Response*, Vol. 1, pp. 105-150.

[375] "First in this Country," *Catholic Citizen* 30 December 1893.

[376] Peplinski, Vol. 1, pp. 95-98.

[377] Monsignor Aloysius Muench relates a visit to Father Joseph Keenan at Sacred Heart Sanitarium, "broken by drink." Muench Diary, p. 106.

[378] Prudence A. Moylan, *Hearts Inflamed: The Wheaton Franciscan Sisters, A History of the Franciscan Sisters Daughters of the Sacred Hearts of Jesus and Mary Saint Clara Province* (Wheaton: Our Lady of the Angels Convent, 1993), pp. 20-27.

[379] Benjamin J. Blied, Ph.D., "Wisconsin's Catholic Hospitals," *Salesianum* 43 (January 1948): pp. 10-19.

[380] Sister M. Francis Cook, O.S.F., *His Love Heals: A History of the Hospital Sisters of the Third Order of St. Francis, Springfield, Illinois, 1875-1975* (Springfield, Sisters of St. Francis, 1975); Heming, p. 963. "Jacob L. Reiss, Benefactor for Sheboygan, Dies," *Catholic Herald Citizen*, 22 January 1955.

[381] Margaret Shekleton, S.D.S., *Bending in Season: History of the North American Province of the Sisters of the Divine Savior, 1895-1985* (Milwaukee: Sisters of the Divine Savior, 1985).

[382] Jerome Schommer, *The Moment of Grace: A History of the North American Province of the Society of the Divine Savior* (Milwaukee: Society of the Divine Savior, 1994), pp. 65-79.

[383] "Another Wealthy Catholic," *Catholic Citizen*, 22 February 1902.

[384] Sister Imogene Palen, *Fieldstones '76: The Story of the Founders of the Sisters of St. Agnes* (Oshkosh: Oshkosh Printers, 1976), pp. 140-142.

[385] John R. Beix, "St. Francis, Wisconsin, The Chief Educational Center of the Church in Wisconsin, 1856-1946," (unpublished M.A. thesis , Marquette University, 1948), pp. 85-91, Sister Margaret Peter, "The History of St. John's School for the Deaf, 1876 to 1976," Centennial Publication, copy in St. John's School for the Deaf, St. John's File, AAM.

[386] M. M. Gerend, "Memories of By-Gone Days," *Salesianum* 7 (April 1912): pp. 6-7.

[387] M. M. Gerend, *St. John's Catholic Deaf-Mute Institute* (n.d.).

[388] Sister M. Eunice Hanousek, *A New Assisi: The First Hundred Years of the Sisters of St. Francis of Assisi,* (Milwaukee: Bruce Publishing Company, 1949), pp. 127-134.

[389] Philip Gleason, *Conservative Reformers,* p. 25.

[390] James Grummer, S.J., "The Parish-Life of German Speaking Roman Catholics in Milwaukee, Wisconsin, 1840-1920," (unpublished Ph.D. diss., University of Notre Dame, 1989), pp.82-83. Grummer also quotes the work of the two well-known historians of Polish America, Thomas and Znaniecki to make the same point about Polish parishes.

[391] *Celebrating a Proud Past-Sharing the Challenges of the Future*, Catholic Family Life Insurance, 1868-1993, memorial booklet.

[392] Dorothy Deer (ed.) *Catholic Knights Insurance Society: The First 100 Years* (Milwaukee: Catholic Knights Insurance Society).

[393] Benjamin J. Blied, "The Catholic Knights and the Seminary," *Salesianum 48* (April 1953): pp. 60-67.

[394] Joseph M. Sevenich, "1883—The Catholic Order of Foresters—1933," *Catholic Herald*, 27 July 1933; "A New Forester's Hall," *Catholic Citizen*, 2 January 1895.

[395] The best history of the Knights is Christopher J. Kauffman, *Faith and Fraternalism: The History of the Knights of Columbus, 1882-1982* (New York: Harper and Row, 1982).

[396] Horton L. Roe, *The History of the Knights of Columbus in Wisconsin from their beginnings in the year 1900* (Oshkosh: Wisconsin State Council, 1952), pp. 43-128.

[397] "Milwaukee K. of C. New Club House Opened," *Catholic Citizen*, 11 April 1916.

[398] Valery P. Schuster, "Catholic Normal School of the Holy Family and Pio Nono College," (unpublished M.A. thesis, St. Francis Seminary, January 1941).

[399] Joseph Rainer, *A Noble Priest, Joseph Salzmann, D.D., Founder of the Salesianum* (Milwaukee: Olinger and Schwartz, 1903), pp. 172-186.

[400] Quoted in M. M. Gerend, "Memories of By-Gone Days," *Salesianum* VII, (July, 1912): pp. 7-8.

[401] Robert J. Schmitt, "A History of Catholic Church Music and Musicians in Milwaukee" (unpublished

M.A. thesis, Marquette University, 1968), pp. 28-54.

[402] The best history of this movement is Ronald Damian, "A Historical Study of the Caecilian Movement in the United States" (unpublished Ph.D. dissertation, Catholic University of America, 1984).

[403] Otto Singenberger, "Compositions and Works of Prof. John Singenberger," *Caecilia* 51 (July and August 1924): pp. 35-40.

[404] Damian, pp. 117-140. J. Vincent Higginson, "The American Caecilian Society," *The Catholic Choirmaster* 38 (September 26, 1942): pp. 104-110.

[405] "Archbishop, Priests and Students at Requiem for Prof. Singenberger," *Catholic Herald*, 5 June 1924.

[406] "Msgr. Traudt Preaches, Otto Singenberger Directs Music," *Caecilia* 59 (June 1932): p. 232; Damian, p. 135.

[407] "Choir of 1,200 School Children in Gregorian Chant at St. Casimir's," *Catholic Herald Citizen*, 3 June 1944.

[408] "To Level Singenberger Mansion for Church," *Catholic Herald Citizen*, 30 August 1958.

[409] William A. Boerger, "Just an Ordinary Trail," autobiographical essay in AAM. Boerger was born in 1875 and died in 1955. He graduated from the Normal School in 1892 and had a varied career as a teacher, journalist, politician in Stearns County Minnesota, author, lawyer, school administrator, novelist, and poet.

[410] Lochemes was ordained in 1883 and had a number of assignments before coming to Pio Nono with Gerend. He kept a diary of his years in the pastoral ministry, including his time at Pio Nono where he records some of the details of his work as a priest. See Albert F. Austen, "An Estimate of Msgr. M. J. Lochemes" (unpublished M.A. thesis, St. Francis Seminary, January 1937).

[411] Benjamin J. Blied, Ph.D., "After Seventy-five Years," *Salesianum* 40 (July 1945): 105-113; Warren C. Abrahamson, "Pio Nono High School, St. Francis, Wis.," *Salesianum* 35 (October 1940): pp. 193-199.

[412] Brother Franklin Cullen, C.S.C., "Sacred Heart College, Watertown, Wisconsin, 1872-1912," (unpublished paper, for Eighth Annual Conference of the History of the Congregations of the Holy Cross, Stonehill College, North Easton, Massachusetts, June 16-18, 1989, in Archives of the Congregation of the Holy Cross, Notre Dame, Indiana).

[413] "His Grace, Mgr. Satolli," *Catholic Citizen*, 9 September 1893.

[414] M. Adele Gorman, O.S.F., "Lay Activity and the Catholic Congresses of 1889 and 1893," *Records of the American Catholic Historical Society of Philadelphia* 74 (1963): pp. 3-22.

[415] "The Gem City of the West," *Catholic Citizen*, 20 October 1894; "Bishop Messmer at the Head," *Catholic Citizen*, 1 December 1894.

[416] "The Work Inaugurated," *Catholic Citizen*, 9 March 1895.

[417] Ralph A. Weber, *Notre Dame's John Zahm: American Catholic Apologist and Educator* (Notre Dame: University of Notre Dame Press, 1961).

[418] "Columbian Summer School," *Catholic Citizen*, 20 July 1895; "A Success Beyond Expectation," *Catholic Citizen*, 27 July 1895; "Coming to a Close," *Catholic Citizen*, 3 August 1895; "Summer School Closing," *Catholic Citizen*, 10 August 1895.

[419] "Defends the School," *Catholic Citizen*, 29 August 1895.

[420] "Columbian Summer School," *Catholic Citizen*, 25 July 1896; "The Attendance Increases," *Catholic Citizen*, 1 August 1896. The highlighted speakers were Eliza Allen Starr of Chicago who spoke on "Catholic Art" and Bishop Thomas O'Gorman of Sioux Falls who spoke on American Catholic history. "Western Summer School," *Catholic Citizen*, 20 March 1897.

[421] "For a New Location," *Catholic Citizen*, 7 October 1899; "Summer School at Detroit," *Catholic Citizen*, 23 December 1899.

[422] Messmer wrote for advice to the bishops of the Chicago, Cincinnati, Dubuque, Milwaukee, St. Louis provinces. Messmer to "Rt. Rev. and Dear Sir," February 18, 1908, Messmer Circular Letters, AAM.

[423] "July Fourth at Spring Bank," *Catholic Citizen*, 11 July 1908.

[424] "Spring Bank Re-Purchased," *Catholic Citizen*, 19 June 1909.

[425] "The Fourth at Spring Bank," *Catholic Citizen*, 10 July 1909.

[426] "Western Catholic Chautauqua," *Catholic Citizen*, 18 June 1910.
[427] "Studies at Spring Bank," *Catholic Citizen*, 8 July 1911; "As a St. Louisan Saw Spring Bank," *Catholic Citizen*, 23 September 1911.
[428] "Town Talk," *Catholic Citizen*, 23 March 1925.
[429] Donald L. Kinzer, *An Episode in Anti-Catholicism: The American Protective Association* (Seattle: University of Washington Press, 1964), pp. 116-118.
[430] K. Gerald Marsden, "Patriotic Societies and American Labor: The American Protective Association in Wisconsin," *Wisconsin Magazine of History* 41 (Summer 1958): pp. 287-294.
[431] "A.P.A.'s in Wisconsin," *Catholic Citizen*, 8 April 1893.
[432] "150 A.P.A. Councils in Wisconsin," *Catholic Citizen*, 22 September 1894.
[433] Kinzer, pp. 116-117.
[434] "Great Anti-A.P.A. Mass Meeting," *Catholic Citizen*, 3 March 1894.
[435] The following account is derived mainly from E. David Cronon, "Father Marquette Goes to Washington: The Marquette Statue Controversy," *Wisconsin Magazine of History* 56 (Summer 1973): pp. 266-283. Other states that chose religious figures for their selection included California, Junipero Serra; Oregon, Rev. Jason Lee; Utah, Brigham Young; and Illinois, Frances E. Willard.
[436] Trentanove also sculpted a statue of the Blessed Virgin for St. Patrick's Church and was consulted about the statues that were planned for St. Josaphat's basilica. "A Marble Statue," *Catholic Citizen*, 13 March 1897; "Statues for St. Josaphat," *Catholic Citizen*, 20 March 1897.
[437] Quoted in Kinzer, p. 211.
[438] "Archbishop Katzer is Dead," *Catholic Citizen*, 25 July 1903.
[439] "Archb. Katzer is Laid to Rest," *Catholic Citizen*, 1 August 1903.
[440] "Who Will Be Archbishop of Milwaukee," *Catholic Citizen*, 1 August 1903.

Part III
Ecce Quam Bonum et Quam Jucundum
1903–1940

Archbishop Frederick Katzer's death came on July 20, 1903, exactly the same day that the nonagenarian Pope Leo XIII departed this life. Rival headlines contended for the precedence, but the funeral and mourning for Katzer was overwhelmed by the pontiff's demise and the election of Cardinal Giuseppe Sarto (Pius X) as his successor in the dramatic conclave of 1903.[1] Milwaukee would wait longer than the universal church for a new shepherd.

As Katzer lay dying in Fond du Lac, Milwaukee's consultors believed the odds-on favorite would be Messmer of Green Bay. Abbelen wrote to the apostolic delegate, "Between Rainer, Schinner and myself, Bishop Messmer is the only logical candidate."[2] But shortly before his death Katzer summoned his consultors, James Keogh and Peter Abbelen. "The arbp. was quite weak," Keogh wrote, "but he roused himself by a special effort and said, 'I have sent for you to tell you before I die that I wish to have Father Schinner as my successor.'"[3] In deference to Katzer's wishes, the archdiocesan consultors met the very day of the prelate's funeral and drafted a *terna* that had Augustine Schinner (*dignissimus*), Sebastian Messmer (*dignior*) and the venerable Joseph Rainer, rector of the seminary (*dignus*). The consultors dispatched this to the delegate in the hopes that their wishes would be fulfilled.

But as they had earlier, the archbishops of the country altered the list by dropping Rainer and switching Messmer to the first spot and Schinner to the second. As the apostolic delegate sorted out the differences between

Archbishop Frederick X. Katzer of Milwaukee [AAM]

Rev. Peter Abbelen [ASND]

the wishes of the Milwaukee consultors (and priests) and the recommendations of the prelates, a host of interesting letters were exchanged for and against the bishop of Green Bay. Most vocal in opposition to Messmer were the English-speaking clergy who feared yet another German. James Keogh of the cathedral, a strong supporter of Schinner, and Francis Ryan of St. Matthew's parish denounced Messmer as a "teutophile" and an "out and out Cahenslyite."[4] The ever-trenchant Father Thomas Fagan, also dismissed Messmer, arguing that "His priests in Green Bay would like to have him leave—he is inclined to change old established ways."[5] Polish priests as well were fearful of the Green Bay prelate who had clashed repeatedly with the large Polish communities of the northern diocese.

Rev. Joseph LaBoule [AAM]

Messmer also had his defenders. Keogh's accusations had been balanced off by praise from Peter Abbelen, who suggested that, despite Katzer's dying wishes, Schinner was "too youthful" and "too familiar with clergy." He warned, "I fear that his great personal familiarity with his confreres would weaken his official authority and even beget contempt in cases of collision." He endorsed fellow German speaker Messmer, and noted that the former university professor would bring important leadership "against the ever-growing socialism and kindred movements."[6] Besides Abbelen, other Milwaukee clergy weighed in on Messmer's side. For example, a strong letter of support came from the pastor of St. Henry's in Watertown, former seminary professor Father Joseph S. LaBoule. He defended the prelate from Keogh's and Ryan's allegations of excessive nationalism, and accentuated Messmer's work as the leader of the multiethnic Federation of American Catholic Societies. LaBoule, who had worked with Messmer on the Columbian summer schools, was assured that Messmer would be the best selection to maintain the fragile archdiocesan unity.[7]

Other bishops added their opinions. James Edward Quigley of Chicago said in support of his fellow bishop, "Bishop Messmer's learning and services to the Church, and his well-known and truly Roman conservativeness [*sic*], are the reasons upon which I base my preference."[8] Likewise, Frederich Eis, Bishop of Marquette, Michigan, urged his appointment for ethnic reasons, "The Germans are by far the great majority of the Catholic population in the Archdiocese of Milwaukee

.... To appoint one not of the German nationality would be a great calamity and detrimental to our Holy Religion."[9] Remarkably, even though he had opposed Messmer's selection for the Green Bay See in 1891, Archbishop John Ireland had little or nothing to say about his succession to Milwaukee. "I am not able to offer any judgement as to their respective merits," wrote the St. Paul prelate. Speaking of the candidates presented to him, "There are reasons for and against each one—so that when things are balanced up I find I have come to no conclusion."[10]

After he received private assurances that English-speaking priests would receive Messmer, Apostolic Delegate Falconio decided for Messmer. The Green Bay bishop's appointment to Milwaukee was made on November 28, 1903 and announced to the public on December 10, 1903.[11] Messmer finally arrived at his Milwaukee post in February 1904.

Messmer would direct the affairs of the Milwaukee See for 26 years until his death in his native Switzerland in August 1930. A new bishop was appointed within a few months. Samuel Alphonsus Stritch, a native of Nashville, Tennessee and bishop of Toledo, Ohio arrived in Milwaukee in November 1930 and remained on the job for 10 years. Documents are not available that provide the details of Stritch's selection for Milwaukee. However, by 1930, the role of the apostolic delegate in the selection of bishops had increased considerably. Moreover, Stritch's metropolitan, Archbishop John Timothy McNicholas, O.P., of Cincinnati no doubt played a large role in Stritch's elevation to the rank of archbishop. His relative youth (43) and Roman education made him a likely successor for the aged Messmer. If Messmer represented the last link with the foreign-born past of Milwaukee's earliest days, Stritch and his successors represented the new wave of Roman-trained bishops that were now dominating the dioceses of the American Church.

In the 36 years of the episcopacies of Sebastian Messmer and Samuel Stritch, an expected maturation took place in the archdiocese. Church life was centralized and coordinated as never before. By 1940, more power and decision-making authority was vested in the archbishop and his growing bureaucracy than ever before. Milwaukee had a host of new departments, agencies and centrally directed organizations that covered every aspect of Catholic life. Messmer's and Stritch's activities left a lasting influence on charities, higher education, the cathedral, clerical life and parish organization. The structure of the Milwaukee Archdiocese had resembled the administrative models of some of the large businesses like Allis Chalmers or Northwestern Mutual Life rather than those of volunteer groups. The transformation was accompanied by the inevitable clashes that attend any form of institutional innovation. For most Milwaukee Catholics the new directions seemed clear and reasonable, and were warmly endorsed. But the virtues of centralization and consolidation were not easily appreciated by the partisans of the archdiocese's strong ethnic and parochial traditions.

Milwaukee's Catholic Church in this period also became steadily "Americanized" as the federal government's restrictions on immigration weakened the linguistic and cultural moorings of Milwaukee's polyglot population. By 1940, the archdiocese of Milwaukee had once again re-tooled itself to confront the changed demographic, social and economic realities of life in southeastern Wisconsin.

Patterns of Episcopal Leadership: Centralization and Romanization

Sebastian Messmer was born August 29, 1847, in Goldach, Canton St. Gallen, Switzerland, a picturesque village on Lake Constance.[12] His father was a minor official in the district of Rohrschach and served on the council of St. Gallen. Sebastian was the eldest of five children. He had a younger brother, Joseph (known as Gabriel after he became a Capuchin Franciscan) who became the provincial of the Capuchins in the United States, and three sisters. (Gabriel preceded his brother to Wisconsin where he joined the Capuchins near Fond du Lac.) Sebastian lost his mother at the age of 10 and was raised by his father and sisters. He entered the seminary of St. George at St. Gallen (it was there that he served Mass for visiting Bishop John Martin Henni in 1862) and then was sent on to Innsbruck for advanced study in 1866. Like Katzer, Messmer became enthralled with the Jesuits and considered joining them. But also like Katzer, he was redirected by the advent of an American emissary, Bishop James Roosevelt Bayley of Newark, New Jersey, who stopped at Innsbruck in 1869 on his way to Rome for the ecumenical council. Bishop Bayley alerted him to the possibility of service in the growing diocese of Newark. Messmer was released from St. Gallen, and after completing his studies was ordained in Innsbruck on July 23, 1871. He celebrated a first Mass for family and friends at St. Gallen a week later (where close friend and future Salesianum faculty member Otto Zardetti preached), and then he departed for America. In September 1871 he was appointed a professor of theology at Seton Hall College in South Orange, New Jersey.[13]

Messmer cut an energetic figure with the young men of Seton Hall. As one later recalled: "He was a young priest full of vigor in mind and body. Not only had he a large fund of correct information which he sought to use skillfully, but he was also physically very efficient. He was a very good horseman, a good marksman, long distance jumper, and an enduring walker."[14] Messmer always looked robust, and he loved to spend summers working in the fields. But in fact, his health was never really good. In 1880 he nearly died of typhoid fever, and beginning in 1908 and continuing throughout his episcopate, he spent long periods away at spas, health resorts and warmer climates.

Messmer taught an array of subjects at Seton Hall, and helped care for the boarding students on the South Orange campus. But his training at Innsbruck gave him a deep love for scholarship and a gift for theological study.

Messmer always cultivated his scholarly pursuits even as a bishop and he missed the life of scholarship and the classroom. When he revisited the campus of the Catholic University in April 1904 for a meeting of the American archbishops, he admitted wistfully to a reporter, "I would like to be back in Washington as a professor in the Catholic University. I was homesick when I saw again the college buildings where I spent so many happy hours in study and teaching.... In Europe, the bishops have more time for study."[15] Messmer remained a productive scholar even after his busy episcopal years began. He edited seven volumes of the writings of John England, the first bishop of Charleston, South Carolina.[16] He also displayed an intense interest in aspects of the history of the archdiocese of Milwaukee. In 1918 and 1919, he produced an edition of Bernard Durward's lengthy life of Martin Kundig, which was written between 1871 and 1878. Messmer's annotated account appeared on the pages of the seminary journal *Salesianum*.[17] In 1924, he produced a biographical series on Father Florimond Bonduel.[18]

As he burnished his academic credentials at Seton Hall, he soon became immersed in the field of canon law. In 1883, he served as a consultant for the bishops of New York who were preparing for a provincial council. Later, his teaching and reading of canon law at Seton Hall enabled him to craft a helpful pamphlet called *Praxis Synodalis*, a sort of "how to" manual on how to hold local ecclesiastical meetings. Other publications on canonical issues came later, including a translation on criminal cases related to clerics to which he contributed.

In 1884, he came to national attention when he was selected to help with the preparations for the Third Plenary Council of Baltimore. He assisted with the drafting and final preparations for the documents to be submitted to Rome, and received as a reward an honorary degree as doctor of canon law in 1886. The year previous he had been awarded the pastorate of St. Peter's Church in Newark, whose German-speaking congregation he had assisted for years. (Messmer also rendered "supply" service to a German Catholic orphanage and to the parish of St. Leo's in

Rev. Sebastian Messmer [AAM]

Irvington, New Jersey). Unwilling to give up his academic work at Seton Hall, however, he maintained both positions until his health problems prompted him to resign the parish in 1886. His prominence as a canonist at the Baltimore Council had positioned him to take over the new chair of canon law at the Catholic University in 1889. Selected by new Rector John J. Keane, he secured permission to pursue more systematic studies in the field, and was sent to Rome where he took in the lectures of noted expert Dr. Luigi Giustini at the Apollinaris.

He returned to America in 1891 and enjoyed only one year of professorship at the Catholic University. The recently-founded university was caught up in the tensions between "liberal" Americanizing bishops and conservative "Germanizing" clerics. The former had been in the forefront of pushing for the creation of the university. The latter mistrusted the creation of a school outside their dioceses and looked warily at faculty appointments to see if German speakers would have their due.[19] Archbishop Heiss was on the original board of the university, but rarely went to meetings and eventually begged off from the responsibility altogether, pleading ill health.[20]

Messmer was quite aware of the controversies surrounding the university, and took a firm but careful stand in favor of his fellow German speakers. In 1891, in the wake of the organization of the German *Priester Verein* and the Milwaukee-based American Catholic Clerical Union, *Catholic Review* editor John Talbot Smith of New York spoke out, accusing these priest organizations of fostering an unhealthy nationalism. Messmer replied to Talbot in a long article printed in the *Review* defending the German organization, drawing a careful distinction between "nationalism," which he agreed was bad, and "nationality," which he considered good. He accused the *Review* of "calculated prejudice."[21] Messmer's words were picked up by Archbishop Ireland's *Northwestern Chronicle* which, accepting his distinction between "nationalism" and "nationality," accused the German priests of the former. Messmer replied to the *Northwestern Chronicle* and admitted that, "We all must become Americanized." But he argued that the day had not yet come, and insisted that the clerical unions could do much to strengthen and further the Catholic faith among the people. Messmer graciously noted, however, that "if ever these unions should impair the spirit of unity, or injure the interests of the Catholic people ... let them be suppressed at once."[22] The *Northwestern Chronicle* editor was relentless, "If Dr. Messmer wants to see some evil results of these clerical unions let him look to Wisconsin .... The Church in Wisconsin presents a sorry spectacle of certain sections of the church and people arrayed in hostile camps, and encouraged in their hostility by the secular press."[23] Faced with the intensity of this invective, Messmer let go of the matter even when asked by his old friend, *American Ecclesiastical Review* editor Father Herman J. Heuser, to write a lengthy article examining the clerical unions. "I earnestly believe the Clerical Unions, keeping within proper limits, would do much good," he wrote to Heuser, but, "Archp. Ireland's main objection, that they keep up the spirit of nationalism, is nonsense." Having said that he retired from the field.[24]

The controversy did not harm his chances for episcopal advancement and Katzer nominated him for his former post in Green Bay. Despite a desultory effort to "break the Wisconsin Union" launched by Archbishop Elder of Cincinnati, Messmer received the nomination at the end of November 1891. Shortly after receiving this news, Messmer filed a plea with the Vatican to be delivered from the episcopate.[25] When Rome refused to turn aside the nomination, Messmer made plans for his episcopal consecration.[26] At St. Peter's Church in Newark on March 27, 1892, Messmer's longtime friend (and former St. Francis Seminary faculty member) Bishop Otto Zardetti consecrated him a bishop, assisted by Bishop Winand Wigger, his ordinary in Newark and Bishop John Keane of the Catholic University.[27] Messmer arrived in Wisconsin in the spring of 1892 and, after a visit with Katzer, set himself to work in Green Bay, maintaining a studied determination to avoid the excesses of the raging nationality debate. Messmer seemed to get along well with Katzer and loyally supported his metropolitan in the various disputes that would bubble to the surface in the context of the contentious 1890s. Messmer felt strongly about the expansion of Catholic schools in the Green Bay diocese—a fact that must have endeared him to Katzer. But he was no "sure vote" for Katzer's alleged Germanizing. The Green Bay bishop had a mind of his own on certain things.

Messmer arrived in Green Bay in late spring and was greeted by his 109 priests. The diocese was prosperous, with 176 churches and 72 schools and a population pegged at 120,000 Catholics. He would remain in Green Bay for 11 years. In those years he was dutifully loyal to Katzer's lead—joining him in thanking Leo XIII for the condemnation of Americanism and insisting that the parochial school decrees of Baltimore III be fully implemented. He despised temperance and denounced the Catholic Total Abstinence League. He suggested instead a more moderate Catholic Temperance League that would be more harmonious with the drinking habits of American citizens and European immigrants.[28]

Bishop Sebastian Messmer of Green Bay [AAM]

He ruled the Milwaukee Archdiocese vigorously, centralizing and coordinating archdiocesan affairs as never before. In 1924 at the age of 77, he suffered the first of a series of debilitating heart attacks that would weaken and slow him until his death in August 1930. After 1925, he began to detach from day-to-day affairs of archdiocesan governance, allowing more leeway for his right-hand man, Chancellor Bernard Traudt. With the help of the bureaucracy that Messmer assembled, Traudt was able to maintain archdiocesan stability, although financial affairs would suffer. More illness beset Messmer in 1925 and sent him for weeks to Sacred Heart Sanitarium. On Christmas Day 1928 he contracted a nearly fatal case of influenza. In 1929, with Traudt still running affairs, he repaired to a sanitarium in Chinchuba, Louisiana, where he appeared to recover. In 1930, he made plans for a final trip to his native Goldach and took his closest clerical friend and companion, Monsignor Augustine Breig. On the way to the East coast, Breig and Messmer paid a courtesy call on Apostolic Delegate John Bonzano. Bonzano gently suggested to the aging and physically decrepit prelate that he ought to prepare for the appointment of a coadjutor when he returned. Messmer took this news hard and steamed for his native soil.[29] In August, he died and was buried in Goldach. The transition in Milwaukee was short, and in November a new archbishop would take up residence in the handsome Pabst mansion that Messmer had purchased in 1908.

Archbishop Sebastian Messmer of Milwaukee [AAM]

Samuel Alphonsus Stritch was born August 17, 1887 in Nashville, Tennessee, the seventh of eight children of Garrett Stritch and Katherine (Katie) Agnes Malley. Garrett Stritch was a native of Ballyheigue, County Kerry and had come to Louisville in 1870.[30] Malley was the daughter of Irish immigrants and had come from Indiana. The young family began its life in Nashville where he

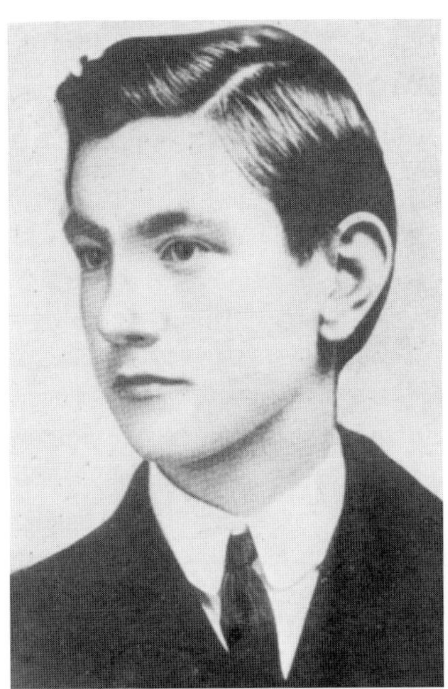

Samuel Stritch at sixteen years old
[Marie C. Buehrle. *The Cardinal Stritch Story,* Bruce Pub. Co., 1959]

secured white collar work with the railroad. He formed an association with Nashville railroad builder, Major Eugene W. Lewis, who headed the Sycamore Powder Company, an explosives firm that blasted roadbeds for railroads. The couple moved around a bit, but then settled in a home at 1121 Summer Street in North Nashville. When "Sammy" was 9-years-old, Garrett died and Katie Malley became, in his words, "the greatest influence in my life." Stritch remained close to "Mama" until her death in 1928.

Growing up Catholic in the South had its liabilities and its advantages. Young Stritch spoke with a southern lilt throughout his days (an accent that priest secretaries attested got stronger whenever he visited his native region).[31] He also had rather benighted racial attitudes, even by northern standards. But Stritch grew up by temperament and social need into a rather flexible and easy-going (on most matters) young man. He was exceptionally precocious and rapidly mastered school lessons in the parish school of Assumption Church in Nashville. By the age of 10 he was ready for high school. Apart from his brothers, his strongest male bonding came with Father John B. Morris (later bishop of Little Rock, Arkansas), a priest of the diocese of Nashville who was related to Stritch by marriage. As Stritch's nephew later suggested, the association with Morris was a bit of good luck. Morris was also connected by marriage to the family of Father John P. Farrelly,

Bishop John Morris of Little Rock
[Archives of the Diocese of Little Rock]

another Tennessee boy who served for many years in Rome and as bishop and kingmaker in Cleveland, Ohio. In the clubby world of Southern Catholicism and in a Romanized system where having a patron in high places meant everything, these connections went a long way in accounting for Stritch's later rapid ascent into the hierarchy.[32]

Stritch served Morris's Mass and Morris in turn encouraged his priestly vocation and convinced Bishop Thomas S. Byrne of Nashville to send the young man first to St. Gregory's Seminary in Cincinnati for his high school and college training, and in 1904, to study in Rome. These years in the Eternal City left their mark on Stritch. He was only 16 when he arrived and was overwhelmed not only by the city's ecclesiastical culture and the cult of the papacy, but also by all things Italian—people, food, and culture—a gift that served him well in Milwaukee where problems with Italian parishes were an ongoing challenge. On May 21, 1910, he was ordained a priest at the Lateran Basilica by Cardinal Pietro Respighi. After an additional year of study he was sent back to Nashville, where he served for a time as an assistant at his home parish. The relative shortage of priests in the Nashville Diocese (which encompassed the entire state of Tennessee) made for quick elevation to a pastorate and he was appointed to head the very large church of St. Patrick in Memphis. In 1916 Byrne summoned him back to Nashville, where the still young cleric was given a series of jobs, some of which he held simultaneously. He was appointed variously episcopal secretary, rector of the Cathedral of the Annunciation, chancellor of the diocese and, the job he loved most, superintendent of schools. Juggling all these tasks was not as daunting as it may seem. In 1921, the year he left for Toledo, there were only 25,000 Catholics in Tennessee and 58 churches and 53 priests. There were only 25 parochial schools that served 5,200 students (a number of whom were not Catholic).[33] As in most Southern dioceses, the tempo of Catholic life was slow and easy.

Bishop Samuel Stritch of Toledo
[Marie C. Buehrle. *The Cardinal Stritch Story,* Bruce Pub. Co., 1959]

On August 10, 1921, at the age of 34, Stritch was named the second bishop of Toledo, Ohio. He was consecrated on November 30, 1921, by Archbishop Henry Moeller of Cincinnati, assisted by Bishop John B. Morris of Little Rock. Toledo was booming in the 1920s and Stritch spent most of his time there using the enhanced resources of the diocese to expand and improve the quality of Catholic life. The "boy-bishop" as the newspapers dubbed him embarked on an active program of reform. Stritch became passionately committed to the improvement of the Catholic schools of Toledo, and insisted that Catholic schools conform in every way possible to the professional standards established by the state of Ohio. He insisted that teachers in the Catholic schools be well–trained in subject matter and pedagogical methods. Uncomfortable with the thought of nuns attending secular colleges and normal schools, he urged religious communities to establish Saturday and summer college sessions in their motherhouses for teaching sisters. At Stritch's urging a new Catholic college, Mary Manse, was established by the Ursuline Sisters.[34]

Stritch also undertook to build a magnificent new cathedral for the diocese—one patterned after the great cathedral of Toledo in Spain. Ground was broken for the cathedral, designed by the Pittsburgh architectural firm of Comes, Perry, and McMullen, at a solemn ceremony in October 1925 attended by Cardinal Edward Czarnoch, primate of Hungary. Stritch lovingly followed the details of the elaborate church's construction and it became a building far more elegant than any that had been seen in Toledo. However, its costs were astronomical, and he left his successor, Bishop Karl J. Alter, with a staggering debt that the prelate had to lift in the midst of the Depression. Stritch forever regretted this bit of extravagance, and lived frugally in Milwaukee and Chicago, approving expensive building projects only reluctantly.[35]

Stritch adjusted to episcopal life after a time. Slow and easygoing, he affected a rather casual manner, a style very much at variance with the austere and remote "CEO" style cultivated increasingly by American bishops. Stritch spent hours reading and sought any occasion to rhapsodize from the pulpit on the subject closest to his mind (he often did this at priest's funerals where he insisted on preaching). His tribute to the recently deceased would occupy a few initial words and then the subject would turn to art, philosophy, and history. Stritch had a hard time keeping a schedule and cherished the informality of sloppy attire, answered his own door and phone and took long walks in his neighborhood. On August 26, 1930, as he was in the midst of work on the cathedral, news reached Stritch that he was to succeed Messmer.[36] Putting his affairs in order, he bid a sad farewell to Toledo, which he had come to love, and arrived in Milwaukee in time for Thanksgiving. Using a new black Cadillac, given to him by the priests, he began his nine year administration of the Milwaukee See.

After the death of Cardinal George Mundelein in Chicago in October 1939, an intense bit of internal politicking went on to select a successor to the now very prestigious and powerful see.[37] By this time a raft of national and international circumstances caused the American government to pay close attention to who ruled the Catholic Church in Chicago. Chicago was also a hotbed of isolationist activity spearheaded by Colonel

Robert McCormick's sharply anti-Roosevelt *Chicago Tribune* and isolationist groups such as the America First Movement, which had its headquarters in the offices of one of the vice presidents of the Chicago-based Quaker Oats Company. Roosevelt had cultivated a public friendship with Mundelein and in 1936, after delivering his famous "Quarantine Speech" against isolationism, visited the cardinal at his private residence.[38] To keep the Mundelein base alive, the Roosevelt administration actively sought the nomination of Mundelein's popular and staunchly pro-FDR auxiliary bishop, Bernard J. Sheil. But to everyone's surprise, the nod went to Stritch, clearly less prominent and more socially conservative than Mundelein. FDR's curmudgeonly interior secretary, Harold Ickes, summed up the administration's reaction to Stritch's appointment when he confided to his private diary, "Well you and I have had a pretty severe blow today."[39] Stritch departed Milwaukee in March 1940 and spent the next 18 years paying off Mundelein's debts and coping with post-war Chicago's city tensions and rapid suburban growth.

Archbishop Samuel Stritch of Milwaukee [AAM]

Coping with Ethnic Diversity

The prescriptions for a more centralized archdiocesan life came to some degree from external sources, especially the increasing demands of Roman authorities. This was all the more accentuated by the changed circumstances of U. S. church life after 1908 when the Holy See declared that the United States was no longer a missionary territory.[40] The practical effect of this was to create lines of direct authority between the American hierarchy and various curial offices, which now assumed direct oversight of American affairs. Likewise, popes from Pius X (1903-1915) through Pius XII (1939-1958) built an increasingly powerful cult around their person and authority that virtually united Catholicism with the will and mind of the pope. The Catholic experience of this period was different from the ecclesiological realities of the 19th century. Autonomy was surrendered to a stricter chain of command that began with the pope and flowed through the curia to local bishops and their bureaus and departments. The apotheosis of this came when a long-awaited codification of canon law was issued in 1917 and declared effective on Pentecost Sunday 1918. The administrative clarity of the "New" Code of Canon Law gave broader powers to Roman and diocesan officials. The resulting ethos had a marked effect on the archdiocese of Milwaukee.

But a second, and perhaps equally potent, reason for insistence on archdiocesan unity under central administration came as a result of Sebastian Messmer's response to ethno-cultural challenges. Immigrants continued to pour into the see until their numbers were stanched by the restrictive immigration legislation of 1921 and 1924. While Germans held their own as the dominant group, the Poles overtook the Irish as the second largest Catholic population in Milwaukee. Although most Poles lived in cities such as Milwaukee, Kenosha, Racine, and Sheboygan, there were also sizeable pockets of Catholic Poles in rural areas. Other ethnic groups began to build on the foundations of the 19th century ethnic patterns. Italians became visible in Milwaukee's Third Ward, and with support from the cathedral parish, found a niche for themselves not only in Milwaukee but also in Kenosha, Racine, Beloit and Madison. Often this took the form of new parishes. Occasionally it meant an active Italian subculture in an existing parish.

Southern and eastern European groups emerged as well. "A Polyglot Church," read the title on a brief notice in the *Catholic Citizen* in March 1907. "The Catholic Church in this city is becoming a cosmopolitan institution," the paper reported. In Milwaukee alone there were 33 churches: "thirteen German, six Polish, nine English, two Bohemian, one Italian, one Slovene, one Slovak."[41] The same ethnic mix was to be found in Racine, Kenosha, and Sheboygan. Other variations occurred in Fond du Lac and Beaver Dam.

Ethnic Equilibrium Disturbed: Messmer the Americanizer

Katzer had indeed left a polyglot diocese. And the Milwaukee See was enjoying a much-needed spell of peace. This was one of the reasons that the priests of the archdiocese and Katzer himself wanted to have Schinner succeed to the episcopal throne in 1903. When James Keogh, archdiocesan consultor and cathedral rector, opposed Messmer's nomination, he used the archdiocese's ethnic peace as his primary motivation: "We are now blessed with a zealous and united clergy, and that the racial question [*sic*: ethnic], which was once acute is now settled at least for the present and that all nationalities work together for the common interests of the church." For this happy state of affairs he gave credit to Schinner, "who has had practical charge of the archdiocese for nearly eight years." He pleaded with the delegate, "The clergy of the Archdiocese, a learned, zealous and successful body of priests see no reason why a stranger should be appointed for their archbishop to endanger the unity and good feeling which now exist among them, and which they feel assured will continue if Father Schinner be selected to rule over them. They see no reason why a bishop from another diocese should be transferred here."[42]

Even Abbelen, who ultimately endorsed Messmer, believed that the nomination of Rainer or Schinner might be better for the preservation of ethnic peace. In the case of the Poles, Rainer's "appointment would be very welcome to the strong Polish element in all the dioceses of our Province, perhaps even a solution, in part at least, of the Polish bishop question." Although he favored Messmer, he also knew that the Green Bay prelate had his liabilities: "He would ... not be so well-liked as either Rainer or Schinner. In the eyes of the Germans and the Poles he stands as one who favors and fosters their de-nationalization sooner too much than not enough."[43]

Abbelen spoke with prescience. Messmer was indeed partial to his fellow Germans and favored the causes they believed in, e.g., nationality parishes and Catholic schools. However, as bishop of Green Bay, he surprised Ireland and others by his emphasis on the "neutrality" of the episcopal office when it came to nationalism. He insisted often that he wanted to be bishop of the entire diocese and not just one nationality.

As bishop of Green Bay, Messmer insisted on using more English in the churches. In 1900 he imitated the example of Bishop Frederick Eis of the neighboring diocese of Marquette, Michigan, and ordered that at least one sermon in English be preached at the Sunday Mass.[44] When questioned about it, Messmer observed that he was only implementing a policy established by Propaganda in 1887 aimed at the children of immigrants, especially "young Polanders or Germans" to make sure that they heard the English language at least occasionally in their churches.[45] Messmer soon became a vigorous advocate of English as the common language of Catholicism in the United States, and sought out others who pressed for transcending ethnic identity.

Just as important as his insistence on English was his support for the multiethnic American Federation of Catholic Societies, which he co-founded in 1901 with one of his former students from Seton Hall, Bishop James McFaul of Trenton.[46] In an address to a gathering of German Catholics in Fond du Lac in the summer of 1900, he cited the need for a general mobilization of American Catholics to combat the problems of the day, "a closed and well-ordered phalanx ready to fight in the battle of the age, under the leadership of their ecclesiastical superiors, for justice and truth, for home and family, for God, Church, and Country."[47] Messmer's identification with the federation was the reason for Father Joseph LaBoule's defense of Messmer from accusations of German nationalism. "In the opinion of serious clergymen of my acquaintance," wrote LaBoule to Apostolic Delegate Diomede Falconio, "there is nothing which has ever done so much in the U.S. toward a 'rapproachment' and a stronger union of the different nationalities in the Church than the Federation of Catholic Societies, which owes its origin and present strength mostly to the patient efforts of Rt. Rev. Bishop Messmer." LaBoule concluded, "The laity either Irish or German or Polish do not want more separation, they want a union of strength for the better good of the church."[48]

Although Messmer came to Milwaukee with an accent and a European "look," he was determined to unite the scattered tribes of ethnic Milwaukee to combat a host of social problems. "The Catholic principle is in its very nature a principle of unity," he lectured in an article on the federation in the seminary quarterly *Salesianum*. "We are not merely called the Federation of Catholic Societies, but the American Federation of Catholic Societies. We are Catholics—yes and we are Americans—yes, to the end of time."[49]

Messmer's efforts to create an American Catholic "phalanx" of united nationalities ran into virulent and at times violent opposition from the Poles in the Green Bay diocese, who were in no hurry to assimilate or submit to a German-speaking bishop. Tensions in Polish parishes in Stevens Point and Manitowoc disturbed his years in Green Bay. In 1897, he tangled with the powerful Polish contingent at the community of Pulaski. Speaking later of the controversy, he identified his feelings toward the Poles to Apostolic Delegate Sebastiano Martinelli: "I trust your Excellency will never know by experience how well these Polish people understand how to turn a line or a word from the bishop against their priest or a word from higher authority against priest and bishop." Messmer struggled with the Poles in Green Bay on a number of fronts. "The worse symptom in every single case has been the open resistance to ecclesiastic [*sic*] authority. The Poles, misled by their newspapers are beginning to carry the democratic principle of American politics into the Church of God and claim for themselves the right to rule and manage at least the temporal affairs independently of Diocesan laws or Episcopal ordinances."[50]

The problems in Pulaski were replicated in Menasha, Princeton, and Stevens Point (here the Poles were so enraged at Messmer they almost stoned him on the street). One of his disgruntled priests bitterly blamed Messmer for making difficult situations worse, saying, "He never can understand the Polish people and character and has created such a disturbance in Polish congregations that he can only blame himself for the rebellious ostentacion [*sic*] shown in his whole diocese."[51] He also faced the possibility of a large defection from the Church by disgruntled Poles–especially when Archbishop Rene Villatte, a schismatic leader of the old Catholic Church made a strong play for those elements to join him.[52] Likewise, in 1897, a major schism occurred between Polish Catholics and the diocese of Scranton, Pennsylvania, resulting in the foundation of the Polish National Church (PNC). The PNC soon managed to garner enough support to create separate parishes in the vicinities of large concentrations of Poles in America. A dissident Polish priest, Francis Hodur, was consecrated bishop for the new community and would establish two successful churches in Milwaukee. The PNC and the old Catholics continuously hovered in the background, anxious to take advantage of any split in Catholic ranks. Messmer brought all of this "baggage" to Milwaukee when he had to confront its even larger Polish population.

Messmer pounded on the drum of archdiocesan unity during his first year. In March he spoke of convening a diocesan synod to review church policies and practices.[53] In April he unveiled a new diocesan seal sporting three fishes on one side and a sheaf of wheat on the other. Beneath the shield was the Latin phrase, "*In Ubertate Terrae*" (In the Richness of the Earth).[54] That summer, his Americanizing goals were made clear when he shocked the German priests at their July retreat by speaking to them in English and letting them know of his concern that some Catholic schools, outside Milwaukee, were not using English in their curriculum. "You see we are in America, an English-speaking country, and English is our language. It should be the prevailing language in all schools...it is well to teach foreign languages . . . but at all times the English language should be supreme."[55] All ethnic groups in the archdiocese must have been a bit unsettled by all of this posturing, but it would be the Poles who would react most violently to Messmer's efforts to downplay ethnic identity.

[AAM]

The battle began almost immediately when he learned that one of his Polish priests, Father Wenceslaus Kruszka, was in Rome lobbying for the appointment of a Polish bishop.[56] If Kruszka's Roman lobbying seemed worrisome, the news brought by Father Anthony Lex, pastor of St. Casimir's parish, seemed even more problematic. In a letter to Messmer in August 1904, he passed on the allegation that Kruszka had sired an out of wedlock child with the housekeeper of St. Casimir's parish.[57] The priests had told Messmer to handle the matter. "They want me to do so myself personally," he informed the apostolic delegate, "as they fear the wrath of the Reverend Gentleman."[58] Indeed, the "Reverend Gentleman's" wrath was worth fearing.

The years between 1904 and 1917 were years of serious internal difficulties in the Milwaukee archdiocese. Factionalism and controversy brought the archdiocese as close to schism as it ever would be. The basic issue is fairly simple to understand. Like the Germans in the American hierarchy at large and the English speakers in the Milwaukee clergy, Poles in Milwaukee demanded some visible sign that they had "arrived." For them, this demand for respect and some degree of autonomy in their affairs crystallized around the call for a Polish bishop. Preferably this bishop would be an ordinary of a diocese. But the Milwaukee Poles were willing to settle for an auxiliary bishop who would take over as pastor of some prominent Milwaukee Polish church, and in effect be the *de facto* ordinary and regular minister of the sacraments to the Poles. What the Poles wanted was what the ill-fated Lucerne Memorial proposed in 1891, a diocese within a diocese, based on nationality and not territory. Sebastian Messmer was opposed to this demand. His position disrupted the equilibrium that Keogh and others had lauded during the Katzer/Schinner years.

Messmer was already aware of Wenceslaus Kruszka's presence in Rome when Apostolic Delegate Diomede Falconio questioned him about Kruszka. Messmer urged caution in dealing with Kruszka. He warned them not to move hastily, telling Falconio, "I intend to address Cardinal Gotti [the prefect of Propaganda] a memorial upon the question of a Polish bishop which undoubtedly involves difficulties with which Rome ought to be fully acquainted." Earlier, he had warned Falconio about allegations that Kruszka had sired a child with a housekeeper and suggested that the other Polish priests in Milwaukee did not totally support their brother in Rome.[59]

The request for a Polish bishop finally reached the new pontiff, who sounded out American bishops. Many registered negative opinions, fearing a recurrence of the tensions that afflicted the American hierarchy in the 1880s and 1890s. Confronted by the insistent Kruszka's requests, Pius X appeared to temporize. He summoned Kruszka and allegedly assured the Wisconsin priest in an audience on April 15, 1904, "It will be decided as soon as possible. Tell the Poles in America that the decision will be made as soon as possible, and it will be according to your wishes."[60] Wiring back exultantly to his half-brother Michael, Wenceslaus Kruszka claimed victory and wrote an article for *Kuryer* which called April 15 "a day of triumph and victory" for Polish Americans. As subsequent events unfolded, it was unclear whether Pope Pius X really gave Kruszka what he was looking for, or had simply made a vague statement to buy more time. However, for Kruszka, the pontiff had made a promise.

Initial Polish hopes were first trained on Messmer's successor in Green Bay. But Messmer threw his support behind the appointment of another German speaker, Father Joseph Fox, who was consecrated in July

Pope Pius X
[AAM]

1904. Hopes among the Poles also burned brightly in early 1904 when plans were afoot to create a new diocese in Wisconsin. Rumors surfaced that the new see would be at Madison, but more astute observers suggested that it would be for the northern third of the state and headquartered at either Stevens Point or Ashland. Here it was hoped that the long desired Polish bishop could be appointed.[61] Eventually, however, the new diocese was headquartered at Superior. Apostolic Delegate Falconio asked Messmer about the possibility of a Polish candidate for the new see. Messmer threw cold water on the idea, laying out his Americanist biases on the whole issue of a national bishop. "With the knowledge of the Polish priests and especially the clergy that we have, we do not consider it opportune to propose a Polish name. We consider it premature as long as the Poles are not more Americanized (in the good sense)."[62] In a 1905 letter to Cardinal Gibbons in Baltimore he repeated the same misgivings: "The Polish are not yet American enough & keep aloof too much from the rest of us." [63]

St. Wenceslaus Church, Ripon [AAM]

Polish anger was reignited when the names on the Superior *terna* leaked out to the *Catholic Citizen.* Of the three names on the list, A. Philip Kremer, vicar general of La Crosse, Joseph Schrembs, vicar general of Grand Rapids, and Milwaukee favorite Augustine Schinner, none were the long-awaited and now promised son of Poland.[64] Still the Poles waited patiently and responded with eagerness when Archbishop Albion Francis Symon of Plock, Poland, was sent by Pius X to inspect Polish conditions in America. He appeared in Milwaukee in June and was present for celebrations in the city's Kosciusko Park, when the Polish community presented an equestrian statue of the Revolutionary war hero to the city. When Symon's visit produced no direct results Kruszka grew bitter. Messmer warned the priest to curtail his agitation. Kruszka disputed the archbishop's accusation and told a friend that "Archbishop Messmer was an enemy of the Poles, for he was an enemy of their most vital cause in America."[65]

Added to the disappointment over the Polish bishop was Kruszka's increasing frustration at being stuck in Ripon. He had been there since 1898 and priests younger than he were being appointed to newly-founded Polish parishes. Kruszka suspected that his efforts to cajole Messmer into giving him a new parish had fallen on deaf ears because the archbishop believed the accusations that Kruszka had sired an illegitimate child. Seeking an outlet for his frustration, Kruszka poured his anger into a series of articles critical of Messmer that appeared on the pages of *Kuryer*. He also linked the issues of a Polish bishop, his own Ripon "exile" and the rapidly declining fortunes of St. Josaphat's parish. Now burdened by a debt that soared to $400,000, the parish was in an economic free fall. In 1906, Messmer met with the parishioners, many of whom had lent money to Grutza for the building, urging them to be patient and not demand their money back right away. *Kuryer* scoffed at the efforts and suggested that finances would improve if Wenceslaus Kruszka were pastor.[66]

Relations between Messmer and Kruszka hit a nadir when an embarrassing incident took place in 1906 involving Kruszka's *History of Poles in America* printed in serialized fashion in the *Kuryer* and later transformed into 13 volumes, each of which carried Messmer's *imprimatur*. Messmer was shocked to find reprinted in the ninth volume (which he had not read) embarrassing correspondence between the superiors of the Polish Resurrectionist Order in Rome and their subjects in Chicago. In these letters, Roman authorities had severely criticized their Chicago confreres. This brought forth howls of protest from Chicago-based Resurrectionist leader Father Francis Gordon. Mortified that he had not discovered the embarrassing correspondence himself, Messmer was compelled to publicly apologize to the Chicago Resurrectionist.[67]

Messmer had already begun to take on Kruszka on the delicate subject of counting the Poles. Since a major premise of Kruszka's history and his demand for a Polish bishop was based on a belief that Poles were dramatically undercounted, Messmer attempted to get an accurate count, and to do this he laid down criteria for counting. Using a request by the Holy See to take an accurate census of foreign-born Catholics, Messmer used more restrictive guidelines in counting than had Kruszka. "The Nationality [*sic*] of a family will be determined by its descent on the father's side and the language spoken in the family. Where three generations of a family were born in this country and the present family speaks the English language only, it may be classified as American. In case of doubt, classify according to general and popular estimation."[68] The effect of these more rigid criteria was to reduce the number of Poles counted to those who truly spoke the language.

Messmer also became aware of the ambivalent feelings many of the Polish pastors had for Michael Kruszka and *Kuryer,* going back to the 1896 PES dispute over the teaching of Polish in public schools. Pastors resented Kruszka's occasional forays into journalistic independence and his willingness to assert certain rights of the Polish laity over and against their pastors. In December 1906, Messmer helped to finance an alternative Polish daily called *Nowiny Polski*. He appointed seminary professor Boleslaus Goral as editor, and wrote a letter to Polish pastors endorsing the new paper and urging Catholics to subscribe to it. *Nowiny* never overtook *Kuryer* in circulation, but it was the single largest rival to the Kruszka paper, and the mouthpiece of Messmer and priests loyal to him in opposing the two brothers. On the

Rev. Boleslaus Goral [AAM]

pages of *Nowiny* and *Kuryer* both sides lobbed verbal grenades at each other—a level of invective that would astound readers today by its virulence and passion. Both Kruszkas opened the rhetorical floodgates when describing Goral, accusing him of public drunkenness and sexual misconduct. Goral replied in kind, attacking Michael Kruszka's earlier efforts to undermine the Polish Catholic schools and pointing out that the editor's daughter went to the "infidel" Downer Normal School. He also unleashed a torrent of invective on his fellow cleric, Father Wenceslaus Kruszka. The fight spun out of control in 1907.

Since Wenceslaus Kruszka was the easier to control, episcopal restrictions were placed on his opportunities to speak and write. In early 1907 Bishop Joseph Fox banned him from preaching in Green Bay at the funeral of a prominent Polish priest. Likewise, Messmer ordered him to stop writing any more articles for *Kuryer*. In the meantime, an ambitious Goral heaped opprobrium on both the Kruszkas, including everything from disloyalty to the Church to vicious personal invective. Michael Kruszka, untrammeled by ecclesiastical obedience, decried Goral's vilification in a 23-page letter to Messmer.

In the meantime, the now-silenced Wenceslaus demanded the opportunity to reply to the accusations leveled against him in the newspaper *Nowiny*. He became even more upset when Messmer issued a *Handbook for Catholic Parishioners* that insisted on the implementation of the rule of the Provincial Council of 1886 "that the children of foreign languages should learn the catechism not only in their own language, but in English as

Kuryer Polski **delivery boys** [Kwasniewski Collection, Archives, UWM Libraries]

well."[69] Kruszka took this as a direct assault on Polish Catholic life and wrote a complaint to Apostolic Delegate Falconio, asking for permission to respond and raising the threat of rebellion. "I do not believe in rebellion against church authorities and so do [nor] the Poles at large—but we Poles believe in *insurrection* for self-defense, especially if the higher church authorities fail to do justice."[70] Falconio urged Messmer to attend to Kruszka's complaints and the archbishop referred the matter to a tribunal of seminary priests who determined to see if Kruszka had genuinely been wronged.

The meeting of the investigators with the parties concerned did not take place until early October 1907. Angered at the delay, Kruszka complained to the apostolic delegate demanding a resolution of the matter. Messmer grew increasingly more hostile to the priest. To one of Falconio's queries about the state of the case, Messmer replied, "The character of this man is shown by the fact that he had the impudence of sending me a bill demanding of me $50 for the 2 trips made in vain to Milwaukee when it could not have cost him more than about $3.00 to come and go." Messmer also raged against "that infernal sheet" *Kuryer Polski*, which was "doing more harm to Catholicity among the Poles than any other paper in the United States." But he admitted that the *Nowiny's* replies to *Kuryer* were sometimes intemperate. "The young editor, Rev. Goral ... sometimes loses his temper and the Polish fighter hits beyond the mark." Messmer promised, "this will stop."[71] In 1908, after two delays of the formal hearing, Falconio finally pressed Messmer for a solution, "As this case has been dragging along now for a long time, it must be settled."[72] Messmer spat back, "That man Kruszka of Ripon is not worth the paper we use about him." He also repeated the damaging information regarding Kruszka's "love child" (one of the reasons he wanted to keep him "on the farm" in Ripon): "This is the same man whose former housekeeper and her mother swear that he was the father of her child some five years ago, just before I came here. He denies it but I know he paid for her support after she left him." Nonetheless, he informed the delegate that the case was near a judgement and that he had promised Kruszka "a better place at the next opportunity." Messmer concluded dryly, "Your Excellency need not bother about him. I will do what is right."[73]

Pressed by an increasingly irate Falconio, the Milwaukee archbishop softened a bit toward Kruszka and attempted to deliver him from his Ripon "exile" by offering the task of organizing a new Polish parish in West Allis. Suspicious of Messmer's "gifts," however, Kruszka brusquely turned down the offer, insisting that Messmer gave it to him "under the impression that West Allis is a booming city." Kruszka complained, that the business panic of 1908 had resulted in the laying off of nearly 11,000 workers from the Allis Chalmers plant, leaving only 22 Polish families and about 20 single Poles. "So at the present time it is impossible to organize a separate congregation there because the few Poles there could not support it."[74] Messmer then tried to interest Kruszka in the pastorate of St. Stanislaus parish in Racine, but viewing it as not much better than Ripon, he turned that down as well. Kruszka appealed to Falconio and begged the delegate to restore his right to publish in *Kuryer* and to make the attacks in *Nowiny* cease. "I demand a better parish in Milwaukee city, just there, because the *Nowiny* wrote I am kept out of Milwaukee 'for punishment.' Let there be justice and there will be peace."[75]

St. Josaphat's Again

In 1908, Messmer decided to mend some fences with the Poles. His change of heart was not based on a new found love and respect for their nationalistic aspirations, but more practically on his need for Polish support in dealing with the escalating problems of St. Josaphat's Church. Since the death of Father Wilhelm Grutza, repeated efforts had been made to shore up the tottering finances of the huge church. These had failed miserably. In 1906, debt stood at $400,000. By 1908 it had ballooned to nearly $700,000. As St. Josaphat's finances deteriorated, criticism descended on the archbishop from every quarter. Many, including the Kruszka brothers, wished to know why someone in authority had not reined in the grandiose schemes of the late Father Grutza. Truly at his wit's end and fearing that the church would have to face the embarrassment of foreclosure and the possible sale to some secular firm, Messmer traveled to Rome to seek guidance about the St. Josaphat debt and the question of a Polish auxiliary.[76] Meeting with Pope Pius X (who certainly got an earful about Milwaukee's Polish problems), Messmer secured permission to invite a religious community to take over the parish who could raise funds on a nationwide basis to succor the financially distressed church. Moreover, their vow of poverty would reduce overhead expenses at the parish.

After much negotiation, Messmer cajoled the Conventual Franciscan Friars of Buffalo, New York, to take over the basilica and $400,000 of the $650,000 debt—$200,000 of which was owed to the parishioners themselves. The rest would have to be raised by the archdiocese.[77] Father Hyacinth Fudzinski, the provincial of the order, assumed the pastorate on January 1, 1910. Within a few days of arriving, he held a tense parish meeting during a blizzard in which he announced a plan to refinance the portion of the debt owed to the parishioners. He asked them to accept only $.75 on the dollar and to forgo any interest they may have had coming. To this the parishioners generally agreed.[78] "I am the busiest man in Milwaukee," Fudzinski told a reporter. And indeed he was as he began to untangle the various fiscal and legal complications that had beset the parish since Father Wilhelm Grutza and his string of hapless successors. Since no one really wanted to foreclose on the elaborate basilica, Fudzinski was able to win time and additional credit. He forestalled the foreclosure proceedings that had been launched by the Fidelity Insurance Company, and secured a second mortgage from a Syracuse Bank that came due in 1915.[79] In his first year alone, Fudzinski paid off over $66,000 of the staggering debt. In 1911, an additional $39,000 was raised that reduced the debt to $294,000.[80] Ultimately, the penny-pinching Fudzinski paid off the reduced debt to the parishioners and consolidated his portion of the remaining indebtedness at manageable rates of interest so that the magic combination of regular parish revenues and the host of fund-raisers (dinners, craft sales, fairs, etc.) would cover the rest. By 1925 the debt would be repaid and St. Josaphat's moved to a new stage of development.[81]

About $250,000 of the debt was assumed by the archdiocese. Messmer allegedly placed a second mortgage on the recently purchased Pabst Mansion, and then assessed each of the parishes a certain portion of the debt. To meet the urgent demands of creditors, Messmer borrowed $120,000 on archdiocesan credit and then turned to the parishes to help him pay off the new debt. He imposed a general collection on the see for the retirement of the debt (absolving archdiocesan parishes from collecting either for the Negro missions or the Holy Land for the duration). "This was the only way to save St. Josaphat's from bankruptcy and the Catholic church in America from a horrible scandal," he lectured in a pastoral letter. He directed a few hopeful words at his critics in the Polish community: "There is no use in asking how such a terrible debt has been created. Those who were responsible for it are dead, and have answered an infinitely just judge. For us there is nothing left but to meet the actual conditions of affairs."[82]

However, eliciting freewill donations for the retirement of the debt was unsuccessful. In 1911 Messmer then ordered the priests to report to their deans and to discuss not *if* but *how* the parishes were going to pay the debt. He even suggested that if cooperation were not forthcoming, the entire amount would be laid on the clergy themselves.[83] Acting under this episcopal goad, an assessment committee composed of respected pastors of every nationality met in the spring of 1911 to determine parish assessments.[84] Numbers were given and parishes began to pay.

The handling of the debt at St. Josaphat ignited a major controversy among the Poles which was waged on the pages of the two rival dailies, *Nowiny* and *Kuryer*. Attributing the St. Josaphat "disaster" to the mismanage-

Rev. Hyacinth Fudzinski, OFM Conv. [*Golden Jubilee Album St. Anthony of Padua Province*, 1956]

ment and lack of accountability of the clergy, Michael Kruszka launched a campaign for greater lay oversight over church financial affairs. To the consternation of the Polish clergy (who had memories of their battles with him over the school issue), he urged Polish Catholics to withhold contributions to churches unless pastors committed themselves to some form of open accounting for the money. He also suggested the organization of a federation of American Catholic Polish Parishes to press for more lay control of parish finances. Polish pastors openly denounced the newspaper editor for encouraging insubordination. However some Polish parishes refused to pay their part of the St. Josaphat assessment. Just as disconcerting, Wenceslaus Kruszka connected the dots between the plight of St. Josaphat's and the need for a Polish bishop. He wrote to the apostolic delegate in 1908, "The only way to save St. Josaphat is to make a Polish auxiliary bishop and appoint him rector there—and all the trouble will be ended .... An energetic Polish auxiliary seated at St. Josaphat's would pay the debts within one year! I guarantee this. Why? He would be the first Polish bishop in America and his church would like-wise be considered as a cathedral of this first bishop and be sure, all the Poles in America, young and old would consider it a point of honor to wipe out the debts of the Cathedral! No doubt about that!"[85]

Bishop Paul Rhode of Green Bay (middle) [Kwasniewski Collection, Archives, UWM Libraries]

There would finally be the long-awaited Polish bishop, but not in Milwaukee. In July a Polish priest of the archdiocese of Chicago, Peter Paul Rhode, was selected by Archbishop James Quigley as auxiliary. Rhode's consecration set off jubilation around Polish America, and Milwaukee Catholics joined in the celebration. Although busy with Chicago's large Polonia, Rhode took to the road, ministering to groups of Polish Catholics all over the Midwest. At Falconio's behest, Rhode used his good graces to end the standoff between Messmer and Kruszka. Rhode went to Milwaukee on Holy Thursday to preside at the blessing of the Holy Oils, and afterwards met with Messmer and Kruszka.[86] He succeeded in getting the priest to withdraw his complaint against Goral and Messmer, and then convinced Messmer to give Wenceslaus Kruszka a plum Milwaukee parish. In September 1909 Messmer appointed Kruszka to the pastorate of St. Adalbert's Church on Becher Street. Kruszka was now close to the heart of the largest concentration of Poles in Wisconsin. Here also he burnished his reputation as a strong leader and preacher, and ensured the financial success of the parish. He remained at St. Adalbert's until his death in 1937.

Once Wenceslaus Kruszka was in his new location in Milwaukee, the brothers resumed their war of words with Goral at *Nowiny*. Accusations of sexual misconduct were hurled at Goral and others of the "Nowiny Ring" by Michael Kruszka. "Their sporting proclivities make them forget their divine calling; most of them consider priesthood merely as a good money-making business and as a profession in which licentiousness is just as much a matter of course as polygamy in Mormonism." It was sweet revenge for his half-brother who had been pilloried for sexual misconduct.[87]

Messmer realized that to help pay off the St. Josaphat debt and restore calm to the archdiocese, he would have to ordain a Polish auxiliary. But he worried that acceding to this demand would create even more problems. Archbishop Ireland, to whom he poured out his problems, wrote back sympathetically, "You have a most serious problem—that of selecting a Polish priest for auxiliary .... You are absolutely right in determining that the Ordinary must always be the Bishop de facto of all his people, of Poles as likewise of others. The least apparent division on national lines is fatal to the unity of government and to the welfare of religion. By all means, hold to the principle of unity at whatever cost." He continued, "To find a Polander who will sincerely and earnestly work to that end is, in my opinion, almost an impossibility. He himself may begin well-intentioned but soon he will yield to influences and almost conscientiously believe [he is] sent [from] Heaven to lead his people .... If you must have a Polish auxiliary, take an older man around whom plottings for future ambitions cannot be built up."[88] Acknowledging that he had to have someone who would appeal to his growing Polish coreligionists, he sought to find a prelate who spoke the language, but who would not set himself up as a rival bishop within the archdiocese. He believed that he had found that in the person of the auxiliary bishop of Cleveland, Joseph Maria Koudelka, a Bohemian. As it turned out, it only made matters worse.

The Battle of the Auxiliary Bishops

Koudelka was born December 8, 1852 in Chlistova, Klatovy, in Bohemia (the present day Czech Republic). He studied the classics at the gymnasium in Klattau, Bohemia. In 1868 he emigrated with his parents to Wisconsin, where he settled in Manitowoc. He attended Mount Calvary and then entered St. Francis Seminary, where his facility with a number of languages (he eventually mastered eight: English, French, German, Bohemian, Slovak, Polish, Slovenian and Russian) made him an academic star. As a "language epidemic" hit St. Francis in the 1870s, Koudelka did duty as a substitute professor.[89] He was also an artist, able to do passable freehand sketches of various people and things. His talents were on display when he designed the scenery for the seminary dramatization of Father Frederick X. Katzer's *Der Kampf der Gegenwart*. Bishop Richard Gilmour of Cleveland enticed the young cleric to come to his diocese while still in minor orders, and he finished his theological training at St. Mary's Seminary where he was ordained a deacon in February 1875.[90] So desperate were diocesan authorities for Bohemian clergy that Koudelka was sent as a deacon to the Bohemian national parish, St. Procopius, and was made pastor shortly after his ordination to the priesthood. Koudelka enjoyed success after success in this first pastoral assignment, reviving a defunct school and bringing back to the church scores of Bohemian "defectors." Koudelka's accomplishments with Bohemian Catholics in Cleveland propelled him into the national limelight. For two years (1881-

1883) he lived in St. Louis where he edited a Bohemian weekly called *Hlas* (*Voice*). He also prepared a series of textbooks for Bohemian Catholic schools (some were used in Milwaukee's St. John de Nepomuc). In 1883 he was recalled to Cleveland, where he founded the German parish of St. Michael on the city's growing south side. He erected a splendid Gothic revival structure (which placed the parish in horrendous debt for years) in which he himself did the art work. He also did troubleshooting for dissident parishes. In 1886 his bishop, Ignatius Horstmann, sent him to settle a quarrel at a Polish church where a riot had destroyed the building. Even with these assignments, he continued to be in popular demand, traveling widely among the scattered Bohemian communities throughout the country. Horstmann designated Koudelka a special vicar general for Slavic peoples in the polyglot Cleveland diocese.

Rev. Joseph M. Koudelka [Michael W. Carr. *A History of Catholicity in Northern Ohio*, Press of J.B. Savage, 1903, p. 252]

Koudelka's talents marked him for episcopal ordination and Bishop Horstmann petitioned the Holy See in 1904 for his appointment. Finally in 1907, his nomination as an auxiliary bishop of Cleveland surmounted all of the bureaucratic hurdles and he was consecrated by Horstmann, assisted by Bishop Michael Hartley of Columbus, Ohio and Bishop Joseph Fox of Green Bay. From the outset, it was understood that Koudelka's appointment was for the Slavic peoples of the Cleveland diocese. Moreover, as the sole Bohemian in the American episcopate, he was in constant demand by Bohemian communities around the United States. If Koudelka had "played his cards" correctly, his ascent in the hierarchy might have merited him a large American diocese.

All the adulation he received must have affected Koudelka's judgement. In 1908 he made a mistake that altered his career forever. When his patron, Bishop Ignatius Horstmann, died, Koudelka took the unprecedented step of voting for himself to be on the *terna* for the Cleveland succession. This stunning show of bad manners was noted by Cleveland Chancellor Thomas C. O'Reilly who later disparaged Koudelka's nomination for the see of Toledo created in 1910, by noting to the apostolic delegate, "I don't wish to say a word against his personal character as

I believe that he is a conscientious man, although his conscience allowed him to do what seemed very strange when he voted for himself in 1908 for a place on the Cleveland *terna*. He seems to have no administrative skill." [91]

Koudelka's goose was cooked when the man who did receive the Cleveland appointment, Bishop John P. Farrelly, heard of his auxiliary's brazen behavior. Farrelly, born of the Tennessee aristocracy, had for many years been the spiritual director of the North American College in Rome.[92] Farrelly took an instant dislike of Koudelka because of his poor judgement in the succession issue. It flared to an active hatred when he became suspicious that Koudelka was making common cause with a cadre of priests who had opposed his nomination. Koudelka's frequent trips also annoyed Farrelly, who expected his auxiliary to stay home and help shoulder the burden of confirmations, banquets, and other episcopal duties. Tensions between Farrelly and Koudelka spilled out at a gathering at the cathedral in April 1910, when the two of them engaged in a violent quarrel within earshot of all who lived in the house. Farrelly shouted so loudly at his subordinate that Koudelka left the room "my heart filled with shame and grief." Incensed that his subordinate had left without being dismissed, Farrelly followed him out of the room, bellowing even louder to the consternation of all in the house.[93] It became evident that Farrelly wanted Koudelka out and Koudelka wanted to go, preferably as an ordinary. But he needed to escape any way he could from the jealous and vindictive Farrelly.

A year earlier, Koudelka's name had been placed on the *terna* for the bishopric of San Antonio. (It was a remote dusty place that the somewhat cultured prelate would have found difficult, but he was willing to accept on the principle of "Better to reign in hell than to serve in heaven.") However, he did not receive this post. Increasingly, he took to the road to find sympathetic ears for his difficulties with Farrelly. One of Koudelka's refuges was Milwaukee, where he volunteered his service to the ailing Messmer.[94] Milwaukee seemed just right, with a substantial Slavic population and pockets of Bohemians in Milwaukee and Racine to provide a support network for other work. Messmer listened sympathetically to Koudelka's tales of woe and graciously allowed the prelate to function in the archdiocese. (In the bitter April 1910 exchange, Farrelly had accused his auxiliary of "parading" himself in Wisconsin as his victim.)[95]

In early 1910, rumors of an impending appointment to the post of auxiliary bishop in Milwaukee surfaced.[96] Virtually all the metropolitan sees surrounding Milwaukee—Dubuque, St. Paul, and Chicago—had auxiliary bishops and the need for additional episcopal hands was evident, especially as Messmer's health suffered through much of 1910. At what point the wisdom of selecting Koudelka dawned on Messmer is unknown, but clearly he had some of the characteristics he hoped would work. Koudelka was 60-years-old in 1911—an age that precluded serious consideration for higher office at that time. He would be able to handle not only the Polish language, but a variety of tongues that were already being heard in the archdiocese. He would also be appropriately beholden to Messmer for rescuing him from Farrelly (and Farrelly would be grateful to have gotten rid of the offensive challenge to his absolute authority). Most importantly, he would not be an ethnic Pole, and therefore could not be a rallying point for Polish separatism.

Messmer's consultors in general supported his decision to nominate Koudelka. The only voice of warning was raised by longtime pastor William G. Miller of Waukesha—urging caution. Miller insisted that despite Koudelka's charm and linguistic abilities, he would ultimately be unacceptable to the archdiocese because of his Bohemian ethnic background.[97] Messmer seemed to acknowledge the truth of Miller's critique when, in petitioning the Holy See for Koudelka's transfer in July 1911, he admitted, "I know, that there will be a very great and bitter dissatisfaction among some Polish priests, and through them among the Polish people. But," he hoped, "I think that this will pass away after some time when they hear Bishop Koudelka preach to them in their own Polish language."[98]

Miller's warning was right. Any possibility that Koudelka's appointment would be accepted was wishful thinking. When Koudelka's transfer was announced in Milwaukee on September 6, 1911, the negative reaction was instantaneous.[99] Wenceslaus Kruszka and his half-brother Michael were loud in their disapproval. Interviewed by the *Milwaukee Daily News*, Wenceslaus commented, "He [the Pope] knew our wishes for a Polish bishop, and I do not think the Pope will so wholly disregard our wishes as to place a Bohemian bishop at the head of our church."[100] On the pages of *Kuryer*, Michael Kruszka laid the appointment to Messmer's "Machiavellian politics."[101] But even more devastating to Messmer's hopes and to Koudelka's future was the dissatisfaction registered by 25 of Messmer's loyal supporters among the Polish clergy—including Hyacinth Gulski and Boleslaus Goral. They drafted a petition that "humbly but emphatically" called on Messmer to appoint a Polish auxiliary to "pacify the present pernicious agitation and restore normal conditions."[102] Wenceslaus Kruszka, emboldened by the swelling discontent with the appointment, went even further. In a speech delivered in Kenosha in December 1911 he declared that "no foreign bishop will enter officially my church, because the Archbishop himself will secure very soon a Polish Bishop in accord with the Pope's promise and wishes, if not, he will kill me and pass over my corpse on the way to my church."[103] The gauntlet had been thrown down. That December, Messmer's chief Polish ally, Hyacinth Gulski, died on Christmas Eve.

Messmer Renews the Struggle

Kruszka's rejection of Koudelka could not go unchallenged. Messmer summoned the priest to his residence and in a series of three meetings insisted that Kruszka undo the damage of his words and publicly declare his willingness to accept Koudelka to his parish. Wenceslaus balked and sought to evade the full impact of what he had said by blaming it on the purported misreporting by a *Kuryer* cub reporter. But by March 1912, however, he was forced to sign a public document admitting his disobedience and retracting his challenge to episcopal authority.

To deal with Michael Kruszka and the forces of the *Kuryer* Messmer issued a pastoral letter condemning the *Kuryer* and Chicago Polish daily, *Dziennik Narodowy*. He even imposed penalties, such as the withholding of sacramental absolution, for any Catholic in Wisconsin who read it. "Should any such Catholics dare to go to confession and communion without confessing or telling to the priest that they still read or keep or subscribe to the papers mentioned, let them understand that by such confession and communion they commit horrible sacrilege," the letter said.[104] Although this did not severely hurt the circulation or financial standing of the paper, it nonetheless created yet another wedge of dissatisfaction in the archdiocese. In retaliation, Michael Kruszka filed a lawsuit against Messmer and the Milwaukee province bishops on February 21, 1913 accusing them of conspiracy and boycott by issuing a letter in violation of Wisconsin statutes that covered injury to business, restraint of will, and pursuit of work. He sought $100,000 in damages. When the civil suit was adjudicated in March 1914, Messmer was compelled to answer questions about the position of the diocese, but court rulings also allowed him to exclude such critical testimony as how he drew up the pastoral letter. Rulings in favor of the bishops were appealed by Michael Kruszka, who eventually gave up the case in 1918. In the long run, the pastoral had a minimal effect on *Kuryer* circulation and revenues.[105]

Messmer received strong support from the Polish clergy in his efforts to punish the Kruszka's for their opposition. At a variety of Polish organizations, on the pages of newspapers and in gatherings of Polish associations, Goral and others defended the archbishop and called down fire and brimstone on the Kruszkas. Some of this emanated from their own personal antipathy to the volcanic and often bullying Wenceslaus. Others detested the lay rebellion advocated in Michael's columns. But this support came at a cost. For as much as some of them disliked Wenceslaus Kruszka, they also had to admit they shared his distaste for Koudelka.

When the Bohemian prelate arrived in 1911, there was little public celebration. Polish priests, on either side of the controversy with the Kruszkas, made it clear that even though he spoke their language, he was not one of them. Koudelka must have been aware of these hard feelings before he came. No doubt Messmer had been warned by Farrelly of Koudelka's penchant for the open road (and Koudelka's use of his episcopal dignity for fund-raising). Messmer attempted to tie the bishop down by making him pastor of Ss. Peter and Paul Church on Milwaukee's upscale East side, hoping the large and prosperous parish would appeal to Koudelka. Koudelka at first seemed to relish the opportunity to resume parish work and immediately developed plans to build a new school for the parish.[106] However, as the Cleveland chancellor had observed, Koudelka had no gifts for administration, and soon turned over day-to-day affairs for the parish to his assistants, including the costly building program. Bored with his parish work and shut out from many of the parishes, Koudelka again hit the road seeking out friendly Bohemian and Slovak communities around the Midwest who welcomed him gladly and gave him some respite from the increasing isolation of Milwaukee. His continued absences were dutifully recorded by the *Catholic Citizen*.[107] Eventually Messmer began to resent his auxiliary's absences from his parish and from the round of confirmations and other episcopal duties Koudelka had gladly taken before he was assigned to Milwaukee. By the end of 1912, it was clear to Messmer that he had erred in bringing Koudelka to Milwaukee, and he was eager to be rid of the wandering prelate.

An opportunity presented itself in 1913 when Bishop Augustine Schinner turned in his resignation as head of the Superior diocese. Messmer urged Roman authorities to appoint Koudelka to the vacant Superior See.[108] Koudelka accepted the inevitable and even tried to make the best of it by claiming that, at age 60, he was now too old to go traveling too much and wanted his own diocese. He was installed in Superior in the summer of 1913 and remained as bishop until his death in 1921. Koudelka's subsequent career was wormwood and gall. He quarreled bitterly with the priests of the diocese, and the Consistorial Congregation (the Roman office in charge of bishops) took away his favorite safety valve, travel, and insisted that he remain in residence in the diocese, even during the bitter winter months.[109] Koudelka spent long periods raising funds for a huge orphanage for the city of Superior. He also built himself an elegant, but drafty house—to the consternation of his priests.

By 1915 things had become so bad that Messmer urged the Holy See to remove

[AAM]

STATE OF WISCONSIN

IN SUPREME COURT

JANUARY TERM, 1916 — No. 17

KURYER PUBLISHING COMPANY, a Corporation,
Plaintiff and Appellant,

vs.

SEBASTIAN G. MESSMER, JAMES SCHWEBACH, FREDERICK EIS, JOSEPH J. FOX, and AUGUSTINE F. SCHINNER,
Defendants and Respondents.

BRIEF FOR RESPONDENTS ON MOTION TO DISMISS APPEAL

This is a motion to dismiss an appeal from an order of the Circuit Court of Milwaukee County, Honorable Lawrence W. Halsey, judge presiding, limiting the examination of the defendant Most Reverend Sebastian G. Messmer, *after issue joined,* under Section 4096.

This is an action brought against the above named defendants on account of a pastoral letter issued by them as Catholic Archbishop and Bishops of the Province of Milwaukee, including the State

Koudelka and make him a kind of floating apostolic missionary for Slavic Catholics in the United States and Canada.[110] This the Holy See rejected and Koudelka was truly condemned to spend the rest of his days in Wisconsin's northernmost city, surrounded by priests who hated him. He came to detest Superior so intensely that before he died on June 24, 1921, he insisted that his remains be carried back to his beloved Cleveland so that he could be interred near his parents.

Even before Koudelka was sent to Superior, Messmer finally understood it was time for a Polish auxiliary, and asked Rome for one. In November 1913, the nomination of Father Edward Kozlowski was announced. Kozlowski was born November 21, 1860, a native of Tarnow, in the Austrian partition of Poland. After his classical and gymnasium training, Kozlowski was compelled to do the mandatory military service that many Poles escaped to America to avoid. He served one year in the Austrian army and in 1885 came to America at the age of 24, settling first in Chicago and then making his way to St. Francis Seminary in Milwaukee. Here he began studies for the priesthood for the diocese of Grand Rapids, Michigan. Ordained in June 1887, he was assigned first to a multiethnic parish in Midland, Michigan, which had one time been an Irish church. His gifts as a conciliator were first used in East Saginaw, Michigan, at a parish that had been closed by Bishop Henry Richter because of violence. In 1889, after pacifying the Saginaw parish, he was sent to an even more violent parish, St. Joseph in Manistee, Michigan. He remained at Manistee for nearly 10 years and in 1900 was sent to St. Stanislaus in Bay City. This parish had been in an uproar for nearly two years and was surrounded by heavily armed guards. Shots had been fired at the pastor who barely escaped with his life. Kozlowski calmed the situation and presided over the formation of two parishes in the city for the Poles, St. Hedwig and St. Hyacinth. Likewise, he helped to procure land and establish places for new

Rev. Augustine Schinner [AAM]

Polish churches in the diocese of Grand Rapids.[111]

But Kozlowski's chief strength, and his appeal to Messmer, was that he was able to negotiate between the demands of Poles in Grand Rapids and the authority of a German bishop, Henry Richter. Messmer sought Kozlowski as the perfect solution to his problems—a bishop the Poles could accept (most of his clergy knew Kozlowski from Polish organizations and the informal network of priests in the Polish "league"), while at the same time one who would understand and work under his authority. Yet, with the Kozlowski appointment, Messmer finally had to accept the fact that he could no longer be considered the absolute authority in his own ecclesiastical domain. Kozlowski would in fact become the center of episcopal gravity for Milwaukee's Polish communities. But as a trade-off, Kozlowski undercut much of the bitterness directed toward Messmer, helped him to avoid the increasingly bitter and unpleasant Polish parish confirmations, and gave some visible support to his supporters in the Polish clergy.

Kozlowski however had made some powerful enemies. Even before Koudelka left for Superior (he would drag his departure out until November), Messmer had Apostolic Delegate Giovanni Bonzano secure opinions about Kozlowski from various sources. His own ordinary, Henry Joseph Richter, praised him as a peacemaker. Boleslaus Goral commended him as "bright, very intelligent, uncommonly eloquent, and conscientious ... a staunch Polish patriot ... although characterized as an adherent of the policy of 'German Bishops.'"[112] But the investigation and Kozlowski's ascent to episcopal ordination was stopped in its tracks when his enemies began to pepper the delegate with stories of clerical extravagance, and that he was a former member of the Carmelite order. Most damning, they raised allegations of sexual misconduct. The source of the worst allegations was a Father Bieniawski of St. Joseph in Manistee who informed Bonzano that Kozlowski had sired at least one and possibly two sons by his housekeeper, Mrs. Valeria Kraskowska, one of whom had become a priest himself.[113] Kozlowski had apparently known Mrs. Kraskowska since his student days in Tarnow and brought her over to serve as his housekeeper when he was ordained. Bienanowski claimed that local Polish papers had carried stories about Kozlowski meeting Kraskowska in a Detroit hotel for liaisons. The stories halted the official naming of Kozlowski. The nomination was frozen until Bonzano received exculpatory evidence from Bishop Joseph Schrembs of Toledo. Schrembs wrote that Bienanowski was part of cabal of priests (among whom was listed Kruszka) opposed to Kozlowski.[114] He shot down the story of misconduct with a simple exercise in math. He informed the delegate that if the story were true, Kozlowski would have had to impregnate Mrs. Kraskowska when he was 14-years-old, since there was only a 15 year age difference between Kozlowski and the young priest accused of being his "son." On September 30, the objections were swept away and Bonzano informed Messmer that he finally had a Polish auxiliary. On October 13, 1913, the *Sentinel* leaked the story of the Kozlowski nomination.[115] Messmer released the official news in mid-November.[116]

Kozlowski was consecrated on January 14, 1914 amidst general jubilation.[117] Like Koudelka, Messmer gave his new auxiliary a parish assignment, posting him as the pastor of the oldest Polish church in the city, St. Stanislaus.[118] In effect, he became Messmer's chief conduit to the Poles. Kozlowski worked hard to heal some of the wounds of the past years, reaching out especially to Wenceslaus Kruszka whose parish he visited and upon whom he lavished praise for his work in agitating for Polish bishops. Messmer left Kozlowski in charge of the diocese when he departed for a visit abroad in 1914. Kozlowski convened a council of Polish priests to help straighten out discrepancies in their salaries (the Polish priests got less from their parishes than their non-Polish clerical counterparts), he endorsed efforts to perpetuate the Polish language, and he called for more Polish bishops.

One final piece of the Polish controversy was the possibility of Roman Catholics joining the Polish National Church, headed by Francis Hodur. Although there were similarities between Hodur and Kruszka (both used an equally strong invective against the oppression of Poles and shared a strong love for Polish language and culture as the mediums of Catholicism), historian Joseph Wieczerak compared the two of them to Luther and Erasmus. One, Hodur, was a radical willing to bring his beliefs to their logical conclusion by breaking with the Roman Church, the other, Kruszka, came close but ultimately was not willing to abandon the Church of his youth.[119]

Polish national churches developed around Milwaukee led by Polish national priest, Francis Bonczerak. One of the most serious sites of Polish national strength was in the industrial suburb of South Milwaukee where St. Adalbert's Church was the center of activities. Disaffected Poles had formed the church in 1897 under the leadership of a schismatic priest named Olszewski who had been ordained by old Catholic bishop Rene Villatte.[120] Factional infighting at the church continued through 1897, but eventually the majority of the parish decided to join the archdiocese and in particular submit to the regulations regarding church incorporation.[121] However, the parish would be subjected to periods of internal disorder related to fi-

Rev. Edward Kozlowski [AAM]

nances and the election of parish officers. In 1913, Messmer placed the congregation under interdict.[122]

Although Messmer expected it at any time (and suggested it occasionally to Roman authorities) Wenceslaus Kruszka never left the Roman Church for the Polish National Church. Not only was there a matter of visceral loyalty to the Church of Rome, but in addition he and Bonczerak did not get along at all. However Bonczerak managed to attract nearly 1,000 members to his church, and may have siphoned off the most intractable cases from the Polish parishes. The Polish National Church would continue to be a small but influential force in Milwaukee, although never a serious rival for the affections of most Polish Catholics.[123]

Bishop Edward Kozlowski of Milwaukee [AAM]

In August 1915, Polish fortunes in Wisconsin took a turn when Kozlowski died from blood poisoning.[124] His death caused shock waves of genuine sadness. However, the gloom lifted when Peter Paul Rhode came to nearby Green Bay as coadjutor to the ailing Joseph Fox. The appointment of Rhode in September set off another round of rejoicing and Rhode became a regular participant in Polish life in Wisconsin. The Polish Church war ended with a whimper.

As we have described, the fortunes of St. Josaphat's improved considerably. In 1914, Conventual Franciscan Father Felix Baran was assigned to the church. He remained at the post until 1942, when he died while offering a Mass for the parish youth in service. Baran wiped out the remaining $272,000 debt that Fudzinski had refinanced after the Franciscans had taken over.[125] Between 1926 and 1927 artist Gonippo Raggi decorated the church's vast interior with frescoes and paintings depicting scenes from the life of St. Francis and other subjects. In 1931, the church that tottered on bankruptcy was elevated to the status of a minor basilica. Baran, known for his exquisite good taste and his devotion to the poor, became a fixture in the neighborhood. After his death, the community named a nearby park in his honor, one of the few

Catholic priests in Milwaukee to receive such a tribute.[126]

The Kruszkas also went on to more peaceful pursuits. The *Kuryer* remained on the list of forbidden reading materials, but after the death of Michael Kruszka in 1918 the paper lost its combative edge. Father Wenceslaus Kruszka remained at St. Adalbert's and built a magnificent neo-Romanesque church in the early 1930s. When he died after Thanksgiving in 1937, more than 10,000 persons filed past his bier at St. Adalbert's.[127] Meanwhile, as a result of reforms imposed by Messmer, the seminary turned out younger priests of all nationalities who were far more docile than their predecessors. Polish parishes coexisted in a kind of informal league, presided over by a senior pastor of a large parish.

Although Messmer kept Boleslaus Goral at his side as a member of his unofficial "kitchen cabinet," Messmer never really felt comfortable with the Polish element in the archdiocese and few other Polish clerics were allowed to come close to archdiocesan administration. This changed dramatically when Archbishop Stritch came to power. In 1931, he appointed Father Anthony F. Makowski, a curate at St. Vincent de Paul's Church, as his personal secretary. When Makowski was dispatched to Rome in 1933 for graduate studies, he was replaced by Father, later auxiliary bishop, Roman Atkielski, an assistant at St. Stanislaus, who would remain a fixture of archdiocesan life until his death in 1968. Father John Wieczorek, an assistant at St. Hyacinth's was also sent to Rome for canon law studies. [128] Stritch also occasionally intervened in seminary affairs to the favor of Polish seminarians. He angered seminary director Aloysius Muench in late 1934 when he suspended seminary rules and allowed seminarians of Goral's St. Hyacinth to leave the campus to attend golden jubilee celebrations at the parish. (Goral had personally asked for the seminarian's attendance.) Raging to his diary Muench wrote, "It is generally known that the Archbishop is 'playing up' to the Poles in order to gain their good will."[129] Muench was essentially correct.

St. Adalbert Church, South Milwaukee [AOSF]

Polish Expansion

The Poles continued to build parishes at a fairly rapid rate in the period between 1903 and 1945. Polish Catholicism became visible in Kenosha in November 1902 when nearly 3,000 people watched Father Augustine Schinner lay the cornerstone for St. Casimir's Church.[130] Planning for the church had begun in 1898 under the auspices of St. George parish. In 1901 a small group of Polish Kenoshans incorporated themselves and organized the parish in early 1902. Land for a new church was secured on the north side of the city along Washington Road (in those days called Division Street), and the purchase of two lots from a Peter Jacobs were augmented by a "sizeable donation" from bedding manufacturer Zalmon P. Simmons, typical of the interest industrialists felt for the welfare of their workers. In 1909 a school run by the School Sisters of Notre Dame began in conjunction with the parish.

Polish laborers in Racine's burgeoning industrial plants also grew in sufficient number to warrant their own parish. Like their Kenosha compatriots, they had found their first spiritual home in the German Holy Name's and St. Mary's parishes. St. Stanislaus had begun with the formation of a Polish devotional society, the Holy Name Society. This group organized scattered Polish Catholics throughout the 1890s and imported clergy to celebrate Mass and hear confessions. One of these occasional visitors, Father Joseph Chylewski, became the first resident pastor. Masses were held in St. Mary's Hall by visiting priests. In 1906 Messmer assigned Chylewski full-time to organize the new parish. Fund-raising took time, but in 1907 a combination church and school costing $16,000 was planned and finally opened on February 24, 1908 at ceremonies directed by Archbishop Messmer. In 1915, the Polish Sisters of St. Joseph from Stevens Point opened the school. By 1936, the church had grown enough to secure the services of a second priest. Father Anthony Czaja.[131]

In Milwaukee, Polish growth and presence took a major step forward when Father Hyacinth Gulski convinced the Polish Sisters of St. Felix of Cantalice, popularly known as the Felicians, to come to Milwaukee to staff a new Polish orphanage.[132] St. Joseph's orphanage was built on vacant land between 18th and 20th and Euclid and Ohio Streets on Milwaukee's south side. The sisters, who already had Wisconsin outposts in Polonia and Manitowoc, were reluctant at first, but eventually Gulski's good will won them over. They contributed $14,000 they had received in a bequest from a Polish priest in Pittsburgh to purchase the land on which St. Joseph Orphan Asylum would be constructed. Ground was broken in April 1907. Designed by Milwaukee architect H. Esser, the three-story red brick building was 150-feet long and 85-feet wide.[133] In May 1908, 46 boys and 39 girls were welcomed into the orphanage. In 1910, the rapidly growing sisterhood was crowded in its Detroit motherhouse and chose to create a new province central in Milwaukee. Milwaukee was chosen, the Felician historian suggests, because there the sisters encountered little rivalry with other

Parish	Year Founded	Church Built	School Begun	Sisters
St. John Kanty	1907	1907	1907	SSND
St. Adalbert	1908	1909/1931	1909	SSND/SSJ
St. Barbara	1921	1924/1960	1924	SSJ
St. Alexander	1925	1926/1967	1926	Felicians
St. Helen	1925	1927	1927	Felicians
St. Mary Magdalene	1925	1926	1925	Felicians
Blessed Sacrament	1927	1927	1927	SSND

Table 3-1

Polish sisterhoods in the continual competition for aspirants.[134] The Mother of Good Counsel Province remained in Milwaukee until 1924, when it transferred itself to Chicago, after having taken over a number of parish schools. In the meantime, however, the Felicians became an important element of the stable Polish community on the south side of Milwaukee. In 1910, they accepted the teaching responsibilities in the Polish parish of Holy Family in Cudahy. Other Polish parishes in the vicinity of their orphanage and motherhouse were also accepted: St. Mary Magdelene (1925), St. Alexander (1926) and St. Helen (1927). Later, these sisters would build St. Francis Hospital across the street from St. Alexander parish.

Important growth continued in the northern part of the city, as a portion of St. Casimir was broken off to form St. Mary Czestachowa in 1907. In the same year, another West Allis parish, St. Joseph's, was incorporated. Disagreements over where to locate the parish slowed its actual formation, but by 1908 a permanent pastor was appointed, and a new church at 64th and Mitchell Streets was begun. Notre Dame sisters came to tend the school that was commenced in the combination church, school, and convent building. By 1925, the parish had grown sufficiently to construct a new church building and to expand its school and church hall.[135]

The remainder of Polish parishes were on the south side of Milwaukee, many of them running along either side of Oklahoma Avenue, which cut from east to west across the entire city. (See Table 3-1.)

The creation of Polish parishes reflected both the maturation of the Polish community and its extension south of Lincoln Avenue. The parish histories that describe the details of the founding of these parishes virtually all refer to the "piggyback" effort each parish made to help launch the other. For example, Ss. Cyril and Methodius collected funds for the building of St. Alexander and St. Helen parishes.

Christmas at St. Joseph Orphanage [Kwasniewski Collection, Archives, UWM Libraries]

Other "Catholicisms"

Other groups of Slavs from southern and central Europe joined the mix of nationalities transforming the face of the archdiocese of Milwaukee around the turn of the century. These migrants from the polyglot Austro-Hungarian empire were recruited first for the heavy mining and industrial work in Pennsylvania, especially Scranton, Reading, and Pittsburgh, as well as heavy labor in Youngstown and Cleveland. Eventually, Wisconsin's booming industries brought them to the shores of Lake Michigan. Slovak Catholics were not numerous at first, and early Slovaks formed a mutual benefit society, First Catholic Slovak Union, *Jednota*, in 1890. Slovaks tended to identify with Bohemian parishes like St. John de Nepomuc in Milwaukee. In 1907, a group of Slovak parishioners at St. John de Nepomuc came together to form St. Stephen's parish at 5th and W. Walnut Street. A school was established there in 1913 which grew rapidly.

Drill Team and Supreme Officers of the First Catholic Slovak Ladies Union, St. Stephen Martyr Church, Milwaukee [AAM]

In 1932 Conventual Franciscans of the Our Lady of Consolation Province took over the ministry at St. Stephens. Already in 1930, the congregation had outgrown the small church and school site; moreover, as the Bohemians had before them, the community also sought to distance itself from the African American community in that part of Milwaukee. Twenty lots were purchased at North 55th and 56th Streets between Leon Terrace and West Congress Streets. However, Archbishop Stritch disliked the parcel because it was riddled by alleys and streets and was not capacious enough for a single parish plant. Moreover, he was reluctant to permit any new building in the midst of the Great Depression, and he refused permission for the parish to relocate. Archbishop Moses E. Kiley found a way out of the impasse by purchasing a new plot that suited the purposes of church and school building. He offered the parish this block between North 50th and 51st Streets and between West Hope and West Marion for $16,000. The parish accepted the offer and, in an amazing display of solidarity, the 20 lots were sold to parishioners who relocated to be near the new church. By 1953, the parish had a new church.[136]

Under similar circumstances, Slovak parishes were created in 1908 in Cudahy (St. Joseph's), in 1910 in Kenosha (St. Anthony's) and in 1914 in Racine (Holy Trinity). St. Stephen's and St. Joseph's both created schools, while the Racine and Kenosha parishes held off school building until after World

War II. Slovak Catholics maintained a strong group identity for many years, reinforced by their mutual aid societies and also by celebrations that linked them with their co-religionists in Europe. For example, in 1934 Milwaukee Slovaks celebrated the 1,100th anniversary of the Christianization of Slovakia by Prince Pribina. This elaborate event on the grounds of St. Francis Seminary included representatives from the Slovak parishes in the see. Organizers dragged Bishop Augustine Schinner out of retirement to preside at the event and even managed to snare Governor Albert G. Schmedeman.[137]

Lithuanian parishes opened in Kenosha (St. Peter, 1903), Sheboygan (Immaculate Conception, 1903), Racine (St. Casimir, 1910), and Milwaukee (St. Gabriel,1913). Slovenian Catholics formed parishes in West Allis (St. Mary Help of Christians, 1909), Sheboygan (Ss. Cyril and Methodius, 1910) and Milwaukee (St. John the Evangelist, 1916). The most interesting transformation took place at the German bastion of Holy Trinity in Walker's Point. Throughout the 1920s the composition of the neighborhood changed as prosperous Germans moved out to new homes and left behind housing for Slovenians who worked in nearby factories. One person who did stay to watch this metamorphosis was publisher William George Bruce, who watched the parish change from one that spoke German, to English, and then to Slovenian and Croatian. In 1935, after the retirement of longtime pastor William Haberstock, the Conventual Franciscan Friars, who spoke Slovenian and other Eastern European languages, took over the parish.[138]

On 7th and Galena Streets, Croatian Catholics purchased an old German Lutheran church and began Sacred Heart Croatian Church in 1917. A second gathering of Croatians in West Allis formed St. Augustine parish in 1928. Both of these parishes were served by an array of diocesan clergy imported by the chancery to serve the needs of the people—with greater or lesser degrees of success. Finally, in 1930, Franciscans from the Croatian Commissariat of Chicago accepted an invitation to come to Milwaukee to assume control of both parishes.

Rounding the medley of parishes was a church for Syrians, St. George, established in 1915. Likewise Hungarians, who began to turn up in sizeable numbers around 1919,

St. George Church, Syrian Rite [AAM]

began to worship at St. Francis parish at 4th and Brown. In 1928 Father Michael Plale, who spoke Magyar, gathered the scattered community to his assigned church at St. Joseph and ministered to them. Later Father John J. Nemon arrived and organized a separate church. The Hungarians worshiped briefly at St. George Syrian Church, but in 1933 scraped together enough money to build their own church at 107 17th Street. St. Emeric's, as it was named, was the first Hungarian church in Wisconsin.[139] The Milwaukee Hungarians were fortunate to be able to organize their parish. Similar efforts to create a new parish for a contingent of Hungarians in Racine were turned down by Archbishop Messmer and Chancellor Bernard Traudt.

St. Gabriel Church, Milwaukee [AAM]

A Portrait of Parish Life

The patterns of development were quite similar to those in other ethnic enclaves: organization, fund-raising and community building (socials, fairs, and bazaars), the celebration of ethnic devotions and customs brought over from the old world—and periodic conflict.

Conflict arose between parishioners and clergy over the use of money, the location of the church site and the admission of people to sacraments. For example, the church historian of the 40th anniversary of Sacred Heart Croatian parish spoke of the three groups within the parish that divided it terribly in its first years, "One group wanted the church on the south side and purchased a piece of land there. The second group wanted the church on the north side and they purchased a church and rectory at 7th and Galena Streets." In addition, he wrote of a third group, "who were against the church [and] did whatever they could to disunite the parishioners. These anti-churchers even managed to get on the church committee and annoy the pastor and parishioners."[140] There was a constant coming and going of pastors who got caught in the crosshairs of these disputes and who often sided with one faction or another. One pastor, Charles Soric, lasted barely six months (June to December 1918). Internal wrangling among Milwaukee's Slovenian Catholics erupted over the location of St. John the Evangelist Church. Originally a Jewish synagogue, the church soon became too small to handle its growing number of Slovenian immigrants who located on the south side. When members of the congregation demanded the right to build a new church in a different location, Messmer and Traudt insisted instead that they relocate to the emptying Holy Trinity Church in Walker's Point.

Occasionally a priest would ban a parishioner from the sacraments if he became "disobedient." Such was the case of Francis Garmus, appointed pastor of Immaculate Conception in Sheboygan. When a Lithuanian family with whom he had clashed attempted to have their daughter married at nearby Holy Name Church, Garmus asked the chancery to stop the proceeding, arguing that the errant parishioner was trying to show him that "a pastor is only a paid servant of the parishioners" and "a man with money can do as he pleases, even with the laws of the church."[141] In a later letter, Garmus described the condition of the Lithuanian parish, "During the 25 years of the parish existence they have had 26 pastors .... In 'changing' pastors the Sheboygan Lithuanians became accustomed to feeling that they were 'bosses' and on my arrival in Sheboygan the treasurer, M. Drasutis, told me that the treasurer of the parish is the 'boss,' for he controls the money and has to see to it that the pastors do no harm to the parish."[142] Garmus eventually surrendered the parish to Father Francis Shlikas, who would lead it into a period of relative calm and stability.

An ethnic disagreement that took place in Kenosha in the 1930s expressed representative "old" and "new" world expectations of parish priest authority, a struggle over the location of community space, and the eventual introduction of religious order priests of a different nationality to calm things down.[143] Holy Rosary of Pompeii parish had been founded in 1904 by Father Joseph Angeletti on the corner of 22nd Avenue and 54th Street in Kenosha. Angeletti, who had been driven from Pompeii parish in Milwaukee, remained a short time and erected a small wooden church in 1905. His successor, Augustino Baudizzone, attempted to build more but failed and returned to Italy in 1913. Another northern Italian, Pietro Perardi, arrived in that year, embellished the wooden church with brick facing, and helped the parish cope with steady growth. But by 1921, he too was deemed unacceptable to the community, and in fact so antagonized parishioners over some detail of church administration that they literally stormed the church and the rectory and sent Perardi fleeing for his safety to nearby St. Thomas Aquinas parish. Messmer placed the parish under interdict in the spring of 1921 and sought to resolve the matter

Immaculate Conception Church, Sheboygan [AAM]

through the intercession of a local Knights of Columbus attorney, Walter C. Burke, and neighboring pastor, Father Francis Pribyl of St Anthony's. The ensuing episode established a pattern between the Italian community of Kenosha and the archdiocese that would replicate itself to some degree in the matter of Father Angelo Simeoni, the next priest at Holy Rosary and the building of a new church.

Messmer was insistent that his rights to appoint clergy be respected and sought a solution that had Perardi come back to the parish for a short time and then be transferred to another location. Burke worked with this proposal and also made efforts to secure Perardi's possessions, locked in the parish rectory. However, Monsignor Traudt grew alarmed at Burke's warnings that active Italian Protestants were waiting in the wings to take advantage of the situation.[144] Moreover, Pribyl's small church was soon overcrowded with Italians seeking the sacraments (the interdict also lasted through the month of July when their traditional festival in honor of Our Lady of Mount Carmel was held). Traudt then capitulated to the demands of the faction of the church opposed to Perardi and removed the pastor while handing administrative duties to Pribyl. Pribyl welcomed the dissenters to his church and promised them that all would be done as they wished: Perardi would never return. Burke, who had worked with the case, was never informed of the change and protested in a letter to Traudt.[145] As was his wont, Traudt became truculent with the attorney and attempted to defend the decision not to bring Perardi back, even for a short time.[146] Not in Holy Orders and hence unintimidated by Traudt's bullying tones, Burke replied, "The more I think of the action of Father Pribyl in holding meetings with dissenting Italians and then going to see you entirely unbeknown to Father Perardi, the more thoroughly disgusted I feel. It would certainly be a great breach of ethics among the professional laity and I certainly deem it much more so among the clergy." But Traudt's bad manners aside, Burke was worried over the implications of the archdiocese's capitulation to the violent and abusive tactics of the Italian faction that wanted Perardi out. "It is a matter of fact which cannot be denied," he declared, "that today the dissenters and disturbers of this Congregation feel they have triumphed over the Archbishop and over the Church, and there is absolutely no question in my mind that when they again desire a change in pastors, they will take whatever action they feel like taking and feel assured of attaining a successful end."[147] Burke turned out to be a prophet.

As Perardi departed in 1921, the Italian "colony" of Kenosha was coming into its own as a strong, rather cohesive community, composed mainly of southern Italians (Calabrians). Many of the leaders of the community had found work in Kenosha's developing service economy. Among the members of this enterprising business elite were men like dairyman Leonardo Montemurro, hotelier, Raffaele Molinaro, and grocers Eugene Madrigrano and Frank Vena. Elected officials included men like Nicholas Conforti, who in 1912 was the first Italian on the Kenosha City Council, and Jasper Gentile who would join the city council in 1932 as a representative of the Non-Partisan League. The next priest at Holy Rosary, Angelo Simeoni, would take his place in this mix.[148]

Simeoni, a native of Verona, Italy, had been a priest since 1899 and had come to America at the direction of his religious community, the Stigmatine Order. A community devoted to the service of Italian immigrants, the Stigmatines had sent Simeoni to a parish in Hazelton, Pennsylvania. When Messmer requested Stigmatine assistance at Our Lady of Pompeii in Milwaukee, Simeoni was sent to Wisconsin. Here the priest soon ingratiated himself with Messmer and incardinated into the Milwaukee archdiocese. In 1916, Messmer sent him to St. Joseph Church in Madison where, as we have seen, he built a new church and school for the capital city's Italian colony. When Perardi was sent packing from Kenosha, Simeoni was sent to take his place. (Perardi went to Madison.)

Using a mixture of tyranny and pastoral solicitude, Simeoni took Kenosha by storm. Among his most memorable accomplishments was the formation of popular marching bands and athletic leagues for Italian youth. A skilled musician, he taught all the instruments, raised money for uniforms, and marched the band in every parade and procession he could find. In athletics, he practiced with young athletes, coached games, and encouraged genuine talent where he saw it. The good will he built up with these activities was necessary to counterbalance his occasional harshness. Women wearing sleeveless dresses at weddings would be publicly ordered out of church. His ultimate weapon against any kind of insubordination from parishioners was to refuse them the sacraments. The effect of this on Italian Catholics was often devastating. Children went unbaptized at a time when common Catholic teaching spoke of "limbo" for children who died before baptism. Exclusion from the highly public occasions of First Communion and Confirmation meant that young children had to watch in sadness as their friends and classmates enjoyed the solemnity, feasting, and gift giving of the day. Occasionally parishioners would thumb their noses at Simeoni and repair to the nearby Slovak parish of St. Anthony for their sacraments. But Simeoni complained loudly enough to cease that kind of poaching. The effects of the sacramental boycott were horrifying to Archbishop Stritch, who discovered in 1932 that there were over 100 unbaptized children in Simeoni's parish and over 200 who had not made their First Communion.[149]

The goal of the parish, and Simeoni's personal dream, was to build an elegant new Holy Rosary Church that would be the pride of the Italian people of the city. He squirreled away money that he had raised over the years through various fund-raisers, collections and band performances. Allegedly, he secretly invested these funds in North Shore Bonds, a company owned by the powerful utilities magnate Samuel Insull.

In 1929, the city of Kenosha approached Simeoni with an offer to purchase his church in order to do some necessary street widening on 22nd Avenue, which had become an important automobile thoroughfare. At the same time, the land-wealthy benefactor of several religious denominations, Nash Motors President W. H. Alford, donated several lots at an area 10 blocks north on 22nd Avenue. Recognizing his golden opportunity in this intersection of events, Simeoni announced that the time had come to build the new church. Archdiocesan officials caught wind of the pastor's planning and insisted that he include a school for the new church. Plans ground to a halt when Archbishop Messmer died in August 1930, but the new Archbishop Samuel Stritch, agreed to visit the colony and examine the prospects.

The hiatus created by the episcopal interregnum gave the Italian community of Kenosha time to think about their new church and the question of its location. Commercial leaders of the colony, especially those who had shops and homes near the church, were reluctant to allow one of the community's anchor institutions to move away. Many people did not have cars and public transit was not easily accessible. Many walked to and from the church. Merchants with shops near the church did a lucrative trade after Sunday Mass, when people stopped to pick up ingredients for the traditional Sunday meal.

Simeoni for his part wanted the church in a new neighborhood to symbolize a new prominence and prestige for Kenosha's Italians. The old church was rickety and small—everyone agreed a new one was necessary—and its location was in an area that many believed would soon deteriorate. Moreover, although he had no intention of building the traditional church/school combination in line with what archdiocesan officials wanted, he quite willingly used this directive in his argument for the new site. There was no space for a school on the old site, so Simeoni sold the church property to the city and believed that there was no turning back.

Stritch visited Kenosha in March 1931, shortly after his installation. He was greeted by warm crowds and, speaking in

Holy Rosary Church Band, Rev. Angelo Simeoni behind bass drum [AAM]

passable Italian, promised to return to dedicate the new church. On that night he filled out papers seeking permission from the apostolic delegation for Simeoni to borrow $65,000. He also gave Simeoni permission to draw up plans for a church and school to be built on the Alford property. Stritch reluctantly acceded to Simeoni's desire to build the church first and a school later. The new Holy Rosary Church began to rise on the former Alford Property. The magnificent Renaissance structure, designed by Florentine architect Francesco Banterle, had a striking facade and an imposing bell tower. But nothing would be easy as long as Simeoni was involved. The pastor plunged into his own soap opera of conflict over the construction. Problems dogged the building every step of the way. Simeoni had violent arguments with the church contractor and suppliers. Frequent shouting matches led to delays and court cases.

At the same time the church was being built, discontent with Simeoni's action galvanized a cadre of unhappy parishioners who took matters into their own hands. Anxious to preserve the original site, a stroke of good fortune came their way when they heard that the city had to discontinue the street widening project due to a lack of money (it was the Great Depression). The dissident parishioners pooled their resources and offered the city $2,000 to repurchase the old church.[150] Once the deeds were inked, the group then announced that they would keep the property as a Catholic church and seek another priest to serve at the site. Simeoni was infuriated by these actions and appealed to Stritch for help.[151] The archbishop agreed that Kenosha could not afford two Italian parishes, and sought an easy way out of the feud by offering to pay back the $2,000 the group had spent for the old property. The Kenosha Italians refused.

The hornet's nest surrounding the new church became so agitated by the middle of 1932 that Stritch worried that disaffected Italians might simply choose to quit the church altogether and attend the small brick *Chiesa Evangelica* that had opened up on 52nd Street not far from the parish. Reluctantly, Stritch agreed to allow the dissidents to keep the church as a chapel to the new parish. But by

Holy Rosary Church, Kenosha [AAM]

Holy Rosary Church, Kenosha [AAM]

this time the dissidents would have nothing of a deal that included any ministrations by Simeoni. Raffaele Molinaro, one of the leaders, wrote to Stritch, "The committee has agreed to all the propositions made, and that you come among us Monday to explain to the parishioners. But we have not agreed to continue under that system which places us under the control of Father Simeoni." He concluded ominously, "To attempt to force the people to that will only result in revolt which will end in a civil war. The people ... will not tolerate being under the control of Father Simeoni."[152] Not only would they not accept Simeoni, but they refused to allow him to take precious items of the church's fabric to the new site. When Simeoni went to the old site to transfer a statue of St. Rocco that was especially precious to the community, a parishioner, Arthur LaMacchia, warned him away with the threat of fisticuffs. When Simeoni backed down, LaMacchia crowed to the mob that their side "was victorious." Indeed, they had won. The group named the former Holy Rosary Church in honor of Our Lady of Mount Carmel and set up a special bank account to hold monies collected for it from those who remained.

Now, despite Stritch's efforts, Kenosha had two Italian parishes. Simeoni tried one last time to assert authority over the situation by locking the old church door and limiting the number of religious services he would conduct (no weddings, funerals or baptisms, just Sunday Mass), but this further inflamed matters. Finally, the bedraggled pastor went to his native Italy for a rest and Stritch used his absence to calm the situation by sending Vicar General Joseph Barbian to find a solution. When Simeoni returned, he found that Stritch had again capitulated to the demands of the dissidents by assigning assistant priests who covered the religious ministry of the mission. One was an Italian, Gino Ferrari, who managed to win the good will of the dissidents. Simeoni had him ejected and Stritch sent two American-born priests, Francis Karwata and Oswald Krusing, to help. Both of them Simeoni treated with contempt and ordered his parish trustees not to pay them or give them room and board. Karwata simply left. Krusing took up residence at the local Catholic hospital, where the Dominican sisters fed and boarded him. Since Simeoni would not assign him duties at Holy Rosary, Krusing worked exclusively at the old church, saying Masses, baptizing, and even setting up a religious education program. The dissidents loved him. Finally, Simeoni agreed to leave the parish permanently and Stritch brought in German Augustinians who spoke Italian to administer Holy Rosary. The Mount Carmel Chapel was to remain a mission of Holy Rosary, but could not have its own pastor.[153]

In the final episode of the drama, the Italians of Mount Carmel Mission "imprisoned" the now popular Oswald Krusing in the old parish rectory. Krusing seemed to love the attention and the people would cheer whenever he came to the window.[154] Eventually the young priest was "freed" by Monsignor Barbian, who showed up with two Kenosha County sheriffs, and the matter ended peacefully. The next Sunday the Augustinians appeared at the mission for Sunday Mass, and calm was restored to the turbulent Italian colony. The mission of Our Lady of Mount Carmel was permitted as a "temporary" solution until passions calmed. The hope was that eventually it would close due to demographic shifts and the deterioration of the building. As late as 1942, Archbishop Kiley was warning communicants at the mission not to raise funds for a new church or to launch aggressive membership drives.[155]

But always underneath the surface of the parish was an intense loyalty to the Mount Carmel site and church. In the meantime, the place began to deteriorate and by May 1946 even the Augustinians felt it was time to close the rickety structure.[156] However, once again, vigorous representations were made to Archbishop Kiley, who despite his authoritarian manner was deeply fearful of any kind of public conflict. Like Stritch, he chose an easy way out by assigning an Italian-speaking priest, Father Raymond Leng, to take care of the mission and even raised it to parochial status in 1947. In 1965, Father Salvatore Tagliavia built a new church on a parcel of land across the avenue from the old Mount Carmel belonging to Columbus Park. The Italian heartland in Kenosha remained intact.

But these parishes represented the last grasp of ethnicity from the "old" immigrants—Germans and Irish—and the "new" immigrants—Poles, Italians, southern and eastern Slavs. As the 20th century dawned, two new groups of migrants altered the character of life in Wisconsin, especially in the industrial cities of Racine and Kenosha—African Americans and Latinos.

African American Catholicism in Milwaukee

The African American population of such industrial cities as Milwaukee, Racine, Madison, and Beloit, within archdiocesan boundaries, grew steadily. In Milwaukee it rose from 980 in 1910 to 2,229 in 1920, to 7,501 in 1930, and 12,773 in 1940—the biggest single concentration of African Americans in the state.[157] Most of these new denizens came from the South and were lured by the prospect of industrial jobs. Historian Joe Trotter notes that by 1930, 80 percent of Milwaukee's African American workers held industrial jobs.[158] By 1930, most of Milwaukee's African Americans lived in an area bounded by State Street and North Avenue and between Third and Twelfth Streets. Within these boundaries, they shared life with Slovaks and Croats, both of whom had Catholic churches thereabouts—churches that would soon move as the first instances of Catholic "white flight."

Latinos, mostly Mexicans, arrived in significant numbers in Milwaukee in the 1920s, largely recruited by the labor agents of the Pfister and Vogel Tanneries who brought 100 young Mexican males to work in the South Side Tannery. This nucleus of workers soon expanded, and in 1930, census figures pegged their numbers at 1,479. However, as historian John Gurda notes, this was certainly an undercount. The Young Men's Christian Association calculated a population of 4,000 Latinos. The Latino contingent grew slowly, but it would ultimately emerge as the most dynamic elements of Milwaukee's growth by the 1990s.

Both of these communities developed lively subcultures in Wisconsin cities. In Milwaukee's African American community there were newspapers (the *Milwaukee Enterprise,* later the *Enterprise Blade*), a chapter of the Urban League, a savings and loan, and various social and entertainment centers. Within the Latino section of the city, mostly in the old Walker's Point neighborhood on the south side, a similar array of social clubs, businesses, and a newspaper developed. For both communities, a key social institution was the church. For African Americans, St. Mark's African Methodist Episcopal Church had been a force on the Milwaukee landscape since 1869. In 1895, Calvary Baptist was opened and Greater Galilee and Mt. Zion Baptist were commenced in 1919. In the Latino community the Catholic church was the anchor of community life.

The response of Catholics to these two new communities was mixed. The Bohemian Catholics of St. John de Nepomuc, located in Milwaukee's sixth ward, found themselves increasingly "surrounded" by African Americans and watched church attendance and school populations decline. In response they relocated their church to Sherman Park in the 1920s. Likewise, racial change was behind the move of St. Stephen's Slovak Church on Galena Street. Catholics in Milwaukee viewed their parish boundaries also as racial boundaries. Eventually, the steady growth of African Americans, especially during and after World War II, transformed the north side of Milwaukee and

Milwaukee industry, Pfister & Vogel Tanner (center image) [Milwaukee Real Estate Board. *Milwaukee. 100 Photogravures,* Art Gravure & Etching Co., 1892]

reworked the demographics of Catholic life in the see city.

The Latino presence was strongest on the south side. As they grew, Latino Catholics eyed the property of St. John the Evangelist Church on 4th and Mineral and inquired about purchasing the church when it was rumored that the Slovenians might move out.

Ministry to African Americans

The origins of Catholic ministry to Milwaukee's African American community can be traced back to 1886 when a white layman named Charles Boetting began working among the small black community in the heart of the city.[159] Boetting brought together a handful of black Catholics to worship at old St. Gall's Church on North 2nd Street and West Michigan Avenue. However, Boetting's efforts transgressed on the turf of the local Jesuits who ran St. Gall's, and he left the city abruptly. (One of the things that inflamed the Jesuits was that Boetting would don a cassock and surplice and deliver "sermons" to the African Americans as though he were a cleric or a priest.) St. Gall's eventually merged with another Jesuit-run congregation, Holy Name on 11th and West State Streets becoming the nucleus of yet another parish named Gesu on 12th and Wisconsin. When Gesu opened its doors in the winter of 1894, black Catholics were urged to attend. However, as they had been at St. Gall's, they were compelled to sit in the gallery. Moreover, Gesu was farther removed from their residences than Holy Name. Racial discrimination also nettled the small group, some of whom had contributed to a chandelier in the new church.

In 1908, an African American Catholic layman, Captain Lincoln C. Valle and his wife Julia, arrived in Milwaukee to take up work among the city's African American community. Lincoln Valle had been an important figure at the Catholic Negro Congresses of the late 19th century and was very active in organizing African American Catholics in Chicago. Shortly after marrying Julia Yoular, Captain Valle headed for Milwaukee to bring Catholicism to African Americans.

The Valles presented themselves to Archbishop Sebastian Messmer who warmly welcomed them and helped them establish a storefront chapel at 530 State Street named in honor of St. Benedict the Moor.[160] Father Nicholas Becker of old St. Mary's also lent a helping hand, celebrating Mass and organizing activities to draw the community together. Only a small handful of black Catholics remained from Boetting's earlier ministrations, and much of the Valle's work involved person-to-person recruiting for the parish and giving instructions leading to baptism or full reception into the church. In December, the *Catholic Citizen* reported, "For the first time in the history of the city, a class of Negroes received First Communion at the mission of St. Benedict the Moor."161 Year after year, the papers carried accounts of large numbers of black converts to Catholicism, virtually all as a result of the efforts of the Valles. They also began a short-lived newspaper called the *Catholic Truth* and opened an employment bureau as well. Valle wrote of

Lincoln Valle [AAM]

his efforts in Milwaukee in a letter to Josephite Father Justin McCarthy: "Our work is moving along nicely here. In fact the success of this work, through my efforts as a layman, has startled this part of the country. I have had the entire management of the work."[162] Valle begged the nearby Capuchin fathers to assist with daily Mass (Becker could no longer help after a while), and he secured the services of the School Sisters of Notre Dame to teach at a Sunday school for the growing number of African American children brought to the mission by their parents. Valle wanted an African American priest to tend to the mission, but in 1911 the Capuchins volunteered their services. With the "take-over" by the Capuchins, the mission was supplied with steady clergy and financial support. Capuchin resources made it possible to move the mission from its storefront site to a location at 1041 North 9th Street.[163] In the next year, the School Sisters of Notre Dame opened a small day school for black children. The Valle's continued their work into 1913 with Mrs. Valle and the Notre Dame sisters opening a trade school for women giving instructions in plain and fancy sewing, embroidering and crocheting.[164] Eventually lay-clergy tensions erupted between the Valles and the Capuchins who like most priests of their time would not abide lay "meddling" in church affairs (especially those dealing with the sacraments). The Valles left the city. A bitter aftermath was the circulation of unsubstantiated rumors that the Valles had misappropriated funds and that the Captain had abused alcohol. Passions subsided, however, and when Lincoln Valle visited the mission again in 1927, he was warmly received by both students and staff.

The Capuchins bought property around the 9th Street location, which was quite close to a large Lutheran church and across from Marquette Academy. In 1912 Valle and the Capuchin pastor began canvassing the neighborhoods for potential recruits for a new school.[165] In 1913, Father Stephen John Eckert, O.F.M., Cap., became the first permanent resident pastor of St. Benedict the Moor mission.[166] Eckert took up the cause of the school, going door-to-door and soliciting African Americans to come to the mission and the day school. In mid-August 1913, he wrote his superior, "I have seen within the last few days, over two hundred colored faces .... They all received me, with a few exceptions, most cordially." Part of the admission to the school was a requirement that children take lessons in the Catholic faith. As a result of this there were a number of conversions.

In 1913, he took into his private residence three orphaned children who also attended the school and these became the nucleus of the boarding school. Eckert soon expanded the boarding school, believing that it was a superior way to educate black youth, whom he thought needed "deliverance" from their environment. Eckert believed, as historian Cyprian Davis has observed of other

Rev. Stephen Eckert, OFM Cap. [AAM]

white priests, in a "paternalistic conception of their [African-Americans] lack of moral fiber."[167] While other priests attributed these "deficiencies" to the debilitating effects of slavery, Eckert attributed them to the deplorable conditions of the urban ghettoes of the north. Appealing for funds from Mother Katherine Drexel, a benefactress of African American Catholics, he described the poor conditions of Milwaukee's sixth ward, where most African Americans lived. "So many live in unfavorable surroundings and … so many are left at sea owing to marriage ties being broken."[168] So intent was Eckert on removing the children from the baleful influences of the city and their broken homes that he nearly wrecked the mission when he moved the school from downtown Milwaukee to a remote location in Corliss (today Sturtevant) in Racine County, where he set up in buildings left vacant by a failed girls academy of the Dominican sisters. One year in the country was enough for Eckert, and he returned to Milwaukee. He had lost the services of the Notre Dame sisters, however, but he managed to persuade Mother Romana Thom of the Dominicans to send a contingent of sisters to work at the school.

Chagrined by the failure of the Corliss venture and warned by Mother Romana that he had to make adequate living provisions for the sisters in order to keep them, Eckert hit the road preaching and doing nonstop fundraising for the mission. He contracted the influenza and died in February 1923 and was interred in Calvary Cemetery.[169] Later when it appeared that his cause for beatification and canonization were being pressed by the

Mother Romana Thom, OP, with children at St. Benedict the Moor Church, Milwaukee [AOP-Rac]

St. Benedict the Moor Church, Milwaukee [AAM]

Capuchins, he was disinterred and re-buried in a tomb next to St. Benedict the Moor Church. His large white marble statue that towers over his grave stands as a lonely reminder of the burly Capuchin who had built on the strong foundations laid by the Valles.

After an interim pastorate, the second most important Capuchin pastor, Father Philip Steffes, came to the leadership of St. Benedict Mission in 1923. Steffes, who would serve as pastor until his death in 1950, was every bit as enthusiastic about the prospects of the mission as Eckert, but he was a bit more realistic. Steffes brought many of Eckert's dreams to reality.[170] In 1924 a chance meeting with brewing mogul Ernest G. Miller, brought a donation of $50,000, a sum large enough to complete a Romanesque-style church designed by Erhard Brielmaier.[171] The church, which had been commenced the year before, was dedicated by Messmer in early March.[172] A solitary statue of St. Benedict the Moor adorned the walls, and by October it was joined by a relief carved from a block of wood by Ermano Moroder, a Tyrolese. This 10-by-12 foot relief depicted the 22 Ugandan martyrs who had been beatified (they would be canonized by Pope Paul VI in 1967) and was set against an exquisite altar that replicated features of the private papal altar in the Vatican's Pauline Chapel.[173] This was only the beginning of the generosity of the Miller family. In 1925, when the Jesuits abandoned the old Marquette Academy for their new building on 35th and Wisconsin, Miller gave the Capuchins $125,000 to purchase the site.[174] This enabled them to expand the school, especially the boarding facilities. Miller asked only that he be acknowledged publicly and that the children of the mission pray for his healing of some malady that kept him in warmer climates for much of the winter. Under Steffes and the Dominicans, the academic program of the school developed. A two-year commercial course was offered, and a full-fledged high school program was set in place in 1938. Enrollments went as high as 400, Catholics and Protestants, and at one time from all parts of the country.

The school influenced Milwaukee life as much as the AME and Baptist churches. St. Benedict's graduates entered professional careers in law, sports, journalism, politics and music. Among the significant alumni were Chicago Mayor Harold Washington, entertainer Redd Foxx and musician Lionel Hampton (who claimed he learned his musical skills from one of the Dominican sisters). The program of conversions which was at the heart of the Valles and the Capuchins continued, and scores of children and their parents were baptized.[175] As with all "conversion" programs, the long term effect of the change varied from person to person. Some abandoned Catholic practice, others remained lifelong adherents. African American children were also inducted into various aspects of Catholic ritual, including altar serving, May crownings, and liturgical processions. The curriculum of the elementary and high school replicated features at all other Catholic schools. However, the students were also exposed to African American history and celebrated Black History Month every February. Outside speakers included African nationalist Marcus Garvey who visited the school in 1916, and poet Claude McKay, himself a convert to Catholicism. Members of the upper classes were permitted to spend an afternoon with entertainer Bill "Bojangles" Robinson when he appeared at the Riverside Theater. In 1919 a general gathering of the city's African American community took place at St. John's Cathedral auditorium to commemorate the 300th anniversary of the landing of African Americans in America. On this occasion Dr. Wilberforce Williams of Chicago gave a lengthy address dwelling on the history of African Americans in the United States. "We want no privileges, but fair play and justice. The Negro is progressive and aggressive if let alone, but most pugnacious if oppressed." In his address, Wilberforce paid tribute to the Knights of Columbus and the Salvation Army "as they treated all alike, irrespective of race or creed." Other leading Catholics followed Wilberforce to the platform, including William George Bruce, attorney Oliver O'Boyle, and Father Stephen Eckert. It was a unique moment when diverse elements of the Milwaukee community met under Catholic auspices.[176]

Already in the 1920s, Father Philip Steffes hoped to build a hospital close to the parish to complement the mission services provided by St. Benedict. Ernest Miller agreed to help pay for it and Steffes began acquiring plots of land on which to build. Miller had insisted

Ugandan martyrs bas-relief, St. Benedict the Moor Church, Milwaukee [AAM]

St. Benedict the Moor School, Milwaukee [AAM]

that nuns run the hospital, and in 1930 the Franciscan sisters of Little Falls, Minnesota, had just been terminated from Milwaukee's Trinity Hospital on 9th and Wells, so they volunteered for service. In December Steffes laid the cornerstone for a 42-bed hospital, and in May 1931 a cast of ecclesiastical luminaries, including Stritch, Apostolic Delegate Pietro Fumasoni-Biondi and Bishop Richard Gerow, were on hand for the dedication.[177]

Despite these efforts racism tinged Catholic efforts on behalf of African Americans. The good intentions of the Capuchins and others, in a later light, suffered from an offensive paternalism. Although most Capuchins loved and respected the people with whom they lived and worked, they also had a sense of "noblesse oblige" in dealing with "unfortunates." Especially odious were the methods of fund-raising for the school which stressed the poverty and supposed social pathologies of the African-American children and their families. While some children were referred to the school from juvenile courts, many of them came from environments as stable, loving and hard-working as white children. Frustration with paternalism reflected itself in sentiments penned by an African American woman named Beatrice Murphy for *Preservation of the Faith Magazine* reprinted in the archdiocesan weekly in September 1937. Murphy took aim at well-intentioned "liberals," asking them to be sensitive to the subtle stereotyping that often occurred in conversations. "If you want to be my friend," she lectured, "don't tell me about the Negro servant who used to work in your household .... Don't tell me darky and pickaninny stories ... please don't talk dialect to me .... I went to the same schools you did and can understand English perfectly .... Please don't use me as a stepping stone to Heaven by flaunting me in front of your friends, 'See, I've done my good deed for today. I've been seen on the street with a Negro. I've fulfilled my Christian duty ....' And please don't preach salvation to me on one hand ... and then snatch the very bread out of my mouth with the other .... Don't forget that I am a human being first, and Negro second."[178]

The Dominican sisters also reflected contemporary biases in some of their approaches, although they also evolved in their attitudes toward their students. However, African-American girls did not find a welcome in their community ranks—and such would be the case with other religious communities in the Milwaukee Archdiocese as well as at St. Francis

Seminary for many years. African Americans could attend Pio Nono High School, but candidates for the priesthood or religious life were told to find a religious order to respond to their vocations.[179] Such was the case of James Bailey, who attended St. Rose and St. Benedict the Moor schools and then in 1943 entered as a lay brother the Dominican Order headquartered in River Forest, Illinois. Taking the name Brother Edward, he was the first African-American brother in the community's Midwestern Province. He made it through his novitiate and temporary vows, but died at the age of 17, being permitted to take his solemn vows on his deathbed.[180] It was not until 1947 that an African American, Sacred Heart Father Herman A. Porter, was ordained to the priesthood in Milwaukee.[181] An African-American seminarian from Madison, Gerry Mills, was the first to enter St. Francis Minor Seminary in the 1950s. A few others followed Mills, but most African-American students chose to enter the Capuchin seminary at Mount Calvary. The archdiocese of Milwaukee would not have African-American diocesan priests until 1975, when Joseph Perry and Marvin Knighton were ordained. The archbishops of Milwaukee other than Messmer had ambivalent feelings as well. Stritch, a born and bred Southerner, still had rather benighted views about blacks. Moses Kiley's approach to African-American Catholics was to maintain existing patterns of segregation in churches and he resisted early efforts to have blacks move into white parishes as their numbers grew. Albert Meyer was equally remote from the condition of African Americans, in part the result of his own upbringing in a hermetically sealed German-Catholic ecclesiastical seminary world. Meyer had a racial "awakening," but not until he went to Chicago where the size and challenge of African-American issues could no longer be avoided. Still, despite the mixed intentions and results, Catholics attempted to do what they could to work with a new community. Adopting primarily the techniques and standards of the ethnic parish, they were content to allow African Americans to have their own churches, schools and priests. Such would be the case also with the Latino community.

Dominican Sisters with students at St. Benedict the Moor School, Milwaukee [AOP-Rac]

Mexican Catholicism

The outbreak of internal disorders in Mexico between 1917 and 1930 created a wave of refugees to the United States in the 1920s. Specifically, the persecution of Catholics by the regime of President Plutarco Elias Calles between 1923 and 1928 led to an armed uprising of Catholic militants, the "*Cristero* Rebellion," and the exile of hundreds of bishops, priests and nuns fleeing from the closure of churches and other restrictions on Catholic practice. Mexican immigrants to the United States tended to hover close to the borderlands of their nation (Texas, Arizona, New Mexico, and California) and many entered the labor force performing tasks formerly done by immigrants from Europe. (The latter had been excluded by the immigration laws of 1921 and 1924.) Eventually, Mexican Catholic immigrants reached Milwaukee where they worked in tanneries and other industrial jobs.[182]

Catholic outreach to the increasing number of Mexicans on the south side came first from the St. Vincent de Paul Society, which visited Mexican homes and assisted them with food, clothing, and finding jobs.[183] The Knights of Columbus provided opportunities for Mexicans to organize clubs and also offered their facilities for social occasions.[184]

Gravesite of Rev. Stephen Eckert at St. Benedict the Moor Church, Milwaukee [St. Benedict the Moor Church]

The needs of the Mexicans were met largely through the efforts of Frank Gross, one of the more engaging figures of Milwaukee Catholic history. Gross (1888-1980) was a Milwaukeean who operated one of the city's most popular church goods stores, the Church Mart. To cultivate his business, Gross participated actively in Catholic club life. He was active in the St. Vincent de Paul Society, the Knights of Columbus and was later one of the founders of the Serra Club, a society of laymen (later including women) who helped cultivate native vocations to the priesthood. Gross had a deep devotion to Our Lady of Guadalupe and through his connection to the Knights took a keen interest in the struggle of the Catholic Church in Mexico. Gross was particularly sympathetic to the cause of the Cristero Rebellion in which a contingent of militant Catholics fought the Mexican government for a short time. Gross became a lifelong student of Mexican and Latin American affairs and spent a great deal of time writing letters to newspapers and magazines refuting criticisms of the Catholic Church and attacking anti-clerical rule south of the border.[185] He became closely associated with a conservative Catholic movement called Synarchism begun in 1937 as a perpetuation of the ideals of the vanquished Cristeros. In its call for a new Mexican government the Synarchists called for the return of an "organic" state where church and state worked in harmony and where democratic institutions were dismissed. Synarchists were among the first groups that pro-Fascist groups (like those supporting Generalissimo Francisco Franco of Spain and also the Nazis) attempted to influence to bring Mexico into closer association with the Axis powers before the war.[186] Despite the misgivings of many American bishops and clerics about the right-wing learnings of Synarchism (including some Mexican clergy) Gross stoutly defended the movement and touted it as "the salvation of Mexico." In fact, he was so visibly active on their behalf that the State and Justice Departments insisted that he register as a foreign agent.[187]

In any event, Gross was the leading figure in providing for the spiritual needs of the growing number of Mexicans coming to Milwaukee. When he brought the needs of the Mexicans to the attention of his Knights of Columbus council, he was appointed to head a committee to oversee efforts on their behalf. Publisher William C. Bruce (son of William G. Bruce) also lent his support to the project and with his interest in rural life kept a close eye on the spiritual needs of migrant workers appearing more regularly at the farms and orchards of the state during harvest season.[188] In 1926 Gross and Bruce secured a storefront church for Milwaukee's Mexicans on 5th and National and after spending $1,600 to remodel it, christened it the "Mission of Our Lady of Guadalupe." The *Catholic Herald* took note of the efforts and reminded its readers that helping the Mexicans in Milwaukee was only a favor returned since funds for the cathedral had come from Mexico and Cuba.[189] Working with Messmer, Gross scoured the country for Spanish-speaking priests. The first priest who came in 1926 was a Mexican national who had studied medicine in Chile before entering the priesthood, Father Ernesto Osiori Aguirre remained only one year. Eventually, Gross recruited exiled Mexican priests from the Mercedarian community to commit to the small Milwaukee mission. When Father Serapio Gonzales died in 1944, one final pastor, Father Fidel de la Puente, was appointed for a few months and then the Mercedarians ended their commitment.[190] It was then assumed by the nearby Conventual Franciscans who had already taken over nearby Holy Trinity parish.

The early pastors lived in the tiny quarters above the storefront church. The Milwaukee Archdiocesan Council of Catholic Women (MACCW) tended to the religious education of the youngsters by forming a branch of the Catholic Instruction League. The Daughters of Isabella (the female branch of the Knights of Columbus) provided sewing and cooking lessons. On December 12, 1926, Messmer blessed the new chapel and the Mexican mission was launched. Even from the start, the church was too small and Father William Haberstock of nearby Holy Trinity Church occasionally permitted larger celebrations within the ample confines of the parish. As mentioned, Gross made some preliminary inquiries about the fate of the Slovenian St. John the Evangelist on 4th and Mineral, but that church was unavailable.

Our Lady of Guadalupe Chapel dedication, 1929, Milwaukee [AAM]

More Mexicans moved to Milwaukee to satisfy the demand for laborers during World War II. Gross goaded the archdiocese into purchasing a large building being vacated by the Wisconsin Telephone Company about four blocks from the mission. The one-story building, with a full basement, was made of brick and steel, and quadrupled the amount of space available. Refurbishing of the building took place throughout the fall of 1944, and it was ready in time for the December 12 Guadalupe celebrations that year.[191] This structure served as the central church and social center for Mexican Catholics until 1965, when they merged with the church of the Holy Trinity.

Since the mission was small, the Catholic press and indeed most of Catholic Milwaukee paid little attention to the Latinos on the south side. However, an interesting glimpse into the growing community was provided in an article published in the *Herald Citizen* in the summer of 1940. The article spoke of interviews with several different Mexicans in Milwaukee, each of them reflecting on the joys and challenges of settling in cold industrial Milwaukee. One, a single mother with eight children, remembered wistfully the days of her youth in Mexico and the revolution that had brought her and her family to the United States and to Milwaukee. Her husband then returned to Mexico leaving her the task of rearing her eight children. "The years of hardship, intensified by the difficulty of learning English and caring for her family alone ... brought gray to her hair and lines to her face .... 'Yes I love Mexico and at times have wanted to go back,'" she admitted to the reporter, "'but I love my children more. This country is theirs, and now it is mine. I have gone to night school and am a citizen.'" A 10-year-old recounted stories told to her by her parents about Mexico. One of 12 children, she spoke of her love for movies and her idol, screen actress Dorothy Lamour. She rattled on about visits to Milwaukee parks on Sundays or movies and parties. Her father worked for the railroad and her brother at sugar beet farms. Margaret herself wanted to be a nurse, "but I probably won't. It costs a lot of money to be a nurse and takes a long time .... Maybe I will be married. But if I do, I would like to have only two children, one boy and one girl. When you are poor and have twelve, it is very hard."[192]

Eventually, the mission to Latinos expanded beyond Milwaukee. As early as the 1930s the Mercedarian priests were visiting pockets of Spanish-speaking Catholics in Waukesha and Fond du Lac counties. In 1942, the number of Mexican farmworkers and migrants increased when the United States began the bracero program with Mexico.

Administrative Centralization in the Archdiocese of Milwaukee: Central Headquarters, the Clergy and the Seminary

The ethnic disputes and the vitality of the various "Catholicisms" of the Milwaukee See took place against the backdrop of a major program of centralization and consolidation of virtually every aspect of archdiocesan life. In fact, the virulence of the Polish Church war can be seen as a bitter reaction to this effort to impose common standards and a stronger centralized leadership. Clearly, the efforts to transform the archdiocese administratively were fed not only by the centralizing prescriptions of Canon Law promulgated in 1918 and the example of a strongly centralized papacy and Roman curia, but just as much by the example of American business consolidation and the increasing professionalization of American life.

Messmer appeared in Milwaukee in February, 1904 and began to take control of diocesan affairs. As we have seen, his appointment stirred some concern given his reputation for forceful and firm leadership in Green Bay. Messmer issued a calming signal in early February when he re-appointed the popular Father Augustine Schinner to the post of vicar general. "There had been the general impression that it was my intention to turn things topsy-turvy," he declared in an interview. "This is a mistaken idea. There will be no radical departure from the policy that has been pursued. I shall let matters drift along in the same groove .... But," he said, "of course, where I see an opportunity for improvement, it will be made."[193] Even if Messmer had wanted to "let matters drift along in the same groove," the changing nature of the archdiocese and the evolving canonical and ecclesiastical framework of his office would not permit it.

The change in the style of transacting the official business of the Roman Catholic

(l to r) Revs. August Schinner, Dominic Thill, James Keogh, Bernard Traudt [AAM]

Church came about gradually. This "Search for Order" or "Organizational Revolution" began with the emergence of big business and in response to a demand for order and specialized service in an increasingly complex market. Businesses that had been run as small organizations, such as by the members of one family, soon required more specialized and standardized methods of operation. These reforms soon appeared in other areas: medicine, education, and even ecclesiastical affairs.

In Roman Catholicism, organizational reforms began in the office of the bishop. Many 19th century bishops had limited time or need for bureaucracies. Many wrote their own letters, took care of meager diocesan finances, and undertook the other aspects of episcopal administration in more informal and sometimes haphazard ways. This changed when dioceses grew and the administrative burdens demanded full-time attention. Many bishops got by with just a secretary who took dictation. Others relied heavily on their vicars general for advice and administrative substitutions.

Archbishop John Martin Henni wrote most of his own letters and managed finances on a "catch-as-catch-can" basis. He relied on his vicars general, Martin Kundig and Leonard Batz. Batz in particular exercised his skills of leadership, especially when Archbishop Heiss was gone from the archdiocese or ill. However, when the post of vicar general became an ethnic appointment, with posts for German speakers and English speakers, the office became honorary and less effective. Eventually the bishop became more central to the day-to-day affairs of the local church and parish. The role of the archbishop's "official family," especially the bishop's secretary and the chancellor, became significant. Heiss had a series of priest secretaries who lived with him, but it was Katzer who made his secretary something of an alter ego in running archdiocesan affairs. In addition, the chancellor (officially a notary and collector of official documents) also assumed the task of administrative oversight for a number of diocesan projects.

One additional bit of change accelerated internal administrative reforms: Roman decrees. Already from the Plenary Councils of Baltimore, dioceses had been called on to improve the quality of their administrative services by creating chancery offices. In the early part of the pontificate of Pope Pius X, a reorganization of the Roman Curia took place which shifted offices and reordered the relations of the Vatican with local churches and with sovereign nations. (In 1908 the United States was transferred from missionary to "independent" status.) The centralization of power in the hands of the Roman Curia set off similar moves in dioceses throughout the world. A new array of Roman-trained bishops (or those influenced by the changes) brought the same dynamic to American dioceses as centralizing and consolidating bishops soon dominated major sees. In Chicago, George William Mundelein set the pace. In Boston, it was William Henry O'Connell, in Philadelphia, "God's Bricklayer," Denis Dougherty, made the transition.[194] Archbishop Messmer, although not Roman trained, knew enough of the development of canon law to impose important changes on diocesan administration in Milwaukee. These included a new structure for the formation of priests, and the organization of charity and schools.

Messmer's first foray into administrative reform was to create a new central headquarters for the Church. Eager to centralize administrative records and personnel into one site, he soon found the old Lynde Mansion at 22nd and Chestnut Streets "rambling" and "unsuitable" for his plans. He discovered that it would take nearly $30,000 to add offices and record keeping areas. Early in his term, Messmer began to look for a new property (one of them was the old Schandein Mansion on Grand Avenue, which became an Emergency Hospital and is now a public school). Messmer made it known that he would sell the Lynde property, and for a time it appeared that the state Normal School might relocate there.[195] In 1908, while he was abroad, his secretary bought the stately Flemish Renaissance mansion of the Pabst family which had come on the market when Captain Pabst's widow died. The sprawling three floor mansion had elaborate rooms for public functions, and ample bedroom space. The 1893 pavilion of the estate (in which it had won the coveted Blue Ribbon for its sudsy brew) was transformed into a chapel. Later, the priests

Pabst Mansion, Archbishop's residence [AAM]

of the archdiocese decorated the new chapel with a handsome altar and stained glass windows. The stable and carriage house on the premises were converted into office space for Messmer's secretary and became the administrative center of the archdiocese until the Pabst mansion was sold in 1975.[196] Renovations on the structure went on into the fall and after Messmer returned from a trip abroad he moved into the new home.[197] The Franciscan sisters kept house, and Messmer lived with his priest secretary in the mansion along Milwaukee's most prestigious street. The old archiepiscopal mansion on Chestnut Street was turned over to the Sisters of Misericordia who transformed it into a maternity hospital.[198]

The person who brokered the house deal and installed the Sisters of Misericordia in the old episcopal mansion was Father Bernard Traudt, one of the key players in the reworking of archdiocesan administrative affairs. Traudt was born in Milwaukee on August 28, 1876, and as a young man entered St. Francis Seminary. Ordained at the age of 22 in 1898, he was chosen in 1901 to serve as Archbishop Katzer's secretary. Messmer retained the young priest, who became his alter ego in running diocesan affairs. Traudt soon rose to the post of chancellor after Augustine Schinner departed in 1905 for the diocese of Superior; and, in 1922, Messmer made Traudt his vicar general, with full powers to administrate in his name while he was away. Traudt brought a firm hand to the administration, an influence that lasted beyond his years in the office through his sister Anna Marie, who kept the diocesan books. He also brought on veteran bookkeeper Harry Inkmann, who also kept an eye on archdiocesan finances. Traudt wielded great power in the archdiocese, especially since Messmer's declining health took him away for long spells at sanitariums in Louisiana or Europe. It was Traudt who brought together the fabled "kitchen cabinet"—a small cadre of senior priests including his classmate Father George Meyer, veteran West Allis pastor Julius Burbach, and Polish loyalist Boleslaus Goral among others, who gathered at the Pabst

Rev. Bernard Traudt [AAM]

mansion and decided archdiocesan policy. Indeed, Traudt did surround himself with cronies. He and Meyer traveled together extensively, played tennis (the two claimed credit for putting in tennis courts at the seminary), hunted and joined others for evening games of the Wisconsin favorite card game, *schafskopf*. He had strong supporters among the clergy, to whom he could be beneficent. One of his fans was the aging and curmudgeonly William Miller, pastor of St. Joseph's in Waukesha, who lauded Traudt as an agent of Messmer's efforts to further Americanize the archdiocese, "Msgr. Traudt is a thoroughly American priest acquainted with the wants of our people, not meaning a specific section of them, but all of them," Miller wrote to Messmer.[199] Traudt could be a fine clerical comrade, but he was no one to be trifled with if he was crossed.[200]

One of his less desirable administrative techniques was to publicly dress down a priest at some highly public occasion like a Forty Hours. One victim of the Traudt wrath was Lithuanian Father Francis Garmus of Immaculate Conception parish in Sheboygan. When Garmus committed the unforgivable "sin" of directly contacting the bishop of Newark, New Jersey to see if he might move there, Traudt confronted Garmus at a clergy gathering after a Forty Hours at Random Lake, and berated him loudly in front of the guests. "The severe reproof with which you spoke to me at Random Lake in the hearing of the other priests," wrote an injured Garmus, "made a very painful impression on me."[201] Traudt only partially apologized for the public humiliation: "I am sorry indeed, if I have left the impression on you that I have any hard feelings against you." However he deliberately held up the priest's nearly completed plans to leave the diocese and warned him, "If you want to leave the Archdiocese of Milwaukee for some other field of labor, you had better wait until the new Archbishop comes and take up the matter with him."[202] He was always on the look out for clerical chicanery in financial matters and used his authority to compel obedience. For example, he refused to issue a proxy for the building of a new rectory to a South Milwaukee pastor until that parish paid its share of the high school assessment. "If you think you are going to make a clown out of me," he thundered, "I want … you to understand you are mistaken." With relish he concluded, "It is a great pleasure for me to write you this kind of letter."[203]

The chickens came home to roost for Traudt in 1925. In February Messmer was stricken with acute angina pectoris and for a time his death seemed imminent.[204] During the crisis, questions were raised about appointing a coadjutor to the 78-year-old prelate. (Indeed, just before the onset of the heart attacks, he had been planning to go to Rome on an *ad limina* visit.) Traudt brushed aside the rumors and Messmer recovered sufficiently to go to Rome and continue his duties. But he realized that he needed help and made an effort to have Traudt appointed as his auxiliary.[205] In a private communication to a number of select priests, he inquired whether he should advance Traudt's name to the Consistorial Congregation. Although the replies that remained in the archdiocesan archives were generally positive, a large number of those surveyed never replied, for fear that Traudt would see what many really thought of him. Others voiced their misgivings to Messmer and the apostolic delegate privately.[206] Traudt never became a bishop.

Rev. Bernard Traudt blessing cornerstone of St. Anthony of Padua Church, Milwaukee [ASAC]

Messmer's own failing health may have accounted for a lack of energy in pushing the nomination. However, Roman officials with long memories also may have recalled Messmer's problems with Joseph Maria Koudelka and his increasing disenchantment with Edward Kozlowski. The only auxiliary Rome would consider would be a coadjutor with right of succession.

Nonetheless, Traudt did much good in his years in office. With Messmer's encouragement, Traudt introduced new business techniques to the task of episcopal administration. The gathering of information was the most important field. In the diocesan ethnic survey of 1905 mentioned earlier, Traudt and Messmer extended the question about ethnic origins to include needed information about parochial finances.[207] Another innovation altered the annual report to include more data on parish life, problems and finances. Pastors initially balked, but Messmer pressed hard for the data which Traudt dutifully tabulated and kept in files.

But Traudt's days of power were over almost as soon as Messmer died in 1930. Although the new Archbishop Stritch retained many of Messmer's appointments, his largesse did not include Traudt, who held the posts of chancellor and vicar general. Stritch almost immediately banished Traudt from any day-to-day administrative tasks. The alleged reason for this was an incident at Stritch's installation when Traudt confidant, Father George Meyer, undiplomatically informed the new archbishop that the priests expected him "to be good to Monsignor Traudt."

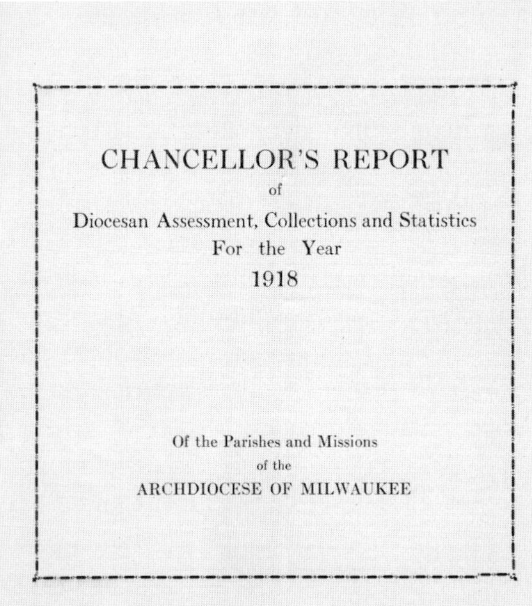

CHANCELLOR'S REPORT
of
Diocesan Assessment, Collections and Statistics
For the Year
1918

Of the Parishes and Missions
of the
ARCHDIOCESE OF MILWAUKEE

[AAM]

Nettled by Meyer's presumptuousness, but also well-informed from his own sources about Traudt's power and compromised relations with many of the clergy, Stritch sent a clear message that he did not want Traudt around. He delayed Traudt's reappointment as vicar general (a pro forma appointment in most cases) and the old warhorse was moved from the episcopal mansion and dispatched to the chaplaincy of Mount Mary College. Even the secular papers began to wonder if he had been demoted.[208] After six months Stritch relented, and renewed the vicar general's title.[209] When Milwaukee's St. Anne's pastor, Monsignor August Salick died in 1934, Stritch appointed Traudt pastor of the magnificent and thriving church.[210] At Christmas of that same year, Traudt was made a protonotary apostolic. Resplendent in miter, ring, buskins and crozier, Traudt presided like a mini-Emperor at St. Anne's (putting his coat of arms in the sacristy windows) until his death in 1945.

Replacing Traudt as the most powerful clerical figure in the archdiocese was Monsignor Joseph Barbian.[211] Barbian was born October 26, 1883 in New Coeln, Wisconsin, a rural community south of Milwaukee (today the site of the Milwaukee Airport), and attended St. Stephen's parish grade school and St. Francis Seminary. He was ordained on June 14, 1908. After two years as an assistant at two German parishes, St. Lawrence and St. Mary's, Barbian joined the faculty of Pio Nono. Here he demonstrated the administrative and fiscal skills that would single him out

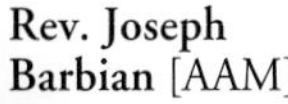

Rev. Joseph Barbian [AAM]

for higher office. In 1916 he came to head Pio Nono, which at that time still included the Holy Family Normal School. After a successful stint at Pio Nono College, he became the archdiocese of Milwaukee's first full-time school superintendent. In this capacity, Barbian won plaudits as a hard-nosed, no-nonsense administrator and set the Milwaukee Catholic schools on the road to a new phase of professionalism and growth. Barbian lived with Stritch and became responsible for more than school matters. His weight in the archdiocese was not to be discounted and might have grown, had he not died suddenly on All Saints Day in 1936. Stritch soon filled other important slots with his own men.

His most important appointment was that of his secretary and housemate, Roman Atkielski.[212] Born August 5, 1898, the son of Francis Atkielski and Catherine Hildenbrandt (Bialasaszewki) Atkielski, Roman Atklielski was educated by the Jesuits at their Prairie du Chien Campion Academy and at Marquette University. He later entered St. Francis Seminary and was one of the first priests ordained by Stritch in 1931. He was assigned to one of the "Polish League" parishes in Milwaukee (an assistant to Father Rudolph Kielpinski at St. Mary Czestachowa on Milwaukee's north side), and then was tapped in 1933 by Stritch to move into the Pabst Mansion and serve as his secretary and later chancellor of the archdiocese. "Romy" as he was affectionately called by Stritch, became more than just a secretary. He tended to every aspect of Stritch's schedule and person, even dusting dandruff off Stritch's shoulders. Even after Stritch was transferred to Chicago in 1940, Romy visited the prelate weekly.

One of Romy's tasks was lifting Stritch out of his bouts of deep depression. Although no clinical diagnosis can be made from this historical distance, Stritch clearly suffered from mood swings and periodic spells of deep melancholy. It is not quite certain what triggered these episodes (although in hindsight they might have been connected with Stritch's penchant for "junk food"—he loved tamales, stick candy and chopped ham sandwiches, and ate indiscriminately).[213] Certainly the depression was also related to a form of Seasonal Affective Disorder (SAD) brought on by the short, gray, cold days of winter. Indeed, he always needed a lengthy respite from the climate and in his later years spent the time between New Year's and Ash Wednesday in Florida. Living near the Great Lakes, he also suffered frequent sinus infections. But whatever the cause, Stritch did suffer from depression his entire life and occasionally his responsibilities overwhelmed him. Aloysius Muench related how on one occasion in 1934, Traudt had found Stritch sitting in a darkened room brooding about something. When Traudt attempted to cheer him up, "he [Stritch] left his study and went into his bedroom. The sister told Msgr. [Traudt] that she found the A[rchbishop] crying in his bedroom."[214] When Stritch was affected in this way, Romy was the one who could often see it coming and either rouse his superior or secure the services of educational psychologist (whom Stritch referred to often as a psychiatrist) Dr. Ralph Bergen. Bergen, who began working for the school department, eventually followed Stritch to Chicago and boosted the prelate's moods with his wise counsel and soothing advice. In any event, as Stritch settled into his Milwaukee routine Milwaukeeans came to know and like him, and often saw him and Romy on brisk walks from his mansion on Wisconsin Avenue to the lakefront.

Stritch settled into life in Milwaukee, creating a new archdiocesan bureaucracy and structure that matched his disdain for desk work (he told William E. Cousins whom he later consecrated as an auxiliary in Chicago and who eventually became archbishop of Milwaukee—"Don't run your diocese from behind a desk").[215] Although the indecisive Stritch had a difficult time in Depression-era Milwaukee, he was much esteemed by rank and file Catholics. He patiently stood in line to greet confirmandi and their parents, gave his pocket change regularly to people who stopped him for a handout, loved to preach at funerals and banquets, and was unfailingly kind and courteous.

Stritch also became highly visible on the national scene through his role in the leadership of the National Catholic Welfare Conference, the chief lobbying and educational arm of the American bishops. Formed after World War I, the NCWC grew slowly as a major force in lobbying for Catholic issues. It also helped sustain Catholic interest in a number of issues, and its departments and staff churned out a host of Catholic positions on social issues.[216] Initially skeptical of the organization (he had a falling out with its executive secretary, Paulist John Burke), Stritch ultimately became one of the NCWC's leading lights and served repeatedly on its administrative board. He forged a strong personal bond with former Ohio colleague, Archbishop John T. McNicholas, O.P., of Cincinnati and Archbishop Edward Mooney of Detroit. The trio shared not only common ideas on many of the challenges facing American Catholic life in the '20s and '30s, but also a mutual interest in advancing the "cause" of Midwestern Catholicism against the entrench power of the older Eastern sees of Boston,

Archbishop Samuel Stritch of Milwaukee (l) and Archbishop Edward Mooney of Detroit [AAM]

New York, and Philadelphia. The three prelates "conspired" over the years to blunt the plans and activities of Archbishop Francis Spellman in New York. Stritch's activities on the administrative board were felt in Milwaukee in various organizational endeavors, especially the hierarchical "takeover" of Catholic Action, but also in a sense of social action that energized Catholic social teaching during the Depression. Stritch was also generous in sending Milwaukee priests to study at the Catholic University of America and for service on various NCWC boards. Two priests who did this, Francis Haas and Paul Tanner, later became bishops themselves.

Programs of Diocesan Centralization

As part of his efforts to centralize and coordinate archdiocesan activity, Messmer undertook to codify an assortment of church policies that had been proposed over the years by the writing and promulgation of the *Handbook for Catholic Parishioners.* Messmer himself probably wrote the lion's share of this 119-page booklet which was distributed in the summer of 1907 to all pastors, all parish trustees and was available to the faithful for $.25 a piece. The purpose of the booklet was twofold, according to Messmer's introduction. "It means to take the parishioner by the hand," he wrote in the introduction, "and lead him on to the faithful discharge of his duty towards the parish."[217]

The subject matter of the pamphlet was quite comprehensive. It included old information about the nature of church incorporation and bylaws. It also laid out in clear detail the duties and powers of parish trustees, and the requirements of congregational membership, especially church support. It included Messmer's expectations for an active Catholic school program and, in its most controversial passage, codified earlier decisions about bilingual education, especially in the teaching of religion. It crystallized archdiocesan policy on church music, marriage celebrations, church burial, membership in societies and fraternals, and spelled out Messmer's regulations regarding the role

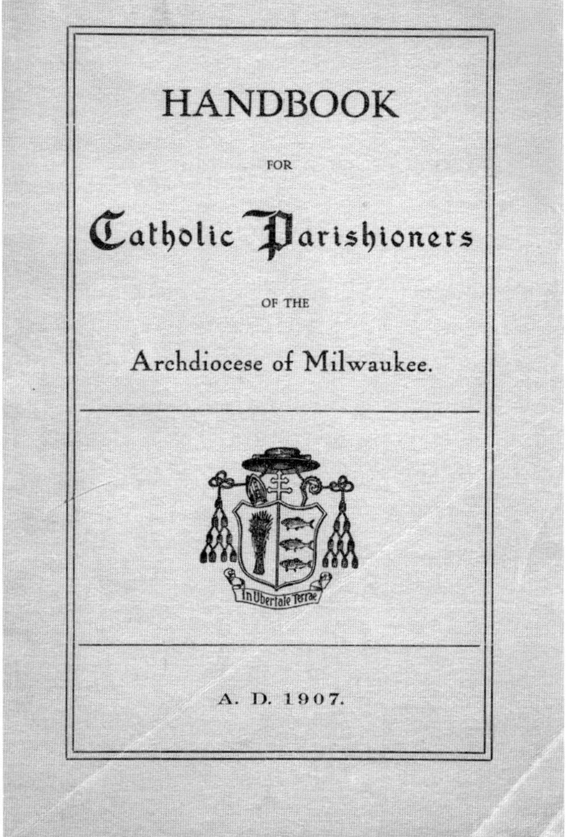
HANDBOOK

FOR

Catholic Parishioners

OF THE

Archdiocese of Milwaukee.

In Ubertate Terrae

A. D. 1907.

[AAM]

of churches in local politics. The pamphlet urged parishioners to be deferential to the authority of the local pastor and likewise insisted that pastors refer disputed or unclear questions to the local chancery. Messmer wrote to the clergy in late September 1907 mandating October 1st as the date that these regulations were to go into effect. He urged that pastors read salient portions of the handbook to their parishioners from October 1 to February 2.[218]

It is difficult to assess just how widely the booklet was received either by pastors or by the faithful, but there are some indications that it was ignored. Messmer sent frequent letters complaining that pastors had not given sufficient attention to the forms requiring information. "I am really tired of repeating the instructions and pleadings addressed to the clergy in this matter during the last five or six years," an exasperated Messmer wrote in late 1911. "It all seems in vain and I do not know what to think of its unless it be that my over-indulgence has given some pastors the idea that this whole business of the annual report is a huge joke for the annual benefit of the Archbishop and his chancellor."[219] Messmer had to continually threaten suspensions, embarrassing publicity and harsh personal letters to eke information out of his clergy (especially as it related to parish assessments).

Nonetheless, despite the opposition by some of the clergy, Messmer's efforts to create a more centralized administrative apparatus were gradually accepted. The new bureaucratic approach to church governance generated scores of statistics related to sacramental activity, parish membership, school attendance, religious instruction for public school children, and finances. Archdiocesan files bulged with this information along with an unending stream of letters to the clergy from Messmer or Traudt related to special collections, public events, and new ministerial endeavors. Other paperwork emanated from the offices at the diocesan headquarters at the Pabst mansion and related to the implementation of Roman directives on catechesis, church music, and the control of the Catholic press.

Confusion over Church Music

Pope Pius X (1903-1914) made a number of important policy changes in areas of direct importance to the average "Catholic in the pew." Unlike other pontiffs, Pius had actually served in a parish and had been the resident bishop of a diocese. In November 1903, he issued the *motu proprio Tra le Sollecitudine.* This decree banned the use of "operatic" or "theatrical" church music and held up Gregorian chant, as sung by the monks of the Benedictine abbey of Solesmes, as the "best" type of church music. Its most controversial element was an insistence on all male choirs. Milwaukee's long attachment to the Caecilian movement and the work of John Singenberger at the Holy Family Normal School ensured compliance with the pope's request on the quality of church music.[220] But the insistence on male choirs clashed with the reality that most of the Caecilian music was composed for male and female voices. In addition, Pius X's expressed preference for the Solesmes version of the Gregorian chant, performed without organ accompaniment, was another blow to the Caecilian music establishment. For them the church organ was the cornerstone of its musical performance. Deeply loyal to Singenberger and fearful of the uproar such a decree could cause, Messmer took a forceful stand against it. At a meeting of the archbishops in late April 1904, he spoke his mind to a reporter on the mixed choir provisions of the new *motu proprio.* "I do not favor the banishing of women from our church choirs. The change of our choirs and the adoption of the church music under the plan originated by the Pope will take time for its ultimate realization." Messmer noted, "I heartily favor the Gregorian chant where it can be properly done. But there are few places where it can be put into effect immediately. The Caecilian society has done much to prepare the way for change .... Rome has been written for instructions. Until they have been received there will be no radical change in Milwaukee Catholic church choirs."[221] These comments drew a swift rebuke from Apostolic Delegate Falconio, who urged Messmer to publicly modify his "suspension" of the *motu proprio.*[222] And clarity was slow in coming.

St. Cecilia Verein, musical society, meeting at St. Francis Seminary [AAM]

Dutifully, Messmer worked with Singenberger to draw up an acceptable list of approved church music that was mandated by order of the archbishop for use in parishes.[223] He later empaneled a committee (with himself as chair, Singenberger and a number of priest-musicians) to lay plans to implement the pontiff's wishes throughout Wisconsin.[224] The "*Guide to Catholic Church Music*" appeared in 1906, and Messmer insisted that every parish have a copy. This guide, no doubt devised by Singenberger, but approved by all of the bishops of the province of Wisconsin, sought to implement the *motu proprio's* demands. It also added a few more details that imposed episcopal control over choir-loft activities. For example it forbade religious sisters from directing mixed choirs and members of one parish choir from joining another. In a blow at a practice in use at some of the ethnic churches around the archdiocese, it ended the practice of singing in the vernacular during the Sunday High Mass.[225] At the same time Singenberger devoted himself to the task of adapting to the Solesmes chant favored by Pope Pius X. In 1907, Messmer devoted a whole section of the *Handbook for Catholic Parishioners* (five-and- a-half single-spaced pages) laying down archdiocesan rules governing church music and the conduct of choirs.

But the question of mixed choirs remained confused. Parishes reacted differently. Women left the choir of St. Francis Church in Milwaukee in September 1906.[226] By 1913, the cathedral choir had been emptied of women. In the *Handbook* Messmer alluded to the demand of the *motu proprio* that women be excluded (rule #8), but then commented later in the text: "In regard to rule n. 8 the conditions in most of the parishes of the Archdiocese make it impossible to dispense with lady singers in the choir. Hence permission is given to continue the present custom until male choirs can be found to render the sacred chant."[227] Figuring out what the pope really meant in the *motu proprio* made it impossible to come to clarity on the issue of women in the choir.

Some bishops thought to ask the pontiff. In early 1906, Messmer received a letter from Archbishop John Keane of Dubuque (his former rector at Catholic University), who described a meeting with the pope on the issue. When asked if the pope urged a "speedy and entire observance everywhere of the *motu proprio,*" Pius X "answered with a smile that while urging the principles [of the *motu proprio*] he took it for granted that its practical enforcement would have to be gradual and even slow." Keane then asked the pontiff "laughingly" whether he really desired to exclude women from singing the praises of God, seeing that the nearest of all to Our Lord were women, "he laughed good naturedly and said he did not wish to exclude women from singing God's praises, but to exclude prevailing scandals."[228] On May 1, 1908, Messmer raised the issue when visiting the pope, pleading for the retention of women in choirs and insisting that if they were banned "we could not have solemn services at Mass or vespers in a great number of our parishes." By this time, the pontiff had probably had enough questions from American bishops, and replied to Messmer sharply, "Well then, let them sing, but let them behave themselves, and do not allow them to sing theatrical and worldly music." [229]

Messmer continued to be a strong supporter of the Caecilians, whose music needed women's voices. In a celebrated letter to Singenberger, which was reprinted on the pages of the journal of the Caecilian society, Messmer used his conversation with Pius X as the authority to give permission for women to continue in church choirs where it would be impractical to do otherwise. He also carefully noted that the permission had been given for Milwaukee directly by the pontiff, and not for the whole country. He praised the pope, noting that his interpretation of the difficult *motu proprio* gave evidence of "the old rule or principle admitted by every wise lawgiver that his law is not meant to bind his subjects when its observance is either impossible, or very difficult or harsh or calculated to do more harm than good." Messmer also vigorously asserted the right of the local bishop to "determine how and in what manner the general law of the church … shall be carried out in the actual given circumstances …."[230]

In the end, mixed choirs remained, although a new emphasis on Gregorian chant soon began to replace the Caecilian music.

It would have been difficult to eliminate the custom of congregational singing, already entrenched in many parishes. For example, at St. Joseph's parish in Racine, Father John Bach had introduced the custom during his long pastorate in the 1920s and 1930s. He even insisted that the altar boys sing the hymns as they held the paten under the chins of communicants at the reception of the Eucharist, a time when most of them would have been expected to be silent. In some parishes, members of the congregation were urged to sing popular hymns that replicated the ordinary parts of the Mass. Other ethnic groups, such as the Slovaks, did the same. Hymnody that paralleled the Ordinary parts of the Mass was also rich among the archdiocese's large Polish congregations. Even ethnic devotions, later scorned as "private" piety, gave Catholics opportunities to sing their faith. For example the Polish "Lamentations"—*Gorskie Zale*—with their hauntingly beautiful tones of sorrow and contrition were sung antiphonally between celebrant and congregation. The popular Sorrowful Mother Novena, and other Marian devotions included popular, if at times saccharine, hymns, such as "Good Night Sweet Jesus," "Mother Dear O Pray for Me," and the ever popular "Holy God We Praise Thy Name," which Catholics could sing with gusto often to the horror of liturgical or musical purists.

The Age of First Communion

Pius X also took interest in the question of first communion, and in 1907 insisted that children who had reached the "age of reason" (about 7-years-old according to the best pastoral wisdom of the day) should be permitted to make first holy communion. There was an immediate disquiet in many parts of the Catholic world over this decree, since first communion had not been permitted until the age of 12 (in part, so that children could endure the requisite Eucharistic fast from the previous midnight before holy communion. Messmer at first resisted this mandate. He believe that at the age of 7 children still did not have a clear understanding of what the Eucharist was. He also worried that children would leave Catholic schools once they had made their first communion.[231] As he had with the question of mixed choirs, Messmer stood on his episcopal rights and began seeking interpretations of the decree from the Holy See. Here his Polish antagonist Wenceslaus Kruszka struck. Anxious to implement the practice with the children of his parish grade school, he fell afoul of Traudt who did not permit him to undertake the practice until the bishops of Wisconsin had come to some common understanding of its implementation. When Kruszka insisted that this was the desire of the Holy See (and preached this from the pulpit) Traudt contradicted his invocation of Roman authority by dismissing it as the work of some "Roman monk." Kruszka reported the matter to Rome and Falconio pounced on Messmer's foot dragging and virtually ordered him to permit pastors to give communion at a younger age.[232] Messmer replied angrily, "Rev. Kruszka has been lying again" and stoutly defended "my good chancellor" who swore "on his honor that he had never made a statement regarding the pope's decree … attributed to him in your letter." [233]Messmer then compromised, permitting the practice of first solemn communion to 10-year-old children. "All children below ten years who are found to be equally well-fitted for holy communion, may be admitted privately in each individual case."[234] Eventually, however, more and more children chose the age of seven, and the practice of first holy communion changed rapidly in the archdiocese. In fact, among its leading proponents were archdiocesan priests who soon formed a branch of the Priest's Eucharistic League to promote frequent communion. In 1911, Monsignor Joseph Rainer spoke to an international Eucharistic Congress on the practice, extolling the wisdom of Pius X who "felt and foresaw that the sooner and the more frequently the children of God's Church would be united with Jesus in Holy Communion the more surely and the more thoroughly the renewal of all things in Christ would be accomplished."[235]

Legal Advice

One major change in archdiocesan life was the recruitment of outside specialists to assist in the running of the archdiocese. To some extent all bishops had sought out professionals in law, architecture, and other areas for *ad hoc* advice and fund-raising help. Among the new lay advisors brought on board by Messmer and Traudt was attorney Henry V. Kane. Kane was a thoughtful attorney who made his debut in archdiocesan life through membership in the Holy Name Society and service on the Board of Directors of the newly founded *Catholic Herald* in 1923.[236] Kane graduated from Marquette University in 1899 and then took advanced study at Georgetown University where he received his M.A., Ph.D. and LL.B. degrees. He was admitted to the bar in 1902 and in 1906 began to handle *gratis* the legal affairs of several Catholic institutions such as the House of the Good Shepherd, the orphanages and the seminaries. Before long a number of Catholic institutions called on Kane for sound legal advice.

Rev. Peter Schroeder with First Communicants at the Little Flower Mission, Milwaukee, in the 1930s [ASAC]

In 1910 he became the archdiocese's first full-time attorney on retainer and would be especially helpful to Messmer and Stritch in the myriad legal difficulties and technicalities that beset the financing and organization of parishes. The legal end of education, charity, cemeteries, legislation, press and parish issues became his main concerns. Kane's methodical style was of great assistance in keeping the archdiocese afloat and out of serious legal trouble during the Messmer, Stritch and Kiley years. After his death in 1948, he was succeeded by Alfred W. Ecks.

Kane's influence over archdiocesan affairs would be felt in a number of areas– especially financial and political matters. He also carefully navigated the Milwaukee See through the web of worker's compensation and unemployment legislation that emerged in the Progressive and New Deal eras.

Gatehouse at Calvary Cemetery, Milwaukee [AAM]

One of Kane's less heralded accomplishments was his management of the growing complexities of archdiocesan cemeteries. Cemeteries dotted the landscape of the archdiocese of Milwaukee, many of them run by local parishes (e.g., St. James in Mequon, St. James and St. George in Kenosha) or by ethnic associations. Remnants of earlier burial grounds run by "ghost parishes" also still existed. For example, Blessed Sacrament Cemetery on West Forest Home Avenue located around the abandoned church continued to be cared for by the sexton of Calvary Cemetery.[237] Among the most distinctive features of the archdiocese's continuing ethnic heritage were the variety of burial customs, the nature of funeral monuments, and the practices surrounding the memorialization of the departed.

The first Catholic cemetery was established by Henni in 1844 when he purchased 10 acres south of Grand Avenue and west of 15th Street for a Catholic burial ground. In 1857, he purchased another 55 acres along Bluemound Road, west of the growing city and this became Calvary Cemetery. In 1865, he purchased land in the Town of Lake and laid out Holy Trinity Cemetery.[238] By 1909, the archdiocese managed five cemeteries located at strategic points around Milwaukee County: Calvary (1857), Holy

Trinity (1865), Polish Union (later St. Adalbert) (1888), Mount Olivet, and later Holy Cross (1909).[239] The Polish Cemetery, which abutted Holy Trinity, had for years been governed by Monsignor Boleslaus Goral of St. Hyacinth's parish. Calvary Cemetery was one of the most beautiful sites in the archdiocese. Imitating the magnificent entrances to the German cemeteries, Erhard Brielmaier erected a turretted gatehouse to the burial ground in 1897 that resembled a medieval castle and added dignity to the somber processions entering the cemetery.[240]

In 1902, the hill that rose in the southern part of the cemetery was crowned by a magnificent burial chapel, intended as the resting place for Milwaukee clergy. The first to be interred was the founding pastor of St. Casimir's Church, Father Aegidius (Giles) Taraszewicz. His legendary funeral procession was headed by 2,200 marchers from various Polish societies, and consisted of 45 carriages carrying various Polish clergy and other dignitaries, the Kosciusko Guard bearing drawn sabers alongside the hearse, followed by 101 carriages containing the grieving parishioners of St. Casimir's. The entire procession took nearly a half-hour to pass any one spot along its route and snarled traffic.[241] Later the hill was flanked by other clergy—including the Jesuits of Marquette University.

Inevitably the existing cemeteries began to fill up and a body of legislation emerged that governed the placement and size of cemeteries, as well as prescribing sanitary burial procedures. The emergence of secular cemeteries and their appeal to Catholics prompted Messmer to include several pages in his 1907 *Handbook* on the matter of Christian burial. He insisted that Catholics be buried in consecrated ground and strictly forbade priests from officiating at graveside ceremonies in secular cemeteries. But he stepped gingerly around the question of ethnic cemeteries. These burial grounds were independently run and reflected the burial traditions of their nationality groups. They also managed large funds given for the purchase of plots and for their subsequent care. Cemeteries soon became big business as these monies were pooled into large endowment funds.

Rev. Giles Tarasiewicz
[AAM]

The 1920s saw the emergence of a more professional funeral industry and the creation of additional secular graveyards that vied for the business of Catholics. In 1925, Traudt was compelled to restate the prohibitions against Catholic burial in unconsecrated ground (the exception being converts and others who had purchased plots in cemeteries).[242] In the late 1920s, Kane worked to unify the archdiocesan cemeteries under central administration by creating an archdiocesan corporation to manage the burial sites.[243] At Messmer's behest, Kane prepared the articles of incorporation and also penned a small handbook that covered policies at Calvary, Holy Cross, Holy Trinity and Mount Olivet cemeteries.[244] Citing the appropriate citations of the newly issued Code of Canon Law, Messmer reiterated his insistence that Catholics be buried in Catholic cemeteries and laid out the strict rules governing the appearance of Catholic clergy at gravesides. Prohibitions against cremation and other departures from Catholic norms of burial were also restated. The handbook went even farther, however, in laying down a common set of policies regarding the layout and procedures for cemeteries under archdiocesan control. The rules regulated the nature and type of funeral monuments, the kinds of things that could be left on graves, and prohibited families from erecting iron fences or other kinds of monuments in addition to the gravestone. Large vehicles were prohibited from entering cemeteries and the cemetery sexton was given authority to make all decisions related to the dispositions of the local grounds. There was now an "official" archdiocesan way of being buried—one more step in the diminution of once thriving ethnic customs. These rather precise regulations regarding the burial of the dead anticipated major improvements in the conduct of cemeteries and funerals in other dioceses across America.

It was left to Archbishop Stritch to incorporate the growing Polish Union Cemetery, renamed St. Adalbert, into the archdiocesan system. Goral, who administered the affairs of the cemetery, had for several years importuned Stritch for a way to relieve him of the task. When union organizers began their efforts to unionize cemetery help, Stritch informed Goral that the archdiocese would be willing to take on the cemetery. "I know that the administration of St. Adalbert Cemetery has been a great burden to you for years. I have been anxious to relieve you of this burden."[245] In the 1930s Kane oversaw the details of the transfer, negotiated a contract with the incoming unions, and set up the structure of the cemetery endowment fund that generated millions of dollars of revenue for the archdiocese. Additional cemetery lands would be procured in other parts of the archdiocese, especially as older parish and city cemeteries filled up. In 1957, Archbishop Meyer added burial grounds in Ozaukee County which he named Resurrection Cemetery.

The Centralization of the Seminary and the New Clerical Culture

Messmer worked hard to raise archdiocesan consciousness among his ethnically diverse flock. This was especially true at the archdiocesan seminary, which underwent important transformations in personnel, leadership and direction after World War I.

St. Francis Seminary had come to something of a crossroads by World War I. It had been under the leadership of the saintly but reclusive Joseph Rainer since 1887. The seminary had grown in size and diversity through his years in office and attracted students from dioceses across the country.[246] As we have seen, Rainer helped the institution adjust to the more diverse ethnic constituencies of the archdiocese by learning to speak Polish, Hungarian, and even some Lithuanian. The seminary's faculty reflected a cross section of old-style European scholars and newer American intellectuals who did some publishing and cut fairly respectable reputations for themselves. In the latter category, Dr. Joseph Selinger from Jefferson City, Missouri, was a highly esteemed teacher of dogma and one of the progenitors of the Neo-Scholastic revival at St. Francis. Dr. Frederick Schulte from Alton, Illinois, wrote the popular and long-used *Manual of Pastoral Theology*. Dr. Charles Bruehl of Philadelphia introduced the study of social teaching into the seminary curriculum.

In 1909 the alumni donated funds to build a separate seminary library, a long-needed building. The new library would allow students to go into the stacks and select books in lending-library style.[247] Benefactions from the ample libraries of Father Thomas Fagan of Bay View and Monsignor Leonard Batz of Milwaukee augmented the collection.[248]

St. Francis Seminary was wired for electrical current in 1895 and received indoor plumbing in 1916. The seminary chapel took on a warmer tone with the installation of new stained glass windows by local artist Marie Herndl. Herndl's talent with glass had first been discovered when her creation "The Fairy Queen" was awarded a bronze medal in a competition at the 1893 Columbian Exposition in Chicago.[249] Introduced to Katzer, who was impressed with her work, she was soon contracted to design and execute the series of stained glass windows that still adorn the main seminary chapel. In 1897, a new zinc statue of seminary patron St. Francis de Sales was solemnly blessed and hauled up to a niche over the front entrance of the building. In 1927, with the help of a hefty donation from the generous Miller brewing fam-

Salzmann Library at St. Francis Seminary [AAM]

ily, a new gymnasium was built for the young men.

But St. Francis Seminary underwent a significant period of transformation to a more Romanized and Americanized institution during Messmer's years. Demographic changes meant that St. Francis was no longer called on to produce German-speaking priests in the numbers required in previous generations. As a result, the number of students from other dioceses decreased proportionately, and the seminary faculty gradually shed the European scholars who once graced its lecture halls. Likewise, bishops from other dioceses who had once lent their priests to the Milwaukee seminary faculty withdrew them as they created their own seminaries.

The most important development affecting the course of seminary education was the condemnation of the "synthesis of all heresies," modernism. On July 3, 1907, the Sacred Congregation of the Holy Office issued the decree *Lamentabili* condemning 65 theological propositions labeled "modernism." On September 8, 1907, Pope Pius X issued the encyclical *Pascendi Dominici Gregis*, in which the condemnations were explained at length. In *Pascendi*, bishops were directed to make sure their seminaries taught scholastic philosophies, and left the pope no room to doubt what exactly that was: "When we prescribe scholastic philosophy, we mean principally—and this is a point of capital importance—the philosophy which has been bequeathed to us by St. Thomas Aquinas." On the basis of Thomistic philosophy, the pontiff declared, "the edifice of theology is to be carefully built."[250] Pius X's insistence on the primacy of neo-Scholasticism reinforced what his predecessor Pope Leo XIII had laid down in the encyclical *Aeterni Patris* (1879) which prescribed the teaching of St. Thomas as the church's primary means of combating modern intellectual errors. By specifying Thomism as the cure for the errors of the Modernists, Pope Pius X set an important parameter for clerical formation, and indeed for Catholic life in general. As historian Philip Gleason observed, "For the next half-century, Neoscholasticism furnished the cognitive foundation for American Catholic intellectual and cultural life."[251]

In 1910, Pope Pius X issued *motu proprio*, the decree *Sacrorum Antistitum*, which elaborated on the provisions of *Pascendi* as they applied to the training of young men for the priesthood. In it the pontiff carefully limited the amount of "secular" course material that could be in the seminary curriculum and insisted that seminarian contact with the outside world be even more strictly circumscribed. "We absolutely forbid them to read newspapers and reviews, however excellent these may be, and we make it a matter of conscience for superiors who fail to take precautions to prevent such reading."[252] *Sacrorum* also insisted on a profession of faith and an oath against modernism of all seminary instructors and candidates for ordination to the priesthood. In 1918 the new Code of Canon Law stipulated new rules regarding the formation of young men for the priesthood. The impact of these canons was, as historian Joseph White has noted, to impose the Tridentine ideal of the priest as the norm for the universal church. A specific priestly spirituality, which stressed the priest as a participant in Christ's sufferings and largely drawn from the models of 17th century French spiritual writers such as Pierre de Berulle and Sulpician founder Jean Jacques Olier, was made normative.[253] In addition, the norms of acceptable and unacceptable clerical behavior were also laid out: priests were to wear appropriate ecclesiastical attire at all times and were prohibited from engaging in business, politics or military service. In 1915 the *motu proprio Seminaria Clericorum* created a new curial congregation to oversee seminaries and universities. A constant flow of papal utterance relative to seminaries continued throughout the 20th century, each of them leaving an imprint on the character of Milwaukee's seminary.

After World War I, Messmer moved decisively to implement the new Roman decrees at St. Francis. The seminary curriculum was restructured to give primacy to the teaching of St. Thomas Aquinas and Milwaukee seminarians learned the principles of Catholic dogma from manuals of theology which distilled the essential points of the angelic doctor. Beginning in 1911, the oath against modernism was administered to Milwaukee seminarians and priests.[254] Messmer also rewrote the disciplinary code of the institution, demanding more clerical obedience (likely a by-product of his struggles with the Polish clergy). A Committee of Vigilance was formed of senior archdiocesan priests who were supposed to monitor the orthodoxy of the local clergy and report violations to the bishop. Milwaukee's committee rarely met and there were no serious outbursts of anti-modernist witch-hunting in the archdiocese. However, Milwaukee was the recipient of one loser in an orthodoxy battle in the Rochester, New York seminary, Father Andrew Breen. Breen questioned the work of fellow faculty member Father Edward J. Hanna on the subject of Christ's self-knowledge which appeared in the progressive *New York Review* (a publication that terminated its existence soon after the issuance of *Lamentabili*). The effect of the accusations was to halt Hanna's appointment to the episcopate. Later, however, Hanna was cleared (he went on to become Archbishop of San Francisco), but Breen was banished in 1918 for his part in the episode. Messmer took him into St. Francis after the dismissal of Father Paul Schaffel and he remained on the faculty until his death in 1938.[255] St. Francis produced a new kind of priest in the aftermath of these changes: one less "foreign," more uniform in

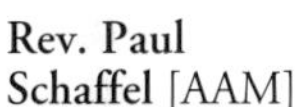
Rev. Paul Schaffel [AAM]

theological training and clerical lifestyle and certainly more reflexively obedient to papal and episcopal direction.

Messmer also dealt with the reality that St. Francis was no longer the major seminary of the Midwest. In 1920 he convoked the bishops of the province and pressed for a major reorganization of the seminary's constitution to make it a provincial rather than a national seminary. The transition seemed logical, given the fact that new seminaries were already being built in Chicago and in other dioceses. In an administrative shake-up in 1920, Messmer deposed the venerable Rainer (to soften the blow he tried to have him appointed a titular bishop but Rome would not agree and so Rainer simply became a protonotary apostolic).[256] In his place he put Father Augustine Breig as rector.

Breig was born in the Black Forest region of Germany in 1872.[257] He undertook studies for the priesthood at the University of Freiburg in Baden and was ordained in 1897. After a year as an assistant in a parish in Basel, Switzerland, he received a doctorate in philosophy from the University of Fribourg in Switzerland. After another stint of parish work, he returned to Freiburg and completed a doctorate in theology. In 1902, he was permitted to study trade unionism in America and ended up for a time in Pittsburgh: but through the influence of a clerical companion he ended up in Cleveland, where he resided and worked at St. Michael's Church, under the pastorate of Joseph Koudelka. Devoting himself to social questions, Breig lectured and wrote extensively and joined with Peter Dietz in founding the *Social Justice Review.*[258] Koudelka brought him to Milwaukee in 1912, and Messmer first placed him at a short-lived academy run by the Dominican sisters of Racine in the town of Corliss, Wisconsin. Here he wrote an analysis of *Rerum Novarum* entitled *Papal Program of Social Reform,* which sold more than 25,000 copies. After the academy closed, Breig was swooped up into the growing chancery operation at the Pabst mansion and served as an understudy to Traudt (he served as acting chancellor while Traudt was in Europe in 1914). Messmer then installed him at the seminary as a professor of dogma and librarian. The aging prelate enjoyed Breig's company enough to have the priest accompany him on his various journeys, especially his therapeutic trips to Louisiana and Switzerland. In all Breig made seven trips to Europe with Messmer.

Rev. Augustine Breig [AAM]

Under the reorganization, seminary courses were differentiated more clearly by age, with minor seminary, philosophy, and theological sections being more clearly separated. An additional year was added to the minor seminary (or classical course). Major changes in the faculty took place as well. For at least a decade prior to the reorganization the seminary faculty had been undergoing a steady transformation. Breig and Messmer began to reassemble a faculty drawn almost exclusively from the ranks of the Wisconsin clergy. Nicholas Maas, pastor of St. John's in Rubicon, became the new spiritual director and its chief liturgist. Joseph Barbian was brought over from Pio Nono to replace Louis Peschong as seminary procurator (business manager). Cathedral curate David O'Hearn, educated in Rome, was drafted to teach canon law and church history. When O'Hearn was made rector of the cathedral, he was replaced by a recently returned veteran of World War I, Father Peter Leo Johnson (also trained in Rome). Johnson's fellow veteran, George Eilers, rejoined the seminary faculty (he had served there briefly before joining the service) and became a professor of English and prefect of studies. To maintain a Polish presence on the faculty, Messmer appointed Ladislaus Bednarski to teach Polish. Acknowledging the increasing importance of educational standards mandated in secular schools, the seminary applied to the State Department of Education for permission to grant high school diplomas and college degrees. Likewise, the affiliation of the seminary theological courses with the Catholic University of America was sought.[259] In another development of the seminary grounds, Messmer sold the lakefront property of the seminary to the city of Milwaukee for $30,000—on the proviso that the land would be used for a public park.[260] City officials purchased the land and ran Sheridan Road, later renamed Highway 32 in front of the venerable Catholic sites.

To further "Romanize" his seminary faculty, Messmer resumed the practice of sending bright young priests to schools abroad to prepare them for service on the seminary faculty. One of these was Father Aloysius Muench, a future papal nuncio to Germany and cardinal of the Church. Muench was a

Rev. Aloysius Muench [AAM]

native of Milwaukee and a son of St. Boniface parish. Ordained in 1914, Muench had been selected for studies at the University of Innsbruck. But the outbreak of World War I detoured him into parish work at St. Michael's in Milwaukee. In 1917, he was appointed to assist Father Henry Hengell at the St. Paul Center in Madison. Muench's work at St. Paul revolved around serving the needs of Catholic students at the University of Wisconsin. However, he used the free moments of his days to study for a master's degree in economics, which he won in 1919. Muench's biographer, Colman Barry, highlights Muench's occasional jousting with militantly secularistic professors on the Wisconsin faculty, such as professor of sociology Edward Aylsworth Ross. [261]

In 1920, Messmer sent Muench to Fribourg where he studied moral theology and wrote a doctoral dissertation on the development of compulsory health insurance in the United States. He supported himself by writing articles for the Jesuit weekly *America*. In 1922, he returned to the seminary staff and taught an array of classes from dogma to social theory. Linking up with brewing mogul and Catholic convert Valentine Blatz, he sponsored a number of charitable projects. One of his more interesting endeavors was his work with a homebound invalid he had met during his curacy at St. Michael's parish, Clara M. Tiry. Tiry suffered from severe bronchial asthma and was virtually imprisoned in her home during the harsh winter months between November and May. In 1926, she and Muench formed an association called the "Apostolate of Suffering"—an organization of the sick and disabled around the archdiocese who would voluntarily offer up their sufferings for the good of the church. Over time, Tiry managed to make contact with over 6,000 people.[262] Later they organized the Good Samaritan Guild, a group of laywomen who devoted themselves to visiting the sick and shut-ins. The movement spread across the United States and was fostered by a small bulletin, *Our Good Samaritan,* which encouraged those who visited the sick and brought consolation to those who were homebound by illness. The organization lasted well into the era of the Vatican Council.

Cardinal Aloysius Muench (center) at a Day for the Sick, sponsored by the Apostolate of Suffering [AAM]

Messmer also sent a significant number of men to Rome for their post-graduate education. Future bishops Albert Meyer and John Grellinger, as well as Oswald Krusing, were dispatched to the Eternal City. Archbishop Stritch, an even more thoroughgoing Roman than his predecessor, sent priests Frank Schneider and John Schulien to Rome. All of these men spent a portion of their youth in the Rome of Pope Pius XI in the 1920s and 1930s, and were educated according to the reigning norms of neo-Scholasticism and deep loyalty to the Holy See. The Roman graduates were, for the most part, either capable teachers or Church leaders. Few of them, however, wrote books or engaged in much original research.

The process of selecting "the best and the brightest" for advanced study abroad continued through much of the history of the Milwaukee seminary. This permitted it to remain the leading intellectual center for church life in southeastern Wisconsin and insured in most cases a respectable quality of classroom teaching. For the young priests chosen for this honor, the years of study in Rome were an unparalleled educational opportunity. Living in an international community of scholars and students allowed them to forge friendships with priests around the country and the world. Their Roman degrees ensured orthodoxy and a definitive word in various theological questions referred to them. Opportunities for travel and cultural exchange also enhanced their lives in ways they could never have dreamed while growing up in Milwaukee, Kenosha, or West Allis. Sometimes these men burned out and failed to live up to expectations. In other cases, the investment of archdiocesan resources paid a handsome dividend.

Such was the case of Kenosha native John Schulien, who taught on the seminary faculty from 1936 until his retirement in 1981. A student of Jesuit theologian (and later consultant to the Holy Office) Sebastian Tromp, Schulien had completed his studies with distinction at Rome's Gregorian University, writing a thesis on the Mystical Body of Christ. He returned to St. Francis and spent the rest of his life teaching hundreds of seminarians the cyclical dogma courses that were the core of the seminary curriculum. "Serene Aquin's verdict no less your own," one former student eulogized him in a lovely poem.[263] Schulien was the perfect model of a seminary professor steeped in the reigning neo-Scholasticism of his day. Apart from Joseph Rainer, few seminary professors stayed as long as Schulien did or could claim as much influence over the intellectual and theological formation of their young charges. Stritch tapped the young priest to serve as an instructor to Catholic nurses and doctors on matters of medical moral ethics.[264] He was also appointed *censor librorum* for the archdiocese—a not inconsiderable task given the fact that America's largest Catholic publishing house, the Bruce Company, was constantly feeding manuscripts to him in order to secure the all-important *imprimatur*. In

Rev. John Schulien [AAM]

this regard Schulien's views on Church censorship of books reflected the extent to which his theological views were carried into action. At a time when even some Catholic academics were beginning to bridle against Church restrictions on research and writing, Schulien cooly defended the Church's right to censor books to a group of Wisconsin Catholic librarians by drawing careful distinctions. Bad censorship, such as practiced by the Nazis or Communists, destroyed human freedom, while Church censorship preserved the human person from fatal errors that robbed them of the truth. "In seeking to reconcile intellectual freedom and censorship, we must distinguish between the legitimate use of censorship which does not conflict with true freedom and the abuse of censorship which destroys genuine freedom." Schulien argued, "truth is one and it is unchanging ... it is not a sign of tolerance to be more tolerant than truth itself."[265]

Rev. Nicholas Brust's first Mass [AAM]

Milwaukee's "Cookie Cutter Priesthood": Aspects of Clerical Culture

The cumulative impact of the changes in clerical education mandated by Rome brought an increasing "standardization" of clerical culture. Various aspects of clerical lifestyle were now carefully stipulated: salary, living quarters, associations with women and "seculars," and clerical attire. The priests of the 20th century were different in many ways from their 19th century counterparts. For example, early Milwaukee priests like Martin Kundig or John Vahey did not seem to wear distinctive clerical attire. Neither were referred to in clerical address as "Father," but more commonly as "Reverend Mister." By the 20th century pastors such as St. Thomas Aquinas founder Edward Blackwell, *Nowiny* editor Boleslaus Goral, and St. Boniface pastor Henry Stemper were all known by their respective clerical titles (Blackwell and Goral were Monsignors, and Stemper was a "Father"). Formal pictures depict them in clerical attire—often a roman cassock, and for street attire a clerical vest and a heavily starched Roman collar. Episcopal regulation of clergy became more direct and priests were held more strictly accountable to the directives of the chancery. Letters of transfer were met with dutiful compliance and violations against rules and insubordination to pastors or chancery could bring the wrath of God on a hapless cleric. Messmer generally delegated the monitoring of clerical discipline to Traudt, who, as we have seen, exercised it quite forcefully at times. When Traudt was removed from power, the task went to Monsignor Joseph Barbian. Archbishop Kiley personally lowered the boom on errant clergy—either lashing them through sharply worded letters or hauling them into his private office at the Pabst mansion and delivering thunderous lectures that boomed through the entire house. ("Get out! Get out!" he was heard to shout at one quaking Polish priest who begged for a pastorate.)

Indeed, Milwaukee clergy of the 1920s and 1930s had significantly internalized the Romanized aspects of priestly life and identity that they learned at St. Francis Seminary—clerical attire was the cassock and biretta (a three cornered hat worn for "strolling around" and taken off at Mass). Lines of authority between pastor and assistants, and between chancery and pastors were sharply drawn and observed.

However, as daunting as a summons from the chancellor or the archbishop himself might have been, Milwaukee clergy could practice a form of passive aggression when it came to compliance with demands from central headquarters. This was evident in their response to episcopal demands for documents, statistics, and regular reports which some turned in late, incomplete or just ignored. Messmer and Traudt raged against this clerical indifference and wrote sharp letters insisting on immediate compliance—but to no avail. As Messmer grew older, sicker, and spent more time away from the archdiocese, clerical discipline flagged. Archbishop Stritch's approach to clerical discipline was not much more successful than his predecessor's. When he came to Milwaukee, he had been warned of the "loose" state of affairs under Messmer, and sought to remedy it by issuing a rather detailed set of rules and regulations for priests.[266] Some of these mandated the wearing of hats in public, stipulated the hours by which the junior clergy had to be at home and

Archbishop Samuel Stritch [AAM]

in bed at night and insisted that in riding with women in the parish automobile the woman was to sit in the back and not the front (to avoid the impression of an illicit association). Stritch also resurrected a rule from the Katzer era that forbade priests from going into taverns and saloons.[267]

But when it came to enforcing these regulations, Stritch could not carry through. As seminary rector Muench noted in his diary, "He has a tendency to make strict rules on the grounds of single and rare cases—rules which are afterward not observed because of their severity, e.g., rules regarding selling alcoholic liquors on church property, taking housekeepers, or other women, even relations in the auto, etc.—general non observance."[268] Muench was right. Early on Milwaukee priests discovered that Stritch was unusually gentle and patient in dealing even with acts of outright insubordination. As noted earlier, Father Angelo Simeoni in Kenosha virtually ignored Stritch's orders to build a church/school combination; and Bernard Traudt spent only a short time in clerical "exile" before being awarded high honors and the pastorate of prestigious St. Anne's parish; and George Meyer who had publicly insisted on good treatment for his old pal Traudt got the equally upscale St. Leo's Church on the near-northwest side. One other feature of Stritch's treatment of priests: he did not hit them hard for money. Muench related Stritch's discomfit with Cardinal Mundelein's penchant of compelling "voluntary" contributions from his clergy and of "keeping a list" of who donated and who did not. Muench related, "he [Stritch] said that no bishop can in conscience put a priest on the black list for not contributing what is asked of him."[269] Indeed, Stritch was always reluctant to ask for money, even for worthy causes. By contrast, his successor Moses Kiley levied assessments on priests without blinking an eye.

Rev. August Salick [AAM]

The variables in clerical life of this era were to be found not in lifestyle or the duties demanded, but in the personality of the pastor, who ruled with a strong hand over all aspects of the parish—finances, schedules, and personnel. The acquisition of a pastorate meant an immediate jump in the financial well-being of a priest. Pastors generally took over the loose change collection and the stole fees from weddings, baptisms and funerals. All priests received a stipend for each Mass they celebrated, but pastors monopolized the more expensive High Mass stipends (Masses celebrated with the singing of the Ordinary parts by a cantor or choir).

Stritch imposed the idea of an irremovable pastor, a concession that had been made to the American Church during the heyday of ethnic squabbling over parish jurisdictional rights. But in fact, most Milwaukee pastors died in their boots. August Salick at St. Anne's shepherded the parish from its inception in 1895 to his death in 1934. So did Patrick Durnin at St. Rose. William Haberstock was baptized, confirmed, celebrated his first Mass and from 1910 to 1935 was the pastor of Holy Trinity parish.[270] Pastors had larger living quarters and office spaces and generally more privacy and leisure time than the "junior" clergy. Clerics lived together in rectories built adjacent to the church and enjoyed a rough approximation of the communal life of religious orders, with house affairs presided over by the pastor who was assisted by one or two housekeepers. The common understanding was that the rectory was "the pastor's house." Younger clergy were occasionally reminded of this by the pastor himself or by the housekeeper (sometimes a blood relative of the pastor), whose loyalty to the pastor occasionally included scolding the younger men or reporting them to the pastor. Rectories were often places of conflict not only because of the difficulties of common living in small confines, but also because of the inevitable clashes of personalities, vanity, and clerical jealousy.

Conflicts between pastors and assistants were the stuff of clerical lore. Father Sylvester Dowling, of Milwaukee's St. Rose, found himself locked in battle with his assistant Father George Durnin whom he accused of conspiring with the superior of the Sinisinawa Dominican sisters who taught in the school.[271] Father Henry Riordan, appointed to the pas-

Rev. Patrick H. Durnin [AOP-Sin]

torate of St. Joseph's parish in Fond du Lac in 1932 went through a stream of young priests sent every year like sacrificial lambs to help him carry the sacramental and instructional load.

Under such conditions the clergy had their share of problems with addictions. Every so often one of their number would "defect" and disappear into the night—never to be heard from or referred to again. Problems were real and, in hindsight, the difficulties and dysfunctions of the rectory life became evident. No one believed, however, there was much one could do about it except shift priests from one place to another and hope that good "chemistry" would develop among the priests. And this did indeed happen. Priests often maintained friendships that they had begun as teenagers in the seminary. They vacationed together, preached at each other's Forty Hours and funerals, and enjoyed an informal camaraderie in each other's rectories—playing cards, swapping stories, and comforting and consoling one another in times of distress. In the rectories where priests got along and worked harmoniously for the good of the parish, the esprit de corps was evident. One Dominican sister at St. James in Kenosha noted the obviously loving interactions of the priests presiding at a Solemn High Midnight Mass on Christmas (Father James Cotter, Victor Kemmer, and Harold Ide): "The celebration of this Solemn High Mass by the three zealous and devout priests of this parish must have added to the joy of the people as well as the priests for there was on this occasion [*sic*] especially a unity between them that even the casual observer could not miss."[272]

Seminary priests in Egypt [AAM]

Ranks and distinctions among the clergy began to grow sharper as the number of priests increased. One factor in clerical prominence, as we have seen, was ethnicity. As English-speaking priests discovered, their German-speaking brothers enjoyed a special status and favor with the first three bishops of the see. Rank within the clergy was also defined by the status and prestige of the parish at which a priest pastored. Larger urban parishes, with enormous church buildings, large schools, scores of assistants, and thriving congregations were emblems of clerical success. Banishment was often to rural parishes or to cities distant from Milwaukee. Fortunate was the priest who was given the chance to build a new church. In an era when building materials were expensive and labor was relatively cheap, it was possible to employ first rate architects who could construct magnificent churches. Such an accomplishment was also a feather in the clerical cap, and the day of the cornerstone laying or church blessing was a golden moment for a proud pastor.

Priests continued to be assigned to parishes based on their ethnic background far into the 20th century. A typical assistant might wait anywhere from twelve to eighteen years for a pastorate (longer for the Poles because of the scarcity of Polish parishes).

When the trend toward Romanization began to take hold in Milwaukee as elsewhere, the conferral of the Roman honor "Monsignor" became more common, and also added another twist to the realities of clerical status in the archdiocese of Milwaukee. Technically, there were three ranks of monsignors: protonotaries apostolic, domestic prelates of his holiness, and papal chamberlains of his holiness. The first Milwaukee priest to receive the honor of "monsignor" was Vicar General Leonard Batz. Later, Father Patrick Donohoe of the cathedral and Father Stephen Muenich, the episcopal secretary, were given the title. As a rule then, the rectors of St. Francis Seminary and St. John's Cathedral were made monsignori. As the episcopal bureaucracy grew, those who received the honor headed departments: the chancellor, the head of the marriage tribunal, and even the episcopal secretary. Messmer began to increase the number of monsignori in the archdiocese. Stritch, who was Roman-trained, opened the spigot for these honors. By 1941, there were 11 monsignori, many of them heads of departments, schools, or pastors of prominent parishes. Archbishop Moses E. Kiley conferred the honor even more liberally than his predecessors.

The most rare protonotaries apostolic would be conferred on a few Milwaukee clergy: Joseph Rainer, Bernard Traudt, James Kelly, and Frank Schneider. This rank allowed the holder to dress as a bishop, replete with miter, zucchetto (the little skull cap worn by bishops), and to be seated at a special throne in the church sanctuary. However, this rank of monsignor was caustically re-

Msgr. James Kelly [AAM]

ferred to as a "mule bishop"—that is one unable to replicate its own. The protonotaries could not ordain men to the priesthood, nor even confirm without permission. Most Milwaukee priests were either honorary or domestic prelates or chamberlains.

The practice of conferring a title, like the decision to send some "favored" away for studies abroad, generated no little amount of clerical envy. In 1906 Messmer secretly confirmed the efforts of the School Sisters of Notre Dame through their cardinal protector to have Peter Abbelen raised to the rank of "Cameriere Segreto Soprannumerario" (although he asked that the honor be scaled back to domestic prelate). In adding his endorsement to the work of the sisters, Messmer begged that his part in the promotion be kept secret. "When the sisters came here to ask me that I should get this honor for Rev. Abbelen, I refused for reasons of policy. You know the jealousy here among the priests of the different nationalities. I have been approached by the Irish and the Poles who want all of their clergy made Monsignori."[273] These feelings had not changed much 28 years later. Aloysius Muench observed of the group of eight Milwaukee priests made monsignors just before Christmas 1934 that "the Irish priests are very quiet" when only one of their number was given the honor, in comparison to six Germans. Stritch took note of the grumbling and Muench noted that it, "told a pointed story on Irish jealousy."[274]

But priests loved the honor and parishioners dutifully celebrated the elevated status given to their parishes by having a monsignor for a pastor. At elaborate installation ceremonies and receptions they donated lavishly to help the new monsignor pay the "taxa" (often $100) for the Roman rescript and to pay for the elaborate robes. Muench, a realistic, no-nonsense kind of administrator, was genuinely touched when Stritch informed him of the honor and insisted, "None deserves it more than you." Muench, who often criticized Stritch, was overcome: "These words acted like a tonic to my timid and bashful nature. I am at times inclined to depreciate my abilities and merits."[275] The practice of conferring this rank on large groups of Milwaukee priests ended in 1965, although individual priests, James Harvey, Fabian Bruskiewitz, and David Malloy, received the honor from their associations with Roman congregations and the curia. Father George Gajdos, who served for years at St. Michael's Ukrainian church, was also honored in this way.

What was the reaction of the laity to their priests? Catholic school and other forms of religious instruction bred a deeply rooted respect for the priesthood in the Catholic laity. Annually, the pastor's name day was celebrated by parish children (who occasionally received the day off for the event). Since priests were invested with the outward trappings of a sacred office, a distinct lifestyle, and a deliberate remoteness from social interaction with parishioners (especially women), Catholic parishioners in the archdiocese probably didn't even think to ask themselves whether they liked or disliked a particular priest. Few parishioners protested the transfer of priests or wrote letters praising the sermons, parish administration or the other duties performed in their parishes. Catholic parishes were territorial, and people did not follow an eloquent preacher or a good and sensitive confessor.

Laity did however express themselves on some matters. A continual subject of complaint was that of parish boundaries. Since archdiocesan rules stipulated the boundaries of parishes and required the permission of pastors for laity to transfer from one parish to another, parishioners on the "borderlands" often found themselves in conflict with the pastors of the parishes they were supposed to attend when they insisted on attending one that might actually be closer or to which they had sentimental ties. Sometimes they attended parishes outside their boundaries because they wished to send their children to the parochial school of a neighboring parish. The pastor who held "boundary" rights was reluctant to let dues-paying members go to a neighboring parish and occasionally withheld marriage and even burial to a parishioner who did not attend or contribute regularly to the church.

Sometimes parishioners complained about certain clerical dysfunctions, such as drunkenness, bad language or abuse delivered from the pulpit. One letter from a disgruntled St. Jude's, Wauwatosa, parishioner complained that pastor J. J. Sullivan "has given us the same Christmas sermon every year that he has been here. Who wants to hear the identical flowery sermon [every year]?" This same parishioner contrasted the high-living Sullivan with his humble predecessor Joseph Hurst, who had seen the parish through the difficult days of the Depression. "When he came here he complained because there was so little house furnishings. Father Hurst paid for everything himself. It is too bad he left his davenport and matching chair, because it was not good enough for this pastor." As the parishioner added to the litany of complaints about Sullivan, he or she concluded, "I have always had a special regard for all priests, but with … conditions of this sort

Creation of New Monsignori 1938 St, Anne Church [AAM]

how can we respect the clergy as we should."[276] Archbishop Kiley, to whom the letter was addressed, could not give any reply since the letter was sent anonymously.

Efforts to Relocate the Seminary: The $5 Million Fund Drive Fiasco

As part of the general reorganization of the seminary, Messmer thought seriously about moving the entire operation away from the madding crowd around the "holy acres" at once remote St. Francis. Moving the seminary had perhaps first entered Messmer's mind when he noted that a number of religious orders were building seminaries out in remote areas. In 1922, the Pulaski Franciscans purchased Holy Rosary Academy in Corliss (later Sturtevant) and transferred their junior seminarians to the site renamed St. Bonaventure Seminary. The same friars purchased 171 acres in rural Burlington where they built a mission style friary and transferred their philosophy department in 1929.[277] In the rolling hills and shimmering lakes of far-off western Waukesha County near Spring Bank and other undeveloped areas more Catholic development took place. In 1910 the Redemptorists purchased the estate of Comptroller of the Currency James H. Eckles on Lac La Belle near Oconomowoc and opened a seminary.[278] Other religious orders, including Claretians and three different groups of Cistercians, came to Okauchee. In 1942, the Augustinians began a seminary on Lac La Belle near Oconomowoc purchasing mansions belonging to the Pabst and DuPee families. The friars cherished the rural character of the area, apart from the contamination of the city, and yet close enough to doctors, rail lines and other accouterments of civilization in nearby Waukesha.[279]

In 1924, the old Catholic Chatauqua grounds, formerly owned by the Spring Bank Company, were deeded to the archdiocese of Milwaukee. The next year, officers of the Catholic Hospital Association bought the property from the archdiocese, and then executed a 99-year lease giving six acres of vacant land and some shoreline to Messmer in gratitude for his role in helping the CHA. Eventually, the rest of the property and the lease were sold to the Cistercians of the Common Observance, who erected a monastery on the grounds.[280] On this Spring Bank property a mansion, once owned by the George Parker family (of Parker pens fame), was used by archdiocesan seminarians as a summer villa.

In Granville, a small rural village north of the Milwaukee, a devout Catholic couple, John and Katherine Klehr, donated 147 acres to the Servites of Chicago for use as a school for boys and a monastery. Construction of a great four-story stone building was begun in 1892 and the first Servite community took up residence at the Monastery of St. Philip in August 1893. The plans for a boys school never materialized, and the Chicago Servites used the property for their novitiate and a residence for their students studying philosophy and theology. Servite formation continued on the site until 1961. The monastery was closed and sold in 1969.[281]

Believing that the unspoiled rural environment and the quiet of the country was more conducive to proper clerical training, Messmer worked hard to raise the staggering sum of $5 million from all the Catholics of the state in order to build a new seminary in the country. He also hoped to provide the needed cash for a number of Catholic charitable institutions in Wisconsin.

The idea of unifying collection efforts had finally come of age during World War I. Impressed by the collective efforts of the government to raise monies through coordinated Liberty Loan campaigns, private organizations developed Community Chest collections in most major American cities as a way to raise a large amount of money for private charities. Since these funds were disbursed on a proportional basis, Catholics in Milwaukee and in other communities drew a substantial portion of their budgets for childcare work and other social provision from the general intake of revenues.

The decision to raise $5 million did not seem so implausible given the fantastic success of the big collection taken up during the war by major denominations. Catholics had received a piece of this "big collection" campaign for their war activities. In early 1919, Milwaukee's Catholic Social Welfare Bureau picked up a whopping $10,000 from the National Catholic Women's War Council in order to establish a community center for girls under Catholic auspices.[282] This home, established in the "Italian district" on 3rd and Jefferson Streets included rooms, assembly halls, and a gallery for traveling art.[283] Eight private colleges, including Marquette University, launched a "union drive" to add to their respective endowments.[284]

Messmer convinced the other bishops of Wisconsin that a statewide collection could work, with monies doled out on a pro rata basis. Although skeptical, the bishops agreed and it was determined to use the Chicago-based fund-raising firm of Ward and Company to raise the $5 million they needed for seminary and other charitable spending.[285] The plan included slick brochures and for the first time a media packet that included a grainy silent film highlighting Archbishop Messmer's call to contribute. The fund-drive was announced just before Thanksgiving in 1920, and the needs of the seminary as well as of the orphan asylums and other social welfare operations were accentuated.[286]

The United Catholic Campaign, as it was called, formally commenced on February 21,

Servite Fathers & Brothers monastery in Granville WI [Servite Archives]

1921. From its headquarters at the Plankinton Arcade in Milwaukee, campaign publicists issued a drumbeat of positive news about quotas reached and goals within striking distance, in order to generate a bandwagon behind the movement. Leading Catholic figures were recruited to head up the various dimensions of the movement to give it even greater momentum. William George Bruce, partially retired from his successful book and magazine publishing career, was the general chairman. The list of supporters included popular Third Ward Alderman Cornelius Corcoran, Judge Michael Sheridan, Milwaukee County clerk of courts Ignatius Czerwinski and Congressman (later Judge) John Kleczka. Bruce confidently predicted that the drive would be oversubscribed by $500,000.[287] One of the most innovative features of the campaign, with the exception of the film of Messmer, was the use of a handsome poster displayed in parishes and other public locations, depicting a nun begging for money. "Your Help–Helps These!" screamed the title, as it listed all the charitable institutions slated to receive money from the drive. The poster, proven effective in recruiting men and women for the armed forces in World War I and generating support for the Liberty Loan drives, reflected the influence of modern fund-raising techniques on the Catholic Church.

[*Catholic Citizen*, April 1921]

Ultimately, Messmer discovered that there was a big void between the promises and the ability of these companies to deliver. Despite all of the efforts and the huge amount of money expended with the fund-raising firm, the United Catholic Campaign was an enormous flop. Sensing this, Messmer desperately appealed to William George Bruce to step forward and rescue what he could of the effort. This the dutiful Bruce did, but came nowhere near the goal of $5 million. One of the reasons for the failure was a brief turndown in the American economy that took place as the nation readjusted to peacetime endeavors between 1920-1923. But internal difficulties were even more decisive. The bishops of the rural dioceses of Superior and Marquette pulled out of the program, citing other pressing needs.[288] Alumni of the Salesianum were not convinced of the need to build a new seminary away from the traditional and now sacrosanct St. Francis site. Some were angry that Messmer had ceremoniously removed the beloved Rainer and replaced him with the "outsider" Augustine Breig.[289] But Messmer came closer to the truth when he blamed the "indifference of some pastors and parishes" for failing to meet the goals of the drive.[290] Indeed, it was a mistaken belief that the fund-raising successes enjoyed during wartime or for specifically local needs, like the Community Chest, could be replicated with a statewide collection for projects that appeared to have no direct bearing or relevance to the lives of the givers. Catholics did give money generously, but most of this was directed to their local parishes. St. Josaphat paid off the last of its bills and elaborately decorated its church, and magnificent new churches were built throughout the diocese. To paraphrase the observation of House Speaker Tip O'Neill, all Catholicism was local.

It is not known how much was raised or how the funds were distributed to the Wisconsin dioceses. After failing to make even half of the goal, the campaign and its materials faded into obscurity, never mentioned again in the newspapers. The campaign materials, including the film and the beautiful poster, appear to have been lost to history. Perhaps an angry Messmer ordered the materials burned at a public bonfire to remove all memory of the failure. The failure of statewide interdiocesan cooperation also left its mark. The bad feelings left over from the withdrawal of the smaller dioceses from the campaign, and the lackluster collections from the ones who remained, killed any future cooperation among the Wisconsin Catholic dioceses. It would not be until a statewide Catholic census campaign in 1957 that anything of this nature would be tried again.

More Seminary Changes

Eventually, Messmer's interest in the seminary began to fade. Breig's inattentiveness to his duties led to his ouster in a "palace coup" that installed Aloysius Muench as rector in 1929. From that point until 1935, when he became bishop of Fargo, North Dakota, the seminary was the beneficiary of intelligent, energetic and purposeful leadership. Muench upgraded the seminary academically and administratively. He established burses (or endowments) for seminary education and improved the buildings by planting and landscaping (he himself helped to plant the stately trees that line the seminary drive). He introduced modern records keeping, archives and other administrative techniques that equipped the seminary for growth. Muench opened up the stacks of the Salzmann library to students and also kept up a lively program of publishing.[291]

Muench was highly visible in the archdiocese. He celebrated Mass each Sunday in Kenosha for his friend, St. Mark pastor, Alphonse Berg. He attended clerical gatherings faithfully and helped to set up the archdiocesan fund for the health care of priests, the St. Michael's Fund. Using his contacts among the many professionals he met (both clergy and laity), he brought in an impressive array of outside speakers to inform the cloistered lads about the "real" world. This roster of speakers included his friend Val Blatz who spoke about the work of the St. Vincent de Paul Societies, Justice John D. Wickershem of the Wisconsin Supreme Court, Father Edwin V. O'Hara of the Catholic Rural Life Movement, and Father Stephen Klopfer who described the work with the deaf taking place adjacent to the seminary.

Although possessed of great talent and obvious administrative ability, Muench could also be brittle and dictatorial. His relationship with Archbishop Stritch was strained nearly to the breaking point at times. He was especially put off by Stritch's somewhat lackadaisical and diffident approach to administrative matters. Relating a conversation with the equally frustrated Joseph Barbian, Muench vented to his diary about Stritch's "lack of decision." "He does not get letters out in time despite assurances and promises. New appointments should have gone out a month ago—they have not been made. An important letter on assessments has not yet been written."[292] Muench was especially disappointed with Stritch because the prelate could not make good on a promise to build a new seminary and to purchase land on 30 acres adjacent to the existing property. "He is afraid that the public might find out, and the reaction would be bad if people learned that we are investing in land in times of distress .... The Archbishop is expending a good deal of his time in keeping his ear to the ground to find out what people might think or say. Priests are beginning to mutter that he knows how to say nice things but does not do anything."[293]

A New Catholic Press

At the same time he was making changes in the structure of the seminary and other areas of archdiocesan life, Messmer also created a separate Catholic newspaper.[294] Since the 1880s, the *Catholic Citizen* under Humphrey Desmond had been the strongest English-speaking Catholic journal in Wisconsin. It also had a strong appeal in other areas of the Midwest. However, Desmond's approaches on certain matters did not sit well with Messmer, particularly on the question of temperance. Desmond eventually fell afoul of Roman authorities. In 1910, he published the account of a controversial trip to Rome made by former Vice President Charles Warren Fairbanks. During his visit, Fairbanks was refused a papal audience because he had first addressed a Methodist congregation in the Eternal City. Desmond expressed disbelief at this report attributing it to the rantings of anti-Catholic journalists and noting that a similar Vatican snub of a French dignitary had brought harsh reprisals on the Church. When the story was confirmed, he went on to ridicule Vatican diplomacy. "We ourselves would welcome the day when all the diplomats shall be sent out of the Vatican and sentenced to teach catechism to the neglected Italians." He dismissed this blunder on "some major domo of the Vatican." [295] This same editorial was run in other Desmond-controlled newspapers, including the *New Century* which circulated in Washington, D.C.

Apostolic Delegate Diomede Falconio read the article and fired off sharp letters to Messmer and Cardinal Gibbons, demanding that something be done about Desmond. To Messmer he wrote, "As your Grace may have observed, the spirit of this paper calling itself Catholic has been for some years a cause of regret and scandal to Catholics and it cannot be tolerated any longer." He commanded, "I beg your Grace to order the editor to withdraw from the title the name "Catholic," or to submit his writing before publication to a censor appointed by your Grace according to the constitution *Officium et Munerum* of Leo XIII and *Pascendi Dominici Gregis* of Pius X."[296] Messmer delegated to Traudt the task of informing Desmond. Stung by the accusations Desmond admitted his criticism of Vatican actions in the Fairbanks affair was out of line (he wished that he had not put in the crack about the Vatican "major domo"). He sought to reestablish his Catholic bona fides by reminding Falconio that he had been a strong promoter of pastoral care of Italians in Milwaukee (a cause dear to Falconio's heart). He urged Falconio to pay close attention to the content of the paper. "I will show you that your interest will be appreciated and that you are dealing with a Catholic editor who welcomes every counsel and direction to make sure his publication is safely Catholic. Not that I can hope to escape mistakes, but then, the Catholicity of a paper must be judged by its *record in the long run*, not by occasional errors."[297] Falconio was not placated. "Permit me to say," he lectured the editor, "that for a Catholic editor to assume the role of censor of the actions and dispositions of the Holy See and to belittle those who by their Sacred and high offices deserve our respect and veneration is an act of presumption which cannot be tolerated." He continued, "I regret to say that for the past few years such a reprovable tendency has been manifested in your papers in many different ways."[298] To save himself, Desmond printed a somewhat coy "retraction" noting his assumption that the whole Fairbanks incident was a misunderstanding. "We of course were mistaken in this conjecture; and a reverend friend who knows his Rome thoroughly advises us that in this instance nothing of the kind could be probable. 'Mistakes do not occur even in the decorum of the Holy See.'"[299] He also published a letter from Milwaukee priest, Father Hiram Fairbanks, a relative of the American vice president, which upheld the right of the Holy See to be critical of Fairbanks's actions, while at the same time insisting that his distant relation was not a bigot.[300]

In 1922, Messmer created a separate publishing arm for the archdiocese of Milwaukee, the *Catholic Herald.* Financing was difficult at first and a plan to merge the paper with the Dubuque-based *Iowa Daily Tribune* fell by the wayside when editor Nicholas Gonner and his daughter perished in an automobile accident.[301] In 1923, the Wisconsin Catholic Publishing Company was established and sold over $100,000 in stock, largely to the Catholic clergy. The paper was initially overseen by Monsignor Joseph Barbian, and a lay editor, John Palange, was brought in to do the actual work. Later a skilled writer and active Vincentian, Al Schimberg, did the editing and writing.[302]

The unmarried Schimberg was a native of Appleton, Wisconsin, and honed his journalistic skills while working as a reporter for the *Appleton Post Crescent* and later the *Dubuque Catholic Daily Tribune.* He studied journalism at Marquette University and took high honors. He became totally devoted to Catholic causes, and in addition to his interest in journalism was also a skilled translator and author. He took a special interest in the claims of the popular Stigmatic Therese Neumann of Konnersreuth Germany, translating highly descriptive German accounts of her sufferings. These were produced by F. Ritter von Lama in three volumes and printed by the Bruce Publishing Company. After World War II, he published *The Story of Therese Neumann* which went into six printings. He authored works on the liturgy, and biographies of St. Francis, St. Coletta and Frederic Ozanam. He was active in the Holy Name Society and the St. Vincent de Paul Society and wrote the account of the charitable organization's work in the archdiocese of Milwaukee.

Al Schimburg
[SVdPSA]

The *Herald* and the *Citizen* competed with one another, even after Desmond's death in 1932. Stritch then moved to acquire the *Citizen* and directed the priests of the diocese to sell or donate their *Herald* stock to provide funds for the transaction. By 1935, the two were blended into the *Catholic Herald-Citizen*, which became the official organ of the archdiocese of Milwaukee. A new corporate structure called the Catholic Press Apostolate was formed under archdiocesan auspices to oversee the direction of the paper. Although the *Herald-Citizen* began with limited resources, Stritch insisted that the paper become self-sufficient through the sale of subscriptions and advertising revenue. Humphrey E. Desmond, son of the former editor/owner, became the general manager. For general editor, Stritch chose archdiocesan priest, Father Franklyn Kennedy. Circulation increased dramatically after the merger, soaring from 34,800 in 1935 to 135,000 in 1956.

Social Welfare

As we have seen, social provision was one of the earliest aspects of archdiocesan infrastructure created by John Martin Henni with the establishment of orphanages and the provision of charity for the poor. The problems generated by the industrial economy demanded more consolidated action. Homes devoted to children and single females began to emerge in response to the rapid growth of industrial cities and the problem of unprotected children and single women. Since 1877 Milwaukee had the House of the Good Shepherd. Located on 25 acres in "rural" Wauwatosa, the Sisters of the Order of the Good Shepherd ran an industrial school where the children spent half a day in school and the remainder of the day at some sort of labor. The more "hardened" females were in a reformatory where they were "reclaimed from their evil lives." Many of these children left the House of the Good Shepherd, but more than a few of the women remained and became members of the Order of Magadelene Sisters.[303] In 1894, at the behest of Mayor John Koch of Milwaukee, the Sisters of Mercy opened a home for working girls on Sycamore Street. By 1913, this home, originally called Mercy Home, was renamed "St. Catherine's Home for Working Girls" and expanded its work by purchasing another home next to the original structure. Three years later, the sisters collected enough donations to build a new facility at Michigan Avenue, near Marquette University.[304]

House of Good Shepherd, Wauwatosa [AAM]

With Messmer's arrival in 1904, the scope of social provision in the archdiocese of Milwaukee was expanded significantly. The care of indigent children and "lost youth" seemed to be a priority. In 1905 he established in the old Falk mansion on 25th and South Pierce, the Catholic Home Finding Society to care for dependent and neglected children. "The homeless urchins of the street will find there a safe shelter and wide training for a life of useful industry."[305] However, this endeavor did not last long, and the home was abandoned temporarily. Father John Daly of the cathedral opened another home for boys that burned down in 1910, and the homeless lads were transferred to St. Aemillian's Orphanage. Not until 1920 was there a replacement, when St. Charles Boys Home opened through the efforts of the St. Vincent de Paul Society. In 1923 a new brick structure with facilities for 40 boys was erected.[306] Later, St. Charles would be turned over to the Brothers of the Holy Cross.

St. Charles Boys Home, Milwaukee [AAM]

In 1908, child care in Milwaukee took another step forward, as Messmer's old home, the Lynde Mansion, became the nucleus for the Misericordia Maternity Hospital, which began its work with out-of-wedlock mothers and adoption placements. The hospital later expanded its medical and surgical facilities to all women. In 1924, the Sisters of Misericordia who owned the hospital began a $350,000 fund drive for a new five-story addition and Messmer commended their efforts to the archdiocese at large.[307] He pressed all parishes to contribute, and sent a special letter to Polish pastors exhorting them to be especially generous since a large number of the charity cases and out-of-wedlock pregnancies were Polish. "There was a larger percentage of Polish girls than of any other nationality." He hastened to add, "This does not mean that more Polish girls fall from virtue than others do. It only means that while others seek help elsewhere, Polish unfortunate girls go to a Catholic institution."[308] The letter had little effect on the Polish community, who continued to maintain their own ethnic institutions. In 1908 they had already welcomed the Felician Sisters of Chicago, a Polish sisterhood, that opened St. Joseph's Orphan Asylum for children of Polish descent. They also continued to agitate for a Catholic hospital on the south side of Milwaukee, a reality the Felicians would bring about after World War II.

A major impetus for change in the methods of caring for indigent children came about after President Theodore Roosevelt hosted a conference on child welfare in the White House. Dominated by social workers who called for a greater coordination of child welfare work, the conference inspired archdiocesan institutions to develop more up-to-date and better coordinated methods of taking care of youngsters. In 1912, a boys camp was organized by Father Joseph Kroha first at Brown Deer and later at the more remote Elkhart Lake. Camp St. Michael, as it was called, claimed the honor of being the first Catholic boys camp west of the Alleghenies. In 1912, Carmelite Sisters of the Divine Heart of Jesus, a Dutch community, led by the charismatic Mother Mary Teresa of St. Joseph van den Bosch, arrived in Milwaukee and when they inquired about opening a foundation for dependent children, they were shown the old home on Pierce Street, which they accepted. Mother Mary Teresa, who saw her new foundations in visions and dreams, helped the community to grow, and waited for just the right house to come available in Milwaukee for her central headquarters. A house she had seen in a dream was shown to her by a Wauwatosa resident on Kavanaugh Place and she purchased the property. She added homes for the aged in Kenosha, and on Galena Street in Milwaukee. In 1913, the Carmelites moved out of the cramped property on Pierce Street to a newly-built structure on 17th between Wells and Wisconsin Avenues.[309] In 1915, the Milwaukee Catholic Home began caring for aged couples under the auspices of the Marquette Women's League.[310] At St. Benedict the Moor parish for African American Catholics, the Capuchins under Father Stephen Eckert founded a day nursery and an employment office. All of these efforts were supplemented and complimented by the return of the St. Vincent de Paul Society.

A Renewed Vincentianism in the Archdiocese of Milwaukee

The St. Vincent de Paul Society returned to Milwaukee in 1908.[311] The Vincentian movement began in Milwaukee in 1843 during Henni's time and lasted until 1874. Parish-based care for the poor and the indigent supplanted the need for the society. Sporadic efforts to bring back the society had failed; for example Father August B. Salick of St. Anne's parish attempted to revive the organization at his parish in 1898.

The stimulus that finally worked was an exhortation by Messmer in the *Handbook for Parishioners* of 1907, that Catholic Aid Societies, like the St. Vincent de Paul Society, be created in the parishes. For some, the need to revive more active social outreach had been stimulated by the tremendous success of socialists in capturing Milwaukee's mayoralty, running especially strong in Catholic wards. Since the Socialists had made social welfare an important part of their bid for office, Catholics moved quickly to shore up their own public visibility in this area. In 1908, the Capuchin St. Francis of Assisi parish led the way for the rebirth of Vincentianism in the Milwaukee See. By 1914 there were 20 new units of the association, cutting across ethnic boundaries as no organization had yet done in Milwaukee.[312]

A general council bound the parish associations together. Through the central council, more coordinated social welfare activity was undertaken. Spiritual ministry to the county institutions was regularized and given to the Capuchins at Holy Cross Church and later to the Pallottines, who took over the parish in 1921. A central office and clothing depot opened in October 1914; it collected scrap of various kinds to support the rent, and then collected food, clothing and fuel to pass out to people down on their luck. Vincentians were assigned to monitor the proceedings of the juvenile court, provide Christian burials for deceased indigents and in some cases provide housing and employment. The chaplaincy of the organization was assumed first by the Capuchins, and in 1915 taken over by diocesan priest Stephen Klopfer, who also managed the School for the Deaf.

Other areas of the archdiocese began to organize parish units as well. By 1934, Racine and Madison each had enough parish councils to create their own councils. In 1938 a Kenosha Particular Council was created, and in November 1939 a Particular Council was

Members of St. Benedict the Moor Conference of the St. Vincent de Paul Society on retreat in Techny IL [SVdPSA]

created in Madison. Racine, Kenosha, and Madison all developed salvage and dispersal centers. In 1934, Archbishop Stritch created an Archdiocesan General Council to even better coordinate the work of the parish-based Vincentians.

The need for more centralization was made clear by the proliferation of social welfare projects, the Carmelites' and Capuchins' independent apostolates, and the quickening of social activity generated by the St. Vincent de Paul Societies.

Centralizing Catholic Social Activity

The same social impulses that helped to create the Progressive movement in Wisconsin also guided the archdiocese of Milwaukee as it developed a professionalized and specialized social bureau.

Indeed, Wisconsin had been on the cutting edge of Progressive reform. Beginning in 1901 with the advent of Governor Robert E. LaFollette's administration, a host of social welfare proposals became public policy—old age insurance, workman's compensation, and the regulation of hours and wages for women and children.[313] The nature of social provision became much more sophisticated and "scientific" in the last half of the nineteenth century and the first decades of the twentieth. Progressive era thinkers and policy makers developed a strong attachment to efficiency, rational planning, the use of scientific experts, central organization, professionalization and the need for institutional as well as individual reform. The relatively modest accomplishments of the Progressives in equalizing some of the inequities and dislocations caused by the industrial expansion and the rise of urban life were later augmented by social safety net proposals in the Depression and in the post-World War II era.

Public policy was influenced by advances in medical technology and new attitudes on the causes of poverty and on the proper ways to raise children. In Milwaukee County, this was evident in the delivery of social services in the early years of the 20th century, particularly in the administration of orphanages and the delivery of care to the poor. In 1915, a former dentist, William Coffey (a devout member of Gesu parish), took over as the leader of the Milwaukee County institutions and introduced reforms that professionalized and expanded the provision of health care, poor relief, care for the mentally ill, and social services for the indigent.[314] Other counties in Wisconsin followed suit, inspired by similar provisions made in the reforming administration of Wisconsin's Progressives. In virtually all counties there was an emphasis on consolidation, specialization, and structured activity to replace the inefficient agencies of the past. In addition, as noted earlier, coordinated efforts to collect funds for social welfare organizations under the auspices of the Community Chest became an important source of support. These monies were essential to the expansion and development of private social welfare agencies. Catholics were among their chief beneficiaries and Catholic leaders endorsed these collections and kept an eagle eye on their disbursement.

The efforts to better coordinate and consolidate Catholic social work in the archdiocese came from a variety of sources. At St. Francis Seminary, the lectures of Philadelphia priest, Father Charles Bruehl, acquainted the seminarians with the world of Catholic social teaching. A native of Germany, Bruehl was educated at Munster and Louvain and joined the Salesianum faculty in 1909. Until his archbishop recalled him to teach at the Philadelphia seminary in 1914, he was one of the most influential and popular professors, and offered the seminarians a respite from the manual dogmatic theology by his own forays into sociology. Bruehl also had "lived" some of the theology he taught, and related at length the social challenges of his parish work in Philadelphia and at working class parishes in London and Glasgow, Scotland. Bruehl gave the seminary a lustrous reputation as a center for Catholic social thinking, and his insistence that the Church had to care for the poor greatly impressed students like Aloysius Muench and Francis Haas, both of whom would later teach social theory and practice in the seminary.[315]

The Marquette Women's League strongly encouraged Messmer to help improve the quality of social provision. The league had come into existence in March 1910, when Father Charles Mouliner, S.J., invited 350 women "to organize a league of Milwaukee women with a view to strengthen by systematic co-operation the personal and corporate endeavors of Milwaukeeans for the betterment of individual society in all literary, artistic, scientific, social and philanthropic lines of activity."[316] The league's first leader was Anna Marie Hackett. Born Anna Marie Conroy, she was educated at the Notre Dame Convent and the Academy of the Sacred Heart in Chicago. In 1900 she married physician James Hugh Hackett and enjoyed the benefits of a well-to-do life. She traveled abroad and was even received in audience by Pope Pius X. She soon devoted herself to concern for public welfare and joined any number of clubs and organizations that promoted her favorite causes.[317] Formed of independent "circles" drawn together into common endeavors, by 1919 the league enrolled nearly 900 women. The league stimulated social thinking and reform in the Milwaukee archdiocese and was one of the first forums for Catholic laywomen to exercise leadership on public issues.

Rev. Charles Bruehl (center) [AAM]

In September 1910, they opened a small office and held a fund-raiser at Milwaukee's Davidson Theater. Eager to project a Catholic voice in the discussion of public affairs, the League sponsored a series of lectures on topics of general interest. In October 1910, the women brought Catholic author James J. Walsh of Fordham University to deliver a talk on socialism at St. John's Cathedral auditorium. Family concerns were also front and center. Speakers who could address issues related to home and family won large audiences. For example, Judge John C. Karel, a local jurist, lectured to a rapt audience on the growing use of the automobile, which he warned "was the instrument of the downfall for boys and girls."[318] One of their favorite subjects was child welfare—a subject dear to the heart of many Progressive era women, Protestant, Jewish, or Catholic.

In 1910 the women invited Father William Kerby to come to Milwaukee. Kerby, an alumnus of St. Francis Seminary, had studied social and political science at Louvain and taken a rather progressive approach on the application of moral theology to the problems of society. In 1910 he founded the National Conference of Catholic Charities, which contributed to the professionalization of Catholic social work nationwide. He was also a staunch foe of socialism. Kerby's address brought home to the women his efforts to improve and upgrade the character and professionalism of Catholic services for children. In 1912, at a conference sponsored by the National Conference of Catholic Charities in Washington, the improvement of Catholic childcare facilities was discussed. One Milwaukee Catholic woman, Katherine Williams, a member of the State Board of Control, addressed the gathering with a talk, "The Poor as Victims of their Moral and Social Environment."[319]

Catholic Choral Club (June 1912) [AAM]

Milwaukee league members were energized by the conference. At the urging of the women, in early 1912, Messmer formed a nine member committee that was chaired by Father Joseph LaBoule of the seminary faculty. Other members were Matthew McEvoy (later the permanent chair), Boleslaus Goral, Anna Hackett, Mrs. Henry Sullivan, Katherine Williams, Judge Michael Sheridan, and J. F. Derse. A newly arrived and social justice oriented priest, Peter Dietz joined this group, which discussed plans "for the unification and centralization of Catholic charities in the city for better and more systematic work."[320] Dietz would play a role in subsequent development, but the real leader was an archdiocesan priest who had been a student of Kerby at the Catholic University, Matthew F. McEvoy.

McEvoy was born in 1877 in Ashford, Wisconsin, a small town in Fond du Lac County.[321] He studied at St. Thomas College in St. Paul and then went to St. Francis Seminary. Ordained in 1902, he spent seven years at St. Rose parish in Milwaukee, and in 1909 he was sent to the Catholic University of America for graduate work in sociology, where he met and studied under Kerby. Kerby urged his students to survey the various problems confronting social welfare work in different dioceses. With Messmer's blessings, McEvoy traveled around the archdiocese evaluating Catholic social welfare work. He presented his report at the first National Conference of Catholic Charities in 1910.

McEvoy noted Messmer's desire to establish some sort of coordinated council for social activity, but, he observed, "there is no fixed system of record keeping." In other parts of the archdiocese professional standards and planning had a long way to go. Of Racine he wrote, "Cooperation among Catholic Charities is not satisfactory. There is no attempt at unification."[322] After McEvoy graduated in 1913 with a doctorate in sociology, Messmer dispatched him to the seminary to teach. He kept his interests alive in the better organization of social work and helped found the Gibbons Club at Wisconsin's State Teacher's College in Milwaukee. McEvoy persuaded the Marquette Women's League to support the coordination of social activities.

Early efforts to consolidate and coordinate social welfare work in the archdiocese floundered for a time. Finally in 1916, a Bureau of Catholic Charities headed by Father Eugene Kroha was established. Kroha did not remain long. When Messmer appointed him to head St. Aemillian's Orphanage in 1918, the task of organizing Catholic charities work in Milwaukee fell to McEvoy. McEvoy tapped Evelyn L. Murphy, a professional social worker, to serve with him in the creation of the new bureau. Murphy was one of the first graduates of the National Catholic School of Social Service founded by Kerby at the Catholic University. She had earlier taught in New York City and served as the head of Catholic Settlement House in Sayerville, New Jersey. She later moved to Milwaukee and served at a small Catholic settlement house in the Third Ward. Murphy began working half-time, helping McEvoy organize the bureau and serving as the director of case work.

In June 1920, McEvoy sent out a questionnaire to all the Catholic social organiza-

Rev. Matthew McAvoy, first director of the Catholic Social Welfare Bureau [AAM]

tions he could find, to assess what they were doing and to see if there was any interest in greater coordination of efforts. Results from the questionnaire were uneven. Few appeared interested in centralized direction, but the survey did point out areas that needed attention, such as a "placing out [adoption] agency" and improvements in the city's drinking water. Most other demands related to distinct needs for new facilities, heating, and an endowment. Only Father Stephen Eckert of St. Benedict the Moor encouraged further consolidation, "Unity gives strength and it is certainly a right idea."

In May 1920, a preliminary meeting to lay plans was held at the episcopal mansion, and in June the Catholic Social Welfare Bureau was officially organized with McEvoy at the head. They created a board to oversee the operation, consisting of publisher William C. Bruce, attorney Katherine Williams, and McEvoy. On October 1, 1920, with the help of a $2,000 loan, the Catholic Social Welfare Bureau began its work in Room 208 of the Pereles Building at 85 Oneida Street. The staff consisted of the director, the field secretary and a stenographer. McEvoy had a difficult time establishing a firm foundation, as independent agencies were reluctant to give up their autonomy and fund-raising to a central bureau. Interestingly, the support for the new agency did not come from archdiocesan subsidy (although some bills were paid by the chancery through 1922), but through a series of fund-raisers and social events. McEvoy cashed in his own insurance policies to help it over its early financial difficulties. He was able to provide a steady stream of revenue when he connected the bureau to the Milwaukee Community Chest. His efforts to centralize and coordinate the childcare agencies of the archdiocese were greatly facilitated by the requirements of state licensure and by a state regulation that institutions that received donations would have to be affiliated with an oversight agency of the sponsoring institution.

McEvoy remained head of the bureau until his death in 1952. Throughout his long career he not only managed the affairs of the various childcare institutions, but he also became an important Catholic voice on public issues related to birth control, public health, and local and state legislation affecting social welfare. He kept a close watch on the recipients of the Community Chest funds, making sure that birth control advocates at Planned Parenthood never got a dime of these monies. McEvoy also played a role in shaping legislation affecting childcare institutions and matters of public health. His understudy, Father Joseph Springob (whose mother had sat on one of McEvoy's boards), carried on in the same direction after his death.

Catholics and Politics: The Struggle with Socialism and State Government

The traditional Catholic emphasis on social provision flowed directly from a desire to maintain the family as the central unit of society and an equally strong desire to resist the state's growing tendency to take over social functions related to birth, marriage and death. The emergence of socialism in Europe in the 19th century, a response to the inequities of industrial capitalism, had been opposed by the Catholic Church. Catholic opposition to socialism was ideological: socialism represented an ideology at odds with the Catholic vision of society as organic. Socialism sharpened class distinctions and tended toward violence as a resolution for pressing social ills. Socialism also called for the construction of a strong, centralized government that assumed many responsibilities for the health, education and welfare of citizens, functions best discharged by families and the Church.

The Church ultimately condemned Socialism because of its materialism and disregard for the supernatural destiny of the human race. "It is the fatal mistake of Socialism and similar theories," wrote Messmer in 1912, "to look at the social question as one of mere economy and material affairs. The radical fault of its philosophy consists in making purely material and economic conditions the source from which religious and moral ideals and principles are derived. The contrary is the truth. It is not a blind and fatalistic evolution of the material world, but the supreme will and law of God, known by the light of reason and revelation, that must regulate all conditions and affairs of the human race if man is to be happy."[323]

Catholics were also aware that socialism itself was a complex phenomenon that manifested itself on a spectrum of points of view. American socialism was in fact quite different from European socialism, and many of the issues raised by the socialists—such as pay inequity and other social ills—merited attention. Dr. Joseph Selinger, a faculty member of St. Francis Seminary, penned an article in the *St. Louis Review* in early 1904, urging just such a careful approach to socialism. He suggested that "methods of combating it be not only effective, but such as will not create misunderstanding or disaffection among working men, otherwise well disposed towards religion." And, he noted, "The Church is not opposed to Socialism of every kind: she is a friend of the poor; she encourages protection and improvement of the condition of the laboring classes; she is not the self-contained arbiter of all disputes between capital and labor, but leaves these questions to those who have the duty and quality to settle them. Sweeping denunciations should not be inconsiderately indulged in this matter."[324] Selinger's words reflected his experiences in Milwaukee while a professor at St. Francis. In fact, Catholic workers in particular were slowly migrating to a socialist party created by Victor Berger, one of the most effective socialist leaders of his time.

Socialism in Milwaukee was found first in the societies of German liberals, particularly in the Turner groups which were dominated by the old Forty-Eighters.[325] After the defeat of Populism in the 1896 elections, a group of Milwaukee socialists coalesced around Austro-Hungarian immigrant Victor Berger, who had himself "converted" to socialism.[326] Berger was an exceptionally skilled organizer and writer (he had founded a newspaper, the *Milwaukee Leader*). Berger's most important skill, however, was adapting the grand and sometimes controversial theories of socialism to fit the needs of Milwaukee's growing desire for urban reform. Since 1898, Milwaukee had enjoyed the leadership of Democratic mayor David S. Rose, a dapper and popular "character." Rose served as mayor from 1898 until 1910, interrupted by a two-year hiatus. He was influential all over Milwaukee, especially among the south side Catholic wards which were heavily dominated by the Poles. Rose would become a Catholic on his deathbed, but his second wife was Catholic and the two had donated a window to the new St. Josaphat's Church.[327]

Milwaukee Mayor David Rose [MCHS]

Between 1898 and 1901, Milwaukeeans became disenchanted with Rose. His regime accomplished many important improvements (including major purchases of land for Milwaukee's system of parks), but it was rife with corruption, as well as being openly tolerant of prostitution (which Rose did not want to eliminate but control), saloons, and gambling houses. Rose defended his leadership, claiming he wanted Milwaukee to be a "live" city—and indeed, conventions and annual meetings, including some Catholic gatherings, were held here in great number. However, Milwaukee district attorney, Francis McGovern turned the spotlight on the corruption.

Meanwhile Berger had founded the Social Democrat Party in 1901 and propagated a version of socialism that abandoned high-flown ideologies, overheated rhetoric of class struggle, and wholesale condemnations of private business. Berger's message was one of reform, honesty, and efficiency in city administration. A key element of Berger's success, and the one that made Catholic participation possible, was an alliance with local labor leaders. Many of them were still smarting from the bitter events of 1886 when workers demanding an eight-hour day were set upon by local troops. Catholic laborers, many of them on the south side, responded warmly to Berger's ideas and rhetoric. Many of them learned of his ideas through flyers and papers disseminated all over the city in rapid time by the "Bundle Brigade." In 1910 disgust with Rose, the rising needs of labor and the general diffusion of Progressive reform on the local, state and national levels allowed Milwaukeeans to elect their first Socialist mayor, a former woodcarver named Emil Seidel.

Catholic response to the political scene in the first decade of the 20th century was mixed. Among Messmer's first acts was halting the use of parish or school halls for political meetings. "For the church to meddle in politics," he lectured, "is not only entirely opposed to American sentiment and the spirit of our laws; but it would also prove injurious and hurtful to the Catholic interests in our country."[328] But the socialist tide was rising in Milwaukee and Desmond at the *Catholic Citizen* noted after the April 1904 elections that Socialists were taking more seats, especially in the German Republican wards. However, he noted, "In the distinctly Polish ward, the Fourteenth, they polled 666 votes, about one-fifth of the total vote." Desmond prophesied incorrectly, "It is probable, however, that this election marks the high tide of Socialism and that the coming fall election will show a tendency to return to old party alignments."[329] As socialism continued to make more inroads among Catholic workers, Messmer took stronger measures to dissuade Catholics to turn away. In the *Handbook*, Messmer warned that "in our days many labor unions are, unfortunately, entirely committed to the false and pernicious principles of socialism." He likewise urged Catholics to lobby against the presence of socialist reading material in public libraries and public sitting rooms.[330]

Milwaukee Mayor and Congressman Victor Berger [MCHS]

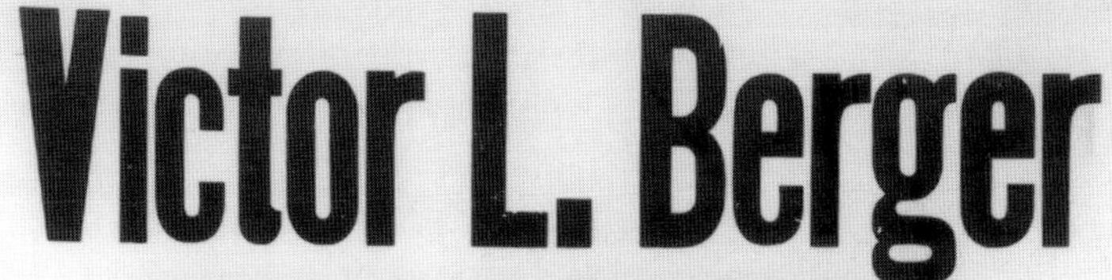

The Socialists triumphed in 1910, electing Seidel mayor, sweeping the aldermanic wards, and sending Berger to Congress. One key to their success was the heavy support in the 14th ward, which had produced a strong turnout six years earlier. As historian Frederick Olson has noted, the Socialist party "devoted special attention [to the 14th] for four elections."[331] He also observed, however, that Catholic support for the party was not monolithic; the socialists lost races in three other strongly Catholic wards in the downtown area and one on the west side. Nonetheless, the *Catholic Citizen* lamented what the socialists would do "with defenceless [*sic*] Milwaukee" by quoting liberally from Berger's press statement: municipal ownership of public utilities, free textbooks (a *bête noire* for Messmer), free public health, the condemnation of slum property as a way to end pauperism and prostitution."[332]

Seidel would serve only one term as mayor. After making important strides in carrying out the socialist agenda, he was driven from office. This happened in 1912 when the legislature changed Milwaukee's charter to permit the creation of the Non-Partisan League—a fusion of Democratic and Republican candidates led by German Lutheran Gerhard Bading. The Non-Partisan League was quite aware of the ethno-cultural dimensions of Milwaukee's politics and made sure that the fusionist ticket contained a Polish Catholic, Louis Kotecki, who ran for comptroller, and P. J. Carney, an Irish Catholic who ran for treasurer. The election of Bading drew national attention. The Omaha *True Voice* noted that the victory of Bading, "taught the old parties the necessity of 'cleaning up.' Let us hope they remain clean." The *Pittsburgh Observer* opined, "It [socialism] has been tried under circumstances most favorable to its success; and it has been found wanting." The Los Angeles *Tidings* compared the ouster of Seidel to similar developments in the City of the Angels, when the "safe and sane" elements of its civic community produced a victory over a socialist candidate.[333] The seminary quarterly *Salesianum* also rejoiced in the ejection of the "stigma on Milwaukee's fair name." But it also noted that the Socialists had pulled nearly 30,000 votes—3,000 more than their 1910 victory. It urged the newly elected Bading regime to pay heed to the demand for good government: "In the interests of religion, the home, and safe and sane economic principles, it is to be hoped that Milwaukee's present administration will give a square deal to all, leaving room for not even the remotest suspicion of prostitution of office for private greed or gain."[334]

Tensions between Catholics and socialists flared occasionally. Desmond of the *Catholic Citizen* pounced on anti-Catholic lapses or comments by socialist leaders or organs. For example, when the socialist weekly, *Milwaukee Leader,* repeated old American Protective Association canards about "Catholic" assassins, naming John Wilkes Booth, the murderer of Abraham Lincoln and Leon Czolgosz, who gunned down William McKinley, Desmond was quick to retort that Booth was probably an Episcopalian like his father and that Czolgosz had given up his Catholic faith when he "embraced anarchism which is a cousin-germ of Socialism." He further taunted, "Why omit the names of other comrades from the list" citing the socialist assassins of Archbishop [Georges] Darboy of Paris, the Empress Elizabeth of Austria and President [Marie Francois Sadi] Carnot of France."[335]

Desmond also fired the occasional blast at the local socialists who geared up for another try at the mayoralty in 1914. The editor accused the *Milwaukee Leader* of sympathies toward the anti-Catholic American Protective Association, when he wrote, "When the Socialists last had control of our city government, the sign 'No Catholics Need Apply' was tacitly hung over the doors of the city hall." Moreover, Desmond noted, when school board elections were held in April 1909, the Milwaukee Socialists sent hundreds of pamphlets through their "Bundle Brigade" urging voters to "Scratch All Catholic Names on the ticket." When the *Leader* replied caustically that it would take more than one blast from Archbishop Messmer's ecclesiastical bugle to throw down the edifice of public education," Desmond replied, "Socialism in Milwaukee is becoming A. P. Aism, impure and crooked. And the comrades don't deny it." He further warned, "No doubt the wiser Socialists would prefer to keep their party free of sectarian squabbles; but at present in Milwaukee, it looks as if the A. P. A. tail were wagging the Socialist dog."[336]

The *Leader* occasionally took potshots at some Catholic effort or matter, but by and large the paper heeded the advice of Desmond and stayed away from too many attacks on religion or priests. In 1916, the Socialists came back into power when they elected Daniel Webster Hoan mayor by a narrow margin. Hoan, who had entered government as city attorney in 1910, survived the purge of the party in the Bading election of 1912 and had earned praise for pressuring the city railway system for lower fares and better service.[337] Hoan may have had distant Catholic roots, being the son of an Irish laborer. Even if he had been predisposed to be antagonistic to Catholics, however, his marriage to Agnes Corcoran, a member of St. Rose parish, may have kept those tendencies in check—as well as the fact that socialists did not control the common council. Catholic voices approved of Hoan, and Desmond explained to his readers that Hoan's work on city transportation and his support for a municipal

Milwaukee Mayor Daniel Hoan [MCHS]

lighting system, "drew to his support many thousand non-Socialist votes."[338] Within a month of his election, Hoan appeared at a Catholic party sponsored by the Catholic Order of Foresters at St. Thomas Aquinas parish. Hoan played cards, danced and, when he was called on by Father Edward J. Blackwell for a few remarks, "responded very pleasingly."[339] Even though Messmer strongly urged Catholics to vote against Hoan in the 1919 election most Milwaukee Catholics simply ignored the dire warnings of anti-clerical and anti-religious radicalism heaped on Hoan.[340] Hoan would hold on to the mayoralty of Milwaukee until 1940 and enjoy peaceful and even amicable relationships with Catholic communities, occasionally even attending Mass with his wife.

Catholics were also reassured by the fact that a non-partisan majority controlled the city's common council, which was chaired by Cornelius Corcoran of the Third Ward.[341] Even if Hoan had been a fire-breathing radical, his ideas would never have passed muster with the council. The political equilibrium, reinforced by Milwaukee's own conservative political stability, reassured everybody. Even more formal Socialist activities in Milwaukee began to lose steam with World War I. Divisions among the Socialists over the war created tensions and accusations of sedition against the *Milwaukee Leader* and Victor Berger. Even though he was prosecuted, Berger never lost his seat in Congress until 1922. He later forged an alliance with Progressive Robert LaFollette, and supported his bid for the presidency on a third party ticket in 1924. But the Socialist party he had forged in Milwaukee petered out by the end of the 1920s.

Engaging the Social Question: One Response to the Socialist Challenge

The rise of socialism, and in particular many Catholics' embrace of it, gave Messmer and others reasons for pause. While they disdained the class consciousness, and anti-clericalism associated with the movement, clearly the popularity of the socialist program responded to real needs. Milwaukee's long tradition of socialism and a social approach to public problems resonated with Catholic social teaching.

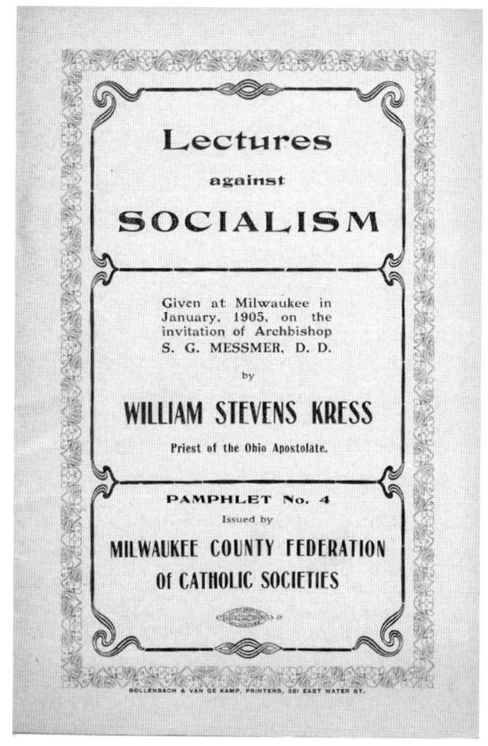

Lectures against SOCIALISM

Given at Milwaukee in January, 1905, on the invitation of Archbishop S. G. MESSMER, D. D.

by

WILLIAM STEVENS KRESS

Priest of the Ohio Apostolate.

PAMPHLET No. 4

Issued by

MILWAUKEE COUNTY FEDERATION Of CATHOLIC SOCIETIES

BOLLENBACH & VAN DE KAMP, PRINTERS, 381 EAST WATER ST.

[AAM]

Catching the spirit of Progressive reform in Wisconsin, some Catholics wondered aloud if they were doing enough to address the cause of "social betterment." Speaking to a civic club on the subject of "The Church and the Laboring Man," City Treasurer J. P. Carney, observed "no man has more forcibly campaigned against socialism in Milwaukee than me," but by failing to lobby for a minimum wage bill in the coming legislative session the Church was guilty of negligence in looking after the welfare of the people "who compose 75 percent of its membership." Carney noted the united effort of many churches to bring a dance hall ordinance before the common council, "How much more ought they to work for the welfare of the people who comprise nearly all of their membership."[342]

Carney's call for a more aggressive social Catholicism was echoed by Messmer who welcomed the U.S. Catholic Church's most effective force against socialism nationwide, Father Peter E. Dietz, who came to the archdiocese in early 1912.[343] Dietz (1878-1947) was born on the lower East side of Manhattan of German immigrant parents. He began studies for the priesthood at the age of 16 and spent a short time with the Society of the Divine Word studying at their seminary in Moedling, Germany. He came back to the United States filled with ambition and enthusiasm for the cause of social justice and economic reform. He completed his studies at the Catholic University of America and was ordained for the diocese of Cleveland, Ohio in 1903. He quickly aligned himself with the new social justice emphasis of the reconstituted *Central Verein*, and wrote for the organization's principal publication, the bilingual *Central Blatt* and *Social Justice* (Dietz wrote in English while another Clevelander and future Milwaukee priest, Augustine Breig, wrote in German). Disagreements with *Central Verein* director Frederick Kenkel, made this a short stop, and Dietz turned his attention to church work with organized labor. His "Militia of Christ for Social Service" was founded to bring Catholic influence to bear on the shaping of American labor organizations, particularly through the American Federation of Labor (AFL). His key emphasis was combating socialist or communist tendencies in these organizations. Active branches of the

Essays in Socialism-I

BY

Rev. Andrew E. Breen, D. D.

Public Interests Committee
Bishop Henni Assembly
Fourth Degree, Knights of Columbus
Milwaukee, Wisconsin

[AAM]

organization (which was never formally linked with the AFL) were to be found in every major industrial city, including Milwaukee. Dietz came to Messmer's attention because of their mutual interest in the American Federation of Catholic Societies which Dietz saw as an important vehicle for social reform. In 1911, he helped create the Social Service Commission to press the organization to implement Catholic social teaching.

Dietz's reputation as a socialist fighter through the Militia of Christ was well-known when he arrived in Milwaukee. Messmer assigned him to Ss. Peter and Paul parish on the east side of Milwaukee, and turned him loose to coordinate Catholic social services in a way that would better serve the poor and working class.[344] Dietz and others coordinated Catholic social services under one centralized administration, but Messmer gave him more time to work on his efforts to arrest socialist advances (now somewhat slowed because of Seidel's defeat) and released him from parish duties to work full-time with trade union issues and writing.[345]

Since the days Charles Bruehl had been on the faculty of the seminary, Catholic social teaching became an important piece of the seminary curriculum. Priests were trained to identify social ills and to propose solutions based on the prescriptions of the social encyclicals. Catholic social teaching as elaborated by moral theologian Monsignor John A. Ryan of St. Paul and others struck a resonant chord in the socially-minded Catholic milieu of Milwaukee. Augustine Breig, who specialized in social thought in his advanced studies in Switzerland, taught it for a time at St. Francis Seminary. It was later picked up by Aloysius Muench who studied social doctrine in Fribourg, Switzerland.

Father Francis Haas, a Racine native ordained in 1916, also was deeply influenced by Catholic social teaching. He impressed Father Robert Roche of Holy Rosary parish in Milwaukee, who promoted him for advanced studies and a teaching position. Roche also urged him to pay close attention to the "little people." He later parlayed a seminary teaching position into an opportunity for advanced study at the Catholic University under Ryan, then returned to teach social ethics at the seminary. He joined Muench on the lecture circuit, with forums provided by the Holy Name Society, the Knights of Columbus, the Councils of Catholic Men and Women, and an array of national Catholic gatherings. Haas became extremely interested in labor relations and mediated strikes in Wisconsin. Later he was appointed head of the National Catholic School of Social Service in Washington, D.C. Working closely with Ryan, who helped him gain the appointment in Washington, Haas also developed close ties to the Franklin D. Roosevelt Administration. In 1935, Muench became the bishop of Fargo, North Dakota, Haas was recalled for a time to head St. Francis Seminary. But later he was permitted to return to Washington, where he resumed his duties at the Catholic University until his selection as bishop of Grand Rapids, Michigan, in 1943.

Both Haas and Muench expressed, in their speaking and writing, a sometimes harsh critique of laissez-faire capitalism, insisting again and again on an organic vision of society that emphasized cooperative action directed toward the common good. Much of this teaching stemmed from the general corporatist thrust of Catholic social teaching elaborated in *Rerum Novarum* and *Quadragesimo Anno*. It would also be fair to say that the atmosphere of cooperative activism present in Milwaukee's German parishes, the network of charities, as well as the coordinated efforts of groups like the Milwaukee Archdiocesan Council of Catholic Women (MACCW) inspired Muench and Haas.

Catholics and Progressivism: Gender, Prohibition and World War I

Catholic support for the politicians of the period 1900 to 1940 is difficult to ascertain. According to historian John Buenker, the traditional ethno-cultural split that had characterized Wisconsin's voting patterns held through much of the early part of the century. Catholics generally supported Democrats and elected local ethnic leaders like Michael Kruszka and Humphrey Desmond to state offices. Catholic support for Robert LaFollette was tepid. LaFollette, who despite his French surname, was not a Catholic, was regarded with suspicion because of his support by rural and university elements, both of which manifested hostility toward the Catholic Church. Still, Catholics like educator Edward A. Fitzpatrick came to work for Progressive regimes, and Catholic officeholders did represent Catholic needs.

Beginning in 1911, the state legislature became more active on a number of fronts, among them child welfare, education and marriage laws. The increased activism of the government required a more coordinated and effective response from Catholics anxious to protect their interests in Madison. As was the case with many state capitals that were not the see city, consultation on Catholic issues often took place with the pastor of the most prominent Catholic church of the city. In this case, the Madison church of St. Raphael and its pastor Patrick Knox was often the port of first call. Later, Messmer appointed Father James J. Oberle as his chief liaison with the legislature. Oberle was born in New York in 1876 and came to Wisconsin when he was 12-years-old. He studied for the priesthood at St. Lawrence in Mount Calvary and St. Francis Seminary.[346] He was ordained to the priesthood in 1898 by Cardinal James Farley and headed to Milwaukee where he was appointed first to St. Boniface and then to Holy Redeemer mission on the still undeveloped north side of Milwaukee. In 1904, he was sent to be pastor of St. Stephen's Church in New Coeln, where he remained for much of his priesthood. During his tenure the church burned twice, in 1908 and 1926. Between fires, however, this rural parish had little activity except on weekends, and so Oberle studied law at Marquette University and graduated in 1913. Although a very large and articulate man, Oberle moved quietly through the legislative halls in Madison. He cultivated a number of friendly contacts, including the very conservative Milwaukee state Senator

Bernhard Gettlman and Eau Claire solon, Roy Wilcox.

As Catholics in Milwaukee contended with socialism, the social ferment of the era reemphasized other questions of social concern: gender and temperance. The question of women's rights, especially the right of suffrage, engaged Milwaukee Catholics. The spearheads of reform in this area were groups of middle-class women, largely of British-American origins, who often linked suffrage with other reforms in American life.[347] In 1869, the Wisconsin Women's Suffrage Association (WWSA) was formed and from 1885 to 1913 was headed by a Universalist Minister, Olympia Brown.[348] The WWSA enjoyed limited support and went through a period of low numbers and limited visibility even as other women's organizations flourished. In 1910, the WWSA's new leaders rejuvenated the idea of women's suffrage. Taking advantage of the sentiment sweeping the country, these new leaders staged marches, reached out to working women (stripping the suffrage question of its former associations with nativism and temperance reform) and put more direct pressure on politicians through parades, and letter-writing campaigns.

Bernard Gettleman [SHSW]

These efforts brought about a suffrage referendum in 1912, and it lost badly in November, carrying only 14 of 71 counties. Historian John Buenker notes that most of the strength for the amendment came from the Scandinavian and Yankee strongholds. Opposition came from liquor interests (who linked suffrage with Prohibition), traditional conservatism among Wisconsin voters and official Catholic opposition to the move. Messmer made his feelings about the nature of women and the question of women's suffrage known in early 1912 as the campaign crystallized. The archbishop questioned publicly why women needed the vote to influence society: "Divine Providence has endowed woman with a quiet, soft and sweet power over man, for good or bad, which seems almost irresistible, a power the sort of which man with all his masculine mind and heart cannot exert over his fellow brother." He continued, "Nor does women need the right of the ballot or of suffrage in order to exert her power to its fullest limit; in fact, she is every way stronger without the ballot." Messmer declared that Catholic women would be better served by the formation of a united league of women that could bring the strengths of their nature to bear on the important problems of the day.[349] In another speech Messmer declared that a "woman's sphere [is] the home" and that her primary task was the rearing of children.[350]

After the referendum was defeated, Messmer amplified his opposition to women's suffrage before a meeting of the Federation of Catholic Societies in Watertown. Quoted verbatim by a *Milwaukee Journal* reporter, Messmer lectured, "A great many of the theories and principles upon which this movement is supported are anti-Christian. A great many of the theories and principles upon which this movement is supported are anti-Christian and infidel. A great deal more is pure sentiment with no reason to support it." Messmer was willing to grant women "a certain modified suffrage" such as election to the school board, but he did not want a woman representative in Washington. Messmer insisted, "The authority of the family rests with the man. Woman was given to him as a helpmate, not as an equal. This absolutely excludes equality between them."[351] Later, Messmer claimed that he had been misquoted by linking equal rights with infidelity. But his position on women's suffrage remained firm and to some extent reflected the feelings of the Catholic flock.[352] But even by the standards of the day, Messmer held fairly benighted views about women. Living in a man's world most of his life and given to blunt speech, Messmer's misogynistic tendencies were evident. For example, in a 1915 circular to the clergy about proper procedures for confirmation, he reiterated his order about the headdress of women who approached the sacrament: "The modern crazy hats for women render a decent performing of the holy ceremony impossible."[353]

The question of temperance, as we have seen, was an issue that divided Catholics among themselves and set them at variance with other elements of Wisconsin's population. The heavily German Catholic population of the archdiocese of Milwaukee, who cherished a weekly visit to the beer garden, opposed any kind of prohibition or temperance legislation. Moreover, the chief proponents of temperance reform, the Women's Christian Temperance Union, which had been founded in Wisconsin, were often white, Anglo-Saxon Protestant women who liberally sprinkled their exhortations to temperance and abstinence with nativist comments and hostility to ethnic Catholics. Catholic opponents of temperance however found themselves in an uneasy league with saloon keepers and liquor interests who also had a vested interest in prohibiting any law that curtailed their livelihood.

The cause of temperance in the archdiocese of Milwaukee lost a powerful voice when Father James Cleary left the archdiocese in the 1880s. However, leadership in the cause of Catholic Prohibitionism was taken up by another archdiocesan priest, Father M. J. Ward. After a short stint at Benton, Ward was appointed to the pastorate of St. Thomas parish in Beloit and spent the remainder of his priesthood there. A 6-foot-7-inch giant, Ward wore a full beard and was a "conspicuous presence wherever he went." The priest became one of Beloit's most beloved citizens, helping to attract industries and a new hotel to the small river valley city. But his strongest efforts were in behalf of the cause of abstinence. He served as president of the Catholic National Total Abstinence Society, lobbied hard in Ohio and Wisconsin for anti-saloon legislation and was one of the founders of the Catholic Prohibition Society.[354] Ward never lived to see the triumph of his effort, dying in 1915, four years before the 18th amendment was ratified in 1919.

Although no friend of saloons and excessive drinking, Archbishop Messmer did all he could to stem the tide of Prohibition, suggesting openly that some of the enthusiasm for it came from Protestants eager to stop the use of sacramental wine. These "sectarian" and "sinister" forces were "trying to profit by this opportunity of attacking her in the most sacred mystery entrusted to her." Messmer sternly forbade any prohibition speeches on Catholic property.[355] The 18th Amendment, passed during the World War as a food conservation measure, did not sit well with Catholic leaders.[356] Adjustments were made under the provisions of the Volstead Act for the securing of altar wine, but the idea of prohibition stuck in the craw of Messmer, who made headlines in 1926 when he publicly denounced the enforcement of Prohibition and urged that the law be modified to permit the sale of beer and wine. "The law of prohibition was absolutely unnecessary to remedy the evil of drunkenness at the time it was passed," he lamented to a *Milwaukee Sentinel* reporter in 1926. "Conditions are now worse than they were before prohibition. Drunkenness was confined to grown-up men; now it assails women and particularly our young people … now at sociables and dances of young people the 'hipper' is a regular attendant."[357]

Messmer, like many other Americans, probably flouted the law. Tales of meetings of the cadre of old pastors called the "kitchen cabinet" who gathered at Messmer's home are replete with rooms blue with cigar smoke and tumblers of spirits. Messmer's suppliers included Father George Meyer of Holy Angels parish and the School Sisters of St. Francis, who brewed a cherry-based violation of the Volstead Act that they passed off as a medicinal beverage called "*kirchenwasser*."[358]

World War I

Both prohibition and women's suffrage passed constitutional muster during World War I. This great conflict deeply divided the citizens of Wisconsin, composed as they were of nationalities on both sides of the war. The heavily German and Austro-Hungarian elements of the archdiocese were naturally concerned about the war. Even the Irish surnamed Catholics could not rouse much support for Great Britain, particularly after the Easter Rebellion of 1916. When the war broke out in August 1914, Messmer was abroad with Traudt and several other priests, making his *ad limina* to Rome and visiting his native Switzerland. In May Messmer conferred for the last time with Pius X, who would die that August. Traudt returned in August, but Messmer stayed on in Europe hoping to secure an audience with the new pope, Benedict XV. When he wrote home, his pro-German sympathies were on display. "Belgium is paying a just punishment for its treacherous conduct against Germany, which is clear proof to show that both Belgium and France have broken Belgium's neutrality even before the war was fully opened," he wrote to Traudt. While he lamented the destruction of the famed library of the University of Louvain, he turned his ire on the Belgians, who fired on the "heroic" German soldiers trying to save the rauthaus (city hall) and the cathedral. "They must have become crazed in their fury against the German invaders." He ridiculed the English and French armies, and noted, "I have followed the beginning of the war very closely and cannot but pray for the victory of the just cause of Austria and Germany."[359] On October 15, he spoke with the newly-elected Pope Benedict for a half hour. Benedict, who would later attempt to broker peace among the belligerents, inquired of Messmer about the state of opinion on the war in his native Switzerland. When he returned to Milwaukee in November, his support for Germany was even sharper. "I do not know whether or not Germany will win this war," he told a reporter from the *Evening Wisconsin*, "but I hope from all my heart she does." When asked if the war was a "sin" Messmer huffed, "A sin?! It was a sin on the part of Russia and England to start it. I feel that England is responsible to a great extent for the war."[360]

Messmer had a bit of difficulty finding passage home on a liner that would brave the war-infested waters of the Atlantic. When he arrived in mid-November, he was greeted with the gift of a new automobile.[361] Milwaukee Catholics followed the war with great interest. One Milwaukee pastor, Father Paul Siska, pastor of St. Stephen's Slovak church, was drafted into the Austrian army, but released in early 1915. Polish Catholic women raised funds for their co-religionists under the direction of Bishop Edward Kozlowksi. By late January they had collected more than $8,000.[362] In the next year, Polish Catholics raised $25,000 for relief.[363] When tensions flared internationally over shipping rights and the sinking of vessels with Americans on board, the Milwaukee County Federation of Catholic Societies sent a petition to President Woodrow Wilson and Senator W. J. Stone of Missouri, chair of the Senate Foreign Relations Committee, urging both to practice restraint so as to prevent "our beloved nation from being drawn into murderous war."[364]

When Emperor Franz Josef died in late 1916, Messmer officiated at a requiem Mass at which Austrian Joseph Rainer preached. Recalling words he had spoken in the Hapsburg court four years earlier on a visit to Vienna, Rainer declared, "Although we Austrians have severed political ties to enjoy the rights of American citizens, our love for and devotion to the Imperial house of Austria and the venerable jubilarian Emperor can be torn from our hearts by no earthly power and by no distance however great."[365] Messmer kept a firm lid on any clerical opinionizing on the war and strictly forbade priests from speaking on the 1916 election, in which the question of preparedness and the war loomed as an important issue.[366]

The coming of war in 1917 silenced Messmer's open support of the central powers, but enthusiasm for the Allies' cause was muted. Messmer continued to clamp down on any clerical sentiments expressed in favor of the Allies. In 1917 Jewish convert Paul Schaffel, a native of Bessarabia in Romania, and an advocate of Romanian freedom from the Hapsburgs, spoke favorably of the Allies at a seminary rally. Messmer summarily removed him from his scripture teaching post at St. Francis, and banished him to St. Joseph's parish in Waupun, including the chaplaincy at the state prison.[367] In the interim before Father Andrew Breen could come from Rochester to take over seminary scripture classes, Messmer taught the subject himself.

On the other hand, Messmer did nothing to stop those who criticized the Allies. Irish Catholics brought to Milwaukee Mrs. Hannah Sheehy Skeffington, a virulently anti-British propagandist whose editor-husband, Francis, had been shot by British soldiers during the Easter Rebellion. She herself escaped from virtual house arrest in Britain. Skeffington who breathed fury against the British spoke to a large crowd in the cathedral auditorium, raising money for the Irish Relief Fund.[368]

The declaration of war in April had been opposed by some Wisconsin legislators, like Victor Berger and Senator Robert LaFollette. Concern about the loyalty of Wisconsin Catholics manifested itself in an unusual incident involving the Federal Bureau of Investigation. An unidentified woman had overheard a streetcar conversation suggesting that there were 1000 rifles hidden in "some German Catholic Church" in Milwaukee. Agents of the F.B.I., led by W. S. Fitch, inspected fifteen German Catholic churches and found nothing. The matter was cleared up when an ordnance officer from the federal arsenal at Rock Island, Illinois, recalled that a group of Slovak cadets at St. Stephen's parish had purchased a few outdated Springfield rifles for drilling. An apologetic Fitch wrote to Father George Meyer of Holy Angels parish, "There was no discrimination in our investigation: we simply followed up the rumor." The text of this letter was reprinted on the front page of the *Catholic Citizen* accompanied by grumbling from Desmond that the "Federal Secret Service [*sic*: Federal Bureau of Investigation] cannot allow anything to pass, overlooks nothing and feels compelled to take cognizance of even the slightest rumors." He expressed gratitude, however, that Fitch's thorough investigation "now gives these churches a clean bill."[369]

Both the ideological and military mobilization for the war found Catholics "doing their bit" to keep "Old Glory" flying. Messmer sought to dispel any doubts about his loyalty by giving a "fervently patriotic" address to Red Cross workers and speedily releasing priests for military chaplaincies. In November 1917 Messmer issued a "War Pastoral" that was read in all the churches of the archdiocese of Milwaukee. He assured some of his skeptical co-religionists that the war was a just war and urged all citizens to do "whatever is necessary to prosecute this war to victory." He urged young Catholic men to enlist in the service and to purchase Liberty Bonds, and he asked Catholic women to supply clothing, bandages and other knitted goods for the soldiers. He enjoined the Knights of Columbus to "minster to the welfare and comfort of our soldiers." He concluded, "Let us pray for the success of our army on the battlefield .... But in doing all this let us not cease to pray to the Lord of Hosts for a speedy and lasting peace."[370] Jesuit Father Charles Mouliner added to Messmer's words when he concluded his reading of the pastoral by saying, "This is not only a just war, in which we may enter—it is a holy war in which we must take part."[371]

Local Catholics began to volunteer for service. Marquette's campus became a drilling ground for young recruits, and Marquette President Herbert Noonan, S.J., gave a strong patriotic speech before a large crowd at the Plankinton Arcade. Flag poles were erected, fraternal orders voted resolutions of support, and Polish Catholic enlisted actively for all-Polish units. "Flags fly from all the Catholic schools and the children are given daily lessons in patriotism," declared the *Catholic Citizen* on May 12, 1917.[372] That November, 6,000 Milwaukee Poles turned out for a huge patriotic rally at the auditorium that highlighted tableaux of patriotic scenes, and an address by the scholarly Father Michael Wenta of Ss. Cyril and Methodius parish. "When the living picture was completed, the audience knelt and renewed allegiance to the cause of the allies."[373]

Chaplains from the archdiocese were recruited to serve the men in the armed forces. Milwaukee had given only a few priests to

Fr. John J. Shanahan [AAM]

chaplaincies. Father Henry Stemper, pastor of St. Boniface, had served with American troops in Puerto Rico during the Spanish American War. But the most famous priest-chaplain of that time was Father Michael Huston, a priest and chaplain of the National Soldiers Home in Milwaukee, who was one of the leading figures in the military. A native of Ireland, he had come to the United States in 1884 and after his ordination served for 10 years at the cathedral. After his parish service, he became the chaplain of the large soldier's home caring for nearly 2,000 veterans of the Civil War. Huston endeared himself to the men and their families and became one of the main contacts with the government in helping to identify chaplains for the world war effort. Among the first Milwaukee priests to join was Father Thomas F. Regan. Regan, of St. Rose parish, had been the son of the quartermaster and postmaster of the Soldiers Home. He was ordained in 1912 after studies in Washington, D.C., and after a brief stint in Racine was sent back to the Catholic University for further studies. From there he entered the United States Navy.

Rev. Michael Huston [AAM]

Other chaplains included Father August Gearhard, a nephew of Bishop Augustine Schinner. Gearhard, was ordained by his uncle in 1917 and within a year volunteered for chaplain duty. He was named chaplain of the 318th infantry serving in France and in the fall of 1918 saw bitter combat. After receiving the Silver Star and three citations for "heroism in action," he was discharged in 1919. In 1924, he enlisted in the Army Reserve and was called back into action in 1942. Named chaplain of the 5th Army Air Force, he entered the combat zones of the Pacific. He rose in the ranks of chaplains, being named brigadier general in 1950 and was deputy chief of chaplains for the U.S. Air Force. Gearhard became pastor of St. Joseph Church in Waukesha and lived long enough to see youthful protestors in his church decrying American military involvement in Vietnam.[374]

Father George Eilers had the love of the military in his veins and had celebrated his first Mass in the chapel of the Soldiers Home.[375] Every Sunday, while he was on the faculty of the seminary, he traveled out to the Soldiers Home to celebrate Mass. At Huston's recommendation he entered the chaplaincy and was attached to the 121st machine gun battalion in the 106th infantry.[376] In July 1918 Eilers was sent to the Ypres Salient in Belgium. There he witnessed some of the most savage fighting of the war as Allied forces broke the Hindenburg line between St. Quentin and Cambria. "The loss was great and day and night the stream of wounded continued, only to give place to the grimmer task of burying the dead .... The fields and hills leading to that St. Quentin canal will always remain in my mind, a scene of ghastly horror."[377] In a piece that appeared in the archdiocesan newspaper, Eilers wrote about saying Mass in a bombed out church for 500 soldiers. "I heard a hundred confessions before Mass," he reported, and during the offertory a lone bugler [*sic*: trumpeter or cornetist] had begun playing the Marian hymn *O Sanctissima.* "In a few moments, all too brief, this had died away, but I could feel the effect it had on all of us." At the *Sanctus*, the trumpeter played "Nearer My God to Thee," "its last echo had just died when the solemn moment of the consecration brought us all in, very fact, nearer to our God." Hiding the obvious terror of the experience, Eilers spoke of the constant shelling that beset his unit, "I have been very fortunate, have only been touched once with shrapnel—only marked my coat, but did not hurt me."[378] In 1924, a grateful Polish government honored Eilers by creating him a Chevalier of the Order of *Polonia Restituta* (an award given to pianist/politician Ignace Padrewski, and Milwaukee clerics, Wenceslaus Kruszka, Boleslaus Goral, Bronislaw Celichowski). "This officer rendered invaluable service during all the battles and engagements of the 106th infantry in Belgium and France," read the award, "displaying courage of a high order under shell fire and often going beyond the call of duty in ministering to the wounded officers and enlisted men of the regiment, his heroism and

Rev. George Eilers [AAM]

good cheer being a constant inspiration to all ranks."[379] As in other wars, letters home from these chaplains gave insights into the reality of the front. Gearhard wrote to his parents in mid-1918 from "Somewhere in France," "The people here are very poor but all are Catholics, and as soon as I told them I was a Catholic priest, they followed me .... The Americans are dead anxious to fight for these people as they loved them at first sight."[380]

When the war ended in November 1918, celebrations took place around the archdiocese. Father Joseph W. O'Keefe of St. Gall's parish in Milwaukee rounded up the school children and paraded all over the north side of the city waving a huge American flag. "Some of the children were hoarse for a week," wrote a Sinsinawa Dominican sister, "but it was worth it to think that autocracy was crushed."[381] Father Henry Hengell of St. Paul's Chapel in Madison, spoke to a huge crowd assembled at the state capitol: "Whistles blew, bells rang, dignified men and women danced about and waved flags. Then as the full meaning of peace dawned upon our minds, we felt like weeping for joy. Now we have assembled in this capitol to celebrate the dawn of a new peace .... Therefore let us sing in our hearts tonight even as the Angels sang on the first Christmas night, "Glory to God in the highest."[382]

Veteran's Day at St. Anthony School, Milwaukee, November 1928 [ASAC]

Hengell urged his listeners to go to their own places of worship and give thanks to God "who has at last given our enemies counsels of meekness." However, church worship was problematic because of the worldwide epidemic of deadly influenza which hit Wisconsin with force in the declining months of World War I.[383] State officials banned large public assemblies during October and Messmer dispensed Milwaukee Catholics from the obligation to attend Mass, but he urged priests to leave side sacristy doors open for people to individually visit the Blessed Sacrament. He also urged them to hear the confessions of any and all who came.[384] Parochial and public schools were later included in those orders, and Messmer banned the celebration of Midnight Mass for Christmas, 1918.[385] The plague ceased nearly as quickly as it started, but the toll of death kept a drumbeat of Requiem Masses going at archdiocesan parishes that fall and winter. Parish life eventually went back to normal, but the war itself was a watershed for the archdiocese in an important way.

One of the casualties of the war was the German language in archdiocesan schools and official business. The reaction in Wisconsin to German culture and language was intense. German language instruction was banned in some public school districts, the popular Deutsch Club in Milwaukee was renamed the "Wisconsin Club," German-speaking citizens were eyed warily as potential Fifth Columnists (the search for guns in the basement at Holy Angels Church being but one example) and even the beautiful statue of "Germania" on the Germania building in Milwaukee was taken down.

However, the world war appears to have only given a final push to a process that was under way. In Milwaukee parishes German was already on the wane by the 1890s. Evidence of this was a mandate from Archbishop Frederick X. Katzer that religious instruction in parochial schools was to be given in the ethnic tongue and in English. Indeed German youth were already unfamiliar with the language and were missing key points in their religious training. What began with the teaching of religion extended to the teaching of other subjects until gradually German was not heard much in the classrooms or even on the playground.

Other instances of the passing of German as a common tongue for Milwaukee Catholics were evident. In 1907 St. Lawrence pastor James Dieringer announced the end of most German language instruction at his school. "In order that the children may become Americanized, it is advisable to have them study German as little as possible." He also noted that "the younger generations do not understand German in every case" and hence he "and several others of the German pastors have an English sermon in our Sunday morning services."[386] The year before, in a move that was intended to reinforce clerical unity, Messmer did away with the practice of separate retreats for German and English-speaking clergy. Hence forward, the archbishop decreed, the entire clergy would attend the retreat and conferences would be given in English. "This rule is a decided innovation," noted the *Catholic Citizen*.[387]

Other bastions of German strength began to change. At the mother German church of old St. Mary's on Broadway, Father Nicholas Becker became the first non-German-born pastor. The neighborhood around the old church had changed dramatically (as had the neighborhood around the cathedral) and it was no longer the popular gathering place for Milwaukee's Germans. Even devout families like the grocery store owning Meyers, who had walked past the cathedral to attend services at old St. Mary's, quit their neighborhood store and moved to West Allis in the 1910s. Between 1916-1918 Becker gave up

[AAM]

on German homilies and mandated that all subjects be taught in English, abandoning the bilingual arrangements that had been in place since the 1890s.[388] St. Anthony's parish on the south side retained its German bilingualism until World War I, when homilies, devotions and school subjects rather abruptly switched to English. St. Anthony's dropped all German language instruction in 1925. Even the organizational culture of these German parishes, with their popular *vereinen*, gave way to the more generic "Catholic Action" groups like the Holy Name and the Knights of Columbus, which brought many different ethnic groups together. Milwaukee would still retain elements of its "Teutonic crust" as historian Bayrd Still observed, and this was true of Catholicism. That there was still a market for German-speaking priests is attested to by Father George Meyer of St. Leo's Church who complained to seminary rector Muench in 1934 that his assistant did not know enough German to hear confessions.[389] Moreover, rural parishes like St. John the Baptist in Johnsburg still had an active German language constituency until after World War II.[390] St. Michael's and St. Boniface in Milwaukee, the two "new" German churches founded in 1888, had emphasized the preservation of German culture, language and identity, but they too eventually gave way to using more English in public ceremony, school and catechetical instruction.

Messmer and Traudt took advantage of the backlash against things German to further tighten their control over the internal affairs of parishes. Monsignor Bernard Traudt quietly passed word to Milwaukee Judge Paul Carpenter and Senator Roy Wilcox of Eau Claire that the Church would not oppose a state enactment requiring the use of English in all official corporate actions. This would compel foreign-language parishes to transact their official business in English and not their mother tongues, which in some instances had "made it impossible for the ecclesiastical superiors to read the original entries except by an interpreter." Traudt wrote, "It seems to me that now is the opportune time for such a bill when everybody is doing away with foreign languages." He further urged, "May I suggest that the bill be brought before the legislature by a Protestant, not a Catholic; and that no mention be made of church corporations, either Catholic or Lutheran, or least of all, of myself."[391] In some respects the proponents of the "English-only" Bennett law of the 1890s and the clerical conspirators who schemed against Heiss's nomination in the 1880s won a belated victory.

Anti-Catholic Interludes

Catholic patriotism during World War I did not completely eliminate vestiges of anti-Catholic feeling in Wisconsin. Even before the war a flare-up of anti-Catholic activity had erupted from the spoutings of former Populist leader Tom Watson of Georgia. *Tom Watson's Magazine*, a personal organ of the vocal and bigoted politician, had begun taking potshots at Catholics and especially the Knights of Columbus. These ravings were picked up by another anti-Catholic periodical *The Menace* which began publication in

Aurora in the Missouri Ozarks in 1911. The *Catholic Citizen* caught wind of the Wisconsin debut of this periodical in February 1913 when stickers advertising it were pasted up all over Milwaukee.[392] Various priests kept an eagle eye out for the publication, and one, Father William Malone, founding pastor of St. Thomas Aquinas parish in Kenosha, managed to thwart the distribution of 500 copies at an industrial plant in Kenosha.[393] In retaliation, local *Menace* agent, Frank Stewart, began spreading a rumor that Malone had "assaulted" a woman in the confessional. Among those with whom he shared this bit of salacious information were the Monteens, a Kenosha family with whom he was boarding. The Stewart rumor soon reached Malone, who immediately went to the offices of the district attorney and claimed that he had been criminally libeled. Stewart was rounded up and incarcerated. Meanwhile, a tearful Monteen admitted that he had heard the slander and passed it on. Eventually, Stewart renounced the lie and Malone pleaded for leniency for the two of them.[394]

Rev. William Malone [AAM]

Another anti-Catholic group that reared its head in Wisconsin were the Guardians of Liberty, one of whose leaders was General Nelson A. Miles, a hero of the Civil War, Indian conflicts and the conqueror of Puerto Rico in the Spanish American War. Likewise, another group known as the Sons of Luther also contributed to a small surge in anti-Catholic sentiments in the state. A battery of anti-Catholic speakers appeared in Wisconsin cities in 1913 and 1914, sounding warnings about papal domination of the public schools and politics. At a meeting in Milwaukee in November 1913, 2,500 cheering and foot-stomping partisans were regaled with stories of tunnels between a nuns convent on Lake Drive and the home of priests.[395] It might have been easy to ignore this shop-worn anti-Catholic screed if it did not coalesce with anti-immigration sentiments that were building in time for the 1914 elections.

Anti-Catholicism played a role in the defeat of Lieutenant Governor Tom Morris of La Crosse, a Catholic, who ran for the United States Senate as an heir to the Progressive coalition assembled by Robert LaFollette.[396] Wisconsin Scandinavians, who had been strong supporters of LaFollette, defected from the Morris candidacy on religious grounds. The Norwegian-language newspaper *Skandinaven* published a blast from one of LaFollette's associates, Herman Akern. "Shall we, as Scandinavians and Protestant citizens of Wisconsin, bestow our confidence upon a Roman Catholic as our representative in Washington? … The history and record of the Catholic power is black, blood-stained and rotten … and remember, it never changes."[397] Thanks in part to the Scandinavian defection, Morris lost to Francis

McGovern. Hot-button religious issues went underground to some extent in the succeeding elections. But they arose again in the 1918 gubernatorial campaign and vetoed the candidacy of state Senator Roy Wilcox of Eau Claire, whose support for the war and careful cultivation of the powerful Anti-Saloon League in Wisconsin were undercut by the fact that he was a Catholic. Wilcox was defeated by John J. Blaine by a vote of 113,001 to 102,199.[398]

The rise of the Ku Klux Klan, which began about the same time as the emergence of the Guardians of Liberty, proved to be a bit more of challenge. Begun in Georgia in 1915, the "new" Ku Klux Klan proved to be remarkably adept at recruiting members through the effective use of the techniques of advertising and the appeal of fraternalism. Klan membership skyrocketed after World War I (fueled in part by the popularity of W. D. Griffiths classic film *Birth of a Nation*) and Klan chapters, called "Klaverns," were organized in a number of northern states by local boosters called "Kleagles." Klan organization began in Wisconsin in 1920 when a group of business and professional men gathered for a meeting aboard a U.S. Coast Guard cutter anchored in the Milwaukee River. A Milwaukee insurance man, William Wieseman, became the "king kleagle" of the badger state and secured a charter from the national organization. Wieseman was replaced by Charles B. Lewis in 1924 and under Lewis the organization was formally chartered by the state of Wisconsin.[399]

The Klan never portrayed itself as a "hate" organization, but rather as a proponent of good order. As native-born Protestants, they saw themselves, their lifestyles and values as the paradigm for "authentic" Americanism. They looked peevishly on the "new" immigrants (southern and eastern Europeans) and supported immigration restriction. They also posed themselves as militant guardians of public virtue and ferreted out instances of illegal gambling, violations of Prohibition, narcotics and the white slave trade. One of their target neighborhoods for moral cleanup was Madison's "Little Italy" also known as "The Bush." Naturally, the majority of denizens in this part of town were Italian Catholics.[400]

Organizers from the Klan began a heavy recruiting campaign in most Wisconsin cities. Even though socialists Victor Berger and Daniel Webster Hoan attacked the Klan in Milwaukee, it managed to organize a "Klavern" that claimed a membership of 7,000 people. Historian Norman Weaver attributes their numbers to the fact that the Klan hated the Catholic Church as much as many socialists did.[401] Large Klan initiation rites were held at Riverview Park. In July 1924, at Racine, the appearance of 35,000 Klansmen and their families was a festive occasion as shopkeepers decorated their stores and Racine County deputy sheriffs wore their Klan regalia with their gold shield badges on the outside to direct traffic. Over 2,000 men were inducted into the order and heard an address by Imperial Wizard Dr. Hiram Wesley Evans.[402] Subsequent pageants, parades and meetings were held in Racine, Oshkosh, and elsewhere. The best estimates of total Klan membership suggest that about 15,000 Wisconsinites were dues-paying members of the organization.[403] A Klan newspaper, the *Badger American* began publishing in 1924.

However, Catholics did not take this lying down. The *Catholic Citizen*, now a veteran of a number of anti-Catholic crusades, began to expose the order by printing the names of its members at initiations and ridiculing Klan anti-Catholicism as un-American.[404] In late February 1924, about 3,000 angry Catholics mobbed the Commercial Hotel in Waukesha located at the Five Points commercial center, breaking windows and doors, smashing furniture and wrecking the hotel cafeteria to get at the Klan organizers.[405] Efforts to bring Klan ideas to politics met an equally strong reaction. When it became known that Wisconsin Secretary of State Fred Zimmerman had joined the Klan in 1922, popular outcry from Catholic organizations was loud enough to make him renounce his membership. By convincing enough Wisconsinites that he had "reformed" he was able to win the governor's chair in 1924.[406]

Concerted Catholic opposition to the Klan came from Catholic organizations such as *Central Verein*, the Catholic Women's Union of America, the Catholic Knights of Wisconsin, the Ancient Order of Hibernians, and most potently from the rapidly growing Knights of Columbus. Local Catholic professionals, like future U.S. Senator and state commander of the American Legion F. Ryan Duffy, spoke out against the Klan.[407] Added to this was the opposition of the state's leading elected officials. Governor John Blaine attacked the Klan as "an organization of hate and haters" and the Milwaukee Common Council, led by Catholic Alderman Cornelius Corcoran, passed an ordinance to limit Klan activities, branding them "an ever-present menace to good order in the community."[408]

Catholics may have found these organizations an annoyance, and occasionally they managed to exert some muscle in political campaigns. However, their impact on Catholic growth and advance was minimal. By 1928, the Klan had virtually disappeared from the state.[409] Catholics turned themselves to growth and development of their parishes.

New Parishes of the 20th Century: English-Only

Anti-Catholic bigots who still managed to stir fears of a "foreign" Catholic Church were not attuned to the changing demographics of Wisconsin life. The parishes that emerged in the 20th century reflected a new set of realities for archdiocesan life. Many of them were constructed on the edges of growing towns and cities. The new parish buildings virtually always began with a combination building that housed a Catholic school, in addition to a place of worship. Catholic identity in the new parishes began to reflect a more heterogeneous Catholic population, and in fact, ethnic identity played a more diminished role than ever.

The steady expansion of Milwaukee northward brought additional parishes. In 1909, St. Leo's on 22nd and Locust was opened and headed by Father Peter Theisen. The new church was soon filled by upwardly mobile Milwaukeeans moving steadily northwest, out of the downtown neighborhoods they had once inhabited. The parish had a growing school run by the School Sisters of Notre Dame. In 1923 Theisen built a huge Romanesque church that was elaborately decorated and contained state-of-the-art sound, lighting and heating systems. St. Leo's Church would soon surge forward as one of the largest and most active parishes on the north side.[410] Later, Father George Meyer assumed the pastorate and oversaw even more development of the church and school.

In 1911, Father Calasanctius Grim O.F.M., Cap., stationed at the Capuchin Holy Cross, established a parish in the tiny industrial suburb of West Milwaukee. Grim had worked closely with a local Catholic layman and well-to-do property owner, Balthazar Haerle, who lent Grim an old public school building for church services. With Messmer's permission it became in 1911 the site of a new parish in honor of St. Florian. Grim was only a temporary appointment, and a diocesan priest, Father Joseph Ritger, was assigned to the new parish for one year. The situation was so financially distressed,

St. Leo School, Milwaukee [AAM]

however, that the Capuchins came back, and using their own resources, helped the parish find a permanent location on 46th and Scott. Eager to relinquish the parish in light of their other needs and duties, the Capuchins suggested that the Discalced Carmelites of Holy Hill, a shrine they operated in Washington County, might be interested in the parish. The community accepted and in 1913, Father Irenaeus Berndl became the first Carmelite pastor of the new west side parish.[411]

Also in 1911, Messmer approved the founding of a new parish in the rapidly opening suburban area of Washington Heights. On land he had purchased in 1909, Messmer sent Father Francis Kleser to create St. Sebastian parish (the one parish named for the prelate). Beginning in 1912, a series of buildings rose on the property located right in the heart of the upscale neighborhood on five acres lying between North 54th and North 55th Streets and between West Washington and West Vine. The land at the time was hilly and ungraded and Washington Boulevard ended at 55th Street. Nearby were the Pabst farms. The parish grew rapidly and on the eve of the Depression, St. Sebastian's built a spectacular new church that befitted the character of its neighborhood. Designed by the architectural firm of Herbst and Kuenzli, the exquisite Gothic church soared over the neighborhood. In 1936, the parish celebrated its silver jubilee with an elaborate booklet, banquets and a series of Masses honoring the memory of the founders and the future of the parish.[412]

In 1911 Francis Kleser was asked to perform double duty in order to organize the scattered Catholics in the adjoining suburb of Wauwatosa. Wauwatosa's strong Protestant establishment had deterred the organizing of Catholics in their midst, but the Catholic population grew anyway and Wauwatosa soon welcomed a more visible Catholic presence.

St. Sebastian Church, Milwaukee [AAM]

The initial meetings of the soon-to-be formed parish were held in the Knights Templar Hall—a fraternal organization in which membership by Catholics had been banned in the 19th century. Bernard Traudt lent a hand when Kleser could not tend to the duties of establishing both parishes, and Messmer sent Catholic University-trained Father John H. Fitzgerald to manage the task of building a respectable Catholic presence. Fitzgerald named the congregation "St. Bernard's," and built a school, rectory and basement church before his health gave way in 1935.[413]

Archbishop Sebastian Messmer (second from left) at St. Bernard Church, Wauwatosa [AOP-Sin]

Western suburbs were not the only ones growing. The village of Shorewood, a residential suburb, had been incorporated as East Milwaukee in 1900, and civic improvements turned the farmland into a village. By 1912, 900 people lived there and Messmer appointed New York-born Farrell P. Reilly to head the new parish. Reilly had moved to Wisconsin in his youth and was one of the few priest alumni of the Watertown College of the Sacred Heart. Ordained in 1904, he became a great favorite of the English-speaking clergy, especially aging Father Hiram Fairbanks and Father Robert J. Roche of Holy Rosary, whom he had served as curate. With Roche's help, Reilly convened Catholics at the Shorewood village hall and by July 1913 had erected, along the unused right-of-way of an old transit line along Maryland Avenue, a 32-by-24 foot rugged frame church that resembled something one would find on a remote frontier. Named in honor of St. Robert of Newminster, the $100 that the humble structure cost was all the parish could afford after purchasing its property from the village. By Easter Sunday 1914, the pioneer period ended for the Shorewood parish and a church/school combination building was erected. The next year a school staffed by the Sinsinawa Dominicans opened. Reilly built piecemeal a rectory, convent, and school addition. By 1929, Shorewood had become the home of some of the most prominent and well-to-do Catholic families in Milwaukee, including brewer and convert Val Blatz, financier Neil Gleason, and chamber of commerce leader Phil Grau.[414]

In the beginning of the Depression in 1931, Reilly began to plan (with his financial experts) a new church. This immediately set off anxiety with Archbishop Stritch and his advisors, who were anxious about any display of church "opulence" while the nation was in such severe economic straits. Stritch's anxiety about the building project was reinforced by the departure of several wealthy parishioners from St. Robert's, including A. J. Kunzelman of the prominent Kunzelmann-Esser furniture firm.[415] Vicar General Bernard Traudt warned Reilly (who had complained to him of a mini-exodus from the parish), "I have a suspicion that some of these good people are asking for a transfer to another parish because of the fact that they fear the contribution which they might be called on to make for your new church building."[416] A nervous Stritch sought to slow Reilly by insisting that he have $50,000 in cash (a nearly impossible feat in the Depression) and $150,000 in pledges before he could build.

For four years, Reilly scrimped and saved and his well-heeled parishioners backed him up. To increase parish revenues, Reilly kept other archdiocesan collections at bay. Indeed, in 1936, Reilly challenged representatives of the archbishop's Emergency Fund, which had begun collecting for the restoration of the recently-burned St. John's Cathedral, by insisting that the cathedral parishioners themselves ought to pay for the restoration. To rebut Reilly, Stritch called on historian Peter Leo Johnson of the seminary to prove that the structure had been built with outside donations and the benefactions of other churches in the archdiocese. Stritch grew so agitated by Reilly's sparring over his responsibilities to the archdiocese and efforts to keep local dollars at home that he exploded at the Shore-

St. Robert Church, Shorewood [AOP-Sin]

wood pastor, "I have reached the conclusion that your Parish should not assume the name Catholic but should call itself Presbyterian or Congregational. It does not seem to acknowledge an Ordinary or to sense its obligations to the Archdiocese."[417] To punish Reilly, Stritch removed him from the list of those to be created monsignori in 1938, claiming disingenuously to Roman officials that Reilly would be embarrassed by the honor.[418]

Nonetheless, by late 1935, Reilly was ready to move. He moved the existing rectory back so that the new church could have room to front Capitol Avenue. To design the new temple, Reilly reached outside the network of Wisconsin architects and contracted the Boston firm of Maginnis and Walsh.[419] They worked along with the old Brielmaier and Sons firm, who signed on as associate architects. Ground was broken in 1936, and Archbishop Stritch arrived in August to lay the cornerstone. In 1938 the church was ready for occupancy. The Romanesque structure with its looming tower seated over 1,000 people. Its magnificence made it a candidate to succeed St. John's Cathedral after the fire of 1935. It also goes down in history as the first Wisconsin Catholic Church to telecast the Mass at Christmas (1950).[420] Once the church was built, Reilly began saving up for a new high school to complete his full design for the parish. On the occasion of his 40th anniversary of ordination in 1944, his parishioners collected an enormous $125,000 for their pastor. This he set aside for a new high school.

Joining St. Robert's parish as a haven for the well-to-do was St. Clement's Church in Sheboygan. Since 1872, the massive fieldstone Gothic Holy Name Church, the work of Father Michael Haider, had stood as the Catholic architectural gem of the city. Other parishes had been split off of the mother church: the German-speaking St. Peter Claver in 1888, the Lithuanian Immaculate Conception in 1903, and the Croatian Ss. Cyril and Methodius in 1910. Agitation for an English-speaking parish no doubt existed among some of the Catholics of Sheboygan, but none had the resources or as much clout with church officials as Anna Mary Reiss, wife of the leading coal merchant of the industrial city. She pressed for the creation of an English-speaking church with a priest friend in nearby Manitowoc. In 1913 a church was organized and young Father Francis E. Murphy was assigned as the first pastor. Land at the intersection of New York Avenue and North Sixth Street was acquired for $15,000, and $70,000 was budgeted for the church. The La Crosse firm of Parkinson and Dockindorf was entrusted with the design, which the parish history called "low Gothic." The 130-foot-long , 500-seat church was a showplace for the Reiss fortune. Anna Reiss donated the main altar of Italian marble and the Stations of the Cross. In 1915 the new church was solemnly dedicated.[421] Other Reiss family members donated the auditorium and the organ (as well as an endowment for its upkeep). The elegant stained glass windows were from both the Reiss and Kohler families. Later a gymnasium and parish center were constructed by a hefty donation of William A. Reiss, who was rewarded in 1949 by being created a Knight of St. Gregory.[422]

In Kenosha, the parish of St. Thomas Aquinas was founded by Father William Malone. The parish represented a new wave of non-ethnic growth in a town with a plethora of nationalities. From it would spin two new churches after the war, St. Mark's and St. Mary's.[423]

In 1914, the guns of August were booming overseas. The European war put a halt to much building, but two new parishes were created. Rapid growth north of Milwaukee created overcrowding in the church and school of St. Boniface which had dominated the area since 1888. Father George Meyer, pastor of St. Louis Church in Caledonia (a fiefdom of this large family, which included the future archbishop of Milwaukee and several other diocesan and religious order priests), was called on to establish the new parish. Securing 18 lots near a hill at 11th and Atkinson, the parish purchased stone from the recently demolished Plankinton House Hotel in Milwaukee and built a typical combination church and school building in 1916, named in honor of the Holy Angels.[424] This was to be the first of a projected five building complex, later to be crowned with a new church. However the parish grew slowly. The parish history noted, "The streets north of Atkinson Avenue, owing to war conditions were not opened until 1920, and consequently there was very slow growth until the year 1926, when a building boom struck this part of town and a great many bungalows were erected north, west, and east of the parish."[425] Eventually, Holy Angels would flourish.

St. Clement Church, Sheboygan [AOP-Sin]

The Parishes of the 1920s

In Milwaukee, the area of most rapid growth was the northwest side of the city. The corridor along Bluemound Road was an artery for development. In 1921, Messmer handed over the administration of Holy Cross parish, directly across from Calvary Cemetery, from the Capuchins who had staffed it since its foundation in the 1870s to the Pallottine Community. The Pallottines, a German-based community had been one of the last new orders to enter the diocese directly from Europe (although they had sponsored houses in eastern dioceses for many years).[426] The first Pallottine pastor of Holy Cross was a German national, Father Peter Schroeder, who had served in Italy and been especially successful working with Italians in Brooklyn, New York. After community politics caused the loss of the Brooklyn parish to another province of Pallottines (and thereby their loss of the parish altogether because the bishop would not accede to the transfer), Schroeder heard that the Capuchins were eager to unload Holy Cross in order to concentrate more resources on their clericate in Marathon, Wisconsin and the newly established St. Benedict the Moor Mission.

Rev. Peter Schneider, SAC [ASAC]

In 1921, Schroeder came to Holy Cross and built a new school. At Holy Cross the sons of Vincent Pallotti cared for the parish, tended to the burials at Calvary Cemetery, took over the care of the county institutions (a task the Capuchins had carried for years) and were permitted to open a house of formation for their new members. A seminary eventually created at Holy Cross was the seedbed of American vocations to the community. Schroeder was full of energy. He established a mission farther down Bluemound and named it in honor of St. Anthony. This would be the site of a popular novena and also the birthplace of the largest Catholic high school of the archdiocese, Pius XI. Later, Schroeder discovered a body of Italian Catholics in Marconi Heights at 92nd and Bluemound, and there established a parish in honor of St. Therese. Schroeder's methods of doing business often skirted the borders of fiscal prudence and he nearly bankrupted the community by his borrowing and spending. But by the time he quit his duties in the 1930s and returned to Germany, he had established a major Catholic presence on the west side of Milwaukee—a virtual Pallottine corridor down Bluemound Road.

Although Schroeder and the Pallottines spoke German, their pastoral task, especially after World War I, was to help make the transition into a new English-speaking community. Messmer still had to hew a careful line, especially with the dominant Poles, in permitting the establishment of foreign-language parishes. In the 1920s, however, the only national parish was the Latino church on the south side.

This new policy was revealed in the charge to Father Peter Dietz, who was sent up to the growing suburb of Whitefish Bay to create St. Monica's parish in 1923. In a complaining letter to Bernard Traudt in December 1929, Dietz worried that his new parish would be carved up before it could attain a secure financial position. He recalled Messmer's words to him when he sent him to Whitefish Bay. In reaction to Messmer's fears that a group of Polish Catholics at the south end of the parish were accumulating enough strength to demand the formation of a new Polish parish, Dietz related, "His Grace told me … that it was his determined policy not to start a *national* parish in the suburbs. It seems to me that a Polish priest knowing English as you or I do and able to hear confessions in Polish should establish an *American* parish when the time is ripe."[427]

Indeed, Dietz did set out to found a new church in a hitherto underdeveloped "resort" area north of Milwaukee. Along the north shore, his and Reilly's at Shorewood were the major parishes for many years. Dietz began St. Monica's by insisting that traditional forms of church support give way to a form of tithing, a practice more common in Protestant churches. He wrote in 1929, "During this six year experiment, I have had no bazaars, card parties, dances, no pew rent, no money at the door, no school money. I have asked that each member contribute one day's income a month and nothing more."[428] But to build a church and school, Dietz had to

Rev. Peter Dietz [Mary H. Fox. *Peter E. Dietz, labor Priest*, University of Notre Dame Press, 1953, p. 3]

scramble like the rest of his clerical colleagues. He argued with wealthy parishioners who beat a hasty retreat to Holy Rosary parish to escape the burden of paying for a new church or who refused to tolerate the discomfort of temporary quarters. The voice that had argued for the rights of laboring men and clashed with bishops over politics wrestled endlessly over finances and the repayment of bonded indebtedness. However, it would fall to Dietz's successor, John J. Barry, to build the church that would match St. Robert's for the prestige of a wealthy community.

Farther west, a less flamboyant story unfolded with another German-based religious community. In 1926 Messmer welcomed the Society of the Divine Savior (Salvatorian fathers and brothers) to establish yet another new parish near Holy Cross Cemetery on Burleigh Road.[429] The Salvatorians had been in Wisconsin since 1896, when Archbishop Katzer had given them control over the vast lands of the Oschwald colony at St. Nazianz in Manitowoc County. There the young Salvatorian province flourished and in 1909 opened a popular minor seminary that educated generations of Wisconsin priests (including a good number from Milwaukee). The province also created a successful publishing department under the leadership of Father Bede Friedrich. Friedrich was a business mogul with all the common sense and business instincts of Pallottine Father Schroeder, but none of his penchant for the extravagant or the risky. Under Friedrich the Salvatorians pioneered the use of direct mail appeals, used by religious communities to this day. They also sold a popular Catholic periodical called *Manna* which a black-habited Salvatorian brother hawked to Catholic schools and which included endearing Catholic stories, riddles and iconography. Many of the stories were penned by Father Winfrid Herbst, S.D.S., a native Wisconsinite, whose "Question Box" column was one of the most popular features in the nationally distributed *Our Sunday Visitor* from Indiana.

Rev. Winfrid Herbst, SDS [ASDS-M]

The new Salvatorian parish, named Mother of Good Counsel, was located at the intersection of Burleigh and Lisbon Avenues and replicated the Pallottine formula: the Salvatorians cared for the parish, and tended to the needs of Holy Cross Cemetery. (One Salvatorian chaplain, World War I veteran Marcelline Molz, buried thousands of Milwaukeeans and in his later years, would often meander across an increasingly busy Burleigh Avenue bringing traffic to a halt and nearly becoming a fatality himself.) The Salvatorians also experimented with creating a house of formation and even having their general headquarters in America at the Milwaukee site, but the establishment at St. Nazianz was more suited—especially since the minor seminary assured a large flow of candidates into its novitiate.

On Milwaukee's south side in 1924, Father Julius Wermuth founded St. Gerard's, a new parish for the English-speaking along Oklahoma Avenue. The next year, Messmer called him to create a parish in the Tippecanoe section of the town of Lake. This community, named for St. Veronica, was built as a virtual replica of St. Gerard's not only in the church/school combination style, but also in its "English-only" policy of ministry. Reflecting on the difference between St. Veronica's parish and older neighboring parishes, the parish history observed that they "had been formed to serve primarily one nationality or language group: Immaculate Conception was Irish, St. Augustine's and Sacred Heart were German, and St. Paul's was for the Polish. Only English was used at St. Veronica's for preaching and instruction."[430]

Continual suburban growth continued directly west of Milwaukee and erratic patterns of land development meant that new churches had to be inserted between existing ones to accommodate increasing populations. In 1928, the parish of St. Jude the Apostle was set midway between the Pallottine St. Anthony of Padua and Wauwatosa's St. Bernard. The parish found space on elegant Glenview Avenue and had as its first pastor

Rev. Marcelline Molz, SDS
[ASDS-M]

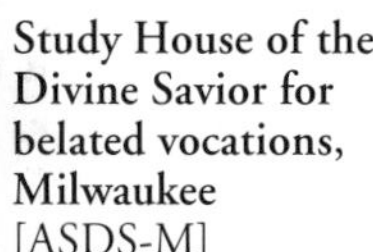

Study House of the Divine Savior for belated vocations, Milwaukee
[ASDS-M]

Joseph Patrick Hurst. Hurst was the founder of St. Bernard's Home, a refuge for working men. He was also one of the liturgical pioneers of the archdiocese, introducing his parishioners to the use of the newly popular hand missal, the dialogue Mass (in which parishioners said aloud the Latin responses of the Mass) and study clubs.

A second parish in Wauwatosa was begun in 1939 once the Depression had subsided. Father Joseph Huepper named the parish Christ the King, in honor of a new feast inserted in the church calendar by Pope Pius XI. Located on 18 lots Messmer had earlier purchased on Swan Boulevard between Clarke and Center Streets, it served the homes that sprouted around it in an area that was "formerly farmlands." By 1956, the parish plant was capped by a large Georgian church designed by the architectural firm of Brust and Brust.[431]

St. Rita Church and Monastery, Racine [AAM]

In 1926 another Sheboygan parish was carved from Holy Name, named "St. Dominic" in honor of the patron of the pastor of the mother parish, Dominic Thill. Located on 20 acres outside the city limits (it was soon annexed by a growing Sheboygan), St. Dominic was restored by Father George Knackert who contracted architect Mark Pfaller to design the church/ school building.[432]

New churches in Racine, included St. Edward's, founded in 1919 "in an open field" on the fringes of the city. Messmer appointed recently returned army chaplain, John W. Bott as pastor. By 1953, the parish could afford a new church.[433]

St. Rita's Church in Racine, began as a monastery conceded by Messmer in 1925 to a group of German Augustinians seeking a foundation in the archdiocese. Messmer offered them a recently vacated convent of Dominicans in Hales Corners and the care of the small congregation of Holy Family in Caledonia, a church founded in 1855. As an alternative, he also offered them the possibility of starting a monastery in the small town of Ives, north of Racine, that could double as a church for the people of the area who were too poor to afford one. The Augustinians chose the Ives settlement and sent priests every Sunday to the little Holy Family mission until 1928, when Messmer ended it. The Augustinians set to work establishing a monastery in Ives, known as the "worst vice resort between Milwaukee and Chicago." In a series of purchases, the Augustinians bought up a series of seedy taverns, whore houses, and a bowling alley to form the parish of St. Rita of Cascia. Pews and altars from old St. Peter's Church graced the new headquarters.[434] In 1938, the friars opened a house of formation that sent students to St. Francis Seminary for theological study. In 1939 architect Henry Slaby was called on to draft plans for a new church and shrine.[435]

Similar expansion of English-speaking parishes took place in Kenosha. The name of St. Mark was once again affixed to a Catholic parish in Kenosha in 1924, when Father Alphonse Berg established a parish in the Allenwood subdivision on the south side of the city. To the west, on the literal edge of Kenosha, Father Raymond Bell was sent from a pastorate in Saukville to establish the parish of St. Mary in 1929. After beginning services in a tavern on Roosevelt Road, he erected the first stage of an extensive parish plant with the characteristic school/church combination. In 1951, the architectural firm of Lindl and Schutte designed a distinctive colonial style church that was built by parishioner Paul Becker.[436]

West Allis as well took on new parish communities as the Allis Chalmers operation boomed. In 1920, St. Aloysius congregation was created to accommodate the growth of West Allis south of 84th Street. Property at 92nd and West Greenfield was chosen for two barracks purchased from Camp Custer, Michigan, for a church and school. The growth was so rapid that the barracks served only until 1926, when a new church and school were erected.[437] As West Allis exploded with growth, St. Aloysius was soon subdivided, and a new parish, also named for St. Rita of Cascia, like the Augustinian foundation in Racine, was created in 1924. A farm was purchased on Lincoln Avenue (at that time a rutted road) and 60th Street and an inauspicious first Mass was celebrated in a tent rented from the nearby state fair grounds. The parish soon constructed a building. It was not until 1929 though that West Allis extended sewer and water lines to this area, and continual adjustments of property took place as portions of it were cut off by road improvements and infrastructure. In this respect, the church preceded the pace of development.[438]

Virtually all of the parishes described above followed the directions of the Third Plenary Council of Baltimore and began schools. The first buildings erected contained room for a temporary church and a school.

St. Mary Church and School, Kenosha [AAM]

Sacred Heart Church, Racine [AAM]

Later, as the parish could afford to build a church, the building was left to the use of the school. Many of these buildings were well-constructed, and are still in use in the archdiocese (although they have undergone renovations and repairs). The construction of these church/school combination buildings represented an "innovation" in Catholic life. The first generations of Catholics built their churches first and schools afterward. Now the environment of sacred worship took a back seat to the need to educate Catholic youth. Unconsciously, the symbolic value of the church structure on the urban landscape (its steeple, windows, cruciform shape, and "sacred" presence) was undercut. The church/school combinations were not unattractive and were certainly visible as religious structures, but they lacked the specific identity of a church structure. In some respects these buildings may have indirectly contributed to the secularization of society. Within, the "temporary" churches were simple, relatively unadorned, and functional. Obviously designed to be transformed into gymnasiums or parish halls, the altar sat on an elevated portion at the end of the building, flanked by two side altars, one dedicated to the Blessed Virgin, the other to St. Joseph. Stations of the Cross adorned the walls, and other saint's shrines were squeezed in as space was available. Wooden confessionals, often made at either St. Aemillian's Orphanage or St. John's School for the Deaf, were placed in the rear of the church for the weekly Saturday night ritual of confession. The collective impact of these relatively impoverished structures on the quality of liturgical observance is a subject well worth pondering. Certainly, the quiet growth of the liturgical movement in Milwaukee and elsewhere might have been fed by the less than desirable liturgical environment in which many parishes operated.

Parish energies were first directed to paying off the church/school combination, and then toward the building of a permanent church. Some parishes, like St. Gerard's and St. Helen's, remained in their church/school buildings. Others, like St. Veronica's in Milwaukee, and St. Mary's and St. Mark's in Kenosha, built permanent churches and remained in their buildings until after World War II. The church/school combination structure remained the norm in the archdiocese of Milwaukee even after the war. By that time, building materials became even cheaper and the new generation of "temporary" buildings seemed even shoddier than the first.

First Communicants, St. Rita Church, Milwaukee [ICCA]

The Reshaping of Catholic Education

If Catholics were willing to wait years for a decent church, they were not willing to wait that long for a Catholic school. The Catholic school network, already strong in the archdiocese because of the Germans, grew even stronger and more unified between 1903-1930. Important changes in the wider field of education had also been taking place since the end of the 19th century.

Historian Philip Gleason has identified the key force in the transformation of Catholic education as an "organizational challenge." The components of this challenge were the emergence of the free public high school as the characteristic agency of secondary education; the increase in collegiate enrollments, which included large numbers of women attending coeducational institutions and women's colleges; the breakdown of the classical curriculum and the increase of new fields of study; the rise of the research university and the professionalization of learning; and the development of voluntary organizations of educators who established and monitored standards of performance at every level of education. "Taken together," Gleason writes, "these and related developments constituted a veritable revolution which reshaped American higher education in the last quarter of the nineteenth and the first two decades of the twentieth."[439] All of these factors were in evidence in the archdiocese of Milwaukee.

One of the first attempts to create a unified school system took place under Archbishop Heiss, who formed an archdiocesan school board to oversee Catholic schools. One of its accomplishments was the drafting of an archdiocesan "Course of Studies" in the 1890s which gave the first outlines of a standardized curriculum for the Milwaukee Archdiocesan schools.[440] In his last year of life Katzer tried to reinvigorate the idea of creating an archdiocesan school system and in 1902 he called for the formation of a new archdiocesan school board and the establishment of local school boards.[441] The most controversial feature of these provisions was the mandate that religious instruction be given in both English and the foreign tongue.[442] In 1903, an archdiocesan committee devised the "Course of Study for the Eight-Grade Bi-Lingual Parochial Schools of the Archdiocese of Milwaukee," which formalized the extension of bilingualism to all of the subjects in the curriculum.[443]

[AAM]

COURSE OF STUDY

FOR THE

EIGHT-GRADE, BI-LINGUAL PAROCHIAL SCHOOLS

OF THE

ARCHDIOCESE OF MILWAUKEE.

By Order of the Most Reverend Archbishop.

MILWAUKEE.
RIVERSIDE PRINTING CO.
1903.

However, parochial schools in the archdiocese were just that—parochial. Local pastors and sister-administrators ran them according to local needs and means. This meant that instructional techniques and equipment varied from school-to-school—as did "requirements" for graduation. School calendars were calibrated to the Catholic sanctoral cycle, the liturgical year, and the personal idiosyncracies of the local leadership. The pastor's name day was often the occasion for a day off from school, but secular patriotic holidays were sometimes ignored. "In 1895," grumped one Notre Dame sister, "according to the orders of the APA, all national holidays had to be observed, so we were compelled to teach on St. Joseph's and also St. Anthony's Day."[444]

Teacher preparation was another issue. The earliest practices of almost all teaching sisterhoods who taught in archdiocesan schools was to attempt to reply to as many requests for parish schools as possible. As a result, young sisters and candidates were assigned to schools with little or no training, or even a minimum of introduction to the demands of the religious order. Sometimes, a young woman would start teaching at a school,

"Minuet Group" at St. John Nepomuk School, Racine [ASSF]

be called away to the motherhouse for clothing in the religious habit and a brief novitiate, and then be turned back into the school system. Teaching sisters, like their counterparts in the public schools, often got their formal education "on the run," and learned the skills of pedagogy on a trial and error basis. These early schools could be stressful places. Unruly students and difficult parents and parish priests made the life of a teaching sister miserable and often unbearable. Physical circumstances usually required the sisters to live in the school buildings until a convent could be built. Some sisters, barely teenagers, broke down physically and mentally under this stress and had to be taken back to the motherhouse, "for a rest." Other sisters endured the privations and managed to do great things for their pupils.

Outside the sphere of Catholic schools, state requirements for education and educators began to be formalized and codified. The major development was the separation of high school students from elementary schools and from collegiate programs. The development of high schools grew rapidly in Wisconsin in the first decades of the 20th century. Between 1890 and 1906 the number of high schools in Wisconsin grew from 169 to 288.[445] The need to establish a curriculum that would allow students to enter the University of Wisconsin without taking an entrance exam led to the definition of clear elementary school and high school curricula. It also led to stricter requirements for high school teachers. Later when the state required mandatory school attendance to the age of 16, the need for more schools and clear policies grew.

Gradually the changes in pedagogy, school organization and teacher training in the public schools began to be felt in the Catholic schools. In many schools, large undifferentiated classes gave way to age-oriented graded classes. Father Dominic Thill of St. Mary's in Milwaukee apparently introduced this into his large school in the late 19th century, and replicated it when he was appointed the pastor of Holy Name Church in Sheboygan. Graded classes became the rule in Catholic schools in large cities, and were accepted more gradually when the parish could not

Classroom at Holy Redeemer School, Milwaukee [AAM]

bear the expense of too many teachers—even poorly paid sisters.

Both the sisters' communities and the archdiocese itself imposed some standardization on subject matter and textbook use. Printed "Notes on Pedagogy" and elaborately plotted curricula for each of the grades were circulated among Notre Dame teachers.[446] A comprehensive text of school instructions appeared in 1889. The School Sisters of Notre Dame held a summer gathering at their Elm Grove Convent to discuss pedagogy, to hear talks from priests on educational matters, and to take the equivalent of "workshops" with skilled senior sisters who had perfected techniques of teaching science, math, penmanship, and religion. The School Sisters themselves developed standards for their schools as well as a pattern of visitation conducted by the mother general, and later by a sister designated to oversee the quality of the school. Other religious communities followed suit.

In order to make sure that Catholic parents were aware of their responsibility to enroll their children in Catholic schools, Messmer's *Handbook* of 1907 repeated the legislation of the Third Plenary Council of Baltimore and insisted that all Catholic children attend Catholic school if they lived within three miles of its location. Many children complied, since parish schools did not charge tuition; however some simply ignored the order—even when threatened with sanctions, such as the withholding of absolution during the sacrament of penance.

The rising tide of educational professionalism led to the formation of the Washington, D.C.-based Catholic Education Association (CEA). This organization was established in 1904 at a special meeting held in St. Louis in conjunction with centenary celebrations of the Louisiana Purchase. It changed later, adding the word "National" to its title and becoming one of the major forces pressing for the professionalization of Catholic schools and teacher training. At the annual meetings of the NCEA, papers were read and ideas exchanged over such topics as curriculum development, teacher preparation, student needs and discipline, relationships with parish and pastor and the development of Catholic high schools and colleges. Milwaukee began sending representatives to the NCEA meetings, and in July 1907, the Jesuits at Marquette University played host to the fourth annual meeting of the organization. In subsequent years, archdiocesan superintendents Barbian and Goebel were influential members of the organization and educators from the Milwaukee See participated actively in NCEA events.

The NCEA was an insistent voice for the upgrading and professionalization of Catholic education and helped to set the standards for the improvement of Catholic schools. It was at their behest that dioceses were urged to create departments of education in chanceries, headed by a professionally trained school superintendent who would oversee teacher training, educational standards, the development of a standardized curriculum for parish schools and the interfacing of the Catholic schools with developments in public education. The latter was quite important, since Catholic grade school children often attended public high schools and colleges. The office of the school superintendency in Catholic circles, like other aspects of the educational program, took its cue from developments in the public schools.[447] Superintendents were chosen by school boards, who generally appointed one of their number to implement the decisions of the board and to monitor compliance with policies delivered by the board.

Among Catholics the idea of a central school "inspector" first came about in New York in 1888, and the idea soon spread to dioceses. It was in conjunction with the NCEA that the small group of school inspectors/superintendents began meeting in 1906 and eventually developed themselves into a larger and more established body of administrators. In fact, a Milwaukee priest, Father John Voelker, wrote the history of the evolution of the Catholic superintendency.[448]

The idea of having a central school supervisor who would oversee curriculum development, assist in textbook selection and supervise the work and progress of teachers also took root among the various sisterhoods around the nation. A religious community of any size generally appointed a senior sister to the office of school supervisor. Her task was to help the younger women, many of whom were removed from the classroom themselves by only a year or two, to make the transition into the large classes and demanding educational routine required by teaching orders. The School Sisters of Notre Dame developed such an office and began to hold annual summer meetings at their Elm Grove convent. Other religious sisterhoods adopted the same techniques. Diocesan structures developed under Messmer gradually coordinated the semi-autonomous aspects of archdiocesan parochial schools to bring them in line with state standards.

Rev. Joseph Barbian, Superintendent of Schools [AAM]

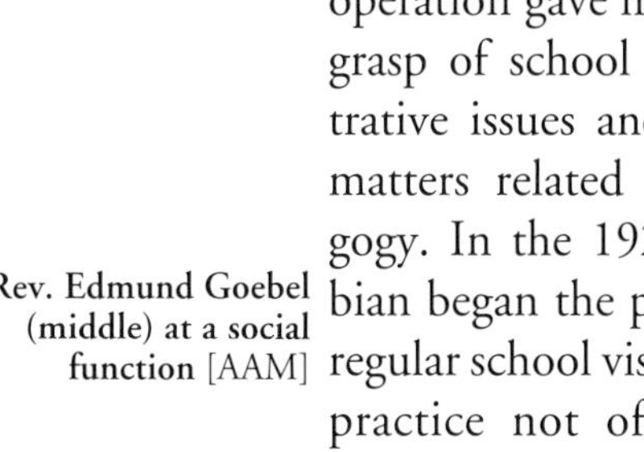

In 1921, Messmer appointed Father Joseph Barbian to be school superintendent for the archdiocese. His 10 years at the Pio Nono/Holy Family operation gave him a sure grasp of school administrative issues and also of matters related to pedagogy. In the 1920s, Barbian began the process of regular school visitation, a practice not often welcomed by either the sisters or the pastor, who feared a one-size-fits-all approach to educational policy. Barbian also managed the archdiocesan efforts to expand and improve high school education. Eventually, Barbian withdrew from day-to-day management of school affairs, as Stritch leaned more heavily on him to oversee wider archdiocesan affairs.

Barbian's successor in the superintendency was Father Edmund Goebel. Goebel was born in Caledonia, Wisconsin on April 4, 1895.[449] He was ordained in 1924 and served one year as an assistant in Janesville until he was appointed to the faculty of Pio Nono. In September 1929, he was tapped to be the principal of Messmer High School and oversaw the transition from the old St. Elizabeth buildings to the new site at Eighth and Capitol. Archbishop Stritch insisted that Goebel take more classes in educational administration and sent him to Marquette University. There he quarreled bitterly with the chair of

Rev. Edmund Goebel (middle) at a social function [AAM]

the Department of Education, Edward Fitzpatrick. His tenure at Messmer was anything but pleasant. Allegations of drunkenness, womanizing, and financial mismanagement dogged Goebel. "What a story of inefficient management of Messmer High school by Fr. Goebel," harumphed Aloysius Muench in his diary. "Domination by a woman, no bookkeeping, wasteful expenditures, etc." Muench repeated in his diary the gossip that circulated in the diocese when Goebel was eased out of the high school and sent to the Catholic University, "The suspicion that the Archbishop sent Fr. Goebel to Washington 'for further studies' to get him away from Messmer appears to have a basis in fact."[450] But even at the Catholic University he ran afoul of university administrators and was nearly dismissed. Nonetheless, he completed his degree, securing a doctorate in education.

Upon his return Stritch assigned him to the chaplaincy of the Sorrowful Mother Sisters in Granville, just north of Milwaukee. Convinced of his rehabilitation, Stritch then appointed him to the Board of Education, making him its secretary, and in 1937 appointed him to replace Barbian. From 1937 to 1970, Goebel ran the education department of the archdiocese. His first headquarters was a suite of offices in the Pioneer Building at 625 North Milwaukee Street.[451] As the operation grew bigger and more sophisticated (and Goebel took on other tasks such as spiritual advisor to the archdiocesan Council of Catholic Nurses and chief liaison with the Catholic hospitals), he secured a 50-year-old mansion once owned by brewing mogul Henry Uihlein at 437 West Galena Street.[452] The elegant old mansion was refurbished for the school department and a raft of other offices (Archdiocesan Home and School Association, Goebel's healthcare operations, the Sodality Union of Milwaukee Archdiocese [SUMA] and the Inter-American Affairs Office) and was renamed "The Calaroga" in honor of the place where St. Dominic received his inspiration.[453]

The Calaroga, Archdiocesan Department of Education building [AAM]

From the major teaching communities of women in the archdiocese, Goebel secured assistants to help him in the annual visitation of schools. Goebel soon expanded his staff by adding representative members of the nine chief religious communities of the archdiocese as school visitators, and appointed a director of religious music, Otto Singenberger of St. Anne's parish. Goebel pressed for a regular budget line from the chancery. Beginning in 1938, Goebel produced an annual statistical report on the state of the Catholic schools. Originally rexographed by his office, this easily readable and succinct pamphlet provided an excellent summary of most of the important developments.[454] Goebel himself remained active in professional organizations, attending meetings of the NCEA and the professional organization of school superintendents. He worked closely with his counterparts on the state and local levels, and became something of a Milwaukee institution.

Goebel supported his office largely through royalties he received for authoring a series of Catholic textbooks that were published by the Ginn and Company and mandated for use in the Catholic schools of the Milwaukee archdiocese.[455] He also raked in profits from the annual archdiocesan teachers conventions begun in 1943. At these gatherings, held at the Milwaukee Auditorium, Goebel charged hefty display fees for book and educational materials suppliers who set up tables in the convention halls. Most of these earnings went to keep up the aging building and to pay the salaries of his growing staff. Goebel himself was a wealthy man, and built a magnificent home on Pewaukee Lake to which he invited guests and friends.

Sisters and Rev. Edmund Goebel entering the Education building on its dedication day [AAM]

The archdiocese complemented the improved teacher training by issuing curriculum guides and purchasing common textbooks in subjects such as history, mathematics and English. The annual visitation of teachers and schools by the superintendent's office and the hosting of an annual archdiocesan teacher convention gave some structure to the disparate and occasionally unique schools of the diocese. Opportunities to share information about common issues of scheduling, hygiene, school construction, and pedagogical matters were very important. Annual diocesan examinations began to be administered to the schools in the 1940s. School diplomas now bore the insignia of the archdiocese of Milwaukee and the signature of the superintendent.

Archbishop Stritch's particular interests led to many important changes in the way education was conceived and delivered. Among his innovations was a program of psychological testing and evaluation that drew on the services of Dr. Ralph Bergen, a clinical educational psychologist. Bergen convinced the prelate that more could be done with children who learned slowly or who were only slightly developmentally disabled. Heeding his advice, Stritch mandated the opening of "opportunity rooms" in schools where there were sufficient numbers of students who could not keep up with the regular program of studies.[456] The reaction to this mandate was mixed. For a while Stritch directed sister communities to provide the room and the extra staff to accommodate the slower children, but he did not pass the mandate along to the pastors who were expected to pay for the additional instruction. Consequently, the sisters were expected to find a teacher for the new room (a difficult task, since the number of schools outpaced the number of trained religious). Pastors sometimes refused to pay for the extra nun, nor did they always willingly reallocate space for the opportunity room. Some large sisterhoods complied grudgingly. Others groups like the Sinsinawa Dominicans refused to implement the reforms. One Dominican sister, the principal of St. John's Cathedral High, insisted that Bergen (who had attended the Catholic University) was "the product of pagan ideas."[457]

The reorganization of the elementary school system presented a new problem: what to do with the elementary school graduates? Few independent Catholic high schools existed, and the appeal of boarding schools was limited by sparse financial resources and parental unwillingness to allow children to leave home. As the archdiocese moved into the 1920s, the *Catholic Herald* observed, "One of the great needs in our diocese is the fostering of Catholic higher education .... The need of Catholic free high schools in our diocese is pressing if we are to have any permanent influence on the graduates of our parish schools."[458] The process of providing Catholic high schools had already begun with the transformation of the archdiocesan academies.

The Emergence of the Catholic High School: Transforming the Academies

Mirroring the expansion of secondary schools in Wisconsin, Catholic high schools developed around the archdiocese. Religious orders led the way by sending the little children to elementary schools, and transforming their old academies into four year institutions. Marquette Academy had separated its programs according to age level in 1906 when Johnston Hall was built for collegians alongside Gesu Church on Wisconsin Avenue.[459] The high school students remained at the old site until 1925, when a generous donation from Ellen Storey Johnston enabled the Jesuits to build a new high school for its all-male student body at 34th and Wisconsin Avenue. By 1926 over 500 boys registered at the school. The curriculum had four separate tracks: classical, Latin-modern language, scientific and commercial. The majority of the students enrolled in the demanding classical courses.[460] The old Marquette academy was sold to the Capuchins of St. Benedict the Moor School, who were able to purchase it with the help of funds from brewer Ernest G. Miller.[461]

The Sisters of Charity of the Blessed Virgin Mary of Dubuque (BVM) had come to the archdiocese in 1885 to establish a Catholic school at Holy Rosary parish. In 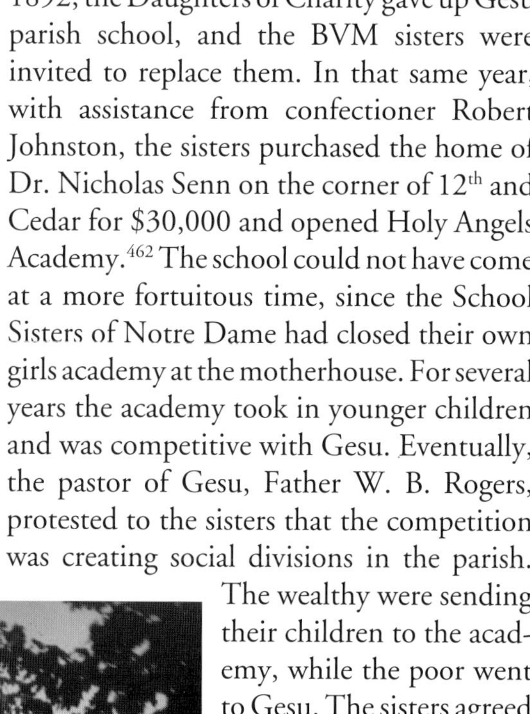1892, the Daughters of Charity gave up Gesu parish school, and the BVM sisters were invited to replace them. In that same year, with assistance from confectioner Robert Johnston, the sisters purchased the home of Dr. Nicholas Senn on the corner of 12th and Cedar for $30,000 and opened Holy Angels Academy.[462] The school could not have come at a more fortuitous time, since the School Sisters of Notre Dame had closed their own girls academy at the motherhouse. For several years the academy took in younger children and was competitive with Gesu. Eventually, the pastor of Gesu, Father W. B. Rogers, protested to the sisters that the competition was creating social divisions in the parish. The wealthy were sending their children to the academy, while the poor went to Gesu. The sisters agreed to discontinue the lower grades and the academy flourished. Generous benefactions came from the Johnston family, as well as a $90,000 gift from Mrs. Charles Knoernschild (whose daughter was a BVM nun). This allowed the nuns to contact architect Barry Byrne of Chicago to design a handsome new academy building which opened in 1928.[463]

St. Mary Academy, St. Francis [AAM]

One important feature of Holy Angels Academy was its accreditation to the Catholic University in 1918, and to the University of Wisconsin in 1915. The term accreditation (or affiliation which was used interchangeably) originally meant a one-to-one association between educational institutions that permitted the graduates of one to be admitted into the program of the other. Most schools in Wisconsin entered into these affiliation arrangements with the University of Wisconsin. However, the term accreditation soon expanded to mean a general approbation of the course of studies, faculty expertise and physical facilities of a school. This latter sense was used by the professional accrediting agencies. It also influenced the programs of teacher-training for nuns.

In 1904, the Franciscan Sisters of St. Francis, Wisconsin, had begun St. Mary's Academy for Girls on their convent property. This was done despite the spirited protests of the seminary faculty next door concerning the presence of females so close to the concupiscible seminarians. Nonetheless, the community erected a small building and took in 60 boarding students. Rising enrollments forced new construction in 1922 and again in 1929.[464] As it happened at many of the transformed academies, the sisters opted to keep the academy female. However, this would not be the case in Racine.

In 1921, the Racine Dominican Sisters discussed with the local clergy the pros and cons of a centralized high school. In February 1922, after she had been reelected, Mother Romana Thom, O.P., petitioned Rome for permission to build a new high school. On March 19, 1922, the Feast of St. Joseph, excavations began at 12th Street and Park Avenue. Barry Byrne of Chicago was given another school-design contract. The handsome three-story brick school was framed in terra cotta and calculated for 600 pupils.[465] In its 1,000 seat theater a mammoth pipe organ was installed; and a library, study halls, and modern science labs were accommodated. Leaving the upper floor unfinished, the project cost to the Racine Dominicans was a whopping $300,000. By the time the building was finished, its costs soared to $500,000. The original plan was to rename the new enterprise St. Thomas High School in honor of the Dominican St. Thomas Aquinas. A statue of the angelic doctor was even installed over the main entrance of the new school. But alumnae of the school demanded the retention of St. Catherine as the principal patron. In May 1924, Messmer traveled to Racine to dedicate the new structure.

St. Catherine High School, Racine
[AOP-Rac]

The Racine Dominicans decided to make St. Catherine's a coeducational rather than perpetuate the all-girls academy that had been in place since 1864. Mother Romana recruited a young diocesan priest, William McDermott, to head the enterprise. Later, conflicts with McDermott over financial affairs led to demands by the sisters that he be removed and he was replaced by Father Stanislaus Witkowiak, who shepherded the school until the 1970s. Although coeducation began with the entering class in 1924, one enterprising young man, Frank Lemanowicz, "argued his way" into the all-female senior class and graduated with the academy members in June 1925. Paying off the huge construction debts required great fiscal discipline and countless fund-raisers sponsored by the sisters, but after 10 years, all the bills were met.[466]

Since 1902, the Sisters of Mercy had expanded their presence in the archdiocese of Milwaukee and by building Our Lady of Mercy Convent on South 7th Street and National Avenue. This structure served as the community's motherhouse, a day academy for girls and housed fifty boarding students. When an earlier convent, at St. Patrick's parish in Fond du Lac, closed, many of the sisters came to Milwaukee and expanded the offerings of the small school. Mother Bernardine Clancy purchased a piece of property on South 29th and Mitchell Streets called Comstock farm and laid plans for a new $400,000 high school. The four-story Mercy High School building designed by Brust and Philips opened in the fall of 1925.[467]

Mercy High School, Milwaukee [AAM]

In Madison, the Sinsinawa Dominican Sacred Heart Academy for Girls still ran a prosperous boarding school with just a few days students. But by 1917-1918 accommodations in the old Washburn-Marshall mansion where the academy was housed were growing tight. In an effort to create space and also a more defined high school program, the sisters dropped all grades below sixth. Mother Samuel Coughlin was hesitant to build unless she had the support of local pastors. With the strong backing of Father Henry Hengell of St. Paul's Chapel (who also lived at the academy), clerical backing was secured. In November 1925 ground was broken for a new Edgewood Catholic High School. Hengell spoke at the groundbreaking, sounding familiar themes of dedication, hard work and the necessity of Catholic schools as an antidote to the secularism of the time.[468]

In 1909, the Sisters of St. Agnes transformed their sanitarium into a girls academy. St. Mary's Springs Academy opened in Fond du Lac with 17 girls in the first class. Interest in a central Catholic school grew over the years, but lack of funds and the crushing of the local economy in the Great Depression made it impossible to think about a separate school for boys in Fond du Lac. Continued complaints and pleas from pastors and families with boys caused Stritch to rethink his opposition to co-education. In 1939, when Agnesian superior, Mother Aloysia Leickem, intimated to Stritch her willingness to accept boys, Stritch approved, noting in a letter to Mother Aloysia the traditional objections to such practice, but realizing: "We are however faced with a practical question, the answering of which will not brook delay until at some future date, at this time recognized by all as distant, we shall be able to provide separate high school education for our boys and girls." He wrote further, "Experience shows how great are the benefits to religion which flow from Catholic Coeducational High Schools in circumstances which do not permit the erection of separate institutions. God in his goodness in such circumstances comes to our aid and marvelously there disappear the inconveniences and drawbacks bound up with co-education in adolescence. These Catholic Coeducational High Schools not only are freer from dangers for our youth than the secular schools, but actually through the special gifts to God to those, who try in difficult circumstances to rear Catholic youth, they succeed in founding adolescents safely on the firm basis of Christian truths and morals."[469]

St. Mary Springs Academy, Fond du Lac [Courtesy of Kevin Wester]

Parish High Schools

Some parishes, had the wherewithal and staff to mount academy and high school programs. The prototypical parish high school was associated with St. John's Cathedral. After long resisting the creation of a Catholic grade school, Father James Keogh turned his attention to creating a network of school buildings on the cathedral block. In 1895, he formed a grade school, in which the Sinsinawa Dominicans taught the boys and the Daughters of Charity the girls. The Daughters also taught in a small girls high school on the property. Grandiloquently named "St. John's Institute," it attained some popularity, even though the area around the cathedral was emptying of residents. In 1905, Keogh reorganized St. John's when the Daughters of Charity decided to withdraw from schools around the archdiocese. He combined the two grade schools and admitted boys to the high school. All of these schools were under the central direction of the Sinsinawa Dominicans. In explaining the transition to the parishioners, Keogh said, "Their work during the past ten years has been more than satisfactory. I have therefore no hesitation in now giving them the whole school with the fullest confidence in their ability to conduct it on the most progressive educational lines."[470]

In 1932, Father Louis Jurasinski, pastor of St. Stanislaus on the south side, opened up a wing of his school building for a high school program. Jurasinski added one year consecutively to the program until 1936, when a four-year program was in place. Eventually it became one of the leading high schools for the entire south side. A later pastor acknowledged its broad appeal and renamed St. Stanislaus High "Notre Dame."[471]

On the northwest side of Milwaukee, a high school program named for the reigning pontiff, Pope Pius XI, was begun in 1927 when a two-year commercial course was added to the program of St. Anthony's school on Bluemound Road.[472] This enterprise, begun by the Pallotine whirlwind Father Peter Schroeder, grew gradually. From the two-year course, Schroeder steadily added additional high school years. At one point Archbishop Stritch, worried about the over-extended finances of the parish ordered it closed. Nonetheless, Schroeder built a new school and secured Stritch's reluctant permission to continue. For many years, Pius XI High School was tethered to St. Anthony parish and resources from the parish would sustain the school. Schroeder was exceptionally lucky in having the generous service of the School Sisters of St. Francis, and also in being in the right location to take advantage of western Milwaukee's growth. Pius XI would one day become the largest Catholic high school in Wisconsin.[473]

Pius XI School
[ASAC]

In 1938, the Capuchins and the Racine Dominicans transformed the two-year high school course at St. Benedict's parish into a four-year program for the African American students. This was done for multiple reasons: Catholic high schools would not admit black students, and parents of the students in the lower grades asked for an extension of the program to include all four years of high school. The Capuchins and Dominicans graduated their first class of students from St. Benedict's High School in 1942.

Some parishes tried to transform small commercial courses into full-fledged high schools. Commercial courses were geared toward teaching pupils skills for office work: typing, shorthand, and bookkeeping. Although many young men took these courses, they were also popular with young women who could enter the workforce as secretarial help. Most graduates of these programs went right into the workforce. Others transferred to regular high schools and finished off their education. In 1908 St. Anne's parish in Milwaukee began a two-year commercial course for its elementary school graduates. In 1919, St. Francis parish did the same. St. Anne's turned out 500 graduates before financial distress closed it in 1934. St. Francis closed earlier as both schools shipped their students to Messmer High School or to other sites.[474] One commercial course that survived and transformed itself into a successful four-year program was at St. Mary's in Burlington. In 1920, 14 students (8 girls and 6 boys), were the first students in a commercial class begun at the Burlington school. After two years, the curriculum of the school was changed to a more classical high school curriculum and St. Mary's students took some of their classwork at the local public high school. In 1926, the parish was able to build a separate high school. In August 1929, the school was accredited to Marquette University and the University of Wisconsin.[475]

A New Central Catholic High School

The successes of the Catholic high school in Racine and the decision to move forward with coeducation stimulated even more interest in a central archdiocesan high school located in Milwaukee. Cautious Milwaukeeans kept an eagle eye on developments in other dioceses around the country. Historian John Augenstein notes that, during the 1920s, annual meetings of the National Catholic Education Association and discussions among the association of school superintendents stressed the need for a centralized location for the growing number of Catholic teens.[476] The recurring concern was that Catholic youth would be "lost" if they left the protective cocoon of the Catholic school environment with its blend of religious instruction, liturgical and devotional life, and, above all, moral instruction. Anxieties over coeducation, were amplified by papal and curial utterances against it. Indeed, most leading Catholic educators were against it, but they were also confronted by the pragmatic reality that dioceses could not always afford to build and equip two distinct Catholic schools. As a result, co-institutional arrangements were often made. It was in this context that

Milwaukee's first central Catholic High School was built.

The origins of the high school begin with Father George Meyer. Meyer began a small high school at Holy Angels parish by moving two used World War I-era barracks on to his property and began classes for students in the 9th and 10th grades. The big demand for these classes prompted Meyer to approach Messmer and school superintendent Monsignor Joseph Barbian with a plea for a new Catholic high school.[477] Barbian and Meyer surveyed the education of 2,214 Catholic grade school pupils in April 1926 and discovered only 540 went on to a Catholic high school. The rest attended public high schools, technical high schools, vocational schools or business colleges, or just went to work.[478] In order to stop this "leakage" Messmer allowed Meyer to begin a high school program in the old grade school buildings of St. Elizabeth parish. In 1926, he recruited the School Sisters of Notre Dame to teach. This would serve as a temporary site for the new Catholic central high school.[479]

Rev. George Meyer [AAM]

The location of the site, on the city's north side, reflected Meyer's preferences. The high school endeavor had begun as an offshoot of his parish and the north side of the city was booming with new parish foundations in the 1920s. However, south side Milwaukeeans felt that they did not have equal access, nor did students in outlying areas, especially since the new school had no boarding facilities—a staple of the earlier academies. Site controversies raged for about a year. An offer from the School Sisters of Notre Dame to start a high school on the northeast side of Milwaukee at 55th and Vliet was considered by an ad hoc meeting of northwest side pastors. But they rejected their offer because "the location is wholly inconvenient as the territory served would be entirely too limited."[480] Finally, in 1927 a large tract on 8th Street and Capitol Avenue near Meyer's Holy Angels parish was purchased by the archdiocese. Messmer would be a north side school.

The St. Elizabeth's site soon became too cramped for the growing high school. However, even though Messmer had begun raising funds for a new high school as early as 1925 the efforts came up short. In 1928 a corporation was formed to oversee the project and raise more money for construction. But when fund-raising faltered again, Traudt secured permission to market $650,000 in bonds to pay for the new high school. Ground was broken in late 1928 for the new Messmer High School, designed by the firm of Herbst and Kuenzli, and it went forward throughout the fateful year of 1929.[481] Meyer was replaced as principal by Father Edmund Goebel, who oversaw the construction of the school. Hundreds of Milwaukeeans converged on the construction site in September 1929, for the cornerstone laying, presided over by

Rev. Edmund Goebel speaking at cornerstone laying of Messmer High School, Milwaukee, 1929 [AAM]

Traudt.[482] In early 1930, the buildings were ready for occupancy and Goebel recruited student help to close down the old facility and to move over to the new school. In February, 1930 the new Messmer High School was opened, and in May an infirm Archbishop Messmer presided at rites of dedication.[483] That fall Messmer High School welcomed a new freshman class and a total enrollment of 507 students. It soon exceeded all expectations for success and by the early 1940s, Messmer was running double shifts to accommodate all the Catholic students who wanted to attend.

Messmer High School, Milwaukee [AAM]

Catholic Higher Education: Marquette University

The separation of elementary and high school students into their own educational programs cleared the way for a major reshaping of Catholic higher education. Once again, the secular academy provided the norms. The standardization of learning and the earning of degrees had led to the formation of credit hours and the restructuring of curriculum to cover certain important areas of knowledge (the core curriculum), a remnant of the old classical education. Harvard University had introduced the innovation of elective classes and with that the prospect of specializing or majoring in particular areas of study. The old fashioned Catholic colleges with their minim departments and classical curricula soon gave way to the four year post-secondary educational experience. In addition, Catholics also attempted to imitate the modern research university.

Johnston Hall, Marquette College [MUA]

In the archdiocese of Milwaukee, Marquette University stood out as the major Catholic institution of higher learning in the state and in the entire Midwest. Marquette began its major transformation in the 1905-06 school year when the high school and collegiate courses were divided into two separate programs. In 1907, the college section moved into Johnston Hall on Grand (later Wisconsin) Avenue.

Father Alexander Burrowes, S. J., was the Marquette president who envisioned the transformation of the small men's college into a Catholic University by the affiliation of self-supporting units.[484] Working together with his vice president, Henry Spalding, S. J., the college acquired a series of nearly bankrupt professional schools which were linked to the new university. In 1906, the Milwaukee Medical College on 9th and Wells Street was "affiliated" with Marquette (it retained its autonomy and oversight of its fiscal affairs, but became part of the Marquette program). Later, when Dr. William Earle who brokered the deal died, Marquette acquired the school outright. In 1907, Burrowes sent Spalding to "affiliate" a struggling Milwaukee law school. This lengthy process spilled over into the administration of Burrowes successor, Father James McCabe and was completed by 1908. In 1910, Marquette began its steady expansion westward down Grand (Wisconsin Avenue) and purchased the Mackie residence on 11th and Grand.[485] Later, colleges of music, engineering and journalism were acquired. A school of dentistry was established with the medical school.

Marquette's efforts to live up to its university status consumed the energy, resources and skills of subsequent Jesuit presidents. In a short time it became Wisconsin's premier Catholic institution of higher learning, and by 1922 had to transfer its annual commencement ceremonies to the civic auditorium to accommodate the 273 degree recipients.[486] By 1928, Marquette registered 4,000 students in its various programs, making it one of the largest institutions in the whole Jesuit system of schools. Its leading rival in Wisconsin was the University at Madison.

In a significant departure from common Catholic practice and in particular the practice of Jesuit schools, Marquette admitted women to its undergraduate programs. Its first female graduate, Daisy Wolcott, received a degree in 1906. Although women were not permitted to live on the Marquette campus until the 1950s, a steady flow of lay and religious women attended the university. The decision for coeducation caused heartburn among some elements of the archdiocesan bureaucracy, including Archbishops Messmer and Stritch, who thoroughly disapproved of coeducation.

Continued expansion "down the Avenue" carved out more space for a growing Marquette. Marquette brought college football to Milwaukee in 1905 and Marquette teams took to the gridiron in a small stadium at 10th and State. The game's popularity took off like a rocket after World War I and the increasing crowds led to the construction of a 15,000-seat stadium (later expanded) on some vacant land at 35th and Clybourn. Local pride in the Marquette team became a staple of Catholic life in Milwaukee and annual grudge matches with the Notre Dame team raised local interest even higher. The same stadium would be used as a site for prayer rallies and other kinds of large archdiocesan demonstrations throughout its existence. Marquette played football in the stadium until 1958.

Marquette Stadium
[MUA]

In 1916, Jesuit President Herbert Noonan launched a highly successful fund-raising campaign that was one of the first in the archdiocese to use professional fund-raisers (as noted earlier it was one of the inspirations for the failed $5 million campaign of Archbishop Messmer). Noonan managed to rake in over $350,000 when all the campaign expenses were made.[487]

Rev. Herbert Noonan
[MUA]

Unfortunately, an effort to endow the medical school by purchasing northern Michigan timber lands in 1920 failed badly. Marquette found itself holding the bad debts of the company that attempted to market the lands to farmers and was even precluded from harvesting the timber rights on the properties because of previously granted concessions to timber companies. The scheme ended up costing Marquette hundreds of thousands of dollars and with the collapse of the farming economy after World War I, left it with remote properties for which there was no market. In 1945, the land was eventually purchased at fire sale prices by the United States government for a forest preserve.[488]

Marquette's claim on valuable urban space grew more visible as time went on. With the proceeds of the 1916 drive, President Herbert Noonan began to purchase a number of private residences, rooming houses, apartments and even mansions along the "Avenue" and to the south of the campus on Michigan Avenue. Some of these Marquette transformed into classrooms, faculty offices and residence halls for men. (Such was the case of the two Plankinton mansions along Wisconsin Avenue.) Some they demolished to make way for new structures.[489]

Marquette Law School [MUA]

It was the ambitious Father Albert Fox who took over in 1922, and shepherded the construction of some of the most beautiful buildings on the Marquette campus. Fox, unlike the reclusive Noonan, was an extroverted backslapper who made quite an impression on Milwaukee's business and civic community. He was determined to link the Marquette campus more firmly into the network of urban life, and in 1923 began a building program that resulted in a new science building, crowned by a distinctive campanile (today Marquette's logo) and a new law school on the corner of 11th and Wisconsin. The "Father Grimmelsman" room of the law school sported an exposed beam meeting room and fireplaces.

He also attempted to secure the site of the Schandein mansion on 24th and Wisconsin, owned by the county of Milwaukee, for a new health center and teaching hospital for the medical school. This proposal stirred considerable opposition among various elements of Milwaukee's populace (including socialists, who wanted a "free" hospital on the site as opposed to a privately run institution, as well as erstwhile Ku Klux Klan members who saw the "land grab" as additional evidence of Catholic domination of county government). In a tumultuous meeting in 1927, Marquette's bid to purchase the Schandein property was rejected. In 1932, after Fox had left office, a new medical school was built.[490] (The school never had a university hospital and was compelled to send its interns to the county and veteran's hospitals.) In 1940, a new engineering building between 15th and 16th and Wisconsin capped a period of university building and growth. The growing complex of buildings along Wisconsin Avenue attracted the generosity of some of Wisconsin's wealthiest men and women. The money to build the law and medical schools came from Harriet Cramer, the generous benefactor of the Gesu.[491]

Even though the archdiocese kept a strict hands-off policy over the internal affairs of the university, the concerns of both intertwined at various times. Shortly after the dedication of the medical school in 1932, the university hit a serious financial crisis. The economic slump caused faculty layoffs and annual operating deficits of over $60,000. Father Raphael Hamilton's history does not blame the crisis on the building of the medical school, because Marquette's finances had been in precarious shape during the 1920s. In these years the institution (like many archdiocesan parishes) had run up huge amounts of bonded indebtedness—$3 million in all by 1928.[492] Father William Magee, the successor of Father Fox, had the task of shepherding the university through a time of grave fiscal crisis when it could not meet payments on its bonded indebtedness or its operating budget. Marquette University was on the brink of financial disaster. It was at this point that the archdiocese stepped in to offer some help.

The relationship between the archdiocese and Marquette had been cordial, even if distant, during the Messmer-Traudt years. Because the school was under the auspices of the Society of Jesus there were limitations on archdiocesan authority over its personnel and policies. Clearly, neither Messmer nor Stritch was happy about the fact that women attended the school. Although Messmer appears to have been concerned about the hiring of non-Catholics on the faculty, he paid little attention to the affairs of the school. Some of this may have been a residue of old German/English-speaking ethnic boundaries. The Jesuits at the university generally steered clear of internal archdiocesan controversies, but were dominated by English speakers. Nonetheless, sometime in the 1920s the archdiocese lent Marquette $26,000, which the university paid back in 1927.[493]

Archbishop Stritch, who had enjoyed warm relations with the Jesuits in the diocese of Toledo, ushered in a new "era of good feelings" between the archdiocese and the university. As he did in Toledo, he called on the Marquette Jesuits to provide a teacher-training program for the religious women of the archdiocese and called on local Jesuit faculty to provide advice in areas of expertise. His daily walks down Wisconsin Avenue took him past Gesu Church and the Jesuit residence at Johnston Hall. In 1932, when Marquette's financial crisis came to a head, Stritch came to the assistance of the beleaguered university. Praising the university to the Jesuit superior general, he laid out a series of proposals that he hoped would do something to alleviate the financial distress. He offered to suspend all archdiocesan assessments on Gesu parish for a period of five years with the proviso that the parish would turn over those monies to the university. He also urged that the community assessments demanded by the provincial of the St. Louis Province (under which the Marquette Jesuits operated) be given directly to the ailing school. He recommended that the Jesuit faculty accept more parish "help-outs" and turn the proceeds over to the school. He suggested a modest fund appeal to the 11,000 living graduates of the university. In his most generous gesture, he permitted the taking of a "Marquette Sunday" collection (timed to the end of July around the feast of St. Ignatius Loyola) in all of the parishes of the archdiocese.[494] In recommending the collection to the parishes he noted, "I shall not have it said that the Archbishop and clergy and people of the Milwaukee Archdiocese failed to give in its hour of need every possible support to Marquette University to which we are so deeply indebted."[495] Throughout 1933 Stritch worked with Magee to refinance the interest on the bonds.[496] When bondholders were compelled to accept a lower rate of interest than what they had originally agreed to, some wrote angry letters to Stritch, who had written in behalf of the new arrangement. He deflected the anger directed at the Jesuits and asked the bondholders for understanding. "We are living in extraordinary times," he informed one irate bondholder, "and extraordinary requests are not unusual."[497] Likewise Stritch interceded with federal officials, including Madison Catholic Leo T. Crowley, the head of the Federal Deposit Insurance Corporation, to secure a Reconstruction Finance Corporation loan for Marquette (this required an alteration of the RFC enabling legislation which Stritch pushed with Senator F. Ryan Duffy).[498] In fact about the only thing Stritch forbade the Jesuits to do was to mortgage Gesu Church properties for the relief of university debts.[499] It would be an overstatement to suggest that Stritch's actions, the collection, and his support in the various refinancing and government loan efforts played a defining role in Marquette's economic stabilization. However, the struggling university did get back on its feet again by the end of the 1930s and managed to move forward on the expansion of its campus and the steady improvement of its academic programs.

It is difficult to underestimate the influence of Marquette faculty and students on the development of Catholic life in the archdiocese of Milwaukee. "This university is a distinct asset to the Catholic Church in Wisconsin," wrote Archbishop Samuel Stritch to the Jesuit general in 1932.[500] In 1950 Marquette president Edward J. O'Donnell compiled a lengthy report on the Social Apostolate of the Jesuits in Milwaukee, laying out the contributions of the Jesuits and the graduates of Marquette University to Wisconsin life. Of the graduates (1,542 in the academic year 1948-1949 alone), O'Donnell wrote, "They form a potent leaven spreading Catholic or at least scholastic philosophical principles to the region." He counted 174 lawyers, 77 physicians, 50 dentists, 250 engineers among the year's graduates, all of whom "have social mindedness inculcated upon them continually while in school."[501] O'Donnell went on to list the number of Marquette graduates in local, state and national politics, the judiciary, journalism (Catholic and secular), the ranks of the priesthood and religious life, and was careful to explain how these products of Jesuit education helped the local church build a cadre of well-educated professionals who over time came to exercise some influence on archdiocesan and parochial affairs.

A Catholic College for Women: Mount Mary

Continued archdiocesan discomfit with coeducation played some role in approving the transfer of a college for women to the see city at the end of the 1920s.

Since the beginning of the 20th century, a number of women's academies run by religious sisterhoods had evolved into colleges for women. One of the first was the College of Notre Dame of Maryland which began as a girls academy in the 1860s and by 1896 had formed a separate liberal arts program for women. Others followed. In 1900, Trinity College in Washington, D.C. opened as the first Catholic college for women that did not evolve from an academy.[502]

Mount Mary College followed the general pattern of development and was the offshoot of St. Mary's Academy, which had begun in the School Sisters of Notre Dame motherhouse under Mother Caroline in the 1850s.[503] In 1872, Mother Caroline opened St. Mary's Institute in Prairie du Chien, where benefactors John Lawler, an associate of railroad mogul James J. Hill, and Peter Doyle, a former secretary of state for Wisconsin, had erected a new building for them in 1877. In 1913, the high school and college departments were separated and St. Mary's College was chartered. New college buildings were erected and the first bachelor of arts degrees were conferred in 1916. By 1921, St. Mary's had been accredited by the National Catholic Educational Association and approved by the Department of Public Instruction for the issuance of teachers' certificates. In 1927, the college won accreditation by the North Central Association of Colleges and was admitted to the American Association of Colleges.

Archbishop Messmer was anxious to have a women's college in the see city and responded enthusiastically to plans by Sinsinawa Dominican head, Mother Samuel Coughlin, to relocate the collegiate portion of St. Clara's Academy at Sinsinawa Mound to Milwaukee. "There is room here, aye, there is a great need for such a girl's and young women's college as you have at Sinsinawa to be established here."[504] But the Dominicans decided to build Rosary College (today Dominican University) in River Forest, Illinois, and it

[AAM]

ST. MARY'S INSTITUTE, PRAIRIE DU CHIEN, WIS.

This Institution, situated on a beautiful eminence overlooking the Mississippi River, in the most delightful part of Prairie du Chien, is under the direction of the School Sisters de Notre Dame. The house is new, large, and commodious; it is furnished with furnace, water, baths, etc.

TERMS.

Board, Washing, Tuition in all English Branches, French, and German, per annum................ $150 00

Music, Drawing, Painting, etc., form extra charges. For further particulars, address Sr. M. PATRITIA, Superioress.

would be the Sisters of Notre Dame who actually made the move.

After World War I concerns were raised about the remoteness of St. Mary's, which was across the state on the Minnesota border. As one college historian wrote in 1963, St. Mary's was "lacking some of the cultural and recreational advantages of a metropolitan area."[505] Likewise, the large number of young girls in the phalanx of Notre Dame schools in and around Milwaukee and the metropolitan area were being lost to secular institutions. Parents of Milwaukee-based parishes were not inclined to send their daughters to the far western part of the state. Perhaps a Notre Dame-run college nearer the feeder schools would have a better chance of success. The community chronicles announced a change: "A most momentous decision was reached in the Spring of 1927. This was the determination of the Superiors of the Order to transfer the College from Prairie du Chien to Milwaukee." The chronicle noted the reason: "on account of the trend of the times toward associating all institutions of higher education with urban life."[506] Over seventy acres of land was purchased in a lightly occupied area on the northwest side of Milwaukee at 92nd and Burleigh.[507] A set of tasteful campus buildings, dominated by a 175-foot English Gothic tower, were designed by the firm of Herbst and Kuenzli. Symbolic of the new location and the new identity, the sisters renamed the women's college "Mount Mary." It would soon mature into a flourishing Catholic college for laywomen and the School Sisters of Notre Dame.

Mount Mary College, Milwaukee [MMCA]

When the cornerstone was laid for the new campus, the principal speaker was the dean of the graduate school of Marquette University, Edward Augustus Fitzpatrick. Fitzpatrick became the chancellor and first president of Mount Mary and played a pivotal role in this and other endeavors in Catholic education.[508] Fitzpatrick was born on New York's lower east side on August 29, 1884. Unable to attend Catholic school because of tuition, he graduated from public grade and high schools and entered Columbia University, where he majored in English literature and won a teaching certificate. This was followed by a master's degree in English and a doctorate in educational administration in 1911, with a dissertation on DeWitt Clinton's theories of education. Fitzpatrick entered the Training School for Public Service launched by the American Political Science Association. In 1913, his friend Charles McCarthy of the Wisconsin State Legislative Bureau had been entrusted with a review of Wisconsin's rural school system on behalf of the Wisconsin State Board of Public Affairs. McCarthy recruited Fitzpatrick to study the issue and because of his work, the Wisconsin legislature enacted a minimum wage law for teachers. During World War I, the United States Army Reserve commissioned Fitzpatrick as a major and he supervised the conscription of Wisconsin men. From 1919 to 1923 he served as the secretary to the Wisconsin Board of Education and enjoyed the reputation of a reformer. However, the board was forced to dissolve in 1923 in the wake of investigations launched by the legislature. This ended Fitzpatrick's work in public education. He next worked for a hospital supply company and took a special interest in issues of hospital administration. In 1924, Father Albert Fox, S.J., invited him to become dean of the struggling Marquette graduate school and director of the school of hospital administration. He also assumed direction of the department of education and offered classes in college and university administration.

It was at Marquette that he met a group of School Sisters of Notre Dame who took his seminar class in 1927 and deemed him to be the appropriate person to help lead the new college program. Mother Stanislaus Kostka Schilling, general superior of the sisters, invited Fitzpatrick to take over the educational administration of the new college. Fitzpatrick kept his position at Marquette, and although he was quite dynamic, the two positions would tax his patience. Eventually the Jesuits fired him in 1938.

Edward Fitzpatrick, President of Mount Mary College [MMCA]

Fitzpatrick worked heart and soul for Mount Mary and used his considerable contacts with federal, state and local government officials to enhance its status. He also worked hard to enhance the college's slender financial situation by tapping into wealthy benefactors in the city and beyond. Fitzpatrick, however, did things that annoyed the sisters. For example his luxurious home on the campus offended the sense of poverty that the sisters practiced.

Other things that Fitzpatrick did revealed the limits to which such lay-religious association could go in those days. In fact, the sisters clashed angrily with Fitzpatrick when his insistence on the highest standards of academic excellence caused him to discard convent-bred ways of academic governance in favor of more modern, efficient, and business-like paradigms of management.

Fitzpatrick strongly insisted that the educational administration of the college be detached from the internal running of the convent. He believed that the sisters should be treated like employees of the school and not view the school as an extension of their convent or internal religious life. At his address at the laying of the cornerstone, in the presence of the Notre Dame commissary general, he declared, "The educational policy of the institution is in the hands of the faculty under the educational leadership of the president."[509] In the printed rendition of the talk, he was even more blunt: "No person, religious or lay, will be appointed to the college who does not have fully the educational requirements for the position."[510] This meant that positions could not be created for sisters out of broad cloth, nor could the convent place them in academic positions if they were occupied by someone else. The implications of this policy soon dawned on the sisters when Fitzpatrick refused to fire a lay teacher when a sister who was capable of doing her work became available (this happened occasionally in parish schools). The distressed sister wrote to her superior, "The real question is this: Does Dr. Fitzpatrick own Mount Mary College? Has it been given over to him for the furtherance of his own personal ambitions and to let his friends share the spoils?"[511] Fitzpatrick's decision was unchanged.

Ultimately, Fitzpatrick held on to his position at Mount Mary, even when he took a leave during World War II to assist General Lewis Hershey administer the draft. He continually promoted the college to benefactors and kept a watch over the quality of its programs and future. One of his most ambitious promotional tasks was to assemble a yearbook of the college's history and life. "We started out Mount Mary College here in Milwaukee ten years ago," he wrote in 1939, "to work out a higher education for women that would be consistent with the best academic practice of American colleges for women, with the clearest insight of an inclusive philosophy of education, with emphasis on supernatural religion." In the lengthy text, embellished with pictures, graphs, and student testimonies, Fitzpatrick launched into a paean to the college and predicted even greater growth and prosperity.[512] He was a prolific scholar and one of the pioneers of a new pedagogical approach to religious education which called for an end to the rote memorization of passages from the Baltimore Catechism. He retired from the college in 1954 after having conferred an honorary degree on another voice that called for the improvement of Catholic higher education, Monsignor John Tracy Ellis of the Catholic University of America.

Fitzpatrick was also at the heart of a number of other endeavors related to Catholic higher education in the archdiocese of Milwaukee—especially to the creation of sisters' colleges.

Doing Something about Teacher Training: The Colleges of the 1930s, St. Clare's, St. Albertus, St. Joseph's, and Mount Mary

The final link in the remaking of the archdiocese's system of Catholic schools revolved around the need to improve the training of teachers, mostly sisters, in the parochial schools. This led directly to the establishment of St. Clare's (later Cardinal Stritch College/ University), St. Albertus (later Dominican College of Racine), St. Joseph's (later Alverno College), and Marian (at Fond du Lac) colleges. Impelling this concerted effort to improve teacher training were not only the directives of Archbishop Samuel A. Stritch, but also the increasing state oversight of education—especially of high school youth destined for admission to the state university. In addition to Wisconsin's requirement, the teaching sisterhoods also had branch houses in many other American states where minimum standards for teachers were in place. In Nebraska for example, the School Sisters of St. Francis had schools at which sisters weren't permitted to teach unless they were certified.

Most of Milwaukee's teaching sisterhoods began to augment the education and pedagogical skills of their young teachers in the late 19th century. In 1887, the School Sisters of St. Francis opened a normal school in their convent. In 1900, the Franciscan Sisters of St. Francis opened a normal school named for St. Catherine. The Agnesians of Fond du Lac had begun summer sessions for teachers at their motherhouse. These normal school programs would be the nuclei of later teacher training colleges.

However, given the multiple demands on the sisters, the limitations of their financial resources and the lack of trained personnel to conduct courses, the normal schools were haphazard operations. As a result, sisters in need of professional training and state certification often took courses at state normal schools in or near their vicinity. Some even attended the state university at Madison, long scorned by the clergy as a bastion of

St. Agnes Convent, Fond du Lac [Courtesy of Kevin Wester]

secularism. Archbishop Stritch succinctly summed up the feelings of many about the University of Wisconsin, "The state University is no place for Catholic students."[513]

When Archbishop Samuel Stritch came to Milwaukee, the matter of the training of teaching sisters was uppermost in his mind. As a young priest in the diocese of Nashville, he had served as superintendent of schools, a job that fit his rather bookish nature. It was in Tennessee, as his nephew attested later, that he became convinced of the need to upgrade the quality of instruction and administration in Catholic schools. When he became bishop of Toledo in 1921, he took steps to professionalize the Catholic schools and improve the training of teachers. He found only one institution of higher learning, the Jesuit-run St. John's University for men. In 1922, Stritch established a teacher's college and had it affiliated with St. John's College. He would later establish a school for women, called Mary Manse, under the direction of the Ursuline Sisters. The St. John's/Teacher's College alliance worked well, offering courses during the summers to part-time students and to a small number of full-time pupils.[514] It provided Stritch with a model he would attempt to implement in Milwaukee.

Each year, as archbishop of Milwaukee, he issued a pastoral letter on the subject of education and insisted that more parishes build schools—even in the midst of the Depression. More than any other bishop, Stritch thought seriously about the nature of education and its desired outcome. True to his Thomistic training, Stritch saw human knowledge issuing in faith and insisted that education that did not lead one to believe in God was something less than desirable. Yet even as he insisted that Catholic school teachers had to match their secular counterparts in liberal education and pedagogical training, he feared the secularizing impulses of contemporary educational theories such as those of John Dewey. Typical of his approach were words he spoke to the School Sisters of Notre Dame, "I don't care how many degrees or I.Q.'s a Sister may have; these do not determine the good teacher. The good teacher is the religious teacher .... The modern educators put too much stress on the meaning of the word "education." They claim that education is a "drawing out" and a development of the instincts of the child. We know, as Catholic Education has always known, that the teacher stands before the child to give him something which the child has not and which the teacher has."[515]

Stritch arrived in Milwaukee in late 1930 and spent a better part of a year getting to know his archdiocese. But from the letters that came from various sisterhoods requesting permission to attend the Milwaukee Normal School or similar institutions, he was soon aware of the "problem" of religious communities sending their members to secular schools. Sisters, he insisted, should be educated under Catholic auspices. On matters of the cloister, he always chose the strictest interpretation and was negative on the idea of too many home visits by the sisters. Speaking shortly after his arrival to the School Sisters of Notre Dame, he spoke of a "silly woman" who urged the sisters to become more engaged in the world. "No," he lectured the sisters, "we would draw our Sisters ever farther away from the world, closer to the Master, so that possessing Him themselves, they may give Him to the children."[516]

Stritch turned his attention to the matter of providing adequate teacher preparation for the sisters. His first hope was Marquette University, where he thought he could replicate the St. John's/Teacher College association in his former diocese of Toledo. Indeed, Marquette offered the greatest hope for a unified teacher training program for the sisters of the archdiocese. As we have seen, since 1906 Marquette admitted women to undergraduate programs and a coeducational summer school began in 1908. The summer sessions, however, were difficult because of the strain and stress this put on the sisters and their Jesuit instructors who only weeks before ended an often stressful academic year. "School is hardly closed when they start summer school. After that they have a few days of retreat, and then it takes just about two weeks to scrub up the house and school starts again," complained one Jesuit. "More than one Father would find it more gratifying to be out giving retreats than to be giving summer courses."[517] Even more vexing, after blocking out courses and time slots (and turning down retreats or parish work that brought in revenue to the community), Jesuits often found themselves without summer students when a solicitous mother general pulled out sisters at the last minute to give them a rest.

Nonetheless, at Stritch's request, the Marquette dean sent out a circular to the teaching sisterhoods asking for suggestions for summer course offerings.[518] In October 1931, Stritch sent letters to the major sisterhoods of the archdiocese urging them to reply to the dean and to use Marquette as the site for teacher training. "I cannot countenance the patronage of secular schools by our Sisters .... Your cooperation to the extent of frankly telling the Rev. Dean just what your sisters need in the field of teacher training will be deeply appreciated both by the University and myself."[519] To arrange for the establish-

School Sister of St. Francis Postulant [ASSF]

ment of a regular teacher training program for sisters at Marquette, Stritch outlined his basic goals and left the details to Superintendent of Schools Joseph Barbian, who worked with Marquette dean, Father William Grace and his assistant, Father Donald Keegan.

Interest was high in this proposal but planning could not get underway for at least a year. In the meantime the financial difficulties at Marquette made university administrators wary. At a September 1932 meeting the Jesuits informed the sisters and Monsignor Barbian that since the university would confer grades and credit, it would have control over the educational programs, and that "the movement would have to be self-supporting." The proposed endeavor sounded good in theory, but as reality set in, the idea fell apart. Sisterhoods were themselves financially strapped, and could not afford the tuition and transportation costs that the program advised.

For example, Mother Mary Samuel Coughlin of the Sinsinawa Dominicans reminded Monsignor Barbian that Stritch had earlier given his permission for sisters to attend the state normal school, although asking the sisters not to broadcast it far and wide. As to beginning a new teacher training college for sisters, Coughlin, who was still getting Rosary College off the ground, noted that the costs involved would be phenomenal ("several hundreds of thousands of dollars for the building, equipment, and partial endowment"). Fearful of losing the schools on which her motherhouse relied for revenue because the sisters lacked proper training, Coughlin begged Barbian to keep the permission secret. "You know it would be disastrous if any report were to be circulated that the Archbishop had given general permission for the Sisters to go to the normal .... No doubt other Congregations with problems similar to ours have already had conferences with His Excellency."[520] The Dominicans continued to attend the normal schools, but eventually shifted their teacher-training program to Rosary College in River Forest, Illinois.

Likewise, the School Sisters of Notre Dame who had just opened Mount Mary College had no interest in participating in this program. Even when a more compact two-year program, approved by the state Department of Education, was presented in 1934, the sisters could not participate.[521]

However, the demands of securing certification for their high schools meant that the sisters could not ignore the need for professional teacher training. Unable to be part of the Marquette plan, individual sisterhoods injected their moribund normal school programs with new life and a network of Catholic colleges took shape. Already in 1932 the Franciscans of St. Francis opened St. Clare's College in their motherhouse, with 23 novices and postulants as its first students. St. Clare's added to its program yearly, winning accreditation piecemeal from the University of Wisconsin. In 1936, St. Clare's began a three-year program leading to teacher certification, and in 1937 received a state charter to be a four-year degree granting institution. In 1946, it began to admit laywomen and renamed the college Cardinal Stritch to honor the prelate under whose auspices it had begun. In 1953, its undergraduate programs were approved by the North Central accreditation organization, and in 1964 its graduate offerings were accredited. In 1962, it moved to a new campus in Fox Point/Glendale.[522]

In 1935, the Racine Dominican sisters began their teacher-training institution in their motherhouse at 12th and Park. The school, named for St. Albert the Great (the sisters used the Latin "Albertus"), admitted only girls. It added a year at a time, securing approval from the University of Wisconsin for its program. Led at first by Sister Demetria Myer, the college added a school of music under the direction of Sister Marian Schwin, and ran a two- and three-year course sequence for music teachers. In 1937, laywomen were admitted to the fledgling college. In 1946 St. Albertus changed its name to Dominican College, and a new dean, Sister Gerold Thome, began to transform the school into a four-year institution. In 1947, the college took in men, whose G. I. Bill benefits paid for higher education. The influx of money and men helped boost the small college. The men were compelled to leave (as it turned out temporarily) when canonical prescriptions forbidding coeducation, suspended during wartime, were reimposed by Church authorities. In 1955, however, the Dominicans built a separate residence hall and instruction center and the men returned. Under Sister Thome, the college began to grow in size and sophistication. Her successor, Sister Rosita Uhen, purchased prime lakefront property north of Racine, and in 1961, Dominican College moved to the lakefront campus. Several years later the Racine Dominican motherhouse was built next to it.[523]

The Agnesian Sisters of Fond du Lac began a summer school for teacher training at their motherhouse. They also received permission to send sisters to the nearby Oshkosh Normal School and to St. Norbert's College in DePere. On September 8, 1936, Marian College was founded in a wing of the motherhouse. The next year laywomen were admitted to the college, and in 1941 the four-year program was accredited by the University of Wisconsin and affiliated to the Catholic University. In April 1960 the college secured accreditation with the North Central and in 1965 it moved to a new campus on National Avenue in Fond du Lac.[524]

In 1936 the School Sisters of St. Francis joined the cavalcade of sisters colleges. They too had begun a normal school program in 1888, but it was poorly staffed and disorganized. Obedient to Stritch's request, they began planning their new college by first consulting with the Franciscans of St. Francis to learn of their experiences in starting St. Clare's College. Convinced that they could start such a program, the School Sister's general superior, Mother Corona Wirfs, commissioned Sisters Jutta Hollenbeck and Augustine Steele to work out the details. It was Sister Jutta who broke the news of the opening of St. Joseph's College to Stritch as she met the prelate and Barbian by chance while waiting for a cab in downtown Milwaukee. Stritch praised the plans and much to the surprise of Sister Jutta urged her to send the sisters away for the best training. In his typical expansive fashion he told her, "The English teacher should be trained at Oxford, the French teacher should go to Paris for her education." When Sister Jutta noted that the costs of European training would be beyond the resources of the congregation, she wondered if it would be possible to send the sisters to the Catholic University in Washington, D.C. To her surprise, Stritch replied, "Send them to Madison ... come to me I will give you permission to send them there. The best is none too good and the training of its members is the soundest investment a Congregation can make."[525] In the fall of 1936, St. Joseph's Teacher's College opened its doors. At the same time, Sister Cherubim Schaefer opened the St. Joseph College of Music offering special courses in liturgical music, organ registration, and choir training. In the next year it was renamed the more Franciscan-sounding Alverno Teacher's College and Alverno College of Music.[526]

School Sisters of St. Francis Musicians Sisters [ASSF]

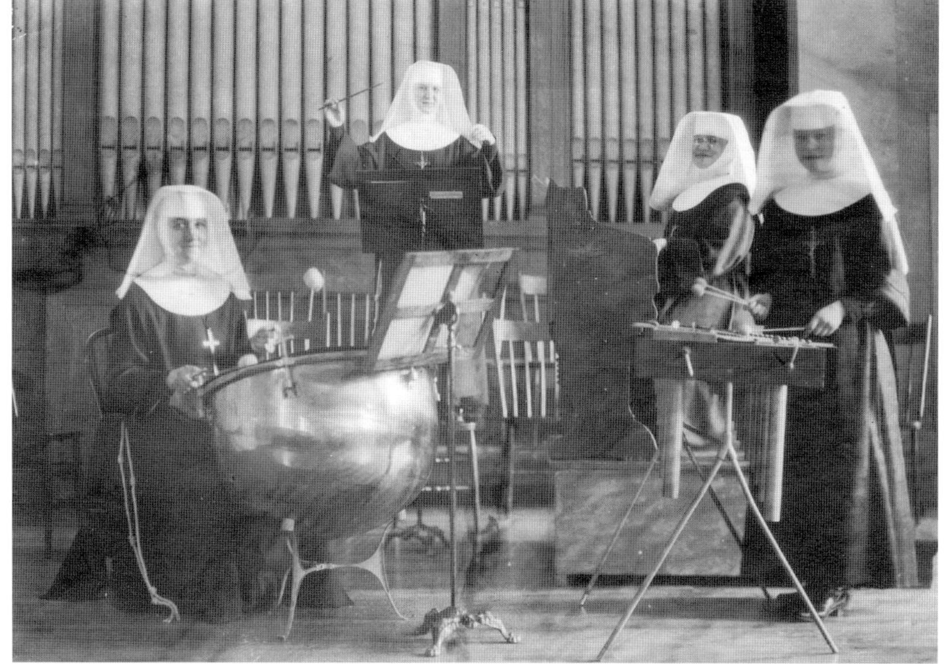

Graduate Dean and Mount Mary President Edward A. Fitzpatrick watched the proliferation of sisters' colleges with concern. He considered it foolish to divide collegiate efforts among communities, none of which on their own could mount effective academic programs and provide the requisite number of trained faculty and facilities to meet minimum accreditation standards. These jerry-rigged colleges with their haphazard academic programs also created unnecessary competition for female students, who would be good candidates for Mount Mary. Years after St. Clare's formation, Fitzpatrick summarized his feelings for the new colleges when he dismissed the Franciscan college as being "built on sand."[527]

Fitzpatrick tried one last time to make Marquette the training site for the sisters of the archdiocese. In unity there could be strength and excellence. He hoped that he could build a successful program that sisterhoods would find attractive and perhaps also make them willing to abandon their dreams of individual colleges before too much money and human effort had been expended. He targeted the School Sisters of St. Francis as the best prospect for his hopes since their plans were still relatively fluid in 1936.

The Franciscan sisters followed on archbishop Stritch's request that they seek affiliation with Marquette and in September 1936 met with Father William Grace, dean of the university. "Father Grace was reluctant about consenting to an affiliation without more information as to what the archbishop has in mind," the sisters confided to their convent annals. Grace probed the sisters about the qualifications of their teachers. "He was more than astonished to learn that they receive merely a high school education." He inquired what the state superintendent of schools would say if he knew this. Sister Jutta Hollenbeck replied, "Up to the present time we had not been questioned."[528]

Despite the negative reaction of Father Grace, Fitzpatrick forged the outlines of an agreement between Marquette and St. Joseph's Teacher's College.[529] The outline was to have the sisters run a three-year liberal arts and professional training program affiliated with the university, and then join Marquette in the fourth year for an accredited degree. Delicate problems of tuition, class requirements and the like were also worked out. Fitzpatrick nudged the proposal further along by suggesting that St. Joseph's College become the School of Education of Marquette University, "into which the School Sisters of St. Francis or any other sisters may insert a unit."[530]

The School Sisters and Fitzpatrick's detailed proposal hit problems with timing. In the fall of 1936, he submitted it to Father William Magee. However, Magee's term as president ended in November and he departed for the presidency of John Carroll University, leaving the proposal to his successor, Father Raphael McCarthy. McCarthy took a skeptical view of the proposal, noting that a similar plan had faltered in St. Louis due to opposition from the North Central accrediting organization. However, he pledged to keep an open mind. In January 1937, Fitzpatrick tried one last push to get it through, arguing to McCarthy, "My direct interest in the problem with the School Sis-

Sister Jutta Hollenbeck, SSSF [ASSF]

ters of St. Francis was to prevent multiplication of teacher training agencies which would necessarily be mediocre in quality. Some cooperative arrangement with the University seems to me to be an absolutely essential basis for competent work."[531]

In early 1937, the plan seemed to be moving forward and the assistant dean of liberal arts, Father Donald Keegan, assumed control of the project. Keegan was somewhat skeptical and seemed even less enthusiastic about the project when he found out that the School Sisters had not even secured recognition from the University of Wisconsin for their program. However, after conversations with Stritch, who was still hopeful that the project could be realized, Keegan's enthusiasm and energy level picked up considerably. At the same time, the sisters set to work securing the approval of the University of Wisconsin for their classes.[532]

Representatives from Marquette's education department worked out curricular details while Fitzpatrick approached the wealthy Sensenbrenner family for donations. Archbishop Stritch, sought and received permissions from Rome to effect the transfer. Even North Central gave a thumbs up to the project.[533] The sisters were elated, hoping among other things that a merger would enable them to save large amounts of money on the 26 full-time and 37 part-time students they had already enrolled.[534] When permission was received from the Jesuit generalate for the proposal, Keegan appeared at the door of the motherhouse of the School Sisters of St. Francis and announced himself as the dean of Alverno College (the name that St. Joseph's had taken).[535]

President Raphael McCarthy, who was intent on stabilizing Marquette's precarious finances and in building new buildings, intervened at this point and derailed the proposal. In July when the merger might have been signed, sealed and delivered, the Marquette president asked for more time to allow the sisters' institution to become more stable.[536] In November 1937 Milwaukee native Father William McGucken, S. J., of St. Louis University, a widely acknowledged expert on higher education and a rigorous proponent of high academic standards, investigated the proposed merger at McCarthy's request and came up with a negative evaluation.[537] McGucken cited the inadequate facilities of Alverno, the poor library, lack of privacy for student study, and the poor credentials of the sisters in the college program. The sisters were offended and noted in their annals, "We appreciate Father McGucken's frankness and realize he has the best interest of Catholic education in view, but we feel he is aspiring just a little too high."[538] McGucken's report ended any interest in the merger proposal.

The School Sisters proceeded forward to expand their own school. In 1946 it first affiliated with the Sacred Heart School of Nursing, and then in 1950 the Alverno College of Music changed its name to Alverno College. It began to admit laywomen in 1947. In 1951 it was accredited by the North Central Association, and in 1953 opened a $5 million facility in the Jackson Park neighborhood of Milwaukee.

Fitzpatrick had walked a delicate line, holding two jobs at Marquette and Mount Mary. From the outset the Jesuits were not happy with the arrangement and had refused to attend the testimonial banquet honoring the beginning of his work at Mount Mary. The Jesuits already thought Fitzpatrick was diverting women from attending Marquette, and the final straw came in 1938 when the Notre Dame sisters publicly complained that Marquette was accepting too many young women. This in turn prompted some sharp questions from Archbishop Stritch, who only tolerated coeducation in post-secondary institutions. Suspecting that Fitzpatrick was leaking information to the suspicious prelate, McCarthy terminated him from Marquette in 1938. Fitzpatrick ended his days as the head of Mount Mary.

A Catholic Presence at the University of Wisconsin

Among the chief reasons for creating separate Catholic colleges and universities was a deep suspicion of state-run institutions. Clearly, these institutions were considered off limits to religious sisters and priests. In Chicago, Cardinal Mundelein forbade his clergy and religious to attend the "red" University of Chicago. Accusations of anti-Catholic behavior or negative estimations of the Church (often coming through history classes that skewered the "Catholic" middle ages and the Spanish Inquisition) were reported as regular occurrences at the University of Wisconsin. However, while bishops and religious superiors could exclude their subjects from going to these places, the attendance of lay persons was another matter. In fact, hundreds of Catholic pupils attended the University of Wisconsin. Tending to the needs of this Catholic diaspora on the secular campus was a leading concern of the Messmer era.

Interestingly, the impetus to construct a Catholic chapel in Madison came not from the church but from the university itself. It was the noted economist Richard T. Ely of the Wisconsin faculty who pressed for the establishment of university chapels, educational centers, and guild halls on or near the campuses of state universities. Concerned about "moral education," Ely even urged his own Episcopalian Church to create such a center.[539] Ely's concern was picked up by President Charles van Hise who addressed a letter to the public signaling the welcome denominational chapels around the Madison campus.

Interest in a Catholic campus presence had been percolating since 1883. An Ohio-born law student, John J. McAnaw, had accused one of his professors, William Francis Allen, who taught a course called "Medieval Institutions," of slandering the Catholic Church. McAnaw voiced his complaints at a Thanksgiving Day dinner held at the home of a benefactor of Catholic students, Mrs. John Melvin. Mrs. Melvin urged the young student to form a discussion group for the "study of Irish and Catholic history and literature." Those present heeded her advice and named the group the "Melvin Club." The "Melvins" kept up a lively club for many years, hosting discussions on Catholic topics both historical and current and also equipping Catholic students with facts and the courage to stand up to professors who appeared to be insulting their baptismal faith. In some instances they won retractions from the errant professors. By 1900, the Melvin Club had developed largely into a social organization, and students desiring more substantive discussions and faith formation formed Bible study and other discussion groups.

In 1903, Father Henry C. Hengell, a curate at Holy Redeemer Church in Madison, stepped forward to help create a new organization for the inquiring Catholic students. Hengell, was a native of Waukesha, born February 26, 1877. A "delayed vocation," Hengell attended public grade and high school and had worked as a teller in a bank. It was apparently a conversation with a Methodist co-worker that convinced him to study for the priesthood. He entered St. Francis Seminary, where he graduated from the classical department in 1899. Because of his age and maturity, he was sent to Eichstatt, Germany for additional theological study. Ordained in 1903, Hengell was sent to the "German" Holy Redeemer parish, and there began to teach the college students seeking additional biblical information.

Rev. Henry C. Hengell [AAM]

He was such a popular teacher that his classes in the Bible and Christian doctrine attracted overflow crowds in rooms rented over a drugstore on University Avenue. Hengell's popularity set in motion efforts to build a Catholic chapel near the University of Wisconsin. At this same time, other secular campuses were erecting Catholic clubs and chapels in their vicinity (some inspired by the Melvins in Madison). In 1904, a former Melvin Club member, attorney L. B. Murphy, drew up an article for the incorporation of "The Catholic Club of the University of Wisconsin" and headed a drive to erect a Catholic chapel near the university. Although this met some resistance from clergy around the state who disliked the university, Murphy and Hengell were undeterred. Hengell surveyed the campus and discovered 300 Catholic students in the student body. In February 1906, Hengell drafted a letter to Messmer requesting permission to commence a Catholic Students Organization. Messmer inspected conditions in Madison, and in September 1906, transferred Hengell from Holy Redeemer, making him the first full-time chaplain in a non-Catholic institution of higher learning in the United States.

Messmer also directed Hengell to create a "Catholic college" attached by the Church to the University of Wisconsin. These *scholae religionis* had been mandated by Pope Pius X in his encyclical *Acerbo Nimis* (1905) as an institution to be run by the Church at or near the sight of major universities. Hengell dreamed not only of a chapel, but also of a thriving educational center. The St. Paul Chapel, as it was called, soon caught the fancy of Messmer, who assisted in the fund-raising, and who even looked on it as an excuse once again to deny a collection for the Catholic University of America. In 1910, a Tudor Gothic chapel was erected on State Street, near the State Historical Society. Later additions followed on the L-shaped structure, culminating in the construction of Newman Hall in 1934. Hengell's years in banking gave him the foresight to create an ample endowment for the center. By 1920, Hengell had erased the $35,000 debt on the building. As the program took shape, Hengell, sought to make the *scholae religionis* mandated by Pope Pius X a reality. He attempted to entice the Sinsinawa Dominicans to open a residence for Catholic girls on the campus, even though he supported their work at the nearby Edgewood College of the Sacred Heart. This portion of his work never came to fruition, although the lecture halls of the center were always busy with various programs.

For many years, Hengell was the leading Catholic voice in Madison. He developed what may be characterized as a "love-hate" relationship with the University of Wisconsin. He blasted professors like E. A. Ross and Max Otto and carried on a running battle with university president Glenn Frank. At one point he even urged listeners in his Madison chapel to send their children to Marquette.[540] However, even as he criticized the University of Wisconsin, he continued to build on to the St. Paul Chapel and left it in excellent financial condition.

Hengell was blessed with a series of assistants, including future seminary faculty members Peter Leo Johnson, Aloysius Muench, and John Grellinger. Grellinger was with him when he became incapacitated in 1936 and resigned from the post to seek a cure at Hot Springs, Arkansas. After his departure he was

St. Paul Chapel, University of Wisconsin, Madison [AAM]

succeeded by Father Alvin Kutchera, who was chaplain from 1936 until his death in 1964.[541] The St. Paul Chapel and the modest lecture halls associated with it would be an important part of the Catholic presence in the state capital for many years. Archbishops of Milwaukee visited infrequently, and communities like the Jesuits of Milwaukee disparaged the allocation of Catholic resources for this kind of work.[542] But the fact was it was necessary, and even ardent proponents of Catholic schools and colleges, like Archbishop Samuel Stritch, found it a pleasant surprise to see the effects of Hengell's work.

[AAM]

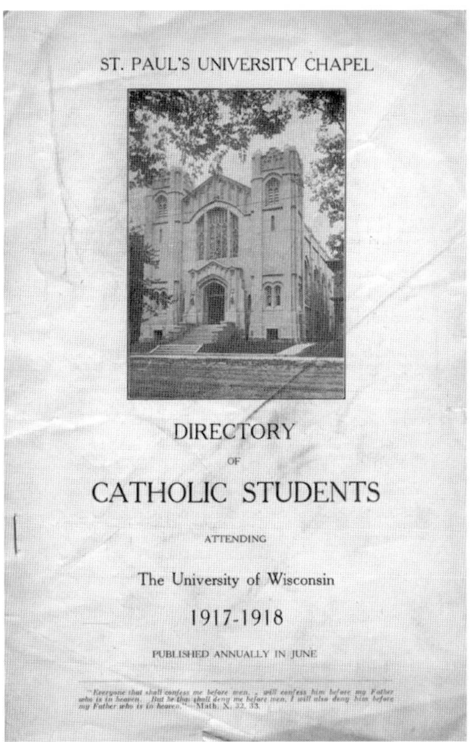

The Catholic Instruction League and the CCD

The concern for Catholic education at its various levels is often obscured by the fact that most Catholic children attended public schools in Milwaukee. Although attendance rates at Catholic schools were comparatively high, a 1936 survey revealed some important data. Stritch calculated the relationship between the number of baptisms and the number in Catholic schools. In 1936, he discovered that 48.3 percent of all children born in Milwaukee County were baptized Catholics. But out of a total of 101,000 grade school children and 34,000 high school students only 32,096 were enrolled in Catholic grade schools and only 3,717 in Catholic high schools. That meant that over 68,904 Catholic students were in public grade school and 30,283 were in public high schools.[543] Stritch constantly reminded pastors about the obligation Catholic parents had to send their children to Catholic school (an obligation that could be enforced by denying parents who ignored it absolution in sacramental confession). He urged parish priests to give the dispensation from attendance at Catholic schools only sparingly.[544] But these kinds of threats were ineffective. Parish priests were unwilling to carry them out and parents truly believed what the Church had long held: that they had the final say in how and where their offspring would be educated.

Assuming that Stritch's rough calculations were correct, and even taking into account the effects of the Great Depression (although many Catholic schools had no tuition, only fees for books and school supplies), the stark reality was that most Catholic children either did not wish to go to or could not get into a Catholic grade school or high school. Certainly some could not pay the tuition or book fees. Some ethnic groups, like Italians, were not predisposed to send their children to Catholic schools. Still others, especially English-speaking parents, refused to send their children to schools that overly emphasized foreign language, culture, and custom. In mixed marriages religious rearing of the children was often a bone of contention. Non-Catholic spouses were not often open to sending their children to Catholic schools. Some parents eagerly welcomed an alternative form of religious education to fulfill the promise many of them made to rear their children as Catholics and to prepare them for the sacraments. Others requiring religious training presented themselves to pastors.

Some children were confined to state, county, and city institutions for bodily or mental ailments. These included children in secular orphanages who could very well have lost their faith if not for some instruction. Older lapsed Catholics who had not been confirmed or even received their first communion needed instruction. Finally, there were children and others in rural areas, a part of Catholic America left behind by the predominantly urban character of U. S. Catholicism, who needed instruction. Rural children often could not attend Catholic schools, and their work schedules often precluded regular attendance even at public schools. The need to provide religious instruction for students who fell outside the pale of Catholic schools became increasingly necessary. Pope Pius X in his encyclical *Acerbo Nimis* (1905) urged pastoral care for youths who didn't attend Catholic schools.

One response came in 1912. The Catholic Instruction League was founded in Chicago by Father John M. Lyons and Lilian Kubic who rounded up 8 or 10 little Italian girls for a sewing circle at which they would impart some religious instruction.[545] The key to their cooperation was Lyons's belief that a lay person could actually convey religious doctrine and instruction to these unlettered children. When Kubic's gentle discussions of doctrine as the girls sewed resulted in six confirmations a few weeks later. When Lyons informed Archbishop James Quigley that he had instructed them through the assistance of lay persons, and not priests or sisters, Quigley approved the plan to continue the program. In June 1912, Lyons opened a center for the "Catholic Instruction League" in a storefront on 20th and Loomis Streets in Chicago, near the site of St. Procopius parish. The first class drew 29 children and soon swelled to 96. Scores of baptisms and confirmations came out of the program and Lyons laid out its goals carefully. These included religious instruction and character formation.

In 1916 Milwaukee became the "eldest" daughter of the Catholic Instruction League. In November 1916, while en route to give a retreat in St. Paul, Minnesota, Lyons shared the story with Marquette University Father Herbert Noonan, S. J. He urged Lyons to explain the program to Archbishop Sebastian Messmer. Messmer responded positively to Lyons's presentation and urged that CIL centers be established not only in Milwaukee, but also in Kenosha and Racine (two cities with large Italian populations and parishes). Responsibility for the CIL in Milwaukee was laid at the feet of another Lyons, Father Leo Lyons, S.J., who imitated the Chicago Lyons by seeking a laywoman to help him organize the program.

Leo Lyons threw himself into the work with gusto. Born in St. Louis in 1872, he had entered the Jesuits in 1891 and had taught in a variety of the community's institutions around the Midwest before coming to Milwaukee. "A manly man," as he was characterized by the Catholic press, Lyons had a love for youth and athletics that made him a natural for work with urban youth. Lyons embraced the Catholic Instruction League work, even foregoing his summer vacation for "off the street" work with local pastors. With Messmer's help, Lyons recruited attorney and state board of control member Katherine R. Williams to head the CIL. She brought with her the support of the Milwaukee Archdiocesan Council of Catholic Women (MACCW). Messmer summoned an organizational meeting of clergy and laity in December 1916, and an even larger meeting followed a month later in the Cathedral auditorium.

The first CIL center was at Our Lady of Pompeii Church and was announced on the day of the convocation. By the end of the year five other parishes volunteered to become CIL centers. Because of Lyons's charisma, Williams' skillful organizing, and the assistance of the MACCW which took the project under its control, the CIL flourished. Within 10 years, 18 parishes and the Milwaukee County Detention Center became outlets for the league and instructed an average of 2,550 children and others per year. Over 800 were admitted to first communion, 1,446 received the oils of confirmation, and over 1,100 attended an annual retreat. Nearly 250 lay teachers volunteered hours to instruct the children. Instruction in catechetical methods was provided by Marquette University, which held evening classes. The league also hosted catechist training sessions. Thanks to Williams the efforts of the CIL were also linked to the active work of the Third Order of St. Dominic headquartered at the Cathedral of St. John.

Lyons died tragically in late 1917 when a railing gave way on the bleachers of the Marquette Athletic Field, causing him to suffer fatal injuries. His funeral, attended by thousands in Gesu Church, reflected the love many young people felt for the popular priest. "He was the best friend I ever had," sobbed one Italian youngster from Pompeii parish.[546]

The program went on nonetheless. Financial support of the league's works came through an annual collection sanctioned by Messmer. Other centers opened in Racine, where statistics revealed that more Catholic children attended public than parochial schools. In Racine, the target communities of the CIL were Italians and Hungarians, who flocked to the CIL's Lakeside center. Here

CIL organizing resulted in the formation in 1925 of an ecclesiastical mission named in honor of St. Lucy, which eventually blossomed into a full-fledged parish. In Janesville and Kenosha, the league was a presence but not as popular. Janesville seemed to be able to deal with its Catholic instruction needs through the parochial schools, and only two centers opened. In Kenosha, the league outlet was founded in 1917 and also targeted the large Italian community of the city.[547] But its center at St. Thomas parish put it somewhat outside the area where Italian Catholics lived. The CIL program involved regular meetings during the year and the hosting of a two-week summer school at some convenient spot. Often these classes were held on Saturday mornings and drew in the sisters of the parish. In many places the bulk of the instruction was carried on by lay persons.

Stritch was a strong supporter of the Instruction League.[548] In 1936 he added impetus to the program by appointing Father Paul Tanner the head of an Office of Religious Instruction, which worked in tandem with the Catholic school department. Stritch instructed Tanner to expand the work of the league, draw in more children, provide free teacher training for catechists, and to further coordinate the catechetical work going on in parishes, CIL centers, high school discussion groups and vacation schools.[549] As he had with Catholic schools, Stritch emphasized the training of lay catechists and provided opportunities for the enhancement of doctrinal knowledge and pedagogical skills.[550]

In 1937, Stritch also began Milwaukee's participation in the program of the Confraternity of Christian Doctrine (CCD). This would eventually supplant the CIL and be mandated for every parish. Begun by Father Edwin Vincent O'Hara, a noted apostle of rural Catholic education and future bishop of Kansas City, the CCD was also a direct response of the call of *Acerbo Nimis* to further the influence of Christian instruction. O'Hara resurrected an old confraternity ideal from the Counter Reformation era and adapted its organizational lines to American realities. O'Hara secured critical support from Roman authorities and the National Catholic Welfare Conference for this ambitious, well-organized effort to provide religious instruction to rural and public school pupils around the country.

The CCD was a parish-based catechetical program that drew heavily on the volun-

Archbishop Albert Meyer (l) with Rev. Paul Tanner [AAM]

teer efforts of laity to provide religious instruction for those who did not attend parochial grade or high schools. The confraternity organization divided a diocese up into districts and was overseen by a clerical representative appointed by the bishop. Religious education materials were produced, some of them written by O'Hara himself. Diocese after diocese formally embraced the program and the CCD became a synonym for after school or Saturday morning religious education for "publics."

Other programs launched by O'Hara included adult discussion groups based on biblical texts and religious programs designed to maintain the allegiance of those who did not enter fully into the Catholic subculture by attending Catholic schools. Archbishop Stritch gradually introduced the CCD to the Milwaukee Archdiocese. His successor Moses E. Kiley moved more aggressively to make sure all parishes had a branch. Kiley appointed St. Mary's pastor, Monsignor Philip Schwab, to spearhead the efforts. CCD would become highly effective, bringing the rudiments of Catholic life to youth, transforming the lives and faith development of the catechists who participated in the programs, and ultimately reaching more youths with the Catholic message than the Catholic schools.

Devotionalism and Popular Religion in Archdiocesan Life

The organization of lay Catholic life in this period built on the accomplishments of the old associations. The parish was the site for the celebration of the most important life passages: birth, adolescence, marriage, and death. The parish church also defined neighborhood and ethnic identity. People defined themselves by their parish membership, identifying a church's distinctive art, architecture, sights, sounds, and smells, as well as their various clergy and religious as a significant part of their religious world.

However, as important as the Mass and sacraments were to Catholics, there was another realm of religious experience that did not require the clergy or the official sanction of the church. We refer here to what historians of religion call "popular religion," loosely defined as the non-official prayers, suffrages, and devotional exercises of believers, linked to but not totally dependent on official church sanction. The faith of the man or woman in the pew also reflected another dimension to the Catholic experience in the archdiocese of Milwaukee.

In German immigrant parishes, but also in those of Poles and other groups, devotional societies provided symbols and occasions to express deeply held beliefs. Virtually every parish had some sort of association like this, although they varied with the ethnicity, size and resources of the parish. Large German parishes generally hosted a number of these associations, separated by age and gender.

Catholic authorities also lent a kind of sacral presence to the blending of cultural life with American identity. The Poles for example worked hard to create public monuments for their great Revolutionary War heroes Tadeusz Kosciusko and Kazimierz Pulaski—and when statues of both were dedi-

Home altar dedicated to St. Anthony's [ICCA]

cated in public parks, Polish clergy presided. The large statue of Kosciusko in Kosciusko Park on Lincoln Avenue was presented to the city by Father Hyacinth Gulski as a gift of the Polish people to the city of Milwaukee. The dedication of other statues of prominent people had both a religious and civic quality and they often found Milwaukee clerics or even the archbishop in attendance.

Devotional life among ethnic Catholics was still very intense. German Catholics continued to demonstrate their public faith through parades, replete with bands, elaborately decorated banners depicting the name of a devotional society, and outdoor liturgical services such as Corpus Christi celebrations.

Public expressions of devotional fervor were particularly strong among Milwaukee's Italians at Pompeii parish. They established a public festival in honor of Madonna del Lume, Our Lady of the Light, a particular form of Marian devotion embraced by a large number of Sicilian Milwaukeeans. Every year in September a parish society would begin making plans for the festival which began with a week-long novena, a solemn high Mass with a florid panegyric, and a street procession with the statue of the Madonna. To the statue were attached the *vota* or prayer requests of the devotees of the parish, usually given with some token cash donation. This practice of *clientelismo*—a powerful feature of Latin spirituality—generally elicited the horror of northern and western Europeans, who saw it as a form of bribery of the Blessed Virgin.[551] The event was climaxed by a day of feasting and dancing. As the years went on the celebration became more elaborate. Similar celebrations took place in Kenosha on the feast of Our Lady of Mount Carmel (July 16) and in Racine on the Feast of Our Lady of the Assumption (August 15).

One interesting adaptation of Catholic ritual with African American cultural religious practice was the so-called "storm novena." This

[AAM]

popular form of Catholic petitionary prayer called for a period of nine days of prayer for some particular intention (storm novenas were made for Ernest Miller and for various financial and personnel crises commended to the children by Father Philip Steffes and the Dominican sisters). The children would come into the church and "storm" heaven with their prayers nine times each day with arms outstretched to heaven—a rather unusual prayer posture for American Catholics until the advent of the Charismatic Movement in the 1960s. Storm novenas were an important part of the cultural life of St. Benedict the Moor Mission. They also helped raise funds as promises of children's prayers often induced people to give to the mission.

Polish Catholics too marched in parades for significant religious or national events. On the occasion of the cornerstone laying for St. Casimir Church in Kenosha in November 1902, a thousand Poles marched from St. George Church to the new site. They included the Knights of St. Theodore from St. Josaphat's Church in Milwaukee, the Knights of King David of Milwaukee, the Polish Holy Name Society, and the St. Martin's Society of Milwaukee. Five hundred men from the Kenosha Catholic societies joined in the lengthy parade. As the cornerstone was set in position, the *Kenosha Evening News* reported "a chorus of a thousand people joined in the singing of a hymn."[552]

The archdiocese of Milwaukee's most important devotional site was a high point in southwestern Washington County called Holy Hill.[553] Part of a chain of hills extending from Door County to the city of Madison, it was originally known as "Lapham's Peak" in honor of Increase Lapham a Wisconsin geologist who explored the ridges. Known also as "Miracle Hill" and "Hermit's Hill" (because of reports that a solitary lived on it), apparently the property had first been acquired in 1855 from the U. S. government by the Catholic Church by Father F. X. Paulhuber, the builder of St. Francis Seminary. However, the deed was never registered and Paulhuber departed Wisconsin never to return. The site was sold again to a land speculator named Martin Cutler in 1856.

Distant view of Holy Hill [Courtesy of Kevin Wester]

The locals seemed unaware that the land had changed hands. In 1857, parishioners of St. Boniface under their pastor J. B. Haselbauer erected a large white oak cross, 5-feet by 7-inches in thickness and 15-feet high. On it Roman Goetz, the maker of the cross, inscribed the words: " Ich bin die Auferstehung und die Leben" (I am the Resurrection and the Life). In the summer of 1862, Father George Strïckner began to erect a small log chapel which he blessed and dedicated on May 24, 1863, the Feast of Mary Help of Christians. In 1868, the trustees of this "St. Mary's Chapel" repurchased the land from Cutler, and in 1876 the land was conveyed to Archbishop Henni by Father Ferdinand Raess of St. Hubert's parish in Hubertus, the church closest to the hill.

Raess also secured a white statue of Mary Help of Christians that had been crafted by the Pustet religious goods studios in New York and featured at the 1876 Centennial Exposition in Philadelphia. In 1878 Raess had it solemnly carried to the chapel in a procession led by 18 young women robed in white, a handful of priests, men on horseback and delegates from every part of the state. The statue was borne seven miles. Along the pathway to the hill, Raess designed Stations of the Cross to be prayed as pilgrims ascended the hill. The numbers of pilgrims increased and in 1879 Raess built a larger chapel on the top of the hill to accommodate worshipers. Raess, like so many well-intentioned priests, spent more on the church and its decorations than he could afford. When his fund-raising efforts fell flat, the debt on the church was assumed by the clergy of Milwaukee by a system of assessments. Subsequent pastors of surrounding parishes made additions to the hill: new stations, altars, a 1,200 pound bell and bell tower. In 1897, a version of the popular Lourdes Grotto was built on the property, and a pipe organ was installed in the church.

These activities set off a minor flurry of pilgrimage—especially in the fall when the spectacular views of changing foliage were an added benefit. The shrine-like quality to the site, seemed tailormade for a religious order's particular devotions and reputation for pilgrimage ministrations. In the 1850s, Henni had tried to interest the Capuchins in the site, but they chose Mount Calvary in Fond du Lac County. In 1876, after he had received title to the hill, Henni invited the German Franciscans from St. Louis to take over the site, but they also demurred. It remained as a diocesan mission for years to come under the direction of pastors at St. Kilian's in Hartford. Mass and devotions were celebrated on Marian feasts and pilgrims continued to come.

In September 1905, Kilian Gutman and Eliseus Mackina, two Discalced Carmelites from Regensburg, Bavaria, came to the United States to establish a house of the order. Like most German religious communities, they considered the *Deutsche-Athen* in Wisconsin a congenial place to relocate. They came to St. Francis where the Franciscan Sisters gave them hospitality. Monsignor Joseph Rainer of the seminary informed them of "Holy Hill," and the two Carmelites traveled to the site in company with Mother Thecla Thren

Proposed Shrine at Holy Hill [Courtesy of Kevin Wester]

and two other sisters. Impressed with what they saw, the Carmelites agreed to take over the property in early July, 1906.[554] The Carmelites soon began to transform the site.[555] The last diocesan pastor, Father J. A. Bertram had purchased nearby farms around the hill, and in 1906, these were deeded over to the Carmelites for $15,000; the rest of the land was given for $1.00. With the help of a contingent of Carmelite brothers and others, the priests built a monastery and a series of church expansions to handle the growing flow of crowds to the hill. In the 1920s, the Carmelites made the hill the center of their religious life and established a novitiate and "college" for the training of new members.

By 1925, the old brick church built by Raess was no longer adequate, so the Carmelites contracted architect Herman Gaul of Chicago to design a grand church that would crown the hill and be seen from all sides. In order to sink a steady foundation for the new church, the hill had to be leveled off 20 feet. In 1926, Messmer laid the cornerstone, and the next year the main body of the church was standing. By 1931, the $250,000 Romanesque church crowned the hill—its steeples spiking 150 feet above the top of the site. The statue purchased by Raess in 1878 was enthroned over the high altar of the upper church, and Archbishop Stritch presided at the dedication. In 1937, the Carmelites began to build their new monastery and again contacted the architect Gaul.

Carmelites at Holy Hill [Courtesy of Kevin Wester]

In the history of the archdiocese of Milwaukee there have been occasions when miraculous events were alleged to have taken place. For example, the School Sisters of Notre Dame attributed the cure of one of their mortally ill members to a blessing given by Archbishop Henni with an image of the Blessed Virgin.[556] In 1926 Pallottine Father Peter Schroeder began a devotion to St. Anthony of Padua. By 1933 over 15,000 people had visited the shrine on Stevenson Avenue and Schroeder's files bulged with 1,000 letters recording favors received by devotees.[557] When Schroeder began holding "healing services" with a relic of St. Anthony and apparently "healed" a young man with the relic, the popularity of the devotion soared.[558] But no place acquired the reputation of being a place of healing like Holy Hill—the Lourdes of Wisconsin.

The thaumaturgic qualities of the hill were already rumored when in 1858 a peddler named Anton Meister received a miraculous healing of his paralyzed arm after climbing up the hill and saying some prayers. After he finished praying he inadvertently used the paralyzed arm to leave a coin and to his delight discovered that he could use it. He quit his peddling job and returned to regular labor in Chicago. Meister's cure inspired a local resident, Louis Marmes, to climb the hill to cure his rheumatism. It took him four hours to accomplish the task, with the help of canes and friends. He made several trips up the hill, feeling better each time, and eventually leaving behind his crutches at the miracle site. In 1886 young Clara Kroeger, daughter of Herman Kroeger, proprietor of a large department store on National and First in Milwaukee, came to the hill also seeking a cure from a degenerative disease of the eyes. She and her father made the Stations of the

St. Anthony of Padua Shrine in Holy Cross Church, Milwaukee [ASAC]

Cross and upon reaching the hilltop chapel, she claimed to be cured. Later, she entered the convent. A year later, Ida Klingl, a resident of Burlington afflicted by an eye disease was healed after nine days of prayer to Mary.[559] In 1893 Fond du Lac resident, Mrs. T. Cale, made the pilgrimage to Holy Hill to seek a cure for a chronic foot ailment. In excruciating pain, she climbed to the shrine and begged help. "I returned to my boarding house," she wrote the *Catholic Citizen*, "and removing the bandages found the foot perfectly healed."[560] Holy Hill's reputation as a place of healing continues to this day as visitors walk past a pile of crutches and canes left behind by those who believed themselves to have been cured by the miraculous intervention of the Blessed Virgin Mary.

Italians San Rocco Festival, Milwaukee [ICCA]

Clerical opposition to Holy Hill and the "excesses" of popular religion are a part of the historical record. The popular belief that apparitions were taking place there set off a mini-debate among the clergy. One of the pastors of nearby Fond du Lac, Father Joseph Keenan of St. Joseph parish (one of the co-conspirators in the "plot" to stop the Heiss nomination in 1878), publicly dismissed the allegations of apparitions and miracles on the hill. He scoffed that they were a money-making fraud perpetrated on suffering people. "The theory that the place is a holy shrine and that the afflicted who come there and pray can be cured of their troubles is pernicious," he snorted. "The imperfections of human nature are easily turned into … revenue by the mercantile spirit."[561]

The popular devotions of the Italians also came in for their share of criticism. Messmer complained to apostolic delegates that the annual Milwaukee *festa* had become "a public scandal," and accused the organizers of pocketing most of the money affixed to the processional statue. He further stated, "I am dealing with Sicilians, whose ignorance in religion is terrible and who stick to their native customs."[562] His successor, Stritch, although more kindly disposed, also stereotyped southern Italians, lamenting once to the apostolic delegate, "The Calabrians do everything by conspiracies."[563] Disgruntled Milwaukeeans complained about the noise and revelry under religious auspices. Referring to celebrations in honor of St. Rocco in the summer of 1935, one correspondent wrote to Archbishop Stritch that the noise of music and fireworks "was almost unbearable," and that the final night's celebration "resembled a battle front and made night hideous for everyone."[564]

But efforts to stop the public outpouring were not susceptible to clerical displeasure. Holy Hill continued to thrive despite Keenan's snide comments. And Messmer learned the limits of his episcopal authority in dealing with the Italians. "Last year I forbade the parish priest to go with this so-called procession and take the statues out of the church," he explained to Apostolic Delegate Fumasoni-Biondi. "Well, they simply engaged a strange priest and borrowed statues from a statuary firm and held their procession."[565]

The Heyday of Catholic Action

Although devotionalism and popular religion were not restricted to ethnic Catholics, a good bit of it emanated from religious customs and practices transferred from Europe. However, as the fires of ethnic self-consciousness began to flicker (although not die out) the nature of the ethnic organizations promoting these practices began to change as well. Many Catholics were undergoing that elusive process called Americanization, and the need to forge bonds with compatriots of the same language and cultural group began to weaken.

Catholic devotionalism continued to flourish. Marian devotions were still an important part of the weekly routines of "American" parishes, along with elaborate Eucharistic devotions, such as Benediction of the Blessed Sacrament, Forty Hours Devotion, and Corpus Christi processions. Novena Catholicism, which we shall cover later, was still strong. At Marquette's Gesu Church devotees gathered faithfully to pray and petition St. Anne, the mother of Mary. In virtually every church of the archdiocese, banks of votive candles burned before images of the Sacred Heart, the Virgin Mary, St. Joseph, and St. Jude. When the young French Carmelite, Therese of Lisieux, was canonized in the 1920s, parishes swamped religious goods suppliers with requests for plaster statues of the saint. Catholic school children absorbed the language of devotionalism which became part of a special vocabulary of faith that added a distinctive quality to their Catholic life, even as ethnicity faded.

New forms of Catholic lay organization and activism emerged during this period. The code name for this new emphasis on organized lay collective activity was "Catholic Action," a term coined by Pope Pius X to refer to an organized Catholic effort to "renew all things in Christ" (his papal motto). Pius X's vision of a reconstituted social order was not unique to him, but as the ideas of a newly self-confident Catholic identity began to take hold among American Catholics, it had a great deal of appeal.

The new non-ethnic approach to Catholic identity came from the clear and distinct ideas of Thomism. Pope Leo XIII had called for a revival of the teachings and ideas of St. Thomas Aquinas in his encyclical *Aeterni Patris* (1878). Aimed at doing "intellectual combat with modernity" the Neo-Thomistic revival resurrected the epistemological optimism of the medieval theologian, and in its popularized versions, resonated well with the common sense ideology and pragmatism of American Catholics.[566] Presented to American Catholics through sermons, college and high school catechetical instruction, pamphlets, and popular speakers, Neo-Thomism brought about a renewed and highly practical sense of order and structure that had practical implications in the creation of a new wave of unified societies that transcended the traditional boundaries of the parishes and ethnicity to form a "Catholic phalanx," as Messmer had described it, to qualitatively affect the social order. Catholic Action became the general rubric under which people could associate with this larger movement.

Farewell event for Archbishop Samuel Stritch at the Milwaukee Arena [AAM]

As the concept of Catholic Action matured, Pope Pius XI, "the Pope of Catholic Action," gave it a more specific definition. Pius declared that Catholic Action was, "the participation of the laity in the apostolate of the hierarchy." By rooting authentic Catholic activity in the validation of the bishop and the clergy, Pope Pius subordinated independent lay initiative to the guidance and direction of the official church. Catholic Action in the archdiocese of Milwaukee took a variety of forms over the years and was highly popular in Milwaukee, drawing together large elements of the archdiocese that might have continued to remain in ethnic enclaves or never ventured out from the protective shadow of the local parish. It was a perfect vehicle for an increasingly more Americanized Catholic population.

Catholic Action in the Private Sector: The Case of the Bruce Family

Since the goal of Catholic Action was to form enthusiastic "lay apostles" to serve the Church in the world, the logical place to look would be the endeavors of private Catholic individuals. In Milwaukee, lay Catholic activity was a constant. From Henni's friend James Johnson through newspaper editor Humphrey Desmond, lay Catholics played an important role in shaping local Catholic culture. Many people could vie for the title of "most" prominent Catholic lay person in archdiocesan history, but virtually all would point to the Bruce family as exemplars of deep faith and action in the Milwaukee archdiocese and throughout the nation. The family became involved in a number of endeavors of enduring value to Catholic life, most especially through their ownership of a local press that became the largest Catholic book publisher in the United States for a time.[567]

William George Bruce (1857-1949) was born in Milwaukee, the son of a German-Catholic mother and Protestant father.[568] In his childhood he was stricken with a hip ailment that disabled him for his entire life. Self-taught in reading and writing, he began work with the *Milwaukee News* and later moved to the *Milwaukee Sentinel*, where he served as assistant business manager. While working for the morning *Sentinel* he took a special interest in school issues and eventually became a member of the city's school commission. Denied a promotion at the newspaper, in 1891 he quit his job and with $600 in savings formed the Bruce Publishing Company. He began his long career in publishing by producing a magazine, *The American School Board Journal*. After a period of struggle, the *Journal* flourished and Bruce expanded into

William George Bruce speaking at the cornerstone laying of St. Camillus Hospital (August 1931) [AAM]

other specialized trade journals. *Industrial Arts and Vocational Education* followed in 1914. In 1920, he provided the Catholic Hospital Association (headquartered in Milwaukee) with its publication, *Hospital Progress*.[569] In 1929, Bruce Publishing purchased and produced *The Catholic School Journal*.

Rev. Peter Leo Johnson and John LaVies in photo taken by William George Bruce [AAM]

Although the Bruce press would later become synonymous with Catholic book publishing, its first books were associated with trade journals. In 1913, the first Bruce book was *High School Buildings* and inaugurated a series of volumes on industrial arts, which were then just becoming part of the curricula of public schools. Not until 1920 did a Catholic book roll off the Bruce presses when as a personal favor to the author, Father Edward F. Garesche's *Vade Mecum* for Catholic nurses was published.

Bruce's two sons, William C. and Frank, joined their father in 1902 and 1906 respectively and gradually assumed more of the day-to-day responsibilities of the press. This freed William George, now nearly 50, for a second career in politics and other public tasks. In 1904, he became secretary to the Milwaukee Association of Commerce, a position he held until 1925. His interest in boosting Milwaukee led him also to become a member of the Milwaukee Harbor Commission, where he served as president of that body in 1913. For 39 years he took a leading role in the development of Milwaukee's port facilities and worked tirelessly for the opening of the St. Lawrence Seaway. Bruce also supported the construction of a respectable civic center to attract conventions and public meetings. The construction of the Milwaukee Auditorium, a popular site for Catholic rallies, conventions and gatherings was the result of this effort.

Bruce, a Democrat and a supporter of Mayor David Rose, received a patronage position as tax commissioner in 1902. He supported the various candidacies of William

Jennings Bryan and took some small part in efforts at banking reform that culminated in the creation of the Federal Reserve in 1913. After the death of the legendary Robert LaFollette, local Democratic politicians prevailed on Bruce to run for the United States Senate. In the midst of all this booster and political activity, he was a prolific author, penning a popular history of Milwaukee, his autobiography and two substantial parish histories.[570]

Bruce was a "cradle-Catholic" and a member of two of Milwaukee's old German parishes, old St. Mary's and Holy Trinity. In his childhood he remembered seeing John Martin Henni puttering in his yard. But by his own admission, his links with Catholicism were formal and perfunctory through much of his youth. "Then came a period," he wrote in 1937, "when I was thrown into contact with hundreds of priests and the higher church authorities in the Archdiocese of Milwaukee." When he wrote these words, the level and intensity of his contacts with the Milwaukee church were at their peak.[571]

Bruce grew especially close to Archbishop Messmer, to whose table at the Pabst mansion he was occasionally summoned to provide advice and bilingual conversation. Bruce listened carefully and respectfully as Messmer discussed theology or church affairs, but he did not hesitate to give his opinion on matters that were within his sphere of expertise. "In our discussions," he recalled, "I would frequently carry his mind into the realms of commerce and trade of community life."[572]

Bruce's innocence of matters theological did not prevent him from taking a higher profile in church affairs, beginning in 1920 when Messmer called on him to rescue the faltering $5 Million Appeal that professional fund-raisers had botched. Bruce stabilized the collection (the actual amount collected was never revealed, but it was considerably short of the overly-ambitious $5 million). In 1923, Bruce's skills for administration were brought to the organization of the Union of Holy Name Societies. Under Bruce, the organization flourished as one of the main associations of Catholic men in the archdiocese and at one point claimed 50,000 active, dues-paying members. As Bruce's contacts with clergy developed, the Bruce home on the south side of Milwaukee and a summer cottage on a nearby lake became a regular watering hole for bishops, priests and religious of all types. Bruce photographed his clerical guests and later sent the pictures with thoughtful notes.[573]

With his increasingly closer ties to Catholic endeavors and leaders he was acknowledged as Milwaukee's most prominent Catholic layman. (Messmer secured for him the prestigious papal honor, Knight of St. Gregory, and Bruce always appended "K.S.G." after his name). He moved easily between the Catholic enclave of Milwaukee and the world of commerce. William George Bruce captured every honor that a lay Catholic could, including the prestigious *Laetare* award given him by the University of Notre Dame one year before his death. When he died in August 1949, he had a massive civic funeral at which Archbishop Kiley preached. Bruce had known all five of Kiley's predecessors.

Bruce's sons reflected another form of Catholic lay activism. Initially, he brought the two boys, William C. and Frank, into the press and helped them apprentice at the many aspects of running such a complex operation. When the elder Bruce "retired" in 1927 the two boys transformed the press into a major Catholic book publishing operation. Later William George Bruce recalled, "I merely built the foundations. My sons built the superstructure."[574] William C. took over as president and editor, while Frank took the posts of publisher and treasurer.

Rev. Peter Leo Johnson and William George Bruce [AAM]

Both boys had been educated by the Jesuits at Marquette High School and University. Frank Bruce recalled vividly how Jesuit scholastic F. X. McMenamy had impressed on him in a humanities class "how we Catholics were making so small a contribution in the arts and sciences, in professions and public life." McMenamy awakened young Bruce to "a culture distinctly Catholic … that *sentire cum ecclesia* [to feel or think with the church] refers to more than dogma … that our culture … is applicable to today's problems … our faith can be taught by today's methods, and that today's problems can be solved by our formulas."[575]

The Bruce brothers purchased the *Catholic School Journal* from Humphrey Desmond's sons Thomas and Joseph. Working closely with Marquette educator Edward A. Fitzpatrick, the brothers changed the magazine's format. It also began to reflect Fitzpatrick's relentless efforts to bring a greater professionalism and excellence to Catholic education. The brothers shared Fitzpatrick's strong views for providing "a theological foundation of education, the need to bring to bear on the educational problems the outlooks of theology in addition to the outlooks of philosophy and of the sciences." A series of articles that Fitzpatrick penned on this theme for the pages of the *Catholic School Journal* were eventually collated into a book, *Exploring a Theology of Education*.[576]

From the school journal the Bruce brothers moved far beyond the eclectic line of Catholic prayer books and small monographs their father had run through the press. Frank Bruce developed a line of Catholic books that was launched in the winter of 1931 with the inauguration of the *Science and Culture* series, edited by Jesuit Joseph Caspar Husslein.[577] Husslein was a Milwaukee native, born in 1873. He graduated from Marquette College in 1891 and entered the Society of Jesus. After his ordination in 1905 he was assigned briefly to John Carroll University in Cleveland and then went to Fordham University, where he received a doctorate in 1919. In 1909 he had begun writing articles for the newly founded Jesuit weekly *America* and in 1911 joined the staff, where he remained until 1927 when he was appointed to teach sociology at St. Louis University. In 1930, his reputation as a Catholic social thinker as well as his belief that Catholic answers could be provided for contemporary issues, made him a natural to help shape the new series being planned by the Bruce Company.

Advertised as "literally a university in print," the *Science and Culture* series enlisted a number of Catholic authors who wrote in the fields of biography, history, literature, education, the natural sciences, art and architecture. In the 150 books of this series, the gallery of stars included major figures in the Catholic Literary Revival of the 1920s and 1930s, such as Hilaire Belloc. "Like the Oxford Movement of another day," wrote one enthusiast about the new line of books, "it represented a return to the fundamentals, an attempt to show the applicability of Christian principles to world problems."[578]

The steady volume of manuscripts coming into the press—and their healthy sales to an increasingly more literate Catholic population—generated another series, *Religion and Culture*. Among its classic titles were Gerard Ellard's classic of the liturgical movement, *Christian Life and Worship* (1933), William Lamm's *The Spiritual Legacy of Newman* (1934) and the tremendously popular *The Man Who Got Even with God* (by Trappist Father M. Raymond Flanagan, a rival to fellow monk Thomas Merton for the "Trappist-conversion" genre). The press also published at least one of Merton's titles *What Are These Wounds* (1950). Local Milwaukee authors like Father James Graham (*Faith for Life*) and a Capuchin favorite, Celestine Bittle (*Science of Correct Thinking*), were part of their program. The Bruce Company became a popular outlet for Catholic historians such as Theodore Maynard, Colman Barry, and John Tracy Ellis, who published his massive two-volume biography of Cardinal Gibbons under this imprint. The canon law tomes of T. Lincoln Bouscaren were published by Bruce, as was John L. McKenzie's classic, *The Two Edged Sword*. In 1943, the Bruces founded a Catholic book club called the Catholic Literary Foundation and adapted the effective marketing strategy pioneered by the Book-of-the-Month Club in the 1930s.

Bruce also dominated the Catholic schoolbook market. In the 1930s Bruce issued the *Highway to Heaven* religion series, hammered out by the School of Education and the

Catechetical Institute of Marquette University to assist people preparing to teach classes in the growing Confraternity of Christian Doctrine programs. Marketed as an alternative to the rote method of the popular Baltimore Catechism, it won a smaller audience than the popular question and answer text, but it offered the first glimmer of what would be an alternative approach to religious education pedagogy.[579] In 1954, the press issued two juvenile series for children ages 3 to 9 and the popular *Catholic Treasury Books,* which illustrated Catholic teaching on faith and morals through the use of heartwarming anecdotes.

The Bruce brothers were also actively engaged in other areas of Catholic life that made Milwaukee a national center for some important movements. Frank Bruce was a leading figure in the work of the St. Vincent de Paul Society and took a major role in establishing the Catholic Rural Life Movement as well as local and international chapters of the vocation group, Serra International. William C., the more reclusive of the two, was also active in the vocations-promotion organization, Serra International, and the National Association of Publishers and Church Goods Dealers. The Bruce family was especially generous to the local church, maintaining a particular affection for Holy Trinity parish which had been the seedbed of the elder Bruce's faith. They ran their company like a small religious community. Every year the Bruce men went on a corporate retreat locally. Seminarians could find employ with the firm during the summer months. Women working with the company were expected to leave once they married.

By 1950, the Bruce press was the largest Catholic book publishing firm in the United States, and the demand for its titles grew dramatically. Anticipating growth, it purchased the nine-story E. R. Godfrey and Sons building at 400 N. Broadway and undertook a renovation to centralize editorial, production, and marketing operations under one roof.[580] In 1950 the new structure opened and the Bruce titles, both trade and monographs of various sorts, rolled off the presses in even greater numbers. The press reached its peak in the 1950s and then declined as the market for Catholic books and materials changed in the wake of Vatican II. In 1968, the firm was sold to Macmillan and Collier. Bruce Pub-

THE LIFE OF
James Cardinal Gibbons
Archbishop of Baltimore
1834-1921

By
JOHN TRACY ELLIS
PROFESSOR OF AMERICAN CHURCH HISTORY
IN THE
CATHOLIC UNIVERSITY OF AMERICA

VOLUME II

THE BRUCE PUBLISHING COMPANY
MILWAUKEE

[AAM]

lishing Company was for a time the largest Catholic book publishing firm in the world and put Milwaukee on the map as a center of Catholic literary and cultural activity. The local chancery provided priest censors like seminary theologian Father John Schulien who read and evaluated manuscripts for doctrinal correctness. They also carried the *imprimatur* [*sic*: let it be published] of the local ordinary. The Bruce family represented the creative impulse of Catholic Action as the energy of this lay-oriented movement (albeit with clerical direction) pulsed through the veins of the local Church.

The Archdiocesan Council of Catholic Women

Two prominent lay Catholic organizations that emerged in this new atmosphere were actually stimulated by the formation of the National Catholic Welfare Conference: the Archdiocesan Conferences of Catholic Men and Catholic Women. The remote origins of this organized lay initiative came from the organization of the National Catholic Welfare Conference (NCWC) and the initiative of Bishop Joseph Schrembs of Cleveland to organize councils of men and women. In March 1920, Messmer sent three prominent Milwaukee Catholic women from the Marquette Women's League—Mrs. James Hackett, Mrs. James Mehan, and Mrs. Minnie Springob—to represent Milwaukee at the organizational conference in Washington. There they heard plans to coordinate efforts of Catholic women around the country. On December 8, 1920, Hackett called a meeting of the women and heads of all women's organizations of the archdiocese, to be held in the cathedral auditorium. This was the birth of the Milwaukee Archdiocesan Council of Catholic Women (MACCW).

After an invocation by Father R. J. Roche of Holy Rosary and the singing of "America" and "On This Day O Beautiful Mother," the more than 200 women present elected Hackett president and chose a slate of officers. Following an address prepared by Paulist Father John J. Burke, general secretary of the NCWC, the women walked *en bloc* to the nearby Pfister Hotel where they heard presentations about the $5 Million Campaign planned by the bishops of Wisconsin "so that they might carry the message back to their homes and interest themselves to create interest and enthusiasm among the Catholic people in their respective localities." After lunch, the women went back to St. John's where Paulist Father E. J. Mallaly of Chicago addressed them further about the nature of the new organization. It was the Catholic moment, Mallaly argued, "for more than fifty years Protestant womanhood has been in the ascendant, being a strong, thoughtful, well-organized body, making its influences felt throughout the country." He warned that without a strong presence of Catholic women social evils would engulf America, "Race suicide, divorce, birth control, and like matters which affect not only the physical but spiritual welfare of our American life .... Therefore our Catholic women must organize for the honor of God and country, and help to stem the tide against these unChristian doctrines and practices."

Messmer then addressed the women, "saying that he was more than happily surprised at the response to the invitations, and that he considered it a happy omen of success." [581]

Hackett and her officers helped the MACCW get off to a strong start. With the assistance of Father Joseph Barbian, who served as chaplain until his death in 1936, the organization swiftly identified areas of need. Messmer recruited members to assist in the provision of archdiocesan charities, and they worked closely with charities head, Father Matthew McEvoy, providing funds and supplies for orphanages and care facilities for the indigent. They also supported his efforts to create a Catholic child welfare program in the state and nation.

Katherine Williams kissing the ring of Archbishop Samuel Stritch [AAM]

In 1923 Katherine Williams was elected to replace Hackett. Williams was one of the first women to enter Marquette University's law school in 1908. Afflicted with an eye disease that seriously impaired her sight, Williams threw herself wholeheartedly into the work of the MACCW and pressed especially for a more active social role for the organization. Unmarried and totally devoted to the Church, Williams had even more time to pour into the programs of the MACCW. Using her contacts in Madison, Williams forwarded resolutions to state legislators and other government officials condemning the birth control movement. She took up the struggle to have delinquent girls assigned to Catholic institutions and helped bring the girl and boy scout movements, under Catholic auspices.

The women assisted the cause of historical preservation by having the old St. Peter's Cathedral moved from the site of Ss. Peter and Paul Church, Milwaukee, to the seminary grounds. There its care and upkeep became an archdiocesan concern until the 1970s, when it was removed to the "Old World Wisconsin" outdoor historical site.[582] To give working-class women a quiet, restful vacation the MACCW purchased the East Beach Hotel on Nagawicka Lake in Waukesha County. They changed the name to Tekakwitha Lodge "after our Indian saint," the "Lily of the Mohawks," and made it a vacation resort for Catholic girls and women. As we have already seen, the MACCW also took a major role in the organization of the Catholic Instruction League.[583]

Catholic Action for Men: The Holy Name Society

In Milwaukee, a male counterpart to the MACCW never really got off the ground. However, the Holy Name Society became the chief outlet of Catholic Action for men.

The Holy Name was originally a devotional confraternity founded in the Middle Ages. Pope Leo XIII had entrusted the Dominican Order with the rejuvenation of the association throughout the world. Two American Dominicans, Charles Hyacinth McKenna and John Timothy McNicholas, transplanted this organization to America. McKenna obtained a rescript in 1896 that allowed the chartering of parish groups, and with appropriate episcopal support the movement began to grow. When McNicholas took control of it in 1908, he pushed it beyond the parish base into a diocese-wide and even national organization. (McNicholas was eager to become a bishop himself and needed the public exposure and name recognition that these nationwide efforts provided.)

As the Holy Name developed in parishes all across the archdiocese, it became a popular outlet for associational and devotional activity. A typical Holy Name organization met monthly for a practice called "Corporate Communion" in which members attended an early Mass and all received communion together. Afterwards, they repaired to the parish hall for breakfast and usually a speaker. The organization generally made itself available to help in parish fund-raisers, fish fries and card games.

By 1920 Milwaukee parishes counted 19 branches of the popular society. To unify this work, Messmer tapped a local Jesuit, Father Archibald Talmadge, S.J., in 1920 and directed him to organize an archdiocesan Holy Name organization. At an organizational meeting held at St. Thomas Aquinas parish in October 1920 the archdiocesan Union of Holy Name Societies was organized with Francis A. Zimmerman as president.[584] After a few years Talmadge recruited William George Bruce to head the organization. Bruce threw himself wholeheartedly into Holy Name for 18 years and dramatically expanded its influence. Annually, the Holy Name men from around the diocese would meet in Milwaukee to celebrate the Feast of the Holy Name in January. Various fund-raising and devotional duties came under the organization's umbrella, helping to unify the archdiocese.

One of the popular things Bruce and Talmadge hosted was an annual production of a passion play (a dramatized rendition of the events

[AAM]

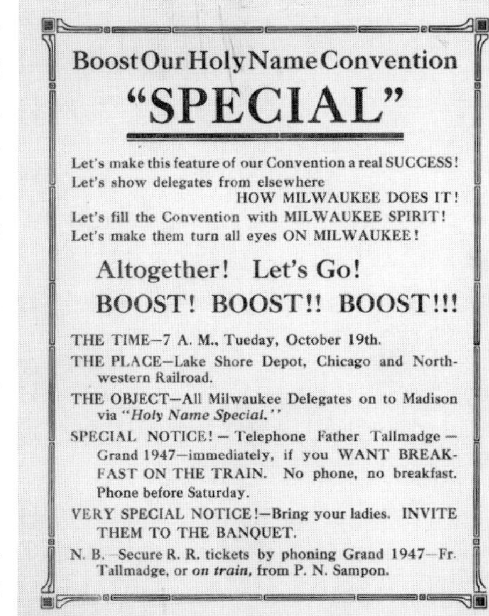

[Courtesy of Earl Reichert]

of Christ's Last Supper, betrayal, trial and crucifixion). Milwaukee Catholics already had a strong tradition of parish and school theatrics, and a passion play had been performed for a large audience in 1921. However, beginning in 1927, the Holy Name put on the play during the Sundays of Lent in some large hall or auditorium. Later, another version of the German script was translated by St. Joseph pastor, Father Joseph Berg. The play recruited actors from parishes around the community and occasionally highlighted a young priest in the coveted *Christus* role. Bruce—who had traveled to the Oberammergau Passion Play and who knew the famous Michael Lang who had played the *Christus* role—took a keen interest in the production.

Other public events sponsored by the Holy Name included mass prayer rallies at the Marquette Stadium and the Vollrath Bowl in Sheboygan and other locations around the archdiocese. In the 1940s and 1950s, the Holy Name was the main organizer of popular "Field Masses"—outdoor celebrations of the Eucharist to commemorate large events. For example when Wisconsin celebrated the centennial of its admission to territorial status in 1936, Catholics in the state hosted a huge field Mass to commemorate the event and to celebrate the Catholic presence in Wisconsin's history.

One of the most popular things the Holy Name did was to mount a highly popular lecture bureau under the leadership of attorney Oliver O'Boyle. Judge Richard Hennessy took over the leadership of the bureau until his death in 1937. Then for many years, St. Robert's parishioner Phil Grau stepped forward to coordinate the bureau. He also served as an important spokesman for the growing society. The lectures, delivered by members of the Holy Name, included discussions of state and local politics, reflections on the challenges of law or business, and exhortations to practice Catholic morality in business and professional affairs.[585]

Leo Dohn and family [AAM]

As the organization grew, the size of its full-time leadership did as well. Talmadge turned over leadership to Capuchin Camillus Becker and a new organizational phase began. Thanks to Bruce's steady recruiting the organization grew rapidly, and in 1929 Becker took on a full-time executive secretary, Leo Dohn, whose family had been longtime members of St. Elizabeth's parish. Dohn was a dynamo and further cultivated the activities of the Holy Name. Eventually a Junior Holy Name was created for youths. Athletic competition in particular became a specialty of the Junior Holy Name. Archdiocesan unity was further enhanced by the competition that pitted parish basketball and baseball teams against one another.

Another organization for youth that came together in the 1920s and 30s was the Sodality. This old Marian association dates back to Counter Reformation days in Rome. Dedicated to praying the rosary and cultivating a personal devotion to Mary, the organization had become inert by the early 20th century. Pope Pius X assigned to the Jesuits the task of renewing the Sodality around the world; in the United States, the task fell to one of the great clerical impresarios of all time, Father

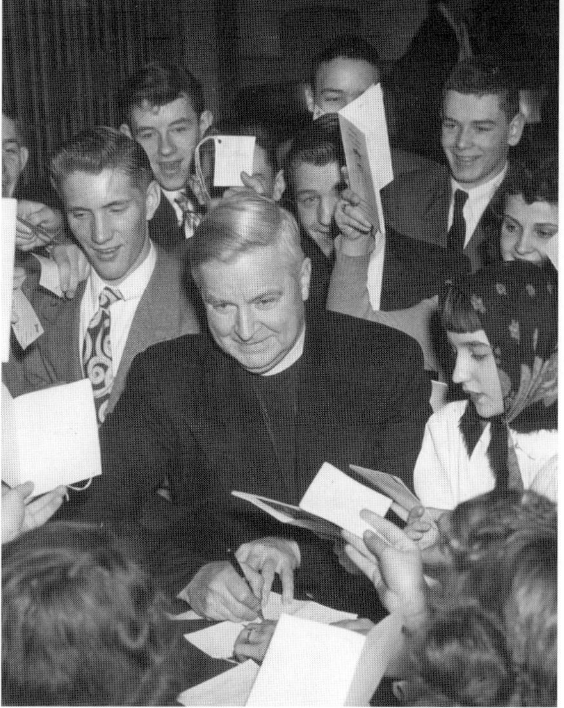

Rev. Daniel Lord, SJ [AAM]

Daniel A. Lord, S. J.[586] Lord had a touch with young people—he was bright, articulate, played the piano, and was blessed with an ability to translate the most complicated Catholic teachings into easily accessible prose. He began writing pamphlets, The *Queen's Work,* for the Jesuit press founded to promote the Sodality movement. The abundance of these gaily colored pamphlets on a variety of subjects, many of them penned by Lord, were often found in racks in the rear of Milwaukee churches. For 10 cents a reader could understand the mysteries of transubstantiation (the theological explanation of how Christ becomes truly present in the Eucharist). He or she could also be informed about how long a kiss between an unmarried man and woman would have to go before it became a mortal sin, and learn the reasons why the Church forbade cremation, membership in the Masons, and discouraged mixed marriages.

[AAM]

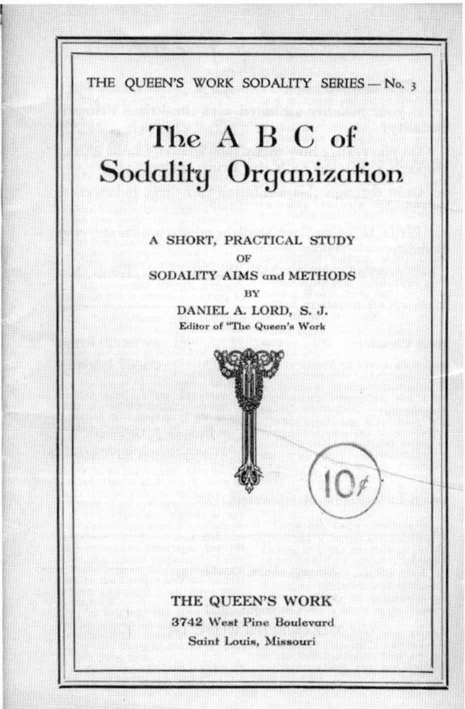
THE QUEEN'S WORK SODALITY SERIES — No. 3

The A B C of Sodality Organization

A SHORT, PRACTICAL STUDY
OF
SODALITY AIMS and METHODS
BY
DANIEL A. LORD, S. J.
Editor of "The Queen's Work

10¢

THE QUEEN'S WORK
3742 West Pine Boulevard
Saint Louis, Missouri

Lord traveled the country promoting the Sodality movement in dioceses and urging the federation of individual parish units into larger bodies. The Sodality Union of the Milwaukee Archdiocese, known popularly by its acronym SUMA, came into existence in 1930 as a result of Lord's efforts.[587] And his syndicated column even graced the *Catholic Herald Citizen.* In the 1940s, Messmer High School faculty member and later principal Father Louis Riedel was appointed the general chaplain of SUMA. Riedel, a Milwaukee native, had been ordained by Stritch in 1933 and served seven years as a curate at Holy Redeemer parish. In 1940 he joined the Messmer faculty and in 1949 was appointed principal. His years working with teens allowed him to develop a good rapport with the large student body.

Riedel enjoyed tremendous success as the SUMA organization won the support of thousands of Milwaukee Catholic youth down to the 1960s. Discussion clubs, devotional activities and well-attended mass demonstrations held at the Milwaukee Auditorium were a prominent part of their highly-publicized activities.[588] Riedel perpetuated the enthusiasm of the Catholic Action mass gatherings of the 1930s and helped to organize the Wisconsin Catholic Action Conferences. The first one was held in 1945 and drew thousands of young people to the Milwaukee Auditorium. Occasionally Lord himself visited Milwaukee to produce one of his extravaganza pageants. The youth loved the grandfatherly Jesuit who played the piano and cracked jokes. In 1947 over 2,500 Catholic teens gathered to hear a who's who of popular Catholic speakers at Milwaukee Auditorium. From Chicago came the charismatic Father Martin Carrabine, S.J., the organizer and mainspring of the Catholic Interstudent Catholic Action of Chicago. Olympic champion Ralph Metcalfe appeared together with Charles Madison, a teacher at St. Benedict the Moor High School, to lecture the conventioneers on interracial issues. Riedel even cajoled F.B.I. division head H. K. Johnson to discuss the work of the bureau. Local priests Joseph Holleran and Vernon Kuehn also spoke.[589] Riedel maintained control of SUMA even after he was appointed the rector of the minor seminary in 1954. But by the time the tall, basso-voiced rector began devoting his energies to building a new minor seminary next to the Salesianum in the 1960s, SUMA was running out of steam.

Samuel Stritch: Catholic Action's Apotheosis

Messmer had an imperfect notion of the finer points of Catholic Action although he had eagerly endorsed its thrust in his episcopate. Stritch, by contrast, had made a careful study of its theoretical aspects, as embodied in papal encyclicals and other utterances. He also had a close association with Archbishop John T. McNicholas of Cincinnati, whose earlier organizational work of the Holy Name Society provided a prototype for translating these principles into action. McNicholas was especially insistent on the need to establish clear lines of hierarchical authority over these movements. The National Catholic Welfare Conference (NCWC) soon created standards for the proper understanding of Catholic Action. Diocesan bishops were encouraged to establish departments of Catholic Action in their chanceries and monitor carefully the use of the term "Catholic Action" as applied to specific activities. As a member of the executive board of the NCWC, Stritch took an active hand in these discussions and implemented them in Milwaukee. "Catholic lay action is the work of the bishop," Stritch told 400 Knights of Columbus: "Catholic lay action presupposes a commission from the bishop of the diocese or from the chief ruler of the flock." [590]

In Milwaukee, Stritch tapped one of his brighter young priests, Father Paul A. Tanner, an assistant at Immaculate Conception Church in Bay View, to serve as secretary of Catholic Action.[591] Tanner had the task of coordinating the activities of the Holy Name, the Knights of Columbus, and various other intra-diocesan organizations, to make sure that they properly reflected the correct understanding of Catholic Action and submitted themselves to episcopal authority.

Rev. Paul Tanner [AAM]

Coordinated Catholic Action had its payoffs. One of its greatest success stories was in the area of youth work. In 1932, after Becker left the Holy Name Society, Stritch appointed Pio Nono principal Monsignor John J. Clark to head the organization and ordered him to survey the Catholic youth and recommend proposals to centralize and expand the outreach to youth. Clark's efforts led to the formation of the Catholic Youth Organization (CYO) in July 1934.[592] This popular parish-based athletic program was created out of the Junior Holy Name, the Senior Men's Sodality and the Senior Young Women's Sodality. In 1937, the many Young Women's Sodalities were brought under the CYO banner. The emergence of this popular sports culture dovetailed with the growth of sports activity, physical fitness and the popularity of spectator sports that grew throughout the 1920s and 1930s. High school athletic competition became an important part of the subculture associated with the emergence of Catholic high schools. Sports helped shape the health, well-being, and sense of belonging of Catholic youth. Attendance at games and athletic rivalry became an important part of the experience of growing up Catholic in the archdiocese of Milwaukee.

Rev. John J. Clark
[AOP-Sin]

A series of Social Action Conferences, based on the Catholic Action thrust, was held for priests and laity in Milwaukee in the 1930s. At the November 1936 meeting of the bishops, an ambitious plan for social education for priests was advanced by Bishop Edwin Vincent O'Hara of Great Falls, Montana. Following the study club method pioneered by other Catholic Action groups, a program of social instructions for priests was structured for month-long seminars to be held in different regions of the country: Milwaukee and Toledo, Los Angeles and San Francisco. The selection of Milwaukee was facilitated by Father Francis Haas, who had been in Washington when the plans were made and who assumed the lion's share of responsibilities for putting together the program. From July 5th to 30th 1937, 122 priests from around the country met at St. Francis Seminary for the summer school of Catholic Action. A variety of theoretical and practical sessions were held, including presentations by heavy hitters like Monsignor John A. Ryan, Bishop Edwin Vincent O'Hara, San Antonio Bishop Robert E. Lucey, and Father Wilfred Parsons, S.J., of Georgetown. The faculty also included local giants like Haas, Father Peter Dietz, Father Joseph Holleran, who was organizing the liturgical movement in the archdiocese, and university campus chaplain Father Alvin Kutchera. Prominent lay Catholics included Judge John J. Kleczka who spoke on minimum wage conditions, Voyta Wrabetz of the state Labor Board, and James Carey of the Congress of Industrial Organizations. This first meeting was judged by all to have been a great success. Subsequent gatherings of priests took place at other locations in the country, generally on seminary campuses, until wartime travel restrictions ended them.

In May 1938, Stritch hosted the first annual National Catholic Social Action Conference, which included lay persons. This three-day meeting was attended by nearly 5,000 delegates from all over the country. But nearly 12,000 attended a pontifical Mass in the Milwaukee Auditorium, and Father Paul Tanner estimated that nearly 40,000 had attended at one point or another. The structure included mass meetings, sectional meetings on subjects such as finance and credit, youth in industry, and reports on labor organizing in the automotive and meat packing industries. Group discussions on the topics followed the sessions. Here too, Father Paul Tanner coordinated the general and particular sessions and worked together with the Holy Name, the CYO and other groups to help accommodate the attendees. Tanner summarized the gathering by noting, "It has been called the most significant Catholic gathering ever held in this country." He hoped that the impact of these days would "diffuse more widely a knowledge of the Christian Social Order." "Action," he predicted, "would undoubtedly follow."[593] Yet another area where the organizing impulse of Catholic Action was felt in Milwaukee was for the rural areas of the archdiocese.

1942 CYO All-Tournament basketball team [AAM]

The Rural Church in the 20th Century

The Great Depression hit rural America especially hard. The general American farm economy had been distressed even during the prosperous 1920s. As farm prices fell through the floor after the collapse of the economy, conditions got even worse. Michael Petrie notes in his study of Catholicism in the North Kettle Moraine, "When the stock market crashed in 1929, a formerly prosperous rural population scrounged dumps for canning jars, pinched pennies to eke out an existence, and dumped milk into pastures." Glenbeulah's St. Fridolin parish sent in only $64 on its parish assessment, informing Archbishop Stritch that "the pew rent arrears amount to over five hundred dollars." The church trustees informed the Milwaukee chancery, "We feel certain that those in arrears will not be able to pay up this year."[594] Farmers and dairymen received some relief with the development of the New Deal's Agricultural Adjustment Administration, which paid government support to regulate the unstable agricultural markets. Nonetheless the flow of population from country to city accelerated. Rural Catholic churches saw a decline in membership. However, even with smaller numbers, Catholic identity continued to burn bright in many of the smaller towns and rural villages of the archdiocese. One such Wisconsin community, Rubicon in rural Dodge County, demonstrated the strength of its Catholic heritage by sending scores of young men to St. Francis Seminary—an accomplishment that was only replicated by urban pastors with large cadres of Catholic youth. At St. John's parish in Rubicon five young men entered the ranks of the archdiocesan clergy, three of them during the 39-year pastorate of Father Francis Weis.

Cross and Plow Club at St. Francis Seminary [AAM]

Archbishop Messmer also sought to perpetuate the rural idyll himself by taking vacations in the countryside and shedding his clerical attire for overalls and a floppy straw hat. Once while visiting his Capuchin brother at Marathon, Wisconsin, he was mistaken for a migrant worker and put to work husking corn for a local farmer.[595] Eventually, the needs of rural Catholics would come under the spotlight of Catholic Action.

The needs of rural Catholics had been publicized by Edwin Vincent O'Hara even while he was a parish priest in Oregon.[596] In 1921, O'Hara established a Rural Life Bureau under the auspices of the Social Action Department of the National Catholic Welfare Conference. The Rural Life Bureau stimulated local associations of rural pastors and organizations concerned with church life in farming areas. Messmer endorsed the work and wrote appreciatively of its principles in the bureau's journal *St. Isidore's Plow*, which appeared in 1922 and was later renamed

Catholic Rural Life. This periodical was edited and produced by Milwaukee priest, Father William McDermott, principal of St. Catherine's High School in Racine.

In 1923 O'Hara developed the National Catholic Rural Life Conference under the auspices of the National Catholic Welfare Conference, and rural issues received sustained attention from the American bishops. In that same year, the College of Agriculture at the University of Wisconsin convened a special "Wisconsin Rural Church Conference," which consisted of 10 days of meetings on rural issues, problems and solutions. Father McDermott urged his fellow priests to pay attention to the needs of rural Catholics in the archdiocese.[597]

In 1932, the executive board of the NCWC urged that Rural Life directors be appointed for all of the dioceses. In September 1933, Archbishop Stritch appointed North Lake pastor Father Louis Zirbes to direct Catholic Rural Life efforts in the archdiocese of Milwaukee.[598] Rural life priorities changed over time. Initially, O'Hara had urged greater attention to rural life because of the superior birthrate of rural families in comparison with urban families. He feared the Church might die out if sufficient attention were not directed to rural churches, and especially to the religious education of youth. In the 1930s the Great Depression changed the focus of Catholic rural activities to a concern for agricultural economics, and Catholic ruralists favored the formation of cooperatives and government aid to farmers. Zirbes worked in these areas, mobilizing Catholic pastors and churches in a loose organization.[599] Rural religious education received a substantial boost with the expansion of the Confraternity of Christian Doctrine in the 1940s. However, the abundance of teaching sisters in Wisconsin allowed for a more equitable distribution of Catholic schools between urban and rural areas. Clearly, urban schools received more money, personnel and attention. But the School Sisters of St. Francis, the Agnesians of Fond du Lac, the Dominicans of Racine, and the School Sisters of Notre Dame all ran rural schools and sent sisters on mission to these locations.

Rural Catholicism required a modification of parish practices that worked well in urban settings. For example Vicar General Traudt urged Father Daniel Wisniewski, O.F.M., of St. Sebastian's Church in Sturtevant to allow more flexibility in confession times to accommodate his parishioners. "In a rural community it is not advisable to insist on confession on Saturday only," he wrote. "In many instances it is very difficult for farmers to go to confession on Saturday."[600] Aloysius Kraus, pastor of St. Martin's in Ashford brought the practicalities of the farming economy home to Archbishop Albert Meyer when he told Meyer that he could not guarantee the safety of the tabernacle (a pet theme of Meyer, who regularly lectured seminarians and pastors on the importance of preserv-

Rev. Louis Zirbes (left) [AAM]

St. John the Baptist Church, Johnsburg [AAM]

ing the Blessed Sacrament from profanation and urged them to keep personal control of the tabernacle key). Kraus wrote dejectedly to Meyer about the sorry state of his tabernacle whose doors could not be locked. "There have been so many things needed here that I have deferred mentioning the tabernacle. Right now with the crop damage and the decrease in farm products, it would be unwise to suggest a new tabernacle."[601]

The needs of Catholics in rural communities, remained, however, a less important priority than the insistent demands of large urban and suburban parishes. Nonetheless, rural churches continued to contribute to the vitality of archdiocesan Catholic life through their own dogged devotion to their parishes. The church buildings in rural communities were some of the architectural gems of the archdiocese. Among the many that stand out are St. John the Baptist Church in Johnsburg and St. Mary's Church in Marytown.

The Johnsburg church had been erected with local stone in 1857. So overcome was Henni when he came to dedicate it that he urged that it be consecrated—an unusual ceremony performed in very few Catholic churches. A later pastor, Father Theodore Tueller scraped together enough money to have artist Paul Klose (who had also decorated the interior of St. Michael's Church (Milwaukee) paint and decorate the interior in 1928. In regular trips back to his native Germany, Tueller, who "loved a

Men's Choir at St. John, Johnsburg [AAM]

rich effect," brought back many elaborate altar furnishings, candle sticks and vestments from Europe.[602]

St. Mary's of the Visitation, founded in 1849, went through a couple of church buildings until a permanent structure was erected in 1897 on top of a hill. The huge stone walls of the church (later magnificently illuminated) presided over the rural countryside. When Father Edward Stehling took over the parish in 1910, he added to the beauty of the interior with elaborate stenciling that complimented the rich woodwork, carved statues and altars and stained glass.

Catholics and the Great Depression

The Great Depression seared the heavily industrialized economy of Wisconsin. Milwaukee, Racine, Kenosha, Sheboygan, Beaver Dam, Janesville and Madison—all cities that relied on industrial wages—soon found themselves with armies of homeless men and women. Historian Paul Glad has described the statistical realities of the economic downturn that began to take hold of Wisconsin's economy. From August 1929 to November 1930 employment in Wisconsin's powerful manufacturing sector fell by almost a fourth, and payrolls declined 37 percent. In 1929 there were 265,000 jobs in Wisconsin's industries. By 1933, there were 159,000. Hardest hit were metalworking, machinery, automobile, and lumber and wood-products industries. Building construction declined 46 percent between 1929 and 1931. Farm income fell from $438 million in 1929 to $186 million in 1932.[603] In most counties, public charity took the form of "outdoor relief." Provisions and victuals were handed out at dispersal centers, where families came with gunny sacks to collect a week's worth of oats, cabbages, meat and other foodstuffs. But by the early 1930s the distress had become so acute that the limited funds for these county efforts (dependent on shrinking property tax revenue) dried up. Ultimately, the implementation of federal New Deal programs restored some stability to the economic system.

Catholics in the Milwaukee Archdiocese were caught up in the larger debate of the causes for the Great Depression. The issuance of the encyclical *Quadragesimo Anno* in 1931 offered not only Pope Pius XI's endorsement of the work of Pope Leo's *Rerum Novarum* (1891), but his own criticism of the unchecked forces of laissez-faire capitalism that had caused the economic collapse. This papal diagnosis of the ills of capitalism also brought with it suggestions for the reconstruction of society along corporatist lines. Few other American bishops were as sympathetic to the "social" and "organic" views of society propagated by Catholic teaching than Samuel A. Stritch.

The archdiocese was the direct recipient of Roosevelt's effort to build good relations with Catholics through his recruitment of Father Francis Haas as a labor mediator.[604] The son of a Racine grocer, Haas's interest in workers' rights and labor organization had been kindled by his father who regularly reported to him on labor issues in heavily industrial Racine. Haas entered St. Francis

Seminary in 1904 and was deeply moved by the lectures of Father Charles Bruehl, who offered an elective course on social justice and contemporary problems. Bruehl's lectures were his first systematic introduction to Catholic social thinking. Ordained in 1913 (interestingly not in the seminary chapel as were most seminarians but in his home parish of St. Joseph), he was first assigned to Father Robert Roche at Holy Rosary parish on Milwaukee's east side. At Holy Rosary he came to know Father Peter Dietz, another important influence on his ideas concerning organized labor. After two years with Roche, Haas was asked to join the faculty of St. Francis Seminary as a teacher of English, and in his spare time worked on his master's degree at Marquette University (he never completed it).

In 1919 Messmer sent him to the Catholic University of America where he came into contact with a stellar array of socially-minded priests including Father John O'Grady, the organizer of National Catholic Charities; Father William Kerby, an expert on social welfare; and the greatest of all, Father John A. Ryan, who was the American Catholic Church's premier social theologian.[605] Ryan, a priest of the archdiocese of St. Paul, had been a bitter foe of socialism (something likely to make him interesting to a priest from Milwaukee). But rather than simply denounce the failings of socialism, he articulated a positive Catholic response to the issues of economic justice generated by the industrial economy. Ryan's books—*A Living Wage* (1906), *Distributive Justice* (1916), and *The Church and Socialism* (1919)—provided a trilogy of well-reasoned Catholic positions on the chief social issues of the day.

Haas studied with Ryan and churned out a dissertation *Shop Collective Bargaining: A Study of Wage Determination in the Men's Garment Industry* which was published in 1922. He returned to the seminary faculty in that same year and was assigned to teach

Rev. Francis Haas [AAM]

English (the social science classes for which he had been trained were taken over by Father Aloysius Muench who had just returned from his studies in Fribourg). He was given permission to take a full-time job teaching sociology at Marquette (in fact he headed the Department of Sociology for a time). He also wrote regularly for the seminary periodical *Salesianum,* which gave him and Muench the opportunity to refine their ideas about various topics.[606] His major contribution to his field was the authorship of *Man and Society,* a sociology text that came from his experiences with students at Marquette and St. Francis. One of his first forays into the arena of public policy took place in March 1923 when he testified before the judiciary committee of the Wisconsin State senate on behalf of an unemployment bill introduced by Senator H. A. Huber.[607] The bill failed to pass, but his public efforts on its behalf, which included writings in religious and secular papers, set the pattern for his future work on behalf of legislation that involved social issues. In 1922 he helped to form an organization to bring Catholic social teaching to a wider audience. The Catholic Conference on Industrial Problems (CCIP) was organized by the National Catholic Welfare Conference under the direction of Linna Bresette, "to discuss and promote the study and understanding of industrial problems." In 1923, Haas helped to bring a meeting of the CCIP to Milwaukee.[608] He also became affiliated with the Catholic Association for International Peace—an organization that stressed church teachings on international justice and urged mediation of disputes.

In 1931, at the urging of his mentor Ryan, Haas was appointed to head the National Catholic School for Social Service in Washington, D.C.[609] Stritch gave him permission to accept the post and he moved to the national capital just as the Hoover era was ending and the new administration of Franklin D. Roosevelt was beginning. This school was an independent entity, but closely linked to the Catholic University of America. Its purpose was to train Catholic social workers. Haas labored diligently to upgrade and expand the curriculum. The school trained primarily women for Catholic charities around the nation.

Haas was not the most capable administrator, and his term as head of the NCSS lasted only four years. However, being in Washington, D.C., during the early New Deal years put the Milwaukee priest at the right place at the right time. When President Roosevelt pushed through the National Industrial Recovery Act (NIRA) in 1933, with its provisions for the protection of organized labor, Haas was appointed to the National Recovery Administration's Labor Advisory Board. This body examined the labor provisions of the various codes of fair competition that industry groups developed. It was Haas's task to see that the labor provisions of the NIRA assured workers a fair wage, eliminated child labor and that the right to organize was guaranteed. This was tedious and mind-numbing work and required vast reservoirs of patience with refractory employers and labor

(l to r) Francis Haas, Archbishop Samuel Stritch, William G. Bruce, Dorothy Day, Katherine Williams [AAM]

groups. The ambiguity of the labor provisions of the NIRA had resulted in a rash of strikes that threatened the goal of industrial recovery. Roosevelt set up a Labor Relations Board and empowered it "to settle by mediation, conciliation or arbitration all controversies between employers and employees which tend to impede the purpose of the NIRA."[610] Haas's work impressed Labor Secretary Frances Perkins, and his widespread contacts throughout the labor movement were also a boon to the new administration. Haas clearly was the most important priest in the Roosevelt Administration.

The Church and Organized Labor in the 1930s

The Catholic Church in the United States was for many years largely a working-class community. As a result, relations between the Church and working people had been close. Catholic leaders were quick to see the importance of early efforts at labor organization. Thanks to the timely intervention of Cardinal James Gibbons in 1886, a Vatican condemnation of the Knights of Labor (an early union) had been averted. Labor organization had been sanctioned by Pope Leo XIII's landmark encyclical *Rerum Novarum* (1891). In order to blunt possible radical or socialist "takeovers" of labor organizations, Catholic bishops and priests had become active in labor issues. Milwaukee's own Father Peter Dietz, as we have seen, played an important role with the American Federation of Labor. The pastor of Milwaukee's first "industrial" parish, Father Thomas Fagan of Bay View, offered some qualified support for the rights of working people during a 1907 strike at the nearby rolling mills. Fagan believed that a strike was the equivalent of war and that at times war was justified. So too, workers should be permitted to resist when a company imposed measures "which were recognized to be unjust and refused to make a change."[611] More often than not, Milwaukee priests found themselves called in as impartial mediators in labor disputes. In 1928, a bitter strike at the Allen Hosiery Company of Kenosha found Father Martin Buenger of St. James parish on a team of interdenominational negotiators to bring peace to the town.[612] In the 1930s, especially after the issuance of Pope Pius XI's *Quadragesimo Anno* in 1931, Catholic enthusiasm for labor's cause burned bright.

The Catholic Action conferences of 1937 and 1938 focused in on Wisconsin's own special issues, especially those related to labor. Father Francis Haas had explained to the priests in 1937 the complex dynamics taking place in the ranks of unskilled labor, as New Deal legislation opened the doors for a new wave of labor organization. The new legislation, he declared, had built on the Norris-La Guardia Act of the early 1930s and Section 7a of the National Industrial Recovery Act and made possible the emergence of an even stronger American labor movement. Unorganized workers in major industries such as steel, auto manufacturing, and meatpacking finally found the opportunity to come together under the umbrella of the Congress of Industrial Organizations (CIO). In 1935, the even stronger National Labor Relations Act replaced Section 7a and set up the National Labor Relations Board to oversee elections in contested industries. Throughout the thirties, the CIO organizers won a stunning array of victories.

After the enactment of Section 7a, a rash of organizing activities began in Wisconsin and so too a season of industrial strife. Efforts on the part of CIO organizers to represent workers met resistance from AFL organiza-

[AAM]

tions and from employers themselves who insisted on maintaining open shops. The economic disruption created by strikes and labor unrest exacerbated already difficult circumstances in Wisconsin.[613] In addition, the strife, bitterness and occasional violence that attended these events was of direct concern to pastors of industrial communities. Parishioners were often turned against each other. Parish revenues (slender as they were during the Depression) plummeted even further. Moreover, thanks to the instruction given at St. Francis Seminary by Bruehl, Breig, Muench and others, Catholic priests of the archdiocese of Milwaukee were aware of the body of social teaching stating that workers had a right to organize. Communist agitators and organizers also injected themselves into labor organizing activities providing another cause for concern. Catholic social teaching rejected class warfare and violence as acceptable strategies to secure the right to organize.

Father Francis Haas was the premier "labor priest" in Wisconsin. When Wisconsin passed the Wisconsin Labor Relations Act in 1937, requiring the establishment of a state labor relations board (Wisconsin Labor Relations Board—WLRB), Governor Philip LaFollette appointed Haas to the panel, and he set up his offices in Milwaukee. He soon won a sterling reputation as an honest broker in industrial disputes. Even before he took the oath of office, he and fellow board members were called on to negotiate a tense situation in Fort Atkinson where local auto workers were attempting to organize the Creamery Package Manufacturing Company.[614] In 1938, he helped to resolve three painful and dangerous strikes: at Allis Chalmers, Nash-Kelvinator in Racine, and Harnischfeger Manufacturing Corporation.[615] In fact work on the WLRB kept him so busy that he neglected his duties as rector of St. Francis Seminary.

A cadre of Milwaukee priests also became quite interested in organized labor. Heavily industrialized Racine had an admirable contingent of labor priests, including Father Anthony Weiler of St. John Nepomuc, Father John J. O'Boyle of St. Rose and Father Henry Schmitt of St. Joseph.[616] Father Henry Riordan, a seminary English teacher like Haas, became pastor of St. Joseph parish in Fond du Lac in 1932 and kept an eye on labor conditions in Wisconsin. To the priests at the

Rev. Anthony Weiler [AAM]

summer school in 1937, he reported a dismal picture of the archdiocese. Citing problems in Port Washington and in Fond du Lac, Riordan noted: "The demand for guidance [on Catholic social principles] is greater in smaller towns than in larger cities."[617]

In December 1934, Father John Boyle, working with Rabbi Aaron Cohen and H. S. Mann, helped to negotiate a settlement of a strike at the Chicago Rubber Clothing Company.[618] The worst labor turmoil in Racine took place when the CIO inspired a strike at the J. I. Case Company, Racine's largest employer. Case had been ravaged by industrial strife for two years, and city officials refused to support the company's claim for an injunction to end strike activities. When CIO activists wanted an election, strong resistance from the company and even violence from members of a competing company kept Racine in the headlines until the strike was settled in the union's favor in early 1937.[619]

Although not a Milwaukee priest, one of the most famous clerical labor negotiators was Viatorian Father John William Rochefort Maguire. Maguire had been born in County Roscommon, Ireland, of Protestant stock.[620] His father soon left his mother. Young John received a classical education and enlisted in the British army. In 1907 he went to Canada and drifted to the western United States. He became a reporter for the Spokane labor paper and covered the labor radical Big Bill Haywood trial in Boise in 1907. His association here led to a lifelong interest in labor issues. He drifted into religion and entered an Anglican seminary. But later he converted to Catholicism after a meeting with a Servite at Our Lady of Sorrows Basilica in Chicago. He made a retreat at a Passionist monastery and was conditionally baptized on February 4, 1908. He entered St. Viator College in 1910 and was ordained December 20, 1916. Like Francis Haas, his studies at the Catholic University of America brought him into contact with the constellation of leading Catholic social thinkers including John A. Ryan and William Kerby, and Catholic Charities organizer John O'Grady. Maguire devoured the "Bishop's Plan for Social Reconstruction," written by Ryan and approved by the American bishops in 1919. It also provided a blueprint for many socially active Catholic priests and lay persons, essentially translating the general principles of papal encyclicals and letters on social matters into a program of action in the United States. This document advocated social insurance, unemployment compensation, equal pay for equal work for women, minimum wage, and reaffirmed Catholic support for the rights of labor to organize and bargain collectively.[621] Maguire devoted himself to labor mediation and pressed for an equal say for both workers and employers in resolving industrial disputes. In 1928 he was made president of his order's St. Viator College and burnished his reputation as a labor priest through highly visible labor mediation, opposition to child labor, and strongly criticized the use of injunctions in labor disputes. When regional labor mediation boards were created by the Roosevelt administration, Maguire was called to serve for the Chicago region.

In his capacity as a roving labor relations mediator, Maguire played a prominent role in settling Wisconsin strikes, including the Milwaukee street car strike (where he worked closely with Francis Haas), the Wisconsin Bridge Company strike, the Northern Refrigerator Car Company strike, the Luick Ice Cream strike, a strike at Menasha Wooden Ware Company, and two glove company strikes. Oftentimes his intervention brought resolution, but his efforts were not always welcomed or appreciated. In March 1934, workers at the Bear Brand Hosiery Company in Beaver Dam went out on strike, demanding the right to organize under the provisions of Section 7a of the NIRA. Eager workers imported Maguire to speak to them, and the priest assured them of their right to organize and bargain collectively. In response, the factory owner refused to deal with any unions and simply shut down the plant, transferring non-striking workers to his other plants in Kankakee, Illinois and Gary, Indiana.

Rev. John Maguire, CSV [SCHRC]

Angry over Maguire's "interference," Father Theodore Rohner of St. Peter's parish wrote to Maguire in April 1935: "It may interest you to learn some of the consequences of the strike. The Bear Brand Hosiery plant is now closed and is not for rent or for sale. St. Peter's Parish has lost 40 very good families—non strikers—and quite a few single members who have been moved to Gary, Indiana and Kankakee, Illinois.... The strikers have dispersed in all directions and if they had moved to Hades no one would care." He further noted the losses in neighboring parishes, chided Maguire for failing to show "the usual courtesy towards the local clergy," and said Maguire's service on the labor board was "outside of ecclesiastical control." He declared, "I am heartily in favor of unions, but unions must also show a sense of responsibility and show a tendency towards a fair settlement of labor disputes."[622] Maguire defended his presence on the labor board and jabbed at Rohner's pompous implication that he [Rohner] was the most important cleric in the town by noting, "I had a long interview with the pastor of the English-speaking parish." More importantly, he refuted Rohner's suggestion that the strike action was the cause for the closure of the plant. "In Beaver Dam, the employees of the Bear Brand Hosiery Co. had a perfect right to organize, if they wanted to; that they had a right to collective bargaining through representatives of their own choosing, and that they had a right not to be fired because of their union activities. Mr. Pope [the factory owner] denied his employees all those legal rights, and when ordered to comply with the law closed down the plant." Maguire regretted that the plant had been closed, "It is of course unfortunate that such things should happen, but the people who are struggling to bring about economic social justice are not to blame."[623]

The Kohler Strike of 1934 and Company Relations with the Catholic Church

Maguire's biggest Wisconsin test came when workers of the Kohler company near Sheboygan attempted to organize.[624] The Kohler family had begun the bathroom fixture company in 1871, creating one of the most important sources of economic life for Sheboygan County. Around the Kohler works, scores of immigrant workers were taken care of by the paternalistic company: housing, insurance, even picnics and other social outings were provided. In the 1930s, Walter Kohler, the son of the company's founder, began to construct a model industrial village replicating the more charming features of an English country village. Most of the owners of these homes were members of management, with industrial workers living in the nearby city of Sheboygan and Sheboygan Falls.

As the Depression worsened, workers looked for a way to improve the quality of working conditions and wages at the Kohler plant. Encouraged by Section 7a of the NIRA, the AFL began efforts to organize workers and sought recognition by the company to negotiate wages and working conditions. Highly toxic working environments (silicosis was a serious problem with Kohler workers) and high temperatures in enameling rooms, not to mention long hours and difficult production expectations, had created serious discontent. Company president Walter Kohler responded to the requests by forming a company union and attempting to thwart labor activism. In July 1934, workers walked out and barricaded the plant, and Kohler vowed not to succumb to the pressure of union organizers. Federal authorities became involved, and Maguire was sent to arbitrate the strike as a representative of the Chicago Regional Labor Board.

Maguire calmed the Sheboygan workers, allowing coal shipments into the beleaguered plants. He hoped that this token of good will toward the company would create an atmosphere of give-and-take at the bargaining table. But the Kohlers were in no mood to compromise. On July 27, 1934, a hundred "special deputies" broke through the picket lines to bring in another coal car. Violence erupted as workers began pelting the factory with rocks and bricks. Kohler's forces responded with tear gas and gunfire. In the melee two strikers were killed and 40 were wounded. Governor Albert Schmedeman called in the National Guard to restore order. In the wake of this violence, Maguire was forced to step away from the negotiations and before he left Sheboygan he issued a blast at the Kohler company in a special report to the Sheboygan County Board. "I have been in many strikes, but I never saw such needless and ruthless killing by supporters of the law," he declared. "As a member of the Chicago Regional Labor Board, I am not going behind fences to say what I have to say. Human lives and human rights are more precious in preserving. They are more sacred than property rights."[625] Maguire was recalled and another took his place. The strike dragged on until 1940 and efforts to unionize were unsuccessful.

Among the important lessons the Kohler management learned from this strike was the powerful effect of Maguire's presence and the consternation caused by his criticism. Sheboygan was a heavily Catholic town and the local clergy were influential with their flocks. The Kohlers believed they paid good wages and generally had good working conditions (although laborers in some divisions strongly disputed this); they were also generous benefactors to the community. However, their largesse in some instances was never purely philanthropic. They paid decent wages as a price for maintaining strict control over their operations and keeping "trouble-makers" at bay. In their charity towards the Catholic Church, they also displayed a regard for churches as essential elements of community stability and there was no doubt a sincere generosity that attended their donations to churches and schools. But gifts of any kind generally indebted the recipient and Catholic churches found themselves caught between a rock and a hard place when their worker parishioners clashed with their company benefactors. In the case of the Kohler company, one of its leading officials, Lyman Conger, was a devout Catholic and a reminder to Catholic priests of their need to be circumspect when dealing with the company. This was especially true in the building of St. John the Evangelist Church in the village of Kohler.[626]

When the village of Kohler was founded, Walter Kohler did not want any churches. He relented, however, and tried to have a site for all the religious groups in the community—something like a military base chapel. This solution proved unacceptable, and Kohler soon became quite interested in helping local churches get started and promised them assistance. In the 1920s, the number of Catholics living in Kohler grew substantially, and Kohler village manager, Anton Braun, organized a petition to have Mass in the village. Messmer approved the idea, and Father George Goesl of St. Mary's parish in Sheboygan Falls began celebrating Mass in the village hall in 1928. Goesl, with the help of two Capuchins, served the needs of the community for a time.

Eager to preserve the architectural integrity of its "model village," the Kohler company made it clear that it would provide substantial support when the church was ready to be built. Meanwhile, the "Kohler Mission," as it was called, had begun the regular pattern of fund-raisers and the assessment of "pew rent" to build up enough money to erect a church. (Unfortunately it had also invested in some of the bonds of the various parishes—St. Jude's and St. Adalbert's—that later teetered in the Depression years.) Nonetheless, by late 1936, the mission had a nice $23,000 nest egg for the church. Two parish trustees approached Stritch with a list of parishioners, a plea for a resident priest, and a reassurance from Kohler of free land and help in taking out a low-interest loan.[627] Kohler offered Stritch a selection from three possible sites in the village and the donation of plumbing and heating fixtures for the new structure.

Stritch demurred, in part troubled because of the unclear legal status of the gift of the property to the archdiocese. He was also hesitant because the Kohlers insisted on building a church rather than the church/school combination that was the practice for new parishes in the archdiocese. Yet while he was privately uncomfortable over the extent to which the Kohlers seemed to dictate the church's programs, he appointed Father John J. Carroll to be the first resident pastor in 1938. Carroll, a native of Platteville, quickly cemented good relations with the company, and brought the process of building a church to completion—largely according to the Kohlers' wishes and minus a school. Carroll raised more money, eliminating the "greasy" fund-raisers by imposing a four percent tithe (he called it the "Budget Plan") on his parishioners. He also added Kohler Company attorney Lyman Conger to his building committee.

Land west of the Valley Road was donated by the Kohler Company. Carroll who, the parish historian noted, "shunned shoddiness in any form," engaged architect Peter Brust, who designed the English Gothic church that fit in with the architectural pattern of the community. The parish borrowed $40,000 which it added to its savings. However, it accepted land, plumbing and heating fixtures, and the landscape service of the Olmstead Brothers as gifts from the Kohler Company.

Carroll had no problem with this, but his superiors in Milwaukee worried that they were being forced to accede to the company's wishes to the long term detriment of the parish. Stritch's misgivings continued: however he left the direct confrontation with the company to his attorney, Henry V. Kane.[628] Kane, objected to the conditions Walter Kohler had placed on the property; it could not use the land for a cemetery and there remained a possibility that it could revert back to the company if the parish ceased to exist. These and other encumbrances, Kane felt, left the church open to potential interference from the company in later days.[629]

When Carroll sought help from Conger to help soothe the concerns, the Catholic attorney left no doubt in the pastor's mind over the proper attitude he and the archdiocese should have in dealing with the powerful company: gratitude and no questions. Conger minced no words: "To begin with," he scolded Carroll, "is the question of the attitude which we should assume in this matter." Suggesting that the Church was ungrateful, he reminded Carroll (and through him Stritch and Kane) that the land for the new church alone was worth $7,700. Taken together with the donation of fixtures for the church and the rectory, the total Kohler gift had come to $10,000. Conger urged an "attitude adjustment" and wrote, "In view of the fact that Mr. Kohler is not a Catholic, these donations most certainly are an expression of friendship and good will, not only to the Kohler Congregation but to the Church as a whole, and should, I believe, be considered in the spirit of appreciation."[630] The Kohler Company made it clear that they called the shots in this community and that churches, like their workers, ought to be grateful for what they received. The veneer of deference to Catholic clergy came off quickly when the company was questioned.

By December the difficulties with the deed had been ironed out with Kohler's gift outweighing other considerations. In 1940, St. John the Evangelist Church (named for Carroll's patron) was ready for dedication. The 400-seat church had warm rafter beams, and elegant stained glass windows by the T.C. Esser Company. Walter Kohler died before the church was dedicated, but his brother Herbert V. Kohler gave substantial cash gifts to the church every Christmas, enabling it to pay off its $40,000 debt to local banks four years ahead of schedule.[631] Father John Carroll dutifully erected a plaque in the new church to memorialize Walter Kohler.

Yet the episode of the Kohler church laid bare some important issues that arose again when the church was asked to take a stand in another Kohler strike. The gifts were not the philanthropy of a disinterested benefactor, but the carefully recorded accumulation of debt that would compromise the Church in future conflicts between the company and workers. By 1954 the Kohlers called in these chits when another strike hit the company.

St. John the Evangelist Church, Kohler [SCHRC]

The clash between church teaching on union organizing and taking gifts from anti-union companies was not restricted to the Kohler Company. It was vividly seen in the buildings at Holy Hill.

Architect Herman Gaul designed a monastery for the Carmelites and then contracted the work out to the Hutter Construction Company of Fond du Lac, a firm that employed non-union labor. In May 1937, after work had begun, 400 members of the Carpenter's District Council of Milwaukee appeared at the shrine on a Sunday in May to picket the Hutter firm. Reporters descended on Stritch to ask his position, and he assured them that "My stand on the labor question is clear and definite." He wanted only union labor in the reconstruction of St. John's Cathedral and for St. Robert's, being built in Shorewood. The Carmelites were "grieved and embarrassed" by the matter and had assumed that architect Gaul had written a union clause into the work. Hutter, who asserted he paid better wages than most union jobs, was unapologetic. "'These union men can't force me .... These farm boys around here have the right as Americans to work. That's one of their civic rights and I shall insist that this right shall not be denied them."[632] However, Hutter was a good Catholic, and so generous to Catholic religious orders that he continued to be used by Catholic firms despite his anti-labor beliefs. His clients included the archdiocese, the Agnesian Sisters of Fond du Lac, and the School Sisters of St. Francis.

The diocesan record on labor was not all bad. Archdiocesan cemetery workers in Milwaukee, for example, were organized by the American Federation of State, County and Municipal Employees. Occasional strikes occurred at the system cemeteries of Holy Cross, Holy Trinity, Calvary, Mount Olivet and St. Adalbert, but unlike other archdioceses, Milwaukee officials did not use seminarians as scabs or strike-breakers.[633]

Taking Care of the Poor within the Diocese

Social provision was an important part of the archdiocesan mission, but these institutions operated at the fringe of Catholic consciousness in the prosperous 1920s. A shelter for homeless men, St. Bernard's Home, for example, was founded in 1917 by the Vincentians and overseen by Father Joseph Hurst. The spiking unemployment rate in Milwaukee brought more and more men to the shelter, and by January 1931, the facility served more than 1,000 meals a day. In addition the shelter provided temporary lodging for 140 men while offering a meager subsidy to shelter 40 to 60 men elsewhere.[634] From December 1930 through March 1931, the shelter served nearly 40,000 meals and gave close to 14,000 nights of lodging, and the end was not in sight. The bills mounted. By early March they had paid out $14,000; by the end of the year, the amount was $43, 000. Even adding 125 beds in the crowded shelter did little to help.[635]

The Society of St. Vincent de Paul did its best to keep up with the staggering increase in caseloads. Local councils brought food, clothing and shelter to the growing number of dispossessed. Thousands of Milwaukee poor converged daily on the salvage and distribution center of the Vincentians on 4th and Walnut to the point that it could no longer

[SVdPSA]

cope with the numbers. In 1936, the Vincentians published a compendium of their most heartrending cases in an edition of the *Catholic Herald Citizen* just before Christmas, listing at the end of each citation the amount of money needed for long-deferred medical treatments, painkillers for a man with cancer, deliverance from improvident fathers and mothers, and supplements to meager relief wages. One typical story was of "Patrick J." and his three sisters whose father's WPA wages were spent mostly in taverns. Through the intercession of a St. Vincent de Paul visitor the errant father was weaned away from the bottle, but more money was needed to feed Patrick and his siblings whose consistent undernourishment left them "fidgety, restless and nervous."[636]

Parishes did their best. St. Mary's in Kenosha began a "Penny Pantry" in the summer of 1932, hosting a Sunday dinner that cost only pennies per entree. It served over 400 people in its first week.[637] St. Alexander's in Milwaukee distributed 31 bushel baskets of food in the parish during the difficult winter of 1932-33.[638] In Waukesha, clergy at St. Joseph's Church helped families overcome the embarrassment of not being able to outfit their children properly for First Holy Communion by simply dressing all the boys in inexpensive cassocks and surplices that could be made from a simple pattern for a mere $1.85.[639]

One additional relief outlet for starving Milwaukeeans came in 1936 when three Catholic women, Nina Polcyn, Margaret Blaser and Florence Weinfurter, aided by Dean Jeremiah O'Sullivan of Marquette's School of Journalism, Leonard Doyle, and Harold Schwartz, established the Holy Family House of Hospitality at 1019 N. Fifth Street. The Houses of Hospitality were the creation of Catholic Worker movement founder Dorothy Day, who had opened a House in New York and in Chicago in 1933. These drop-in centers for the poor and destitute provided a free meal and a night's lodging.

Milwaukee's interest in the Catholic Worker Movement was first stimulated by Father Franklyn Kennedy, a curate at St. Matthew's Church, and later editor of the *Catholic Herald Citizen*. From contacts in New York he had stumbled on the small penny paper, the *Catholic Worker* produced by Dorothy Day and her colleague, Peter Maurin. Kennedy bought a bundle of 400 papers every month for distribution to the parishioners, teachers and pupils of St. Matthew's. In 1934 Kennedy's friend, O'Sullivan brought Dorothy Day to Marquette to speak at a campus event. Day stayed next door to St. Matthew's at the home of parishioners, the Polcyns. The young daughter of the couple, Nina Polcyn, became fast friends with Day, and spent a summer at the New York House of Hospitality. She related her experiences to the Milwaukee Archdiocesan Council of Catholic Women and others who were taken by Day, Maurin, and the ideology of the Catholic Worker. In 1936, the Holy Family House of Hospitality opened and became a source of public charity. To feed the large number of Milwaukee poor, the Catholic Workers received generous donations of food from the School Sisters of St. Francis. The sisters fed the poor from their own convent kitchen for many years during the Depression until, as Polcyn recalled, "the neighbors grew upset." When the Holy Family House opened, the sisters shipped their "excess" food to the House where it provided sustenance for many. Day came back to inspect the work in 1937 when she delivered a talk at the National Catholic Social Action meeting at the Milwaukee Auditorium.[640] Indeed, until Holy Family House closed in 1941, it continued to feed the poor.[641]

Dorothy Day [ASSF]

In addition to providing food and shelter, the Workers embarked on an intensive educational program—a progenitor of programs that would later be run by Father Russell Beix and his associates at the Cardijn Center. Beginning in 1937, a series of popular speakers came to speak under the auspices of the House. At a rented room in the Turnverein Hall, popular Redemptorist Father Raymond Miller discussed the liturgy. Father Paul Hanley Furfey, a sociologist at the Catholic University, spoke on poverty, and lay activists Leonard Doyle and Ammon Hennacy

Sisters in front of Holy Family House [ASSF]

spoke on peace. Father Gerard Smith, S.J., of Marquette University's department of philosophy, led spiritual exercises for the group. The House continued until 1941 when divisions within the movement over American entry into the war and the return of prosperity made it difficult to continue.[642]

Parish Credit Unions

One way parishes found to help with the failure of the American economy was through the formation of credit unions. Credit unions are self-managed, cooperative savings and loan associations which help people save money, take care of short-term credit problems at decent rates of interest, and help in the management of funds. Begun in Germany, they were no doubt the product of several different cooperative endeavors, but are traditionally attributed to the work of Frederick Raiffeisen, a burgomaster of Flammersfeld, Germany. Raiffeisen's idea of a credit cooperative caught on in Germany and soon sprouted a host of "Raiffeisen Banks." The idea spread to the United States and became popular with different occupational groups such as railroad and textile workers, government workers, and others. Religious congregations soon saw the wisdom and relative ease of establishing credit unions. The first parish organization was begun in 1909 at St. Mary's parish in Manchester, New Hampshire. Even before the Great Depression, parishes all over the country saw their value, and parish credit unions helped to finance home purchases that in turn established a stable community around the parish. In addition, many of the depositors in the parish credit union were school children, who learned lessons of thrift along with their regular subjects. As these organizations grew, a body of state regulatory law developed to monitor them.

The credit union was slow to come to Wisconsin. One of the first Milwaukee archdiocesan credit unions was created by Father Peter Dietz at St. Monica's parish in Whitefish Bay, who had observed how well they operated in Canada.[643] Strongly advocated by seminary professors Francis Haas and Aloysius Muench, the parish credit union movement swept the archdiocese of Milwaukee during the Depression decade.[644] A Wisconsin Catholic Parish Credit Union organization was formed under the leadership of August Springob, head of the Family Life Insurance Company which provided the pros and cons of having a parish credit union, and also helped fill out the paperwork required for a state charter. Working in conjunction with *Central Verein*, a number of Milwaukee's leading German parishes soon began to follow the example of St. Monica's. In 1933, St. Anthony parish opened a credit union. Three years later, the three Teutonic bastions of St. Michael's, St. Leo's and St. Boniface followed suit.[645] Immaculate Conception in Bay View began its Credit Union on March 10, 1936.[646] Eventually, a number of parishes throughout the archdiocese adopted these successful cooperatives. Although the return of stability to the banking system undercut their popularity, many parishes have retained these simple lending institutions to the present time.

Preserving the Diocese from Financial Ruin

The archdiocese itself received bad financial news in the summer of 1931, when its chief bonding company, Hackett, Hoff and Thiermann went bankrupt.[647] The loss of this firm, which had overseen and underwritten the construction bonds for a score of Milwaukee parishes during the prosperous 1920s, soon caused a panic. Bonding responsibilities were soon transferred to the Marshall and Ilsley Bank of Milwaukee, and this corporation began to look out for the well-being of bondholders. Messmer and Traudt's reliance on bond issues to fund parochial building and expansion had seemed to make sense when fund-appeals had fallen short. The bonds had seemed to be a quick and manageable way to raise large sums rather quickly. But Hackett, Hoff and Thiermann's failure left Stritch with the task of refinancing the massive indebtedness of many parishes.

Stritch needed new financial advice. Monsignor Bernard Traudt, who had overseen finances in the past, was out of the chancery loop. Stritch then turned to Neil J. Gleason, an employee of the Northwestern Mutual Life Insurance Company and the archdiocesan attorney Henry V. Kane for advice and direction. With Gleason doing much of the negotiating, and Kane checking the fine print, the refinancing of the debts of 13 congregations went forward.[648] The total indebtedness was $325,000 in bonds.

Case by case, each parish that found itself in a bind submitted its financial data to Stritch and Gleason who would devise ways to help the parish out of their plight. Sometimes this worked out fairly well. For example, Holy Family in Cudahy, which had just dedicated a new church, found itself in arrears. Its revenues were shrinking, and the church had little money to pay the principal or interest on its loans or to accumulate savings to make dated payments to bondholders. Holy Family's biggest single debt, $16,000, was owed to parishioner George J. Meyer, owner of a bottle cleaning plant in Cudahy. When Holy Family began to default on their bond payments, which came due every year on June 1, church officials pleaded with Meyer to grant the parish some extra time to pay. Meyer's complaint was that the pastor, Father John Kalcynski was incompetent, and that he would not do anything until

Kalcynski was gone.[649] News of Meyer's opposition to the pastor leaked out, and Kalcynski's partisans drafted petitions of support. This sorry state of affairs dragged on from 1933 until late 1937. Finally, faced with the ruin of the parish, Stritch replaced Kalcynski with Father John Stencil. Stencil persuaded Meyer to accept a new bond issue in place of his mortgage. Meyer was so impressed with the new leadership that he not only agreed to the terms, but remitted the $3,400 interest he had coming on the delinquent mortgage.[650] Stritch confided to Kane, "Fine! I have long prayed and expected this turn of events. For long I sensed that good Mr. Meyer was dissatisfied with the administration of the Parish and that once he was sure it was in able hands he would be the first to cooperate."[651]

But other situations would not be as easily resolved. Such was the case of St. Jude's in Wauwatosa. Father Joseph Hurst had founded the parish in 1928 and borrowed heavily to build a $60,000 combination school and church which was dedicated in January 1929.[652] Efforts to pay off St. Jude's huge indebtedness were further complicated by the fact that Hurst had (like many other pastors in the archdiocese) stopped paying the salaries of the teaching sisters in his schools. Many of the religious communities were able to swallow the loss. Some, like the Sisters of the Visitation from Dubuque who staffed St. Jude's school, had serious financial needs that did not allow them to miss a payment from the parishes they served. When a fire destroyed a great part of their Dubuque academy and the convent laundry, Mother M. Catherine Gough, the general superior of the sisters began to call in as many overdue bills as possible. In 1936 when St. Jude's indicated that it could no longer pay, Gough withdrew the sisters from the school (they were replaced by the Agnesians of Fond du Lac). To retrieve the back salary, Gough wrote a series of letters to Stritch (and presumably Hurst) requesting payment of $2,000 (at 4.5 percent interest). Hurst tried to hold off the sisters by referring to some arrangement whereby a debt incurred by Dubuque was remitted by the sisters foreswearing their salaries to St. Jude. But the doughty Mother Catherine didn't buy it.

St. Jude Church and School, Wauwatosa [AAM]

Stritch assured the sisters that St. Jude was on the verge of straightening out its financial affairs and getting back on its feet. Refinancing the debt became impossible, however, and the parish teetered on bankruptcy. Gough was unmoved by the plight of the parish and continued to demand from Stritch the wages plus interest brushing aside Stritch's reminder that "Our own Sisters, during the period of the Depression, reduced in fact their salaries and in the settlement of balances due from Parishes which suffered heavily in the Depression have been generous."[653] Eventually, though Gough scaled back her request to just one-fourth of the bill in cash. St. Jude's could not even come up with that.

Conditions at St. Jude's went from bad to worse. Hurst often had to close the school due to lack of money for fuel, and foreclosure proceedings by the First National Bank of Wauwatosa began. Other companies with overdue bills also lined up to retrieve what they could from the insolvent parish. Even lawyer Kane, who had been through many of these matters, felt that little could be done to stave off the inevitable. Kane urged Stritch to press parish members to pay their debts: "They use the church premises which really belong to the bondholders; they have allowed a Judgement to go against their church for oil that they have used on a long overdue account, and their Protestant neighbors who own these notes, have really been aiding in the financing of them for a number of years."[654] After transfers of money from archdiocesan coffers paid St. Jude's bills, Stritch called the trustees of the parish to his residence to devise a plan to retire the debt. Ultimately, after Hurst left the parish, St. Jude got its fiscal house in order. But it would not be until the 1950s that the parish could afford a church.

At the end of the 1930s, Stritch had had enough of bonds and bonding agencies. "In my opinion," he wrote Neil Gleason, "it is for the best interests of Religion gradually as we can to retire church loans from the Bond field .... Experience has brought to the fore the disadvantages of such financing and the fact that sometimes it has given engagement to salesmen more intent on private gains than exact representations."[655]

The sometimes harrowing experiences of seeking re-financing for the heavy indebtedness of parishes wore heavily on Stritch. When he appealed to parishes to support Marquette University in 1933, he confessed, "The necessities of the parishes and other institutions have emptied my purse and taxed my ingenuity to the limit."[656] But in 1933, he was only beginning the struggle to maintain the financial solvency of the archdiocese of Milwaukee.

At the same time he struggled to keep parishes from going under, Stritch had to contend with shortfalls that developed in general archdiocesan finances. In 1931, Stritch had to nudge the parishes to pay their annual assessments. "I am very sorry at this time when your revenues are reduced by the existing economic conditions, [but] I must ask for a payment of these amounts ...."[657] Even more ominously, annual collections to fund the general works of the archdiocese, particularly the network of charitable organizations, faltered as well. In addition, transfusions of funds from the Community Chest slipped drastically. In 1932, Stritch called together a panel of experts, including publisher William

C. Bruce, brewer Val Blatz, and seminary rector Aloysius Muench, to seek solutions. The group urged Stritch to begin a fund campaign under his personal direction—it was called the Archbishop's Charity Appeal—in order to stabilize the rapidly faltering finances of the archdiocesan charitable institutions.[658] The fairly modest sum of $75,000 was asked for the first appeal. A general campaign organization was created, headed by paint dealer Frank Surges and a network of teams and captains were dispatched to collect pledges and actual donations. The results exceeded Stritch's wildest imaginings. The fund took in over $100,000, from which Stritch skimmed off the initial $70,000 for the strapped charities. "The Good God gave us more than we asked in this campaign," he wrote to his priests.[659] The idea was initially to be a one-shot collection, but it was so popular that it was continued annually. Stritch enjoyed petitioning for it ("I am going out with my little tin cup," he loved to say) and it became an important part of the more elaborate archdiocesan fund-raising appeals. In 1934's campaign, Stritch set the goal at $250,000 and came in with $270,198.53, and in 1936 nearly $330,000 was raised.

Samuel Stritch accepting a check for the Archbishop's Fund Appeal [AAM]

Stritch shifted funds to the St. Michael Priest Fund and refinanced the heavy bonded debt on Messmer High School, so as to avoid imposing more burdens on the parishes which had all but given up contributing to the general high school fund put in place by Traudt. Stritch had to hold down spending in every way possible, and this he attempted to do by his own personal austerities (he never was one for fancy dining or high living), and by reining in pastors who wanted to spend lavishly even during the Depression. As he had been "difficult" with pastors who built elaborately in the Depression decade, or who wanted to push him into land-buying schemes, so also he was hesitant about rebuilding his own cathedral church.

At 1:30 on the morning of January 28, 1935, cathedral rector Monsignor Francis E. Murphy was awakened by shouts of "fire." To his horror he saw the flames leaping from the historic structure.[660] The fire was so intense that it not only destroyed the roof, but it burned out the support beams under the altar in the sanctuary, so that it went crashing to the basement—tabernacle and all. Fortunately, the destruction did not touch the resting place of Archbishop John Martin Henni. Cathedral parish operations were transferred to the church hall; and in the

Fire damage at St. John Cathedral, January 1935 [AAM]

interim before reconstruction was complete, Stritch and his successor Kiley used large churches, Gesu, St. Anne's, and St. Anthony's as temporary cathedrals. Stritch apparently toyed with the idea of abandoning the site altogether. In 1936, however, he decided to rebuild, and with excess money from the charity drive, he contacted a Pittsburgh architectural firm that had helped him build the elaborate Cathedral of the Holy Rosary in Toledo. But the final rebuilding would not be complete until his successor Kiley was on the episcopal throne.

The Archdiocese of Milwaukee and the Politics of the Thirties: Father Coughlin and the Coming of World War II

As members of a large industrial archdiocese Milwaukee's Catholics felt the brunt of the Depression. They could not remain aloof from the wider national debate on the causes of the economic calamity, nor could the shock wave of nationwide events leave Milwaukee Catholics undisturbed.

The presidency of Franklin Roosevelt was of special concern to Catholics. Indeed he made the cultivation of them a key part of his strategy to weld a winning electoral coalition for the Democratic party. The appointments of Catholic heavyweights to his official family like Montana Senator Thomas Walsh (who died before he took office), Frank Murphy and even Wisconsin Catholics like Federal Deposit Insurance Corporation head Leo T. Crowley and Monsignor Haas, went over well with Wisconsin Catholics.[661]

Leo T. Crowley [Horton Roe. *History of the Knights of Columbus in Wisconsin,* Knights of Columbus, 1952, p. 264]

Archbishop Stritch was also an enthusiast for Roosevelt, at least at first. As a Southerner and a Democrat by birth, he disliked the Republican party that had socially and economically exploited the South after the Civil War. As a Catholic, he detested the uncritical embrace of laissez-faire capitalism embraced by the pro-business Republicans during the 1920s. Although generally circumspect about public officials, he once condemned former President Harding as having a "bungalow mind," and he heaped equal scorn on his successor Coolidge.[662] Although he prohibited priests from speaking from the pulpit on any economic issue, Stritch himself regularly lambasted the greed of businessmen who he believed caused the Great Depression.[663] He approved of such Roosevelt programs at the National Industrial Recovery Act which sought to bring harmony to labor and capital by cooperative action. Both archdiocesan newspapers proudly carried the Blue Eagle of the National Recovery Administration (NRA.) and proclaimed "We Do Our Part."[664] He endorsed programs of public relief that relieved the plight of the unemployed. "The Archbishop is in close contact with the unemployed in Milwaukee and throughout southern Wisconsin," he wrote in a proposal to the Federal Emergency Relief Administration in 1933. "He sees the need for employment and the necessity of public welfare ...."[665] Stritch also wrote to a Kenosha pastor, praising "the intelligent and courageous leadership of the president."[666]

In 1933, Stritch submitted a proposal to the Federal Emergency Relief Administration (FERA). He proposed to turn over portions of Catholic schools rent free to unemployed public school teachers who could conduct non-sectarian instruction in fields such as home arts, drama and speech, English, math and reading.[667] With the endorsement of Governor Albert G. Schmedeman, Katherine Williams of the MACCW and Voyta Wrabetz, head of the State Industrial Commission, Stritch took the proposal to Washington. However, opposition to the plan came from Milwaukee Vocational School Superintendent Robert Cooley, who suggested that if any education programs were to be held they ought to be in his underused building downtown. To Stritch's disappointment officials in Washington excluded unemployed public school teachers from the constituencies to be covered under the FERA program.[668]

Stritch assigned priests to New Deal agencies. Haas was his most famous appointment. But he also permitted ministry to Civilian Conservation Corps camps in the Milwaukee archdiocesan boundaries (Camp Estabrook, Milwaukee, Camp Mt. Horeb, Mt. Horeb, Camp Madison, Madison, Camp Devil's Lake, Baraboo, Camp Whitnall Park, and Hales Corners). The one priest he did send to serve in the camps in the diocese of Superior, Giles Zynda, was compelled to resign when his superior officer found him frequenting taverns and dances and not performing religious services.[669]

But like his fellow southern Democrats, Stritch soured on Roosevelt as time went on. Like many Southerners and Catholics who embraced the principle of subsidiarity, Stritch was distrustful of too much governmental centralization. He complained to the National Catholic Welfare Conference's executive secretary, Monsignor Michael Ready, about the requirements of the Social Security Act passed in 1935. Specifically he worried about what provisions would be binding on the Church and lamented the invasion of privacy suggested by the provision of a social security number and information about people's incomes. "The Washington Bureaus are firm in making each institution give rather definite information regarding its finances and holdings. Personally, I do not like this massing in the public archives of all this information." He concluded, "Before complying with this ruling, I intend to carry on further negotiations. Of course, I may be forced to comply, but I shall not do so until forced."[670] His disillusionment with FDR even extended to his service on the Administrative Board of the NCWC where he took a low profile in official dealings with the Roosevelt White House. Stritch refused the pleas of prominent Catholic layman and personal friend, Leo T. Crowley, the head of the Federal Deposit Insurance Corporation, who pressed Stritch to lobby Senator F. Ryan Duffy to support the president's plan for court reorganization.[671]

Senator F. Ryan Duffy
[*Wisconsin Blue Book,* WI Legislative Reference Library, 1933]

Stritch's feelings toward the president were most evident in the anti-Roosevelt tone of the diocesan newspaper. After the merger of the *Herald* and the *Citizen* in 1935, the paper occasionally criticized Roosevelt's policies and appointees. For example in 1937 when FDR attempted to "pack" the Supreme Court, the paper wrote, "President Roosevelt's well known stamp-collecting hobby has not suffered since he entered the White House. He has added to his collection a rubber stamp Congress and now he is out to get a rubber stamp Supreme Court."[672]

The paper also regularly endorsed the work and ideas of Father Charles Coughlin. By the time Stritch came to Milwaukee, Coughlin was a well-known radio personality whose Sunday broadcast reached millions, Catholic and non-Catholic. Coughlin had begun as an ardent Roosevelt supporter. ("Roosevelt or Ruin" he bellowed from his radio perch during the 1932 campaign. He later proclaimed that the "New Deal was Christ's Deal.") Coughlin believed he had played an important role in electing FDR, and was eager to push forward schemes to lift America out of the Depression. His chief goal was monetary inflation through the additional coinage of silver.[673]

[AAM]

Roosevelt kept the popular radio priest at arm's length, and eventually Coughlin broke with the president he had "elected," claiming that the New Deal had not gone far enough. His popularity made him a source of worry to the president, who faced other challenges from his political left. These fears were amplified when Coughlin put his national publications and the resources of his National Union for Social Justice behind an effort to run a third party candidate to oppose Roosevelt in 1936. FDR's political advisors scanned far and wide for a Catholic priest or bishop of sufficient reputation to rebut Coughlin's bitter attacks, and thereby maintain the Catholic vote for the Democratic party. Ultimately, Monsignor John A. Ryan of the Social Action Department of the National Catholic Welfare Conference stepped forward to confront the "Radio Priest" in a broadcast, paid for by the Democratic National Committee. In retaliation Coughlin sarcastically dubbed Ryan "the Right Reverend New Dealer."[674] Roosevelt kept Ryan in public view, and Milwaukee's own Francis Haas's visibility in the administration was also intended in part to deflect criticism of Roosevelt as anti-Catholic.

Milwaukee's response to Coughlin is difficult to judge. Many Catholics listened avidly to his Sunday afternoon broadcast over radio station WTMJ. In April 1936, the *Catholic Herald Citizen* urged Milwaukeeans to subscribe to Coughlin's hard-hitting periodical *Social Justice*. The defeat of Coughlin's candidates in the 1936 election took him off the air for a time, but by 1937 he was back—to the plaudits of the *Catholic Herald Citizen.*[675] Whatever criticism there was of the radio priest was muted. Even the normally outspoken Aloysius Muench only gently poked at Coughlin's monetary inflation schemes in a lecture given to the St. Rose Home and School Association. "Despite the splendid objectives of Father Coughlin to lend aid to the reconstruction of society," he declared, "his program of money and banking is unsound. He advocates cheap money by a return to bi-metallism. Everyone knows … that wherever bi-metallism has been tried—even in our own country—it has proven a colossal failure."[676]

It is probably more the result of his chronic indecisiveness that Stritch did not insist on a more critical line toward Coughlin in his archdiocesan paper. (His successor Kiley had no qualms about calling in general editor Father Franklyn Kennedy and banning certain articles or ideas from the paper.) Stritch did not like Coughlin for a variety of reasons, but perhaps most importantly because he tread on his own "sacred authority" by purporting to speak for the entire Catholic Church. Commenting on Ryan's 1936 address attacking Coughlin, Stritch noted to Father John Burke of the NCWC: "It would have been so much better had he [Ryan] given his talk under other auspices [than the Democratic National Committee], but I think the talk did serve to bring out in the clear that Father Coughlin does not voice the teaching of catholic [*sic*] economics, and that his interpretation of the Encyclicals is not above criticism."[677]

Gradually, however, as Coughlin became more and more intemperate in his hatred for Roosevelt, Stritch went public with his misgivings. In his address to the Catholic Social Action Conference of 1938, Stritch indirectly lambasted Coughlin, whom he believed had turned away from the proper interpretation of Catholic social teaching. Stritch criticized "the panderers of social nostrums. It is not that they reject the pharmacon of the Church but that they know nothing of it."[678]

Rabbi Joseph Baron [Milwaukee Jewish Historical Society]

Stritch became even more blunt in 1939 when the radio priest became openly anti-Semitic. Stritch then publicly identified himself with a program for good will and civic virtue sponsored by the National Catholic Welfare Conference, aimed at blunting some of Coughlin's intemperate rhetoric. In May Rabbi Joseph Baron of Milwaukee, who had publicly criticized Coughlin, wrote to Stritch, expressing "my own appreciation, and that of many Jews with whom I have spoken, of the splendid spirit of that statement .... It is good to have an authoritative spokesmen of Christendom repeat the words of Pope Pius XI, 'It is not possible for Christians to take part in anti-Semitism.'"[679] Stritch thanked Baron and wrote, "In these times when nefarious propaganda is bringing untold sufferings ... it is highly important that sane men keep cool heads. If there are certain individuals who, to gain and hold a popular audience, degrade themselves, and abuse the trust reposed in them by misquoting, half-quoting and actually insinuating untruths, sane men, who know full well that in the end truth does conquer, must guide public opinions in safe channels." This message was communicated by Baron to Rabbi David de Sola Pool, president of the Synagogue Council of America. It was likewise disseminated by the National Catholic Press bureau.[680]

Stritch and the Coming of War

Adolf Hitler's accession to power in January 1933 and his consolidation of dictatorial powers the next year resulted in repeated church/state clashes. Not only did the *Catholic Herald* openly criticize the Nazi regime, but it also began warning Catholics about the plight of the Jews in Germany.[681] German persecution of Jews, including those who had converted to Christianity, led to a flood of Catholic refugees who fled to Holland and Switzerland. When this human tide overwhelmed local charities, German and Dutch Catholic bishops implored their American counterparts for financial assistance and help in relocating hundreds of displaced clergy and religious. At the November 1936 meeting of the administrative board of the National Catholic Welfare Conference, Stritch was appointed to a committee chaired by New Orleans Archbishop Joseph Rummell to raise $150,000 to aid the Dutch hierarchy.

The work of the committee put Stritch in the position of hearing more about Nazi atrocities against the Jews and against the Catholic Church than average Americans. Regular reports from refugee bishops and nuns told tragic stories about conditions in Germany.[682] Stritch bided his time, but when his neighbor in Chicago, Cardinal Mundelein, created international news in 1937 by deriding Hitler as an "Austrian paperhanger and a poor one at that," Stritch took courage. In 1938 the *Catholic Herald* criticized the famous *Anschluss* plebiscite, which added Austria to the German Reich. "Austria ... for centuries a thoroughly Catholic state, has fallen in the hands of the Nazis and like the rest of Germany will be subject to their paganistic ideology."[683] Stritch himself had noted with sadness the affirmation Cardinal Theodore Innitizer of Vienna had given the Nazi takeover, writing to Archbishop Rummel, "I had hoped for something more from Cardinal Innitizer who is a brilliant man and my friend. Maybe he was too confident, but then one must make every sacrifice for religion." Holding out hope that Hitler might be affected by Catholic pressure to mitigate some of his more offensive actions, Stritch wrote, "I am praying that when he goes to Rome 'Der Fuerher' will kneel at the feet of our Holy Father and listen to wisdom."[684]

Austria was not the last straw, however; Czechoslovakia was. After the summit at Munich in September 1938 where the British and French acceded to Hitler's demands for the Sudetenland in exchange for "peace in our time," Stritch lent his name to a public statement that decried the "indirect means" by which the Nazis were attempting to abolish Catholicism.[685] After reports of the brutal *kristallnacht* attacks on Jewish merchants and residences in November 1938, Stritch finally raised his voice against Nazi leaders on the occasion of the 50th anniversary of Milwaukee's German St. Boniface Church. In an address broadcast over the radio on the parishes' regular weekly hookup, Stritch turned his rhetorical guns on the Nazis: "This paganism," he said, "… has the same concept of life found in the senseless leaders of Nazi Germany … in Germany men are persecuted because of their religion, thrown into concentration camps for daring to follow their own consciences." Referring specifically to the *kristallnacht* brutalities that resulted in the imprisonment of 20,000 German Jews, he declared, "We see a spectacle that makes our hearts bleed, the inhuman persecution of the Jewish people there. All the things Christianity has stood for these leaders have cast to the winds."[686]

Yet even as Stritch grew more belligerent toward the Nazis and as rumbles from Asia brought stories of Japanese persecution of Catholic missionaries in China (including the members of several religious orders based in Milwaukee), Stritch had ambivalent feelings about American intervention. Like most bishops of Irish extraction he was wary of an American intervention that might aid Britain and her colonial empire.[687] He was not alone. There were others in the American Catholic community who shared Stritch's misgivings, and a vocal and active anti-war movement that watched the Roosevelt administration carefully. A series of neutrality laws had been passed in 1937, 1938, and 1939 to limit the power of the president to make war. However, as time went on, President Roosevelt managed to bring about alterations that allowed him to assist American allies. Many worried that FDR was leading America into war with these changes. In September of 1939 the local papers printed a rumor that Stritch was against a "cash and carry" revision of the neutrality laws that was sought by President Roosevelt. Although this probably reflected Stritch's true feelings, he was embarrassed by the publicity. Moreover he did not want his name associated with more militant Roosevelt critics, like Archbishop Francis J. L. Beckmann in nearby Dubuque, Iowa who openly sided with isolationist pressure groups. Stritch issued a public disclaimer on the front page of the *Herald Citizen:* "The archbishop has not approved, authorized or in any way encouraged any effort to influence the Congress of the United States in its action on neutrality legislation. He holds fast to his policy of abstaining wholly from political action."[688] But Stritch's efforts to remain unengaged on the neutrality issue were certainly not reflected in the editorial policy of the *Herald Citizen,* which was under his direct control.

In fact, with Stritch's tacit endorsement, the official Catholic newspaper maintained a consistently isolationist position. The *Herald Citizen* had strongly supported the cause of the pro-Franco, German-backed Falangists in the bloody Spanish Civil War of 1936-37. Leftist attacks on convents, priests and churches further intensified American Catholic support for Franco and his forces. To the consternation of Catholics, U. S. policy inclined more toward the leftists—a factor that alienated some from Roosevelt. The paper had taken the lead in condemning most of Wisconsin's congressional delegation for expressing sympathy for the leftist cause in Spain.[689] When supporters of the leftists in Spain pushed to modify neutrality laws to permit some U.S. aid to the anti-Franco forces, the *Catholic Herald Citizen* carped, "Busy-bodies—the majority of them pink-hued or gullible—are intent on changing the present neutrality policy of the United States ... with the possible result of embroiling the United States in the Spanish conflict." The paper contained a clip-out form letter protesting the change, and urged readers to send it to their representatives in Washington.[690] The paper also lobbied vigorously against the Burke-Wadsworth conscription bill, which narrowly passed Congress in September 1940.[691]

Peace Rally at Marquette Stadium [AAM]

Adding his voice to the opponents of conscription was the redoutable Father Peter Dietz. From his pulpit in Whitefish Bay, he thundered denunciations of the legislation, declaring, "there is no moral justification for this country getting into the European war."[692] This was not the first time Dietz had raised a controversial message about war-related activities. In 1933 he publicly praised Hitler for controlling the press, the theater and the taverns in Germany. He went on record extolling Francisco Franco as a "defender of Christianity" and when Archbishop Stritch was indirectly criticizing Coughlin, Dietz blasted Milwaukee Rabbi Joseph Baron for attacking the radio priest.[693]

As 1939 dawned, Stritch still hoped that the disintegrating European situation would not lead to war. Indeed, he planned to visit

Europe that summer. However, he would never make the trip. On September 1, 1939, Hitler's Panzer divisions roared into Poland from the west and the Soviet army invaded from the east. As Britain and France honored their treaty commitments to protect Polish freedom, war declarations plunged Europe into conflict. In Asia, war had already begun in 1931 when Japan marched into the Chinese province of Manchuria and later invaded Chinese coastal cities. Shortly after the invasion of Poland, Stritch led 60,000 Milwaukeeans gathered at Marquette Stadium in a candlelight vigil for peace.[694]

Even after the fall of France and the Battle of Britain, the Catholic press in Milwaukee still bitterly criticized those who urged American involvement in the conflict. The *Catholic Herald Citizen* wrote, "It's too bad that we can't hang a quarantine sign around the necks of those American citizens who are clamoring for our entrance into the war. The sign should read 'Traitor.' Then the rest of us could shun these war fanatics as they deserve to be shunned."[695] Other voices, however, were heard in the increasingly intense debate among Wisconsin Catholics. In speaking to 3,200 no doubt nervous students at the 1940 fall convocation, Marquette University President Father Raphael C. McCarthy urged them to pray for peace. "But we must recognize the possibility of our being involved in it [the war] and prepare accordingly ..." he said. "We must abjure the fatal and futile complacency that betrayed France and Britain, so that they were not ready when the supreme test came."[696]

The onset of war affected Milwaukee deeply. The battle zones of central Europe, especially in Poland, left many Milwaukee Catholics anxious about the fate of relatives and friends in their former homelands. "The report of the persecution of the Church in Poland by the Nazis makes as gruesome and horrifying reading as the Red attack on the Church in Spain," wrote Franklyn Kennedy for the *Herald Citizen*.[697] In June 1940, the first of many collections for the relief of Polish Catholics was taken up by local Polish groups with Stritch's enthusiastic endorsement.[698] Subsequent collections for Polish relief raised thousands of dollars from sympathetic Milwaukeeans of all nationalities, but especially from the strong league of Polish parishes in Milwaukee and other archdiocesan cities. Judge F. X. Swietlik, a former law school dean at Marquette, was a familiar figure in organizing events and publicity for Polish relief and representing Milwaukee's efforts on the national level.

In October 1939 Cardinal George Mundelein died in his sleep. The large Chicago Archdiocese, raised to a new height of prominence by Mundelein's leadership, needed someone now to pay off the huge debts the cardinal had left behind, and to manage the affairs of the very large diocese. In early 1940 the news arrived that Stritch was to be transferred—the first time a Milwaukee bishop would leave office in something other than a coffin. Milwaukee was *sede vacante* until January 1940, when the bishop of Trenton, the biblically-named Moses Elias Kiley, was chosen to succeed Stritch.

Notes

1 "Archbishop Katzer Is Dead," Pope Leo XIII Passes Away," *Catholic Citizen*, 25 July 1903; "Cardinal Sarto Elected Pope," *Catholic Citizen*, 8 August 1903.

2 Peter Abbelen to Diomede Falconio, August 6, 1903, #4315, Del Ap. USA, IV, Archivio Segreto Vaticano (hereafter ASV).

3 James Keogh to Falconio, August 10, 1903, #4315, Del. Ap. USA, IV, ASV.

4 Ryan's and Keogh's accusations were included in a letter from Father Joseph LaBoule. Laboule to Falconio, October 12, 1903, #4315, Del. Ap. USA, IV, ASV.

5 Thomas Fagan to Falconio, August 7, 1903, Del Ap. USA, IV, ASV.

6 Peter Abbelen to Falconio, August 6, 1903, Del. Ap. USA, IV, ASV.

7 Joseph S. LaBoule to Falconio, October 12, 1903, Del. Ap. USA, IV, ASV.

8 James Edward Quigley to Falconio, August 31, 1903; Archbishop James A. Ryan of Philadelphia also supported the Messmer nomination, Ryan to Falconio, August 16, 1903. Most important, Gibbons in Baltimore, America's "ranking" prelate, endorsed Messmer as well, Gibbons to Falconio, September 26, 1903, Del Ap. USA, IV, ASV.

9 Eis to Falconio, September 18, 1903, Del. Ap. USA, IV, ASV.

10 John Ireland to Falconio, August 16, 1903, Del. Ap. USA, IV, ASV.

11 "Report of Bishop Messmer Selection," *Catholic Citizen*, 28 November 1903.

12 Steven M. Avella, "The Era of Sebastian G. Messmer," *Salesianum* 83 (Spring/Summer 1988): pp. 8-13; "Sebastian G. Messmer and the Americanization of Milwaukee Catholicism," *U.S. Catholic Historian* 12 (Summer 1994): pp. 87-107; Benjamin Blied, *Three Archbishops of Milwaukee* (Milwaukee, 1955), pp. 82-148.

13 Otto Zardetti was a native of Rohrsbach, St. Gall and was educated at Innsbruck. Ordained a year before Messmer, he served as a seminary instructor in St. Gall and then came to America in 1881 where he served as an instructor in dogma on the faculty of St. Francis Seminary until 1886. While he was on the seminary staff he propagated a special devotion to the Holy Spirit that won wide acceptance and formed a student confraternity that lasted until 1921. In 1886 he became the vicar apostolic of northern Minnesota and in 1889 was consecrated the first bishop of St. Cloud, Minnesota. He remained in America until 1894 when he became the archbishop of Bucharest. That appointment lasted only a year and he ended his days in Rome in 1902. See Benjamin Blied, "The Most Rev. Otto Zardetti, D.D., 1847-1902," *Salesianum* 42 (January 1947): pp. 54-62; see also Joseph Chinnici, *Devotion to the Holy Spirit in American Catholicism* (New York: Paulist Press, 1985), pp. 64-72.

14 Quoted in Nicholas Mass, "Alumni Notes and Clerical Changes," *Salesianum* 24 (January 1929): pp. 60-64.

15 "Archp. Messmer Discusses Several Topics Interestingly," *Catholic Citizen*, 30 April 1904.

16 Sebastian G. Messmer, et al. (eds.) *The Works of the Right Reverend John England* 7 vols. (Cleveland: Arthur H. Clark, 1908).

17 S.G. Messmer, "Chips for a Kundig Block: Biographic Sketch by B. I. Durward," *Salesianum 13* (January 1918): pp. 1-26; "The Ohio Mission," *Salesianum* 13 (April 1918): pp. 1-17; "Chips for a Kundig Block: The Detroit Mission," *Salesianum* 13 (July 1918): pp. 1-27; "Chips for a Kundig Block: Stray Pieces from Detroit and Milwaukee," *Salesianum* 14 (October 1918): pp. 1-16; "Chips for a Kundig Block: Stray Chips from Wisconsin," *Salesianum* 14 (January 1919): pp. 1-11; "Chips for a Kundig Block: The Wisconsin Mission," *Salesianum* 14 (April 1919): pp. 1-23; "Chips for a Kundig Block: The Wisconsin Mission," *Salesianum* 14 (July 1919): pp. 1-28; "Chips for a Kundig Block," *Salesianum* 15 (October 1919): pp. 1-14.

18 S. G. Messmer, "The Reverend Florimond Joseph Bonduel, Wisconsin Pioneer Missionary," *Salesianum* 19 (April 1924): pp. 1-16; "Detroit Mission," *Salesianum* 19 (July 1924): pp. 1-21; "Mackinac Mission," *Salesianum* 19 (October 1924): pp. 1-26; "The Green Bay Mission," *Salesianum* 20 (January 1925): pp. 1-24.

19 C. Joseph Nuesse, *The Catholic University of America: A Centennial History* (Washington, D.C.:

Catholic University of America Press, 1999), pp. 67-80.

[20] Ludwig, pp. 491-493.

[21] Colman Barry, *The Catholic Church and German Americans*, p. 125.

[22] Quoted in Barry, p. 126.

[23] Ibid.

[24] Barry, p. 127.

[25] "Has Appealed to Rome," *Catholic Citizen*. 26 December 1891.

[26] "Father Messmer's Declination Refused," *Catholic Citizen*, 6 February 1892.

[27] "Both Bishops Named," *Catholic Citizen*, 19 December 1891; "Bishop of Green Bay," *Catholic Citizen*, 26 March 1892; "Rt. Rev. Bishop Messmer," *Catholic Citizen*, 2 April 1892.

[28] Blied, *Three Archbishops*, p. 99.

[29] This was related to the author by Rev. Raymond Fetterer, longtime seminary librarian who worked closely with Breig.

[30] Thomas Stritch, *The Catholic Church in Tennessee: The Sesquicentennial Story* (Nashville: The Catholic Center, 1987), pp. 232-236; Steven M. Avella, "Stritch: The Milwaukee Years," *Milwaukee History* 13 (Autumn 1990): pp. 70-91; Marie Cecilie Buehrle, *The Cardinal Stritch Story* (Milwaukee: Bruce Publishing Company, 1959).

[31] Interview with Msgr. James Hardiman, Oak Law, Illinois, March 1986; Interview with Most Reverend Cletus F. O'Donnell, Madison, Wisconsin, May 1983.

[32] Stritch, pp. 226-230.

[33] P. J. Kenedy, *Official Catholic Directory*, 1922.

[34] Lawrence A. Mossing, S.T.D., *Young Shepherd in the Diocese of Toledo: A History of Most Reverend Samuel A. Stritch, D.D., Second Bishop of Toledo* (Toledo: Diocese of Toledo, 1988).

[35] For this insight into Stritch's spending habits see the author's *This Confident Church: Catholic Leadership and Life in Chicago, 1940-1965* (Notre Dame: University of Notre Dame Press, 1993), p. 18.

[36] "Bishop of Toledo Succeeds Archbishop Messmer," *Catholic Citizen*, 4 September 1930; Charles T. Lucey, "Milwaukee's New Archbishop," *Catholic Citizen*, 6 November 1930.

[37] Avella, *This Confident Church*, pp. 28-29, 44.

[38] Edward Kantowicz, *Corporation Sole: Cardinal Mundelein and Chicago Catholicism* (Notre Dame: University of Notre Dame Press, 1981), pp. 217-236.

[39] Harold Ickes, *The Lowering Clouds: The Secret Diary of Harold Ickes*, Vol. 3 (New York: Simon and Schuster, 1955), p. 110.

[40] "The New Decree," *Catholic Citizen*, 11 July 1908.

[41] "A Polyglot Church," *Catholic Citizen*, 2 March 1907.

[42] Keogh to Falconio, August 10, 1903, Del. Ap. USA, IV, ASV.

[43] Abbelen to Falconio, August 6, 1913, #4315, Del. Ap. USA, IV, ASV.

[44] Philip Gleason, *The Conservative Reformers: German American Catholics and the Social Order* (Notre Dame: University of Notre Dame Press, 1968), p. 49. Eis, a graduate of St. Francis Seminary, was questioned by local priests when he attended feast day celebrations at the Salesianum. In reply he claimed the edict was misunderstood. "The order was not directed against the speaking of Polish or any other foreign language in churches, but was rather intended for the children, particularly American born children. My idea was that the coming generation of Americans should be aided in every possible way to acquire the fluent use of their own language, and with this end in view my order was that the instruction be given at two low masses each month .... I did not take away from the Polish or other foreign congregation the use of their beloved mother tongues ...." "Bishop Eis on His Edict," *Catholic Citizen*, 2 February 1901.

[45] "Is Nothing New," *Catholic Citizen*, 5 June 1897.

[46] Alfred Juan Ede, *The Lay Crusade for a Christian America: A Study of the American Federation of Catholic Societies, 1900-1919* (New York: Garland Press, 1988), see also Gleason, pp. 60-66.

[47] Quoted in Gleason, *The Conservative Reformers*, p. 61.

[48] Joseph S. LaBoule to Falconio, October 12, 1903, Del. Ap. USA, IV, ASV.

[49] Sebastian G. Messmer, "The Principle of the Federation," *Salesianum 8* (October 1912): pp. 34-43. Messmer also drew inspiration from the encyclical *Graves de Commune* of Pope Leo XIII (1901) which

urged unity among Catholic groups for the sake of pursuing the common good.

[50] Sebastian G. Messmer to Sebastiano Martinelli, January 12, 1897, #3964, Del. Ap. IV, USA, ASV.

[51] Q. Zielinski to Martinelli, November 29, 1897, Del. Ap. USA, IV, ASV. Zielinski's viewpoint may have been somewhat skewed since he was one of the participants in the Stevens Point controversies and claimed that his back salary had been denied him.

[52] William M. Hogue, "The Episcopal Church and Archbishop Villatte," *Historical Magazine of the Protestant Episcopal Church* 34 (1965): pp. 35-55.

[53] "To Call Diocesan Synod," *Catholic Citizen*, 19 March 1904.

[54] "A Diocesan Seal," *Catholic Citizen*, 16 April 1904.

[55] "Must Teach English," *Catholic Citizen*, 10 September 1904.

[56] "A Polish Bishop," *Catholic Citizen*, 16 January 1904.

[57] Kuzniewski, *Faith and Fatherland,* p. 61.

[58] Messmer to Falconio, January 22, 1904, Del. Ap. USA, IV, ASV.

[59] Messmer to Falconio, January 22, 1904, Del. Ap. USA, IV, ASV.

[60] Quoted in Kuzniewski diss., p. 242.

[61] "A Polish Bishop," *Catholic Citizen*, 16 January 1904.

[62] Messmer to Falconio, November 12, 1904, #7455, Del. Ap. USA, II, ASV.

[63] Quoted in Kuzniewski, *Faith and Fatherland*, p. 59.

[64] "Diocese of Superior," *Catholic Citizen*, 22 April 1905. Schinner is mentioned first in the list in a news story in the *Citizen* on 27 September 1905.

[65] Quoted in Kuzniewski, *Faith and Fatherland*, p. 60.

[66] Kuzniewski, *Faith and Fatherland*, pp. 63-64.

[67] Ibid., pp. 64-65.

[68] Messmer to "Rev. and Dear Sir," February 8, 1906, Messmer Papers, AAM.

[69] *Handbook for Catholic Parishioners*, Archdiocese of Milwaukee, 1907, pp. 62-63.

[70] Kruszka to Falconio, September 6, 1907, #15695, Del. Ap. USA II, ASV.

[71] Messmer to Falconio, November 22, 1907, #16245-e, Del. Ap. USA II, ASV.

[72] Falconio to Messmer, January 15, 1908, 16811-c, Del. Ap. USA II, ASV.

[73] Messmer to Falconio, January 22, 1908, 16826-c, Del. Ap. USA II, ASV.

[74] Michael Kruszka to Falconio, February 5, 1908, #17003, Del Ap. USA, II, ASV.

[75] Wenceslaus Kruszka to Falconio, July 15, 1908, #18469-c, Del. Ap. USA II, ASV.

[76] "Archbishop Presented with $6,000," "Problem of St. Josaphat's Debt," *Catholic Citizen*, 25 April 1908.

[77] "To Arrange for St. Josaphat's," *Catholic Citizen*, 24 June 1909. Immediately on hearing of this "arrangement" one of the basilica's creditors, the Windsor Trust Company of New York, sued the congregation of St. Josaphat in federal court to retrieve $25,000 it had borrowed from the Fidelity Funding Company of New York in an effort to refinance its debt in 1907. "St. Josaphat's Sued," *Catholic Citizen*, 31 July 1909; "St. Josaphat's Transferred," *Catholic Citizen,* 9 January 1910.

[78] "St. Josaphat's Paying 75 Percent," *Catholic Citizen*, 22 January 1910; "Father Fudzinski Explains," *Catholic Citizen*, 29 January 1910. A new incorporation for the parish filed in Madison placed the property under the ownership of the Franciscan Conventual Friars. "St. Josaphat's Transferred," *Catholic Citizen*, 19 March 1910.

[79] "St. Josaphat's Foreclosure Prevented,"*Catholic Citizen*, 7 May 1910.

[80] The record of debt reduction is contained in the corporate minutes of the parish, St. Josaphat Parish Archives, Milwaukee.

[81] "Pay St. Josaphat's Creditors," *Catholic Citizen*, 4 June 1910; "Will Pay $70,000 of Debt," *Catholic Citizen*, 19 November 1910; "St. Josaphat's Parish Ends Holy Year by Wiping Out Last of Debt," *Catholic Herald*, 7 January 1926.

[82] Sebastian Messmer to "Dearly Beloved," November 8, 1909 (General Pastoral Letter) Messmer Papers, AAM.

[83] Messmer to "Rev. Dear Sir," April 28, 1911, Messmer Papers, AAM.

[84] Assessment Committee: H. Gulski, H. F. Fairbanks, D. F. Thill, W. G. Miller, P. H. Durnin, B.G. Traudt, W. Haberstock, J. H. Szukalski, B. E. Goral, P. B. Knox, and J. B. Pierron. To "Rev. Dear Father," June 10, 1911, Messmer Papers, AAM.

[85] Wenceslaus Kruszka to Falconio, April 27, 1908, #17642 Del Ap. USA II, ASV.

[86] "Bishop Rhode Coming," *Catholic Citizen*, 3 April 1909.

[87] In this scathing letter to Falconio, Michael Kruszka accused the pastor of his own parish, Father Bronislaw Celichowski, of carrying on sexual liaisons with women in Chicago and in his own parish. Goral he accused of being "very closely connected with a divorced woman, joy-riding in automobiles, sometimes at night with women, is his favorite past time." Michael Kruszka to Falconio, April 23, 1910, 5098-d, Del. Ap. USA II, ASV.

[88] Ireland to Messmer, April 11, 1908, Messmer Papers, AAM.

[89] M. M. Gerend, "Memories of By-Gone Days," *Salesianum* 7 (October 1911): pp. 1-8. Gerend's jocund recollections were charitable to the maximum. Others did not have such pleasant memories of the young Koudelka. One was William G. Miller, a Wisconsin native who was a longtime pastor of St. Joseph's parish in Waukesha. When Messmer queried him as a consultor about appointing Koudelka to the post of auxiliary bishop, he recalled "I only know the present Bishop Kaudelka [*sic*] as a theological student at the Seminary, I think just after his arrival from Bohemia. Of course I am willing to concede that since that time he may have broadened out considerably ... but he had then a disability in the way of stammering that, with another disagreeable snarling twang, made his conversation unpleasant ... it was pretty difficult to know what particular language he was speaking." Miller reiterated that over the years these traits "may have toned down," but if not, "I could not see for the life of me how he ever could have been selected as being fit episcopal timber." William Miller to Messmer, June 17, 1911, Messmer Papers, AAM.

[90] Koudelka's Cleveland career is summarized in Michael J. Hynes, *History of the Diocese of Cleveland: Origin and Growth (1847-1952)* (Cleveland: Diocese of Cleveland, 1953), pp. 244-246.

[91] Thomas C. O'Reilly to Bonaventure Cerretti, December 13, 1910, Del. Ap. USA, IV, ASV. Cerretti was holding the post between the departure of Diomede Falconio and the advent of Giovanni Bonzano.

[92] Stritch, pp. 226-230.

[93] The details of this embarrassing incident and Koudelka's refutation of Farrelly's accusations of disloyalty are found in a letter Koudelka sent to Farrelly on October 7, 1910, Del. Ap. USA, II, ASV, a copy of which is in the Apostolic Delegation files under "Koudelka."

[94] Koudelka first visited Milwaukee in August 1909 when he visited St. John Nepomuc Church. "Bohemian Bishop Here," *Catholic Citizen,* 14 August 1909. He returned again in October to confirm, "Bohemian Bishop Here," *Catholic Citizen*, 16 October 1909; Koudelka was featured on the front page in the *Catholic Citizen's* "Who's Who Among American Catholics Series," which graced every front page for many issues. See "Rt. Rev. J. M. Koudelka," *Catholic Citizen*, 28 May 1910; "Bishop Koudelka Here Again," *Catholic Citizen* 18 June 1910, had him confirming in Racine, Auburn, West Bend, Beloit, Barton and Campbellsport

[95] Koudelka to Farrelly, October 7, 1910, Del. Ap. USA II, ASV. Copy in Apostolic Delegation files.

[96] "An Auxiliary Bishop for Milwaukee," *Catholic Citizen*, 12 February 1910.

[97] William G. Miller to Messmer, June 17, 1911, Messmer Papers, AAM.

[98] Messmer to Falconio, July 25, 1911, 1600-d, Del. Ap. USA II, ASV.

[99] Not everyone was unhappy with the Koudelka appointment. At his alma mater, St. Francis Seminary, the quarterly *Salesianum* ran a warm welcome to their returning distinguished alumnus, "Bishop Koudelka," *Salesianum* 7 (October 1911): pp. 34-36.

[100] "Pope Names Bohemian to Aid Messmer," *Milwaukee Daily News,* 6 September 1911; "Milwaukee's New Auxiliary Bishop," *Catholic Citizen* 9 September 1911.

[101] Quoted in Kuzniewski, *Faith and Fatherland*, p. 85.

[102] Ibid.

[103] Ibid, p. 86.

[104] "To Our Beloved Brethren of the Clergy and the Laity," February 1, 1912, copy in Messmer papers, AAM.

[105] Kuzniewksi, *Faith and Fatherland*, pp. 111-114.

[106] "Ss. Peter and Paul's New School," *Catholic Citizen,* 23 March 1912; "Ss. Peter and Paul's New School," *Catholic Citizen*, 20 April 1912.

[107] Just a sample of Koudelka's wanderings during the years 1912-1913. In February 1912 he was in Chicago delivering a mission at St. Michael's Church; in June he traveled to North Dakota to speak to Russian-Bohemians and at the end of the month took an ocean liner to Europe to attend a Eucharistic Congress. In February 1913, he was off to New Jersey for a mission and March found him in Uniontown, Pennsylvania. "Ss. Peter and Paul's Church," *Catholic Citizen,* 10 February 1912; "Bishop Koudelka's Engagements," *Catholic Citizen*, 16 June 1912; "In Catholic Circles," *Catholic Citizen*, 15 February 1913; "Is Bishop Five Years," *Catholic Citizen*, 1 March 1913.

[108] Messmer's role in ejecting Koudelka from Milwaukee to Superior was revealed in an exchange of letters with the new apostolic delegate, Giovanni Bonzano over Koudelka's mishaps in Superior. Bonzano wrote in reply to Messmer's forwarding of complaints about his former auxiliary to the Apostolic Delegation. "The appointment of Bishop Koudelka to Superior was made principally to satisfy your desire to be freed of him." Bonzano to Messmer, December 14, 1915, 123-e, Del. Ap. IV, ASV.

[109] The Holy See imposed this on Koudelka as soon as he got to Superior. Koudelka attempted to seek some modification of the prohibition–asking that he be allowed to give missions to Bohemians during the winter months. Koudelka to Bonzano, November 9, 1913, Del. Ap. USA IV, ASV. When the Consistorial Congregation forbade this, Koudelka turned down the requests by informing the petitioner that Rome had insisted on this. Embarrassed by this, Apostolic Delegate Bonzano insisted that Koudelka make no allusion to the prohibition of the Holy See. "To make known to the public this disposition of the Holy See does not seem to me to be either prudent or becoming. Hence in the future I think it would be better for you to give some other reason for declining to accept the invitations to give missions ... and not to mention the Sacred Congregation." Bonzano to Koudelka, November 14, 1913, #147679-d, Del. Ap. USA, IV, ASV.

[110] Messmer to Bonzano, November 19, 1915, 123-3, Del. Ap. USA IV, ASV.

[111] "Bishop Kozlowski," *Salesianum* 9 (January 1914): pp. 1-11; "The Bishop-Auxiliary of Milwaukee," *Catholic Citizen*, 27 June 1914.

[112] Richter to Bonzano, August 4, 1913; Goral to Bonzano, August 6, 1913, Del. Ap. USA IV, ASV.

[113] A. Bienanowski to Bonzano, September 16, 1913, Del. Ap. USA IV, ASV.

[114] Joseph Schrembs to Bonzano, September 26, 1913, Del. Ap. USA IV, ASV.

[115] "Pole is Selected Auxiliary Bishop," *Milwaukee Sentinel*, 14 October 1913.

[116] Bonzano gave the permission to release the news on November 13, 1913, Bonzano to Messmer, November 12, 1913, #14665-d, Del. Ap. USA IV, ASV.

[117] "Consecration of Bishop Kozlowski," *Catholic Citizen*, 17 January 1914.

[118] In effect Messmer gave Kozlowski his own cathedral. He soon set to work to create St. Stanislaus as a center of Polish worship. Early he attempted to organize a boys singing choir that replicated the famous Paulist Choristers begun by Father Francis Finn of Chicago. "Bishop Kozlowksi," *Catholic Citizen*, 7 March 1914.

[119] Joseph W. Wieczerak, "Father Kruszka and Bishop Hodur: A Relational Sketch," *Polish American Studies*, 44 (1987): pp. 42-56.

[120] "Not a National Church," *Catholic Citizen*, 13 November 1897.

[121] "Come Into the Fold," *Catholic Citizen*, 5 February 1898.

[122] "St. Adalbert's Under Interdict," *Catholic Citizen*, 25 January 1913.

[123] Stephen Wlodarski, *The Origin and Growth of the Polish National Church* (Scranton: Polish National Church, 1974), p. 114.

[124] Ladislaus P. Krakowski, "The Right Rev. Edward Kozlowski, D.D.," *Salesianum* 10 (October 1915): pp. 1-6.

[125] "St. Josaphat's Parish Ends Holy Year by Wiping Out Last of Debt," *Catholic Herald*, 7 January 1926.

[126] "Death of Father Felix Baran Mourned by Confreres and People," *Catholic Herald Citizen*, 4 July 1942. There is a street named for Archbishop

Moses E. Kiley and the 16th Street Viaduct is named for Father James Groppi.

[127] "Thousands in Last Tribute to St. Adalbert's Pastor," *Catholic Herald Citizen*, 11 December 1937.

[128] "Father Atkielski Named Archbishop's Secretary; 3 Priests Going to Rome," *Catholic Herald Citizen*, 5 October 1933.

[129] Muench Diary, p. 65.

[130] "Cornerstone Laid Great Crowd Attends Blessing of the Cornerstone of the New Polish Roman Catholic Church," *Kenosha Evening News*, 10 November 1902.

[131] "St. Stanislaus, B.M., Church, Racine, Wisconsin. 1907-1957, Golden Jubilee," parish history file, AAM.

[132] M. Charlene Endecavage, CSSF, *The Chicago Felicians: A History of the Mother of Good Counsel Province of the Felician Sisters* (Chicago: Felician Sisters, 1999), pp. 116-117.

[133] Raymond A. Punda, "History of St. Joseph's Orphanage in Milwaukee," (unpublished M.A. thesis, St. Francis Seminary, 1939).

[134] Endecavage, p. 141.

[135] "St. Joseph Congregation, West Allis, 50th Year Jubilee, 1909-1960," parish history file, AAM.

[136] "St. Stephen Martyr Church, 1907-1982," parish history file, AAM.

[137] "Mass on Seminary Grounds Opens Slovak Archdiocesan Celebration Here July 20," *Catholic Herald*, 19 July 1934.

[138] William George Bruce, "Holy Trinity Parish in Transition," *Catholic Herald*, 17 August 1936.

[139] "Hungarian Catholics' Own Church, St. Emeric's Dedicated Oct. 29, First One in the State of Wisconsin," *Catholic Herald*, 2 November 1933.

[140] "Souvenir Book of the 40th Anniversary of Sacred Heart Croatian Catholic Church and the Dedication of the New Parish School," September 15, 1957, parish history file, AAM.

[141] Francis Garmus to Bernard Traudt, September 22, 1930, Garmus File, AAM.

[142] Garmus to Traudt, October 29, 1930, Garmus File, AAM.

[143] The foregoing story is contained in the author's article, "'For the Welfare of My Italian Children': Samuel Stritch, Angelo Simeoni and Religious Ethnic Conflict in Kenosha, 1924-1934," *Salesianum* 86 (Spring/Summer 1991): pp. 6-17.

[144] Walter Burke to Traudt, July 2, 1921, Holy Rosary File, AAM.

[145] Burke to Traudt, July 21, 1921, Holy Rosary File, AAM.

[146] Traudt to Burke, July 22, 1912, Holy Rosary File, AAM.

[147] Burke to Traudt, August 23, 1921, Holy Rosary File, AAM.

[148] Raffaele Molinaro's role is discussed by John Buenker, "George Molinaro: A Labor-Ethnic Politician," in Nicholas C. Burckel and John Neuenschwander (eds.) *Kenosha Retrospective* (Kenosha: Kenosha County Bicentennial Commission, 1981), pp. 244-245; Buenker also discusses the upward mobility of Kenosha's Italians in "Immigration and Ethnic Groups," in John Neuenschwander (ed.) *Kenosha in the Twentieth Century: A Topical History* (Kenosha: Kenosha County Bicentennial Commission, 1976), pp. 33-35.

[149] Stritch to Amleto Cicognani, November 6, 1934, Holy Rosary File, AAM.

[150] "Proceedings of Kenosha City Council," September 6, 1931, Kenosha Historical Society.

[151] Simeoni to Stritch, September 13, 1934, Holy Rosary File, AAM.

[152] Raffale Molinaro to Stritch, May 14, 1932, Holy Rosary File, AAM.

[153] Simeoni was on sick leave from 1934 to 1937. He then returned to Wisconsin and was assigned to Holy Family Church in Reeseville with the mission of St. Columbkille. There he remained until 1951 when he retired. He died in Madison in 1959. "Father Simeoni Dies; Had Been Priest 59 Years," *Catholic Herald Citizen*, 6 September 1958.

[154] Interview with Rev. Oswald Krusing, March 1990.

[155] Kiley to Frederick A. Brossler, O.S.A., October 6, 1942, Holy Rosary File, AAM.

[156] Brossler to Kiley, May 7, 1947, Holy Rosary File, AAM.

[157] John Gurda, *The Making of Milwaukee* (Milwaukee: Milwaukee County Historical Society, 1999), pp. 257-260.

[158] Joe William Trotter, *Black Milwaukee: The Making of an Industrial Proletariat, 1915-45,* (Urbana

and Chicago: University of Illinois Press, 1985), pp. 46-47.

[159] Steven M. Avella, "African-American Catholicism in Milwaukee: St. Benedict the Moor Church and School," *Milwaukee History* 17 (Autumn-Winter 1994): pp. 70-87.

[160] Messmer's attitudes on racial matters were typical of his day. He regarded African Americans as suitable for conversion to the Catholic faith, dismissing their inherited slave religion as "a mixture of low-grade Protestant Christianity and superstition." He believed Catholics could make great inroads among African Americans, "If the Catholic Church cannot convert the negro, then she is not the church of God." He relied on the racial stereotypes of his day to characterize all African Americans as "warm-hearted, naturally religious people; big children if you will, with the tantalizing weaknesses of children, forgetful of favors and of injuries alike, patient and long-suffering, having an abiding faith in the 'Lord Jesus'." He concluded, "The colored people are what slavery made them. It robbed them of their power of self-direction and took from them the great civilizing power of the family life." "Negro and the Church," *Catholic Citizen*, 29 May 1909.

[161] "Negro First Communion Class," *Catholic Citizen*, 11 December 1909.

[162] Lincoln C. Valle to Justin McCarthy, June 2, 1910, Josephite Archives, Box 31, Section D, Letter Nine.

[163] "Plan Negro Catholic Church," *Catholic Citizen*, 14 October 1911.

[164] "St. Benedict's Trade School," *Catholic Citizen*, 15 February 1913.

[165] "St. Benedict's School," *Catholic Citizen*, 27 July 1912.

[166] For more biographical information about Stephen J. Eckert see, Berchmans Bittle, *A Herald of the Great King* (Milwaukee: St. Benedict the Moor Mission, 1933). Officials of the Capuchin Order and the archdiocese of Milwaukee began the process of canonization for Eckert in the 1950s. These efforts were stopped.

[167] Cyprian Davis, *The History of Black Catholics in the United States* (New York: Cross Road, 1990), p. 184.

[168] Stephen Eckert to Katherine Drexel, January 26, 1915, copy in Archives of the Dominican Sisters of Racine.

[169] "Father Stephen, O.M. Cap., Pastor of St. Benedict the Moor Dies Friday; Funeral Tuesday," *Catholic Herald* 22 February 1923.

[170] "New Home of St. Benedict the Moor Mission to Be Memorial to the Late Father Stephen," *Catholic Herald*, 14 June 1923.

[171] "Ernest Miller Chief Donor to Negro Mission Building," *Catholic Herald*, 21 February 1924.

[172] "Negro Mission to Be Blessed Next Sunday," *Catholic Herald*, 28 February 1924; "Negro Mission Dedicated by Archbishop Messmer on Sunday," *Catholic Herald*, 6 March 1924.

[173] "Hand-Carved Relief Distinguishes New High Altar at St. Benedict's," *Catholic Herald* 2 October 1924.

[174] "Announce Generous Second Contribution to Saint Benedict's," *Catholic Herald*, 17 June 1924.

[175] "Sixty Colored Children Will Be Baptized Feb. 16 at St. Benedict's Mission," *Catholic Herald*, 7 February 1924.

[176] "Colored People's Anniversary," *Catholic Citizen*, 29 November 1919.

[177] Celestine N. Bittle, O.M. Cap. *A Romance of Lady Poverty: The History of the Province of St. Joseph of the Capuchin Order in the United States* (Milwaukee: Bruce Publishing, 1933), pp. 450-455; "Papal Representative Visits Milwaukee Archdiocese," *Catholic Herald Citizen*, 14 May 1931.

[178] Beatrice M. Murphy, "Negress: 'Please Don't Use Me As A Stepping Stone to Heaven," *Catholic Herald Citizen* 18 September 1937.

[179] "Priesthood is Goal of Young Negro Who Was Pio Nono Pupil," *Catholic Herald*, 17 July 1924.

[180] "Young Milwaukee Negro Takes Dominican Vows on Deathbed Nov. 7th," *Catholic Herald Citizen*, 18 November 1944.

[181] *Catholic Herald Citizen*, 19 July 1947. Archbishop Moses E. Kiley ordained Porter on June 7, 1947 with other members of the Sacred Heart Community. The newspaper carried a picture of Porter celebrating his first Mass at St. Elizabeth parish in Chicago. He eventually left the Sacred Heart community and was incardinated into the Chicago Archdiocese.

[182] Jan Bazant, *A Concise History of Mexico* (New York: Cambridge University Press, 1977), pp. 126-155; 167-168. See also Manuel G. Gonzales, *Mexicanos: A History of Mexicans in the United States* (Bloomington: Indiana University Press, 1999), pp. 113-138.

[183] Gary Pokorny, "Ministry to Hispanics in the Archdiocese of Milwaukee," in Steven M. Avella (ed.) *Milwaukee Catholicism: Essays on Church and Community* (Milwaukee: Knights of Columbus, 1991), pp. 108-110.

[184] "Club for Mexicans Organized in City By K. C. Committee," *Catholic Herald*, 21 February 1924.

[185] Gross wrote letters to such magazines as the *Saturday Evening Post, Harpers Bazaar,* and newspapers such as the *Milwaukee Journal.* Copies of these are in his papers at the Marquette University Archives (hereafter AMU).

[186] Nicholas Cheetham, *A Short History of Mexico* (New York: Thomas Y. Crowell Co., 1970), p. 260.

[187] Gross to Joseph Thorning, February 20, 1943, Frank Gross Papers, FG, Series 1, Box 1, AMU. Copies of Gross's annual registration forms with the Department of Justice are also included in his papers.

[188] Gross's interests in affairs south of the border made him a strong advocate for the Mexican Synarchist movement,

[189] "Seek Store Building for Mexicans' Chapel on Lower South Side," *Catholic Herald*, 2 September 1926; "Mexicans Here Await Dedication of Their Chapel Next Sunday," *Catholic Herald*, 9 December 1926; "Chapel of Mexicans Blessed on Sunday Feast of Patroness," *Catholic Herald*, 16 December 1926. "One Good Turn," *Catholic Herald*, 23 September 1926.

[190] The Mercedarian pastors included, Father Pedro Nolasco Barres, Father Adelmo Obregon, Father Serapio Gonzalez and Father Fidel de la Fuente.

[191] "Milwaukee Mexican Parish Acquires Building to Serve As Social Center," *Catholic Herald Citizen*, 23 September 1944.

[192] "Mexicans Cling to Their Memories, Put Faith in God and New Country," *Catholic Herald Citizen*, 3 August 1940.

[193] "Vicar-General Schinner Reappointed," *Catholic Citizen*, 6 February 1904.

[194] See Kantowicz, *Corporation Sole* and James O'Toole, *Militant and Triumphant: The Life of William Henry O'Connell* (Notre Dame: University of Notre Dame Press, 1987).

[195] "May Sell Episcopal Residence," *Catholic Citizen,* 26 January 1907; "Archbishop's House for Normal School," *Catholic Citizen*, 11 May 1907; "Cannot Purchase Archiepiscopal Residence," *Catholic Citizen,* 15 January 1907.

[196] "New Archepiscopal Residence," *Catholic Citizen*, 23 May 1908.

[197] "Archbishop Messmer's Return," *Catholic Citizen*, 11 June 1908.

[198] "Former Residence of Milwaukee Archbishops on Misericordia Hospital Grounds," *Catholic Herald Citizen*, 19 July 1958.

[199] William G. Miller to Messmer, June 10, 1925, Traudt File, AAM.

[200] "Death Takes Msgr. Traudt, Archdiocesan Vicar General," *Catholic Herald Citizen*, 28 July 1945; "Archdiocesan Vicar General Buried in Calvary Cemetery," *Catholic Herald Citizen,* 4 August 1945.

[201] Garmus to Traudt, October 29, 1930, Immaculate Conception File, AAM.

[202] Traudt to Garmus, October 29, 1930, Immaculate Conception File, AAM.

[203] Traudt to John Peschong, August 13, 1929, Peschong File, AAM.

[204] "In Local Catholic Circles," *Catholic Citizen*, 21 February 1925; "Archbishop Messmer Precariously Ill," *Catholic Citizen*, 28 February 1925.

[205] "In Local Catholic Circles," *Catholic Citizen*, 7 February 1925.

[206] Dominic Thill to Messmer, June 10, 1925; William G. Miller to Messmer, June 10, 1925; Edward Blackwell to Messmer, June 13, 1925; Peter Holfetz to Messmer, June 12, 1925; Traudt File, AAM.

[207] Messmer to "Rev. Dear Sir," February 8, 1906, Messmer Papers, AAM.

[208] A series of undated clippings from the secular papers in Traudt's file suggest that a period of waiting was over for the vicar general. "Traudt Again Chosen as Vicar–Action Sets to Rest Rumors He was to Be Appointed Mount Mary Chaplain," "Msgr. Traudt is Reappointed Vicar General."

[209] Stritch to Traudt, April 9, 1931, Traudt File, AAM; "Msgr. Traudt is Appointed Vicar General," *Catholic Herald Citizen*, 16 April 1931.

[210] Stritch to Traudt, March 5, 1934, Traudt File, AAM.

[211] "Msgr. Barbian's Death Mourned by Archdiocese," "Archdiocese Mourns," *Catholic Herald*, 7 November 1936.

[212] David F. Wilbur, "Alumni Notes and Clerical Changes," *Salesianum* 42 (October 1947): pp. 179-180; "Scholarship and Hard Work Marks Career of New Bishop," *Catholic Herald Citizen*, 16 August 1947.

[213] Interview with Thomas Stritch, July 1991.

[214] Muench Diary, p. 45.

[215] Interview with Most Reverend William E. Cousins, May 1989.

[216] Earl Boyea, "The National Catholic Welfare Conference: An Experience of Episcopal Leadership, 1935-1945," (unpublished Ph.D. dissertation, Catholic University of America, 1987).

[217] *Handbook for Catholic Parishioners of the Archdiocese of Milwaukee* A.D. 1907, copy in AAM.

[218] Messmer to "Rev. Dear Sir," September 25, 1907, Messmer Papers, AAM.

[219] Messmer to "Rev. Dear Sir," December 20, 1911, Messmer Papers, AAM.

[220] Damian, "A Historical Study of the Caecilian Movement," pp. 83-116.

[221] "Archbp. Messmer Discusses Several Topics Interestingly," *Catholic Citizen*, 30 April 1904.

[222] Falconio to Messmer, May 8, 1904, #6209, Del. Ap. USA IV, ASV

[223] "To Catalogue Church Music," *Catholic Citizen*, 13 August 1904.

[224] "Committee on Church Music," *Catholic Citizen*, 2 December 1905. The committee consisted of Messmer, Singenberger, Charles Becker, Norbert Dieringer of Milwaukee and priests from Green Bay, La Crosse and Marquette dioceses.

[225] "Church Music," *Catholic Citizen*, 6 January 1906.

[226] Fleischmann, *St. Francis*, p. 70.

[227] *Handbook*, p. 76.

[228] John J. Keane to Messmer, January 20, 1906, Messmer Papers, AAM.

[229] "Women in Church Choirs," *Catholic Citizen*, 6 March 1909.

[230] Ibid.

[231] Falconio to Messmer, March 25, 1911, #8378-d, Del. Ap. USA IV, ASV.

[232] Ibid.

[233] Messmer to Falconio, March 28, 1911, #8452-d, Del. Ap. USA IV, ASV.

[234] "Public First Communion at 10 Years," *Catholic Citizen*, 20 May 1911.

[235] Joseph Rainer, "Holy Communion, Its Effects on Adults, Particularly Converts," *Salesianum* 7 (October 1911): pp. 15-22.

[236] Kane occasionally penned thoughtful articles for the *Catholic Herald*. H. V. Kane, "Minority Judicial Rule," 10 July 1924; "Crime and Punishment," 4 September 1924. See also "Last Rites for Henry Kane, Archdiocesan Legal Counsel," *Catholic Herald Citizen* 31 July 1948.

[237] Kane to Atkielski, August 25, 1943, Cemetery Transfer File, AAM.

[238] "The First Cemetery," *Catholic Citizen*, 26 April 1913; "Milwaukee's Catholic Cemeteries," *Catholic Citizen*, 18 August 1925.

[239] "Now Five Cemeteries," *Catholic Citizen*, 5 June 1909.

[240] "New Cemetery Entrance," *Catholic Citizen*, 20 February 1897.

[241] "A Big Funeral," *Catholic Citizen*, 3 June 1903.

[242] "Burial in Secular Cemeteries Forbidden," *Catholic Citizen*, 4 April 1925.

[243] Kane to Messmer, January 9, 1928, Kane File, AAM.

[244] *Handbook of Calvary-Holy Cross-Holy Trinity-Mt. Olivet Cemeteries, Milwaukee Wisconsin, A.D. 1929*, copy in AAM.

[245] Stritch to Goral, July 14, 1937, Cemetery Transfer File, AAM.

[246] By the seminary centennial in 1956 St. Francis had produced six archbishops and 34 bishops. Subsequent episcopal ordinations of St. Francis Seminary alumni include Leo J. Brust (1969), Richard J. Sklba (1979), Raphael Fliss (1979), Fabian Bruskiewitz (1994), Joseph Perry (1998) and James Harvey (2000). Johnson, *Halcyon Days*, pp. 394-395.

[247] "To Erect $30,000 New Library," *Catholic Citizen*, 8 February 1908.

[248] "Seminary Gets 17,000 Volume Fagan Library," *Catholic Herald* 18 October 1923. Fagan left a huge $62,000 estate, $47,000 of which went to Immaculate Conception parish, $7,000 to St. Francis Seminary and the rest to relatives and for Masses for the repose of his soul. "Late Father Fagan Leaves $47,000 to Parish He Founded," *Catholic Herald* 31 July 1924.

[249] "Windows for St. Francis," *Catholic Citizen*, 20 July 1901; "Death of Miss Herndl," *Catholic Citizen*, 18 May 1912. The windows cost about $550 a piece.

[250] *On the Doctrines of the Modernists (Pascendi Gregis Dominici)* (Daughters of St. Paul), p. 57; White, *The Diocesan Seminary*, pp. 260-264.

[251] Philip Gleason, *Contending with Modernity: Catholic Higher Education in the Twentieth Century* (New York: Oxford University Press, 1995), p. 16

[252] White, p. 264.

[253] Ibid., pp. 269-271.

[254] "Priests Renew Fealty to Rome," *Catholic Citizen*, 7 January 1911. The chancery mailed a copy of the oath to all of the priests of the archdiocese in late 1910.

[255] Massey, p. 36.

[256] Messmer made this request directly to the Consistorial Congregation which referred the matter to Apostolic Delegate Giovanni Bonzano. Bonzano dismissed Messmer's praise of Rainer as exaggeration and claimed that Germans had for too long dominated the episcopal selections of the archdiocese. The record of this incident is recorded in an aide memoire of Bonzano to the Consistorial Congregation, Scatola 241 "Joseph Rainer" Del. Ap. USA IV, ASV.

[257] David F. Wilbur, "The Rt. Rev. Msgr. Augustine C. Breig," *Salesianum* 42 (October 1947): pp. 200-202.

[258] The best source on Dietz is Mary Harrita Fox, *Peter E. Dietz: Labor Priest* (Notre Dame: University of Notre Dame Press, 1935).

[259] "Msgr. Rainer Resigns, Father Breig Now Rector," *Catholic Citizen*, 3 July 1920; see also Robert Massey's description of these substantial changes in "St. Francis Seminary, 1855-1981: One Hundred and Twenty-Five Years of Continuity and Change," (St. Francis Seminary, 1981), pp. 34-41.

[260] "Town Talk," *Catholic Citizen*, 13 December 1920.

[261] Colman Barry, *American Nuncio: Cardinal Aloysius Muench* (Collegeville: St. John's University Press, 1969), pp. 15-16.

[262] "Cheering of Sick is Woman's Mission," *Milwaukee Journal*, 1 October 1949; "Why We Must Suffer," *Catholic Herald Citizen*, 14 June 1958; "Apostolate of Suffering," pamphlet in Apostolate of Suffering files, AAM.

[263] Ronald O. Crewe, "Dolce Far Niente, for John Schulien," reprinted in *Salesianum* 86 (Spring/Summer 1991): p. 83.

[264] Stritch to Schulien, October 10, 1938, Schulien File, AAM.

[265] "Church Has Right to Censor Dr. Schulien Tells Librarians," *Catholic Herald Citizen*, 20 November 1954.

[266] These prescriptions are found in Stritch's circular letter file, AAM. In 1948, Archbishop Kiley issued extra-synodal legislation in the form of a brief *Liber Manualis* which contained a series of rules pertaining to the life and conduct of clergy. Copy in AAM.

[267] "Must Shun Saloons," *Evening Wisconsin*, 14 July 1892.

[268] Muench Diary, p. 62.

[269] Muench Diary, p. 76.

[270] "Resigns Pastorate of His Baptism, First Communion, First Mass," *Catholic Herald*, 17 January 1935.

[271] Sylvester Dowling to Mother Mary Samuel Coughlin, n.d., Coughlin Papers, AOP-Sin.

[272] Annals of St. James Convent, Kenosha, Wisconsin, December 21, 1956, AOP-Sin.

[273] Messmer to Falconio, December 6, 1906, #13342-c, Del. Ap. USA IV, ASV.

[274] Muench Diary, p. 100; "Holy Father Honors 13 Priests of Milwaukee Archdiocese," *Catholic Herald Citizen*, 27 December 1934.

[275] Muench Diary, p. 98.

[276] "Disgusted Member of St. Jude's to Moses E. Kiley, February 1946, Sullivan Deceased Priest file, AAM.

[277] "History of the Assumption B.V.M. Province, Pulaski, Wisconsin," Archives of Franciscans of Pulaski, Wisconsin. The friars also assumed control of St. Sebastian's parish when they came to Sturtevant in 1922. Subsequent additions to the

seminary property were made in 1930 and 1957. The friars also opened a novitiate in Lake Geneva when they purchased the former Lasker mansion and added individual cells and gathering areas. The former coach house of this property, circular in design, became a library.

[278] "Redemptorists Buy Eckels' Home for Seminary," *Catholic Citizen*, 26 May 1910.

[279] "Former Du Pee Estate Dedicated as Seminary for Augustinian Fathers," *Catholic Herald Citizen*, 5 September 1942; "Archbishop Kiley Will Dedicate Augustinian Seminary on June 8th," *Catholic Herald Citizen*, 3 June 1944.

[280] Memo Leo J. Brust to Rembert G. Weakland, August 2, 1990, Chancery Property Files, AAM.

[281] "St. Philip's Monastery, Granville," Servite Archives, Chicago.

[282] "Catholic Social Service Work," *Catholic Citizen*, 12 April 1919.

[283] "Catholic Social Settlement House," *Catholic Citizen*, 24 May 1919.

[284] "Eight Colleges Plan Union Drive," *Catholic Citizen*, 7 June 1919.

[285] For details of the fund drive see William George Bruce, *I Was Born in America* (Milwaukee: Bruce Publishing, 1937), pp. 385-387.

[286] "Wisconsin Catholic Launch $5,000,000 Drive for Seminary and Charities," *Catholic Citizen,* 20 November 1920.

[287] "United Catholic Drive Is On," *Catholic Citizen*, 19 February 1921.

[288] Circular Letters August 26, 1920, September 14, 1920.

[289] Blied, *Three Archbishops*, pp. 121-122.

[290] Messmer offered this post-mortem in a fund-raising letter to all Catholics which he ordered to be read from the pulpit. Messmer to Our Catholic Clergy and Laity, April 11, 1924.

[291] A sample of Muench's articles in the *Salesianum* include, "The Priest and Social Study," *Salesianum* 18 (January 1923): pp. 20-32; "The Ethical Aspect of Wages," *Salesianum* 18 (October 1923): pp. 25-37; "The Ethics of Wages in Relation To Business," *Salesianum* 24 (July 1929): pp. 9-13; "Liberalism and Capitalism: Causes of International Unrest," *Salesianum* 25 (January 1930): pp. 6-16; "Sound Money or Inflation," *Salesianum* 28 (October 1933): pp. 16-26; "Strikes and the Recognition of Unions," *Salesianum* 29 (July 1934): pp. 1-7; "Labor's Struggle for Collective Bargaining," *Salesianum* 29 (October 1934): pp. 8-15.

[292] Muench Diary, p. 63.

[293] Muench Diary, p. 45.

[294] Thomas T. Brundage, "The Development of Catholic Journalism in the Milwaukee Archdiocese," (unpublished paper, St. Francis Seminary, 1985).

[295] "That Fairbanks Incident," *Catholic Citizen*, 12 February 1910.

[296] Falconio to Messmer, February 15, 1910, #4363-d, Del Ap. USA IV, ASV. See also Falconio to Gibbons, February 15, 1910, #4364-d, ibid.

[297] Desmond to Falconio, February 24, 1910, #4464-d, ibid.

[298] Falconio to Desmond, March 1, 1910, #4464-d, ibid.

[299] "Wisdom of the Holy See," *Catholic Citizen*, 5 March 1910; Desmond also published another report about Fairbanks that suggested he did not know that priests were celibate. "Blunder of Mr. Fairbanks," ibid.

[300] "The Fairbanks Incident: Father Fairbanks' View," *Catholic Citizen*, 9 April 1910.

[301] "Nicholas Gonner and Daughter Killed in Automobile Accident," *Catholic herald*, 7 December 1922.

[302] "Funeral for Al Schimberg at St. Catherine Friday," *Catholic Herald Citizen*, 26 November 1949.

[303] Heming, *Catholic Church in Wisconsin,* p. 935.

[304] Pat Illing, RSM, *Foundations of the Regional Community of Chicago,* (Chicago: Sisters of Mercy, 1994), n.p.

[305] "Benefit Concern for Catholic Boys Home," November 25, 1905, unidentified clipping, Milwaukee County Historical Society.

[306] "Saint Charles Home for Boys Gets Building," *Catholic Citizen*, 16 August 1923.

[307] Messmer to "Rev. dear Sir," March 11, 1924, Messmer Papers, AAM.

[308] Messmer to "Rev. dear Sir," April 14, 1924, Messmer Papers, AAM.

[309] Anna Maria Tauscher van den Bosch, *The Servant of God: Mother Mary Teresa of St. Joseph, Foundress of Carmel of the Divine Heart of Jesus: An Autobiog-*

raphy (Berchmans Bittle, O.F.M. Cap. trans., Carmelite Convent, Wauwatosa, Wisconsin, 1953.)

[310] "Catholic Home for the Aged," *Catholic Citizen*, 2 October 1915. This facility located on 544 Astor Street was a former residence and donated by an anonymous benefactor. It was refurbished by the Marquette Women's League and had accommodations for 30 residents. It cost $500 per person to get into the home and at its opening only 14 applicants were welcomed.

[311] Albert Paul Schimberg, *Humble Harvest: The Society of St. Vincent de Paul in the Milwaukee Archdiocese, 1849-1949* (Milwaukee: Bruce Publishing Company, 1949).

[312] Schimberg, p. 48.

[313] Buenker, pp. 431-514.

[314] Steven M. Avella, "Health, Hospitals, and Welfare: Human Services in Milwaukee County," in Ralph M. Aderman (ed.) *From Trading Post to Metropolis: Milwaukee County's First 150 Years* (Milwaukee: Milwaukee County Historical Society, 1987), pp. 196-254.

[315] For the influence of Bruehl on Muench and Haas, see, Colman Barry, *American Nuncio: Cardinal Aloisus Muench* (Collegeville: St. John's University Press, 1969) p.12 and Thomas E. Blantz, C.S.C., *A Priest in Public Service, Francis J. Haas and the New Deal* (Notre Dame: University of Notre Dame Press, 1982), p. 17.

[316] *Catholic Citizen*, 15 March 1910.

[317] "Our Catholic Women Leaders," *Catholic Herald* 23 February 1922; "Mourn Passing of Mrs. Hackett," *Catholic Herald Citizen*, 18 June 1937.

[318] Undated Clipping in Scrapbooks of Marquette Women's League, Marquette University Archives (hereafter MUA).

[319] "Child is their Theme," clipping in Marquette Women's League scrapbooks, MUA.

[320] "Unification of Catholic Charities," *Catholic Citizen* 16 March 1912.

[321] John M. Murphy, "The Rt. Rev. Msgr. Matthew F. McEvoy," *Salesianum* 52 (July 1952): pp. 157-58.

[322] Quoted in Eldred Lesniewski, "History of the Catholic Social Welfare Bureau, Milwaukee, Wisconsin, 1920-1959," (unpublished M.A. thesis, Fordham School of Social Service, New York, 1960), p. 38.

[323] "Archbishop Messmer on a League for Women," *Catholic Citizen*, 27 April 1912.

[324] "Combating Socialism," *Catholic Citizen*, 5 March 1904.

[325] Sally M. Miller, "Casting a Wide Net: The Milwaukee Movement to 1920," in Donald T. Critchlow (ed.), *Socialism in the Heartland* (Notre Dame: University of Notre Dame Press, 1986), pp. 18-45.

[326] Sally M. Miller, *Victor Berger and the Promise of Constructive Socialism, 1910-1920* (Westport: Greenwood Press, 1973).

[327] John Gurda, *The Making of Milwaukee*, pp. 199-202; "Ex-Mayor Rose Calls Priest, Dies Catholic," *Catholic Herald*, 11 August 1932. Rose made his profession of Catholic faith to Father Michael Huston, chaplain of the Soldiers Home. His funeral was held at St. John's Cathedral in August 1932.

[328] "Politics Barred," *Catholic Citizen*, 9 April 1904.

[329] "Socialists Poll Big Vote," *Catholic Citizen* 9 April 1904.

[330] *Handbook for Catholic Parishioners*, pp. 109-110.

[331] Frederick I. Olson, "The Milwaukee Socialists, 1897-1941," (unpublished Ph.D. diss. Harvard University, 1952), p. 185; "Catholic Socialists: Milwaukee's Most Catholic Ward Goes Socialist," *Catholic Citizen*, 19 November 1910.

[332] "Tell What They'll Do," *Catholic Citizen*, 23 April 1910.

[333] "Catholic Papers on the Milwaukee Election," *Catholic Citizen*, 13 April 1912.

[334] "Socialism in Milwaukee," *Salesianum*, 7 (April 1912): pp. 30-31.

[335] "A Socialist A.P.A. Yawp," *Catholic Citizen* 19 October 1912.

[336] "Socialist Daily Pleads Guilty," *Catholic Citizen*, 10 January 1914.

[337] Gurda, pp. 220-221.

[338] "Again a Socialist Mayor," *Catholic Citizen*, 8 April 1916.

[339] "Socialist Mayor At Catholic Card Party," *Catholic Citizen*, 31 May 1916.

[340] Messmer to "Rev. Dear Sir," March 27, 1919, Messmer Papers, AAM.

[341] "Ald. Corcoran Buried from St. John's Cathedral," *Catholic Herald Citizen*, 29 February 1936.
[342] "The Church and Social Betterment," *Catholic Citizen* 31 December 1912.
[343] Fox, *Peter E. Dietz,* passim.
[344] "Unification of Catholic Charities," *Catholic Citizen*, 16 March 1912.
[345] "Fr. Dietz Heads Charities Bureau," *Catholic Citizen*, 29 June 1912.
[346] "Fr. Oberle Honored on Golden Anniversary of Ordination December 26," *Catholic Herald Citizen*, 1 January 1949.
[347] Theodora W. Youmans, "How Wisconsin Women Won the Ballot," *Wisconsin Magazine of History* 5 (1921-1922): pp. 2-32; Buenker, pp. 345-352.
[348] Later, when the Racine Dominicans sold a portion of their Dominican College campus to the Racine public school system, the school located in the old college buildings was named for Olympia Brown.
[349] "Archbishop Messmer on a League for Women," *Catholic Citizen*, 27 April 1912.
[350] "Archbishop on Woman's Suffrage," *Catholic Citizen*, 10 February 1912.
[351] "Equal Rights Infidel Move," undated clipping Messmer Papers, AAM.
[352] "Archbishop Misrepresented," *Catholic Citizen*, 21 May 1913."Opposes Women's Suffrage on Religious Grounds," *Catholic Citizen*, 31 May 1913.
[353] Messmer to "Rev. Dear Sir," May 18, 1915, Messmer Papers, AAM.
[354] "Death of Father Ward," *Catholic Citizen*, 10 April 1915.
[355] "Archbishop Messmer Forbids Prohibition Speeches in Catholic Halls," *Catholic Citizen*, 29 June 1918.
[356] Hennesey, pp. 231-232.
[357] "Messmer Condemns Dry Law," *Milwaukee Sentinel* 13 February 1926.
[358] Mother Stanislaus Hegner to Messmer, January 24, 1930, 1-003, Box 1a, Folder 8, ASSF.
[359] "Archbishop Messmer on the War," *Catholic Citizen*, 3 October 1914.
[360] "Archbishop Messmer Hopes Germany Will Win War," *Evening Wisconsin*, 14 November 1914.
[361] "The Archbishop Returns," *Catholic Citizen*, 21 November 1914.
[362] "Notes and Personals," *Catholic Citizen,* 23 January 1915; *Catholic Citizen*, 30 January 1915.
[363] "$25,000 Raised for Poland," *Catholic Citizen* 22 January 1916.
[364] "Make a Plea for Peace," *Catholic Citizen*, 31 May, 1916.
[365] "Mass for Franz Josef," *Catholic Citizen*, 9 December 1916.
[366] Messmer to "Rev. and Dear Sir," n.d., 1919, Messmer Papers, AAM.
[367] "The Reverend Paul Henry Schaffel, D.D., S.S.L.," *Salesianum* 53 (October 1958): pp. 195-196; "Fr. Schaffel Dies; College Chaplain," *Milwaukee Sentinel*, 11 October 1958.
[368] "Mrs. Sheehy-Skeffington's Lecture," *Catholic Citizen*, 7 April 1917.
[369] "No Arms Hidden in Catholic Churches; Report of Secret Service," *Catholic Citizen*, 28 April 1917.
[370] "Archbishop Messmer's War Pastoral," *Catholic Citizen,* 17 November 1917.
[371] "'A Holy War' Says Fr. Moulinier," *Catholic Citizen*, 24, November 1917.
[372] "Milwaukee Catholics and the War," *Catholic Citizen*, 12 May 1917.
[373] *Catholic Citizen*, 24 November 1917.
[374] "Monsignor Gearhard Dies at 80," clipping from *Waukesha Freeman,* 20 March 1974 in Gearhard File, AAM.
[375] "First Masses of Priests," *Catholic Citizen*, 23 March 1912.
[376] "Fr. Huston Retires, Fr. Eilers Becomes Soldiers' Chaplain," *Catholic Herald* 15 December 1932.
[377] "The Rev. George Corbett Eilers, Captain, Chaplain, U.S.A.," Eilers File, AAM.
[378] "Wisconsin Priest Writes from War Front," *Catholic Citizen* 9 November 1918.
[379] "Rev. George Eilers, Army Priest, Made Chevalier by Poland," *Catholic Citizen*, 20 August 1924.
[380] "An Army Chaplain's Letter," *Catholic Citizen*, 22 June 1918.
[381] Annals of St. Gall Convent, Milwaukee, November 11, 1918, AOP-Sin.
[382] "Speaks on Peace," *Catholic Citizen*, 16 November 1918.
[383] Steven Burg, "Wisconsin and the Spanish Flu Epidemic of 1918," *Wisconsin Magazine of History* 84(Autumn 2000): pp. 36-56.

[384] "Catholic Churches Closed Last Sunday," *Catholic Citizen*, 12 October 1918.

[385] "Influenza Regulations," *Catholic Citizen*, 14 December 1918; "In Catholic Circles," *Catholic Citizen*, 21 December 1918.

[386] "Abandoning German," *Catholic Citizen*, 12 October 1907.

[387] "All Retreats in English," *Catholic Citizen*, 26 July 1906.

[388] Donald Hying, "The Americanization of Milwaukee's German Catholic Church," (unpublished paper, St. Francis Seminary, 1987).

[389] Muench Diary, pp. 17-18.

[390] At St. John's, historian Benjamin Blied notes that German was on the way out already in 1934. In 1948 when he came as pastor and intoned the Angelus and Divine Praises in German he "elicited a response feeble enough to convince him that the German language had become extinct except for confession." Benjamin Blied, "A History of St. John the Baptist Congregation, Johnsburg," pp. 67, 76-77, parish history file, AAM.

[391] Traudt to Roy Wilcox, March 5, 1919, Messmer Papers, AAM.

[392] "'Menace' Stickers," *Catholic Citizen* 15 February 1913.

[393] "Father Malone in City," *Catholic Citizen*, 10 June 1914.

[394] "Priest Forces Menace Agent To Retract Foul Slanders," *Catholic Citizen* 10 June 1914; "Slander Alleged," "Stewart Discharged," "Sink Probe Deeper," undated and unidentified clippings in St. Thomas Aquinas, Kenosha, Parish file, AAM.

[395] "A Sample Anti-Catholic Lecture at Milwaukee," *Catholic Citizen*, 15 November 1913.

[396] Buenker, pp. 653-654.

[397] Quoted in Herbert F. Margulies, "Anti-Catholicism in Wisconsin Politics, 1914-1920," *Mid-America* 44 (January 1962): pp. 51-54.

[398] Wilcox received the endorsement of the *Catholic Citizen*. "Hon. Roy P. Wilcox," *Catholic Citizen*, 21 August 1920.

[399] Norman F. Weaver, "The Knights of the Ku Klux Klan in Wisconsin, Indiana, Ohio and Michigan," (unpublished Ph.D. dissertation, University of Wisconsin, Madison, 1954), pp. 50-52. Wisconsin revoked the Klan charter in 1946, claiming that there had been no corporate activity by the organization since 1930. "Klan Charter in Wisconsin Is Revoked," *Catholic Herald Citizen*, 14 December 1946.

[400] Robert A. Goldberg, "The Ku Klux Klan in Madison, 1922-1927," *Wisconsin Magazine of History* 58 (Autumn 1974): pp. 31-44.

[401] Weaver, pp. 74-78.

[402] "How About it Racine," *Catholic Citizen*, 2 August 1924.

[403] Kenneth T. Jackson, *The Ku Klux Klan in the City* (New York: Oxford University Press, 1967), pp. 236-239. Weaver places the total at 75,000–a bit of an exaggeration.

[404] "Center of Klan Strength Shifting to Middle West, 15,000 at Wisconsin Meet," *Catholic Citizen*, 4 August 1923; "The Klan Organizing in Wisconsin," *Catholic Citizen*, 10 January 1924; "Kluxers Meet Near Milwaukee," *Catholic Citizen*, 21 June 1924. In November the *Catholic Citizen* put out a special anti-Klan edition.

[405] "Ku Klux Kicked out of Waukesha," *Catholic Citizen*, 1 March 1924.

[406] "Is Secretary of State Zimmerman a Member of the Ku Klux," *Catholic Citizen*, 26 April 1924; "Klan May Enter State Politics," *Catholic Citizen*, 5 July 1924; "The Ku Klux as an Issue in Next Week's Primary," *Catholic Citizen*, 26 August 1924.

[407] Michael Jacobs, "Selling Fraternalism in the 1920s: The Economic Rise and Decline of the Ku Klux Klan in Milwaukee," (unpublished paper in possession of author).

[408] Quoted in Paul W. Glad, *History of Wisconsin: War, a New Era, and Depression, 1914-1940* (Madison: State Historical Society of Wisconsin, 1990), p. 123, n. 69.

[409] Weaver, pp. 67-69.

[410] "St. Leo's Silver Jubilee," parish history file, AAM.

[411] "Golden Jubilee, St. Florian Parish," parish history file, AAM.

[412] "25th Jubilee, St. Sebastian Church," parish history file, AAM.

[413] "St. Bernard's Parish, Silver Jubilee, 1911-1936," parish history file, AAM.

[414] "History of Saint Robert Church, 1912-1953," parish history file, AAM.

[415] A. J. Kunzelmann to Reilly, July 28, 1931, Reilly File, AAM.

[416] Bernard Traudt to Reilly, November 27, 1931, Reilly File, AAM.

[417] Stritch to Reilly, November 10, 1936, Reilly File, AAM.

[418] Amleto Cicognani to Stritch, January 3, 1938, Reilly File, AAM. Reilly eventually secured the honor in 1944 from Archbishop Moses E. Kiley.

[419] Charles Maginnis was a native of Londonderry, Ireland who came to Boston in 1888 and designed a number of prominent New England Catholic churches. His contributions to Catholic architecture were so great that he received Notre Dame's prestigious Laetare Award. "Who is Maginnis?," *Catholic Citizen*, 12 April 1924.

[420] "Mass is Telecast First Time in State from St. Robert's Church, Milwaukee," *Catholic Herald Citizen*, 23 December 1950.

[421] "Dedication of New St. Clement's Church at Sheboygan, Wis.," *Catholic Citizen*, 29 May 1915.

[422] "St. Clement's Parish, Sheboygan, Wisconsin, 1914-1954," "St. Clement's Parish, Sheboygan, Wisconsin, 1914-1964," parish history file, AAM.

[423] "St. Thomas Aquinas' New Church," *Catholic Citizen*, 18 May 1912; "Golden Jubilee, St. Thomas Aquinas Church, Kenosha, Wisconsin," parish history file, AAM.

[424] "Dedication of Holy Angels Church," *Catholic Citizen*, 20 November 1916.

[425] "Souvenir of the Silver Jubilee of Holy Angels Congregation, Milwaukee, Wisconsin, 1914-1939," p. 15, parish history file, AAM.

[426] Steven M. Avella, *Like an Evangelical Trumpet: A History of the Mother of God Province of the Society of the Catholic Apostolate* (Milwaukee: Society of the Catholic Apostolate, 1999), pp. 28-56.

[427] Peter Dietz to Traudt, December 10, 1929, Dietz File, AAM.

[428] Ibid.

[429] Jerome Schommer, S.D.S., *The Moment of Grace: A History of the North American Province of the Society of the Divine Savior* (Milwaukee: Society of the Divine Savior, 1995). V.1, pp. 148-150.

[430] "St. Veronica Parish, 1926-1976," parish history file, AAM.

[431] "Christ the King Congregation, 25th Anniversary," parish history file, AAM.

[432] "St. Dominic Parish, Sheboygan, Wisconsin, 1928-1953," parish history file, AAM.

[433] "St. Edward's Catholic Church Golden Jubilee, 1919-1969," parish history file, AAM.

[434] "St. Rita New Name of Ives in Racine Co.," *Catholic Herald*, 15 May 1930.

[435] "The Order of Saint Augustine and the Dedication of Saint Rita's Church and Monastery," parish history file, AAM.

[436] John W. Bailey, "St. Mary's Parish, Kenosha, Wisconsin, 1919-1979," parish history file, AAM parish histories.

[437] "Fifteenth Anniversary, St. Aloysius Parish, 1935," parish history file, AAM.

[438] "Saint Rita Church, West Allis, May 5, 1964," parish history file, AAM.

[439] Gleason, *Contending with Modernity*, p. 21.

[440] "Standards of the Schools of the Archdiocese of Milwaukee," Katzer Papers, AAM.

[441] "Important Letter Issued by Archbishop Katzer," *Catholic Citizen*, 19 April 1902.

[442] "Catechism in English," *Catholic Citizen*, 3 March 1902.

[443] "Course of Study for Schools," *Catholic Citizen*, 27 June 1903. A copy of these regulations are found in ASND. The text was printed by the School Sisters of Notre Dame and issued on May 11, 1903.

[444] Chronicle of St. Anthony Convent, 1872-1959, ASND.

[445] Buenker, p. 371.

[446] Copies of these are in ASND.

[447] John J. Augenstein, Ph.D., *Lighting the Way: The Early Years of the Catholic School Superintendency, 1908 to 1935* (Washington,D.C.: The National Catholic Educational Association, 1996).

[448] John M. Voelker, "The Diocesan Superintendent of Schools: A Study of the Historical Development and Functional Status of His Office," (Washington, D.C.: Catholic University of America, 1935).

[449] Chancery Death Notice, Monsignor Edmund Goebel, June 8, 1973, Goebel File, AAM. "Funeral Service for Msgr. Goebel," *Catholic Herald Citizen*, 12 June 1973.

[450] Muench Diary, pp. 82-83.

[451] "Archdiocese Opens Downtown Office for Catholic Schools," *Catholic Herald Citizen*, 17 August 1937.

[452] H. Carl Mueller, "Mansion Faces Destruction," 10 March 1975, unidentified clipping Milwaukee County Historical Society.

[453] "Archdiocese Acquires New Education Office," *Catholic Herald Citizen*, 26 April 1947.

[454] Copies of these are available in AAM.

[455] Father Harold Ide, who worked at the school department under Goebel, related that subject matter of these Catholic texts were parceled out among the various superintendents in Wisconsin. Goebel drew the texts for social studies and history. Father Paul Esser, also closely associated with school work, verifies the observation that these texts were probably authored by religious sisters and "gone over" by Goebel who attached his name to the work.

[456] The resistance of the sisters came from Stritch's demand that they provide the opportunity room with existing faculty—meaning one sister would have to take on additional work in covering a grade. Sisters protested the extra work and the space difficulties that it entailed. Stritch nonetheless remained adamant. For an example of this see Stritch to Mother Mary Samuel Coughlin, March 22, 1937, Stritch Papers, AAM.

[457] Joseph Barbian to Mother Samuel Coughlin, November 22, 1934, GA-12, Box 8,3/322, AOP-Sin.

[458] "Parochial Schools in Archdiocese Show Commendable Growth," *Catholic Citizen*, 20 April 1922.

[459] "New Marquette College," *Catholic Citizen*, 24 February 1906.

[460] "Catholic High Schools and Academies Here Begin Year with Increased Attendance," *Catholic Herald*, 23 September 1926.

[461] "This Year's Class Last from Old Marquette Building," *Catholic Citizen*, 18 June 1925.

[462] "Senn Property Bought," *Catholic Citizen*, 3 September 1892.

[463] A picture of the architect's rendering is found in "Splendid New Holy Angels High School," *Catholic Herald*, 4 November 1926. M. Jane Coogan, B.V.M., *The Price of Our Heritage: History of the Sisters of Charity of the Blessed Virgin Mary* v. 2 (Dubuque: Mount Carmel, 1978), pp. 236-239.

[464] Hanousek, *A New Assisi,* pp. 123-126.

[465] "Beautiful New St. Catherine's High School," *Catholic Herald*, 26 July 1923.

[466] Mary Hortense Kohler, *Rooted in Hope* (Milwaukee: Bruce Publishing, 1964), pp. 196-205.

[467] "New High School and Motherhouse for Sisters of Mercy," *Catholic Herald*, 27 March 1924; "New Home of Mercy High," *Catholic Herald*, 23 July 1925.

[468] Sister Mary Eva McCarty, *The Sinsinawa Dominicans: Outlines of Twentieth Century Development, 1901-1949* (Dubuque: The Hoermann Press, 1949), pp. 159-160; 426-427. "History Made at Edgewood When Ground is Broken for Dominican Sisters' New High School There," *Catholic Herald*, 12 November 1925.

[469] Stritch to Mother Aloysia Leickem, May 24, 1939, St. Mary's Springs, Fond du Lac File, AAM.

[470] Quoted in M. Eva McCarty, *The Sinsinawa Dominicans: Outlines of Twentieth Century Development, 1901-1949* (Dubuque: The Hoermann Press, 1949), pp. 28-29.

[471] "The Notre Dame Story" St. Stanislaus Parish History, 1976, parish history file, AAM.

[472] "Parish School Bears Name of Pope Pius XI; is Richly Blest By His Benevolence," *Catholic Herald*, 21 December 1933.

[473] Steven M. Avella, *Like an Evangelical Trumpet*, pp. 51-54, 122-125.

[474] Chronicle of St. Anne Convent and Chronicle of St. Francis Convent, ASND.

[475] Chronicles of St. Mary Convent, Burlington, ASND; "Burlington High School Blessed Last Sunday," *Catholic Herald*, 9 September 1926.

[476] Augenstein, pp. 50-52.

[477] "Msgr. Meyer of St. Leo's Celebrate's 50th Jubilee as Priest Dec. 8th-12th," *Catholic Herald Citizen*, 4 December 1948.

[478] "High School Survey Begun Here Monday," *Catholic Herald*, 15 April 1926; Joseph F. Barbian, "Catholic High Schools," *Salesianum* 23 (April 1928): pp. 1-5.

[479] "Diocesan High School at St. Elizabeth's," *Catholic Herald*, 3 June 1926.

[480] Minutes of Meeting, B. Traudt, A. Salick, E. Blackwell, S. Bernard, Schiltz, P. Flasch, Knitter, Pius Stuzer, O.F.M., Cap., Sylvester Groff, Messmer High School File, March 24, 1925.

[481] "Modern New Catholic High School," *Catholic Herald*, 23 May 1929.
[482] "Messmer High Cornerstone is Laid Today," *Catholic Herald*, 12 September 1929; "Work Progresses on Messmer High School," *Catholic Herald*, 12 September 1929.
[483] "Messmer High Dedicated to True Training," *Catholic Herald*, 15 May 1930.
[484] Raphael Hamilton, S.J., *The Marquette Story* (Milwaukee: Marquette University Press, 1953), p. 77.
[485] "Marquette Acquires New Property," *Catholic Citizen*, 18 June 1910.
[486] Hamilton, p. 245.
[487] Ibid., pp. 133-139. The final amount realized after the books were closed on the drive was $340,462.98.
[488] Ibid., pp. 178-184.
[489] Ibid., pp. 192-195.
[490] Ibid., pp. 210-215.
[491] Ibid., pp. 245-246.
[492] Ibid., p. 215.
[493] Traudt to F. Gosiger, S.J., Marquette University File, AAM.
[494] Stritch to Vlodimir Ledechowski, September 9, 1932, Marquette University File, AAM.
[495] Stritch to "Dear Reverend Father," July 14, 1933, Stritch Papers, AAM. Stritch later approved the taking of an archdiocesan-wide collection for the erection of the school of engineering. Stritch to "Dear Reverend Father," May 31, 1939, ibid.
[496] Stritch to Magee, May 3, 1933, Marquette University File, AAM.
[497] J. J. Welte to Stritch, August 24, 1933; Stritch to Welte, August 27, 1933; Stritch to F.W. Gloeckner, November 27, 1933, Marquette University File, AAM.
[498] Magee to Stritch, December 11, 1933, Magee to Stritch January 5, 1934, Stritch to Magee, January 6, 1934, Stritch to Ryan Duffy, January 6, 1934 (copy), Marquette University File, AAM.
[499] Stritch to "My dear Father Provincial," January 21, 1933, Marquette University File, AAM.
[500] Stritch to Vlodimir Ledechowski, S.J., September 9, 1932, Marquette University File, AAM.
[501] "A Report on the Social Apostolate of the Jesuits in Milwaukee," March 1950, Marquette University File, AAM.
[502] Gleason, *Contending with Modernity*, pp. 89-95.
[503] Edward A. Fitzpatrick and Sister Mary Dominic, (eds.), *The Autobiography of a College* (Milwaukee: Bruce Publishing, 1939), pp. 8-11.
[504] Messmer to Coughlin, January 21, 1914, GA 12, Box 8, 5/4, AOP-Sin.
[505] "On This We Build: A Brief History of Mount Mary College Over the Past Fifty Years, 1913-1963," copy in Archives of the School Sisters of Notre Dame (hereafter ASND).
[506] Chronicle of St. Mary's Institute, p. 41, ASND.
[507] "Tower Will Dominate Gothic Buildings on Campus of New St. Mary's College," *Catholic Herald*, 10 May 1928.
[508] Ronald Rutkowski, "E. A. Fitzpatrick and Catholic Education," *Journal of the Midwest History of Education Society,* 21 (1994): pp. 159-171. See also William M. Lamers, "The Public Service of Edward A. Fitzpatrick," (Milwaukee, 1937), Fitzpatrick File, Marquette University Archives.
[509] Edward A. Fitzpatrick, "The Foundations of St. Mary's College," Address at the Laying of the Cornerstone, St. Mary's College, Milwaukee, Wisconsin, September 12, 1928, copy in ASND.
[510] Ibid.
[511] Unknown Sister to Mother Stanislaus Kostka, January 6, 1933, Mount Mary File, ASND.
[512] Fitzpatrick and Mary Dominic, *The Autobiography of a College,* vii.
[513] Stritch to Vlodomir Ledechowski, September 9, 1932, Marquette University File, AAM.
[514] Mossing, pp. 13, 15-16.
[515] "Address Given by Our Most Reverend Archbishop on the Occasion of His Welcome to Our Motherhouse," December 1, 1930, ASND.
[516] Ibid.
[517] "Report of the Diocesan Committee At Marquette University" September 2, 1932, copy in the Archives of the Sisters of St. Agnes (hereafter ASA).
[518] W. J. Grace to "Dear Sister Superior," October 8, 1931, copy in Marquette University File, AAM.
[519] These letters were sent to the mothers general of all the major teaching sisterhoods in the Milwaukee Archdiocese. See Stritch to Mother Samuel Coughlin, October 22, 1931, GA 12, Box 8, 5/4, AOP-Sin; Stritch to Ven. Mother Stanislaus Kostka, October 22, 1931, copy in Marquette University File, AAM.

[520] Mother Samuel Coughlin to Joseph Barbian, Coughlin Papers, 1304-8, 4/11, AOP-Sin.

[521] W. J. Grace to Stritch, June 7, 1934, attachment "Proposal for Two Year Teacher Training Program for Elementary School Teaching in Parochial Schools," Marquette University File, AAM.

[522] Hanousek, *A New Assisi*, pp. 174-82; Robert Francis Flahive, "Cardinal Stritch College, Yesterday, Today and Tomorrow," (unpublished Ed. D. dissertation, Marquette University, 1973).

[523] Kohler, pp. 232-236.

[524] Sister M. Vera Nabor, *With All Devotedness: Chronicles of the Sisters of St. Agnes* (New York: P. J. Kennedy and Sons, 1959), pp. 233-237.

[525] SSSF Daybook, May 9, 1936, MS 005, Archives of the School Sisters of St. Francis (hereafter ASF).

[526] "College of Music Opened to Public," *Catholic Herald,* 29 August 1936.

[527] SSSF Daybook, October 7, 1947, MS 005, ASF.

[528] SSSF Daybook, September 3, 1936, MS 005, ASF.

[529] Mother Stanislaus Hegner to William Magee, S.J., August 18, 1936, Magee Papers, Archives of Marquette University (hereafter AMU).

[530] Donald J. Keegan, S.J., to William Grace, S.J., November 2, 1936, AMU; Skeleton Agreement with the School Sisters of St. Francis, n.d., AMU; Some of these arrangements are discussed in Barbaralie Stiefermann, O.S.F., *Stanislaus: With Feet in the World* (Baltimore: Gateway Press, 1990), pp. 212-215.

[531] "The Teachers' Training Program," Memo to the President, No. 404, January 27, 1937, McCarthy Papers, AMU.

[532] SSSF Daybook, March 13, 1937, MS 005, ASF.

[533] Donald Keegan to George A. Works, February 11, 1937, AMU.

[534] SSSF Daybook, January 4, 1937, MS 005, ASF.

[535] Telegram, P. A. Brooks to Raphael McCarthy, August 20, 1937, AMU; SSSF Daybook, September 4, 1937, MS 005, ASF.

[536] SSSF Daybook, July 2, 1937, MS 005, ASF.

[537] "Fr. McGucken, Native of Milwaukee, Jesuit Educator, Dies at 54," *Catholic Herald Citizen*, 13 November 1943.

[538] SSSF Daybook, November 18, 1937, MS 005, ASF.

[539] John Whitney Evans, "The Newman Idea in Wisconsin, 1883-1920," *Wisconsin Magazine of History* 54 (Spring 1971): pp. 204-219.

[540] However, the complaints of one of the students who took his advice revealed that Marquette had its problems too—in fact she accused it of being a secular campus run by the Jesuits. From that point on Hengell never promoted the Jesuit university again and frosty relations marked the two until the 1930s when Jesuit retreat master, Father Archibald Talmadge, broke the impasse and preached at the Madison chapel.

[541] "Father Hengell Will Retire; Father Kutchera in Chapel Post," undated clipping, Milwaukee County Historical Society; Dr. Hengell, First Student Chaplain, Dies," *Catholic Herald*, 29 May 1937.

[542] Gleason, *Contending with Modernity,* p. 24.

[543] Stritch to "Dear Reverend Father," September 2, 1937, Stritch Papers, AAM.

[544] Stritch to "Dear Reverend Father," Feast of St. Bartholomew, 1937, Stritch Papers, AAM.

[545] Gabriel Ward Hafford, "The Activities of the Catholic Instruction League in the Milwaukee Archdiocese," (unpublished B.A. thesis, St. Francis Seminary, January 1929).

[546] "Sad Death of Father Lyons," *Catholic Citizen*, 20 October 1917.

[547] "Instruction League Work Grows," *Catholic Citizen*, 1 December 1917.

[548] "Archbishop Urges Expansion of Instruction League; Need More Centers, More Teachers," *Catholic Herald*, 22 December 1932.

[549] Stritch to "Reverend and Dear Father or Venerable Sister Superior," November 28, 1936, Stritch Papers, AAM. Yet another by-product of this concern for students in public schools was the formation of a Junior Newman club which received support from the cathedral clergy, hosted dances and socials and received financial support from the Knights of Columbus.

[550] Stritch to "Reverend and Dear Father," January 27, 1937, Stritch Papers, AAM.

[551] For a complete discussion of the role of these kinds of celebrations in Italian life see Robert Orsi, *The Madonna of 115th Street: Faith and Community in Italian Harlem* (New Haven: Yale University Press, 1985). A bit less sympathetic but insightful is

Rudolph Vecoli, "Cult and Occult in Italian American Culture: The Persistence of a Religious Heritage," in R. M. Miller and T. D. Marzik, *Immigrants and Religion in Urban America* (Philadelphia: Temple University Press, 1977).

[552] "Cornerstone Laid Great Crowd Attends the Blessing of the Cornerstone of the New Polish Roman Catholic Church," *Kenosha Evening News,* 10 November 1902.

[553] Sister M. Eugenia Heppe, O.S.F., "A History of Holy Hill, Washington County, Wisconsin," (unpublished M. A. thesis, DePaul University, Chicago, June 1941).

[554] "Carmelite Fathers Here," *Catholic Citizen*, 6 January 1906.

[555] "Carmelites at Holy Hill," *Catholic Citizen*, 7 July 1906.

[556] This occurred in April 1871 when Henni blessed the seriously ill Sister Mary Elpis with an image of Our Lady of Perpetual Help and she soon recovered. Motherhouse Chronicles, Vol. 1, ASND.

[557] "One Thousand Letters Tell of Favors Received by St. Anthony Clients," *Catholic Herald*, 21 December 1933.

[558] "Miracle Man," *Milwaukee Journal*, 13 August 1922.

[559] These and other Holy Hill miracles are described in J. M. LeCount, *Holy Hill: Its History—Authentic, Legendary and Pre-Historic in Prose and Poetry* (Hartford: J.M. LeCount and Son, Printers and Publishers, 1891), pp. 189-214. The Kroeger's were an intensely Catholic family. "Death of Herman Kroeger," *Catholic Citizen*, 24 June 1916. One son, Joseph, joined the Jesuits after his graduation from Marquette in 1900. See "Former Milwaukee Priest Dies," *Catholic Citizen*, 21 March 1925.

[560] "Miracle at Holy Hill," *Catholic Citizen*, 30 October 1893.

[561] "Doesn't Believe in Holy Hill," *Catholic Citizen*, 15 August 1903; "For and Against Holy Hill Shrine," *Catholic Citizen*, 22 August 1903; "Hits Holy Hill," *Catholic Citizen*, 19 August 1905.

[562] Messmer to Pietro Fumasoni-Biondi, April 3, 1928, Blessed Virgin of Pompeii File, AAM.

[563] Stritch to Amleto Cicognani, November 6, 1934, Holy Rosary File, AAM. Stritch's comment was about the Calabrians in Kenosha.

[564] Edward P. Sherry to Stritch, August 20, 1935, Blessed Virgin of Pompeii File, AAM.

[565] Messmer to Pietro Fumasoni-Biondi, April 3, 1928, Blessed Virgin of Pompeii File, AAM.

[566] William Halsey, *The Survival of American Innocence* (Notre Dame: University of Notre Dame Press, 1980).

[567] "Milwaukee's First Citizen Has 90th Birthday Sunday," *Catholic Herald Citizen*, 16 March 1946; "City Mourns William George Bruce, Pioneer, Statesman," *Catholic Herald Citizen*, 20 August 1949.

[568] William George Bruce, *I Was Born in America* (Milwaukee: Bruce Publishing, 1937), passim.

[569] William George Bruce, "Twenty Five Years of *Hospital Progress*," *Hospital Progress* 26 (May 1945): pp. 152-153.

[570] William George Bruce, *History of St. Mary's Church* (1921); *The Story of Holy Trinity Parish, 1850-1950*, both available in parish history file, AAM.

[571] Bruce, *I Was Born in America*, p. 381.

[572] Bruce, *I Was Born in America,* p. 389.

[573] Bruce's papers in the State Historical Society of Wisconsin are filled with numerous letters to and from priests. The author has seen the heavy photo albums with numerous pictures of bishops, priests and nuns who enjoyed the Bruce family's gracious hospitality.

[574] "Frank Bruce, Book Publisher Stricken," *Catholic Herald Citizen*, 28 February 1953.

[575] Frank Bruce, "An American Challenge and Opportunity," *Irish Monthly* 61 (November 1933): pp. 729-731.

[576] Edward A. Fitzpatrick, "Twenty-One Years in Retrospect: The Catholic School Journal, 1929-1949," (Milwaukee: Bruce Publishing, 1949).

[577] George G. Higgins, "Joseph Caspar Husslein, S.J., *Social Order* 3 (February 1953): pp. 51-53. "Editor of Catholic Book Series," *Catholic Herald*, 31 December 1931.

[578] Howard Smith, "The Bruce Publishing Company," *Catholic Library World* 28 (January 1957): pp. 171-174. Husslein contributed a selection to the series by writing a "diary" of the Holy Family.

"Fr. Husslein Adds New Diary to Book Series," *Catholic Herald Citizen*, 2 February 1946.

[579] "The Religion in Life Curriculum: A Graded Course for the Elementary School," Edward A. Fitzpatrick Papers, Marquette University Archives, Box #2, "Article and Speeches, 1934-1939."

[580] "New Era for House of Bruce," *Catholic Herald Citizen*, 18 February 1950.

[581] "Synopsis of Proceedings of the Organization Meeting of the Milwaukee Diocesan Council of Catholic Women," December 8, 1920, MACCW File, AAM.

[582] "You're Invited to Cornerstone Laying At First Cathedral," *Catholic Herald Citizen*, 26 August 1939; "Academy of Church History Erected," *Catholic Herald Citizen*, 2 September 1939.

[583] Mrs. Thos. O'Meara, "Retrospect of the first Eighteen Years of the MACCW from 1920 to 1938," MACCW Papers, AAM.

[584] "Local Holy Name Societies To Hold Joint Meeting," *Catholic Citizen*, 17 January 1920; "Archdiocesan Union of Holy Name," *Catholic Citizen*, 16 October 1920; "Record of Catholic Action Achievement," *Catholic Herald Citizen*, 26 January 1946.

[585] "Phil Grau New Chairman Holy Name Speakers," *Catholic Herald Citizen*, 10 April 1935.

[586] Thomas F. Gavin, *Champion of Youth: A Dynamic Story of a Dynamic Man, Daniel A. Lord, S.J.* (Boston: St. Paul Editions, 1977), pp. 67-83.

[587] "SUMA Begins Thirteenth Year with Announcement of Season Discussions," *Catholic Herald Citizen*, 25 September 1943.

[588] Riedel to Kiley, April 26, 1943, Riedel File, AAM.

[589] "Youth Needs Christ, Action Convention Told," *Catholic Herald Citizen*, 11 September 1947.

[590] "Hierarchy Leading, Laity Helping Constitutes True Catholic Action," *Catholic Herald Citizen*, 21 December 1935.

[591] "Msgr. Tanner New Gen'l Secretary of the N.C.W.C.," *Catholic Herald Citizen* 11 January 1958.

[592] "Youth Work to Holy Name Society," *Catholic Herald Citizen*, 18 January 1934; "Youth Movement Leaders are Named," *Catholic Herald Citizen*, 17 May 1934; "The Program for Boys," *Catholic Herald Citizen*, 24 May 1934.

[593] Paul Tanner, "The First National Catholic Social Conference," *Salesianum* 33 (July 1938): pp. 115-122.

[594] Quoted in Michael Petrie, "Catholicism in the Northern Kettle Moraine: The History of St. Fridolin's Mission," (unpublished paper in author's possession).

[595] Blied, *Three Archbishops*, p. 146.

[596] Timothy Michael Dolan, *Some Seed Fell on Good Ground: The Life of Edwin V. O'Hara* (Washington: Catholic University of America Press, 1992), pp. 58-110.

[597] McDermott's views on rural issues were explained in "The Wisconsin Rural Church Conference," *Salesianum* 18 (1923): pp. 5-13.

[598] Stritch to Louis Zirbes, September 11, 1933, Zirbes File, AAM; "Countryside Apostolate Asked by Archbishop in Address at Rural Life Conference Dinner," *Catholic Herald* 26 October 1933.

[599] Louis N. Zirbes, "The Diocesan Rural Life Bureau," *Salesianum* 31 (July 1936): pp. 116-121.

[600] Traudt to Daniel Wisniewski, OFM, December 20, 1927, St. Sebastian Parish File, AAM.

[601] Aloysius Kraus to Meyer, July 16, 1954, Kraus File, AAM.

[602] Benjamin Blied, "A History of Saint John the Baptist Congregation," p. 66, in parish history file, AAM.

[603] Glad, pp. 356-257.

[604] Blantz, *A Priest in Public Service*, pp. 1-21.

[605] Francis L. Broderick, *Right Reverend New Dealer: John A. Ryan* (New York: Macmillan, 1963); Blantz, pp. 22-46.

[606] A sampler of some of Haas's articles include, "Social Insurance and Health," *Salesianum* 23 (October 1928): pp. 38-48; "Poverty and Wealth," *Salesianum* 26 (April 1931): pp. 49-55; "Economic Security," *Salesianum* 26 (July 1931): pp. 37-43; "Catholic Doctrine and Industrial Practice," *Salesianum* 27 (January 1932): pp. 1-9; "Freedom Through Unionization," *Salesianum* 28 (October 1933): pp. 7-15.

[607] "Doctor Haas Argues in Favor of Huber Unemployment Bill," *Catholic Citizen*, 11 March 1923.

[608] Francis Haas, "Catholic Conference on Industrial Problems," *Salesianum* 17 (April 1923). "Conference on Industrial Problems," *Catholic Citizen*, 23

June 1923; "Mass Meeting Closes First Annual Meeting of Catholic Industrial Conference," *Catholic Citizen*, 5 July 1923.

[609] H. G. Riordan, "Father Haas Goes to Washington," *Salesianum* 26 (October 1931): pp. 43-44.

[610] Ibid., p. 91

[611] "Talks of Strikes," *Catholic Citizen*, 24 August 1907.

[612] Leon Applebaum, "Turmoil in Kenosha: The Allen-A Hosiery Dispute of 1928-29," *Wisconsin Magazine of History* 7 (Summer 1987): pp. 281-303.

[613] Darryl Holter, "Labor Spies and Union-Busting in Wisconsin, 1890-1940," *Wisconsin Magazine of History* 68 (Summer 1985): pp. 242-265.

[614] Blantz, pp. 156-157.

[615] Ibid., pp. 163-170.

[616] "St. John's Parish Honors Father Weiler," *Catholic Herald* 1 December 1932. This account alludes to Weiler's arbitration of labor disputes in Racine during his pastorate.

[617] Rev. Henry Riordan, "Organization in Local Industry," in "Economic Organizations," *Proceedings of Summer School of Catholic Action for Clergy, St. Francis Seminary, July 5-30, 1937* Vol. 4, copy in AAM.

[618] "Strike Settlement at Racine Largely Due to Fr. O'Boyle," *Catholic Herald*, 6 December 1934.

[619] Rev. Henry Schmitt, "A Local Strike," ibid.

[620] No biography of Maguire exists. My information is drawn from a timeline of his life and a brief sketch written by his former student John Tracy Ellis located in Viatorian Archives, Arlington Heights, Illinois. See Maguire File, Viatorian Archives.

[621] A good overview of the 1919 pastoral is Joseph Michael McShane, *Sufficiently Radical: Catholicism, Progressivism and the Bishops Program of 1919* (Washington: Catholic University of America Press, 1986).

[622] Theodore Rohner to Maguire, April 24, 1935, Maguire Papers, Archives of the Viatorian Community.

[623] Maguire to Rohner, April 26, 1935, Maguire Papers, Archives of the Viatorian Community.

[624] Paul W. Glad, *The History of Wisconsin: War, a New Era, and Depression* (Madison: State Historical Society of Wisconsin, 1990), pp. 426-435; see also Walter J. Uphoff, *Kohler on Strike: Thirty Years of Conflict* (Boston, 1966), pp. 2-10.

[625] Quoted in Uphoff, p. 77.

[626] Conger in fact seemed to have some quite sophisticated theological views. At a Holy Name breakfast meeting to honor the fifteenth anniversary of St. Dominic's parish in Sheboygan, Conger reviewed the history of the parish and commented that "all parish life centers around Christ, the Sun and Center of each parish member's life, not in church only but also in all other phases of daily living. In all departments of life, he said, God's commandments and sanctions determined the welfare of the individual and of the community." Conger called for a "spiritual awakening" that would lead to an application of the great moral principles to governmental activities. "St. Dominic's Parish, Sheboygan, Observes Its Fifteenth Birthday," *Catholic Herald Citizen*, 16 January 1943.

[627] Aide Memoire, "Kohler Parish," November 12, 1936, St. John the Evangelist Parish File, AAM.

[628] Architect Peter Brust dutifully submitted his plans to Stritch who rhapsodized somewhat vacuously about the structure of the church, and felt satisfied that he had made his contribution to the final product. Brust to Stritch, May 18, 1938, St. John the Evangelist File, AAM; Stritch to Brust, May 27, 1938, St. John the Evangelist Parish File, AAM.

[629] Henry V. Kane to Carroll, February 6, 1939, St. John the Evangelist Parish File, AAM.

[630] Lyman Conger to Carroll, February 18, 1939, St. John the Evangelist Parish File, AAM.

[631] Delores Flader, "St. John the Evangelist Church, Kohler, Wisconsin," n.d., copy in AAM parish histories.

[632] "Pickets At Holy Hill; Monks Not to Blame," *Catholic Herald*, 8 May 1937.

[633] One of the longest strikes by archdiocesan cemetery workers lasted over two weeks in 1957. "10 Day Cemetery Strike Remains in a Deadlock," *Catholic Herald Citizen*, 20 April 1957; "Cemetery Strike Ends; Work is Resumed," *Catholic Herald Citizen*, 27 April 1957.

[634] "Society of Saint Vincent de Paul and St. Bernard's Home Feeding Hundreds of Homeless Men Daily," *Catholic Herald*, 22 January 1931.

[635] "St. Bernard Home Adds 125 Beds to Help Jobless Men," *Catholic Herald* 31 December 1931.

[636] "Some of Milwaukee's Needy Families," *Catholic Herald Citizen*, 19 December 1936.

[637] "Kenosha 'Penny Pantry' Has Over 400 Customers During Its First Week," *Catholic Herald* 21 July 1932.

[638] "1700 Garments, 31 Bushel Baskets of Food to Parish Poor," *Catholic Herald*, 5 July 1933.

[639] "Waukesha Parish Solves First Communion Clothes Problem in an Economical Manner," *Catholic Herald*, 8 June 1933.

[640] "Ex-Communist To Speak at Local Parley," *Catholic Herald Citizen*, 8 May 1937; "Convert from Reds Tells of New Venture," *Catholic Herald Citizen*, 15 May 1937.

[641] Letter of Nina Polcyn Moore to author, October 2, 1992.

[642] Ibid.

[643] "Saint Monica Establishes Credit Union," *Catholic Herald*, 28 February 1929; "St. Monica Credit Union Statement Reveals Growth," *Catholic Herald Citizen*, 25 January 1936.

[644] "Credit Unions in the Parish," *Salesianum* 24 (April 1929): pp. 15-21; Paul Tanner, "Parish Credit Union Opportunities in Wisconsin," *Salesianum* 31 (July 1936): pp. 122-128. See also Edmund Bettinger, "The Parish Credit Union," (unpublished B.A. thesis, St. Francis Seminary, January 1931).

[645] "3 Parishes Seek Credit Union Charter," *Catholic Herald Citizen*, 28 November 1936.

[646] "Bay View Parish Will Form Credit Union on March 10th," *Catholic Herald Citizen*, 29 February 1936.

[647] This firm had been taken over by Max Thiermann at the end of the 1920s and had done a healthy business in stock transactions, bonds and finance. It was assumed that financial difficulties in the firm were linked to the stock market crash of 1929, but when Thiermann committed suicide by leaping out of the 8th floor window of Milwaukee's Goldsmith building, a John Doe probe found that he had been embezzling money since 1926. "Thiermann 'Juggling' Since 1926 is Charged," *Milwaukee Sentinel*, 9 August 1931; "Thiermann Took Firm Cash to Buy Control," *Milwaukee Sentinel* 13 August 1931; "A Lone Silent Dictator is Picture of Thiermann," *Milwaukee Sentinel*, 5 August 1932.

[648] Holy Family (Cudahy), Blessed Sacrament, Sacred Heart, St. Francis, St. Helen, St. Alexander, St. Paul, St. Francis, St. Veronica,Carmelite Sisters, Misercordia Hospital, St. Ignatius, St. Joseph, St. Adalbert (Milwaukee), St. Jude (Wauwatosa), St. Mark, St. Mary (Kenosha). Neil Gleason to Stritch, August 21, 1937, Stritch Papers, AAM.

[649] Gleason to Stritch, October 21, 1933, Holy Family Parish File, AAM.

[650] Kane to Stritch, December 29, 1937, Holy Family Parish File, AAM.

[651] Stritch to Kane, December 31, 1937, Holy Family Parish File, AAM.

[652] "St. Jude's To Be Dedicated Next Sunday," *Catholic Herald*, 24 January 1929.

[653] Stritch to Gough, September 20, 1937, St. Jude Parish File, AAM.

[654] Kane to Stritch, December 9, 1938, St. Jude Parish File, AAM.

[655] Stritch to Neil Gleason, July 20, 1938, Pio Nono File, AAM.

[656] "Stritch to "Dear Reverend Father," July 14, 1933, Stritch Papers, AAM.

[657] Stritch to "My dear Reverend Father," September 1, 1931, Stritch Papers, AAM.

[658] Stritch to "Dear Reverend Father," March 30, 1933, Stritch Papers, AAM.

[659] Stritch to "Dear Reverend Father," July 10, 1933, Stritch Papers, AAM.

[660] "St. John's Cathedral Wrecked by Fire; Will Be Restored," *Catholic Herald Citizen*, 31 January 1935.

[661] Stewart L. Weiss, *The President's Man: Leo Crowley and Franklin Roosevelt in Peace and War* (Carbondale: Southern Illinois University Press, 1996); "Crowley's Record Hard to Beat for Quiet Efficiency," *Catholic Herald Citizen*, 27 October 1945; "Archbishop Kiley Confers Papal Award on Crowley," *Catholic Herald Citizen*, 12 January 1946.

[662] Interview with Thomas Stritch, July 1, 1988.

[663] Stritch to "Dear Reverend Pastor," March 3, 1933, Stritch Papers, AAM. An example of Stritch's sometime trenchant social criticism is "Archbishop Messmer's Heart Revolted at Unjust Social Order,

say His Successor," *Catholic Herald*, 10 August 1933.

[664] "The New Deal Comes Home," *Catholic Herald*, 27 July 1933; "Archbishop Stritch Asks Support of National Recovery Program," *Catholic Herald*, 7 August 1933.

[665] "Plan of the Most Rev. Samuel A. Stritch, Archbishop of Milwaukee for Work Relief in Education in Milwaukee and Southern Wisconsin," NCWC Legal Department Files, ACUA.

[666] Stritch to Angelo Simeoni, October 21, 1933, Holy Rosary File, AAM.

[667] Plan of the Most Rev. Samuel A. Stritch, D.D., Archbishop of Milwaukee for Work Relief in Education in Milwaukee and Southern Wisconsin, Legal Department Files, Archives of the Catholic University of America (hereafter ACUA).

[668] Memo, William Montavon to John J. Burke, October 26, 1935; Montavon to Burke and Michael Ready, December 14, 1933, ACUA.

[669] Peter F. Meyer to Stritch, September 4, 1938, Giles Zynda File, AAM.

[670] Stritch to Michael Ready, March 20, 1937, Ready Papers, National Catholic Welfare Conference Papers, Catholic University of America.

[671] Because of problems with Coughlin the Roosevelt administration was wary of other Catholic critics. Apparently Stritch's difficulties with the White House were noted by the president himself who allegedly referred to him as a fascist. That the administration had serious misgivings about Stritch became evident when the episcopal vacancy opened in Chicago. Through Attorney General Frank Walker, FDR's concerns were expressed to Archbishop Spellman of New York who phoned Stritch and asked directly if the Milwaukee prelate was favorable to the Roosevelt administration. Stritch heatedly denied that he opposed the president and wrote a lengthy letter to Spellman exonerating himself which Spellman passed on to the president. See Avella, *This Confident Church*, pp. 44-45.

[672] "Men and Affairs," *Catholic Herald Citizen* 13 February 1937.

[673] Charles J. Tull, *Father Coughlin and the New Deal*, (Syracuse: Syracuse University Press, 1965). Alan Brinkley, *Voices of Protest: Huey Long, Father Coughlin and the Great Depression* (New York: Random House, 1983).

[674] Broderick, *Right Reverend New Dealer*, pp. 211-243.

[675] "Father Coughlin Returns," *Catholic Herald Citizen*, 18 December 1937; "Fr. Coughlin Returns to Air in 60 Stations," *Catholic Herald Citizen*, 8 January 1938.

[676] "Msgr. Muench Sees Peril in Fr. Coughlin's Plan," *Catholic Citizen*, 11 May 1935.

[677] Stritch to John Burke, October 26, 1936, Burke Papers, National Catholic Welfare Conference Papers, ACUA.

[678] "Religion and Economic Life," *Pontifical High Mass Sermon*, Proceedings of First National Catholic Social Action Conference, May 1-4, 1938, copy in Salzmann Library, St. Francis Seminary.

[679] Joseph Baron to Stritch, May 18, 1939, Stritch Papers, AAM.

[680] Baron to Stritch, June 5, 1939; Stritch to Baron, June 25, 1939, Stritch Papers, AAM; "Archbishop Decries Slanders of Jews, Says Catholics Sympathize," 24 July 1939, NCWC News Service Clipping, NCWC Archives, Catholic University of America.

[681] "Herr Hitler's Mistake," *Catholic Herald*, 6 April 1933.

[682] Copies of these reports are in the Stritch Papers, AAM.

[683] "Spain and Austria," *Catholic Herald Citizen,* 2 April 1938.

[684] Stritch to Rummell, April 19, 1938, Stritch Papers, AAM.

[685] Undated clipping in Stritch Papers, AAM.

[686] "Paganism Rampant in U.S. Same As Nazi Leaders are Foisting on German People," *Catholic Herald Citizen*, 19 November 1938.

[687] George Q. Flynn, *Roosevelt and Romanism* (Westport, Conn: Greenwood Press, 1976) chronicles the rocky relationship of the Roosevelt administration and American Catholics on issues of foreign policy.

[688] "No Official Stand on Neutrality Statement," *Catholic Herald Citizen*, 23 September 1939.

[689] "5 Wis. Congressmen Praise 'Red' Spain," "Citizens of Wisconsin," *Catholic Herald Citizen*, 12 February 1938.

[690] "Let's Keep the U.S. Neutral,"*Catholic Herald Citizen,* 31 December 1938.

[691] "'The First Attack on Religion," *Catholic Herald Citizen*, 10 August 1940; "Wisconsin Congressmen Favor Exempting Clerics From the Draft," *Catholic Herald Citizen* 24, August 1940.

[692] "Father Dietz Is Dead Here," *Milwaukee Journal*, 12 October 1947.

[693] Ibid.

[694] "Candles Light Field as 60,000 Pray for Peace," *Catholic Herald Citizen*, 16 September 1939. Other rallies, sponsored by the Archdiocesan Union of the Holy Name, were held in Kenosha and East Bristol.

[695] "We Don't Want War," *Catholic Herald Citizen*, 21 December 1940.

[696] "Pray for Peace But Face Reality, Father McCarthy Tells Marquette Students," *Catholic Herald Citizen*, 12 October 1940.

[697] "Poland's Way of the Cross," *Catholic Herald Citizen*, 3 February 1940.

[698] "Archbishop Pleads for Aid to Poles; Collection Sunday," *Catholic Herald Citizen*, 1 June 1940.

Part IV
"Milwaukee Continues to Boom"
1940–1958

As the nation edged toward war, Milwaukee gave its first archbishop to the see of Chicago and in his place received a dour old Roman insider, Moses E. Kiley. This scowling son of Nova Scotia administered archdiocesan affairs with a almost Manichean grimness. His episcopal motto, "*Ut Sim Fidelis*" (That I Might Be Faithful), was not St. Paul's plaintive plea for fidelity to Christ to the end, but the mental whiplash of an autocratic dictator who viewed his duties as a relentless forced march.

Kiley was succeeded by his protege, Albert G. Meyer, the first son of the archdiocese to lead the Church. Meyer too embodied the hyper-serious purposefulness of Kiley, but without the ponderous authoritarianism that made his predecessor far more feared than loved. Although both were educated in Rome and reflexively obedient to Roman direction, neither of them had ever totally absorbed the sentimentality and easy grace of Mediterranean Catholicism. The episcopate consumed any personal preferences and forbade all but the rarest human expressions of warmth and sociability. If all was dependent on their leadership skills, vision, and personalities, Milwaukee Catholicism would have atrophied seriously under their leadership. However, by its centenary in 1943 the Catholic church in southeastern Wisconsin was so large and dynamic that it could not be easily reined in or slowed.

The Church, which had negotiated competing claims of ethnic identity and created a centralized and distinctively Catholic presence, now faced a re-ordered society. It also had to work in the context of the new relationship between Americans and their government. The federal government made home ownership possible on a scale never before seen in American history. It poured funds into decaying cities, built a massive interstate road system that encouraged the wide use of automobiles, funneled dollars into health care and education and gave impetus to massive social changes in race and gender relations. Within this setting, Catholics once again had to stake their claim for visibility.

The Roman Line Continued: Moses Kiley and Albert G. Meyer

On New Year's Day, 1940, Moses Elias Kiley, bishop of Trenton, New Jersey, received notice that he was to succeed Samuel A. Stritch as archbishop of Milwaukee.[1] On March 7, the Feast of St. Thomas Aquinas, he received the pallium at installation ceremonies held in Gesu Church, since St. John's Cathedral was still in ruins.[2] Archdiocesan Catholics were immediately aware of a change. Accustomed for years to the short and paunchy Stritch, their new leader stood 6-feet-6-inches tall and favored tall miters that accentuated his height. Unlike the gentle southern lilt of Stritch, Kiley spoke in a "sepulchral" basso—often mimicked by priests. The gregarious Stritch walked the streets of Milwaukee, gave money to beggars, stood for long hours with confirmants and regaled in parish suppers. Kiley was remote, austere and authoritarian, preferring the company of a few friends, smoking a cigar after dinner, taking a pinch of snuff and allowing the occasional discussion of baseball statistics as his only form of recreation. There could not be two more diverse men. Kiley reigned (and the word is chosen deliberately) for 13 years, bringing to its high water mark the program of centralization begun by Messmer and Traudt early in the century.

Archbishop Moses E. Kiley and Msgr. Philip Schwab [AAM]

Moses Elias Kiley was born November 13, 1876, one of nine children of Irish immigrants John Kiley and Margaret McGarry. The Kileys had come to Inverness County near Cape Breton, Nova Scotia. Later they moved to the eastern shore of the island to the resort area of Baddeck, made famous by the visits of Alexander Graham Bell, who conducted experiments in aerodynamics from one of the higher elevations in the vicinity. The Kileys were farmers and by most accounts a rather sober-sided Irish family. As the elder brothers of the Kiley clan moved away, Moses became an indispensable farmhand. ("I could ride a horse as soon as I could walk," he confessed to a reporter years later). He appeared to be the family member designated to stay at home and take on the small family farm.[3] By the time he was 15, the tall and lanky-framed Kiley was a perfect farmhand, capable of long hours of arduous manual labor.

When the farm failed in 1894, however, the family moved to the industrial town of Somerville, Massachusetts, where some of the older boys had established a fairly successful carriage factory. "Mose" went to work in this shop and became a skilled woodworker. Religious faith ran deep in the Kileys and an older brother, Myles, had already entered the seminary as a candidate for the priesthood in the archdiocese of Boston. Moses's uncle on his mother's side, Holy Cross Father Moses McGarry, for whom he was named, was an important role model as well. At age 27, Moses decided to follow what must have been his heart's calling for many years, and entered the seminary.

Unfortunately, his age precluded acceptance into priest-rich Boston, and he had to search high and low for a diocese to accept him. Father McGarry helped his acceptance into the Holy Cross-run College of St. Laurent in Montreal (McGarry was president). During the summers, Kiley did odd jobs to earn his college tuition, including a stint as a motorman on the Boston transit lines in 1905 and 1906. He kept his motorman's badge and license for the rest of his life and in rare moments of personal self-revelation related stories of his work on the streets of Boston.

Upon Kiley's graduation in 1906, McGarry helped him get into St. Mary's Seminary in Baltimore, where he completed his philosophical studies and was "adopted" by the "western" archdiocese of Chicago. Since Chicago had no major seminary at that time, Archbishop James Quigley sent him for further studies in Rome in 1907. There he became acquainted with a seminarian from Nashville at the other end of the age spectrum, 20-year-old Samuel A. Stritch.

Moses Kiley as a young priest [AAM]

Kiley had come to Rome just as the twin thunderbolts of *Lamentabili* (July 1907) and *Pascendi* (September 1907) were hurled by an angry Pius X at "the synthesis of all heresies": Modernism. The strong emphasis on doctrinal orthodoxy and utter loyalty to the Holy See (reinforced by the kindliness and popular appeal of "Papa Sarto") impressed Kiley and Stritch deeply. As we have seen, the developments along the banks of the Tiber would be felt on the western shores of Lake Michigan. Messmer and Stritch proceeded to reform the seminary and the formation of the clergy according to the framework of these anti-Modernist dicta. The sternness and intensity of this anti-Modernist campaign reached its apogee in the Kiley years. Milwaukee has not had a bishop before or since so instinctively attuned to the demands of Roman imposed orthodoxy. Years later, his personal secretary and future Cardinal John Carberry recalled of his years with Kiley in Trenton, "He loved to speak of his days in Rome, and of his great love for Pope Saint Pius X. He was truly a Roman."[4]

Kiley was ordained to the priesthood in Rome a year after Stritch, on June 11, 1911, by the patriarch of Jerusalem, Giuseppe Ceppatelli. That year the 35-year-old priest was assigned to St. Agnes parish on the south side of Chicago where he lived in a newly built rectory with Father Newton Hitchcock, himself a "delayed vocation." After five years as a curate, a new archbishop, George W. Mundelein, assigned Kiley to establish a mission for homeless men in Chicago's "Hobohemia" on West Madison Street. Mundelein purchased a six-story grocery warehouse that Kiley himself helped renovate (his skills as a woodworker came in handy), and he opened a shelter known as the Holy Cross Mission.[5] The mission was a great success, providing succor to nearly 250 men at a time. Kiley lived on the site and was occasionally called to physically eject someone who may have come in drunk or was out of control. Mundelein was sufficiently impressed with his work and appointed him to head the newly reorganized Catholic Charities Bureau in 1917.

[AAM]

In this work, Kiley got his first taste of the challenge of diocesan-wide administration. His task was raising funds for diocesan charities and regularizing the distribution of monies by the active St. Vincent de Paul parish conferences. Kiley kept an eagle eye on the requests for money that came from the various parishes, investigating and scrutinizing the claims. He also took note of the reluctance of some parishes to contribute to the charities' general fund or participate in fund-raisers. Mundelein was compelled to borrow money from downtown banks to keep Kiley's welfare works viable.[6] No doubt at Kiley's urging, Mundelein stepped in and took over the lackluster fund-raising operation, using the full weight of his episcopal authority to compel reluctant pastors to contribute. Mundelein's use of brass-knuckled episcopal power to shake donations out of his unwilling subjects had an important effect on Kiley. As Roman theology and ultramontanism helped to define Kiley's mentality, so also did Mundelein's insistence on unflinching clerical obedience. A submissive and responsive clergy was an essential component of the "Mundelein vision" for Chicago, and it would be transferred to Milwaukee by Kiley.

Kiley was created a monsignor in 1924. In 1926 at the urging of his old classmate in Rome, North American College rector Eugene Sebastian Burke, Kiley was tapped to become the spiritual director for the seminarians at North American, replacing Edward Mooney. Mundelein approved Kiley reluctantly, lamenting, "We have nobody just ready to 'fill your shoes.'" However, Mundelein saw a benefit in having Kiley in Rome. "You have the opportunity," he lectured Kiley, "of doing splendid work and rendering a great service to the Church in this country by helping to mold the spiritual side of these young men away from their homes and families for so long a time, and sent to the center of Christendom .... You know my mind on the subject." But he also kept his hooks in the young priest, "I need not tell you that from time to time when we need your services in Rome for any purpose, I will not hesitate to call on you."[7]

Kiley arrived in Rome on March 26, 1926, and set about the task of directing the spiritual lives of the seminarians.[8] It must have been Kiley's sober mien, mature age and austere piety that recommended him for the task. North American Collcgc historian Robert F. McNamara gently characterizes Kiley's conferences to the young men as "less brilliant than some which the Collegians had heard, but nevertheless solid." Kiley occasionally "spiced up" his talks with "homely illustrations—such as the way a pulley works–a reflection of his mechanical past."[9] Another reading of these preserved talks reveal often depressing rants on the grimness of priestly life. He portrayed the vocation to which many of these bright young men had surrendered their freedom, virility and opportunities for successful "secular" careers as, more often than not, a distasteful task that had to be carried out without question or hesitation.[10] Again and again he stressed the personal unworthiness of the candidates for the priestly state, and emphasized repeatedly that any good that came from their lives was attributable to God's grace alone. No Puritan divine ever preached more intensely on the sufficiency of grace and the unworthiness of the human condition. Kiley himself modeled what he preached. Seminarians coming to the chapel in the pre-dawn light found the spiritual director there ahead of them rapt in prayer.[11]

He did not fraternize with his young charges, or even much with the other priests in the house. His grim demeanor must have kept many a young man at bay. But he was also a lodestar to many others. Those who did find the courage to approach him, even with doubts about their vocation, found him to be a gentle and compassionate counselor. On trips home, he took pains to visit the parents

Moses Kiley en route to Rome [AAM]

Msgr. Kiley entertaining Roman guests [AAM]

of his charges, many of whom were not permitted to leave Europe until their studies were complete. His austerity, loyalty to the Church and commanding presence inspired young seminarians like Albert Meyer (who imitated Kiley's early morning chapel appearances when he was rector of St. Francis Seminary) and John Grellinger.

Kiley also volunteered his services to the Roman curia and, at the behest of Cardinal Mundelein, squired important visitors around Rome. His work in charities brought him a slot on the pontifical board of the Society for the Propagation of the Faith. In 1929, he was designated a consultor to the Pontifical Commission on Russia. He also "moonlighted" for the Congregation of the Council, a position in the Vatican comparable to an executive post in the U. S. Department of the Treasury. He would later recall of this post, "It was a listening post for the financial problems of dioceses throughout the world, and of course we got the worst problems."[12] His services were required for the powerful Consistorial Congregation which selected bishops. In the late 1920s he opened a channel of communication with Baltimore Archbishop Michael Curley, with whom he exchanged Roman gossip and passed on to various officials Curley's opinions of episcopal appointments around the country.[13] He returned to Chicago briefly in the summer of 1926 to serve as an aide to Apostolic Delegate John Bonzano, who presided at many of the events of the Eucharistic Congress that summer. Like a good Roman he carefully cultivated contacts in Roman dicasteries and with an array of prelates with whom he corresponded relative to his work at the North American college. Kiley's biggest patron appeared to be Raphael Rossi, the Carmelite Cardinal who headed the Consistorial Congregation (the congregation that appointed bishops).

Kiley's next career step came in 1934, when Bishop John Joseph McMahon of Trenton, New Jersey died after a brief four-year episcopate. No doubt with Curley's patronage, Kiley was appointed to succeed him.[14] Rossi consecrated the 57-year-old spiritual director in the American church of Santa Susanna in Rome on St. Patrick's Day in 1934. Kiley sang in basso profundo the "Volo" and "Credo" responses to the preliminary Latin examination of the consecration rite. After celebrating a pontifical Mass for the students of the college and being given a farewell ceremony in the North American's opulent "Red Room," Kiley debarked for the challenges of episcopal administration in America.[15]

Like many dioceses (including Milwaukee), Trenton had serious financial problems during the Great Depression. McMahon had left the diocese in financial straits—in part because of the building spree of his predecessor Thomas J. Walsh, archbishop of Newark. Kiley came into office and imposed rigid austerity, foreswearing even his own salary and turning away seminarians because he had no funds to subsidize their education. Like Stritch, Kiley spent a great deal of time with bankers and mortgage brokers trying to renegotiate the nearly $10 million in debt left from the Walsh and McMahon regimes. Ultimately, with the help of a government-backed Reconstruction Finance Corporation loan and the assistance of his able vice chancellor, Richard T. Crean, he brought down the interest on the remaining debts from 6 to 3 percent.

If his conscience would have permitted it, he may have grumbled against Archbishop Walsh for having left such a fiscal mess. To make matters worse, Walsh dealt him another blow when he engineered a split in the New Jersey dioceses that detached six counties (whose income he desperately needed) to form the diocese of Camden. This deprived the diocese of 75 diocesan priests, 49 parishes, 30 parochial schools and a Catholic population of 105,246.

Kiley kept a low profile during his six years in Trenton. When he left the diocese in March 1940, the *Trenton State Gazette* noted: "By reason of a retiring disposition and an intense preoccupation with the spiritual and temporal duties of his office, Bishop Kiley had not become well-known to the people of Trenton during his six years of labor here." The paper further stated, "He has remained aloof from public life."[16] Kiley later related to one of his secretaries that someone in Rome had told him that the local bishop should appear in the local press twice, once when he came and the second time when he died or left.[17] One of the young priests recruited by Kiley for secretarial help was a Brooklyn seminarian he met in Rome, John Carberry. After Carberry's return to Brooklyn, he had been sent for advanced study at the Catholic University of America in canon law. Upon finishing his degree, the Brooklyn bishop "lent" him to Kiley who needed a canonist in 1935. Carberry later became Kiley's personal secretary and traveled with him.[18]

Moses E. Kiley, Bishop of Trenton NJ [AAM]

Kiley's appointment to Milwaukee was a bolt out of the blue—inexplicable to anyone until Roman documents are released. About all that can be said is that Kiley had sufficiently powerful Roman contacts who must have paved his way for the appointment. Likewise, his refinancing and austerity programs helped to pull ailing Trenton's finance into the black. On March 7, 1940, Kiley took control as the sixth archbishop of Milwaukee.[19] In his inaugural address to the clergy he made one rare effort at humor: "Some remarked today that man proposes, God disposes, and the Holy Father sends Moses." But lest his subordinates think that he was too lighthearted, he lectured them: "Of the future one thing is certain. We will do our duty, for we cannot be altogether faithful to God, unless we do our best."[20] The new episcopal crest, with its motto, "*Ut Sim Fidelis" (That* I Might Be Faithful), became the hallmark of his regime.

Into his official family he invited a new generation of younger priests, many of whom had already been singled out by Stritch. They assumed administrative tasks at the episcopal residence and offices. Among them were Father Joseph Emmenegger, a native of Monroe, Wisconsin. A bright young man, he had been sent abroad to Rome by Stritch to finish his theological studies, but he had to return home during World War II. He finished his theological studies at the Catholic University of America and came back to Milwaukee, where he joined the chancery staff. Emmenegger returned to Rome in the 1950s to serve as vice rector of the North American College on Via dell'Umiltà (The House on Humility Street). Later he returned to the "Casa" during Vatican II. Meanwhile, Father John Wieczorek handled the marriage tribunal and Father Mark Lyons was Kiley's personal secretary. Father Leo Brust also joined the new Kiley team. Remaining on the staff was Stritch's friend and confidant, Monsignor Roman Atkielski. Stritch had actually wanted to take "Romy" with him to Chicago, but Atkielski wisely refused, believing that his presence would be resented by the Chicago clergy. Instead he made weekly visits to Chicago to see Stritch and "cheer him up" when his manic depressive moods took over. In 1947, Kiley selected him to be Milwaukee's third auxiliary bishop. Atkielski was consecrated by Kiley in St. John's Cathedral and eventually given the pastorate of prestigious St. Sebastian's and later Christ the King parish in Milwaukee; while at the same time tending to the duties of confirmations, cornerstone ceremonies, religious professions and unending banquets.

Installation of Archbishop Kiley [AAM]

Atkielski, occasionally choleric and prickly, played to mixed reviews among the Milwaukee clergy. His familiarity with them led some of the older ones to occasionally scold him when his new episcopal status caused him to forget his humble origins.[21] His confirmation appearances were often dreaded by pastors and children because of his harping on the perils of communism. Nonetheless, Atkielski was a generous man who donated large sums secretly to Catholic schools, youth programs, and to the African American St. Benedict's Mission. He served three archbishops dutifully and faithfully (Kiley, Meyer, and Cousins).

Kiley was especially hard on his staff. He took few vacations and expected them to follow his lead. He could thunder violently at some quavering priest. (He once made his secretary, Father Mark Lyons, open and close a door a number of times when he suspected the priest had slammed it too emphatically).[22] He so demoralized Father Joseph Emmenegger that at one point the young cleric lamented at the funeral of a priest that he wished he [Emmenegger] were in the coffin instead of the deceased![23] A hectoring micromanager, Kiley followed carefully the reconstruction of the cathedral, phoning every day to check on its progress and dropping in unannounced to see that the work was being done properly. When he launched a major renovation of the major seminary buildings, he so browbeat rector Albert Meyer over minor details that the normally unflappable Meyer would occasionally come back from meetings with Kiley puffy-eyed.[24]

Bishop Roman R. Atkielski (center) at his consecration [AAM]

Kiley's 13 years were perhaps the most administratively rigid the archdiocese had ever known. Yet the same Kiley had a softer, gentler side that took people by surprise. For example, he could be moved to tears at the

Msgr. Joseph Emmenegger meeting Pope John XXIII [AAM]

mere mention of motherhood or when he evoked memories of his own mother. At times he blubbered uncontrollably before large groups. Likewise, even though priests feared him, they all attest to his gentleness in dealing with erring clergy who drank too much—"the good man's disease," he called it—and would seek help and rehabilitation for "fallen clergy."

Kiley's health began to falter in the early 1950s, and saw a steady weakening and loss of weight that made the tall prelate seem at times like a walking corpse. When ill health finally landed him in St. Mary's Hospital, he behaved like a caged tiger. Everyone felt his wrath, including the hapless John Grellinger who dropped in for a visit and suggested that Kiley receive the anointing of the sick (Extreme Unction), "telling him of the temporal effects" [of the sacrament] (i.e., physical healing). Kiley rejected the suggestion firmly and remained peeved at his former student for some time. "Some time I get the impression that he isn't very pleased with me for suggesting the anointing,"[25] Grellinger wrote Albert Meyer. Grellinger nonetheless kept coming back and watched Kiley's steady decline. "He is … still very gaunt, almost like Abraham Lincoln."[26] But Kiley's refusal to accept graciously the solicitude of his fellow bishops was coupled by his insistence on holding on to power until he was dead. Apart from liturgical duties, Kiley refused to delegate anything to his auxiliary bishop, Roman Atkielski. Week after week the chancery staff brought him documents to inspect and sign in his increasingly illegible script. He was even rigid in the application of liturgical rules to the very end. When the hospital chaplain appeared daily with the Holy Eucharist, Kiley insisted on getting out of bed and on to his knees to receive the sacred host.[27] Yet the same polarities between harshness and tender sentimentality remained with him to the end. At the time he was so hard on his official family, his nurses attested that he sang Irish ballads and shared nostalgic moments of his youth with them. When he died on April 15, 1953, his eulogist in the seminary magazine, *Salesianum*, spoke diplomatically and generously of the difficult Kiley years: "One cannot write of the greatness of a man until he

An ailing Archbishop Kiley at the dedication of St. Frederick Church, Cudahy [AAM]

sees his eternal success; until he sees as God sees; for *homo videt in facie, Deus autem in corde.* [Man sees the appearance, God sees the heart.] One can judge the sympathy of this man of God by his gift of tears; his justice by the sternness given whenever necessary and to whoever deserved it; his spirituality by his hours of prayer each day, and his insistence, against all advice, in receiving Christ in communion while he knelt on the hospital floor."[28]

After a brief "widowhood" Milwaukeeans learned in mid-July that their new archbishop was to be a native son. Albert Meyer, the first man to have been born and reared in the Catholic culture of the archdiocese of Milwaukee, was now to be the seventh man to administer the affairs of the see.

The Hometown Boy Comes Back: Albert Gregory Meyer

In a move unusual for the episcopal politics of the day, Albert Gregory Meyer returned to his native archdiocese of Milwaukee to be its seventh archbishop. He was born March 9, 1903, the fifth and youngest child of Peter Jacob Meyer and Mathilda Thelen, and was delivered above his parents' grocery store on Warren Avenue on the lower east side of the city. His roots in Wisconsin go back to his grandfather, one of the first German settlers in Caledonia in Racine County, Peter Jacob Meyer, a native of Kalenborn in the German Rhineland.[29] After purchasing land in Caledonia, the elder Meyer returned briefly to Germany in 1847 and picked up more family members before beginning his career as a successful farmer. In 1851 he married Angela Eppers, the daughter of another Caledonia farmer, and sired 12 children. The 10th of these was Peter Jacob, the father of Albert. One of the Meyer brothers, Theodore, would become a priest. [30]

In 1894 Peter Jacob married Mathilda Thelen, the daughter of a large Caledonia farming family that had roots as far back as the Meyers (Peter's brother John also married a Thelen sister). The Thelens too had priests in their family (Leonard Thelen who was Mathilda's brother). Between the Meyer and Thelen branches of the family, Albert Meyer had 101 first cousins. Peter Meyer had moved to Iowa shortly before he got married and attempted to lure Mathilda to the "hawkeye state" for a new life. But Mathilda had had quite enough of the drudgery of farming and wanted to move to the city.[31]

The Meyers moved to Milwaukee and purchased a small grocery store at 179 Warren Avenue and began having children right away. Edmund (1895), Norbert (1897), Olivia (1899), Louise (1900) and Albert (1903). Peter and Mathilda ran a strict German household and spoke a combination of German and English, typical of many Milwaukee households. In later renditions of the family life, the Meyers appeared to be a happy-go-lucky family that prayed often, held occasional family sing-alongs and cherished close ties throughout their life. Most of this was true, but it would be stretching the point to consider any of the Meyers "fun-loving" or "easygoing." Taciturnity was a family trait, and the family's reserve and lack of comfort with small talk were more characteristic of their upbringing. Although never harsh or unpleasant, the Meyers were not social or garrulous.

The religious orbit of their existence was old St. Mary's Church on Broadway; the church was a bit of a hike from the Warren Avenue grocery store, past the Cathedral of St. John, but worth it for the German church service and schooling. Young Albert entered St. Mary's School in 1909 and was instructed by the School Sisters of Notre Dame. He served Mass for the sisters daily at the nearby motherhouse (occasionally being made late for school by the length of time it took the aging and nearly blind Peter Abbelen to get through the Mass). The characteristic cursive handwriting style taught by the Notre Dame sisters never left him during his entire life. Olivia Meyer, Albert's older sister, entered the convent, taking the religious name Sister Alberta in his honor.

Young Albert G. Meyer [AAM]

Before he was 14, Meyer was tall, reserved and studious. It did not take much prodding from the sisters for young Albert to consider a priestly vocation. He had "reverend uncles" on both sides of his family, and sisters in the convent (in addition to Olivia, his sister Louise became an Agnesian). When he finished eighth grade, he and James Graham, a classmate, began taking Latin lessons from assistant chaplain Father Peter Schnitzler.[32] He desired to go into the seminary at St. Francis right after eighth grade, but Peter Meyer lost the grocery store in 1912 and until the debt was discharged he was compelled to go to work for one of his creditors, the Shaw Manufacturing Company, a condiment company. Albert's older brothers, Edmund and Norbert, then had to make up the financial deficit in order to support the family. Family finances were really not stable until Peter found work with Edmund at the Chain Belt Company in West Allis in 1916. The family moved that year and bought a new home in the growing suburb.[33]

To assuage the disappointment, Albert received a scholarship to Marquette Academy that enabled him to remain in school. But his seminary dreams were only deferred a year. In the interim, Mother Borgia Meek of the School Sisters found a benefactor (likely the sisters themselves) to pay the $125 per year tuition at St. Francis. He entered the high school program "on schedule," his Latin lessons with Schnitzler and his work at Marquette making him ready for the seminary course.

It was September 1917 when Albert entered the classical department of St. Francis Seminary. There were 315 boys and men living in the single seminary residence. The long-serving Joseph Rainer was in his last years as rector, to be replaced in 1920 with Augustine Breig. Studious and un-athletic, Meyer got on well with his classmates (occasionally playing the mandolin and cello for them), but he preferred solitude. While the other seminarians rough-housed on the playing fields or basketball courts, he was absorbed in his books. He made a few lifelong friends at St. Francis, including a young Lebanese student named Joseph Macksood whom Meyer often brought home for holidays (Macksood lived in Detroit). Macksood eventually left the seminary and became a successful surgeon. John M. Voelker became a good friend, but Meyer's closest seminary companion was a young seminarian from Algoma, Wisconsin named William Groessel. Groessel, like Meyer, was quiet, serious and kindly—the two of them were a temperamental match and remained close for the remainder of their lives. Years later when Meyer lay dying of a brain tumor in Chicago's Mercy Hospital, Groessel moved into an adjoining room and communicated with his old friend by a series of hand-squeezes.[34]

Meyer's academic excellence singled him out for advanced study abroad, and in September 1921 he was dispatched to the Propaganda University in Rome with residence at the North American College. During his years of study Meyer counted among his teachers such future ecclesiastical luminaries as Domenico Tardini, a future secretary of state for Pius XII; Enrico Dante, a specialist in rites and rubrics; Ernesto Ruffini, a scripture teacher who would become archbishop of Palermo; and Gregory Agagianian, an Armenian priest who would ascend to the Roman curia and be actively considered as the first non-Italian candidate for the papacy in

Rev. William V. Groessel [AAM]

centuries. Many of these same men would be his peers in the Sacred College of Cardinals, and even his opponents during the debates of Vatican II.

Meyer absorbed more than the theological study that was given daily to students sitting on backless benches in the Propaganda aula. In the atmosphere of anti-Modernist Rome (only slightly mitigated by Popes Benedict XV and Pius XI) he breathed in the very air of Romanità—a love for things and ideas Roman, and an unquestioning obedience to papal authority and for any words that came from the lips of the Holy Father. He came to know priests from around the nation and the world, many of whom became bishops at the same time he did. He also met and befriended fellow Wisconsin student, John Grellinger.

Msgr. Moses E. Kiley, Spiritual Director, North American College [AAM]

Life as a student in Rome in the 1920s had its moments of excitement. He was present for the death and burial of Pope Benedict XV, and for the ensuing conclave and election of Pope Pius XI. He witnessed the canonizations of St. John Vianney and St. Therese of Lisieux in 1925. Later, as a student at the Pontifical Biblical Institute, he witnessed the signing of the Lateran Treaty in 1929 which ended years of hostility between the Holy See and the Italian state. His visits to the shrines of Europe and other sight-seeing tours gave him a feel for European culture. If moments of loneliness overtook him in his early years, he had the presence of his Capuchin cousin, Father Dominic Meyer, who had entered the order in 1915 and was in Rome studying at thc Gregorian.

In July 1926, Albert Meyer was ordained to the priesthood by Cardinal Basilio Pompilj at the Church of Santa Maria Sopra Minerva in Rome and then he completed his last year of classes. In his last year at the North American College he met Monsignor Moses Kiley, the tall and solemn spiritual director of the North American College who had replaced Monsignor Edward Mooney. He and Kiley became closely associated (it would be difficult to call Kiley a friend, since he did not permit that level of association). Kiley served Meyer only one year as spiritual director, but he later became the young seminarian's patron. Kiley visited Meyer's parents in West Allis when he returned to Chicago on vacation.

Meyer finished his licentiate in theology in 1926, and in 1927 received his doctorate after completing a thesis on the indwelling of the Holy Spirit. He was permitted a brief visit home in 1927 to say his first Mass in Milwaukee and to visit his ailing sister Olivia, who was slowly dying of cancer at the Notre Dame convent.[35] While Meyer was in Rome, Pope Pius XI issued the *motu proprio Bibliorum scientiam* (1924) which required professors of scripture studies to have degrees from the Pontifical Biblical Institute or the Pontifical Biblical Commission in Rome.[36] In October 1928 Messmer sent Meyer back to Rome to begin classes at the Pontifical Biblical Institute and to reside at the Anima, a residence for German priests in Rome. The four years at the Biblicum included extensive work in ancient semitic languages as well as in Latin and Greek. Among his teachers was Jesuit Agostino Bea, a German Jesuit who would become a confessor to popes and a cardinal. Meyer studied for a summer in Palestine (growing a beard, to the horror of his mother, and dressing in a caftan and headdress). Here he came into contact with Dominican Marie-Joseph LaGrange and imbibed enough knowledge to teach a standard course on biblical archaeology and geography at St. Francis, known as "Dan to Beersheba." Before he finished his work in 1930, Meyer had also met Bernard Alfrink a future cardinal in the Netherlands; William Newton of Cleveland, a founder of the American Biblical Association; and Rudolf Graber, a student from Eichstatt, Germany, who later became the bishop of Regensburg.

He returned to Milwaukee in the summer of 1930, just as Messmer was departing for what would be his last sojourn abroad. The uncertainty caused by his death and the advent of Stritch in November resulted in Meyer's being assigned to St. Joseph's parish in Waukesha. The one year of "seelsorge," as he later called it, would be his only exposure to parish life. His sermons from the pastoral year in Waukesha—carefully written in a tiny "Notre Dame cursive," were tightly reasoned and often larded with lengthy quotations from papal encyclicals.[37] Meyer was never a dynamic speaker, and extemporaneous comments were not his forte. In 1931, Stritch appointed him to the seminary faculty, and St. Francis Seminary would be his home for the next 16 years.

As did most junior professors, Meyer taught an array of classes in every branch of the seminary program. He taught religion to high school students, Latin and biblical archaeology to collegians and dogma to theologians. Italian was added to his class load in the 1933-1934 school year. He also taught Greek,

Albert Meyer, Seminary rector
[AAM]

Hebrew, and ascetical theology. Meyer's students remember him as a careful, well-prepared and thorough teacher. His imposing 6-foot-4-inch figure was a commanding presence in the classroom, and he maintained discipline with a bug-eyed stare or by peering over the rim of his glasses.[38] His classroom performance, however, suffered in comparison with those of his colleagues Aloysius Muench or Francis Haas. Like his Waukesha sermons, his lectures were dull and uninspiring. One student of those years called them "leaden." He never inspired student familiarity, nicknames or friendliness. His chief emotional outlets appear to have been playing the cello parts to recorded music and the mandolin for his friends and the students at the summer seminary villa. He visited his parents every Sunday, with the equally taciturn William Groessel (one wonders if their get-togethers weren't more like Quaker meetings with one waiting on the spirit to move the other to speak). He also was friendly with John Grellinger, who returned to the seminary as an instructor in philosophy in 1936.

With the exception of one major project, Meyer was not a research scholar. In 1936, he was recruited by a fellow Biblicum classmate, Father William Newton of Cleveland, to participate in a team gathered to re-translate the Rheims-Challoner version of the vulgate for the new Confraternity of Christian Doctrine version of the bible sought by CCD patron and sponsor, Edwin Vincent O'Hara.[39] Working under the direction of Sulpician Edward Arbez, Meyer's task was to translate the Epistles of St. John.[40] He was also to produce a readable essay giving the basic principles of exegesis and some interpretation for confraternity readers, who would be using it for catechetical instruction. Meyer worked from 1936 to 1937 on the translation and even longer on the commentary, which was so lengthy that the editors had to pare it down. His skills as a translator must have not been quite what the reviewers expected. When the new scriptural text and the translation appeared in 1942, Meyer confessed to John Grellinger that the editors had so thoroughly revised his work that he barely recognized it when it did come out in print.[41]

This work on the Johannine epistles constituted Meyer's most ambitious scholarly effort based on his doctoral work in Rome. By contemporary standards they would be unacceptable, but they were typical of the kind of apologetic style taught at the Biblicum and elsewhere, prior to the introduction of historical-critical forms of exegesis.

Apart from a biblical geography class he taught younger students at the Salesianum. He rarely taught scripture or exegesis to major seminarians, since Father Andrew Breen, who had been teaching scripture since 1918, was still very much alive. By the time Breen died, Meyer was rector and only able to teach a light load of classes; most of the scripture courses were "farmed out" to Redemptorist Edward Mangan. Meyer produced a few articles for the seminary journal *Salesianum*—largely works of exegesis and no doubt papers he had done while a student in Rome.[42] As a professor he did supply work in parishes and provided liturgical services to the Italians of West Allis.

Meyer served first under two rectors, Aloysius Muench and Francis Haas, before assuming the job himself. When Haas went back to Washington, D.C., Stritch called in the 34-year-old Meyer, and appointed him to head St. Francis Seminary.[43] Meyer turned to Muench for advice, and the bishop of Fargo urged him to delegate tasks and not try to do everything himself, "You will relieve yourself of work that can be well done by others, and … you will flatter them with the attention you pay them," Muench wrote. He let on as well, "I found 'the pest house' in the Infirmary a quiet place to get a little rest on afternoons when bells or other rest-disturbing noises on the third floor prevented me from taking a nap." Finally he counseled, "You will find the first year difficult because of the strangeness of the work and the adjustments which you will have to make. I hope you will not carry your work into the vacations."[44] Meyer adjusted well to the role of seminary rector, and in 1938 was made a monsignor.[45]

Rev. Andrew Breen [AAM]

The 1930s were a time of transition for American seminaries. Pope Pius XI issued two decrees that reshaped theological study: *Deus Scientiarum Dominus* (1931) and *Ad Catholicii Sacerdotii* (1935).[46] The former urged seminaries to tighten the academic and intellectual integrity of their programs. The second document, *Ad Catholicii Sacerdotii,* rehashed much of what the pontiff had said in earlier letters and directives on the priesthood and priestly formation, but also made a strong appeal for the cultivation of the inner life of the priest. Meyer was enthralled with the language of *Ad Catholicii* (in fact, he even had a saying from the encyclical engraved on his tombstone at St. Mary of the Lake Seminary in Mundelein). In his conferences to seminarians and his approach to the spiritual life of the seminary, Meyer drew heavily from the ideas embodied in this text. In 1938 and 1939 the pontiff ordered a general visitation of seminaries throughout the world. One of the results was a decision to separate the minor and major departments. In fact, Stritch had anticipated this, and on the night he made Meyer rector, he expressed his desire to make this happen. However, the financial outlay involved and Stritch's departure made this impossible.[47] When Kiley arrived, these plans were formalized and the Pio Nono buildings behind the seminary were transformed into St. Francis Minor Seminary; the younger boys were transferred from the old Salesianum building.[48] The major seminary also came in for some long overdue renovations and upgrading.

The new St. Francis Minor Seminary was to be headed by Meyer's friend Groessel and would have a distinct faculty, although some professors from the major also did duty at the minor. To pay for the renovation of the building, Kiley showed how different he was from his predecessor and levied an assessment of $160,000 on the clergy (which caused muted grumbling). Nothing escaped Kiley's eagle eye. The major seminary renovation included the transformation of two existing dining rooms into one large refectory, the large dormitories of the high school and college into private rooms, and the installation of an elevator. Kiley went over every aspect of the plan and insisted that seminary procurator Father Nicholas Brust send him detailed reports of the progress of the building and the money expended. When he discovered that rubber flooring was being installed by the contractor and not the seminary workmen, he raged at Brust and insisted that this work be done by local labor in order to "save the hard-earned money of the clergy." He made it clear to Brust and Meyer that not only was he watching their every move but so were all the priests "who can pay only ten or fifteen dollars per month."[49] Dutifully, Meyer was compelled to trudge to the archbishop's office to explain expenses and occasionally to be warned about "extravagance." Kiley also upbraided the rector for appointing Grellinger as the seminary secretary without his approval.[50] He ordered professors to change textbooks in mid-semester, abolished a separate dining

Ordinations to the priesthood [AAM]

room for the faculty (a *sine qua non* for the harried professors who lived with the young men); and insisted that the faculty all be present for the mind-numbing ritual of reading the long list of rules of the seminary.[51] Kiley could be utterly erratic in his behavior, approving one privilege for the minor seminarians and denying it to the major seminarians.[52]

Yet despite the challenge of coping with Kiley, Meyer loved St. Francis and his work as rector. He moved the seminary through the accelerated courses required to maintain draft deferments through World War II, and was the soul of kindness to young men discovering they had no vocation. To each of the ordination classes he gave special conferences and a small gift that many of them treasured. The students reciprocated his kindness by inviting him to preach at their first Masses and according him a respect and reverence that was not readily given to his successor, Monsignor Frank Schneider.

If he found anything distasteful in the job, it was probably the public relations tasks attached to it. He was called on to speak to lay groups around the diocese and to preach at large archdiocesan events and rallies, such as the popular prayers-for-peace rallies at Marquette Stadium and elsewhere. He assumed the moderatorship of the local Serra Club and met with the pious men monthly to drum up support for priestly vocations. These forays into the world of backslapping bonhomie must have tested him severely. No one was happier to turn his automobile back up the seminary drive than Meyer after one of these sorties.

Perhaps the most interesting aspect of Meyer's career, given his austere personality, was his "secret" attachment to utterly sentimental forms of Latin piety, particularly to the Sacred Heart of Jesus. He was particularly fascinated with the passionate and garrulous Father Mateo Crawley-Boevey, a Chilean-born priest of the Sacred Heart.[53] Father

Rev. Mateo Crawley-Boevey, SSCC [Marcel Bocquet. *The Firebrand,* Corda Press, 1966]

Consecration of Albert G. Meyer [AAM]

Mateo, who had been healed at the Sacred Heart shrine of Paray-le-Monial in France, had devoted his life to spreading devotion to the Sacred Heart of Jesus. His specialty was promoting a program called "night adoration" in which people would spend nights in prayer before a special picture of the Sacred Heart that had been enthroned in the home by the parish priest. Crawley-Boevey came to the United States in 1940 and Kiley recruited him to deliver the clerical retreats in 1942. Meyer was so moved by Crawley-Boevey's "soul stirring eloquence" that he had him deliver the seminarian's retreat that year. In a semi-darkened chapel, Father Mateo lectured the impressionable young seminarians in dramatic, sometimes barely audible tones. He would then abruptly change the pitch of his voice and bark out one word like "love," "death," or "sin." Some students could barely stifle their amusement at the retreat master's histrionics, but Albert Meyer and Archbishop Kiley regarded him as a saint. At the end of the seminarian's retreat, Father Mateo formally "enthroned" a picture of the Sacred Heart in the seminary dining room. As he did Kiley broke down in tears.[54]

With Kiley's permission, Mateo traversed the diocese, often with Meyer as his chauffeur, to preach night adoration and the enthronement doctrine.[55] Some of the seminarians were equally enthralled. Others dismissed him as a pious fraud and wondered how he could have wormed his way into the confidences of two such frigid personalities as Meyer and Kiley. Meyer for his part never lost his affection for Father Mateo, who died in 1960. When he became bishop, Meyer chose as his motto "*Adveniat Regnum Tuum*" (Thy Kingdom Come) in imitation of Mateo's penchant for beginning his rambling letters to him with a bold-printed ADVENIAT! Meyer wrote in a collection of Mateo's works that appeared after the priest's death (*Father Mateo Speaks to Priests*) that "I have always considered it one of the special graces of my life to have known Father Mateo."[56]

Meyer also cultivated a special respect and secret attachment to the Italian stigmatic, Padre Pio, whom his Capuchin cousin Dominic Meyer had served as secretary since 1948. Meyer actually had intended to visit the Capuchin at his monastery in Foggia, Italy in 1953, when he received the appointment to Milwaukee. When the prospect of succeeding Kiley overwhelmed him, he implored his cousin to ask Padre Pio for prayers. "I have felt so weak of body the last few days that I wondered at times whether something would not perhaps break. I surely would not wish to get sick now." He further begged, "I ask you to recommend this petition to Padre Pio's prayers, that through the 'Novena iresistibile al Sacro Cuore de Gesu' I may be given the grace of bodily health and strength as well [as the] grace of total dedication to the new apostolate assigned to me by the Will of God through the mandate of the Holy Father."[57] When he did finally make the trip to Italy in 1954 for the canonization ceremonies for St. Pius X, Meyer slipped away to Foggia to confess to the saintly stigmatic and to visit his cousin.

In February 1946 Meyer received the news that he had been named to succeed Bishop William Patrick O'Connor in Superior. Although sentiments of unworthiness are part of the "drill" for all those nominated to the Roman Catholic episcopate, for Meyer they appeared to be genuine. Meyer really did not wish to leave the safe cloister of the seminary, fearful of the tremendous social demands the new job placed on him. On April 11, 1946, he was consecrated bishop of Superior by Kiley, assisted by Aloysius Muench and Bishop O'Connor in the recently restored St. John's Cathedral.

Three days later he performed his first confirmations at Gesu Church and at St. John's School for the Deaf. On May 8, 1946, he arrived in Superior and was enthroned in the Cathedral of Christ the King. He would spend seven years in the diocese, attempting to bring about some unity among its far-flung parishes and highly individualistic presbyterate. These 16 counties of northwestern Wisconsin contained 60,893 Catholics (out of a total population of 321,219), 149 priests and nearly 600 sisters. There were 86 parishes, 61 missions, four Catholic high schools, 32 grade schools and 28,000 persons in Superior, the largest city. The ethnic medley was similar to Milwaukee's: Polish, Irish, Slovak, Italian, French and German congregations. In addition two Indian reservations for the Chippewa at Bayfield and Red Cliff were also sites of Catholic activity and the work of Indian priest Philip Gordon.[58]

The problems Meyer inherited in Superior were in part based on its remoteness and poverty. The area had no strong industrial base and relied heavily on some minor industries, seasonal lake shipping and recreation. It had been saddled with a huge debt in the 1920s when Bishop Joseph Gabriel Pinten erected the Cathedral of Christ the King, a virtual replica of the church of St. Lawrence Outside-the-Walls in Rome, but nearly impossible for the tiny Catholic population to pay for. The episcopate of Pinten's successor Kentucky-born Theodore Revermann, also made matters difficult. Revermann was a man of erudition and good training, but he found the Superior See difficult to take and was incapacitated by heart problems and financial worries (aggravated by the Great Depression). His scrupulosity on sacramental matters caused him to refuse to ordain men to the priesthood—men who were desperately needed to fill in at mission stations and parishes throughout the widespread diocese.[59] O'Connor tried to get matters on track, but when the opportunity came to escape, he quickly jumped to the new diocese at Madison, created in 1946.

Meyer came to these problems with his deliberate manner and the experience of running a seminary. He took up residence in the old drafty episcopal mansion at 1108 East Second Street that had been built by Bishop Joseph Maria Koudelka; and with limited staff, set out to "present himself" to the problems of Superior as they came to his desk. His first months were lonely. He confided his longing for the seminary to his cousin Dominic Meyer, who consoled him: "I can well understand that you miss the teaching .... Your great consolation—the chapel—and you have a nice quiet devotional retreat in your house chapel. Prayer, as you say is the only thing that counts."[60] Given the shortage of clergy and the lack of money to hire secretarial staff, he had no choice but to immerse himself directly into diocesan administration, typing his own letters, answering his own phone, and traveling without a master of ceremonies for official duties. He soon gathered around him a group of trusted priests, including Alphonse Kress, whom he moved into the episcopal mansion. Kress admired and respected the bishop, but found Meyer's inability to indulge in much small talk unnerving.[61] Kress was frequently rescued from long silent dinners by Monsignor Joseph Annabring, a graduate of St. Francis Seminary and a native of the area. Annabring, the cathedral rector, was gracious and gregarious and one of the most astute priests of the diocese. Meyer worked hard to have him appointed his successor in 1953.

Meyer stumbled a bit in his early days when he attempted to implement Kiley's dictum that no young priest should own a car, and by insisting that each priest pay back the diocese what had been expended for their seminary education. Both policies raised tensions with the local clergy and revealed how little the "city-boy" Meyer knew of the distances traveled in rural dioceses and of the limited finances on which priests worked in the poor see. After a short

Episcopal Residence, Superior WI [AOSF]

time, he backed away from both.[62] To bring some unity to the Superior clergy, he adapted many of the techniques of seminary administration: holding clerical conferences that he conducted like seminary classes on topics related to priestly ministry (e.g., canonical issues, devotion to the Sacred Heart, etc.). He also attempted to centralize certain diocesan activities and created the Superior Diocesan Council of Catholic Women and even provided a Superior Diocese edition of the Milwaukee *Catholic Herald Citizen.* While he continued to rely heavily on the Franciscans and Benedictines who served in diocesan parishes, Meyer was fortunate to share in the vocation boom of post-war Catholic America. By the time he left Superior in 1953, tiny Superior counted 50 seminarians in different phases of formation and a string of priestly ordinations that took place every year to begin to erase the damage created by Revermann's priestless years.

Superior's long winters gave him the opportunity to do the writing that he never had time to do at St. Francis. Over the course of several winters Meyer drafted a series of sermon outlines based on the readings of the Mass prescribed for the day. These outlines contained extensive information for Sunday sermons (in those days sermon topics were determined in some dioceses by the bishop and announced in the Catholic newspaper).[63] Kiley liked the texts so much that he had them reproduced and used in Milwaukee's churches. Meyer intended them only as guides and stimuli for the independent work of the priest sermonizer. Some priests in Milwaukee and elsewhere simply read them verbatim from the pulpit.

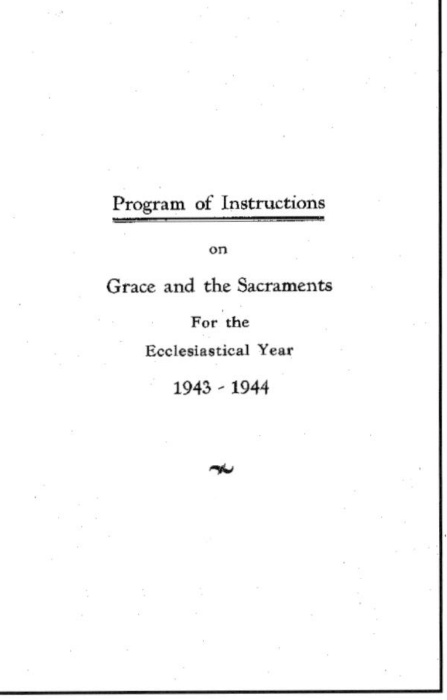
Program of Instructions

on

Grace and the Sacraments

For the

Ecclesiastical Year

1943 - 1944

[AAM]

The years in Superior went quickly. Meyer returned to Milwaukee to assist in the consecration of Monsignor Roman Atkielski as Kiley's auxiliary in 1947, and in 1949 was in the sanctuary when his friend Grellinger was consecrated an auxiliary bishop of Green Bay. He visited Rome on an *ad limina* visit in 1949. In 1952, the health of both of his parents declined badly. Peter Meyer pulled out of the slump, but Mathilda died on January 21, 1953.[64] Likewise, Kiley's health, in steady decline since 1949, also gave way. Meyer was in attendance on April 15, 1953, when Kiley died, cradling the prelate's head in his arms when he gave up the ghost.[65] Meyer participated in the solemn requiem, giving one of the absolutions over Kiley's remains, and then he returned home to Superior.

In July 1953 some Milwaukee friends came up for an annual fishing expedition. The day they were scheduled to depart, Meyer's secretary brought a packet of mail that contained a letter from the apostolic delegate. Excusing himself, he went to another room and read of his appointment to Milwaukee.[66] The news of the nomination was given to the press during a meeting of the St. Francis Seminary Alumni Association on July 28, 1953. Prepared for the interviews and questions, he calmly pulled a statement from his cassock pocket and read: "I am returning to those who remember me as one of their own. This establishes an immediate bond between us which, with the help of God's grace, I hope will continue to grow and prosper."[67] Within he was fearful, and confided his concern to Grellinger, who wrote back, "I suppose it does take quite a while to adjust oneself to the idea of being Archbishop of Milwaukee. MEK [Moses Elias Kiley] seemed to be such a Rock [*sic*] that one thought of his abiding forever, and it must seem strange to succeed him."[68]

Meyer finished out his affairs in Superior and said farewell at a Mass held in the Cathedral of Christ the King on September 22, 1953. The question of his successor was one of the first he had to deal with as the new metropolitan archbishop of the Wisconsin province. The decision was difficult, since his friend, John Grellinger, now an auxiliary bishop in Green Bay, desperately wanted a diocese of his own. Grellinger subtly pressed his candidacy on Meyer, hinting that he was already tired of serving as an understudy to Bishop Stanislaus Bona.[69] However, even a lifelong friendship with Grellinger did not deter Meyer from doing what he felt was right. Instead of Grellinger, he recommended the appointment of cathedral rector Monsignor Joseph Annabring as his successor. Unlike any other Superior bishop, Annabring, a native of Turtle Creek, Wisconsin, was a son of the diocese. Meyer returned in 1954 to consecrate Annabring and hoped that he would bring growth to the struggling Superior diocese. When Annabring died unexpectedly in 1959, Meyer lamented to a former colleague in the diocese, "I hoped that we would have given the diocese a good bishop for years to come."[70]

Consecration of Bishop John Grellinger [AAM]

On September 24, 1953, Meyer stood once again at the center of attention in the sanctuary of St. John's Cathedral, where he was solemnly enthroned by Apostolic Delegate Amleto Cicognani. In a 44-minute sermon, carried live by radio and television, Meyer told the assembled multitudes, many of them priests he had instructed at St. Francis Seminary: "The ties which bind me to the glorious past of the history of the archdiocese of Milwaukee are many and varied; forming both a personal and an official heritage on which it shall be my responsibility to build. As seventh in the line which begins with the name of John Martin Henni, in the words of the biblical proverb quoted by Our Lord, 'I have been sent to reap on that which I have not labored; others have labored, and I have entered into their labors.'"[71] The work of administering the rapidly growing Milwaukee archdiocese was more than Meyer could handle and in the spring of 1954 he suffered some kind of physical breakdown precipitated by a case of the flu. The diagnosis for public consumption was that Meyer was suffering from an ulcer, but in reality, the loss of his mother and Kiley as well as the barrage of demands in his new job had induced a "mild" nervous breakdown. However with diet and some attempts at exercise along with his own highly disciplined personality, Meyer was able to overcome the setback.[72]

In the 18 years of Kiley's and Meyer's administrations, the challenge of Catholic visibility returned, but with a twist. The archdiocese hit its centenary mark in 1943 and could look back on a successful experience of adapting the Catholic presence to social and economic life in Wisconsin. Scores of churches commanded acres of prime urban property, presided over bustling industrial towns, and still towered over villages and communities. The systems of school and social provision had been substantially expanded and reformed to meet the changing framework of educational philosophy and the demands of new theories of health care and the needs of dependent children. The archdiocese of Milwaukee had produced a Catholic culture large and generous enough to provide sons and daughters to serve the needs of the Church. Although ethnic elements remained in clergy and laity, the preponderance of archdiocesan Catholics were now American-born and rooted in the neighborhoods of Wisconsin. They spoke in the idiom of their communities, took their points of reference from the industrial culture around them, and knew the value of time and money. They cherished few doubts (thanks to their theological formation) about the nature, purpose and identity of Catholic life. Coping with World War II was their first task. Later, the shifting currents of the post-war world would be taken on without missing a beat.

Rebuilding the Cathedral

Kiley's installation at Gesu Church brought home to him one of the first priorities of his administration, the rebuilding of the Cathedral of St. John. After the fire, rumors circulated that Stritch considered abandoning the cathedral, and either building a new structure on another site or designating an impressively large church like Gesu or St. Anne's as the new cathedral of the archdiocese.[73] Likewise, some speculated that he allowed Shorewood priest Farrell P. Reilly to proceed with his elaborate Romanesque church with the idea that this too might be the new church of the Milwaukee See. Building anew was quickly ruled out because of expense and the possibility of arguments over location. However, fearing that a change to a parish church might stir up residual ethnic jealousies, Stritch decided to rebuild St. John's. He began to raise funds for the new cathedral in 1936 by turning over a portion of the now annual Archbishop's Emergency Fund to the task.[74]

Cathedral fire, January 1935 [AAM]

Stritch was the first bishop since Henni to stress the primacy of the cathedral, "as the mother church" from which all other churches and chapels take their canonical standing and meaning. Reaching into the church's past, he insisted that "No church guarantees apostolicity and catholicity like a cathedral." Of the $300,000 goal of the annual appeal, Stritch pledged $125,000 for the cathedral rebuilding.[75] In 1937, he directed architect William Richard Perry of Pittsburgh, whom he had employed to build Toledo's Cathedral of the Holy Rosary, to come up with some sketches for the restored structure.[76] Perry lengthened the structure by 55 feet (this was made possible by the removal of the old Bishop's Hall that stood on the east side of the property) and capped it with a new and higher barrel-vaulted roof. The new roof required slightly higher walls and the addition of pillars on each side of the cathedral. This dramatically altered the inner space of the church and made it look more like a Roman basilica than the building architect Victor Schulte had intended.

The transfer of Stritch and the "settling in" time of Kiley slowed the project, but no doubt Stritch pressed the completion on to his successor. In May 1941 cathedral rector Monsignor Francis Murphy reignited interest in the project by revealing that over $200,000 had been spent to restore the site.[77] In September, Kiley said another $250,000 was necessary to complete the job.[78]

In 1941 local artisans at the T.C. Esser Studios were commissioned to design windows to go into 53 openings of the newly enlarged walls.[79] But the project slowed, as $206,000 was eaten up by the roof and the extension. In November 1941 Kiley targeted the 1943 archdiocesan centennial as the date for the completion of the cathedral renovation. Financial conditions were improved to the point where he could launch a $500,000 "Centennial Fund Drive" to pay for the re-

Cathedral rebuilding [Courtesy of Kevin Wester]

mainder of the project and to support archdiocesan charities.[80] An artist's sketch of the new cathedral interior appeared in the *Catholic Herald Citizen* before Christmas 1941 as an inducement to give.[81]

Kiley hired the firm of Schmitt and Son as the general contractors. By mid-1942, a photo essay in the Catholic newspaper showed Kiley and Stritch inspecting the progress of the cathedral.[82] Steady advance continued despite wartime building restrictions. On

Repairing the Cathedral clock [AAM]

September 16, 1942, the cathedral tower clock, stopped since the fire in 1935, was restarted—at 4:23 P.M. Additional details of the renovation were provided in mid-October, 1942, when it was predicted that the church might be ready for Midnight Mass at Christmas. Terrazzo floors had been installed, and even before the altar furnishings were in place, the outlines of the extended sanctuary were evident. On each side of the sanctuary was a "sister's loft," which would look down on the scenic design of the sanctuary marble. (For years photographers would use this perch to capture the symmetry, or lack thereof, of the various classes of ordinandi lying prostrate before the altar.) Ornamental plaster adorned the tops of new pillars with Corinthian capitals, yet another departure from the original style of the interior.[83] In late October Kiley unveiled the first of T.C. Esser's stained glass windows. The image, composed of 5,408 pieces of glass, was of the cathedral's patron, St. John the Evangelist. Ambrose Esser described for *Herald Citizen* readers the creation of the windows from the charcoal "cartoons" of design artist Leo Cartwright to the skilled work of master craftsman Erhard Stoettner. Subsequent months saw the addition of more windows as they were produced by the artists and artisans of the Esser Studios.[84] The new interior design appeared in the *Catholic Herald Citizen* which printed an elaborate drawing showing plans for a baldacchino over an imported marble altar.[85]

By December 1942 the altar was being installed, with promises that the baldacchino would be ready for Easter. Elaborate descrip-

The new Cathedral windows [AAM]

tions of the new sanctuary appointments revealed that altars were constructed of several different types of marble (Breccia Violetta, Breccia Serravezza, Giallo Siena, Bianco Chiaro, all quarried at Carrara, Italy).[86] When Kiley sang the Midnight Mass of Christmas, demand was so high that tickets were handed out to a select number. Shortly after Christ-

Cathedral baldacchino [AAM]

Between October 7-10, 1943, Kiley showed off St. John's Cathedral on the occasion of the archdiocesan centenary.[89] Each day's events began with a Pontifical Mass celebrated in the church, the first being by Archbishop Stritch and highlighting choirs of women religious and school children from the archdiocesan schools. Bishops from around the country marveled at the building. The celebration of the centenary was deliberately modest in view of wartime restrictions. Apart from the cathedral ceremonies, few other archdiocesan celebrations took place. Seminary historian Father Peter Leo Johnson produced *Centennial Essays*, a compilation of essays to commemorate various aspects of the archdiocese's foundation.[90] The muted cel-

mas, the hyper-dramatic Apostle of the Sacred Heart, Father Mateo Crawley-Boevey, conducted a holy hour in the restored church. In March 1943, ordinations to the priesthood took place in the refurbished church, permanently transferring them from the seminary chapel.[87] By Wednesday of Holy Week the baldacchino was complete, in time for the solemn chanting of Tenebrae, and Easter celebrations took place in the full glory of the new sanctuary.[88]

Rebuilt Cathedral interior [AAM]

ebration occurred during a period in which scores of requiem Masses were offered up daily for those slain in the war, and fervent prayers for peace went on nonstop.

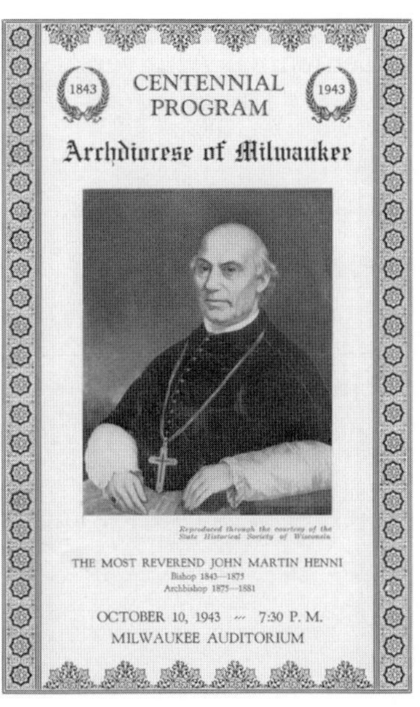

[AAM]

Milwaukee During the War

Wisconsin's Catholics—especially those of Polish and German descent—were on a war-footing even before Kiley arrived in early 1940. As we have seen, Stritch had genuine misgivings over American involvement abroad, but his increasingly vigorous denunciations of Nazi repression had heightened archdiocesan awareness of looming international issues. The huge prayer rallies for peace organized by the Archdiocesan League of Holy Name Societies and held at Marquette Stadium were for many a hope that America could dodge the bullet.

There was no poll of archdiocesan Catholics on the question of involvement in World War II, but they probably reflected the division of opinion that existed among Catholics across the United States. Some Catholics leaned toward Roosevelt's increasingly more aggressive policy of helping the British fend off Hitler. The collapse of Poland in 1939 had been followed by the fall of the Netherlands, Belgium, the invasion of Scandinavia and in June 1940 the capitulation of France. The Battle of Britain began to rage in the summer of 1940.

Within the Catholic world, voices like those of St. Augustine Bishop John Patrick Hurley urged Americans to be aware of the dangers of appeasing the rapacious Third Reich. In a July 1940 radio broadcast, Hurley had called on all Americans, but particularly his co-religionists, to support Roosevelt's plan for preparedness and urged firmness with Hitler.[91] On the other side of the issue was the head of Milwaukee's neighboring archdiocese of Dubuque, Francis J. L. Beckmann, who warned Americans not to be taken in as they had been in World War I by somber warnings of impending disaster.[92] Anti-interventionist sentiment had been strong in America and grew stronger after the 1940 election when Roosevelt engineered the Lend-Lease Act of 1941 to funnel military goods and material to Britain and after June 1941 to Soviet Russia.

The America First Movement, which began in Chicago, included among its list of headline speakers Father William O'Brien, a highly successful Newman chaplain at the University of Illinois and a leading convert-maker. O'Brien came to Milwaukee's auditorium in October 1941 to urge locals to stay out of the war. At times Milwaukee clerics weighed in on the question, although this diminished rapidly as Kiley renewed Messmer's prohibitions on clerical commentary on political topics.

Wisconsin Catholics were as shocked as the rest of the nation when radio broadcasts were interrupted on September 7, 1941, to inform Americans that the naval base at Pearl Harbor had been attacked. Press reports were quick to note the death of two local men, Cornelius John O'Donnell and Norbert Fliss. Concerns were raised about the 18 sisters and seven priests who hailed from Wisconsin and were now in the Pacific war zone.[93] One former Milwaukee priest, Father James Cherne, the founding pastor of Ss. Cyril and Methodius in Sheboygan who had returned to his native Slovenia in 1938, was arrested by the Germans and placed in the Laufenberg prisoner of war camp in Bavaria.[94]

The one lone clerical voice who dared to defy Kiley's ban on making political statements was the somewhat eccentric Father Leonard Koehring, pastor of St. Augustine Church in Janesville, whose passion for non-intervention continued beyond Pearl Harbor. The hapless Koehring brought a firestorm of criticism on himself when in a sermon given one week after Pearl Harbor, he declared that Japan was "justified" in her attack on Pearl Harbor, because the United States had "declared economic war" on the Asian nation.[95] The ensuing uproar eventually resulted in Koehring's transfer to the rural St. Mathias Mission in Auburn, where his outspoken behavior continued, but was far removed from local newspapers.

As in World War I, the nation was called on to mobilize militarily, economically and ideologically. Recruiting stations in Wisconsin cities were jammed. Civil defense officials drew up black-out plans and conducted air raid drills and other preparedness activities. As men left the factories and machine shops, their places were taken by older men and a cadre of women. The Catholic Church in Milwaukee sought to adjust to the challenges and disruptions of war.

Rev. Harold O. Prudell [AAM]

War Chaplains

Milwaukee's Catholic men and women responded to the call for service, and by July 1942 nearly 10,000 archdiocesan men had enlisted.[96] Priests were also caught up in the patriotic fervor. The day after Pearl Harbor, Father Mark Lyons later recalled that nearly 20 clerics volunteered for service in the military.[97] In 1941 young Father Harold Prudell, the son of a retired army captain, had already entered the armed forces and was the youngest chaplain in the army.[98] Among the first to join the fray was World War I veteran Father August F. Gearhard, whose reserve unit was called up.[99] Kiley was not eager to allow his priests to go into the military, fearing shortages in supplying parishes, but the call of duty and the demands from Archbishop John J. O'Hara, head of the military ordinariate, left him little alternative. By February 1942 seven Milwaukee priests were in the military. By the end of the war, 37 Milwaukee clerics had entered various branches of the armed forces. Kiley's worries about being shorthanded were allayed by the acceleration of the seminary program, which ran year-round during the war to maintain the draft exemptions of the young men.

One of the most famous Milwaukee chaplains, Father Mathias Zerfas, an assistant at St. Mary's in Fond du Lac, had already joined the army in 1940 and was assigned to the 26th Cavalry Regiment in the Philippines before hostilities began. Zerfas soon drew attention because of his capture in the Philippines during the notorious Bataan campaign and "death march."[100] Although the Twin Lakes native survived the march, he met a watery death when the Japanese prisoner ship bearing him to imprisonment in Taiwan was sunk by American planes during a raid on Takao Harbor.[101] Zerfas's memory was kept alive by frequent remembrances in the diocesan newspaper, by sentimental accounts in the seminary magazine *Salesianum* and even by noted author John Hersey.[102] Another chaplain, Ladislaus A. Polewski, assigned to the Mars Task Force in Burma, contracted a fever and died in early 1945.[103]

Some archdiocesan priests drew less hazardous military experience. In Florida St. Augustine Bishop Joseph Patrick Hurley invited eight seminary professors to join other priests in helping him to minister to the 75,000 servicemen assigned in his diocese.

Rev. Mathias Zerfas [AAM]

Among these were dogmatic theology professor John Schulien, who actually considered entering the service during the war. The eight priests went down to Florida at Christmastime, dividing themselves between locations in northern and southern Florida.[104]

Closer to home, liturgical services were held for German prisoners of war imprisoned behind barbed wire at General Billy Mitchell Field located south of Milwaukee. Serving the Catholics fell to the fathers of the Sacred Heart from Hales Corners. Father Angelico Koller celebrated Mass for the POWs, and with donations of German prayer books and benches from St. Anne's parish, as well as other charitable donations he solicited, attempted to take care of the men so far from their German homeland.[105]

Rev. Eugene Kapalczynski [AAM]

The Milwaukee Chaplains

Letters from the chaplains to Archbishop Kiley report not only spiritual statistics (numbers of confessions, communions, etc.) but also tales of exotic cultures (especially those accompanying troops in the far-off Pacific). Bernard Scholzen was stationed in Assam, India, flying with pilots over the "Hump" to take supplies to Chiang Kai Shek's [Jiang Jieshi] Nationalist Chinese. Oliver Zinnen accompanied MacArthur's forces in New Caledonia, New Guinea and the Philippines. David Ryan was in Africa, and Eugene Kapalczynski was in Saipan. Those who worked with American armies in Italy had an opportunity to see Catholicism's "central headquarters." Raymond Vint, who received his chaplain's commission in 1943, was the first American chaplain to enter Rome when American forces liberated the Eternal City in 1944. He saw the grateful Pius XII stand on the balcony of St. Peter's, welcoming the liberators with his arms outstretched. Vint celebrated Mass at the tomb of St. Peter, toured the catacombs and various Roman churches and shared a meal with the head of the Congregation of the Council, Cardinal Francesco Marmaggi.[106] In 1945 Vint joined the forces that landed on the shores of southern France at San Tropez. "My first act was to place the men of the Regiment under the Protection of Our Lady," he wrote Kiley, "and we attribute many successes to her intercession." Vint relayed in great detail the advance of the army up the Rhone Valley, past the former papal palaces at Avignon. He spoke sadly of the destruction of churches in France and Italy, but noted the generosity and devotion of the young men in his regiment. "When asked for the cause, I have given my conviction that it lies in the Catholic school system."[107]

The demands of chaplain life challenged the norms for liturgical observance priests had learned at St. Francis Seminary. Mass without vestments, without an altar stone or even without a chalice and unleavened bread were "permitted" during the war. So were general absolution of sins without auricular confession, and dispensations from fast and abstinence. Chaplain David Ryan wrote from Africa, "I received a veil [antimension], about the size of a corporal to be used in place of an altar stone." He noted with appreciation, "It will cut down the weight of the Mass kit considerably."[108] The celebration of Mass in the afternoon and evening was also an innovation to a generation of priests who had never celebrated a Mass after noon. "Among the many new experiences I have enjoyed," wrote army chaplain George Holzem, "possibly the greatest is the privilege of saying evening Mass." He noted approvingly that the request for the evening service had come from a group of men who wished to receive communion every day. "The evening was the only time they could do it. And it is inspiring to see them come for communion when it means that they have to miss their supper to do it."[109] The practicality of the evening Mass became evident on the home front as schedules were changed by wartime conditions. In 1953 Pope Pius XII permitted the celebration of afternoon or evening Masses based on the discretion of the local ordinary.[110] Other chaplains acted as vocation directors for men who discovered a priestly calling during the war years. "Since I have been at Ellington Field [Texas]," wrote air force chaplain John "Ty" Cullen, "several men have approached me as to the proper procedure of getting into seminaries after the war."[111] Many of those young men would begin studies for the priesthood, swelling the numbers of vocations to all-time highs. Others would never return from combat.

Chaplains came home from the war changed men. Some of them had seen horrible brutality, coped with immorality and fear among their own men, and written countless letters home to the parents, wives and sweethearts of deceased soldiers. Some of

Rev. John T. Cullen [AAM]

these priests became alcoholics or chronic smokers; some never were able to wash the memories of the carnage and sorrow out of their minds and hearts.[112] Virtually all of these men, most of them Wisconsin-born and bred, had a rare opportunity to travel and see the world. One chaplain wrote after service in the Pacific, "This past winter was my second without snow. Where I was we had rain instead. I guess I'll have to get Wisconsinized all over again when I get back."[113]

Catholics and the Home Front

Catholics at home in the archdiocese responded to war as did most others, by supporting patriotic drives to conserve and provide support for fighting men and women abroad. They also launched crusades of prayer which turned out thousands to pray for the safety of loved ones, the return of peace and even the victory of American forces.

Parishes sponsored an array of wartime activities. Red Cross chapters popped up, knitting garments for servicemen, cutting and rolling bandages, and preparing materials for USO clubs. Thousands of hours of service and goods were produced: St. Wenceslaus parish in Milwaukee reported in 1943 that its chapter had knitted 600 garments and rolled 10,000 surgical dressings. St. Sebastian's noted 18,000 hours of knitting, sewing and bandage rolling. Monsignor Traudt at St. Anne's Church insisted that the Notre Dame sisters convert their flower beds into a Victory Garden.

Parochial schools built war and patriotic consciousness through readings, plays and the collection of scrap and paper. At St. Boniface School, girls knitted scarfs and afghans for servicemen and collected toilet articles "for this noble cause." Others pooled their funds to purchase the small "Father Stedman's Missal" for soldiers, and helped to outfit a "chaplain's kit."[114] The sale of defense stamps, the dissemination of memorial flags by the war and treasury departments, and junior Red Cross activities marked the pattern of the school year. By 1944, the Catholic press reported that archdiocesan school children had bought $2.3 million in war bonds and stamps. Milwaukee's St. Thomas Aquinas

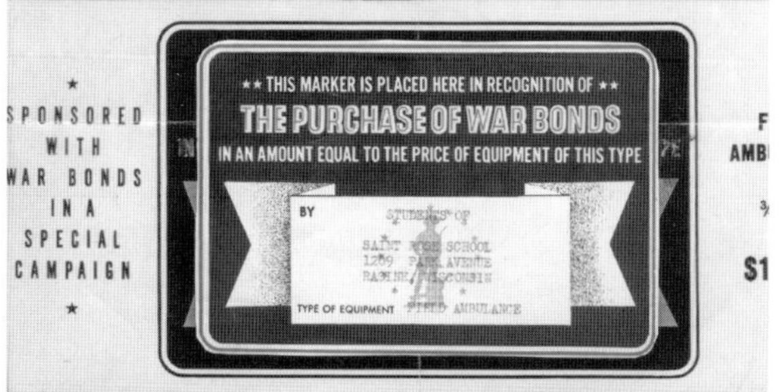

[AAM]

school children topped all others in the entire state by purchasing $25,279.15 in war bonds and stamps—enough to "purchase" a Fairchild PT-19 training plane, three jeeps, a Grasshopper plane, two field ambulances, two life vests and one walkie-talkie.[115]

Crusades of Prayer

One of the most important ways in which the Catholic Church helped people cope with the war was through prayer rallies. These expressions of popular piety were frequented by thousands of anxious archdiocesan Catholics. Archbishop Kiley continued to use the large rallies sponsored by the Holy Name Society and the Knights of Columbus. In January 1942, the Holy Name Society organized four patriotic rallies—three in Milwaukee churches and one in Kenosha—at which speakers linked allegiance to the name of God to allegiance to the nation.116 Kiley celebrated a Pontifical High Mass in Racine and urged 1500 members of the Holy Name to pledge allegiance "to the name of God and to the [American] flag" during the time of crisis."[117] In September, he invited Stritch to preside at a rally of 25,000 in Marquette Stadium. Two days before that rally, the two prelates hosted another in Madison that was attended by 10,000 shivering Catholics. Rallies in Racine and Kenosha to pray for peace touched a similar outpouring of attendance and support.

Religious orders such as the Dominican Sisters of the Perpetual Rosary on Stevenson and 68th in Milwaukee held a monthly prayer vigil for peace. The Jesuits transformed Gesu's annual Novena of Grace into a prayer for servicemen. Blessings of service flags, ceremonies for Gold Star families, and of course

Peace prayer rally, Marquette Stadium [AAM]

the regular occurrence of the somber Requiem Masses for those who fell in battle were part of the rhythm of Milwaukee Catholic life. In one parish alone, Holy Redeemer on Milwaukee's north side, 270 men fell in battle.

The accounts of activities on the day of the 1944 D-Day invasion reflected an unflagging devotion to the cause of the war, even after it had raged for nearly three years. The first to hear of the invasion of Normandy were those who attended the 6:00 A.M. Mass at Gesu celebrated by Father Richard Cahill. "There were tears in many eyes as Father requested special prayers for victory and peace," noted a reporter. Perpetual Help devotions, usually held on Tuesdays, were more crowded than ever and "a majority of those who prayed in the churches were women with coats thrown over their house dresses as thoughts of their men in service had pulled them away from their work." Youngsters at St. Robert's in Shorewood received maps to help study the invasion territory, while aged Catholics received the news personally from the Little Sisters of the Poor, who went room-to-room to pray the rosary with the elderly in their facility on Wells Street.[118]

[AAM]

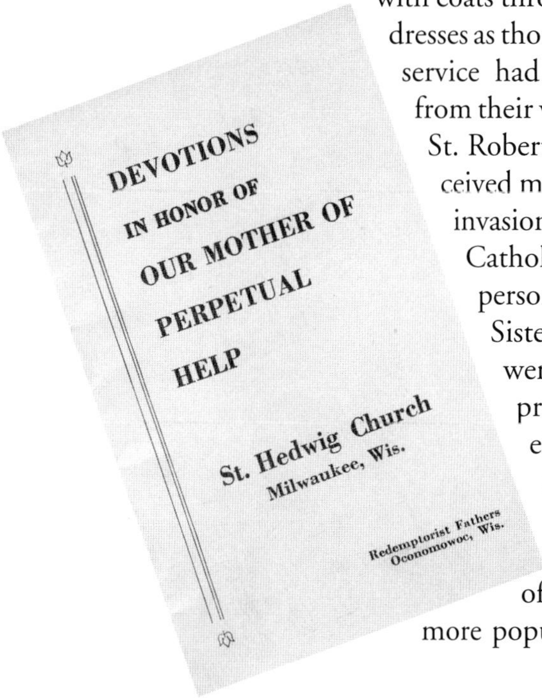

The flourishing novena crusades of the period grew even more popular during the war. Thousands flocked weekly to their parish churches to beseech God for an end to the conflict and the safety of loved ones. In particular the novena to the Sorrowful Mother, begun by the Servite Fathers in Chicago in 1937, became one of the most popular devotions in Milwaukee history. It had been prayed at the Servite monastery, Mount St. Philip in Granville, and from there it was commenced at St. Louis parish in Caledonia. Later it spread throughout the diocese. Two parishes, St. Boniface and St. Elizabeth in Milwaukee, began the novena in late 1938 when two visiting Servites led the first exercises.[119] The attendance at St. Mary's in Kenosha was so large that two back-to-back services had to be scheduled to accommodate the overflow.[120] In 1939, St. Anthony's on Mitchell Street also began leading the prayers, attracting nearly 2,000 people every Friday night.[121] On the fifth anniversary of the novena at St. Anthony's, Kiley attended two services given in honor of Gold Star mothers. At both events, pastor Charles Keyser handed out a booklet entitled "*Thoughts of Mary from the Foot of the Cross*" to help console the grieving women.[122]

The appeal of the novena to a suffering Mary was quite obvious to those who sought her help and intercession during the *sturm und drang* of the Depression and World War II. For those who could not easily go to church, the novena was broadcast from the cavernous Basilica of Our Lady of Sorrows on Jackson Street in Chicago by the powerful transmitters of station WCFL. Interestingly, the experience of praying together, and even singing the cloying "Good Night Sweet Jesus" at the end of the service, planted seeds of popular participation that would be harvested by liturgical reformers seeking to promote active participation at Mass. Even the secular *Milwaukee Sentinel* reported, "It is in this novena as in no other service of the Catholic Church that the people themselves participate in the devotions. The congregational singing alone is a novelty in a Catholic Church, but it is one of the things that has intensified the fervor of the novenites."[123]

Milwaukee made an original contribution to the novena craze by launching a new devotion to Mary under the title "Our Lady of Victory." St. Stanislaus parish had erected an outdoor patriotic shrine to "Our Lady of Victory" with a mural painted by Notre Dame sister Mary Roman Obremski. Under the mural was a roll of honor bearing the names of 153 parish members who had already enlisted in the armed forces.[124] Assistant pastor, Father Raymond Punda, penned nine days worth of prayers and petitions to the Virgin Mary. He gave the credit for his inspiration to his pastor Monsignor Bernard Kobelinski, who declared to the press that the devotion was "something new, something keyed to the emergency." He observed as well that the novena was necessary to help mobilize moral support behind the crusade to fight Hitler and the Japanese, as well as to provide comfort for those sending sons and daughters to the war zones.[125] At the opening of the novena in late May 1942, 1500 people jammed into the church on a rainy Wednesday night.[126] Punda eventually condensed his material into a small pamphlet that was published and disseminated by the popular *Queen's Work* press of the Jesuits of Missouri. The novena sold thousands of copies and netted Punda royalties. Punda himself joined the army, serving in the Pacific with the 145th Infantry and won the Silver Star.[127] With his troops he prayed the novena to Our Lady of Victory.[128] As "novenites" crowded St. Stanislaus to pray for their loved ones and for

Archbishop Kiley blessing gold star banner [AAM]

AAM

victory over the Axis, the Dominican Sisters of the Perpetual Rosary turned their chapel over to anxious souls and inaugurated a 24-hour monthly vigil for peace that featured common recitation of the rosary, sermons and other devotions.[129]

Devotion to peace took other forms. At summer sessions in the sisters' colleges, courses covered the peace proposals offered in a series of Christmas messages of Pope Pius XII. Ultimately these and other papal statements on war and peace, were compiled into a large volume by Archbishop Samuel Stritch of Chicago and published by the National Catholic Welfare Conference. These so-called papal peace points were next distilled into popular study guides and discussion club proposals that found a place in the summer curricula in such places as Mount Mary.[130]

Shoring up international relations with neighbors in Latin America was also undertaken by Milwaukee religious. Two Franciscan sisters, Frederick Lochemes, and Patrice McNamara, participated in a joint endeavor devised by the National Catholic Welfare Conference and the Latin American desk of the Department of State to increase cultural contacts between North and South America by the exchange of visits of Roman Catholic bishops, priests and religious. Lochemes and McNamara, both veteran educators, were dispatched on a whirlwind tour of Latin American capitals in 1944, not only gather-

Sisters Frederick Lochemes and Patrice McNamara, OSF, on South American tour [AOSF]

ing information for classes and workshops on inter-American relations, but also indirectly acting as good will ambassadors from the United States.[131] Lochemes and McNamara compiled the details of their journey (truly remarkable, given the restrictions for cloistered sisters) in a book called *We Saw Latin America* which was published by Bruce and Company of Milwaukee.[132] They also injected a required unit of study on Latin America into the curriculum of Catholic schools and freely shared their experiences in a variety of formats.[133] However, Lochemes and McNamara were always guarded in their subsequent discussions about their dealings with Latin American diplomats and political leaders, to whom they made ceremonial visits in the company of the local papal nuncio.

Coping with the Sorrow

It was the task of Catholic pastors and others to console the bereaved and to provide the final rites of the Church for hundreds of Milwaukee Catholics who died in the war—even if their bodies were interred overseas. The archdiocese's newspaper published weekly lists of Requiem Masses mourning the war dead. Sister organists pumped out the doleful *Dies Irae* in Mass after Mass as clerics garbed in funeral black commended the sons and daughters of grieving parents to the Almighty.

On the omnipresent service flags proudly displayed in churches, the stars sewed in for members in the service were changed to gold when that person died in battle. These included men like Pfc. Elroy J. Petrovic, 20-years-old and a graduate of St. Aloysius School, killed in infantry action in France on August 10, 1944; it numbered Corporal Casper Damato, a member of St. Rita's Church killed in France just six days after Petrovic and Marine Private Albert Heinrich of St. Mary's in South Milwaukee, killed in action on Saipan.[134] Memorials to these fallen family members flooded into churches in the form of chalices, statuary, church windows and innumerable plaques that were affixed to altars, devotional sites and the walls of church vestibules and the lobbies of schools.

The sadness of war also bridged denominational boundaries. When Father Vincent Thomas learned of the death of the son of a couple in the small town of Eden, he was the first person to go to their home to offer condolences. The grateful couple, Mr. and Mrs. John Montgomery, wrote a brief note of gratitude to Archbishop Kiley for Thomas's "comforting words and kindness." They explained further, "We are members of the Anglican Church and Father Thomas certainly was a Christian to be of such comfort as he was at such a terrible time."[135] Even two years after the war was over the ministry of consolation continued. When the remains of Francis Dunne and John McWilliams were brought back to Milwaukee's St. Rose Church for burial, the school children of the parish "lined the street and stood in reverent silence as the bodies were driven to church."[136]

The Search for Inner Peace: Milwaukee's Contemplatives

Sister Miriam of the Holy Spirit (Jessica Powers), Carmelite Sister [Carmelite Archives]

In the disturbing years of the Depression and the war, hunger for religious peace surged among people of all denominations. Intense local interest attended the entrance of poet Jessica Powers into the Carmelite convent on Wells Street in Milwaukee.[137] Powers, a native of Mauston, was born February 7, 1905. She had grown up on a farm and attended Marquette University for one year and spent another year as a secretary in Chicago before she returned to Mauston to care for her family after the death of her mother. In 1937 she moved to New York, where her gifts for poetic expression matured as she did menial work. There she joined the Third Order of St. Francis and became a daily communicant. In New York, she grew close to Jessica Pegis, the wife of Fordham philosophy professor Anton Pegis, whom she had met through correspondence. She moved in with the Pegis family, who nurtured her faith and poetic gifts. Her poetry soon was accepted by not only Catholic periodicals like *America* and *Commonweal*, but also by secular journals such as *Harpers, American Mercury*, and even the *New York Times*. Her first book of poems, *The Lantern Burns,* was published in 1939 by the Catholic Poetry Society. Responding to the stirrings of a religious vocation, in April 1942 she was clothed with the habit of a cloistered Carmelite nun at a ceremony presided over by Monsignor Albert G. Meyer of St. Francis Seminary (Meyer himself had a cousin in a Carmel). It was Meyer who bestowed the new name by which Jessica Powers would be known henceforth: "Sister Miriam of the Holy Spirit."[138] The Carmel of the Mother of God on Wells Street welcomed its share of visitors seeking the "peace that surpasseth understanding." In 1957, the nuns purchased seven acres overlooking Pewaukee Lake and built a new $375,000 cloister.[139] Jessica Powers would disappear only for a time behind the Carmel walls. Her poetry and her search for God in the quiet of the cloister was a harbinger of the hunger for peace that would send a number of men and women to the doorsteps of convents, monasteries and seminaries after the war. Indeed, it prefigured the reaction that would greet the writings of another contemplative—Thomas Merton—who entered the Abbey of Gethsemani just a few months before Powers entered Carmel.

Merton's autobiography *Seven Storey Mountain* skyrocketed to the top of the Catholic best-seller list and stimulated an interest in prayer, contemplation and monasticism. Trappist monasteries burgeoned, as new foundations were planted around the country. Several Milwaukee men entered Trappist life, including young John McCabe, a 1952 graduate of Marquette High School and a parishioner at Milwaukee's St. Thomas Aquinas. McCabe, who was known as Brother Bernard in his religious life at New Melleray Abbey in Peosta, Iowa, returned to secular life and became a longtime and beloved professor of English at Marquette University.

Trappist Thomas Merton with Salvatorian Sister Therese Lentfoehr
[ASDS-W]

Abbot Richard Felix, OSB
[Benedictine Archives]

Other monastic foundations in the Milwaukee Archdiocese included the Cistercians at Spring Bank; actually, three different nationalities of the order (German, Dutch and Hungarian) occupied the property over the course of its existence.[140] These monks were not the Strict Observance made famous by Merton, but the Common Observance, which allowed them to interact with visitors who came to their chapel to hear them chanting the Divine Office.

In 1945, another monastic foundation of a different kind for men began in Kenosha County in a portion of Salem Township named "Benet Lake," established by Father (later Abbot) Richard Felix, a monk of Conception Abbey in Missouri.[141] Ordained in 1918, Felix was taken by the possibilities of home mission work during a graduate school stay with the Paulists in Washington, D.C. When he returned to his abbey, he was assigned to two Missouri parishes where he had a chance to experiment with various catechetical techniques. To combat the local Jehovah's Witnesses he began a series of innovative radio broadcasts called "Highway to Heaven," which consisted of 15 minutes of catechetical instruction given in the form of a dialogue between a priest and a young man or woman. In 1933, he organized a publishing firm called *Defenders of the Faith* and began producing a series of small leaflets that began with "Why?" These handouts explained basic Catholic doctrine and were widely distributed to CCD organizations, penal institutions, and bus and railway stations. Called back to his monastery, Felix expanded the work of *Defenders of the Faith* by sending St. Benedict medals to military men and collecting donations for his work. He hoped one day to establish a large monastery that would serve as a central headquarters for a network of dependent houses and lay organizations (something on the model of the famous medieval French Abbey of Cluny) to conduct evangelical work in the United States.[142]

Benedictine Community, Benet Lake WI [Benedictine Archives]

In 1945 his abbot gave him permission to pursue this goal and he traveled to Milwaukee where Kiley received him and informed him of a parcel of land in Kenosha County on the Illinois border that was owned by the Catholic Women's Order of Foresters in Chicago. The property was situated next to a lake (alternately called Paschen Lake and Lake Shangri-la), and had a large residence on it. Felix purchased this tract with $100,000 he had saved from his *Defenders of the Faith* organization (a purchase that raised some concerns at Conception Abbey), and then he proceeded to transform the land into a major monastic center. Felix renamed at least a portion of the lake Benet Lake (an old name for St. Benedict), and ran a small farm and print shop to sustain the operation. He changed the name of the operation to *Our Faith Press* and organized it all under the umbrella organization of the Missionary Associates of St. Benedict. Taking a page from his successes in rural Missouri, Felix took to the airwaves once again, broadcasting his homey explanations of Catholic doctrines using actors and actresses to engage him in dialogue. Felix's radio program was carried by hookup to over 120 stations. Seeking to imitate the pilgrim-tourist trade at Benedictine monasteries abroad like Monserrat in Spain and Einsiedeln in Switzerland, Felix encouraged "pilgrims" to come to the monastery where he built a series of dioramas depicting biblical scenes. Once the number of monks hit 60, he borrowed $250,000 from the

Wheaton Franciscans and built a larger monastery.

In 1952, the monastery attained the status of an independent abbey and Felix began multiplying houses. Offshoots of the Benet Lake abbey included houses in Pecos, New Mexico; Hingham, Massachusetts; and Atwater, Ohio. He opened priories in Mexico, El Salvador, Costa Rica and Nicaragua. Felix was eventually forced to step down in 1964, as his own monks began to weary of his constant activity and scheming. St. Benedict's Abbey continued as a retreat center.

The retreat movement in Milwaukee had started already in the 1920s as one of the important outreaches of the growing Catholic Action movements. The Holy Name Society had been in the forefront of encouraging its members to take a spiritual retreat at some out of the way place as a form of spiritual rejuvenation. The Jesuits took the lead with Messmer's approbation and a strong letter of encouragement was read from Milwaukee pulpits. In 1925 a branch of the Laymen's Retreat League was formed. J. A. Fitzgerald became its president and Neil Gleason its vice president. Later Edward Fitzpatrick would become the leader of the group.[143] This organization soon scheduled a series of retreats at Spring Bank lasting from Thursday to Sunday nights and directed by Father Charles Mouliner, S.J. Messmer encouraged the movement and sent to all the priests a pamphlet by Jesuit Edward Garesche, S.J., describing the spiritual value of retreats. He also invited pastors to a meeting to discuss further ways and means of promoting this particular spiritual practice.[144]

Stritch was also a fan of the retreat movement and soon pressed local religious orders of men to provide facilities for retreats. The Capuchins were among the first to provide a retreat house for men of the archdiocese in 1931, when they turned over a portion of their recently vacated clericate at St. Francis parish (the house of formation had moved to Marathon, Wisconsin).[145] Later, minor seminaries at St. Nazianz, Mount Calvary and elsewhere opened their doors to retreatants during the summer months.

Retreat facilities for women were problematic at first. Convents were cramped for room and their religious rules discouraged the sisters from mixing with "seculars." Consequently, retreat facilities for women were restricted to the facilities of the MACCW on Lake Nagawicka. In 1943 the Sisters of the Cenacle opened a retreat house for women in a converted mansion on Wauwatosa and North Avenue (they would later move to a site on North Lake Drive). Twenty-eight women came to the first retreat. The reporter who related the details of the house and the conferences dwelt less on the subject matter of the Jesuit retreat master, and more on the images "the warm fragrance of baking bread ... the sheltered feeling that came when thunder roared and lightning burst in the sky outside ... crackling fresh sheets on beds." The reporter observed of the whole experience, "There was nothing of the fretfulness of life within the Cenacle walls."[146]

Rearranging Lives: Gender, School, and Church Schedules

Many shortages occurred during the war years, but most especially the shortage of men. Numbers in Catholic schools and the seminary dipped as men enlisted to fight the Axis. The dearth of men in the workforce led to the hiring of women for industrial jobs. In the Catholic community, a gender line was broken when women were invited to join the fund-raising efforts of the Archbishop's Appeal. "We sincerely appreciate the assistance the women have volunteered to give us," noted longtime fund-raising organizer Frank Surges.[147] In late October 1942, Milwaukee County Sheriff Joseph J. Shinners traveled to St. Joseph Convent on Layton Boulevard to bestow certificates and air raid wardens' armbands to 135 School Sisters of St. Francis. Judge Roland Steinle called the nuns "angels of civilian defense."[148]

Catholic disciplines touched many aspects of home life [AAM]

The demands of the war and the long arm of the draft brought about important changes in the programs of Catholic schools, colleges and universities. Colleges, universities and seminaries were compelled to accelerate academic schedules to preserve student deferments or to help students finish high school before enlistment.[149] St. Francis Minor Seminary, St. John's Cathedral and Messmer High School ran school year-round and graduated a steady stream of students at midterm.[150] Courses were added in military science, such as pre-aeronautics, physical fitness and mathematics. As noted earlier, students at St. Francis Seminary were compelled to take classes all year round in order to retain their draft exemptions.[151] The accelerated pace of school meant an "irregular" run of ordinations as priests finished their requirements earlier than planned. For example in 1944, there were ordinations in January and October.[152] The class scheduled to be ordained in May 1946 had its ordination date pushed up to September 29, 1945.

Other accommodations were made to the changed conditions of life. Milwaukee finally broke the iron grip of the Great Depression as war orders flooded the city's industries. The requirement of 24-hour production required alteration of Mass schedules to accommodate workers. Masses at shift changes such as 3 or 4 o'clock in the morning or even in the evening were now allowed. Confessions too were scheduled at "odd" hours to meet the needs of the reorganized work patterns in industrial cities like Racine, Kenosha, Milwaukee, and Fond du Lac.[153] Rationing and food shortages led to a mitigation of the laws of fast and abstinence, although the scrupulous Kiley insisted on the traditional Friday abstinence and the fasts for the vigil of Christmas, Ash Wednesday, Good Friday and Holy Saturday morning.

The War's End

The end of the war came in 1945. The collapse of the Third Reich was complete by early May and the war in the Pacific hurtled to a conclusion during the spring and summer. When the atomic flash went up over Hiroshima and Nagasaki in August 1945, the hostilities ceased. One of the Sinsinawa Dominicans at St. John's convent in Milwaukee laid a Marian template on these events: "The war which began on the eve of the Feast of the Immaculate Conception (December 7) 1941, ended with V. J. Day, August 15 (the feast of the Assumption)." She observed, that "the celebration was joyous but subdued" and noticed the immediate uptick in noisy automobile traffic around her urban convent.[154]

Interestingly, in Milwaukee only a few Catholic observers discussed the morality of using the bomb. One was Jesuit Edward McGrath, a professor of philosophy at Marquette. He declared in a lecture to the University Physics Club that "the use of the atomic bomb has caused much controversy, even among theologians and moralists." While acknowledging the difficulties posed by the bomb and other weapons of mass destruction he argued that the use of the bomb was legitimate on the moral principle of "double-effect." He insisted that the evil of the bomb was outweighed by the good effects it produced: "One million American lives were saved as well as a quarter of a million British lives. Evil was not intended, but it could not be avoided."[155] The unidentified Sinsinawa sister that had seen the Blessed Virgin Mary's hand in the end of the conflict, provided another perspective on the use of the bomb: "This victory was the result of the use for the first time in history of the atomic bomb based upon the faction of atoms of uranium .... Its destruction is so tremendous as to make future military or naval engagements thoroughly obsolete." She wrote with emphasis, "May it never again be used."[156]

Postwar Transition: A New Catholic Visibility

The war was a watershed for the archdiocese of Milwaukee. Clearly the men and women who came back from the conflict were never the same. One important difference in American life was the changed relationship between individual citizens and the federal government. Government decisions and policies affected American citizens as they never had before. These decisions were felt in housing, education, and social provisions, especially health care and social relations. Just as important, a spike in the general population, the so-called "baby boom," provided a new social and demographic context for the postwar years. Accommodating the newcomers, building churches and schools and expanding the Catholic presence occupied the Catholic community.

The postwar growth of the Catholic Church in Wisconsin was substantial. Catholic numbers in the archdiocese of Milwaukee stood at 310,000 in 1930. In 1940, records show 457,000. A slight drop was registered in 1950 with 421,308 (due largely to the detachment of the diocese of Madison in 1946), but in the 1950s growth was rapid as the baby boom hit its crest in 1955. In 1953, there were close to 500,000 Catholics, 300,000 living in Milwaukee County alone. There were 227 parishes, 36 missions, 533 diocesan priests and 348 religious order priests. Over 4,500 religious sisters lived and worked in the archdiocese. There were two diocesan seminaries and 13 seminaries and scholasticates of religious orders; 176 parochial schools accommodated 62,316 pupils, and 423 diocesan. Parish and private high schools enrolled nearly 10,000 students. Marquette University and five small Catholic colleges enrolled nearly 10,000 students as well. There were 14 general hospitals run under Catholic auspices, four special hospitals and sanitaria, five orphanages and infant asylums, four protective institutions and 14 homes for the aged. In 1960 Milwaukee's Catholic population stood at nearly 600,000.[157]

Bishop William P. O'Connor (center) [AAM]

In January 1946, a public announcement was made by the Vatican that seven counties (Marquette, Green Lake, Columbia, Dane, Jefferson, Rock and Green) were to be detached from Milwaukee, and four (Sauk, Iowa, Grant and Lafayette) from La Crosse, to form a fifth Wisconsin diocese headquartered at Madison.[158] The new diocese was officially created on March 12, 1946 in ceremonies at Madison's St. Raphael's Church. It contained 80,900 Catholics and 134 diocesan and 13 religious order priests. The bishop of Superior, former World War I military chaplain and philosophy professor William Patrick O'Connor, was chosen as the first bishop of the newly erected see. The Milwaukee Archdiocese was left with the 10 counties of southeastern Wisconsin: Dodge, Fond du

Lac, Kenosha, Milwaukee, Ozaukee, Racine, Sheboygan, Walworth, Washington and Waukesha. New Catholic churches and schools began to be built as Catholic numbers soared.

Postwar Church Construction

Shortages of building materials continued into the immediate postwar period and some parishes made use of surplus war materials. For example, St. James parish in Franklin, formerly a mission of St. Stephen's in New Coeln, moved in surplus barracks upon which they perched a steeple and inserted stained glass windows to create a church and school. At the same time they received Father Francis Drabinowicz as their first resident pastor.[159]

Once building restrictions were lifted, church and school building took off at a rapid pace. The most common form of building was the postwar version of the church/school combination that was typical of the construction of Milwaukee parishes prior to the Great Depression. However, the architectural quality of these buildings was quite different from their pre-1920s predecessors. Building materials, many of them pre-fabricated and similar to the materials used in suburban housing,

Sacred Heart Church, Fond du Lac first Sunday Mass in public school gymnasium [AAM]

St. Mary Church, Kenosha [AA]M

were relatively inexpensive, but labor costs were quite high. As a result, the church/school combinations of the postwar era were far less solid and aesthetically pleasing than the pre-Depression generation. In fact, the architecture of suburban churches embraced the distressing sameness of the housing tracts around them. Often constructed by the Brust and Brust company, the single-level schools and parish buildings were built with a minimum of traditional ecclesiastical adornment and were often flat, functional structures. One builder defended the new structures, noting, "The use of steel and aluminum have reduced the 'massive' feeling. Churches today can be more clean and direct without the confusion of excessive detail."[160] Builders often faced these structures with weather-resistant brick, but interiors were constructed of simple plasterboard walls, linoleum tile floors and a wonderful fireproof substance that proved worth its weight in gold as insulation for water and heating pipes: asbestos.

The worship space was ordered in a building that was ultimately destined to be a gym. The altar was at the far end of the "court," marked off from the nave by a communion rail and filled with pews that flanked each side of a central aisle. Sometimes the "temporary" church had a small balcony in back for the parish choir. On either side of the sanctuary small devotional altars in honor of Mary and Joseph were set up. Altar furnishings were simple, sometimes blonde oak or wood of lesser quality. One innovation that was adapted into a number of these "temporary" churches was an infant's "crying" room. The first Milwaukee parish to use this was St. Rita's in Racine.[161] Other parishes adapted the small room with a glass pane and developed speaker systems to pipe in the audible portions of the Mass. Likewise, new churches built on more expansive suburban lots allocated space around the new structures for automobile parking. Older parishes allowed use of parish school playgrounds for cars.

Compared with older urban churches, the suburban churches were devoid of images, symbols or other accouterments of Catholic culture. "Symbolism is all too often lacking in our churches today," lamented one architect in a newspaper survey. Another summed up the major architectural differences between the older and newer churches by writing, "In older churches construction took place when labor was cheap and materials expensive. Today the reverse is true. Money is always a factor in construction today, so machine-made materials are used whenever possible. Today's design of churches requires a suitable combination of materials and methods. An expensive piece of stone can be much cheaper than a simple piece of carved wood or stone."[162] School additions were necessary as well as Catholic school numbers skyrocketed. Inexpensive building materials were used to add on to existing school structures or older churches. Here the vivid contrasts between architectural styles and building materials was most evident.[163]

The rapid expansion of schools put pressure on parishes to build new churches to free up space needed in the old church/school combinations of the 1920s for the growing number of students. In Kenosha, St. Mary's decision to establish a high school in the parish school increased the number of students and made a gymnasium a necessity. At Christmas 1952, Father Raymond Bell opened the new double doors of St. Mary's Church for its 950 families. The $450,000 colonial-style church was a cream-brick edifice with natural oak beams, and a high clock tower from which a 1,000-pound bell chimed the hours. In deference to actual colonial style, Bell did not install stained glass windows and kept traditional statuary and other "Romish" accouterments to an absolute minimum.[164] In 1956 Archbishop Meyer blessed the new Blessed Sacrament Church on Oklahoma Avenue. Designed by Herbst, Jacoby and Herbst, the new building was one of the most innovative examples of church architecture at the time. Its most powerful element was a huge mural-like stained glass window that was 55-feet wide and 37-feet high. Designed by the Conrad Pickel studio of Waukesha, the window depicted the life and role of the Virgin Mary in honor of the Marian Year 1954 (the year construction on the church had begun).[165]

Blessed Sacrament Church, Milwaukee
[AAM]

Suburbia

Suburbia sang a siren song to postwar urban dwellers. Like the immigration of old, the demographic transition to the suburbs had pull and push factors. Historian Kenneth Jackson points to the confluence of government policy, cheap and inexpensive housing, and automobility as the keys to understanding the tremendous burst of suburbanization after World War II.[166] The desire for suburban living was also driven by the need for space and the possibility of independent home ownership for young couples with growing families. It was also accelerated by racial succession and the whites' fears of living with African Americans who were growing substantially in most northern cities, including Milwaukee.[167]

Milwaukee's suburban boom began shortly after the war. The older suburbs, such as Wauwatosa, West Allis and Shorewood, annexed land to cope with the new demand. Nearby pastures and orchards were so rapidly transformed that eight new suburbs were incorporated either as cities or villages between 1950 and 1957. To the north, this included Bayside, Brown Deer and Glendale and to the south were Franklin, Greenfield, Hales Corners, Oak Creek and St. Francis. In adjacent Waukesha County, Brookfield became a city in 1954 and Elm Grove a village in 1955. New Berlin became a city in 1959. To the north, in Ozaukee County, the town of Mequon was incorporated. Meanwhile, the city of Milwaukee annexed an additional 46 square miles, including the rapidly growing northwestern corner of the county where the Town of Granville billed itself as "Milwaukee's suburb in the city."[168]

St. Gregory the Great Church, Milwaukee [AAM]

Catholic officials responded slowly to the demographic shifts. The first stirring of growth in older parishes brought requests for building additions and new structures. Building restrictions during the war were lifted, but shortages of materials continued. Archbishop Kiley moved slowly, reluctant to focus on more than the rebuilding of the cathedral and the renovations to the seminary buildings. Nonetheless, some new churches slipped through, such as St. Catherine's at 51st and Center. Likewise Kiley created 11 new parishes.

Archbishop Albert Meyer caught the brunt of the building program in the 1950s. Growth demands had been so insistent that new parishes were called for annually during the five years of his term. Meyer wrote to Father Joseph Emmenegger in Rome in early 1956, "Milwaukee continues to boom and the problems of procuring new parish sites continues to occupy a lot of attention. The building activity seems to be without end."[169] Before Meyer departed for Chicago in 1958, he would create 25 parishes, bringing to 36 the number created between 1940 and 1958. The following chart gives an idea of how many new structures Meyer and his auxiliary Atkielski blessed between 1953 and 1957 (this includes cornerstone ceremonies).

Year	Schools & Additions	Churches	Convents	Misc.
1953	11	6	4	2
1954	17	3	2	0
1955	12	6	4	2
1956	14	7	5	2
1957	12	9	1	1
Date Unknown	17	8	15	12

Table 4-1 [Source: Compilation in Meyer Papers, AAC]

The process of land acquisition consumed increasing amounts of time on the part of chancery officials. Eventually, many of these tasks fell to Father Leo Brust, a native of New Coeln, who had been ordained in 1942. Genial, humble and dutiful, he had served first as vice chancellor of the archdiocese and lived in the episcopal residence. Brust schooled himself in the intricacies of land acquisition and in particular learned how to predict the path of urban growth by poring over utility surveys and other materials from local government offices.[170] On his recommendation, approved by the Board of Consultors, thousands of acres were purchased at what he deemed to be strategic locations for the establishment of new parishes, or in locations he believed were destined for growth.

Each of the 10 counties of the archdiocese registered significant growth between 1950-1960. The following chart (see Table 4-2, page 622) gives some idea of the total population growth of the coun-

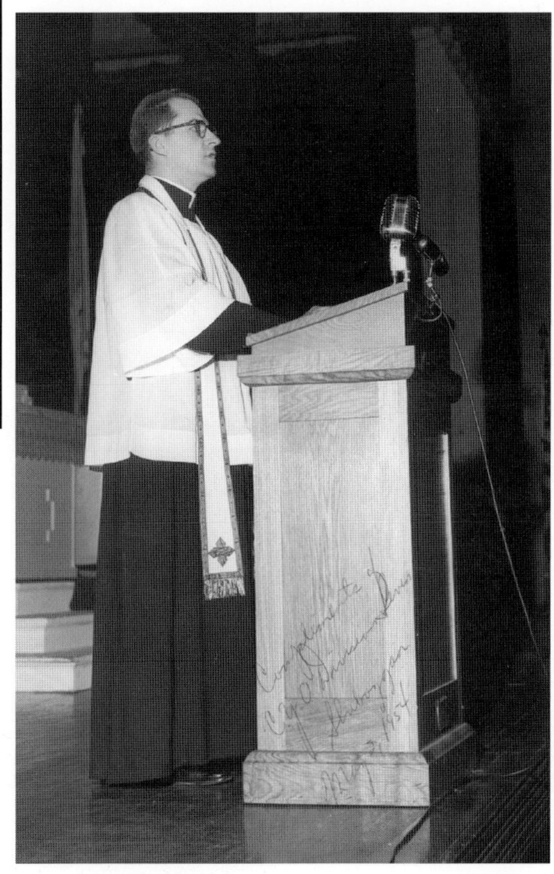

Msgr. Leo Brust [AAM]

Table 4-2
*Indicates mission raised to parish status
[Sources: *Milwaukee City and County: A Statistical History* (Milwaukee Public Library, 1955); H. Yuan Tien (ed.). *Milwaukee Metropolitan Area Fact Book, 1940, 1950, 1960; Status Animarum Reports, Archives of the Archdiocese of Milwaukee.*]

County	1950	1960 (% increase)	New Parish	School or New Addition (1953–1958)
Dodge	55,611	63,170 (9.6)		St. Andrew, LeRoy; St. Mary, Lomira; St. Peter, Beaver Dam
Fond du Lac	67,829	75,085 (20.7)	Sacred Heart	St. Mary, Eden; St. Matthew, Campbellsport; Presentation, North Fond du Lac
Kenosha	75,238	100,615	St. Therese	St. Anthony, Kenosha; Holy Rosary, Kenosha; St. Mark, Kenosha
Ozaukee	23,361	38,441 (64.6)	St. James*	St. Cecilia, Thiensville
Racine	109,585	141,781 (29.4)	St. Lucy*	Sacred Heart, St. Rita, St. John Nepo., Racine; St. Louis, Caledonia; St. Mary, St. Charles, Burlington, St. Charles
Sheboygan	80,631	86,484 (7.3)		Holy Name, St. Peter Claver, Sheboygan; St. George
Walworth	41,584	52,638 (25.9)		St. Andrew, Delavan
Washington	33,902	46,119 (36.9)	St. Frances Cabrini, West Bend	St. Hubert, Hubertus
Waukesha	85,901	158,249 (84.2)	St. Bruno, Dousman*; Good Shepherd, Menominee Falls; St. Leonard, Muskego; St. Dominic, Brookfield*; St. Anthony, Pewaukee*; St. William, Waukesha*	St. Joseph, Big Bend; St. Therese, Eagle; St. Jerome, Oconomowoc; Vistation of Mary, Elm Grove; St. Mary, St. Anthony, Pewaukee

ties outside of Milwaukee. Here, as we see, the rates of growth varied, and the major increase in institutional growth came primarily in the addition of or rebuilding of schools. Only in four counties, Fond du Lac, Kenosha, Washington and Waukesha (which was in the Milwaukee metropolitan area) were there actual new parishes. In Ozaukee and Racine (as in Waukesha), mission stations became parishes.

The most dynamic growth was in Milwaukee County (see Table 4-3, below).

Table 4-3

Milwaukee County	1950	1960	Percent Increase	Parishes
Milwaukee	871,047	1,031,681	18%	
Far North	29,314	62,335	113%	Corpus Christi, St. Philip Neri, St. Albert
Fox Point/River Hills	3,152	7,072	124%	St. Eugene
Northwest	37,656	67,293	78%	St. Margaret Mary, Our Lady of Sorrows
Brown Deer	3,500	6,136	75%	St. Bernadette
West Allis	54,602	65,616	20%	Mary Queen of Heaven
Southeast	49,242	59,968	20%	St. Roman
Jackson Park	28,832	50,978	77%	St. Gregory, Our Lady of Lourdes

Typical of this growth was the creation of a thriving parish in Brookfield, directly west of Milwaukee. Until World War II, the area, had been the home of truck and dairy farms. The Catholics had been adequately served by a tiny chapel erected during the days of Henni. Considerable postwar population growth prompted archdiocesan officials to raise the mission to parochial status in 1956. Its first pastor, Edward Grohall, didn't even try to enlarge the existing building but purchased a multi-acre farm and by 1959 had a capacious gym-church built on the site.[171]

The implications of the suburbanization of Catholic life did not immediately occur to church officials struggling to keep up with the tremendous expansion. Officials generally assumed that the patterns of urban Catholic life (church, school, convent, and rectory) could simply be replicated in suburban neighborhoods with little essential change. It became clear in the 1950s, however, that the major energies and resources of church life were being transferred to this suburban frontier and that the church was slipping the moorings of its traditional identity in urban neighborhoods.[172]

The Postwar Urban Parish

While the most dynamic growth was at the urban perimeter, still there were building projects—churches and schools—in the city. In Milwaukee, St. Catherine's Church on 51st and Center patiently waited for the war's end to begin construction of a $350,000 church designed by W. G. Herbst. The state-of-the-art church had seating for the disabled and a crying room.[173] Other urban parishes added on or built structures.

The shift of Catholics to the suburbs raised concerns about the fate of once-thriving urban parishes, especially in Milwaukee. The declining numbers were felt in virtually every urban parish: slipping collections, fewer weddings and baptisms and a greater proportion of funerals that were for aged parishioners. School enrollments began to slide as well, leaving huge buildings with fewer and fewer youngsters. Urban transit systems faded, largely because of competition from automobiles. Shopping centers, such as the popular Southgate, which opened on the fringe of the city in the 1950s, and new supermarkets, began to replace the downtown emporiums, green grocers and butcher shops.

In the period 1945-1955, the cities of the Midwest underwent significant changes.[174] Coping with the decline of urban parishes, pastors and religious who lived and worked there did what they could. Parish societies met, feast days were celebrated, schools continued to educate. But urban geography changed in postwar cities of the archdiocese. These dynamics were most evident in Milwaukee, but could also be detected to some degree in cities like Racine and Kenosha, and to a lesser degree in Fond du Lac, Beaver Dam and Sheboygan.

The key change in urban living, especially in Milwaukee, Racine and even Kenosha, was racial. People of color came in increasing numbers to Milwaukee and most other industrial cities of the archdiocese during and after the war, at the same time as many whites were leaving for the suburbs. Since African Americans, the largest group of the new urban dwellers, were not predominately Catholic, urban parishes lost numbers in the pew benches and saw vacant school desks.

The Challenge of Race: From Conversions to Interracialism

In 1940 African Americans were concentrated in a few centers in the state of Wisconsin. Nearly 90 percent of them lived in Milwaukee, Beloit, Madison, Racine, and Kenosha. More than four-fifths lived in Milwaukee. At the onset of World War II the number of African Americans coming to Milwaukee rose, but *de facto* segregation kept them confined to a tight enclave bounded by Kilbourn Street on the south, Eighth Street on the west, Walnut Street on the north and Third Street on the east. Within this small island, the African American population reached 10,000 in 1940. Soon the enclave grew north to Wright Avenue and west to 12th Street. Industries that had steadfastly refused to hire African Americans before the war gladly took them on to handle the abundance of war-related work orders. Moreover, white landlords who had not previously rented to blacks or who had employed restrictive covenants to keep them out of white neighborhoods soon gave way.[175]

Segregation was also a way of life in other cities within the archdiocese. The largest number of African Americans living in Racine lived on the south side or near the city's grimy factory district. In Beloit, there were several distinct districts for African Americans, many of whom worked at the Fairbanks, Morse & Company. Madison was considered a congenial place for African Americans, but the population was small and transient. None of the Catholic churches in these cities appeared to make any special accommodation for African Americans, to convert them to Catholicism or educate them.

During the 1950s, the growth in Milwaukee was phenomenal. A combination of steady work and the presence of a relatively benign city administration under Mayor Frank Zeidler saw record numbers of African Americans making their home in the city. The pace of neighborhood transition picked up considerably, aided by block-busting real-estate agents who bought cheaply from anxious white homeowners and sold at a high cost to eager African American buyers.[176] The former German neighborhoods steadily emptied their white inhabitants. African Americans who may have desired to purchase in other areas of the city were blocked by the red-lining policies of banks and savings and loans, which simply refused to make loans on property in some sections of the city. Home ownership, an important aspect of Catholic identity, was lower among African Americans in Milwaukee and elsewhere in the 1950s than among whites.

Home ownership was at its worst in the most dilapidated sections of the older cities. In Milwaukee, the ownership rate was better and the quality of housing was better too.[177] By 1950, the African American population had soared to 23,000, and the boundaries of the black district stretched north to Locust Avenue and west to 20th street. (By 1960, the number would nearly triple to 63,000, a gain of 274 percent.) African Americans who were only 3.4 percent of the city's total population in 1950 comprised 8.4 percent of the populace a decade later.[178] Yet, there were limits with regards to where African Americans could settle. Few blacks ventured across the Menominee Valley, which separated the north and south sides of the city, or across the Milwaukee River, which separated the northwest from the upscale east side and north shore of the city.[179]

One issue that changed dramatically in Milwaukee was the nature of racial tolerance and acceptance. Historian Joe William Trotter has noted a pattern of acceptance and limited interracialism in Milwaukee as long as African American numbers were relatively small and "contained" vis-à-vis the white populace. But when numbers grew bigger, acceptance and tolerance gave way to anxiety about property values. Resistance took the form of either blunt refusal to allow blacks to live in certain areas or, more commonly in Milwaukee, "white flight." African Americans did not receive a warm welcome at Catholic churches in Wisconsin, and for men like Capuchin pastor Father Philip Steffes of St. Benedict the Moor, this posed a serious stumbling block.

Catholic Responses to African Americans in Milwaukee

Building on the foundations left behind by Lincoln and Julia Valle, Father Stephen Eckert and other Capuchins, efforts continued through the 1930s and 1940s to convert African Americans to Catholicism. Newly ordained "padrini" were sent to canvass neighborhoods and bring people to the faith. The *Catholic Herald Citizen* recorded the numerous African American baptisms that took place at St. Benedict. On one occasion in 1927, 100 African American children were baptized in one ceremony on a Friday and received their first communion the following Sunday.[180] Children in both the day and boarding schools embraced the Catholic faith in substantial numbers. Results began to show. In 1931, Archbishop Stritch reported that there were only 350 Catholics out of 12,000 blacks in the diocese. By 1939 Stritch bragged to Bishop Bartholomew Eustace of Camden, New Jersey, that "no other group in the archdiocese is better taken care of than the Negroes."[181]

St. Benedict the Moor School [AOP-Rac]

But the conversion strategy had always had its limits. Most Capuchin visitors found the African American people of Milwaukee friendly and receptive, but with little interest in becoming Catholic. One young Capuchin complained, "It seems far easier to make Catholics out of pagans than Catholics out of Baptists, Methodists or Holiness People. To a Buddhist or a Fetish worshiper, a missionary can preach Christ and the Gospel, but these Protestants have already heard the Gospel in garbled form; they know that they are 'forgiven and saved' and miracles almost seem required to disentangle them from the errors in which they are enmeshed."[182] Indeed, Milwaukee's African American community never converted in the number that the Capuchins or others may have hoped.

One stumbling block was the Catholic teaching on divorce and remarriage, which conflicted with the actual marital situations of many with whom the Capuchins spoke. Many had been married at an early age and had been divorced or abandoned by their spouses. Moreover, the prevalence of mixed marriage among African Americans was considerably higher than in the homogeneous Catholic ethnic communities of Milwaukee. The unwillingness of Church authorities to abridge canon law on divorce or remarriage or move through marital annulments (a virtual impossibility in those days) no doubt caused many potential converts to lose interest when they were told they could not participate in the sacraments.[183]

The other issue was the entire question of social justice as it applied to the treatment of African Americans. In 1932 Aloysius J. Muench would be among the first Milwaukee priests to bring attention to the seriousness of the race question and the clear Catholic principles which applied to it. Decrying the economic exploitation of African Americans and the faulty economic theory that had rationalized slavery, he urged a just wage and the removal of barriers to discrimination in hiring and firing. "He [the African American] is the last one to find a job; and having one, the first to lose it. In some large cities, in a number of instances, misguided individuals have made the proposal of relieving unemployment by discharging Negro workers and substituting in their places white workers," Muench wrote.[184]

But while Muench turned the spotlight of racial injustice on society at large, the Capuchins were aware of discrimination within the Church itself. Even as Stritch was trumpeting to his fellow bishop in New Jersey about the "care" blacks were getting, Father Philip Steffes noted, "In Wisconsin, just as elsewhere in the United States, the Negro is here to stay .... In decades to come there will not be less but more colored in Milwau-

Transfer of the remains of Rev. Stephen Eckert, OFM Cap. [AAM]

kee and in all Wisconsin. The question confronting the Church is this: Will the number of Negro Catholics keep pace with the growth of the Negro population? There are many reasons to hope it will." But he noted the difficulty that blacks faced in other parts of the diocese: "The only reason to fear that the Negro will be lost to the church is the old and bitter evil of segregation. The Negro is not welcome except in Negro churches and schools .... There is little encouragement for a colored man to join the Catholic church in Wisconsin if he knows that he can be a Catholic in Milwaukee at St. Benedict's but it is impossible for him to be a Catholic in Madison and Beloit." Steffes urged: "At the risk of being deemed an extremist let me say that the white Catholics must be converted first to the Colored cause, and then the conversion of the Negro will quickly follow. As long as white Catholics are unwilling to give practical expression to the belief in the Catholicity of the Church by extending the hand of fellowship to the Colored Members of Christ's Mystical Body, for so long there will exist a barrier to conversions among Negroes."[185]

Change was already taking place as Steffes wrote. In the 1930s, a modest move north and west by the African American community brought it into the proximity of two parishes. One, the formerly all-German St. Francis at Fourth and Brown, which was run by the Capuchins, had begun admitting African American students in its school and its instruction programs. The other, diocesan-run St. Joseph's at 11th and Cherry eventually accommodated itself to the few blacks who sought to attend the church and send their children to the school. The Irish St. Rose also had African American members.

After the war, as the black community grew and housing restrictions gave way, African Americans appeared in formerly all-white parishes. By the late 1940s, there were 2,500 black Catholics out of a total Catholic population of over 400,000.[186] With the African American population moving north and west, St. Benedict the Moor was on the periphery of the black enclave of Milwaukee. In September 1954, the Sinsinawa Dominican sisters of St. Gall's noted, "For the first time children of the Negro race were enrolled in the school. During the past years parish boundaries have included residents of this race." They were aware that historical patterns of urban Catholicism were about to be altered. "Considering the recent statistics showing only five percent of the nation's Negro population to be of the Catholic faith, one realizes the changes that will ultimately incur in St. Gall's Parish."[187]

A Last Attempt at Segregation

Confronted by this growth, the first response of the Milwaukee Archdiocese was to make one last attempt to maintain segregation in the churches by providing a mission church for African Americans under the direction of the Capuchins. When the Croatian community of Sacred Heart moved west to 49th Street, Kiley offered the Capuchins the site at Seventh and Galena, considerably north of the St. Benedict site, with the promise of archdiocesan subsidies to repair the decaying buildings. The mission, named for the Dominican brother, Blessed Martin de Porres, soon became a beehive of activity under its Capuchin pastors Julian Phelan, Joel Tuller and Matthew Gottschalk. Although lacking a school, Blessed Martin's offered athletic and summer programs that attracted scores of African American youth. It also trained future diocesan priests, such as activist James Groppi, who succeeded to the service of urban black parishes in the late 1950s and the 1960s.[188] One of the most popular programs was "Father Stephen's Day Camp," begun in 1953 and funded by Miller Brewing Company heir Harry John. Recreational, craft, and field trip activities provided social outlets for African American youth.

Meyer continued to support the efforts at Blessed Martin's and endorsed the canonization of Father Stephen Eckert.[189] He also intervened to prevent the transfer of Father Julian Phelan from Blessed Martin Mission.

Philanthropist Harry John with school children [Marquette University]

But Meyer was perhaps the first to note that the changing demographics of Milwaukee's African American population made it impossible to segregate the African American Catholics from the larger community. African Americans were living in diverse areas around the city's north side.

Officials of the city Housing Authority had approached Meyer in 1955 with preliminary plans to demolish the structures in the Blessed Martin area for urban renewal. Urban renewal chief Richard W. E. Perrin asked the archbishop what his future intentions were for the mission in light of the redevelopment plans. Consultation with the Capuchins brought the question to a point right away: "Whether to discontinue the church at this location and thereby integrate Negro communicants into other larger Catholic churches in the city."[190] For the time being, Meyer wanted the mission to stand and informed the Housing Authority that he would not consent to its demolition. Yet despite the decision to retain a separate African American church, segregation of white parishes was already ending.

Blessed Martin de Porres Mission, Milwaukee [AAM]

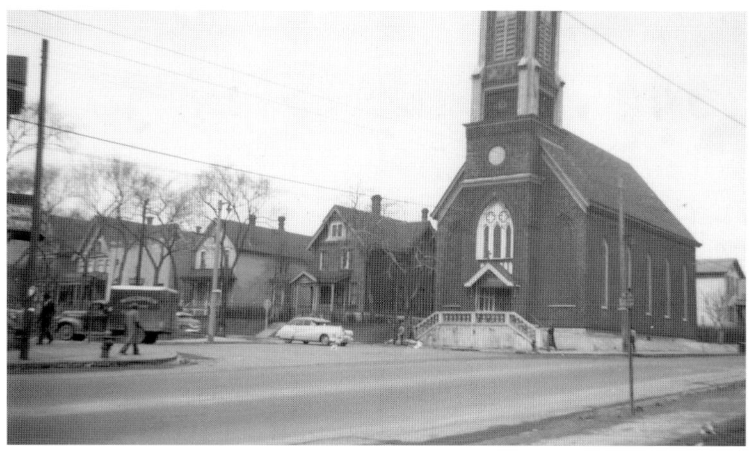

This was especially evident in the area directly north of the Hillside area where Blessed Martin's was located. Here the black population shot up 1,583.9 percent in the 1950s, and fanned into four Catholic parishes, including some of the most populous of the old German *Deutschum*, which were seeing black faces in their neighborhoods and in the schools and pews.[191] On the near west side of the city, similar changes affected four parishes. African American incursions into upscale Sherman Park marginally affected two long-established parishes.[192] Parishes in the path of African American movement steadily lost membership and school enrollment.

Confronted with African American communicants, some pastors like Monsignor George Meyer of St. Leo's shooed them back to St. Benedict's and welcomed the opening of Blessed Martin in 1950 as a safety valve for black Catholics. But without much fuss or discontent, formerly all-white churches began to admit black children into the school and into parish membership.[193] One of the first to do this was the old German parish of St. Boniface on 11th and Clarke Streets. Under the leadership of Father Lawrence Kasper, 32 black children were enrolled at St. Boniface, and in 1958, 181 black children attended school there.[194] St. Boniface, which had been the headquarters of the most conservative elements of Milwaukee's once dominant German community, became by the 1960s the central command of the most militant proponents of the civil rights movement in Milwaukee. Other north and west sides parishes followed.

If any section of the city actively discouraged black in-migration, it was the city's heavily Polish south side. Block-busting real-estate agents did not operate there. Moreover, local politicians kept a vigilant eye on possible minority settlement. Such was the case in the 1950s when a number of blacks tried to move into the south side's 17th ward and found determined opposition from Catholic alderman Joseph Schmidt, who withheld zoning approvals from their planned development.[196] Other evidence of south side resistance to African Americans is revealed in the reply of Brother Daniel Sharpe, S. M., principal of Don Bosco High School to his superior regarding the placement of an African American brother at the school. "There seems to be a possibility that the Archbishop [Meyer] would welcome a Negro Brother .... it is not an easy situation here, you know, but with time and preparation designed as a target date, there are those who believe the problem possible of solution." Later, Sharpe admitted that it would take a year-and-a-half

Interracial First Communion, St. Boniface Church, Milwaukee, 1952 [AAM]

to prepare the way at Don Bosco for an African American brother. None was ever assigned.[197] Awareness of these racial tensions within the Catholic community were brought home forcefully by two advocates of interracialism.

In the 1940s, Jesuit Father Claude Heithaus and Monsignor Franklyn Kennedy stepped forward to insist that Catholic social teaching be applied to racial relations in Milwaukee. In February 1944, Heithaus delivered a major address to the students of St. Louis University, calling on the Jesuit institution to reject racism and admit African American students.[198] Within months the Jesuits lifted the ban on African American admissions, becoming the first institution of higher learning in Missouri to do so. Later, due to Heithaus's lobbying, Archbishop Joseph E. Ritter mandated an end to segregation in Catholic colleges and schools of the archdiocese of St. Louis. Heithaus came to Marquette in 1947 as a professor of Archaeology and Classics (in part some guessed because of his role in the integration decision in St. Louis). But his academic work was only a perch to pursue his real interests on behalf of racial justice. Indeed, his highly visible efforts suggest that his classes probably received relatively short shrift. Shortly after his arrival in Milwaukee Heithaus presented a series of lectures on "Catholics and White Prejudice" as part of a summer program at Marquette. These hard-hitting speeches exposed white racism among Catholics in the north. "We do not lynch Negroes in Milwaukee," Heithaus declared, "[but] we torment [them] in a thousand other ways."[199] He attacked white racism as "repugnant to Catholicism," and enjoined his listeners, "We must set our faces against it with uncompromising determination lest we give scandal."[200]

Heithaus was soon in high demand on the lecture circuit and spent his summers speaking on racial issues at summer schools for nuns and various conventions. He soon formed a Marquette Interracial Club which grew to 100 members. Weekly meetings welcomed an array of interesting speakers. The club also sponsored plays that highlighted

Rev. Claude Heithaus, SJ [MUA]

themes of racial justice, and hosted all university "mixer" dances which brought 900 to 1000 students together for what was then considered the rather "shocking" spectacle of interracial dancing. The Interracial Club stood as a guardian against incidents of racial discrimination on campus and included under its umbrella not only the small number of African American students on the campus but a smaller group of Asian students.

Heithaus carried his passion for racial justice to the larger community. He joined the Milwaukee County Interracial Federation and served on its executive board and program committee. In 1948, barely one year after he arrived at Marquette, the federation honored him as "Man of the Year."[201] Mayor John Bohn appointed him to the Mayor's Commission on Human Rights which gave him ample opportunity to survey the city's record on racial discrimination and provided a framework to sponsor educational events that would break down racial stereotypes. One of Heithaus's favored exercises was the "Rumor Game" in which he would depict a hypothetical situation of a clash between an African American and a white citizen and note how the passage of the story from one person to the next would bring embellishments often untrue and always uncomplimentary to the African American.[202] Heithaus's work was given strong support by Father Franklyn Kennedy of the archdiocese.

Kennedy was born in 1904 in Monticello, Wisconsin and went to school in Sheboygan and at St. Norbert's College in DePere.[203] After ordination in 1929 he served in the ring of Irish parishes in Milwaukee—St. Rose, Immaculate Conception and St. Matthew's—and became engaged in a number of social issues, especially labor organizing in the 1930s. Moreover, as we have seen, he helped establish a Catholic Worker house in the city in the 1930s. In 1935, Stritch appointed Kennedy to be the editor of the newly merged *Catholic Herald Citizen*. Kennedy pursued his social justice interests on the pages of the newspaper in concert with Milwaukee's other leading Catholic journalist, Dean Jeremiah O'Sullivan of the Marquette School of Journalism.

Kennedy's interest in racial justice was the longest thread of his career. Kennedy, like Heithaus, relied on the egalitarian principles that flowed from the Catholic teaching on

Msgr. Franklyn J. Kennedy [AAM]

the mystical body of Christ to undergird his own deeply held beliefs on integration and against prejudice. Beginning in 1947, Kennedy turned a search light on the issue of housing discrimination by decrying the development of a "black belt" in downtown Milwaukee.[204] Again and again, Kennedy hammered on the basic equality of all before Christ, and used the *Herald Citizen* to extol the wonderful effects of social and cultural interaction among the races. For example, in 1949 he wrote at length of a trip he made to a Vincentian-run summer camp at Pigeon Lake near Drummond, Wisconsin, which included both black and white youngsters. He described the fun of campers and counselors of both races, and allowed the words of Mary Klein, a young student at Cardinal Stritch College, to sum up his own beliefs on interracialism: "This camp has proved conclusively to me that all people, regardless of their racial heritage, can live together in complete harmony. If Catholics really applied the Church's doctrines on the Mystical Body of Christ, there would be no need for publicity about a camp of this nature, for all races would be living together and such a camp would be an accepted thing."[205]

Kennedy became active in Catholic Interracial Council activities in Chicago and joined any number of organizations dedicated to racial justice in the city and the state. In 1945 he became a member of the Milwaukee County Interracial Federation, a private organization to promote racial harmony. In 1948 he was appointed to Milwaukee's Human Rights Commission, and a year later to the Governor's Commission on Human Rights. From the pages of the *Herald Citizen* and in public addresses, Kennedy hammered away at the need for more attention to racial issues and justice. Two important incidents highlight Kennedy's devotion to racial justice.

The first was his ringing condemnation of the American Bowling Congress, whose national headquarters was in Milwaukee. In 1946 the Milwaukee County Industrial Union Council sponsored a bowling tournament and allowed people of all races to register. Acting on pre-World War I Jim Crow rules, the bowling congress forbade the organization of any affiliated league that was not composed exclusively of white males. In a lengthy editorial that was later reprinted in pamphlet form, Kennedy wrote: "I have Christian principles to judge by. I know racial intolerance is morally wrong. I have specific facts about the discriminatory practices of the ABC [American Bowling Congress]. In the light of Christian principles, I am forced to conclude that the discriminatory practices of the American Bowling Congress are MORALLY WRONG." [206]

In 1949 naval veteran Albert J. Sanders came to Milwaukee with his family to enroll in the Milwaukee School of Engineering, but he could not find a residence in the city. Directed to a Greenfield trailer park he found a spot there, but the day he moved in, a group of residents circulated a petition to have him ousted. Opponents of the petition and supporters squared off for combat, and a mob gathered in front of the Sanders's trailer hurling insults and threatening violence. Despite police protection, Sanders and his family left the camp.[207]

The next morning Kennedy and Heithaus joined human rights commissioner Bruno Bitker, African American attorney James Dorsey, Urban League president William V. Kelley, and Milwaukee Ministerial Association president Norman Ream to publicly pressure Milwaukee County District Attorney William J. McCauley to protect the Sanders family under state civil rights laws. McCauley readily agreed. Meanwhile at the trailer camp the two factions continued to be at loggerheads. Heithaus drove the Sanders family back to their trailer and waited with them inside while Bitker spoke to the crowd outside urging them to allow the Sanders to settle in peace. Heithaus also emerged from the trailer to inform the demonstrators, "Those who instigate intolerance are betraying the principles of Christianity."[208] Sixty-five sheriffs were required to maintain order in the camp. In the meantime, Kennedy and Heithaus circulated among the camp factions and managed to calm tensions and even win over a majority of those who opposed the Sanders moving in. By the middle of July, even the ringleaders were convinced that it was wrong to discriminate against the Sanders and tendered a public apology to them.[209]

One of the persons active in the resolution of the Greenfield Trailer Park incident was African American attorney James Dorsey. Dorsey was born in 1897 in Missoula, Montana.[210] The son of a carpet cleaner, Dorsey attended Loyola Catholic High School in his hometown and in 1919 entered the University of Montana, where he majored in psychology and cultivated interest in sports and art. At Montana he excelled on the gridiron and often spoke of the influence of his coach on his desire to excel and to make something of himself. After graduation, he entered the law school at Montana and after getting his degree traveled east to Des Moines, Iowa; St. Paul, Minnesota; and finally Milwaukee. He was admitted to the Wisconsin Bar in 1928. After working as a janitor for a time, he got his footing in the legal profession in Milwaukee. He opened his own law office and became one of the leading African American professionals in the city.

Dorsey loomed large as one of the leading political figures among African Americans in Milwaukee's sixth ward and was an unsuc-

James Dorsey (center) [MCHS]

cessful candidate for an aldermanic seat.[211] He was also a faithful parishioner of St. Benedict the Moor parish, where he joined the Holy Name Society. Dorsey was in high demand in Catholic circles as a speaker in the Holy Name lecture bureau. Audiences in Burlington, Sheboygan, Mount Mary College and Marquette University heard Dorsey describe the difficulties of his upbringing and the discrimination he encountered in the Catholic Church (he was given a scholarship to a Catholic college only to have it withdrawn when they found out he was black). But, thanks to his association with Jesuit interracialist, William Markoe, Dorsey learned that Catholicism really did stand for racial justice and against discrimination. Dorsey was one of the pioneer activists in Milwaukee for desegregation. In 1941, he led Milwaukee's first civil rights march when with 700 African Americans he marched from Seventh and Walnut down to Lake Drive to protest discriminatory hiring practices in defense jobs. When Wisconsin created a Fair Employment division in the state Industrial Commission, Dorsey was selected to be on its advisory committee. Dorsey also served as a board member in the Milwaukee Urban League and lent his legal expertise to the Milwaukee chapter of the National Association for the Advancement of Colored People. Dorsey would be front and center in the dispute with the American Bowling Congress. Between 1945-1958, Dorsey served as a member of the Governor's Commission on Human Rights. Dorsey was perhaps the most visible lay African American Catholic since Lincoln Valle. His efforts to combine his Catholic faith with the cause of racial justice won him the James J. Hoey Award of the New York Catholic Interracial Council in 1957.[212] The next year he was a featured speaker at the meeting of the National Catholic Conference for Interracial Justice, held in Chicago. In 1966, Dorsey died in a tragic house fire in a futile attempt to rescue his daughter.

Ministering to Latino Catholics

Another focus of urban transition was in the city's growing Latino population.

The Latino community of Milwaukee was the hub of Spanish-speaking Catholicism. Since 1944, the Guadalupe Mission had been under the direction of the Conventual Franciscans, an eastern European group that adapted nicely to the language and cultural challenges of the new arrivals.

A new wave of Spanish-speaking men and women came into the archdiocese in the 1950s from the American Territory of Puerto Rico.[213] Puerto Rico had become an important recruiting ground for labor after World War II, and Puerto Ricans began to make their presence felt in many East Coast cities. In Milwaukee Puerto Rican Catholics came in large numbers in the early 1950s and settled mostly on the east side of the city, near the parishes of old St. Mary and St. John's Cathedral. Steadily, Puerto Rican families moved west into the St. Benedict the Moor and St. Rose neighborhoods. They also migrated to Holy Trinity and St. Patrick's on the south side. In Waukesha they began attending St. Joseph's Church. Because of serious priest shortages in Puerto Rico, the church affiliation of many of the newcomers was tentative. Less than half of the Puerto Ricans in Wisconsin attended church services, and of these only 17 percent attended services in Spanish.[214]

Unwilling to create a new ethnic parish downtown, Meyer secured the services of Roberto Rodriguez, a seminary student from Monterey, Mexico, whom he brought to Milwaukee in 1951 to finish his studies at St. Francis Seminary. He became Milwaukee's first Spanish-speaking diocesan priest. Ordained in May 1953, Rodriguez was sent to old St. Mary's in 1954 and began walking through the neighborhood contacting Spanish-speaking residents. The noon Mass at old St. Mary's soon became designated for the Spanish-speaking, and catechetical and other religious education programs were established with the assistance of three School Sisters of Notre Dame and two laywomen. A conference of the St. Vincent de Paul Society was also formed to provide assistance of various kinds.[215]

Rev. Roberto Rodriguez [AAM]

Meyer hoped that the ministry to Puerto Ricans would be transitional, but other priests grew interested in work with Spanish-speaking residents. Two seminarians, John Richetta and Paul Witteman, took Spanish lessons during a villa season for the seminarians at Okauchee and used the language in their priestly work. From the nucleus of Guadalupe and old St. Mary's, the increasing number of Spanish-speaking in Milwaukee proper altered the character of parishes on the west side (e.g., St. Rose) and later in the Polish bastions on the south side.

Beyond Milwaukee, the ministry to Spanish-speaking involved keeping up with migrant laborers, who came to the state during the planting and harvest seasons. Redemptorist Father Santiago (Jimmie) O'Connell arrived in the 1940s, traveling up from his home base in Texas as he followed the Mexican migrants. Residing at the Oconomowoc seminary of his community, he set up shop in the state for six to eight weeks, visiting migrant camps, celebrating Mass and helping where he could. With the help of Fond du Lac Latin teacher Ursula Cannon who was fluent in Spanish, religious education programs were set up in migrant camps at Eldorado, Rosendale, Ripon, Alto, Randolph, Cambria, Brownsville, Oakfield, Lomira, Rubicon, Jackson, Richfield, and Hartford. Cannon and O'Connell recruited 20 girls to teach the migrants and a bevy of nurses from the St. Agnes School of Nurses to care for the health needs of the workers.[216] O'Connell also visited the migrant workers, who settled in Delavan in the 1950s and worked for the Rodriguez Brothers. Redemptorist seminarians assisted him in this work. In addition, O'Connell was one of the first to mobilize Hispanics diocesan-wide by sponsoring the popular pilgrimage to the Carmelite shrine at Holy Hill. Beginning in 1953 this became an annual event.

In 1951 a colony of migrant workers decided to remain in the Sheridan Woods area of Racine, just south of city. These came to the attention of Monsignor Henry Schmitt of St. Joseph's parish in Racine and the dean of the area who then opened Guadalupe Chapel on Durand Road, just north of this barrio. Religious and social services, catechetical instructions and other services were provided. Eventually the mission was absorbed by St. Lucy's Mission.

As with all other ethnic groups, fears of rival denominations "moving in" on Catholic people stimulated action and organization. Archbishop William Cousins appointed Father George Kolanda, pastor of St. Joseph's Slovak parish in Cudahy, to coordinate efforts on behalf of Spanish-speaking Catholics. Kolanda was later assisted by Father John Maurice, a missionary recently returned from Peru who was stationed at St. Joseph's in Waukesha. Spanish-speaking Father Paul Witteman scoured the Kenosha and Fond du Lac areas for migrant camps and served them as best he could.

Catholic Churches: Urban Renewal and Freeways

The demographic shifts in urban neighborhoods changed the character of the Catholic Church in the Milwaukee See. Added to this (indeed intersecting with the whole issue of racial succession) were the efforts of the federal government to supply aid to cities which desperately needed help rebuilding after the Great Depression. The advent of freeways as well literally resculpted the face of cities.

Federal programs for cities began with the housing programs of the 1930s, which built public housing to help house the homeless of urban America. These public housing tracts appeared in every Wisconsin city of any size, and their presence soon became a point of controversy when their appeal to the poor was perceived to be a threat to urban land values. Public housing battles were bitter and hot as neighborhoods, real estate developers, and local politicians fought to keep them out of their bailiwicks.

In addition to public housing, the federal government also began to provide funds in the late 1940s to rehabilitate deteriorating portions of cities. Incentives were given in the form of federal funds to encourage cities to clean up blighted areas and to remake portions of the city into thriving commercial or residential areas. In Milwaukee, the head of these efforts was Richard W. E. Perrin, an urban historian and head of the city redevelopment agency. Some church buildings, like Blessed Martin in Hillside, stood in the midst of targeted redevelopment areas.

Early redevelopment efforts revealed serious flaws in planning. For example, serious concerns were raised about the fate of residents when the dilapidated buildings in which they lived were torn down. Many were poor and could not afford higher rents in other parts of the city. Racial exclusion kept others out. If a church were not slated for demolition, the destruction of the neighborhood was just as lethal to its future. This affected Catholic parishes, territorial by nature (or even ethnic parishes around which a good number of communicants resided) more so than Protestant denominations, which left the city and followed their congregations to the suburbs. Catholic parishes, tied to a particular parcel of land and with heavy investments in church buildings, convents, schools, and rectories, could not easily close down and move.

For these and other reasons, a popular backlash set in against urban redevelopment in the late 1950s and 1960s. Churches sometimes resisted efforts to destroy the neighborhoods and the church buildings. For example, in Merrill Park, Monsignor John J. Clark of St. Rose organized 250 area residents into the "Community Beautification and Stabilization Committee." These "neighborhood conservation" efforts included paint-up and clean-up programs that fixed up deteriorating structures around the church in order to spare it the wrecker's ball. St. Rose even gave away construction supplies, and from the pulpit its pastor prodded sloppy landowners to fix up their property.[217] At the same time, they resisted being yoked with property owner's groups that resisted the whole idea of urban renewal because of the involvement of the local government.[218]

At Blessed Virgin Mary of Pompeii Church, the resistance to urban renewal was

St. Rose of Lima Church, Milwaukee [AAM]

even more forceful. The leader was Scalabrinian Father Anthony Cogo who was assigned to the parish in 1954. Perrin had already been in touch with Archbishop Meyer regarding the fate of Pompeii Church as the city developed elaborate plans to remake the old Third Ward. Meyer directed them to meet with Cogo and Monsignor James Kelly of the cathedral who agreed to act as his emissaries.[219] Whatever happened at the meeting angered Cogo who may have heard similar stories from his Scalabrinian confreres of Italian churches in other big cities who were being summarily removed by redevelopment plans. Even though Pompeii had declined dramatically in membership over the years, it still had a devout following of about 250 souls who came from various parts of the city to Sunday Mass. Others returned to have children baptized, make first communion or to solemnize their marriages. Cogo fought urban renewal by recruiting former seminarian-turned-lawyer Dominic Frinzi to halt the proceedings and even to challenge the whole urban renewal program. In November 1955 Frinzi and the other attorneys launched a phone-calling campaign to the Common Council to oppose the planned destruction of the church.[220] Cogo's and Frinzi's efforts were successful and the demolition of the church was averted—at least for a time. Ultimately, freeway expansion took the venerable structure down.

Formal urban redevelopment programs were altered and slowed over the course of time, but American cities continued to be literally reshaped by the advent of the expressway system. Nothing did more to disrupt traditional patterns of neighborhood, church and community than these super-

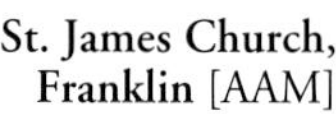

St. James Church, Franklin [AAM]

highways that literally demolished thousands of homes and destroyed neighborhoods on which churches relied for members and support.

The initiative to build freeways came from the increasing American attachment to the automobile and the concomitant decline of once heavily used streetcars, busses, and inter-urban rail lines. Americans had fallen in love with the automobile in the 1920s, and resumed their love affair after World War II when wartime savings and good jobs allowed American families to own at least one vehicle. In the 1950s the Eisenhower administration subsidized the construction of a massive system of interstate freeways (packaged under the guise of the need for military roads and passed by hefty majorities in Congress). The federal interstate system began to bisect Wisconsin in the fifties, as old U.S. highways and state roads were widened and expanded to welcome increased automobile ownership. No Wisconsin town was exempt, but Milwaukee experienced the most dislocation.

One of the first parishes to be affected by the widening of roads was St. James Mission in Franklin. In existence since 1857, the church had been a dependency of St. Stephen's in New Coeln. A small church and cemetery existed together with a school on several acres along the old Green Bay Road (now 27th Street) that linked Milwaukee with Chicago. Facing increasing traffic congestion, the state of Wisconsin expanded the old military road into Highway 41 in 1930-1931 and purchased a right-of-way through a portion of the St. James property in 1931. The old school building and garage were sold and the church was hoisted and moved to a position north of the cemetery. Continued growth in the area led Kiley to raise the mission to parochial status in 1946 and appoint Father Francis Drabinowicz to head the new community. Drabinowicz convinced the parish to build a new parish center on seven acres he purchased from the Baum estate, directly across from the original site of the church which included an old farmhouse that dated back to 1834 (erected by Cyrus Curtis a pioneer resident and the father of a later owner of the *Saturday Evening Post*).[221] Drabinowicz and his parishioners redecorated the Curtis house for the rectory. To provide a new church and school building, Drabinowicz took advantage of some surplus buildings being dismantled at the nearby prisoner of war camp at the county airport. Securing the former administration building of the camp for a little over $1100, he transported the structure to hold a six-room schoolhouse, a sisters convent, and a 350-seat church. In 1951, the old church, a relic of the days of Henni was sold. St. James Church became one of the first communities radically altered by the transportation and demographic shifts of the postwar era.[222]

The extension of Highway I-43 through the south side and over the Menominee Valley radically disrupted the parish life of St. Stanislaus, St. Josaphat and St. Patrick's parishes. These churches lost hundreds of members as their homes were taken away to make way for the new super highways. As noted earlier, Our Lady of Pompeii, which had earlier resisted the demands of urban developers, also fell to the wreckers ball to make room for a freeway. The venerable St. Joseph's Church on 11th and Cherry, a fixture of Milwaukee Catholic life since the 1850s, also fell—although the parish title and some original artifacts were transferred to a new Wauwatosa site off Center Street. At the time, apart from a few distressed souls who hated to see their beloved churches destroyed for "progress," few took note.

Archdiocesan Catholics also loved and relied on the automobile—an article of faith for suburban life. Catholic churches of this new era had to include large parking lots and reschedule Mass times to make sure that traffic jams did not take place outside the church. The "privilege" of owning an automobile, generally restricted to pastors who could afford them (or to the occasional young priest who had well-to-do parents) was now, perforce, extended to the parish assistants, who could no longer rely on public transport to transact pastoral duties. Kiley dragged his feet on giving permission for auto ownership to junior clergy, and Albert Meyer foolishly tried to impose that restriction on his priests in Superior. Slowly and quietly during the 1950s and early 1960s, most parish priests acquired cars.

Catholic Schools in the New Era

A polio epidemic in the late 1940s closed all the schools for a few weeks, but public health officials re-opened them when the danger appeared to pass.[223] From that point the number of children seeking entrance into Catholic schools grew astronomically, spurting past the 100,000 mark in 1957 for the first time in archdiocesan history.[224] The growth of the decade is evident in the following statistics:

Table 4-4
[Source: Annual School Reports, AAM]

Year	Enrollment (Elementary/ High School)
1945	61,063
1950	62,742
1955	83,927
1960	108,869

The following provides statistics in the growth of schools:

Year	Elementary Schools	9th Grades	High Schools
1945	204	15	22
1950	174	24	21
1955	190	19	22
1960	218	7	24

Table 4-5
[Source: Annual Reports, AAM]

The building of schools preceded the construction of churches and virtually every year of the postwar era saw new schools

St. Lawrence School, Milwaukee [AOSF]

open—even in parishes that had been established for many years. In Kenosha, St. Anthony and Holy Rosary opened schools in the 1950s. Each year Monsignor Goebel's annual report recorded the new school buildings that welcomed Catholic children each fall.[225] Slowly as well, the capacity of high schools increased to meet the needs of the rapidly growing teenaged population. Rooms were crowded with large numbers of students, but the religious personnel to staff them fell far behind the needs.

The Teaching Sisterhoods

In 1950, more than 4,600 religious sisters served in the archdiocese of Milwaukee. This number jumped past 5,000 by 1960. This sampling of the major sisterhoods in the archdiocese reflects how their numbers grew:

Table 4-6
[Source: Archives of Sisterhoods]

Order	1940	1950	1960
Notre Dame	2,132	2,158	2,125
Franciscan (OSF)	710	847	929
Franciscan (SSSF)	2177	2453	3018
Salvatorian	274	336	433
Dominican (Racine)	482	530	570
Dominican (Sinsin.)	1,399	1,611	1,896
Agnesian	697	701	804
Sisters of the Sorrowful Mother	613	652	680

The growth in these teaching sisterhoods was phenomenal as large numbers of young women annually entered the convents in large investiture and profession ceremonies.

New Aspirants, Racine Dominicans, 1952 [AOP-Rac]

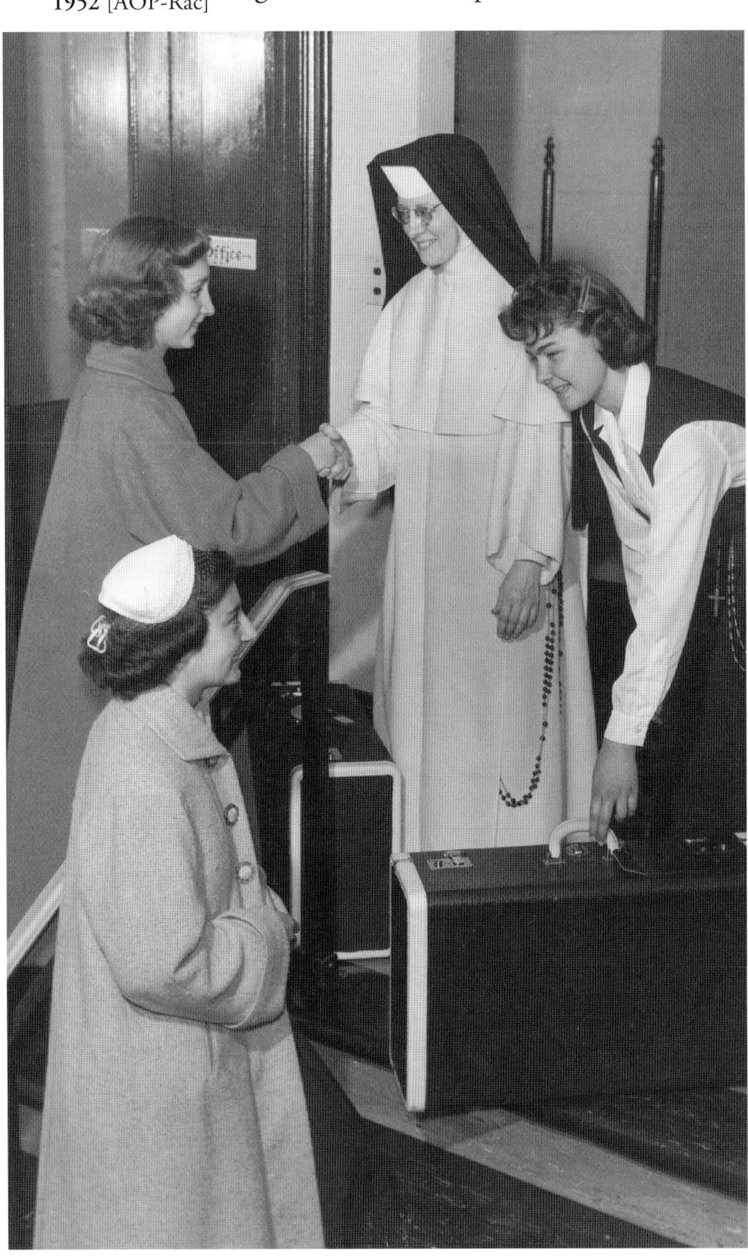

To cope with the need for space, the teaching orders moved college programs begun in the 1930s out of the main convent buildings and into separate institutions (this was also done to secure accreditation). New modern motherhouses were built by the Notre Dame, Racine Dominican and Sinsinawa Dominican communities that contained large wings for novices, newly professed sisters (called "juniors"). They also included antiseptic infirmaries, large dining halls with state-of-the-art kitchens, and elaborate new chapels which highlighted new architectural styles. Other communities simply added on new building additions or expanded and redecorated chapel areas (for example, the Franciscans of St. Francis).

Although the sisters were governed by rules that prescribed in great detail their day, life in convents varied. Certainly religious life in the motherhouses, under the eye of the mother general and her advisors, differed from the life in convents where a local superior directed daily life, tasks and religious exercises. Sisters worked hard to maintain a balance between their life of prayer and their life of work, and most of them rose early to pray and celebrate Mass, spent long hours in the classroom and then went home for additional schoolwork, supper and evening study. Many sisters did not have the leisure of a summer "off," but almost as soon as they shut down their classrooms for the year were trundled off to college classes, retreats or work at the motherhouse. Sisters received their annual "missions" or assignments, in various forms—some by spoken order from the community hierarchy, others in colored transfer forms (one community called the letters "bluebirds"). The similarity of lifestyles among religious sisters was evident to some. In one "diary" composed for the Catholic newspaper, an anonymous Notre Dame sister took the reader through a typical day of religious exercises, school challenges and problems. In the section titled "Twilight Hour," she wrote, "I reached the convent door of Home Sweet Home just as the bell was ringing to take me straight to God once more. As I knelt for the opening prayer, I wondered how many other Sisters in the city, in the archdiocese, in the state, and in our time belt were praising God and our Lady with me in this twilight hour."[226]

Changes within convents required a new style of leadership. Commissary General Fidelis Krieter of the Notre Dame Sisters, Corona Wirfs of the School Sisters of St. Francis, Olympia Heuel of the Salvatorians and Bartholomew Frederick of the St. Francis Franciscans were strong, resourceful and expansionist leaders. In many of these convents, the tradition of the chaplain or spiritual director as the *de facto* director of much convent life (especially in the matter of buildings and temporalities) gave way to an unfettered hand by the sisters. The School Sisters of Notre Dame no longer had a Peter Abbelen type to "advise" and "direct" them. Neither did the Racine Dominicans. However, the tradition of a strong chaplain continued for a while yet with the School Sisters of St. Francis who allowed Monsignor Adolph Klink and later his nephew of the same name to direct their affairs.

The brunt of the work in sustaining the sisterhoods financially and accommodating the large numbers of applicants (many of them from high schools run by the sisterhoods) fell to the elected mother generals. Additional funds were needed to pay for the care, education, feeding and clothing of these

Profession ceremonies, School Sisters of Notre Dame [ASND]

young women. Continual struggles ensued over the salaries paid to religious sisters in parishes. An archdiocesan standard was set, but parishes often could not make the payments. For a time some sisterhoods often owned the convent buildings and paid for their upkeep. Later, many of these properties were sold to individual parishes and the sisters received a salary for their teaching duties as well as other duties they assumed around the parish. In some parishes the sisters took care of church music and the sacristy as well as performing janitorial duties.

Slowly but surely however, the sisters began to draw boundaries around what they would and would not do in their schools. "We have discontinued taking care of the furnaces and also the supervising of the sweeping and cleaning of the schoolrooms, as well as the church in all of our missions," wrote the School Sisters of St. Francis to Father Ferdinand Falbisoner in 1930.[227] The Notre Dame sisters first determined a fee schedule for their various services in 1915. Contracts for services were also written out. But different parishes worked out the details in alternative ways. Some parishes provided certain services to the sisters in lieu of cash payment (for example, giving food or paying utility bills), and others allowed sisters to supplement their income by holding fund-raisers, socials and openhouses. In 1915 when the Sisters of Notre Dame appealed for higher wages, they noted that the amount given for their services had not changed in 20 or 30 years. "You understand," the sisters wrote to the pastors, "that one of the most essential obligations of our Community is to provide for the education of efficient teachers, to supply the present demands of the parochial schools. You realize that this obligation, not to mention the care of the sick and the support of the aged and infirm, entails heavy expenses."[228] Salary demands would often be sidetracked, but the sisters nonetheless kept up their work. Generously, the sisters often foreswore salaries during the De-

Racine Dominican teacher [AOP-Rac]

pression and often had to wait while a pastor found the funds to pay them. In some places, like St. Mark's in Kenosha, the School Sisters of St. Francis had to wait for months before the pastor Father Alphonse Berg would pay them. At St. Anthony of Padua School in Milwaukee, Father Peter Schroeder tried to pay the sisters with canned goods.[229]

The mothers general and their consultors fielded an ever-increasing demand for sister-teachers not only for all the Milwaukee schools, and also for other dioceses where their community had missions. At the same time, for a variety of reasons, the sisterhoods began to back away from their custom of sending untrained teaching sisters into large classrooms. They made this decision at a time when demands for their services were higher than ever. Nonetheless, years of sometimes disastrous experiences for young women with overwhelming numbers of children and the demands for professionalism caused the sisters to change direction. This had implications for parishes.

In the 1948-1949 school year, the Notre Dame sisters notified pastors that for every seven sisters, the parishes had to hire and pay for a lay teacher. The demand brought immediate squawks from pastors and an appeal for relief to the archdiocesan school board. The board's secretary, St. Leo pastor Monsignor George Meyer, complained to Commissary General Mother Fidelis Krieter that the new rule would require the hiring of 35 lay teachers in the Milwaukee and West Allis schools alone at the cost of $56,000. Meyer and the board tried to hand responsibility for hiring new lay teachers back to the sisters and insisted that they be paid out of the funds given by the parish to the sisters. Meyer concluded his letter to Mother Fidelis: "It does seem strange, however, that you find it necessary suddenly to withdraw so many sisters from our city that has helped the Notre Dame Sisters to gain the position that they hold today and had undoubtedly given the Order many hundreds of its daughters to the Notre Dame Community."[230]

Mother Fidelis was not easily intimidated. "We realize Monsignor, that our plan will place a financial burden upon the parishes," she wrote. "However, may we remind you that during the Depression we provided one or more teachers free to many for the parishes in Milwaukee and that for several years we furnished five high school teachers for Messmer without any salary, which meant the saving of many thousands of dollars to Milwaukee." Mother Fidelis took on Meyer's argument that the Notre Dame sisters "owed" the archdiocese because they had taken so many vocations from local parishes. "The fact is, Monsignor, that Milwaukee has not contributed sufficient numbers of vocations to Notre Dame to take care of its own needs." She needled the St. Leo pastor by pointing out that just to supply his large parish school, "St. Leo's should have furnished 24 vocations yearly to replace working personnel, or a total of over 200 over the ten year period." "Actually, there have been 79 members or 40% of the quota received from this area during that period of time." Finally, while offering to assist in the selection of new lay teachers,

Mother Fidelis firmly rejected the notion that the sisters should somehow assume financial responsibility for paying the lay teachers. "We are asking that it be taken care of by Pastors or parish trustees," she wrote, "We shall be happy to repeal this emergency measure as soon as the necessary increase in vocations enables us to do so. We therefore beg all the reverend clergy to pray and work zealously that the Lord may send more good laborers into His vineyard."[231] In the end, a compromise of sorts was worked out on a parish-by-parish basis but overall, Mother Fidelis's will was enforced. By 1958, over 500 of the 2,400 teachers in the Milwaukee archdiocesan system were lay persons. One new school opened that fall with nine new lay teachers and only four nuns. In addition, the number of men teaching on the elementary school level began to rise steadily. Fifteen men reported to classrooms in 1958.[232] Parishes picked up the tab for the higher expenses by charging tuition—something that had been avoided in archdiocesan elementary schools to this point.

Although conflict did sometimes mar the relationships between pastors and teaching sisters, the general experience was one of satisfaction and fulfillment with the work of the sisters. "We pastors realize how futile would be our ministry without the teaching Sisters in our parish schools," observed Monsignor Bernard Kobelinski, pastor of St. Stanislaus, in 1943. As he reflected on the 75 years the Notre Dame sisters had served at St. Stanislaus, he saluted them "not as the Brides of Christ—no you are more than that—you are truly co-ministers with the priests of the Catholic Church."[233] In that same year, Holy Name spokesman Phil Grau paid tribute to the Dominican sisters at St. Rose during a Friday evening broadcast over radio station WEMP. "For five decades they have seen go from the portals of that school fine types of boys and girls who now grace every walk of life, economic, professional civic and religious," Grau declared. "Their teaching is interwoven with this city's historical development in a pattern of high ideals and noble unselfish service."[234] In 1947, the centenary of Notre

Aspirants in class, Racine Dominicans [AOP-Rac]

Dame order was celebrated with great fanfare with a Mass at St. John's Cathedral. Thousands of young voices from all the Notre Dame schools combined to chant the magnificent Gregorian Mass Number VII at the celebration attended by Mother General Mary Almeda, and Commissary General Mother Fidelis.[235] "In the hearts of the countless numbers who have been trained by these Sisters, there is gratitude," wrote Franklyn Kennedy at the *Herald Citizen*.[236]

The Catholic High School

The other major development that built on the accomplishments of an earlier era had been the proliferation of Catholic high schools. In fact, the high school now came into its own as an established feature of larger educational life. The success of Messmer High School and the variety of order-run private high schools made them one of the prime areas of expansion. "At present our schools are crowded," wrote Superintendent Goebel in his 1942-43 annual report, "but this should not deter us from developing a program that ultimately will provide every elementary school graduate an opportunity to attend a Catholic high school." Addressing Kiley's suggestion that the creation of ninth-grade classrooms around the city would alleviate crowding in high schools, he concluded, "His Excellency, Our Most Reverend Archbishop, has also emphasized the necessity of providing additional facilities in the Milwaukee area. Though this project must await the peace, plans are being made to hasten this work as soon as it is feasible."[237]

All of the private schools, Mercy, St. Mary's Academy, Holy Angels, and Marquette High registered strong enrollments. St. John's Cathedral High also soared in enrollment and would make substantial additions to its aging property in the 1950s. Messmer High School was running double sessions to accommodate its overflow. The following chart gives some idea of the spike in Catholic high school attendance between 1940 and 1960:

Year	# HS Students	# High Schools
1940	5,222	15
1950	9,298	23
1960	15,113	24

Table 4-7
[Source: Annual Reports, Catholic School Department, AAM]

Shortly after the war, Goebel placed the need for high school expansion on the front burner of the educational agenda. Noting in 1945 that the existing ten Catholic high schools could accommodate only 1,250 of the 3,900 eighth-grade graduates, he wrote, "It is imperative that additional Catholic high school facilities be provided."[238]

Kiley began collecting for two new Catholic high schools. Taking advantage of the popular feelings toward recently returned

Sinsinawa Dominican Sister receiving an honorary degree from Rosary College, June 1937 [AOP-Sin]

war veterans, he launched the "Archbishop's Memorial Building Fund Campaign" to memorialize in brick and mortar those who had fallen in battle.[239] In early August, 1945, Kiley's distinctive voice was heard on WTMJ urging Catholics to give $750,000 for the new high schools and a new boys home as well.[240] On Easter Sunday afternoon in 1948, Kiley broke ground for the new Catholic Memorial High School in Waukesha in the rapidly growing western part of the archdiocese.[241] In 1949, an ebullient Kiley, just returned from his *ad limina* in Rome, sped to

Archbishop Kiley breaking ground for Catholic Memorial High School, Waukesha [AAM]

Waukesha to dedicate the building, the first Catholic high school built since Messmer in 1930. Catholic Memorial opened its doors with Father John Voelker as principal.[242]

Diocesan high schools were expensive and were possible only if a religious order agreed to staff, entirely or in part, the faculty and often the administrative positions. At the same time Kiley was begging for money for new high schools, members of the Society of Mary (Marianists) were recruited for high school service. The first contingent of brothers served as teachers in the crowded Messmer High School during the 1944-1945 school year.[243] During that year the archdiocese remodeled the old West Becher Street School on Milwaukee's south side, and in September 1945 opened Don Bosco High School for boys, which relieved the overcrowding in nearby St. Stanislaus High School.[244] In 1949 Kiley approved a large expansion of St. Catherine's High School in Racine. In 1950 the Sisters of the Divine Savior built a new high school for girls on the northwest side of Milwaukee. For the small group of students on the upper east side, a new high school operated by the Sisters of St. Joan Antida opened in 1954, welcoming 48 students from 18 parishes to the newly built school on Cass Street. In 1958 the Salvatorian fathers opened up Francis Jordan High School near their parish of Mother of Good Counsel.

Sister Aquinas Petro, St. Catherine High School, Racine [AOP-Rac]

Divine Savior Holy Angels High School [AAM]

Interestingly enough, religious orders were eager to acquire high schools after the war. These schools not only provided an apostolic outlet for their growing numbers, but they also were prime recruiting grounds for future members.[245] Sisters' high schools in particular often included aspirancy and even postulant sections for young girls who had already decided in eighth grade that they had a religious vocation. For religious orders of men, the transition from the high school to a novitiate was fairly easy and was often facilitated by faculty members. Religious orders drew a great number from the Milwaukee youth they taught in high schools. The largest numbers were to be found in the religious sisterhoods that had motherhouses in Milwaukee. Male orders that drew heavily included the Society of Jesus, the Marianists and the Pallottines.

Efforts at Central Catholic High Schools: St. Joseph's (Kenosha)

Sponsoring and funding Catholic high schools became an important priority of the Catholic community. Virtually every community wanted to have a Catholic high school nearby, but the archdiocese could not afford it. Consequently, groups of parishes, usually in cities like Sheboygan or Kenosha, attempted to pool resources to build a Catholic high school. Sometimes these efforts came to naught, as in the case in Sheboygan where they failed to realize elaborate plans to build a new high school in honor of St. Thomas Aquinas.[246] In other communities, like heavily Catholic Kenosha, such a project got enough steam to begin St. Joseph's High School, but eventually surrendered the project to the control of a more financially secure religious community.

For many years, Catholic high schoolers in Kenosha made a long shuttle to St. Catherine's High School in Racine. A ninth grade was opened in St. George School, but in 1948 St. Mary's pastor, Raymond Bell, added a wing to his large school building to phase in a high school operated by the Racine Dominicans. Bell's high school soon became a big hit with Kenosha Catholics, and he then laid plans for a new high school building once he had completed a new church.

Bell's plans were lukewarmly received by other pastors. Father Ralph Altstadt of neighboring St. Mark's, complained that Bell's "lone-wolf" approach jeopardized the formation of a central school at a "neutral location" that would be supported by all the parishes. Altstadt took his complaints to Archbishop

Rev. Ralph Altstadt [AAM]

Kiley, who called on Bell to cooperate with the plans spearheaded by Altstadt. Acting with Kiley's consent and later with Meyer's, Altstadt organized the central Catholic High School in Kenosha and began collecting funds from the priests of the city (except Bell).[247] He purchased within the boundaries of his own parish, a plot of ground on the site of what had been a Kenosha amusement park. Bell's death in August 1956 removed any major stumbling block from the local clergy. Altstadt took the lead in creating St. Joseph's High School and recruited the School Sisters of St. Francis, who ran his parish's own parochial school, to direct the new enterprise. Building plans were laid and the firm of Pfaller and Pfaller were chosen to construct the new building.

But problem upon problem with the new edifice drained money and the parishes' enthusiasm. Excavations revealed that the St. Joseph's site sat over an underground stream. Some had warned Altstadt of this, reminding him that as youths they had skated on a pond that sat on the property, but he pressed on nonetheless. Spending to shore up the soggy earth and fortify the foundation used up all the money Altstadt had collected. To rescue the project, Altstadt assessed the Kenosha parishes for more money. This created unrest since several were in the midst of or had just completed expensive building projects. St. Anthony's and Holy Rosary had just built new schools; St. George had made an expensive addition to its buildings; St. Peter's Lithuanian parish had relocated to the north side of Kenosha. The fledgling St. Therese parish was still so strapped for funds it wasn't even required to contribute, and St. Mary's had just built a new church.

Fearful of seeing the high school plan collapse, Altstadt persuaded Mother Corona Wirfs of the School Sisters of St. Francis to purchase the school. Winning the consent of her council for the proposal, the doughty mother general dramatically re-worked the plans for the high school, adding elaborate marble floors in its entry way, a state of the art little theater, and a huge convent set up to

First faculty St. Joseph High School, Kenosha [ASSF]

accommodate 50 resident teaching sisters. The school opened in 1957, with diocesan priest Father Leslie Darneider at its head. Local parish priests took turns teaching in the school's religious programs. A small corps of lay teachers joined the Franciscan Sisters and the priests at the growing high school.

The Parish High School That Became Diocesan: Pius XI

Sometimes the process of high school formation began with a parish-sponsored school. Some like Father Bell's efforts at St. Mary's faltered. Others, like St. Mary's in Burlington, managed to hang on and serve a small constituency. One of the archdiocese's largest high schools (indeed the largest Catholic high school in Wisconsin) began as a parish school. Its dynamic growth soon made it a magnet for hundreds of other pupils from neighboring parishes. Before long it had grown into a diocese-wide high school. Only after the sponsoring parish grew weary of subsidizing the school, did its status change.

Groundbreaking Pius XI High School, Milwaukee, 1948 [ASAC]

Pius XI High School had begun in the 1930s as the parish high school of St. Anthony of Padua parish on Milwaukee's west side. It was just one part of the expansionist activities of St. Anthony's hyperactive pastor, Father Peter Schroeder.[248] Schroeder had begun the school on "a wing and a prayer" and ran a rather amateurish operation. At one point Archbishop Stritch threatened to shut it down when he noted that the poor facilities and weak academic program would not pass muster with an accreditation team sent by the University of Wisconsin. Schroeder begged for more time and then worked hard to turn things around. Eventually he built new buildings and upgraded academic programs that ensured the high school's continued existence.

Schroeder left the United States in 1937 and died in 1939. His successor, Father Joseph DeMaria, a lovable and highly effective pastor, devoted his considerable energies and talents to building and expanding the Pallottine presence in Wisconsin. He was the first American provincial of the Midwestern

Mother of God Province of the community, and under his aegis the Pallottines began a successful minor seminary in Madison that trained a number of future Madison priests and some members of his own community. As pastor of St. Anthony of Padua parish, he helped push through a major expansion of the high school. Eager to build big and to claim a share of the growing high school "market," DeMaria envisioned a massive high school that would replace the buildings Schroeder had erected. The $1.6 million plans drawn by architect Mark Pfaller in 1948 included classrooms, labs, and a student dining room. It was to be the largest Catholic high school building in the state.[249] DeMaria financed this not only by securing a $400,000 loan from the Catholic Knights Insurance Company, but also by securing Kiley's help in wringing donations out of nearby parishes such as St. Sebastian's and Holy Assumption in West Allis, who had begun sending students to the school.

In a manner unthinkable today, DeMaria also added funds from the parish of St. Anthony, and the parish transferred hefty subsidies to the high school until the 1960s. This delayed for many years their hopes for a new place of worship. In November 1949 Kiley came to dedicate the new building which already registered 1,082 pupils. By the next year the number increased to 1,240 and by 1954, more than 1,500 students attended Pius XI. In 1955 DeMaria broke ground for what was originally intended to be a two-story addition, but ended up becoming a six-story, 40 classroom wing and convent.

As Pius XI matured, Franciscan Sister Beatrix Wolsfelt attempted to professionalize school administration and improve curriculum. In these efforts she constantly tripped over the well-intentioned Father DeMaria. He still thought of Pius XI as an extension of his parish and interfered with school policy by handing out candy, declaring free days and overruling decisions of teachers and administrators. Tensions between Wolsfelt and the other Pallottines on the faculty flared when they occasionally imposed harsh punishments on the students similar to the ones they had received in German schools. At one point Wolsfelt nearly succeeded in ejecting the Pallottines from their own school when Archbishop Meyer invited the Christian Brothers of the St. Louis province to take over the teaching of the boys.[250] However, the Pallottines fought back and retained control of the school they had founded. When Wolsfelt lost these battles, she retired. How-

Pius XI High School [ASAC]

ever, a new professionalism did take hold of Pius XI's administration, and DeMaria's hand was eventually removed from direct control over the high school and the parish. Pius XI became an archdiocesan school in 1964.

One other Catholic high school—Dominican High School in the upscale suburb of Whitefish Bay–had altogether different origins. This high school went back to the grand planning and design of Father (Monsignor) Farrell P. Reilly of St. Robert Church in Shorewood. After he had built his magnificent church, Reilly wanted to crown his colony of Catholic buildings with a high school that could be available to the growing number of pupils on Milwaukee's north shore. On the occasion of his 40th anniversary of ordination in 1944, the parish awarded him a $142,000 purse, which he promptly put into a fund for a high school. This grew to a $300,000 nest egg. Since there was literally no room in Reilly's parish, his plans were put together with those of Father Peter Dietz of St. Monica in Whitefish Bay to build a school on his grounds. Dietz did not have money to undertake the project, and even the $300,000 Reilly bequest was not enough. Eventually, the Dominican Sisters of Sinsinawa stepped forward, at Reilly's request, to help bring the pieces of the deal together.

Dietz's successor, Father John J. Barry, wanted the new school to complement the huge church he had built. He too began to work with the Sinsinawa Dominicans and helped them through zoning battles fought against local residents who were skeptical of the presence of a large school in their nice neighborhoods. In 1952, Barry deeded the land to the Sinsinawa Dominicans on the promise that they would start building before 1955. Engaging the firm of Brielmaier, Grellinger and Rose, the sisters drew up plans for a $3 million building capable of holding 500 students.[251] The original name, "Farrell P. Reilly High School," gave way to the more prosaic "Dominican High School," and it opened its doors in September 1956.[252] Father Robert McCormick was the first principal.

Groundbreaking Dominican High School, Whitefish Bay [AOP-Sin]

The proliferation of Catholic high schools offered the Catholic Church a new opportunity for visibility in yet another changing dimension of life: the emergence of a distinctive youth subculture.

The Ethos of the Schools and Postwar Youth Culture

The expansion of the Catholic high school system in Milwaukee was in keeping with similar developments in Wisconsin and the rest of the country. Catholic schools of Milwaukee after the war were in many respects the same as in previous times. Children from a neighborhood trooped to the school attired in a distinctive school uniform. Lay teachers, unknown in Catholic schools since the 19th century, reappeared in the classrooms in the 1950s. Most of the faculty, however, were still teaching sisters, attired in the distinctive habits of their respective orders. The office of Catholic schools had imposed a degree of standardization on the schools, in part to conform to the requirements of accreditation agencies, but also to reflect the growing consensus among educators on matters of childhood development, curriculum, pedagogical techniques, and the physical layout of school buildings. Much of what the children learned in Catholic schools was similar to what their public school counterparts learned. There were no "Catholic" mathematics, phonics or science courses.

The teaching orders did have specialties. The School Sisters of St. Francis had a reputation for being excellent music teachers (private lessons were available to children at most schools), the Racine Dominicans excelled at teacher training, and the Franciscan Sisters of St. Francis were specialists in reading.[253]

The distinctive aspects of Catholic education entered into the lives of students not only through course work in religion, but also in regular sacramental practice—Mass was part of most school days. The sisters encouraged a lively sense of devotion in the classroom throughout the year. Students were introduced to novenas, the rosary, and the special saints and heroes of the orders of sisters who taught them. Dominican schools made a great fuss over St. Dominic, St. Thomas Aquinas and St. Catherine of Siena; Franciscans rhapsodized over the virtues of the Poverello of Assisi and St. Elizabeth of Hungary. Lessons in purity were given through St. Dominic Savio (a popular youth patron) and St. Maria Goretti whose resistance to the sexual advances of a lustful young man led to a brutal martyrdom.

One of the capstone experiences of the year in most Catholic schools was the May Crowning. This event, highlighting a major devotional celebration, saw children compete for the honor of perching a crown on top of a statue of the Blessed Virgin Mary. Often the celebrations were reverent and joyful. Sometimes they were disasters. In 1945, the May Crowning at St. John's Cathedral was a series of mishaps. First a torrential rain "played havoc with congregation, punctuality, light dresses and order," wrote an exasperated sister-chronicler. Even worse, the chosen "Queen," Alice Sierachi, was so late that the procession started without her, and her place and veil were given to another. When the out-of-breath Sierachi arrived and demanded her place in the line, she tried to get the veil off her substitute, who would not give it up. "Alice persevered, however," wrote the sister, "joined the group at the altar and then proceeded with the usual acts. When she turned to descend the steps after the coronation we were all horrified to see her fall heavily to the stone floor of the sanctuary." The sister concluded, "Fortunately, she was not hurt, but there was a good indulgence in nervous, tense weeping after all was over."[254]

The impact of these sacramental and devotional exercises may have been lost on the young children at first, but through steady reinforcement the occasions of sacramental celebration, especially first communion and confirmation, formed milestones in a child's life. Catholic school children learned to mark time by the liturgical year, absorbed the militant self-confidence of the Catholic theological world of the day and learned a lively sense of right and wrong. Sacramental confession, while intended to be a source of peace and to reinforce virtue, did have its negative aspects. Fully believing that one was capable of "serious sin" by the time of the age of reason (generally pegged at age 7), teachers drilled students in lists of sins and penetrating examinations of conscience more suited to adults than to children. The darkness of the confessional, the invisible voice coming from behind a screen, and the worry that one might forget a mortal sin also added to the worry of the children. Occasionally confessors were hard and cruel with children (and adults), but more typical, even for priests with reputations for being harsh, was a dramatic transformation once they stepped into the confessional. In truth, despite the elaborate midrash spun by literary figures and stand-up comics who related funny memories about "growing up Catholic" or boozy stories spun at class reunions about hard-of- hearing priests whose voices could be heard throughout the church, probably few people were really "yelled at" or scolded. Such was the case with the authoritarian Archbishop Kiley who could be uncharacteristically gentle with erring priests. So too the roaring voice of Fond du Lac's Henry Riordan was stilled to a gentle whisper in the confessional and in personal counseling. Catholic school children saw their priests regularly as the young assistants appeared to teach religion, instruct the altar boys, or play basketball or baseball with the boys. In some parishes, the pastor's name day was a mini-feast day, sometimes accompanied by a day off from school. Christmas was a time for priests' gifts of holy cards to school children.

May Crowning, St. Mary Academy, St. Francis [AOSF]

Summer brought swimming and baseball outsings for the altar boys.

The dramatic bulge in the birth rate soon created a large body of teenagers in the country, and these young people developed their own distinctive youth culture. Social historians have noted that the term *teenager* became popular in the 1940s and the early 1950s, as adolescents began to separate themselves in a variety of ways from their parents and their younger siblings.[255] The outward signs of this were different tastes in hairstyles, clothing and above all music. The heroes of this new youth culture often came from movies or popular entertainment. Young movies stars like Marlon Brando (*The Wild Ones*, 1954) or James Dean (*Rebel Without a Cause*, 1955) enthralled young people and filled their parents with alarm. Rock music, born of a mixture of rhythm and blues and jazz blared from record players and radio. Bill Haley's Comets began the transition with their bouncy "Rock Around the Clock" (the theme song of another popular movie from 1955, *Blackboard Jungle*, starring a surly young Sidney Poitier); but other pop music stars loomed large, especially a young singer from Mississippi named Elvis Presley. Presley's unabashedly sexual gyrations and the suggestiveness of his crooning created frenzy wherever he appeared, and loathing and fear in parents and elders. (Television variety show host Ed Sullivan would not permit his cameramen to film Presley from the waist down when he appeared on his show in 1955.)

Teenagers' perception of themselves as rebels were reinforced by industries that catered to their clothing, hygiene and entertainment desires. The youth culture's attitudes toward premarital sexual behavior caused anxiety among parents. Stars like Presley, Brando, Dean and others sent strong signals of liberated sexuality that young people imitated. The rituals of courtship and "going steady" were soon transferred to teenage romances, including the exchange of rings. Dancing, always a concern for those worried about inappropriate relations between the sexes, became more frenzied and passionate and slow dancing drew young boys and girls together in what appeared to be inappropriate proximity. The tendency of young people to form cliques and gangs also worried parents and educators. Urban youth in particular renewed a trend to stake out urban turf and challenge opposing groups of teens to fight them. Scrapes with the law, fighting, even murder were reported in lurid detail, and anxieties about juvenile delinquency were circulated through popular media, including women's magazines, human interest inserts in Sunday papers and increasingly on television.

Catholics were already concerned about youth culture in the 1930s. A survey taken by the *Catholic Herald Citizen* in 1937 of young Catholic men and women revealed a somewhat roseate view, but also noted their tastes in funny papers and music, dating preferences, and religious practices (one in 25 girls was a daily communicant and 114 boys indicated an interest in the priesthood). Most notably, the boys indicated that they had no intention of following in the footsteps of their mostly working-class parents.[256] These concerns continued into the postwar era and were focused around the behavior and dress of students in Catholic high schools. In 1945, superintendent of schools, Edmund Goebel, issued a series of regulations governing the holding of proms (end-of-year dances that were becoming occasions for drinking and sexual activity). Goebel surveyed 3,000 parents and devised rules that both strengthened security (students were not to leave the prom hall and were to go home in the company of their parents), and also made sure that the prom was affordable (a $3 ceiling was placed on prom admission).[257]

But concern about "wild youth" continued. In November 1950, the *Milwaukee Sentinel* carried a lengthy series about "Be-Bop" activities in Milwaukee's public high schools.[258] "Be-Bops" were young people of both genders who wore distinctive hairstyles (the boys "duck tails" and the girls long straight hair combed behind the ears) and clothing (the boys brightly colored trousers pleated at the waistline and the girls long, dark skirts, and field jackets for boys and girls). The article commented negatively on the gang activities of these young people, "which include[d] stealing, disobedience to authority, and immorality culminating in

Sodality Union Mass, Milwaukee Auditorium [AAM]

interracial [activity]." It even suggested that the young people were being influenced by the Communist party. A Sinsinawa Dominican writing about this noted that Goebel had given orders to expel such types if they showed up at Catholic high schools. "Thank God, we have no one to expel," she wrote, "although two girls were expelled a month ago."[259]

Catholic schools worried especially about the impact of the sexual messages received through the medium of television, movies and novels. Celibate priests' and nuns' preoccupation with pre-marital sexual activity was, like the experience of confession, caricatured by comics and others with recollections of a Catholic childhood. But there was an element of truth to these accounts. The content of Catholic teaching on sexual morality was occasionally legalistic and abstract. Moreover, in the admirable desire to teach children the beauty and dignity of human sexuality, the processes of sexual maturation sometimes were accentuated as an occasion of sin. Strong messages on abstinence, chastity and the morality of "venereal acts" were regularly transmitted to Catholic youth in both written and spoken form. Catholic high school classes stressed chastity as one of the highest of virtues and sought to reinforce sexual purity. Priests were urged to be strict in the confessional. Worrying that young priests were taking too easy an attitude on matters "*de sexto*," Archbishop Stritch ordered the seminary to be "stricter than the moral theologians with regard to solitary sins [masturbation].[260] Messages appeared to be targeted primarily at girls. Speaking to young girls who had just made an act of consecration to the Virgin Mary after their confirmation at St. Anne's parish in Milwaukee, Archbishop Stritch extolled the superior virtue of women. "Men may sit in front of kings, they may gather around council tables, but who can measure the tremendous influence of women?" But, he warned, if women became "bad and depraved ... there is not a demon in hell who can do her work." He exhorted the young women to chastity and to embrace the Blessed Virgin as their model. "Don't ever kneel at the shrine of Venus; do not go to the bathing beach or to the movies to find your ideal."[261] These messages were continually repeated by Stritch's successors, pastors, and sisters who urged young girls to be the ones to say "no" to the passionate urges of boyfriends. Stritch's directive to take the Virgin Mary as a role model was translated into action. Catholic high schools had contests among the girls who vied for the most "Mary-like" dress, and the perpetual virginity of Mary was extolled as the true model of purity. Likewise, the elevation of the celibate state as superior to marriage was a signal received by large numbers of young men and women who entered convents, seminaries and religious orders.

On the archdiocesan level, a renewed effort to attract youth to large-scale Catholic activities found expression in the Sodality Union of the Milwaukee Archdiocese (SUMA), which began having youth rallies in 1945 centered on Marian themes which stressed youthful chastity and purity. In addition, the 1950s saw a rejuvenation of the athletic programs of the Catholic Youth Organization (CYO), which provided "wholesome" social opportunities for young men (women's sports were not accepted as yet).

Milwaukee Catholic officials also endorsed the efforts of the Legion of Decency, an organization founded in the 1930s as a cooperative endeavor between the Catholic Church and Hollywood producers to curtail offensive depictions of sexuality and the glorification of crime in motion pictures.[262] The weekly *Catholic Herald Citizen* printed lengthy ratings of popular movies. Annually priests led parishioners in a pledge crafted by the league to foreswear attendance at entertainment dangerous to faith and morality. In 1947 Kiley led boycotts of Milwaukee theaters showing a scantily clad Jane Russell in "The Outlaw" and the equally racy "Forever Amber," a story of a British prostitute.[263] In 1956, Archbishop Meyer joined scores of other American Catholic bishops in condemning Elia Kazan's "Baby Doll" released by Warner Brothers.[264] (The Catholic press, however, did push attendance at favorable movies like the Bing Crosby hits, "Going My Way" and "The Bells of St. Mary's" as well as devotional classics on the Marian apparitions

Marian rally, CYO, Sheboygan [AAM]

at Lourdes and Fatima.)[265] Catholic parents also launched campaigns against "suggestive" reading materials, which in those days included comic books that glorified crime or portrayed comic figures in scanty attire.

In May 1956 Archbishop Albert Meyer addressed the concerns of youth culture in a widely circulated (and admired) pastoral letter titled *Decency and Modesty*. Drawing on themes from the 1954 Marian year, Meyer shared with the Milwaukee flock his concerns about the state of morality in the See and urged Catholics to greater vigilance in matters of dress, reading, entertainment and "company keeping."[266] Meyer's words won for him unique national acclaim as the pastoral was reported on the National Catholic News service and requests for additional copies flooded the Milwaukee Chancery.

Another effort to reach Catholic youth came through the publication of a youth magazine called *Hi Time*. This widely-circulated tabloid was the brainchild of Henriette Mackin, a graduate of the University of Wisconsin and an educational reporter for the *Milwaukee Journal*. One of ten children from a devout Catholic family (her brother William became a priest of the archdiocese), Mackin had become intrigued with the idea of a catechetical text for high

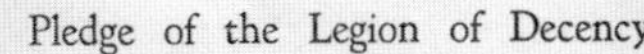

Pledge of the Legion of Decency

Pope Pius XI said in his Encyclical on Motion Pictures: "All pastors of souls will undertake to obtain each year from their people a pledge similar to the one already alluded to which is given by their American brothers, and in which they promise to stay away from motion picture plays offensive to truth and Christian morality.

The Bishops at their annual meeting in Washington, 1938, requested all Ordinaries to have the Pledge of the Legion of Decency taken by all the faithful at all Masses, in all churches and chapels throughout the United States, on the Sunday within the Octave of the Feast of the Immaculate Conception.

The request is now made that the Bishops may take practical measures to carry out the wishes of the late Pontiff, Pope Pius XI, regarding the following Pledge of the Legion of Decency on Sunday, December 14th, the Sunday within the Octave of the Feast of the Immaculate Conception.

IN THE NAME OF THE FATHER AND OF THE SON AND OF THE HOLY GHOST. AMEN.

"I CONDEMN indecent and immoral motion pictures, and those which glorify crime or criminals."

"I PROMISE to do all that I can to strengthen public opinion against the production of indecent and immoral films, and to unite with all who protest against them."

"I ACKNOWLEDGE my obligation to form a right conscience about pictures that are dangerous to my moral life. As a member of the Legion of Decency, I pledge myself to remain away from them. I promise, further, to stay away altogether from places of amusement which show them as a matter of policy."

8

[AAM]

Henriette Mackin (far right) with *Hi-Time* board
[Coutesy of Michael Vogl]

[Courtesy of Michael Vogl]

school students when she spent a brief time with the Catholic Pflaum Publishing company in Ohio. Pflaum had pioneered the use of small periodicals like the *Young Catholic Messenger* and *Treasure Chest* which replicated the format and appeal of the popular *Weekly Reader* handed out to grade school children. Mackin returned to Wisconsin determined to create a similar tool for high school catechesis. As her plans matured, she envisioned a journal that would incorporate religion, social studies and geography, and could be used by Catholic high schools in their religion or history classes, as well as by the rapidly growing CCD. She broached her plans to Auxiliary Bishop Roman Atkielski who not only endorsed her but gave her money to get off the ground. She likewise secured the support of Archbishop Meyer and Cardinal Stritch. In 1954, the pilot issue of *Hi Time* rolled off the presses and Mackin took the sample to Catholic high schools in Milwaukee and elsewhere. The interest of these schools got her fledgling operation off the ground (it had begun in the garage of her home in Big Bend, Wisconsin), and on March 6, 1955, she began operations with headquarters in a rented office space on 76th and State Streets in Wauwatosa.

Mackin herself did the layout of the first issues and using her extensive contacts in the publishing business employed artists and others to help design the text. The name, *Hi Time,* was conferred on the periodical by Catholic high school students. Her goal of creating a more attractively packaged catechetical text was enhanced by the snappy writing of Father John M. Murphy, a seminary English professor and clerical youth idol. She also recruited another clerical heartthrob of the day, the ruggedly handsome Father Richard Madden, a Carmelite from Holy Hill. Madden was one of the most popular "youth priests" of his time, and traveled the country giving talks, retreats and days of recollection for youth. Among other things, he authored a popular "Life of Christ" written for young people that first appeared in serialized form on the pages of *Hi Time* and later was put together in book form. Other archdiocesan priests penned articles for the magazine: Eldred Lesniewski, Roger Roensch, and Monsignor (later Bishop) Jerome Hastrich. Mackin found other talent for her growing journal and pieces from well-known theologians like Gerard Sloyan, Eugene Maly, and Andrew Greeley appeared from time-to-time.

Mackin's operation reached out to the archdiocesan CYO and to all parts of the youth market in the archdiocese. Pius XI high school requested 1,000 copies of *Hi Time* a week. Notre Dame High School did likewise. The Milwaukee-based periodical soon caught on in every state of the union and even sent copies to Canada and Australia. By the late 1960s and early 1970s over half a million copies were printed every week.[267] Mackin's staff grew as the demand for *Hi Time* increased. In 1965 she bought a new center at Bluemound and Elm Grove Roads, and kept in her employ 12 full-time editors, 12 in the circulation staff and had a large mail room facility. Mackin died in 1983 and the company continued until 1998.

Efforts to throw the protective blanket of Catholic subculture around archdiocesan youth were partially successful. Indeed, the proliferation of youngsters in Catholic high schools made it easier to counter "youth culture" messages that came from the popular media, especially television and magazines. Popular nuns and priests could convince young people to remain chaste until marriage and could reinforce it with devotions and warnings of eternal damnation. Vigilance at dances and other social events included warnings from priests and nuns "to leave room for the Holy Spirit" when young people danced a bit too closely, and rigid enforcement of clothing and hairstyle codes sent many a Catholic teen home to let down the hem on a hiked up skirt, to un-peg pants, to comb the hair properly or to remove lipstick and make-up. That Catholic youth

Reception of Elena Chavez as Salvatorian Sister [ASDS-W]

responded (or reacted) to these requests is beyond a doubt—since many did follow their religious mentors to seminaries and convents. The fact that they joked about these things later in life was to some degree evidence that they took them seriously.

In the last analysis, however, the media of popular culture, especially television, was much stronger at sending cultural messages than Catholic schools were. Rock music, condemned by elders for its volume and suggestive lyrics, came to be regularly played at Catholic school dances and proms (with the occasional priest or nun boogieing to the beat, to the delight of the teenagers); clothing styles allowed for more freedom and flexibility, especially for young women; and concerns about "going steady" soon faded as educators realized there was not much they could do about the desire of a young man and woman in a mobile society (teens began driving when they were 16) to get together away from the gaze of parents or educators.

The youth of the archdiocese of Milwaukee were, in most respects, typical teenagers of their time. Those who did attend Catholic high schools cherished the memories and maintained close ties with fellow graduates, many of whom had been with them since the first days of school. In a development that certainly pleased parents and educators, many Catholic young people met their future life partner in a Catholic high school. Some of them even attended college together.

Reception of Salvatorian novices [ASDS-W]

Catholic Higher Education

Several factors helped to reshape the face of higher education in the archdiocese of Milwaukee. The first was the Serviceman's Adjustment Act of 1944, also known as the G.I. Bill of Rights. The liberal educational and living benefits given to veterans produced an unprecedented stampede to higher education, creating a boom and almost incessant demands for more classes, classrooms, teachers and buildings.

Marquette University felt the brunt of this change right away. Once the university had thrown off the burdens of its bad debts in the 1930s, it embarked upon a program of expansion made possible by the generous benefactions of alumni and local industrialists. Marquette's campus was more sharply delineated on the city landscape by bigger and better classrooms, laboratories, a new library and a student union.[268] By 1958, the expansion of programs in undergraduate and graduate areas brought nearly 10,000 students to Marquette, making it one of the largest private institutions in the state and in full-time students and total enrollment the largest Catholic university in the United States exceeding Notre Dame, Boston College and St. Louis University.[269]

The sisters' colleges founded in the 1930s also underwent a period of tremendous growth and even greater professionalization. This caused shortages of nuns in the schoolrooms, exactly at the time that student numbers were growing. But among the sisters themselves there developed a firm determination to secure the kind of religious and professional training that was required not only by state requirements and accreditation agencies, but by their own sense of pride in the quality of their work as educators. Bringing this to expression was the Sister Formation Movement, spearheaded by St. Mary's Notre Dame president, Sister Madaleva Wolff, C.S.C. In a famous 1949 talk called *The Education of Sister Lucy*, the theologian-poet-president urged teaching sisterhoods to concentrate on preparing their sisters for lives of scholarship

Two views of Marquette University in the 1950s [MUA]

and ensuring proper training for religious.[270] Milwaukee sisterhoods complied with the exhortations of "Sister Lucy" and sent delegations to various sister formation conferences and in August 1958, hosted a regional session of the movement at Marquette University.[271] Virtually all of the new motherhouses constructed in subsequent years contained capacious novitiate facilities, designed for sisters to remain a full canonical year. In addition, these new convents included "juniorates" or places where young sisters in collegiate studies could live, study and recreate apart from the demands of the classroom. Each order's educational supervisor carefully monitored the progress of the sisters, attempting to coach them in the skills of teaching and providing in the schools of their respective communities demonstration schools—special parish schools staffed by the community's best (and most patient) master teachers who mentored the young nuns.

Other developments among the sisters were harbingers of changes yet to come. Great ferment among religious began in the 1950s as the Conference of the Major Superiors of Women Religious were organized at the behest of the pope. Likewise, Pope Pius XII insisted on some reforms in cloistered religious life, beginning with modifications in religious habits, which were often uncomfortable, unsanitary and cumbersome in the work of teaching.[272] A rash of minor modification of habits took place in the 1950s that seemed in those days to be quite shocking. Nonetheless, the ferment among religious women, the increase in their professional training, the acquisition of advanced degrees and the introduction of lay staff to parochial and high schools began gradual changes in convent life. Within a decade, most religious sisterhoods had a strong corps of sisters who held masters and even doctoral degrees in a variety of subjects. Although securing the undergraduate degree still took years of summer courses, many of the younger sisters were sent directly to colleges and universities to be professionally prepared before they stepped into the classroom.

One final influence on the shape of Catholic higher education came from within the ranks of Catholic educators themselves. In the midst of all the expansion some asked if Catholic colleges and universities were really able to mount serious academic programs. Could they provide the libraries, laboratories and sufficiently trained faculty to win accreditation and also to provide their students with a respectable education? Some questioned whether Catholic intellectual methods, shaped heavily by Thomistic theology, discouraged research, writing, and standards of scholarly life common among professors at secular universities. Many of these concerns were brought to expression by Catholic University of America historian, John Tracy Ellis, who addressed these issues in a famous talk, "American Catholics and the Intellectual Life," given to the Catholic Commission on Intellectual Affairs in 1955 and reprinted in the Jesuit journal *Thought*.[273] Although Ellis understood the historical reasons why the Catholic educational system lagged behind (immigrant roots, lack of funds, separation of church and state), he indicted Catholic intellectual methods as substandard and insisted that if Catholic institutions were to gain any semblance of respectability that scholars and teachers had to be free to compete effectively with their peers in the secular academy. This meant a renewed emphasis on scholarly research in all fields and the concomitant financial support to sustain genuine collegiate and university status. Ellis was scornful of the proliferation of Catholic colleges that operated on a shoestring—a barb that could have been directed at Milwaukee. Catholic educational administrators in the archdiocese responded as best they could to demands to upgrade and improve their collegiate offerings. But Ellis's troubling indictment of the neo-scholastic underpinnings of Catholic education (i.e., his suggestion that "truth" was not always self-evident and had to be revealed by a long process of inductive research) did not sit well with many Catholic critics. His suggestion that the deductive methodologies of Catholic theologians and others were somehow intellectually deficient struck Archbishop Albert Meyer as wrong.

Archbishop Albert G. Meyer [AAM]

In 1957, the National Catholic Educational Association held its annual meeting in Milwaukee and Meyer chose the opportunity to reply to Ellis's critique. Admitting that "examination of conscience is considered one of the most important exercises of religion," he noted: "Ordinarily, however, it is not conducted in such public fashion as to lower us in the esteem of others, or to give occasion to our enemies to undermine our mission or to distort the good results of our work." He went on to declare that "our Catholic schools, especially our institutions of higher learning, can be charged with indifference to intellectual excellence, an indifference which some writers call anti-intellectualism." Defending the methodology of Catholic scholars, he went on: "Her chief duty in the field of scholarship, it is true, is to preserve and to explain the Deposit of Faith." However, he observed: "she has ever fostered profane knowledge too, because growth in it is good for men and aids her to explain the Deposit of Faith better." Even more profoundly, Meyer raised the larger issue engendered by the debate over intellectual life in the Church: "To what extent can her [the Church's] children mingle en masse with the members of an alien and often hostile culture, and make themselves acceptable to it, without losing the vigor of their Catholicity, or even their Catholicity itself?" He concluded: "If the Church had to choose between living in a ghetto with the faith of her children preserved, and mingling with the secularists with the faith of her children lost, she would prefer to live with them in the ghetto. But that is not her mission, nor must she make that choice."[274] Ellis received much negative response from Church hierarchy and educators over his criticisms—some of them blunt and threatening. But he never alluded to Meyer's publicly delivered rebuke at the single largest gathering of Catholic teachers. The archbishop's feelings about Catholic intellectual life were no doubt taken seriously by the growing cohort of Catholic college and university teachers in Milwaukee, but in the long run, Ellis's insistence on upgrading and improving Catholic intellectual life struck a sympathetic chord with archdiocesan educators.

New College Buildings

With the great increase in students and the large numbers of young women seeking admission to convents, the location of sisters' colleges in motherhouses became untenable. In addition, accreditation agencies insisted that college programs provide libraries, labs, and proper classrooms for students. As a result, all of the sisters' communities built new college facilities.

In Racine, St. Albertus had begun taking in "seculars" in 1941 and launched a successful music program. In 1943, it was determined that sisters should remain at the college for two full years before going out into teaching. In 1946, a new face in the college administration, Sister Gerold Thome, took over as academic dean and began to transform the scope and breadth of the small college.[275]

Dominican College, Racine [AOP-Rac]

Thome dedicated herself to the task of making St. Albertus a respectable four-year liberal arts institution. She convinced her superiors to rename the institution "Dominican" (an easier title than the Latin "Saint Albertus") and plotted a four-year curriculum. Thome made sure that the college's program was approved by the Wisconsin Department of Education and won approval to grant the bachelor of science and bachelor of music degrees. In 1947, she added five members to the faculty and invited laymen to begin attending the college. Soon the number of men taking classes from the white-habited sisters soared to nearly 200.

The unexpected bulge in the number of men attending the college led to a revisiting of the original permission for men to attend (granted initially as a wartime concession). Eventually nervous canonists caused the sisters to eject the laymen, insisting that Roman rules precluded men from attending classes in a convent. However, in 1955 the men were eventually welcomed back and Dominican proudly advertised itself as a coeducational college. In 1948 Thome assembled a governance board that consisted of Kiley (who never attended meetings) and some of Racine's most prominent citizens. On this board were banker Ben Beakley of the First National Bank and Trust; George Wheary of Wheary Incorporated; real estate developer and insurance kingpin Milton LaPour; and Western Publishing Company owner, William Wadewitz who served as chairman. The growing number of students pushed the sisters to acquire property around the motherhouse and St. Catherine's High School for expansion. They also purchased local homes for student residences and took over the old Holy Name School building when a new structure was erected in the 1950s. But even though the sisters held title to 13 acres near the high school, they realized that more land and space would be needed for a new college building.

In 1955, at the same time men were readmitted to the college, real estate agent Milton LaPour informed Sister Gerold that a 25-acre site on the north side of Racine, on Lake Michigan, had come on the market. A hastily convened meeting of the board of trustees approved the purchase of a tract that had been on the market for $90,000, but whose sellers were willing to let go for $29,500. The sisters contacted a professional fund-raising firm and began to raise $1 million of the nearly S2.5 million needed. The firm of Barry and Kay from Chicago devised a master plan that would transform the lakefront property into a campus, able to accommodate 600 students. The Dominicans of Racine made a direct appeal to the Catholic parishes to contribute. Despite strong support from Meyer and a letter read to the congregations of the city in 1958, contributions were disappointingly slow.[276]

The chief fund-raising task rested on the shoulders of William Wadewitz. He helped raise funds to open the first part of the new college in 1960. Archbishop William Cousins came to dedicate the new buildings in the fall. Dormitories for women and men were constructed later. Sister Gerold Thome died shortly after the new college opened, and the new president Sister Rosita Uhen steadily built the quantity and quality of its faculty and library holdings. In early 1961 the Camillan Fathers, who had built a scholasticate nearby attached to an old mansion owned by Samuel Johnson (Windhover), decided to sell the property to the sisters, giving them an additional 87 acres and a lake frontage of 2,200 feet. On this property, the sisters later built a modernistic motherhouse replete with large wings for a novitiate and a juniorate.

Marian College, Fond du Lac [AAM]

At Marian College in Fond du Lac the admission of laywomen had been a given from the very start in 1937.[277] The first lay graduates had received diplomas in 1939. In 1941, the small college secured the accreditation of their course work with the University of Wisconsin and the recognition of their courses in the training of elementary and secondary school teachers. Later the Department of Public Instruction certified their work. Over the years the college helped provide for the rural areas that dominated Fond du Lac County by providing a convenient evening session, which allowed teachers to make progress toward state-required certification. This program lasted until 1958. Likewise, using its St. Agnes hospital as a training site, Marian College trained nurses and developed course work in medical technology.

Organizationally, however, the college took time to mature. Despite affiliations with the Catholic University of America and the National Catholic Education Association, until 1951 the college still kept the Mother General of the Agnesian Community as the president. Mother Albertonia Licher, elected in June 1951, ended that practice, and appointed sisters as president and dean. In addition tentative first steps were made toward securing accreditation from North Central. A preliminary report done by the former mother general laid the ground work for a serious self-study. Under the presidency of Sister Fidelis Karlin, C.S.A., the march toward accreditation began in 1955. Lengthy studies were hammered out in 1957 and 1958, but they were rejected by North Central for lack of sufficient evidence for evaluation and for the lack of a master plan. In 1959 the sisters invited representatives from North Central to help them draft an acceptable report and prepare for visitation. The report was accepted and the visitation made in the fall of 1959. The sisters waited on pins and needles, and their hopes sank as the decision, to have been made in March 1960, was deferred until July. In July, however, the coveted accreditation was secured and Marian was poised for its next stage of growth.

Building colleges in Racine and Fond du Lac was comparatively easy because the local sisterhoods dominated the "education market." In Milwaukee, however, the need to build often found sisters bumping into each other. It also called on the intervention of archdiocesan authorities to make sure that colleges, high schools and hospitals were not built in such close proximity as to set up unhealthy competition for the same pool of students or patients. The creation of Alverno College by the School Sisters of St. Francis on the south side of Milwaukee provides a case study of inter-community skirmishing.

Franciscan versus Franciscan: Competing South Side Colleges

In May 1944, financier Neil Gleason brought to the attention of the School Sisters of St. Francis the availability of a 50-acre tract called Fischer Farm, located between Oklahoma and South Morgan and between 39th and 43rd. Since 1933, the sisters had been looking for a site to build a hospital for Catholics on the south side. They soon learned, however, that the Felician Sisters had already made a bid to build a new Catholic hospital on the south side—in part a response to the efforts of the Lutheran Church to build a new St. Luke's Hospital at 27th and Oklahoma. Nonetheless, the School Sisters of St. Francis did not quite give up on the idea of a hospital, but purchased the land with Archbishop Kiley's permission, suggesting the possibility of a hospital and a new Catholic college on the site. They also thought of building a new hospital in West Allis. Throughout 1944 and 1945, the idea of a hospital and college percolated. Kiley wanted the sisters to build in West Allis, but he was open to a college-hospital arrangement and urged them to go along with their building plans. In July 1944 the *Catholic Herald Citizen* carried a story that the School Sisters planned to build a 250-bed hospital on that site.[278] However, the idea of building a school for the training of sisters of all congregations, was also held out as a possibility for the land. Kiley had warned against building "another Mount Mary," but he was supportive of the prospect of a sisters' college "like the one in

Washington D.C."[279] By the end of 1944, it was on record that there was the possibility of a college on the Fischer tract, although not as clearly as it would later seem in hindsight.[280]

What to do with the Fischer tract came into sharper focus after the war when the need to do something with the rapidly expanding Alverno Teacher's College became urgent. Alverno was changing. In 1946 the various schools sponsored by the School Sisters of St. Francis—the school of music, the teacher training school, and the nursing school associated with Sacred Heart Sanitarium—were combined with the college and simply renamed Alverno College. In 1947 laywomen were admitted. At the same time, the huge motherhouse was filling with postulants and novices. Space was at a premium.

Also in 1946 similar energies were being expended for St. Clare's College on the motherhouse grounds of the Franciscans of St. Francis. Symbolic of new energies, the sisters renamed their college "Cardinal Stritch," in honor of the elevation of Archbishop Samuel A. Stritch to the rank of cardinal in the first postwar consistory in February 1946. They too began taking in laywomen in 1946. As a part of the plan to reorganize the college, the Franciscans had purchased four square blocks between 35th and 39th on Oklahoma Avenue. They engaged the firm of Brielmaier and Sons (one of the sisters, artist Thomasita Fessler was the granddaughter of Erhard Brielmaier) to draw plans for a campus for 400 residential and commuter students and which would include classrooms, labs, studios, a reading clinic and a model elementary school.[281] The site was only a few blocks from the plot purchased by the School Sisters of St. Francis.

Fisher Farm [ASSF]

The news that the Franciscans of St. Francis planned to build on a site adjoining the still undeveloped Fischer Farm tract sent Mother Corona Wirfs and her educational director, Sister Jutta Hollenbeck, scurrying to the office of Archbishop Moses Kiley. Kiley, the School Sisters recounted "was taken aback" when he saw on a map how close the Franciscan Sisters property was to the Fischer Farm. Wirfs next produced architectural drawings of a hospital with the college

Mother Corona Wirfs, SSSF [ASSF]

in the background. "He promised to do what he could for us," the corporate minutes reported.[282] Kiley summoned the St. Francis Franciscans' Mother Bartholomew Frederick and urged her to work out an arrangement with the School Sisters on the issue of the property. Frederick respectfully defended her community's prior rights to college building in the area, noting to Kiley that she had bought the property on the assumption that the School Sisters intended to build a hospital, not a college.[283] Nonetheless, the two sisterhoods agreed to meet, and Mother Corona and an assistant visited Mother Bartholomew at the Franciscan motherhouse on the evening of June 24, 1946. A friendly exchange took place, as Mother Bartholomew expressed surprise at the proximity of the purchase and noted that "two colleges across the street from one another would not do." She did suggest that perhaps the School Sisters might look elsewhere. After all, Frederick observed, the School Sisters of Notre Dame had bought and sold three times before deciding on the site of Mount Mary.[284] Mother Corona left without promising anything.

Mother Bartholomew sought advice from her advisory board, composed of sisters and lay persons associated with the community. They urged her to plow forward, insisting that "we acted in good faith when we purchased the land, we should go ahead with our plans." She further insisted that even people who did know that the School Sisters' land was nearby assumed that it was for a hospital. Mother Bartholomew seemed to suggest as well that both Kiley and the chancery were aware of and approved their plans.[285] Upon hearing this news, Wirfs immediately appealed to Archbishop Kiley. The archbishop upbraided Mother Bartholomew for moving

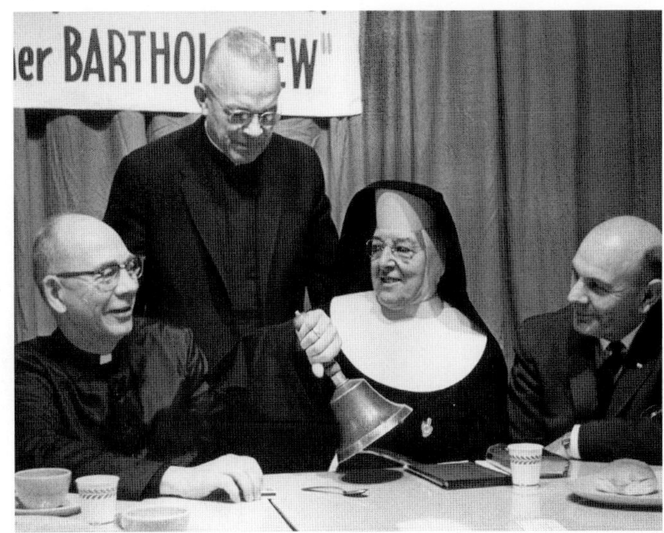

Mother Bartholomew Frederick, OSF [AAM]

Alverno College campus [ASSF]

ahead with the college and accused her of "contempt for the archbishop" and of not consulting him with their plans. He must not have read his own archdiocesan paper, for he suggested that the idea that the School Sisters intended the property for a hospital was "gossip," and refused to believe that the Franciscans of St. Francis had bought the property in good faith.[286] Mother Bartholomew accepted the criticism in good humor, but insisted, "To my knowledge, either I or the President of the College, Sister Mary Ignatia, consulted with Your Excellency at every step of this undertaking." But, she concluded, "We have no intention of going contrary to your wishes in this or in any other matter."[287]

By early 1947 the Franciscans gave up hope of building the new Cardinal Stritch on the land in southwestern Milwaukee. Instead, Kiley gave them permission to transfer St. Mary's Academy to the Oklahoma Avenue site and to expand their college on the motherhouse grounds. Bitterness ruled the day, as the School Sisters recounted that their "confidential sources" had revealed the Franciscans had abandoned the idea of building on the south side tract. "The gentleman who gave us this information remarked that the Sisters [Franciscans of St. Francis] are of the opinion that we 'turned our guns on them.'" They noted, "We did nothing but hold our own since we purchased the property between 39th and 43rd Streets long before they purchased theirs, and we had the permission of the Archbishop to build a college on this plot."[288] Having lost their property, the Franciscan Sisters eventually did build up St. Mary's Academy on their own grounds, and continued to operate the college there for a time. In 1949, the press announced that the sisters had relocated their plans for a new college on a 60-acre tract on Milwaukee's north shore, on the boundary of Glendale and Fox Point.[289] The new campus opened its doors in 1958.

In the meantime the School Sisters were free to advance their plans for a college. In 1947, they were informed by Edward Fitzpatrick that they could not rely on accreditation if they intended to run a school only for other sisters: the enrollments would be too low. He urged them to open it up to laywomen. In the late fall, 1947, they nervously approached Kiley and asked if they could have permission to admit laywomen and build on the Oklahoma site. Unexpectedly Kiley gave permission, something he had banned earlier in deference to Mount Mary. "It was a day of rejoicing for us because we feared we would not receive the desired permission to admit lay students, and with the small number of students now enrolled, it would be difficult to secure North Central accreditation," the sisters wrote.[290]

In 1950, with accreditation going forward on one front, the sisters engaged the St. Louis architectural firm of Maguolo and Quirk to design the campus. The best construction bid, $5.4 million, came from the James McHugh Construction company. In January 1951 construction began.[291] At almost the same time as the basement was being excavated, the North Central Association announced that Alverno had received accreditation.[292] The sisters were so delighted that Mother Corona assembled the entire motherhouse community in the chapel and recited the *Te Deum* and had the sisters sing "Holy God We Praise Thy Name."[293] Auxiliary Bishop Atkielski presided at the October 19, 1952, cornerstone laying.[294] On April 21, 1954, Cardinal Stritch traveled from Chicago to see what had become of the institution he had helped establish back in the desperate days of the 1930s.[295] Stritch lauded the college as one more Catholic effort to stanch the decay of western civilization. On the dais with him were Governor Walter Kohler, Mayor Frank Zeidler, and Father Frederick Arnold of West Allis, a generous benefactor of the sisters and the college. The new Alverno College was launched.

The Church and Politics

Catholic engagement with the great body of new laws regarding schools, social welfare and employees was led by exceptionally busy archdiocesan attorney Henry V. Kane. An important challenge arose in the 1930s when Father John Bach of St. Joseph's parish of Racine demanded disability payments to help compensate him for a serious eye injury suffered on the job.[296] Bach's request to be considered under the provisions of a state disability act provoked questions as to the "right" of a cleric to consider himself an employee of the parish or the archdiocese. Stritch was vehemently opposed (and pointed to it as an instance of how social welfare legislation could cramp the rights of the Church). Diocesan clergy were ultimately defined as "self-employed" and hence ineligible for employer-mandated considerations.

Similar concerns were expressed over the extent to which employees in parishes would have to be covered by mandated social insurance, such as social security, unemployment and disability. Periodic challenges emanated from the state legislature and elsewhere threatening Catholic tax exemptions, or promoting morally offensive programs like sterilization.[297] For many years, Milwaukee's chief legislative broker was Father James Oberle, pastor of St. Stephen's parish in New Coeln. Oberle had been felled by heart attacks and his own parish church burned twice during his pastorate. He retired in July 1939 and spent his remaining years in convalescence.

Rev. James J. Oberle [AAM]

The gregarious Stritch was willing to deal with legislators and politicians and his files were full of letters from high government officials such as Leo T. Crowley, head of the FDIC and FBI official (and former Dominican brother) Edward A. Tamm. Kiley, by contrast, steered clear of politicians and felt it his bounden duty to keep the Church out of any political quarrels. Nonetheless, issues came before the state legislature that impinged on Church concerns in education, health care and child protection. At Kane's urging, in 1941, Kiley retained Madison lawyer, William H. Spohn of the firm Spohn, Ross, Stevens and Lamb. Spohn worked closely with the Wisconsin bishops to help protect Catholic interests in the legislature and promote bills that had a positive effect on Catholic institutions. Working with Spohn was the secretary of the archdiocesan school board, Monsignor George Meyer. Meyer also apparently was Kiley's liaison with local government.[298] Neither Spohn nor Meyer kept a high public profile in their political work. In fact Spohn was so low-key that when William Patrick O'Connor took over as bishop of Madison in 1946, he was surprised to discover that the archdiocese had a lobbyist in place.

The largest single issue affecting Catholics before state government related to education. Litigation over the issue of public support for education loomed large in the 1940s and several cases reached the United States Supreme Court. Catholics in Wisconsin and elsewhere accepted the notion that some accommodation could take place between church and state despite the non-establishment clause of the constitution. This was opposed by a loose coalition of secular humanists, and Protestant and Jewish organizations who insisted on the "wall of separation" between church and state articulated by President Thomas Jefferson in his 1802 letter to the Danbury, Connecticut, Baptist Association. The question of aid to parochial schools was a hardy perennial.

One important issue was the bussing of private school students. Wisconsin Catholics had an oar in the water on the bussing issue since 1944, when Spohn and legislative allies such as state senators Bernhard Gettelman of Milwaukee and Edward Hiker of Racine, secured passage of a ballot initiative amending the Wisconsin constitution to allow state-funded bussing to be extended to children in parochial or private schools. In 1946, the proposal went before the people of Wisconsin in a statewide referendum.[299] Kiley laid aside his allergy to secular politics and campaigned vigorously for a "yes" vote on the proposal. The proposal seemed to generate a great deal of support and even won an endorsement from the *Milwaukee Journal* and a number of state papers.[300] At Spohn's direction, the Catholic press stressed the rights of Catholic children (hinting that a vote against the amendment was an act of discrimination against Catholics), and also took pains to educate Wisconsinites that all kinds of publicly-funded services were already available to parochial school children: police and fire protection, public health, etc.[301] Despite all these efforts, the initiative went down to defeat in the November elections. However, Wisconsin Catholics were slightly consoled less than a year later, when the Supreme Court in *Everson v. Board of Education* upheld a New Jersey statute which permitted municipalities to reimburse parents for costs in using regular bus lines to transport students to non-public schools. In its 5-4 decision, the court upheld the "individual benefit" theory which insisted that individuals were the beneficiaries of this kind of funding and not the religious schools they attended.[302]

Other court decisions linked to the relation between public and private schools came down from the high court. In 1948, the U.S. Supreme Court issued *McCollum v. Board of Education* in which it disallowed religious education in public schools. In 1952, however in *Zorach v. Clauson*, the court upheld "released time," religious education programs outside public school buildings.

Few other legislative goals would be met in the Kiley-Meyer years, but neither man had an appetite for partisan politics. Secular political activity was largely reactive and defensive. Both archbishops had all they could do to manage the intricacies of politics among their own clergy.

Clerical Life and Discipline

Writing to Joseph Emmenegger in 1956, Archbishop Meyer lamented, "Practically every new parish within a short time requires an assistant or two, and the old ones don't seem to want to give up any. Then the requirements of our high schools continue to increase. So I believe that I will continue to talk vocations just as much in Milwaukee as I used to in Superior."[303]

Viewed from the perspective of priest shortages in the 21st century, Meyer's statement of a vocation shortage seems unbelievable. Indeed, priestly ordination classes were very full. In 1955, Milwaukee gained 30 new priests, the highest number ever in archdiocesan history. The seminary "Centennial" class of 1956 was next with 29 ordinands.[304] The following chart indicates that the number of Milwaukee archdiocesan priests was on the rise in the postwar era.

Table 4-8 [Source: OCD]

Year	Total Diocesan	Total Religious	Grand Total (including externs, retired, misc.)
1950	585	344	971
1955	505	354	913
1960	587	423	1057

Yet, despite this steady growth, scores of letters from other bishops, teaching sisterhoods and others attest that there was a fear that the numbers of trained clerics and religious was insufficient to keep up with the increasing demand for schools and parishes. In 1953, there were 655 seminarians in the major and minor seminaries of the archdiocese of Milwaukee. Various religious orders of men had 739 seminarians under formation in the archdiocese. There were 34 communities of religious women in service to the archdiocese with a total of 4,516 sisters. By 1958 the number had grown to 693 seminarians, 504 being students for Milwaukee and the rest students for other dioceses who studied at St. Francis Seminary. There were 541 religious order seminarians and 4,551 sisters representing 45 communities. The numbers were indeed large, but the rate of growth did not match the dynamic needs of the parishes and schools. Indeed, Meyer and others were right to lament the number of vocations.

St. Francis Seminary had changed little since Meyer left the rector's chair seven years earlier. His successor, Monsignor Frank Schneider, had brought a different tone to the leadership of the venerable institution.[305] Schneider was born one of six children in Milwaukee in 1904. His father was a prosperous real-estate agent and young Frank received his early education at St. Anthony's

Archbishop Meyer ordaining [AAM]

School on Mitchell Street and at Marquette Academy. In his youth he was active in St. Anthony's flourishing Holy Name Society which he noted in later years had encouraged him to study for the priesthood. After two years at Marquette University, he entered the major seminary in 1924 and was ordained in 1930. He spent five years as an assistant at St. Michael's parish in the city, and Stritch then sent him to the Gregorian University in Rome to study for a doctorate in theology while living with the Maryknoll fathers. When he returned to the seminary faculty in 1938, he taught fundamental theology and a course on homiletics, but his speciality was moral theology. In addition to this, between 1943 and 1946 he administered a small mission parish of St. Cecilia in Thiensville in Ozaukee County and served as moderator of the Salzmann Correspondence Course, a mail-in catechetical program staffed by the seminarians. Although Schneider could be noisy and bumptious, Meyer tried to have him appointed vice rector in 1943, but Kiley insisted that the second role go to an Irish-surnamed priest to keep the ethnic balance of appointments. Father John J. Barry, the seminary's English teacher took the post and remained in it until he succeeded Peter Dietz at St. Monica Church in Whitefish Bay. In 1946, at Meyer's recommendation, Schneider succeeded Meyer as head of St. Francis Seminary.

Rev. Frank Schneider
[AAM]

The first thing seminarians noticed was that the new rector was far more talkative and in some respects more approachable than Meyer. Schneider was a more gregarious man, given to joking around and possessing a ready

Msgr. Frank Schneider
[AAM]

wit. Yet seminarians also found out that he could at times be unreasonably legalistic, strict and forbidding. Although many recollections of Schneider have been filtered through the anti-authority ethos of the 1960s and 1970s, it is fair to note that Schneider did not elicit healthy respect. After men were "safely" ordained, they mimicked his penchant for punctuating every sentence with a hurried "Naturally, of course, of course" and made fun of his officiousness. Schneider was never hated, but he was not loved. His passing from the seminary scene in 1965 was greeted with relief by many.

Schneider also changed the role of the seminary rector. The introverted Meyer viewed his work at St. Francis as primarily in-house, observing and instructing the seminarians and overseeing the administration of the buildings and grounds. Hence, apart from Sunday help-outs and the occasional trip to visit a classmate, Meyer left the building only when he had to, and he was always the first one in the seminary chapel in the morning. Schneider was content to leave the day-to-day work of dealing with students to Barry and the faculty, and appointed himself the chief public relations officer. In a way not seen since the days of Muench, he was constantly on the road at meetings of the Serra Club, Forty Hours, priest's funerals, national commissions, and conventions, forever plumping the Salesianum and encouraging donations. Early in his term, Schneider had attempted to emulate Meyer's pre-dawn presence in the seminary chapel, but his late-night activities and the weariness he felt while sodden with food and liquor made it difficult to continue this practice.

Under normal circumstances, as it had been with Muench, Haas, and Meyer (as well as rectors Heiss, Flasch and as had been attempted with Salzmann and Rainer), the rector's chair at St. Francis was a gateway to episcopal ordination. Schneider, with his Roman education, probably expected it to be the case with him after an appropriate interval of administrative experience. However, his penchant for spouting off turned out to be his downfall. Meyer had been willing to tolerate Kiley's incessant meddling in the inner life of the seminary and did not protest when the prelate made some new demand. Schneider talked back to Kiley, suggesting for example that the prelate's concern with seminary minutiae was not helpful to discipline or faculty morale. Likewise, Schneider outright refused the archbishop's request to advance some students to priestly orders before they finished their studies. Faculty members may have silently cheered this standing up to Kiley, but Kiley resented it, and it may have put an end to any hope that Schneider had of becoming a bishop. Schneider tangled even more violently with Auxiliary Bishop Roman Atkielski. After he left the seminary in 1965, Schneider did get the consolation prize of a protonotary apostolic and the right to wear a miter and ring and to have a coat of arms. He even erected a tiny baldacchino in the sanctuary of St. Robert Church in Shorewood where he became pastor. But as he lay dying in 1972, he accused Atkielski (who had died in 1969) of "blackballing" him.[306]

A separate minor seminary had been established shortly after Kiley's arrival.[307] Headed by Father (later Monsignor) William V. Groessel, the high school and junior college students were resettled on the campus of the old Pio Nono College in Salzmann Hall that Stritch had erected in 1932.[308] In 1954 for reasons of health, Groessel left the minor seminary post for a position on the faculty of the major seminary and was replaced by Messmer principal Louis E. Riedel. He was assisted by Fathers Leonard Busch and James Doheny who served as vice rector and spiritual director respectively. Groessel and Riedel assembled a crew of young priests to teach the high school and junior college courses, provide spiritual direction and support, and make sure that the boys enjoyed as many of the pleasures of adolescence as were possible for young men who had already made a commitment to the priesthood after graduating eighth grade. Enrollments skyrocketed as hundreds of young men applied for admission to the seminary.

Year	1945	1950	1955	1960
# of Students	384	463	404	375

Table 4-9 [Source: OCD]

St. Francis Minor Seminary departed from the custom of similar institutions of the day and allowed seminarians the option of boarding at the school or attending as day students. Many students chose the latter, hanging on to the comforts of family life until it came time to go to the "major." The combination of high school and college-aged students in the school created its own set of challenges and opportunities. Obviously the age differences and levels of maturity had to be measured by the hard-working faculty. On the positive side, the older men served as mentors and guides for the younger—realizing that the best reinforcement of a priestly vocation was the example of other men and friends who took that road.

Other aspects of life in the minor seminary, derived from the pages of *Via*, the seminary annual that began publishing in

Minor seminary procession, All Souls Day [AAM]

clergy. Row after row of these seminarians, attired in natty bow ties and formal wear for their graduation pictures were a snapshot of the future of Milwaukee clergy.

The swelling growth of seminarians at the minor and major seminaries challenged the facilities of the major to their limit. (The minor escaped the terrible crowding because of its day scholar option.) The major seminary building had been equipped to hold 190, but enrollment crept past 200 by 1952. In 1953, when projected enrollments seemed even higher, the faculty voted to place a limit of 280 students. No more could be jammed into the tiny rooms designed for two that now slept four, nor could the creaky wooden floor of the chapel and the limited tables and chairs in the dining room and recreation areas hold any more.

Kiley had begun to plan for additions to St. Francis and in 1949 built a new power plant. However, he got lost in raising money for St. Aemillian's Orphanage, and the seminary was put on the back burner. Meyer reignited the expansion plans, of which the power plant was the first phase.[309] He contracted the architectural firm of Brust and Brust to draw up blueprints for a dining hall, an expanded auditorium and music facility,

1955, note the absence of such high school rituals as dances, homecoming, pop culture and the like. But many of the pictures suggest that athletics played an important role in the overall formation of the young men in preparation for the priesthood. In 1954, faculty athletic director Father Gerald Hauser cajoled his brother Art, a middle linebacker for the Los Angeles *Rams*, to play a pre-game warm up on the grounds of the minor seminary with the local favorites, the Green Bay *Packers*. Seminary students were thrilled to see many of their favorite players close-up and waited in line to collect the autographs of the famous Elroy "Crazylegs" Hirsch and "Tank" Younger.

Seminary friendships begun in high school perpetuated themselves in lifelong nicknames that followed the men into their years in the

Msgr. John Schulien with Theologians
[AAM]

and a much needed residence hall with a chapel. Meyer broke ground for the $3 million additions on the seminary's patronal feast, January 29, 1955, and they were ready for the solemn dedication ceremonies on September 11, 1956, when Stritch was welcomed back to the campus together with Bishops O'Connor and Muench. The residence hall, the largest of the buildings, was christened Heiss Hall. An old gymnasium was transformed into a stage and musical hall named for Joseph Rainer. Opinions varied about the new buildings, which were so stunningly different in style and quality from the elegant main building or even the library and gymnasium. One clerical wag quipped of the residence hall, which sported tiled wall: "One hundred years ago men of culture and learning came to this

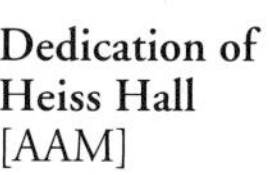

Dedication of Heiss Hall
[AAM]

spot and built a beautiful seminary. Frank Schneider has built us a four-story basement."[310]

The New Catholic Thought: Cardijn Center

Clerical training was locked in the grip of the neo-Scholastic theological manuals that had become standard at St. Francis Seminary in the 1920s. Yet, even in the intellectual straitjacket of the manual theology, creative energies bubbled under the surface. As priests learned to apply the tenets of Thomism to social issues, they were able to weave the "perennial teaching" of the Church into new patterns. Although theology was pretty much a clerical preserve, the application of theological concepts to "real-life" issues began to engage religious sisters and the laity.

One of the key "breakthroughs" of the theological world at the time was the theology of the mystical body of Christ. This approach to understanding the nature of the Church and the character of its identification of Christ in the world drew heavily from Pauline texts stressing the essential unity of the Christian community with Christ as its head. The images used stressed an organic connection between Christ and the Church and a similar interlocking character of the relationship of the members of the Church with one another. The key principles of this highly evocative ecclesiology had been discussed by theologians for many years, but they were most carefully elaborated in Pope Pius XII's encyclical *Mystici Corporis Christi* in 1942. This document gave great inspiration to a whole host of Catholic activists who worked to make real the unity and interconnectedness suggested by the theological framework.

For most reformers, the mystical body of Christ was most powerfully experienced at the weekly celebration of the Mass. Likewise the unity experienced at Mass was to be shared with the "outside" world. Catholic liturgical worship was by its nature social, not individualistic. Society was intended by God to share this same vision. Human beings were part of a family, organically interconnected with one another, and responsible for each other's well-being.[311] For example, these were the ideas that inspired the work of interracial activists like Monsignor Franklyn Kennedy and Jesuit Father Claude Heithaus, who insisted on racial justice as a corollary of belief in the essential unity of human kind. A new generation of Catholic thinkers, writers and activists began to translate the teaching of the mystical body into action. They formed a series of specialized movements that drew on the old Catholic Action theme but required an even more intense commitment to personal and societal transformation through study, reflection and action.

In Milwaukee the Specialized Catholic Action movements in the late 1940s and 1950s became an important conduit for this new awareness of the Christian role in the reconstruction of society. As we have seen, the term "Catholic Action" had been used by popes as a shorthand for a broad movement of energizing the laity to participate in the work of remaking the world according to

Christian principles, and had been adapted by the bishops of the United States. Archbishop Stritch used his office as bishop to coordinate the activities of lay Catholic groups like the Holy Name Societies, the Knights of Columbus and other Catholic organizations.

Unlike the hierarchically directed devotional or fraternal organizations, Specialized Catholic Action worked through age and occupational groups and formed small, highly committed "cells," or groups of priests, sisters and laity who were challenged to change their environment. These movements and their particular methodology were spawned in Europe at about the same time that the larger Catholic Action thrust was being defined and disseminated. Chief among its pioneers was a Belgian priest, Canon Joseph Cardijn who sought to reclaim disaffected European Catholics by forming tightly knit and well-instructed groups of lay apostles who would be like the scriptural "leaven in the dough." [312]

Two groups—the Young Christian Workers and the Young Christian Students—took root in Europe and America. Their methodology, based on a direct application of St. Thomas Aquinas's writings on the virtue of prudence, directed the young apostles to "observe, judge, and act" in order to give witness to their Christian faith. Believing as they did in the organic interconnection of all people in Christ, no act was too small or insignificant to change the world. Priests who had studied in Europe introduced these movements to American Catholics in the late 1930s. Chicago would be an important center for these movements inspired by Monsignor Reynold Hillenbrand, the rector of the St. Mary of the Lake Seminary from 1937-1944.[313]

Milwaukee's own apostle of Specialized Catholic Action was Father John Russell Beix. Beix was a native of Burlington, Wisconsin,

Rev. John R. Beix
[AAM]

who had studied at St. Francis Seminary and was ordained in 1935. His first assignment was to St. John's Cathedral as an assistant to Monsignor Francis Murphy. He had first heard of the activities of Canon Cardijn and others when a well-known afficionado of the movements, Australian layman Paul McGuire, lectured in Milwaukee in the 1930s. In 1939, while attending a labor school held at the

Mundelein seminary, he met Father Louis Putz, C.S.C., one of the handful of priests who had learned of the specialized movements abroad and introduced them to American audiences. Deeply impressed by Putz, Beix came back to Milwaukee and began the first "cell" of Young Christian Students at Cathedral High School.

Beix, a hardworking and energetic man, had a deep interest in social issues and was one of the first Milwaukee priests to take an interest in organized labor. He introduced the Association of Catholic Trade Unionists, a national organization headquartered in Detroit, to the archdiocese in 1940. In 1941, he was transferred to Sacred Heart parish in St. Francis and the next year moved across the street to the minor seminary, where he taught and coached. There too, and at nearby St. Mary's Academy, he organized "cells." Sympathetic priests such as Father Vernon Kuehn, principal of Messmer High School, and Father Eugene Bleidorn, also of the seminary staff together with Fathers Francis Eschweiler and John Michael Murphy recruited a small group of adherents who were eager to "bring Christ to the market place" by their "observe, judge, act" methodology. Beix also won the support of *Catholic Herald Citizen* editor, Franklyn Kennedy, who covered these movements with great sympathy.[314] The Young Christian Students of these institutions evoked a range of reactions—from curiosity and interest to outright hostility—from their fellows.

Canon Joseph Cardijn (center) with Milwaukee priests [AAM]

Beix and his growing cadre of followers began to form "cells" of Young Christian Workers, which met on Saturdays and also in the evenings to learn Catholic social teaching, read papal encyclicals and to study the liturgy. The number of adherents grew so quickly that in late 1948, Beix asked Archbishop Kiley for permission to establish a central location where these groups could meet, and also for permission to be their chaplain. Kiley agreed, and Beix and his group found space in the upper story of a deserted flophouse at 787 North Water Street. Repairs to the building were soon completed, and in February 1949 the "Cardijn Center" opened its doors. More than 250 people squeezed in to hear talks by the staff of *Integrity,* a periodical devoted to the movements, Bernard Bauer of the South Bend Christian Family Movement, and Eugene Lawler and Jerry Quinn of the Milwaukee Catholic Family Movement.[315]

The Cardijn Center served as a meeting place for the "cells" of Young Christian Workers and Young Christian Students. These two movements had some impact on the young and found a raft of dedicated younger clergy quite willing to be chaplains. A series of interesting programs were hosted by the Cardijn Center staff, which drew "volunteer faculty" from all over the city. From the outset the center sponsored days of recollection and summer study weeks. By 1953, the center was running a full array of programs: days of recollection, a lecture bureau, a library and cooperative bookstore, a bookmobile to carry good Catholic literature far and wide, a tape-playing station where listeners could hear recorded talks from visiting lecturers or radio addresses of Fulton Sheen and a school of social studies that focused on the message of the social encyclicals, foreign policy, organized labor and the social implications of the Eucharist.[316]

The center stimulated an interest in liturgy that had been percolating throughout the archdiocese since the 1930s.

[AAM]

Milwaukee and the Liturgical Movement

Liturgical reform had been brewing in the Catholic Church since the middle of the 19th century. Spearheaded by the Benedictine monks of Solesmes and a renewed appreciation for the Church's liturgical life, European Benedictines had delved deeply into the history of public prayer and found in the treasury of ancient documents a rich tradition of practices and customs that had fallen by the wayside or had been supplanted by the 16th century revision of the liturgy by the Council of Trent and Pope Pius V. Monastic communities studied the nature of early Church celebration of the sacraments (especially the Mass and the sacraments of initiation—baptism, confirmation and Eucharist) and found a marvelous variety of expressions and rituals that brought the deeper meaning of these events to life. They also studied the origins of church architecture, pondering such things as the placement of the altar, the arrangement of the faithful in relationship to the sanctuary and the ways in which the celebration of Mass changed over time. Liturgical scholars and reformers of the 19th century did not consider themselves "innovators" but recoverers of an ancient liturgical "treasure in the field." The riches of the liturgical past, especially active participation in the Mass, needed to be given back to the faithful in order to quicken Christian life and spirit and to combat the acids of modernity.

Eventually these changes moved from the monasteries to the church communities of the Catholic world. In 1946, they received a general (although circumscribed) approval by Pope Pius XII in his encyclical *Mediator Dei*. Pius XII would in later years take the first steps toward a general re-evaluation and renewal of liturgical life by revising laws on the Eucharistic fast and restoring the Easter Vigil to its proper time in the evening. (It had been celebrated throughout the western Catholic world on Holy Saturday morning). Later, Vatican II embraced many of the liturgical movement's key ideas and principles in its Constitution on the Sacred Liturgy.

The modern liturgical movement in America began with the efforts of Benedictine Virgil Michel of St. John's Abbey in Collegeville, Minnesota.[317] Michel had studied the movement as it developed in several Benedictine abbeys in Europe and was particularly taken with the insights of Dom Lambert Beauduin, O.S.B., whose lectures he attended at Mont Cesar Abbey in Belgium, and who insisted that liturgical reform would bring about a more just social order. In 1926, after he had returned to Collegeville, Michel and two associates, Father Martin Hellreigel, a priest of the Archdiocese of St. Louis, and Jesuit Father Gerard Ellard, founded the American Liturgical Movement and its chief organ, *Orate Fratres*. This journal served as an important medium of communication with interested Catholics (clerical, religious, and lay) throughout the United States. Its articles included introductions to the rich liturgical past of the Church.

The trio of Michel, Hellreigel and Ellard stressed all of the key ideas of the European movement. But they added a special emphasis on the liturgy as a source of social justice. They insisted that the "corporate" worship of the Mass was the wellspring and model of a restored social order. Again and again, in their writings they railed against excessive individualism at Mass and in public life. Human solidarity was God's plan for the world and the liturgy continually held that up as the terminus of all human endeavor.

One important "innovation" that sought to re-invigorate popular participation in the liturgy was the introduction of the hand missal, a small Bible-sized book that contained English translations of the Ordinary and Proper of the Mass. Those who purchased these books were encouraged to "pray" the Mass along with the priest-celebrant (if they could figure out where he was in the silence of the ritual). The English translation of the rites offered Catholics an opportunity to see just what was being prayed in their name. Although epistles and gospels were often proclaimed in the vernacular after the priest had read them in Latin, the other proper parts of the Mass (Introit, Gradual/ Tract, Alleluia versicle, Offertory and Communion verses) were also translated. As the missal explained, at one time these had been sung by the faithful.

It is hard to know when hand missals were first introduced to Milwaukee Catholics, but there is evidence that by the 1920s some parish priests were urging their use. Convents also provided entering sisters with these books and urged them to follow the Mass in this manner. Whatever was communicated to the sisters often found its way to the Catholic classrooms, and school children were also introduced to the use of the missal. Soon it became a first communion practice to give a missal to a young communicant instead of a book of popular prayers. Another "innovation" urged by liturgical reformers was the *missa recitata* or recited Mass. In this format, the faithful were trained to recite the Latin prayers of the Mass in response to the audible prayers of the priest-celebrant. Also known as the "dialogue Mass," this caught on more slowly throughout the archdiocese.

The reception to these innovations by priests was mixed. Among the most effective instruction at St. Francis Seminary had been courses in liturgical rubrics. Young Levites were compelled to undertake very thorough studies of church rituals. Such books as former St. Francis rector Innocent Wapelhorst's 19th century study of the liturgy were standard fare for seminarians until well into the 20th century.[318] Seminarians were urged by a series of spiritual directors who doubled as "liturgy" teachers to follow the rubrics of liturgical observance without deviation.[319] Years and years of watching the practice of seminary professors who approached the "proper" celebration of sacred ceremonies with an emphasis on exactness that bordered on the scrupulous, reinforced solemn warnings never to "tamper" or "innovate" with the Mass and its rituals.

But other priests showed a receptiveness to the literature coming out of Collegeville. As the pages of *Orate Fratres* revealed, a wide network of priests, religious and laity sought to disseminate the core ideas of the liturgical movement. A particularly strong center of liturgical innovation was in Chicago. There, St. Mary of the Lake Seminary's rector, Monsignor Reynold Hillenbrand, introduced principles and practices of the movement to seminarians. Chicago's active lay movements also caught the liturgical spirit, and Chicago priests

Novices, School Sisters of Notre Dame [ASND]

worked closely with groups that celebrated the *missa recitata*, discussed the import of the scriptural readings at the Mass and sought to translate the corporative energy of worship into social action.

One of the closest readers of Virgil Michel's work in Milwaukee was Father Joseph Holleran. Born in Milwaukee in 1903, James Joseph Holleran (he later inverted the order of his first two names) was baptized at the cathedral and began his grade-school

Rev. Joseph J. Holleran [AAM]

education with the Sinsinawa Dominicans. When he was 10, his parents moved the family northwest to 21st Street where they joined St. Leo's parish and where his intellectual gifts were cultivated by the School Sisters of Notre Dame. Holleran began seminary studies at the Salvatorian minor seminary in St. Nazianz, and then moved on to St. Francis Seminary where he was ordained by Bishop Joseph Gabriel Pinten in the seminary chapel in February 1930.

Holleran had developed an interest in liturgical reform during his years at the seminary, and in his first assignment at St. Sebastian's parish in Milwaukee he received mention in the chronicle section of *Orate Fratres* when he introduced the use of the hand missal in 1935. Two years later, while stationed at St. Patrick's Church in Janesville, Holleran invited Michel to come for a two week liturgical retreat. Michel, who would die shortly after the trip to Janesville, remarked favorably on the breadth of Holleran's interest and knowledge of the liturgical sources. In 1939, Holleran was chosen by Stritch to go to the Catholic University of America for studies in theology. He finished his course work in 1941 and returned to Milwaukee where he taught sociology at the seminary. Although Holleran was most prominent in advancing the agenda of liturgical reform in the archdiocese of Milwaukee, other priests also read the same Collegeville materials and had long years of experience in bringing about popular participation in liturgical life.

One of the ways of disseminating information about liturgical issues was through day long seminars on the subject that featured both outside and local speakers. In March 1941, Milwaukee's first "liturgical day" was held at the convent of the School Sisters of St. Francis with an attendance of 380 people.[320]

After that gathering, four citywide meetings used the momentum gained at the liturgical day to promote other projects.[321] The next year's gathering was held at St. Mary's Academy and doubled the number of participants. Using the theme "Liturgical Life in Church and Home," it included among its featured speakers Monsignor Martin Hellreigel of St. Louis, as mentioned one of the founders of the liturgical movement in America.[322]

One of the most enthusiastic promoters of the liturgical movement was Father Henry Velte, pastor of St. Boniface Church in Milwaukee. Like many liturgical enthusiasts, Velte's interests had been prompted by the holding of a novena that encouraged widespread participation. In his case, it was the Sorrowful Mother Novena. Velte's services drew hundreds to the large church and in 1936 radio station WTMJ broadcast his Mass and the concerts of his boys choir each week.[323] In one notable by-product of the enthusiasm generated by the liturgical days, Velte held a solemn public baptism of five converts—Henrietta Collins, Margaret Koepel, Roy Roeglin, Elmer Mierow and Raymond Helbert—on the evening of June 20, 1941, rather than baptizing them privately in the small baptismal chapel. The event filled the cavernous St. Boniface Church with liturgical enthusiasts, curious onlookers and parishioners excited about Velte's own enthusiasm for a restored liturgy. Velte explained the meaning of each rite and translated the prayers into English as Father Joseph Stagl performed the rites. Joseph Holleran preached about the history of the ceremonies. The versicles and songs normally read in Latin by the priest were chanted by Stagl and the huge St. Boniface choir.[324] Years later, what Velte had done in a spectacular manner in June 1941

Rev. Henry Velte [AAM]

would be standard operating procedure among Milwaukee parishes at the Easter Vigil.

Liturgical reform advanced cautiously in the archdiocese of Milwaukee (neither Stritch nor Kiley understood or appreciated it too much). Nonetheless, sustained interest in various aspects of the movement continued to be discussed among the priests. Father John A. Schulien, the main instructor of dogma at St. Francis Seminary, had written his doctoral dissertation at the Gregorian University in Rome on the mystical body, under the direction of Father Sebastian Tromp, S. J., who later was the "ghost" author of Pope Pius XII's 1943 encyclical on the subject, *Mystici Corporis Christi*. One of Milwaukee's most brilliant priestly sons, Racine native Father John Lawrence Murphy, while serving as a curate at busy St. Thomas Aquinas parish, also published a book, *The Living Christ* (1952), on the meaning of the theology of the mystical body. Coming out under the Bruce Publishing imprint, it received wide circulation and high praise in U.S. Catholic circles.[325]

Liturgical ideas were also popular with sisterhoods, seminarians and other Catholic Action groups. College campuses with their active Sodality groups also became enamored with liturgical practices such as the "dialogue Mass." In 1950 Kiley gave permission for the dialogue Mass at the request of the Sodality at Marquette University. He later withdrew the permission, however, and his displeasure with the Mass was so firm that no one dared to ask him for renewed permission. When Meyer came, a group of sororities, fraternities and other organizations at the campus received permission and the dialogue Mass was begun in February 1954 at 10 A.M. in the basement church of Gesu. It was placed under the supervision of Father George Ganss, S. J., who had trained 40 student leaders in the responses and placed them strategically around the basement church. As the Mass went on, the students responded and Ganss gave a running commentary of the Mass.[326]

[AAM]

On the national front, Joseph Holleran continued to be the most visible Milwaukee presence in the liturgical movement. In 1940 the first annual liturgical week was held in Holy Name Cathedral in Chicago. The next year, when the second of the national liturgical weeks was held in St. Paul, Holleran was invited to give the closing address. Urging conference participants not to rush into liturgical reform, he suggested a slower, more gradual process of building. "People's minds have been cast into a mold of personal individual devotion. To break not only the habits of thinking, but the religious practices of a life-time is not an easy thing. People must be trained away from intense individualism in religion to the social viewpoint, not by sudden changes, but by a slow, painstaking reinterpretation of the dogmas of the church."[327] Holleran spoke eloquently in his address about the various parish societies and organizations that could be connected more and more to the liturgical heart of the parish.

In 1955, after a period of teaching and administration of archdiocesan programs, he was appointed to the pastorate of St. Jude Church in Wauwatosa. He immediately set to work to educate the parish in the principles of liturgical life and reform, insisting, as did most reformers of his day, that rites be carried out with dignity. Characterizing beauty as "the fifth mark of the church," Holleran sought to bring home the richness of the liturgical tradition by attention to the quality of liturgical vessels, vestments and religious art.

Holleran had a rare opportunity to translate some of his liturgical vision into brick and mortar when he undertook the construction of a parish church for St. Jude's in 1957. The architectural firm of Grellinger and Rose listened carefully to Holleran as he insisted that the church be modest but beautiful. "The high altar will dominate the whole church," Holleran related to the *Catholic Herald Citizen* as the structure was rising. "It will emphasize that the church is built for the altar and the altar is the focal point of all spiritual life. The baptismal font to the right as people enter the church from the vestibule will be passed by everyone entering for Mass. Thus the baptismal font will bring attention to bear on Baptism which is the sacrament of bringing divine life to human souls and the altar on which the Holy Eucharist, which perpetuates both Christ's sacrifice and His presence in our midst."[328]

The resulting $600,000 church featured a large black marble altar, set on three triangular marble bases. The traditional side altars were much smaller than the main altar of sacrifice so as not to distract from the main altar, and even the traditional statuary of the side shrines was constructed to point back toward the altar. Holleran directed that the baptismal font be made of the same black marble as the altars, connecting baptism and Eucharist. Over the altar stood a huge 17-foot high crucifix made of black

Interior St. Jude Church, Wauwatosa [AAM]

wood on which hung an 8-foot corpus. Holleran wove his own focus on corporate worship into the elegant stained glass, the handsome reredos behind the altar and other devotional areas. All of these functioned as subsidiary agents to help worshipers enter into the saving mystery of the cross that was made present in the Eucharistic sacrifice.[329]

In the same year as the new St. Jude's went up, another pastor, Father Oscar Winninghoff tried his hand at what he termed "a conservative contemporary" design of church architecture when he built a new St. Aloysius Church in the industrial suburb of West Allis. Winninghoff insisted on a free standing altar that faced the people (*versus populi*) similar to the one used in the great Roman basilicas.[330] Although the final execution of the ambitious West Allis design did not come off as well as Winninghoff hoped (his blending of "conservative" with "contemporary" mixed two clashing liturgical visions and theologies), these two churches remain as architectural monuments of the first stirrings of liturgical reform among Milwaukee Catholics.

[AAM]

In 1954, Holleran helped play host to more than 1,300 visitors when Milwaukee put on the liturgical week in hot August. Participants represented a range of those involved in the liturgical movement around the country. Days of talks were held at Holy Angels Academy, the Marquette University Library and the newly built Brooks Memorial Union. Sessions for laypersons, priests, religious women, and seminarians packed the four days. Dialogue Masses were celebrated nearly every day with a special 8 P.M. Mass held at Gesu on the final day of the national convention. Milwaukeeans participated when Archbishop Meyer celebrated a Mass in the newly built county stadium on Sunday afternoon.[331]

Other liturgical reforms took root throughout the archdiocese. Prior to the summer 1954 liturgical week, Pope Pius XII had permitted the restoration of the Easter Vigil to Holy Saturday evening and allowed local bishops to implement the practice at their discretion. During the Easter Triduum of 1954, 60 archdiocesan parishes and institutions held these late evening/early morning ceremonies.[332] The next year permission was extended and even more parishes joined in the practice.[333]

Reactions to the new ritual were generally positive. A Sinsinawa Dominican at St. James parish in Kenosha reported enthusiastically on the level of participation in April 1953: "The true Easter Vigil was kept in our parish for the first time in the history of our parish .... It is interesting to note that all present in the church took an active part in the chanting of liturgical prayers."[334] Similar enthusiasm was expressed by the sisters at Sheboygan's St. Clement school who trained their eighth grade choir to provide music for the Holy Saturday services. At St. Gall's parish the new rites were not introduced until 1956. A Dominican sister noted the experience with some restraint: "The restored Holy Week services were different but beautiful. It seemed strange to receive our Divine Lord so late in the afternoon and evening."[335]

The comments of the St. Gall's Dominican sister provide an important perspective on the progress of liturgical renewal in the archdiocese of Milwaukee. Although the evening celebration of the Easter Vigil soon became mandated practice throughout the archdiocese, many pastors did not embrace the change with much enthusiasm and performed the rites in the same manner and spirit that they had performed the early morning Holy Saturday rites. For other communities, devotional practices specific to ethnic communities or introduced in the mid-20th century continued to be a focus of common prayer life. Some Catholics did not like the dialogue Mass when they found it in their parish or on the Catholic campuses. At Marquette University, for example, some students found it too confusing or more commonly "distracting" (a common complaint of those who resisted the transition from Latin to English and the mandate for popular participation of Vatican II). For others, the occasional explanations of the details of the Mass reminded them of the wordiness of grade school teachers.

If occasional stories in the *Catholic Herald Citizen* were any indication, people still were intrigued by stories of "exotic" liturgical practices, including some reported by military chaplains on the front of World War II or the Korean War. But those stories could be explained as wartime exigencies.[336] Practices that anticipated genuine liturgical reforms were often written in the fashion (not the style) of "Ripley's Believe It Or Not!" These included stories about priests who used liturgical vessels made of glass or stone or having a different artistic design than the traditional bell-shaped cup, said Mass with leavened bread, gave communion under both kinds, had lay persons read the day's epistle in English or who wore the flowing gothic style vestments rather than the more familiar Roman (or "fiddleback" vestments).[337] The Tridentine liturgy in use in Milwaukee (with ethnic variations) was still the standard by which all else would be judged.

These attitudes were in evidence in Catholic parishes of different rites. Such was the way that Melchite (Syrian) Catholics celebrated at St. George's Church. So also was the case of St. Michael's Ukrainian Catholic Church, founded in 1950 on Milwaukee's south side for a colony of displaced immigrants from the Ukraine, Germany, Austria and England who were permitted to come to America under the Refugee Relief Act. Meeting first in a classroom of St. Rose Hall, the cleric from Chicago, Myroslav Ivan Lubachivsky (later to become a cardinal), provided the first services. He was succeeded by Father Wolodymyr Wozniak. In 1952 the community received its first resident pastor, Father

St. Michael Ukranian Catholic Church, Milwaukee [AAM]

Ivan Oleksiuk. In 1952, Oleksiuk purchased a former Polish National Church on 11th and Washington and began holding services singing the Byzantine Rite in old Slavonic. Additional purchases added a rectory and a hall. Ongoing interior decorations in the church adorned the building with exquisite icons. The presence of the Eastern-rite Mass intrigued some Milwaukee Catholics, who attended the lengthy services and received communion under both species.[338]

Milwaukee and the Response to the Family

The emphasis on the "social" dimensions of the Roman Catholic Mass intersected with concerns about the basic unit of society: the family. After World War II, a lot of young Catholic men and women were getting married. Their need for solid instruction in the theology of Catholic marriage became a pressing pastoral necessity. In addition, wider societal concerns prompted renewed efforts to shape family issues.

Among the issues that truly alarmed Catholics was the growing acceptance of divorce, made possible by a major renovation of state laws. Divorce obviously tore at the fabric of the family, and Catholic proscriptions against the practice deterred it for many years. Divorced and remarried Catholics were barred from the sacraments, although some did raise their children as Catholics and often went to church, obediently abstaining from the Eucharist as their children went forward. In 1956 Archbishop Albert G. Meyer's pastoral *Decency and Modesty* included a lengthy section outlining the dangers of "company keeping" (which he identified in most cases was a cause of sin) with the divorced. Citing the impossibility of a future valid marriage for divorced persons, "company keeping is illicit and sinful" and "a penitent who persists in such kind of company-keeping is not properly disposed to receive absolution."[339]

Divorced and remarried Catholics, regardless of the causes for the divorce, were often shunned. This created heartbreaking scenes such as the case of William Janssen, who was given a divorce from his wife in May 1940, and was also awarded custody of his child, a student at Pius XI High School. Janssen also had a daughter in the Franciscan convent. He worked as a funeral director for a mortuary that did extensive business with Holy Ghost parish in Milwaukee, but Janssen's divorced status made him so unwelcome in the church that the pastor Father Leo Gabriels refused to admit him into the building, even when he was sent there on funeral business. Gabriels seemed to be the only one who had a problem, as Janssen was readily admitted to St. Lawrence, St. Patrick's and St. Anthony's. The secretary of the Milwaukee County funeral directors association called Gabriels's cruelty to the attention of Archbishop Kiley. "We absolutely believe that this so-called persecution is beyond all reason and fairness," he wrote. Invoking the wartime four freedoms, he appealed for justice for Janssen, "We are stressing tolerance, and trying to abstain from religious or racial hatred. That is one of the fundamentals our boys are fighting for in the present conflict."[340] There is no record of Kiley's reply.

Likewise artificial birth control, formally and publicly condemned by Pope Pius XI in his 1937 encyclical *Castii Conubii,* was also deemed an offense against the natural law and the family. Seminary moral theologians, such as Father Frank Schneider, sternly warned future priests against permitting these "unnatural acts" in marriage, and confessors were urged in some cases to probe whether a family used birth control. The sharp drop in the Catholic birth rate during the 1930s in the Milwaukee Archdiocese suggests that some did use birth control. Nonetheless, Catholics waged war collectively on any efforts to liberalize access to contraceptives.[341]

Editorial cartoon in ***Catholic Herald-Citizen*** [*Catholic Herald-Citizen*]

None So Blind

For years Catholics were the chief nemesis of Planned Parenthood, effectively denying them any share in Community Chest funds. Catholic opposition to artificial birth control was still strong in the 1950s. In response to a prediction by Everett W. MacNair, pastor of Plymouth Congregational Church and a strong supporter of the Milwaukee chapter of Planned Parenthood, that "the Catholic Church is going to liberalize [on the issue] of birth control sometime," Catholic Family Life director Joseph Holleran replied, "It is a waste of time to speak of liberalizing laws on birth control, since neither the Catholic church nor anyone else has the power to change the laws of God written deep in the human heart." Charles O'Neill, local executive secretary of the Society of St. Vincent de Paul, added, "The Catholic Church will always uphold the natural law, to say that the church will 'liberalize' in this regard is simply ridiculous."[342]

The concern for marriage and family that burst forth after World War II found its expression in the Christian Family Movement. This too had taken some inspiration from the work of Canon Cardijn and had blended with newer understandings of the meaning of Christian marriage. The CFM grew out of the Catholic Action groups operating in Chicago, New York, South Bend (Indiana), and even Milwaukee. Monsignor Reynold Hillenbrand, the chief devotee of Specialized Catholic Action, was the movement's first "protector" and organizer, but Chicago attorney Patrick Crowley and his wife, Patricia, as well as Bernie and Helene Bauer of South Bend and Father Louis Putz, C.S.C., created the framework for a national organization. A 1949 meeting at a Catholic Action retreat house in Wheeling, Illinois, called "Childerly," developed a national coordinating committee with the Crowleys at the head. At a second meeting at St. Procopius Abbey in Lisle, Illinois, the Crowleys were designated the executive secretary couple, a position they held until 1970. The organization adopted a newsletter already in existence called *ACT* as the mouthpiece of the movement, and drafted a guidebook called *For Happier Families: How to Start a Catholic Action Family Section*, known as "the little yellow book."

From the central headquarters in Chicago the executive committee dedicated itself to the "observe, judge, act" methodology of the Specialized Catholic Action movements and provided materials that "served," "educated" and "represented" families. Each CFM unit was autonomous and free to adapt materials sent by the central group, but the themes chosen in the annual booklets put out by the movement included "Economics and Family Life" and "the Family and World Crisis." The Milwaukee branch of the CFM was initiated by the Cardijn Center's John Russell Beix who was in contact with movement developers in Chicago. The CFM was originally designed with a strong social thrust, focusing on the union of liturgy and social action and the "transformation of the social order." Beix contributed to the intellectual heft of the programs by inviting speakers of national and even international renown to the Cardijn Center and by providing a rich array of books and contemporary religious articles and artwork.

[AAM]

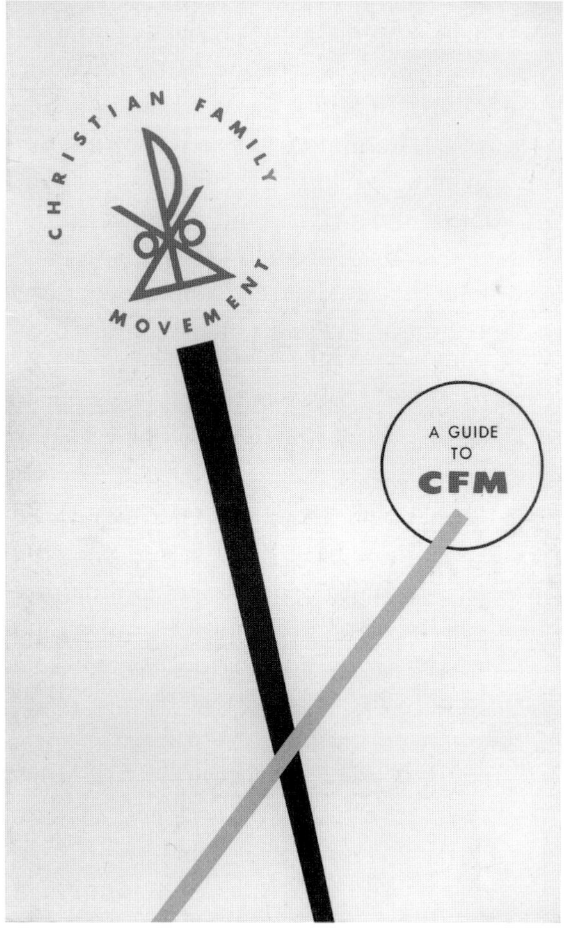

The adult education activities of the Cardijn Center were among its most innovative offerings. At a time when most religious education was confined to grade school and high school catechetical training, these programs offered ongoing religious education to Catholic adults. Moreover, the content included the latest and best information coming from European and American scholars—things many Americans, including students at the seminary and even in the religion courses of college, did not hear in the classroom or from the pulpit.

The groups that met at the Cardijn Center used the same meeting pattern: 15 minutes of reading and shared meditation from scripture, 15 minutes to review the liturgy for the coming week, and then a discussion of a problem under review and always a determination about what to do about the problem. Among the courses were scripture, personal sanctification, lay spirituality, church history, social problems, labor history, local Milwaukee housing and racial issues, international affairs and personal growth and development.

The old headquarters had a powerful effect on those who came through the door. Eugene Bleidorn, who played an important part in these and other movements in archdiocesan history, recalled how he helped create a powerful symbol of the work of the center after a trip to the United Nations building in New York. On an unfinished section of wall at the center where old lath, plaster and wood were covered by a piece of glass was this: "There is always unfinished business in the world that calls for the Christian's attention." The other image was a mural of Christ with a poem urging followers to work in the city, using the most difficult cases to bring the light of Christ to those who needed it most.[343]

Beix, Bleidorn and others attracted some of the most influential speakers in the Catholic intellectual and social action circuit. In the first year alone, the center brought in hundreds to hear Anton Pegis, Jacques Maritain, Maisie Ward, Louis Putz and even Fatima crusader Stephen Oraze. In later years Dorothy Day visited the center. So also did the Baroness Catherine de Hueck Doherty, founder of the interracial Friendship Houses. In 1948 and 1949, the center published a monthly magazine called *Vivant* that focused on marriage and family life. In 1959 Bleidorn estimated that 15,000 to 20,000 people had walked through the door of the Cardijn Center since its opening in February 1949, about 5,000 had taken part in days of recollection (mini-retreats given in the course of a single day), and 3,000 had joined in various study days sponsored by the center.[344]

Yet for all the enthusiasm and goodwill of the young people and their clerical advisers, Specialized Catholic Action did not enjoy universal support in Milwaukee. The earliest opponent was Frank Gross whose Church Mart was located near the center. He disliked the competition from the cooperative bookstore. Gross apparently took his fears to Frank C. Bruce of the Bruce Publishing Company, who likewise looked on the bookstore and the center with disdain and refused to allow it the same generous 33 percent discount he allowed "pagan" bookstores like the popular Schwartz bookstore in Milwaukee.[345] The movement also antagonized Mother Madeleine Heimann, superior of the Franciscan Sisters of St. Francis, who banned Beix from St. Mary's Academy when overly-zealous Young Christian Students began challenging the classroom instruction of academy chaplain Father James Graham. She was also disconcerted to find evidence that the tenets of Specialized Catholic Action had made some inroads among the young novices of the community.[346]

An even more formidable barrier to complete acceptance were the confusing attitudes of Archbishop Kiley and the priests of the diocese. Although he had given permission to Beix to open the center, Kiley was wary of groups of lay people, and had insisted on monthly reports. Kiley, really too ill to do much beyond the strictly liturgical and administrative demands of his office, never visited the center. Priests of the diocese took this as a cue about the prelate's discomfort with the things happening on Water Street. Many priests supported Beix, but others disliked the programs of the movement that transcended parish boundaries and occasionally, as happened at St. Mary's Academy, caused someone full of zeal associated with the movements to criticize a Sunday sermon or offer some unrequested bit of advice on running a parish. Petty clerical politics and pure jealousy at the obvious success and attractiveness of Beix's efforts were also part of the mixture. Priests could be brutal to one another.

Cana and the Catholic Family Life Bureau

In addition to his work with the seminarians and the budding liturgical movement in Milwaukee, Father Joseph Holleran also took to the hustings, delivering well-received speeches on marriage under the auspices of

Rev. Joseph Holleran speaking to Cana gathering [AAM]

the Committee on Family Life of the Milwaukee Archdiocesan Council of Catholic Women.[347] In 1948, Kiley appointed him to begin the Cana Conference Program in Milwaukee.[348]

This program for married persons originated in a series of New York retreats given by Jesuit John P. Delaney, who adapted from European sources a series of exercises known as "Family Renewal Days." Similar retreats conducted by Jesuit Edward Dowling in St. Louis gave the retreats the sobriquet "Cana Conferences," relating them to the wedding feast described in the gospels. Unlike the rarefied devotional or spiritual exercises of the popular retreat movement, Delaney and Dowling spoke to the real life experiences of the participants, attempting as best they could to use the nitty-gritty difficulties of marriage as fodder for their talks. Moreover, the retreat format was relaxed and informal, and provided an opportunity for discussion with the couples who attended.

The Cana idea caught on like wildfire in Chicago, where it was approved by Cardinal Stritch and was put in the charge of Monsignor John J. Egan, one of the most energetic organizers of the day. Egan was extremely helpful to Joseph Holleran in helping launch the Cana Movement in Milwaukee.[349] Later, a program for the engaged, called Pre-Cana, was developed by Father James Voss and layman Clem Lane of Chicago; it too became popular among Catholic laity. Introduced to Milwaukee in 1948, the Pre-Cana conferences drew 1,228 persons in 1953 to five weekly sessions drawing from 84 parishes in the archdiocese. Other sites for meetings were set up in Racine, Kenosha, Sheboygan, Waukesha, Beaver Dam, Hartford and Port Washington.[350]

Holleran's strong organizational skills and the support of priests helped the movement grow. In October 1948 he updated Kiley on the progress of the work, writing that its beginnings had been "slow and steady" and that "it receives its main stimulus from the lay people who have been helped to see their Marriage more in the light of Catholic truth." Holleran admitted that some people wondered if the four-hour format was too long, and whether it could be a lugubrious rehash of the traditional "four last things" of a parish mission. "But when they hear that the Cana approach is quite different in that it presents doctrine on marriage in a popular and everyday manner, they are more willing to come. And if they go home stimulated and encouraged, they in turn tell their friends and this is like the leaven."[351] Holleran explained his approach on the pages of *The Compass,* a magazine for the Cana Conference organizers: "The technique in Milwaukee, in common with that elsewhere, tries to interpret the Catholic doctrine on Marriage in every day experience, to show the beauty of truth in action." [352]

Monsignor James Kelly of the cathedral pressed Kiley to create a Catholic Family Life Bureau. In 1948 Kiley gave the job to Holleran while insisting that he remain on the seminary faculty. Kiley instructed the priest: "There are so many developments in the family life field that I do not want any splinter growths.

I am appointing you director. I want you to go out and win cooperation."[353] Holleran's appointment and the beginning of the Catholic Family Life Bureau were announced in the diocesan paper. The next year Holleran was relieved of full-time duties at the seminary and given the chaplaincy of St. Mary's convent, the provincial center of the Sisters of the Divine Savior on 35th and Center. He was ably assisted by Sister Mary Francis Berg, S.D.S., who served as his secretary until her untimely death. The convent chaplaincy made it possible to support himself (Kiley gave him no salary nor budget for the bureau), and to provide early offices for the bureau, whose activities began to grow significantly.

Rev. Joseph Holleran meeting with Family Life experts [AAM]

Holleran was the mainspring of the movement. An engaging and eloquent speaker, he hosted study days, days of recollections, and retreats. He made the rounds of forty hours and spoke with priests about the structure of the bureau and the resources he could make available. The Catholic Family Life Bureau remained at St. Mary's convent until 1955 when Holleran was asked to take over St. Jude's parish in Wauwatosa. Between 1948 and 1951, two separate family life programs were functioning: the Christian Family Movement, which emanated from the Cardijn Center, and the Cana and Pre-Cana Movements, which were directed by Holleran. Eventually simmering discontent erupted between the Christian Family Movement, one of the more popular programs of the center, and the Catholic Family Life Bureau. Kiley had given permission for both, but differences between the two movements' approaches, coupled with clerical complaints and parochial disputes with some devotees, led to a heavy-handed episcopal intervention that ended CFM as an effective force and seriously undercut the growing appeal of the Cardijn Center.

A Struggle, Reorganization and Suspicion

The serious disagreement between the Cana and Christian Family movements centered on the nature of instruction and the pace of change. Cana philosophy viewed family life as a kind of sanctuary from the evils of the age; but the CFM, with its Cardijn-inspired "observe, judge, act" taproot, called on families to be agents of social change. [354] Moreover, the swelling demands of young families and their obvious interest in religious instruction and a deeper Christian life made the CFM advocates eager to respond with alacrity. As he had in introducing the liturgical movement, Holleran's Cana Conference adopted a "go-slow" attitude, building up a good reputation among priests and overcoming negative feelings among lay persons over the length of sessions and what would be covered. Holleran also slowed down the acceptance rate by insisting that he was the only one who could give the conferences. This left many eager parishes waiting for long periods until his busy schedule could be cleared for them. By contrast, Beix was adept at finding skilled lay leaders and a wide array of priests whom he trusted (and who did not have to be perfect) to help guide the sessions.

The generally positive image of the Cardijn Center and the reputation of its programs for being "down-to-earth" was at variance with the Cana Conferences where Holleran had to constantly confront and convince people that Cana was worth a Saturday afternoon. As a result, attendance at CFM soared and units of the movement were set up across the archdiocese. Eventually the competition for the family life "market" led to conflict between Holleran and Beix.

The matter soon became jurisdictional. Who had authority to speak in the name of the diocese on family life matters, Beix or Holleran? Kiley temporized for a time, but when complaints about Beix came from senior priests like West Allis St. Rita's "Fritz" Arnold, Joseph Emmenegger recalled that Kiley grew disaffected.[355] He finally called the priest into his office in 1950 and sternly informed him that the CFM was under Holleran's jurisdiction from that point on. Beix accepted it meekly and transferred materials to Holleran.[356] Holleran, still running the Catholic Family Life Bureau almost single-handedly (although he had the occasional help of Monsignor Sylvester Gass of the marriage tribunal), simply ignored the existence of the organization and continued to devote himself primarily to the Pre-Cana and Cana Conference Movements.

The CFM did continue, largely with "rebellious" lay people who refused to accept Holleran's "takeover." They were assisted by priests who grumbled about Holleran's bureaucratic "triumph." In 1956, after Holleran had taken over a parish, CFM was restored under the direction of Father Joseph Strenski, the librarian at the minor seminary, and one who had been involved with the Cardijn project from the start. Strenski, performed his task well, resuscitating the movement first by sending out a questionnaire and finding a local couple, Eugene and Joyce Mary Lawler, to serve as coordinators for the movement. Holleran's management, however, had seriously harmed the CFM in Milwaukee. Cardijn Center priest and later chaplain, Eugene Bleidorn noted in his memoirs, "When the Archbishop took CFM away from the Cardijn Center, he removed one leg of a three-legged stool [Young Christian Students and Young Christian Workers being the other two 'legs']. CFM slowly began to fade." He wrote, "I believe the priests who were unable or unwilling to support Cardijn Center's programs, including YCS and YCW programs, viewed them as a threat to clerical authority and power in the parishes."[357] When the center closed in 1961, Bleidorn gently criticized the "conservative" archbishops of Milwaukee who defined their task as preserving and conserving rather than initiating new things.[358]

The center stumbled on, but Beix was clearly a broken man. He died of leukemia on March 19, 1952. His funeral Mass at Burlington's Immaculate Conception Church amazed Kiley who, sitting somberly in the sanctuary, was agog at the large number of young persons approaching the communion rail to receive Eucharist. Frequent communion had been part of the liturgical lessons taught at the Cardijn Center. Miraculously, Kiley did not scuttle the entire operation. He gave Father Vernon Kuehn permission to continue as chaplain but warned him to be wary of lay persons on the board of the center. In the few months of life that Kiley had left (he died a little more than a year after Beix) he tried to maintain closer control over the center and insisted that speakers be approved by his office. Occasionally he vetoed them.

When Meyer became archbishop in 1953, he trod cautiously around the dispute, recognizing the strong feelings of Holleran and his supporters and also the injured feelings of the Cardijn devotees. In 1956, when Kuehn became principal of Messmer High School, Meyer appointed Father Eugene Bleidorn to be the Cardijn chaplain, moved him to the major seminary and reduced his teaching load. He also made efforts to reinvigorate the CFM throughout the diocese, calling on many of the priests who had worked with Beix. Yet he also insisted on being kept informed monthly of things happening at the center and even visited it twice, although he would not permit pictures to be taken of him doing so. Later, as archbishop of Chicago, he warmed to CFM considerably and by the end of his life he could call the organization his "strong right arm."[359]

The Cardijn Center lasted a while under Bleidorn who, strapped by years of hard work at the high school seminary and the increasing demands on his time made by those who visited the center, eventually moved into parish work in rural Bristol in 1960. The center was taken over by seminary classics professor Daniel York, but most of its programs had either withered or were taken over by other diocesan agencies. All that was left was a bookstore which later relocated to a small shop directly across from Gesu Church on Wisconsin Avenue. Run for years by Catholic actionist Florence Weinfurter, it eventually passed into other hands. Finally Marquette University purchased the stock and

Archbishop Aloysius Muench visiting Cardijn Center [AAM]

ran it until the building was demolished in the 1990s. For many years this bookstore was the chief provider of progressive Catholic books and literature, high-quality religious goods and cards. Stuffed to the walls with stock, it did a respectable business—at least enough to keep Weinfurter afloat.

The Cardijn Center's approach in many respects anticipated the lay participation encouraged by the reforms of Vatican II. The interest in experience-based religious instruction that made religion relevant to the struggles and joys of the human experience reflected a dissatisfaction with the highly intellectual and doctrinally heavy programs of catechetical and convert instructions common in those days. Although the truly committed core of Cardijn Center devotees was small relative to the entire population of the archdiocese, the organization had a very powerful effect. Scores of men and women, who later became the first wave of commentators, lectors, and religious educators in their parishes after Vatican II, traced their interest in church life to their association with the Cardijn Center. The center's emphasis on social action inspired others to enter local politics. Cardijn's importance is also symbolic of the type of Catholic experience that was emerging in the postwar period. Cardijn devotees were often young men and women, removed maybe by two generations from immigrant status. Most were high school trained and many college bound. Some of them were suburbanites, struggling to raise families away from the framework of the traditional neighborhood parish that had defined Catholic life and identity. Cardijn programs, like the CFM and other lecturers and speakers, provided some guidance. Likewise, they also reflected the impact of the postwar religious revival in the archdiocese of Milwaukee.

An additional lay Catholic center that entered the archdiocese of Milwaukee in 1956 was Opus Dei, then a secular institute approved by Pope Pius XII. This group of lay persons and clergy were committed to developing an intense spirituality placed at the service of bringing the gospel to the secular arena. Begun in Spain in 1926 by the charismatic Jose Escriva de Balaguer, a lawyer turned priest, this association flourished worldwide. It came to Madison in 1955 to set up a House of Study (the name of its centers) near the University of Wisconsin and was warmly welcome by Bishop William P. O'Connor. The next year he endorsed their efforts to begin a House of Study in Milwaukee. Irish-born Father Paul Cummings (a former engineer) arrived in Milwaukee in late 1956 and purchased "an obscure brick and frame house" at 2175 South Layton Boulevard. The 10-room, two-story building called the Layton House of Studies attracted a number of men and women to their combination of spiritual exercises, personal direction and religious training.[360]

Social Provision: Child Care and Hospitals

Needs in social provision and health care also concerned the archdiocese after the war. New thinking about how to care for dependent children emerged in the 1930s and

1940s, prompting changes in the archdiocese's orphanages. Essentially, child experts and others moved away from the asylum and institutional model and toward treating each child as an individual case. These new insights were complemented by a declining need for ethnic orphanages and a stream of bad stories and rumors of abuse that appeared in the press and even on the silver screen. Even the best orphanages came to be associated with an unhealthy "warehousing" of innocent children. As a result, dependent child care turned more to encouraging adoption, foster care, and smaller group homes where children could receive individual attention and care. These changes were made in the orphanages of Milwaukee County as well as across the country.

In 1950 Catholic Charities head Monsignor Matthew McEvoy reported that the Catholic Church took care of 2,564 dependent children.[361] Most of them had been referred from the juvenile and family courts, from parents and relatives, and from other social agencies. To help the children leave the orphanages, he developed a network of foster homes for certain children, placements with relatives and even adoptions. Yet the network of institutions—St. Vincent de Paul Infant Asylum, St. Aemillian's, St. Rose's, St. Joseph's Homes, as well as the Carmelite Home for Boys, St. Margaret's Guild, St. Charles's Home and the House of the Good Shepherd—continued to extend care to children. Virtually everyone seemed to know that the orphanage had seen its last days except Moses E. Kiley and his consultors.

Kiley decided in 1951 to rebuild St. Aemillian's orphanage on a new location. The venerable institution had burned in 1931, and the orphans had scattered to other sites and to a "temporary" shelter at 60th and Lloyd Street.[362] Even though orphanage superintendent Monsignor Eugene Kroha had begged to have the facility restored, plans to rebuild it had faltered because of the Depression. Rebuilding the cathedral took precedence when Kiley arrived, and then wartime building restrictions halted any idea of working on the orphanage. After the war, the demand for new high schools and expanded parishes and hospitals was given priority. In 1951, however, the State Industrial Commission forced Kiley's hand. It inspected the 60th and Lloyd site and deemed it unfit unless a host of costly repairs were made immediately.[363] Kiley then pressed forward with fund-raising for a new orphanage.

Apparently, specialists in Catholic Charities attempted to dissuade the prelate from building a large "asylum-style" institution for Catholic orphans[364] but such institutions (like the Felician-run St. Joseph Orphanage) continued to exist in the archdiocese. Moreover, Kiley's advisors, largely leftovers from the late Messmer era—Monsignors George Meyer, Julius Burbach, Frederick Arnold and others—may have shared the prelate's enthusiasm for rebuilding St. Aemillian's along its former lines. In the summer of 1951 Kiley announced a million dollar fund-drive to build the new orphanage.[365] An expanse of undeveloped land between 88th and Capitol on Milwaukee's northwest side had been secured.[366] Here a significant amount of Catholic building was in the works: St. Anne's Home for the Elderly run by the Little Sisters of the Poor, Divine Savior High School and ultimately a new parish named for St. Margaret Mary and to be headed by former army chaplain Raymond Vint.

Kiley accumulated nearly a million dollars in the St. Aemillian fund, but his fatal illness ground the process to a halt. When Meyer took over as archbishop, the St. Aemillian's decision was one of the first ones on his desk. The Catholic Social Welfare department, especially Monsignor Joseph Springob who had succeeded Matthew MacEvoy as the head of the agency, suggested that the new orphanage not be built. When Meyer laid this before the aged consultors, virtually all balked at any alteration of Kiley's plans, insisting that to do so would be a breach of trust with the people who had given the money in the belief that their funds were going to a new St. Aemillian's.[367] Meyer capitulated and broke ground for the orphanage in December. The large "e-shaped" building, designed by the E. Brielmaier firm, was to accommodate 100 boys in two large dormitories. Recreation halls, dining rooms, a kitchen and a chapel with a handsome memorial bell tower were included in the plans.[368] At groundbreaking ceremonies in December 1954, Meyer justified what was certainly a controversial decision. "This was one of Archbishop Kiley's most treasured ambitions—a new St. Aemillian's."[369] Meyer dedicated the facility in October 1956.[370] However, Springob's warnings about the future of child care were on target. All of the archdiocesan orphanages phased themselves out of existence, and by the 1980s, the archdiocese had a white elephant at 88th and Capitol.

New St. Aemilian Orphanage [Courtesy of St. Aemilian-Lakeside, Inc.]

Changes in the method and delivery of social welfare were accompanied by important changes in medicine and the delivery of health care. Medicine grew increasingly more professionalized and specialized throughout the 20th century. Improvements in medical technology, surgical techniques and nursing skills continued the transformation of American medicine. During and after the war, considerable federal investment in medical research and technology reflected itself in the formation of the National Institutes of Health. Millions of federal dollars flowed into research and development, medical education, and even hospital building. Public awareness of healthcare issues rose even higher when finding cures for public scourges, like polio, tuberculosis and cancer became the objects of large publicity campaigns.[371]

Catholic health care also reflected these same trends. The Catholic Hospital Association which had been founded in Milwaukee in 1915 by Jesuit Father Charles Mouliner, regent of Marquette University's medical school, became one of the chief agencies encouraging on-going improvement in Catholic hospitals.[372] (Mouliner, it may be remembered, was also the inspiration behind the Marquette Women's League and the centralization of Catholic social welfare work early in the 20th century.) Messmer had signed on as a sponsor of the new organization and defended its goals and activities in its formative years. The CHA brought a higher degree of professionalism and standardization. It also served as a liaison between professional groups of physicians and hospital administrators and religious communities that made health care part of their general apostolic work. Not only were hospitals substantially improved, but greater attention to nurses' training was given by such groups as the School Sisters of St. Francis and the Sisters of St. Agnes, both of whom ran very large nursing schools. The training of nurses professionally and theologically was a prime objective of the CHA. Edward A. Fitzpatrick of Marquette (and later Mount Mary) insisted regularly in the pages of *Hospital Progress* that nursing schools be well-funded and connected with a teaching hospital. In Milwaukee, Archbishop Stritch made School Superintendent Edmund Goebel responsible for the religious education of nurses working in archdiocesan hospitals. Goebel provided oversight of the network of private hospitals within the archdiocesan boundaries and regularly recruited local priests, like seminary faculty member Father John A. Schulien, to teach theological and medical-moral courses in nursing schools.

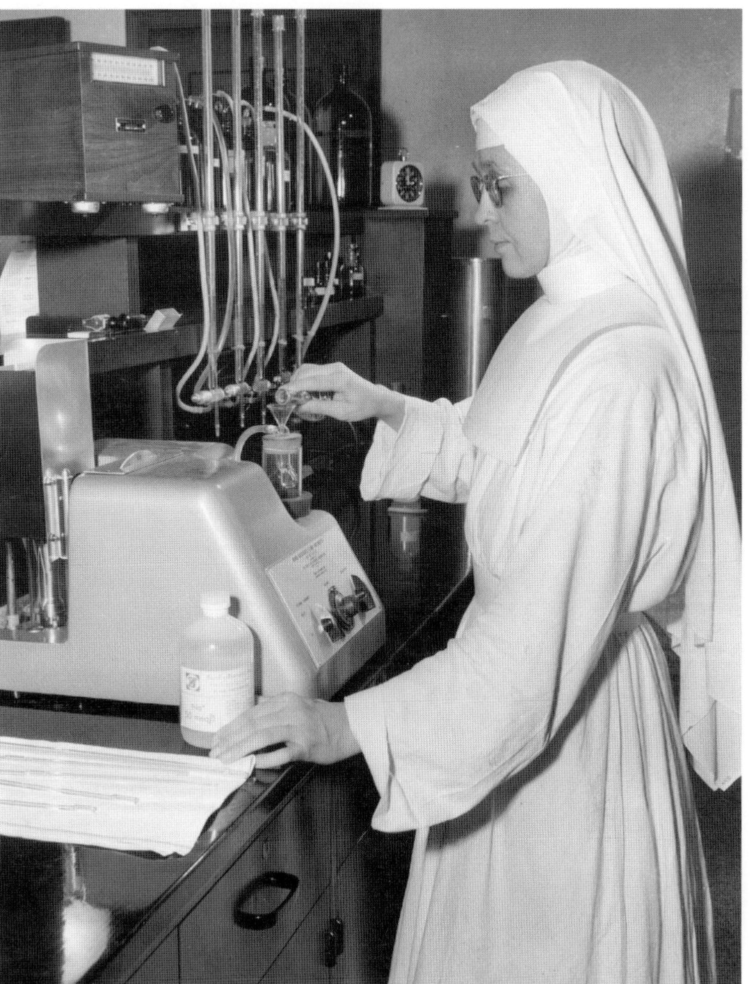

Salvatorian Sister nurse [ASDS-W]

World War II brought advances in medical technology, such as antibiotics. The first stirrings of moves on state and national levels to provide national health care found Catholic leaders wary, worrying that the use of federal funds for health care would drive people away from private hospitals (where they might not be permitted to use the funds). They also feared that government subsidy meant interference in the distinctive practices of Catholic hospitals, especially in the sensitive issue of medical ethics. The preference of Catholics for private health insurance firms was manifested in the work of archdiocesan attorney Henry V. Kane, who helped establish Blue Cross Insurance in Wisconsin, a private insurance firm that was acceptable to Catholic hospitals. This company would later be headed by Northwestern Mutual Life financial advisor, Neil Gleason.

New Hospitals

The most obvious effect of the professionalization of health care was manifested in the construction of hospitals. As hospitals became an increasingly important part of the delivery of health care, local officials kept an eagle eye on the number of hospital beds relative to the general population. Large for-profit hospitals began to be erected in many cities. Catholics had fewer financial resources but, with the support given by religious orders, they managed to mount a fairly impressive hospital building program to keep up with needs.

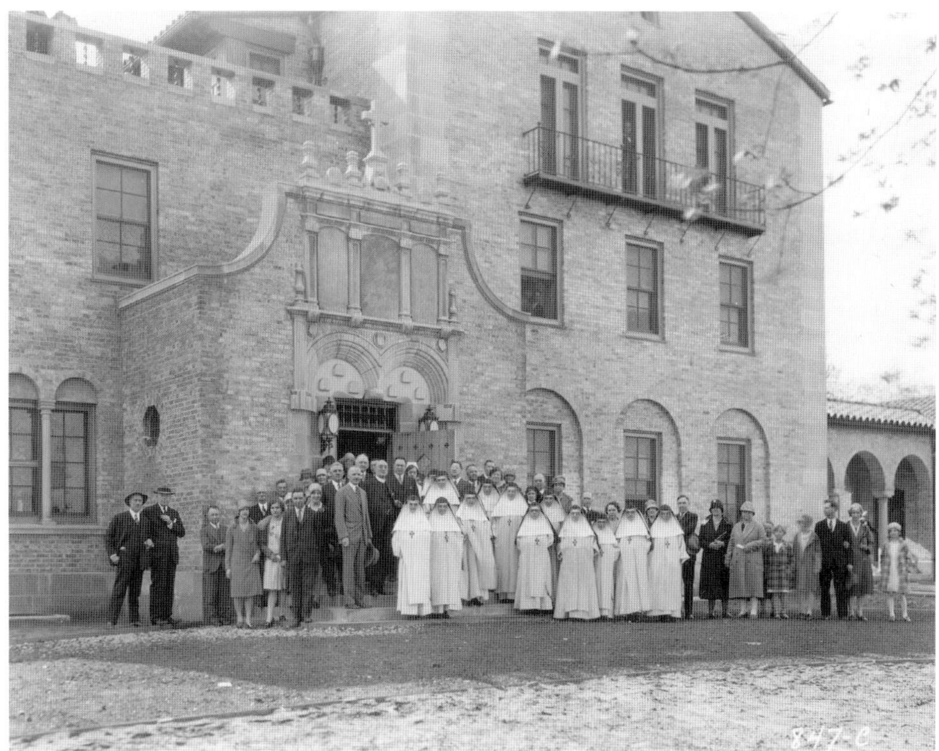

St. Catherine Hospital, Kenosha [AOP-Ken]

The archdiocese of Milwaukee's hospital growth had been considerable during the 20th century. Two new hospitals begun by orders who devoted themselves to this task came to the archdiocese—St. Catherine's Hospital in Kenosha and St. Camillus Hospital in Milwaukee.

St. Catherine's Hospital was founded by a group of Dominican sisters exiled from revolutionary Portugal early in the 20th century. They had come over to America and established schools and hospitals on the west coast. In 1916 they were offered land in Kenosha. Meeting with Archbishop Messmer they decided to accept the offer and moved to the city in August 1917. Their initial foundation was a hospital they established in a

St. Camillus Hospital, Wauwatosa
[Camillan Archives]

former boarding house on Howland and Prairie Avenue (60th Street and 22nd Avenue). The small facility filled up rapidly and within a year the sisters were looking for a new site. Fortune smiled on them when Kenosha hydrotherapist, Dr. Nelson A. Pennoyer, offered to sell the nuns his large sanitarium and equipment along with 15 acres of land and three cottages on the shore of Lake Michigan for $70,000. The Pennoyer Sanitarium had been a Kenosha institution since 1857, advertising the therapeutic benefits of an artesian well on the lakefront property known as the "Kenosha Water Cure." With fund-raising help from Kenosha citizens, the sisters were able to purchase the facility and transform it into St. Catherine's Memorial Hospital in October 1919. The sisters cultivated good relations with the community by setting aside beds for wounded veterans of World War I. Beginning in 1924, piecemeal additions were made to the rapidly deteriorating Pennoyer building culminating in a 110-bed addition in 1960.[373] At the same time they moved to Kenosha the sisters transferred their novitiate to the new site. In 1951 the community formally separated from its Portuguese roots and created a separate congregation with general headquarters in Kenosha.

In the 1920s, the archdiocese of Milwaukee welcomed a religious community devoted exclusively to health care, the Camillans. Founded in Rome in the 16th century by St. Camillus de Lellis, the Order of the Servants of the Sick, known popularly as the Camillans, grew rapidly in Europe. In 1919, through the instrumentality of a priest of the diocese of Omaha, the German branch of the order, was invited to come to Wisconsin to take over "Durward's Glen" in Baraboo, left by artist and poet Bernard I. Durward to the Milwaukee See, with the proviso that it be used for some charitable purpose. The Baraboo property was never formally taken by the archdiocese because of the remoteness of the location. However, the Camillans were interested, and sent over Father Michael Mueller to meet with Father James Durward, the proprietor of the estate and to check out the possibilities for a new apostolate in America. En route to America in 1921, Mueller met Archbishop Messmer and revealed to him the plans. Messmer expressed great interest in the work of the Order and mentioned that health care needs in Milwaukee were great. He was especially in need of a facility to care for old and chronically ill men. Mueller proceeded to Baraboo, but found it too remote, and found also that healthcare needs there were adequately cared for by the Sisters of the Divine Savior who had a hospital in nearby Portage. Mueller returned to Milwaukee and decided to take advantage of Messmer's offer to come to the see city. Messmer placed him temporarily at St. Anthony's parish in Menominee Falls. In February 1923 Mueller purchased a house on South 26th Street. With the assistance of many friends he refurbished the structure and in 1924 three Camillan brothers and three priests arrived to begin work. They purchased the house next door to their residence and transformed it into a rest home for men. In 1925 they purchased seven acres in Wauwatosa, and in 1931 broke ground for a new hospital that would house 65 invalid and incurably ill men. Later, the Baraboo property, which they had first rejected, was deeded to them, along with an endowment and possession of a number of Bernard Durward's paintings. In 1939 the American Camillans became a separate province and expanded from their Wisconsin headquarters. In 1942, 14 archdiocesan cities had Catholic hospitals (see Table 4-10).

After World War II, the growth of the population required a dramatic addition of hospital beds. All hospitals, public and private, undertook extensive building campaigns that were the first act of the ongoing reorganization of American health care in the late 20th century. Even the smaller communities in southeastern Wisconsin improved their hospitals. Millions of dollars were spent in this expansion of the archdiocese's healthcare "system."

Table 4-10

City	Hospital/Date
Beaver Dam	St. Joseph, 1930
Columbus	St. Mary, 1913
Fond du Lac	St. Agnes, 1896
Hartford	St. Joseph, 1920
Janesville	Mercy, 1907
Kenosha	St. Catherine, 1919
Milwaukee	St. Mary, 1848; St. Joseph, 1884; Sacred Heart, 1893; Misericordia, 1908; St. Mary Hill, 1912; St. Anthony, 1931; St. Camillus, 1932; St. Michael, 1937
Monroe	St. Clare, 1939
Portage	Divine Savior, 1917
Port Washington	St. Alphonsus, 1940
Racine	St. Mary, 1882
Sheboygan	St. Nicholas, 1890
West Bend	St. Joseph, 1930
Watertown	St Mary, 1914

An important stimulus for the riot of hospital building was the federal government. In 1946, Congress passed the Hospital Survey and Construction Act, also known as the Hill-Burton Act, which provided generous federal subsidies for the construction of new hospital facilities.[374] This funding went to over 700 private hospitals, including a number in Milwaukee. While the funds were helpful, however, most of the monies for new hospital construction were raised by the sisters who sponsored the hospital, either through fund-drives or by loans.

Older hospitals built additions. St. Mary's in Milwaukee planned an addition that added additional beds to its structure. St. Agnes Hospital in Fond du Lac invested over $2 million to enhance its 300-bed hospital.[375] In 1947, a new addition had been made to the growing St. Anthony Hospital.[376]

A number of new hospitals were also established in the archdiocese after World War II. Leading off was a new Catholic hospital on the south side of Milwaukee. Although Sacred Heart Sanitarium existed on the south side, the need for a larger general hospital had been evident for some time. As noted earlier, the School Sisters of St. Francis expressed some interest in beginning a hospital on the south side. However, the Felician Sisters announced plans in 1947 for a hospital that adjoined their thriving St. Joseph's Orphanage on Euclid and Ohio Streets.[377] Fund-raising would lag, however, and the 254-bed hospital would not be built until 1956.

In 1951 the School Sisters of St. Francis opened a new hospital in Waupun.[378] Government efforts to coordinate the dispersal of hospital building funds led to the creation of the United Hospital Fund Appeal in Milwaukee County in 1952. Five existing hospitals were to be expanded with a *pro rata* share of the proceeds. Two new hospitals received these funds: St. Francis Hospital on the south

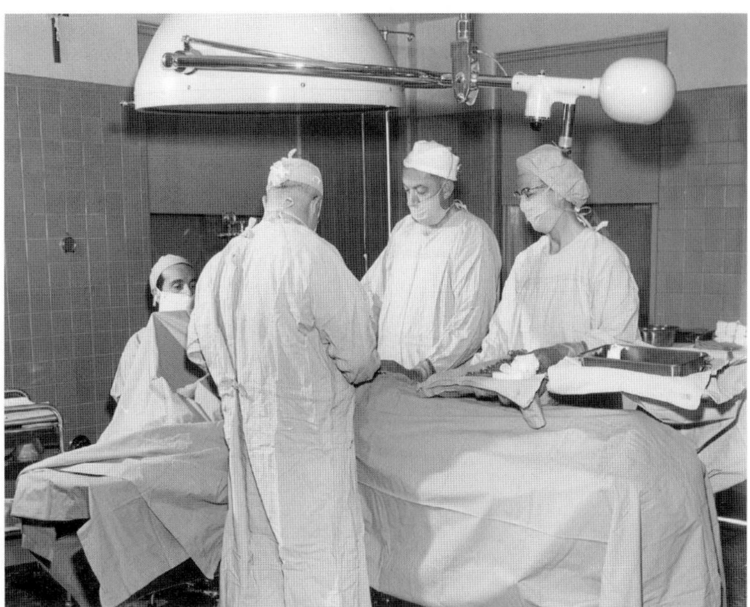

St. Anthony Hospital, Milwaukee [Courtesy of St. Benedict Church]

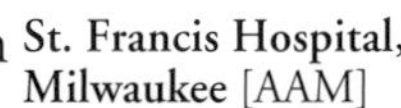

St. Francis Hospital, Milwaukee [AAM]

side and St. Michael's, built on Villard under the direction of the Franciscan sisters who ran St. Joseph's Hospital. The name "St. Michael" had been given to the old St. Joseph facility on 4th and Reservoir when St. Joseph's opened its new facility on 58th and West Chambers Street in Milwaukee's Sherman Park Area in 1928. The sisters sold the old facility, but in 1937 it came back into their hands and they reopened it as an annex of St. Joseph's. In 1940 they separately incorporated the old site as "St. Michael's." A number of clinics—maternity, dental, eye, pediatric, ear, nose and throat care—providing curative and preventive services for low-income groups and others unable to afford private care and ineligible for public relief opened at the facility. It also provided services for alcoholic rehabilitation and was one of the first Catholic sites for the Alcoholics Anonymous program which gained popularity in the 1940s and 1950s.[379] Eventually, the need for a modern hospital became evident. The Franciscan sisters acquired land on Villard Avenue between 23rd and 25th Streets. The new St. Michael's Hospital was dedicated in 1957 and the old facility demolished.[380] By this time the use of walk-in clinics had been adopted by other hospitals in the area.

In November 1953 the Franciscan sisters of the Immaculate Conception announced plans to open a Catholic hospital in Cudahy named for the Holy Trinity. Trinity Hospital, as well as St. Francis and the new St. Michael Hospitals, received $1.7 million in federal funds.[381] A survey of the American Medical Association revealed in 1953 that Catholic hospitals had 44 percent of the beds in the general hospitals within the boundaries of the archdiocese of Milwaukee. Of the 31 hospitals in the area, tallying 4,719 beds, Catholics operated 13 with 2,072 beds.[382]

St. Joseph Hospital, Beaver Dam [ASSF]

The expansion and development of Catholic health care in one sense was a continuation of the traditional Catholic theme of visibility. Catholics were expected to go to Catholic hospitals. Certain surgical procedures such as sterilizations or the termination of pregnancies were to be handled in ways consonant with religious teachings. Each hospital had a chapel and a resident chaplain who

St. Alphonsus Hospital, Port Washington [AAM]

provided sacramental services 24 hours a day. Likewise, the influence of the Catholic Church on the practice of medicine was quite extensive. Many of the doctors who worked in Wisconsin's healthcare establishment were graduates of the medical school of Marquette University. Schools of nursing attached to Catholic hospitals provided other healthcare professionals for the region. Catholic sisters who ran the complex facilities acquired the skills and experience that made them some of the best administrators in the field. Sister nurses influenced the vocational decisions of young women, some of whom joined religious communities to become nurses.

Catholic hospitals were swept into the larger tide of standardization and professionalization. The doctors who comprised the medical staffs of these institutions insisted that Catholic hospitals be run according to "regular" standards and that sisters be trained professionally. This included not only nurses, but also pharmacists, X-ray technicians, physical therapists and even food service and laundry personnel. Religious art, crucifixes in rooms, the presence of a chapel and a chaplain, morning communion calls with a small bell signaling the presence of a priest with the Blessed Sacrament and the omnipresence of sisters in habits assured some kind of Catholic visibility and identity.

A Militant Catholic Culture: Anti-Communism and Piety

The Cold War between the capitalist United States and its leading economic and military competitor, the communist Soviet Union, defined international and national politics after World War II. Each side, armed with nuclear weapons, regarded the other side with distrust. The threat of mass destruction hung over the two nations, and the notion that a conflict in an allied nation might set off a chain reaction of nuclear war undergirded the thoughts of a generation of Americans.

The Catholic Church had long opposed communism, going back to the critique of Marxist ideas in the 19th century. Catholics resisted communism not only because of its ideology of state control (particularly over education and marriage), but even more so because of its militant atheism. The Bolshevik takeover of Russia in 1917 elicited revulsion from the Vatican, which was cordially returned by the new Red masters of the Kremlin. Soviet leaders closed churches, expelled or persecuted clergy, and forbade public worship. Wherever church-state conflict erupted, Catholics often laid the blame for Church persecution at the feet of Bolshevik or Red sympathizers—for example, in Mexico in the 1920s.[383] In 1937, Pope Pius XI's encyclical *Divini Redemptoris* scathingly attacked communism, both in theory and in practice. American Catholics loyally supported their Church's revulsion for communism, which was doubly odious because of its state-controlled economic system. Milwaukee Catholics—in pulpits, at lectures and in printed materials—echoed this disdain for the Soviets and their atheism and looked askance on any person or ideology that seemed to mirror the communist line.

Most Catholics plugged their nose when the United States made league with Soviet dictator Josef Stalin to defeat Hitler in World War II.[384] Suspicions re-emerged after the war when Stalin organized a *cordon sanitaire* around the recently devastated Soviet Union, which included dominating, if not outright conquering, Eastern European states like Poland, Czechoslovakia and the Balkans, areas of central Europe that had sent scores of its sons and daughters to the United States and to the Milwaukee Archdiocese. It was not difficult to stir up anti-communist fervor in America after World War II, but among Eastern European Catholics, anti-communist militance and suspicion of espionage and subversion by Soviet agents in America ran especially high. American politicians of all stripe, but especially in the long out-of-power Republican party, quickly seized on the worry that there were Soviet or communist sympathizers in our midst. A climate of anxiety was created by such events as the Soviet detonation of an atomic bomb, the fall of China to the communists in 1949, the stunning conviction of Alger Hiss, and the discovery that American nuclear secrets had been given to the Soviets by leftist spies. A number of politicians seized on these fears to advance their careers, most notably California Representative (and later Senator, Vice President and President) Richard M. Nixon and Wisconsin's own Senator Joseph R. McCarthy, a Wisconsin Catholic.

Milwaukee Catholics of all nationalities were caught up in anticommunist fervor in the late 1940s and early 1950s. Even before the end of World War II, concerns were raised about Soviet occupation of the Baltic States which they had seized in 1939. Over 500 Lithuanian Catholics had gathered at Milwaukee's St. Gabriel parish hall and passed resolutions expressing their concern over the treatment of 4,000,000 Lithuanians by the Soviet Union.[385] Articles and editorial cartoons in the *Catholic Herald Citizen* and frequent visits and talks by missionaries (including local sisters and priests) who had escaped the "Red Hell" of Communist China in 1949-1950, or who had braved communist regimes in Eastern Europe, fed the sense of a Church beleaguered. Catholics heard of Pope Pius XII's opposition to communists and his efforts to forestall a potentially embarrassing Communist victory in the 1948 elections in Italy (American Catholics had funneled thousands of dollars to the anti-communist effort through the Central Intelligence Agency).

Editorial cartoon, *Catholic Herald-Citizen* [*Catholic Herald-Citizen*]

Bishop Aloysius Muench of Fargo, North Dakota, was appointed papal nuncio to war-torn Germany and warned of the potential for West Germany to "turn communist" unless efforts were made to shore up the destroyed German economy and infrastructure. Polish Catholics had raised thousands of relief dollars during the war under the leadership of a former dean of Marquette's Law School, Judge Francis Xavier Swietlik, who continued his advocacy for embattled Poland after the war. Marquette University hired Hungarian emigré Bela Varig for its political science department, which became a bastion of anti-communist activity; Varig provided a stream of analysis about the horrors of communism.[386] At the insistence of Pope Leo XIII in the 1880s, Catholics in Milwaukee had added a series of devotional prayers to the end of the Mass for the conversion of Russia. More spiritual weapons for this combat with the communist anti-Christ would be forthcoming in the postwar era.

Fear of communist nuclear strength was evident as well. Milwaukeeans devised emergency plans and had air raid drills; church basements often sported the black and gold civil defense logo and provided a port in a potential atomic storm. Fears of nuclear destruction in Milwaukee eventually led to the mounting of Nike defensive missiles on the lakefront (on the current Summerfest

APPENDIX I
CIVILIAN DEFENSE REGULATIONS

As long as there remains the threat of enemy attacks by air, Civilian Defense Regulations are a necessity in every school. Each student is to acquaint himself with the following Civilian Defense Regulation, so that he will know what to do in an emergency.

INTRODUCTION:

Civilian Defense is the organization and the preparation of our people to take care of themselves and of others in case of war, enemy attacks, bombings, etc. Every school is expected to publish a set of defense regulations, telling both students and faculty what they are to do in case of any emergency such as those mentioned above. The purpose of these regulations is not to alarm people, but to prepare them. All must hope for the best but be prepared for the worst. The necessity for these Civilian Defense Regulations is based upon recent developments in world affairs. It is folly to imagine that the destruction of another world war will not reach the United States. It is only prudent to be prepared for any emergency that might come. Panic is caused by the unexpected. In an emergency, panic and hysteria are the greatest obstacles to efficient aid for those who need it. In an emergency remain cool, calm, and silent, and follow orders. Our American people are very slow to realize that they face possible emergencies in the days to come. Let us be fully prepared here at St. Francis. Many lives may be saved thereby. Keep these Regulations handy, save them for future reference, and read them over frequently, so that you will be thoroughly acquainted with them. Each student will be held responsible for a working knowledge of the regulations. Regular, unannounced drills, based on these regulations, will be held regularly.

SECTION ONE—WARNING SIGNALS.

The warning signal for an emergency will be given over the regular school bell system. The fire horns will not be used, except for the regular fire drills. For an emergency, the bells will be rung three times, five seconds each time, with a pause of one second between the ringings: thus:

Ring 5 seconds pause Ring 5 seconds pause Ring 5 seconds

This three fold ring will be repeated as often as is deemed necessary. If the electricity has already been turned off at the time the signal is to be given, (which is not likely to happen), a verbal warning will be sent to each classroom and study hall, and to each group of persons on the campus.

SECTION TWO—SHELTERS.

Upon receipt of the signal described in Section One of these regulations, all persons on the Minor Seminary grounds are to hurry to the following places of shelter:

All Day Students — Day Students Locker Room.
All Resident Students — Library (Key is in the school office).
Professors — Basement corridors of building in which they live. Those living in laundry building, in kitchen corridor.
Sisters — Long corridor of basement in their building.

SECTION THREE—SILENCE:

All are to go to the designated places in silence, so that any orders or instructions given, will be clearly and instantly understood. Silence is important. The welfare of many may depend upon it. When the order to "be at ease" is given, talking will be permitted, bu no loud noises or shouting.

SECTION FOUR—BOMBING:

The most likely type of emergency is a bombing. When the actual bombing comes, lie flat on the floor, away from windows as much as is possible. Be sure to

— 21 —

cover your head, at least with your hands. If possible, get beneath a table or desk, or anything else that might break the force of falling objects, masonry etc. In any case do not stand. Lie down. Remain thus for 10 seconds after the crash, unless you are in the path of falling debris.

SECTION FIVE—ATOM BOMBING:

If a terrific flash precedes an explosion, it is likely an atomic bomb. In that case, follow the instructions given above in Section Four, with these additional points for safety: 1. To avoid flash burns, look away from the flash, and cover all exposed parts of the body, (head, face, arms, hands), if at all possible; 2. Stay out of the line of flying glass, (which does great harm in atomic bombings) by being sure that glass will pass over you or merely fall upon you after its force has been spent; 3. Do not go out into the open for about 10 minutes, to avoid atomic radiation. Do not eat or drink anything that was exposed to the explosion. Use only canned and bottled food and drinks, until assured that other foods are safe.

In case of an under water atomic explosion, remember that the water is contaminated by atomic radiation. It will fall like rain. Stay out of it by all means. Such contamination can be very dangerous for as long as 24 hours. It is important to listen to the directions and the advice that will be given over the radio in such emergencies.

SECTION SIX—UNEXPLODED BOMBS:

If an unexploded bomb is discovered, be sure to follow these hints: 1. Remove all persons from the vicinity. 2. Do not move the bomb. 3. Inform the nearest Fire Department. 4. If it is inside a building open all doors and windows to disperse the force of a possible blast. 5. Surround the bomb with mattresses, sand bags, books, or like materials. This barricade should be built some distance from the bomb, and not straight, (vertically), but at an angle. The purpose of the barricade is not to stop the force of the explosion but to deflect it. 6. Remove inflammable materials. 7. Be prepared for fire fighting and first aid. 8. If the bomb must be moved, avoid turning or upsetting it, and do not jar or shock it. Keep a heavy pad or mattress between the bomb and the person handling it. 9. Never use water on an unexploded bomb.

SECTION SEVEN—INSTRUCTIONS TO PARENTS:

Parents of students are to be urged to remain calm in an emergency. They should be assured that all precautions have been taken and will be taken to safeguard the welfare of their sons. The students will find a better and a safer shelter in the concrete and steel constructed buildings of the Minor Seminary than in any private home. The seminary basements are ideal shelters. Parents are asked to remain away from the Minor Seminary until an emergency is over, and are asked not to phone the school during an emergency. The phone lines must be kept open for communication between the school and Civilian Defense Offices, Fire Departments, Police Stations, Emergency Squads, etc. Parents should be reminded too that a completely equipped infirmary, with all first aid requirements, is to be had at the Minor Seminary, together with a group of students trained in first aid.

SECTION EIGHT—FACULTY:

The professors are not given a definite assignment during and immediately after an emergency, so that they may move freely among the students, advising and counseling them and ministering to their needs as such needs arise. If an emergency alarm sounds during a class of study period, the professor is to go to one of the shelters designated for the boys of his class. If the alarm sounds outside of a class or study period, he is to follow the instructions given in Section two — "Shelters."

— 22 —

[AAM]

grounds). Bishop John Grellinger, who was called on by Archbishop Moses Kiley to make preliminary sketches for an addition to the nearby seminary in 1952, made one effort to dissuade Kiley from building on the site: "Now that we are living in the atomic age with Milwaukee a primary military target and the Lakeside Power Plant, adjacent to the seminary very vulnerable to attack, a question arises as to whether one should plan any more buildings for the present Seminary site, thus exposing twelve years of vocations to danger."[387]

One of the chief vehicles for Catholic anti-communism was Marian piety. Milwaukee's Catholics did not need prompting to honor the Virgin Mary. Marian devotions of various ethnic groups—whether it was the annual celebrations of Madonna del Lume of the Sicilians of the Third Ward, or the deep devotion to Our Lady of Czestachowa among the Poles of the south side—had long been an element of Milwaukee's culture. In 1950, 35 archdiocesan parishes were named for Mary.

Annual SUMA conventions also provided an occasion for large public demonstrations in honor of the Virgin Mary. Thousands of SUMA members gathered annually or more often at the Milwaukee auditorium for public rallies, Masses, recitations of the rosary and listening to inspirational speakers such as Daniel Lord (who died of cancer in 1955) and others. The living rosary, practiced at many gatherings of young people, called on students to arrange themselves as a rosary tableaux of 50 beads and to recite the rosary at a public event.

Living Rosary, St. Boniface Church, Milwaukee [AAM]

Father Donald Weber, an assistant at St. Mary's parish in Racine, recalled one such living rosary at the large Memorial Hall on Racine's lakefront. He "invited the parents and families to see their lovely daughters (or blood sisters) in colorful formals taking a Hail Mary in the Rosary. Naturally the boys were the Our Fathers." He noted further, "This event became a highlight for the young people."[388]

Novena booklet [Courtesy Sister Mary Roman Obremski]

One particular Marian devotion practiced often was to Our Lady of Fatima. This related to purported apparitions of Mary at Fatima to three Portuguese children believed to have taken place between 1915 and 1917.389 Mary's call for prayers for the conversion of Russia seemed especially timely when the United States and the Soviets entered the Cold War. Her exhortation to pray the rosary for world peace seemed a fitting Catholic response to the threats of nuclear war after the Soviets detonated a nuclear device in 1949. The Fatima cult was eventually given ecclesiastical approval and soon became an important Catholic response to the Cold War.[390]

Devotion to Our Lady of Fatima developed rapidly among Catholics in the archdiocese, with parishes holding special devotions in her honor. At St. Stanislaus parish, no sooner had World War II ended when parishioners switched their weekly novenas from Our Lady of Victory to Our Lady of Fatima.[391] Images of Our Lady of Fatima began appearing in archdiocesan churches, chapels and in the corridors of schools and convents. Nationally-known Fatima apostles, such as former G.I. Stephen Oraze, descended on Milwaukee in early 1950 to deliver eight hard-hitting lectures to packed audiences. In dire tones, he warned Milwaukee Catholics that World War III was imminent unless they heeded the call of Mary to do penance and pray the rosary. Through his widely circulated *Scapular Magazine*, Oraze reached even more homes with his Fatima message.[392]

In 1957 the Pilgrim Virgin statue, a traveling image of Our Lady of Fatima, made the rounds of the churches of the archdiocese. The visiting priest who accompanied the statue on its worldwide tour met with the

Sinsinawa Dominican sisters at St. Rose convent to share "specific incidents and policies, not known by the general public, that indicate forcibly the need of recourse to Our Lady of Fatima as the sole means of saving our country from the diabolical schemes and influence of Communism."[393] In April 1948 large crowds jammed the Cathedral of St. John, spilling out into the cathedral square, where many knelt for a holy hour to Mary of Fatima held on the eve of the traditional communist holiday of May Day.[394] Also in 1948, thousands of Milwaukee Catholics shivered in the rain as Auxiliary Bishop Roman Atkielski dedicated a huge outdoor shrine to Our Lady of Fatima built next to the grounds of the convent of the Sisters of the Perpetual Rosary.[395] Funds for the shrine had been gathered by the sisters, and by Monsignor Adolph Klink, chaplain to the School Sisters of St. Francis. Designed by Leonard Schmidt, the shrine was built of ledge rock and had streams of water flowing through it. Five carrara marble statutes of Mary, the visionaries, and the sheep were hoisted into their niches in the park. In 1949 rosary priest Father Patrick Peyton, C.S.C., led the exercises before the shrine as 8,000 people attended.[396]

Other parts of the diocese shared the Fatima fervor. Father Donald Weber recalled the first Catholic entry in a Racine civic parade on the fourth of July in the 1950s was a float of Our Lady of Fatima with live figures and sheep. The next year he chose Our Lady of Lourdes and recalled the growing competition among the teenage girls of the CYO group to be selected as the Blessed Mother.[397] In Kenosha, Conventual Franciscan friars led by Father Dominic Syzmanski purchased the Allen estate in the southwestern part of the city and established "Marytown" a center of Marian piety inspired by the Auschwitz martyr, Maximilian Kolbe. "Our Lady of Fatima" friary became an important center for Marian literature, public and private devotion and days of recollection for area Catholics.[398] At St. Helen's parish in Milwaukee parishioners and school children raised over $2,500 for a Fatima statue.[399]

Marian year celebration, 1954
[AAM]

So intense was this blending of anticommunist and Marian themes that many Wisconsin residents believed that a new apparition of Mary had appeared in the Juneau County town of Necedah. In August 1950, over 100,000 went to Necedah on the day Mary was scheduled to speak to a visionary,

Mrs. Eugene Van Hoof.[400] The "apparition" was eventually judged unworthy of belief and Catholics were enjoined to stay away—but the popularity of the apparition was worth considering. This gathering, which included at least 60 priests and nuns may have been the single largest religious gathering in Wisconsin history. Among them were thousands of Milwaukee Catholics who continued to believe in the validity of Mrs. Van Hoof's visions, and in particular heard through her Mary's warnings about the communist threat.

In Milwaukee local concerns about communist subversion were not traditionally directed at institutions of higher learning, as was the case with the University of Wisconsin in Madison. Milwaukee's leading institutions of higher education, like Marquette, had burnished a reputation of being staunchly anti-communist, and Marquette students participated actively in Marian devotions and welcomed the regular run of anti-communist speakers. The Jesuits themselves found it easy to tie into this, since many of their houses and members had fallen victim to Red persecution.

Auxiliary Bishop Roman Atkielski often denounced Communism in his public addresses [AAM]

Catholics in Wisconsin also tended to support one of the most famous anti-communist politicians of the era, Senator Joseph R. McCarthy. McCarthy hailed from a devoutly Catholic family near Appleton, Wisconsin and was a graduate of Marquette University's law school. In his two campaigns for the senate, the Republican McCarthy won the support of a good number of Catholic voters who normally voted Democratic. Yet it is important to note that his support was not monolithic, and even more importantly that McCarthy rarely linked his religious beliefs with his crusade against communist subversion in America.[401] He had close friends among the clergy, for example Jesuit Edmund Walsh, founder of the school of diplomatic service at Georgetown University and Bishop Joseph Patrick Hurley of St. Augustine, Florida. However, there were few clergy in Wisconsin who openly supported him, and there does not exist a single letter between the Wisconsin senator and archbishops Kiley or Meyer—even on routine matters. The Catholic press, although militantly anti-communist, said very little in favor or against Senator McCarthy.

Where Catholics had serious concerns about leftist or even communist infiltration was in the labor movement. The struggle, begun in the 1930s and temporarily stopped by the war, was resumed after the war. Working men and women, who had held back demands for higher wages in deference to wartime needs, now wanted and needed raises. A new season of industrial conflict loomed, and in the Catholic Church, which had gone "on record" during the 1930s as an advocate of organized labor, the issues were sharp. Desires to support organized labor were also tempered by fears of communist subversion and takeovers of the unions. In the main, Catholic clergy treaded softly on matters of strikes after the war.

The Cause of Organized Labor

Anti-communist fervor flavored the reaction of some in the archdiocese to the cause of labor organization. In the 1930s, the feelings of Milwaukee Catholics over communist activities in revolutionary Spain had been stirred by the reporting of the Spanish Civil War in the *Catholic Herald Citizen.* Concerns over communist subversion and the presence of radicals in the growing labor movement among industrial workers concerned Catholic pastors, and in particular caught the attention of Father Franklyn Kennedy of the *Catholic Herald Citizen.*

Catholic concerns about communist infiltration of labor unions was a major impetus for Church action in the labor movement. Within groups of industrial workers, communist elements and Catholic priests dueled over control of the unions and the proper approach to conflicts between labor and management. As we have seen, Catholic labor schools developed in industrial communities. Catholic priests, like Father Francis Haas, worked with laborers to resist communist or radical takeovers of unions and to avoid violence and class warfare while pressing for better wages and working conditions.

Catholic concerns about communism in labor unions became an important part of the labor issues at the huge Allis Chalmers plant, Wisconsin's largest private employer. Workers at the plant had already organized under the banner of the AFL. However, United Auto Workers Local 248, headed by Harold Christoffel, was attempting to swing the workers to the CIO. As elsewhere in the labor movement, Communist sympathizers and organizers were active in CIO activities and this gave Catholics cause for concern. A considerable portion of the Allis Chalmers workforce were Catholics who attended the seven large parishes in the vicinity of the sprawling plant. In late 1937, Kennedy picked up news that a Chicago communist paper was promoting itself as an organ of the Congress of Industrial Organizations and urging that it be made available to the rank and file of the West Allis workers.[402] Objecting that the association of the communist newspaper with the cause of the unions harmed the legitimate cause of labor, Kennedy began a campaign to keep an eye on the activities of Local 248, and spread stories, later circulated by other Catholic figures, that Christoffel was a communist. Later, a front-page story related in detail how Sam Gandelman, a representative of the offending paper, the *Midwest Daily Record,* suggested that the paper ought to be the official CIO paper. In response Kennedy fired off a letter to CIO chieftain John Brophy asking him if the *Midwest Daily Record* was a part of the CIO. Brophy wrote back that it wasn't and that the CIO was going to issue an official weekly paper from its Washington headquarters.[403] Kennedy kept up his criticism and insisted that they drop any kind of affiliation with the offending *Midwest Daily Record* and anything remotely resembling communism.[404]

Kennedy's persistence brought a rebuke to the local union from Nicholas Fontecchio, the regional director of the CIO affiliated Steelworkers Organizing Committee who also disavowed the *Midwest People's Daily* as a legitimate labor paper. By the end of the year, Homer Martin, international president of the United Auto Workers, pledged an investigation of the paper.[405] However, leftist elements were not about to give up. When leaflets urged "Brothers and Sisters of the Catholic faith" to make common cause with communists against fascism, Kennedy condemned the "daringly dishonest" propaganda techniques that suggested there was common ground between the two groups.[406]

The accusations by Catholic sources of communist influence among the workers of the plant were music to the ears of the company's managers. They had worked assiduously to keep an open shop, and they made a very narrow interpretation of Section 7a of the National Industrial Recovery Act, which permitted organization and collective bargaining. Allis Chalmers's vice president, Harold Story, the company's point man against the union, welcomed the Catholic critique. In an industrial forum sponsored by the Milwaukee Archdiocesan Council of Catholic Women, he assured his listeners that "big business has met its social responsibility in the past and will continue to take care of it in the future."[407] Kennedy's anti-Red policy drew a sharp retort from a communist group that met at the auditorium to celebrate the first issue of the *Midwest Daily Record.* Sigmund Eisenscher condemned the *Catholic Herald Citizen* as a "traitor to its own people" and attacked its "vicious editorials." He urged listeners to reply to the Catholic weekly by writing letters of support to Senator Philip LaFollette lauding his support of the Loyalist (pro-leftist) cause in the Spanish Civil War.[408]

Kennedy's Red-baiting took place against a backdrop of labor tension. By early 1938 the CIO had become the dominant force among Allis Chalmers workers. In late April Christoffel informed Governor Philip LaFollette that 8,000 workers intended to walk off their jobs unless the company agreed to a closed shop and to union demands that seniority play a role in layoffs. A tense standoff ensued between the company and its workers and state labor board mediators struggled to find a resolution before a strike would be called. Father Francis Haas was eventually called in to help mediate the differences and, despite some sit-down activity by workers that disrupted work in all departments, Haas kept plugging for a compromise that would avert a large-scale walkout. By May 7, Haas had helped bridge the difference and both Christoffel and Story emerged from the negotiations singing the priest's praises.[409]

In 1940 an organization known as the Association of Catholic Trade Unionists was founded in Detroit to coordinate Catholic efforts in this regard. This organization was introduced to Milwaukee's Catholic unionists by Father John R. Beix and Father William O'Connor.[410] Kennedy became an important supporter of the ACTU.[411]

In early 1941, with war orders pouring into the plant, Christoffel again led the workers into period of confrontation with Allis Chalmers officials that resulted in a lengthy strike and renewed efforts by Francis Haas to try and compose matters once again. Acts of violence marred the proceedings and Christoffel led his workers out in January 1941. Efforts by the government to mandate the reopening of the plant were met by strong opposition and violence by workers who threw stones at the car of Governor Julius Heil who had come to try and bring a resolution to the matter. In April the strike ended abruptly.[412]

Allis Chalmers would again become a troubled labor site after World War II when a bitter eleven-month strike lasted from 1946 into 1947. Catholic activities played a role again in the unfolding drama when accusations that UAW 248 head Harold Christoffel was pro-communist were made by two former communists, Louis Budenz, a lapsed Catholic who had come back to the fold, and Farrell Schnering, a member of the Catholic Worker Movement. Budenz had made his charges against Christoffel at a February 1947 speech given at Mount Mary College.[413] As a result, many churches in West Allis remained quiet during the strike, not wanting to take the side of union workers whose leaders, Christoffel and his successor Robert Buse, had been linked to leftist politics and communism. This was also in keeping with the policy Kiley had demanded in regards to Church "mixing" in secular politics.

However, not all followed the strict anti-communist line nor Kiley's prohibitions. The loudest pro-labor voice was Father Francis Eschweiler. Ordained in 1935, Eschweiler was one of three priest brothers in the archdiocese of Milwaukee (his older brother Carl

Former Communist, turned Catholic, Louis Budenz [AAM]

had been ordained ahead of him and his younger brother Edward was ordained in 1948). Eschweiler was deeply influenced to support organized labor by his seminary studies with Francis Haas. At the beginning of his priesthood at his first assignment at St. John Nepomuk in Racine, he came under the influence of Father Anthony Weiler, known as a good friend to labor unions in Racine. Next came a stint at St. Michael's parish in Milwaukee, where Eschweiler's discussions of the social encyclicals among the unemployed raised the eyebrows of his pastor, the magisterial Sebastian Bernard.[414]

When the Allis Chalmers strike began Eschweiler was a teacher at the minor seminary and became drawn to the striker's cause.

Rev. Francis Eschweiler [AAM]

At a meeting of the West Allis-Greenfield Merchants in late 1946 he urged a settlement of the strike. One angry merchant complained to Kiley that Eschweiler had come into the meeting "uninvited by the group" and had urged a "campaign of heckling the Allis Chalmers officials by phone." At the meeting Eschweiler had dismissed concerns that Buse was an "ideological communist" even though Buse associated with them. "I don't see how a Catholic priest can say such things, condoning communism," wrote one meeting attendee. He asked Kiley, "Do you permit such appearances? Or approve them?"[415]

Eschweiler's boldest move on behalf of the workers came when union vice president Joseph Dombeck warned him that violence was about to erupt among the workers. Eschweiler, who knew many on the bargaining committee, immediately jumped into action and tried to calm the workers. He recalled later, "I kept talking to Joe, trying to show him that non-violence was the right way.... I ate beans with the men on the picket line and I got a chance to reason with them. There was some violence, but we averted a break-in which could have really been a bloodbath."[416] Eschweiler then took the "radical" step of addressing the shop stewards in the UAW union hall, without seeking Kiley's permission.

Complaints against Eschweiler's pro-union stands must have intensified, because in March 1947 he was abruptly transferred in the middle of the seminary school year to rural Kewaskum in Fond du Lac County. There is some evidence that Allis Chalmers officials pressured Kiley through pastors sympathetic to the company like St. Rita's pastor Frederick Arnold and Holy Assumption's Julius Burbach. Moreover, the Allis Chalmers company took out large ads in the *Catholic Herald Citizen* that did not allude to the strike, but that portrayed the company in a very positive way. Harold Story, the Allis Chalmers vice president who stood fast against the union, also played a large role in Kiley's nonstop fund-raising to build high schools and to provide for charities, and was one of the leading figures in raising substantial sums for Kiley's pet project, the rebuilding of St. Aemillian's Orphanage.[417] Eventually the "Reds" of the union were purged by UAW national president Walter Reuther and labor peace was restored.

The Catholic Church acted as a conservative force in labor matters. As bitter as the Allis Chalmers strike was, the stakes were even higher in another industrial battleground where the forces were re-engaged after a long period: Kohler, Wisconsin.

Kohler Strike II

Although Kohler Company attorney Lyman Conger called the period from 1934 to 1954, a period of "uninterrupted labor peace," pro-union historian W. J. Uphoff refers to the period as more like a "cold war" between the powerful Kohler Company and its workers.[418] The triumph of the company union in 1934 was short-lived; and disaffected workers, particularly those who worked in the most hazardous parts of the huge fixture and bathtub plant pressed for more aggressive union representation on the matters of wages, hours, working conditions, pensions and job security. Company leaders thwarted early efforts to organize, but in 1953 the United Auto Workers gained the right to organize the Kohler workers, and negotiated a temporary contract that was to expire in early 1954.

The success of the United Auto Workers set the stage for a period of bitter confrontation. The Kohler Company, now headed by Herbert V. Kohler, the son of the man who had broken the 1934 strike, stockpiled arms, mounted searchlights on the buildings and made arrangements to hire non-union labor. Negotiations between the company and the union began in early 1954. Company antagonism flared toward workers (some of them former officials of the docile company union) who had helped to bring the UAW, and there was resistance to "communist" unions telling owners what to do. Difficulties centered around the work in the super-heated enameling room, where workers were compelled to eat their lunch in 2 to 5 pauses between putting in and taking out bathroom fixtures in the kilns. In April 1954, the breakdown of negotiations between Kohler and the UAW was complete and when the company fired 12 enamelers, the workers went out on strike. Herbert Kohler did not wait out the cooling off period, but shored up his labor force with "scabs" hired from a variety of different places, mostly from farms. The importation of the scabs inflamed the UAW, which had pondered long and hard before the strike, but once committed threw in millions of dollars to support the strikers. The polarization in the community was immediate. Some 500 union workers rejected the union and simply went back to work on the company's terms. They claimed that the wages were good and that with the exception of a few areas in the plant (such as the enameling room) conditions were good. Kohler's paternalism had provided them with enough benefits and they did not want to go without work.

Bitter relatives and friends, some of whom had survived the 1934 strike, could not tolerate the disloyalty. Public events such as church picnics soon became occasions for heated arguments and even violence. The point man for the company in the negotiations was Lyman Conger, the company attorney and a prominent member of St. John the Evangelist parish in the village of Kohler. Given the high number of Catholics on both sides of the Kohler fence, and with remembrances of Viatorian labor mediator John A. Maguire's and Father Francis Haas's unsuccessful efforts in the 1934 strike, it was inevitable that the Church would be drawn in. Sheboygan and Kohler became a war zone where the union and the company tolerated no neutrals.

St. Mary Church, Sheboygan Falls [SCHRC]

Labor union discontent with the Catholic Church was common during the tremendous building spree after the war. Although the Church had established a clear teaching on the rights of labor to organize and bargain collectively, there was no concomitant commitment to hire union labor to build the schools, churches and seminaries that were popping up.

In 1949 angry members of the AFL-affiliated Sheboygan Building and Construction Trades Council had written to Archbishop Kiley protesting the decision by Sheboygan Falls pastor, Father Anthony Knackert, to build a school with contractors who did not use union labor. When Knackert replied that he wanted to give the work to residents in Sheboygan Falls, union representatives pointed out that union members within his parish had not been contacted or offered the right to make bids on the job. "We of the Sheboygan Building & Construction Trades Council know that the Catholic Church has championed the cause of labor," wrote Herman Graenzig to Kiley, "and ask you to use your good offices so that those contractors will at least give us the courtesy of an interview."[419]

Knackert caught wind of the letter and, in formalizing permission to build his new school, he noted, "I hope our labor unions haven't given you any more troubles. The truth of the matter your Excellency is that my heating man, my electrician, my plumber and a number of the subcontractors are all union men." But he revealed his basic attitude toward the unions when he wrote, "The only non-union man I have is the general contractor, and one of the reasons I took him was just because a group of labor dictators tried to tell me I couldn't take him. By their threats they forced me to do as I did, in order to see whether we still have some of our freedoms, or whether we are slaves of labor." He boasted, "I will not lose out in this controversy, no matter how high this group of small fry intend to go."[420] Kiley never answered the union members' letter, and the disgruntled union men sent a similar request to Stritch, who gave it only a perfunctory answer.[421]

Knackert ignored the tempest and later moved to become the head of Sheboygan's largest Catholic church, Holy Name, in 1950. Two years earlier, Father John Carroll, founding pastor of St. John the Evangelist, had taken over St. Clement's parish in the city. Carroll and Knackert were the most powerful pastors in the city. From his years in Kohler, Carroll knew most of the Catholics who were managers at the Kohler Company. Knackert also knew them but his two parishes, St. Mary's in Sheboygan Falls and Holy Name, contained more workers than management. It is difficult to characterize the attitudes of both these men toward organized labor. Carroll clearly had little to do with union workers. Knackert's disposition toward the union was revealed in his attitude toward the "labor dictators" in his school building controversy.

The clergy of Sheboygan had mixed feelings on the relationship of the company to its workers. But it was clear that the attitudes of

Rev. John J. Carroll [AAM]

Knackert and Carroll, hardly sympathetic to the union, held the day. The Catholic Church was deeply beholden to the Kohlers for a number of reasons. Kiley and his successor Meyer hewed to a policy of absolute neutrality in the Kohler strike, and sought to keep clergy as far removed from the limelight as possible.

Archbishop Meyer heard of the events largely through Father John Carroll, who was his point man on the scene. Catholic clergy watched with dismay as the town polarized further and negotiations failed. Publicly they determined to maintain a strict neutrality and to avoid speaking in any way that would give comfort to either side. Instead, they devoted themselves to prayers and novenas to end the strike, hoping that perfervid prayer would soften the hardening of issues.[422]

Eventually, the initial bargaining had brought the issue to a fine point: Would Kohler be willing to take back the 12 men in the enameling room who had walked out? The union made this the symbolic issue and the company dug in its heels and refused to take them back. Two county circuit judges, F. H. Schlichting, whose family owned the Piggly-Wiggly shopping chain, and Judge A. R. Murphy, were on the cusp of much of the action since disputes related to violence and vandalism came before them—as well as efforts for injunctions. Schlichting and Murphy secretly asked Carroll and Canon William Elwell of Grace Episcopal Church, both of whose congregations contained the main Kohler management, to hold a meeting with company officials to see if they could bring about an end to the strike. Meyer gave permission for Carroll to attend, and in September 1954 he met with Kohler, Conger and L. L. Smith, another official of the company. A spirited two-hour discussion took place.

Skilled by long years of being obsequious to the company as the best way to gain their cooperation, both Carroll and Elwell tipped their hand as to their feelings about the strike. As Carroll admitted in a report to Meyer, "At the outset we postulated the power of the Company's position right now .... We started with the position that the Union had lost the strike as of now." Although Carroll admitted that "we weakened our cause argumentatively by agreeing with them on the strength of the Company's position," he felt that was the situation as in "truth and reality we view the situation." He urged the corporate masters to be generous and give some small concession to allow the union to save face. Kohler and Conger refused, perhaps happy that they had neutralized the clergy enough to admit the company's "victory," noting that the scab workers they had hired feared reprisals from the union men when they came back. Even more, Kohler and Conger refused to give even a hint of concession which the labor people could "spin" as a victory. They believed they were doing their part to uphold the rights of property owners everywhere. They did not want to deal with the union and no force could make them. "We are really fighting Communism," they informed Carroll and Elwell, "and its influence right here in our community."[423]

Carroll admitted failure to Meyer, who was alarmed that at one point Carroll invoked the archbishop's authority for the negotiations, and compelled Carroll to withdraw the "endorsement." Murphy urged Carroll to hold a similar meeting with union officials, but the priest demurred, observing "that if I were to be of any influence with the Company I should stick to my position of not dealing with the Union."[424]

But clerical "neutrality" did not last long. When Judge Schlicting sentenced a union member, William Vinson, to a particularly harsh term at the state prison in Waupun for beating up a "scab," UAW secretary-treasurer Earl Mazey criticized the judge for his harshness and called for a boycott of Piggly-Wiggly food markets in which Schlichting owned considerable interest.[425] Organizations around Sheboygan County rose in defense of Schlichting. One of them was the Catholic clergy which issued a statement, their first public statement on a strike-related matter, on the front page of the *Sheboygan Press*. "There comes a time when silence is imprudent, and may even be harmful to a community. For Sheboygan the time is now." The ad thwacked Mazey, who "has attacked the integrity of a major court of this country, and deserves to be called decisively to task for his insolence."[426]

Mazey fought back during an emotional speech given to 2,200 workers at a labor rally. Still insisting that Vinson's sentence was unduly harsh, Mazey lashed out at the clergy, "I'm not seeking a quarrel with the clergy, the bar association … but I think its only fair and proper to ask these gentlemen the following questions: Why were you silent with the disclosures by Herb Kohler that he had guns, clubs and tear gas and planned on using them, if necessary against Kohler workers?"[427] Mazey was cheered loudly by the assembled union workers and this in turn set off a wave of letter writing to Archbishop Meyer who wondered about the activities of the Catholic clergy if their stance was supposed to be "neutral." In a lengthy letter to Meyer a delegation of union men calling themselves a "Catholic Action group" and hailing from various parishes wrote, "A furor among the Catholics, such as Sheboygan, and surrounding communities has not been witnessed in history, accured [*sic*]." They noted as well that the letter had brought about "a loss of respect" for the clergy, a "weakening" of the faith among members and more painful, "Accusations that regard the financial and monetary needs were paramount rather than

UAW Local 833
And Kohlerian
REPORTER

AMERICAN FEDERATION OF LABOR & CONGRESS OF INDUSTRIAL ORGANIZATIONS AFL CIO

Vol. 19, No. 21 Friday, December 14, 1956 Price 5 Cents

Mazey Rips Kohler Co.

EMIL MAZEY, UAW Secretary - Treasurer, as he addressed Detroit businessmen last Tuesday.

[SCHRC]

Msgr. Henry Riordan [AAM]

justice as taught by the church." They noted as well, the presence of "accusations that the Catholic clergy is anti-labor, fostering the cause of the Kohler Company, and seemingly condoning the action of the Kohler Company in its total disregard for its employees, and for the community." "Why," they demanded to know, "was the clergy silent during all this time the company has refused to recognize its responsibility and settle the dispute, thus ending all the problems, tensions, hardships, and harm to the employees and to the community?"[428] Meyer sought to deflect a public position on the strike by empaneling a special committee of local pastors who could respond to the complaints. The workers and the priests met with the group in late January, 1955, but as Carroll reported, "Nothing great was accomplished." But, he hoped, the meeting "created a definite atmosphere of better feelings between them and us."[429]

But the efforts by Meyer and the clergy to remain quiet during the strike took their toll. The priests of the city witnessed day by day the division in the community and could not help but be affected by it. One priest, Father John A. Risch of Kohler, allowed the stress of the strike to let his diabetic condition get out of control. "Father has parishioners on either side of the fence," a physician from Sacred Heart Sanitarium wrote to Archbishop Meyer, "and both come to him and relate their stories. He has been under severe tension because of this. If the strike should continue," the physician counseled, "it might be well that Father be transferred to another assignment."[430] Even more, priests themselves found their words and actions rigidly scrutinized for any trace of sentiment for or against labor or management. Even the novenas offered in local churches for peace and resolution of the strike were seized on by one side or another as "proof" of support or disloyalty.

Most clergy just kept their heads down and proceeded with routine pastoral affairs. However, as the letter condemning Mazey had put them in the public spotlight, another brother priest called them to task for their silence. This was none other than the volcanic Monsignor Henry Riordan of St. Joseph's parish in Fond du Lac. Riordan had been on the seminary faculty with Haas and was a close student of union affairs. He ruled his Fond du Lac parish like a Russian tsar, and his penchant for purple prose from the pulpit and in his rexographed bulletin were legendary. (He once allegedly eulogized an apostate fireman at his funeral service by observing "He won't be able to put out the fire where he's going.")

On June 19, 1955, Riordan attacked the Kohler Company for "dragging on the yearlong crucifying of its employees." He took dead aim at his clerical brethren: "Apparently the local clergy and ministerial groups are content to sit back and allow this struggle to continue .... Why are those groups silent? .... What can possibly seal their lips from expressing a desire to see this struggle settled fairly and justly?" Riordan's comments were repeated with glee by the weekly striker bulletin which wrote, "He is interested in justice and the dignity of man and is very outspoken in his opinion .... He is evidently more interested in the cause of justice for the working man than he is in donations of sinks and wash bowls for any contemplated building projects."[431]

Riordan's blast was followed by another incident that occurred as the company attempted to have a Norwegian ship unload a cargo of special English clay at the Sheboygan docks. The UAW sought to stop the unloading, and a large crowd gathered at the dock on July 5th. Some pushing and shoving took place along with some vandalism of the trucks brought to take the clay to the plant. Although the situation was tense and had the potential for violence, company officials called it a "riot."[432] Other Catholic forces noted the disorder in Sheboygan. The La Crosse diocesan paper took the opportunity of a successful labor negotiation between the UAW and the La Crosse-based Northern Engraving & Manufacturing Company to criticize the obduracy of Herbert Kohler. "Kohler of Kohler, is making a spectacle of itself before the world .... The results of Kohler's attempt to return to the area of the 'yellow dog contract' are evident in the hatred and violence, disorder and confusion in the Sheboygan area."[433]

Criticism of Kohler's efforts to break the strike brought a counter-response from other Wisconsin industrialists. Walter Harnischfeger (also the object of a UAW drive) wrote bitterly to Cardinal Samuel Stritch of Chicago to defend the company and urged "that every effort ought to be made to give the Kohler management the maximum amount of moral support."[434] Local coal magnate William Reiss sputtered in rage over Riordan's letter. Fearing that union pressure would prevent the unloading of his coal at Sheboygan's docks, he convened a meeting of the local clergy to discuss a response. When none of the Catholic clergy showed up at the July meeting, Reiss's son, William Reiss Jr., dashed off an angry letter to Carroll: "Your decision to avoid the meeting caused my father no little embarrassment ... and I believe did not help to erase the harm to the Catholic Church occasioned by the June 19th Catholic Church bulletin issued in Fond du Lac."[435] Carroll replied courteously, but hewed to his decision not to attend the meeting as a sign of neutrality. Riordan continued to comment *ad libitum* on the strike. He compared Kohler to Soviet dictator Stalin and, as was his wont, consigned the recalcitrant industrialist to the flames of hell. UAW strikers repeated these blasts verbatim in their weekly strike bulletin. Reiss Jr. again rose, this time to his fellow manufacturer's defense, and demanded that Archbishop Meyer launch an investigation of Riordan[436] If Meyer was leery of speaking forcefully to the Kohler Company, he may have been positively terrified of taking on Henry Riordan. Meyer never confronted Riordan directly on the matter of his statements. In 1960 newly-installed Archbishop William E. Cousins urged Riordan to ease off his running commentary on the Sheboygan situation, "in the hope that your evident interest in the settlement of Fond du Lac's strike be manifested in less incendiary methods."[437]

At the same time Carroll tried once again to bring the warring parties to a quiet meeting out of the glare of publicity. The union had readily consented, but the company refused, saying that the "word of the Union that the meeting would be completely sub rosa cannot be accepted."[438] As time went on, the priests realized that their "neutrality" was not helping the situation, and begged Meyer for permission to issue a public appeal for the resumption of negotiations. Meyer refused and stuck to his preference that Carroll handle on-site matters, asking that he be kept informed.[439]

Rev. Robert M. Hoeller [AAM]

Meyer traveled to troubled Sheboygan in August 1956 to preside at an outdoor rally sponsored by the Holy Name Society at the Vollrath Bowl. In his address, he touched indirectly on the bitterness engendered by the strike. "To harbor hatreds, rancor, disagreements, quarrels and all the other enemies of charity is surely contrary to everything that our belief in the Eucharist emphasizes, teaches and symbolizes," Meyer declared to several thousand area Catholics on the warm summer night.[440] But Meyer's word fell on deaf ears as yet another controversy erupted—this one surrounding a new Catholic school. The source of the problems stemmed from a UAW boycott of Kohler products. In Racine, the boycott had cost the company thousands of contracts, including the Elmbrook Shopping Center. In Milwaukee, strong efforts had been made to keep Kohler fixtures out of the newly relocated St. Luke's Hospital on 27th and Oklahoma.

Catholics found themselves between "a rock and a hard place" as they coped with the boycott. The need to keep down costs made the donation of the expensive fixtures attractive to church buildings. In fact, just before the boycott was announced the new St. Francis seminary additions used the fixtures in the lavatories of Heiss Hall. The use of the fixtures in the seminary created some backlash, but more attention was paid to St. Peter Claver parish in Sheboygan, which began building its new school in 1956. Union members had petitioned the pastor, Father Robert Hoeller, not to install Kohler products. Hoeller allegedly agreed to hold off, but he faced escalated construction costs as well as demands from other clergy to be neutral on the strike. He hit on what he thought was an appropriate solution in June as the building was nearing completion: install Kohler products in half the building and the rest with products from another company.[441] Hoeller promptly left on a lengthy vacation, leaving his flummoxed assistant, Father John Litzau, to take the heat at an angry parish meeting where the hapless associate had to defend a decision that was not his. Angered parishioners petitioned Meyer to stop the Kohler installation and one anonymous correspondent wrote: "Our Church people are upset. The working class make up the majority of our members. We want to be heard. We want the Kohler-ware removed as we will hold back our financial assistance to our parish." The letter-writer signed it: "Disgusted." The letter reflected a feeling that was crystallizing among the strikers: the clergy were really not neutral at all, but on the side of the company. "Rev. Hoeller has been against labor since the C.I.O. strike," "Disgusted" wrote. [442] A similarly strong letter to Meyer about the St. Peter Claver incident came from the executive board of the Local UAW 833.[443] Eventually the church decided to stop the installation of Kohler products, but not to pull out what had already been put in place.

Perhaps alarmed by the furor created by the angered parishioners in Sheboygan, not to mention the strong union support still existing among parishes in Milwaukee, the archdiocese endorsed efforts at mediation. The origins of the last initiative by the clergy to help end the strike are unclear. Monsignor Anthony Knackert suggested in personal correspondence to the author that the idea had emanated from union members who came to him quietly (some he had known from his two parish assignments in the area) and suggested securing help from clergy outside Wisconsin. They proposed Father John Cronin, an assistant director of the Social Action Department of the National Catholic Welfare Conference. Knackert warned the union men that there would be no prospect of a solution, since the company would never take back the strikers they had fired. If the unionists were hopeful, however, he promised to support the idea and suggested that meetings be held at Father John Carroll's more capacious rectory at St. Clement's. He further suggested that Carroll take the initiative, since he had good ties with Archbishop Meyer (something Knackert felt he did not have).

The union members approached Carroll who in turn enlisted Meyer's help in securing Cronin and a team of negotiators that included Rev. Dr. Cameron P. Hall, executive director of the department of Church and Economic Life of the National Council of Churches, and Rabbi Eugene J. Lipman of the Social Action Commission of the Union of Hebrew Congregations.[444] All of Cronin's expenses were to be defrayed by the Sheboygan clergy. Guaranteed privacy and a zone of comfort in Carroll's St. Clement's rectory, both sides agreed to come to the table. In an important move, Carroll excluded the sometimes bumptious Anthony Knackert from most meetings.

The negotiations which began on February 12, 1957, were off to a rough start as local media learned of the gatherings.[445] Meyer hastily wrote Herbert Kohler, assuring him "none of this premature publicity came from our office." But he hastened to underscore his own confidence in Cronin's competency and fairness, and assured Kohler that "I was happy to invite him here, for the great contribution which I was confident he could make."[446] The group met six times in New York, Chicago and Sheboygan between February and April, and substantial progress was made. UAW president Walter Reuther himself offered to participate in the negotiations and help conclude the matter. But in late April, as matters looked on the verge of being composed, Kohler and his lawyer, Conger, sensed that they were winning (the public was against organized labor) and refused any more compromise. Cronin and the other negotiators retired from the field in defeat. It was the last effort by the Church to try to bring about labor peace.[447]

One last blast at the Sheboygan clergy came from UAW Secretary Treasurer Earl Mazey when called on in 1958 by Congress to testify before the McClellan Committee about the Kohler strike. (The hearings brought the matter to even greater national attention, warranting a trip to Sheboygan by majority counsel member Robert F. Kennedy that January. (After attending Mass at Lithuanian Immaculate Conception, he said he thought he was back in Europe.) When cross examined about his attack on Judge Schlichting, Mazey once again assailed the "neutrality" of the clergy who had remained silent on such Kohler Company offenses as stockpiling arms and refusing good faith efforts at negotiation. He noted sarcastically that their only public statement was a condemnation of the union. Senator Barry Goldwater, the company's leading defender on the committee, took Mazey to task for condemning the clergy "just because they disagreed with you."[448] Later Mazey sent a telegram of apology to the offended clergy. Just before Easter, Father John Carroll sent his parishioners a lengthy letter that he begged not be construed as "a condemnation of either the Kohler Company or the UAW-CIO." He recounted how he and the clergy had tried to be "as objective as humanly possible, not only in action and statement, but even in the formation of personal opinions."

Nonetheless, in language that certainly must have pleased Kohler lawyer and his former parishioner Lyman Conger, Carroll revealed his suspicions of Mazey and suggested that the vandalism that had occurred during the strike years was the union's fault.[449] Carroll died two years later, without seeing the end of the strike. Kohler remained unwilling to reinstate the workers fired at the outset of the strike, and the matter went to mediation in the federal courts. In 1962 the courts ruled for the union.[450] Appeals kept the process going until 1965 when the final decision was again in favor of the union. This longest and most bitter strike in U.S. labor history came to a quiet end. For its role, the archdiocese of Milwaukee left a mixed, but mostly negative heritage.

The decision for neutrality by the Sheboygan clergy was flawed from the outset. Neutrality worked for the company and was correctly interpreted by the union supporters as a public relations boon for Conger. Indeed, as a validation of Mazey's critique, the only public statement any of the Sheboygan clergy made on the strike was critical of the union—the Schlichting case. Never once did they call public attention to the violations of the Kohler Company vis-à-vis the workers—as did Riordan and the La Crosse paper with the consent of Bishop John Patrick Treacy. Union workers had every right to be suspicious of clergy who were dependent on company largesse—Carroll being the case in point—and who could fiercely denounce sexual indecency, but be strangely quiet on matters of economic justice.

The Kohler strike reflects the Milwaukee clergy at its worst moment: the rush to silence, the insistence on working behind the scenes long after it was apparent that this would not work, the utter unsuitability of Carroll, who had spent most of his clerical career pandering to the Kohler Company, Knackert's well-known disdain for "labor dictators," Hoeller's lamebrained compromise over school fixtures (and his cowardice in leaving the explanations to his assistant), and Meyer's rabbit-like timidity in refusing to make a public statement about the strike in light of Catholic social teaching. It was left to the sometimes unstable Riordan and others to fill in the void in this disgraceful vacuum. John Maguire's words about the company in 1934 were prophetic: Kohler was willing to use whatever means necessary to keep unions out of its shop. With the collusion of the silent Sheboygan clergy, Lyman Conger and others neutralized a force that could have brought a degree of public relations pressure on the company to settle the strike. The result of this cowardice was a contribution to the polarization of the community that the clergy wished to avoid. Sheboygan became known as "Heartbreak City."

January 1958 found Cardinal Samuel Stritch of Chicago on his annual vacation in Hobe Sound, Florida. Since going to Toledo in 1921, Stritch had suffered from the dampness of the Midwestern winters and sought relief and therapeutic sunshine in Florida. While he was there an unexpected letter from the Vatican Secretariat of State arrived in a pile of letters sent down by his chancery staff. Stritch ignored the letter until an irritated call from the apostolic delegation was transferred from Chicago, asking why the cardinal had not replied to the letter. Stritch pawed through his mail, discovering to his horror that he had been caught in the gears of Vatican politics and had come out appointed "Pro-Prefect" of the Congregation for the Propagation of the Faith. Nearly 70-years-old, still subject to bouts of manic depression and unwilling to move to Rome, Stritch begged for a reprieve, but Pope Pius XII simply "thanked him for his dutiful obedience," and the crestfallen cardinal packed his bags for Rome. Stritch had been suffering pain in his right arm even before he arrived in Italy. Once he got there, he was in deep distress and was rushed off to the hospital, where his arm was amputated. He seemed to be on the road to recovery, but then took a turn for the worst and died on May 27, 1958, suffering from the shock of the transfer as well as the major surgery that removed his right arm.

Chicago was now *sede vacante*—and indeed had been since Stritch's transfer. Archbishop Meyer attended the funeral in Chicago and then came back to Milwaukee the

Departure of Albert Meyer to Chicago, 1958 [AAM]

same day to bless the new Cardinal Stritch College (which had opened its first buildings on its new site in Fox Point/Glendale). In the summer of 1958 Pope Pius XII himself entered his death throes, gasping desperately for breath as an unstoppable case of hiccups began to convulse his already over-drugged body. One of his last episcopal appointments in America was to Chicago, and it was Albert Meyer. Only days before the pontiff's death, Meyer's transfer to Chicago was announced. On November 14, 1958—the feast of his patron St. Albert—he was installed in Holy Name Cathedral.

By that time, a new successor to Peter was on the papal throne, Angelo Giuseppe Roncalli, the former patriarch of Venice, who had taken the name John XXIII. Among his first duties was filling the vacant seat in Milwaukee, and finally, fifty-three years after a previous effort had failed, a bishop of Peoria, William Edward Cousins, came to the Milwaukee See.

Installed by his predecessor in ceremonies of customary pomp, the gregarious Cousins took over as Milwaukee's eighth archbishop.[451] His episcopate began as the see was at its height in population and prospects were bright for even greater growth. In the works were plans for a new minor seminary and building plans for a host of new parishes and schools, and huge new convents and colleges.

As Milwaukee was gearing itself to another episcopal personality, an almost hidden event took place in late January at the great basilica of St. Paul Outside the Walls in Rome. At the fabled old Benedictine church, during the Chair of Unity Octave, Pope John announced three things: a new synod for Rome, a revision of Canon law—-and an ecumenical council. Cousins's life and that of the entire church of Milwaukee would be changed in ways yet to be revealed.

Notes

1 Steven M. Avella, "'We Will Do Our Duty,' The World of Moses E. Kiley," *Salesianum* 80 (Fall/Winter 1985): pp. 12-16.

2 "The Archdiocese of Milwaukee Welcomes its New Shepherd," *Catholic Herald Citizen*, 30 March 1949. "Archbishop Kiley Dies," *Catholic Herald Citizen*, 18 April 1953.

3 "Our Roving Reporter Goes to Trenton," *Catholic Herald Citizen*, 13 January 1940.

4 Letter of Cardinal John J. Carberry to author, November 15, 1984.

5 Kantowicz, *Corporation Sole*, pp. 135-136.

6 Ibid.

7 Cardinal George Mundelein to Kiley, January 27, 1926, Kiley Papers, AAM.

8 For the details of Kiley's service as the spiritual director of the North American See, see Robert F. McNamara, *The American College in Rome* (Rochester: The Christopher Press, 1956), pp. 509-510.

9 Ibid., p. 509.

10 Copies of these are in the Kiley Papers, AAM.

11 Interview with the Most Reverend John Grellinger, November 29, 1980 and October 12, 1983.

12 "At 72, the Archbishop is Still Working Hard," *Milwaukee Journal*, 14 November 1948.

13 Michael Curley to Moses E. Kiley, December 29, 1927; Michael Curley to Moses E. Kiley, January 27, 1928; Michael Curley to Moses E. Kiley, February 6, 1930, Curley Papers, Archives of the Archdiocese of Baltimore.

14 Vincent E. Kane, "Fifth Bishop: Moses E. Kiley, 1934-1940," in Joseph E.Shenrock (ed.) *Upon This Rock: A New History of the Trenton Diocese* (Trenton, Diocese of Trenton, 1993), pp. 147-154.

15 McNamara, pp. 554-555.

16 Quoted in Keane, "Fifth Bishop," p. 153.

17 Interview with Monsignor Joseph Emmenegger, October 7, 1983.

18 Letter of Cardinal John Carberry to author, November 15, 1984.

19 "Archbishop Kiley to Be Enthroned Here March 28," *Catholic Herald Citizen* 23 March 1940; "The Archdiocese of Milwaukee Welcomes Its New Shepherd," *Catholic Herald Citizen*, 30 March 1940.

20 "Newly Enthroned Archbishop Feted," *Catholic Herald Citizen*, 6 April 1940.

21 Interview with Monsignor Joseph Holleran, October 8, 1983.

22 Interview with Father Mark Lyons, October 19, 1983.

23 Emmenegger interview.

24 In one famous episode, Kiley upbraided Meyer over the type of flooring that was being placed in the refurbished corridors. The information about Meyer's demeanor after his sessions with Kiley came from the interview with Bishop John Grellinger.

25 Grellinger to Meyer, November 29, 1952, Meyer Papers, AAC.

26 Grellinger to Meyer, December 11, 1952, Meyer Papers, AAC.

27 Emmenegger interview.

28 John M. Murphy, "The Most Rev. Moses Elias Kiley, D.D.," *Salesianum* 48 (April 1953): pp. 98-100.

29 Father Dominic Meyer, O.F.M., Cap., compiled a very lengthy family genealogy. A copy of the Meyer family tree can be found in the Meyer Papers in the Archives of the Archdiocese of Chicago (hereafter AAC). "Death of Peter Meyer," *Catholic Citizen*, 26 July 1913.

30 The relatives of Peter Meyer included a bevy of archdiocesan priests. In addition to his son Theodore, Peter Meyer counted among his relations in the priesthood: Father Alfred Meyer of Iowa, Father George Meyer, later pastor of St. Leo's in Milwaukee, Father Edward Meyer of Plymouth, Father Peter Stumpfel of West Bend, Father Philip Schweitzer of Watertown, Father Adam Arents of Thorp, Wisconsin, and Fathers Bernard and Adam July, of Mazomanie and Campbellsport respectively.

31 Interview with Norbert Meyer, November 22, 1980.

32 James J. Graham, "The Elementary School Days of Albert Cardinal Meyer," *Salesianum* 71 (Spring 1976): pp. 30-31.

33 Norbert Meyer interview.

34 Groessel interview.

35 All during his studies abroad, Meyer had received continual reports of the declining health of his

sister Olivia and hoped that she would hang on until he came home. When Messmer's offers of biblical studies came, Albert accepted, but asked if he could slip in a home visit to celebrate his first Mass and see his dying sister at the Notre Dame convent. The problem was money. Meyer's mother had received pledges of support from Breig, Father Julius Burbach of Holy Assumption parish, and her brother Father Leonard Thelen and her brother-in-law Father Theodore Meyer to help finance her son's return. Mathilda Meyer to Albert Meyer, March 21, 1927, Meyer Papers, AAC. However, Messmer agreed to lend the young cleric money to finance his return trip. Messmer to Meyer, March 25, 1927, Meyer Papers, AAC.

[36] White, *The Diocesan Seminary in the United States*, p. 273.

[37] The originals are in the Meyer Papers, AAC.

[38] Interview with Reverend Gerald B. Hauser, October 10, 1983.

[39] See Gerald Fogarty, *American Catholic Biblical Scholarship: A History from the Early Republic to Vatican II* (San Francisco: Harper and Row, 1989), pp. 188-217; Albert G. Meyer, "The Revision of the Vulgate," *Salesianum* 30 (January 1935): pp. 10-22; "The Catholic Biblical Association of America," *Salesianum* 33 (July 1938): pp. 106-110.

[40] "Milwaukee Priest Translates 3 Books of New English Bible," *Catholic Herald Citizen*, 1 March 1941.

[41] Grellinger interview.

[42] Albert G. Meyer, "Daniel 9: pp. 24-27 and Its Interpretation: The Seventy Weeks Prophecy," *Salesianum* 27 (January 1932): 33-42; "Daniel 9: 24-27, Part II," *Salesianum* 27 (March 1932): pp. 33-42; "More than a Prophet," *Salesianum* 31 (October 1936): pp. 182-188; "Sabbato Ad Laudes II," *Salesianum* 35 (January 1940): pp. 1-10.

[43] "51 Priests Are Given New Posts–Dr. Meyer is New Head of Seminary," *Catholic Herald Citizen*, 18 September 1937.

[44] Muench to Meyer, September 30, 1937, Meyer Papers, AAC.

[45] "Pope Pius XI Honor 3 Milwaukee Priests for Exceptional Work," *Catholic Herald Citizen*, 19 March 1938.

[46] White, pp. 277-281.

[47] St. Francis Seminary Chronicle, February 21, 1940, Archives of St. Francis Seminary.

[48] "Plan Separate Minor Seminary at St. Francis," *Catholic Herald Citizen*, 3 May 1941.

[49] Kiley to Nicholas Brust, September 17, 1941, Kiley Papers, AAM.

[50] Grellinger interview.

[51] Minutes of Faculty Meetings, September 19 and November 3, 1941, Archives of St. Francis Seminary.

[52] Interview with Monsignor William V. Groessel, May 26, 1980 and October 17, 1983.

[53] Marcel Bocquet, SS.CC. *The Firebrand: The Life of Father Mateo Crawley-Boevey, SS.CC.* (Francis Larkin, SS.CC., trans.) (Washington: Corda Press, 1966). See also Mateo Crawley-Boevey, SS.CC. (Francis Larkin trans.) *Father Mateo Speaks to Priests* (Westminster: Newman Press, 1960).

[54] Hauser interview.

[55] "Father Mateo Will Conduct Cathedral Holy Hour Sunday," *Catholic Herald Citizen* 26 December 1942; Albert G. Meyer, "You Are My Friends: The Spirit and Practice of Night Adoration in the Home," *Salesianum* 39 (July 1944): pp. 91-100.

[56] Crawley-Boevey, p.v.

[57] Albert Meyer to Dominic Meyer, August 2, 1953, Meyer Papers, AAC.

[58] P. J. Kennedy, Official Catholic Directory, 1947. *Catholic Herald Citizen,* 6 April 1946. For information on Gordon, see Paul Delfield, *The Indian Priest: Father Philip B. Gordon, 1885-1948* (Chicago: Franciscan Herald Press, 1977).

[59] Interview with Father George Gleason, September 18, 1983.

[60] Dominic Meyer to Albert Meyer, November 10, 1946, Meyer Papers, Archives of the Archdiocese of Chicago (hereafter AAC).

[61] Interview with Monsignor Alphonse Kress, September 19, 1983.

[62] Gleason interview.

[63] Copies of the Sermon Outlines can be found in AAM.

[64] When he returned to Milwaukee his father had been placed in St. Camillus Hospital, but he grew difficult in that environment and so Albert moved his father into the episcopal residence for a time and engaged a Camillan Brother to sit with "Papa" and

take care of his hygienic and other needs. Meyer and other members of the household kept the elder Meyer company with games of checkers and cards. Peter Meyer died in July 1956. Edmund Meyer to Albert Meyer, July 29, 1952, Meyer Papers, AAC.

65 Holleran interview.

66 Grellinger interview.

67 "Meyer Appointed Archbishop Here," *Milwaukee Journal* 28 July 1953; *Catholic Herald Citizen*, 26 July 1953.

68 Grellinger to Meyer, August 19, 1953, Meyer Papers, AAC.

69 Grellinger was rumored as the odds-on favorite to succeed Meyer in Superior–a fact that the Green Bay auxiliary mentioned jokingly in letters to Meyer. At one point, when a letter from the apostolic delegate arrived, Grellinger opened it "with misgivings" only to discover it was a warning against attending the World Council of Churches meeting in Evanston in 1953. Grellinger's name may have been on the *terna* sent by Meyer to the Apostolic Delegate and at one point Grellinger may have tried to pry out of his old friend some idea if he was going to Superior. When Meyer deflected the inquiry, Grellinger wrote back apologetically for his fishing expedition. In 1959, when his hopes of getting a diocese seemed dashed forever, Grellinger wrote to Meyer dejectedly, "I have no ambitions as these are usually understood in connection with auxiliaries. I am not gifted among other things with the knack of inspiring confidence in those who work for me." Grellinger to Meyer, February 1, 1959. See also Grellinger to Meyer, August 11, 1953 and December 4, 1953, Meyer Papers, AAC.

70 Grellinger interview.

71 "Archbishop Meyer Enthroned in Solemn Rite," *Catholic Herald Citizen*, 26 September 1953.

72 Brust interview.

73 Stritch's nephew, Thomas Stritch, was visiting the prelate on the night that the cathedral burned. As he rode to the rail station with his uncle, the young Stritch lamented the disastrous fire. Archbishop Stritch smiled and suggested that the destruction of the building was a blessing. Later, however, he changed his mind. Interview with Thomas Stritch, July 15, 1989.

74 "Restoration of Cathedral Urged By Archbishop; Names Heads of Districts for 1936 Drive," *Catholic Herald Citizen*, 1 February 1936.

75 "Cathedral," *Catholic Herald Citizen*, 14 March 1936.

76 Stritch also relied on the advice of Father Thomas Plunkett, a Josephite priest whom he had brought with him from Toledo and who had some expertise in church architecture.

77 "Cathedral Restoration Cost Announced by Msgr. Murphy," *Catholic Herald Citizen*, 24 May 1941.

78 "Archbishop Kiley Announces Plan to Complete St. John's Cathedral," *Catholic Herald Citizen*, 13 September 1941.

79 "Windows Installed at Cathedral," *Catholic Herald Citizen* April 1941.

80 "Seek $500,000 Centennial Fund for Cathedral Rebuilding and Charities," *Catholic Herald Citizen*, 8 November 1941.

81 "Sketch Shows Beauty of Cathedral's Interior Plan," *Catholic Herald Citizen*, 6 December 1941.

82 *Catholic Herald Citizen,* 25 July 1942.

83 "Majestic Proportions and Simple Beauty Mark St. John Cathedral," *Catholic Herald Citizen,* 17 October 1942.

84 Dorothy Witte, "5,408 Pieces of Glass Form First Window Installed in Cathedral,"*Catholic Herald Citizen*, 24 October 1942; "St. Peter, St. Matthias, St. Jude Windows Are Installed in Cathedral," *Catholic Herald Citizen*, 24 April 1943.

85 "St. John Cathedral New Altar," *Catholic Herald Citizen*, 19 December 1942.

86 "Cathedral's New Altar Ready for Masses on Christmas," *Catholic Herald Citizen*, 19 December 1942.

87 "Archbishop Kiley Ordains 18 Priests," *Catholic Herald Citizen*, 27 March 1943.

88 "Pontifical Mass at New Altar will be Climax of Cathedral Paschal Rites," *Catholic Herald Citizen,* 24 April 1943; "Cathedral's Main Altar is Surrounded by Semi-baldacchino Dome," "Imported Marbles Used in Sacred Heart, Blessed Virgin Altars," *Catholic Herald Citizen*, 1 May 1943.

89 "Pontifical Mass at Cathedral Opens Centennial October 7; Children's Pageant October 10," *Catholic Herald Citizen* 18 September 1943; "Note Centennial of Archdiocese Here Oct. 7-11," *Catholic Herald Citizen*, 2 October 1943.

[90] Peter Leo Johnson, *Centennial Essays for the Milwaukee Archdiocese, 1843-1943* (Milwaukee: Centennial Committee, 1943). The book contained a foreword by Kiley, and complimentary copies were sent far and wide. Large stocks of these books were still available and were stored at the seminary by librarian Raymond Fetterer as late as the 1980s.

[91] Charles Gallagher, "Patriot Bishop: The Life and Times of Joseph Patrick Hurley,"(unpublished Ph.D. dissertation, Marquette University, 1998).

[92] For Beckmann's troubled career see, William E. Wilkie, "Seeds Must Die," in Mary Kevin Gallagher, *Seed/Harvest: A History of the Archdiocese of Dubuque* (Dubuque: Archdiocese of Dubuque, 1987), pp. 79-108. Beckmann got in trouble over financial matters and an investigatory committee headed by Kiley made a report to the Holy See. Beckmann was given a coadjutor, Ralph Hayes of Davenport. Beckmann eventually resigned and returned to Cincinnati.

[93] "Local Boys Killed In Jap Attack," *Catholic Herald Citizen*, 20 December 1941.

[94] Cherne was released from Laufenberg and allowed to settle in Salzburg, Austria. He was permitted to return to the United States in 1945 and came back to Sheboygan in poor health. He spent three years as a patient in St. Nicholas Hospital until his death in 1948. "Former State Priest Prisoner of Germans in American Camp," *Catholic Herald Citizen*, 20 November 1943; "Fr. Cherne, Sheboygan Parish Founder, Buried," *Catholic Herald Citizen*, 25 December 1948.

[95] "U. S. Provoked By Japan Priest Declares," clipping from *Janesville Gazette*, 15 December, Koehring File, AAM.

[96] *Catholic Herald Citizen,* 25 July 1942.

[97] Interview of Father Mark Lyons with Francis X. Malloy, October 22, 1984. Cited in Francis X. Malloy, "Maturation and Mobility: The Milwaukee Archdiocese, 1939-1949," (unpublished M.Div. Thesis, St. Francis Seminary, December 1984).

[98] "Milwaukee Priest Is Youngest Chaplain in the U.S. Army," *Catholic Herald Citizen*, 4 January 1941.

[99] "Father Gearhard Leaves Friday to Be Chaplain in His Second World War," *Catholic Herald Citizen*, 3 January 1942.

[100] Hersey mentions Zerfas' heroism in *Men on Bataan* published by Knopf in 1942. "Regiment's Valor Citation Mention in Book on Bataan Shared by Chaplain Zerfas," *Catholic Herald Citizen*, 19 December 1942. See also"Bearded Priest From Wisconsin With Hero Force in Philippines," *Catholic Herald Citizen*, 14 February 1942; "Wisconsin Priest in Philippines Shares Citation for Valor," *Catholic Herald Citizen*, 21 February 1942.

[101] "Milwaukee Chaplain Father Zerfas, Killed," *Catholic Herald Citizen,* 4 August 1945.

[102] Joseph Springob, "A Classmate Remembered: Matthias Zerfas," *Salesianum* 83 (Spring/Summer 1988): pp. 18-20.

[103] Ladislas Polewski File, AAM.

[104] Interview with Monsignor John A. Schulien, September 25, 1985. Malloy, p. 35.

[105] "Mass Behind Barbed Wire in Kenosha County," *Catholic Herald Citizen* 23 June 1945.

[106] "Fr. Vint First American Chaplain to Enter Rome; Sees, Hears Holy Father," *Catholic Herald Citizen*, 8 July 1944.

[107] Raymond Vint to Kiley, February 1, 1945, Vint File, AAM.

[108] David Ryan to Kiley, n.d., Ryan File, AAM.

[109] George Holzem to Kiley, February 2, 1943, Holzem File, AAM.

[110] "Afternoon or Evening Masses in 13 Archdiocesan Churches," *Catholic Herald Citizen*, 8 May 1954.

[111] John T. Cullen to Kiley, October 20, 1944, Cullen File, AAM.

[112] Donald F. Crosby, *American Catholic Chaplains in World War II.*

[113] Oliver P. Zinnen to Kiley, May 2, 1945, Zinnen File, AAM.

[114] Chronicle of St. Boniface Convent, 1945, ASND.

[115] "Pupils of Archdiocese Buy War Bonds, Stamps Totaling $2,300,000," *Catholic Herald Citizen*, 12 February 1944; "Local Parish School, St. Thomas,' Tops All In War Bond Campaign," *Catholic Herald Citizen*, 11 March 1944.

[116] "Allegiance to Name of God, Flag of Country is Pledged Anew by Thousands Sunday," *Catholic Herald Citizen,* 17 January 1942.

[117] Quoted in Malloy, p. 25.

[118] "D-Day Turns Milwaukee Catholics to Prayer for Victory and Peace," *Catholic Herald Citizen,* 10 June 1944.

[119] "Milwaukee Will Help Novena Reach Half-a-Million Mark," *Catholic Herald Citizen*, 15 October 1938. For a full story of the popular novena see John M. Huels, O.S.M., *The Friday Night Novena* (Berwyn, Illinois, Easter Province of Servites, 1974).

[120] "Two Novena Services At Church in Kenosha," *Catholic Herald Citizen*, 3 September 1938.

[121] "Parishioners Wonder How Father Keyser, 'Does It,'" *Catholic Herald Citizen*, 16 June 1945.

[122] Chronicle of St. Anthony's Convent, 1944-45, ASND.

[123] Quoted in Huels, "The Friday Night Novena," p. 39. He offers a full description of the impact of the novena on the cause of liturgical participation on pp. 38-40. The Servites later produced a film called "The Eternal Gift" which provided viewers with a close-up of the "secret" actions of the priest at Mass (i.e., the parts they did not see because the priest's back was to them). A helpful commentary was provided to explain the various parts of the Mass. A copy of this film is in the Archives of the Servites in Chicago.

[124] Sister Mary Roman Obremski recalled that the painting had been commissioned by Father Punda for the novena and later adorned the cover of the novena booklet he had published in 1942. An art student of Sister Mary Roman did the illustrations that adorned the inside of the booklet. "St. Stanislaus Victory Shrine Will Be Dedicated on Saturday," *Catholic Herald Citizen*, 2 March 1942.

[125] "World Premiere of Novena to Lady of Victory Opens Here," *Catholic Herald Citizen*, 16 May 1942.

[126] "Local Victory Novena Begins to Sweep Nation," *Catholic Herald Citizen*, 30 May 1942.

[127] "Fr. Raymond Punda Serving as Chaplain in North Carolina," *Catholic Herald Citizen*, 19 December 1942; "Silver Star Awarded to Fr. Raymond Punda," *Catholic Herald Citizen*, 27 October 1945.

[128] "Report of Chaplain: Raymond A. Punda," August 1944, Punda File, AAM. Later, during the Korean conflict, Punda composed another manual of prayer for men in the armed forces. "G. I.'s Prayer Manual Issued by Fr. Punda," *Catholic Herald Citizen*, 16 June 1951.

[129] "Crowd Chapel for First Peace Vigil," *Catholic Herald Citizen*, 23 May 1942.

[130] "No Vacation for Teacher; 1,500 Sisters Registered in City Summer Schools," *Catholic Herald Citizen*, 7 August 1943.

[131] "U. S. Travel Grant Sends Sister to Latin America," *Catholic Herald Citizen*, 27 February 1943; "Local Sisters Visit Cradle of Spaniards' Conquest in Americas," *Catholic Herald Citizen*, 11 March 1944; "Franciscan Sisters Return After 25,000-mile South American Trip," *Catholic Herald Citizen*, 1 April 1944.

[132] Frederick Lochemes, O.S.F., *We Saw South America* (Milwaukee: Bruce Publishing, 1947). "Milwaukee Nuns Relate South American Tour," *Catholic Herald Citizen*, 15 March 1947.

[133] "Franciscan Nuns Conduct Inter-American Institute," *Catholic Herald Citizen*, 14 July 1945; "Respect Latin America Nun Tells Rotarians," *Catholic Herald Citizen*, 8 November 1947; "Inter-American Catholic Unity Strongest Link for Hemisphere, Students Told," *Catholic Herald Citizen*, 13 December 1947.

[134] "Requiems Offered in Local Church For Men Dead in Action," *Catholic Herald Citizen*, 16 September 1944.

[135] John P. Montgomery to Kiley, December 4, 1944, Thomas File, AAM.

[136] Annals of St. Rose Convent, November 1947, AOP-Sin.

[137] Regina Siegfried, "Jessica Powers, the Catholic Revival, and Wisconsin as a Locus of Community," *American Catholic Studies* 111 (Spring-Winter 2000): pp. 51-59; Delores R. Leckey, *Winter Music: A Life of Jessica Powers: Poet, Nun, Woman of the 20th Century* (Milwaukee: Theological Book Service, 1992).

[138] "The Story of Jessica Powers and Her Search for Happiness," *Catholic Herald Citizen*, 25 April 1942; "Friends Crowd Small Chapel for Investiture at Carmel," *Catholic Herald Citizen,* 2 May 1942.

[139] "Cloistered Carmelite Nuns Build New Monastery Near Pewaukee," *Catholic Herald Citizen*, 9 November 1957; "Formal Enclosure, Blessing of

New Carmelite Nuns' Monastery," *Catholic Herald Citizen*, 20 December 1958.

[140] "Cistercian Community Comes to Spring Bank," *Catholic Herald*, 9 August 1928; "Two Reverses Fail to Daunt Okauchee Cistercians," *Catholic Herald Citizen*, 28 July 1951.

[141] "Benedictines Open New Monastery in Archdiocese," *Catholic Herald Citizen*, 24 March 1945. Joel Rippinger, "The Monastic Vision of Richard Felix," *American Benedictine Review* 48 (1997): pp. 372-395.

[142] Elise Lavelle, "Benedictine Records Convert a Day Through Home Study Work," *Catholic Herald Citizen*, 15 November 1947.

[143] "Retreat League," *Catholic Citizen*, 31 January 1925; Edward A. Fitzpatrick, "Retreats–A General Principle of Life," *Salesianum* 26 (April 1931): pp. 41-48.

[144] Messmer to "Rev. and dear Father," February 4, 1926, Messmer Papers, AAM.

[145] "Retreat House for Laymen Opens at St. Francis Monastery on Sept. 11th," *Catholic Herald Citizen*, 13 August 1931. Stritch also sent a letter to clergy urging them to have parishioners make use of these and other facilities for retreats. Stritch to "Dear Reverend Father," August 12, 1931, Stritch Papers, AAM.

[146] "First Cenacle Retreat Draws 28 Women to 'Weekend With God,'" *Catholic Herald Citizen*, 21 August 1943.

[147] "1942 Cathedral, Charities Campaign to Have Help of First Committee of Women," *Catholic Herald Citizen*, 24 January 1942.

[148] "Nuns Receive Air Warden Certificates," *Catholic Herald Citizen*, 31 October 1942.

[149] "Messmer High Plans Double Shift; Adds Brothers to Faculty," *Catholic Herald Citizen*, 29 July 1944; "Double Shift Next Year at St. Catherine," *Catholic Herald*, 28 April 1945.

[150] "Minor Seminary, Saint John's Messmer Have Midwinter Graduations," *Catholic Herald Citizen*, 27 January 1945.

[151] "Seminary Adopts Study Speed-up as War Measure," *Catholic Herald Citizen*, 3 April 1943.

[152] "Ordains Priests Early So That More May Enter Chaplain Corps," *Catholic Herald Citizen*, 15 January 1944.

[153] "War Workers Given Chance to Confess at Extraordinary Hours," *Catholic Herald Citizen*, 17 April 1943.

[154] Annals of the Convent of St. John, August 1945, OP-Sin.

[155] "Atomic Bombing of Hiroshima, Nagasaki Held Justified On Moral Grounds By M.U. Jesuit Professor of Philosophy," *Catholic Herald Citizen* 29 September 1945.

[156] Annals of the Convent of St. John, August, 1945, OP-Sin.

[157] P. J. Kenedy, "Milwaukee," *Official Catholic Directory*, 1941, 1951, 1961.

[158] "See Has 80,900 Catholics, 147 Priests and 100 Parishes," *Catholic Herald Citizen*, 19 January 1946.

[159] "New Church-School Marks Oak Creek Parish's 95th Year," *Catholic Herald Citizen*, 29 July 1950.

[160] "Church Architecture—Today and 100 Years Ago; the Same Guiding Principles in New Development," *Catholic Herald Citizen*, 26 April 1958.

[161] "Church-Monastery Near Racine Will Be Dedicated on May 24," *Catholic Herald Citizen*, 23 May 1942.

[162] Ibid.

[163] Additions to St. Anne's, St. Veronica's, Immaculate Conception and Ss. Peter and Paul, all in Milwaukee made in the 1950s are evidence of this. See special construction issue, *Catholic Herald Citizen*, 30 March 1957.

[164] "Bishop Atkielski Dedicates St. Mary's Kenosha, Aug. 15," *Catholic Herald Citizen*, 15 August 1953.

[165] "New Blessed Sacrament Church to be Dedicated Sunday July 1," *Catholic Herald Citizen*, 30 June 1956.

[166] Kenneth T. Jackson, *Crabgrass Frontier: The Suburbanization of the United States* (New York: Oxford University Press, 1985).

[167] Ibid., pp. 289-290.

[168] Frederick I. Olson, "City Expansion and Suburban Spread: Settlements and Governments in Milwaukee County," in Ralph M. Aderman (ed.) *Trading Post to Metropolis: Milwaukee County's First 150 Years* (Milwaukee: Milwaukee County Historical Society, 1987), pp. 54-68.

[169] Albert G. Meyer to Joseph Emmenegger, June 25, 1956, Meyer Papers, AAC.

[170] Interview with Most Reverend Leo J. Brust, December 16, 1983.

[171] "St. Dominic Parish History, 1981," Copy in Archives of Archdiocese of Milwaukee (hereafter AAM).

[172] One of the first to discuss the impact of suburbanization on American Catholic life was Andrew Greeley, *The Church in the Suburbs* (New York: Sheed and Ward, 1959). Other views included Neil P. Hurley, "The Church in Suburbia," *America* 98 (November 16, 1957): pp. 194-199 and Paul Brindel, "A Pox on Suburbia," *Voice of St. Jude* 22 (April, 1957): pp. 6-10.

[173] "Saint Catherine's Ready to Build $350,000 Church When War Ends," *Catholic Herald Citizen*, 20 January 1945.

[174] Teaford, *Cities of the Heartland*, pp. 174-252.

[175] Trotter, *Black Milwaukee,* pp. 147-194.

[176] Interview with Mayor Frank Zeidler, February 17, 1996.

[177] Thompson, pp. 354-55.

[178] Paul Geib, "From Mississippi to Milwaukee: A Case Study of the Southern Black Migration to Milwaukee, 1940-1970," *Journal of Negro History.*

[179] Zeidler interview. Zeidler was mayor of Milwaukee during the period of the heaviest African-American in-migration (1948-1960) and towards the end of his term commissioned a study of the impact of the changing racial demographics of the city. See "Mayor's Study Committee on Social Problems in the Inner Core Area of the City-Final Report to the Honorable Frank P. Zeidler, Mayor" (Milwaukee, Wisconsin, April 15, 1960). Inasmuch as Trotter's book ends its study in 1945, this report continues to be the best synthesis of the changing racial situation in Milwaukee after World War II. Copy in Frank P. Zeidler Papers, Milwaukee Public Library, Milwaukee.

[180] "Sixty Colored Children Will be Baptized Feb. 16 at St. Benedict's Mission," *Catholic Herald*, 7 February 1924; "Baptism of a Hundred Children Here Friday," *Catholic Herald,* 10 February 1927; "Eleven Priests Baptize Ninety Six at St. Benedict the Moor Mission," *Catholic Herald* 16 February 1928; "Mother and Three Children Among 75 Baptized at Mission," *Catholic Herald*, 10 March 1932.

[181] Stritch to Bartholomew J. Eustace, December 20, 1939, St. Benedict the Moor File, AAM.

[182] Unidentified report, n.d., in St. Benedict the Moor Parish Files, AAM.

[183] Interview with Father Matthew Gottschalk, O.F.M., Cap., June 22, 1987.

[184] Aloysius J. Muench, "Forgotten Fundamentals in the Race Question," *Salesianum* 27 (April 1932): pp. 7-15.

[185] Steffes to Stritch, January 6, 1940, St. Benedict the Moor Parish File, AAM.

[186] These numbers and percentages are derived from the annual reports of the African-American parishes in the archdioceses of Milwaukee and Chicago, AAM and AAC.

[187] Annals of St. Gall Convent, AOP-Sin.

[188] Avella, "Milwaukee Catholicism, 1945-1960: Seed-Time for Change," Avella (ed.), *Milwaukee Catholicism: Essays on Church and Community* (Milwaukee: Knights of Columbus, 1991), pp. 165-166.

[189] Eckert's body was exhumed from Calvary cemetery on the 25th anniversary of his death in February 1948 and sent back to St. Benedict's for burial. The next year a seven-foot carrara statue depicting the Capuchin was placed over the grave and Capuchin postulators began working to develop a cult of veneration that was intended to lead to his beatification and canonization. A thousand people attended a ceremony in May 1949 to dedicate the new statue. "Priest Who Pioneered City's Negro Mission 'Coming Home,'" *Catholic Herald Citizen*, 27 December 1947; "Marble Statue of Father Stephen to Mark Grave," *Catholic Herald Citizen*, 12 February 1949. A picture of the dedication ceremony is in the *Catholic Herald Citizen*, 7 May 1949.

[190] Richard W.E. Perrin to Meyer, April 13, 1955, Blessed Martin Files, AAM.

[191] Ibid. Seeking to account for this rapid neighborhood transition, former Mayor Frank Zeidler (1948-1960), a close student of urban life, has observed that ethnicity may have played a role in the nature and intensity of racial tensions. The areas first claimed by the expanding black community of Milwaukee were predominantly German and, for whatever reason, Germans did not resist and more

easily vacated the neighborhoods to the newcomers.

[192] Gottschalk interview.

[193] Gottschalk interview. Gottschalk, a Capuchin priest, was assigned to St. Benedict's shortly after his ordination in the early fifties.

[194] Interview with Father Lawrence Kasper, March 13, 1983. Kasper, a priest of the Archdiocese of Milwaukee was pastor of St. Boniface from 1953 until 1965. Other records and impressions of the coming of African American children to St. Boniface can be found in the Chronicles of St. Boniface Convent of the School Sisters of Notre Dame, Archives of the School Sisters of Notre Dame, Milwaukee.

[195] This is not to say that there were no unpleasant incidents. Gottschalk relates a few anecdotes without mentioning names. Gottschalk interview. However, one Milwaukee pastor, veteran pastor Monsignor George Meyer apparently warned African Americans away from St. Leo's.

[196] Zeidler interview.

[197] Quoted in Christopher J. Kauffman, *Education and Transformation: Marianist Ministries in America Since 1849* (New York: Herder and Herder, 1999), p. 229.

[198] "Jesuit Says College In U.S. Must Open Doors to Negroes," *Catholic Herald Citizen*, 26 February 1944.

[199] "Racism is Laid to White Folk," *Milwaukee Journal*, 16 July 1947.

[200] "Racism is Repugnant to Faith, Says Jesuit," *Catholic Herald Citizen*, 26 July 1947.

[201] W. J. Doyle to Ann Harrigan, January 22, 1948, Friendship House Papers, Box 4, January-February 1948, Chicago Historical Society.

[202] "A Report on the Social Apostolate of the Jesuits of Milwaukee," Jesuit File, AMU.

[203] "Msgr. Kennedy Dies at 62," *Milwaukee Journal* 4 June 1967.

[204] "Segregation," *Catholic Herald Citizen*, 6 December 1947.

[205] Franklyn Kennedy, "All Questions Asked Are Answered at Vincentians Yearly Interracial Camp," *Catholic Herald Citizen*, 3 September 1949.

[206] Franklyn J. Kennedy, "Why Catholics Fight 'White Only' Bowling" *Catholic Herald Citizen,* 4 February 1950; "Who Dictates 'Whites Only' Rule for American Bowlers?" *Catholic Herald Citizen*, 11 February 1950; William F. Thompson, *History of Wisconsin, Continuity and Change, 1940-1965* (Madison: State Historical Society of Wisconsin, 1988), p. 329.

[207] "Given Pledge of Protection," *Milwaukee Journal*, 8 July 1949.

[208] "Negroes Stay at Camp After Unruly Meeting," *Milwaukee Journal*, 9 July 1949.

[209] "Apologies End Outburst of Racial Row in Camp," *Milwaukee Journal*, 13 July 1949; "Greater Milwaukee Shows The Way," *Catholic Herald Citizen* 15 July 1949.

[210] The biographical information is taken from the James Dorsey Papers, Milwaukee, County Historical Society.

[211] Trotter, pp. 210-217.

[212] "James Dorsey and George Meany Win Interracial Justice Awards," *Catholic Herald Citizen*, 12 October 1957; "Civic Responsibility Key to Overcoming Racial Injustice," *Catholic Herald Citizen*, 2 November 1957.

[213] Gary Pokorny, "The History of Hispanic Ministry in the Archdiocese of Milwaukee," (unpublished paper, St. Francis Seminary, 1985).

[214] "The Puerto Rican Organization of Wisconsin, A Survey of the Puerto Rican Community on Milwaukee's Northeast Side in 1976." (Milwaukee: Milwaukee Urban Observatory, 1977), p. 15.

[215] Joseph Kneeland, "Pastoral Care of Puerto Ricans Bridges Barriers of Traditions," *Catholic Herald Citizen*, 20 March 1954.

[216] "Challenge to Teacher Six Years Ago Start of Program for Migrants," *Catholic Herald Citizen*, 9 August 1958.

[217] "St. Rose Parish Leads Its Own Neighborhood Clean-Up Campaign," *Catholic Herald Citizen*, 26 April 1958.

[218] Kevin Smith, "'In God We Trust': Religion, the Cold War and Civil Rights in Milwaukee, 1947-1963" (unpublished Ph.D. dissertation, University of Wisconsin, Madison, 1999), pp. 205-208.

[219] Meyer to Perrin, November 9, 1954, Blessed Virgin of Pompeii Files, AAM.

[220] Smith, "'In God We Trust,'" pp. 214-216.

[221] "Curtis House Built in 1834 Now Serves Parish Rectory," *Catholic Herald Citizen*, 27 September 1947.

[222] "St. James Parish, Oak Creek To Mark Centennial Sept. 15," *Catholic Herald Citizen*, 14 September 1957.

[223] "Polio Affects Church and School Attendance," *Catholic Herald Citizen*, 2 September 1944.

[224] "Enrollment in Schools Tops 100,000 Figure," *Catholic Herald Citizen*, 5 January 1957.

[225] Each year the *Catholic Herald Citizen* would issue a listing of all the building projects around the archdiocese. School construction led the way as typified in this 1952 report, "Extensive Catholic School Construction Under Way in Wisconsin," *Catholic Herald Citizen*, 10 May 1952.

[226] "Suppose that Nuns Kept Diaries," *Catholic Herald Citizen*, 7 June 1947.

[227] School Sisters of St. Francis to Ferdinand Falbisoner, July 7, 1930, 2-011 Box 9 F28, ASF.

[228] Mother Marianne Haas to "Reverend and dear Father," July 24, 1915, copy in ASND.

[229] Two examples of the difficulties of the School Sisters of St. Francis in receiving their pay were at St. Mark's parish in Kenosha and St. Anthony of Padua parish in Milwaukee. In Kenosha, Sister Winfrida Hopp had to inform Mother Stanislaus Hegner, "Regarding the salary the parish is owning, I regret very much to be obliged to inform you that it is absolutely impossible for the parish to meet this obligation." Winfrida Hopp to Stanislaus Hegner, April 25, 1935, MS 013, Box 12, ASF. Mother Stanislaus had to pressure Father Peter Schroeder of St. Anthony who decided to pay the sisters with foodstuff. "You will not take it amiss, Reverend Father, for you realize as well as I that the Sisters cannot live on canned peas, corn, and bread." Hegner to Schroeder, February 20, 1933, Box 10 Folder 12, "St. Anthony File," ASF.

[230] Copy of Letter of Monsignor George Meyer to Mother M. Fidelis Krieter, May 13, 1949, ASND.

[231] Mother M. Fidelis to Monsignor George Meyer, May 16, 1949, copy in ASND archives.

[232] "Archdiocesan Schools to Have Full Staffs," *Catholic Herald Citizen*, 24 July 1958.

[233] Chronicles of St. Stanislaus Convent, 1943-1984, 1943, ANSD.

[234] Annals of St. Rose Convent, AOP-Sin.

[235] "6,600,000 Pupils Record of Sisters," *Catholic Herald Citizen*, 26 April 1947.

[236] "School Sisters of Notre Dame," *Catholic Herald Citizen*, 26 April 1947.

[237] *Annual School Report, Archdiocese of Milwaukee, 1943-44*, p. 12, AAM.

[238] "Report Shows Need for School Building Program," *Catholic Herald Citizen*, 7 July 1945.

[239] "Youth Training Plans Outlined by Archbishop Kiley," *Catholic Herald Citizen*, 7 July 1945.

[240] "Archbishop Asks $750,000 for Youth Building Fund," *Catholic Herald Citizen*, 4 August 1945.

[241] "Our Duty to Teach God's Truth, Says Archbishop at Waukesha," *Catholic Herald Citizen*, 3 April 1948.

[242] "Waukesha's New Catholic High School Blessed," *Catholic Herald Citizen*, 4 June 1949.

[243] "Messmer High Plans Double Shift; Adds Brothers to Faculty," *Catholic Herald Citizen*, 29 July 1944.

[244] This was not the first time the Marianists had come to the Milwaukee See. In the 1850s they had staffed a school at Germantown. For the full story of Marianist ministries see Christopher Kauffman, *Education and Transformation*, passim. "Don Bosco High Ready for 200 Boys on September 5th," *Catholic Herald Citizen*, 25 August 1945. A gymnasium built several years later was aided by a $15,000 donation given by newly consecrated auxiliary bishop Roman Atkielski. "Bishop Atkielski Gives His Gift of $15,000 to School," *Catholic Herald Citizen*, 30 August 1947.

[245] In a news report in 1952, it was noted that 14 students from Messmer had gone to the convent or seminary, eight graduates from Don Bosco, seven boys from Marquette High School entered the Jesuit novitiate and one, John McCabe, became a Trappist. Two girls joined the sisterhood from Divine Savior High School, six girls did the same from St. Mary's Academy, and three students from Pius XI High School tested religious vocations. "Many Diocesan High School Grads Have Chosen Convent or Seminary," *Catholic Herald Citizen*, 27 September 1952.

[246] "Announce Plans for High School in Sheboygan," *Catholic Herald Citizen*, 1 June 1957. Corporation

papers for this high school and correspondence regarding its planning are to found in AAM. Letter of Monsignor Anthony Knackert to author, August 1, 1983.

[247] "Archbishop Authorizes Kenosha High School," *Catholic Herald Citizen*, 19 December 1953.

[248] Avella, *Like an Evangelical Trumpet,* pp.122-125, 176-188.

[249] "New Pius XI High School to Accommodate 1500 Students," *Catholic Herald Citizen*, 17 May 1947.

[250] Brother Irenaeus Philip to Meyer, May 12, 1956, Pius XI File, AAM.

[251] "Begin Work on Whitefish Bay's Dominican High School," *Catholic Herald Citizen*, 6 March 1954.

[252] "New Dominican High in Whitefish Bay to Hold First Registration," *Catholic Herald Citizen*, 25 February 1956.

[253] "Alverno's School of Music One of Nation's Best," *Catholic Herald Citizen*, 23 August 1952; "Reading Hard? Stritch Clinic Makes It Easier," *Catholic Herald Citizen,* 23 August 1952.

[254] Annals of the Convent of St. John the Evangelist, May 1945, AOP-Sin.

[255] Grace Palladino, *Teenagers: An American History* (New York: Harper Collins, 1996).

[256] "The 'Teen-Age Girl,' What Is She Like, What Does She Like," *Catholic Herald Citizen*, 10 April 1937; "The 'Teen Age Boy'—His Likes Differ From Those of His Sister," *Catholic Herald Citizen* 17 April 1937.

[257] "Regulations for High School Proms Issued by Dr. Goebel," *Catholic Herald Citizen* 2 April 1949.

[258] Richard S. Davis, "Why Do Boys Go Wrong? Parents and Home Hold Key," *Milwaukee Journal*, 5 November 1950.

[259] Annals of the Convent of St. John High School, November 5-11, 1950, AOP-Sin.

[260] Muench Diary, p. 62.

[261] Chronicle of St. Anne Convent, 1929-1935, ASND.

[262] Gregory D. Black, *The Catholic Crusade Against the Movies, 1940-1974* (Cambridge: Cambridge University Press, 1998); see also James M. Skinner, *The Cross and the Cinema: The Legion of Decency and the National Catholic Office for Motion Pictures, 1933-1970* (New York: Praeger Publishing, 1993).

[263] Kiley to "Reverend Dear Father," December 9, 1947, Kiley Files, AAM. The story was the subject of a best-selling historical novel by Kathleen Winsor and had been thoroughly condemned by the Catholic press when it first appeared in 1944. "'Forever Amber' Labeled, 'Disgraceful Performance,'" *Catholic Herald Citizen*, 11 November 1944.

[264] Meyer to "Dear Reverend Father," December 19, 1956, Meyer Papers, AAM.

[265] A full page ad featuring Jennifer Jones playing Bernadette Soubirous in 20th Century Fox's "Song of Bernadette," appeared in *Catholic Herald Citizen*, 13 March 1944. A similar ad in the *Catholic Herald Citizen* featuring a smiling Bing Crosby as Father O'Malley, the star of "Going My Way" appeared on September 2, 1944. *Herald Citizen* editor Franklyn Kennedy acknowledged some of the errors in the film, but reported that the film had been received with acclaim and was the talk of Milwaukeeans. "Going What Way," *Catholic Herald Citizen*, 14 October 1944. A similar treatment was given to the sequel "The Bells of St. Mary." "'Bells of St. Mary' Has Everything," *Catholic Herald Citizen*, 1 December 1945.

[266] *Decency and Modesty: A Pastoral Letter of His Excellency the Most Reverend Albert G. Meyer, S.T.D., S.S.L., Archbishop of Milwaukee, May 1, 1956*, copy in AAM. "Archbishop's Pastoral Asks Crusade For Decency, Modesty in Daily Life," *Catholic Herald Citizen* 26 May 1956.

[267] Phone Interview with Michael Vogel, November 4, 2001. Vogel, a 1955 graduate of the Marquette School of Journalism, began working for Mackin in 1956.

[268] "Marquette Proceeds with Expansion Plan," *Catholic Herald Citizen*, 10 May 1952.

[269] "Marquette Leads All Catholic Enrollment," *Catholic Herald Citizen*, 18 January 1958.

[270] Marjorie Noterman, *From Framework to Freedom* (Lanham: University Press of America, 1993). See also Mary Lea Schneider, "American Sisters and the Roots of Change: The 1950s," *U.S. Catholic Historian* 7 (Winter 1988): pp. 55-72 on sister formation.

[271] "More Thorough Education of Nuns Studied at Marquette Workshop," *Catholic Herald Citizen*, 9 August 1958.

[272] Sister Mary Margaret Modde, "A Canonical Study of the Leadership Conference of Women Religious (LCWR) of the United States of America," (unpublished Ph.D. dissertation, Catholic University of America, 1977).

[273] John Tracy Ellis, "American Catholics and the Intellectual Life," *Thought* 30 (Autumn 1955): 351-388. See also, "No Complacency," *America* 95 (April 7, 1956): pp. 14-25; "Intellectual Standards Among American Catholics," *American Ecclesiastical Review* 135 (November 1956): pp. 323-336.

[274] Most Reverend Albert G. Meyer, "Education and Communication," Sermon, Pontifical High Mass, 54th Annual Meeting of the National Catholic Education Association, Milwaukee, Wisconsin, April 23-26, 1957, reprinted in *Bulletin Report of Proceedings and Addresses, 1957.*

[275] "Dominicans Found New College in Racine," *Catholic Herald Citizen*, 26 April 1947; Rachel King, "Joy Marked Efforts of College Founder," *Racine Journal Times*, 2 July 1978; "Sister Gerold, Dean of Dominican College, Dies," *Catholic Herald Citizen*, 2 December 1955.

[276] "Plan New Campus College Plant for Racine Dominican, Fund Drive in May," *Catholic Herald Citizen*, 26 August 1958.

[277] Sister M. Vera, C.S.A., "A Quarter Century Span, Marian College, Fond du Lac, Wisconsin," December 8, 1961, unpublished pamphlet, in Archives of the Congregation of St. Agnes.

[278] "School Sisters of St. Francis Plan 250 Bed Hospital, Nursing School," *Catholic Herald Citizen*, 15 July 1944.

[279] Kiley to Mother Corona, n.d., School Sisters of St. Francis File, AAM.

[280] SSSF Daybook MS005, November 22, 1944, ASF.

[281] "New Cardinal Stritch College Building Plans Announced; Classes to Begin This Fall," *Catholic Herald Citizen*, 22 June 1946.

[282] SSSF Daybook, MS005, June 20, 1946, ASF.

[283] Holleran interview.

[284] SSSF Day Book, MS005, June 24, 1946, ASF.

[285] Synopsis of Letter from Mother Bartholomew to Mother Corona, June 29, 1946, in SSSF Daybook, MS005, June 1946, ASF.

[286] Kiley to Mother Bartholomew, July 9, 1946, Franciscan Sisters File, AAM.

[287] Mother Bartholomew to Kiley, July 18, 1946, Franciscan Sisters File, AAM.

[288] SSSF Day Book, MS005, March 13, 1947, ASF.

[289] "Stritch College Acquires Tract North of Milwaukee," *Catholic Herald Citizen* 12 March 1949.

[290] SSSF Daybook, MS005, October 10, 1947, ASF.

[291] "Sisters of St. Francis Plan New Alverno College," *Catholic Herald Citizen*, 19 August 1950; "$5 Million Building for Alverno College," *Milwaukee Journal*, 12 January 1951.

[292] "Alverno Is Made Accredited School," *Milwaukee Journal*, 3 February 1951.

[293] SSSF Daybook, MS005, March 29, 1951, ASF.

[294] "Five Unit Building to House Alverno College," *Catholic Herald Citizen*, 18 October 1952.

[295] "Cardinal Stritch Dedicates New Alverno College," *Catholic Herald Citizen*, 1 May 1954.

[296] The question of Bach's entitlement to unemployment compensation after he suffered an on the job injury to his eyes at St. Joseph's parish in Racine led him to file a lawsuit against the parish for his claims under terms of the state's unemployment and disability laws. This engaged the issue as to whether priests or nuns could truly be considered "employees" of the Church. Henry V. Kane did much of the investigation regarding Bach's claims and the all-important issue of his status and concluded that priests and nuns were not "employees" in the strict sense of the word. See Kane to Barbian, February 17, 1934 and February 19, 1934, St. Joseph, Racine File, AAM.

[297] "State-Wide Organization Backs Just Bus Law," *Catholic Herald Citizen*, 5 October 1946; "Archbishop Asks Apostolate of Catholic Men," *Catholic Herald Citizen*, 17 January 1948; "Catholic Maternity Guild Battles Pagan Propaganda," *Catholic Herald Citizen*, 23 October 1948.

[298] Former Mayor Frank Zeidler and others attested to the behind the scenes political "clout" of George Meyer. Unfortunately few documents can verify his contacts or the issues to which he gave his attention. Interview Mayor Frank Zeidler to author.

[299] "Legislature Opens Way for Pupils Transportation to Parochial Schools," *Catholic Herald Citizen*, 23 June 1945; "Facts You Should Know about the 'Bus Bill,'" *Catholic Herald Citizen*, 5 October

1946; Henry V. Kane to Kiley, April 16, 1945, Kiley Papers, AAM.

[300] *Milwaukee Journal*, 13 October 1946; "State Daily Papers Back Bus Amendment Referendum, Urge Affirmative Vote," *Catholic Herald Citizen*, 19 October 1946.

[301] "Vote Yes on School Bus Referendum," *Catholic Herald Citizen*, 5 October 1946; "Protection for All Children Common Practice," *Catholic Herald Citizen*, 12 October 1946; "Shall Catholic Children Be Denied Rights," *Catholic Herald Citizen*, 2 November 1946.

[302] "Transportation of Pupils to Parochial Schools," *Catholic Herald Citizen*, 15 February 1947.

[303] Meyer to Emmenegger, February 16, 1956, Meyer Papers, Archives of the Archdiocese of Chicago (hereafter AAC).

[304] "Ordain 23 for Archdiocese of Milwaukee May 14 at Cathedral," *Catholic Herald Citizen*, 7 May 1955. In all Meyer ordained 28 men that day, three Camillan Fathers, one Cistercian and one for the Diocese of Superior. The remaining Milwaukee priests were students abroad and were ordained with their classes at their respective institutions.

[305] Gabriel Ward Hafford, "The Rt. Rev. Msgr. Frank M. Schneider, S.T.D.," *Salesianum* 50 (April 1955): pp. 55-63; "Alumni Notes and Clerical Changes," *Salesianum* 41 (October 1946): p. 192; Gabriel Ward Hafford, "Our Eleventh Rector," *Salesianum* 60 (July 1965): pp. 103-106; "Msgr. Frank Schneider dies; was seminary rector, pastor," *Catholic Herald Citizen*, 29 December 1973.

[306] Holleran interview.

[307] Prior to the establishment of St. Francis Minor Seminary in 1941, the only other institutions in the state were the Mount Calvary Seminary of the Capuchins and the Salvatorian Seminary in St. Nazianz. Eventually, Green Bay and LaCrosse both opened minor seminaries after the war and the Pallottine Fathers opened a seminary that was used by the diocese of Madison until Holy Name Seminary was built. All of these seminaries were feeders for St. Francis Major Seminary which drew students from all over the state and even some other Midwestern dioceses into the 1980s.

[308] "Salzmann Hall at Pio Nono School to Be Dedicated April 4," *Catholic Herald*, 31 March 1932.

[309] Gabriel Ward Hafford, "The Building Program," *Salesianum* 51 (October 1956): pp. 173-178.

[310] Attributed to Father William Wallaik.

[311] Joseph J. Bluett, "Current Theology: The Mystical Body of Christ, 1890-1940," *Theological Studies* 3 (June 1942): pp. 261-262.

[312] Mary Irene Zotti, *A Time of Awakening: The Young Christian Worker Story in the United States, 1938 to 1970* (Chicago: Loyola University Press, 1991), pp. 1-4.

[313] Robert Tuzik, "The Contribution of Msgr. Reynold Hillenbrand (1905-1976) to the Liturgical Movement in the United States: Influences and Developments," (unpublished Ph.D. dissertation, University of Notre Dame, 1989).

[314] Other clerical supporters included Walter Dean, Salvatore Tagliavia, Donald Reiff, John Donovan, Edward Eschweiler, Adrian Race, Louis Reidel, Joseph Litzau, Joseph Strenski, Leo Lambert, James Johnson, Robert Mueller, Edwin Grendzielewski, Francis Bleidorn and George Zwadzich. See Beix to Kiley, n.d.

[315] "Cardijn Center to Open Soon for Milwaukee Lay Apostles," *Catholic Herald Citizen*, 29 January 1949; "Large Crowd at Opening of Center," *Catholic Herald Citizen*, 19 February 1949.

[316] Lois Edna Goeden, "Doorway to Christian Living," *Voice of St. Jude* 18 (January 1953): pp. 6-9.

[317] The classic work on Virgil Michel is still Paul Marx's *Virgil Michel and the Liturgical Movement* (Collegeville: Liturgical Press, 1957). A more recent account is Keith F. Pecklers, S.J., *The Unread Vision: The Liturgical Movement in the United States of America: 1926-1955* (Collegeville: Liturgical Press, 1998).

[318] Innocent Wapelhorst, *Compendium Liturgiae Juxta Ritum Romanum* (New York: Benizger Brothers, 1887). There were numerous subsequent editions of this text.

[319] Michael G. Witczak, "Liturgical Formation of Milwaukee's Priests," in Avella (ed.) *Milwaukee Catholicism*, pp. 173-194.

[320] "Liturgical Day on March 12 Will Be First One in City," *Catholic Herald Citizen*, 1 March 1941; "Plan Mass and Talks to Arouse Interest in Church's Liturgy," *Catholic Herald Citizen* 8 March 1941; "380 Represent Fifty-Two Parishes at Liturgical

Program on Sunday," *Catholic Herald Citizen*, 15 March 1941.

[321] "4 City-Wide Meetings Planned to Spread Liturgical Movement," *Catholic Herald Citizen*, 12 April 1941.

[322] "Liturgical Life in Church and Home is April 19 Theme," *Catholic Herald Citizen*, 11 April 1942.

[323] "First St. Boniface Broadcast Sunday," *Catholic Herald Citizen*, 1 February 1936. Velte's inaugural sermon was "Candles and Their Use in the Liturgy of the Church." See also *Orate Fratres* 15 (1940-41): p. 284.

[324] "Five Converts Baptized In Solemn Public Rites at St. Boniface Church," *Catholic Herald Citizen*, 28 June 1941.

[325] "Milwaukee Priest Tackles a Tartar," *Catholic Herald Citizen*, 12 April 1952; "Fr. Murphy's Book Much-Needed Study," ibid.

[326] "Dialogue Mass Gives 'Viewers' Chance to Take Part Actively," *Catholic Herald Citizen*, 16 October 1954.

[327] A copy of Holleran's address is found in Diane Perrone (ed.) *No Trumpets Before Him: Father Joseph J. Holleran's Philosophy of Priesthood in the Spoken and Written Word* (Milwaukee, 1994), pp. 8-16; *Proceedings of the National Liturgical Week*, (Newark: Benedictine Liturgical Conference, 1942), pp. 231-237.

[328] "Begin Construction of New St. Jude Church, Wauwatosa," *Catholic Herald Citizen*, 19 November 1955.

[329] "St. Jude Has First Permanent Church," *Catholic Herald Citizen*, 27 April 1957; Holleran Interview.

[330] "Conservative Contemporary Design for New St. Aloysius Parish," *Catholic Herald Citizen*, 26 January 1957.

[331] "Liturgical Week, Aug. 16-19 To Deepen Knowledge of Mass," *Catholic Herald Citizen*, 7 August 1954; "Liturgical Week Conference Deepens Appreciation of Mass," *Catholic Herald Citizen*, 21 August 1954.

[332] "60 Parishes, Institutions to Have Easter Vigil Services," *Catholic Herald Citizen*, 17 April 1954.

[333] "Extend Faculty to Transfer Easter Vigil," *Catholic Herald Citizen*, 22 January 1955.

[334] Annals of St. James Convent, Kenosha, April 17, 1953, AOP-Sin.

[335] Annals of St. Gall Convent, Milwaukee, March 28, 1956, AOP-Sin.

[336] An example of this style of curiosity is to be found in "Barefoot Priest Used Drinking Glass as Chalice for Mass," *Catholic Herald Citizen*, 2 October 1954.

[337] One of the local sources for Gothic-style vestments were the Franciscan Sisters of St. Francis that produced full sets of this increasingly popular liturgical apparel out of their convent tailor shops.

[338] "Latin Not Used in this Milwaukee Catholic Church," *Catholic Herald Citizen*, 15 December 1956.

[339] Albert G. Meyer, *Decency and Modesty*, pp. 27-28.

[340] Henry Dobratz to Kiley, June 16, 1944, Leo Gabriels File, AAM.

[341] "Now Comes a 'Clinic,'" *Catholic Herald*, 14 July 1932.

[342] "Birth Control Rejected by Catholics, Lutherans," *Milwaukee Journal*, 24 May 1950.

[343] Eugene F. Bleidorn, *In My Time: Aspects and Perceptions of Personal Experiences* (Milwaukee, 1994, self-published) pp. 29-30.

[344] Bleidorn, p. 31.

[345] Beix to Kiley, February 20, 1949; Beix to Frank Bruce, n.d. 1949, Beix File, AAM.

[346] Beix to Kiley, June 1949, Beix File, AAM.

[347] "Fr. Holleran To Give MACCW Marriage Series," *Catholic Herald Citizen*, 22 September 1945; "To Many 'Adolescents' In Marriage, Says Priest," *Catholic Herald Citizen*, 27 October 1945; "Fr. Holleran Talks at Service on Holy Family Feast," *Catholic Herald Citizen*, 19 January 1946; "Fr. Holleran Repeats Marriage Talks in Kenosha," *Catholic Herald Citizen*, 26 January 1946.

[348] "Archbishop Inaugurates Cana Conference Program, Appoints Fr. Holleran to Direct Work," *Catholic Herald Citizen*, 27 March 1948.

[349] Interview with Monsignor Jack Egan, October 18, 1981; Holleran interview.

[350] "Pre-Cana Notes Large Increase in Enrollment," *Catholic Herald Citizen*, 12 June 1953.

[351] Holleran to Kiley, October 27, 1948, Cana File, AAM.

[352] "The Cana Program in Milwaukee," *The Compass* 29 (April 1949): p. 4.

[353] Holleran interview.

[354] This difference is brought out in Jeffrey Burns, "American Catholics and the Family Crisis, 1930-1962," (unpublished Ph.D. dissertation, University of Notre Dame, 1982).

[355] Emmenegger interview.

[356] Holleran interview.

[357] Bleidorn, pp. 33-34.

[358] Bleidorn to "Dear Leo," April 28, 1961, Cardijn File, AAM.

[359] Avella, *Confident Church,* p. 173.

[360] "'Model of Secular Institutes' Open New House in Milwaukee," *Catholic Herald Citizen*, 15 December 1956.

[361] Janet Imse, "Children, 2,500 of Them, Wards of Catholic Welfare," *Catholic Herald Citizen*, 11 March 1950.

[362] "Present St. Aemillian's is a Makeshift Structure," *Catholic Herald Citizen*, 4 August 1951.

[363] "Plan Million Dollar Drive for New Orphanage," *Catholic Herald Citizen*, 14 July 1951.

[364] Emmenegger interview.

[365] "Plan Million Dollar Drive for New Orphanage," *Catholic Herald Citizen,* 14 July 1951.

[366] "Site for New Orphanage 55 Acre Plot in City's Northwest Neighborhood," *Catholic Herald Citizen*, 22 September 1951.

[367] Emmenegger interview; Interview with Monsignor Joseph Springob, March 5, 1985.

[368] "Will Build New St. Aemillian's Next Spring," *Catholic Herald Citizen*, 19 December 1953.

[369] "Calls New Orphanage Memorial to Late Archbishop," *Catholic Herald Citizen*, 18 December 1954.

[370] "Archbishop Blesses St. Aemillian Home," *Catholic Herald Citizen*, 6 October 1954.

[371] The best source on the evolution of the American hospital is Paul Starr, *The Social Transformation of American Medicine* (New York: Basic Books, 1982).

[372] Christopher J. Kauffman, *Ministry and Meaning: A Religious History of Catholic Health Care in the United States* (New York: Crossroads, 1995), pp. 168-192.

[373] Sister Mary Thomas, *The Lord May Be in a Hurry: The Congregation of Dominican Sisters of St. Catherine of Siena of Kenosha, Wisconsin* (Milwaukee: Bruce Publishing, 1967), pp. 155-164.

[374] Starr, *Social Transformation of American Medicine*, pp. 347-351.

[375] "Plan Eight-Story Addition to St. Agnes Hospital, Fond du Lac," *Catholic Herald Citizen*, 16 January 1954.

[376] "Archbishop to Dedicate St. Anthony's Addition May 10," *Catholic Herald Citizen*, 26 April 1947.

[377] "Plans for South Side Hospital to Be Aired at Meeting on Sunday," *Catholic Herald Citizen*, 9 December 1944.

[378] "Archbishop Kiley Blesses New $1,750,000 Hospital at Waupun," *Catholic Herald Citizen*, 7 July 1951.

[379] "Old St. Michael's Hospital to End 74 years of Service," *Catholic Herald Citizen*, 25 May 1957.

[380] "Doctors Give Fund for New St. Michael Hospital a Good Start," *Catholic Herald Citizen*, 13 December 1952.

[381] "Catholic Hospitals Get Grants of $1,377, 372," *Catholic Herald*, 17 March 1956.

[382] "Have 44% of Bed Capacity of All General Hospitals," *Catholic Herald Citizen*, 26 September 1953.

[383] Francis Clement Kelley, *The Book of Red and Yellow, Being a Story of Blood and a Yellow Streak* (Chicago, 1915).

[384] For a solid treatment of the impact of Roosevelt's foreign policy on Catholics see George Q. Flynn, *Roosevelt and Romanism: Catholics and American Diplomacy, 1937-1945* (Westport, Conn.: Greenwood Press, 1976).

[385] "For Lithuania," *Catholic Herald Citizen*, 11 November 1944.

[386] "Hungarian Underground Leader in Nazi Days to Teach at M.U.," *Catholic Herald Citizen*, 3 December 1949.

[387] John Grellinger, "A Study of the Building Needs at St. Francis Seminary, 1952," Meyer Papers, AAC.

[388] Donald N. Weber, *Priesthood: A Happy Journey* n.d., self-published.

[389] "Fatima" in Richard McBrien (ed.), *Encyclopedia of Catholicism* (San Francisco: Harper Collins, 1995), pp. 520-521.

[390] Steven M. Avella, "Let Us Pray for the Conversion of Russia: The Fatimization of American Marian Piety," (unpublished seminar paper, University of Notre Dame, 1983).

[391] "Novena to Our Lady of Fatima at St. Stanislaus," *Catholic Herald Citizen*, 29 September 1945.

[392] "Fatima Forgotten?" *Catholic Herald Citizen*, 28 January 1950.

[393] Annals of St. Rose Convent, February 1957, AOP-Sin.

[394] "Largest Crowd In Years Jams Cathedral in Holy Hour of Prayer to Mary," *Catholic Herald Citizen*, 8 May 1948.

[395] "Thousands Brave Rain to Witness Dedication of Shrine to Lady of Fatima," *Catholic Herald Citizen*, 22 May 1948.

[396] "8,000 in Annual Procession Rite at Fatima Shrine Here," *Catholic Herald Citizen*, 21 May 1949.

[397] Weber, p. 17.

[398] "Our Lady of Fatima Friary, 'Marytown,'" Kenosha, Wisconsin, in *Sursum Corda: Silver Jubilee, 1939-1964* (Lake Forest: St. Bonaventure Province, 1964), p. 90.

[399] "St. Helen's Builds Fatima Shrine," *Catholic Herald Citizen*, 4 October 1958.

[400] For the complete story of this event see Thomas Kselman and Steven Avella, "Marian Piety and the Cold War in the United States," *Catholic Historical Review* 62 (July, 1986): pp. 403-424.

[401] Thomas Reeves's excellent study, *The Life and Times of Joe McCarthy: A Biography* (New York: Stein and Day, 1982) makes few allusions to the role of McCarthy's religious beliefs as a source of his militant anti-communism.

[402] "Unions Must Be Vigilant," *Catholic Herald Citizen*, 27 November 1937.

[403] "Expose Effort of Red to 'Use' Milwaukee CIO," *Catholic Herald Citizen*, 4 December 1937.

[404] "A Badly Deceived Union," *Catholic Herald Citizen*, 11 December 1937.

[405] "CIO Official Was Misled by Reds' Trickery," *Catholic Herald Citizen*, 18 December 1937; "Martin to Probe Local C.I.O. Aid for 'Red' Paper," *Catholic Herald Citizen*, 25 December 1937.

[406] "Communists Are Caught Again in Bold Trickery," *Catholic Herald Citizen*, 15 January 1938.

[407] "Big Business Sees Its Duty Says Labor Forum Speaker," *Catholic Herald Citizen*, 19 February 1938.

[408] "Rap Herald Citizen at Reds' Meeting Here," *Catholic Herald Citizen*, 19 February 1938.

[409] Blantz, pp. 163-164.

[410] "Catholic Trade Unionists Form Milwaukee Chapter of ACTU," *Catholic Herald Citizen*, 29 March 1941.

[411] This history of the Association of Catholic Trade Unionists is Douglas Seaton's, *Catholics and Radical: The Association of Catholic Trade Unionists and the American Labor Movement from Depression to Cold War* (Lewisberg: Bucknell University Press, 1981), pp. 56-57, 165.

[412] Seaton, p. 165.

[413] Kiley forbade the reporting of controversial subjects in the archdiocesan newspaper so the report of Budenz's talk did not carry the remarks about Christoffel. "U.S. Greatest Physical Obstacle to Russian Aggression, Church Greatest Moral Obstacle," *Catholic Herald Citizen*, 22 February 1947; Frank Gross to Louis Budenz, March 1, 1947, Frank Gross Papers, FG 1, Series 1, Box 1, AMU.

[414] Paul Wilkes, "Father Francis Eschweiler," reprinted in Fran Eschweiler, *Fire in the Heart* (Milwaukee: Hi Time Publishing, 1992), pp. 9-27.

[415] Joseph E. Roche to Kiley, October 1, 1946, Francis Eschweiler File, AAM.

[416] Eschweiler, p. 13.

[417] Story was also joined by such anti-union notables as George Hutter of Fond du Lac, head of Hutter Construction, and Fred Salditt, vice president of Harnischfeger Corporation. See "James T. Barry Heads Campaign for Orphanage," *Catholic Herald Citizen*, 21 July 1951.

[418] For an account rich in detail but highly sympathetic to the strikers, see Walter Uphoff, *Kohler on Strike: Thirty Years of Conflict*, (Boston: Beacon Press, 1966); for a contrary account see Sylvester Petro, *The Kohler Strike: Union Violence and Administrative Law* (Chicago: Henry Regnery, 1961); see also P.M. McMahon, "Heartbreak Town," *Catholic Digest* 20 (November 1955): pp. 99-105 which was a reprint of a lengthy article that appeared in the *Milwaukee Journal*.

[419] Herman Graenzig to Kiley, July 9, 1949 (copy), Kiley Papers, AAM.

[420] Anthony Knackert to Kiley, December 21, 1949, Knackert File, AAM.

[421] Herman Graenzig to Stritch, November 25, 1949, Stritch Papers, AAC.

[422] A letter extolling the novenas was sent to the *Sheboygan Press* by Henry Winkle. "Editor's Mail Bag," July 3, 1954.

[423] Carroll to Meyer, September 14, 1954, Carroll File, AAM.

[424] Carroll to William P. O'Connor, September 27, 1954, Carroll File, AAM.

[425] Uphoff, p. 349.

[426] "Catholic Clergy Has Statement on Mazey," *Sheboygan Press*, 12 November 1954.

[427] Quoted in Uphoff, p. 350.

[428] Arthur Bauer et al. to Meyer, December 3, 1954, Carroll File, AAM.

[429] Carroll to Meyer, February 14, 1955, Carrol File, AAM.

[430] William L. Herner to Meyer, July 7, 1955, Risch File, AAM. Risch died in April 1958, "Rites for Fr. John Risch in Sheboygan," *Catholic Herald Citizen*, 19 April 1958.

[431] Facsimile Copy of Striker's Bulletin, Carroll File, AAM.

[432] Uphoff, pp. 226-243. The clay was not unloaded from the ship in Sheboygan and Mayor Frank Zeidler did not permit it to be unloaded in Milwaukee. Eventually it was taken to Montreal, unloaded and shipped by rail.

[433] Clipping from *LaCrosse Sunday Tribune*. 17 July 1955, in Stritch Papers, AAC.

[434] W. Harnischfeger to Stritch, July 22, 1955, Stritch Papers, AAC.

[435] W. A. Reiss, Jr., to Carroll, July 7, 1955, Carroll File, AAM

[436] William A. Reiss, Jr., to Meyer, October 27, 1955, Carroll File, AAM.

[437] William E. Cousins to Riordan, September 13, 1960, Riordan File, AAM.

[438] Carroll to Meyer, July 14, 1955, Carroll File, AAM.

[439] Carroll reported the results of his conversation with Meyer on this subject when they were together at a school blessing in Caledonia. See Carroll to Fathers Knackert, Wieshaupl, Koren, Hoeller, Shlikus, Risch, and Neu, September 26, 1955, Carroll File, AAM.

[440] "Holy Hour Plea for Love Among Men made by Archbishop Meyer," *Sheboygan Press*, 20 August 1956.

[441] Uphoff relates this incident without naming Hoeller, p. 252.

[442] "Disgusted Parishioner to Meyer," July 28, 1956, Carroll File, AAM.

[443] R. H. Kohlhagen to Meyer, August 18, 1956, Carroll File, AAM.

[444] "Hold 'Exploratory' Meeting on Strike, *Sheboygan Press*, 16 February 1957.

[445] "Make New Attempt to End Strike," *Sheboygan Press*, 20 February 1957; "Strike Settlement Talks Continuing," *Sheboygan Press*, 21 February 1957; "Union Weighs New Kohler Proposal," *Sheboygan Press,* 22 February 1957.

[446] Meyer to Herbert V. Kohler, February 17, 1957, Meyer Papers, AAC.

[447] "Report on the Kohler Strike Mediation Effort," February 12-April 26, 1957, Carroll File, AAM. Robert Wallace, "A Long Strike's Human Face," *Life*, 20 May 1957. This excellent article summarized the efforts up to that point and included a consideration of the failed mediation effort by Cronin and his associates.

[448] Uphoff, p. 351.

[449] Carroll to "My Dear Parishioners," Passion Sunday, 1958, Carroll File, AAM.

[450] George Higgins, "Kohler Strike Ends, Peacemaking Begins," *New World* 6 July 1962.

[451] "Bishop Cousins of Peoria Named Archbishop of Milwaukee," *Catholic Herald Citizen*, 20 December 1958.

Appendix

The Lakeshore Counties

Manitowoc County had been devoid of a Catholic presence until the 1850s, but its subsequent growth, spurred by heavy immigration was reflected in an explosion of Catholic parish life. In 1852, two parishes opened at Kellnersville (St. Joseph) and Two Rivers (St. Luke). The next year, Holy Maternity was opened at Manitowoc Rapids. In 1854, Holy Family at Cooperstown and St. Isidore at Meeme capped three years of church expansion. Manitowoc County paused for about three years and began another spate of parochial formation in 1857 with new sites at Mishicot (Finding of the Holy Cross), Maple Grove (St. Patrick), and in Manitowoc itself, St. Boniface. The next year, St. Peter opened at Northeim and St. Wendel in Cleveland. In 1860, St. Anne was founded for the people of Francis Creek while a quasi-utopian colony under the Bavarian priest Ambrose Oschwald founded a new church and religious commune at St. Nazianz in Eaton Township. In 1864 parishes opened at Kiel (St. Peter), a second parish at Meeme (St. Fidelis), and St. George in Centerville. In the following year, the parish at Cooperstown was named for St. Wenceslaus, the parish at Mishicot in honor of St. Mary, and St. Ann at Kossuth opened its doors. The tremendous burst of expansion finished in 1866 when St. Mary's in Clark's Mills began.

Sheboygan County also experienced dynamic growth in the fifties and sixties. St. Patrick in Adell was begun in 1853. In 1854, St. Mary in Random Lake entered the lists. St. Joseph in Schwarzald was commenced in 1856 and St. John in Rhine the next year (later renamed in honor of St. Andrew) along with St. George in St. George. In 1858, St. Michael began in Mitchell and St. Mary in Cascade. A long pause ended in 1864 when St. John the Baptist in Plymouth opened, St. Rose began appropriately in Lima, and St. Mary in Silver Creek. St. Fridolin began in Glenbeulah in 1866.

Ozaukee County registered slower growth. St. Mary opened in Belgium in 1851. The next year, St. Stephen opened in Port Washington and St. Joseph in Grafton. In Fredonia, Mater Dolorosa began in 1860 and the parish development paused in 1861 after the foundation of Immaculate Conception in Saukville.

In Milwaukee Country, the year 1851 saw the formation of parishes in Wauwatosa (St. Ambrose), St. Matthias on the Beloit Road and St. Barnabas in Greenfield. In the see city itself, a new German church opened in Walker's Point named in honor of the Holy Trinity while the same architect, Victor Schulte put the finishing touches on the Cathedral of St. John the Evangelist. A new German parish would open in the far western part of the city in 1855 named in honor of St. Joseph. Four years later, in rural Greenfield, a new church in honor of the Holy Sacrament opened its doors. The efforts of circuit riders and the steady increase in Milwaukee's population resulted in permanent foundations in Granville (St. Catherine), Oak Creek (St. Matthew), and St. Martin (Sacred Heart of Jesus).

Racine County as well continued its steady pattern of growth. In 1851 German farmers erected the church of St. Louis in Caledonia township and in 1857 a second church named in honor of the Holy Family was erected. A year later in Yorkville, a church in honor of St. Andrew was opened. A church for Germans sprung up in Racine named in honor of St. Mary. In 1864, the old church of St. Sebastian in Burlington was named in honor of the Immaculate Conception.

Kenosha registered strong growth as well in all parts of the county. In Brighton, St. Patrick's Church opened in 1851. Two years later a parish named in honor of St. Wendelin opened in Paris. In 1864, the church was renamed in honor of St. John the Baptist. Farther west, St. Elizabeth opened in Wilmot and in 1860 it was renamed in honor of the Holy Name of Jesus. That same year, the town of New Muenster opened a parish in honor of St. Alphonsus Liguori. In Bristol, St. Michael Church welcomed worshipers in 1867.

The Second Tier Counties

The counties adjoining the lakeshore were especially dynamic in their growth, providing some of the strongest Catholic communities in the state.

Catholicism in Walworth County, slow to get off the ground, grew rapidly in the 1850s. In Sharon, St. Aloysius began in 1851 and a church also opened in Big Foot Prairie. The next year at Sugar Creek another church opened as well. In 1855, St. Thaddeus commenced in East Troy. The next year, St. Patrick began in Whitewater. In 1858, St. Kilian opened in Lyons. In 1865, St. Lawrence in Elkhorn was erected.

Waukesha County saw St. Bruno open in Dousman in 1851 and St. Theresa in Eagle in 1852. Four years later a parish opened in Delafield. In 1858 a new church opened in New Berlin while St. Catherine began in Mapleton. In Duplainville, Ss. Peter and Paul began in 1860 and five years later St. Mary began in Pewaukee.

Washington County saw a renewal of parish formation in 1852 with a church in the county seat of West Bend named in honor of St. Matthias and a church in Jackson named to honor the Irish saint Bridget but was changed to St. Augustine in 1855. In 1853, Richfield opened a church in honor of St. Augustine but the next year changed it to the Church of the Holy Maternity. In 1854, Holy Immaculate Conception opened in West Bend. In 1855 at Newburg, Holy Trinity was formed and a year later at Allenton, St. Anthony Church was founded. In 1857, the march of church openings continued with St. Bridget in Wayne, St. Peter in Farmington (changed to St. John of God in 1864), and St. Peter in Slinger. St. Michael opened its doors in Kewaskum in 1858, being renamed Holy Trinity in 1864. In 1860 Immaculate Conception in Barton was begun and in 1865, Holy Angels began in West Bend and St. Kilian in Hartford.

The most dynamic growth took place in Fond du Lac county which sustained a tremendous burst of church formation. Indeed, so thick were the church settlements that the area is characterized to this day as the "Holy Land." In 1851, Holy Visitation of the Virgin Mary opened in Marytown, while French-speaking Catholics began Fond du Lac's first parish named in honor of the saintly Franciscan tertiary, St. Louis of France. Four years later, Calvary Church was opened at Marshfield (later renamed in honor of St. Joseph in 1857) and Holy Mary of Help at Springvale. In 1856, St. John the Baptist was founded in Johnsburg and St. Martin in Ashford. The next year Dotyville opened a church in honor of St. Virgil (later renamed St. John the Baptist in 1866). Osceola dedicated a church in honor of the Immaculate Conception (renamed in honor of St. Matthew in 1861), Holy Ascension opened in Eden, and St. John in Byron. The advent of the Capuchin Franciscans brought a new burst of parish formation in the county. Holy Cross opened its doors at Marshfield in 1864 and later moved to the village of Mount Calvary. Churches in honor of St. Patrick were built in Fond du Lac proper and in Ripon, while in Auburn St. Matthias Church began welcoming worshipers. In 1867, three new Fond du Lac county parishes opened: St. Mary's in Fond du Lac, St. John the Baptist in Woodhull, and St. Matthew in New Cassel. By the time of the split of the dioceses, the heavily Catholic character of Fond du Lac County was established.

The North Lakeshore/ Lake Winnebago Counties

This admittedly artificial grouping comprises those counties that were tied to the economies generated from the commerce of Lake Michigan and the activity around Wisconsin's largest inland lake, Lake Winnebago. They comprise, Kewaunee, Door, Brown, Outagamie, Calumet, Winnebago and Waupaca counties. Fond du Lac, at the foot of Lake Winnebago could have been included, but its orbit, because of transportation routes was towards Milwaukee. Later these would become the nucleus of the diocese of Green Bay.

Kewaunee County also registered strong Catholic growth all through the 1860s. St. Hubert parish began at Rosiere in 1861. The next year parishes at Luxemberg (St. Mary) and Franklin (St. Lawrence) began. In 1863, St. Louis parish was created at Dycksville. In 1865, Holy Trinity opened its doors at Slovan and St. John Nepomocene at Coryville.

Door County, Wisconsin's future resort area, saw the foundation of St. Adella Church in Belgium in 1858, St. Odilia Church in Sherytown in 1860, and St. Mary ad Nives in 1866.

In Brown County, destined to become the headquarters of the diocese of Green Bay in 1868 a strong burst of Catholic activity was evident. In 1852, St. Kilian began at New

Franken. Three years later, in Green Bay, the church of St. Mary was founded while at Holland, St. Francis Seraph was created. In 1858 Holy Cross was founded at Bay Settlement, St. John the Baptist at Duck Creek, and St. Bernard in Green Bay. The next year at DePere, St. Ignatius Church opened its doors. In 1861, St. Joseph Church was created at Robinsonville while in 1864, St. Francis Xavier was founded at DePere. In 1866, five new parishes began: Holy Martyrs of Gorsum in Preble, St. Patrick and St. Willibrord in Green Bay, St. Bridget in Marrison and St. Patrick at Askeaton.

Outagamie County grew rapidly as well. In 1852, St. John Nepomocene opened in Little Chute. In 1857, churches at Freedom (St. Nicholas) and Kaukauna (Holy Angels) began their work. St. Mary at Bear Creek opened in 1860. The next year, St. Edward in Mackville and St. Mary of the Seven Dolors, Appleton were created. St. Peter in Snyderville opened its doors in 1864. Immaculate Conception in Greenville was created in 1865 while St. James in Hortonville opened in 1867.

In Calumet county, growth was modest. St. Catherine in Stockbridge and St. Maximilian in Chilton were founded in 1857. St. John the Baptist was created in the town of St. John in 1864 and in 1867 St. Martin Church in Charlestown was opened.

Winnebago County had steady growth. In 1852 St. Malachy at Clayton and St. Peter in Oshkosh opened their doors. In 1854 a church opened at Black Wolf, and five years later a second parish opened in Oshkosh. St. Charles in Menasha opened in 1860. St. Thomas in Poygan began services in 1864.

Waupaca County's first church opened in 1859 at Northport and was named in honor of St. Francis. In the rural farming village of New London another church was titled in honor of St. Francis in 1864. In nearby Lebanon, a church named for Irish St. Finbar opened in 1866.

The Third Tier Counties

The collection of counties that constitute this third tier represent virtually all agricultural counties and the state capital of Madison (Dane County). These counties extend beyond the Fox-Wisconsin axis into the areas of the north of Wisconsin. Wide variations existed among their respective Catholic populations, giving a heterogeneous texture to Wisconsin's religious geography.

In Rock County, the city of Janesville would be an important center of Catholic life. In 1851, St. Cuthbert Church opened in that community. Just as significant would be the border town of Beloit and important commercial and educational crossroads of Wisconsin. In 1854, St. Thomas Church opened in that city. In 1855, a church in honor of St. Michael was begun in Porter. Parish formation would be on hold until 1864 when St. Joseph Church would be founded in Edgerton. In 1866, a second Janesville parish in honor of St. Patrick opened. A year later, St. Augustine in Footville was commenced.

Green County included only two Catholic settlements, St. Victor in Monroe, founded by Swiss immigrants and St. Francis De Sales in Albany opened in 1864.

Dane County, home to Wisconsin's state capital, continued to have aggressive growth in this period. St. Francis Xavier began in Cross Plains in 1864. St. Joseph began in Sun Prairie in 1856. In 1857 Holy Mother of Consolation began in Oregon while St. Patrick opened in Cottage Grove in the same year. St. Simon began in Vermont in 1861 and the next year St. Barnabas in Mazomanie commenced operations. St. Margaret began in Vienna in 1863 while a year later, Sacred Heart of Jesus and Mary began in Sun Prairie and St. Anne in Deerfield. That same year (1864) St. Peter opened in Ashton and Holy Savior in Perry. Westport was the site of St. Mary of the Lake in 1867 while in that same year, St. Bernard opened at Paoli.

Jefferson County likewise was an important site of Catholic growth. St. Henry became the major parish in Watertown in 1853. Three years later St. Malachy began in Crawfish River. A year later the parish was renamed in honor of St. Raphael. In 1859, St. John the Baptist began in Jefferson. In 1867, St. Wenceslaus opened in Waterloo.

Dodge County sprouted a number of Catholic establishments in this period. In 1853, St. Isidore parish began in Clyman. A year later, St. Mary Help of Christians began in Sullivan. In 1856, Beaver Dam gained a second parish in honor of St. Mary, while at Elba, St. Columbkille began its existence. The next year, St. Malachy opened its doors at Horicon and St. Mary in Mayville. A third Beaver Dam parish, in honor of St. Peter, began in 1860. St. Joseph parish in Waupun and St. Patrick in Beaver Dam began in 1864. St. Joseph began in Richwood in 1865.

Columbia County counted six new establishments in this epoch of growth. St. Simon began at the future resort area of Wisconsin Dells in 1851. Six years later, in 1857, St. Jerome began in Columbus. A church was founded in Marcellon in 1858 and a year later, St. Augustine opened in Wyocena. St. Kieran opened in the village of Dekorra in 1860. In 1864, St. Cecilia in Kilbourn City began.

Tiny Green Lake County had a small Catholic population. St. Mary opened in St. Marie in 1854. Holy Trinity in Berlin began a year later.

Marquette County had an equally slow pace of development. Gethsemane Church was founded in Montello in 1853, St. Pius in Briggsville in 1860, and St. Andrew in Buffalo in 1864.

Waushara County had a church at Oasis in 1858 and another unnamed church at Saxeville in 1860.

Sauk County had a healthy Catholic growth. In 1858 the city of Dellona witnessed the creation of All Saints Church and a year later, a church in honor of St. Bridget. In 1859, the city of Baraboo, home of the Ruengling family of circus fame, saw the creation of St. Michael Church. In 1860, a church in honor of Our Lady of Loretto opened in Honey Creek. St. Luke Church opened in Plain in 1861. St. Fridolin Church began in Ironton and St. Alphonsus in Westfield in 1864. St. Patrick in Marble Ridge began in 1865

Juneau County, to the north of Sauk, saw the city of Mauston open St. Patrick Church in 1859. In 1864. St. Paul opened at Lisbon, and Immaculate Conception at Lyndon Station. At Lindina, St. Michael parish opened in 1865 and in the same year, St. Theresa at Union Station.

The Mining Counties

By this epoch of diocesan life, the mining frontier in southwestern Wisconsin had been depleted and the earlier vitality of Catholic life in the region is reflected in the relatively slow pace of growth in these counties.

In Grant County, abutting the river and near the heavily Irish Catholic outpost of Dubuque, Catholic life was at its strongest. In 1852, St. Mary Church was founded in Platteville. In 1859, St. Charles Church in Cassville was commenced. Three new Grant county churches emerged in 1864: St. John in Patch Grove, St. Lawrence O'Toole in Mount Hope and St. Clement in Lancaster. In 1866, St. Sebastian Church in Glenhaven began.

Crawford County to the north continued to be dominated by St. Gabriel in Prairie du Chien. In 1864, St. Patrick opened in Seneca, St. Philip in St. Philip's.

Vernon County saw St. James Church in Liberty Pole open in 1857 and ten years later St. Charles in Genoa.

Richland County saw two new churches formed in 1866. At Cazenovia, St. Anthony parish began and in Keyesville, the Nativity of the Blessed Virgin Mary.

Iowa County registered strong growth. In 1855, new churches at Mifflin (St. John the Baptist) and Ridgeway (St. Bridget) were formed. St. Michael's Church was formed in Highland in 1864 and a year later renamed in honor of St. John Nepomocene. In 1866, St. Malachy Church at Clyde and St. Patrick Church in Hollandale were opened.

Lafayette County had two churches added to their lists in 1852 at Elk Grove (St. Rose of the Prairie) and at Wiota. In 1857 St. Pius was opened at Kendalltown. In 1864, St. Michael was founded at Darlington.

The North Counties

These counties spanned the length of the state from west to east and included LaCrosse, Trempeleau, Monroe, Jackson, Buffalo, Pierce, St. Croix, Pepin, Dunn, Chippewa, Eau Claire, Wood, Marathon, Portage, Waupaca, Shawano, Menominee, Oconto and Marinette counties.

LaCrosse's development was the most prodigious. In 1856, the church of St. Mary was erected in that city. The next year, a church in honor of St. Joseph (later to become the cathedral) was founded in 1857, as well as St. Alphonsus Church in Woomata. In 1859, St. Mary Church in Boswick Valley opened and a year later another church in honor of St. Joseph was erected in LaCrosse.

Trempeleau County, destined for fame as the site of an important study on the validity of Turner's frontier thesis, saw a new church in Pine Creek (Most Sacred Heart) established in 1864. Two other churches, St. Wenceslaus in Trempeleau and St. Bridget in Ettick were opened in 1865.

Monroe County had a few parishes established. St. Mary's in St. Mary began in 1856. In 1865, St. Finbar's in Ridgeville and in 1867 St. Patrick's in Sparta welcomed worshipers.

St. Croix County enjoyed some of the healthiest Catholic growth in the northern part of the state. In 1852, an establishment was made in the Mississippi River town of Hudson. In 1857, at Hudson, St. Mary on the Lake was created. A year later, St. James was opened in the same city. St. Ann in Somerset began in 1859. A year later, St. Joseph opened in Somerset. One additional parish, St. Patrick, at Erin Prairie was begun in 1860.

Some counties had only two parishes. Pierce County saw the establishment of Nativity of the Blessed Virgin Mary in Big River in 1859. A log church, later named for Our Lady of Perpetual Help was begun at Clayfield in 1863. Dunn County had St. Francis in Menominee and St. Peter in Eau Galle which opened their doors in 1863. Chippewa likewise had two parishes, St. Mary in Chippewa Falls in 1857 and St. Peter in Tilden in 1864. Likewise, Eau Claire had two parishes. St. Peter in Eau Claire began in 1859 and St. Patrick in the same city in 1864. Waupaca County had St. Francis parish in Northport in 1859. In the Irish settlement of New London, another St. Francis opened its doors in 1864.

Marathon County had a more sizeable Catholic population because of migration to the lumber mill city of Wausau. St. Mary of the Immaculate Conception began as a mission chapel in 1857. St. Benedict in Marathon City began in 1859. In 1864, Nativity of the Blessed Virgin Mary began in the same city. Portage County welcomed St. Stephens parish in Stevens Point in 1857. In 1865, St. Joseph parish in Polonia began.

Some of the far northern counties had but one parish for the entire population. Jackson County had one solitary Irish settlement, St. Columbkille in Shamrock founded in 1866. Buffalo County had one parish, St. Joseph in Glencoe opened in 1865. Wood County had one parish in Grand Rapids, Exaltation of the Holy Cross, founded in 1857. Shawano County had one parish founded in 1863. Menominee County had one parish at Keshena founded in 1853 in honor of St. Michael. Oconto County saw the commencement of St. Peter Church in 1857. In 1866, Assumption of the Blessed Virgin Mary began at Marinette. Pepin County had a small Catholic presence. St. Mary in Durand began in 1860.

Index

B

C

E

F

G

H

I

J

K

N

O

Q

R

S

Index compiled by
Betsy Schoeller